Packard

A HISTORY OF THE MOTOR CAR AND THE COMPANY

AN
AUTOMOBILE
QUARTERLY
LIBRARY
SERIES
BOOK

A H

AND

Packard

HISTORY OF THE
MOTOR CAR
THE COMPANY

Beverly Rae Kimes, Editor

STAFF FOR THIS BOOK

Associate Editor
for Chapters 1-6 and 24-31:
RICHARD M. LANGWORTH

Contributing Authors, Historical Text:

JAMES J. BRADLEY, STAN GRAYSON,
GEORGE HAMLIN, DWIGHT HEINMULLER,
RICHARD M. LANGWORTH, C. A. LESLIE, JR.,
TERRY MARTIN, RICHARD K. PHILLIPS,
DON E. WEBER, L. MORGAN YOST

Contributing Authors, Appendices Sections:

ROGER ABBOTT, CHARLES BETTS,
MENNO DUERKSEN, GEORGE HAMLIN,
JOHN B. MONTVILLE,
W.C. WILLIAMS, BOB ZIMMERMAN

Packard Portrait Photographers:

RUSSEL W. BERRY, HENRY AUSTIN CLARK, JR.,
STAN GRAYSON, BUD JUNEAU,
RICHARD M. LANGWORTH, RICK LENZ,
STROTHER MACMINN,
MARC MADOW, DON VORDERMAN

Produced by the staff of AUTOMOBILE *Quarterly* Magazine
in association with Princeton Institute for Historic Research.

General Edition

Typesetting by Kutztown Publishing Company, Kutztown, Pennsylvania;
printing and binding by South China Printing Company, Hong Kong;
color separations by Lincoln Graphics Incorporated, Cherry Hill,
New Jersey, and Graphic Arts Corporation of Ohio, Toledo, Ohio.

Library of Congress Catalog Number: 78-71063
ISBN 0-915038-11-0: AUTOMOBILE *Quarterly* Publications

AUTOMOBILE QUARTERLY PUBLICATIONS

Book Designer
THEODORE R. F. HALL

Editor	Art Director
LOWELL C. PADDOCK	MICHAEL PARDO
Managing Editor	Associate Art Director
CHRISS BONHALL	DAVID W. BIRD II
Associate Editor	Chief Photographer
JOHN F. KATZ	ROY D. QUERY
Associate Editor	Librarian
JULIE M. FENSTER	LOUIS TORRES
European Editor	Archivist
GRIFFITH BORGESON	HENRY AUSTIN CLARK JR.

President
GLENN F. JOHNS

Founding Editor and Publisher
L. SCOTT BAILEY

PREFACE

It was in late 1972 when thoughts at Automobile Quarterly turned to Packard. To Packard as a book, that is. Packard had been on our minds for a long time before that.

On July 2nd of 1962 by official decree of the Studebaker-Packard board of directors the name Packard died because, as a company spokesman said, it no longer held magic. Pragmatically, there was at that time perhaps no compelling reason to continue its use. The cars had, after all, already passed into history. But Automobile Quarterly was just beginning then, we were perhaps ingenuously idealistic; pragmatism seemed a poor excuse to render into oblivion one of the grandest hallmarks of the American automobile industry. No magic in the name? We were appalled. "Muffled drums bestilled," we said. We mourned its passing. Packard was the subject of Automobile Quarterly's first marque history. And it was the first automobile to be the sole photographic feature on the cover of our magazine. The car was a 1934 Dietrich convertible victoria. The issue was Volume I, Number 3, fall 1962.

Ten years later the "proud name of Packard" remained no less compelling to us. And to virtually everyone else who cared about superb automobiles; the passage of time had utterly negated the contention that the name held no magic. But remaining, too, were the "many and varied suppositions as to why the Packard motorcar is no longer with us and the unanswered questions" which we noted in 1962 would "keep Packard mourners busy for years." We hope this book will answer them.

But it is equally the intention of this volume to celebrate the life of Packard as to examine the reasons for its death. For Packard seems to us to be much more than an automobile. There has always been an intangibility about it, at once intriguing yet definable. For nearly a half century the motorcars from East Grand Boulevard provided a metaphor for that strata of the contemporary social scene which reflected the finest that was America. No other automobile so well expressed this young country's striving for an elegance, a tradition, a heritage to match the centuries-old culture of Europe. It is telling in this regard to note that to European connoisseurs of the automobile the name Packard presents precisely the same image as it does to Americans, perhaps even more emphatically. And it was for this reason, because for such an extended period Packard was so intrinsic a factor in American society, that a detailed examination of the marque seemed important. Packard's rise, and indeed its fall, mirrors a considerable portion of American history of the Twentieth Century.

Thus the Packard book had long been a dream for Automobile Quarterly when, in 1972, the formulation of it was begun. It was our intention from the outset that Packard would be our most ambitious book to date. (It remains that today, a number of Automobile Quarterly Library Series books later—and probably it always shall.) One realization struck us immediately. So vast was the task con-

templated that the selection of one author for the project was virtually impossible. Ultimately a multi-authored approach was decided upon, with the book's sections entrusted to Packard historians and enthusiasts with interest and expertise in the various motorcars and eras which make up the whole of the Packard history. A press release to the automotive news media dated March 2nd, 1973 announced our plans and asked those interested in contributing to the project to write us. By October 1973 many of the contributing authors had been enlisted and the first bulletin to them was issued that month outlining the project. During the spring of 1974 the first 10,000 words of historical text were submitted, followed by further cascades throughout 1975, 1976 and 1977, the last copy arriving early in 1978. The more than 500,000 words which are the end result here were accompanied during this period by at least five times that many in communications to contributing authors and researchers, to coordinate the text sections, to cross-check facts, to secure illustrations and photographic documentation. It would require a volume this size to narrate the saga which has been this Packard book.

It would not be an exaggeration either to state that the accumulated years of research represented here is considerably more than the equal of the Packard Motor Car Company's lifetime. Terry Martin began delving deeply into the Warren years of the company soon after he made that town his home; Morgan Yost's experience with the marque dates back a half century; C.A. Leslie's and Dick Phillips' enthusiasm was early born; George Hamlin and Dwight Heinmuller were barely into their teens when Packard became an important part of their lives; Don Weber has long been fascinated with the Dominant Six era of the marque, and Jim Bradley has been intimately involved with Packards since that day in 1956 when, after the company announced its move to South Bend, he and several associates drove to the plant to rescue for the Detroit library what proved to be truckloads of historic photographs. In correlative areas, both Roger Abbott and Bob Zimmerman have been collecting and documenting Packard literature for years, John Montville's interest in the truck industry dates to his youth, as does Charlie Betts' in racing and Stan Grayson's in early aircraft; Menno Duerksen has long been interested in Packard and Bill Williams' dedication to mascot history extends back to the Sixties. More than a half decade was required to give birth to this Packard book. Many more decades of research, however, are represented in the overall effort.

Selection of the authors and the original outline for the book itself were the work of Richard M. Langworth. As a member of the staff of Automobile Quarterly, he directed the Packard project from 1973 until his departure from the magazine in January 1975. In addition to his authorship of two chapters, he was responsible for the first editing of chapters one to six and twenty-four to thirty-one—and he was an important consultant for further of the historical text sections of the book. In this regard as well, the continuing and valuable advice and counsel of Jim Bradley, George Hamlin and C.A. Leslie should be mentioned; their contribution to the total project extended considerably beyond the individual chapters which bear their names as author.

Some note should be made regarding the format of this book. The Packard Motor Car Company—it will be agreed by anyone who has looked into the subject—did not bear the historian in mind as it coursed through the decades. The inconsistencies, the contradictions Packard left in its wake are monumental, the official Packard record a tangled web. Much of the history which follows is new—if history can be termed such, and if not, the word in this instance is apt in any case. It is not so much that the Packard saga is being rewritten—this is not a revisionist volume—it is simply that a good deal of history is being set down for the first time. It is remarkable that so venerable and tradition-bound a company as Packard would have chosen so often to ignore or obfuscate its own past. But it did.

And sometimes, even when it did not, the results remain open to varying interpretations, all of which have the seeds of historical truth. Packard was too confounding a company to lend itself to matter-of-fact analysis—and its history was too complex to allow for a strictly-adhered-to calendrical approach. Consequently, although to a general extent, the Packard story herewith is followed chronologically, there are several excursions which carry the narrative out of the specific years and into a specific subject. It is important, for example, that for an overall understanding of the place of the prewar Junior Packards in the company's history that these cars be examined by themselves and in the context of the prevailing social forces which prompted their introduction. Likewise the Clipper, another departure from the traditional and carefully traveled norm of the company and one which bridged two distinct eras of the firm's history, is best detailed in the context of the prevailing forces within the industry which brought it into being. And an individual examination of the Twin Six/Twelve of the Thirties allows both for a detailed telling of that car's intriguing "pre-history" as well as a closer look at Packard's varying policies regarding custom coachwork during the classic years.

Note should be made too regarding style usage in this book. The Packard Motor Car Company chose to confuse itself—and probably the public then and the enthusiast ever since—with a Kafka-esque labyrinth of designations for its cars which has to be quite unique in the annals of the American automobile. The sorting out of its history was perhaps easier on occasion than determining how to designate a particular Packard for a particular year. Riddle. When is a One Twenty not a One Twenty? When it is a One-Twenty or a 120—or for that matter an Eight, as Packard was occasionally wont to call it. Consistency is best served for reader understanding; history is best served by allegiance to the mode chosen at the time by Packard; explanatory footnotes abound in the text, in the interest of both accuracy and comprehension.

To begin to list here the scores of persons interviewed by the sixteen authors in the preparation of this work would be a task fraught with difficulty, as well as diplomatic peril. As with any volume of history the composition of which is the result of primary source material solely, this book represents a roster of contributions and contributors which cannot with justice be qualitatively assessed or given priority. All sources and contributors are listed in the bibliographic section of this book, and our profound gratitude is extended to each of them for their assistance in this massive project. It would benefit the reader here, however, to be given an inkling of what lies ahead, as well as an idea of the manner in which this book was approached, and to accomplish this a sampling of primary sources might be instructive. For Packard's earliest years, for example, Roger Turreff White and Belva Hatcher Sanford, grandson and daughter respectively of George Weiss and William Hatcher who, with the Packard brothers, started it all in 1899; Warren Packard, grandson of William Doud Packard; Mrs. Myron C. Summers, niece of James Ward Packard; Carolyn Kirkham Raymond, daughter of George Kirkham, who bought the first Packard sold in 1900; David Blackmore, son of George Blackmore who became the company's first dealer that same year; Ward Schryver and Wesley Fetch, son and nephew respectively of Henry and Tom, Packard's chief mechanic and Old Pacific's transcontinental driver; H. Jay Raymond who as a boy worked in the Packard factory in Warren. Providing their Packard reminiscences through the years were Henry B. Joy, Jr., Alvan Macauley, Jr., Edward Macauley, Jr.; sales managers and administrators of the classic years, Hugh Hitchcock, Jr., Wayne Bellows, Harry T. Gardner. And the designers: Ray Dietrich, Alexis de Sakhnoffsky, Howard Darrin, Al Prance of Briggs, Duncan McRae of Studebaker, Enos Derham, son of the founder of Derham, Tom Hibbard and Alex Tremulis. The memories of the chief stylists:

John Reinhart, Richard Teague, William D. Schmidt. The engineers: William D. Allison, William H. Graves, Forest R. McFarland, Ross Taylor; Eleanor Paton, daughter of Clyde Paton; Nicholas Van Ranst, son of Cornelius Van Ranst; Charles H. Vincent, brother of Jesse Vincent and doyen of the Packard Proving Grounds, and his successor at Utica, Roy Frailing. Executive staff personnel of the postwar years: James J. Nance; Roger Bremer and Richard Stout of Product Planning; James Marks and Robert Laughna of Purchasing; plant managers Arne A. Kesti and Richard Collins. And Studebaker president Harold Churchill; from Henney, president Charles Russell Feldmann, sales manager Newell Steinmetz, stylist Richard Arbib, engineer Norman Pinnow and chief inspector Clarence Hibst. The list could go on and on.

Equally lengthy would be the list of documentary sources consulted. Again, the reader is referred to the bibliography. Suffice to say here that sources ranged from the late Nineteenth Century diaries of James Ward Packard (the Tom Summers Collection) and William Doud Packard (the Packard Electric Company Archives) and the early Twentieth Century correspondence and memoranda of Henry B. Joy (Henry B. Joy Papers, Bentley Historical Library, The University of Michigan), through board minutes dating from Packard's earliest years and the Alvan Macauley correspondence of the classic era to Jim Nance's alternately desperate and poignant letters and memos of the late Fifties as the Packard company was collapsing all around him (Studebaker-Packard Papers, George Arents Research Library, Syracuse University). Packard literature consulted was in the thousands of pieces; it would be impossible to more closely estimate it than that.

Most of the photographs accompanying the text of this book are historic, never before published and originally were the property of the Packard Motor Car Company. They are now part of the National Automotive History Collection of the Detroit Public Library. Neither the incredible historic value of that collection nor the important part the Detroit library played in this Packard book project can be underestimated. The nucleus around which the Packard collection of the library was built was the acquisition in 1956, as earlier mentioned, of the Packard photo archives upon the company's move to South Bend. Augmenting this was the discovery by L. Scott Bailey a short while later of sixty further cartons of Packard photographs in South Bend which, upon the company's transfer of manufacturing operations to Canada, were spirited away to the Detroit library as well. Further to this was the arrival later of still more historic photographs, many of these smuggled out of the plant during what one gentleman who was there at the time has described as the "last days in the bunker."

Numerous others contributed photographs and illustrations for this book; they are noted individually in the credits section. Special mention should be given Automobile Quarterly's chief of research Henry Austin Clark, Jr., who combed his vast photographic collection for us on many occasions; to Brad Skinner, who contributed additional research and documentation equally often; and to the good people of Harrah's Automobile Collection who offered invaluable assistance throughout the project. Special mention should be given the ten photographers whose Packard portraits appear in the color portfolios, the owners who graciously prepared their cars for the photography sessions, and the numerous others who contributed illustrations, reminiscences and counsel. A cliché it may be, but a book such as this one owes so much to so many. Our profound thanks go to everyone who helped.

One feels during the writing of this preface that the reader is perhaps being too long delayed from the story that follows. So on with it, the glorious and compelling saga of Packard. Allow me first, however, to introduce you to the authors who will relate it for you.

—Beverly Rae Kimes 7

In 1954 TERRY MARTIN, at age seventeen, bought his first antique car, a 1929 Buick for thirty dollars. He joined the Antique Automobile Club of America in 1957, assisting in the organization of the West Virginia Region that year and becoming its vice-president. Under his editorship the region's newsletter won several AACA awards. He spent eight years collecting and restoring automobiles with his father, their number ultimately running to fifty, comprising numerous American marques ranging in model years from 1900 to 1951 and including both a single-cylinder and an eight-cylinder Packard. In 1962, with his wife and their three children, he moved to Warren, Ohio. It was in 1968, at the annual Hershey meet, that he saw for the first time a Packard which had been built in Warren, the 1900 Model B from the Harrah collection. Returning home—and realizing that the Warren years of the Packard company had been the least chronicled in the company's history—he placed an article in the *Warren Tribune* requesting local residents who had been associated with the company to contact him. It was the beginning of more than a half decade of correspondence and interviews with descendants of Warren, Ohio Packard owners or workers from as far away as Texas and California.

A native of Wisconsin, with a master's degree in Library Science from Carnegie Institute, JAMES J. BRADLEY has been curator of the National Automotive History Collection of the Detroit Public Library since 1958. The Packard archives in the library—doubtless the largest collection of Packard documents and illustrations in the world—are in his care. He is a frequent author and contributor to automobile books and magazines, and he has been research-writer for the last two editions of *Automobiles of America*, the volume published by the Automobile Manufacturers Association. In addition to numerous assignments as a consultant in the field of automotive history, he is a member of the advisory committee of the National Motor Sports Hall of Fame, the chairman of the Cugnot Awards Committee of the Society of Automotive Historians and a field judge for the annual Greenfield Village Old Car Festival. He lives in Royal Oak, Michigan with his wife and three children.

The former owner of a 1948 Custom Eight sedan affectionately named "Fat Albert" and disposed of when he concluded what he really wanted was a prewar open Packard, RICHARD M. LANGWORTH has been writing professionally about the cars from East Grand Boulevard, among numberless others, for nearly a decade. Joining the editorial staff of *Automobile Quarterly* in 1970, his first story for the magazine, "The Glorious Madness of Kaiser-Frazer," and extensive further research on that subject led to his first book, the award-winning *Kaiser-Frazer: Last Onslaught on Detroit*. Leaving *Automobile Quarterly* in 1975 to become a freelance writer, shortly thereafter he ventured as well into publishing, establishing Dragonwyck Publishing Ltd. That company produces Packard Automobile Classics' quarterly magazine, *The Packard Cormorant*, and in 1977 published its first book, *The Hot One: Chevrolet 1955-1957*. Feature editor for *Car Classics* and classic car editor for Consumer Guide Publications, he is a contributor to such other magazines as *American Way*, *Automobil Cronik* and *Special-Interest Autos*. Richard Langworth has authored books on the postwar Chrysler, Hudson and Studebaker, and has co-authored, with Graham Robson, a definitive history of Triumph. He lives in New Hampshire with his wife Barbara.

Born, raised and educated in Texas, DON E. WEBER resides in Corpus Christi today and spends many of his avocational hours in aesthetic and cultural pursuits, which interests doubtless sparked his dedication to the Packard marque. He has owned a 1929 645 sport phaeton by Dietrich and a 1939 Packard Twelve touring

cabriolet by Brunn. His collection today includes a 1914 Model 1448 seven-passenger touring car, and it is the pre-World War I Packard which has become his special interest in historic research and literature collecting. A member of ten automotive clubs including Packard Automobile Classics, Packards International and the Society of Automotive Historians, he is a past director of the Lone Star Region of the Classic Car Club of America. An independent oil producer, real estate investor and general partner of Southwest Exploration Company, he holds directorships in the Art Museum of South Texas and the San Antonio Museum of Transportation, and the chairmanship of the Public Broadcasting Service's technical committee and the South Texas Educational Broadcasting Council, among numerous other organizational affiliations.

Since 1968 and his graduation from Pennsylvania State University with a master of arts degree in English, STAN GRAYSON has pursued a career in writing and photography. A Vietnam veteran who served as an Army newsman and photographer, he spent a year after his discharge in Germany as a newspaper reporter and freelance photojournalist. His photographs have appeared in *Time*, *The Washington Post* and diverse other publications. A lifelong car enthusiast who worked as a mechanic during his university days, he joined *Automobile Quarterly* magazine in 1973. Since then his research and writing have focused on automobiles of all types and eras. In addition, aircraft and aircraft engines, particularly those of World War I and earlier, have been an enduring interest of his for many years. He admits to liking all sorts of cars equally well but with a preference for sporting machinery of any vintage. He is senior editor of *Automobile Quarterly* magazine and lives in Princeton, New Jersey.

For over fifty years, L. MORGAN YOST has owned and driven Packards, beginning in Kenilworth, Illinois with his father's 1927 club sedan. He bought his own first Packard—a used 733 roadster—in 1932. As a youth he amassed literature from Chicago automobile shows and showrooms, this material forming the nucleus of his extensive Packard library. During high school days, he designed and built a speedster body for his Model T Ford, and he planned to become a custom body designer, which ambition was revised to the profession of architecture in college days. But his interest in automobiles never lagged. Setting out in 1950 to gather together a representative selection of Packards, he has owned some thirty-seven models, his collection now honed to ten ranging from a 1910 Model Thirty to a 1952 Pan American, and including a 1933 Twelve Dietrich sport phaeton (a 100-point car and multi-prize winner), a Second Series Twin Six landaulet, a Dietrich convertible coupe on the 243 chassis, a 734 boattail speedster and a two-off 1936 Hibbard coupe de ville on the One Twenty chassis. A member of the major automobile clubs, he served as president of the Illinois Region of the AACA for three terms. A few years ago he retired as an architect, moved from Kenilworth to Cherokee Village, Arkansas, built a new lakeside home, and a garage for his Packard collection.

On Labor Day weekend of 1967, C.A. LESLIE, JR. realized a dream he had held for nearly thirty-five years. He discovered and purchased a 1932 Twin Six dual cowl phaeton. Since then his collection has grown to include four more Twin Sixes from 1932 (a phaeton, a seven-passenger touring car, a rumble-seat coupe-roadster, a five-passenger sedan) as well as a 1933 Twelve sedan-cabriolet, a 1930 734 speedster roadster by Heaton, a 1932 Standard Eight phaeton and, for variety, a 1928 Hudson with town car coachwork by Murphy. He is a member of eight automobile clubs, a past director of the Oil Belt Region of the Classic Car Club of America, charter member and president of the Cimarron Region of the Antique

Automobile Club of America and past president of the Oklahoma Corvette Club. In 1969 he founded the Packard Twin Six Association. A charter member and past president of the Oklahoma Chapter of the Society of Manufacturing Engineers, he is president of Aico Corporation (manufacturer of aircraft valves, cylinders and accessories, also components for computers and tape transport mechanisms) and Architectural Hardware, Inc. He lives in Oklahoma City with his wife Mary K., their three sons and his Packards.

The first car RICHARD K. PHILLIPS owned was a 1937 120-C convertible coupe with 75,000 miles on a broken speedometer and bought in the fall of 1952 for two hundred dollars as a better way than the streetcar to commute to classes at the University of Pittsburgh. His earliest memories, similarly, were of Packard—helping his father wash a new 1936 One Twenty. A Packard family, the Phillipses would ultimately own eleven examples of the marque, including a 1939 Super-8 coupe, a 1942 Clipper, a 1947 Clipper Super Eight and a 1951 Patrician 400. The collegiate convertible coupe, sold in 1953 for a low-mileage 1948 Super Eight, was repurchased in 1959 (for seventy-five dollars this time), having been traced through a labyrinth of five owners and discovered in shameful disrepair in a tin shack in Glassport, Pennsylvania. It was painstakingly restored in subsequent years, became a prize winner—and Richard Phillips has since become a devoted enthusiast and historian of the Junior Packards of the prewar era. He is district sales manager of the Fiber Glass Division of PPG Industries and lives in Souderton, Pennsylvania with his wife and four children.

A resident of Maryland since 1962, GEORGE HAMLIN was born in Des Moines and graduated from Iowa State University. He has been a member of Packard Automobile Classics since 1964, and has served on its board of regents since 1966. He currently holds the post of vice-president for regions. He is a frequent contributor to, and senior editor of, Packard Automobile Classics' magazine, *The Packard Cormorant*. His work has also appeared in other automobile publications. He assisted in the founding of the Professional Car Society and the Milestone Car Society, and belongs to several other automobile associations including the Society of Automotive Historians. He has been a Packard owner since 1956 and has owned fifteen cars ranging from model years 1936 through 1956. A technical writer for the U.S. Navy, he lives in the country with his wife Bee, two cats and, as he notes, "sundry aging vehicles."

Born in Baltimore on May 16th, 1948, DWIGHT HEINMULLER was driven home from the hospital in his father's 1941 Super-8 One-Sixty. Two decades later he once again became intimately involved with Packards, and has remained so ever since. A member of Packard Automobile Classics since 1969, he has been its projects vice-president since 1970; a member of Mid-Atlantic Packards also since 1969, he was a director from 1975-1977 and the editor of the club's publication "Hexagon" from 1971-1974. He has been associated with the Old Dominion Packard Club since 1971, and was tourmaster of Packard Automobile Classics' National Meet in 1973. His extensive research into Packard Motor Car Company history began in 1971 with long-distance phone calls. From 1967 to 1978 he was manager for Giant Food, Inc. in Maryland. During the latter year he moved to Bar Harbor, Maine where today he is proprietor of Reynolds Mens Wear. His collection of Packards includes five examples of the marque from 1948 to 1956.

Having acquired an absorbing interest in railroad and automotive history by age eight, JOHN B. MONTVILLE began collecting automotive material in 1940 and has specialized in gathering research on the truck industry since about 1950.

For a number of years he worked full time as an accountant and later tax advisor, but recently has subordinated his financial consulting work to his commitment to the study of commercial vehicle history. In 1970 he contributed the complete truck section for Automobile Quarterly's *The American Car Since 1775*. And in 1973 he authored the book *Mack*, the definitive history of the company, which received the Cugnot Award of the Society of Automotive Historians. His home and his commercial vehicle archives are in Poughkeepsie, New York.

A newspaperman by profession and a "committed Packard man" by his own admission, MENNO DUERKSEN apprenticed in automotive machine shops at age fourteen, later did a bit of dirt track racing in Oklahoma and the Southwest, worked for the U.S. Office of War Information during World War II and United Press in Europe for several years thereafter. For the past fourteen years, avocationally, he has written an historical column for *Cars & Parts* magazine. He lives in Memphis, Tennessee, and recently acquired the sixth Packard he has owned in his lifetime, a One Twenty club coupe.

His collection currently including three Packards (a 1947 Custom Super Clipper, a 1951 200 Deluxe and a 1953 Caribbean) as well as thousands of advertisements covering the company's entire history, ROGER ABBOTT has been active in the old-car hobby since the late Fifties, has been involved in mechanical restoration work on historic cars since the early Sixties, and in a reproduction parts enterprise since the early Seventies. A member of Packards International, as well as four multi-marque clubs, he lives in Pasadena, California, and is ever on the lookout to "collect anything connected with Packard."

A native and lifelong resident of Akron, Ohio, and a power plant electrician for the Goodyear Tire & Rubber Company for the past twenty-four years, BOB ZIMMERMAN has had a lifelong interest as well in Packard. His was a Packard-owning family, he learned to drive on a 1950 model and he worked two summers while in high school at a Packard dealership. In the mid-Sixties he began collecting automobile literature, deciding early on to specialize in Packard. A past president of the Midwest Region of Packards International and presently editor of its newsletter, he is a member also of Packard Automobile Classics among other automobile clubs. He owns and is currently restoring a 1954 Patrician.

His interest in automotive history dating back to the early Twenties, CHARLES BETTS has always harbored an especial enthusiasm for motor sport, and through the years has amassed an impressive library on the subject. In 1948 he compiled and published the book *Auto Racing Winners*, and since 1950 he has been on the staff of the official publication of the Antique Automobile Club of America, *Antique Automobile*, being honored in 1954 for his services to that magazine with the Thomas McKean Memorial Trophy. He was one of the founders of the Society of Automotive Historians in 1969 and has served as its secretary since 1976. He lives in Yardley, Pennsylvania with his wife Vicki.

Beginning his collection of automotive mascots in the early Sixties simply to remain "active in the hobby during the winter months when my Rolls was in storage," W.C. WILLIAMS turned his avocation into his profession several years ago. His Pulfer & Williams company specializes in supplying emblems, nameplates, mascots, et al. to automotive restorers, and he has spent the last half dozen years in intensive research into the history of the ornaments which have graced automobiles through the years, a book on this subject to be published soon. He lives in New Hampshire with his wife Dorothy and their four children.

CONTENTS

CHAPTER ONE

THE PACKARDS OF WARREN

The Years Before the Marque

AUTHOR: TERRY MARTIN

History is often made with but a single phrase. Surely in the chronicle of the automobile there exists no more sterling example of this than what Mr. Winton is supposed to have said to Mr. Packard one balmy day during the spring of 1899. Probably no other conversational exchange in automobile lore has so captured the fancy of historians—and none, one might project, has been so widely reiterated. Indeed most histories of the Packard automobile begin with this famous meeting. And—by doing so—leave a good bit of Packard history untold.

Emerson's dictum that "there is properly no history, only biography" merits some qualification, of course, but to present the history of the Packard automobile as welling up from one casual meeting with one feisty Scotsman is to contextually put the car in an historical vacuum. Some biography is in order, some background to lend perspective, to place in context the events leading up to the Packard resolve to build an automobile. Before one has Mr. Packard meet Mr. Winton, one must first meet the Packard family.

For the past one hundred fifty years the Packards of Warren, Ohio have been intimately associated with the history of that city and the Trumbull County area. A Packard was a pioneer settler south of Warren, a Packard was a pioneer in the commerce of Warren, and two Packards were pioneers in its industry.

The Packard family had been in America since the Seventeenth Century, the first to arrive in the Colonies being named Samuel, who traveled from England in 1638 in the good ship *Diligence* and settled at West Bridgewater, Massachusetts. Long before Horace Greeley suggested it, the descendants of Samuel Packard were going west, from Winchester, Virginia; Washington, Pennsylvania and other points east into the Western Reserve. By 1825 their number included William Packard who arrived that year in the Austintown area of Ohio, just south of Warren and at that time part of Trumbull County. Shortly thereafter he and his wife Julia relocated in Lordstown, five miles south of Warren, to take up farming and begin raising a family. Their first child, Warren, was born on June 1st, 1828. There would be quite a few more.

In the years between 1828 and 1847, William Packard fathered nine children—and then developed a bit of wanderlust. In 1849, at the age of forty-six, he left his wife and children, aged two to twenty-one, for California. Gold had been discovered—and William Packard would spend the rest of his life looking for it and other means to a fortune, never to return to Lordstown. After a while his family heard he was dead and stopped writing—while he, who was very much alive, assumed he had been abandoned. Contact was lost, for nearly twenty-five years. Finally, three years before his death four of his now-grown sons learned of their father's whereabouts and visited him in a cabin at the foot of Greenhorn Mountain in California. William Packard never found the gold he was looking for. The Packard family Bible records that at his death on December 11th, 1877, he was a judge in Kernville County, California.

His was a life like many others of that era: the farm, the large family, the desertion of a past for a future filled with promise, the promise unrealized. Were it not for his paternity, William Packard would have been altogether forgotten. But among his nine children was Warren Packard who would be one of the towering figures in the early history of the town for which he was named—and among Warren Packard's children would be two sons who would make the family name famous the world over. First, the father.

In 1846 Warren Packard left the Lordstown farm to seek his fortune at the county seat of old Trumbull. Eighteen years old, he trudged into Warren, all his earthly possessions tied in the proverbial cotton handkerchief. Though his father was three years away from his decision to seek a fortune in gold, young Warren had probably already made up his mind that for him a less precious metal was the key to success. Through the influence of a brother-in-law, Eli K. Weisell, he obtained a position with Milton Graham who was then operating the pioneer iron store in that area. During his first year in Warren, he attended school much of the time, paying his board by doing chores nights and mornings, and on Saturdays driving Mr. Graham's team to Niles and Youngstown to buy iron and nails for sale the following week at the store. His duties also included taking care of the team, as well as one or two cows, sawing stove wood for the house and shop, and at the noon hour "tending store" while everyone else lunched. It was a long day—from five in the morning till nine at night, but apparently young Warren thrived on it, for he was to maintain the same exacting schedule until his death. The rewards would be ample.

During his second year with Graham, Warren received board and a hundred dollars in wages. Four years later he owned the Graham store, as well as the shop started by Charles Reuben Harmon in competition to it. "Busy till night, pleasing myself mightily to see what a deal of business goes off a man's hands when he stays by it," Samuel Pepys had recorded in his diary a couple of centuries previous. Warren Packard didn't keep a diary. He probably didn't have the time. The following year, on September 21st, 1852, he paused long enough to get married, to Sylvia Camp, daughter of Alanson Camp of Warren.

In 1854 Warren, with brother John R. and uncle Dr. Daniel B. Packard, established Packard & Company in Greenville, Pennsylvania, subsequently incorporated as Packard Hardware Company in 1892. By 1863, with the acquisition of the Thomas H. Morely store in Warren, he was proprietor of the largest iron and hardware business between Cleveland and Pittsburgh. And he was only beginning. There followed, in 1865, Packard, Cook and Company, Warren allying himself with another brother, B.F. Packard, and Madison W. Cook, that firm

On the pages preceding: Warren at the turn of the century, the Packard home sited below church. Above: The town's busiest street, circa 1871.

becoming Warren Packard and Company with Cook's retirement six years later. In 1865, too, he became the largest owner in Austin Flagstone and a partner in R.H. Barnum & Company, which was renamed The Packard & Barnum Iron Company and, with a rolling mill added to its steam forge in 1867, rolled the first merchant iron in Warren.

One day Warren Packard was summoned to New York City by Jay Gould. The Wizard of Wall Street informed him of his desire for a half interest in Packard & Barnum, in return for which Gould would sell all the scrap iron on his Erie Railway to Packard's company. "You can weigh the scrap yourself," Jay Gould said. Somehow, despite the attractiveness of the proposition, Warren found himself saying no to Gould, no mean feat in those days. Perhaps later he wished he hadn't. His venture into iron manufacture was not made at a propitious time. Many iron mills would soon be operated without profit, his included. Eventually he lost almost all of the $200,000 he had invested. Another loss was suffered with his W. & A.J. Packard Company, A.J. being yet another brother. This firm successfully supplied the "Hardware Block" in Youngstown until the panic of '73 and a fire combined to scuttle the venture.

But Warren Packard had so well diversified his enterprises that failure in one or two did not spell financial ruin. Far from it. By the 1860's Warren Packard was a lumber man as well.

All this began during the building of the Atlantic & Great Western Railroad (later the Erie System), for which Warren Packard furnished probably half the lumber, in collaboration with S.L. Abell. They had bought the Stowe Mill in Braceville (outside Warren) in 1862, and a year later brought Harmon Austin into the enterprise and began establishing a solid reputation. When the Titusville & Pithole Plank Road people wanted three million feet of plank in three months during the oil excitement, they knew right where to look. Packard-Abell-Austin got the job. Thereafter, in collaboration with either Austin or Abell, Warren Packard established several more mills around Warren, by the 1870's owned others at Charleston and Huntington, West Virginia, and in 1876 associated himself with Will Payne and J. W. Spangenberg in eight thousand acres of timber land in Kentucky where two saw mills were put to work in 1887.

This flurry of activity might lead one to question whether Warren Packard knew the meaning of the word recreation. Actually he did. True, his tour of Europe in 1867 was largely to lay a foundation for the direct importation of hardware, which branch of his business he operated profitably until prohibitive U.S. tariff laws were enacted. And much of the 1874 winter he spent with his family on the Pacific Coast—ostensibly a vacation—was devoted to securing valuable trade connections. But his

The father and his sons, photographed in the early 1890's. From the left, Warren Packard, James Ward Packard and William Doud Packard.

vacations at Chautauqua Lake, New York were more relaxing. He built the first cottage in the region and with associates purchased the farm upon which the delightful little village of Lakewood—with its plethora of summer homes today—is sited.

His personal life was, sadly, flawed by tragedy during his early years in Warren. He and his wife Sylvia had two sons born to them: Harry who died at the age of ten months, Rollo who didn't survive two years. His wife died on December 4th, 1856, when she was but twenty-three. Happily, within a few years Warren Packard discovered Mary E. Doud of Mendham, Morris County, New Jersey—and they were married November 20th, 1860. Five children were born to them: William Doud, James Ward, and three daughters, Alaska, Carlotta and Cornelia Olive.

Warren Packard died on July 28th, 1897, his second wife six years later, on October 9th, 1903. His had been a full life, as only befits a man possessed in equal measure of vision and optimism. He dared always, he faced reverses boldly, ofttimes turning them to his advantage. Probably no man was held in higher esteem in the Warren area. Association with him was a mental tonic, and his enthusiasm was contagious to others who had taken up the industrial and commercial life of the Mahoning Valley. And, most significant, was the effect of the father upon his two sons. Warren Packard's life of work gave the boys a solid foundation upon which to build. They started doing exactly that early. William Doud and James Ward were very much their father's sons.

William Doud Packard was born in Warren—where he would spend the whole of his life—on November 3rd, 1861. He was educated in Warren public schools and at Ohio State University. Early on, he gave evidence of having inherited his father's business acumen. As a boy, he and his younger brother sold newspapers and established a small printing office in the family home, using the earnings thus accumulated to pay expenses for a visit to Philadelphia's Centennial Exposition in 1876. He also learned telegraphy, of which he was soon to make practical use.

Immediately after leaving college in 1882, William Doud took a position as bookkeeper and salesman in his father's hardware store. When the store became the Warren agent for American Union Telegraph and the U.S. Express Company, the young man was made express clerk and telegraph operator. Later he would serve the same function, and operate a newsstand, at his father's hotel at Lakewood. (Apparently the elder Packard didn't *completely* relax during vacations at Chautauqua Lake.) And he would join his father in the planing mill at Warren as junior member of the firm of Warren Packard & Son.

William Doud's younger brother, James Ward, was born on November 5th, 1863. His aptitude for things mechanical was shown as early as his brother's commercial sense. He was educated in Warren public schools and later, in 1884, graduated with a mechanical engineering degree from Lehigh University in Bethlehem, Pennsylvania.

James Ward kept a daily notebook beginning in his college days which has fortunately survived. In it are notes of his bicycle trips to Allentown and Easton, and reminders of the fact that he had drawn $545 and $706 in 1883 and 1884 respectively from his father's account to cover the costs of his last two years in college.

After leaving Lehigh on August 4th, 1884, James Ward entered the shops of the Sawyer-Mann Electric Company in New York City, a pioneer incandescent lamp manufacturing concern later to be absorbed by Westinghouse. He started in the dynamo room at a dollar a day, but a month later both his wages and his responsibilities were increased when he was made superintendent of the dynamo room, and by November foreman of the mechanical department. Subsequently he applied for the first two of many patents he would earn during his lifetime—the first for a magnetic circuit and the second for an incandescent lamp bulb which would later be sold to Westinghouse. At Sawyer-Mann, James Ward gained a practical knowledge of the electrical industry, and after six years there decided it was time to move on. In 1890 he returned home. As wise decisions go, his was a particularly good one.

His brother was, James Ward knew, a consummate business man. With whom better might an ambitious young inventor team in the founding of a new company? For his part, William Doud was already well

The house Warren Packard built, High Street and Mahoning Avenue, 1874.

aware of his brother's mechanical aptitude. The familial ties that bind would find a very practical application. When James Ward asked, William Doud readily assented, both aware that their father's stature in Warren would be a boon to ready acceptance of their venture.

The official announcement of the new firm appeared in the *Warren Tribune* on June 3rd, 1890. The headline read:

NOW IT'S ASSURED
PACKARD ELECTRIC CO.,
THE NEWEST OF WARREN'S NEW ENTERPRISES

And the story went on to reveal:

"The lot is bought, the contracts are let, and the dynamos will soon be a-going. The Packard Electric Company has secured a property of two hundred feet front on North Avenue—the road to the Tube Works; two hundred feet from Park Ave., and running back two hundred feet to the Nypano, giving opportunity for a switch.

"The contracts for two buildings, one of wood, 40 x 80, two stories in height, and one of brick, one story, 16 x 30, with a boiler shed, have been let, work will be commenced immediately, and it is the hope of the proprietors that the machinery will be running by September.

"Associated with the Messrs. J.W. and Wm. D. Packard in their enterprise will be a gentleman who has been engaged in the sale of electrical goods, and in all probability also Messrs. C.F. Clapp, M.B. Tayler, and Jacob Perkins of this city, making a company of such strength, both of ability and finance, that when the wonderfully rapid development of electrical manufacturers is considered it would seem that it could not fail of success.

"As has already been stated in these columns, the new company will probably make dynamos, lamps, and electrical specialties. Mr. J. Ward Packard is not only an eminent electrician, but a mechanical engineer as well, and it may be just as certain that in the construction of the new plant some valuable improvements will be introduced. For one thing, the power will be conveyed to the different machines not by belts or steam pipes, but by electric wires, the motive power of each machine being its own dynamo."

Several notes of interest arise from this newspaper report. First, the scarcely concealed enthusiasm of the editors for the enterprise. Second, the early use of electric motors for each individual machine. This was obviously a forward-thinking concern. (From ten employees in 1890, Packard Electric grew to 13,000 today and status as one of the largest automotive wiring suppliers in the United States. It became part of the General Motors family in the early Thirties.) And third—though no one knew it at the time—that forty-by-eighty two-story wood structure would house the nascent Packard automobile.

On June 5th, 1890, in the downtown Warren office of notary public

A NEW DEPARTURE

In the Hardware Trade!

:o:

WARREN PACKARD & CO.

:o:

IN this, the 29th year of our business, taking it for granted that we have "touched bottom," and we can safely extend our business, we have resolved to trim our sails, throw our banner to the breeze, and "go in," with renewed vigor and confidence,

FOR THE CAMPAIGN OF 1879!

in order to concentrate our means, and give our business here our undivided attention, we have closed our Youngstown store and removed the Goods to Warren. In addition to the above we have exchanged a lot of real estate with parties East, for a

LARGE AMOUNT OF

Miscellaneous Hardware & Agricultural Implements.

This and the Youngstown stock we have placed in our 2d story and warehouse, separate from our other goods, and shall proceed to convert them into cash. To accomplish this result speedily, we shall offer them at prices

BARELY COVERING THE COST OF MANUFACTURE!

This stock may be classified as follows: I.—A large lot of Whips, Halters, some Saddlery, Carriage Goods, Buggy Wood Work, Plows, Cultivators, and Coffee Pots, not kept by us regularly.

ALL NEW, IN GOOD ORDER, AND WILL BE SOLD AT MANUFACTURERS WHOMESALE PRICES!

You can buy a Whip from us at 40c. that you can buy *anywhere* for 75c.

We Have 60 Dozen Genuine Westenholm Knives at 19c. Each.

THEY CANNOT BE IMPORTED NOW AT THIS PRICE—BOYS, COME IN!

3.—A big lot of bulky stuff, such as Baskets, Tubs and Pails, Coal Scuttles, Lanterns, etc., which we have no room for, and will sell at cost, as we *must* have the room.

IT WILL PAY YOU TO BUY THESE GOODS NOW!

TO USE WHEN GRANT GETS HIS THIRD TERM.

4.—A car load of Miscellaneous Goods, old stock, odd sizes, damaged goods, some of them got wet, and odds and ends generally. The statement that Old Ben Wade made about the Cleveland *Leader* would apply with force to this lot, to wit: "It is the d——dest meanest" lot of goods in Ohio. These goods will be sold for anything we can get.

LAST, BUT NOT LEAST!

OUR GENERAL STOCK OF

Builders' Hardware, Iron, Nails, Lead and Oils, Miscellaneous Goods, etc., will be Kept Full and Complete.

:o:

OUR PLANING MILL

Will be kept runnine in the interest of our customers. We are prepared to furnish bill direct from our mills in Pennsylvania, or from our yard here, and will not be undersold.s

We Mean This!

Come and look over the Youngstown stock, whether you want anything or not.

WARREN, Ohio, May 1st, 1879. WARREN PACKARD & CO.

Advertisement in The Mahoning Dispatch, *June 6th, 1879.*

Advertisement appearing in the city directory of Warren, 1894.

Thomas H. Gillmer, six men met to draw up the Packard Electric Company's incorporation papers. In addition to the five mentioned in the *Tribune* story, there was Justin W. Spangenberg, he presumably being the gentleman identified in the report as having been "engaged in the sale of electrical goods." The newspaper erred in that regard, Spangenberg, as we've seen, instead having been associated in the saw mill business with the Packard brothers' father. He had been associated with other Warren businessmen as well, one particular partnership being with the Austin & Pendleton machine shop and foundry, producers of saw mills and steam traction locomotives.

The designer for the latter concern was Edward P. Cowles, who in 1878 had vied his 14,255-pound steam road vehicle named The Green Bay Machine against The Oshkosh steamer during trials held in Wisconsin concomitant to that state legislature's offer of a $10,000 reward to any citizen who could come up with a mechanical conveyance which would be "a cheap and practical substitute for use of horses and other animals on the highway and farm." Cowles lost the 201-mile race (the winner averaging a little over six miles an hour), but apparently not his enthusiasm for finding a substitute for the horse. He would head the drafting department at Packard Electric—and he would also assist James Ward Packard with his first designs for an automobile in 1896. Spangenberg, incidentally, would retain his association with Pendleton, and the two of them would produce their first automobile in the shops of Trumbull Manufacturing in Warren in 1899—the same year as the first Packard appeared.

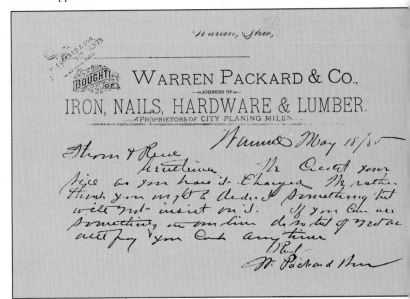

Warren Packard & Co. business correspondence from May of 1885.

Above: The first Packard Electric building, 1894, also home of The New York and Ohio Company; the first Packard automobile would be begun in the addition on the right. Below: The house built in 1898 alongside the factory, to serve as an office for Packard Electric.

Historians have often stated that Cowles joined Packard in 1893, and collaborated with James Ward that year in designing a horseless carriage which never left the drawing board. Recent examination of James Ward Packard's handwritten diary, however, proves conclusively this was not the case. There is no mention whatsoever of any desire to build a horseless carriage during 1893 or 1894, and Cowles was not hired in 1893, but 1896.

Of Packard Electric's other directors, M.B. Tayler was a twenty-nine-year-old Warren banker with an especial interest in promoting local businesses, C.F. Clapp was vice-president of the Second National Bank of Warren, and Jacob Perkins was a wealthy landowner, controlling most of the land in the northern section of Warren. It was Perkins who had sold Packard Electric the land on which to build. And the new factory was completed exactly on schedule in September, the first meeting held there on October 6th, 1890.

Several months later, on January 27th, 1891, the same group of men decided that if one corporation was good, two would be even better, and they met to do something about it. Unfortunately, their call to Warren citizens to subscribe stock toward the enterprise produced meager results, and James Ward Packard made an appeal to some former associates and acquaintances in New York for the desired financial aid. It was soon forthcoming, and the new firm's name logically followed. It was called simply The New York & Ohio Company.

The New York & Ohio Company—incorporated, for tax advantages, in the state of West Virginia, its predecessor having Ohio incorporation—was begun for the purpose of manufacturing Packard incandescent lamps and transformers. John W. Peale of New York was elected president, W.D. Packard secretary-treasurer, and J.W. Packard general superintendent. At this time the Packard Electric Company moved out of its original building and leased both it and its equipment—for one year and a rental of $425 a month—to the new corporation. (Packard Electric would move into a new addition to the plant completed in July.) It was the new company to which William Doud Packard devoted most of his energies, traveling as its salesman and factory representative to every large city from St. Louis to Boston in the 1890's and into the new century to promote Packard products to city-owned and private lighting companies. And, on occasion, he looked around for engines with which his younger brother might experiment back in Warren.

If there be one keynote to James Ward's career, it is that he was always adamant in securing sufficient provision for testing and design. No matter the endeavor, he was quick to establish laboratories for research work, departments for formulating improvements, experimental rooms for building and testing models. A fascination for original work led him repeatedly into new adventures.

It is scarcely surprising that the horseless carriage was one of them. It would not be untoward to assume that a man of James Ward's vision could look ahead to a horseless age, though neither steam nor—surprisingly—electric power seemed to interest him.

The first note in his diary of any mechanical conveyance was on February 16th, 1892, when he wrote: "In New York bought 25' 4 HP naptha launch of Gas Engine & Power Co. price with fittings $1095.50." James Ward kept this launch and others he bought later at the Chautauqua Lake property, but the only indication of his desire to delve into its workings was in August 1894, when he "took launch engine apart and cleaned valve parts."

The Panic of 1893 put a damper on the electric business, and for a while operations were halted because of litigation, concerning the Edison patents, brought against Packard Electric by the General Electric Company. This lawsuit would be fought until the patents expired, and for the duration James Ward Packard found himself frequently on the road to Cleveland and the courtroom.

But the electric lamp business, while interesting, didn't stir one's blood—certainly not James Ward Packard's anyway. And the horseless carriage was fast aborning. William Doud attended the World's Columbian Exposition in Chicago in 1893 and saw a Daimler, a Benz and the few other automotive vehicles there. In Warren, the local newspaper carried stories about French electric carriages. The *Warren Chronicle* also featured ads for gasoline engines, one local dealer advertising a variety of them from one to twenty horsepower. These were really portable or stationary engines intended for farm, not automotive, use, but their existence could easily inspire an inventor's imagination. In 1895 came the *Chicago Times-Herald* contest, which is generally recognized as the signal event that spurred inventors to intense efforts in bringing America into the horseless age. And late in 1895, there finally occurred the one event above all others that convinced James Ward Packard to build an automobile.

Later, in the 1920's, William Doud's son Warren* would recall the occasion for Packard salesmen: "In the year 1895, my father . . . made a trip to Europe visiting both England and France and looked over the various automobiles running at that time. After returning, I am sure a good discussion followed with his brother, of what he saw, and they soon sent for a French tricycle, a de Dion-Bouton. They were very anxious to see how it would run over the rough American roads and also see what made it run. It proved to be more of a quadricycle than a tricycle. In place of the front wheel was added a cross between a motorcycle side car and a

dentist's chair which held the passenger. The driver sat behind on a regular bicycle saddle and steered with handle bars. The motor was a single cylinder air-cooled vertical engine geared direct to the back axle. J.W. called the French tricycle a thing of pain and sorrow. It was hard to start, made a lot of noise, was hard riding, faulty ignition, poor lubrication, gave him tire trouble, bucking carburetor and had breakages—still as crude a mechanical contrivance as it was, it held Packard's fascination and gave him something to experiment on, make improvements on, all adding to his horseless carriage experience."

Fascinating it must have been, for James Ward now exhibited real enthusiasm. On January 2nd, 1896, he subscribed for $2 to *The Horseless Age*, fledgling exponent of the automobile, and on January 6th he hired the aforementioned Edward P. Cowles as a "draftsman and pattern maker" who "commenced work in factory @ 22½ cents per hour," though on what James Ward didn't record. On May 16th, however, the diary notes: "Engage Cowles to work on motor wagon @ $12 per week 8 hrs per day," which was three dollars more than Cowles started with, "Expenses to be divided between Howry, W.D. and J.W.P." J. H. Howry was president of the Packard Electric Company Ltd. of St. Catharines, Canada, though how he became involved in the project is not stated.

Then, on January 15th, 1896, the Packards made a short trip down to New Brighton, Pennsylvania, "and examined Dr. Booth's Motor Carriage at works of Pierce Crouch Engine Co." (Carlos Booth had begun construction of his vehicle in Youngstown, Ohio, intent upon entering it in the 1895 *Chicago Times-Herald* contest, but it hadn't been completed on time.) The Booth was an assembled vehicle joining motor to a standard horse carriage, but what James Ward thought of it he does

James Ward notes his plan to do something about his automotive idea.

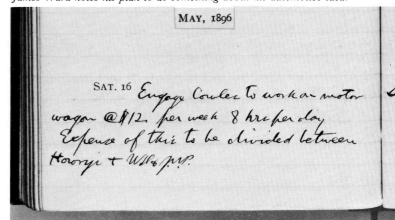

MAY, 1896

SAT. 16 Engage Cowles to work on motor wagon @ $12 per week 8 hrs per day Expense of this to be divided between Howry + W.D. & J.W.P.

---

*Warren Packard, named for his grandfather, was the only son of William Doud and Anna Storer Packard. He was born October 5th, 1892 and died in a plane crash near Detroit in 1929.

not record. And as suddenly as it had peaked, his enthusiasm seemed to temporarily ebb, for no further record of his interest in the horseless carriage appears in his diary for 1896. But late in the year a significant personage had arrived by the name of Henry A. Schryver.

Schryver was an expert machinist who tended the manufacturing equipment at the Packard Electric and New York & Ohio companies, and who later ran his own shop in Warren. Most importantly, however, he did most of the machine work on the first Packard car.

In his daily log book, Schryver noted that on January 1st, 1897, he had done some drawings of a horseless carriage for James Ward. One cannot be sure whether these were for a new machine or improvements on the De Dion. On January 4th, he related: "Started to repair J.W. Packard's naptha engine," and further entries show that he worked on it until he finished on January 21st. Again, he did not note from whence the engine came, nor what it was possibly for, and did not mention it again that year. Eighteen ninety-six must stand, however, as the year James Ward first began working on a motorcar, although his decision to actually go into business building automobiles was still three years in the future. (The Packard Motor Car Company ran an ad later, in the April 16th, 1903 *Motor Age*, stating that "Packard knew what he was doing when he started with the 1 cylinder 7 years ago.")

Despite all this documentation, and to the surprise of this writer, there is not one word about a horseless carriage in the 1897 diaries of James Ward or William Doud, nor in the minutes of the Packard Electric Company. We can only assume that there was nothing significant to report. Having learned everything he could from the De Dion, James Ward discarded it. (Eventually it was given to young Warren to play with.) And having exhausted the educational possibilities of the various engines he

Below: The 1898 model Winton that James Ward Packard bought. Right: The men of Winton Motor Carriage Company, photographed in 1898.

and his brother had procured, James Ward was now ready—and anxious—for something new and different with which to experiment.

Just about this time an inventive fellow named Alexander Winton decided to go into the automobile business in Cleveland.

One is confronted now, of course, with the episode which began this chapter. It is one of the most enduring legends in the history of the automobile—and some historians think today it is just that and no more, doubting the conversational exchange did indeed take place. In the December 28th, 1901 edition of *The Autocar*, however, correspondent Hugh Dolnar, in writing about the new Packard motorcar, gives his version of what happened, which is interesting in the extreme: "Mr. Packard, of Ohio, feeling a desire to enter the ranks of practical automobile users too strong to be resisted," he related, "went to Mr. Winton, of Cleveland, Ohio, for a waggon, and explained to him that while he regarded the Winton as a most admirable creation, there were yet some details in which he wished his prospective vehicle to embody certain more or less novel ideas of Mr. Packard's own. Mr. Winton, who is English born, replied with all the suave consideration of a true British manufacturer to the effect that the Winton waggon as it stood was the ripened and perfected product of many years of lofty thought, aided by mechanical skill of the highest grade, and could not be improved in any detail, and that if Mr. Packard wanted any of his own cats and dogs worked into a waggon, he had better build it himself, as he, Winton, would not stultify himself by any departure whatever from his own incontestably superior productions."

Mr. Dolnar, who was to become perhaps the most noteworthy American automotive journalist of the pre-World War I era, erred in a couple of particulars in his account, as we will see, but it is nonetheless fascinating to have such early documentary evidence, second-hand though it may be, as to the exchange of remarks between the two men involved. And since in Mr. Dolnar's long article about the Packard he mentions James Ward's corresponding with him, it is not hazardous to assume that it was James Ward himself who told Dolnar of the episode. And Dolnar obviously exercised a little poetic license in its retelling.

William Doud fleshed out the circumstances of the episode even more in his daily notes, and these provide fascinating reading as well, beginning with an entry in late May 1898 which introduces us to Tom Fetch. Fetch was then superintendent of the Jefferson Light & Power plant which the Packards owned and some years later would be immortalized as the man who piloted Packard's Old Pacific across the continent, breaking the Winton record. On this occasion, however, Tom and William Doud were on two wheels, bicycling from Jefferson to Ashtabula, a little less than ten miles away. The elder Packard brother was an enthusiastic cyclist, traveling to and from work usually by bicycle and joining friends for Sunday rides of twenty to thirty miles. Tom Fetch,

apparently, was a bicycling devotee as well.

But William Doud's enjoyment of bicycle travel was of necessity curtailed during this period. He was having problems with his eyes—and was spending considerable time in Caulfield Hospital in Cleveland. No doubt his extended stays there well versed him in the goings-on at Alexander Winton's establishment, information he passed on to his brother. From his hospital bed, on Friday, July 22nd, 1898, he recorded in his daily log: "Ward here at 10:30 to investigate the Winton Motor carriage—out riding with Mr. Winton." In James Ward's diary of the same date is this remark: "To Cleveland tried Winton Motor carriage—fine price $1000.00—immediate delivery."

It is interesting to note that Winton gave the demonstration himself. Rumor had it that he had already contacted James Ward regarding the latter's providing the wiring for his new car. Even though Packard Electric did not then make automotive ignition cable, the company did do electrical work involving some kind of wiring, though not yet the waterproof variety which later made it so popular.

William Doud obviously couldn't have joined his younger brother on that first known Packard visit to the Winton factory. He remained in the hospital into August, but on the 4th—a Thursday—he was allowed a reprieve to take a ride with George Weiss, one of Cleveland's first automobilists and the organizer of that city's first automobile club, who was then working very closely with Alexander Winton in getting Winton's automobile business started. Could William Doud have been thinking ahead? One can well imagine the conversation on that afternoon's drive, the elder Packard brother casually eliciting as much information as he could about the Winton enterprise.

While still in the hospital, William Doud noted in his daily log:

Front seat from the left: Winton, George Weiss and William Hatcher.

JULY, 1898

FRI. 22 To Cld Ale Tried Winton Motor Carriage — fine price $1000. Immediate delivery. WDP & self to Buffalo by boat & to N Cat

AUGUST, 1898

SAT. 6 To Cld went out with Geo A Weiss in Motor Carriage great. Ordered one fm Winton M C Co $1000.
WDP. retd to Warren

SAT. 13 Went to Cld & came down in new Motor Carriage — hard trip — towed in Hesser, Winn & Hafer fm Cin here. Closed deal for transformer orders

MON 15 Burt Hatcher mechanic fr W M C Co working on motor

WED. 17 Cary here to look over paste joints & msfd pumping decided to adopt it
Got motor running
Hatcher retd to Cld

FEBRUARY, 1899

SAT. 4 Mr Winton here PM to look over my carriage

MARCH, 1899

TUES. 28 Man fm Winton Motor C Co here to help put motor together.

FRI. 31 PM Winton's man retd to Cld. Motor very noisy & not running very well

APRIL, 1899

TUES. 4 Loaned Chas Rye $10. to be paid in "a week or two"
Went to Cld saw Winton re exchanging motor promise to write

MON. 17 Went out for first country ride in motor Roads horribly rough — gave it up

SAT. 22 To Miller with Motor rough

MAY, 1899

MON. 1 Occasional thunder showers very warm Vegetation coming out wonderfully fast

TUES. 2 To Cleveland saw Winton will make carriage "good as a new one"

SAT. 6 Went to Cld saw Winton Co Carriage not quite only

FRI. 12 To Cld with Gilbert to run motor home trouble with tyre went bad at Ashtabula left machine there Cld to Ash 9 & to L PM Retd via Youngstown Lake Shore

SAT. 13 Had Winton man put spare tyre on motor

"Saturday (August 6th) Cleveland. Ward here this a.m. and after further investigation of the motor carriage, purchased one." James Ward noted: "To Cleveland went out with George Weiss in Motor Carriage. Great. Ordered one from Winton Motor Car Co. $1000.00." Later that day, his eyes much improved, William Doud returned to Warren by train with his brother. Two days later Winton was paid a $200 deposit, and five days after that James Ward went back to Cleveland to pick up the new Winton carriage. His journey home would not be without its difficulties.

As William Doud indicated in his notes of August 13th, his brother didn't arrive back until about 11:00 p.m. after ten or eleven hours on the sixty-five miles of road separating the cities. The last part of the trip was spent behind a horse team. As William Doud wrote, "Machinery broke down abt 3 miles from home and he had to be towed in." James Ward's notes are briefer, exasperatingly to the point: "Saturday, August 13, 1898 went to Cleveland came down in new motor carriage—hard trip, towed in.... Winton carriage balance pd. $800.00."

Of the twenty-one automobiles sold by the Winton company in 1898, the Packard sale—of car number twelve—was the only one to an Ohioan. Apparently Winton wanted this particular customer to be pleased, because James Ward's diary finds Winton foreman William Hatcher in Warren the following Monday, August 15th, repairing Packard's car. Hatcher had the engine running on the 17th, and on the 19th, Friday, James Ward returned the "motor," as he called it, to the stable back of the Warren Packard house at 2 High Street. James Ward also records making an agreement with a Mr. Burnes to take care of the Winton—rather as one would a horse, it seems—and by Sunday, the 21st, the car that embarrassed him ten days before was his pride and joy: He took one of his Packard Electric stockholders for a twenty-mile ride to Bloomfield, and describes the experience in his diary as "great."

In its August 24th edition the *Warren Daily Chronicle* shared James Ward's delight: "A novelty in the vehicle line is an automobile carriage that J.W. Packard has just brought to Warren. The motor uses naptha, and drives the carriage at a high rate of speed. The rig weighs 1400 pounds." James Ward continued showing off his new vehicle, taking two local businessmen for rides on September 5th. November 17th found him returning to the Winton factory, apparently not for repairs, but possibly to further satiate his interest and enthusiasm.

James Ward must have spent some time with George Weiss on his second trip to Winton, for he records that on November 30th Mr. and Mrs. Weiss arrived in Warren, using his Winton while visiting. James Ward again returned to the factory on December 3rd—meeting George Weiss beforehand and taking him along—and discussed "failure of the dynamo igniters" with Mr. Winton. During December, too, he records installing new batteries in the carriage at a cost of $13.23, and making another small repair for $11.55.

Eighteen ninety-nine dawned, and brought no decrease in James Ward Packard's visits to the Winton plant. He was there on January 2nd and March 15th, and on March 28th Mr. Winton sent a man to Warren "to help put motor together." Obviously the recovery of James Ward's Winton had been followed by a relapse. After three days Winton's man left, and James Ward notes that the engine is "very noisy and not running very well," so he returned again to Cleveland and discussed exchanging the engine. Mr. Winton promised to write.

James Ward's and William Doud's diaries are the best sources there are, and it is a fair deduction that the classic encounter between James Ward and Alexander Winton did not occur in 1898—J.W. was obviously still enthusiastic. But by the same reasoning one can assume that the face-off was approaching, because as 1899 moved along, Packard's Winton continued to displease.

The Packard diaries do not reveal if James Ward received his new Winton engine, though he does record trying to take a ride in the country in mid-April and giving up because of road conditions. On April 22nd he drove five miles to Niles, commenting that the motor ran rough. So it was back to Cleveland again on April 27th, this time with close friend and Packard Electric employee Slew Chadwick. Wrote Packard: "Left at 8:00 a.m, arrived Winton works 4 p.m. Roads part way good and part way bad. Staying at the Hollender Hotel and the next day went over to the Winton works.... Came home on train."

Slew Chadwick later remarked of this trip, "the biggest problem was keeping water in the radiator, and the fact that autos were so new. It drew a crowd to the curbs along Euclid Avenue in Cleveland." For an ailing car it must have been a gruelling trek, which was surely why James Ward was returning it to the factory.

By this time his face must not have been the most welcome sight at the Winton establishment. On May 6th he was back again, "carriage not quite ready." On Monday, May 9th, he picked up the car, but had to take a train home because of rough roads. Subsequently, on the 12th, he returned to Cleveland and began the trip home, but "tyre" trouble delayed him in Ashtabula and the car was left, again with a Winton man, to mount a spare tire. Finally on May 14th, "went to Ashtabula via Cleveland left Ashtabula at 11:00 a.m. arrived in Warren at 3:30. One run away [horse] above Orwell, no one hurt." The Winton was back!

And so was James Ward—on June 10th, 1899—when he paid his last visit to the Winton factory as a customer and enjoyed "supper and evening with George Weiss." Probably it was during that visit that the exasperated Winton owner and the cantankerous Scotsman had it out, Winton responding to James Ward's suggestions for improvements with something like, "well, if you're so smart, maybe you can build a better machine yourself." Doubtless James Ward already thought he could—and he would persuade a couple of Winton's men to help him.

CHAPTER TWO

THE FIRST OF THE MARQUE

The Models A, B, C, E and F

April 1899–December 1901

AUTHOR: TERRY MARTIN

The defections from the Scotsman's camp came quickly. The first to come over to the Packard side was George Weiss. He had been born in Allentown, Pennsylvania, on February 19th, 1862, his father a mine and wagon shop owner and inventor of several mechanical devices, including a lever brake for light buggies. Settling in Cleveland in 1888, George Weiss' involvement with Winton came nine years later. On March 23rd, 1897, he received a letter from Winton's secretary and manager, George Brown, who hoped to interest him in investing in that company as "one of the biggest things in the country." Weiss was convinced, and in fact contributed considerably more money to Winton than he did to Packard; on June 17th, 1899, just before joining the latter, he divested himself of 170 shares of Winton stock valued at $12,000. He would put only $3000 into his Packard investment.

James Ward, as already mentioned, was in close touch with Weiss throughout early 1899. It was to Weiss, in fact, that he apparently first wrote of his desire to enter automobile manufacture. This important letter, dated April 11th, 1899 and preserved by Weiss' grandson, Roger White, refutes the suggestion of some historians that the first Packard was merely an avocational exercise arising out of James Ward's interest in mechanics generally. In it, Packard not only mentions going into business but strongly implies that he wants Weiss to be part of it: "I must go [to Cleveland] sometime this week on business and I hope that you will be at home. I am quite anxious to talk 'horse' with you. I have got Will [his brother] making a special investigation on the other side [Europe] but have not had a report from him yet. I believe that this report would be of some value to anyone contemplating starting into the business here. It is a branch of work which has a very great fascination for me and it is not impossible that I may go into it someday. With this possibility in view I should like to talk matters over with you . . ." Carefully worded as it is, the letter certainly makes James Ward Packard's intentions clear.

Although Weiss was quick to join Packard, he would not change his residence. His wife Laura Turreff Weiss and their two children, Edith and Harold, would remain in Cleveland, as would he much of the time. He was elected vice-president of the local automobile club there in January of 1900 and owned a number of cars at the time, Edith Weiss Dingle remembers, and she recalls too that her father began selling Packard automobiles from their home during 1900.

The second defector from Winton was William A. Hatcher, an inventive mechanic who had been born New Year's Eve of 1871 in South Bend, Indiana, who was largely self taught, having left formal schooling after the eighth grade, and who was serving as Winton's shop foreman. James Ward's diary notes after a visit by George Weiss to Warren on June 29th, 1899, that they decided "to put up three thousand dollars (each) if we can engage Hatcher." Apparently Mr. Winton was not the

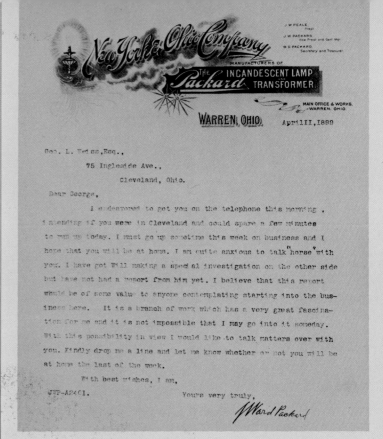

The first Packard, being contemplated above, being built below (note use of two levers) and during testing near machine shop in November at the right (now with single lever but no H shifting box). On the pages preceding: William Doud takes his car out during early spring of 1900.

most endearing of employers, and Hatcher quickly accepted the Packard-Weiss proposition. On July 3rd he agreed to report for work in Warren by the 15th to develop "a practical Motor Vehicle, at the earliest possible date . . . and if the first machine proves successful, to immediately proceed with say six more sample machines, for the purpose of development." The Packards and Weiss agreed to furnish the necessary capital and to pay Hatcher $100 per month plus, "if a Company is formed," $5000 worth of stock and the opportunity to purchase a reasonable amount of additional shares. In return, Hatcher agreed to apply for any ensuing patents under the name of "Packard & Weiss."

It should be noted here that Packard & Weiss and The New York & Ohio Company were separate in name only. Work was carried on in the latter's building, and after December 30th, 1899, Packard & Weiss became the "Automobile Department" of New York & Ohio. The stock in the two companies was never merged, but New York & Ohio obviously supplied the support for Packard & Weiss. James Ward notes two New York & Ohio partners, "Rem and J.W. Peale," arriving from New York on July 15th and deciding to "increase stock to 200,000, making stock dividend of 50m. Decide to continue New York & Ohio to put up machine shop."

No time was wasted in getting to work. Until the new machine shop was completed, machining would be done at The New York & Ohio Company, and its drafting room was now turned over to Hatcher. On July 7th, 1899, he completed the first drawings for a new carriage. Many more followed, some made and never used, others tried and then revised. Parts were quickly made up and tested, and on July 26th James Ward noted that George Weiss made a visit to Warren and was "well pleased with progress on the carriage." Although Packard worked closely with Hatcher on the project, it was the former's name which generally appeared on the drawings, along with the names of other New York & Ohio draftsmen from time to time. These included one A.C. Nelson from Berea, Ohio, who was added as a second motor carriage draftsman at two dollars a day on July 19th.

As the new carriage entered the construction stage, James Ward dispatched Hatcher to Cleveland to see to patterns and castings, which were made there. Interestingly, Packard continued to motor about in his Winton during this period, with little more befalling him now than the typical problems of contemporary automobiles.

On October 30th the first completed engine was ready for testing. James Ward noted: "Auto engine on new machine tests out 7.1 h.p." This is quite a bit less than the 9 hp this car has always been said to produce, though it is possible that its horsepower was increased later. On November 2nd, James Ward records a "ball" to celebrate the opening of the new machine shop, as well as his "last ride in old carriage." He was about to forsake his tired Winton for the first Packard.

On November 6th the new car was ready for the road. One can well imagine the pace of activity in that small wood-frame building. Indeed neither Hatcher nor James Ward—a man who knew the value of a patent and already had a number to his credit—had been able to find the time during this frenetic development period to do the necessary paperwork to protect their new project. It was not until January 16th, 1900 that J.W. finally applied for the first of his automotive patents (issued February 12th, 1901). Both it and five subsequent patents awarded to Packard and Hatcher covered parts used on the first Packard automobile of 1899.*

The first official word on the new automobile appeared in Warren newspapers on November 7th, one day after the machine's first road test. As the *Warren Daily Chronicle* reported: "The 'auto' worked satisfactory, and save in one or two minor features, was found to be fit in every respect for exacting road work. The motor, which is the essential feature is pronounced superior to any on the market, and the entire vehicle marks an advance in similar construction." The news provided in the *Warren Tribune* varied: "The automobile completed by W.D. Packard was given its first test this morning. It proved satisfactory in every particular. It was expected the car would make 30 miles an hour and can easily go 35 miles. The successful completion of the machine will probably mean a factory for automobiles in this city."

The *Tribune* erred by crediting the car to James Ward's elder brother, but the newspaper was exactly on target about just what the vehicle meant to the city of Warren. The next day the *Tribune* gave another pat on the back to the enterprise: "The successful test of a horseless carriage, all made in Warren representing a new industry, [brings] to the city another manufacturing concern which will doubtless be heard from in the industrial and commercial world."

The interchangeable use of the words "automobile" and "horseless carriage" in these reports indicates that one couldn't yet be entirely certain as to how to designate the new motorized vehicle. Two weeks later, on November 22nd, a magazine whose title reflected how its editors viewed the new era, spread word of the first Packard automobile. *The Horseless Age* gave the news but minor mention, however, and again

---

*On August 25th, 1899, incidentally, Edward P. Cowles had likewise applied for a patent on an automobile he devised. Cowles, who had helped James Ward on his first automotive designs in 1896, was still in the Warren area—though no longer employed by the Packard brothers. Conceivably he may have returned to his former employers, Spangenberg and Pendleton, who were associated with Trumbull Manufacturing. This company, the only other Warren concern to build a complete automobile, would produce a grand total of seven cars from 1899 to 1904. Obviously, if Cowles had planned to stay in the automobile business, he would have been better advised to have stuck with Packard.

The H-gate shift lever, installed in first Packard after November test run.

The first Packard, left, photographed on November 7th, 1899, the day George Weiss arrived to see it. Packard number five, center, with H-gate shift lever.

erroneously credited its building to William Doud Packard. The Warren newspaper articles and this one national mention were the only public announcements in 1899 of just what the Packard brothers were doing.

George Weiss missed the first day's run of the new car, but as James Ward noted he did arrive on the 7th, "apparently pleased with machine and progress made. Decide to go ahead on present partnership basis and make 6-8 or more machines. W.D. and J.W. paid 250.00 toward carriage stock"—the first investment in Packard shares.

Until the recent discovery of the original Packard-Weiss-Hatcher agreement of July 3rd, and the original factory blueprints, it was thought that only one Packard automobile was produced in 1899, and this may be so as far as it goes. But if more were not produced, more were at least *started*—and altogether there were *five* Model A's. This will be a surprise to tradition, for it has always been assumed that only one Model A was built, in 1899. But the facts are plain. The July 3rd agreement clearly stated that if the "first machine proves successful," the company would "immediately proceed with, say six more sample machines. . . ." And there is further evidence.

The first car had a ram's horn-shaped front frame member supporting the spring mounts. This is shown on an August 14th, 1899 drawing by Hatcher. But that drawing carries on it as well a note dated December

24th, 1899, indicating the change to the 1900 style straight-type spring support. Recently discovered photographs show four other cars—in addition to the first Packard—with the ram's horn. This, as we shall see, solves a number of perplexing questions regarding this early period of the Packard automobile story. Many historians, and even the Packard company itself in later years, concluded that only one car was begun during 1899 and that only five were made during all of 1900. Instead the first five cars were made or started before the latter year even began.

The Warren years of the Packard automobile saw many changes in body style and model. Often these occurred within a given model year. Chassis, for instance, were designed in groups of from five to twenty, allowing the company ample time to experiment with the first models from each group and then make the necessary improvements for the next series. At other times certain characteristics were shared by different models. The first bodies, spanning Models A and B, were all built by a local buggy manufacturer, Morgan and Williams, located off the courthouse square about five blocks from the Packard plant.

In the first five 1899 Model A's, one can see the development of three completely different body styles. The very first car—the one now on permanent display in the Packard Engineering Building at Lehigh University—was designed to carry four passengers, though in later years it was

This car was sold to George Kirkham on February 3rd, 1900, and was photographed, right, in front of Kirkham's house; the straw basket was for his lunch.

never pictured with the rear seat. It sported a leather dash as well. The second car carried the same body design and was the personal conveyance of William Doud Packard, driven by him (sometimes as far as Lakewood, New York) over the period of almost a year. His was the first Packard to have the lower front axle, and featured a rich-looking wood-paneled dash with a padded emergency seat and a brass rail. Inside the dash was a compartment for the storage of crank and tools. The third Packard was built exactly like it.

Then, cars four and five bore the look of the 1900 Model B, featuring a smooth curved dash with rail on top, the spade handle steering lever and a rear seat styled exactly as the Model B would be. This rear seat, incidentally, came complete on the rear deck lid, all in one piece.

The final events in 1899 were recorded by James Ward Packard in his diary: "Sat. December 30 George Weiss and his father here, sign partnership agreement." Apparently this formalized the July 3rd agreement and set up Packard & Weiss as the Automobile Department of The New York & Ohio Company. And on December 31st, in a day when the only type of rear wheel automobile drive was by chain, James Ward noted: "flexible shaft driving in place of chain."

There are few mentions in the Packard diaries of problems with the new motorcars save carburetor troubles in January—in one case James Ward noted that the carburetor was "blown to pieces." But on January 28th, there were "new and larger carburetors put on engines with little backfiring, apparently makes it a success."

Now, which of the five Model A Packards represented the company's first sale? For years historians have reported that one George D. Kirkham bought the original Model A Packard on January 3rd, 1900, for the sum of $1200, this purchase prompting the Packards to decide to enter motorcar manufacture. If one had visited the company that month, however, one would have seen from a half dozen to a dozen Packard automobiles in some stage of construction. The Kirkham story obviously is in need of modification.

George D. Kirkham was a Warren businessman, residing on Park Avenue, one block south of where the cars were built on North Avenue. The Packard brothers passed his house daily en route to their home on High Street in the center of Warren. There is no doubt that George Kirkham did buy one of the first Packards, but it was car number five, the last Model A. A photograph in the possession of George D. Kirkham, his grandson and namesake, proves this. It also solves the mystery, long puzzled over, regarding how the Packards retrieved the very *first* car they built from Mr. Kirkham. They didn't, because they didn't have to; he never had it. Doubtless that car was never out of their ownership.

35

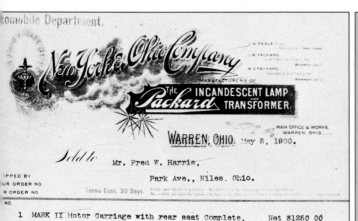

*Packard gets into production. An early invoice, above,
prior to the formation of the automobile company; curiously,
the car was referred to as a "Mark II" and not a Packard.
However they were termed, the first Packards were admirably
tested prior to delivery, as indicated by a photograph
from May of 1900 showing one of the cars on the test rig.
The first full-page advertisement for Packard automobiles
published in* The Horseless Age, *November 7th, 1900.*

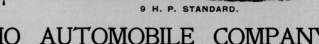

The Kirkham episode proves, too, that at least one of the five Model A Packards was sold. Only Kirkham could have first dispassionately answered the later Packard clarion call—"Ask the Man Who Owns One." And it would seem, too, that he *was* asked—for in a few months an order for a Packard automobile would be forthcoming from someone at the Harris Automatic Press in nearby Niles, Ohio. George D. Kirkham was part owner of that company.

The year 1899 was devoted to experimentation by the Packard company, the year following would see the next big step. And we know the exact date on which that step was taken: April 13th, 1900. In the afternoon edition of the *Warren Daily Chronicle* that day was the announcement: "The New York & Ohio Co. this morning shipped its first automobile to a Cleveland gentleman. The Co. will ship six more machines this month and has the same number of machines under construction at its manufactory. The autos are as fine as any made and tests have proved them superior in many points to the other machines."

The Packard automobile was in production. Of course, it must be admitted that the Cleveland gentleman indicated in the report as the recipient of the first production Packard was none other than George Weiss who was rather intimately connected with the company. But why mention that in the newspaper?* Mr. Weiss was no doubt anxious in any case to drive the new Packard around the streets of Cleveland, and perhaps nonchalantly take a turn round the Winton factory.

That month, too, *The Horseless Age* carried the latest news from New York & Ohio of Warren, that the company "has been working for the past year developing and perfecting a gasoline motor vehicle and have now commenced regular deliveries. They start out with a capacity of two carriages per week which will be rapidly increased. We are promised photos and a complete technical description of the machine which the company states is in no way experimental, in the near future. Numerous patents have been applied for, some have been allowed. Inventors are Messrs. Packard & Hatcher."

This reference would indicate that so busy had the Packard enterprise been in getting the car into production that the idea of promotion had scarcely been considered. No advertising of any kind had appeared thus

---

*Interestingly, on the same day the *Chronicle* had mentioned the shipment to Weiss in Cleveland, the paper also reported that James Ward had received a gasoline motor tricycle "made in France" but assembled in Massachusetts by the Waltham Manufacturing Company. (This was a De Dion-engined vehicle, priced at $450.) It was probably one of the last of the many carriages from other manufacturers James Ward bought for experimental purposes, and compared with the vehicle he was building at the time it must have seemed rather a toy. But James Ward had been known to purchase a complete automobile in order to study only its carburetor or spark mechanism.

far. Indeed the next Packard press mention would again be a news story, this one the purchase of the first Packard production car by an outside source. The purchaser was Charles Harris, of the aforementioned Harris Automatic Press. Harris placed his order on April 17th, was promised a May 1st delivery, and got it. Big news in those days.

Within a month after the first production car was sold, at least eight Warren citizens joined the ranks of Packard owners. In May they banded together to demand their rights as automobilists, rights they believed were being usurped by Warren horse lovers. They hired attorney W.W. Smiley to represent their interests. That they had good cause for complaint is indicated by Warren Packard's reminiscences of motoring in those days: "Another duty of mine was to act as lookout for broken glass and nail studded boards which farmers would place on the road to ruin our single tube bicycle tires. To keep our tires running, in desperation we filled them with various kinds of dope. One I remember was a mixture of glue and chicken feathers. This stopped a small hole pretty well but if too many of the farmers' nails went through at one time we were likely to get a shower of this remarkable concoction and return with car and passengers looking as if they had been tarred and feathered."

For the Packard company, the angry reactions of local horse lovers was a minor concern. Paramount was bringing the Packard name to the attention of automobile fanciers outside Warren. Even before the sale of the first twelve machines it was decided to go ahead with twelve more in March and this was increased to twenty-four in May. And that month too the company found the time to let the rest of the country in on what had been virtually a secret heretofore. Photographs of the Packard and a news release were sent to the various U.S. automotive publications. It seems fitting that this important historic automobile, the 1900 Model B, be described by the company which built it:

"It is solidly built, to endure high speeds on rough roads, and the workmanship is thorough and first-class. The wheels are 34 in. in diameter, with 3-in. pneumatic tires . . . The frame is of seamless steel tubing, made flexible by ball joints. . . . Double elliptic springs support the body at the rear, and a reversed elliptic spring carries the front end.

"The engine is of the horizontal, single cylinder, four-cycle type, with a high compression for full load and a throttling control. By an automatic device the lead of the ignition, which is of the jump spark type, is shifted to correspond to any speed at which the engine may be running. The engine is designed to run at a normal maximum of 800 revolutions, and at this speed, with a full charge, it will brake 9 h.p. All ordinary grades can be climbed with the ordinary gear. A spring transmission is interposed between the engine and the gear shaft, which prevents binding in the bearings and relieves the wheels of the 'kick' of the explosion.

"A gear and chain drive is used. The reverse is a slow speed, giving with varied speeds of the engine from 6 to 10 miles per hour. The hill-climbing gear is approximately the same speed. . . . The high or working speed gives a range of 7 to 20 miles or over per hour. . . . The speed of the engine is controlled through a pedal operated by the right foot of the driver. The two forward speeds, the reverse and the brake are controlled by a single lever in the right hand of the driver. Any one of these operations can be performed by the lever instantly . . . if the brake has been applied and it is desired to put on the high speed at once, it is not necessary to pass through the slow speed, which, if the carriage was running, would make a very unpleasant, if not dangerous, check to the speed. Steering is done by a lever in the left hand. In addition to the hand brake, a powerful foot brake acting on the rear axle is provided. The chain is a special nickel steel roller chain which, under the most severe tests, has shown no appreciable wear and an ample margin of strength. . . .

"The body of the carriage shows the best possible coach work and upholstering, and the aim has been to get rid of the 'horse wanted' appearance. The leather dash is not used, but instead a boot or box forming a part of the body. In this is ample space for parcels, waterproofs, etc. The mudguards are ample and are designed more with a view to utility than to carriage appearance. A complete outfit of all necessary tools, wrenches and oilers is supplied with each machine. A chime foot bell is fitted and a single special automobile lamp is affixed to the center of the front spring.

"All machines are given a thorough test before they leave the factory. [With the testing apparatus] the rear of driving wheels of the machine under test are supported on a pair of endless belts running over pulleys on two parallel shafts. One of these shafts is provided with a brake pulley by means of which any desired load can be applied. A tachometer is attached to the engine, indicating at all times the exact speed, and while on this tester numerous indicator cards are taken from each engine. The machine is run under varying loads and speeds for one or two days [and is then] taken out for a further and final test on the road. Thus, when the highly finished body of the carriage is fitted, all of the mechanism has been thoroughly tested out and is in perfect running order."

What the foregoing description did not include, of course, was the historic significance of some of the Packard features. Though it is a dangerous course always to state categorically that someone was first with something—someone else might come along and discover an earlier "first"—it is not irresponsible to note the areas in which the Packard pioneered. The automatic spark advance, for example, was a feature not to become common on other automobiles for a number of years—and note should also be made of the rotating governor built into the automatic spark, which at maximum speed would pull the rotating cam on the shaft beyond the point of contact so as to stop the spark. (The rotating cam also had a tapering operative face, to bring the wider portion of the cam into operation as the speed increased and the narrower portion as the speed

George Blackmore and the 1900 Model B he bought in September 1900 (left); factory guidelines for the construction of the 1901 Model C (below), this drawing having been tacked up on the wall of the Packard drafting room. A 1901 Model C surrey (right), the body style ordered by John D. Rockefeller.

decreased.) The "H" gear slot, patented by Packard, would become the most generally used pattern in years to come. And certainly not many vehicles of that era could boast a foot pedal to control engine speed.

On George Weiss' Model B, James Ward was particularly careful and anxious to incorporate improvements. On May 9th he wrote Weiss to say he had just received a lighter pair of flywheel springs and was sending them to Cleveland, along with a man to put them on. (Such springs took the shock of piston firing, the transmission and crankshaft not being connected directly.) "It is not at all surprising that these small alterations have to be made," Packard wrote Weiss on May 14th. "We have been learning something on the carriages in use, but I am pleased to say that nothing has proved radically wrong or weak. . . . The probabilities are that a month from now you will have a better carriage than you have at present. I will be very glad, however, the first part of next week to take some rather lengthy trip with you." He wasn't kidding.

On May 18th, James Ward and William Hatcher left Cleveland in the Weiss Packard at 1:00 in the afternoon and arrived in Warren at 6:15. Discounting the hour and a quarter for stops to allow horses to pass and other necessities, the run of over sixty miles was made in just four hours. Three gallons of gasoline were used, the extra can of fuel carried in the car not being necessary. There hadn't been a single mishap, and Packard made the front page of the *Warren Tribune* for the first time; the newspaper called the car "a flying road cruiser." A little more than a week later, James Ward was back in Cleveland to pick up Weiss, and on Saturday morning, May 26th, they left Cleveland bound for Buffalo, New York, stopping in Ashtabula that morning and again in Erie, Pennsylvania for dinner. The roads, they found, were generally good, and the car hit speeds of ten to twenty-two miles an hour at times, encountering no trouble at all during its thirteen-and-a-half-hour journey, the last thirty miles of which were made after dark on strange roads. The pair arrived in Buffalo that night, stained and begrimed, and were almost refused accommodation at one of Buffalo's better hotels. But after explaining their appearance, and the fact that theirs had not been a pleasure trip but a thorough testing of the long distance capability of the car they manufactured, they were allowed in.

Sturdy construction and the reliability demonstrated by such drives became a Packard trademark. Still, the first cars were not without their teething problems. One area of the original design which gave some trouble arose because the undercarriage was made of seamless tubing and fastened to the front axle with ball joints, so that when one wheel hit a hole, the other would be raised in such a manner that the spade handle might be pulled from the driver's grip.

Warren's first automobile accident occurred because of this, and Charles Harris was the victim. The news made the Warren papers. On June 21st Harris was driving from Niles to Warren and "while rolling along at a fair speed a rut in the road jolted the machine and jerked the steering lever from Mr. Harris's hand." The automobile took a quick swerve into a ditch, and its passenger, John McNutt, was thrown out. Happily, his only injury was a badly sprained ankle. Harris escaped injury, but the Packard did not. It was rather badly in need of repair.

But one mishap didn't deter Warren motorists. On June 27th Mr. and Mrs. A.F. Harris gave an "automobile party"—a trip to Lordstown (five miles away), followed by a supper at the Hotel Nuhenberger. The list of guests resembled a Who's Who of Warren, most of them Packard owners: Fred Harris, Charles Harris, J.P. Gilbert, George Kirkham, John McNutt (probably limping), W.W. Smiley—and wives. More sedate certainly was the afternoon social some days later given at the Harris residence by Mrs. George Kirkham and Mrs. Al (A.F.) Harris. Three hundred ladies were in attendance, among them Elizabeth A. Gillmer. Miss Gillmer would, in a few years, become Mrs. James Ward Packard.

At this point, however, James Ward found himself rather heavily occupied with business matters, with no time for romance, for on July 20th, 1900 the Packards, Weiss and Peale had proposed to organize a corporation with $100,000 capital, Peale himself offering to put up $30,000 of that amount. Deciding that his engineering department could do with a little expanding as well, James Ward contacted the Case School in Cleveland and they recommended a man named Russell Huff. He was

exactly the person Packard was looking for. An ambitious student who had worked summers for Lincoln Electric in Cleveland and who had finished his college course before the end of the year, he had taken a job with a Cleveland lamp company while waiting for an opening in the mechanical engineering trade. This training would prove beneficial later, for he would invent the famous rear light for Packard automobiles. Huff's first two years with Packard saw him acting as the company's entire design engineering department—doing drafting, tracer and blueprints, all of which filled a long twelve-hour day. As other draftsmen arrived, Huff stepped up in position, to head draftsman.

A large question mark has always surrounded the number of cars Packard produced in 1900. The frequently-cited five figure is obviously incorrect. Other estimates have placed the number as high as twelve. According to the notebook kept by James Ward Packard, however, a total of *forty-nine* Model B Packards was produced from April 13th, 1900 to the end of that year. Exactly when the last 1900 Model B was sold is not known, but the car was on display at the first automobile show in New York in November along with the 1901 Model C. The Model B was retained for sale as a "lower horsepower" car not to be used "for high speed" as the 1901. It was termed the standard 9 H.P., whereas the 1901 Model C was listed as the special 12 H.P.

Packard sales totaled about twenty-five cars through August of 1900. No advertisements had appeared. In fact, no literature of any kind was available from the factory. The news reports, the various runs, one satisfied customer telling another—this was the extent of the Packard promotion. All effort was put to the Model C. Its development most likely started as early as June 1900. The August 28th issue of *Motor Vehicle Review of Cleveland,* called it "the new racing machine," by virtue of its hotter engine. In appearance it was changed only slightly from its Model B predecessor.

Mechanical changes, too, were few, save for the cylinder which was revised from a square casting with flat copper sides for cooling to the new—and soon to be patented—round copper cooling jacket. The major change was the steering wheel, which tilted forward for ease of entrance and egress on the first group of twelve Model C's produced. For an extra charge, the wheel steering could be fitted to the standard nine-horsepower vehicle, though no photos are extant indicating that this was done. A rare photograph does however show a Model C with tiller steering. Apparently the company would be as flexible on this matter as the customer desired.

Standard to the Model C was a rim brake, which was a channel tacked to the inside of each rear wheel. When the two hardwood blocks came in contact with the rim, the car would come to the requisite stop. The brakes could also be locked upon leaving the car. The Model C retained the smooth, single-tube tire of its predecessor though its width was now four

inches instead of the original three.

What remained unchanged—and would so for the next few years—was the Packard policy regarding customer service. The company was so concerned that the purchaser be satisfied that it sent one of its men to accompany every new owner to his home, provided said owner lived within driving distance of the Warren factory. If the car was shipped by boxcar directly to a customer, then the company's representative would himself accompany the car and see that it was properly unloaded and in good working order. One must remember, of course, that often in those days customers might be riding in and driving a horseless carriage for the first time when their Packards were delivered.

Henry Schryver, the machinist and mechanic who had worked with James Ward during the experimental period of the mid-Nineties, was the man assigned to this job. And, at those times when an owner might need repairs, find himself without a suitable mechanic in his area and call upon the factory for help, Henry Schryver was the man who answered. As an example, he kept records of a trip to New York on August 28th, 1900 to fix the vehicle of A.F. Harris (of the Harris brothers of Niles, who happened to break down during a trip): "I was sent to the Crowell Clutch & Pulley Co., Westfield, New York. Left Warren 10:15 on Penna. for Ashtabula. (fares $1.35, dinner and car fare $.55) Left Ashtabula for Westfield 12:51 (fare $2.00) Adjusted vaporizer, gave carriage thorough inspection and put on tire. Carriage O.K. at noon 29th. Al Harris gave a few friends a ride after dinner. At 2:00 P.M. started for Ashtabula (hotel bill at Westfield $2.00, soldering valve $.05) made run from Westfield to North East 15½ miles in sixty minutes. Stopped ½ hour, then made the run to Girard, Penna. stopped for supper then started for Ashtabula. Arrived at 10:15 where we ran into the viaduct, smashed both front wheels and bent rear left hand axle. Put up at the Stall house telephoned for repairs which we received at 1 P.M. the 30th. At 6:10 we started for Warren, arrived at 10:40 making 136 miles in 12 hours actual driving time." The total cost to Mr. Harris was $5.95 for expenses and Schryver's time, not to mention the fraying of the mechanic's nerves.

Selling Packards was an adventure of less formidable proportions—and the company soon appointed its first outside agent. Prior to September 22nd, 1900, Packards could be bought only at the factory, or from George Weiss, who was cheerfully selling them from his home in Cleveland. But now George Blackmore of Painesville, Ohio was given the Packard agency for that city.

Blackmore was a well-known Painesville businessman, the owner of a men's clothing store on Main Street, who about 1886 added the Western Toy Company's high wheel bicycles to his line. In 1900 he became interested in establishing a motor bus line between Painesville and Fairport but sometime that summer his attention was drawn elsewhere.

Packard owners had found Painesville a handy resting place on their various runs—indeed even Packard and Weiss stopped there on their journey to Buffalo. George Blackmore became very interested.

In either late August or early September, Blackmore made a trip to Warren to investigate. He bought the thirtieth Packard. As impressed as he was with the car, James Ward Packard must have been equally impressed with him. He became the first Packard dealer either right there on the spot, or very shortly after taking the car home. The latter happened a couple of weeks after his first trip to Warren. He returned to the factory, and with a mechanic at his side (probably Henry Schryver) made the fifty-mile trek back to Painesville. Waiting at home was his very anxious eleven-year-old son David.

David Blackmore remembers that day well. The mechanic, he recalls, stayed with the Blackmores a few days to acquaint his father with the vehicle. His father would be driving much of the time, allowing the mechanic to take over only when necessary, as for example the time they slid into a gutter and stalled. The mechanic took over then, instructing in the ways of getting the car started and out of the gutter without turning it on its side.

Two trips in the Packard are remembered especially by David Blackmore. The first was to the Pan American Exposition at Buffalo in 1901, only two weeks before President McKinley was shot. The only trouble encountered was buying gasoline, the only place selling it in Erie being a drug store which stored it in a barrel in the basement. The second was an ill-starred trek, an attempt to drive around Lake Erie during the summer of 1902. A reporter from the *Painesville Telegraph* had decided to tag along with the father and son to report the happenings. Unfortunately there were plenty of those, and most of them had to do with the axle. The trip was initially stopped at Norwalk, Ohio for three days awaiting a new one from Warren. George Blackmore saw to the repairs himself in a farmer's barn. More difficulties were hit at Toledo, but these were overcome, the car making it to Detroit where the journey was ultimately abandoned because of yet another axle breaking. Thence the car was shipped back by boat to Cleveland. Packards, even the company agreed, were not perfect.*

Neither was the firm's administrative set-up, its founders concurred. The Packard automotive effort had up to now been rather casually handled. It was simply a Packard-Weiss partnership operating out of The New York & Ohio Company. On August 20th, 1900, however, the

---

*The Blackmore story has a happy and very contemporary ending, incidentally. The faithful one-cylinder Packard that served them for so many years will some day soon be driven on the streets of Painesville and Warren once more. Its remains were recently returned to its birthplace by the writer and in the next few years the car will be born again.

The New York to Buffalo run, 1901: James Ward with George Weiss (unseen behind the wheel) above; William Hatcher (with observer) below.

certificate of incorporation decided on in July was drawn up for a new concern to be called the Ohio Automobile Company. It was forwarded to William M.O. Dawson, West Virginia's secretary of state. On September 10th the company was duly incorporated. The sum of $100,000 was subscribed, $10,000 being paid in, with the privilege of selling additional shares to increase capital stock. Shares of a hundred dollars each were awarded as follows: James Ward and William Doud Packard, thirty-three shares each; George L. Weiss, thirty-two shares; James P. Gilbert (a Packard Electric stockholder), one share; William A. Hatcher, one share.

The first stockholders and directors meeting was held October 24th, and its conclusion saw James Ward elected president of the board and general manager, his brother treasurer and George Weiss vice-president.

The Packard people were now becoming cognizant that theirs was a business with a bright future, and a little planning and sense of order would go a long way to assuring its success. The previous month the company had produced its first piece of promotion, a four-page leaflet describing the Models B and C and the philosophy that had produced them. *The Horseless Age* published the leaflet verbatim in their October 3rd issue as "A Model of Business Literature." Advertising was now

begun, half and full page ads appearing in the same magazine—the Packard people knew a good friend when they had one.

The often-heard-of sale to W. D. Sargent of Chicago really did take place, as so many Packard histories have reported. On October 24th, 1900, James Ward Packard's diary notes: "Sold big machine to W. D. Sargent, Chicago for $1750." This car has frequently been described as a special just for Sargent—it was a special, all right, one of two modified models of the 1901 Model C Special. James Ward often referred to it as the "big model," meaning the twelve-horsepower car instead of the nine.

About the same time came the first unsolicited testimonial from a satisfied Packard owner. On November 5th, 1900, Dr. S.P. Ecki of Mansfield, Ohio sent a letter, noting that he had been thinking of writing for some time about the Packard he had received six weeks before: "I have given it all manners of tests, such as hill climbing, long distance runs, and making professional calls. Made quite a run the week before, from this city to Dayton, Ohio, a distance of 126 miles, taking eight hours with four people in the carriage. As for hill climbing, the car can beat them all. I have gone over the notorious Mohawk Hill, which is half a mile long, average grade 30%. It never stopped with three people in the carriage. Have investigated all the different styles and makes and frankly believe I have the best machine on the market."

This man who owned one didn't change his mind about the Packard, because two years later, on December 22nd, 1902, he wrote the company again to update his experiences with the car: "It took me about sixty days to learn the machine thoroughly, so if anything went wrong I could locate it readily. As to practical use of auto, will say that thirty days after purchasing auto I sold my horses and have had no use for them since.

"I use my machine in all kinds of weather, rain or snow, hot or cold and strange as it may seem I have no trouble to start my machine in cold weather; seems to fire as readily when 15 below zero as it does at 90 in the shade which is very satisfactory. When I see others giving five or six turns of the crank before getting an explosion, and the Packard, my machine, invariably fires first compression. This is a very important feature for a physician as we are obligated to stop frequently."

As we have seen, thus far most Packard sales—Dr. Ecki's car was probably number thirty-five—were to customers in Ohio, most of whom were made aware of the car by friends or other Packard owners. The company had begun a little advertising, it is true, but something more was needed, something that would bring attention to the car on a larger scale. The Automobile Club of America was about to provide that something. Around April of 1900 the club let it be known that from November 3rd to the 10th that year, it would sponsor the first national automobile show in Madison Square Garden. New York City beckoned, and the Ohio company was determined to be there.

One can perhaps overemphasize the automobile and the "plaything-

The first use of a famous slogan, from Motor Age, *October 31st, 1901.*

Packards

Are built for combined *reliability* and *speed* over any roads. Ask the man who owns one. Our machines can and do *prove their efficiency* in every detail. Descriptive catalogue free. :: ::
We shall exhibit at the New York show.

OHIO AUTOMOBILE CO.
Warren, - - - - - **Ohio**

for-the-rich'' theme. But it is nonetheless true that the wealthy had the wherewithal to purchase this grand conveyance, that purchase of a particular machine by one glittering nabob oft led to that particular vehicle being favored by other members of the social set, that the East Coast abounded with moneyed types—and that, to put it in contemporary parlance, Packard wanted a piece of the action.

So Packard went to the automobile show with a vengeance —displaying its cars inside, stationing two more outside for giving demonstration rides to prospective buyers. William D. Rockefeller noticed. He bought two Packards, the beginning of a long love affair he would have with the marque. (Previously he had owned five Wintons, as well as a number of European cars.) Boston's Hollis Honeywell noticed too, and bought one of the Packards on display. Historically, these two sales to social leaders were most significant. They would set a pattern for Packard promotion and merchandising for many years to come.

The company did not, of course, have a dealer in New York at the time, so the Packard booth was in the charge of George Weiss. He did a good job. His pat little speech to answer inquiries of reporters was disarming: "We have no million dollar factory, but we are turning out thoroughly practical road vehicles for delivery, which is more than many who are making bigger claims are doing. Our desire in bringing out a gasoline motor vehicle has not been an endeavor to make anything radically new or especially light and cheap, but has had in mind the attainment of perfect service under ordinary American roads." It was a becoming modesty that could but impress reporters whose ears were continually bent with the grandiose proclamations of other manufacturers and dealers. It was Weiss, incidentally, who would be doing most of the traveling for the company in the setting up of dealerships. Though James Ward did attend the shows, he preferred staying in Warren. He was the archetypal quiet inventor. And as general manager of the factory, he would soon be busier than ever anyway.

The two Packard types displayed at the show were the Model B (Standard) of nine horsepower and the Model C (Special) of twelve horsepower. The latter, Weiss' car, had wheel steering. Save for racing and very heavy machines, most of the other vehicles exhibited in New York featured a lever steering system, and to one reporter that was the way it should be. "A few here have adopted that foreign freak, the wheel," he wrote. "It appears to be popular on the other side, but for what purpose is beyond my reasoning faculties, unless it is due to their love of inconvenience and complications. In my opinion nothing can compare with the lever which requires only one hand and can be moved for the sharpest turn instantly, and one knows when it is brought back to straight without looking at the wheels."

Despite Packard's radical step in featuring such an awkward contrivance on the larger model, the cars made a splendid showing at Madison Square Garden. The show was a benchmark for the company. From Warren, Ohio, Packard would now move out into the world. Four days later the eastern headquarters of the Ohio Automobile Company would be opened, managed by George B. Adams and located at 487 Broadway—"Automobile Row" in New York City. The first production Model C—Packard number fifty-six—would be sold to Charles C. Otis of Yonkers. Fifteen of the next nineteen Model C's would go to New York State residents. And one of these new Packard owners—Ellicott Evans of Buffalo, secretary of that city's automobile club—went to Warren several months later to inquire about taking on Packard sales in his area. Shortly thereafter he did just that.

By early January the Ohio Automobile Company had over $40,000 worth of orders on hand. This amounted to about thirty-three cars, a mind-boggling number for the little company, one that couldn't be handled by its small workforce. Word passed around on this, and from all over Ohio machinists answered Packard's call. E.P. Clay of Barberton accepted the company's offer of "25 cents per hour for machine work and 27½ cents per hour for floor work, either day or night." Fred March, who had learned his trade at Trumbull Manufacturing, joined up. And Tom Fetch came over on April 8th, 1901.

Outside of Ohio some very influential people were being drawn to the Packard banner. Albert R. Shattuck, president of the Automobile Club of America and partner in one of the East's most prestigious automobile emporiums, H.B. Shattuck & Son of Boston, was one of them. On March 27th he sent his representative, Ben Smith, to Warren, and George Weiss promptly assigned to the Shattuck enterprise the selling of Packards for the entire northeast territory. On June 15th Shattuck entered a twelve-horsepower Packard in the first annual race meet of the Automobile Club of New England at the Brookline Country Club. On July 31st he opened a second showroom in Newport, Rhode Island, and three weeks later William Doud Packard visited him, first in Boston where both Smith and Shattuck complained that they weren't getting the Packards as quickly as they thought they should, and then in Newport where Shattuck picked him up at the railway station in an electric carriage to drive the point home. When William Doud stopped marveling at the opulence of the mansions and the minions of automobiles of all kinds in the area—he would write home that it was the greatest show he had ever seen—he explained to Shattuck that Packard's was, after all, a small establishment and they were expanding as quickly as they could.

By early spring of 1901 George Weiss arranged for Alden S. McMurtry to join George Adams in partnership of the New York branch of the Ohio Automobile Company. Soon thereafter, on April 20th, McMurtry was driving a Model B—his Model C had met with an accident only moments before—in the Long Island Automobile Club's hundred-mile endurance test. Beginning April 26th McMurtry was in Warren (so William Doud's notes tell us), visiting with the elder Packard and driving to Cleveland with the younger.

Centering on McMurtry is the little known one-off Packard Model E. According to James Ward Packard's list of motor numbers and owners, C-70 was a "special" ordered by McMurtry. The very next order listed by J.W. is for the one and only "E," model E-71. McMurtry apparently declined it, because James Ward lists himself as the buyer and notes that it was "a special carriage all around. Practically all parts different from others." No record has ever been found, incidentally, indicating there was a "D" Packard.

McMurtry left Warren on April 26th for Cleveland in a new Model C, returning two days later, and then he headed for New York in the Waltham tricycle James Ward had purchased in 1900. He was arrested in Pittsburgh and fined for speeding, an incident that has been reported in every Packard history as having taken place in Warren. Many have thought this stunt was to publicize the opening of the new New York agency, but of course by this time that dealership was well under way.

About the time of McMurtry's visit, the Packard factory was just beginning to be divested of a lot of its presold cars. A good many of its sales were now going to the Northeast, and in this area it was a common practice to put a car on blocks during the months when driving it would be less than pleasurable. Thus winter deliveries were seldom made, and more often than not the factory was expected to store the car until such time as the owner desired it. Thus, too, spring was a happy time at Packard, both because the removal of the cars gave the company some breathing room and because their disposition brought to company coffers the rest of the purchase price. (In general, down payments only accompanied orders.) Sometimes, during the pleasant months, the new owners would travel to Warren to pick up the cars themselves. Two who did so in 1901 were Dr. T.J. Martin and John M. Satterfield, both purchasers of Model C's. Actually it is not known whether Satterfield drove the car back to Buffalo himself, but Dr. Martin did. The Martin car, incidentally, was the third Model C to sport the new wood spoke wheels and a white body. Satterfield's car was blue with red running gear. At that time, choice of color was entirely the purchaser's prerogative.

The Ohio Automobile Company was moving along well. But aside from its automobiles it had very little that it could call its own. It leased the buildings of Packard Electric and borrowed the machinery of New York & Ohio. On September 30th, 1901, there would be some changes made. At the stockholders meeting that day it was decided that the buildings of Packard Electric would be bought by Ohio Automobile for the sum—in cash—of $13,000. This included the original building built by Packard Electric, and the addition of 1891. It was decided, too, that additional land next to the property would be purchased "on the best

terms available" from Jacob Perkins. Further, New York & Ohio offered to sell all the machinery, tools and fixtures now being used by Ohio Automobile for the sum of $15,602.02—and this offer was accepted. The Packard automobile would now stand alone.

On that afternoon it was also concluded that all the business credits and obligations of the firm of Packard & Weiss would be taken over by Ohio Automobile, and authorization was made thereby to issue to William Hatcher a certificate for fifty shares of capital stock, this having been the agreed upon figure in the original contract for the automotive venture of July 3rd, 1899. (It is curious that it took a full year after the incorporation of the Ohio Automobile Company for the partnership of Packard & Weiss to be finally dissolved.) The five patents heretofore accrued were now transferred to Ohio Automobile for the sum of $30,000—or three hundred shares of stock, one hundred each to be issued to William Doud Packard, James Ward Packard and George Weiss. The last two mentioned also received $5000 (and twenty-five shares of stock) for their work of the two years previous, neither of them having been paid up to that time for their efforts. This would seem to indicate that once James Ward had settled on the idea of manufacturing an automobile, it was he and George Weiss who saw to the particulars, with William Doud taking over The New York & Ohio Company and devoting only incidental time to the automotive side of the business.

Indeed William Doud would remain in Warren during the Packard's week of triumph on the East Coast in September 1901 for the six-day endurance run from New York to Buffalo sponsored by the Automobile Club of America. The terminus city was the site of the Pan American Exposition then in progress and, it was hoped, would provide a spectacular finish to this first long distance endurance run in the United States since the *Chicago Times-Herald* contest of 1895.

The Ohio Automobile Company entered three cars in the event: one to be driven by James Ward Packard with George Weiss, one by William Hatcher with a passenger by the name of Olwer, one by A.L. McMurtry representing the New York office. Two privately entered Packards also enlisted, their drivers we've already met: Dr. T.J. Martin who would take Buffalo Packard dealer Ellicott Evans along for the ride, and John M. Satterfield who preferred to travel alone. The McMurtry car would be registered as a fourteen horsepower, the Martin car as a sixteen. Packards during this period could be provided owners with a choice of horsepower—from nine to twenty-four, as the advertisements stated.

The purpose implicit in this contest of 390 miles over roads seldom traveled before by automobile was simple: to prove that American manufacturers were best equipped to produce automobiles for American roads. Of eighty starting entries, only five were European makes, only two of which finished—both Panhards, one driven by David Wolfe Bishop, the other by Albert R. Shattuck, the Boston Packard dealer who

The Packard stand at Madison Square Garden, November 1901.

George Weiss and his wife in the W.D. Sargent car in Cleveland.

had many allegiances obviously. Fifty-four of the entries were gasoline automobiles, twenty-six steamers. Size ranged from a 78-pound motor bicycle entered by the E.R. Thomas Company to a 10,189-pound steam truck entered by the American Bicycle Company. The run began Monday, September 9th.

On the Wednesday before, the Ohio Automobile Company shipped its cars to New York. (They would be competing in Class C, 2000 pounds and over.) James Ward and William Hatcher left the following evening, to give themselves a few days to socialize and look over their competition. Not since the Madison Square Garden show had so many motor vehicles been gathered together in one spot in America.

At 8:00 a.m. on the appointed day, the vehicles were dispatched up Fifth Avenue amid appropriate fanfare. When the smooth streets of the city disappeared, the trouble began. Getting lost was just one of the problems. Around Tarrytown the sand was eight to ten inches deep and covered stones that gave all the vehicles severe shocks, sometimes throwing the occupants from their seats. Some of the bridges had loose planks that would tip up after the passage of one vehicle and fall back, hopefully, just in time for the next. High grades were taken as efficiently as possible, the cars coasting down the other side at high speed to make up lost time. Sharp turns at the bottom of such hills taxed the nerves.

In addition to the run that first day, a climb up Nelson Hill was also staged, and the primary challenge here soon proved to be negotiating

past the many stalled cars. All five of the Packards made it. Poughkeepsie was the layover stop that night.

Tuesday dawned bright, with Hudson the intended stop for lunch. That morning's run, however, saw the total loss of one machine, the Victor steamer which overturned at speed, resulting in the loss of most of his teeth for the driver. From Hudson to Albany the Panhard competitors decided to turn the endurance run into a race—something the organizers had feared—and a Gasmobile and Haynes-Apperson joined in. All were duly reprimanded at the next control. But the urge to race was hard to quell—for some. The Packard team resisted the temptation.

By now reporters began filing interim reports on the adventure, noting with nationalistic pride (and perhaps a bit of chauvinism) that the foreign machines, particularly the De Dions, seemed to be shaking themselves to pieces. As for the Packards, they were seen to be as smooth running as any of the entrants, and particularly impressive for "wasting little power in transmission." The only problem any Packard suffered on the way to Albany was a minor one, a hot crank pin on the Satterfield car. One reporter mentioned that loss of time and necessity of repair seemed to grow in proportion to the number of cylinders a vehicle possessed, this no doubt delighting James Ward Packard who was already a supporter of the one-cylinder engine.

Leaving Albany on day three, the rains came—and now the run turned into a different kind of endurance: keeping the vehicle pointed in the right direction and out of the gutter. Most of the cars were as high as they were wide and rode on tires that were treadless. Traction became a definite problem, and some competitors wrapped rope around the rear wheels to effect same, then found the ropes worn completely through by the next stop. Only one car on the run was provided with any special device to prevent slipping, and this was Dr. Martin's Packard. It was a mysterious arrangement, straps fastened to each side of the tires and running around the tread every six inches. However strange, it worked—and Dr. Martin arrived in Syracuse in good condition.

Already, however, others had decided the adventure was no longer fun; John Jacob Astor, tired of fighting the cold and the rain and the mud to the hubs, left his Gasmobile in the hands of his chauffeur and returned to New York. Only one of the Packards failed to make it to the control that evening before closing time. William Hatcher, coasting down a steep hill turned too sharply, skidded, and the result was two rear tires off their rims. He made the necessary repairs, and arrived late. Drivers and passengers regaled themselves meantime with thrilling tales of near disasters on the edge of cliffs and miraculous escapes from collision. The run was over for the motorcycles, however, the rain had done them in.

The night was something to behold. Express offices were filled to bursting with parts for the different cars—spare tires, wheels, running gears, batteries, everything. The De Dion people had a repair van

William Hatcher giving the Packards' sister Olive and company office girls a ride in the 1901 Model C styled as a rear entrance tonneau.

following their contingent, as did Gasmobile. Some company owners joined chauffeurs in working all night to repair broken axles, springs and steering. As for the Packards, Satterfield tightened up his crankshaft connecting rod and Hatcher put on another tire.

The fourth day's run from Herkimer to Syracuse saw rain again and fifty-five competitors still on the road. Oneida, the noon stop, was shortened to a half hour to allow a run straight through to Syracuse where the night control was opened at 1:30 in the afternoon. Not even Bishop in the Panhard made it there by that time. Roads no longer permitted racing, in fact it was now more of a plowing contest. All five of the Packards made it to the control on time, the last being Satterfield who had broken a rear axle after skidding into a hole, but he'd repaired it quickly enough to arrive in Syracuse by 7:53. Forty-eight out of the fifty-five starters were still in the contest.

The following day's run was to Rochester, eighty-seven miles away. The roads were bad and so was the weather. Only thirty-nine cars made it to the control on time that evening. James Ward's Packard was second, behind Bishop's Panhard. Then Edgar Apperson, a Locomobile steamer, and Hatcher. The only Packard experiencing difficulty that day was McMurtry—a carburetor adjustment and blown out spark plug porcelain held him up, but he arrived.

The last day's run was to be to Buffalo, with a curtain call at the Pan American Exposition. But while the cars had been wending their way toward Rochester, President McKinley was shot at a reception at the Exposition. "A beautiful type of manhood, a great loss to our country, a fair man to all parties," William Doud Packard would write in his daily notes. The organizers of the event met the following morning and decided to abandon the tour at Rochester. The three Packard factory cars were shipped back to Warren immediately.

"Ward and Hatcher home tonight. We probably won highest American honors," William Doud noted in his daily log. And he was exactly right. The highest average speed from start to finish was maintained by the Bishop Panhard, next came James Ward Packard, then William Hatcher, then the cars of the Apperson brothers. All the Packards, save Satterfield's, received first class certificates for averaging twelve to fifteen miles per hour; Satterfield received a second class certificate signifying a ten to twelve mile an hour average. The latter's accident, by the way, would be alluded to by the company's New York office: "the rapidity with which repairs were effected, enabling Mr. Satterfield to make Syracuse within the time limit, demonstrates the recuperative powers of the Packard and its susceptibility of quick road repairs." Only half the vehicles that started the contest finished it—but every one of the Packards did. It was a record of which any company might boast.

And Packard would. Until now company advertisements had been generally limited to a recitation of technical specifications and manufacturing philosophy. Now Packard would have more to say. And the

47

The Packard office building, 1901. Talking business matters over on the porch, right, and upstairs working in the drafting room, left.
Packard Model F's stored in the factory during the winter of 1902, most already sold and awaiting delivery to their new owners in the spring.

phrase, "Ask the Man Who Owns One" was born. It first appeared within the text of an ad in the October 31st, 1901 edition of *Motor Age:* "Packards—Are built for combined reliability and speed over any roads. Ask the man who owns one. Our machines can and do *prove their efficiency* in every detail."

The origin of this famous slogan has become the stuff of legend, a couple of them as a matter of fact. The most popular has James Ward Packard's secretary entering his office with a letter from a Pittsburgh man desiring information about the Packard car. "What shall I tell him?" the secretary asks. To which Packard replies, "Tell him I'll be over to talk with him—no, wait, just tell him to ask the man who owns one." Another version has James Ward returning from the New York automobile show to find his desk piled high with inquiries about his car. Since as yet the company had produced no literature, his beleaguered secretary is given the famous response as answer to an obvious dilemma.

Either of these incidents might have happened. And again they might not. Perhaps the explanation is a simple one. Obviously that *Motor Age* ad was predicated on the handsome showing of the Packards in the New York to Buffalo endurance run five weeks earlier—and the excellent performance of the two privately entered cars might easily have prompted the slogan. Somehow, however, one does prefer the legend.

On September 16th, 1901 William Doud noted in his log that the first tests of the new Model F had been completed and that it was running beautifully. The Packard had now changed substantially, from a high buggy-like car to a lower, more streamlined affair with longer wheelbase and sleeker body, "distinctly Frenchy lines," some would say. Soon the company would be offering the first of its rear entrance five-passenger models. Previously Packard had experimented with the idea by placing a pair of front seats facing each other on the rear deck and even coming up with a very early example of a surrey-style side entrance version.

The major chassis change now was the addition of a third gear between low and high, and the change to a sliding gear system from the previous two-speed planetary. The body was hung low on a drop frame, ingeniously constructed without an underframe as in years previous. The radiator was out front now. Tires were larger, at four by thirty-four. And the company had decided upon red as the standard color.

On October 30th, William Doud noted that the factory had shipped two of the new Model F's to New York for the automobile show. This followed a seven-week strike by Packard machinists, the first to hit the automobile plant. On November 3rd, James Ward left for the show, which had begun the day before at Madison Square Garden. Just one of the new F's was put on display, alongside the still available C. (One of the latter, had been sold to Victor Buck of Los Angeles a couple of months previous, the first Packard to be shipped to California.)

There was some talk at the show about the optimum number of cylinders a car should have. James Ward Packard felt he had the answer: one. He was convinced his was the right engine for his particular vehicle, and his particular vehicle the right car for American roads at that time: "In the past year we have seen no valid reasons for abandoning our general system. . . . The objections to the single cylinder we frankly acknowledge, but these apply to machines constructed on the old lines entirely. By our system of spring drive and automatic firing control their objections are, we believe, entirely overcome. We have, of course, heard the popular clamor for multiple cylinder engines placed upright in front of the carriage so as to be readily accessible. We acknowledge the necessity of easy accessibility with these multiple cylinder machines, but we state positively that our own engine and all its appliances are as readily accessible as in the other type. We also as positively affirm that it is unnecessary to get at the parts for constant tinkering. There is a decided advantage, too, in the underhung engine with fly wheel and main weight near the center of the car, in the improved stability and in the proper distribution of weight. This distribution of weight is with more than half of the weight on the rear wheels, giving the greatest possible freedom from skidding and maximum traction which is noticeably lacking at times in those machines having the engines up front."

Packards were selling well now—and right off the floor at the automobile show. The response proved so enthusiastic that bigger headquarters were needed for the New York agency. Adams & McMurtry moved to 317 West 59th Street on December 11th, 1901, where the showroom would remain until November of 1904.

When George Weiss was asked by a reporter at the show about the total Packard production, he replied with a figure of 165. This correlates with figures in James Ward's personal notebook: five Model A's, forty-nine Model B's, eighty-one Model C's. James Ward also listed two Model F's as having been produced before the end of the C's production, the first in September for testing, the second just before the New York show. Apparently Weiss included the one Model E and two dozen or so Model F's then in some stage of manufacture to arrive at his 165 total.

It had been a busy two years for Packard, from the well-made Model B to the proved-in-practice Model C. Nineteen one had seen the beginning of a dealer network which would grow into one of the largest in the motor world—and the adoption of a slogan that would, and will, endure as long as men love motorcars. The marque had already earned the respect of automobile journals across the country. And from the small Ohio town in which it was born, the car was now finding its way to owners on both coasts. But perhaps most important the fact of the Packard as a high quality automobile had been firmly established. That would remain, though all else would change.

Nineteen one would be the last year that the men who founded the company would control its destiny. Henry Joy was coming to town.

CHAPTER THREE

ON TO DETROIT

The Models F, K and M

January 1903 - October 1903

AUTHOR: TERRY MARTIN

It is of significance that by the turn of the century the town of Warren, Ohio was not particularly sympathetic to the automobile. It was a quiet, residential place and preferred to remain so. Mechanics recruited by the automobile department of The New York & Ohio Company had difficulty finding places to live, and the city council even enacted a law to prohibit workmen from carrying lunchpails up "millionaire row," Mahoning Avenue. But the Packard car was growing, in both sales and sophistication, so some resolution seemed necessary as the company faced 1902. That the resolution came in the form of capital and managerial interests from Detroit was possibly the luck of the draw at the time, although as later years told this would be fortunate for Packard. The capital from Detroit was considerable. Its funneling into the company was largely directed by Henry B. Joy.

Henry Joy was part of a wealthy Detroit family—his father, James F., had made a fortune with the Michigan Central and Chicago, Burlington and Quincy railroads. Naturally the son was educated at all the right schools, Phillips Academy in Andover, Massachusetts, and the Sheffield Scientific Institute at Yale University. In 1886 Joy began his business career as a clerk in the Peninsular Car Company of Detroit; he was shortly made paymaster, and then assistant treasurer. In November 1890 he became secretary of Fort Street Union Depot, in 1891 he took over the Depot's treasury as well, and by 1900 he was its president. His other interests included Utah mining and he was an official of the Peninsular Sugar Refining Company of Caro, Michigan as well.

In 1898 Joy became intrigued by the horseless carriages being put together by one Henry Ford, and wanted to buy one. Mr. Ford told Mr. Joy he should wait for the next model because it would be a lot better. But as Ford was having financial difficulties at the time, Henry Joy never took delivery—if he had, Packard's future might have been different.

For Joy, of course, the horseless carriage lust remained, and he began investigating a variety of vehicles then being made throughout the country. New York was considered the best place to find the widest selection of horseless carriages; Joy went there often. One day in 1901, while he and his brother-in-law Truman Newberry were inspecting a steam-driven machine, a glass tube indicating the boiler water level exploded in Newberry's face, and this ended Joy's interest in steam as a motive force. Later on the same day, he and Newberry visited Adams and McMurtry's agency, in front of which were two carriages made by the Packard brothers—about which Joy and Newberry had already heard much. Mr. Joy was fascinated.

One of the big selling points of steam cars in those days was their consistent ability to start—this in fact had attracted Joy to the steam vehicle before his mishap with the level indicator—and the Detroit millionaire's first question about the Packard was, "Will it start?" Of course it would,

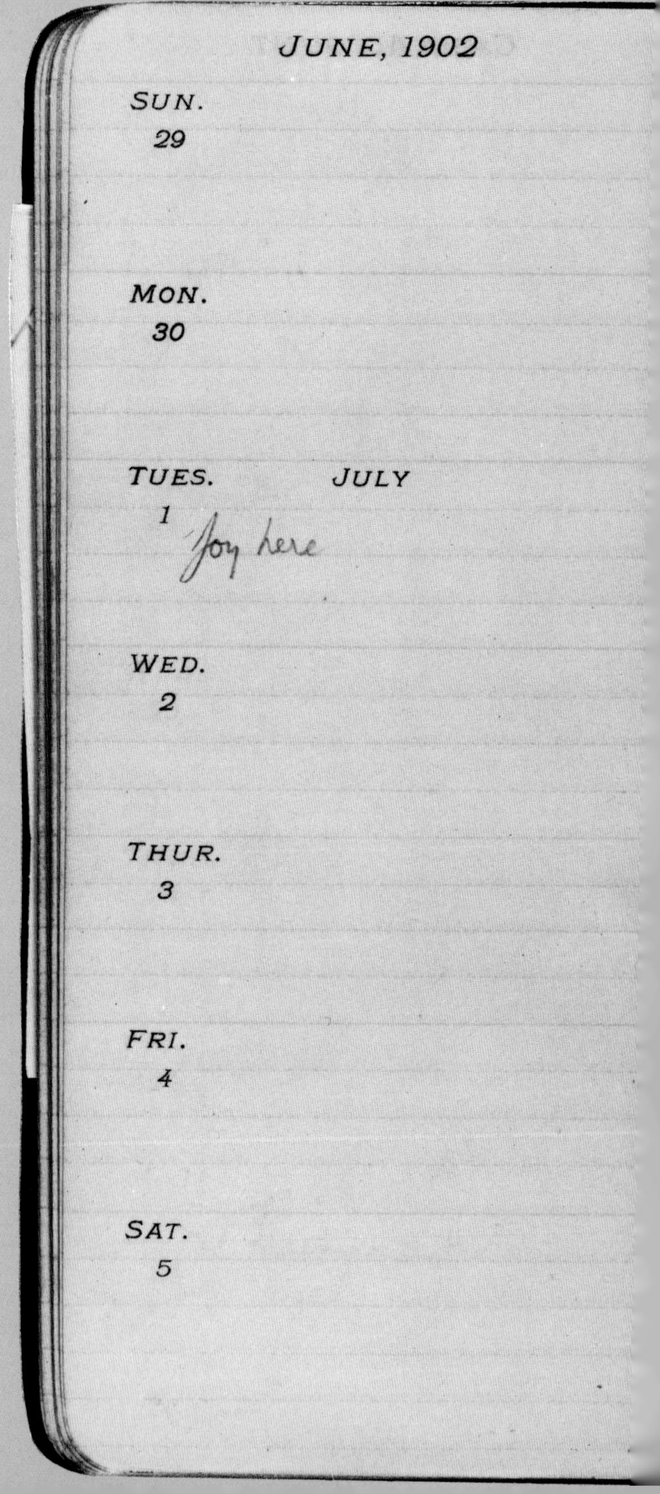

52

On the pages preceding: The 1902 Model F in production.
Right: James Ward's diary noting an historic visit in 1902.

JUNE, 1902

SUN.
29

MON.
30

TUES.   JULY
1   Joy here

WED.
2

THUR.
3

FRI.
4

SAT.
5

came the somewhat surprised reply, and just then the two Packards proved it. A fire apparatus came clanging down the street, and the drivers of the two cars leaped to the machines, pushed switch buttons, gave quick spins to the starting cranks and set off in pursuit, trailed by deep-throated noises from each of their single cylinders. Mr. Joy was delighted: Not only did these Packards start, but they did so when their drivers commanded. Right on the spot, Henry Joy became a Packard owner.

This episode has often been represented as occurring at the time of the New York auto show held November 2nd to the 9th, 1901, and one report is that the Packard Joy bought was a 1901 Model C which he had first offered to Newberry, who also wanted a car. The date is correct, but the car was actually a leftover 1900 Model B chassis with tiller steering, fitted with a 1901 Model C body—not a standard Packard offering and probably the only such vehicle built. The Detroit *Free Press* of December 8th, 1907 pictures Mr. and Mrs. Joy in the 1900 Packard and states that it was the first car Joy owned. At the time of purchase, too, Joy told the press of his taking delivery of a year-old model and simultaneously ordering a new 1902 Model F, which car was delivered to him the following March. His publicity was not generated without a purpose.

Joy was quick to realize that the Packard car was, as he put it, "one of the best in this country." And just before he wrote and mailed the

Below: The car that convinced him—Henry Joy's first Packard, a Model C with 1900 Model B chassis and steering.

The last of the Packard Motor Car Company factory buildings in Warren, Ohio, the brick structure completed in January of 1903.

newspapers his story, he purchased 100 shares of stock in the Ohio Automobile Company.

On January 23rd, 1902, Joy bought another 150 shares for a total investment in Packard of $25,000. A year later, when a reporter asked him to explain his enthusiasm, he replied that it "got so that if I were given my choice of losing either my legs or my Packard, I didn't know which I would rather have kept."

The coming of Henry Joy marked a significant watershed in Packard history. As a stockholder and enthusiast, he would make many a trip to Warren in the next several months, where he'd consult with James Ward Packard about future development, investigate the chances of his becoming further involved in what looked like a very promising business, and even suggest to James Ward his next engineer and designer—of whom more shortly. Joy's name does not appear in the minutes of the Ohio company until October 1902, but he was present earlier, on January 24th for example, when he and Weiss were in town for a stockholders meeting following the opening of the third factory building.

The new edifice was the penultimate one erected by Ohio Automobile for the purposes of building cars—the fourth, of brick construction,

would be built in the autumn of 1902. The building was a two-story wooden structure measuring 100 by 60 feet and the *Warren Tribune* commented generously that it was "a fine addition to the factory and shows what everyone felt sure of, that anything undertaken by Messrs. J.W. and W.D. Packard is bound to expand."

Whenever Henry Joy visited, he must have been encouraged by all the work going on. With its new addition, the Ohio Automobile plant was among the top auto factories of the day, equipped, as *The Horseless Age* put it, "with every labor saving device known to the art [which] will suggest two things. A very complete machine and the greatest care in the construction and testing of every detail." The reference, of course, was to the new 1902 Model F, introduced on September 16th, 1901.

The Model F reflected a steady growth in the product that could be traced progressively from the original. The Model A had sold for $1250, and was mounted on a 71-inch wheelbase chassis, its engine displacing 143 cubic inches with a bore and stroke of 5½ by 6. The 76-inch wheelbase Model B sold for $1750, the 75-inch wheelbase Model C for $2000, but the latter had a larger engine, 6 by 6½, 184 cubic inches. The Model F, on an 84-inch wheelbase, came in at a weighty $2500—the highest price for a Packard yet—though it used the same engine as the Model C. Its body, however, was considerably different.

Main distinguishing features of the F were its larger fenders and blunter front end appearance. Also, its body offered different configurations through the use of a removable rear tonneau. Packard advertising illustrated the possibilities: Without the rear tonneau mounted, the F was a speedy-looking little roadster; with it, extra seating was provided behind the front seat. One entered the tonneau through a small rear door, the center rear seat cushion lifted to allow access. It took a brave soul, though, to lean back against the rear door, which was held closed only with a small brass latch.

James Ward Packard built himself a special Model F which was described in the August 13th, 1902 edition of *The Horseless Age*. Coincidentally, this article provides a useful description of some features of the standard model. J.W.'s car, said the magazine, "is substantially their 12 horse power model 'F,' but with an arrangement of seats after the style at present becoming popular in France.... In addition to the oil side lamps, this machine is equipped with two acetylene headlights, as Mr. Packard is an enthusiastic night driver.

"A new departure in this vehicle is the adoption, after a long series of tests, of 2 inch hollow steel axles, running on bearings consisting of ⅞ inch steel balls. Each axle has a 1 inch hole running through its entire length. The hub brakes are of new design, double acting and very powerful, [and there is] a very effective single acting brake on the end of the transmission shaft, operated by throwing the clutch lever forward. The transmission is the same as on the model 'F,' giving three speeds ahead with but two gears in mesh at any time, and a reverse.

"The carburetor is of the float feed pulverising type, and one set gives a uniform mixture for all variations of engine speed. The fenders are of aluminum, painted and striped to match the body. The steering is by worm and segment, with a special cushioning device for relieving the worm of the shocks produced on the wheels by bad roads. The forward seat might, in the estimation of some, be changed with advantage to individual seats, but the arrangement adopted is preferred by Mr. Packard on account of its roominess."

While the Model F wasn't built on an assembly line, each stage of production was isolated in specialty shops. After the chassis was constructed, the water and fuel tanks, oiling system and miscellaneous components were put on. Smooth, all-white Goodrich tires were mounted, and the chassis was rolled to the next building to be mated to the correct body style. Before assembling, body and chassis would be painted the requisite colors, then the car rolled from the paint shop to the wiring department. One man worked half a day assembling the harness. From there the car went out onto North Avenue, where it was driven up and down to ensure that everything operated properly. The test mechanic carried out all necessary corrections and thought nothing of removing the body again if an adjustment was required before shipment.

With production averaging one F a day and sales increasing rapidly, Packard retail outlets now required additional facilities. In those days most city car agencies had limited capacity; in Chicago for example, where 600 cars were in use, there were only four agency-stations. In New York, the hotbed of motoring, perhaps 2000 horseless carriages were running, yet there were only about twenty agencies and stations, with capacities varying between twenty and 150 machines.

In January 1902, the New York Packard agency of Adams and McMurtry moved from its old Fifth Avenue location to 317 West 59th Street. Its new premises were featured in *The Automobile* of June 21st, 1902, as "a model repair shop. It is not merely a place for the accomplishment of ordinary repair which necessitates little machine work, but is fully equipped for any and all jobs which may be needed, even in the face of inability to quickly obtain duplicates or injured parts. In fact, so well is the place fitted for making new parts that no stock of new duplicates is carried or sought. Unfinished forgings are kept in stock, and when needed are finished to suit the occasion. The power of the shop is a 20 horse power vertical gasoline engine, which also drives an electrical generator furnishing the establishment with its lighting current.

"The machine tool equipment comprises two engine lathes, a universal milling machine, a shaper, a small sensitive drill, a regular drill press, a back saw and an energy power grinder. They also have a forge and equipment. For convenient handling of work underneath vehicles a hoisting frame or platform, on which a carriage may be jacked and then lifted as high above the floor as desired, has been devised. This permits the workman to stand upright under the vehicle and directly upon the repair shop floor, which is obviously more convenient than standing within a pit."

J.W. and W.D. Packard visited Adams and McMurtry about six times each during 1902, calling it their "eastern branch." One could see a great deal of the Packards' forward thinking in the New York facilities. Adams and McMurtry probably had the first automobile hoist in town, and in a comparatively short time had become an exceptionally well equipped station. Packard always prided itself on its dealerships and service centers; Adams and McMurtry merely set the standard.

Chicago was quick to join in. In March 1902 Pardee Company was organized at 1404 Michigan Boulevard—just in time, as it happened, for Chicago's first automobile show, which William Doud attended. On March 8th, he noted in his diary that "after looking over all the autos, I am better pleased than ever with our Machine."

Shortly after the Chicago agency opened, a dealer named Rudolph Winslow added Philadelphia to the list of cities where Packards could be purchased. Winslow located at 302 North Broad Street, becoming the fifth big city Packard store after Boston (Shattuck), Buffalo (Evans), New York (Adams and McMurtry), and Chicago (Pardee). In September the total increased to seven, with Chippen and Church in Los Angeles and A. B. Costigan and Company in San Francisco.

There were also some smaller dealerships. Blackmore, for example, was still selling Packards in Painesville and running his own ads in *The Horseless Age.* And according to *The Packard* of June 1910, C.J. Bousfield of Bay City, Michigan added to the count, visiting Warren in July of 1902 and securing his own franchise.

On March 14th Henry B. Joy's new Model F arrived in Detroit, that city's *Journal* announcing the event with the headline, "It's a Blue Devil." Said the paper: "It is a gasoline road machine with blue body, red wheels and plenty of brass work, giving the machine an elegant appearance. Mr. Joy secured it this week from Warren, Ohio having sold his runabout to F.S. Stearns. The only other [Packard] in Detroit is the red devil owned by Truman H. Newberry. Mr. Joy says his 'blue devil' is not intended for racing and has a maximum speed of 25 miles per hour. It is a two seated affair and one of the most expensive automobiles in

Detroit." (Actually there were three Packards in Detroit at the time: A Model C was sold to a Miss Fletcher there in early 1902.)

It is hard to believe that a city soon to become the motor capital of the world boasted only three Packards and still didn't have a Packard agency, but Henry Joy was attending to that. He was already trying to convince James Ward Packard to put up a Detroit store and had also introduced him to an engineer who would prove significant in Packard's future development and eventual move to that city: Charles Schmidt.

A Frenchman with over eight years' experience designing cars for

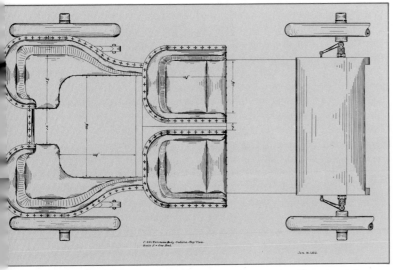

The new 1902 Model F, the car William Doud called the "Red Devil."
Underneath the "Red Devil," the chassis of the 1902 Model F.
Factory drawing of the rear entrance tonneau of the 1902 Model F.

firms in his native country, Schmidt had been most recently with the Mors factory as plant superintendent and part-time racing driver. His work on the Mors chassis attracted Joy's attention, and on one of James Ward Packard's visits to New York, Henry Joy effected a meeting. Packard's diary records: "Sunday April 6 15 hp Mors Bronx Park, Schmidt & Joy." (No confirmation can be found of the rumor that Schmidt was later arrested in Greenwich, Connecticut for running over a dog, and subsequently bailed out by James Ward and Joy.)

On Saturday, April 12th, James Ward, Joy and Schmidt had breakfast together in Warren, along with George L. Weiss. The future of the Packard was discussed, and Schmidt was hired at four dollars a day—both Packard diaries confirm the event. Schmidt began work five days later in Warren.

The contemporary Mors was powered by a flat twin of 850 cc, so Schmidt was evidently not wedded to James Ward's idea of a single-cylinder engine. It has been suggested, however, that Joy hired Schmidt to effect the change resulting in a Packard four, and as we see from the diary notes, this was not done without the consent of the Packards and George Weiss.

Eighteen days after he began work, Schmidt was given full charge of the Ohio company shops in addition to engineering and design duties. He would perform all these jobs until C.J. Moore—of Westfield, Massachusetts—was hired as factory manager on March 8th, 1903. Moore, like Schmidt, was a man of real ability who would be instrumental in solving problems arising from the later models K and M, while at the same time trying to maintain production of the popular F. But his most important role was to undertake the move of the entire plant from Warren to Detroit. We are, however, getting ahead of our story.

The one-cylinder Packard still had quite a while to live, and proved its prowess again at the second Long Island Automobile Club's contest on April 26th, over a course beginning at Jamaica, extending through Flushing to Oyster Bay, and returning south through Massapequa to the starting point. This year's entries were more numerous, and the weather better. New York's Alden McMurtry represented the Ohio Automobile Company, along with Fred C. March of Warren in a second Packard, and both were among the twenty-one finishers awarded blue ribbons for covering the 100-mile course without a stop.

Another 100-mile endurance run was held by the Automobile Club of America on May 30th, 1902, the route running from New York City to Southington, Connecticut and back. Unlike the Long Island contest, no gasoline vehicle was entitled to an award unless it made the entire trip without a stop—excepting, of course, "tire trouble, police orders, problems with horses, closed railroad crossings, blocking of the road or the demands of nature." An official observer was on hand to record all stops and caution drivers about speed limits—eight miles per hour in the city, fifteen in the country. On the first day of the run the A.C.A. would hold a double trial and for the second a speed trial. Four bright red Packards were the Ohio Automobile Company's entry at the Plaza Hotel starting point, A.C.A. headquarters.

Two Packards bearing numbers 2 and 3 were entered by Adams and McMurtry Company, Fred March driving one and Adams and McMurtry manager W.S. Ions the other. Only Ions made a penalized stop, but from starting in sixteenth position he ended up as ninth. March had troubles with an overheating bearing, started seventeenth and finished thirty-fourth. Another Packard, number 32, was driven by Harlan W. Whipple. He started eighteenth, and with only one stop due to valve trouble finished third. The fourth Packard was owned by one Osborn W. Bright, who did not complete the run, and none of the Packards that did qualified for awards because all had made non-permitted stops. But Whipple's Packard had put in quite a performance, rendered all the more impressive in that it carried three passengers besides the driver for a total weight of over 3000 pounds—its curb weight was only 2200.

One of the longest runs by an automobile to date was recorded by a Packard in August 1902, a Model F driven by Chicago businessman E.B. Martin from that city to New York. On August 9th Martin set out in his yellow tourer and on the 22nd reached his destination, where the car was seen by a representative of *The Horseless Age*. Evidence of severe usage was plain—the tires were deeply pitted and cracked—but after being worked on by Adams and McMurtry the machine bore no sign of deterioration. This was quite a testimonial.

Yet another Packard triumph was provided by Model C owner H.E. Clapp of Attleboro, Massachusetts, who had read about F.O. Stanley and other steam car exponents ascending Mount Washington in New Hampshire during 1899-1902. Clapp decided that anything steam could do, gasoline—and Packard—could do better. On August 2nd his Model C became the heaviest vehicle yet to scale the peak and the only one so far driven by gasoline. In addition, he had a passenger, one R.C. Reed.

Back in Warren, the Ohio Automobile Company continued to grow, the aforementioned fourth and last plant building being announced on July 2nd. This red brick edifice measured 200 by 60 feet; it was located just east of the other shops, and it effectively doubled plant output. The building was often pictured by the company on later anniversaries as the birthplace of the first Packard, which of course it was not, though many famous models were built there in 1902 and 1903.

The brick building was still standing in 1965, serving as a warehouse for the Ohio Lamp Plant of General Electric, which had bought it and the rest of the lamp business from the Packard brothers back in 1910. Some employees realized it was part of the original Packard factory, and after GE decided to tear the building down that year began looking around. Out of sight in an old closet they found some of the tools used to

build the first Packard and others up to 1902, labeled with the names of New York & Ohio and Ohio Automobile. GE placed the tools in a vault in the basement of its plant, but recently this writer convinced the plant manager to allow them to be displayed with other Packard items of the period in the Packard birthplace museum in Warren. Outside the GE plant, a plaque provided by Packard on the occasion of its Fiftieth Anniversary attests to the location as the birthplace of the marque.

Up to this point in its history, nearly everything that went into the building of the Packard automobile was made in the Warren factory, this because very few outside products completely satisfied James Ward and his brother. The exceptions were wheels, the wire for which came from Weston-Mott in Ithaca, New York; wood spoke hubs from the American Ball Bearing Company in Cleveland; and most castings.

In 1931 *MoToR* magazine published an article by Walter Hackett, who had served William Doud Packard as secretary in the late Teens and early Twenties. W.D. often spoke to Hackett about Packard's early problems: "Our troubles were almost entirely with the materials rather than design. There were continual breakages. We soon began making our own materials because we could not get the quality we demanded. . . On several occasions we rejected so many of the parts we got into trouble on production. For example, the people from whom we were buying our wheels refused to make any more for us because we rejected so many of them. We had trouble with our bearings. For our gears, the only steel we could find that would do was that made for armour-piercing shells for the Navy. We got some of these forgings made for wheels to make gear blanks but because the best that we could get from commercial sources were not good enough for us, shell steel was also used for our cylinders.

"Another trouble which involved both design and materials came when we put a governor on our spark. We were afraid to let the engine run too fast and so had the spark stopped at what we thought was a safe speed. One of our car owners learned that he could move the governor and after he did so, ran circles around everybody else in town for some time. Finally, he speeded a little too fast and the flywheel flew off, making a very nasty wreck."

But most owners including William Doud enjoyed their one-cylinder Packards and praised them highly. It's a wonder, really, that James Ward finally let that engine be replaced at all—he once told a reporter that "more than one cylinder on a Packard would be like two tails on a cat—you just don't need it." His company even published a little booklet on the advantages of a single versus more complex configurations. Titled "Six to One, or Wasted Pride, Perspiration, and Profanity," it bore no byline, but could have been written by James Ward himself:

"Now I want it clearly understood that I'm patriotic, ride American machines, with 'PACKARD'S' Yankee Doodle Single Cylinder. For American roads 'PACKARD' automobiles have no peers. When I see a

French machine go gliding by and a friend says: 'Oh, isn't that fine.' I can't help but think—six—six—what a mix. Really you observe I'm a trifle prejudiced. France—glorious France. France for paintings, sculpture and vin ordinaire, don't you know,—but that's 'bout all.

"Before entering upon an automobile existence, look around you. Get a machine that will stand the wear and tear, the bumping and thumping. Get one, not so complicated but that you can understand it without a polytechnic course. Get one as good as the 'PACKARD' and you will get all that's coming to you. 'Ask the man who owns one.' "

After testimonials such as this, it must have shocked quite a few readers of *The Horseless Age* to find a description in its September 3rd,

1902 issue of a new Packard two-cylinder engine, even though it only looked like two singles joined. Whether Charles Schmidt had much to do with this engine is questionable. Drawings of it had been completed before he arrived at Packard and thereafter he was at work on one even more ambitious—a four—but in any case Packard built the two, and the car it was put into was called the Model G.

The first Model G had a detachable rear tonneau, like the F, and another variation with a fixed rear seat, "which makes a surrey of the machine" as well, was available as an option. The wheelbase was ninety-one inches—Packard's longest yet—and its thirty-six-inch wheels were larger than either the Model C or F. The front wheels ran on ball

James Ward Packard posing in the special 1902 Model F he had built for himself. The rear seat accommodation was "said to be very comfortable."

A.L. McMurtry, ready to roll in the 100-mile endurance run sponsored by the Long Island Automobile Club on April 26th, 1902.

bearings, the rear wheels being keyed to the shafts that drove them. The Model G frame was made of channel steel and rested on semi-elliptic front springs and full elliptics in the rear, each spring forty inches long. "The employment of semi-elliptics in front in place of an inverted elliptic spring," said the magazine, "constitutes a departure in 'Packard' construction. To obtain a boot of considerable depth it was necessary to resort to this practice."

The Model G engine, of course, drew the most attention. It was described by *The Horseless Age* as "a horizontal, opposed double cylinder of 24 horse power, located under the body. The crank shaft is parallel with the axles, the cylinders are located on the left side of the centre line of the vehicle, and the flywheel is located on the right hand side. . . . Each cylinder of the engine has a separate carburetor, and the timing of the spark is done by a centrifugal governor, which revolves with the cam shaft and shifts the two ignition cams. . . . The ignition is by jump spark. A three cell storage battery in the front boot furnishes the current to the igniters. . . . There are two water tanks under the main seats, which hold approximately four gallons each. One of the gasoline tanks is located under the boot and the other below the body at the extreme rear." The tanks were connected by a stop cock and tube.

The Model G's fenders were of aluminum, and front seats were attached to the body individually. All seats were upholstered in tufted leather, and "to afford the passengers additional comfort the footboards are inclined." The Model G, said *The Horseless Age*, could carry eight persons if the tonneau was substituted for the rear seat option. And this load would apparently not tax the brakes too badly as there was a new double acting brake on the "secondary change speed shaft" and a foot-operated brake in the differential drum.

James Ward recorded that the first Model G was completed on June 28th. Three days later Henry B. Joy was in town to look it over, and the car was purchased—even before it was announced—by William Rockefeller. The latter had a lot of faith in Packard. He would also be in the vanguard of four-cylinder buyers a few months later. Another Model G buyer was Harlan Whipple of New York, who had driven in the 1901 Long Island run with his Model C. It fell to Whipple to achieve the Model G's greatest feat: the New York to Boston Reliability Trial.

The Trial was set up by the Automobile Club of America. The round trip covered a distance of 500 miles, through Norwalk, New Haven, Hartford, Springfield and Worcester, and sixty-eight of the seventy-five cars that started completed the route. The rules were tougher than the

The two-cylinder 1902 Model G with those stupendous bronze hubs, the car above purportedly the one delivered to William Rockefeller.

roads, however. Cars were required to average fourteen miles an hour for the six days. Should a car fall behind by a fraction of a minute it would lose a mark at each observation point, the same should it gain time. Most automobiles by then could easily achieve the speed figure—though full power was sometimes needed on hills—but as George Weiss later remarked, holding the average wasn't easy. "It takes a man who knows his machine exceedingly well," Weiss said. "The inclination is to let the car out a little on good level stretches, but if you do, you make it still harder for yourself to keep within the time limits on the rest of the way to the control. Running on the high gear, as a good driver is naturally inclined to do whenever he can, there are times when the motor is barely turning over, and in throwing in the lower gears you take more chances of ignition and other motor troubles. My driver frequently warned me that the motor would be liable to balk and cause a penalized stop if I persisted as I did, in picking my way up some of the steep hills on the high gear, relying on working the clutch for keeping both the motor and the car going. You know, of course, how this can be done right along on account of the speed limit. . . . When it is kept up for six days the mental strain is something enormous."

Weiss, obviously, was one of the Packard drivers, with a Model F

loaned him by Adams and McMurtry. Henry Joy was along too, with his personal Model F, writing back to all the Detroit papers about it and simultaneously coaxing Goodrich to advertise the fact that the Packard ran on its rubber. Fred C. March, in another Adams and McMurtry Model F, was the third Packard, and yet another was entered by Boston dealers H.B. Shattuck & Son and driven by their Ben Smith. The fifth Packard was, of course, Harlan W. Whipple's Model G.

Model G's were uncommon, and Whipple's drew considerable comment. Fitted with the standard rear entrance tonneau body style, it stood out with its four huge bronze hubs, each as big as a beer cask. It topped the scales at nearly 4000 pounds, and including driver it was to carry no less than seven people. Whipple's big G drew the scorn of *The Automobile and Motor Review*, which called it "ponderous . . . a true leviathan, turning the scales at 3950 pounds, and propelled by an opposed cylinder engine . . . rated at 24 horsepower. Pneumatic tires support this massive car, whose raison d'être must be found in the caprice of the purchaser rather than in any apparent advantage to be gained by its enormous weight." Mr. Whipple, of course, was about to prove them wrong—his Model G had plenty of advantage.

"Few persons have any idea of what it means for a manufacturer to

The only photo extant—taken from a broken glass negative—of the 1903 Model F delivery car, only one example of which was produced.

enter a machine very much heavier than anything previously built by him in a contest of this kind," remarked George Weiss, defending Whipple and the Ohio company. "But people don't look into those things very deeply. They like to have a fling at anything they have not seen before.

"There are certain vital points in automobile construction where you cannot afford to take chances; and the steering knuckle is one of them. Besides, when you put the wheels, under a heavy car like that one is, on ball bearings, you must protect those bearings. Now, in this car it was particularly desirable to have the steering pivots as close up against the hub as possible and nearly in line with the plane of the spokes, so as to reduce the leverage on all strains and thereby the chances for mishaps and mis-alignments of the wheels as well as the knuckles. In order to obtain this effect it was necessary to reduce the extension of the hub on the side toward the car, and if we had not extended them correspondingly on the outside, the width of the ball bearings would have been insufficient." But *The Horseless Age* wondered about "the stupendous destruction which would result if two of these vehicles should try to pass on a narrow country road and accidentally 'lock horns.' "

Harlan Whipple fortunately didn't meet another Model G on the run. He merely won one of only two President's cups awarded at the conclusion of the Trial for the highest number of points possible. Packard also won the other cup, and the gold medal, with Weiss' Model F.

Only a few Model G Packards were built, despite Whipple's im-

pressive performance. A 1921 Packard truck brochure does illustrate what appears to be a Model G, with truck body, being used by the factory in 1903—so this low production model not only ranks as a Trial winner but as the basis for Packard's first commercial vehicle. The only other truck verified to have been built in Warren was a 1903 Model F, fitted with a lovely panel delivery body and beautifully striped, with "Packard Motor Car Company" painted on its side. It would have had to have been produced after October 13th, 1902, because that was the date when the Ohio Automobile Company changed its name.

Meantime, William Doud hinted at the need for outside investment, and even, possibly, getting out of the car business. On September 24th, 1902, while in Chicago to promote New York & Ohio lamps, he had supper with his cousin Levi, a banker. W.D. noted in his diary: "Levi says it is not bad business to borrow money for your business, provided you have the tangible assets. Levi also says if we care to sell stock in the auto company he would probably like to take some."

Two days later W.D. was back in Warren, and the Packard brothers had a meeting with F.S. Terry of the National Electric Lamp Company. The subject—possible sale to Terry of The New York & Ohio Company. It is not known if this was a move to refinance the automobile business—the Packards were trying to buy two electric companies around the same time—though it might have been. The meeting was inconclusive, and New York & Ohio stayed a Packard enterprise.

But apparently the Packards were exploring their options: An offer to buy half interest in the company arrived on September 29th from H.B. Wick of Youngstown. Wick, according to *The Horseless Age*, had just built his own first car, and offered according to W.D.'s notes "$50,000 now and balance later." This offer was not accepted, and what the balance was is lost to history.

The refinancing of Packard therefore fell to Henry B. Joy, who doubtless wanted to handle it anyway. On October 13th's special stockholders meeting in Warren, the name was officially changed from the Ohio Automobile Company to the Packard Motor Car Company. William Doud offered the motion, it was unanimously carried. It was further resolved to elect a new board of eight directors at the annual stockholders meeting on January 1st, 1903, and at a directors meeting that same day—October 13th—2500 additional shares of capital stock were authorized for sale. Joy and some of his colleagues were the buyers.

Was the name changed to ease the transfer out of Warren? Very possibly so. "Packard Motor Car Company" was not a name that bespoke Warren, Ohio, and the Packards were not such egotists to change the name simply out of vanity. The additional stock offering, at $100 a share, also allowed Joy to bring into the company other prominent Detroit colleagues to the tune of a quarter of a million dollars—and Joy had the connections to bring the money in fast.

H.E. Clapp taking on Mount Washington in August 1902 with his Model C, the first gasoline car to make it to the summit.

Joy's wife was the former Helen Hall Newberry, daughter of John Newberry, one of Detroit's most distinguished citizens. Truman H. Newberry, Joy's brother-in-law, was, as we know, a satisfied Packard owner too, and Joy and Newberry both had friends in Detroit whom they could easily convince to become fellow investors. Joy's name didn't appear on corporate documents until the 13th of October, yet he was earlier asserting considerable influence on the company—particularly in the hiring of Charles Schmidt. Doubtless Joy told James Ward of the powerful financial backing he could recruit should the Packards decide, as W.D. earlier intimated, to invite more outside investment.

It should be pointed out too that James Ward Packard was not a total stranger to the group of investors Joy and Newberry were lining up. He made a number of visits to Detroit earlier in 1902, and noted in his diary for April 26th a visit to the moneyed Grosse Pointe country club with Joy and his colleague Russell A. Alger, Jr.

Alger was the first Joy associate to invest, putting up $50,000, and was followed by Fred M. Alger with $25,000. Joy himself put in an additional $25,000—making his total share $50,000—and a brother, Richard P. Joy, added another $10,000. Truman H. and John S. Newberry each offered $25,000. The additional investors were C.A. DuCharme, $10,000; D.M. Ferry, Jr., $5000; Joseph Boyer, $25,000; and Phillip H. McMillan, $50,000.

Each investor paid in cash one half of his total subscription at the time of buying the shares; this totaled $125,000. Adding Joy's original $25,000, this gave the Detroit investors majority interest, since the Packards and Weiss had invested a total of $125,000 including the original $3000 each. After the Detroiters paid their full amounts, their investment towered at $275,000, better than double that of Warren's original principal. It was obvious who would henceforth be running the company.

Good investors, of course, were intrinsic to the Packard Motor Car Company throughout its early history, helping Packard to rise to its position of sheer dominance in the luxury car field by its golden age, the mid-Twenties. In the beginning, the firm needed lots of money, but the need was never so great that it outstripped the ample fortunes and almost unlimited credit of Packard's backers. Thus Packard never felt the pinch for money that drove many a manufacturer to court ultimate disaster by sacrificing the quality of its product for temporary profits. Never, that is, until much later.

The day following the decisive meetings, October 14th, a reporter from the *Warren Tribune* asked James Ward if the new situation meant a move to Detroit was in the offing. There were no such plans, J.W. replied. The subject was in fact not even "brought up among the stockholders, and it is not likely that a large and already well equipped plant will be dismantled and another built." The reporter replied that

The New York to Boston Reliability Trial sponsored by the Automobile Club of America, and held October 1902. Left: Harlan Whipple and his

this would be good news to Warren—he apparently didn't mind the lunchpails on Mahoning Avenue—because Warren couldn't afford to lose any enterprise involving the Packard brothers: "They have done a great deal for the city in many ways and young men who are uniformly enterprising and successful are what Warren needs more of." The *Tribune* noted cheerfully that the motorcar would still be called the "Packard," and that soon the present output of one car a day would be increased to ten times that.

Not everyone was so easily mollified. W.A. Hatcher resigned on January 27th, 1903. George Weiss was also unhappy. On November 15th he turned in his resignation as director and vice-president. Weiss apparently didn't like the way things were going, with Joy and the other Detroiters—and the feeling was mutual. In a letter to James Ward Packard dated December 29th, 1902, replying to a suggestion by J.W. that Weiss continue on as part of the business, Joy wrote, "we think it would be wise for the company not to take on again, any business relations with Mr. Weiss. Mr. Weiss has severed his business relations with the Packard Motor Car Co. and we think, if it meets with your approval, that it is best that no more trouble should be incurred, through renewing business relationships." The "with your approval" thinly veiled Joy's ability to get what he wanted: "I do not like to feel," he continued, "that your letter of Dec. 27 advises the appointment of Mr. Weiss

because I feel that you ought to be able to get along to a better advantage without him, in as much as he seems to create friction . . . he may sell [his stock] to anyone whom he pleases. We are doing our level best to . . . make that stock valuable to him. I think we should succeed."

A few days later William Doud ran into Weiss on the Cleveland train, and recorded, "Weiss very much disgruntled with the policy of the Motor Car Co." In March Weiss inquired if the company would exchange machines for his capital stock, but Joy said it would be "impractical for this company to exchange from a legal point of view." Finally, records James Ward's diary of March 30th, 1905, Weiss severed all connections with the company he had helped start by trading his 300 shares for twelve leftover 1904 Model L's, which he no doubt sold from his home in Cleveland. Possibly as the years went by, and Packard prospered, he had cause to regret his decision.

Next to its birthday, October 13th, 1902 must stand as the most important date in the history of the Packard automobile. Detroit managers were now in charge—by a comfortable majority. Under the Packards and Weiss, the firm built fine cars but was small and relatively secluded. No one can say what its future would have been had it remained so, but many similar small auto manufacturers outside of Detroit gradually ebbed away as the years passed. Under Joy and his colleagues, however, a mighty corporation would emerge.

ackard Model G with those lethal bronze hubs. Center and right: George Weiss behind the wheel of his Packard Model F entry.

CHAPTER FOUR

THE COMING OF
HENRY JOY

The Models F and G

January 1902 – December 1902

AUTHOR: TERRY MARTIN

When James Ward Packard told the reporter a move to Detroit was neither in the works nor being considered, it was a case of either good public relations or letting the board of directors play its own hand. In any event there is little doubt that the subject came up early. In December of 1902, a scant six or eight weeks after the October 13th invitation to Detroit investors, Joy wrote James Ward saying, "I am much interested in having your views as to the size and extent of the new factory about which we have talked some . . . we are ready to cooperate in the manner to the fullest extent. You have mentioned sketches of the building at one time which I have never seen, but suppose you are both excessively busy"—the "both" included Sidney Waldon, J.W.'s assistant and Packard's advertising manager.

The way Joy wrote, the decision to build a plant in Detroit was already fait accompli. "I am strongly in favor of the new plant being built with the knowledge you now have of what such a plant should be. The removal can be accomplished in the dull season when the new works is finished and can be done expediently with a period of shutdown cut to a minimum. In order to do this we must act at once preparing plans, specs and details for new machinery, even though at present the matter may not be decided. I urge you thus to the consideration of these matters because to me they are paramount for the permanent security of our investment and success."

Once the Detroit investors joined the company, too, any idea of retaining some facility in Warren was abandoned. The Warren buildings simply didn't fit any of Joy's plans. They were all under different roofs, and wedged between the railroad tracks and the streets on two sides. The only way to expand was laterally, in one direction. This could have influenced James Ward's acquiescence, although the Detroit investors' majority stockholdings probably was the paramount factor. Detroit was calling the shots.

In early January 1903, James Ward requested Henry Joy to send an architect to Warren, and the man Joy sent represented Albert Kahn. Accounts of how Kahn came to Joy's attention vary, but the most plausible is that one of Kahn's commissions was the remodeling of a shop for Joseph Boyer, a Packard stockholder. Joy was so impressed he persuaded the board to retain Kahn as the architect for the new Packard plant.

In Albert Kahn, Packard had picked another brilliant collaborator. Born in a Westphalian village in Germany in 1869, the son of a wandering rabbi, Kahn came with his family to Detroit in 1884, where he attended art classes conducted by Julius Melchers, the city's foremost sculptor. At twenty-one Kahn won a $1500 traveling scholarship to Europe in a contest sponsored by the *American Architectural Magazine*; he returned to Detroit, and in 1895 formed his own company. At his death in 1942, Kahn was still designing Packard facilities. He had also

On the pages preceding: The 1903 Model F, posed on North Avenue in Warren, just down the street from the plant. Below: Construction ongoing in Detroit for the new factory, this photograph indicating the progress made by late summer of 1903. Left: An eerily moody portrait of the much lamented Model K.

served as Ford's architect for a third of a century, as Chrysler's for almost twenty years, and designed 150 major plants for General Motors. It is estimated that some $2 billion worth of Kahn-designed factories dotted the world's industrial landscape before his career ended.

On January 9th, 1903, Joy made his representations to Kahn's office, and wrote James Ward to say Kahn had been hired. "We want a good shop," he wrote, and offered some suggestions for J.W., such as a steel-reinforced roof, whitewashed brick instead of glazed tile for the interior. The first plans were made without a known site, so in March Joy told James Ward he was "asking for sketches as to the character of the buildings and the space designed at present, with everything laid out with a view to extend, for the future." A few days later he suggested "a one story with a light benefit thus covering say a plant of sufficient capacity to make two model 'M' machines a day and such K's as we would want to put through." Joy stuck to his one floor idea even after it was decided to use more than one; he later questioned "the advisability of putting heavy machinery on the second floor, thinking of the cost of raising and lowering of equipment. Wouldn't it be better that a complete ground floor machine shop be built with proper roof light?" In this Henry Joy was a half century ahead, because one of the reasons Packard would abandon this plant in 1954 was the contemporary notion that such factories should be one-story affairs.

Joy also reminded J.W. to "figure the cost of items that can not be moved from our present establishment, and the cost of moving present machinery and setting up, plus the additional cost of new machinery, to turn out the quantity of automobiles as mentioned before. Will you let me know how soon in advance of the need for the necessary machinery will it have to be ordered say to be set up and operating by Oct. 1. I must insist on your earliest possible consideration of these matters as we don't want any slips to hold us up." Plan, build and occupy a brand-new factory in a little over six months? Yes, that was the program. And amazingly enough Henry B. Joy wasn't far off the mark.

The plant site Joy finally bought, on May 19th, 1903, is today so swallowed up by the city of Detroit that it's hard to imagine it was first a cow pasture. Joy paid $19,434 for the 66.4 acres, then still outside the city limits on what was called Grande Boulevard. On the same date the board approved purchase of a strip of land the full length of the proposed factory, to be used to connect it to the Michigan Central Railway. And the plans submitted by Albert Kahn were approved and accepted.

Meanwhile, back in Warren, the Packards called a special meeting of stockholders on January 29th for the purpose of electing eight directors, as stipulated in the October 13th meeting. Only four stockholders were present—William Doud, James Ward and Sidney Waldon of Warren, Robert Gorton from Detroit, presenting the proxies of the Detroit investors. The directors elected, each to a one-year term, included the Packard brothers and Waldon and five Detroiters: Joy, Russell Alger, Joseph Boyer, Truman Newberry and Phillip McMillan.

While Detroit plans blossomed, there was still a business to run in

Left: The Model F of 1903, photographed during that summer. Right: The car Henry Joy loved to hate, an experimental chassis of the Model K.

Warren. One of its first activities in 1903 was something new to the industry in which Packard can rightly claim a pioneering role: a school for mechanics. The program consisted of a series of lectures to Packard employees on the principles of construction and operation of the parts which go into an automobile. One magazine called it "one of the best things that an automobile firm has ever done." At the suggestions of its classes, the company also started a library including "the standard works on automobiles and a copy of each of the trade papers."

On January 16th Fred March and Sidney Waldon left for New York to set up Packard's display at Madison Square Garden's 1903 automobile show, scheduled for the 17th through the 24th. Waldon managed the booth for the entire week, with Joy and J.W. Packard stopping by several times. The company had taken over the Adams and McMurtry retail outlet in New York in October 1902, so some representation from Warren was doubtless desirable.

Another reason Joy wanted Packard in New York that January was to attend a meeting of the new Association of Licensed Automobile Manufacturers with the Electric Vehicle Company, holder of the famed Selden Patent. This association, represented by men like Packard and Joy, George Pierce, Elwood Haynes, Edgar Apperson and others, was organized to deal as a body with royalty claims exercised by Electric Vehicle on behalf of George B. Selden. Selden had been granted a patent in 1895 on "gasoline automobiles," and demanded royalties from most manufacturers, suing those who objected. Nearly everyone, including Henry Joy, felt the patent was unfair, but preferred paying the royalty to wasting time in court, though he happily noted to J.W. that with the A.L.A.M., at least Electric Vehicle would have to deal with an association representative.

At the same time several non-member companies led by Ford were banding together to fight the Selden claims and, in 1911, they finally won. Until then Packard displayed Selden Patent plates, and James Ward's diary records that his company agreed to pay Electric Vehicle one half of one percent of the retail price of each Packard sold.

Back at the automobile show, Joy asked Packard if some of the department heads from the upholstery, body and machine shops might attend the exhibit and relieve Waldon, whom he felt ought to be paying more attention to the overall promotion program. Joy was similarly asking Waldon when he was going to start advertising the new models, and complained that new copy was being run with old (1902) Model F's.

As time passed, Sidney Waldon became abundantly active in various publicity stunts including some incredible record and test runs, which probably pleased Joy. To Waldon, too, goes the credit for Packard's first-published periodical, "Strong Talk," a newsletter sent out for the first time in December 1902, containing letters of praise from satisfied customers, but no photographs. Next came "Packard Pointers," printed on fine quality paper; it was still being published at least as late as July 1903. This little sheet was forerunner to *The Packard* magazine.

The New York show exhibits included the well-known Model F, altered for 1903 with a longer hood, but using approximately the same removable type tonneau and featuring only minor mechanical changes. The Packard Model G was not present. Joy mentioned "turning the big G into money" to Packard in one letter, but regretted that so many were at the New York dealership, and suggested making trucks out of them back in Detroit. (We have already noted the 1921 truck brochure showing an apparent Model G with truck body.) The big G was fading rapidly; even ever faithful Harlan Whipple offered to trade his, plus $2500, for a new Model K. But at least one Model G survived in private hands, because a 1914 issue of *The Packard* noted that one J.T. Robinett of Farmersville, Illinois wrote for parts and "received the same treatment for his two cylinder veteran as the owner of an S-48 limousine." The only Model G known to exist today—and probably this same car—is owned by Lindley Bothwell of California.

The Model F wasn't new, of course, so the big news at the New York show was the just-released Model K—Packard's first four-cylinder car—a rear entrance tonneau touring model. Though the K was on the road the previous fall—and Schmidt had been working on it since his arrival the previous April—New York was its first formal appearance.

Of the Model K, *The Automobile* said its "workmanship, design and finish is easily in the front rank of all the American cars shown, and may be regarded as registering its makers conviction that the French type is after all 'the thing' for those who can pay for it." They were referring to the price—a whopping $7500—which put Packard on top of literally everybody else at the time. (William Rockefeller iced the cake by paying $8160 for his K, with a special body—his ninth Packard.)

The Model K featured a sloping, Renault-like hood, a 91-inch wheelbase, a bore and stroke of 4 by 5 inches, and 24 horsepower. The credit for producing it has often gone to Henry Joy, but, as we shall see, he was for the type of vehicle that would sell best, regardless of the number of cylinders. And he thought the K was pretty terrible.

Joy's first ride in a K, which he called an "experimental model," was in Warren on February 25th. The next day he wrote James Ward saying that it "misses, due to excess of oil in the cylinders, due to splash feed lubrication. I am and always have been opposed to the splash feed lubrication in the crankcase although it might be used in Europe. The operation of the 'K' machine in Warren was a disgrace to the Packard Company and is better to be scrapped if it can not be made to run, and the rest of them treated in the same manner. [Splash lubrication] destroys a gasoline engine by getting oil where it is not wanted on the spark plugs. Do you believe me I can prove it?" In a subsequent letter Joy says he had never seen a Model K run with any satisfaction: "The certain positive operation of the F is not like the K.''

James Ward Packard replied, saying the K was not a splash feed. Joy retorted, "It certainly is," and he was probably right—after the dash-mounted oiler had dumped all its oil through the various oil lines into the crankcase. Joy suggested using baffle plates to keep the splashing out of the cylinders, and told Packard he would come to Warren, New York or Chicago to drive the car, "when they get it running right."

That must have rocked Packard's founder. On March 9th Joy apologized, but didn't back down. The K, he said, was put together with the best of interest, yet he'd never seen it operate except in "the most discreditable manner. No. 1 K misses with delightful irregularity and the noise of the exhaust is heart rending, these are defects for which I can see no cause and there ends my experience as I have never seen No. 2 K."

But Henry Joy was an astute businessman, and despite his complaints he realized that to recoup an investment the Model K would have to be sold—twelve of them were to be built in 1903—and if it was to be sold it would need be promoted. In April he asked if No. 1 K might not be sent up to Detroit for publicity purposes, and this was done. In the meantime he ordered another K, for delivery by June 1st, planning to continue his promotion campaign, and take the car with him and Truman Newberry on vacation to Watch Hill, Rhode Island, in July.

But the poor Model K was destined not to please Henry B. Joy. New York's W.S. Ions drove No. 1 K to Detroit in May; the batteries were dead, he told Joy, but on inspection it was found only that the wires were crossed. The carburetor was fouled, though, and Joy had to tinker with it himself. "Ions is a good mechanic and machinist," Joy wrote James Ward, "but he is not an electrician and knows nothing except in an ignorant way." Tom Fetch was sent to help. "Fetch did a far better job than Ions on tuning up the K," remarked Henry.

"I think the changes that Schmidt can make on the cam and gear case should be made first or we will have old K's on our hands like the old F's," was the vice-president's next comment. (This must have been received less than happily in Warren.) "I think the next work on the K should be on next year's model." (Ditto.)

Back in Detroit, No. 1 K ran well for a few days. Then it dropped its driveshaft. Schmidt later said this occurred when the K struck a sudden rise in the road while the brake was on, "causing the rear axle to twist down, allowing the shaft to drop." Joy was quick to write: "The shaft is insufficiently keyed for a transmission of so much power. I would hope you would remedy the problem before you sell me one of those cars. It must be on others already out." Packard wouldn't, and it was.

Truman Newberry had taken delivery of another Model K in July, and had driven it out to Watch Hill. Joy wrote James Ward with familiar news: Newberry's driveshaft had dropped out. Twice.

Newberry wrote a letter too. Unfortunately it is lost to history, but one can guess what it said, for James Ward Packard noted in his diary for July 18th, 1903: "Letter from Newberry today causes me to decide to withdraw from the Packard Motor Car Company."

Packard had, of course, not exercised executive authority for some time—at least not since the October 13th, 1902 board meeting. That had been left to Joy, and James Ward had in fact read a statement of resignation as president to the board earlier, on June 16th. But he had remained plant manager, and his role was still important.

Packard's announcement quickly reached Henry Joy—and caused some soul searching. To Truman Newberry, Joy wrote: "I hardly know how to express my feelings in regard to your action in writing such a letter as you did to the Packard Motor Car Co. at Warren . . . It seems to me that you have taken the functions of the board into your hands by having written such a letter . . . insulting Mr. Packard and throwing aside all due regard to whether or not your associates might wish to drive Mr. Packard out of the company which is the effect your letter has had."

Russell A. Alger arrived in Warren on the 20th to try to change J.W.'s mind. Packard told Alger, "I will continue for the present." That didn't bode well, so Joy finally wrote James Ward himself: "I can only state to you that I have never been so shocked and so severely chagrined that any of my associates should write such a letter as this to you with utter disregard for decency not only with reference to you but to [plant superintendent] Moore, and your company. I can not find words to express to you how deeply I feel about the matter and your efforts for the company against your will. I have the greatest respect for you. . . ."

What was meant by "efforts for the company against your will?" Had Packard told Alger that, after all, he had been against a four-cylinder car

Ready for what doubtless would have been a chilly outing, the Model K of 190

from the very beginning? Had he told Alger that he would have preferred to keep the company in Warren, and was only going along with the Detroit move in the firm's best interests? Had he said he was fed up with the whole Detroit lot of them? Possibly. Judging by the tenor of Henry Joy's comments about the Model K, he had a right to be.

Joy's letter to Packard was his last before leaving himself for Rhode Island—one wonders what he had determined to say to Newberry there—but all the bite was out of him, at least this time. He suggested that Packard not wait for him to test his own K at Watch Hill, and that James Ward go ahead now with any changes to the car that J.W. felt necessary. At Watch Hill he would only need two extra tires. But around the same time Joy was admonishing the New York agency, which was shipping his K to Rhode Island, to "keep it in a glass case."

Joy drove his Model K in New England that summer and made several runs to Newport to show the car's speed. In September the car was shipped back to Detroit without further incident. Joy had stopped taking pot-shots at the Model K, all right. And very possibly, the heart had gone out of James Ward Packard.

In the beginning of 1903, Detroit still didn't have a Packard dealer. With control of the company—and ultimately the company itself—vested there, this would never do. Joy and Russell Alger suggested in January that the Models F and K from New York be shipped to Metzger & Company in Detroit, where they could be used in the local automobile show from February 9th to the 15th. Metzger was already the agent for Winton, Cadillac and others, but was willing to take on Packard, if he could get it. Metzger didn't get the New York cars, as it turned out—there apparently wasn't any desire by New York to ship them away

A Packard in seeming peril, probably the Model M ready for testing, May 1903.

—but he did become Packard's Detroit representative in April. Just before the Detroit show opened, Joy wrote Waldon saying, "Wintons are not in top notch popular favor in Detroit," and mentioning that the Model F would be well received there. "But in order to do so it must, of course, be introduced by the agent and Mr. Alger and I think Mr. Metzger is the best recognized agent. I don't know what territory we could give him or arrangement with him, if any is made. But I think it is desirable. . . . If you make any arrangements with Metzger it should be distinctly understood, that as to territory, he should be protected under sales from the factory. He will doubtless insist on this." We see that even as early as 1903, dealer territories had become important. So too had product planning, and 1903 was to prove a year when Packard would try, and revise or replace, several products.

In 1903 alone, no less than five and possibly six different models were built and driven for tests: Models F, G, K, M and L—the L being of course a 1904 model—and one other car suggested by Joy: a small one-cylinder runabout to compete with the Olds. How far the latter project proceeded is not known, though one unidentified photo of May 1903 shows a smaller model different from the others in frontal styling.

Alphabetical order suggests that the Model L was laid down before the M, but it was common practice to "reserve" model designations in advance and to build another model with a later designation first. This may have been the case with the missing Models D, H, I and J, and as noted earlier only one Model E was built. Then at some point before production, the machines might have proven unworkable, or the company might simply have chosen not to produce them, and they were dropped. The Model M was built, but it didn't last long.

The M design was approved at the first board meeting in Detroit, on February 5th, 1903—this probably stemmed from Joy's approval a month earlier of "the $1500.00, 1500 p-d machine" which he hoped "could be gotten on the road as soon as possible." If it ever did get on the road, it was only in test form, for Joy's letters record the birth and death of the M in the short period from February through June 1903.

No drawings, specifications or photos now known show us what the Model M looked like. All Joy says of it was that it was a one-cylinder water-cooled casting without the copper jacket like the other one-cylinder Packards, and was rated at fourteen horsepower. In a letter to James Ward Packard dated February 26th, Joy inquired if it is "not possible to lubricate the crankshaft and cylinder of the M machine as is done on our F? I do not like the splash system and feel it will interfere with the ignition." It is not likely that the M had a vertical cylinder, which meant it used another horizontal single like the contemporary and successful Model F. And, since the F produced twelve horsepower and the M only two more, it's hard to understand why the company would experiment with such a close design in the first place.

73

The Old Pacific saga. Taking on the sand hills in Utah and seeing to a tire near Reno, with N.O. Allyn on the left, Fetch the right, Krarup behind the camera.

On March 10th Joy asked James Ward for some sketches and outlines of suggested Model M bodies. "No possible effort [should] be spared to make this machine pleasing to the eye and easy to manipulate and in fact a jewel which at a glance a person will say there is the most attractive thing I have ever seen. You can do this if you will. I know positively, and such is my firm faith in you."

Later in March Joy had another idea: "I feel our next vehicle must be the two seated type runabout. If we can get up such a machine and get it right, use single cylinder like the Olds, it would be an excellent car. Sell it for $900 to $1000 suitable for physicians or businessmen's use. I believe we can make a machine far better than any on the market today." The little curved dash Oldsmobile was everywhere in Detroit at the time, and obviously inspired this thought; though the M then being developed wasn't exactly like the Olds, it was a step in the lower-priced direction.

On April 9th Joy wrote that he was anxious to go to Warren to see the M as soon as it was completed, and that he hoped to get settled with James Ward on what next year's plans would be. "Surely we should be able to make money with the 25 hp K, 14 hp M or a single cylinder runabout." Joy appeared to be frustrated by the proliferation of models being built or developed, and apparently wanted to settle on one or two.

Throughout April the factory had difficulties obtaining good castings for the M engine, effectively delaying the entire project. Joy asked Moore to send a man to Detroit to see if the castings could be poured there, then asked Moore to talk with Schmidt about changing the design to use a copper water jacket like the F, and a simpler casting. In the meantime, Joy arranged for more castings to be made in a Detroit foundry.

The delay had its effect on May 7th, when Joy wrote, "We feel that it is okay to make up a few more M machines, one of them to be in the form of a delivery wagon. Newberry and Alger think the M machine should be kept very quiet and not offered to agents at all this year, and possibly late in the season, allow some private owners to get the machine known for next year." This apparently referred to early prototypes or test models. Joy asked James Ward for his impressions of the M on May 13th, and according to J.W.'s diary the M was "out and running" on May 21st.

Possibly a Model M did take commercial form as Joy had suggested, as a photo does exist of a 1903 panel delivery made in Warren, with a P.M.C.C. sign painted on its side. Another model has the look of a 1902 Model F chassis roadster body and seat, but with a completely different Mercedes-type hood, unlike the 1903 Model F panel delivery which we do know was built. It looks unakin to any other Packard, and could indeed be the Model M; the date when it appeared in "Packard Pointers" coincides with the M's completion date.

By June 9th, still only one Model M had been tested. James Ward noted it was "not very promising." He then sent a report to Joy, who replied that "the difficulties enumerated in the M machine lead to the

Sand, mud and desolation. A bit of a problem encountered in Nevada and working to extricate themselves from yet another near Thompson, Utah.

conclusion that the proper machine is the four cylinder vertical, where there is a proper place for everything and everything can be in its place.''

Joy's last letter to J.W. concerning the M leads into the beginnings of the first model to be sold in Detroit—the Model L. "The more you rub elbows with the M machine," he wrote, "the more you will come to what I understand is your model L sketch in my judgment. It is not too late to change, I learn from all sides more and more that manufacturers are universally considering the four cylinder vertical for anything above the little runabout class.'' This letter was dated June 11th; at a board meeting in Detroit on the 16th, James Ward writes that "the decision is made in favor of the four cylinder cars.'' Thus ended the Model M, and Packard's last attempt to produce another single-cylinder car.

The remainder of the year, except for the development of the new Model L, would be spent perfecting the four-cylinder K and continuing to produce the faithful F, which would be sold alongside the Models K and L into the beginning of 1904. It is interesting that until the Model M, all the Packard singles were designed by William Hatcher—with great success. Hatcher had resigned from Packard in January 1903, and Schmidt turned some of his efforts to developing the Model M—which was not his kind of engine. This no doubt had a lot to do with its failure.

The 1903 Model F was not much different from its 1902 predecessor. The body had higher seats—which probably were the result of Joy's complaints about his 1902's seats hitting him in the middle of his back—and the front boot took on a longer, lower-slipping bonnet to cover the oil, water and fuel tanks previously mounted over the motor, in the rear. Early 1903 Model F's displayed three brass filler caps on their front hoods, so that the tanks might be filled without raising the lid. Possible body movements doubtlessly proved to pull the necks loose,

because later Model F's did not have these visible.

Model F sales were what kept the factory going and money coming in during 1903. Somewhere around 150 were sold that year, for a grand total of close to 400 single-cylinder Packards in the four years of Warren production. But the F later caused a production bottleneck. Due to the problems in getting out the four-cylinder Model K in late 1902, the 1903 F was held back and the 1902 overproduced. Henry Joy saw some of these '02's in Warren, and wrote J.W. and Waldon to move them out, imploring them to plan ahead on the 1903 cars so that they would not be left with old models at the end of that year. In any case, the Warren factory was keeping a lot of men working.

One of those employed at Warren during the last year of manufacture was Jay Raymond, a young lad who had taken a summer job at the company before finishing his fourth year of high school. The writer encountered Mr. Raymond quite by accident, having intended to talk to his wife—who was the daughter of George Kirkham, buyer of the first Packard sold back in 1900. Needless to say, his reminiscence of those days at Warren was fascinating, and is the only eyewitness account to goings on at the factory in the final year of production.

"My job was to be the making up and installation of electrical cables," he remembered. "I recall one hot August afternoon—daresay I had probably been over at Danceland for refreshments—I was tired and had my fanny up on the bench. Suddenly a voice behind me bellowed out, 'Young man, if you aren't strong enough to stand on your two feet you should not be working in this factory.' It was the voice of top superintendent C.J. Moore. This man could never remember my name and always called me Clarence."

Raymond worked in the two-story frame building which was located

A railroad crossing (left) and a stop for necessities and a fresh supply of gasoline; a cattle crossing (right) and for a short while the trekkers were not alone.

beside the assembly building, completed in January 1902. Here the wooden bodies were constructed, the copper tanks and cylinder jackets formed, wood patterns for castings made, the bodies upholstered and painted. But even with the new buildings just completed, the Warren plant was having difficulty meeting demand, which helps explain the need for a move which occurred during late 1903.

The factory brochure for the 1903 Packard Model F marks the beginning of Packard's long line of superlative auto literature. A beautiful red cover bore the title, "The Highest Pinnacle," in what looked like gold inlay, and the brochure took the reader on a beautifully illustrated tour of the Warren plant complex. It ended with a familiar challenge: "There are two ways for you to make dead sure a Packard will give you satisfaction: Ask The Man Who Owns One, and Buy One." It was without doubt the prettiest piece of literature produced in Warren. But Warren's role in the history of Packard was now waning rapidly. So too was James Ward Packard's.

After the July 18th decision by James Ward to completely leave the company, and his temporary stay of that decision upon the visit of Russell Alger, Joy left for Watch Hill, Rhode Island. His secretary wrote him there, saying Alger was disappointed that he had left without resolving the situation—before he had left, it is noted, Alger and Newberry had asked him to take over management of the company, which his secretary said had come about practically at the request of James Ward and Waldon. Boyer and McMillan had already approved, and the only votes remaining were William Doud's and Joy's himself. But as Joy did not indicate he would assume the management of the company before leaving, Alger wondered if he was declining? If he was not, Alger and Newberry felt, he should be taking charge of things at Warren—at once.

Henry Joy's quick shift to his summer home may have been a case of Caesar turning away the crown. For it was pretty obvious that he would take over full managerial authority—had in fact taken it over, unofficially, some months before. It also seems likely that Newberry purposely wrote a rough letter to Packard in an attempt to bring the situation to an immediate conclusion—but that is mere conjecture. It is odd, though, that Joy didn't assure Packard he would rebuke Newberry.

Joy finally said yes, of course, and James Ward's diary records his arrival to "take full charge of P.M.C.C." on September 11th, 1903. Three days before this, officers were elected, with Alger becoming vice-president and Phillip H. McMillan as secretary-treasurer. James Ward was again elected president, and would be through 1909—the board was having none of his resignation, though whether this was in his honor or the interests of the company is subject to debate. Perhaps each director had his own private thoughts. Regardless, the real change was Henry Joy's becoming general manager of the company, now officially in charge of all operations in Warren, and the coming plant in Detroit.

Joy had thought it wise to either cut back on the new Detroit plant or borrow some money to help finance it, to keep from biting too deeply into working capital. This was done. After a board meeting in mid-June, the plans and specifications by Kahn had been approved and the contracts to build the plant authorized, the cost not to exceed $117,309, plus $5000 more for washroom fittings. James Ward as president issued contracts to the firm of Teakle and Golden of Detroit, who undertook to have the completed factory, four times the size of Warren, ready for occupancy in September or October of 1903. Soon Packard would pass away from Warren and James Ward Packard, to Detroit under Henry Bourne Joy. But Warren had yet two more great achievements to offer—two cars

No welcoming party, but chances were anyone emerging from the house Fetch and Old Pacific were approaching would be seeing their first automobile.

vastly different from one another, but which jointly made the name of Packard renowned throughout the world: Old Pacific and Gray Wolf.

On June 20th, 1903, around the time construction began on the Detroit factories, Warren sent one of its 1903 Model F Packards on a trip across the American continent. Until then, no automobile of any kind had made this trip successfully, though many had tried and failed. The only trip known at all was by one Tom Stevens on a bicycle, Stevens riding this unlikely vehicle between oceans as part of a round-the-world trip in 1885. In July of 1903 George Wyman was to make the trek with a motorcycle, but he would estimate that he pushed his vehicle fully 1500 miles through sand, snow and mud. A perfect highway, as the Automobile Club of America wrote at the time, was still "a dream, one which makes one tingle with pleasurable anticipation."

The first tingle came between May 23rd and July 26th, 1903, when Dr. H. Nelson Jackson from Burlington, Vermont, and his mechanic, Sewall K. Crocker, drove from San Francisco to New York City in a used two-cylinder Winton. Jackson did it on a bet, and his sixty-three-day trip saw a rod coming out through the crankcase, but nothing else of any consequence. Numerous reports noted that the Winton had been helped along by rail shipment part of the way, but Winton fought these reports and in fact offered a $10,000 reward to anyone who could prove them. The good Doctor added $15,000. No one ever claimed the money.

The fact that Winton was in the act may have awakened a spark in James Ward Packard; certainly the idea of trying a transcontinental run in a Packard came from Warren, originated by J.W. and advertising man Sidney Waldon. A month before the Winton began its trip Joy had written Waldon saying he wished to do advertising that would keep Packard's name on top, and had talked to Mr. Alger "relative to the cross country trip Waldon and Mr. Packard have had in mind for so long. Mr. Newberry thought the money could be spent more wisely on the back cover of Colliers because traveling about the country by automobile is not as much of a novelty as formerly [but] it is not our plan to oppose or restrict your plans for advertising. I want to have people crying for Packard machines and not put a veto on any plans to advertise the Packard and if in the judgment of yourself and Mr. Packard . . . [this] is the plan you want and [you] can make a lot of noise about it, go ahead." Joy also reminded Waldon to do efficient newspaper work and have photographs made of the machine in all sorts of circumstances. Waldon did. It is estimated that close to 750 photographs were taken.

Back in March, James Ward Packard had proposed that the editor of *The Automobile*, Marius C. Krarup, be informed of each day's run for the purpose of a weekly report in his magazine. But circumstances provided better than that—Krarup came along. A guide hired to accompany the car failed to show up, and Krarup took advantage of the vacancy to hop aboard—he wasn't much of a guide, but he was ideal for publicity.

Tom Fetch of the Warren plant was selected to pilot the car, a Model F which, according to the *Warren Tribune* of June 8th, "had been taken from stock and is very similar to the one they make and sell every day." Its extra equipment was, however, fairly comprehensive: There were two extra fuel tanks, a lower first gear, variable combustion chamber for high altitudes, repair materials and two small valises for personal belongings. Instruments included a compass, thermometer, barometer, gradometer and extra cyclometer, along with a portable camera for taking all those photos. To deal with mud and sand there were a pair of boots, a stout shovel, two 6 by 20 foot canvas strips and some heavy logging chains. And a .38 caliber revolver was holstered on the dash—there were still Indians in them thar hills.

All luggage and an extra axle, plus a three-gallon can of drinking water, were strapped to the sloping rear deck. A camping outfit was bought after the start, and somewhere along the way a large umbrella was also added as protection from sun and rain. A little canvas awning was built over the front end of the car to shield the radiator coils.

The start was made by Harold W. Larzalere, Packard's Pacific Coast agent, at 5:00 p.m. on the 20th. Fetch and Krarup drove up to Cliff House for a last look at the Pacific before turning east for New York, 3000 miles away. Actually it would be 5600 miles up, down and around before they saw Manhattan. As they swung over to the route of the Southern Pacific, whose line they would follow on the first leg across the Sierras, they decided on the name for their car: Old Pacific.

The Sierra was crossed via Truckee and the Southern Pacific route took the travelers to Reno, Nevada, then on to Ogden, Utah. From Ogden the course was laid through Salt Lake City; crossing the Rockies at 11,000 feet was a "first" in a motorcar.

Road maps, signs and route numbers were unknown in those days, and the only published guide of any kind was a Union Pacific railroad map. There were no roads or bridges, except those built by railroads, west of Denver. When Fetch would follow a good road, it often ended in someone's farmyard, so he began avoiding these and sticking to the compass and open country. He didn't often ask for directions either, as most people had never traveled further than a day's drive in a horse and buggy. Gasoline was shipped ahead by rail to the various destinations, since it could not be bought along the way.

As Old Pacific would pull into many western towns, people would be seeing an automobile for the first time. At Carson City, Fetch and Krarup arrived shortly after a murder had occurred, and everyone including the sheriff left the scene of the crime to look at the car. In another town they arrived on a Sunday morning, and caused an entire church congregation to run outside, leaving the pastor with rows of empty pews.

Many accounts of the trip tell of the close calls Fetch had coming down the mountains, trying to keep the Packard from running away. One reporter told of an 80 mph plunge down into Carson City, and Fetch related the occasions they bounded down narrow mountain trails, each man holding on for life, and how often at the bottom of a hill he would "spit on the brake band to watch it bounce."

The worst roads, Fetch said, were encountered through Utah, "between Carlton and Grande Junction. The Nevada desert was not as bad as told to us, but Utah was seven times worse. At Glenwood, Colorado, it rained and the water made the alkali roads like soap, making steering impossible. The front wheels instead of steering slid, and one of the party would walk alongside the front and help guide the machine. Gullies across the roads in the alkali plains were without doubt the worst of the whole trip. Appearing about every 100' throughout the desert we had to take them as they came, as we found when we got off the road there were more. The strain going down into the gullies on the machine was awful and I was afraid something was going to break, but Old Pacific stood it all."

Welcoming parties would meet Fetch outside most of the larger towns and escort him in. The first such group, at Denver, included three new 1903 Model F Packards like Old Pacific, and George Gorton from the Warren office was among the party. On August 11th, the Fetch Packard pulled into Chicago, and was met by Colonel Pardee, the local dealer, and Sidney Waldon, who paraded with thirty cars to the auto club.

When Fetch was to pass through Ohio the Packard Company set off a gala celebration, closing the Warren factory so folks could give Tom a reception in Jefferson, his hometown. They didn't want Fetch to drive to Warren; competitors would then say the stop was for repairs.

On August 14th the Cleveland Auto Club met Fetch and escorted him to its headquarters, but he didn't waste much time there; he was only thirty miles from seeing his wife for the first time in about two months. On Saturday, August 15th, he arrived home in Jefferson, a public hero. The next morning he left for Buffalo.

By August 21st Fetch had reached Tarrytown, New York. There he was greeted by some two hundred cars, and a huge motorized caravan proceeded south toward New York, with Old Pacific leading. "The machine was bending all the 8 MPH speed limits going into New York City," commented *Motor Age*, and afterward Fetch admitted he was getting anxious. "From Herkimer N.Y. I drove almost steadily for 40 hours. I continually had to fight off sleepiness and the effects of road glare, but the thought that I was on the last lap kept me going!"

Old Pacific arrived in New York on the evening of the 21st, having cut the Winton's time down to sixty-one days. That must have pleased James Ward Packard. During the entire 5600-mile trip, the car needed no major repairs, and N.O. Allyn, who had joined Fetch and Krarup in Reno, had left in Denver after traveling the distance between on the rear deck with the luggage—he got bored, having nothing to do. A front spring

Taking a well-deserved break and meeting some Sunday strollers (above). An overnight stay at Beck's ranch in Edward, Colorado, west of Denver (below).

broke in Sterling, Colorado, Fetch had to grind an exhaust valve at Marengo, Iowa, and at Lyon, New York, the drive chain broke. But that was all. One of the original four tires was still on the car.

"The entry into New York was a veritable triumphal procession," said *Motor Age*, "with the brilliant lamps on the machines shining through the dark and all the occupants were singing. At the Packard headquarters on West Fifty-ninth St. the tourists were surrounded by newspapermen, automobilists, and tradesmen, where until the late hour they were kept busy answering questions. Old Pacific had only the thick dust and coated mud of travel to point to, as ear marks of an achievement that will make its name famous in automobile annals." How true.

On August 22nd, the *Warren Tribune* banner headlined: "Fetch and Old Pacific Have Finished Their Journey! . . . Greatest Trip on Record"—and in a subsequent edition turned to the pragmatic: "It demonstrates the superiority of the Packard machine over all other models, and this will be worth all the thousands of dollars it has cost the company." Never before had the little town of Warren had so much publicity. Tom Fetch's remarks on finishing the trip were more to the point: "Thank God It's Over!"

The many photos helped Old Pacific receive auto magazine coverage in record proportion, sometimes three or four pages to an issue in those days when issues were slim. Krarup, of course, covered it for *The Automobile* in lavish fashion. But Tom Fetch said, "Even photos can not do the trip justice. It was hard, very hard, and I do not care to make the trip again. Not only the physical part but the mental strain worrying over the bad outlook at times was immense." Fetch—and Old Pacific—had become legends. (Old Pacific is on display today at the Henry Ford Museum in Dearborn, Michigan.)

In view of his promotional flair, it is rather strange that Henry B. Joy wasn't more exuberant about Old Pacific's trip, though he did write Packard that he thought it was "doing splendidly." Perhaps this was because it wasn't his idea. Neither did James Ward comment in his diary on the Fetch trip, which is stranger still since he was one of those who thought of it. He talked instead about matters nearer at hand, the new factory in Detroit, the decision to build four-cylinder cars, and the racing car they were working on in Warren—the Gray Wolf.

Being powered by a Model K four-cylinder engine, the Gray Wolf had a 25 hp rating, but did become more square in engine configuration with a new 4-3/16th-inch bore instead of four inches as on the stock Model K. Unlike the four-speed K, it had only two speeds, which was part of engineer Schmidt's weight-saving technique, as was the aluminum body, which was pretty sparse from the dash to back. There were a pair of very low, small bucket-type seats and a pointed rear fuel tank having only a six-gallon capacity behind the driver. Instead of a heavy steel-plated and wood frame like the stock Model K, the Gray Wolf used a pressed steel frame, and featured spidery 34-inch wire wheels with 3½-inch tires instead of the 36x4-inch wooden artillery wheels of the passenger car. At 1310 pounds total weight, against 2200 in the passenger K, it was enormously successful in its weight reduction, but it was placed at first in the 1800-pound class with cars of forty and fifty horsepower.

When Packard entered oval dirt track racing, only a handful of auto companies were sponsoring cars. Among these were Winton and his Bullets, Ford with his 999, the Peerless Green Dragon, and Oldsmobile's Pirate. Most other cars were privately entered by individuals who simply removed their touring bodies and rode the track in a stock chassis with a seat attached.

The incentive to improve American racing cars probably came from the influx of foreign machines used by rich Americans and foreigners on U.S. tracks. Many of these cars had been successful in road racing, but in America they faced a different set of circumstances—American auto racing was done on oval horse tracks. It took a certain kind of nerve to drive a 1903 car at about 60 mph around one of these ovals, and horse

Offering aid to a Winton in trouble at Grand Canyon entrance (left); taking the Nebraska tall grass and in a little trouble themselves near Clark (below).

tracks that had had the same fence for years soon found out that a number of feet of same had to be replaced after every auto race.

Some two months before the Joy correspondence over Old Pacific, James Ward Packard and Sidney Waldon had conceived of a racing car for the same purpose—publicity. In this case too, Joy was less than enthusiastic: "If we can sell our output without that expense the matter need not be pursued with any particular haste." Fortunately, again, Joy's advice wasn't taken, and on March 14th the board decided to make a racing car out of one of the first group of Model K's. Perhaps its Model K base was the reason Joy wasn't enthusiastic . . .

Schmidt, with racing car experience behind him from his Mors days, took charge, with James Ward closely following his progress, on what they first called the K Special. On May 7th J.W.'s diary noted the ordering of "some light rims for the K Special and 3½" racing tires." In early July he invited Henry Joy to come to Warren to see the car, and on July 30th James Ward recorded its first trial.

Another test occurred on Saturday, August 8th, 1903. This time the K Special was taken to the Warren fairground track a few blocks from the factory, and there, James Ward notes, the car did a mile in 1:26. On August 19th, James Ward ordered more tires.

On August 28th, the Trumbull County Fair Board announced that Tom Fetch would be on hand with Old Pacific and that Charles Schmidt would run an exhibition mile in the K Special racing car. According to the *Warren Tribune* of September 3rd, Schmidt "circled the track ten times in the excellent time of 6:36.5 and his best mile was caught by many watches at 1:16. This is a remarkable time for a half mile track and showed that the Packard Co. had a very speedy machine." The *Cleveland Plain Dealer* of the same morning called the car the Gray Wolf for the first time, and the following Monday James Ward refers to it by that name for the first time. No explanation is given for the selection, but the car was gray in color and it did look like a crouching wolf, waiting to spring on its prey, so that probably was the basis for it.

Schmidt's first big event after Trumbull, subject of the *Plain Dealer* report, was the Second Annual Cleveland Auto Club race meet at the Glenville race track in Cleveland on September 4th and 5th. Only two foreign cars and the Olds Pirate, aside from the Gray Wolf, were out of town entries, but Oldfield was there with Winton Bullet No. 2 and W.C. Baker entered his Torpedo Kid, so the competition was formidable.

Schmidt had an unfortunate accident in practice, just after clocking his best time of twenty-seven seconds for the half mile. Entering a turn he swerved to avoid a large touring car and crashed broadside into the inner fence, breaking the Gray Wolf's cooling pipes and wheels and three of his own ribs. At exactly the same time Oldfield in Bullet No. 2 had thrown a rod, which stopped his car instantly; had he not, some said, he would have run into the crowd around Schmidt's demolished machine. Oldfield

won the race, but many reports said it would have been a bit more difficult for him had Schmidt been there to race against him.

The Gray Wolf was quickly repaired and taken to Grosse Pointe for another event the following Monday, with Detroit racing driver Harry Cunningham subbing for the injured Schmidt. This race was won by Tom Cooper in Ford's 999, but not without an epic dice between Oldfield and Cunningham for second spot, which Cunningham eventually won. *Motor Age* was impressed: "With but a few hours practice, and that on a wet track, this young man took a new racer out and made the other drivers and cars work to beat him."

The Gray Wolf went on to Providence on September 19th, with Schmidt at the wheel again, then to the Empire City track in New York and the Brighton Beach races on Long Island. Albert Champion, son of the spark plug Champion, took a turn at the wheel at Brighton Beach, but the car got away from him, crashing against the fence. The Gray Wolf was then sent to Detroit to be rebuilt for Florida.

Preliminary speed trials were held on the Ormond-Daytona Beach course the first week of January 1904, in anticipation of races to be held there later in the month, after the New York show. On January 2nd Charles Schmidt in the Gray Wolf broke Alexander Winton's straightaway record of 4:46.5 with the Winton Bullet No. 1, Barney Oldfield's Los Angeles track record of 4:40.5 with the Bullet No. 2, and the world's record for the 1430-pound class, all in the five-mile straightaway. He also broke all American records for all weights in the one-mile straightaway, covering same in 46.4 seconds (77.6 mph), though on the 12th Henry Ford broke it again with 39.4 seconds on the ice of Baltimore Bay, near Detroit with his 999.

During the summer the Gray Wolf was prepared for the Vanderbilt Cup road race on Long Island, and by the time it appeared on race day, October 8th, it was a different looking car from the day it had been born. The front axle was now attached to two fore/aft springs on each side of a squared-off front frame, giving the car a more stable front end over the road course, and its wheelbase was extended from 92 to 104 inches. The hood was extended another eighteen inches, making an already long bonnet unbelievably lengthy now, and the cooling tubes formerly placed along the frame were relocated above it. For clearing the road, a bulb horn was fastened to the outside of the body on the mechanic's side, and some small alterations were made to the engine.

Unfortunately the Vanderbilt didn't distinguish the Gray Wolf, partly because Charles Schmidt was so busy waving to friends he didn't hear the start. The race was strictly between George Heath in a Panhard and Albert Clément in a Clément-Bayard. Schmidt and four others were still lapping the circuit when the race ended and the crowd began to disperse on the course—which made things decidedly dicey for the remaining racing cars—but the Gray Wolf finished without a mishap.

The Vanderbilt was the last race for the Gray Wolf while in the hands of Packard. The showing it made was fine, finishing fourth overall, second among American entries. It might have been even better had Oldfield been driving—in April 1904 he had replied to Joy's suggestion that he take the car on for the Long Island race by saying he would, if Joy would give him a contract for the season. Apparently this was too much for Joy, so Schmidt and Cunningham campaigned the car instead.

In Henry Joy's scrapbook is a newspaper clipping dated January 1905, saying that the Gray Wolf had been sold to a rich motorist for a great price. This could have been the Colonel Green, or E.R. Green, said to have owned the car when it was raced on May 30th, 1905 at Chicago with Jesse Ellingsworth driving. This is the last record of the Gray Wolf in its racing days.

In its November 1913 issue, *The Packard* published a letter from one F.W. Ford asking for information on the Gray Wolf. He said he was using it as an outside attraction "for racing reels and moving picture theaters in Dallas, Texas." Packard did answer his letter, telling of the car's early racing accomplishments, but evinced no further interest in it. Fortunately, it was finally acquired by Barney Pollard of Detroit, who finished its restoration to original condition in 1972.

Thus the final days of the Packard Motor Car Company of Warren, Ohio, were rich with glory and the pride of accomplishment. If there were any who looked sadly on the move that was coming—and James Ward Packard may have been among these—they had at least some distractions in Old Pacific and the Gray Wolf that were worthy symbols of all that Warren had brought to the world of motoring. But even while the Gray Wolf was racing, on September 8th, 1903, Henry Joy was taking James Ward Packard's place, and on the 11th he was in Warren to see when all operations could be stopped for the move to Detroit. Coincidentally perhaps, Packard's first dealer George Blackmore drove his car to Warren the day Joy arrived; in a November issue *The Automobile* announced that Blackmore would take on the Winton franchise.

On September 14th, the *Warren Chronicle* noted that the company "this morning began tearing out machines for shipment to Detroit, Michigan." This was the only public notice of any kind on the move, though everyone obviously knew of it. Packard employed 300 men at the time, and as the target date of October 10th approached a few quit, but more decided to move with the company.

Summer rains had rendered the mud hub-deep and washed out bridges, as below near Grinnell, Iowa, but at last the sun was beginning to shine and the end in sight.

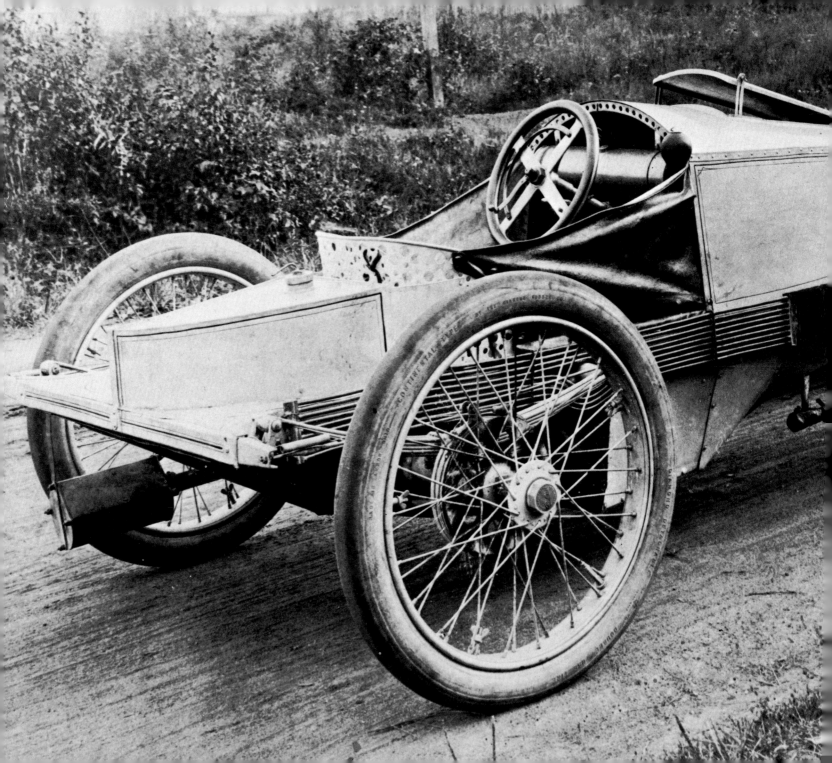

Born in July of 1903, the Gray Wolf was baptized the following month by Charles Schmidt with a mile in 1:16 at the Trumbull County Fairgrounds.

Histories have for years pointed the finger at Warren's city government for driving the company out of town. Alluded to already in this text was the antipathy generated by citizens against the automobile. And there were stories too of restrictions on new housing, which allegedly kept workers out of the wealthy residential area. Still, not all the brickbats tossed at Warren were well founded, for just a block beyond the factory a new zoning allotment had been opened in 1903 where people were invited to build. The newspapers were continually reporting what a fine place Warren—with its three different railroads—was to bring one's business, and just a day after Packard moved out, the Fredonia Automobile Company from Youngstown tried to raise enough money to move in. This did not occur, however, and it may be conjectured that Warren preferred small business to large manufacturing and heavy industry. Whatever the case, resolution of the confrontation between automobile factory and town was now reached, and the factory lost.

Much beyond the concerns of Warren, though, were those of the new managers of the company to make Packard larger, and to themselves provide the capital with which to do so. By every act and every letter, Joy and his associates demonstrated this from the day they took over effective control in October 1902, and though Henry B. Joy was a man of honor and integrity, it seems evident that he didn't object overstrenuously to his less polite associates aiding the cause by whatever method they chose, including Newberry's berating of James Ward over the Model K. James

85

*Harry Cunningham (above and left) at Grosse Pointe track, September 1903.
...bert Champion (below) diced with a fence and lost at Brighton Beach, October.*

Ward and William Doud did support the move to larger quarters in a large manufacturing city. But they had no plans to move with it.

The Packard Electric Company had continued to grow and develop, and had started producing waterproof wiring for the whole borning auto industry. It was in need of more attention. The New York & Ohio Company was selling light bulbs as fast as it could produce them, and at the time of the Detroit move William Doud was working toward the sale of this company to the National Electric Lamp Company, which in turn was to become part of General Electric. Both the Packard brothers were needed in Warren, their full interest required in the management of both companies for some years to come.

While the machinery was being taken apart and hauled away, the *Warren Tribune* noted that one last Packard was in for service—none other than Old Pacific, to be fitted with new bushings and chain in preparation for the big endurance contest in October from Cleveland to Pittsburgh, with Fetch to do the driving. As an honor to him and Old Pacific, Tom Fetch was allowed to lead the competing cars through Warren—to the cheers of many a resident, who thought he was leading the pack! Fetch must have talked with F.B. Stearns during the run, for he was hired away from Packard shortly afterward at a better price. The *Warren Tribune* told of a touching and affectionate farewell Fetch gave his old Packard—witnesses say he actually shed a tear.

Fetch in fact drove the Stearns car back through the Pennsylvania hills to New York after the run, but it was not many years later when he would rejoin Packard, for whom he would work in Detroit into the Teens. Later Tom would return to his home town of Jefferson, where he never failed to enjoy reliving those 5600 miles through sagebrush, sand and mud driving Old Pacific across the continent. He died in 1944, one year after the fortieth anniversary of his run and a dinner held in his honor by an old friend and fellow Packard employee, Barney Pollard.

Charles Schmidt moved with the company to Detroit, and remained with it until January 1905, when he left to accept a similar position with the Peerless Motor Car Company in Cleveland. He was making $5000 a year at Packard; Peerless thought enough of him to offer $10,000. Schmidt replaced Louis P. Mooers, the designer of Barney Oldfield's famous Green Dragon. Henry Joy gave a dinner in his honor at the Detroit Club, and expressed his regret at Schmidt's leaving.

To finish the move the company would still have a few more details to attend to in Detroit: On September 30th Joy wrote Moore saying Detroit could not possibly have steam in three weeks, and as late as that date they were still waiting for sprinkler systems, roads into the plant to get them out of the mud, board walks to walk on temporarily, heating plants for the buildings. Henry Joy certainly had his hands full, and was writing a number of letters daily through September to supplier firms, advising all that the equipment would be arriving from Warren by October 15th. At

On Long Island in October of 1904, Charles Schmidt posed with the Gray Wolf prior to the inaugural running of the Vanderbilt Cup classic. Alas, when the race started he was posing still—and waving to friends.

the same time he was working with the Everitt Auditing Company of Chicago in Warren, setting up a new bookkeeping system.

Joy contacted two railroads for shipping rates from Warren to Detroit. One suggested hauling from Warren to Cleveland, then boating the material across the lake to Detroit, unloading at Detroit and switching to another line out to the new plant. Too complicated, said Joy, who knew something about railroads. It was decided to ship around the lake and save the cost of switching in Cleveland and Detroit.

By October 5th, the time for the move was very close at hand. Joy sent a letter to W.D. Densmore of the Warren office, telling him to please have printed a small clip or notice insert for all letters reading as follows: "on or after Oct. 10 address all communications to the Packard Motor Car Company, Detroit, Michigan." Also, Joy said, "send these to everyone with whom we do business. Please make the necessary arrangements and carry them out for the removal of the office of the P.M.C.C. Warren, Ohio, to Detroit, Michigan so that the shipment can leave Warren on Oct. 10 as we talked." The next day he wrote Waldon who was in New York, saying he had ordered the removal of his office from Warren and that when Waldon arrived in Detroit his new office would be ready for him.

88

But once under way, Schmidt was completely serious, as these shots taken from one of those photographic flip-books so popular during this era reveal. Among American cars, only a Pope-Toledo finished better.

On Saturday, October 10th, 1903, the *Warren Chronicle* noted that "the P.M.C.C. today shipped by express two car loads of office furniture to Detroit, Michigan. A large number of the workmen leave for the same place this evening." Thus ended the life of the Packard Motor Car Company of Warren, Ohio.

October 8th had found James Ward Packard in Detroit, attending the last board meeting held before completion of the new offices. William Doud was in St. Louis, on New York & Ohio business. Early Friday morning, October 9th, J.W. received word that his mother had passed away. He left for Warren immediately, arriving at 4:30 in the afternoon. William Doud left St. Louis at noon, arriving at 9:00 a.m. on Saturday. Mrs. Packard "was in good health until evening," he wrote, "when she attended a dinner at the church. She passed away at 2:35 a.m. Friday. I have lost a mother and the world a good woman."

And Warren had lost Packard. It must have been a melancholy moment for the brothers Packard, the simultaneous departure of their mother and their automobile. They were at the funeral, of course, and were not present to witness the removal of the last of the equipment. Mrs. Packard was buried on Sunday. On Monday each member of the family went his own way for a little time alone.

CHAPTER FIVE

AT EAST GRAND BOULEVARD

The Models L, N and S

November 1903 - July 1906

AUTHOR: JAMES J. BRADLEY

It wasn't really an industry yet, this business of building automobiles, or so most thought. Around the turn of the century, *The Literary Digest* prophesied that although the price of the horseless carriage would "probably fall in the future, it will never, of course, come into common use as the bicycle"—and in 1900 its manufacture was deemed by the U.S. Census Bureau as "miscellaneous" enough to be so categorized, together with sundry other ephemeral ventures likely as not to be miscellaneous again a decade hence.

But each year into the new century had brought gains to technology's new baby. True, what the vehicle's optimal motive force might be hadn't been decided yet—steam cars and electrics were quite as numerous as gasoline cars—nor where, for that matter, it might most advantageously be built. Albert A. Pope scattered his empire among Hartford, Connecticut; Hagerstown, Maryland and Toledo, Ohio. Alexander Winton was still holding forth in Cleveland, joined there of late by the White, the Peerless, the American, the Hoffman. In 1903 there were, among the myriad, the Grout in Orange (Massachusetts), the Jones-Corbin in Philadelphia, the Rambler in Kenosha, the Yale in Toledo, the Prescott in Passaic, the Century in Syracuse, the Thomas and the Pierce-Arrow in Buffalo, the Graham in Chicago, the Haynes-Apperson in Kokomo. And the Packard in Detroit.

Between 1903 and 1904 automobile sales throughout the United States would double, from some eleven to twenty-two thousand, the figures modest but telling—and within a decade of that, the sorting out of powerplants would largely see the decision made for the gasoline car. The decision for Detroit would take longer, but already its ascendancy was being marked.

The Middle Western advantage over New England had been simply its preponderance of hardwood forests and the consequent concentration there of carriage and wagon manufacturers, many of whom logically progressed into motorcar manufacture. The pinpointing of Detroit was predominantly due to the men who took up manufacturing there. Ransom Olds with his curved dash, built into the several thousands by 1903. Henry Martyn Leland who took what Henry Ford had left of the Detroit Automobile Company and turned it into Cadillac. Henry Ford in turn who procured for himself a new company in the same city. William Crapo Durant who later would be thinking big in Detroit. And, contributing with all these, Henry Joy's bringing the Packard to town.

Of historic significance, too, he put the marque in a plant which would represent a whole new idea of what a factory should be. All prevailing concepts of automobile plant design were brusquely turned aside—as well they deserved. Most factories at the time tended toward makeshift arrangements at best, with poor lighting and ventilation, little attention to such details as sanitary facilities, and scarcely more to the sort of structure most appropriate for automotive manufacture. Safety factors were

On the pages preceding: A full day's Model N production returning from a test run. Above: The factory as opened in 1903 at the top, and with the addition of a full second story at center. Below: The original building of reinforced concrete. Right: Where the Packard business was conducted

ill considered, and a good many plants were simply death traps. Already there had been several disastrous fires. With good reason, one reporter in 1903 characterized most automobile factories as "prison workshops."

Packard's, however, would be different. Turned over to its owners on September 22nd, 1903, only ninety days after construction had started, it was laid out in a hollow square of buildings, 363 feet wide and 402 feet deep. The outward areas were for manufacturing; production would progress from raw materials to finished vehicles around the square, ending up in the finishing buildings in the center.

Interestingly, it has been thought for decades that the factory as moved into by Packard in 1903 represented the first industrial use in Detroit of reinforced concrete construction. It would represent that, but not in 1903. The interesting facts are these, recently unearthed through careful research by historian C.A. Leslie. The first Packard buildings—eight in number—were of conventional mill construction, using edge-grained wood block flooring and heavy wood beams to support the roof or, in the case of a second story, to support the upper floors, with pilasters of brick integral with an exterior brick wall. Such construction, however, restricted distances between columns and disallowed the unobstructed floor space necessary for efficient automobile production. Moreover, the

wooden floors associated with same tended to become oil soaked and quite combustible, as noted earlier. And so, for Building No. 10 constructed in 1905 (and Building No. 9 which would be built after it), Albert Kahn turned to his brother Julius, who had joined the architect's firm in 1903 as chief engineer, following his graduation from Michigan University and several years of engineering experience both in the United States and Europe. Albert Kahn had experimented with elementary forms of reinforced concrete following the turn of the century, but it was Julius Kahn who had perfected the proper position of reinforcing rods for better structural strength, and with this background, Packard Building No. 10 went up—and so did the fortunes of the Kahn architectural enterprise. The "Kahn system" would become the factory *de rigueur* following the Packard lead, with a flurry of companies—Hudson, Chalmers, Ford, Dodge, GM among them—thinking concretely in their subsequent plant planning.

What reinforced concrete construction meant also was ease of expansion, which would serve Packard well. The structure could be added to not only horizontally, but vertically, without disturbing the existing buildings. Packard would prefer the upward approach—whether by choice or by necessity occasioned when the land surrounding East Grand

E.F. Roberts on the left, Sidney Waldon on the right, returning from a test run with the new Model L. The weather friendlier, the roads not, as the Packar

became expensive or appropriated for other use—and the company would be given to off-hand comments thereafter like "a destruction gang . . . tearing down a squatty structure" as it proceeded to replace every original building in the complex—save the blacksmith shop—with structures "of a more modern type" by 1916. And, a lot more were added.

Even in its original guise, however, the Packard factory was quite something—certainly the most attractive manufacturing facility in Detroit and doubtless the most advanced factory in the world for building cars. The press was lavish in its praise. *The Automobile* called the occasion of its opening "a memorable one in the history of the Packard company" and the plant "perfect in every detail." *Motor Age* noted a less apparent but still important benefit by reminding its readers, "When a man buys a Packard he gets a machine that was made by workmen who toil in pleasant surroundings, for if there is one thing more than another which characterizes the new factory . . . it is the bright, cleanly and cheerful aspect of the different departments." Individual lockers and forty-four-foot-long wash troughs were provided for 600 employees—about 350 more than were on the payroll after the move—and except for a few areas, heating by warm air and a special ventilating system assured a change of atmosphere every thirty minutes. The layout of the plant had

left little doubt that Packard confidently expected to expand in the near future. The boiler room, for instance, had two 200-pound McNaul boilers set so another pair could later be placed in line with them. The engine room was much larger than necessary, and featured a 280-hp tandem compound Ball engine placed with room for additions.

The Motor World summed it all up when its editors allowed that the facility was "constructed almost without regard to expense"—$117,000 was a lot of money in 1903. It remained now only to begin making Packard cars. Henry Joy was convinced that whatever they were, they would not be anything like the Model K.

Joy had castigated the K incessantly. In addition to comments already cited, he wrote James Ward that "I can see no reason for sending out a part to a customer which does not fit the carriage . . . someone ought to be responsible for things of this sort." At one point, Joy concluded, "The 'K' machine . . . is simply a disgrace to the company."

Whatever James Ward's private views on more than one cylinder, he had endorsed the design of a new four at the February 1903 board meeting, and the last of the singles was the ill-fated Model M, which didn't see production. In early June, Joy told Packard that it "is not too late in my judgment to change," recommending that all possible effort be

. . . es on the Glidden Tours. A Packard family abroad, the Hamilton Carhartts posing in their sturdy Model L on a very cold day in 1904 in Naples, Italy.

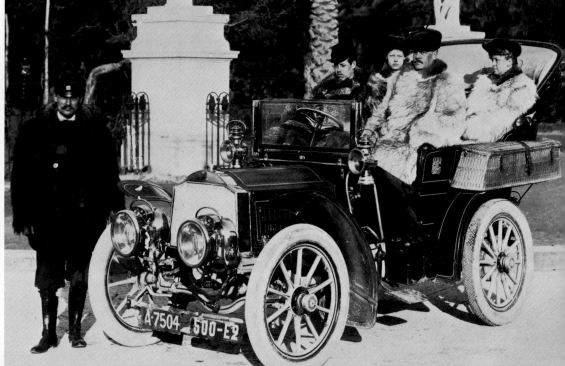

put into the L model. On June 24th, he wrote Waldon about a Mercedes he had seen in New York, suggesting "a machine like that with storage batteries would be a great disadvantage I think in next year's market." By September he was overflowing with ideas for the Model L.

On the 26th of that month Joy sent Moore in Warren "a picture of the Peugete [Peugeot] 12 hp car . . . notice the pretty light design of the wheels, as you see the wood fellows (sic) are cut away between the spokes. I want as near a wheel as you can get for the L cars with 3½" tires to fit. The body is also a good style." That same day Waldon wrote Joy with "an estimate of cost of manufacturing of the L model, being the Packard 18 to 22 hp touring car of the 1904 model," noting also that "many details of construction being yet undetermined . . . [The Model L] will be a very able and excellent car, one if it had been on the market this past year would have readily brought $4000. . . . I am certain that the competition for 1904 will be much more strenuous than in 1903. It does not seem that it would be safe to go below the $3000 price for the

standard model L." The project continued apace.

At least one Model L was probably completed in Warren before the move, as an October 13th, 1903 advertisement illustrates one, probably the prototype model or first production car. On October 6th, Joy had written Warren's manufacturing department to "prepare specifications of parts complete and quotations received on parts of L cars so far as possible for consideration by the directors and hand to me by the 6th." After the L had been officially presented in late 1903, James Ward Packard recorded in his diary that on January 23rd, 1904, the company decided "not to push beyond 200 machines at present. (Sales at the New York show numbered forty-seven.) On July 5th he noted, "101 cars shipped. Co. will have 78 more on hand if all was shipped." On September 1st, "Authorized go with parts for 200. Springfield Metal Body Co."—apparently constructors of some parts of the Model L.

The press had never been given any doubt that it was the Model L upon which, as *The Automobile* reported, "the company will pin its faith

The first attempt for the 1000-mile nonstop record ended badly for the new Model L when driver Jack Boyd diced rather disastrously with a fence rail.

during the season of 1904 . . . [its design] very carefully worked out by Charles Schmidt." Schmidt had thought a little smaller for the L: 3 ⅞ by 5 ⅛ bore/stroke dimensions for developed horsepower that Packard brake tested at 20 at 750 rpm, with an easy 22 at 900. *The Horseless Age*, noting, not exactly accurately, that the Gray Wolf was its "racing prototype . . . with practically the same cylinder dimensions," commented further that "the car probably carries more power in proportion to its weight than any other car of its class." Packard rendered the same thought promotionally—"one horsepower for every 85 pounds of loaded weight . . . ahead of the most advanced European practice."

The Model L weighed in at 1900 pounds, about midway between the stock K and the racing Gray Wolf. Schmidt had toured Europe in 1903, discovering that of the "15,000 motor cars in Paris, over 70 per cent are of the type of voiture legere, averaging one horsepower for every 100 pounds of loaded weight"—and this concept of a "lighter and more nimble brother" to the heavy touring car idea remained his resolve. There

was a certain cachet in the European reference, of course, and Packard played upon it—the Model L was Packard's "Voiture Légère," the company remembering, most of the time, to include the accent marks in the designation. And further, Packard noted that its cylinder castings were imported from Paris "as . . . it has been found impossible to obtain castings of the proper quality in this country." An old problem.

The company also touted what it called the L's avoidance of "almost one-third of the ordinary four-cylinder chassis"—this realized via the simplicity of combining the speed-changing mechanism, bevel driving gears and differential into a complete transmission unit, the whole being supported by the rear axle and enclosed in two aluminum cases bolted together. This eliminated the separate gearbox usually suspended in the middle of a chassis from a "false frame" with shafts running to the motor and rear axle—and contributed, of course, to the light weight aim.

Two independent braking systems—internal expanding and external band, the former operated by side lever, the latter by pedal, and both in-

After the second try, its results assertively advertised, drivers Eddie Roberts and Charles Schmidt struck the determined pose that won the day.

The Model N of 1905: A touring car with full glassback canopy (left), a limousine (right) and the cozy accommodations of the roadster (page opposite).

terconnected with the clutch to automatically disconnect the engine before brake application—stopped the L. Speed changes were wrought by a progressive sliding gear arrangement, with three speeds forward for 10, 25 and 40 mph, though Packard insisted, "This car is practically a one-speed machine. From a maximum of over 40 miles per hour it can be controlled upon high speed down to four miles per hour and be made to turn continuously in a thirty-foot circle and again accelerated to its maximum speed by engine control alone. Both the spark lever and throttle selector are placed on top of the steering wheel, and consequently the operator has no cause to remove his hands from the steering wheel except when shifting his gears from a standing start." The progressive sliding gear would remain a Packard standard for many years, as would the automatic speed governor which had been introduced on the first Packard. It comprised a rubber diaphragm which prevented the engine from racing when the clutch was lifted or when the car stood idle and was operated by the pressure of the water system.

The pressed steel frame, whose two side members and four cross bars were built by the Federal Manufacturing Company and assembled in the Packard shops, was substantial and looked heavy, though it weighed but 110 pounds. Long, semi-elliptic rear springs were hung to the frame by projecting pins and shackled at the rear; at the front, one transverse inverted semi-elliptic spring was secured at the middle by a strong clip to the frame, with the ends shackle-bolted to the axle close to the steering

knuckle, providing the three-point frame suspension. This, with the flexible running gear, thirty-four-inch wheels with four-inch tires and ninety-four-inch wheelbase contributed, as Packard said, "toward an ease of motion that is akin to luxury."

The Model L was an entirely new-looking Packard, the sloping Renault-like hood replaced by a yoke-shaped radiator with what architects call "cusps" at its upper corners—the first of several Packard design trademarks, one that was to persist on all models to come for an incredible fifty-five years. That the Model L body reflected the latest European styling practice was not surprising, nor was the radiator shape's familial resemblance to the French-made Mors. Charles Schmidt was European-conscious in the extreme, and, of course, he had worked at Mors before coming to Packard. And doubtless Henry Joy was averse to the L looking anything like the K in any case.

As Waldon had recommended as a minimum, the L was priced at $3000, which was more than triple that of a Cadillac though half what a Peerless cost. For his money, the buyer also received as standard equipment two side and rear oil lamps, a complete tool kit, and front and rear storm aprons. The body was aluminum over a light wood frame, the crankcase, fenders and hood also of aluminum. The body and hood were painted a dark Richelieu Blue, striped with cream—the same cream color, with a black striping, was repeated on the running gear. Initially, only a five-passenger rear entrance tonneau body was offered, but soon thereafter a surrey type joined it in the marketplace.

Besides the regular series of shop and road tests to which every car was subjected, Packard ran many one-time tests. In January 1904, an L was taken out on East Grand Boulevard when "it was a sheet of glare ice for the fourteen miles of its length. We repeatedly drove our model 'L' around sharp right-angled turns at speeds from fifteen to twenty-five miles per hour and never once could we make it skid," a result, Packard declared, "of the perfect proportioning of weight upon the front and rear wheels. We do not mention this because we think any one will have the opportunity or want to try it, but because it evidences one of the many qualities which make this car unique and gives its operation a charm of its own." But not all the tests ended so happily.

On June 20th, 1904, the company sent a stripped-down L to the Grosse Pointe track, intending to make a 1000-mile nonstop run. Shortly after midnight, with 223 miles complete, all but one of the car's four sets of lamps failed. The driver, Jack Boyd, miscalculated a turn and smashed through a wooden rail. Charles Schmidt, riding as mechanic, was thrown out and suffered two broken ribs when the car ran over him. (It was reported they were the *same* ribs broken via the Gray Wolf in Cleveland the summer before.) But the setback was only temporary.

A month and a half later there was another attempt, this time with Schmidt, Waldon and a fellow by the name of Edward F. Roberts going for the thousand. Roberts, who had apprenticed in his native Champlain, New York as a toolmaker, was relatively new to the Packard organization. He had assisted in the move of the plant to Detroit—and had already proved himself a scorcher of a test driver. In 1903 he was arrested for speeding—fifteen miles an hour when the legal limit was six —while testing a Packard in Schenectady, New York. He was caught by the sheriff on a fast trotting horse and fined $3.40. There would be no sheriff lurking at the Grosse Pointe track fortunately, and this time everything went smoothly.

At nine minutes and 37.6 seconds after midnight on August 8th, it was Schmidt behind the wheel as the tape marking the completion of the trial—nonstop except for tire changes—was ceremoniously driven across. Packard claimed a first for the feat, and notarized statements from observers testified that during the run only one pint of water was consumed. At no time "did the motor get sufficiently hot to prevent the mechanicien from laying his hand upon the side of the cylinder and holding it there." The test was heartening corroboration of Packard's belief that its first Detroit car had been built well.

If the Model L was impressive on the level, Packard promised it was as noteworthy when the terrain became hilly. "Most anything will travel downhill fast, but in our Model 'L' is offered a new sensation—the ability to ascend all ordinary hills faster than you would usually descend them. The same combination which defies the laws of gravitation also

enables the car to pass from zero to maximum speed with a rapidity hitherto unknown." The Model L, the company averred, had "the flexible control of the steam car with power and speed to spare at all times." Promotional copy for the car didn't mince words, and interestingly the company did suggest that its hard-sell touting might lead a reader to one of two assumptions: that the copy writer was "a lineal descendant of Annaneas or that our car is by all odds the best." The company apparently was convinced the correct conclusion would be drawn.

Throughout the spring and early summer of 1904, the Model L participated in many local reliability runs. Then, in July, a tour which fired the imagination of the country was organized by the American Automobile Association: 1218 miles across five states in seventeen days, culminating in St. Louis where a celebration was under way marking the centennial of the Louisiana Purchase. Starting from New York City, the caravan was swelled daily by motorists joining in en route. But only ten cars successfully completed the entire trek, and one of these was a Model L driven by Tom Fetch, who had by now returned to Packard. Fetch reported that his car performed perfectly all the way from New York to just before St. Louis. As he neared the approach to the bridge leading over the Mississippi, however, his batteries short-circuited, but after a short delay for replacements, he was able to finish the trip.*

A more private, and romantic, tour for the Model L came a month later. In his diary entry for August 31st, James Ward Packard wrote simply: "Married—to Lakewood on Model L fine trip." With due

---

*Another finisher, Charles Glidden, was so impressed with what the trek had demonstrated in the way of motoring possibilities that he proposed what later became the famous Glidden Tours.

Further variations on the Model N of 1905: The touring car with victoria top.

respect to the car, doubtless the bridegroom's enchantment centered more upon the lovely Miss Gillmer whom he had just wed.

The exact date on which Packard ceased production of the Model L is not quite clear. The company advertised it well into 1905—though its specifications remained the same and it was clearly a carryover model. The evidence suggests that it and its successor, the Model N, were made concurrently for a short time. *The Horseless Age*, in its report of November 4th, 1904, noted that the "Model N . . . has been completed for some time, and the factory has actually been engaged in its production since the beginning of October, but has purposely refrained from premature announcements regarding it." The two cars could easily have been built alongside one another, since the Model N incorporated no radical changes; Packard wasn't anxious to trifle with a good thing. The N was strictly evolutionary.

With this car, Packard was firmly locked into a one-model policy, which had been hinted at by Joy in earlier correspondence. "Instead of scattering our energies over a line of different cars," announced Packard in late 1904 and early 1905, "we have concentrated on this one type. . . . We offer a car that has graduated from the school of hard knocks, that has no single piece in it but has stood the test of at least a year's use in the hands of the public. In other words—a car refined and beautifully seasoned and, because we are specialists in this one thing, better than anything else of its kind in the world. The price of the Model 'N' (with standard equipment) is $3,500 f.o.b. factory."

The Model N rode on a wheelbase of 106 inches, twelve inches in excess of the Model L, and featured double side entrances, "the most noticeable change," the press said. The radiator shape introduced with the Model L was retained and only slightly modified. Horsepower, with a bore increase to 4 1/16 inches, was up to 28 at 900 rpm; the float feed carburetor, with single gasoline jet and auxiliary air intake, was called Packard's "1000-mile type [a reference, of course, to the Grosse Pointe run] . . . capable of perfect operation at motor speeds from 200 rpm up to 1200 rpm." Suspension remained unchanged from the L and, as *The Automobile* reported, "the power transmitting mechanism has been found by the Packard Company so satisfactory during the past year that no change" was made there either. The brakes remained "calculated to leave as narrow a margin as possible for accidents." On all models except the limousine, 34x4 clincher-type Diamond tires were standard; the limousine came Goodrich shod. Artillery type wooden wheels, twelve spokes in the rear and ten in front, were fitted, with a place under the body for a spare tire, this feature so "your car doesn't look like an ambulance when you take it out." Packard also claimed the Model N would deliver eighteen miles per gallon.

Prices for the double side entrance tourer, Packard's "standard car," were up $500 from the previous Model L, and the limousine was added as the season progressed at $4000, then an enclosed brougham at $4100 and a sporty two-passenger runabout. It is possible to conclude that the beautiful array of custom cars which was to be Packard's hallmark in future years began with the Model N. In the summer of 1905, a semi-limousine was delivered to Clifford Elliott of Detroit whose "idea had governed the design of the car," the Packard shop having translated his notions into a canopy-top body with conventional limousine seating. Elliot's design, however, employed low rear doors, as in a touring car, with extra large rear quarter windows. The result was better air circulation than a regular limousine afforded, and in case of bad weather all openings could be closed with glass windows or curtains.

The mountains of Pennsylvania, with Joy and Alger setting new records between Philadelphia and Wilkes-Barre, were the scene of the Model N's first test. A standard touring model was driven over an especially dreadful combination of roads at as high a rate of speed as safety allowed. The idea, Joy said, was to break or injure the running gear if possible. The only casualty was the car's cape top which had been strapped down; all the steel bows which held it to the body were broken.

Schmidt undertook another trial, one to rate the design of the engine. In brake tests ranging from 400 to 2500 rpm, he satisfied himself that the powerplant would meet the requirements "of rational motorists."

Finally, the connecting rods of an N were loosened so each had about 1/25th of an inch play. Packard engineers believed that the resultant hammering and pounding on the road would bring out any weak spots in the engine. It didn't. (Since the drivers were Packard products too, it is interesting to speculate whether their nerves and ear drums were as impervious to the hammering as the motor was!) In another run, to Chicago and back, a Model N test car averaged 21 mph and performed above expectations.

As the accounts were totted up at the end of the 1904-1905 fiscal year, the Packard stockholders waited nervously for results to become known. In December 1903, the company had been forced to raise $250,000 by issuing 2500 shares of $100 common, and in addition had to mortgage the factory for another $250,000. Packard had been unable to pay anything save interest on the mortgage note. In spite of a handsome financial cushion on his entrance into the auto industry, Joy found that the company had lost over $200,000 on the 192 cars built during the 1903-1904 season, but he remained undaunted. He had raised high sights to 400 cars for the season following, prompting stockholder Joseph Boyer to declare, "If you lost $200,000 in building 200 cars, you'll lose $400,000 in building 400 cars." Joy was unimpressed by Boyer's logic: The latter's shares were promptly bought up by Packard officials at fifty cents on the dollar. Boyer's reasoning may have been syllogistically sound. But his conclusion was in error. In the 1904-1905 year, Packard turned the corner with a $216,137 profit and even paid a dividend. The

company would not see red ink again until 1921. James Ward Packard visited the Detroit factory in mid-July. His diary notes summed up the situation: "at factory, good shape."

Still, it was obvious that 1903-1904 had been a severe strain upon everyone at Packard. The Model K fiasco lingered.* As Sidney Waldon would remember in 1911, "We [had imported] all of the skilled foreign engineering talent which we could get hold of and we let that talent produce us a four-cylinder world-beater as it pleased, with the result that we bought back every one of the twenty-five that were sold and put them in the scrap pile. It was a severe lesson. Financially, the venture was a failure. . . . [That fiscal year's figures] also strained our optimism, but it did not affect our imagination, our energy or our co-operative spirit"—which by 1905 was turning to the idea of entering Packard into the commercial vehicle field. (An experimental three-ton version would be ready by 1906.) Obviously the success of the Model L raised Packard's hopes—and allowed it the luxury of thinking ahead, and expanding.

The company had determined meanwhile that the calamity of the K would never be repeated. No Packard would ever perform again so abysmally, no Packard would be allowed to damage the company's reputation, none would reach an owner's hands that was not as good a car as Packard could possibly make it. The press helped in getting this point across; after Berne Nadall of *Motor Age* visited the factory, he reported his findings with enthusiasm: "No part of the Packard car

*And would for a long time thereafter—so much so that a 1911 Packard-produced "facts" booklet excised the model completely from its list of Packards produced since 1901. Like Orwell's "non-person," Packard had come up with its "non-car."

And perhaps the most piquant of all body styles, the coupe version of the N.

leaves the works without first passing some official inspection; by that is meant that every part must be recorded and hall-marked by the proper official who does nothing else. He is paid for what he knows and not for what he does, so it is obvious that if perfection is to be secured the Packard company will not be the last to gain it."

The "severe lesson" taught by the Model K had also resulted in the inauguration of the Packard Experimental Branch in 1903, following the company move to Detroit. The department was located in the north wing, and consisted at first of ten men and a shop foreman directed by Russell Huff. Huff, a graduate of the Case School of Applied Sciences, had joined Packard in 1900. A driving, tireless engineer, he usually worked a twelve-hour day or more. During his first two years, he was a one-man show, doubling as a designer, draftsman, tracer and blueprint man. In the autumn of 1903, Huff became assistant engineer under Schmidt, whom he succeeded in 1905.

Establishment of the Experimental Branch carried forward Packard's soon-to-be-legendary engineering prowess. The automatic spark advance, independent hand and foot throttle, the "H" gear slot, all dating from Warren days and the spiral bevel gear to come in 1913 were but a few of the Packard engineers' developments in these early years. Many were soon adopted by other manufacturers and the problems of patent control and infringement began to require special attention. Enter the able Milton Tibbetts.

Some indication of Tibbetts' talent is apparent in a thumbnail biography from a 1911 Packard publication: "At the age of twelve, Milton Tibbetts was owner, editor and distributor of the Weekly Bulletin, a story paper designed to divert the young idea in Washington from the doings of Congress. The Bulletin didn't keep the press going fast enough, so Tibbetts hung out a sign, 'Job Printing.' He was a grand worker and studied law nights. The printing business kept right on working when he went to the University and it paid his way through. He practiced law in Washington and worked for the patent attorneys (Foster, Freeman, Watson & Coit) representing . . . Packard."

Tibbetts was to serve Packard more than forty-five years, the last twenty-one as vice-president. He was particularly active in seeing that important inventions produced by Packard's employees were patented and in obtaining patents from sources outside the company. In 1910 he even thought a while of challenging Charles Yale Knight because of Packard's "basic patents on sleeve-valve engines." By 1929 Dewey, Bacon & Company, members of the New York Stock Exchange, estimated that Tibbetts had collected approximately 1000 patents for Packard and that "these patent holdings are reliably believed to bring in not only enough income to cover the expense of a well equipped legal department but also to carry a substantial net to the surplus account."

Joy, especially, was keenly aware of the benefits of protected patents.

As we have seen, he was active in the negotiations which led to the 1903 formation of the Association of Licensed Automobile Manufacturers, serving as its first secretary and treasurer. The A.L.A.M. eventually came to control the Selden Patent, for which Joy had no particular brief, but which he realized was useful in controlling the proliferation of the gasoline automobile. It was Joy, in fact, with Frederic L. Smith of the Olds Motor Works, who refused to grant the Ford company an A.L.A.M. license, precipitating the Selden Patent suit.

Tibbetts often pointed to his company's huge expenditures in engineering as the *raison d'être* of his patent department. When Packard refused to join a cross-licensing patent agreement in 1914, Tibbetts said, "We could never see any fairness in our granting a license under two to three hundred patents to another automobile company that never had any engineering department and never did any work in return for a license under no patents from that company."

By 1911 Packard's Experimental Branch would grow to 150 men and would be spending over $300,000 a year. Five separate divisions were established, encompassing a general machine shop to make new parts, a general assembly room where cars were put together, tested and maintained, a complete body manufacturing shop where all experimental body designs were developed, a motor testing room, and a pattern shop to make patterns and wood models for experimental work. A laboratory completely equipped to handle chemical and physical research augmented the work of the various divisions. Packard neatly summed up the rationale for all this with a statement which has the ring of a modern day Madison Avenue slogan: "We test ideas. We build results."

By now Packard had decided that it liked the closed bodies the company had introduced with the Model N. In 1907, in fact, it began advertising that a touring car owner could ship his vehicle back to the factory for conversion into a "handsome, elegantly appointed, luxurious, up-to-date Packard limousine body which will fit either an '06 or '07 Packard chassis." The body was priced at $1750 and offered in Packard Blue, Packard Maroon or Packard Green. For those affluent enough to own both bodies, most dealers set aside space to store the one not in use.

The quality to which Packard aspired could not, it was said, be attained by relying on outside suppliers for bodies, and the firm dismissed manufacturers who did not produce their own coachwork as mere "assemblers." By 1912 Packard would claim that $750 was expended to build a typical Packard body, though had the company wished to stoop to suppliers it "could have purchased bodies for a third the price"—such a course, however, only leading to the placing of Packard and its patrons "at the mercy of the parts makers."

Calling its enclosed body builders "the aristocrats of the woodworking trades," Packard held that "the erection of a limousine body is like building a fine house, but we don't recommend the formula for persons of modest means who are saving to buy a bungalow." (That was modest enough.) The company's "timber scouts" cruised the forests of North America, and even down through Mexico and over the sea to Tobago for suitable woods. Ash was required for the frames, considered to be the hardest and strongest of woods and the best holder of glue. The soft, even grain of poplar made it ideal for paneling, and also for coupe pillars, intermediate partitions of closed bodies, and the lining and floorboards of tonneaus. The heavier, curved pieces in the rear corners of limousine frames were generally rock elm, a wood that bends and stays bent. For the high permanent finish that Packard window sashes and dashboards needed, mahogany was the only thing, while roof bows over the driver's seat were of birch, because of its strength and suppleness. Packard noted that its limousine bodies contained exactly seventeen aluminum panels.

The curved pieces were bulged first with power hammers, then finished by hand-hammering, and their interior surfaces were painted with corrosion resistant red lead before being fixed to the wood paneling. After hand rubbing with emery paper and a run-over with a file, the body was ready for the paint shop—assuming, of course, that it could pass the scrutiny of a corps of inspectors who "were the most skeptical and exacting obstructionists to be found around the plant."

On June 9th, 1905, an enterprising photographer snapped a flashlit picture of Packard's new model for 1906, a mud-splattered touring car behind the wheel of which was an equally besplattered Sidney Waldon, now Packard's sales manager. Accompanying Waldon was one of the company's newer but most renowned dealers, Boston's Alvan T. Fuller, and three men from the Packard plant. They had just driven through the

Milton Tibbetts (at the wheel) and Russell Huff in a 1901 Model C repurchased from its owner for use as testimony in a lawsuit in 1910.

most severe rainfall in Michigan history, complete with numerous tornado sightings, on a Detroit-Chicago-Detroit test—by now an annual affair—with no more delay than one stop for a punctured tire and another for gasoline. Packard would later boast that before the new car was accepted by the company, "three [were built and tested for] 21,000 miles over every kind of road and grade that existed" between Michigan and Massachusetts. "It was driven by every man who could be prevailed upon to take the wheel . . . ," Packard recounted. "No one not having toured this region can appreciate its priceless value as an automobile testing ground. Man has added 'thank you, ma'ams,' to nature's magnificent collection of rocky roads and sandy grades. At Wilkes-Barre a day was spent ascending and descending the famous Wilkes Barre Mountain, and in the lowering of the previous record for the climb to the summit, from 8 minutes 30 seconds to 3 minutes 44 seconds." The car that did it was the 1906 Packard Model S.

The S or, more popularly, the 24 (for 24 hp at 650 rpm) was in-troduced early in September 1905. Independent sources noted that the engine was powerful enough to develop 40-50 hp at higher speeds. It was a larger car than its predecessors, with a wheelbase of 119 inches, and it offered seven body styles ranging in price from $4000 to $5225. The bore and stroke were 4 ½ by 5 ½ inches, an increase of around twenty percent, and one technical writer observed that the 24 easily gave "25 per cent more power with only about 5 per cent increase in weight, making the Packard touring car of 1906 equal to a mile a minute on a straightaway track." Only a few years before Schmidt had achieved that speed in the Gray Wolf to the utter amazement of everyone. Packard was making rapid progress.

Hugh Dolnar, of *Cycle & Automobile Trade Journal*, was one of America's first writers to report anything comparable to today's road tests. He confirmed the mile-a-minute potential of the new 24 in late 1905. With three others, Dolnar set out in a touring model along North Woodward Avenue toward Pontiac. After testing and recording

Alphabetically it was the S, numerically it was the 24 (for horsepower), this touring car from 1906 exemplifying the already traditional Packard craftsmanship.

acceleration, handling, braking and other performance factors, Dolnar moved to the tonneau to check on comfort. The roller-coaster 55 mph ride in the hills around Birmingham created moments when there was nothing but empty air between the passenger and the seat, but Dolnar soon adjusted. The car was so long, he wrote, that the drop of the front wheels gave the tonneau passengers enough warning to "make use of the foot-rail before the rear wheel bump comes. This foot-rail, a conception of Mr. Waldon's, is emphatically the most desirable addition to the security of the tonneau passenger at high speeds that has ever come under the notice of the writer. The brass foot-rail, about 1¼ inches in diameter, is placed crosswise so as to catch the shoe-heel, and thus enable the passengers to make the lift of the body needful to avoid being tossed in the air when the car jumps out of a severe road depression."

The longer wheelbase of the new car allowed for more generously sized rear doors, twenty-two inches wide, and gave tonneau passengers a more liberal legroom of thirty-seven inches. Dark blue, water-grained

Dramatically photographed, the chassis and engine of the 1906 Model S or 24.

A contemplative Henry Joy pondering Packard Motor Car Company good fortunes in a Model 24 roadster while visiting the firm's New York City showroom.

leather over curled hair and spiral springs provided one of the best up-holsteries on the market, and neatly complemented the standard Packard Blue body. The front springs were now changed to a lengthwise position, semi-elliptics that extended well past the frame. The Eisemann magneto ignition was adopted, the rear tires at 34x4 ½ were larger by half an inch than the front tires. The valves were separated by being placed on both sides of the cylinders instead of a single valve chamber. Splash lubrication was retained. And the 1906 carried a new idea by Russell Huff: knife-type switches by means of which the spark plugs made connection. To trace a misfiring problem, the switches could be raised one at a time, identifying the faulty plug.

With the Model S, or 24, came the famous hexagon-shaped, red-painted wheel hubs that were to distinguish Packards for fifty-two more years. This feature was reportedly another idea of Huff's, designed to accept a six-sided tool which covered the rear wheel hubs during removal—shallow indentations on the front hubs were for cosmetic reasons only. The hexagon was black on the Model S, and remained so until 1913 when it changed to red. Some versions of history have it that the change occurred when inspectors dabbed the hubs red to show the car had passed inspection, which seems a tedious way to so indicate. Another report is that the red paint signified the car had been back to the factory for rebuilding. Whatever its origin, the black and later red hex became an intrinsic part of the Packard mystique, so much so that in 1940 when a slight modification to it was proposed, loyal Packard owners complained

Meanwhile, in New England, also in 1906, Albert Shattuck of the Boston Packard agency gets behind the wheel of a Model 24 prior to a competitive run.

so loudly that the company decided to shelve the alteration.

One variant of the 1906 model should be mentioned, a racy-looking runabout with optional rumble seat and a special 108-inch wheelbase instead of the standard 119. At first glance, the runabout seemed a close cousin to later speed cars of the Mercer and Simplex stripe. Its radiator and motor were set to the rear of the front axle, its steering column tilted at a rakish thirty-seven degrees. Adding to its sleek look were long fenders, rising from the bottom of a short side step to the top of the wheels up front, and its streamlined cowl and divided seats, in a passenger compartment set much lower and further back than the regular Packard line.

Doubtless it was a swifter machine than the standard touring car, but the latter deftly demonstrated its mettle at the Cincinnati Automobile

Club's hill climb on Paddock Road in mid-May of 1906. One O.F. Pogue had removed a few speed-hindering appurtenances on his Model S and took off, a "volley of cheers" greeting his 1:01 speed—the best of the day—a second faster than the second-place finisher, W.S. Balke, in another Packard Model S. Five seconds further back was a Stearns.

When Packard first moved to Detroit, Joy estimated that if the company would build 200 cars its profit should be $200,000 or $1000 a car. As noted earlier, only half this equation proved out; close to 200 cars were made the first year but Packard recorded sizable losses instead of a profit. But with the new S, Joy's formula worked with textbook precision. On 728 sales in 1905-1906, the company's profits were $721,569.

One wonders what Joseph Boyer was thinking now.

107

CHAPTER SIX

A GENTLEMAN'S CAR, BUILT BY GENTLEMEN

The Models Thirty and Eighteen

August 1906–February 1912

AUTHOR: JAMES J. BRADLEY

Good profits and increased production called for more expansion, and the plant on East Grand Boulevard easily obliged. By 1906 its original 100,000 square feet of floor space had grown to 325,000, with 30,000 more planned by the end of the year. "This space will produce the 1907 output," said *Motor Age*, "but plans have already been drawn and preparations started for the increase of the factory, within the year, by 225,000 square feet, so that for the production of 1908 cars, beginning June, 1907, there will be a total of 580,000 square feet . . . over 13 acres devoted to building Packard motor cars."

By the end of 1905, with the 24 successfully introduced, and the company well into the black, Packard was ready for the next step in its automotive development. Alphabetically its new car would have been called the Model U—the "T" having been given over in 1905 for the Packard truck—but this sobriquet was never used in advertising. The letter did serve to identify it in company documents as the 1907 model, and successively as the UA through UE for model years 1908 through 1912. It was a Packard that more than any other would be responsible for helping put the marque in company with Peerless and Pierce-Arrow as the famed "Three P's," America's ultimate motorcars. Popularly, the name selected denoted horsepower: the Packard Thirty.

The first Thirty prototype was built in the winter of 1905-1906, and by early February it had picked up the nickname Gasoline Gus. Engineering ran Gus night and day, probing for weak spots, then turned the car over to those hard-to-please self-appointed testers, Joy and Waldon. Later the sales people had a go at it. After Gus had logged about 50,000 miles, the Packard Thirty was scheduled for production.

Henry Joy confidently stockpiled enough materials to produce 900 of the cars during 1906-1907, though it wasn't publicly announced nor were the favorable test runs reported initially. As *The Horseless Age* noted, "The new model was twice sent over the road from Detroit to Chicago and back during May. . . We are informed that the news of this run was purposely withheld until all of the 1906 models had been disposed of." Two and a half months later, Packard was ready to tell it like it was, when it happened. "Packard Designer Takes 1907 Runabout Through from Detroit to New York in Jig Time," headlined *Motor Age* of the latest trek just completed. A representative of *The Automobile* had gone along, and in his on-the-spot observations during a stretch of "macadam of an unkempt kind" noted that "Russell Huff, designer of this '07 Packard—bigger and more speed-daring than any of its forebears—grumbles at the way a bit, then presses on the foot accelerator, perhaps in spite; perhaps to show me that his pet has no fear of roughened going. Then the dancing hand on the speed-meter jumps ahead in its wavering and does its little jig over the figure '60.' " The only untoward incident during the trek was the bending out of shape of the right rear mudguard after being caught in a loose tire chain—and, in-

terestingly, the entire distance (778 miles) was covered without a fan, Packard being anxious to test the efficiency of the water circulating system "under trying conditions."

News of this run and the first announcement of the Thirty were released about the same time, early in August. "Straight as an arrow through ten years of consistent progress can be traced the ceaseless pursuit of Perfection to its culmination," Packard advertised on the front cover of *Motor Age*. The press referred to the car as "the matured development of the Packard 24."*

Castings for its engine were made in France and, according to Charles H. Vincent who later was placed in charge of the Packard Proving Grounds, were "seasoned about two years in the open air in Packard's back lot. These castings were so fine that the fit could be very close and an engine would produce almost as much power without the piston rings as with a full set. In fitting these pistons, each individual piston had to be free to move, but could not drop through its own weight. And we never had scored pistons. I don't think it is possible to produce cast iron of this quality anywhere today."

The Thirty's bore and stroke measured 5 by 5½ inches for 432 cubic inches—and was said to produce about 55-60 brake horsepower "according to American standards," though its rating was "established on the French basis." The entire top of the cylinders and valve chambers was substantially flat, as opposed to the dome-shaped configuration of the 24 engine. A three-piece cast aluminum crankcase was used, the lower part being a removable oil well. Mechanically operated inlet and exhaust valves were positioned on opposite sides of the cylinders, as in the 24, but were slightly larger in accord with the increased cylinder volume. At this point Packard's machinists were operating under a system of tolerance limits that compared favorably with other automobile plants: Pistons and cylinders, for example, were machined to approximately ± .003 inches. According to some sources, Joy himself was seen to smash to bits parts which had slipped through without meeting the limits.

Front wheels now ran on ball, instead of roller, bearings. Otherwise the Thirty was much like the 24: The carburetor was water-jacketed, with copper float feed and a single vertical breathing nozzle, ignition was via Eisemann magneto supplemented by storage battery for starting. As *The Motor World* commented at show time in January of 1907, with the Packard reputation "now at high water mark . . . no novelties . . . were required." *Motor Age* pointed out the Packard appeal of a car "each succeeding model [of which] is an outgrowth of the preceding one . . . [with] no experimenting in the hands of the customer."

---

*During its debut year, the Thirty was referred to in Packard advertising as the "30"—and would be again for 1912. In the years between, the model designation was almost invariably spelled out, as it will be here.

On the pages preceding: Henry Joy and the Thirty. Above and below: The Packard team and Gasoline Gus—Thirty chassis, S body—during test runs.

The Thirty's 121¾-inch wheelbase carried touring ($4200), limousine ($5500) and landaulette ($5600) bodies; there was later a 108-inch wheelbase runabout available for $4200, "a correct car of the kind," Packard said, "not a touring car with the tonneau left off." The additional length of the Thirty over the 24 was entirely in front of the dash, making for a longer bonnet, which was longer still in the runabout model, with the radiator and motor moved further back for proper balance and the steering column raked at a lower angle. On the touring model, the tonneau was enlarged, and the back seat made several inches lower than the 24, with thicker seat cushions. The touring carried 34x4 tires in front, 34x4½ rear, the runabout 34x3½ and 34x4 respectively.

There was no question in anyone's mind that the Thirty was the most perfected Packard yet. Sales reflected this conclusion, and 1129 1907 Model Thirty Packards were built when production was halted for the 1908's on May 23rd, 1907. It hadn't been easy. As a *Motor Age* journalist saw it, "Even with the enormous increase in floor space built to take care of the output of the 1907 car, every inch of room has been crowded to its utmost, and in many departments greatly overcrowded." Still, the last 1907 was completed twenty-nine days ahead of schedule and *The Automobile* reported, " 'Bill' Birmingham, head tester, [is] the happiest man in Detroit, and every Packard man, from the manager down to office boy, [is full] of pride of accomplishment . . . .

"When this last 1907 Packard 'Thirty' had been tested, tuned and adjusted to its smallest detail; had passed the scrutinizing judgment of the head tester, and was ready to be washed and painted, the small army of hypercritics who compose the Packard testing corps roughly painted the rig in national colors, decorated it with all available flags and banners, crowded themselves into it, and paraded the streets of Detroit.

"Each season the Packard company has progressed in the working out of a policy of one model a year, a definite number of cars of that model, and a definite schedule of manufacture and delivery. Last winter it worked against weather conditions which seemingly made the testing of cars on the road impossible. . . . Back of 'Bill' and his testers, however, was a system, with Henry B. Joy at the head, S.D. Waldon in charge of the sales organization, and Factory Manager Moore, with his assistants, working out the designs of Engineer Huff."

Nineteen seven saw Packard rise to eighth place in the automobile industry with 1403 cars for the calendar year—a position it would achieve only once again, in 1909. Mass production would soon cause other marques to far outdistance Packard, but for 1908 it ranked behind only Ford, Buick, Reo, Maxwell, Rambler, Cadillac and Franklin. And none of these were of all-out luxury caliber in those days. "The Packard factory gradually turns from old work to new," continued *The Automobile*. "Four experimental 1908 cars are on the road, going through a trial of many thousands of miles."

Actually, one experimental 1908 Thirty had been undergoing tests for quite a while, beginning early in 1907 with a frigid run from Detroit to Chicago and back in quest of a new driving time record—Waldon had posted twenty hours thirty-six minutes, about thirty miles an hour, the year before. Like its predecessor, the experimental '07 named Gasoline Gus, this prototype also received a nickname: Hiram.

The christening, it seemed, occurred on the way back from Chicago, at Mottville, where Waldon had repaired to fix a broken spring. The blacksmith and leading citizen was, unremarkably, Mr. Mott. Waldon had handed him some scrap steel to pound into shape when his hammer paused in mid-air. "By catnip! If them ain't those there gosh-blamed irons that Hi Smith brung in to fix up his plow with!" That did it. Waldon and his passengers, including "A. Passenger" representing *The Automobile*, bestowed the car with the name Hiram and christened it "properly, with a half-empty bottle of chill-eradicator."

The Thirty didn't break the record, but it came close, and Waldon assured the press he really wasn't trying because of the cold weather. At East Grand Boulevard, the car was hoisted to the second floor, and driven, mud and all, into the experimental room. "All the factory workers gathered to pass comment on our appearance and ask leading questions," Waldon recounted. "It had been a great ride, but only the first. The car and three others, now being made, must go more miles—miles by the thousands—that qualities which are new may be tested on the rough road before they become standard. Even now is 'Hiram' wallowing in the melting-freezing mud between Detroit and Cleveland under the guidance of Russell Huff."

The testing continued apace. In May Waldon drove another 1908 car from New York to Boston and back by another road, thence to Philadelphia and Pittsburgh—"an eleven-hundred-mile automobile tour over a thousand kinds of roads, but during one continual kind of weather in the form of a spring rainstorm." No problems were encountered, the new Thirty was nearly ready. Introduction was set for mid-June 1907, making it one of the first 1908 cars. By now, the new additions to the factory were nearly complete. "To anyone who has not visited the home of the Packard, this immense space may seem absurd, when the output is only 1500 cars, and only one model at that," an unnamed Packard official told *Motor Age*. "Fifteen hundred cars could be turned out without this [addition] but they could not be Packard cars."

In external appearance, the 1908 closely resembled its predecessor, although the wheelbase had been slightly lengthened to 123½ inches and thirty-six-inch wheels were now used. The frame was hung slightly lower than in 1907, the rear axle cleared by raising its side members somewhat. And that was about it. As *Motor Age* said, "Rather than relegate its four-cylinder motor, expanding clutch, rear axle transmission, frame, running gear and many other parts to 'thankful oblivion,' as

Certainly the most refined Packard produced to date, the 1907 Model Thirty, touring the Michigan countryside.

is the annual house-cleaning of many motor car builders, this Wolverine concern takes these many parts and all others making the summa summarum—sum total—of the machine and passing them in review before the engineering, executive, factory and selling staffs pronounces which is free to take its place in the new model and which must be slightly altered, refined a little here, strengthened a little there and lightened a little in another place, before becoming part and parcel of 'next year's model.' "

The Automobile termed the car "thoroughly Packard," and its description of its holdover engine underlined what that meant: "The crank shaft is cut from a solid billet of hammer forged, high carbon, open hearth steel, is oil tempered and supported in three bearings of liberal size. The connecting rods are drop forgings, bushed at the lower ends with Parsons white bronze, as are also the main crank journals."

On some of the later 1907's, Packard had introduced a newly designed radiator cap. Joy, piqued with trying to unscrew the cap on his car, developed a bayonet instead of screw-thread attaching method, which was used on the 1908's. A new body also appeared in mid-season on the 1908 Thirty, a close-coupled touring arrangement carrying four passengers midway between the front and rear axle. If the owner wished

to drive, there was room for the chauffeur in a rumble seat at the rear.

No one factor contributed more to Packard's success than the strong dealer and distributor system it cultivated. As a matter of policy, Packard began insisting that anyone wishing to handle its cars must locate his outlets where the socially prominent resided. And, if the company was not being represented by a dealer in the way it wished, the dealer was soon replaced. In 1903 Joy wrote to Waldon, "We must ride a high horse with agents. If one agent won't do, get another." Then, too, the company recognized its responsibility. In another letter to Waldon, Joy said, "Please be sure to keep your word absolutely good with Mr. Pardee [Chicago] or anybody else and don't forget any special arrangements you have made, but think twice before making them in the future. We wish to maintain the highest possible reputation for correct and fair dealing. . . ."

The aforementioned Alvan T. Fuller, who was found on many experimental and record runs with Waldon, probably epitomized Joy's idea of the compleat Packard dealer. He was one of the most successful Packard ever had—and one of the more colorful. Born in Malden, Massachusetts, he began selling bicycles from his uncle's barn at age seventeen and opened his own bicycle store in 1896, then set up a shop in

Production of 1403 cars for the calendar year 1907 involved a certain amount of paperwork, of course. The Packard offices were kept rather busy.

Boston a few years later. Unable to resist the lure of the automobile, he opened an agency in 1902 for the Northern car.

"The first we ever saw of Alvan T. Fuller," Sidney Waldon later wrote, "was in the fall of 1903, when he came to the Packard factory with the most peculiar smile it had ever been our pleasure to see, and a check for $2400 that he deposited on an order for ten Model 'L' cars. The check was drawn on the First National Bank of Malden and was O.K. Shortly afterward the president of that bank asked Fuller what he got for his twenty-four hundred and Fuller showed him the contract with the Packard company. Drawing himself up to his full height and making a rapier plunge at the presidential desk with the presidential fore-finger, the president duly informed Mr. Fuller that the First National Bank of Malden did not care to continue business with such a reckless plunger." The president would live to regret that statement.

In 1904 Fuller sold eighteen cars. By 1910 the figure was 389. His salesroom on Commonwealth Avenue, *The Packard* recorded, gave to the prospective customer "a glimpse of Packard's ideals as soon as he steps in the front door. The business has been dignified by harmonious quiet, elegant surroundings, where beauty but emphasizes the efficient, careful arrangement for the proper conduct of the day's business." The building was set in a lovely wooded park-like area, surrounded by a stately wrought iron and concrete fence, and was ultimately larger than the factory Packard moved into in 1903. The salesroom was a showplace, seventy feet deep, with twenty-eight-foot-high ceilings. Full length windows and hanging chandeliers provided the lighting. Floors and walls were finished in quarter sawed and light fumed oak. Mahogany chairs and tables with writing materials were set aside in plush carpeted areas for visitors who wished to dally. Scattered about the room were the latest Packard cars, along with catalogues, upholstery sample cases, and similar paraphernalia. A grand staircase wound to a mezzanine containing offices, and on its landing stood a huge grandfather clock—not only to tell time but to remind employees that "there is always enough time for courtesy."

In common with many other early dealers, Fuller originally sold several lines of cars—Cadillacs, in the beginning, as well as Packards. But he was an unquestioned Packard fanatic, and he finally concentrated only on the latter. "Her art is music," he said of his wife, "and mine—mine is Packard." Fuller's enthusiasm peaked behind a Packard wheel, and his various escapades were notorious. On one occasion he was arrested after "a hot chase" in New York, charged with speeding and put in jail. He attempted to bribe the jailer. When that failed he sent an S.O.S. to his New York Packard colleague on the letterhead of the New York Department of Correction: "My Dear Mr. Hurlburt, Just get me out please as soon as you can. Very truly, Alvan T. Fuller."

Somewhere along the line, the restraining influence of provincial

With flags flying, Packard Thirty production began and ended for 1908.

Boston must have tempered Fuller's high spirits. He served as a trustee of Boston University, the New England Conservatory of Music, the Boston Museum of Fine Arts and the Boston Symphony Orchestra. In 1917 he was elected to the Massachusetts legislature. He became lieutenant governor of the Commonwealth in 1921, governor in 1925, and again in 1928. Fuller was the living personification of Joy's early vision when he began building Packards: "A gentleman's car, built by gentlemen."

The gentlemen congregated around the marque abroad, too. The first Packard seen in Russia was a Thirty driven 14,000 miles around the country by writer Charles J. Belden in 1908. The car suffered no mechanical problems, but one of Belden's guides was stabbed with a pitchfork during an argument with some infuriated peasants who had never seen a car before. In 1910 a Packard Thirty touring model for President Diaz was one of the first cars shipped to Mexico.

It was in France, however, with its long tradition of fine cars and the most highly developed road system in the world, where Packard made its greatest overseas impression. In 1907 the company set up a Paris office at 177 Boulevard Perière, to service American tourists traveling on the Continent. By 1908 the office had registered forty-five Packards. Two years later the figure had grown to 250, and by 1914 it was just over 500. The Paris office stocked a large number of parts, kept a mechanic in residence and provided touring information. Packard owners who were planning a trip to France were issued instructions and advice by the company, including the fact that they would need two front lights (left green, right white) and would have to pay a duty deposit of $5.50 per hundred pounds of car on landing.

Packard had good reason to insure adequate service for its cars, because in those days the quality among non-aligned mechanics and agencies varied enormously. Sears, Roebuck and Company in 1911, for example, issued the following warning in the owner's manual for its vehicle: "By all means try to keep your car out of the hands of repairmen in local garages, especially in small towns, as there are more cars ruined by them than there are by all the owners of cars put together. . . . Nine times out of ten you will get far better results by reading these instructions carefully . . . and [correcting] the trouble yourself." Sage advice for a person driving a two-cylinder motor buggy, but not appropriate for the owner of a $5000 Packard, though Packard did print some of the most complete owners manuals to be found. However, a Packard agency was where the firm encouraged owners to go for any serious work, and the dealers were urged in turn to maintain a full service operation with an extensive stock of spare parts. The company even refused to discount parts sold to independent garages, a policy not abandoned until the mid-Thirties. It was not unusual for a dealer to stock a half million dollars worth of parts, and the company promised that those not used could be returned for full credit. As late as 1910, Packard boasted that its factory could expeditiously supply any part for any model it had ever made.

In that year, too, Packard sent this inspirational message to its dealers: " 'Ask the man who owns one' is perpetuated not only by the continued interest taken by the parent company and its dealers in the service rendered to all Packard cars regardless of the year of manufacture. . . . Every dealer employs a technical expert who makes it his sole duty to keep all Packards in that territory tuned to their highest efficiency. . . . A still further good is the knowledge that a visiting owner from another dealer's territory is to receive the same uniform service, treatment and courtesies as are accorded a local owner. A Packard owner is a member of the family and is received and accepted as such in every dealer's establishment in the country."

Packard expected more than a perfunctory nod to this ideal. Zone representatives periodically evaluated the level of service in agencies under them. In addition, the factory required semi-monthly reports from every technical superintendent, showing the service his shop had rendered. If he couldn't handle the shop work and the paper work, Detroit had a suggestion: assign him a stenographer. The reports were intended as checks against the efficiency of the individual shops and as a way to alert the factory to potentially serious mechanical problems. They also served another purpose. In what must have been an overwhelming record-keeping project, Packard as late as 1912 asked that "as complete a personal history and record of each car we ever manufactured" be kept, "as the itinerant habits of people and cars will permit."

Besides conventional service, Packard urged agencies to do minor tune-ups and adjustments free, to see that cars were thoroughly washed before being returned to their owners and to provide an area where owners, or their chauffeurs, could do their own repairs. The Chicago branch added a little frosting to the cake. It set aside a do-it-yourself section in its plush Michigan Avenue building, with three experts in attendance at all times to help the amateur mechanics. A careful record of the work performed was kept and when the owners were ready to leave they were given a "no charge" bill.

Packard directed agencies *not* to sell used Packards unless they were repainted and overhauled. Further, the cars were to be sold for a standard price and carried the same guarantee as a new Packard. Just how enforceable this policy was is a moot point, but it indicates the company's fierce determination to keep the image of a Packard, even though not new, bright and shining. Another Packard policy required new car buyers to place a deposit when ordering. This served various purposes: to make the contract a serious matter, allow an orderly schedule of production, let the dealer know how his sales stood, and protect the bona fide buyer against speculators. At the height of the Thirty's popularity, it was reported that "premiums as high as $1000 to $1200 were paid to speculators by customers determined to have one at any price." To show

that no one was exempt from the deposit requirement, the company publicized Joy's order for a new car for his wife in 1912—accompanied by a $500 check.

There is good reason to believe that with the Thirty, dealers were adhering closely to factory advertised prices. One dealer's confrontation with the company's obduracy in this respect was published in a 1910 house organ. In January of that year, Packard exhibited a special silver-trimmed limousine at the New York show, priced at $6208.50. The car moved to the Baltimore show, where a prominent society lady offered to buy it for $6200 if Mr. Hamil, the local dealer, would throw in a Warner speedometer. Hamil phoned the offer to sales manager Waldon, who later related, "Of course, I replied that the price was $6208.50 without a speedometer and that to throw off the $8.50, to say nothing of attaching a speedometer, would abrogate a business policy of the Packard company; that in preference to doing this the Packard company would rather lose the sale of the car and have it returned to the factory, restored to standard, and sold at the regular price even though, in addition to the freight from Baltimore to Detroit, the restoration to standard would mean a loss of $1000." Two hours later the lady bought the car for $6208.50 and was enjoying telling her friends how Packard would have sacrificed the sale rather than cut its price. "The experience," said dealer Hamil, "cured me forever of any thought of concession in price or equipment."

As 1908 progressed, sales of the Packard Thirty were seen to be up —the year would finish with over 1800 units built from January through December. The record runs continued, of course, and Packard had a field day equivalent to Tom Fetch's cross-country trip in the old single-cylinder when Jacob Murdoch drove his Thirty from sea to sea.

Murdoch wintered in Pasadena, home of another pretty fair transcontinental driver, L.L. Whitman, who had made the trek in an Oldsmobile in 1903 and a Franklin in 1904. Encouraged by Whitman, Murdoch proposed the trip to Packard, where it met with raised eyebrows—the year before Packard had refused to enter the New York to Paris contest on the basis that it was an insane project. But the firm finally went along with Murdoch to the extent of sending spare parts ahead of him, and on April 24th, 1908, he left Pasadena with his wife, two daughters aged fourteen and eighteen, and son Milton, aged ten—along with about 1200 pounds of supplies and equipment.

The Thirty struggled over the usual assortment of horrible semi-roads, mud holes, sand beds and snow storms, but made New York in twenty-five days. In commemoration of the trip, Packard printed a handsome thirty-two-page illustrated booklet called "A Family Tour from Ocean to Ocean." Subsequent trips by the Murdochs were featured in advertisements, as the Fetch trip before them.

Another Thirty trek of '08 was perhaps even more memorable. Early in the year the irrepressible Sidney Waldon donned mufti and motioned to a couple of others at Packard to come along—and they took a Packard to Cuba for a week's tour. "It was wonderful. Even this country of wars, oppression and insurrections had heard of no such thing. Motor cars they knew the great Americanos had to skip over country where there were roads. Here there was no road." It ended well, the intrepid trio "conquered in their Packard Thirty the alleged impassable obstructions of the wild interior of Cuba—they had made good and did not care a rap that they had no clean clothes in which to appear before the elite of Sancti Spiritus." In surroundings of more amenity, if a steady downpour, a few months previous, a Packard Thirty driven by one E.L. Miller captured the Brazier Cup in the eighty-four-mile "legal-speed-limit" run of the Automobile Club of Philadelphia. Second place went to a Winton.

Officially, the Model UA of 1908 was superseded by the Model UB, the 1909 Thirty (UBS for the short-wheelbase runabout), though the cars were now universally known by the numerical figure. A cellular radiator was substituted on the '09 model, replacing the traditional tubular type, and the separate reverse lever which had been a Packard feature since 1904 was eliminated.

At the bottom of the twenty-one-gallon copper gasoline tank, Packard added a four-gallon reserve tank; hooded front fenders and a mud apron between the frame and running boards to give passenger protection completed the changes for the 1909, and Packard completed the 1907-1908 period of Thirty production with an increase to 1470 units. It would be up again for 1908-1909, with the help of a new model at a more affordable price: the $3200 Packard Eighteen.

With a smaller 112-inch wheelbase, the Eighteen seemed to represent a departure from Packard's oft-stated policy of concentrating on a single model at a time, which had been in effect since 1906. The company's

The Packard Motor Car Company didn't consider a vehicle finished after it had been built; the car had to be tested next, and Packard found the perfect hill for that.

rationalization here was that the Eighteen was not really new, rather a smaller Thirty made to the same standards and quality "for use in the city where the extra weight and power of the 'Thirty' is not needed." Officially, the first series of 1909 Eighteen models was designated the NA.

The Eighteen *was* finely finished and constructed, thus it never compromised Packard's prestige. And it did not represent an expansion into the mass market as it was priced at double and sometimes triple that of the popular Fords, Maxwells, Oldsmobiles and similar volume makes. Also, it was continually outsold by the Thirty, by about three to one.

Deliveries of Eighteens began in the summer of 1908. The cars were finished as standard in Richelieu Blue, further identifying them with the Thirty, and featured a four-cylinder 326-cubic-inch (4-1/16 by 5-1/8) engine developing 18 rated horsepower at 650 rpm. In keeping with its smaller size, the Eighteen rode on thirty-four-inch tires, and used a smaller, eighteen-gallon fuel tank. In addition to the standard touring model, there was a limousine at $4400, a landaulette at $4500 and a jaunty runabout at $3200 on a shortened 102-inch chassis. By December an inside-operated coupe—for both Thirty and Eighteen—was announced, "a special body . . . interchangeable with the regular runabout body without alteration of levers or other mechanical parts."

Painting the Eighteen (and Thirty) Richelieu Blue with cream striping and running gear was no whim. It was as much a part of creating Packard's visual mystique as its by now well-established radiator grille. "The man who buys a Packard usually wants it to look like one," the company said. Meanwhile a number of orders for bright colors were coming in, especially from the West Coast.

There Earle C. Anthony was holding forth as Los Angeles dealer for Packard, an assignment he had taken upon himself in 1905 at age

Photographed under test here were five of the nearly 4000 Packards produced during fiscal year 1909-1910, a production record which would stand for four years.

twenty-five. Fulsomely as colorful as Alvan T. Fuller, the peripatetic Mr. Anthony would involve the marque in numberless publicity-garnering exploits, including the treks of the cars known as Cactus Kate into the wilds of desert and canyon, the latter the Grand one—as well as photographing as often as possible members of the burgeoning film colony in and around Packard cars. It was doubtless his efforts which saw so many examples of the marque in films as year passed year. Anthony claimed for himself the distinction of opening the world's first gasoline station—late 1903 or early '04, and a dubious claim—by installing gasoline pumps on a curb in Los Angeles and calling the result the "Red and White Filling Station." While traveling in Europe, he met Claude Neon and imported what might have been the first three illuminated signs to the United States—one of them reading "Packard" of course. During the Twenties he would become interested in radio, and build the powerful KFI, famous pioneer West Coast broadcasting station—and use it to advertise Packards. Whether Anthony's promotional gambits occasionally gave pause at East Grand Boulevard is moot. In the early Teens, however, one factor caused mild consternation. Earle Anthony thought the customer was always right. In 1911 he supplied a client a phaeton with black hood, frame and fenders, a body of light violet, and white moldings topped off by a white basketwork monogram. Back in Detroit, Packard viewed such extravagances as a result of the climate, or possibly "the Latin mixture in the blood."

In 1911, when Packard finally did introduce a new standard paint scheme, it rated prominent coverage as "big news." But the new finish was still conservative, with bodies and door panels in Packard Blue, striped with Packard Gray, and black moldings, frame, hood, radiator, fenders, battery and tool boxes. Wheels, axles and below-frame parts were gray striped with black on open cars, the reverse on closed vehicles. That was about as far out as Packard colors became in those strait-laced days. Special paint jobs remained available, of course, initially for the $50 extra that had been the charge for the L, for only $25 on the later Thirty. But "under no circumstances" would special color requests be honored for the radiator surface, top bow sockets straps and grease boots—they had to remain black. Packard still had the last word.

Dignity, conservatism and consistency also spread early to Packard advertising. The greatest boost in these directions came in 1907 when thirty-one-year-old Ralph Estep became advertising manager, relieving Sidney Waldon, who had gone to sales on a full-time basis. Before Estep took over, Packard ads verged on the amateurish—loudly assertive of feats, runs, reliability trials and speed records. Or just simply loudly assertive. The company had only graduated from trade press to general circulation magazines with an advertisement in *McClure's* in 1902. All this was to change. Estep quickly imparted to Packard advertising the same aura of class and sophistication the company tried to implant in its sales agencies and the cars themselves.

One of his first efforts was a catalogue for the 1908 Thirty, one of the most opulent pieces of its kind ever produced—and far in advance of the similarly magnificent catalogues of the Twenties and early Thirties. It was a twenty-eight-page publication with illuminated hand-lettering in

Packard Motor Car Company's resident outdoors man had his product suitably adapted "for roughing it in the sparsely settled sections of the far West."

Old English. On the frontispiece, a color engraving of a Packard Thirty was tipped in by hand. The booklet was enclosed in a flap covered with white vellum and embossed with a grid of Packard radiator designs in gold ink. It cost thirty-five dollars per copy to produce, signifying the company's willingness to spend sizable sums for promotion. In a few years Packard would be allotting $40,000 annually for advertising.

Around 1910-1911 another theme reflecting the "who" of Packard ownership began to creep into Estep's advertising. An ad in the September 16th, 1911 *Saturday Evening Post*, for example, related how fourteen percent of all parties registering at the swank Elton Hotel in Waterbury, Connecticut were driving Packards—twice as many as any other marque. Underscoring the idea that Packards were favored by the wealthy and prominent, the advertisement smugly noted that from April to July 1911, fifty-three percent of all cars driven by American tourists abroad were Packards, a three-to-one lead over any other manufacturer.

One of the greatest single tributes to the marque's name was the creation of two distinctive typefaces, "Packard" and "Packard Bold," by Oswald Cooper in 1913—the only typefaces ever named for an automobile. The patent was assigned to the American Typeface Company, distributor of the lettering which of course was found on many Packard documents and publications including the company's own magnificent house organ, *The Packard*, founded by Estep in 1910.

This publication has already been mentioned in these pages, has been quoted from, and will be quoted from again, but one cannot overemphasize the beauty of it, nor the priceless record it contains of the

And looking perhaps less than presidential, Henry Joy suitably adapted himself too.

Packard's elegant New York showroom in 1909; Barney Oldfield behind the wheel of a 1908 Thirty in Syracuse; a storm covering on yet another 1908 Thirty.

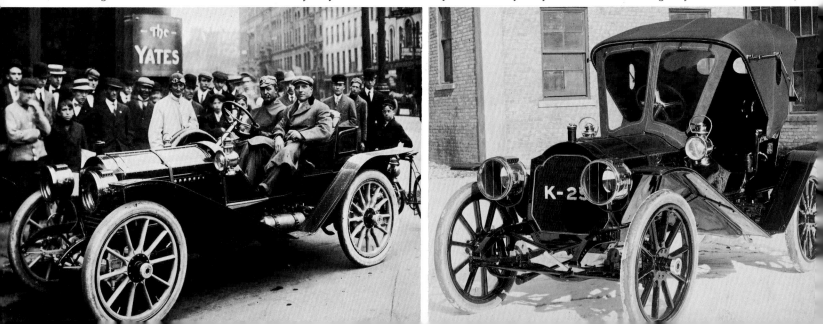

young company's aspirations and philosophy. It featured detailed reports of technical developments, lengthy stories on the construction of everything from car bodies to steering wheels, accounts of cross-country trips in Packards, dealer news, essays on the efficacy of square dealing, and advice to owners. *The Packard* was also made to order for Estep's effervescent sense of humor, which resulted in some atrocious puns. A dealer who had switched from Texas to Alabama was reported to be "now down Old Mobile selling Packards." Once Estep noted plans to class enclosed body parts as either animal, vegetable or mineral. Buckram and duck would, he said, go into the animal section because "if buck, ram and duck are not animal, what the deuce are they?"

Estep was not above publishing humorous caricatures of Packard's leading lights—and the mustachioed countenance of Henry B. Joy appeared in *The Packard* often. On other occasions Estep would indulge in versifying, sometimes with limericks joshing Packard dealers and owners. The lines for C.C. von Hamm, of the moneyed and aristocratic von Hamm family of Honolulu, read:

A Packard in old Honolulu
Bowled over a man called Zululu
The poor wretch said, "Damn,
I bet that's von Hamm."
But it wasn't, tra la tra la lu lu.

The unflappable Cuyler Lee, of San Francisco, was the subject of another Estep effort:

Aristocrat, right, Cuyler Lee
In fact a highbrow, between us three;
His city went up
In awful erup
Said Cuyler, "This is most annoying to me."

One of the brightest gems created by Estep was a Packard-published hard-cover book called *El Toro*, a properly dramatic account of the Cuba trip, of which Estep was a member. He related that the vehicle was christened El Toro by the natives when its powerful engine repeatedly tore the car from seemingly impassable mud holes and rock-strewn trails.

Only minor changes distinguished the 1910 models, which were officially designated Model UC for the 123-inch wheelbase Thirty and UCS for the 108-inch wheelbase runabout, and NB for the Eighteen. Slightly larger fenders were used in front, with a deeper apron between them and the body; a larger steering wheel appeared, on which the wood rim extended to cover the entire periphery of the wheel itself plus a portion of the spokes. But one long-time standard ended when a dry plate clutch replaced the expanding ring variety that had been around for five

years, "a radical departure from previous Packard practice," *The Automobile* said. Designed to afford gradual enlargement and operating without lubrication, thus providing the same action in cold as in warm weather, the new Packard clutch featured a special lining material between plates to insure, it was claimed, its remaining nonflammable even under severe usage. A new phaeton body was also provided the Thirty, this introduced as "a practical vehicle meeting the demand for a fast, powerful car with low seats and small tonneau."

Shortly after the 1910's were introduced in mid-1909, a rumor circulated that General Motors was after Packard. The *Detroit News* reported that "a man closely associated with the Packard company's affairs" had said no negotiations were pending, and that Packard stockholders were not very strong on selling a good thing. Nevertheless, said the paper, "it is known that the General Motors people have had feelers out, endeavoring to ascertain just how the Packard company would entertain the proposition. The Packard Motor Car Company is regarded as one of the strongest automobile concerns in the country. The stockholders are possessed of great wealth and the plant has been doing a phenomenal business." This clipping is found in Henry B. Joy's scrapbook, which does seem to indicate something serious was going on. Interestingly enough, later in 1909 GM did buy a company—though it was not then in Packard's class. Its name was Cadillac. How different history might have been had the purchase gone another way.

Packard had an especially good fiscal year in 1909-1910, the 3990 vehicles produced in that period standing as a record for four more years. Madison Square Garden was chosen to introduce the new cars, following previous sequence with the designations UD and UDS for the Model Thirty and NC for the Eighteen. Two new bodies were on hand, a coupe and a brougham. Packard called the latter a "swagger car, because we think people go to an automobile show to see things they have not seen, rather than the things they are familiar with." The brougham's high, eighty-six-inch body carried four passengers—five with a jump seat—and had a right-hand door opening to the rear seat and a left-hand door to the front. The car was finished in blue and deep gray, all metal parts were nickel plated, and the interior was done in gray checked cloth.

Throughout the open cars of 1911, and in the front seats of closed cars, upholstery was black, hand-buffed, straight-grain tufted leather. Rear compartments of closed cars were trimmed in blue broadcloth from the roof to the seat boards, or a buyer could optionally elect blue goatskin instead of the broadcloth, no extra charge.

Also for 1911, Packards acquired foredoors for the first time, in the limousine and landaulet bodies. Riding qualities were improved by adding three short leaves to the base of the rear springs. A large battery box, accommodating a second battery, was added optionally to take care of yet another new option: combination oil and electric side and rear lamps.

The company cautioned that the second battery was "absolutely necessary," since the added electrical equipment would quickly exhaust a single battery. In 1912, however, the extra battery and combination lamps became standard.

The tireless Waldon continued to keep Packard's basically unchanged cars in the news with record runs. One of his best was reported in an early issue of *The Packard*: Pittsburgh to Philadelphia with only one stop, in twelve hours and fifty-one minutes. Two years before, he'd done it in fourteen hours, one minute. The record breakers were greeted by E.B. Jackson, manager of the Philadelphia agency, "who indicated by his manner that he would set the crowd up to a big feed at the Bellevue-Stratford lunch room." *The Packard* proudly advised that the 23.6 mph average was maintained without ever driving the car over forty-five; the motor was never stopped, and "no dog or chicken or other living thing was hit on the entire trip." As for the driver, he "says he is vice-president of the Packard Motor Car Company when he is washed."

In August the Thirty was in the news again. W.G. Irwin, president of the Indianapolis, Columbus and Southern Traction Company, had rigged one to run on rails, and had reached as high as 60 mph. "Woodrims made by a pulley company fit into the standard rims of the automobile," reported *The Horseless Age*, "and in place of the pneumatic tire there is a flanged steel car tire. These parts are bolted together in such a way that when the car is wanted for road use the special equipment can easily be removed and standard automobile tires attached in its place." The Thirty, it seemed, could do anything well. Henry Joy himself had a "prairie schooner" body mounted on another Thirty for "roughing it in sparsely settled sections of the far West."

Again there was little new about the Thirty and Eighteen for 1912, though the "S" sub-designation had been deleted and the runabout placed under the UE category for the Thirty. Skipping ND, the Eighteen became the NE. The most important change was mechanical—the clutch was combined with the motor by housing both the clutch and flywheel in a rigid extension of the crankcase. This, Packard said, would permanently align the rear bearing of the clutch shaft with the motor.

Body styles did, however, proliferate in 1912. The line now included touring cars, phaetons, coupes, limousines, landaulets, runabouts and broughams priced from $4200 for the touring and runabout to $5650 for the Imperial limousine on an extra long 129-inch wheelbase. There was also a landaulette touring car, with add-on glass rear quarters, back window and windshield between the front and rear compartments. Joy made note of the fact that the $4200 price for the standard touring hadn't changed since its introduction in 1907—and a 1912 tourer provided a bonus of $785.45 worth of equipment which hadn't been there five years before, including top and side curtains, twin gas headlights and piping, a six-volt battery, shock absorbers, removable folding seats, gas tank,

Packard

Ninth Number
September 3, 1910

Ralph Estep was described during this era as the "pioneer developer of scientific automobile publicity." But he brought his sense of the aesthetic to Packard as well. Prior to his efforts, company advertising had been usually boisterous and frequently crude. It was Estep who created the formidably grand catalogue for the 1908 Model Thirty, who founded that remarkable house organ called **The Packard,** *and who brought an aura of dignity and elegance to all the company promotions.*

demountable rims and a monogram. The actual cost of building the Thirty in 1911, Joy told dealers, had risen by $352 over 1910.

There had been a lot of other changes too. In 1909 James Ward Packard had relinquished his by now completely honorary position as president. His diary documents his waning interest in the company he founded. During 1908 his visits to Detroit were infrequent though apparently congenial—"harmonious" is the word he used often to describe them. Even after giving up his Packard presidency, he would return to the factory occasionally—on March 30th, 1910 he paid a courtesy call and on the 21st attended a "meeting at Mr. McMillan's office. Everything very pleasant and satisfactory." But more often, diary entries now recorded matters unakin to Packard, the death of Mark Twain in April, of King Edward VII of England in May, the flight of Glenn Curtiss from Albany to New York also that month, and during the summer the visits to Warren of Albert Kahn who was engaged to build James Ward a brand-new house.

Meantime Henry B. Joy succeeded James Ward in the office which he had by now so deservedly earned. The dynamic part Joy had played in nursing Packard through its early years cannot be understated. He believed strongly in developing a favorable climate for research and invention, and brought Milton Tibbetts in to protect Packard's position through patents. He insisted on standardized accounting methods and sent company representatives into the field to help agencies set up the system he wanted. He closely scrutinized manufacturing, and in 1909 invited Frederick W. Taylor, the country's leading time-and-motion expert, to talk to Packard's top managers about efficiency.

In that year, too, he made another move, in the cause of efficiency, among other matters. On September 1st, Packard Motor Car Company became a Michigan corporation, succeeding the West Virginia company. While under the latter charter, Packard had grown generally in respectable gradation, its original 5000 shares reduced to 2500 in 1901, increased to the original 5000 in 1902, to 6500 in 1905, to 10,000 in 1906, to 15,000 in 1907, to 15,500 in June of '08 and 30,500 in August that year—all shares of $100 par value, with each increase in authorization accompanied by issuance of stock sufficient to absorb the entire increase. Obviously Henry Joy's perpetual factory building program—despite more cars built and more profits made—had to put something of a strain on the corporate coffers. This was alleviated by the changeover to Michigan charter with an accompanying augmentation in capital stock to $10,000,000, $5,000,000 cumulative preferred, $5,000,000 common—this increase made, so *The Horseless Age* reported, "to meet the company's needs for enlargement of floor space and additional facilities generally [and] to enable the company to avoid night work." It would also take care of any financial pinches Henry Joy was feeling.

By August 31st, 1911, Joy could report favorably to the board that

...ody styles, and styling ideas, proliferate at Packard Motor Car Company.
Far left from the top: A runabout Model Eighteen from 1911, the
...wagger car" Model Thirty brougham of 1910, a Thirty coupe from 1912.
Left from the top: The landaulet version of the 1912 Model Eighteen,
...snugly proportioned Thirty coupe of 1911, the close-coupled Model Thirty
...touring of 1911 with its "tiger seat." Above: A many-windowed 1912
...ghteen brougham. Below: The Thirty's close-coupled touring car of 1912.

Packard had never been healthier. The floor area of the plant had now increased to 1,642,212 square feet covering 37.7 acres—against thirteen in 1908. "Packard Factory Spreads In All Directions," *The Automobile* had enthused. There were 7575 men working—against 2500 in 1909. The maximum monthly payroll, in August, was $524,407. Total assets amounted to $16.1 million, working capital $3.7 million; net profits for the fiscal year were $1.4 million, 12.1 percent of sales. The year next would see $1.8 million made on $14.6 million sales, or 12.6 percent. "Mr. Joy points out," said *The Horseless Age*, "that when a company manufactures all of the parts of its cars itself, instead of merely assembling parts made elsewhere, it can turn over its capital approximately once during a fiscal year." A little honey, perhaps, to sweeten the disposition of Packard stockholders.

Packard had truly done well. While its share of the luxury market during its four-cylinder era had increased from only 1.1 to 1.6 percent, percentages are misleading—Packard was now building many more cars, employing many more people, and making much more money. Of course, it was competing for a very tiny section at the top of the price pyramid, and its output of 3000 cars in 1910 was minuscule in the light of Ford's and Buick's 30,000 units apiece.

But the prize was worth the effort, and Packard was in a prime position to snatch it. At least twenty-three of its American luxury car rivals, for example, were priced higher, comparing figures for standard touring cars—these ranged from an Alco at $4500 to E.R. Thomas' big six-cylinder Model K at $6000. Packard's closest rival in this period was the excellent Pierce-Arrow—both in prestige and production. In 1905 Pierce sold about 300 cars to Packard's 481; by 1911 the figures were 2200 and 2521 respectively.

Soon, too, Packards would be wending their way in increasing numbers beyond American shores. Exporting began in 1908 when Von Hamm-Young Company, Ltd. of Hawaii became an "overseas distributor." Within four years Packards were being sold in Paris, London, Spain, Holland, Puerto Rico and Cuba as well. Three years after that, South America, previously the province of European car importation almost exclusively, was invaded by Packard, with distributorships set up in Buenos Aires, Rio de Janeiro and other large metropolitan centers.

But now—in 1911—new horizons lay ahead. Packard, as the world would soon learn, was about to move out of the four-cylinder field for good. But consistency would be served. As Sidney Waldon allowed, "Cars will change and cars will improve. There will be no radical changes. As Patrick Henry said: 'I have but one lamp by which my feet are guided and that is the lamp of experience. I know of no way of judging the future, but by the past.'"

The future would be judged equally as brightly as the past. Henry Joy had hired a new general manager, and his name was Alvan Macauley.

CHAPTER SEVEN

ALVAN MACAULEY AND THE DOMINANT SIX

The Models Six, 48, 1338, 1448, 1438,

4-48, 2-38, 5-48 and 3-38

April 1911–September 1915

AUTHORS: RICHARD M. LANGWORTH AND DON E. WEBER

None of the great men we have already met in this story, nor any whom we will meet, surpassed Alvan Macauley as the very embodiment of Packard—its integrity, its dedication to excellence, its care for reputation, its determination to be always best. In every way he represented what Packard probably thought of as its typical owner/driver, traveling in aristocratic company, respected as a leader of his community as well as his profession. A patron of the arts, Macauley owned paintings by Reynolds, Raeburn, Bronzino and Van Cuelen, and his library was a massive floor-to-ceiling collection of many thousand contemporary and classical works. All was housed, after 1928, in his magnificent home in Grosse Pointe Shores, designed by Albert Kahn, meticulously adapted from English Cotswold architecture and put together by a team of Scots artisans directed by a Cotswold foreman. Macauley collected guns, and was a crack shot, particularly from a duck blind; he was also an ardent fly fisherman and golfer. His closest friends were pillars of the Packard community like Alvan T. Fuller, Sidney Waldon and Henry B. Joy.

Richly dressed, but never natty, Macauley bestrode Packard's story for well over a third of a century, first as general manager, later as vice-president, finally as president and board chairman. He was also president of the Automobile Manufacturers Association from 1928 to 1945, and upon stepping down was called by the press "perhaps the last of the great pioneers of the industry which has made Detroit and the nation world renowned." As Packard's president from 1916 to 1938, he was called "the only gentleman in the automotive business." One of his contemporaries commented, "In some respects, it might be possible to compare him with the car. In working hours, at least, he is like a well oiled, carefully adjusted, trim appearing piece of machinery . . . you can feel his reserve power."

Born James Alvan Macauley in Wheeling, West Virginia on January 17th, 1872—he dropped the first name at an early date—Packard's future leader was heir to a family of distinguished Scots ancestry. His father, James Alexander, had been born in 1840 and spent his youth in Glasgow, sailing with his family at age ten for a new home near Bloomfield, Ohio. James served in the Union Army during the Civil War, then sought a law degree in 1865. He was also an amateur inventor, a trait that would later appear in his son.

James married Rebecca Jane Mills of Wheeling in November 1865, a lady of genteel Irish parentage who "possessed the poise, charm and innate graciousness that reflected her fine background." According to the Alvan Macauley memorial book, "she was of great help to James in his law studies and encouraged him to enter political life."

After passing his bar examinations in 1868, James became a clerk in the Wheeling Post Office, but shortly moved to the state treasurer's office. He was elected West Virginia's treasurer in 1869, and in 1871

Alvan Macauley: With James Ward Packard at the factory in 1915 and (pages preceding) at home in his library in the late Teens.

moved to Washington to accept an appointment from President Rutherford B. Hayes as examiner in the U.S. Pension Bureau. He worked at the Bureau until his retirement, and he and Rebecca raised five children.

Alvan was the second of two sons. His older brother, John Blair, attended Johns Hopkins University and became examiner-in-chief of the U.S. Patent Office and later a patent attorney. All of the Macauley children moved in patrician company; of the three daughters, May married a hospital surgeon, Elsie a Washington cigar and tobacco merchant, Anna a vice-president of Libby-Owens-Ford Glass Company.

From an early age, young Alvan showed an interest in tools of all kinds, and the first fifty cents he ever earned was used to buy a whetstone to sharpen his old knife and the family woodworking tools. Later, an issue of *The Packard* was to feature his wood shop in Grosse Pointe, admirably equipped with tools and machinery, where Packard's president spent many of his leisure hours.

Alvan also displayed a love of mechanics and invention, so it followed that he would enter an engineering college. He chose James Ward Packard's alma mater, Lehigh University, spending two years there, then entered law school at George Washington University. His first five working years were spent as a patent attorney, like his brother, at the prominent law firm of Church and Church, in Washington.

Macauley's first salary at Church and Church was $2.50 a week, of which he was able to save about a dollar. After he had saved a small amount, his bank asked him to close out because small accounts weren't worth carrying. Thirty years later the same bank contacted him at Packard, in the hope that his company would open an account with them; he was too much a gentleman to remind them of their attitude of three decades before, but the incident always amused him.

An opportunity to apply his legal talents in the mechanical and engineering fields arose in 1896—following his marriage in November 1895 to Estelle Littlepage of Washington—when Macauley accepted a patent attorney position with the National Cash Register Company in Dayton, Ohio. He remained there for four years, when the next major opportunity was presented to him—"a managerial post of great responsibility" with the American Arithmometer Company of St. Louis. There he encountered his first industrial scuffle.

When Macauley arrived in St. Louis, a battle was raging for control of the company. Finally its president was overpowered by the board, which dismissed him, and he left with fifty-two key employees. The new president, Joseph H. Boyer, turned to Macauley to reorganize the firm. This was the same Joseph Boyer who had been a disgruntled stockholder in the Packard Motor Car Company.

Alvan Macauley worked a twelve-hour day in St. Louis, finally sorting out the company's manifold production, sales, training and organizational problems. Business improved, but circumstances prevented much expansion in St. Louis, so one night Macauley moved the whole corporation, including 400 workmen and their families, to Detroit. He had paved the way by setting up some machinery there in advance, and the next day the company was back in full operation. It then changed its name to the Burroughs Adding Machine Company, later Burroughs Corporation.

Ensconced in Detroit, Alvan Macauley continued his whirlwind pace and, in addition to managing Burroughs, found time to invent various mechanical improvements to its products and make a comprehensive survey of marketing methods and practices. By 1910 Burroughs had one of the most powerful sales organizations in the country.

Henry Joy probably first heard about Alvan Macauley from Boyer, with whom he remained friends after the latter's pull-out from Packard. He certainly must have taken note of Macauley's faultless transfer of Burroughs to Detroit. Boyer had also told Macauley of his sell-out of Packard stock back in 1904, and remarked that, as Packard fortunes now stood, he was more and more regretting that decision.*

The job of actually recruiting Alvan Macauley as Packard's general manager fell to Sidney Waldon. Macauley's decision to accept the offer wasn't an easy one; he had come a long way at Burroughs. After a few sleepless nights, however, Macauley said yes in April; Burroughs paid him a tribute in its house magazine, and wished him well.

Henry Joy could now leave the general managership of Packard to a skilled associate and concentrate strictly on being Packard's president. This would give him time for other pursuits, including the campaign for constructing the Lincoln Highway, of which he was a leading booster. Joy's interest in the product, though, never faltered, and he and Macauley vociferously paid tribute to the newly announced Packard Six.

Though Packard was preeminently a luxury car, Joy and Macauley made short work of any who felt cars were only for pleasure. "You might as well talk of bird's wings as 'pleasure wings'," Macauley said. "The bird, of course, enjoys flying. But its wings, nine-tenths of the time, are purely business wings, helping to do what is necessary. So it is with the automobile, which gives health, relaxation, education, holds families together, makes an hour do the work of four hours." If a four-cylinder Packard could do the job better than a single, Macauley might have reasoned, a six would do it even better. And a six was already well along when he reported for work at East Grand Boulevard.

The idea for it had come some seven years before. "Waldon says Moore saw [the vision of a six] first," records *The Packard*. "Moore

---

*Boyer never really stopped being a skeptic about cars, however. When his son, Joseph Jr., entered the Indianapolis 500 a number of years later with a Packard, Boyer cabled, "Congratulations. Now let's do something worthwhile."

avers that Huff was the pioneer and Huff passes the credit to Joy. It was in 1905 . . . [then in 1906 an] experimental station was established near Mr. Joy's summer home at Watch Hill. . . . Joy, Waldon, Huff and [sales branches manager] M.J. Budlong seized upon every procurable six-cylinder motor, of European and American make. They dissected it. They searched out its weaknesses and recorded them. They pitted the four-cylinder, as it was, against the six-cylinder as they believed it could be developed—and the six won.

"Those were dynamic years from 1906 to 1910. Russell Huff crossed the Atlantic eight times with the vision for a traveling companion. The others spent months at a time in Europe, absorbing the best offerings of the foreign engineers. In the spring of 1910 the idea had developed to the stage where it was regarded as worthy to bear the Packard seal."*

As chief engineer, Russell Huff was responsible for directing development of the six, though by the time it appeared he had been relieved by Jesse Vincent and had become a consulting engineer to Packard. Huff was assisted by manufacturing engineer C. J. Moore. The body and chassis were handled by A.J. Neerken and Allen Loomis respectively.

---

*The Packard board minutes gave it the number 36 on July 25th, 1910, to wit: "Management was authorized to plan to get out the '36' as fast as possible." The linking numerically of the six to the Thirty was significant; many parts on the two cars would be interchangeable, "not only to simplify manufacturing," Packard would say, "but to facilitate Packard service. The plan was carried out as far as an entirely new type and model of car would permit."

Promotional road testing of the new Six (below) and advertising it (right) in Life *magazine in April 1911, together with the two models which preceded it.*

During and after the development of the six, Packard continued to sell fours. "After a discussion of the question of price and equipment, on 1912 cars," read the board minutes, "it was the sense of the meeting [on January 21st, 1911] that all models be fully equipped; that the prices of the '18' and '30' be raised a sufficient amount to take care of the additional equipment; that the price of the '36' be fixed at $5,000.00. . . ." In February, Sidney Waldon told the board "that the 1912 program contemplates: that all cars be equipped with electric lights; that the '30' with 37 x 5 tires; an output of 250 cars a month, with allotments to dealers 10% in advance of the sales program and prices as follows: '18' $3,-200.00; '30' $4,200.00; '35' $5,000.00." (The "35" was undoubtedly a typographical error.)

Unofficially, word broke on the new Packard Six in *The Motor World* of March 30th, 1911 under the headline, "Packard Finally Embraces the 'Six.' " The magazine admitted that no one at Packard openly confirmed it, but "some of the Packard people themselves have dropped intimations broad enough to remove the slightest doubts." No doubt Henry Joy was again plying the press in his inimitable way. By April 6th, *The Motor World* reported the Six "well advanced, with deliveries in limited quantities to start by summer." A few weeks later, Packard made it official.

The 1912 Packard Six was mounted on a sturdy ladder chassis with a track of 56 ½ inches, a standard (139-inch) and close-coupled (133-inch) wheelbase, and a 121 ½-inch wheelbase for the runabout. In design the bodies were noticeably sleeker and better-proportioned than preceding models, though the Thirty and Eighteen remained in the 1912 line and received similar body treatment. New lines lent themselves well to two toning: Standard colors were Packard Blue for the body, and Packard Gray for wheels and running gear, with black bonnet and fenders.

Following the trend toward a wide selection of bodies that had begun with the Thirty and Eighteen, the new Six offered no less than thirteen variations: touring, phaeton, runabout and close-coupled at $5000 each; touring with leather victoria top, $5250; phaeton, with the same, $5215; touring with full glass canopy, $5445; limousine, $6250; landaulet, $6350; Imperial limousine, $6450; Imperial landaulet, $6550; brougham, $6300; coupe, $5700.

Tradition was served by placement of the transmission, final drive and differential together in the rear axle housing. Packard said this was all the more important with six-cylinder construction, which put more load on the front wheels, and it helped insulate the passengers from noise, produced less torque reaction in the lower gears, allowed a lighter chassis and a more accessible clutch, and provided better balance. The engine itself was a 525-cubic-inch (4 ½ by 5 ½ bore/stroke) T-head rated at 48 A.L.A.M. horsepower. It provided, the company said, "The Fastest Getaway—60 Miles an Hour in 30 Seconds from a Standing Start."

The four main bearing engine featured three pairs of cylinder castings, each with integral water jackets and valve chambers. Connecting rods were drop forged, all bearings were ground, all bushings carefully and accurately fitted. The mechanical valves were interchangeable, with the inlet and exhaust valves on opposite sides of the engine. The cast aluminum crankcase was built in two horizontal sections, the uppermost an engine base, the lower section an oil reservoir in the bottom of which were an oil pump and strainer.

The new Six carburetor was of Packard design and manufacture, combining float feed and automatic mixture and fitted with a primary air intake shut-off valve to assist starting in cold weather. Fuel was fed by gravity from a copper tank mounted under the front seat; a three-way valve controlled the twenty-one-gallon main supply, five-gallon reserve and shut-off. On runabouts, phaetons and close-coupled models,

however, gasoline was pressure fed through an air compressor with automatic regulator on the engine and also a hand compressor for initial pressurizing or emergency.

Packard Six ignition was a Bosch dual system, current supplied by a Bosch high tension magneto and a storage battery for "starting on the switch or for reserve." Lubrication was force-feed by gear pump to the motor, gear, crankshaft and lower connecting rod bearings. Cylinder walls, camshafts and other motor parts were splash lubed from the connecting rod bearings. The transmission and differential ran in oil, the universal joint was encased and packed with grease. Other running or wearing parts were fitted with grease cups, oil holes or oil cups.

The transmission was designed for light weight and as few as possible moving parts. There were three forward speeds and a reverse, the gear lever contained in a single quadrant with a forged casing. Rear axle, final

drive and differential gears were run on annular ball bearings. Brakes acted on the rear wheels through external contracting bands operated by foot pedal. The emergency brakes were lever-operated.

All these expensive features were readily recognized in the marketplace. Packard Six sales were high—as were sales of the remaining Thirty and Eighteen models. At the June 21st, 1911 board meeting, "Management was authorized to contract for material for 250 more '30's'; [as well as] 500 additional 'Six's' if, in its discretion, this should seem wise." At about the same time, the company announced that seventy-seven percent of the anticipated 1912 production had already been sold; the Six was well accepted everywhere.

The Six's power was not lost on those outside the law. "No longer may we ignore the ironical suggestions that have poured in since homicide by motor car has come into prominence in New York," said *The Packard* in

The 1913 Packard 48, its chassis photographed, and the interior of the limousine model showing respectively the bucket and folding seat variations.

September 1913. "Newspaper pictures of the 'gray murder car' show unmistakably that it is a Packard, an unknowing and innocent accomplice of 'Lefty' Louie, 'Dago' Frank and the rest. Our friends intimate that the lightning like getaway has recommended the Packard to the dark uses of the powers that prey. Jesse James, Dick Turpin and other outlaws of yesterday and the day before used the best horses obtainable. . . . The selection of the Packard by the gun men of New York is, we insist, a matter of evolution and no reflection on the integrity of the car."

If it wasn't, the Packard Six was nevertheless a popular way of evading the firm hand of justice. In 1913 Harry Kendall Thaw, millionaire murderer of architect Stanford White, escaped from the Matteawan State Asylum for the Criminal Insane in a Six, "at a speed of eighty miles an hour to the Connecticut State line, where he is immune

The second folding seat is in its tucked-in position along the side (below).

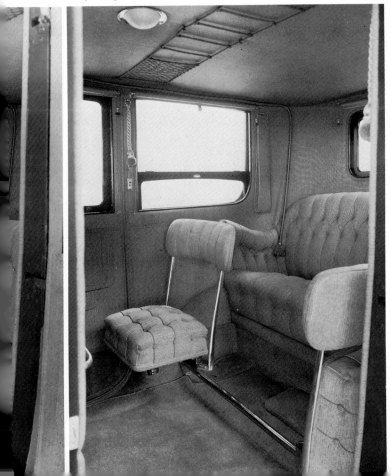

from arrest." His giant black Six touring was seen by early risers in Stormville, New York, ten miles east of Matteawan, Thaw and three accomplices "crouching low to escape the sweep of their rush through the air . . . Stormville marveled at their speed and watched them melt away in the distance." (This according to newspaper accounts.) Pressing a fast car into service, armed guards gave chase, but the Six rapidly increased its lead and pursuers finally gave up. Remarked *The Packard*, "When dependability is vital, when high speed is necessary, when a fast getaway is absolutely imperative, Ask the Man Who Owns One."

Not all celebrity drivers of the new Packard Six were of the nefarious sort, however. A young vaudeville star by the name of Al Jolson, then wowing them at New York's Winter Garden, drove his—with watch manufacturer Julius Schwab and two other friends—from Manhattan to San Francisco during 1912 in less than eighteen days, which didn't establish a transcontinental record, but impressed the man who would give the world "Mammy" mightily.

By the end of 1912, Henry Joy could report a very big year. In the 1911-1912 season, 3617 Packards were sold, against 3047 the previous twelve months. Dividends were declared, wages were increased, and a total surplus of nearly $5 million was reported. Now a new scheme of manufacturing was announced: "The former endeavor was to bring out two models of chassis of two sizes at the same time," *The Automobile* reported, "in order to have them ready for the market at the same time, both models going together through the factory [like the Thirty and Eighteen]. This has proven impracticable for many reasons, and causes delayed deliveries and restricted output. Under the [new] scheme, one model of chassis is developed and manufactured at a time, and offered to the market when ready."

Packard would soon build a smaller six, successor to the Eighteen, but this policy meant it would not normally be built simultaneously with the big six. For the present, however, Packard merely concentrated on the improved 1913 successor to the 1912 Six, which it would name after its A.L.A.M. horsepower rating: the 1913 "48."* At the October 6th, 1911 board meeting, "the following Manufacturing Program was agreed upon: To continue the present Program of 3100 cars for the present season,

*Packard's practice was to surround this designation in quotation marks, as it had all Packard cars preceding and those models to follow during the Dominant Six era. This device was used by many manufacturers during this period. Contemporary grammatical practice and editorial considerations of readability, however, not the least of which would be the flurry of the single and double quote marks when the designation is used in the possessive, have dictated our dropping the device hereafter, confining the use of quotation marks for uses of emphasis or clarification, although, of course, retaining them when they are cited in Packard board minutes or other references from that period.

manufacturing the same at the rate of ten a day; when it becomes necessary to add to this program in order to keep the factory going on a basis of ten cars a day, that the addition be in 1913 'Six's'."

Interestingly, Alvan Macauley at this time favored building more fours. "The foregoing plan was put to a vote, all present voting in favor of it excepting Mr. Macauley, who favored the addition of 250 '30's' instead of confining the addition to 'Six's'. In order to carry out the foregoing plan, the Management was authorized, in its discretion, to order stock for 1,000 new 'Six's'."

The 1913 48 was introduced in the summer of 1912; its rated horsepower designation was misleading, the developed was actually 82 at 1720 rpm, eight more than the 1912 model. Although no reason for the increase was mentioned, it may have stemmed from different test readings. Whatever the case, the car sold heavily from the start. Later this car was designated the "2-48" by Packard, since it was the second of what would ultimately be five 48 hp models built during the four model years 1912-1915. Packard even called its 1912 predecessor the "1-48" in certain board minutes, for the same reason—and as model proliferation set in, these designations would prove handy indeed.

Like the 1912 model, the 1913 48 retained right-hand drive and most of the other established Six features—with certain improvements. Among these were direct lubrication of the piston pin bearings, the overflow from which lubricated the piston and cylinder walls. Splash lube, Henry Joy's old nemesis, was substantially eliminated by the adoption of baffle plates under the cylinders, and an auxiliary oiling system supplied more oil to the cylinder walls through a check valve. Unlike the 1912 model which used gas light, the 1913 48 featured electric headlights. It retained the use of combination oil/electric sidelights and taillights, but the "bails" or handles of the sidelamps were now set into the sides of the lamp bodies instead of overhead, an identifying feature. Other changes included the relocation of the fuel tank from under the seat to the rear of the car, eliminating odors and easing fuel supply on grades, and the removal of the battery and tool box from the running board to positions under the driver's seat.

Again like the 1912 Six, the 1913 models used aluminum bodies built over white ash frames. The touring body, however, was now on a 139-inch wheelbase, and the main body panel of the rear compartment extended in one piece from door to door. The use of aluminum did not, incidentally, signify light cars: The touring model weighed 4560 pounds, the phaeton 4450, and the runabout 4010. The 1913 bodies were about six inches wider, and extra seats of the folding or Pullman chair type were now available on touring and enclosed models.

The 1913 Packard 48 followed a tradition Henry Joy had proclaimed with the Thirty: offering an improved car for less money. The line was uniformly priced below the 1912's, as follows: touring car, $4850; phaeton, $4750; runabout, $4650; limousine, $5850; landaulet, $5950; Imperial limousine, $6050; brougham, $5800; coupe, $5100. These were as much as $600 below 1912.

According to *Motor Age* of January 9th, 1913, supplies of the 1913 48 "were soon exhausted," only one thousand or so being produced before Packard, in accord with its new policy of building two different models alternately, announced in the summer of 1912 a new, smaller six.

The new model was named 38, again after its A.L.A. M. horsepower, though, like the 48, it developed more—close to 60 bhp. As *The Packard* related, the new 38 had been in incubation for quite awhile—since "the fall of 1910," to be exact. The reasons for its long gestation are easy to understand: The Thirty and Eighteen had continued to sell well, the new Six had been a hit, and—most important—the 38 would introduce a host of new features, which took time to perfect.

The wait was worth it, as the new 38 was brimful of forward thinking notions. Its engine was an L-head, cylinders still cast in three blocks of two but featuring a seven main bearing crank—the 48 was a T-head, with four main bearings. The 38 had a 4 by 5 ½ bore/stroke for 415 cubic inches and was equipped as standard with Packard's first self-starter, in combination with generator. The car itself featured left-hand drive, predicting all Packard models to follow. But its most interesting original feature, at least in hindsight, was its centralized "control board," bringing every detail of car operation—starting, lighting, ignition and carburetor control—within easy fingertip reach of the driver.

The control board was conceived by none other than Henry Joy. Attached to the steering column under the wheel, its wire leads were protected by a metal tube. A lock was built in, surrounded by ignition controls, where the ignition key was inserted. To the left was a column of buttons for lights—speedometer, head-side-tail-license lamps. On the right was a wheel control for carburetor fuel mixture. Said *The Packard*, "it makes the operator absolute master of the car without leaving the driver's seat. The only attachments which appear on the dash are the oil and gasoline [tank pressure] gauges [and ammeter], and a button operating the acetylene primer valve, which is to facilitate starting in extremely cold weather."

The starter-generator, purchased from Delco, nudged one Joy commandment by being of outside manufacture, and would prove to have some problems. It wasn't the first of its type to be considered: As early as 1908, Huff brought "a pioneer specimen" back from England, but Packard's high tension magnetos had never made the adaptation of such a device an urgent matter. The starter was energized by a pushbutton on the control board and actuated by stepping on the starter pedal. If necessary, said Huff, it would "crank a motor for half an hour. A car can actually be run several miles on power from the battery."

As for left-hand drive, Packard said this was "simply the triumph of

A summer's day and a phaeton, the 1913 Packard 48.

common sense over custom, the natural accompaniment of a positive self-starter. The two features in combination enable the driver to reach his seat and start his car without stepping into the road." Why American cars weren't left-hand drive from the beginning is curious—we always drove on the right side—and, as Packard pointed out, a man could see better from the left when passing, and could better signal for the "dangerous left turn." The right turn was safer, Packard said, because "you are protected by the curb." Which of course made perfect sense.

The 38's new L-head motor was also a significant departure from the T-head 48. Unlike the latter, its valves were all placed on the right, enclosed by aluminum covers. But like the 48, it used positive pumped oil supply, and was fed fuel from a rear-mounted tank, though 38's were afforded only twenty gallons.

The 38 engine received extensive tests before being okayed for production. Huff and his colleagues had taken a prototype to Long Island in 1911, to a place they called the "Bumblebee's Nest" because "it was in the midst of thick brush, hidden completely from the main line of travel. . . . Engineers taxed their ingenuity to devise racking shop tests—ran the engine at high speed for two hundred hours." Then they installed it in a disguised Thirty and drove all over the eastern United States, for "about half the distance to the moon." Finally, on January 7th, 1913, the old endurance pilot Waldon ran his Chicago-Detroit course in less than ten hours, beating his time with the Thirty by close to an hour. Waldon concluded, "This car is true blue." (His new record didn't stand long; research engineer Frank Trego topped it with another 38 in February 1913, in just over seven hours—a 41 mph average.)

In May of 1913, Packard announced a 200-hour test of the 38 motor at the Automobile Club of America in New York City. This was an attempt to break the steady running record then held by a sleeve-valve Knight engine, with 132 hours back in 1909. A 38 touring car was driven from the Cleveland agency to New York, where it was set up to pound away at 1200 rpm. The throttle was wired open, the spark fully advanced, and A.C.A. lab technicians kept constant record of its performance: They calculated it ran the equivalent of 888 miles a day.

Eight days and a few hours later, the 38 had hummed right on past the 200-hour mark, so the lab decided to try for 300. The engine offered no objection. When finally shut off on May 16th, it had run exactly 12½ days, turning over 21.7 million times, and scoring a mileage equivalent of 11,000, using 1438 gallons of gas. News of this, of course, was trumpeted loudly by Packard.

The 1913 Packard 38, also called the 1338, shown (below) in an interesting depot wagon variation—and the principles which lay behind its production

Like the 48, the 1913 38 offered a wide range of body styles, each priced about a thousand dollars less than the 48—a ratio which would remain pretty much constant in later years. On a short 115½-inch wheelbase was a runabout, the least expensive 38 at $4050. A brougham ($5200) and four- or five-passenger phaeton ($4150) were mounted on a 138-inch wheelbase chassis, while other styles used a 134. These were the touring car at $4150; limousine, $5200; landaulet, $5300; Imperial limousine, $5400; coupe, $4500; and Imperial coupe, $4900. A bare chassis was also listed, for $3500.

On open 38's, hand-buffed black leather was standard, but one could order a special color for twenty-five dollars extra on the touring and phaeton, or ten dollars on the runabout. Closed car interiors featured black leather in driving compartment and Packard Gray cloth in the rear, with all bright metal parts except foot rests finished in silver plate. Sterling silver mounted toilet articles were standard equipment; two-compartment models had speaking tube, folding foot rail, hat and parcel carrier, toilet case and smoking set. Packard Blue was again the standard finish, and Packard recommended that all exposed wooden parts (except wheels), the bonnet and fenders be finished in black. Options, typical of the period for Packard, included a trunk rack, Warner speedometer,

ove right) as published in the elegant brochure accompanying the model's introduction.

Production body styles for the 1913 Packard 38 (clockwise from top left): coupe, cabette, phaeton runabout, limousine, landaulette, brougham.

Winter motoring in the 1914 1448, the phaeton runabout among the less expensive body types for this model ($4700), mounted on the 139-inch wheelbase.

Klaxon horn, two tire covers, bumper, lady's hat box, trunk with three leather suitcases, power tire pump, set of extra lamp bulbs, and seat covers for the open models—one could order all these for about four hundred dollars total.

Despite an August 1912 announcement, the 38 was held up considerably—much to the ire of dealers and customers—apparently to allow the new Delco starter-generator to be perfected. Henry Joy's report to directors for the fiscal year ending August 31st, 1913, notes that "The electric cranking device created a revolution in design. In our own case, we delayed our [38] output during September, October and November of 1912 in order to properly and mechanically make a satisfactory installation of this device. It was good judgment, and while the delay vexed our customers as well as ourselves, we are able to say today that 'our electric cranker is basically good.' " Further, "a curious complication due to an electrical engineering error in magneto construction has caused much uncertainty and varied annoyances for some months. This is now happily being overcome by the magneto manufacturers [Bosch], and satisfaction and enthusiasm is taking the place of passive accept-

ance." The 38 was thus delayed until mid-December 1912, but it was a small price to pay for the Delco starter and Joy, of course, knew it.

Since the 38 was the car that first caused Packard to drop model year designations in favor of series designations, it is important to consider nomenclature. In its introductory booklet—*Facts About the "38"*—dated September 14th, 1912, Packard referred to the new smaller six as the "1338." The first two digits obviously stood for model year. The *Handbook of Automobiles* for January 1913 refers to it as the 1913 "38." But delays, stemming from electric starter problems alluded to by Joy prevented scheduled production of 38's during September-November 1912. By the time they *did* get into production, then out into the hands of customers, it was well into 1913. And around March or April of 1913, they were being joined on the marketplace by the next series of 48's, which were 1914 models. Certainly no dealer could justify selling brand-new 1913 and 1914 models side by side, so something needed to be done about nomenclature.

It is apparent that in order to keep the 38 current, Packard began to refer to it as a 1914 model. Although there is no "break" in serial numbers to indicate exactly when this changeover occurred, if one assumes that it happened when the new 48 for 1914 appeared, it is possible to conclude that only 38's built in 1912 and January-February 1913 were considered "1338's." The rest were "1438's." A total of 678 were produced in this period, from serial number 38000 to 38679. That *some* subsequent cars were indeed labeled 1438's is proven by Packard's owner's manual—*Information [on] The "1438"*—describing exactly the same model.

It was around this time, the spring of 1913, that saw Packard switch over to series designations. Board minutes for April 5th, for example, refer to "the present model '38' (138) car" and "the next model of '38' cars (238)." When in due course the 238 appeared, the facts book for salesmen explained that it was so named because it was the "second 38, and too early to be the 1538." (Packard directors were temporarily confused: On April 21st they referred to the forthcoming "238" as the "1438"—which Packard's own "1438" information booklet was contradicting around the same time!) Whatever confusion remained was cleared up by August, with the arrival of the 238. By this time, Packard was referring in board minutes to the first "38" as the "138" (or "1-38") and even to the original 1912 Six as the "1-48."

Early in 1913 Packard introduced its third model 48, last of the T-head sixes, and a car that remained current longer than any other 48 model. This new 48 appeared at Packard's stand at the Madison Square Garden automobile show on January 11-18th, 1913, and Sidney Waldon had test-driven one in October 1912, though shipments didn't start until March or April. The Garden car, a seven-passenger touring, was "a special job made up to show the public what the car would look like," implying that its release was still some months off. It was displayed alongside the 1-38 model, which owing to the aforementioned delays was still being built at the time. Packard first promised the "New 48" in February, then March, and finally had to settle for April before the cars were in dealer showrooms.

Because this car adopted the 1-38's left-hand drive, combination starter-generator and steering column control board, among other features, it was announced in the press, sales brochure and owners manual as the "New 48." Later, in the board minutes for June 28th, 1913, for example, it was designated the "1448," in line with its smaller linemate the "1438." Once the switch to series nomenclature had been established toward the autumn of 1913, it finally received its most logical designation: "3-48," meaning that it was the third distinct type of 48 produced by Packard.

Owing to the 3-48's T-head engine configuration, identical to the 1-48 and 2-48—and its early introduction (despite the fact that it wasn't sold until much later), this car has often been referred to as a 1913 model. It was not. Aside from the obviousness of the 1448 designation, the car was

NEW PACKARD WORM BEVELS MEAN A SILENT REAR AXLE

PACKARD WORM DESIGN GIVES SMOOTH SILENT ACTION BETWEEN PINION AND BEVEL GEAR

WORM BEVEL GEARS HAVE PRODUCED AT LAST THE SILENT REAR AXLE—THE AIM OF BUILDERS SINCE HIGH GRADE CARS WERE FIRST MADE—NOW AN EXCLUSIVE FEATURE OF THE NEW PACKARD CARS.

Advertising a Packard advance, from MoToR *magazine, September 1913.*

consistently referred to in the press as a 1914 model, and so indeed by Packard itself. At its Garden debut in January 1913, however, it was not specifically called a 1913 or 1914—which has helped create some of the latter day confusion. It was certainly rather early to be introducing 1914 cars at that time. And the series designation 3-48 was still some months off. But any question about its model year was dispelled in March, when the press carried its description, *Motor Age*, for example, under the headline "Packard '14 Model Out." It was still quite a lead time.

"Although it may seem rather early to many to come out with the so-called 1914 car when the 1913 season is not yet mature," explained *Motor Age*, "this is due to the new scheme of manufacturing now in vogue in the Packard shops. One model is developed and manufactured at a time, the complete quota of that particular type being manufactured before another model is commenced. Accordingly, the new 38 made its appearance last fall, followed this spring by the 48." Again, Packard's new alternate manufacturing policy was having its effect.

Whether one calls it a 1448 or a 3-48, the car was particularly interesting, being transitional between the 2-48 of 1913 and the 4-48 to follow. Like the former, it retained the T-head engine "in order to make parts interchangeable with previous models," but, like the latter, it featured left-hand drive, accomplished mainly by repositioning the engine in the engine bay. The 2-48 had a generator with no starter, the 3-48 had a combination self-starter and generator (Delco system number 20), the 4-48 would feature a separate starter and generator by Bijur. Introduced on the 3-48 as well was a profusion of exterior colors—something new for Packard—and a vast array of optional equipment items.

The big 525-cubic-inch engine was only mildly modified; crankshaft

Introducing a new body style, the twenty-first in Packard's repertoire.

The Packard - SALON BROUGHAM - Three Window Type

AN enclosed carriage of new design has been added to the Packard line, making a total of twenty-one body styles now available for attaching to the "2-38" and "4-48" six-cylinder chassis. The new style is called the Salon Brougham, three-window type, and carries four passengers. It fits the phaeton chassis. The new type of Salon Brougham follows the general outline of Packard six-passenger cars, with sloping roof, narrow body and square corners at the rear. The smartness of design is accentuated by extremely low roof and three spacious windows. The effect is strikingly different from the more conventional types.

The Salon Brougham is a particularly smart equipage for the owner-driver. Only a limited number of these cars will be built, and patrons who order early will avoid disappointment.

Ask the man who owns one

end thrust was now absorbed by the rear bearing, and the flywheel was reduced in diameter to mesh correctly with the self-starter gears. At the rear axle, for the first time, was a set of spiral bevel gears.

"For years," reported *The Packard*, "we had been attempting to design a quiet rear axle. Many types of driving gear were tried and discarded. . . . This was not due to poor workmanship on the part of the craftsmen. The gear design was at fault. . . . The gear shop was nearing the end of its tether when it was suggested that an attempt be made to cut a gear with spiral teeth."

Packard engineers milled a gear, cut the spiral teeth by laborious hand filing, then fitted it to an experimental car. It worked beautifully—and silently. Tool drafting foreman Sam Ayr was then asked to design machines to make the spiral gears and matching pinions in quantity; he reconstructed some machines, and built some new ones. More tests were run, several for more than 100,000 miles on a car. Finally they were ready for the 1448, completely eliminating backlash, "that looseness between the teeth of straight bevels which causes the noise in the differential housing."

Other mechanical changes on the new 48 were relatively slight. The Delco combination starter-generator was bolted up, and the turning radius shortened somewhat by using the 38's worm and nut steering.

The body lineup was considerably altered. Open bodies on 1448's were not interchangeable with 1913 versions, as they were wider and had only one (right-hand) front door. However, Packard did note that they "could be made interchangeable, except on the Imperial coupe." The Imperial coupe also opened only on the right. All bodies had wider sills, "to get an even more substantial attachment to the frame," and windshields were equipped with short brace rods. The short wheelbase was eliminated and 139 inches became standard, save for 121½ inches on the runabout. Body styles were still on the increase, and to save confusion were now designated with their passenger capacity. In the lineup below, the capacity is in parentheses:

Touring (7)	$4850	Landaulet (7)	$5900
Phaeton (5)	$4750	Cabette (4)	$5800
Phaeton Runabout (2)	$4700	Brougham (4 + dropseat)	$5900
Runabout (2 + rumble)	$4650	Salon Brougham (4)	$5850
Limousine (7)	$5900	Coupe (2 + dropseat)	$5400
Imperial Limousine (7)	$6100	Imperial Coupe (4)	$5600
Salon Limousine (7)	$6050	Touring, Victoria top (7)	$5065
Chassis	$4100		

The Cabette was "intended for those who require a compact, small capacity car of exclusive design. This body will only be available in very limited quantities." A few were provided for 38's also. Features of the Cabette style were a roofless driver compartment, wide rear doors, two-person rear seating. The "Salon" designation for broughams and limousines simply meant that the front and rear compartments were undivided, with walk space between front seats.

Generally, 1448 closed models were of the same finish as the 1913 48, with the option of folding or Pullman type seats as in open bodies and "cab side" door construction with retractable door windows. The touring and phaeton, however, used single instead of double rocker construction and eliminated outside door handles. Wire wheels were optional at $150 on all models. The aluminum sheet bodies were mounted on wooden frames. The raised edges were brass, the sills under the doors wood. Available rear axle ratios included 3.53, 3.28 and 3.05.

Color and trim options marked the departure of the 1448 from the past, and the variety was so enormous it is worth setting down, if only to show how Packard's thinking in this area had changed. Note that black was not among the offered body colors:

<u>1448 Paint Colors</u>
Blues: Packard, Alice, Azure, Coach, Holland, Rich
Reds: Armenian, Carmine, Derby light, medium and deep, Runabout

The Packard 1448 (Series 3-48) introduced at Madison Square Garden in January 1913, with first deliveries to dealers' showrooms that April.

Yellows: Chrome, Chrome Orange, Cream, Gold Ochre, Naples, Permanent
Packard Violet, Packard Maroon, Violet Purple
Vermillions: Packard, English
Browns: Packard No. 1, Packard Golden, Golden, Hazel
Grays: Packard, Blue, French light, medium and deep
Greens: Packard, Brewster, Bronze, Coach Painter's, Emerald,
M.F., Moss, Olive light and deep, Pea

<u>1448 Leather Colors</u>
Blues: Packard, Holland, Rich
Reds & Maroons: Packard Maroon, Derby light and deep, Vermillion
Browns: Packard Golden, Hazel
Greens: Packard, Coach Painter's, Emerald, Moss
Blue Gray, Packard Gray, Black

Packard described its painting process as "conducting a color symphony." After the body was thoroughly prepared and undercoated, the base paint was applied followed by coloring varnish—"Lillian Russell doesn't recommend this lacquered effect but we consider it quite necessary." Three "massage treatments" were next, the last with decayed, powdered pumice—"the stuff is all right but it's rotten." Then the body was upholstered. The men who painted monograms on the doors, Packard noted, were on the payroll as artists, not painters; together with the stripers, they were the only ones "privileged to display temperament." After upholstering and detailing, a coat of pale amber varnish was applied, with two cups—one to dip the brush into, one to cleanse it, "an antiseptic precaution to guard against a speck of infection." Plus a mysterious "Mennen's talcum powder rub which adds a certain quality to the luster, but this is one of the beauty secrets that we are very jealous of and at the present it is not being syndicated."

Painting the chassis was yet another display of craftsmanship, in a room where "the air is heavy with turpentine and oil. The men are in extreme negligee and are working with feverish energy." Chassis came in from testing, filthy with grime, to "an old fashioned wash with soap and water." Then "a man armed with a putty knife and a stiff lead mixture goes over it inch by inch and fills up every minute pore in frame and wheels. When the surface is sanded it feels like a piece of plate glass." Two coats of lead were applied, then a foundation color, then the final color and two coats of varnish. Wooden parts were coated with a filler to kill the grain, sanded, shellacked, painted, varnished, then rubbed again with "a very refined medium consisting of rotten stone, pulverized and mixed with ill smelling oil. The final French dressing is alcohol applied with the bare palm. The manicure lady working a regular customer is a mere dilettante compared with these hand polishers."

All this mirrored the pervading philosophy of Henry Joy and Alvan Macauley, their dedication to excellence, their command of loyalty. The latter they said was "the most valuable part of our personal capital. It is

the thing that makes the daily work stand out. No taskmaster can command loyalty; no salary can buy it. It must be inspired."

The company was also good to employees, repaying their loyalty richly. In the board minutes for July 7th, 1911, Alvan Macauley "brought to the attention of the Board the case of one Schneckenberger who, while employed at the plant, had been injured, and later died. His death, however, not having been entirely due to the injury received at the plant. The General Manager stated that Schneckenberger left a widow and three children, who were in great need of help and, on motion duly made and seconded, the Management was authorized to give to Mrs. Schneckenberger such financial assistance as it might be thought wise. . . ." In the days before Workmen's Compensation, this evidenced particular concern for a corporation. At Packard it seemed routine.

Meanwhile, the manufacturers of "The Dominant Six" were really rolling. By June 1913, *Motor Age* could report that the factory was turning out twenty-one cars a day, six commercial vehicles and the remainder Sixes, at a rate keyed to 3000 vehicles a year, of which 1800 would be trucks. The plant now covered nearly forty acres of work area, 6000 to 7000 men were on a payroll accounting for $20,000 a day, the work week was 52½ hours. A single shift sufficed, except in two machining

The 2-38 touring car (below and right) in front and driver compartment view.

Further body styles on the Packard 2-38 chassis: The phaeton (above) with victoria top, and the phaeton runabout (below) as viewed in rear three- quarter.

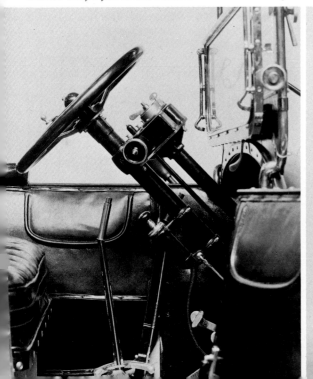

departments, "where it has been necessary to work nights to take care of the extra output due to the introduction of commercial cars in the line."

The assembly of a 38 or 48 engine took seventy-two hours, and was done on a special rotating rack which allowed the motor to be tackled from above or below. The 38 engines were required to develop 40 to 48 hp at 1200 rpm, the 48 engines 60 hp before they were road tested—if not, they were sent back for reassembly. The road test itself never lasted less than four hours.

This whole incredible system of building automobiles was the wonder of most visitors to East Grand Boulevard in those days, and many probably wondered why Packard bothered. "The temptation arises from time to time to change policy and make vehicles of cheaper character," said Henry Joy, "but the conclusion is always reached that such a change in policy would not give 'Packard' results to our patrons upon which the permanent solidity of our business depends. . . . We have just one way of doing things. We are going to keep right on along the same lines as long as we stay in business."

With Packard's exclusive clientele, this policy was obviously the best one. And it paid off. New England's 1912 registrations of the "Three P's," for example, were 943 for Peerless, 1610 for Pierce-Arrow, and 3396 for Packard. That spoke pretty much for itself.

At the end of the fiscal year, on August 31st, 1913, Henry Joy was able to report a record production of 3994 vehicles—four more than the previous high of 3990 set in 1909-1910—and a "startling" total of $81,-650,721.14 brought to Detroit over the ten years of operation. The com-pany had "not a dollar of floating debt." Packard made $2.2 million during the year, on $15.1 million sales. Though minor changes would accrue on future 38's and 48's, they would be only that: "We cannot substantially make them better." Packard, Joy said, had now settled on certain manufacturing principles through the long process of trial and error—and observation of "freak mechanical devices, such as curious 'drives,' ingenious electrical 'controls,' unmechanical valve systems, abnormal devices to do everything." But the Dominant Six was "possibly a better service car as it is, without added complications.

"We have learned at great expense that the right place for the transmission is neither on the motor nor amidships, but attached to the rear axle*. . . . We have learned that the transmission must have only the sliding unit connected up to the clutch, for the best gear-shifting results. We have learned that the high piston speeds are only practical when accompanied by pressure oiling to all engine bearings. . . . We have learned that no car we can make without the hydraulic governor is as pleasing to handle as one with the hydraulic governor. . . . We have learned not to make an expanding service brake; nor to use four-point suspension on a long motor bolted into a flexible frame and driven over uneven roads. We have learned not to tie the entire system for igniting, lighting and starting, up into one unit. We have learned that the public

---

*Eventually Packard would drop this theory and go to conventionally mounted gearboxes. Universal joints used in the rear transmissions didn't hold up well against increasing engine torque loads.

Formidably impressive, the Packard 4-48 runabout on the gargantuan 144-inch chassis. There was never a larger two-seater made at East Grand Boulevard.

will not stand for the gasoline tank inside the body. . . . We have learned not to try to make a four-cylinder engine meet six-cylinder requirements." These features "are not crystallizing; they have crystallized."

Next to crystallize was the 2-38, in September 1913, successor to the sold-out 1-38. Although we have noted the use of the designations 1-48, 2-48, 3-48 and 1-38 after these cars were introduced under different names, by now series designations were firmly established. Thus the 2-38 was introduced under series designation from the start; it was too soon, as we've seen, to be called the 1538, and in addition to that, Packard wasn't using model year terminology anymore. The 2-38 was, simply, the second 38. And Packard said so.

Of the new car, Sidney Waldon waxed eloquent: "It is liquid velvet. It moves as if drawn by a silken thread. There is no harsh sound or action in it, and driving at ordinary speeds may be likened to a dreamless sleep. There's no suggestion of a mechanism but only a murmur, like the sigh of the wind through the tree tops at night." One would think the car was altogether unique—but of course it was only the old 1-38, updated with new spiral bevel gears and a new engine. Retaining the 1-38's 415-cubic-inch displacement, the 2-38 cylinders were now cast in two blocks of three instead of three blocks of two.

Minor mechanical changes in the 2-38 included enclosed secondary wiring, concealed pressure oil leads except on ends of the motor, integral motor bed webs and radiator splashers, improved pressure-feed lubrication to thirty-five points, dual exhausts, accelerator pedal moved to the right of the brake pedal, improved clutch brake, water-jacketed intake header, and seventeen-inch brakes.

The 2-38's wheelbase was lengthened to 140 inches, and this single measurement served all bodies with either a phaeton or a touring chassis. Again body styles proliferated, no less than twenty being made available. With passenger capacity in parentheses, and the initials "C.S." designating cab sides, they were as follows:

Touring (7)	$3850	Landaulet (6)	$4900
Salon Touring (6)	$3850	Landaulet (7)	$4950
Special Touring (6)	$3350	Landaulet, C.S. (7)	$5000
Phaeton (4 or 5)	$3750	Imperial Limousine (6)	$5100
Runabout (2)	$3750	Imperial Limousine (7)	$5150
Limousine (6)	$4900	Salon Limousine (7)	$5100
Limousine, C.S. (6)	$4950	Brougham (6)	$5000
Limousine (7)	$4950	Salon Brougham (6)	$4950
Limousine, C.S. (7)	$5000	Coupe (3)	$4450
All-Weather Convertible (7)	$4525	2-38 bare chassis	$3100

All bodies were distinguished by a new tapered bonnet, blending more smoothly than before into the cowl, and a left front door was now added, as was a rear tire carrier. A rear trunk rack was therefore unavailable, but one could be carried on the running board. The six-passenger styles were new, slightly lower in cost with cozier seat arrangements. They also featured square corners (seven-passengers were rounded) and "one man tops" on landaulets. On open six-passenger cars, the side curtains now opened with the doors.

The new bodies for the 2-38 were an all-weather convertible and a special tourer, the former built by the Springfield (Massachusetts) Metal Body Company. The special tourer was priced five hundred dollars below a 2-38. Before concluding that this violated Henry Joy's admonition against building down to a price, one should consider that the body for this model was not built by Packard, did not carry the Packard guarantee or service warranty. It was a Fisher body, and costs were cut in certain obvious ways. Upholstery, for example, was machine-buffed pebble grain leather, instead of Packard's standard hand-buffed straight grain. Fisher's it may have been, but the model gave Packard entry into a price field heretofore closed to it—and simultaneously provided one of 1914's great bargains—a Packard 38 as much as $1800 below what other models cost.

The non-Packard body was not, however, successful. Henry Joy would later report that "sales were not satisfactory. When a patron saw the two types of bodies . . . standing side by side in our own establishments, and could himself verify the differences in quality by direct comparison, he practically invariably purchased the Packard quality body in preference to the special or contract body. It has been an expensive experiment, but it has proved conclusively that the Packard clientele

Barney Oldfield, with Harvey Firestone, taking delivery of his 4-48.

demand the most superior product . . ."

Many of its customers doubted that Packard's second 38 could really improve on its predecessor. "I have a 1-38 bought two months ago," wrote John Hawkins of Pittsburgh, "and for power I doubt whether a 2-38 will equal it. The motor is absolutely perfect and the same can be said of the entire car." B.A. Behrend of Boston noted that the 2-38 motor "does not run as sweetly" as the 1-38, but that it had more power. Most owners felt the 2-38 was the ultimate, though, or, as C. Ford Seeley wrote, "the last word in 'Motor Cardom.' "

By February of 1914, Packard had turned its attention to the 48 again, which had now evolved to the fourth series of its type. The 4-48, as it was therefore called, "conforms in engineering development with the 2-38."

The 4-48 had "all the refinement and luxury of the '2-38' plus a bigger margin of reserve power." Its wheelbase was increased to a huge 144 inches, five more than the 1448—and, like the 2-38, it offered only one wheelbase for all body styles. One hundred forty-four inches would be Packard's longest wheelbase for many years—a runabout of that length was a sight to behold.

As usual, advancements on the preceding 38 were incorporated into the newest Packard: It was now a seven main bearing L-head, cast in two blocks of three, displacement remaining the same. And like the 2-38, it offered an optional high speed rear axle ratio, 3.28:1 against 3.53:1 standard—which in turn was the optional ratio on the smaller model. The engine was now water- and mud-proofed, lubrication was improved along 2-38 lines, dual exhausts were fitted, the brakes increased to seventeen inches, and the bonnet tapered to meet the cowl.

The 4-48 was designed to accept the same bodies as the 2-38, and all those available on the smaller model were thus available on it—all except the Fisher-built special tourer, which was doubtless felt somehow inappropriate here. Pricewise, each model was exactly a thousand dollars more than the corresponding 2-38 model, even the bare chassis following this pattern. A new body style, the Salon Brougham with three windows, was added in May 1914. Packard body styles now numbered twenty-one.

With the 4-48, Packard made many previously optional items standard. These included a Warner speedometer, Waltham clock, Klaxon horn, power tire pump, rear tire carrier, non-skid tires, gasoline tank funnel, a set of extra lamps. The only thing left out, it seemed, was a map. "It's the boss," Packard said of the 4-48. "Touching the accelerator is like stepping on the tail of a tiger. It travels with the speed of the wind and the grace and ease of a bird. It is the power of the storm, obedient and in harness. It's the man."

Unlike the 3-48, which had appeared almost exactly a year earlier, the 4-48 was not pre-dated as next year's model, by Packard or anyone else. It was a 1914 car, and the reason was obvious: It had to sell alongside the 2-38, which Packard had said was "too early to be named 1538" and was therefore established in the public mind as a '14 model. If Packard wasn't using model years per se, they were still necessary for registration and sales purposes and, regardless of company policy, people naturally referred to '14 or '13 or '15 models.

In February 1914, Packard issued a letter over Joy's signature adjusting its selling season, a plan *Motor Age* said would meet nearly all orders without delays as in recent years. "In 'peak load' months [March-June] the factory was able, by running consistently all winter, to meet the demand for cars that came with the spring. Again in the fall [September-November], demand for closed cars becomes very heavy and this demand must be met by production during the dull periods of the summer. In order to allow chances for necessary alterations, factory adjustments, etc., no deliveries will be made during July and August. Deliveries of '38' enclosed Packards will begin September 1 and deliveries of enclosed '48' cars on October 1." Packard had gone back to producing two models

The seven-passenger limousine version of Packard's Series 3-38 for 1915.

THE NOMENCLATURE O

Packard Six-48   (525 cubic inches, bore & stroke 4 ½ by 5 ½, 74 brake horsepower for the 1-48, 82 horsepower thereafter)

Series	Year	First Called	Engine	Touring Price	Serial Span	Wheelbases
1-48	1912	"Six"	T-head	$5000	23001-26000	139, 133, 121 ½
2-48	1913	"48"	T-head	$4850	35026-37999	139, 133, 121 ½
3-48	1914	"1448"	T-head	$4850	50026-52000	139, 121 ½
4-48	1914	"4-48"	L-head	$4850	63026-66000	144*
5-48	1915	"5-48"	L-head	$4850	78026-78586	144*

simultaneously; except for a brief overlap of 3-48 and 2-38 production, this had not been in vogue since the days of the Thirty and Eighteen.

The autumn 1914 cars were the last of the Packard Sixes, called the 1915 3-38 and 5-48, respectively the third and fifth series of 38 and 48 models. Interestingly, Joy's statement claimed that "our present design promises to remain substantially unchanged for several years," which was plainly a misnomer—a brand-new Packard was already on the way—but one may put this to either the old promoter's instinct for good copy or an honest lack of knowledge of just how close the new car was.

"You can get a Packard in September," the company promptly advertised that summer. The 2-38 supply had been exhausted in April, 500 units short of demand, and very few 4-48's were left by May, so no shipments were made during the summer as Packard stockpiled bodies and chassis for the fall.

The 1915 3-38 and 5-48 were the least evolutionary of all Sixes —indeed Packard had by now rendered them just about unimprovable. The only mechanical change of significance was a higher (lower numerical) high-speed rear axle ratio for the 5-48, 3.11:1 instead of 3.28. The main exterior identifying feature of both cars was the headlight design, incorporating a smaller "auxiliary head light" and a new "combination rear lamp and license tag illuminator."

The Packard Six was never sold as a performance car, its early claim of 0-60 in thirty seconds notwithstanding, but it was nevertheless one of the fastest passenger cars of its day. This Packard proved in unquestionable terms in June 1914 when an advance production 3-38 and 5-48 were tested for an hour each at the Indianapolis Speedway.

Assistant research engineer W.R. McCulla was the driver, first turning twenty-nine laps in the 5-48, falling below 70 mph on only three of them. He was timed at a fantastic 70.447 mph average. Next McCulla hopped into the 3-38, and ran it for an hour, and twenty-six laps, scoring a 62.4 mph average and doing the last two laps at over 67 mph. McCulla weighed nearly 200 pounds, the cars were normal phaetons in the usual touring trim, with tops and upper half of the windshield lowered, spare

Two views of the six-passenger landaulet body style of the Packard 3-38.

HE DOMINANT SIX

Packard Six-38 (415 cubic inches, bore & stroke 4 by 5 ½, 60 brake horsepower for the 1-38, 65 horsepower thereafter)

Series	Year	First Called	Engine	Touring Price	Serial Span	Wheelbases
1-38	1913	"1338"	L-head	$4150	38000-42000	138, 134, 115 ½
	1914	"1438"				
2-38	1914	"2-38"	L-head	$3850	53026-56000	140*
3-38	1915	"3-38"	L-head	$3850	75026-76999	140*

*Phaeton and touring.

tires deleted and running tires mounted on Rudge-Whitworth wire wheels. Ray Harroun, the racing driver, was quick to praise the feat: "Seventy miles in one hour seems nothing short of a miracle."

The Packard proudly carried the testimonials of a dozen racing drivers besides Harroun. René Thomas cabled, "Felicitations. Really fine performance for stock car." Arthur Duray said, "You evidently have the power and speed." And Ralph De Palma telegraphed, "It will make some of the manufacturers who spend thousands of dollars racing cars sit up and take notice. Why do it when a Packard out of stock will do all that?" De Palma may have been referring to Mercer. Its highly touted Raceabout ("a mile in 51 seconds") could guarantee no better than the Dominant Six from East Grand Boulevard.

Private owners proved the Packard performance point too. In Pennsylvania, at the Uniontown hill climb in June of 1915, one Charles Johnson, the local automobile association president, traveled up the three-mile mountain grade of 7.75 percent in the free-for-all in a bit less than three and a half minutes—nearly twenty seconds faster than the runner-up, a Simplex. Interestingly, he nicknamed his Packard the "Greyhound," in remembrance perhaps of the Gray Wolf. The Greyhound vanquished a rather well-known racer that day as well. Ralph De Palma had magneto trouble and finished sixth in his Mercedes Special.

And the Dominant Six was doing equally as well in the marketplace. In the fiscal year ending August 31st, 1914, some 3612 vehicles were produced, an above three-thousand-a-year figure the usual thing for the company—and one of the cars built that August was the 25,000th Packard in its history. The company made $1.2 million on $12.6 million sales. The following April, sales of $3,047,811 would provide the biggest month ever for the company. And fiscal 1915 would produce yet another record—$15,547,165 gross sales, with a net profit of $2.3 million.

"We are unable to turn out cars," the company magazine noted with pride, "in sufficient quantity to supply patrons." Truly Packard had arrived at the auto manufacturer's nirvana.

Packard would never build a car larger than the mighty 38 and 48 again. Only one more model would ever be built with as much painstaking hand labor, and possibly no other Packard in all the history of the marque would ever be built so well as these slow turning, lazily powerful Sixes. But their time was passing. Packard was facing involvement in a world war which would distract it from cars for a time, but not before it came up with the eagerly awaited successor to the Six. For this, Packard turned to another man of legend, with a longevity at the Boulevard that would surpass even that of Alvan Macauley. His name was Jesse Gurney Vincent. His car was the Twin Six.

Czar Nicholas II's 1915 "Dominant Six"; the coming of the 5-48 for 1915. Packard was modest in its horsepower claim; eighty-two was actually developed.

THE "5·48" IS ON THE WAY

VINCENT says: "Be careful how you step on this one. It leaps like a projectile."

Deliveries of the Packard "5·48" will commence October 1. This superlative six develops a maximum of 80 horsepower.

The Packard "5·48" is the car which rolled up seventy miles within the hour under official observance at Indianapolis.

BOSS OF THE ROAD

IMPERIAL Limousine of the six-passenger type—a French style often seen on Fifth avenue.

CHAPTER EIGHT

PRIDE OF JESSE VINCENT

The Twin Six

May 1915 - June 1923

AUTHOR: RICHARD M. LANGWORTH

It strains credulity now, but there was a time when the president of an automobile company thought nothing of testing a new model by driving halfway across the country—being photographed on his back in a foot of mud, checking the undercarriage. But such was *de rigueur* in 1915, at least for Henry B. Joy. He did so in late May and early June on a run from Detroit to San Francisco. One might think he trusted no one else to evaluate Packard's latest car, but more likely he just wanted to see if everything Jesse Vincent said about it was true. It was. Said Joy, the new Twin Six was "the greatest piece of machinery that ever went upon the highways."

That Packard's replacement for the Six would feature double the number of cylinders had been hinted at for some time. Though Vincent had joined Packard in mid-1912, and had contributed to the refinement of the 38 and 48, his main concern from the start had been with the successor to these models, a project for which he was well qualified.

Pages preceding: Joy and Vincent at Sheepshead Bay with the new Twin Six.

Jesse Vincent's childhood in some ways paralleled that of Alvan Macauley. He was born on a farm near Charleston, Arkansas, on February 10th, 1880, and like Macauley he took an early interest in things mechanical. His first gainful work, at the age of ten, was in his own blacksmith shop repairing farm equipment. Vincent received little more than a grammar school education, and at seventeen was temporarily taken off the mechanical track when he joined a St. Louis grain company as a salesman. But he studied engineering in the evenings through an International Correspondence School course to hone his technical talents. *The Packard* best takes up his story from here:

"Vincent's primary impulse was to wrestle with mechanical forces. He jumped his fancy waistcoat job to go to work where the wheels went around. That impulse developed until 'the wonder grew that one small head could carry all he knew.' Thereupon, Vincent entered the employ of a firm of experimental machinists in St. Louis and engaged in developing the mysteries of the early adding machines. [This, of course, was the same American Arithmometer Company, later Burroughs Corporation, that employed Alvan Macauley; Vincent arrived there in 1903.] While there he evolved a method of boring about all the holes in the mechanism at one operation. The next day it was Superintendent Vincent.

"It may have been the fact that Vincent had no higher education to carbonize his cerebral cylinders, but nevertheless he soon knew more about the mechanical dice boxes than any other man in America.

"The adding machine was fast developing into full bloom and it wasn't long before Vincent was trailing along to Detroit with Joe Boyer and his menagerie of trained numerals. He became Superintendent of Inventions [and] was traveling at such speed at this period that he [had to] find a way to double efficiency. It resulted in the duplex adding machine for trial balances, the first of the Vincent Twins.

"But Vincent had a newer and better job. As a side line he had himself made foreman of the Burroughs Garage and made all the adjustments and repairs to officials' cars. Working days and working nights Vincent soon found himself with money enough to buy a car of his own. [But the] cars at his disposal wouldn't travel fast enough. So he straightway decided to go to work for their builders and tailor them to suit himself."

To say Jesse Vincent and Alvan Macauley had something in common would be an understatement. Two years were yet required, however, before they would team up. Macauley left Burroughs in April 1910 for Packard, Vincent departed eight months later to become chief engineer of Hudson. But Macauley wasn't long in his new job before he knew he wanted his old Burroughs associate—and Vincent reported for work at Packard on July 29th, 1912. The next day he was made chief engineer. He would remain with the company, save for wartime interruption, for over forty years.

When Vincent joined Packard, the idea of adopting more cylinders for improved power and smoothness in cars was well accepted already. But most engineers felt the steps should come in two-cylinder quantities. "The six-cylinder motor is but a stepping-stone to the eight-cylinder V-type for higher powers," Cecil H. Taylor of Martin & Company, consulting engineers, told the industry around that time. "I believe [that] up to 50 horsepower, or say 5 ½-inch bore, the four-cylinder motor will hold its own, but that beyond this power the eight-cylinder, V type, will drive the six from the field. . . . The six-cylinder motor is not only educating the public, but the constructors as well, to the point where the eight-cylinder idea can be commercially put in practice."

Jesse Vincent had another idea.

As *The Packard* records, "one day the executive session was broken up by the engineering chief's laconic: 'I've got something to read.' There were thirty-five pages of it. Joy, Macauley, Beall, Hills et al., listened first with respect, then with astonishment. Those pages contained a complete and convincing presentation of the Packard Twin Six* motor."

The presentation, in condensed form, became a Vincent specialty. One of its best-known versions was in a talk to Packard salesmen, which the company published in a booklet entitled, "How Many Cylinders?" It remains the most lucid elaboration of Jesse Vincent's philosophy.

"From the time when the first practical car made its first run on the road," Vincent wrote, "there have been three things which every motorist asked for—MORE RANGE OF ABILITY, GREATER SMOOTHNESS and LESS NOISE. . . . Today the demand is still the same, though we have come much closer to Absolute Quietness, Absolute Smoothness and the

---

*Again, Packard's policy regarding this designation wavered through the years, the words Twin and Six frequently being hyphenated in advertising and brochures. The style used here—and throughout this book—is that used generally in company records and reports.

eft: The 1-35 touring equipped and the 1-25 brougham Twin Six. Below: Right side of the Twin Six engine showing the valve aisle between the two blocks of cylinders.

Maximum Range of Ability desired.

"The single cylinder gave way to the two, *because* the latter came nearer to satisfying the demand. So did the two go out before the four, and the four, in turn, vanish at the perfection of the six, for the same reason. All the way, the tendency has been to make each impulse, each explosion in the motor, smaller in magnitude, but to get the power by many impulses in quick succession.

"A six-cylinder motor is theoretically in absolutely perfect balance, but this is because the vibratory forces due to the rise and fall of one piston are neutralized by equal and opposite forces due to another. The pistons form what mathematicians call a 'system of bodies,' and the forces existing in each individually have no effect on the whole lot considered together, because of the cancelling of one force against another force. Now it is only possible to cancel out forces in this way if they are tied together strongly"—and Vincent went on to point out that the smoothness and quiet of the Six could only be achieved through weight—a heavy crankcase and crankshaft, a rigid flywheel, to keep the bearings from whipping or bending. And the Six wasn't enough: "We want not only the present ability, but we want a greater range of ability. So the only way out is to have more pistons."

More pistons would mean not only more power, but the same degree of rigidity and smoothness as a comparable displacement six, with less piston, crankcase, flywheel and crankshaft weight. But Vincent wanted a heavy crankcase, which implied a one-piece block. How far should one go? Vincent first addressed himself to the V-8 configuration, what he called the "Twin Four."

"Most high efficiency European motors have 3- to 3¾-inch bores and 5- to 6-inch strokes. For the purpose of comparison, let us consider that we desire a motor of about the same cubic inch piston displacement as our Packard 3-38 six-cylinder motor, which is 4-inch bore by 5½-inch stroke and contains 414.7 cubic inches. It would be entirely practical to design a Twin Four motor of practically this same cubic inch displacement within the above mentioned desirable bore-stroke limits . . . a motor of 3-7/16-inch bore by 5¾-inch stroke will contain just over 53 cubic inches per cylinder, or a total of just over 424 cubic inches. Such a motor would have certain advantages and disadvantages."

The advantages, Vincent said, would be more torque, less weight (due to shorter crank and lighter pistons), a little more smoothness at moderate speeds. On the minus side, a V-8 would produce more vibration at higher speeds, and render components like the generator, water pump* and starting motor less accessible, since they could not be mounted alongside the engine but either below the frame or between the cylinder blocks—the former exposing them to moisture, the latter making the valves inaccessible. The V-8 engine would also require a wider frame, with an increase in turning radius, and a steering gear that would be "very difficult" to assemble or disassemble.

"All things considered," Vincent wrote, "it was obvious that along with the acknowledged advantages obtained from the Twin Four, the characteristics of the Four which the Six was designed to overcome would

---

*The Twin Six water pump wasn't very accessible either, its removal required raising the engine four inches.

reappear, and our search for further refinement was therefore insistently pressed, as it was desired to obtain the advantages of the small bore, high-efficiency, multi-cylinder motor without inheriting any disadvantages."

The Six, Vincent admitted, was already "in absolute theoretical and practical balance." Its only disadvantage was that "in order to get a reasonable size motor the crank shaft must be rather long, and the inertia forces are rather large owing to the necessarily large pistons. Since a single six-cylinder motor is in perfect balance, however, there is no reason why we cannot combine with it another six-cylinder motor, V-type, and still have a motor that is in absolute . . . balance."

There is no substantiation of the old legend that Vincent rushed home to design the Twin Six after a pretty girl he'd been dancing with one night looked into his eyes and said, "I see Twins." Jesse Vincent obviously put a lot more preliminary thought into the Twin Six than that.

According to *The Packard*, Vincent's presentation of his idea occurred in early 1915, but that appears to be mere public relations designed to show that Packard thought fast; the board had planned rather further ahead. First mention of the new model (initially referred to as the "28" and "29") appears in the board minutes for September 17th, 1913, at which time management was authorized to enter a stock order for one thousand units. But later in the same meeting, this decision was reversed; the next stock-ordering authorization was moved on May 27th, 1914, and this time it was approved. Five hundred units was the figure envisioned. Then on December 14th, the company geared up for as many as 5000 cars, "with the privilege of stopping off at three thousand."

By early 1915, when Vincent read his Twin Six paper, the car's production was therefore *fait accompli*. Also by early '15, said *The Packard*, Ormand E. Hunt, "the human dynamo of engineering," had pattern makers at work on a wooden model, "another Vincent invention which cuts out one month in the development of new models." Hunt was Vincent's chief assistant, and shortly after Jesse was appointed vice-president for Engineering in 1915, Hunt became chief engineer.

"Ten weeks later," continued *The Packard*, "the first of the experimental cars was in road test. Vincent had succeeded in blending the dominant Packard characteristics into a new type of engine. His middle initial stands for Galvanic. We swear it does."

The Twin Six production engine embodied all of Vincent's ideas for practicality and efficiency. It featured two banks of L-head cylinders, vee'd at a narrow 60-degree angle, allowing accessories to be bolted to the usual spot just inside the frame, protecting them from road hazards and keeping the valves accessible. The small angle made the engine about seven inches narrower overall than a comparable 90⁰ V-8. Bore and stroke were 3 by 5 inches respectively for 424 cubic inches and 85 bhp at 3000 rpm. Rockers were eliminated, with a separate cam for each valve, and all valves were located inboard of the cylinder blocks. A short, light

crankshaft ran in three main bearings. Lubrication was improved, normal oil pressure of 20-30 p.s.i. increasing with engine speed.

"An advantage of small cylinders," remarked *The Automobile*, "is that a high compression can be used and good fuel efficiency obtained thereby. For example, on a recent run made in this car the average for nearly 200 miles in Michigan was 11 miles per gallon. To get this small cylinder with a high enough compression calls for a small combustion space, while the need for large valves demands the opposite. In order to reconcile these two warring conditions, the valves are inclined as regards the cylinder bore which gives room for big valves and yet calls for only a small area of pocket. This has been done before, but it is troublesome on account of the separate setting on the machines needed to bore the two operations out of parallel. [This is avoided] by making everything parallel except the cylinder bore, so all operations such as drilling and facing locate in the same jigs."

Packard used a triangular chain to drive the cam, generator and water pump, said to be "the first silent chain drive installation having a simple adjustment." *The Automobile* called the chain configuration "novel and somewhat daring," because "the generator sprocket was allowed to drive the generator through a large Oldham coupling. The sprocket rides on the outside of an eccentric bushing surrounding the generator driving spindle so that turning the bushing shifts the sprocket relative to the other sprockets but doesn't move the generator . . . . This can not be beaten for neatness and, as the surfaces are large, it ought to work out very well."

The end result of all this technology was, in Vincent's words, "perfection in every way." Torque was "50 percent better than it would have been with a V-8, and 100 percent better than the six. Six impulses per crankshaft revolution blend together so closely as to make it absolutely impossible to distinguish any pause between impulses, even at very low engine speeds pulling through traffic on up grades. The only thing I can liken it to"—Vincent concluded somewhat impishly—"is the action of steam." Packard promotion added that the Twin Six was 400 pounds lighter than the Six: "We believe that this motor will run longer without overhauling than any gasoline motor that has ever been produced."

Other features of the Twin Six specification were less radical, emphasizing Packard's evolution over the last several years. Ignition was supplied by a 120 amp-hour storage battery, generator charged, with a reserve dry cell battery mounted on the left frame side member. An ignition timer and distributor were mounted containing a separate circuit breaker and distributor for each set of six cylinders. These were operated by a common breaker cam, driven for synchronization at crankshaft speed. Separate transformer coils for each bank were sealed in Bakelite cases and all ignition wires were enclosed. A governor in the base of the timer housing regulated spark advance, with an auxiliary hand advance for high-speed conditions. Starter and lights were electric.

he chassis of the Twin Six, 1915.

East Grand Boulevard and the home of the Packard Motor Car Company as it appeared at the close of World War I, the factory as yet incomplete.

Spiral bevel gears were of course standard on the Twin Six rear axle. But in a break with tradition, the gearbox was now moved up front with the engine. Just a few months before, Henry Joy had reported that one of the things Packard had learned was never to do this! On the other hand, the lighter weight of the Twin made placement of the gearbox at the rear less critical for good weight distribution.

The rear axle itself was much lighter than the Six's. "The even torque of the twelve," *The Horseless Age* reported, "eliminates all risk of rattle in the constant mesh gears and [they] are taking pains to lighten the axle as much as possible to reduce unsprung weight to a minimum." The three-speed gearshift lever and handbrake were still mounted on the left side, and the clutch remained of the dry plate type. But a new locking device was added to keep both shifting arms from being used at the same time, and "there is practically no more flywheel than is needed to carry

the clutch and to take the gear teeth for the cranking motor."

Modernity was now appearing in many Packard features: The unit motor and gearbox, the between-banks placement of the carburetor, and the mounting of accessories low on either side of the engine are still present in cars of today. Cooling, too, was progressing toward its contemporary form: The Twin Six featured "a water pump [to keep] fluid circulating, and it encompasses a thermostat which controls its action."

Also relative to cooling was the radiator cap holding clamp, which had appeared earlier, but had an interesting background. Henry Joy had suggested it, after experience with a fruit jar. Henry Joy, Jr. told enthusiast Brad Skinner that Joy, Sr. got a flash one day as he watched his mother open a glass Ball or Mason jar, its metal clasp holding its top tightly in place. Suddenly Joy exclaimed, "That's what I've been looking for to hold down the radiator cap on a Packard." The clasp was produced

More stories would ultimately be added to the two-story building on the left.

in the familiar Packard radiator shape—and it worked. Vincent later used it on the first Liberty airplane engine oil drain. Atop the cap, First Series Twin Sixes featured motometers, bearing a Lincoln Highway emblem, to measure the coolant temperature. Other motometer designs included an airplane in flight—after the Liberty engine was out, this motif was a proud one.

The introduction of the Twin Six on May 1st, 1915 (Sixes were sold into September) was the greatest single announcement made by Packard thus far in its history. Everywhere one appeared, crowds followed to gawk at it. Police often had to be called in to quell the unruly. With a lower price compared to the Sixes, and Packard's increased production plans, more men than ever would now have a chance to own one. "Packard will undoubtedly attract more attention than was ever given to a new model," said the *San Francisco Chronicle*. "The Twin Six marks

the greatest advance in this big industry."

The Automobile drove a Twin Six early, and reported that "no vibration was perceptible up to a road speed of well over 60 miles per hour and the motor is hardly audible even at full revolutions . . . perhaps the most remarkable feature of the running is that there is no sense of effort whatever in opening up from 3 miles on high gear. In a series of trials run against the watch it was found that it was easy to accelerate from 3 miles an hour to 30 miles in 12 seconds on a level cement road and on second speed in a much shorter time. Still, it is not likely that the low gears would be used for more than a decimal percentage of the running."

The company board minutes had revealed the disposition of remaining Sixes, the January 13th, 1915 meeting authorizing management "to stimulate the sale of the remaining 48's and 38's by a sales contest . . . and also to extend to dealers additional discount beyond 20%, and not exceeding 25% [later the Board allowed 30] . . . until the entire program of 38's and 48's is disposed of . . . in order to allow an early announcement of [the Twin Six] 1-25's and 1-35's."

Still, Packard wasn't missing an opportunity to make a dollar on the old Sixes. At the March 18th board meeting, management accepted orders from Russia for 600 trucks and 300 3-38 touring cars, and was hoping for an additional larger order from France. The board authorized filling of these orders, realizing this might "delay for a considerable period the production of one-ton trucks, and also probably for several weeks the production of the new type 1-25 cars. . . . These delays will undoubtedly work a serious hardship on our dealers who will have nothing whatsoever to sell and deliver for a period of . . . three to four months.

"Acceptance of the war orders was authorized in view of the above facts only in view of our plan to devote a substantial portion of the profit from the war orders as a gift to the dealers who were thereby deprived of a source of revenue." One hundred thousand dollars was voted "to assist deserving dealers through the financial stringency . . . to tide them over . . . ." Packard, as always, took care of its own.

Since management feared a delay until as late as July, the Twin Six press announcement in May 1915 was probably a trifle in advance of deliveries to dealers. Because of this early announcement, First Series Twins have sometimes been represented as 1915 models. They of course were not. Packard generally introduced the next year's model nine or ten months before the year began, this practice owing to the company's basing production on the selling season.

The price spread between the 1-25 (125-inch wheelbase) and 1-35 (135-inch wheelbase)—as per listed retail prices excluding taxes and transportation— was not nearly so wide as had existed between the 3-38 and 5-48, since both Twin Sixes shared the same engine. The lineup for 1916 was as follows, with passenger capacities in parentheses and the letters "C.S." standing for cab sides:

1-25		1-35	
Touring (7)	$2750	Touring (7)	$3150
Salon Touring (7)	$2750	Salon Touring (7)	$3150
Phaeton (5)	$2750	Phaeton (5)	$3150
Salon Phaeton (5)	$2750	Salon Phaeton (5)	$3150
Runabout (2)	$2750	Limousine (6)	$4550
Coupe (3)	$3700	Landaulet (6)	$4550
Limousine (6)	$4150	Brougham (4)	$4600
Landaulet (6)	$4150	Limousine (7)	$4600
Brougham (4)	$4200	Limousine, C.S. (7)	$4650
chassis only	$2350	Landaulet, C.S. (7)	$4650
		Imperial Limousine (7)	$4800
		chassis only	$2650

This line of bodies was identical to the previous Sixes and, with the exception of a much shorter hood due to the shorter Twin Six engine, they looked the part of a Packard. Twin Six styling would be gradually altered as the years went by, however. As with their predecessors, standard colors were Packard Blue with Packard Cream Yellow striping. Open car wheels were cream striped with black, closed car wheels blue striped with black. Nickel was the only available finish for bright metal parts. Tires were 36x4 ½ front, 37x5 rear.

Later, two more 1-35 models were listed: a seven-passenger landaulet at $4350 and a salon limousine at $4550. The prices quoted are September's, incidentally—the touring model 1-25 was first announced at $2600, the 1-35 at $2950, but these figures didn't endure.

Demand was brisk whatever the price—indeed the cars were many hundreds less than the Sixes—and Packard had to work to meet it. *The Automobile* reported the Packard workforce at 10,886—a fifty percent increase over the year previous. New machinery and special tools were "coming in almost daily" in August, and in September Packard expanded its plant again, paying $75,000 for 12.8 more acres. The property now exceeded 100 acres and was seeing six new additions being built at a cost of $1.5 million. *The Horseless Age* declared that business was "growing so fast that the officials [find] it will be necessary to further expand in order to cope with the future." Manufacturing vice-president F.F. Beall even chartered a locomotive to deliver a special milling machine from Massachusetts when the railroad refused to guarantee delivery. Packard needed that equipment!

Other changes were not so pleasant: In 1916 Packard lost the services of the unflappable Sidney Waldon, who was enticed over to Cadillac Sales. Many of his duties at Packard were taken over by Frank Eastman, who had been editor of *The Packard* since 1912. Eastman had as wry a sense of humor as his predecessor, Ralph Estep. In late 1917 he published an ad which was sent to all Packard owners: Under a handsome Twin Six runabout, Eastman noted, "We build a good car and charge a good price for it, to which must be added the dealer's discount

. . . ask the man who owes for one."

Plenty of people did—Twin Six sales were titanic compared to the Packard Six before it: 3606 1-25's and 4140 1-35's were built during 1915-1916. This gave some people the idea that the company was abandoning its time-honored hand assembly methods and using more proprietary components, which was not really the case. A Packard body frame, for example, was much more complicated, with many more compound curves than, say, a concurrent Fleetwood body frame. But this was not the first time such a rumor circulated, and Henry Joy had a pat reaction: "This company is not an 'assembler.' We do not believe in it. We undoubtedly build more of the completed automobile than any other maker. . . . We are not 'going after a cheaper line' in competition. We will make the selling price of our vehicles as low as we can consistent with a fair profit. Our quantity of vehicles probably permits us to go further in this direction than any other high grade manufacturer can afford to go." Joy sent these words to an inquiring customer, and made copies for all his dealers. For the latter he appended a note: "I want you to read this!! I want to know you have read it!! Stand squarely on your Packard feet."

One of the Twin Six's best testimonials came from the home of Rolls-Royce, of all places, in a letter from one "W.W." in the *Illustrated London News*, promptly reprinted in *The Packard*. "For twenty years the Packard car has held the reputation of being in America what the Rolls-Royce is in England. Although not so many years ago one could say that it was comparatively easy for a car to be the best produced in America for the reason that, to use a slang expression, it had 'nothing to beat,' those days have gone by . . . .

"Certainly the Packard Twin Six has nothing to fear from comparison with anything that is produced on this side of the Atlantic. Indeed, I am not so sure but that comparison would be all to its advantage. One dislikes saying this, naturally, but it is nothing but the plain truth. Recently I had a day on the road with one. . . . It is not enough to say that the car is silent, or that it runs smoothly; when we are talking about the 'Twin Six' we have to find some other manner of describing these essential qualities. The only approach I can make to it is that the twelve cylinders give such a near approximation to uninterrupted impulse that there is no sense of any mechanical effort.

"It is said that the car has a range of speed on the top gear from 3 to 70 miles an hour. This sort of thing is often claimed, but performance is not always the same thing as the claim. Without giving away our law-breaking performances too blatantly, I should say that in the case of the 'Twin Six' there is something in the claim. Anyway, it is a very fine car indeed." Frank Eastman commented, "Very good of you. . . . Perhaps you don't know that we operate a Rolls-Royce occasionally, just to make sure that we aren't outdone."

Few would think that. One enthusiast was still singing its praises long

Page opposite: Profile and interior of six-passenger limousine 2-25; clover leaf runabout 2-25. Above and below: 2-25 coupe, 2-35 landaulet.

after his Twin Six was new: "I love my old Bus. It has 12 cylinders but I only need four. The rest of them came with the engine and I just let 'em run. The starter starts and the generator gens and the battery bats and the brakes brake and the seats seat and the top tops and the lights light. It will go from .001 miles per hour to 75 on the same high gear. I love my old Bus."

Though the old bus was not commonly found on race tracks, Ralph De Palma made an early test of one at the Chicago Speedway in July 1915. Two Twin Six touring models were supplied, one direct from East Grand, the other Joy's Pacific Coast test car. With the top down and the windshield up in one, De Palma averaged 72.7 mph over a ten-mile, five-lap heat. Then he added five passengers and did it at 69.8 mph. Said *Motor Age*, "the test again disproved the contention once prevalent that touring cars cannot get into the mile-a-minute class." And even at these speeds, A.A.A. officials determined that the Twin Six had recorded a remarkable 13.3 miles per gallon.

In August the patent conscious company did something relatively uncommon: Packard bought the American rights to the English Lanchester vibration damper. Engineering had noticed a small periodic vibration at a certain rpm in the Twin Six, which though not sufficient to warrant a larger crank, would benefit by damping. There was a natural period of vibration when the explosion sequence coincided with the natural vibration period of the engine. Lanchester's device was a small flywheel and disc clutch mounted on the front of the crank. The inner clutch member was made fast to the shaft, the flywheel rode free, and when the crank twisted forward, the inertia of the flywheel rim caused it to maintain a steady speed through the clutch. Packard planned to grant licenses to other American manufacturers for the inexpensive product in exchange

Third Series Twin Six. The seven-passenger limousine 3-25 photographed in front view, the driving compartment of the 3-35 seven-passenger landaulet.

for a small royalty paid to Lanchester.

A new venture for the growing company came in December, when Packard began an association with the government. The V-12 concept had intrigued the War Department, and experimental work was assigned on a "Twin Six type" motor for airplanes. Joy was behind the move. "It is probably a little out of the ordinary," he said, "for a corporation to go out of its way to produce such military devices as airplane motors because the demand for them will probably be very uncertain. Yet our directors feel that it is [the] duty of manufacturers in this country to mobilize their facilities into such form that they might be available . . . . We are inclined to feel that our government is going to find important need of cooperating in the development of what would be the serious wants of our country in time of military trouble." World War I had been in progress in Europe for over a year.

Joy could not have foreseen the heavy involvement of industry and government in the future—though his evaluation of the perils of doing business with Uncle Sam was to be proven disastrously factual for Packard many years later—but the possibility of U.S. involvement in the war was very real. To Joy's credit, he made use of the lead time remaining to him, and when the country called, Packard was ready.

Back in the car business, Packard was now happily on schedule. In July 1916, the 1917 Twin Six was announced, designated 2-25 and 2-35. The most significant mechanical improvement in this Second Series was its cooling. "In place of the water being expelled from the forward ends of the cylinder blocks," noted *The Horseless Age*, "the gas intake manifold has been cored out to permit all water from the cylinder jackets to be circulated through this manifold and thence to the radiator through a single tube at the center [eliminating considerable ducting, and causing] the water to surround the gas intake header while at the highest temperature. . . . Instead of being placed on the water pump, the thermostat is now located in the upper tank of the radiator, so that the thermostat by pass [prevents] circulation through the radiator until the water has reached the proper temperature."

New also were detachable cylinder heads, "to insure a more perfect machining of the combustion chamber with a consequent greater uniformity of compression [and] to keep the cylinders free from carbon and do away with the necessity of valve chamber plugs." The generator also was altered, running faster than the First Series; the carburetor was raised three-quarters of an inch to get it further from the exhaust manifolds, the distributor used less current, foot brake tension was reduced, the gear lever was redesigned and equipped with a ball end.

Packard pointed also to improved fuel consumption on the new series. "Far be it from our intention to start anything with the Standard Oil Company," quipped Eastman in *The Packard*, referring to the trust-busted but still vigorous corporation of the Rockefellers. "That is an ex-tra hazardous occupation. But everybody knows that the gasoline now being marketed is extremely punk, and no one should object to our saying so." To handle the punk petrol, gas intake passages were shortened to allow maximum heating from the circulating water, and fuel now flowed uninterrupted from carburetor to cylinders. The carb itself was warmed by its placement between the cylinder blocks (as before), while the thermostat's location added to more accurate control of engine temperature.

In appearance the Second Series Twin Six looked considerably lower, with smaller 35x5-inch wheels all around—the radiator was an inch higher, and an inch-and-a-half hump was removed from the rear upper body edge. Headlight bezels were now black painted steel, and sidelights had lost their green side lenses of 1916, became smaller and were now fastened directly to the cowl. The 2-25 received a wheelbase increase, to 126 inches. All chassis were beefed from a six-inch depth to seven and a

The runabout 3-25 and a 3-35 semi-collapsible cabriolet by Fleetwood, 1918.

A new series? Yes, but nothing much. We are sure the Flivrolet will give you *more* trouble for *less* money. ❡ We *think* it will run but you can't be *sure* of anything. ❡ It's a Twin-Six to be sure but that's only a pat phrase for twelve cylinders. One cylinder will take you there and bring you back. ❡ The lines are the best we could do but styles will change anyway. ❡ The Packard has a good reputation and some people say it pays to advertise. ❡ We build a good car and charge a good price for it, to which must be added the dealer's discount.

Ask the man who owes for one

Packard's sense of humor (above) and a Third Series Twin Six sedan (right).

half inches, and reinforced over the rear axle to better prevent body distortion. A new body was the four-passenger runabout, with individual front seats. With capacity in parentheses and "C.S." designating cab sides, the lineup was as follows:

2-25		2-35	
Touring (7)	$2865	Touring (7)	$3265
Phaeton (5)	$2865	Salon Touring (7)	$3265
Salon Phaeton (5)	$2865	Phaeton (5)	$3265
Runabout (2 or 4)	$2865	Salon Phaeton (5)	$3265
Coupe (3)	$4265	Limousine (6)	$4665
Limousine (6)	$4315	Landaulet (6)	$4715

Landaulet (6)	$4265	Salon Brougham (4)	$4715
Brougham (4)	$3965	Limousine (7)	$4715
chassis only	$2465	Limousine, C.S. (7)	$4765
		Landaulet (7)	$4765
		Landaulet, C.S. (7)	$4815
		Imperial Limousine (7)	$4915
		Salon Limousine (7)	$4865
		chassis only	$2765

The fiscal year ending August 31st, 1916 was a particularly good one. Compared with earnings of $2.3 million the year before, Packard better than doubled its take with $6.2 million. Company assets at $33.6 million represented an increase of nearly $12 million—and the Packard surplus was a hefty $10,823,717. Capital stock was increased from the $16 million to which it had been raised during 1913 to $21 million. But the Second Series Twin Six—some 9000 would be built—was to be the last model, and this the last fiscal year under the aegis of Henry Bourne Joy.

Henry Joy was forever expansionist-minded. His famous phrase, "Let's do *something*, even if it's wrong," though not definitely known to have been said, fits his personality entirely. And, as his company prospered, it became attractive to outsiders. As we have already seen, General Motors expressed an interest as early as 1909. In 1916 another offer was made, by two men recently departed from General Motors: Charles W. Nash and James J. Storrow.

Nash and Storrow were toying with the idea of becoming a GM of their own—Nash had only just stepped down as that corporation's president—and began scouting for a plant. They approached Packard, Joy was interested. But the Packard board wasn't, or at least not enough members of it. Joy had turned over the presidency to Alvan Macauley that summer, "to let a younger man take over," the trade press said, but had remained chairman. On December 13th, 1916, the Nash/Storrow bid was turned down. A year later, Joy resigned as chairman and as director, and sold his stock in the company, some say because he continued to seek mergers against the inclination of the board.

The role of Henry B. Joy in nursing Packard from an almost cottage industry to America's first luxury marque was a gargantuan one. To Joy goes the credit for bringing Packard to Detroit and for expanding its financial base; for hiring Albert Kahn and seeing the great factory built on East Grand; for espousing the cause of more cylinders, more smoothness, more power and luxury; for helping to pioneer such important breakthroughs as Packard's control board and spiral bevel gears; for insisting always on quality first. Through Joy, Packard acquired Alvan Macauley, and through Macauley, Vincent. It can be fairly said that Packard's first crucial decade, after James Ward Packard had launched his first few models, was really the doing of Joy—the businessman, the promoter, the seer. Now he was gone. But he had built well.

Third Series Twin Six roadsters (above), with custom body and special headlamps for Mrs. Hardeman of Greensboro, North Carolina (above right). Series 116 Single Six roadster (below right).

Though Joy and Macauley followed similar marketing philosophies, they couldn't have been more different personally. Joy was often held a "country club boy." He was outspoken and sometimes considered brusque; Macauley was described as shy and soft-voiced. But he was never shy about command. He energetically took the Packard reins.

In May 1917 management was allowed by Macauley and the board to reduce plans for the next series of Twin Six. "Changed conditions due to the war make it doubtful that . . . 6000 new cars can be marketed within the season," read the board minutes. "It is wise to avoid being overstocked if possible at this late date." Jesse Vincent was now given a three-month leave of absence, to serve the Council on National Defense, furthering the development of the airplane engine—he was actually to be gone for over two years. As a gift upon his leaving Packard's employ, management presented Vincent with a Third Series Twin Six.

The 3-35 and 3-25 models were the final series for the cars, one that would take them into 1923 and cover six full years of production. Mechanical changes included a redesigned electrical system with a grounded return, instead of a two-wire system. The engine now featured improved heads for better breathing plus more water for cooling and a "Fuelizer" in the intake manifold to help vaporize inlet gases with the help of its own spark plug. (Fuelizer kits were also provided for earlier models.) The vibration damper used a smaller fan drive pulley, later enlarged for mountain driving. More significant was the relocation of the gear lever to the center of the floor; the frame was tapered at both ends for greater strength, stamped running board brackets replaced by forgings, the speedometer drive changed from the front wheel to the rear of the transmission, and springs lowered. Wheels were made interchangeable through pressed-in stampings which eliminated the former right- and left-hand threading. Tires remained at 35x5 all around. Horsepower was now rated at 90 brake, 43.2 by A.M.A. formula.

Packard publicity worked diligently on the series image: "It is a mistake to assume [the company] presents an entirely new model every year. It does not. Many features of the car are not changed. But a constantly-working engineering department produces a certain number of improvements in the course of a year. These improvements, thoroughly tried out and proved, are accumulated and put into the car once a year."

One change of more importance than the mechanical details was body styling, Packard's recognition thereof and exploitation of same. To give an added impression of length, wheelbases were up to 128- and 136-inches respectively. This was accompanied by "a remarkable accomplishment in body designing [to match] the achievement of the epoch-making Twin-six motor. . . . The shoulder lines of the characteristic Packard radiator are carried straight back, narrowing slightly, and merge into the cap moulding of the sides and doors of the open cars. In enclosed cars it turns upward into the front pillars."

The Third Series Twin Six was offered as follows commencing June 1st, 1917 and through 1919. Interestingly, the smaller wheelbase 3-25 was now offered in the larger number of body styles:

3-25		3-35	
Touring (7)	$3450	Touring (7)	$3850
Salon Touring (7)	$3450	Salon Touring (7)	$3850
Phaeton (5)	$3450	Limousine (7)	$5400
Salon Phaeton (5)	$3450	Landaulet (7)	$5450
Runabout (4)	$3450	Imperial Limousine (7)	$5600
Coupe (4)	$4800	Brougham (7)	$5500
Limousine (7)	$5000	chassis only	$3350
Landaulet (7)	$5050		
Imperial Limousine (7)	$5200		
Brougham (6)	$5050		
Brougham (7)	$5150		
chassis only	$3050		

Custom bodies had been offered, sparsely, on previous models, but now the Twin Six began to feature them in earnest. The Philadelphia agency, for example, listed on 3-25 chassis a Derham coupelet, limousine with removable windows, brougham landaulet and landaulet with removable front roof; a Judkins touring limousine; a Fleetwood runabout; a Caffrey limousine; and other bodies by Rubay and Kimberly. For the 3-35, a Derham limousine and landaulet, Judkins touring limousine and Fleetwood cabriolet were listed. Fleetwood was, in this period, in earnest pursuit of Packard's business—it did not become part of General Motors until 1929—and built at least one Twin Six "show" model demonstrating such advanced features as steel disc wheels and drum headlights in 1919. (This car, formerly owned by the Atwater-Kent family of Philadelphia, is pictured in color in these pages).

Earle C. Anthony, the Los Angeles dealer, was another early entry in

A Twin Six phaeton, 1920, custom built by Fleetwood for actress Marilyn Miller (above); a Third Series Twin Six roadster and coupe from 1919 (page opposite).

the custom body marketplace and featured several "standard" customs with special names. There was a "Midwick" runabout with large rear compartment for luggage or extra passengers, a "Pasadena" coupe de ville, and a rakish "Annandale" close-coupled four-seater.

Packard owners were as extraordinary as the vehicles. Oklahoma oil made the Osage Indians wealthy; one chief paid $7000 for a custom-bodied Twin, smashed it an hour after taking delivery, and telephoned the dealer for a replacement. Another found all the cars sold when he arrived at the Tulsa agency, so he settled pleasantly for a white hearse. Chang Tso-lin, warlord of Manchuria, paid $35,000 for an armored limousine with priceless wood inlaid interior, and in the sunset of the Russian Empire, Czar Nicholas II and his brother, Grand Duke Michael, both owned Twin Sixes with the front wheels replaced by skis in snowy weather. Heads of state selected them often: In 1921 Warren G. Harding motored to his inaugural in a new Twin—the first automobile so employed. In Tokyo, the first model to arrive caused a less polite stir—mechanics took it on a joy ride, ditched it in the moat of the Imperial Palace and were fined for "disturbing the royal goldfish."

After the war, 3-25 models diminished—the salon body style and Imperial limousine were dropped—and rose in price by close to $2000 a car. The 3-35 offerings remained intact but also rose, topped by the Imperial limousine at a towering $7350. But 4181 3-25's and 5406 3-35's were built through 1919, and Packard profits continued to zoom, with the help of defense contracts. They peaked at over $6 million in 1916—the 1911-1920 average was only $3.65 million—and continued above the $5 million mark through 1919. By 1918 the company announced that the Twin was now perfected, that it would be produced without substantial change indefinitely.

By September 1918, however, Packard had ceased car production temporarily to concentrate on war work. But as Macauley reported to the board a few months later, the strife ended "with startling abruptness," and Packard had to hastily reconvert for auto manufacture again. In a meeting on October 10th, 1919, the board noted that a few prewar Twins were still unsold, and approved construction of 2000 postwar cars bearing the same serial number span and unchanged entirely except for price and the deletion of the aforementioned models. More would follow after the depth of the market had been ascertained.

Alvan Macauley remarked that the car making facilities were "wholly disrupted," but the company had maintained service on its trucks and the 45,000 Packards then on the road. It had actually increased parts and accessory stocks at agencies. The president also mentioned that work was progressing on "a new light car," a sample of which was expected by January 1920. Internally, Macauley said, Packard was "able to cope with anything" except in Engineering where both Vincent and Hunt had departed for the war's duration in August 1917. A goodly number of

their subordinates had been drafted or otherwise recruited, "but many of these are starting to drift back in. I think it is likely that Mr. Hunt will rejoin the organization soon, but whether Col. Vincent will do so depends on his inclination and attitude."* Vincent, of course, did rejoin the company in early 1920, and was present again at a board meeting on May 5th for the first time since his departure.

On October 4th, 1919, another venerable name was consigned to history with the passing of corporate secretary Phillip H. McMillan, one of the original investors in the Warren company. His death, said Alvan Macauley to the board, "marked the first break in the ranks of the small group of men who conceived, organized and laid the foundations of the Packard Motor Car Company."

By the end of 1919 the board had approved the design of the new light car at a rate of 20,000 cars per year. The only outlay recorded for it thus far, however, was $317,000 in September, quite a small amount, even then. The firm also decided to contract with the Buffalo Body Company for the first 1250 postwar Twin Six bodies, but had second thoughts when Buffalo advised it lacked working capital, and a delay ensued.

In board minutes the 1920-1923 Twin Six is often referred to as the "fourth series," but its specifications were unchanged and in the record books at least it remained the 3-35—the 3-25 was phased out. The cars and their prices for 1920, 1921 and 1922, with passenger capacities in parentheses, were as follows:

3-35	April 1920	June 1921	February 1922
Touring (7)	$5500	$4850	$3850
Phaeton (5)	$5500	$4850	$3850
Runabout (4)	$5500	$4850	$3850
Coupe (5)	$7750	$6600	$5250

*Hunt might have returned to Packard, but if so, it was only to pack. And the reason was Emlen S. Hare—lately of the Packard Motor Car Company of New York—and whom, the board minutes record, was made a vice-president in Detroit on October 17th, 1918. His tenure at East Grand Boulevard was brief; he resigned July 29th, 1919, apparently with some empire-building on his mind. On February 27th, 1920 he formed Hare's Motors, an operating company to control jointly three distinguished and respected companies in the field: Locomobile, Mercer and Simplex (Crane-Simplex). He took several Packard people with him: O.E. Hunt; chief engineer of the truck division H.D. Church; general carriage sales manager Henry Lansdale and general transportation engineer F. Van Z. Lane. Doubtless all rued their decision. Hare's Motors was a quick disaster, contributing significantly to the ultimate demise of three fine American marques. O.E. Hunt survived handsomely however, going over to Kelly-Springfield in November of 1920, a year later joining Chevrolet as chief engineer and rising through GM ranks to executive vice-president by 1942.

Duplex Coupe (5)	$7750	$6600	$5250
Sedan (7)	—	$6600	$5400
Duplex Sedan (7)	$8000	$6600	$5400
Limousine (7)	$7900	$6650	$5275

Rumors that the car would be discontinued by now had been making the rounds of the trade press. On January 8th, 1921, *The Autocar* cautiously allowed that it "is not beyond the bounds of possibility that, some time in the future, [the Twin Six] engine will be abandoned in favour of a high efficiency six or a straight eight. . . ." Packard mounted a stout defense. Fred Cardway, vice-president and general manager of Packard Export sent a quick reply to the magazine: "The purpose of this letter is . . . not to point out to you the superior quality and extraordinary performance of the Twin Six, but definitely to refute the inference (which is no doubt made in entire good faith) that Packard is uncertain as to its goal. We wish forcefully to emphasize that Packard is by no means considering abandoning the twelve-cylinder motor car. . . . "

But the Twin Six was gone by early 1923, and there has been much conjecture since about the reasons for its demise. The best source of fact is doubtless Packard's own board minutes, which survive intact. It has been said, for example, that by 1921 Packard was more concerned with the high volume light car (the Single Six) but the minutes do not show this. It has been said also that the Twin Six became too expensive to manufacture, which may be indirectly true: Its price fell by as much as $2625 between 1920 and 1922, and possibly by February 1922 it had indeed become unprofitable to sell at the current price level—although at that point it was incontestably a bargain. After price slashing had resulted in

The parading Twin Six: Wilson and Harding in the 1921 Inaugural, Einstein in New York, 1921 (page opposite); Lloyd George in New York, 1923 (below).

sales gains for the light car, the minutes record the same tactic was then used for the Twin Six and the Packard trucks—without the same success. So the question of being "too expensive to make" is irrelevant; the public simply wasn't buying the car in sufficient quantities at any price. The minutes for September 1920 note demand "greatly below" the 300-per-month manufacturing schedule. In the old girl's defense, she was by now six years old, and the competition was on to newer ideas as well. A longer wheelbase Twin was considered, but not acted upon. Single Six stocks were stabilized at a production of 500 per month, Twins set at 300 were overstocked. By early 1922, Macauley was reminding the board of still more threats to the Twin from increased competition by "Ford owned Lincoln," and Packard's own Single Six, selling at about $1500 below the Twin.

Macauley also noted in early 1922 a plan for a "modified type of the present Twin Six at a considerable reduction in list price with no modification in design." After discussion, Alger moved that the price be reduced on a $1000 basis for the touring. The "new light twin" was under consideration again in May, and actually progressing toward production in July with plans to build 500 per month by the spring of 1923. But the car apparently didn't work out satisfactorily, and in October 1922, minutes record the first mention of a "new eight" being considered simultaneously. Neither the light twin nor the eight was ready for production, the minutes state, but the latter was "showing up in such a way that it seemed probable that after it had reached a slightly further stage of development its adoption as a new model would be recommended." This fairly sealed the fate of the old Twin; later in October the board authorized management to use "its best judgment in cleaning up the remaining stock of Twin Sixes and trucks at as early a date as possible." The last Twin Six was moved out in June 1923.

If any single model of a distinguished line could be said to have most greatly affected the standing of Packard, it would probably have to be the Twin Six. It was in production longer, with higher quantities built, than any other Packard to date. It introduced a radical and successful new V-12 that eclipsed in its time the rival V-8's from America and abroad. Twin Six chassis carried the early forerunners of a brilliant array of custom bodies; Twin Six owners more cohesively than any other group reflected that certain lifestyle which would come to be associated particularly with Packard during the Roaring Twenties: the moneyed, the eccentric, the conservative, the flamboyant. They all loved the Old Bus, and many examples of it would still be in faithful service long after its peers had faded from the roads.

The Twin Six fostered something else too, quite unrelated to Packard's standing as an automobile, which ultimately contributed as much or more to the reputation of the company in the eyes of the industry and public. It was an engine called Liberty.

CHAPTER NINE

IN THE CAUSE
OF LIBERTY

Packard in World War I

AUTHOR: STAN GRAYSON

The British had a name for it, for the month the United States entered World War I: They called it "Bloody April." On Easter Morning, they launched an attack aimed at the northwest tip of the Hindenburg Line near Arras. There, south of Flanders, 84,000 British and Canadian soldiers died in what was considered, by World War I standards, a successful campaign. In the skies above the tortured armies, German pilots grouped into *Jagdgeschwader* (fighter squadrons) knocked down 151 British aircraft while losing less than thirty of their own. Life expectancy in flying time for British pilots was just ninety-two hours as south of the British lines, the French launched a huge offensive in mid-April between Soissons and Rheims. The battle ended a month later with 120,000 men lost, a convulsion followed by mass mutiny within the stricken French Army and the ouster of the campaign's architect, General Robert-Georges Nivelle.

Declaration of war by the United States on April 6th promised relief for her beleaguered allies. Now, there would be new soldiers going to fight, fresh and untainted by fruitless years on the battlefield. There would be shells and supplies and guns. And airplanes too. In the United States, politicians and industrialists talked of "darkening the skies over Europe" with a vast airfleet. The U.S. announced that it could produce twice as many planes as the 22,465 suggested by the French. But when officials looked around for a suitable combat aircraft in the U.S. arsenal, an engine, or even the necessary pilots and mechanics, matters took on a new, rather more grim complexion.

The facts of the situation, thinly hidden by grandiose rhetoric, did not inspire confidence. In 1917, fourteen years after two inventive bicycle mechanics made that historic flight at Kitty Hawk, the United States ranked only fourteenth among the world's nations in aircraft production. Less than 700 airplanes had been built in this country by then, the most sophisticated being the Curtiss Jenny used in a vain attempt to catch Pancho Villa during the punitive Mexican Expedition of 1916. But the stable, gentle 75 mph Jenny was not remotely in the same league as the 115 mph SPAD's, Nieuports, Fokkers and swooping Albatrosses which, with their spitting machine guns, had been contesting the skies over Europe's horrific trenches. Further, although some young Americans had entered the French or British air force before their own country joined hostilities, the number of qualified pilots in the Army's Signal Corps totaled twenty-six. Few of them had ever seen a combat airplane.

Ignorance of the airplane's true military significance was pervasive in the United States. With the notable exception of Colonel George O. Squire, attaché to the British Army during 1916, and a young officer named William Mitchell, there were simply no high-ranking U.S. Army officers who knew what military aviation was all about. Not until a year later, after the U.S. entered the war, did the general staff conclude the Army should delete its regulation that pilots wear spurs.

Ultimately, the country which gave the world mass production managed to produce a total of only 3227 combat airplanes before the war ended. Of these, 1885 were shipped to France and 667 made it to the combat zone where they earned a mixed reputation. Still, America's effort to manufacture and field an air force in time to relieve her allies was the stuff of which legends are made. And the country's premier technical achievement of that war became, for better or worse, a legend in its own time. It is a story bound indelibly to the Packard Motor Car Company though Packard itself was partly responsible for being forgotten when the story of the U.S.A. engine was told. Then too, the Packard gentleman most responsible for the engine was charged after the war with

profiteering. The charges stemmed from an investigation of graft and in-efficiency in the nation's aircraft production effort, headed by jurist and 1916 Republican presidential candidate Charles Evans Hughes. Hughes had been appointed to head the investigation by President Wilson.

Nevertheless, Packard was among the very few American firms which could conceivably have helped the government out of its airplane engine dilemma, mainly because by 1917, the company had been experimenting with prototype aircraft engines for three years. And for the last two of them, Jesse G. Vincent had been devoting increased amounts of time to development of a series of twelve-cylinder racing car engines based on the Twin Six and intended ultimately for aircraft use.

Testing the 299-cubic-inch Liberty prototype. Left: Bill Rader, Frank Farber, Jesse Vincent after a 100 mph lap at Indy, 1916, Above and below: De Palma at Sheepshead Bay—a match race with Chevrolet's Frontenac (No. 54) and the Oldfield Miller; during a test session; posing before a race.

Gear reduction and cast cylinders, the first 905 V-12 and Packard personnel in the company's test lab, the photograph dated December 28th, 1916.

It was a project instigated in 1914 by then Packard president Henry B. Joy. Joy believed in the flying machine's future and, patriotism aside, saw commercial possibilities for a Packard-built airplane engine and he successfully urged company directors to authorize its development.

The first of Vincent's series of new engines was completed in December 1915 and can be considered the prototype of the paradoxical powerplant which became known as the Liberty engine. A 60 degree V-12 with cylinders cast in blocks of three like the Twin Six, the engine had a bore of 2-21/32 inches and a 4½ inch stroke for a 299-cubic-inch displacement. With its spur-gear driven overhead camshafts—one per cylinder bank—and four valves per cylinder, the engine developed 100 hp at 2300 rpm, 130 hp at 3300 rpm and weighed 500 pounds. Given a power to weight ratio of one horsepower per each five pounds, its specifications as an aero engine were not impressive but considering the engine's understressed state of tune, it was a hopeful beginning.

This engine, equipped with battery ignition, was installed in an at-

tractive boattailed single-seater. On August 4th, 1916, the car became the first in the 300-cubic-inch class to lap the Indianapolis track at more than 100 mph, turning in a one-minute, twenty-nine-second lap at an average 116 mph. Later, in November 1917, Ralph De Palma used the racer to eclipse a six-hour speed record set four years earlier by three drivers in a Sunbeam at Brooklands. At Sheepshead Bay Speedway, De Palma drove 616 miles in the allotted time: The Sunbeam had covered 566 miles. "De Palma and Packard Beat World's Records," headlined *The Horseless Age*. The magazine singled out the car's powerplant, already recognized as the forebear of something that had become special: "Of course the fact that the Packard engine incorporated the essential features of the new 'Liberty Motor' had not a little to do with the results." The car's competition days ended with the 1919 Indy 500 where De Palma nursed it home in sixth spot. Although a twelve-cylinder Ferrari was entered in the 1952 Indy 500, the Packard remains the only twelve-cylinder racer ever to finish the classic contest.

The wooden mock-up of the Liberty V-8 in Washington for examination by government officials; note June 17th, 1917 date on placard beneath engine.

Meanwhile, those "essential elements" noted in *The Horseless Age* account of De Palma's six-hour record had soon been incorporated by Vincent into a second, larger prototype engine. Development of this powerplant, built in the autumn of 1916, was abetted by the addition of Vincent's younger brother Charles to the Packard staff. Charles Helm Vincent had been working as chief final inspector at Hudson where, in 1915, he also developed the Super-Six engine that won the first Pikes Peak hill climb. "I was happy with Hudson where the management was very fair and progressive," he recalled. "But . . . I took a job as experimental engineer with Packard . . . where I was tempted by the opportunity to do development work on three racing chassis and two aircraft engines, one a twelve of 299 cubic inches and one with 905."

The development of the prototype 905-cubic-inch engine by Packard is just one confusing part of a generally hectic story. The confusion, unfortunately, stems largely from the company itself. In 1919, Packard published a little booklet dangerously mistitled *The Real Story of the Liberty Motor*. The evolution of the Liberty as depicted in the booklet contains several errors which have been passed down through history and it was only recently that Bradley Skinner—a Liberty engine enthusiast—began to fill in some missing pieces. Basically, the company's evolution sequence is incomplete and out of chronological order. The sequence followed here is published for the first time.

The very first 905 prototype does not appear in Packard's evolution at all but only as an unrelated photograph on a different page. It differed from subsequent prototypes primarily in its use of cast en bloc cylinders—like the Twin Six and the 299—and had a three main bearing crankshaft. Like subsequent prototypes, it was fitted with gear reduction to relieve the crankshaft of stress caused by out of balance propellers.

"The out of balance that exists in propellers is, I believe, responsible for crankshaft breakage in the direct-driven outfits," wrote Vincent in the June 1916 issue of *The Automobile*. "Out of balance is bound to exist in spite of fine workmanship."

177

Occasional crankshaft breakage was, in fact, a problem with the early Liberty twelve-cylinder engines which had reverted to direct drive to save weight. Charles Vincent, however, redesigned the engine's crank, modifying the cheeks and shaving off thirty-seven pounds of crank weight at a time when the heads of bolts were being drilled out to save ounces.

What became of the first Packard 905 is unknown and perhaps the only photo of it was published in *The Packard* and in the company's history of the Liberty engine. It is incorrectly captioned in the latter, however. Only Packard personnel are included in the photo, not government advisers and the engine is not identified. The engine was probably built sometime in early or mid-1916 and some of its parts including its pistons may have been used in the next version. This second prototype 905—now at the Smithsonian Institution—was also a three bearing unit but the cylinders were now machined from forgings rather than cast. The cylinders and their water jackets were welded up in groups of three and mated to the crankcase with a ground fit, no gasket used.

The built-up cylinder technique was pioneered by Mercedes and first used by the German company on its 1914 GP racing cars. Jesse Vincent was not unfamiliar with the advance: He had rather closely examined the Packard-sponsored De Palma Mercedes which won the 1915 Indy 500. The new cylinder construction saved about 100 pounds over the previous cast en bloc 905. Bore and stroke for the 905 were four by six. The

engines employed fork and blade type connecting rods, the rods themselves drop forged and machined and affixed by clevis pins.

On May 21st, 1917, the second 905 engine was dyno tested at Packard and delivered 230 hp with its 1.82:1 reduction gearing. In late July, the engine was put into a Packard racer and taken to Sheepshead Bay where Bill Rader broke all existing circular track records from a quarter mile to ten miles—the former in 13.95 seconds for 129 mph, the mile in 28.76 seconds for 125.1 mph and the ten in 4:50.88 for 123.7 mph. Later, in February 1919, this car brought the unofficial land speed record to the United States. On the 12th of that month, De Palma made a one-way run of 149.9 mph at Daytona Beach to eclipse Bob Burman's 141.73 mark set in 1911 with his Blitzen Benz.

"It is a complete aviation engine with the propeller removed and an electric starter installed because no man could crank it by hand," said *Motor Age*. De Palma's effort with the Packard was first in the monumental series of between-the-wars records, culminated by John Cobb who in his Railton sped 369.74 mph at Bonneville, Utah in 1939.

The last 905 prototype was built in May 1917 and lightened further by deletion of the electric starter and generator. Its cylinders were grouped in pairs and it had four main bearings. Packard engineers experimented with a magneto ignition system but it failed regularly and was replaced by battery ignition on the Liberty. The V-angle of the 905

Testing a Liberty V-8 prototype at Packard and Pikes Peak. Right: The patriarchal Henry Martyn Leland and Macauley dyno-testing a V-8 in 1917.

engine was forty degrees, widened to forty-five on the Liberty series.

By now the United States had been at war for some seven weeks and in an effort to help bring U.S. engineers and military planners up to date on aircraft design, allied commissions were brought to America. At the same time, U.S. delegations journeyed abroad to take a first-hand look at what aerial combat had become since a clear April Fools Day in 1915. Then, a French aviator named Roland Garros had fixed steel deflector plates to the propeller of his monoplane, mounted a Hotchkiss gun on the cowl behind it, and quickly shot down five hapless German planes to become the world's first ace. Later in April, after Garros was forced down and captured behind German lines, Anthony Fokker invented the synchronized gun that could fire through a spinning propeller without hitting it, and the air war began in earnest.

On May 26th, 1917, a French and English military delegation arrived in Detroit to inspect the various automobile factories. Jesse Vincent conducted them through Packard's aircraft engine department and described the three prototypes which had been constructed and tested.

"They seemed to be very much pleased with the quality of the work and the general design of the Packard Aircraft Engine, and stated it would be a very fine engine for certain kinds of work, but that its horsepower was too small for it to be of any real value in a fighting airplane," Vincent wrote in his history of the Liberty's development. The latest 235 hp engine without water or radiator weighed a little under three-and-a-half pounds per horsepower.

That night Vincent dined with Commission members at the Detroit Club and the evening's discussion convinced him that there was no single concern in the country building an aircraft engine that was competitive with the powerplants then used in combat.

"I did not sleep very much that night," Vincent later recalled. "It is a peculiar circumstance that when I got up the next morning, I found a new copy of *The Automobile*. The magazine contained an article noting that about thirty-seven different kinds of aircraft engines are manufactured in England and some forty-six in France." The multiplicity made for both high price and low production and created a spare parts problem for air units scattered across the front. "As an engineer and manufacturer, I realized the very great importance of this article and considered it in the light of a warning," said Vincent. "I immediately jumped in a car and drove up to the residence of the [Packard] president."

Vincent described the problems experienced by the French and English with their diversity of airplane powerplants to Alvan Macauley and suggested that Washington should be apprised of the danger before it fell into a similar situation. Macauley saw the point at once and made reservations for Vincent on the noon train to Washington where Vincent arrived on the morning of May 28th. The jumble of events which would lead to the design of the nation's first combat aircraft engine had begun.

That morning Vincent met with government officials who had the responsibility for ruling on ideas like his, including Howard Coffin of Hudson, now chairman of the Aircraft Production Board, and his associates Colonel Edward A. Deeds and Sydney Waldon; the latter by now had left Detroit to supervise government aircraft production.

"I told them that if the automobile industry is to build large numbers of . . . engines, they must be furnished with proper standardized designs . . . I pointed out the fact that the Packard engine was too heavy but that this could easily be remedied by simply changing the factors of safety [i.e., tuning the engine for more power] . . . A fighting machine must be equipped with an engine with the lowest possible factor of safety that will run satisfactorily for a reasonable length of time."

By 1917 Packard had spent $400,000 on its airplane engine program. Now, Vincent said, Packard was patriotically willing to abandon—for a time at least—all claim to origination of the motor and offer it to the government as the basis for a standardized series of engines which could be produced by the nation's automakers. The offer was accepted.

At the same time, the hard-driving Deeds—who had already been considering just such a project—suggested that Vincent work together with Elbert John Hall of the Hall-Scott Motor Company. Hall had come to Washington to promote his own company's engine, the 824-cubic-inch six-cylinder, 125 hp A-5 then in use by several countries including Russia, China, Japan and England as well as the United States. Hall was thus uniquely qualified to work with Vincent and on the morning of May 29th, with an admonition from Deeds to hurry, the two newly introduced engineers occupied suite 201 at the Willard Hotel. There, with just-purchased drafting tables and instruments borrowed from the Washington branch of the S.A.E., the two men began making drawings.

While Vincent and Hall were laying out transverse and longitudinal sections of America's new engine in their Washington hotel, events in Europe had remained sobering for allied airmen. Still reeling from Bloody April, the British were stunned when their brilliant twenty-one-year-old ace Albert Ball was sent plummeting out of a gray-green and misty sky. On May 25th, Gotha bombers began the first of a series of raids on England itself, killing fifty-six women and children in a market and twenty-nine other people. In France, aviators found themselves harried by the Germans even on the ground as the Gothas gave French aerodromes a constant drubbing. Summer approached and the allied airmen carried grimly on while awaiting delivery of the new Sopwith Camels, SE-5's and SPAD XIII's that would begin to turn the tide in their favor.

"On the evening of the 29th, Mr. Deeds called a session in his rooms at the Willard Hotel at which members of the French Commission were present," wrote Vincent of the Liberty engine's frenzied birth. "Mr. Hall and I had specific questions that we wanted to ask and they were

answered quite firmly by French officials."

The next morning Vincent and Hall received a helper, J.M. Schoonmaker, an engineering friend of Deeds from Pittsburgh who was impressed from his honeymoon visit to the capital to help with drafting the new engine. "He had done no drafting work for a number of years," wrote Vincent. "But nevertheless, he did not hesitate to take off his coat and go to work." Schoonmaker's help gave Vincent time to prepare a report to the Aircraft Production Board describing the new engine and how it would be tested.

Vincent delivered his report on the afternoon of May 31st at a meeting in General Squire's—the former colonel whose ideas about airplanes had once been scoffed at had been promoted quickly—office in the Army and Navy Building. "In laying down this engine, we have without reserve selected the best possible practice from both Europe [from De Dion, Rolls-Royce, Hispano-Suiza, etc.] and America," Vincent said. "Practically all [its] features have been absolutely proved out by experimental work and manufacturing experience in the Hall-Scott and Packard plants. . . . We are, therefore, willing to unhesitatingly stake our reputations on this design providing we are allowed to see that our design and specifications are absolutely followed."

The engine itself was a direct drive 45 degree V-8 displacing 1100 cubic inches with a five-inch bore and seven-inch stroke. It was designed to deliver 275 hp at 1700 rpm and incorporated individual two-valve cylinders machined out of steel forgings. Vincent was confident that weight could be kept to no more than 525 pounds.

Most important, it would be one of a series of powerplants. "In laying down this design, we have had in mind the extreme importance of interchangeability as a well-laid comprehensive program . . . the cylinder, for instance, can be used to make 4, 6, 8, and 12 cylinder motors." In addition, engine parts were designed for mass production. By contrast, European powerplants included complex parts which required skilled craftsmanship to make and might take up to two weeks to build.

After receiving Vincent's report, the board immediately ordered him to continue with his work and he quickly returned to the hotel. On June 1st the drafting work was speeded by the addition of two skilled draftsmen from Detroit bringing the little team in the hotel room to five. By June 4th the engine's drawings were basically complete: The new motor, thanks to Vincent's and Hall's previous engineering experience, had been designed in five days. In the end too, only their foresight in providing for a complete series of engines enabled the United States to field a combat-ready plane before the close of World War I.

In all, creation of the new engine was an effort chock-full of opportunity for government propagandists eager to excite the public with colorful tales about their country's war-making ability. "During those feverish days of war, George Creel, director of the government's publicity

A 905, probably the very first, undergoing test in the winter of 1916. A subsequent 905 compared to a Liberty. A Liberty V-12 on the dynamometer.

bureau, gave out a press story which thrilled the world—at least that part of it which was fighting Germany," wrote Theodore F. MacManus and Norman Beasley in their book, *Men, Money and Motors.*

"In breathless language, the war propaganda told of the summoning to Washington of aircraft engineers—of midnight sessions with the War Department—of locked doors in the Willard Hotel—of soldiers patrolling the corridors—of five days through which engineers worked, eating little, but consuming vast quantities of coffee or whatever it is engineers consume to keep themselves awake and over their drawing boards . . . of how these wizards of pencil and blueprint went into their chambers unimpeded by even an idea and came out with a full set of plans for the Liberty motor . . . The public swallowed it." In fact, the unembellished truth would have been enough.

The series of engines which Vincent called the U.S.A. Standardized Aircraft Engine, comprised powerplants projected for use in trainers, fighters, reconnaissance aircraft and bombers. It included the following:

Type	Rated hp	Max. hp	Weight, lb.	Weight per hp lb.
4	110	135	375	2.7
6	165	205	490	2.3
8	225	275	535	1.9
12	335	410	710	1.7

Deeds authorized construction of five eight-cylinder and five twelve-cylinder engines and Vincent immediately had the necessary drafting work begun in Detroit. On June 6th Alvan Macauley arrived in

Early stages in the assembly of Liberty V-12 engines at the Packard factory.

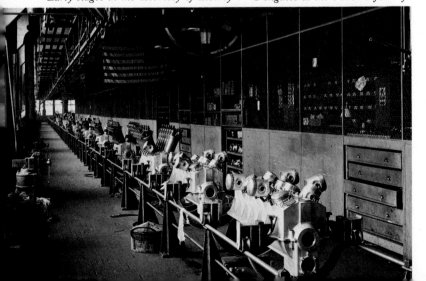

Washington and, in discussion with Deeds, he offered Vincent's services to the government for three months stating that the engine would be put ahead of anything in the Packard factory. Further, Packard's president agreed to finance the engine out of company funds until the government could arrange for payment. Although the new engine was based on Packard research and all prototypes and their testing would be conducted primarily by Packard, Macauley again affirmed the idea for a standardized line of engines—initially relinquishing any plans to call the powerplant "The Packard Engine"—to be built by several manufacturers. "It meant passing up the long-cherished dream of making Packard Aircraft engines as famous in the United States as Mercedes is in Germany, Rolls-Royce in England, etc. . . . ," noted Vincent. Such was the patriotic spirit of the time.

On June 7th Vincent, accompanied by Hall, returned to Detroit, hurrying immediately to the Packard factory. There, chief engineer O.E. Hunt had already secured steel billets for the engine's cylinders and work on some of the engine's detail drawings had begun.

"I realized," wrote Vincent later, "that in order to get the first engine quickly, we must have detail drawings almost immediately and I therefore called for volunteers from the various drafting departments of the Packard organization to work Saturday and Sunday. Every man volunteered with the result that we had a very large force working." In a day and a half, 150 Packard draftsmen completed about eighty-six percent of the detail drawings for the new V-8 engine.

As soon as the drawings were finished on vellum, blueprints were made and sent to manufacturers all over the country and the project began to assume nationwide proportions. From the General Aluminum and Brass Manufacturing Company in Detroit came bronze-back, babbitt-lined bearings. From Hall-Scott in San Francisco came the engine's bevel drive gears. Ball bearings were produced in Philadelphia by the Hess-Bright Manufacturing Company; camshafts came from L.O. Gordon in Muskegon and valve springs from the Gibson Company there. Crankshafts were made in Cleveland at the Parke Drop Forge Company and pistons by Aluminum Casting Company in the same city.

While drawings were being completed and parts ordered, the pattern shop at Packard worked day and night on wooden parts for a model which was completed and shipped to the Bureau of Standards on June 16th. The next day Vincent left for Washington himself, this time at the head of a complete twenty-five-man engineering team drawn from Cadillac, Dodge, Pierce-Arrow and Packard. Within a week the group had settled into offices at the Bureau of Standards and began checking over drawings for the V-12 version.

Back at Packard and at parts suppliers around the country, necessary parts for the first engine were being completed with feverish haste. On July 2nd, a Mr. Hause of the Packard Traffic Department wired Vincent that all the V-8 parts were on hand and had been shipped to Washington. Twenty hours later, after being shunted from one train to another with Packard workmen hurriedly adding final bits and pieces, the engine arrived. It had been just over a month since its conception in the Willard Hotel: It was July 3rd.

The date's significance was not lost on Admiral D.W. Taylor. He suggested that the engine be called the Liberty to commemorate Independence Day and Deeds, who had privately been calling it the All-American engine, agreed—as did everyone else. The Liberty appellation became the engine's official trademark in June 1919, the first instance of the U.S. government registering a trademark under its own laws or the laws of any other country.

Of that first engine, Vincent said, "I admit that we were all surprised at the very clean-cut appearance of every piece. There was no indication anywhere of slighted work simply to put the job over. I asked my engineering department to work on July 4th as I thought there was nothing better they could do to show their patriotism."

That first engine delivered to Washington was not intended to run but rather to show that an actual in-the-metal engine had been developed, and to serve as a basis for final suggestions and modifications. By July 5th, 3600 blueprints including the latest changes had been made and sent to the various factories where parts for five more eight- and five twelve-cylinder engines were to be made. With this work under way, Vincent paused to note the comments of other engineers. "Not one of them," he wrote, "has seriously criticized a single point of design. This also applies to the various French and English officials, who have examined either the design or the sample engine or both." Although Vincent had no way of knowing it, this was just the calm before a storm that would later break over nearly every aspect of the Liberty engine, from its cylinder arrangement to the design of its oil sump cover.

But in early July, Vincent's problems centered around getting a lot done in a little time. In England, the Gotha raids were continuing and Vincent carefully noted an editorial in *The Washington Post*. "The raid upon London yesterday by German airplanes is merely another urgent hint to the United States to get busy and take command of the air," it read. "Germany may be building a huge airfleet but whether she is doing so or not, the United States should be doing so. . . . " Yet, though there was a lot of talk about appropriating money for such a task, Vincent, now in the midst of governmental bureaucracy, was finding it difficult to get ten dollars worth of blueprint paper paid for.

"Germany knows that we have the money and genius in this country to make us a dreaded foe," Vincent advised in a July 9th letter to General Squire. "But she is banking on our not being able to get together and use efficient methods. . . . Can we not get together and fool her?"

On July 24th, 1917, Secretary of War Newton D. Baker's approved plan for a $640,000,000 military aviation program was quickly passed by Congress. The next day, July 25th, after the engine had been broken in by hand-cranking, the first operable Liberty V-8 barked to life under the careful scrutiny of Packard engineers.

Vincent was satisfied with the first tests which showed the engine to be a smooth runner and that, despite its newness and low compression pistons, it developed 214 hp at 1350 rpm. "It thoroughly proved out my contention that even a large bore eight-cylinder motor could be made smooth by setting the cylinders at an included angle of 45 degrees," he wrote. The engine had started readily—a noteworthy feature of all Liberties—with its battery ignition system, and its cooling system also proved adequate. On July 27th, after being removed from the dynamometer and mounted on a Packard truck, the engine was demonstrated to Alvan Macauley, Henry B. Joy, Henry Martyn and Wilfred C. Leland and engineers Charles King and Glenn Martin. The whole rig was then loaded aboard an express train to Washington on July 29th and Vincent followed the next day, his own journey delayed when the train derailed thirty miles north of Baltimore.

When he arrived in Washington, Vincent immediately made preparations to demonstrate the engine to government officials. By August 6th, Waldon, Deeds, the Joint Technical Committee of the Army and Navy, members of the House and Senate, and allied military commissions had all seen the Liberty V-8 perform. It was then dismantled, found to be in fine shape, rebuilt and shipped to Pikes Peak, where high altitude tests would be conducted. Vincent now recommended the engine's manufacture, concurrent with ongoing development.

"Up to this time, this sample engine has run more than fifteen hours

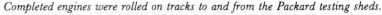

Completed engines were rolled on tracks to and from the Packard testing sheds.

I AM 900 FOR OCT. SHIPPER. DONT STOP ME OR ANY AHEAD OF ME, BECAUSE "WE ARE AFTER THE KAISER"

CHAMPION LIBERTY MOTOR BUILDERS

under wide open throttle conditions," he said, "without a single change or adjustment having been made since the engine left the assembling floor. I certainly believe that this is a world record for a new engine."

At about this time, the government decided the whole project would be insured of continued speed if the chief civilian members were commissioned as Army officers. Both Vincent and Hall were appointed majors in the regular Army and Vincent was later named commander of McCook Field in Dayton, Ohio where development and flight tests of the engine would be conducted. By the end of the war, the Packard engineer had been promoted to lieutenant colonel.

On August 13th, a prototype V-12 Liberty was run under its own power on a special arrangement of two Sprague dynamometers, linked together by Charles Vincent to handle the big machine's great power. It had been rushed into the testing stage when reports from the battlefront suggested that its extra power would be needed, especially since the aircraft selected for American production by the Bolling Commission—sent to Europe in mid-June 1917 to gather information and make recommendations about the direction America's aircraft production should take—was the de Havilland 4. This two-seat light bomber and reconnaissance machine, with its sturdy plywood-covered fuselage, required the 5 by 7, 1750-cubic-inch V-12's power if it was to give adequate performance. It became the only American combat plane of the war.

The decision to concentrate on the DH-4 was preceded by an ill-considered effort to install the V-12 in Britain's redoubtable Bristol Fighter. The engine was too heavy for this aircraft, as Vincent had predicted, but it required the crashing of several Bristol Fighters before the project was abandoned. It seems likely that the crashes did the Liberty's reputation no good and may have prompted later British criticism that the engine was too heavy.

The first sample twelve-cylinder Liberty finished its first official fifty-hour run at 1:30 a.m., August 25th, 1917. Though such runs normally took five days, the Liberty completed the test in just fifty-five hours, a record according to Vincent. The government inspector present during the tests, Lynn Reynolds, began his report: "A consideration of data collected, we believe, will show the fundamental construction is such that very satisfactory service with a long life and a high order of efficiency will be given by this powerplant, and that the design has passed from the experimental stage into the field of proven engines."

During the test, not even a spark plug was changed and the engine averaged 315 hp, producing a maximum of 346 at 1800 rpm. When Reynolds dismantled the engine, he found all parts to be in good condition and suggested only a new-style babbitt bushing for the lower connecting-rod bearings—to preclude cracking at high speed—and an intake manifold change: Two Zenith duplex carburetors were used.

Obviously though, some development was needed before the engine would produce its called-for 400 hp. Initial changes included an improved intake header and increased valve lift. These, in turn, required additional changes in other engine parts to handle the increased output, including changes to the connecting rod bearings, piston-pin retainers and crankshaft. It was at this point that Charles Vincent reduced the weight of, and strengthened, the drop forged, seven-bearing crank.

In November 1917, the first V-12 was delivered to the government at McCook Field. In keeping with the coincidence which had seen the first Liberty V-8 arrive in Washington in time for July 4th, the V-12 reached McCook on Thanksgiving Day, wrapped in an American flag.

Further tests of the new engine revealed that its scupper-type lubrication system, patterned after both Hall-Scott and European designs, was inadequate for the Liberty. Although it gave excellent oil economy, the system, Vincent realized, had a potential flaw. "Due to the fact that the large holes through the crankshaft are open, all oil drains out when the engine is stopped, except in those crankpins which are near the bottom. This does not make much difference when the engine is started. But under cold weather conditions, trouble results and bearings are likely to be burned out, particularly if the throttle is opened quickly after starting." The system was changed to a full pressure feed type.

Actually, the oil itself proved to be something of a problem too. Hiram Bingham, the renowned explorer who had learned to fly at age forty-one and became directly responsible for the Signal Corps' Aviation Section after being commissioned a lieutenant colonel, noted that America had no lubricant, save one, that could stand up to the Liberty's power: "The lubricant from the castor-oil bean . . . proved the sole exception."

Unfortunately, America had inadequate supplies of the promising beans and it was only after a special arrangement with Great Britain that a cargo of them was shipped to the U.S. from Bombay. Meanwhile, a Castor Oil Board was appointed on October 8th, 1917 to oversee American bean cultivation. Eventually, a mineral-based lubricant —Liberty Aero Oil—was developed, thus circumventing the problem.

Final run-to-destruction tests of the V-12 at full throttle were held in November 1917. They indicated the need for some further changes including chrome exhaust valves to preclude burning and new Ford-made bearings for the beefed-up, forked rods.

By February 1918, the engine had achieved an average of 404.9 hp, its problems had seemingly been ironed out, and seventy units were built. According to Vincent, those engines made during the early months of 1918 could not really be considered production powerplants. "The first several hundred engines were made more or less by hand to get out a reasonable quantity at the earliest possible date," he wrote, "and thus permit extensive tryouts." However successful subsequent versions of the Liberty engine were, these early examples were largely responsible for its less-than-excellent reputation when first introduced.

One of the factors that impeded initial mass production was the cylinder design. "In the first Liberty motor, the cylinder had to be machined from the solid," reported the *Scientific American*, "an operation that was very costly in time and money. This, however, was a copy of the best foreign practice."

Deeds and Waldon found the Mercedes-like cylinder-making process "tedious and laborious" and decided to approach the master of mass production about an alternative. They went to the maker of the Model T. Henry Ford turned the problem over to three of his engineers with the admonition to work fast. C. Harold Wills, John Findlater and Carl Emde did just that.

In their history of Ford, historians Allan Nevins and Frank Ernest Hill described Henry's engineers' conclusion. "The solution was reached by substituting steel tubing for the billet. This tubing, of required thickness, was shaped to cylinder size, cut off on a bias and the upper portion folded down at the top to form the head and provide space for the [two] valve ports. The side and the top were welded."

Although government inspectors initially viewed the process with some distrust, it proved viable and the cost per cylinder was reduced from $24.00 to $8.25. Ford was subsequently asked to produce all cylinders for the Liberty engine and delivered 415,000 of them. In addition, Ford also produced about twenty percent of all engines built during the war.

While the twelve's development progressed, the V-8 was installed in an LWF biplane which made its first flight on the afternoon of August 29th, 1917. The engine ran well, carrying the plane to 17,000 feet and a top speed of 104 mph. Tragically, this first plane was destroyed in a crash in January after its pilot began executing an inexplicable series of loops and tailspins culminated by a nosedive into the ground that killed both him and his passenger. There was talk of sabotage; one man was arrested by Army intelligence, but he was not convicted. Vincent believed the crash was caused by pilot error or mechanical failure.

In October 1917, the third prototype V-12 Liberty had been installed in a Curtiss HS-1 flying boat and the craft made its first flight at Buffalo, New York, home of the Curtiss Company. That winter, in February 1918, a DH-4 powered by a Liberty lifted off on its maiden flight.

As production of Liberty twelves—known as the Model A—got under way at different manufacturing plants in 1918, continuing engineering changes caused difficulties for its makers and, inevitably, delays. Design changes averaged a hundred per week, noted Phillip S. Dickey III in *The Liberty Engine 1918-1942*, and affected twenty-five percent of the engine's parts: "The impact on production was so great that manufacturers wrote letter after letter to the Chief of Aircraft Production, attempting to obtain some relief."

Manufacturers with contracts to build the engine included Ford, Buick, Cadillac, Nordyke-Marmon, Trego and Lincoln. The latter's

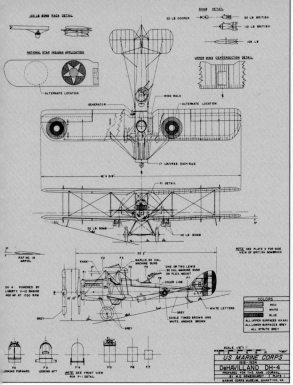

The predominant American-made warplane of World War I, the DH-4. Installing a Liberty engine in a Le Pere in September 1919 at the Packard shops.

directors, Henry M. and Wilfred C. Leland, had quit their jobs at Cadillac when the pacifistic William Crapo Durant initially refused to produce the warplane engine—a decision he later remanded. But Packard, as the originator of the engine, suffered perhaps more than other manufacturers with the Liberty's teething problems, especially in early 1918. The history of the Bureau of Aircraft Production includes the following: "In early February, this effort to produce engines under conditions of constant change, and in response to the insistent demand for them on the part of the government, had resulted in chaos in the Packard shops that was almost unbearable. Changes were so frequent that it was almost impossible to get tools finished and hand-made parts made necessary by lack of tools were well below the desired standard, and the personnel were consequently being educated in the wrong standard."

Shortages of tools, construction jigs, cylinder grinders, water jackets and even spark plugs accounted for an estimated fifty percent delay during the early months of production according to Dickey. Wartime shortages of coal, lumber, gas and electric power forced some plants to shut down completely for a time. Skilled workers were in short supply too, most having been drafted and thus creating the problem of training those who had to take their places.

The problems with the early engines had unforeseen results for the company which had spawned the Liberty and unselfishly devoted its time, personnel resources and money to pave the way for other manufacturers. According to Dickey, "The results of Packard's patriotism in submerging its role as the developer of the Liberty were unfavorable to the company. The developmental engines they had built caused the Packard image of quality to become tarnished, as they were not of the quality of later production; they were used . . . due to the vital need for engines."

Jesse Vincent and Alvan Macauley were unhappy that although Packard had taken care not to tout itself for its pioneering role in the engine's development, other manufacturers were not so concerned with faceless service to their country. "The Packard Company . . . are about the only people seldom heard of in connection with the Liberty engine," Vincent unhappily wrote Deeds in October 1917.

In December, Packard was forced to accept a new government cost estimate for engines of $5000 cost plus $625 profit based on quantity production. Macauley doubted whether the company could come within two hundred dollars of the cost on its first 6000 engines, considering how much Packard had spent on development. Other manufacturers had not, of course, incurred similar expenses.

The sturdy Le Pere built by Packard, and powered by the Liberty V-12 engine, was not fully tested in time to take part in the First World War.

Charles Kettering, who had perfected the Liberty's battery ignition system, was amazed to find that the engine's early production difficulties had led to wild rumors. "National issues have developed out of the length of a bolt and the depth of a radiator to an extent I did not believe possible," he said. Kettering was once confronted in the assembly facility at Dayton by two Chicagoans who had come to him with charges that "this Liberty motor is a failure, a great joke perpetrated on the American public." The men, whose sons were in the Air Corps, were astounded to be shown a completed engine when they believed none existed. "My God," said one. "Have they got one done?" In answer, Kettering showed them an entire row of completed Liberty twelves.

"The Liberty engine cannot read; it has no ears; therefore it does not know anything about the criticism that is going on about it," Kettering told the Society of Automotive Engineers in July 1918. "Otherwise, I do not know whether one of them would get off the ground."

The controversy about the engine was further heated for a time when sculptor Gutzton Borglum—creator of the Mount Rushmore Monument—procured a letter from his friend President Wilson to unofficially investigate the Aircraft Production Board. "His charges of incompetence and waste in the production of aircraft were, for the most part, complete-

ly false," wrote Dickey, "but they served to set up a hue and cry against the aircraft-production effort. As a direct result, investigations were launched in quick succession by H. Snowden Marshall, the Chamberlain Committee of the Senate, and finally the famous Hughes investigation." Borglum, however, was discredited when it was learned that he planned to form his own aircraft company to take advantage of the government contracts lost by those he was attacking.

Packard itself was not seriously affected by Borglum's wild muckraking or by the other investigations, though the company did publish a special edition of its magazine depicting Packard's selfless role in the Liberty's development. But Jesse Vincent did suffer. He had neglected to dispose of his Packard stock when he began working for the government and was charged by the Hughes investigators with profiting illegally from the Liberty engine.

His obvious innocence of criminal intent or guilt was shown by the mere $55.00 his stock had earned him. But although presidential intervention halted any action against him, Vincent never received the same Distinguished Service Medal awarded to E.J. Hall.

Despite charges that the Liberty engine had design flaws, really needed a magneto, used too much fuel and oil, and the Borglum

Adjustments being made to De Palma's Packard 299 during tests prior to the running of the 1919 Indianapolis 500. The car finished sixth in the race.

witchhunt, the engine was duly installed in a combat-bound DH-4 and carried out its first sortie on August 2nd, 1918. Just as the Liberty's introduction had been hampered by production difficulties, the debut of the American-built DH-4 had been delayed when it proved necessary to largely rebuild the machines in France because of production errors.

Even then, the DH-4 met with a mixed reception from American pilots. An otherwise good design, it possessed one fatal weakness, the location of its fuel tank. Installed between pilot and gunner to give the pilot a good view forward and downward for bombing purposes and the observer a wide field of fire for his twin guns—the pilot also had two forward-firing guns—the tank's position made the DH-4 a terrible plane to crash. Aaron Norman, author of *The Great Air War*, described the likely results of a DH-4 crash. "It always came down nose first, and upon impact, the gasoline tank would tear itself loose from its moorings and smash into the hot engine, cutting the pilot in half and then, as a rule, ex-

ploding." It was for this reason that the plane acquired its dreaded nickname, the "Flaming Coffin." Despite this appellation—which the DH-4 had earned before the Liberty was installed in it—no greater percentage of the machines went down in flames than other types according to statistics. If you asked the man who flew one, though, it's likely he would not have been sympathetic to the quoting of percentages.

Deserved or not, the plane's reputation wore off on its new engine. Quentin Roosevelt, son of Teddy and a lieutenant in the A.E.F., wrote of the Liberty, "It's going to be a long time before one gets to the front, and tho' I'm not crazy about the bus I'm flying (a Nieuport 28), I'd be much more comfortable in it than I would in a Liberty." [The DH-4 and the Liberty engine had apparently become synonymous to pilots.] "They have no right to send the things over here, tell people in the states how wonderful they are, and then expect us over here to work with them when every new flight shows some defect to be remedied. Of course, they're all minor defects but. . . ."

Such defects together with aerodrome accidents resulted, however, in fully 249 DH-4's—over a third of the planes that reached the combat zone—being crashed before the Armistice.

British aircraft equipped with the Liberty, primarily the DH-9A, also suffered problems and some English critics, perhaps remembering the early American efforts to put the engine in Bristol Fighters, termed the Liberty "a fairly bad job, too heavy and unreliable." Coastal units which received Liberty-engined patrol planes during the late summer of 1918 did not use their machines over water because they considered the engine's valve gear unreliable for such flights. Initially, British pilots also looked askance at the engine's battery ignition system and were generally derisive of the powerplant, having heard too many melodramatic stories—the U.S. government's public relations effort had mixed results—about its creation. Once the engine was better understood, however, and its early problems ironed out, it remained in service with the British well into postwar years.

Of the 2250 engines ordered by the British during the war itself, though, only 980 were delivered before the Armistice because of the early production delays. It was in one of the early Liberty-powered DH-9A's that American captain Merian C. Cooper—who survived the war to film the original *King Kong*—planned to photograph a mock dogfight involving Eddie Rickenbacker and a captured German Hannover. Stephen Longstreet described what happened in his book, *The Canvas Falcons*. The "American Liberty motor," he wrote, "never too trustworthy and known to balk at the wrong time" died as the plane lifted off the ground and the machine crashed. As neither Merian nor the pilot were injured, a new Liberty-engined plane was readied and this time, things worked better and Merian happily got his shots. Still, the episode nearly ended in tragedy when a group of French aircraft unexpectedly appeared, wanting to join the fray. Only Rickenbacker's frantic hand signals convinced the newcomers that he was bringing the "enemy" down to surrender. Merian's film of the entire incident became a favorite in America where some viewers believed they were seeing Rickenbacker fending off a whole German squadron.

Late in 1918 it was decided to produce a new model of the DH-4 which would eliminate the plane's dangerous fuel tank location. The DH-4B was similar to its predecessor except that the pilot and gas tank positions were reversed. The first examples of this model reached the front on November 12th, 1918, exactly one day after the Armistice was signed. By then, the DH-4's war record had been written. One hundred fifty bombing raids had been completed and some 140 tons of bombs dropped by U.S. flyers. American pilots in the twelve U.S. observation, day-bombing and pursuit squadrons equipped with DH-4's scored a total of fifty-nine victories in their machines. Thirty-three DH-4's were lost to

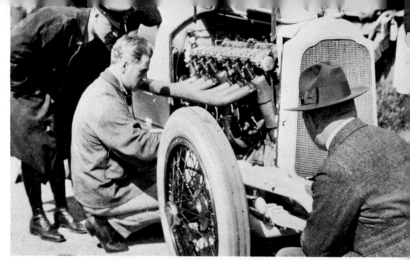

De Palma checks the engine of the Packard 905-cubic-inch racer. The car appeared in streamlined form to set a land speed record at Daytona in February 1919. Its engine is now on display at the Smithsonian Institution.

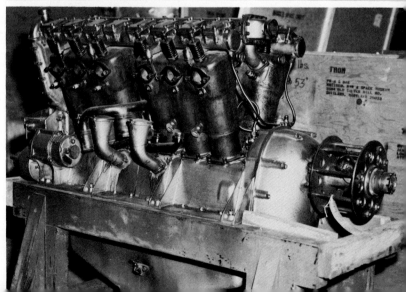

enemy action. Top speed of a Liberty-engined DH-4 was 125 mph, altitude 19,500 feet, better than previous versions. Although the performance of the DH-4 Liberty was considered respectable, it was outclassed by similar machines powered by the magnificent though very complex Rolls-Royce Eagle VIII. DH-4's equipped with this 375 hp engine could do 143 mph and reach 22,000 feet.

Jesse Vincent would have preferred to produce the DH-9 initially. It already incorporated improvements made to the DH-4B, but the newer plane was not available at the time U.S. companies were ready to tool up for plane production. Although the DH-4 eventually proved itself a viable compromise, Packard moved to produce an entirely new aircraft for use by American pilots. The company obtained the services of French engineer, Capitaine G. Le Pere, who designed a striking two-seater designated the Le Pere U.S. Army Combat 11 (LUSAC 11). Powered by the Liberty twelve, this rugged plane with its plywood-covered fuselage, fully-cowled engine and faired-in axle was capable of 132 mph. Two of

Workmen posing with the last Liberty to leave the line, October 1918. By then Packard production had accounted for forty-three percent of all Liberties built.

these machines were in France undergoing trials—and Packard was busily completing twenty-seven more—when the war ended. A further 995 planes were on order from Packard at the time but the contract was cancelled. Pilots who flew the LUSAC 11 found it maneuverable and very promising but suggested that extensive cooling system and fuel-feed modifications would be necessary before it was combat ready.

Still, the Le Pere made a name for itself when, on September 6th, 1919, Major Rudolph W. Schroeder set a world altitude record for a plane carrying pilot and one passenger. Wearing electrically heated clothing, Schroeder flew his Le Pere, fitted with a supercharged Liberty twelve developing 440 hp, to 28,500 feet. He later flew still higher, to 33,000 feet on May 1st, 1920, though carbon monoxide fumes, trouble with his oxygen system and near blindness incurred by his cold-chilled eyes caused him to lose consciousness and fall six miles to 3000 feet before he regained control and managed to land the machine. On September 28th, 1921, another supercharged Le Pere, this one flown by Lieutenant John A. Macready, left McCook Field and soared to nearly 35,000 feet, setting a record and adding further evidence that supercharged engines could play a valuable role in Army aviation.

Briefly during 1919, Packard considered producing a commercial version of the Le Pere airplane. Based on the assumption that "in this country there are hundreds of wealthy sportsmen to whom flying would appeal," *Motor Age* reported in March that "the Packard Company has designed and brought out its first line of commercial airplanes . . . . Packard is not in production on this plane but will probably go ahead with its manufacture." The plane was to be marketed through Packard's regular dealer organization and be available with either the Liberty eight or twelve. Although the company got as far as letting out information about the plane's projected price—$15,000—no sport-type Packard Le Peres were built. The machine's projected cost and the size and power of its engine would have put it far out of the market for postwar sport planes. Later, in 1923, Packard again considered an airplane but it was smaller and less expensive than the Le Pere. It was not produced either.

By the end of World War I, 20,478 Liberty V-12 engines had been produced, 6500 by Packard, a like number by Lincoln, 3950 by Ford, 2528 by Cadillac and Buick and 1000 by Nordyke and Marmon. Engines built by the Trego Motors Corporation were substandard and never used. In addition to the 980 delivered to the British, 405 Liberty engines were delivered to the French out of an allocation of 3575. Besides powering the DH-4, five Caproni three-engine bombers were Liberty-powered as were ten Martin bombers. The latter machines took part in Billy Mitchell's momentous sinking of several battleships, an achievement that failed to significantly impress U.S. military observers.

The smaller versions of the Liberty engine saw little use. Fifty-two six-cylinder engines were built by Thomas Morse and Wright. One of these was installed in a Curtiss PN-1 night fighter but the machine proved barely faster than the bombers it was intended to intercept and the project was abandoned. According to Dickey, the final disposition of the six-cylinder engines is not shown in government files. Fifteen eight-cylinder Liberties were built by Buick but serious vibration troubles coupled with competition from Marc Birkigt's superb Hispano-Suiza V-8 abruptly halted production. A few four-cylinder engines were built by the Hudson company, though none got off the ground.

The postwar career of the Liberty was varied and colorful and included the first transatlantic flight (made by a U.S. Navy flying boat), the first aerial circumnavigation of the globe, and the nation's first airmail service. Eddie Rickenbacker planned to fly Republican presidential candidate Warren G. Harding around the country in a DH-4 equipped with a rear seat canopy for Harding. But when the Democrats accused the Republicans of having a five million dollar slush fund, the expensive idea was shelved. Instead, Rickenbacker used a DH-4 to pay visits on dealers selling the car which bore his name.

The Liberty also found its way into postwar land speed record cars, racing boats and military vehicles. In World War II, Liberties powered a whole series of British tanks, as well as the Christie-inspired tanks used by the Russians who had been building the Liberty without license and calling it the M5.

Packard's development of the Liberty was followed by several subsequent designs including a 350 hp model labelled 1A-1237, a 600 hp 2025-cubic-inch powerplant intended primarily for commercial aviation, and a nine-cylinder diesel radial designed by Lionel Woolson and the brilliant Hermann Dorner who had been chief engineer of the German Hannover Company during the war. Another big Packard V-12 was used in the "Water Wasp" torpedo boats of World War II.

Whatever Packard's accomplishments in aviation, however, the Liberty engine will remain the most meaningful, not just to the history of the company, but to the country as well. In only one year, Packard helped move the United States away from its moribund aviation program and into a position of some prominence. Now America was ready to enter the Air Age. "It stands as a monument to the capacity of the country to change," wrote Dickey of the Liberty, "and in changing, to move a giant step beyond its peers in the development of an infant technology." Of all the statements pro and con about the Liberty, perhaps one of the most meaningful was made by one of the two brothers who had given America a headstart in aviation only to helplessly watch it fall far behind. "It was the finest airplane engine produced up to its time," said Orville Wright. By the time development of the Liberty engine was complete though, it really needed no defenders. Whatever its growing pains, the record of service achieved by the perfected Liberty engine spoke for itself.

MOTOR CARS FROM THE COMPANY

Color Portfolio I
1899-1925

1899 Model A, the first Packard built

1900 Model B Runabout with Dos-a-Dos Seat

1901 Model C Runabout with Dos-a-Dos Seat

1902 Model F Detachable Tonneau

1903 Model F Touring with Detachable Tonneau

1901 Model C Two Seats, Fixed Rear Seat

196

1904 Model L Touring

1905 Model N Touring

1908 Model Thirty Seven-Passenger Touring

199

1909 Model Eighteen Runabout

1910 Model Thirty Limousine

1912 Model Eighteen Runabout

1912 Model Eighteen Landaulet

1912 Model Thirty Seven-Passenger Touring

202

1912 Model Thirty Seven-Passenger Touring

1913 Model 1338 (1-38) Phaeton

1914 Model 1448 (3-48) Seven-Passenger Touring

1914 Model 1448 (3-48) Seven-Passenger Limousine with Cab Sides

1914 Model 4-48 Seven-Passenger Touring

1915 Model 5-48 Seven-Passenger Touring

1914 Model 2-38 Salon Touring

1915 Model 3-38 Runabout

1916 Model 1-35 Twin Six Five-Passenger Touring with California top

1917 Model 2-25 Twin Six Runabout

1916 Model 1-35 Twin Six Salon Touring

209

1920 Twin Six on a custom-built 145-inch chassis with Town Car coachwork by Fleetwood

1920 Model 3-35 Twin Six Limousine

1921 Model 116 Single Six Touring

1922 Model 3-35 Twin Six Special Runabout

1922 Model 3-35 Twin Six Seven-Passenger Touring

214

1922 Model 133 Single Six Seven-Passenger Touring

1922 Model 3-35 Twin Six Special Runabout

1923 Model 126 Single Six Runabout

1923 Model 126 Single Six Sedan

1925 Model 136 Single Eight Coupe

215

216

1925 Model 236 Eight Holbrook Coupe

Owner and Photographer Credits

1899 Model A, the first Packard built
Lehigh University   Photograph by Stan Grayson

1900 Model B Runabout with Dos-a-Dos Seat
Harrah's Automobile Collection
Photograph by Rick Lenz

1901 Model C Runabout with Dos-a-Dos Seat
Frederick C. Crawford Auto-Aviation Museum
Photograph by Stan Grayson

1902 Model F Detachable Tonneau
Harrah's Automobile Collection
Photograph courtesy of the Collection

1903 Model F Touring with Detachable Tonneau
Harrah's Automobile Collection
Photograph by Rick Lenz

1901 Model C Two Seats, Fixed Rear Seat
Harrah's Automobile Collection
Photograph courtesy of the Collection

1904 Model L Touring
Harrah's Automobile Collection
Photograph courtesy of the Collection

1905 Model N Touring
Harrah's Automobile Collection
Photograph courtesy of the Collection

1908 Model Thirty Seven-Passenger Touring
Owner: Burton H. Upjohn
Photograph by Don Vorderman

1909 Model Eighteen Runabout
Owner: W.P. Snyder III
Photograph by Henry Austin Clark, Jr.

1910 Model Thirty Limousine
Swigart Museum
Photograph by Henry Austin Clark, Jr.

1912 Model Eighteen Runabout
Owner: Ernest W. Gill
Photograph by Henry Austin Clark, Jr.

1912 Model Eighteen Landaulet
Long Island Automotive Museum
Photograph by Henry Austin Clark, Jr.

1912 Model Thirty Seven-Passenger Touring
Owner: Frank D. Saylor III
Photograph by Henry Austin Clark, Jr.

1912 Model Thirty Seven-Passenger Touring
Owner: Phil Hill   Photograph by Rick Lenz

1913 Model 1338 (1-38) Phaeton
Harrah's Automobile Collection
Photograph by Rick Lenz

1914 Model 1448 (3-48) Seven-Passenger Touring
Owner: Don E. Weber
Photograph by Rick Lenz

1914 Model 1448 (3-48) Seven-Passenger Limousine
Owner: Edward H. Marion
Photograph by Don Vorderman

1914 Model 4-48 Seven-Passenger Touring
Owner: Stan Tarnopol
Photograph by Richard M. Langworth

1915 Model 5-48 Seven-Passenger Touring
Owner: Frank H. Gardner
Photograph by Henry Austin Clark, Jr.

1914 Model 2-38 Salon Touring
Owner: H. Roy Davis
Photograph by Rick Lenz

1915 Model 3-38 Runabout
Owner: Phil Hill   Photograph by Rick Lenz

1916 Model 1-35 Twin Six Five-Passenger Touring
Owner: James A. Cook
Photograph by Rick Lenz

1917 Model 2-25 Twin Six Runabout
Owner: Howard G. Henry
Photograph by Don Vorderman

1916 Model 1-35 Twin Six Salon Touring
Owner: William Scripps Kellogg
Photograph by Rick Lenz

1920 custom-built Twin Six Town Car by Fleetwood
Owner: Stan Tarnopol
Photograph by Richard M. Langwoorth

1920 Model 3-35 Twin Six Limousine
Harrah's Automobile Collection
Photograph by Rick Lenz

1921 Model 116 Single Six Touring
Owner: Chester Kelsey
Photograph by Henry Austin Clark, Jr.

1922 Model 3-35 Special Twin Six Runabout
Owner: Burton A. Yale
Photograph by Rick Lenz

1922 Model 3-35 Twin Six Seven-Passenger Touring
Owner: Dr. William E. Donze
Photograph by Henry Austin Clark, Jr.

1922 Model 133 Single Six Seven-Passenger Touring
Owner: Richard E. Harms
Photograph by Rick Lenz

1922 Model 3-35 Twin Six Special Runabout
Estate of Paul Baldwin
Photograph by Henry Austin Clark, Jr.

1923 Model 126 Single Six Runabout
Owner: Dr. B.J. Page
Photograph by Richard M. Langworth

1923 Model 126 Single Six Sedan
Owner: Raymond Magalski
Photograph by Rick Lenz

1925 Model 136 Single Eight Coupe
Harrah's Automobile Collection
Photograph by Rick Lenz

1925 Model 236 Eight Holbrook Coupe
Owner: James E. Silvey   Photograph by Rick Lenz

CHAPTER TEN

PACKARD
RE-DISCOVERS
AMERICA

The Single Six Model 116
September 1920 - March 1922
The Single Six Model 126-133
April 1922 - December 1923

AUTHOR: L. MORGAN YOST

The Armistice was signed November 11th, 1918. The War to End Wars was over. The world was weary. In America a small-town newspaperman by the name of Warren Harding captured the mood of the nation with four words: "a return to normalcy." No one was quite sure what that meant, save perhaps good times, prosperity. Harding was elected President of the United States.

But normalcy could scarcely characterize the decade that was to follow. America was no longer a debtor nation, the war's course having changed it to a creditor, with Europe owing this country some ten billions of dollars by its end. Across oceans new concepts in society and government had been wrought by revolution and political strife, in Russia, in Germany, in the old Austro-Hungarian Empire. Nothing would ever be quite the same again.

This was as true for the individual member of society as well as the societal fabric as a whole. The old distances which had kept people apart were quickly being broken down. By communications: The telephone was no longer a source of mystery, and soon after East Pittsburgh radio station KDKA had its first broadcast on November 2nd, 1920, there was a rush to the airwaves. By mobility: The motorcar had arrived as a cogent social force and everyone knew it. Except the bankers.

The impediments to the automobile's progress were being swiftly erased. The war had emphasized good roads—long a cause of former Packard president Henry B. Joy—as a national necessity. Any politician now wanting to be elected had to favor them, enthusiastically. More money would be spent on their construction—some 300,000 miles in all—and on buildings during the Twenties than anything else.

And inside the buildings was another revolution, factories would double production in the decade without a material increase in workforce. The machine was king. It could put your breakfast in a box, or make you a car, just like that, or so it seemed. The advent of mass production, the trustworthiness now of lower priced cars and their economic availability to larger numbers of people brought with it a new definition of what an automobile was—or could be. The old "get out and get under" syndrome was replaced by "get in and go"—Henry Ford's Tin Lizzie, for all its idiosyncracies, had started something. Good living in this period of "normalcy" was seen by most Americans as their inherent right, and part of good living was owning and driving a motorcar. By August of 1920 women in America had been given the vote, and a goodly many thought they should have the wheel as well. In substantial numbers during the war—with the men away—they had settled themselves into the driver's seat and liked it. Here was another big market for the motorcar.

Despite the unbridled optimism all this suggests, the going still would not be easy for the automotive manufacturer. The automobile's early years had seen a flurry of companies founded on nothing more than a screwdriver and a hunch—and occasionally such unfettered presump-

tion met with success. It would take more than that now. Most of the companies dropping out of the arena henceforth would fail for one reason—lack of financing. The production of cars was perforce a volume operation and it took money as well as experience and background to compete. The industry had a lot to learn, about a lot of things.

During the business boom following the war, prices—especially of automobiles—skyrocketed. A depression followed. During 1920 nearly two million passenger cars were produced in America—the highest yearly production so far—but most of those had rolled off assembly lines before the depression hit. When it did, thousands of them remained unsold, cluttering up factories and dealer inventories. Total passenger car production in 1921 fell to a little over 1.5 million.

High prices and no business, that was the Twenties' first roar. Bankers, while cheerfully granting loans on motor trucks for businesses, would not finance the purchase of so-called "pleasure" cars. Potential buyers held off buying because they felt prices would soon be lowered, while manufacturers countered with hints they might raise them instead, reasoning that to do otherwise might incur the wrath of customers who had purchased at the more inflated prices. It was all a bit of a tangle.

To most manufacturers, it would seem, cost of production had little to do with pricing—it was a matter of what the traffic would bear. Certainly this was the case at Packard. Some sources have said that the company's profit margin was an easy thousand dollars per car. Obviously a substantial amount was included for name and reputation. Probably not without justification. But the times were changing.

Chief competitors for the Packard Twin Six had been Pierce-Arrow and Peerless. Cadillac was down a notch or two on the prestige scale, but that car had proved itself smooth and dependable, with a beautifully designed chassis; if its appearance was a mite stodgy by Third Series Twin Six standards, it was nonetheless in the luxury vein.

A look at the two companies—General Motors and Packard—in the year 1920 is fascinating. The former's history thus far had been turbulent. Its founder, William Crapo Durant, was a genius of promotion but no master of moderation. Upon organization of the corporation in 1908, he had gone on a shopping spree that was verily mind-boggling; companies were brought into the GM fold with a signature on a piece of paper and an exchange of stock. Some were valuable, others worthless; and by 1910 Durant had lost control of the GM mushroom. But he was back by 1915, having organized the Chevrolet Motor Company in the meantime, deftly using it, eastern money, and purchase of General Motors stock to propel himself into the driver's seat once more. The irrepressible Billy was soon up to his old tricks, however, and by 1920 Walter Chrysler (head of Buick at the time) abruptly left, convinced that Durant would spend the corporation into disaster. "Everything I have in this world," he said, "is in this company and I don't want to lose it." He

Pages preceding: Twin Six and Model 126 Packards lined up by Aurora, Illinois dealer for 1922 state fair. Above: The Model 116 Five-Passenger Sedan from 1920.

sold his GM stock and left for Willys-Overland.

Durant didn't bankrupt General Motors as Chrysler predicted, but he lost it millions. When the 1920 depression struck, GM stock plummeted and Durant poured his personal fortune into the company and borrowed heavily. By the fall of that year he knew neither how much he owed nor where he stood. When this was unraveled, Billy Durant was once again out of the corporation, this time irrevocably. The du Ponts—whom Durant had interested in GM some years before—acquired two and a half million General Motors shares, Pierre du Pont became president of the corporation, and he in turn appointed Alfred P. Sloan, Jr. as executive vice-president. Sloan quickly went to work and would ultimately devise an astoundingly effective reorganization, making each separate company an operating division responsible for its own success, with research, financial and sales policy divisions available to all. But in 1920 that was not the GM reality. The reality was a corporate snarl.

By contrast, the affairs of the Packard Motor Car Company that year were a model of serenity and good judgment. The firm was recognized to be one of the best managed in the industry, as a glance at the figures following indicates.

Year ending	Net Profit After Taxes	Dividends Paid	To Surplus
1917	$5,400,691	$1,470,636	$3,930,055
1918	$5,616,707	$1,270,388	$4,346,319
1919	$5,433,634	$2,099,244	$3,334,390

For the fiscal year ending August 31st, 1920, the figures were equally impressive: net profits, after taxes, of $6,395,468, dividends on common and preferred stocks totaling $2,511,441. The company had five million dollars in bank loans—but no debts. The volume of business for the year had been $62,579,240; assets added up to $62,808,277. Whatever Packard might do next, it would be leading from a position of strength.

Packard's strength was apparent, too, in the men to whom was entrusted the running of the organization, many of them to devote their entire working lives to the company. E.F. Roberts, with Packard since Model L days, became vice-president of manufacturing in 1920. Vice-president of distribution was Dr. Herbert H. Hills, whom Billy Durant had discovered practicing medicine in 1906 in Flint and talked into putting down his stethoscope and joining Buick as assistant sales manager. He joined Packard soon thereafter, and worked his way up through the ranks. Now doing that as well was Frank H. McKinney, a law school graduate who had entered the Packard factory training program and was dedicating himself to truck sales, soon to be elevated to overall advertising manager. From Packard trucks too—and previous to that work at Garford Motor Truck—R.E. Chamberlain was advancing himself toward Packard's general sales managership. Relatively new to the organization was a fellow with the intriguing name of Merlin A. Cudlip, as secretary. Al Moorhouse had replaced O.E. Hunt as chief engineer; J.R. Ferguson, whose Packard days would stretch from 1905 until the plant closed in 1956, was in charge of chassis work, and Archer L. Knapp bodies. Ranking over these gentlemen, of course, was Jesse Vincent who could do just about anything—or so it was thought, and the press had a good time tweaking him on those occasions in which it was discovered he wasn't invincible. When he fractured his leg in January of 1923, *Automobile Topics* winked, "The mishap occurred while the veteran automobile driver, flier and speed boat enthusiast, was endeavoring to master the use of the ski." He was soon back at his desk in a cast. Fortitude was the mark of the men of Packard, it seemed. When Alvan Macauley fell ill in early 1925, he attended a meeting he deemed important, in a wheelchair, then checked into the Ford Hospital to be made well again.

In retrospect, it was to the company's good fortune that mishap or malady didn't befall the Packard personnel during 1920, for there was much to do—and no time to waste. Perhaps Alvan Macauley sensed already that his car's principal competitor in the years ahead would be the Cadillac, but he was convinced now in any case that Packard's future as a leader in the fine car market could no longer rest upon the production of a few thousand very expensive cars a year. The war and the Liberty engine had brought the company experience in large-volume production. Macauley was sure that a machine, a proper machine, could do finer work than the hand alone, while producing more cars at the same time, so sure in fact that he plunged every dollar of the company's $10 million war profit plus another $7.5 million raised by stock issue into converting Packard to coordinated machine methods. And he would soon abandon truck production entirely to make room for the giant presses and other machinery of a completely new body plant.

All this rendered the Twin Six irrelevant. It could not be adapted to mass production in any sense of the word, and as *Fortune* magazine later pointed out, "smaller motors had grown proportionally more powerful and were much less costly to build," factors Alvan Macauley stressed in board meeting after board meeting. Moreover, the Twin Six was by now an old car. The successful Cadillac V-8 was about half its price, the phenomenal Model T Ford about a tenth—or in general figures down

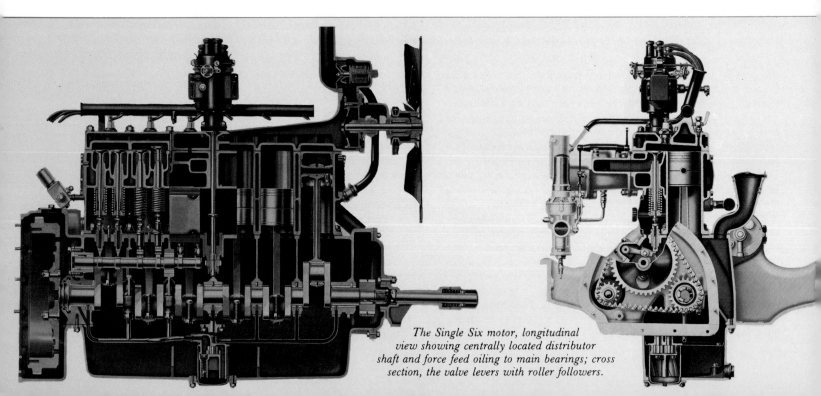

The Single Six motor, longitudinal view showing centrally located distributor shaft and force feed oiling to main bearings; cross section, the valve levers with roller followers.

the scale, $5000 to $2500 to $500. Packard would be taking aim near the middle figure. The rumors started. A new, smaller, less expensive Packard was about to debut. It was the talk of the industry. In September of 1920 the talk became reality when Alvan Macauley announced what was to become the most influential yet least known of any Packard automobile in its history: the Single Six, Model 116, the car which formed the basis for Packard six- and eight-cylinder engine design for the next nineteen years. Even the short-stroke One Twenty of 1935 was to borrow much from it.

Upon its introduction Packard men could not have foreseen its long tenure, but they had planned carefully anyway. Eight years before Jesse Vincent had proposed to then Packard president Joy that a light six-cylinder car be developed, one that would be comfortable, reliable, silent, free of vibration and weaknesses that would require recurring repairs, one that would be fast and quietly elegant in appearance, and one that could be sold at a price somewhat under premium. Joy had responded characteristically, "It has to be done whether it can be done or not."

It wasn't done right away. Neither Models 38 nor 48 were small cars, of course, and the Twin Six was another unabashed step in the all-out luxury direction. With Alvan Macauley's taking over the Packard presidency in 1916, Vincent, however, was put back to the quality light car task. The war interrupted him, but not the idea. In the board minutes of October 17th, 1918, Macauley announced that the project was "proceeding with all proper diligence." It was code-named Single Six, to differentiate it from the Twin. Macauley hoped to "have samples to submit [to the board] for consideration within ninety days."

From 1909 through 1912 Packard had produced the Model Eighteen, a smaller companion to the Thirty, this experience demonstrating that a reduced version of the same car cost nearly as much to produce as the paradigm: the same operations, the same number of parts, the same sales and overhead costs. Packard had sold its Eighteen for a thousand dollars less than the Thirty. The company could do that because its mark-up was substantial, but the conditions prevailing then no longer obtained.

The lesson was remembered. The new Packard engine could not be a small version of the Twin Six. Although board minutes indicate that some officers of the company thought about it a while, a twelve would simply have been too complicated for a light economical car. A V-8 had been rejected immediately, largely because Cadillac had introduced its version shortly before the debut of Packard's Twin Six. A V-8 from East Grand Boulevard now might appear a venturing into the enemy camp—and Packard didn't want Cadillac salesmen chortling at its expense.* The Packard fours were long gone, and to have reverted to that number of cylinders for a new car was unthinkable during this era of swing to sixes and eights. Jesse Vincent had said for years that "a six cylinder type has the smallest number of cylinders that can be arranged

in perfect running balance so as to eliminate vibration." Unquestionably, a six it had to be—and had been concluded as such for years before it finally arrived.

A half dozen different experimental motors were built: one for utmost power for the size, another to exploit the strides aluminum had made during the war, yet another to develop optimum silence without sacrifice of power, and so on. Vincent overlooked nothing. In France Capitaine Le Pere—with whom Packard worked during the Liberty adventure—had developed a new aeronautical engine then highly regarded in the industry. Packard paid $75,000 for the design and built an example in accordance with its plans, an overhead valve powerplant which was powerful, but powerfully noisy as well, the latter less objectionable in the air than on the ground. Further consultations with Le Pere in an attempt to quiet the engine down were unsuccessful, but the experience with the design did make a contribution to the final Vincent and company result.

In the meantime the new car's chassis had been developed and tested, using motors of the competition. When the two—new Packard engine and new Packard chassis—were put together, it seemed a felicitous union. Less amiable was the weather condition. The new Packard was ready for road testing in the winter of 1919-1920, one of the worst Michigan had experienced in years. There were no snowplows to clear the roads, save for those attached to the fronts of some streetcars. Salt, that friend of the junkman, was then only a table seasoning. For sixty-seven days the car was driven hard and constantly. Temperatures averaged between twenty-nine degrees above to three degrees below zero, and sleet, deep snow, ice and rain made matters worse. Two drivers kept the car going by turns, sand bags in the rear seat making up for two more passengers.

A few changes were made during this testing period, for improvement of performance or durability, or to facilitate production. Packard never divulged the nature of these, but they were apparently minor. Throughout, the car was not held up for repairs for a single day and no inherent defect was found. During the entire 25,000-mile run, the valves were not ground, nor was there need to remove carbon, or clean or replace spark plugs. The average gasoline mileage was 17.8 over the entire trip—after carburetor design changes it was 20.3 mpg for the last 9000 miles. Oil consumption was one quart each 2040 miles.

At the test's end, the car still had a maximum speed of 60 mph, and on the last day the car accelerated from five to thirty in fourteen seconds in

*For public consumption, however, Vincent commented only that a V-8 was rejected because "it is not inherently balanced, due to the characteristics of the two four-cylinder motors of which it is composed." He said nothing about a straight-eight. That would have been tipping his hand; he was thinking about it certainly, but for another car altogether.

223

high gear, a good mark. But the Single Six wasn't finished yet. Thence it was to the Indianapolis track for a speed run, this having been impossible on Michigan roads. After five miles on the track, the radiator boiled. Back to the experimental lab it went. For a week, Vincent, engineer Lionel M. Woolson and staff worked on the problem—and solved it. They said not how, but probably it was in the pump and water distribution, both of which were changed in the next model. Suitably fixed, the car was driven at the track for a full hour covering 62.5 miles with top up, windshield in place—and no problems whatsoever.

President Macauley and other Packard officials met the car next for a last few miles of driving, a first-hand impression and their stamp of approval. It was given. The Single Six, they concluded, was precisely the car Jesse Vincent had enthusiastically proposed to Henry Joy eight years before. They were convinced everyone else would think so too.

This was the car introduced September 1920. Its motor was the focal point of interest by the trade press and engineers. It was more or less a conventional L-head type, but improvements in detail were many, the simplicity of design was remarkable, and the accessibility of parts admirable. Cylinders were cast in a single block, with bore and stroke of 3⅜ by 4½ inches; rated horsepower was 27.34, developed was 39 at 1600 rpm, 52 at 2400 rpm (which was below the peak of 2750 rpm). The cast iron cylinder block was bolted to a cast aluminum crankcase, as was the oil pan, the latter removable without disturbing the crankshaft bearings or any other mechanism. (This was not the case with the engines of many Packard competitors; some combined block and crankcase in one casting but the entire unit then was of heavier cast iron.) Further, Packard's separate block casting made it possible to core the casting for larger water jacket volume. And the cast iron cylinder head was detachable, not only for ease of valve grinding but also to permit the uniform machining of all combustion chambers.

Pistons were also of cast iron allowing a smaller clearance between piston and cylinder walls. Piston slap—"that noise which was not discovered until smooth silent engines as the Twin Six"—was overcome by setting the piston pin 3/32-inch below the center of the piston, thus lessening the angle of side thrust. The crankshaft was of seven bearings, the camshaft a single forging with cams integral. Both crankshaft and camshaft were hollow for a full force feed lubrication by the oil pump in the crankcase.

The valve mechanism was most interesting. The cam lift was amplified by a lifter finger pivoted at one end and operating the valve tappet at the other with the cam follower—a roller operating in the lifter finger—between. The pivots were in assemblies of six, detachable from the side of the crankcase by removing stud nuts holding the integral cover housing.

The oil pump and the distributor mounted atop the cylinder head at midpoint were driven by a vertical shaft from spiral gears at the center of the camshaft. Camshaft and generator were driven by a link chain at the front. The generator had no integral bearing at the drive end; its head was machined to fit an auxiliary bronze bearing plate which centered the generator shaft and carried the generator shaft sprocket. The splined end of the shaft fit into the sprocket. The generator was bolted to the crankcase through slotted holes in the generator flange to permit taking up slack in the chain. (The first time you take one of these out, incidentally, you are sure you will drop the sprocket into the soup, but a spring inside maintains its pressure against the bronze plate.)

The Atwater Kent starting motor used Bendix drive and was located on the left side of the engine. Both units were finished with sand blast aluminum heads and shells of smooth black enamel. (The crinkle finish came later.) The starting switch was mounted on the flywheel housing to extend through the floorboard for foot operation.

Baffles in the oil pan prevented surging of the oil, and oil guards attached to the main bearing support webs kept too much oil from splashing up into the cylinders, a major factor in cutting down oil consumption and preventing "oil pumping" or leakage past the pistons which would result in fouled plugs, carbon deposits and knocks.

The water pump was integral with the cylinder head up front, the forward end of the pump shaft carrying the fan and the pulley by which the unit was driven by link belt from a pulley on the front end of the camshaft. This unit received particular praise from the press for its clean design and accessibility. There was, however, considerable service objection to the necessity of removing the headlight assembly, loosening and tilting the radiator, taking off the fan belt by unscrewing the one connecting link, and disconnecting the water by-pass pipe, only then being able to remove the cylinder head with pump and fan attached.

The carburetor was equipped with the Fuelizer, a device used and proven on the Twin Six. It had been the result of an inspiration which had come to engineer Woolson over his pipe at home one evening while mulling a pesky problem: the need for a method of heating the gas before it entered the cylinders for more complete vaporization, so that, in other words, the mixture entered as a dry gas rather than a combination of air and liquid particles. With the Fuelizer, a small portion of the mixture was by-passed into a side chamber where it was ignited by a special spark plug, burning with a steady blue flame which could be seen through a glass peephole, always an entertaining curiosity to non-Packard people. The major part of the mixture passed around this burning chamber reentered the manifold, mixing with the charge going to the cylinders.

Ignition was "Packard-Delco." The distributor contained two contact breakers, each with its own condenser and synchronized together: one for the ignition circuit, the other for the Fuelizer circuit. Thus there was practically a reserve ignition set for use in emergency, since the engine could be operated without the Fuelizer. And there was an automatic advance built into the distributor, relieving the driver of having to use hand spark control except under extreme conditions.

In his aircraft experience, Colonel Vincent had learned that an ordinary T shape in the intake manifold, leading up from the carburetor and branching to fore and aft groups of cylinders, produced turbulence and surging of the gases, giving symptoms of stalling or uneven performance. He eliminated this by splitting the vertical lead with a partition before branching. This was incorporated in the Single Six manifold.

It is interesting to compare this new engine of 1920 with the Packard 1-38 of 1913. The latter had about twice the displacement, yet produced only the same horsepower. And for the same horsepower, the comparative weight of the engines was cut in two. The earlier version, to be sure, operated at 1800 rpm compared to 2400 for the later, but the results of development in the intervening years were nonetheless obvious and dramatic.

The new Packard's clutch was of the multiple dry disc type with seven eight-inch plates, the transmission a sturdy three-speed selective. Drive was taken through a torque arm connecting the rear axle housing to the center frame cross member where it was attached with a spring buffer, this arm taking up the rear axle reactions of driving and braking. Both front and rear springs were semi-elliptics, the rear springs using the tension or hung shackle.

The chassis of the Single Six was conventional, with strong seven-inch-deep side rails. At front and rear, connecting opposite frame horns, was a torsion tube. Wheelbase was 116 inches, wheels wood spoke mounted with 33x4½ cord tires. Brakes were on the rear wheels, drums 14⅜ inches in diameter. The foot brake was external contracting, the emergency brake internal expanding on the same drum. The hand brake was on the driver's left. (This location was to be a Packard characteristic for years to come, and it gave a neater and roomier aspect to the front compartment. Most manufacturers placed their hand brake adjacent to the shift lever.)

Bodies were steel over a wood frame, all purportedly built in the Packard shops. (Though the public was not told, many bodies for the 116 and some open versions for the Twin Six were produced by the Pullman Company, the manufacturer of railroad cars in Chicago.) Open cars were upholstered in leather, the closed bodies in whipcord save for leather front seat and doors. The chassis was priced at $3000, and the four body styles available as follows: Touring Car, five passengers, $3640; Roadster, two passengers, $3640; Sedan, five passengers, $4950; Coupe, four passengers, $4835.

And that was the new Single Six Packard. It didn't sell.

The company was sure this new car would find purchasers at the ready. And purchasers were no doubt ready for a new Packard, but not

Packard chief engineer Al Moorhouse, the portrait taken February 1920.

this one. They were disappointed. It looked like a Packard, but not grandly so. It was easy to drive, for its day, but it did not feel like an expensive car. And it *was* expensive, more so than Packard had originally intended. Board minutes from November 18th, 1919 indicated a general agreement on a price not to exceed $3000; by February of 1920 it was up to $3275; by July 27th up further to $3650. A scant ten dollars had been lopped off the last figure by introduction time.

Moreover, there wasn't a seven-passenger car in the line, and the pleasure driving much in vogue included relatives and neighbors often numbering more than the five allowed for in the biggest Single Six. Buick had a seven-passenger car, so did Studebaker—and both were priced far less than the Single Six. Cadillac had a seven-passenger as well, and it sold for a little less than the Single-Six five-passenger. And, too, even the prospect who didn't desire a seven-passenger probably wanted the look of more car at the Packard price. The company tried to assuage by advertising both the Twin and the Single together, hoping prestige would rub off onto the latter. It didn't work.

Initially Packard thought only the price was wrong. The board of directors met October 30th, 1920 and told itself that in essence the Single Six was "all that could be desired," but dealers were clamoring for a touring car under $3000, and they would have it, despite the possibility—it was sorely lamented—of the "factory having to manufacture the car without profit for a considerable period." Two weeks later the company announced its new prices: the Touring and Roadster down to $2975, the Coupe to $4150, the Sedan to $4250. That was more like it. It would help—some. On October 7th, incidentally, Packard had stated

that it would guarantee against price decreases before July 1st, 1921 and did promptly refund the difference to those who had purchased cars at the higher prices. There weren't many, but the gesture didn't hurt the Packard image.

Packard was hurting though. On October 28th, 1919, prior to the Single Six introduction, the board of directors had authorized production at 20,000 cars per annum. Now general distribution manager George R. Bury advised the press that the economies of this large production had made the price decrease possible. Which would have been true, of course . . . if the cars were selling. By November 9th President Macauley was already talking longer wheelbase, but no one was agreeing yet. On December 2nd the headlines told another story: "NEW FINANCING AND INCREASED PRODUCTION PUT OFF BY PACKARD." Alvan Macauley reported to his stockholders that "nearly 50 percent [of the Single Sixes] are in Packard's own branches including export. Completed vehicles valued at $8,145,208, equal approximately to one-tenth of total shipments for the year ending August 31st, are still on hand." But that tenth was based on Twin Six production before the depression. Only 316 Single Sixes were produced to October 31st, November production was but 450—the total for the entire year was 1042. A sad welcome for the new prince.

The men who put the car together, however, were considerably more impressed. Early in 1921 Alvan Macauley told his board that "a number of employees desire to purchase Single Sixes on special terms"—naturally, even these Packards were considerably outside the price range of the fellows who built them—and this was authorized "at such prices and on such terms as might in [the board's] discretion be profitable." But Packard still had the problem of selling the car to those outside the company organization. The effort was valiant: big, round nickeled headlamps, nickeled radiator shells, cowl lamps, bumpers—accessories all intended to make the cars look bigger and more like the Twin Six. A standard Single Six touring car was specially equipped with, as Packard demurely spelled out, "six hundred forty-six dollars" of luxury extras and exhibited at the 1921 National Motor Show in Chicago.

Meanwhile life went on in the automobile industry, depression or no. Studebaker stopped building wagons, selling its business to the Kentucky Wagon Company. The Heine-Velox Twelve, a $17,000 car from the Pacific Coast, was announced, an anachronism supreme. It failed. February 3rd, 1921 saw a headline, "OPTIMISM RETURNING."

Not for Packard, quite yet. Manufacturing vice-president E.F. Roberts announced that same day that Packard was shutting down to balance stocks. Three thousand employees were affected. The "slump in the west, also a strike of body finishers resulting from alleged reduction in wages of 44c per hour, caused the shutdown," he said. By February 17th the Packard company was under way again, non-union workers

Chassis for the Single Six Model 116; note water pump atop cylinder head.

replacing those striking, with operations at twenty-five percent of normal, to be expanded if "sales continued to increase." The schedule for April was 1000 Single Sixes, expected to double in May. It was wishful thinking. The entire production of Single Sixes for 1921 would be only 6374 units.

In April of 1921 the Packard Motor Car Company issued $10 million in coupon bonds, the funds to be used as working capital. The issue was fully subscribed in two hours. Packard could not sell its Single Six, but it could still sell Packard.

Personnel changes came quickly now. Advertising manager W.H. Holmes left to open his own agency. In July Earle Anthony announced that George Bury would join him on the coast. (He would serve well there, accounting for much of Anthony's success for many years following.) Passenger car sales manager Harry T. Gardner had also resigned. No reason was given. He had previously been executive secretary of the Automobile Dealers Association—and had come to his Packard post in September of 1920, with the promotion of the Single Six in his charge . . . .

By July Packard board minutes recorded authorization "to inaugurate a campaign of advertising to stimulate sales of the Single Six particularly," and the company reduced prices further, the Single Six Coupe to $3750, the Sedan to $3975. Pierce-Arrow announced a second quarter loss of $828,866. Packard wasn't the only one having trouble. Billy Durant meantime was raiding General Motors and others (probably the former with more relish) for executives for his new empire. In July, too, it was reported that even Earle Anthony would be brought into his fold, to handle Durant cars as well as Packard.

Packards weren't selling, but the company was making sure the public was aware the cars were being produced as painstakingly as ever. An *Automotive Industries* article described the Packard testing: a five-hour engine run-in by electric motor; a two-hour dynamometer test in a silent room (where measurements of power developed, compression and fuel consumption were made, and mechanical variances and noises located); each completed car road tested, the test drivers responsible not to a factory foreman but Alvan Macauley himself. It was good press. Good too was the carburetion improvement, a two-range or double jet carburetor, still with the famous Fuelizer. (Apparently the mileage Packard had publicized on the introduction of the Single Six could not be obtained under customer conditions with the original carburetor. Not only did the company immediately equip all new cars with the improved carburetor but also provided it without charge for Single Sixes already in service. It was said to provide twenty miles per gallon under favorable conditions.)

By September Cadillac production was back on a 20,000 per year basis. Packard rather soft-pedaled the news of its 6000 figure for the Single Six, and the following month reduced prices again, this time by

$625 all around. During an automobile salon in December the Twin Six was displayed in several coachbuilt examples, but there wasn't a single Single Six in sight.

At Packard's annual meeting in November it was revealed that the company had an operating loss of $987,366 for the fiscal year preceding. Its financial condition still was excellent, however, surplus having been reduced by $4,833,766 to a—mere—$15,923,895. Of the 12,143 vehicles Packard produced in 1920, only 1042 had been Single Sixes. The remainder were the high profit Twin Sixes and trucks. For 1921 the production of even these was down too, by about seventy-five percent each. Doubtless no one at Packard rued a wish that "we'd just stayed with Twins and trucks." But something had to be done with the Single Six; until it could, however, the Model 116 went on, into 1922: about 1384 cars that year for a total production of 8800 116's.

Early in February that year there was a propitious "news leak." Packard would announce new models of its Single Six "this month." Actually the announcement didn't arrive until April, but in the interim the excitement grew. The new car would have a longer wheelbase, that much was acknowledged—a revelation which might have caused many a prospect to delay another car purchase until the new Packard could be seen.

"Minor Changes in New Packard Single Six" was the *Automotive Industries* headline when the car arrived. Minor perhaps but most important. The new model looked like a new car, but to call it that would have admitted the errors of the 116. The company stressed instead the continuity, pointing out discreetly the changes which careful attention to public comment had wrought. The most obvious of these was the wheelbase length of 126 inches, and the addition of seven-passenger cars to the line, on a wheelbase of 133 inches.

Moreover, body styling was all new. The little 116 had been a product of the short-lived "straight line and bevel" era. The fenders had square drop sides and a sharp peak along the center. The rears of the bodies were squared off, doors and windows square too and surrounded by raised moldings interrupting the body surfaces. Hood louvers were square ended and boxed out, the radiator shell square edged and flat faced. Even the instrument bezels were octagonal. All these design characteristics, applied to a short and high form, produced a boxlike result. The 116 looked like a tiny Twin Six, and it just had not worked.

But the new Single Six had a lithe grace. Here were Packards long and sleek—and pace-setting. The open cars sported a belt molding extending from the radiator through the length of the body, a feature soon to be imitated throughout the industry. For all its design freshness, however, the marque's continuity was not broken in the least. The revised car was indubitably a Packard. The difference was that it sold, like the proverbial hotcakes.

Some $10 million in retail sales was generated during its first forty days. As President Macauley jubilated to his board on April 22nd, "all branches and distributors [are] asking for more cars than it [is] possible for Packard to provide." Within a month of introduction, the company set the production rate at 1000 units per month, only to increase it to 2000 by June. Orders on the books as of June 1st covered all the Single Sixes that could be built in the next three-and-a-half months. Truly the depression was over for Packard.

It was pretty much over for the rest of the country too. Men on commuter trains now discussed the length of time necessary to wait for delivery of their new cars, not whether it would be wiser not to buy them. But some feared too rapid a recovery might bring over-production again. From the Rickenbacker company, Barney F. Everitt advised, "Caution is still necessary in returning the industry to full strength." Pierce-Arrow was not doing well, remaining as it did with just its large, ultra expensive six. There were merger talks between Pierce and LaFayette involving sale of stock to pay off bank loans of both companies, but the idea was abandoned after a few weeks. Pierce-Arrow never would fully recover its position. Others did, at least for the time being. Forty-eight manufacturers had reduced car prices in January for the shows, with more following in mid-1922. This seemed to clear the air. The uncertainty of pricing had hindered sales. Prospects for the future, in business generally, looked very good.

In addition to the obviously seen changes in the new 126 and 133 Packards, there were a number of others, among them: an increase in the stroke to five inches; four driving plates for the clutch; a more forward location for front axle and radiator (the cylinder head now removable without disturbing the radiator); a new radiator shell with convex front surface relieving the severity of the old sharp corners; the water pump now mounted in front of the cylinder block with water forced through the cylinders by the pump. The piston and connecting rod assembly could now be pulled out through the top of the cylinder after removing the cylinder head, rendering unnecessary the removal of the block. (Consider the small boy who could not get his hand out of the cookie jar because he would have to let go of the cookies.) And a new cover was provided for the starter motor to secure quick and easy access to the commutator brushes. Further, the mounting provided for the starter motor driving spring was redesigned, this ostensibly to eliminate any trouble with breakage of the driving spring screws.

What sold the new Single Six, though, was not so much its fine mechanicals, but its looks and the prestige of the marque. And its attractive prices. As one of the ads burbled, "Packard Re-Discovers America—America Re-Discovers Packard." The objects of this rediscovery were eight, as listed here, with passenger capacity in parentheses:

On the 126-inch wheelbase		On the 133-inch wheelbase	
Touring Car (5)	$2485	Touring Car (7)	$2685
Runabout (2)	$2485	Sedan (7)	$3525
Sport Model (4)	$2650	Sedan-Limousine (7)	$3575
Coupe (4)	$3175		
Sedan (5)	$3275		

There were no color options. Though the dealers would repaint to a special color on extra order, this was not often asked for, probably because it would have entailed an additional delay and Packard was already running far behind in deliveries. The open cars were Packard Town Car Blue striped in gold. Closed models were black above the belt line—meaning window frames and rear quarter; closed cars did not have the continuous belt molding—with bodies of the darker Standard Packard Blue, also striped in gold. Fenders, belt mold, apron and chassis were black enamel. Wheels were wood spoke, save for the discs on the Sport Model, and painted the body color. Striping was a restrained 1/32-inch wide. On open cars it was a continuous line one-half inch below the raised black belt mold. Closed bodies carried a stripe one-half inch below the bottom of the superstructure, extending rearward from the windshield post and around the back.

The Touring Car for five was the Single Six's best seller initially, though the Five-Passenger Sedan was soon to overtake it. Closed cars would be coming into increasing favor, eliminating the trauma of the top—it cracked when folded and folding was a mammoth undertaking seldom attempted by one lone man. Side curtains were less than admirable as well, flapping in the wind and making the interior dark and uninviting. Packard did call attention to the outside door handles of its open cars—"an appreciated convenience—and a protection to gloves and cuffs in inclement weather." (Lesser cars had inside handles only and one had to insinuate his hand under the side curtain to reach them from the outside.)

The reason the Touring Car was leader of the line was simply its lower cost—$790 less than the Sedan. Only those with sporting blood really preferred an open car, which was pleasant only on a balmy summer day. An improved cowl ventilator, "instantly adjustable in three positions," cooled the driver's feet. Upholstery was heavy wholehide black leather with long grain bright finish tailored in a flat pleated pattern—and how hot *that* would get in the sun when the top was down!

The gem of the line was the Sport Model, sleek and agile, with a narrow four-passenger body negating any family car connotations. With its lowered—by two inches—body, radiator and hood, its lower-angled seat and steering wheel, and its disc wheels, it was a rakish proposition.

The Runabout, or roadster, body style was generally regarded in the industry in those days as a utility car for salesmen or others who traveled alone and had samples or paraphernalia to carry in the locked luggage

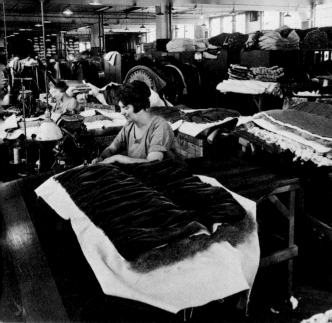

The upholstery shops of the Packard Motor Car Company, these photographs taken during the early 1920's, when both the Single Six and the Twin Six Packards were in production.

In their Packard offices during the early 1920's. Above: H.H. Hills, vice-president for distribution. Below: E.F. Roberts, vice-president for manufacturing.

compartment under the rear deck. Packard thought so too—"suited to business or recreation," the company said, though by the latter was meant hunting, fishing and camping, not country clubbing. The day of the sport roadster had already dawned—but without Packard. Such exemplifications as the Kissel Speedster, the Templar, Wills Sainte Claire and H.C.S. roadsters, and the Jordan Playboy, would become the rage among college students. Actually, Packard thought its four-passenger Sport Model provided the answer, though that was not the ideal of the university crowd. Joe College wanted a personal car, one that obviously wasn't Dad's borrowed for the evening. When double-dating, the coziness of four in the front seat might have had a certain attraction, but the rumble seat in cool weather encouraged an acquaintanceship with better facility. Packard's Runabout had the basic lines to appeal to youth, but it needed a touch of the wand to give it magic. What a knockout it would have been with the lower radiator, hood and body line of the Sport Model. But that was not to be.

The Coupe for four passengers followed the prevailing style of a small enclosed car for town use with the driver's seat somewhat askew and crowded to the left, and behind it a box with a top lid for packages. This was, as tradition had had it for some time, a popular body style for doctors and professional men.

The Five-Passenger Sedan was a straightforward practical car with a chaste interior. As the catalogue said, "Lacings and bindings have been omitted wherever possible in favor of the smart tailored effect gained by welted seams and covert tacking." All cloth upholstery and linings were broadcloth, with envelope type pockets on all doors but the left front. Interior door pulls were cloth covered as were the side arm rests. (There were no center folding arm rests.) The robe rail on the back of the front seat was a cloth-covered cord. About the only exposed hardware, silver plated, was the door glass adjuster handles and the rim of the center dome lamp, which provided the only interior illumination other than instrument light. There were roller shades of silk on the rear and rear quarter windows. The Seven-Passenger Sedan had the same specifications, with the extra seven inches of wheelbase allowing for two comfortable jump seats in the tonneau. The addition of a plate glass partition to this body transformed it into the Sedan-Limousine.

To these eight body styles presented in April of 1922 were added two more in October: a Coupe and a Sedan-Limousine, each for five passengers. The former had hinged front seat backs allowing access to the rear seat, and at $3550 was seventy-five dollars more than the Five-Passenger Sedan. Touted as the "Sport Model of the enclosed cars," it was compared by many to the coach produced by Hudson, a similar two-door body arrangement sold at a low price and as responsible a factor as any other in swinging the market to closed cars. Had Packard wished, the company could have made its Five-Passenger Coupe a higher produc-

tion, less expensive car too—but the rest of the line was selling so far ahead of capacity, the decision was to stay with prestige. "A neatly designed luggage trunk adds a clever sports touch," said the catalogue. The Sedan-Limousine was, as the name suggests, merely the Sedan with adjustable plate glass partition installed, the same unit as in the seven-passenger. This body was put into production with no additional dies or jigs, and was priced only $50 above the Sedan, at $3325.

On June 14th, 1923 yet another body style was introduced. It was Packard's attempt—one also made by many other manufacturers—to improvise an enclosure which would easily convert an open car into a closed one. It was priced at $2750, only $265 more than the Touring Car and $525 less than the Sedan, and it was called the Touring Sedan. It had no provision for luggage. It sported a fixed top, leatherette covered, higher body sides than the Touring Car and wider doors which joined at a single pillar, allowing a glazed panel above each door with only a stanchion between. Packard said, "It provides ready convertibility from an open car to a closed car and vice versa. It is designed as a unit, and all the lines harmonize perfectly, from the headlamps to the tire carrier. Detachment and storage of windows are both easily and quickly effected." One must read all that to mean that a window could not be opened except by taking the window frame panel off from the door. The rear quarter window could not be removed at all. There was no way to extend the arm for hand signals, stoplights were not then regular equipment, and turn signals practically unknown. A bit of a problem. Ventilation could be had—save by removing window panels—only through the cowl ventilator or the top-hinged windshield. One owner told this writer that he used his car all winter with no window on the driver's door because he chewed tobacco. No figures remain on the units built, but probably they were minimal. No such car has survived. This type was, incidentally, carried through into the next model series, but its name was changed to Permanent Top Touring Car. The catalogue description added the line, "Especially adapted to localities where extremes of temperature are not great."

The industry strike of auto body workers adversely affected neither Cadillac nor Packard. Cadillac had its own plant, while Packard controlled the output of its two body makers, one of which was the Pullman Company. In 1921 and '22 this firm had orders for 13,655 bodies for all 126-133 series cars except the seven-passenger sedans and limousines. The breakdown is rather interesting in that it indicates the relative numbers of various closed and open types, to wit: Five-Passenger Touring, 5685; Seven-Passenger Touring, 3820; Runabout, 700; Sport Model, 450; Four-Passenger Coupe, 1550; Five-Passenger Coupe, 450; Five-Passenger Sedan, 1000—10,655 open cars, 3000 closed.

These orders did not cover all of the 126-133 production which totaled 26,560 for the full term—about sixteen months. In fact, Pullman ap-

parently received no further orders after 1922 and for whatever reason summarily dropped out of the automobile coachbuilding business, though the company did make up an all-steel brougham mounted on a Packard Single Six 133 chassis for display at the Custom Salon at the Drake Hotel in Chicago during January of 1924. Packard, seemingly, had been Pullman's only customer in its automotive diversification. Other than this special Salon car, which was not sponsored by Packard, all Pullman-built bodies were of conventional wood frame construction, doubtless following Packard's own drawings.

About this time too, there was a flurry of interest in fabric-covered bodies, the Weymann being the best known, its advantages reputed to be light weight and adaptability to curves without expensive dies. Packard wasn't much interested. One textile company did have a special custom body made up on a Single Six chassis using a product called Meritas, an imitation long grain landau leather material. The car, quite handsome with its black finish and formal rear quarter with opera windows, was exhibited by its maker at the Chicago show in January of 1923. Packard still wasn't interested.

Meantime, however, Packard was becoming very interested in another idea. The notion of buying for other than cash was perfectly suited to the Twenties—and it caught on like wildfire as a practical way to translate expensive dreams into viable reality. Installment buying could but benefit Packard measurably. The company was well aware of this, but its dealers apparently required a little coaxing. Packard general sales manager R.E. Chamberlain would admonish them in the April 18th, 1925 issue of *Packard Inner Circle*: "You will recall that we ask an owner to state whether he has bought his Packard for cash or on the time sales plan. Reports indicate that surprisingly few are taking advantage of the latter method. So few, in fact, that we wonder if you are going after this vast field of potential sales in the right way. The *good business* aspects of this important matter are many. But unless all of us are sold on the idea that it *is* good business, it is going to be hard to step a prospect up to the Packard class when there exist misgivings as to the time-payment means, which make it possible for him to reach his desire. . . . We consider buying on monthly payments as a badge of distinction in a sense. The man who buys on this plan receives a compliment that bespeaks his integrity and high standing in the community [and] he has the added advantage of being able to own those good things which he needs. This is a sales point not to be overlooked." Like all directives to dealers from this era, the admonition was strictly low-key—but it would change some dealers' minds and subsequently the idea of selling a Packard on time enjoyed at least a respectable measure of acceptance.

Accepted now too (and at last) was the pleasure car industry by the banking community. During the business downturn, the bankers who had been loath to lend money to the industry felt themselves smugly justified. The economic upswing changed minds.

Unchanged through all this was the collective mind of the press with regard to Packard for, by now too, the critical reaction to the new Single Six was in. Probably the most ecstatic of its reviews arrived from London, in the April 11th, 1923 issue of *The Tatler*, wherein the critic, after allowing that "generally speaking, I am not enamoured of American cars," went on to relate: "It has to be a pretty good Yankee, therefore, that can overcome my initial prejudice; but when after doing that it contrives to fill me with an uncontrollable lust for possession, then I can assure you it is something right out of the common rut. [The Single Six is], in my humble opinion, as near being the very best car in the world as makes no difference. This is heavy praise, I know, but it can't be helped—I must speak as I find. If I had leisure and one of these cars, I would like to drive it round Coventry and Birmingham and Manchester, and other places where motors are mostly made, and take British managing directors out for a run, just to show them, you understand. The plain fact is that this is a car in which I simply cannot find fault. It is as docile as an angel, but goes like the very devil. It is supremely well sprung, it is uncannily silent, it is a miser on petrol, it steers no heavier than a wisp of cigarette smoke, it climbs like a chamois—in short, it just does anything that it should, and does most things a good deal better than you would think possible." One is reminded, of course, of the fulsome praise from Blighty accorded the Twin Six. England liked the Single Six even better.

And so did most of America, though encomiums in this country were generally a bit more homespun. When Walt Mason, a popular humorist and poet of the day, bought a Single Six sedan in California, Earle Anthony's advertising manager talked him into versifying about it. Packard was sufficiently delighted with the result to publish it, noting, "Just consider the word 'Packard.' A good name, yes; but shades of Byron, Shelley, and Keats, what a sticker for which to find a rhyming phrase! Many a poet would chew his pen in despair. Not so with Walt Mason. When Genius questions, Muse replies. 'Lacquered' (with all apologies to Mr. Roberts and his Manufacturing Department) possesses the full rhythm, the proper swing and cadence. . . ." Or, as the ebullient Mr. Mason wrote,

> When we're riding in our Packard,
> With her fenders nicely lacquered,
> And her cylinders all hitting, fine and true;
> When she's going like the devil
> Up the hills or on the level,
> Then the world seems pretty good to me and you.

The world was looking pretty good to the Packard company too. And it was about to look even better.

Page opposite: The Model 126 Six being road tested in California, 1923.
Above and below: The Five-Passenger Touring Car and Coupe of the Model 126.

CHAPTER ELEVEN

THAT BENEFICENT TYRANNY CALLED REPUTATION

The Single Eight Model 136-143
June 1923-February 1925
The Six Model 226-233
December 1923-February 1925

AUTHOR: L. MORGAN YOST

There is an iron tyranny which compels men who do good work to go on doing good work. The name of that beneficent tyranny is reputation." The advertisement carried the signature of Alvan Macauley. But the prose belonged to Theodore F. MacManus. The ad would be republished in booklet form, with reprints running into the millions; it would be translated into many languages, and become a model of clear rhetorical expression studied by students in many classrooms. The only reason that, historically, it has not the importance of Cadillac's "The Penalty of Leadership"—also written by MacManus—is that the Cadillac ad preceded it by seven years. Packard's "Reputation" appeared in November 1922.

Since 1921 MacManus, Inc. had been Packard's advertising agency, responsible for promoting the "new, larger, more beautiful Single Six," an assignment it accomplished with a deftness leaving no doubt as to what the revised car represented, overcoming the poor impression left by the little 116, yet without derogating it. MacManus was a master.

Following quickly upon "Reputation" was Packard's official release of its fiscal state of affairs—handsomely bolstering the image the advertisement had defined. For the six months ending February 28th, 1923, the company reported factory sales totaling $25,773,923, with a gross profit of $5,725,775. Assets and liabilities were $55,317,770, surplus $7,969,583. The company had redeemed the ten-year eight percent gold bonds dated April 15th, 1921 in the amount $5,915,000 and had $13,-758,950 in cash and marketable securities. During that half year, a seemingly small $1,216,674 had been paid out for plant machinery and tools, largely for a brand-new model. Trucks and Twins would be phased out in 1923. The decks were being cleared. A new Packard was coming. It arrived in June of '23, "lifting the veil on what, to the trade," as *Automobile Topics* said, "has for some little time been no secret."

"It Is a Single-Eight" heralded *The Packard*, putting to rest the rumors that the company would instead be building a new sixteen, a smaller Twin Six, a bigger Six, even a four. At least one of these had been seriously considered. As the board minutes of October 24th, 1922 noted: "management did not feel that it was yet in a position to definitely recommend to the board the adoption of either the new eight or the new light twin to take the place of the present Twin Six in the company's line of products but the new eight was showing up in such a way that it seemed probable that after it had reached a slightly further stage of development, its adoption as a new model would be recommended to the board . . . ." That it was, but what it was to be called remained a question as late as March 26th of 1923, Alvan Macauley pointing out then that "heretofore the trade names adopted for our models were so indicative of the design of the motor that when the design was changed the name of the model necessarily had to be discontinued and [suggesting] that in adopting the name for the new model car to take the place of the Twin Six the name be

adopted which would distinguish the new car from the Single Six but would not be indicative of the type of motor used." Macauley would be overruled on this point, or perhaps convinced otherwise, for the new car would be named for its engine or, as Packard said, the arrangement of its cylinders. A straight eight placed its in tandem fours, 0000 + 0000; the Packard's single eight in effect "cut one four cylinder motor in half, and put a half at either end of another four cylinder motor" for 00 + 0000 + 00. Engineering rationale aside, doubtless Packard decided finally to take promotional and continuity advantage of the Single Six designation

Pages preceding: The main switchboard at the Packard Motor Car Compan

SINGLE-EIGHT
A New Production by
PACKARD

The striking thing about the Single-Eight is that it does the things which are vital, in a more positive, effective way, than they have ever been done before.

These striking contributions to safer, surer, smoother motoring, are not hidden refinements, but very definite qualities quickly discernible.

It is not just a generalization but a fact,

that in comfort, acceleration, flexibi[lity] brake-action, steering and ease of c[on]trol, the Single-Eight has gone beyond previous practice.

The instant and enthusiastic [ac]ceptance of these facts renders it [cer]tain that the Single-Eight will d[omi]nate its own particular field j[ust] as unmistakably as does its c[om]panion car—the Packard Single-[

Furnished in Nine Distinguished Body Types, Open and Enclosed, at Prices Ranging from $3650 to $4950—at Detroit
Packard Single-Six Furnished in Eleven Popular Body Types, Open and Enclosed

236

which had by now become part of the motoring vernacular. But there was a rather quick corporate change of mind. Before the year was out the name had become Straight Eight in advertising, by February the Single Six quietly became the Packard Six and the bigger car the Packard Eight. However the latter was designated, it was an engine configuration which Packard would build into 1954, thirty-one years (excepting war's hiatus), a longevity exceeding that of any other manufacturer.

The new Packard was a very important car, and for reasons more than its motor. Eight in-line powerplants and four wheel brakes had been sub-

jects of considerable discussion in the trade press for some time. Both had been in use in Europe on expensive cars, Isotta Fraschini notably; in America the Duesenberg Model A had been introduced with such equipment. But prior to June of '23 no volume producer of motorcars had given both its stamp of approval. Packard was the first.

Pre-production testing of the car had been as rigorous as that accorded the Single Six—or as *Automobile Topics* reported, "a characteristic amount of preliminary work, so that, like all of [Packard's] productions, it may be set forth as a highly finished piece of engineering, refined to the

Below: Advertisement from September 1923; the Model 143 Touring Car with Winterfront (note finned brake drums); transverse section of the new Single Eight motor.

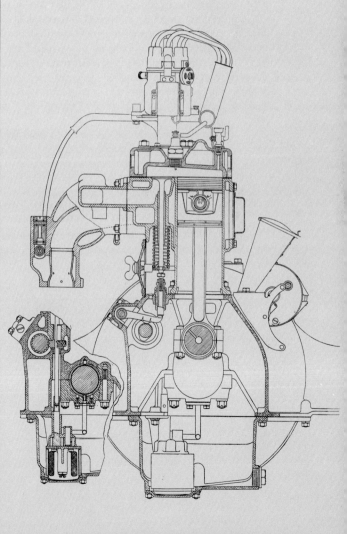

last detail." *The Packard* was more explicit: "Sand storms, rain storms, snow storms and more storms were regular parts of the diet handed out to the Single-Eight on its test trip through the west. . . . Packard engineers deliberately mapped out a route over the worst roads available. They had to do considerable charting and planning to locate them, but find them they did. [How things had changed since Tom Fetch, Old Pacific and the Packards of Warren! Now one could travel all the way from New York to Kansas on paved roads.] Then, adding insult to injury, they drove the new Packard over stretches which should have made Macadam turn in his grave, *all during the month of March*." Into Death Valley at seventy-five miles an hour ("The motometer's mercury scarcely showed the red . . ."); through 600 miles of mud and 300 of ruts ("Would the four wheel brake adjustments 'stay put,' they asked." They would.)—and on for 7000 miles of driving. At its end a test driver identified only as "Red"—a veteran of such wringing out for every new Packard since the Model Thirty—commented laconically, "My first tour." That said a lot.

The new Single Eight was an intelligent car, at once new and daring yet at the same time tried and steady. Much of it was identical to the Single Six, a manufacturing coup which eliminated duplication of many parts for assembly as well as repair. Very little new tooling was required—and production could be easily shifted from Eight to Six as dealer demand required. Manufacture of the Six had endured the shakedown trauma, much of that process was unnecessary for the Eight. Packard, naturally, did not point out the similarities between the two cars to the public, and many people assumed the Eight was heavier and of higher quality throughout because of its heftier price, $1375 more on most models.

The Single Eight surely looked bigger and more impressive than its companion car. It was ten inches lengthier, a 136-inch wheelbase com-

The Model 143 Custom Brougham by Brunn ordered by W.K. Jackson of Buffalo.

pared to 126, and 143 inches as opposed to 133 for the seven-passenger models. And those ten inches were all put in one place—the hood. It was astonishingly long—like a rifle barrel over which one sighted to guide the car. It signified lots of engine and speed and power. And it did not disappoint.

The straight-eight motor had the same general cross section as the six. Cylinders and pistons were the same size—3⅜ by 5 bore and stroke for a displacement of 357.8 cubic inches. The compression ratio was 4.51 to one. The engine developed 85 hp at 3000 rpm—considerable in those days—and did it smoothly via its nine-bearing construction, heavy balanced crankshaft and the Lanchester vibration damper fitted on the front end of the crankshaft. Large diameter main (2.37 inches) and crank pin (2.12 inches) journals minimized torsional deflection. On the shaft the cranks for pistons three, four, five and six were in a plane lying at a right angle to the plane of the cranks for one, two, seven and eight. Pistons initially were slotted aluminum alloy but reversion to cast iron (as in the Single Six) was made by December when aluminum was found to suffer from warpage, piston slap and wear. The engine was mounted in the frame at four points to mitigate the effect of torque reaction. Smoothness was the byword. And for a good and competitive reason.

Cadillac, with its V-8, had a characteristic vibration around 40 mph. With better roads now and consequent higher speeds as well as the greater number of closed cars which amplified and contained the drumming of motor impulses, this had become a negative sales factor for Cadillac.* And now here was the new Packard with a straight eight seemingly as silken as the Twin Six and styling which placed it among the handsomest cars on the road. An effective competitor, surely. Cadillac rushed its V-63 model for introduction in September 1923. Its engine had been redesigned with a two-plane counterbalanced crankshaft to eliminate much vibration. But it would take time to get that point across. Packard had the initial sales advantage.

Cadillac's V-63 also had four wheel brakes, incidentally. There had been a rush on the bandwagon after the Packard announcement: Rickenbacker first (that company having considered four wheel brakes when its first car was drawn up in 1919, but concluding the public wouldn't accept them), followed by Buick, then Oakland, then Cadillac. As announcements for their 1924 models were made, Marmon, Chalmers, Elgin, Paige, Locomobile and others joined in.

---

*The writer has immense respect for the engineering and construction of the V-8 Cadillac, having restored and driven a 1918 Model 57. But the periodic vibration was more than noticeable and carefully avoided by judging speed requirements to travel above or below the critical 40 mph speed. Such "babying" has never been necessary, however, in the writer's Packard Twin Six or Eight 243.

Still *MoToR* cautiously allowed in January of '24, "The next four months will tell the story of four wheel brakes in this country. January, February and March with their wintry weather and difficult driving conditions of roads will give [them] a test which the factories, even with their highly developed experimental and road organization, have been unable to give." Not every manufacturer was convinced of the worth of four wheel brakes. Studebaker ran full page ads stating it would not use them. Even Rolls-Royce was not above casting a slur on their effectiveness. It would be several years before the industry altogether had become assured that the four wheel brake was the only way to go—or, more accurately, to stop.

Packard was sure, at least by half. As vice-president of distribution Hills explained, "Four wheel brakes permit faster and safer driving speeds and acceleration by offering the factor of more rapid and more effective speed reduction. This is the reason we have adopted [them on the Single Eight], a car distinguished for its high speed range and power. On cars of relatively light weight and low speeds they are of less importance for actual safety in normal traffic, but they offer an important factor of safety in heavy traffic and on wet pavements. They are more costly and the public will decide whether the initial cost objection is to be overcome . . . thus far the company has not considered their use on the Single Six because of its lighter weight and lower speed range, conditions which make conventional brake types satisfactory." Words to be eaten soon.

But Hills was quite right in warning against poorly designed or cheap four wheel brake systems marketed without sufficient testing: "Types of brakes which under certain circumstances may interfere with steering, or which are susceptible to derangement, leaving the car without braking of any kind, offer dangerous possibilities to manufacturers, and might have the effect of discrediting the entire four wheel brake theory in the public mind. This can be avoided by careful analysis and by not attempting to go into four wheel brakes on a low price basis. Only good brakes can have a lasting place in the industry."

The system on the new Packard was a good one, as refined through that first model year. Initially, the brakes were mechanically operated internal expanding type, the circumferences of the drums on all four wheels finned (or "ribbed," as was said then). The service brake pedal operated a planetary gearset which stepped up the motion so the operating crank moved 90 degrees to a 26 degree movement of the pedal. Motion was transmitted through equalizing cables on sheaves. On the front, one end of the cable was attached to the operating arm for one wheel, the cable then was run back to a sheave on an arm at the end of a cross shaft and thence through the hollow cross shaft over a similar sheave on an arm at the other end, and then forward to the operating arm for the other wheel brake. The cross shaft was rotated by the brake pedal. A similar arrangement operated the rear brakes.

This system of cables on sheaves for equalizing both front to rear and also the pairs of wheels was changed in December 1923 to a more conventional system using T-arms equalizers. Apparently, the cables had not been flexible enough to give the actual free run over the sheaves that would be necessary to provide the theoretical equalization. The sheaves would bind with use and lack of lubrication, and the cables were subject to wear and fraying.

A stub shaft, with universal joints on each end, connected between the frame and the operating cam of the individual front brake. This shaft, which telescoped to compensate for relative movements of wheel and frame, carried an arm attached to the brake cable, which, when pulled, operated the cam inside the brake drum, and then the brake shoes. The hand brake operated the service brake shoes on the rear wheels only and, as was standard Packard practice, its lever was at the driver's left.

In December 1923 external contracting brake bands were added to the rear wheels, to be operated by the hand brake separate from the service brake. This eliminated the fins on the rear drums, so they were eliminated on the front as well. They would reappear in 1930, but on the Speedster only. (In those days it was thought the rear brake should do most of the work, at about a sixty to forty ratio. It would be many years before it was realized the front brakes should carry a heavier work load, particularly since inertia of the car threw more weight on the front wheels when braking, even when weight distribution was not concentrated over them as in today's practice.)

Four wheel brakes distinguished the new Packard from the original Single Six, of course, but although the general motor design and materials were the same in both cars, there were a number of differences which should be noted. The valve rocker levers were of the same layout but the cam follower was a boss located approximately in the center of the

Gilda Gray with her chauffeur and her new Model 143 Seven-Passenger Sedan.

lever, not a roller as on the 116. The inlet valves were of 1 5/8-inch diameter, while the exhaust valves were 1 1/2 inches. (In the Single Six both were the latter.)

Fuel supply was by a vacuum system from a rear-mounted tank, but a Stemco gasoline gauge was mounted on the instrument board, a rarity in those days; most gas gauges were located on the rear tank itself. Motor lubrication was full pressure. The water pump in the front of the cylinder block as in the Single Six 126-133 was retained although of larger capacity. A Motometer and a Winterfront with automatic thermostat-operated shutters were standard. There was also a sylphon thermostat in the water outlet in the motor head. The Winterfront, however, seemed superfluous so it was discontinued in December, and could be had only as an accessory. Such a device was popular for quicker warming up of the engine on cold winter days. But Packard's Fuelizer took care of that.

The company made another change early in Single Eight production.

Initially the car's radiator shells were of brass on both Six and Eight, an admirable base for nickel plating, but trouble was experienced in forming it into the sharp edges that were the Packard characteristic; the brass blank would split at the corners and necessitate brazing which was time consuming and often resulted in pin holes in the plating—and consequent rejection. Steel could be drawn to shape with no difficulty, so a new plating process was developed which resulted in "a coating of increased depth and greater hardness." The new steel shells were also copper plated prior to the nickel.

Generator and starter motor were made by Owen-Dyneto but were of the same general design as the Atwater Kent used on the Six. Ignition was Delco, as on the smaller car. The battery was mounted in a new and distinctive location—a box sunk into the right front fender. Its removable aluminum cover and this outside location away from heat proved most practical, and the feature was retained by Packard through 1932.

The Single Eight Model 136 Two/Four-Passenger Runabout, with rumble seat, golf bag compartment, pricetag of $3850—and that long Packard hood.

"Binding posts have been provided at the front of the dash to facilitate the removal of all wires and conduits when the body is removed," advised the Packard literature, this notation a holdover from the days, not distantly past, when a limousine body was exchanged for a phaeton at the appropriate season. Packard no longer quoted body prices for this purpose, however. The practical solution for those who could afford to change bodies was a second car—perhaps, Packard hoped, a Single Six.

Packard touted widely its new three-fold (three-bulb) system self-contained in the headlamps: one for town driving or parking, the second a diffused light that "offers no glare which gives enough light to permit of driving with safety up to 25 miles per hour," the third "designed for high speeds and for use on unfrequented roads . . . the beams of the powerful headlights [shooting] straight ahead." In truth, they weren't very good, and wouldn't be until the advent of sealed beams in the Forties. The headlamps themselves were large and cylindrical, more massive than the lamps on the Six which carried the Packard shape on the bezels. They were nicknamed by some "cake" lamps, as they reminded one of a three-layer iced birthday cake, placed on edge of course. More properly they were designated drum lamps. The Macbeth lenses were also distinctive, and after some years in the sun would turn that purple hue which glass bottles left in the desert acquire. (It is amusing today to note ads in the enthusiast magazines seeking these lenses, for restoration purposes, in "the original purple color.") A combination taillight and stoplight was standard equipment, Packard being among the first manufacturers to provide such. The stoplight switch was actuated by the brake pedal.

Though not generally realized, the gearset, clutch, the universal joints and the rear axles were the same on both Eight and Six. Wheels were demountable steel disc as standard on all Eights, using 33x5 rib tread tires on the front, nonskid on the rear. Wheel size was twenty-three inches. (The Single Six used a 33x4½ tire, giving the same outside diameter but necessitating a larger twenty-four-inch wheel. The question is now often asked why the Six, a shorter car, would have a larger wheel. The same outside diameter allows the same road clearance—ten inches—gear ratios and other proportions throughout. Even the springs were the same sizes on both cars.) Balloon tires, 33x6.75 on twenty-one-inch rims, were offered at "reasonable extra cost" in December. Watson stabilizers were used as rebound absorbers front and rear.

Among the attention-garnering features of the new car were the front and rear bumpers, provided as standard and mounted on brackets which were forged integral with the front and rear spring hangers. Conceivably, this also was a Packard first. Most automobiles were not given bumpers at the factory, though dealers would try to sell at least a front one as an accessory, mounting it by drilling holes in the frame—often disastrous—or by "universal" clamps—a makeshift arrangement at best. The bumper Packard supplied on the Eight (all Six advertising illustrations showed no bumpers of any kind) was a steel channel, mounted on spring steel back bars. It was simple, did not detract from the lines of the car and was usually painted black, as the chassis, though an occasional nickeled one could be seen. In December the conventional two-bar bumper replaced it; the new style had a partial facing of nickeled brass bands and was to continue through 1929.

The comparative worthiness of bumpers in those pre-government-crash-test-legislation days was not, however, a subject of much discussion. Other matters weighed heavier, most particularly the factor of seeing where one was going or, conversely, what was coming. Reflections in the windshield of lights from the rear were troublesome, especially since headlights were so dim. Slanted windshields were widely advocated. Though usual on open cars, these were difficult on closed types because of the location of door hinges on the windshield post. (It would be a decade or so before extended or offset hinges, hidden in thick body side panels, would come into prominence.) Some closed cars had triangular glass panes to fill in between windshield post and door frame, but these were expensive and, some thought, cluttered in appearance. Packard clung to the vertical windshield on closed models and said nothing about it. Almost all closed cars, even Fords, had roller shades on the rear window at least, ostensibly to eliminate reflections but also a guarantor of privacy when desired while parked.

One purportedly learned discussion—published in *Automotive Industries* in July 1924—advocated a "vision slot" as an improvement to allow a driver to see "a sufficient stretch of the road ahead of the car without being seriously annoyed by rain, snow or cold air. This slot is obtained by dividing the glass horizontally and tilting the upper plate slightly forward." This was balderdash, of course; we know now—and most drivers discovered then—that the divided windshield always leaked in the rain (whether the upper panel was open or closed) and it certainly was not wise to depend upon seeing through the aforementioned slot in inclement weather. Nevertheless, Packard employed this type of windshield but, perhaps itself questioning its efficacy, never bothered to suggest the reason why. And Packard did provide as standard equipment a built-in windshield wiper. It was hand operated, but still better than rubbing plug tobacco on the windshield to get a glycerine coating, or opening the glass that inch at the horizontal division to get an eyeful of rain along with the view. Vacuum operated or electric wipers were on the market already, but Packard objected to them, as did a lot of others, reasoning that they were distracting, possibly hypnotic and thus a potential cause of accidents.

Packard had determined, however, that seeing behind was a pretty good idea. A rear-view mirror—center mounted interior type—was standard. Standard too, on the Eight, and a real boon, was the power tire pump, mounted at the transmission, actuated by turning a slotted head control in the floorboard, the hose connected to a stem protruding through the left splash apron. The rear-mounted spare wheel was clamped, through the center hole, between the carrier and a screw cover operated by a T-shaped handle in which was fitted a barrel lock. Gone was the receptacle carrier with hold-down straps of old, and no longer available either was a side-mounted spare, though an extension could be had for a second rear-mounted spare.

Bodies, styles and prices for the new Single Eight were as follows:

On the 136-inch wheelbase	Body No.	Price
Touring Car (5)	244	$3650
Runabout (2-4)	234	$3850
Sport Model (4)	246	$3800
Coupe (4)	239	$4550
Coupe (5)	242	$4725
Sedan (5)	237	$4650
Sedan-Limousine (5)	243	$4700
On the 143-inch wheelbase		
Touring Car (7)	245	$3850
Sedan (7)	240	$4900
Sedan-Limousine (7)	241	$4950

Coachwork was the same as the corresponding styles in the Single Six line—but the trim and upholstery were considerably more elaborate. Closed car interiors were in grey-blue broadcloth, with widelace trim, more braids and welting, fancy arm rests, gathered front door pockets, even shirred-front seat cushions. The hardware was more grandiose. There were vanity cases and smoking sets. Deeper pile carpets. The open cars had brown, hand crushed Spanish leather upholstering, instead of the black, long grain of the Single Six. The Packard Single Eight was, in a word, luxurious.

Closed models were painted Packard Blue striped with Twentieth Century Red Medium. Fenders, chassis and the body above the belt were black. In December the striping was changed to azure blue. Open models were completed in Dust Proof Gray deep, striped in Extra Permanent Vermillion with the striping on wheels and bonnet louvers edged in black. Again, fenders and chassis were black. The Sport Model, introduced in December, was the gray in a lighter shade, with disc wheels in the vermillion. Dust Proof Gray, incidentally, was exactly that, a brownish gray which actually did mask the road dust of which there was considerable in those days. It was a sophisticated off-color, strikingly in contrast to the reds and yellows of most sport cars, and a forerunner of the earthy tans, greens and blues of the classic era.

The Runabout now had a rumble seat, upholstered in leather, and the ubiquitous golf bag compartment. The lines of the Eight Runabout were

the same as those of the Six—but that long hood made a big difference.

So did the car itself—on Packard's financial picture. The company's fiscal year ended August 31st, 1923, a little more than two months after the introduction of the Single Eight. Packard sales had peaked at 21,571 vehicles, compared to 14,420 from the fiscal year previous, and, with trucks, aviation and marine engines, parts, et al. included, totaled $55,-670,464. Net profit was $7,081,875—or an eye-popping 12.72 percent of gross! In his annual report to stockholders, Alvan Macauley said in part: "The working efficiency of this organization is indicated by the fact that with very little increase in plant investment the company has been able to develop and perfect the straight-eight; to successfully introduce it upon the market; to get it into full production, and to produce the greatest number of vehicles in the company's history." It was quite an achievement.

New owners of the Single Eight were convinced the car was too: "My 'dream car' is the name I have given it because during my twenty-seven years' association with the automobile, I fancied and dreamed of such a car . . ." was the word from Chicago. "I have been driving the best that Europe and America produce in the way of motor cars for nearly fifteen years, and I know of nothing which even remotely approaches the performance of the Packard Eight" from New York City. "A gondola on a Venetian canal would hardly glide along any smoother, nor more graceful, nor much less cheaply than this car has done" from Kansas City. "To say that the Packard Eight is the car supreme is putting it mildly, as it is beyond my expectations in every way" from Los Angeles. Packard, naturally, took promotional advantage of such testimonials and for those who might remain unconvinced, the company inaugurated a rather novel selling idea during the summer of '24, "full size, best quality" phonograph records available to prospective customers with encouraging words being heard from Colonel Vincent, "Doc" Hills, E.F. Roberts and general service manager H.N. Davock. "Technical subjects have been avoided in all of the talks and every effort was made to make the records as interesting as possible. There are 22,000,000 phonographs in America and it was considered by officers of the Company that everyone who drives a motor car owns a phonograph." A reasonable assumption.

As noted, there had been a number of changes in the new Single Eight in the six months from its introduction to December of 1923. But to have called the car a new model at Christmas would have reflected unfavorably on its predecessor of June. So Packard didn't, incorporating the improvements but not referring to them as such. That was fine for the Single Eight. But the Single Six had been around since April of '22, about twenty months, and a new model was called for. Even clamored. It had by now become exceedingly difficult for Packard dealers to explain away the absence of four wheel brakes on the Six.

Dealers had been besieging the company for them, and in December of 1923 got them—front wheel brakes on the new 226-233 Packard Single Six.

Austin Bement and the Model 226 "official Lincoln Highway Packard" photographed on the "ideal section" in Lake County, Indiana in June of 1924.

The Cadillac V-63 had them, as we've seen, as did a number of other cars, most significantly the new Buick, and it was a solid hit. Its promotion had been masterfully executed with "teaser ads" and aided-and-abetted word of mouth, all before any photographs of the new car were released in August of 1923. When the car arrived, more than a million people visited Buick showrooms for a look. It had four wheel brakes, rounded rear roof lines—and it looked rather like a Packard, unmistakably . . . and with a pricetag about twelve hundred dollars less than the subject of its imitation. Packard salesmen were distraught. It was not so much the price differential—prestige took care of that. But the men of Packard had been placed in a very ambiguous position. At Studebaker, for example, the company gambit could be simply that four wheel brakes were dangerous. Packard could scarcely say that.

And so there was a collective sigh of relief—from 798 Packard distributors, an increase of nearly a hundred over the year previous—when the new 226-233 Packard Single Six was announced in December of 1923, with four wheel brakes. Five months of possible competition with the lower-priced Buick had been quite enough, thank you.

The industry—and Packard—had another contender, however, introduced that same month. It was called a Chrysler, and initially most people had trouble pronouncing the name. (Billboards phoneticized it a while.) Walter Percy Chrysler was well known in the industry, as the former manager of Buick, rebuilder of Willys-Overland and reorganizer of Maxwell-Chalmers. Now he had a car of his own, courtesy of (among others) Fred Zeder, Owen Skelton and Carl Breer. Its appearance fell into the public liking and its performance was the envy of the industry. It was called the Chrysler 70 because that figure was the speed at which it would travel with ease. It had balloon tires to make the ride smooth while doing so, and four wheel hydraulic brakes to bring it to a stop. It was a small, handy car with enough class to gather plenty of sales in the Buick price range—and possibly the Packard's as well. The idea of performance which the Chrysler represented gave it a cachet which would make it an attractive proposition for the well-to-do automobile purchaser, if not as a first car then as a second or third. (Interestingly, here was a smallish car—no seven-passenger model yet available—which would prove a considerable success. Three years previous the Packard 116, possessing many of the same attributes, was a resounding flop.)

The Chrysler diversion, as well as the Buick's, was good for the people at East Grand Boulevard. Though a price class removed, the cars did have the effect of disallowing Packard the comfort of complacency. And the company did have a tendency to be less then venturesome, this the result probably of its venerable position within the industry—and the fact that imitation of Packard, as it was, was quite widespread.

One didn't have to look very far to find it. Late in 1924 the Ambassador Drive It Yourself sedan, manufactured by the Yellow Cab Manufacturing Company, appeared with a radiator much like the Buick's—which meant, of course, like the Packard's. (This car later became better known as the Hertz.) In 1925 the Star, Billy Durant's contender for the Chevrolet market, and in 1926 the Flint Junior Six, also a Durant product, affected the Packard shape, with discreet modifications. The most blatant copying came from the Dagmar of 1922-1924, manufactured by the Crawford Automobile Company of Hagerstown, Maryland. Except for a decided narrowing, both exterior and interior contours of the radiator shell followed Packard's, angle for angle, curve for curve. The Dagmar adopted the red hex in the hubcap, too, though this was soon discontinued when Packard's legal department gently advised that it was a registered trademark. Very few Dagmars were made. The reigning Miss America for 1924 was presented with a yellow roadster by her Philadelphia sponsors. Most onlookers thought it was a special-built Packard.

More talk and rumor resulted from the Buick plagiarism, however. In May of 1924 that firm found it necessary to make an official statement—without mentioning Packard by name, of course—that any purported lawsuit for design infringement was pure poppycock. Which it was, by then. In truth, Packard patent counsel Milton Tibbetts did consider a suit, but management decided against it, preferring the flattery of imitation. Alvan Macauley had a heightened sense of noblesse oblige.

And the situation too provided a rather effective selling point, as witness an advertisement first published in October of 1924, and repeated the following year in *National Geographic*:

The Packard you buy today will not
look out of date in 1935

unless Packard is successful in doing

that which others have been unable
to do—

improve on Packard lines.

If the industry, competing within
itself, has been unable to improve
on Packard lines

but rather, has appropriated them,

then, Packard has set an enduring
style.

And, in an enduring style your motor
car investment is best protected.

Furthermore, the episode evoked a slogan used in Packard advertising

Frank McKinney in the 226 Sport Model admiring the view along the same road.

for many months, usually composed in a distinctive circle: "Only Packard can build a Packard."

The changes and improvements which characterized the 226-233 six-cylinder car which Packard was building now were the same as corresponding features of the Packard Eight. This model of the Six was in the nature of a half step to get it and the Eight marching along together. At the next changeover—February of 1925—new models of both the Six and Eight would be announced at the same time, as they would be from then on. And improvements and changes would generally be common to both. The new Six retained the admired characteristics of its predecessor, and practically the same appearance. The big difference, of course, was its borrowing of the Eight's four wheel braking system. (The Six used the revised system; none were built with the unsatisfactory cable layout of the early Eights 136-143.)

Other than the length of hood, the visual contrast between the Six and Eight was had in the wheels, wood spoked for the former, steel disc for the latter. The new Sport Model Six, however, still retained the disc wheels of its predecessor. In addition to cost, and the wish by management for a small but obvious difference between Six and Eight, the reason for staying with wood wheels on the Six could have been the noise factor. A six-cylinder engine has more noticeable impulses than an eight, setting

The Single Six Model 226 Four-Passenger Coupe and the Model 233 Seven-Passenger Sedan, which sold for $2585 and $2785 after the price reductions.

up a drumming, a reverberation, in a closed car that could be disagreeable and which was increased by the rigidity of the wheels. Pavement or road noises were also transmitted to the car more readily through disc wheels than the more resilient wood, especially as tires were still high pressure narrow 4½-inch cords. In an open car, as the Sport Model, the noise factor was not particularly apparent. A prevalent idea—call it a superstition—also held that heavy disc wheels had a gyroscopic action that not only hindered braking but also made it difficult to steer. The popular toy gyroscopes easily demonstrated how this notion came about. Though the principle did pertain, the actual effect was negligible. More important was the greater unsprung weight which made for a harder ride with high pressure tires.

Other points of change for the new Six were a gasoline gauge on the instrument panel, a tonneau light in the open cars, vanity case and smoking set in closed cars, a windshield cleaner and rear-view mirror in both, a stop signal built in with the taillight, a battery box inserted into the right front fender. Easier steering was provided by ball bearing steering knuckles and a larger eighteen-inch steering wheel. The new Runabout model followed the successful rumble-seat/golf-bag-compartment design of the Eight Runabout, its color remaining dark blue.

Operating economy of the Six was emphasized in all Packard literature, "16 to 18 and even 20 or more miles to the gallon of gasoline, 15,000 to 20,000 miles or more to a set of tires, 500 or more to a gallon of motor oil and, with all this . . . a comparative freedom from adjustment and repairs that is a revelation." It was not overstatement.

Prices were a hundred dollars higher on each model, said to cover the four wheel brake addition. The Runabout's rumble seat put that model's pricetag up three hundred dollars.

Nineteen twenty-four turned out to be a slow year for the automobile industry, and Packard was not excluded. Only 9,505 Sixes were built

during the calendar year, compared to 15,900 the annum previous. (Foreign sales were up, however, twenty-five Packards sold in France during a three-month period ending November 1924 was a distinct improvement over the mere one during the corresponding period the year previous, and fifty-eight Packards found their way into German hands as well—most of these European sales being the Eights.) Packard's net profit for the fiscal year ending August 31st declined to $4,805,174 (from the previous year's $7 million), total sales to $46,003,679 (from the previous $55.7 million). But the last quarter of 1924 had been one of the best in Packard's history, with earnings of $1,872,753. To Alvan Macauley, this indicated good times ahead again. And he celebrated with a price cut. The comparative pricetags, for the December 1923 introduction and the January 1925 reduction, were as follows:

Model 226	Body No	12-27-23	1-2-25	Decrease
Touring Car (5)	220	$2585	$2585	—
Runabout (2-4)	223	$2785	$2785	—
Sport Model (4)	224	$2750	$2750	—
Coupe (4)	222	$3275	$2585	$690
Coupe (5)	230	$3450	$2685	$765
Sedan (5)	221	$3375	$2585	$790
Sedan-Limousine (5)	231	$3425	$2785	$640
Sedan, Touring (5)	232	$2850	Discontinued	
Model 233				
Sedan (7)	228	$3625	$2785	$840
Sedan-Limousine (7)	229	$3675	$2885	$790
Touring Car (7)	225	$2785	$2785	—

These price reductions came at the time of the New York Automobile Show in January 1925, just a month before the introduction of the Third Series cars, and their enactment might have been assumed a clearing-out-the-stock-on-hand maneuver. Such was not the case, however, as the new prices would remain in effect for more than two years.

In the board meeting of April 16th, 1924 Alvan Macauley had "brought up for discussion the future of the Six requesting the board to suggest any policy to revise or improve it in any way." No one could think of a thing. Packard's president sailed on the *Homeric* the month following to look over the company's export business, now up to about $4,000,000 a year, and returned a few weeks later on the *Majestic* convinced that, domestically, "what we really want to do is sell enough of the Packard Sixes to make it possible, through reduced prices, for more people to own them." He convinced management too—and the result had been the Packard price reduction surprise, "one of the most talked-about developments in the present status of the industry," the press said—and one that would provide Alvan Macauley the pleasure, as early as the board meeting of January 5th, of displaying a hefty pile of telegrams from distributors and dealers ordering trainloads of the cars.

With reduced closed car prices it was no longer desirable to produce the Permanent Top Touring Sedan which had merely been an expedient anyway. By now Packard had developed elaborate steel jigs for assembling wood body frames accurately. This saved time and cost not only in that operation but also allowed body panels, hardware, instrument board and other assemblies to be placed without adjustment or hand fitting. Packard had been making most of its own closed bodies since the truck manufacturing area became available.

The open car had become the luxury speciality rather than the backbone of the line during the three years thus far of the Single Six. Packard recognized that it was fast disappearing from the scene, and perhaps wistfully was rather sorry to see it depart. "Sedans may come, limousines go, coupes roll on forever, but for the zest of the Open Road the Open Car beats all comers," *The Packard* rhapsodized in telling of the fleet of five roadsters and Sport Models owned by one Charles G. Rupert of Wilmington, Delaware. Price reductions weren't necessary on open cars; those who still desired them would pay whatever the price. The potential for greater sales lay obviously in lower-priced closed cars. Packard was sure of it.

So, for that matter, was Cadillac. At that same New York show in January, it had announced a new coach model, a two-door sedan with spartan trim, for $3185, the same price as Cadillac open cars. The idea, of course, was to undersell the Packard Six Coupe at $3275. But Packard's surprise price cut on all its closed cars would effectively take the wind out of Cadillac's sales.

By now Cadillac could but be aware that Packard was and would remain its principal competitor. Packard had no doubt. During Twin Six days, this had not been the case, with, for example, the Cadillac Type 55 seven-passenger touring at $2080 and the Packard 3-25 at $3700. But

The Single Six Model 233 Sedan-Limousine, featuring the optional disc wheels.

with the introduction of the Single Six in 1920, and especially the 126-133 Six in 1922, the picture changed. Then a Packard five-passenger touring could be had for $2485, as compared to the Cadillac's $3150. The latter's salesmen adopted the stance that the two cars were not competitive; the one a six, the other a V-8, the Cadillac assuredly a notch or two above the Single Six. Actually this was not entirely the case, particularly with the revised Single Six and its pace-setting styling in striking contrast to the Cadillac's somewhat stodgy look. And too there was the burgeoning preference for closed cars. A Packard five-passenger sedan at $3275 was an attractive proposition over a Cadillac touring car at $3150. (The Cadillac sedan listed at $4100.) There could be a reverse twist to this too—some customers preferring to "make do" with a Twin Six touring car at $3800, being warmed by prestige in the cold weather, rather than being enclosed in a Cadillac sedan at the aforementioned forty-one hundred dollars. With the advent of the Single Eight in 1923, the competition would become even more keen.

It is interesting to compare Cadillac and Packard passenger car production figures during this period, to wit:

Year	Cadillac Production	Packard Production
1921	11,130	7,684
1922	22,021	15,377
1923	22,009	18,897
1924	17,748	15,098
1925	22,542	32,027
1926	27,340	34,391

The figures reflect several things. First, Packard's disappointing Model 116 Single Six venture. Second, the slump overall in 1924. And third, the indisputable fact that Packard was really going places now.

CHAPTER TWELVE

CARRYING PRIDE
WITH APLOMB

The Six Model 326-333, The Eight Model 236-243
February 1925-August 1926
The Six Model 426-433, The Eight Model 336-343
August 1926-July 1927

AUTHOR: L. MORGAN YOST

New models of both Packard Six and Eight began coming through to dealers in early 1925. Factory records indicate the Six 326-333 and the Eight 236-243 were priced with an effective date of February 2nd, 1925—but advertising made no mention of it. February was just a month after the price cut announcement on Six closed models—and at that time it had been reported there would be no changes in Packard cars save for a redesign of the steering gear from worm and nut to worm and sector for the Eight, "which change was made in the interest of easier and more positive steering." And also, one might suspect, to make one more item standard to both cars for economy and efficiency of production.

Nor were Packard stockholders apprised of the new models. In an almost complacently confident letter to all 7174 of them in January, Alvan Macauley advised as to the reasons for the price cut, the "refined and perfected" status of the Six which would render unnecessary for some time to come any change in its appearance or fundamentals, and the "more advantageous production situation" Packard now enjoyed. There was no way a stockholder sitting in his living room in Paducah could assume that the Packards rolling out of the factory a month later would be new models. *Sotto voce* was a Packard tradition.

There might have been a practical reason for Packard's silence now, however. The new models weren't advertised simply because the factory was already overloaded,* and management deemed it appropriate to hold its surprise for use in a possible later lull. But such a lull, it would turn out, would not occur for several years.

On March 11th the company did make one announcement: price increases of $100 to $150 on the Eights. It was somewhat enigmatic that the standardization of body production that had brought such dramatic price cuts to the Six line would not carry over to the Eight which used the same bodies save for trim. The Eight Five-Passenger Sedan at $4750 was $2165 more than the corresponding body style in the Six. There were too many identical parts, too many identical manufacturing operations, too many similar costs, to make logical the great difference in price. But practical logic had nothing to do with it. The difference wasn't a rational one. Doubtless purchasers of the Six wanted the Eight to be significantly more costly; it reflected well on them. Buyers in the Eight's realm couldn't have cared less about pricetags. That car's longer wheelbase, larger engine and greater resulting weight did make for a discernible difference in comfort and performance. And there was that long, long hood. And the aura of top-of-the-line Packard. Packard preferred not talking about prices anyway, at least in its advertising—it's a rare ad that deigned to give them. It was the Age of Ballyhoo, but that wasn't Packard's image.

No longer promoting that image, however, would be MacManus, Inc. Packard's advertising agency since 1921 asked to be released from its contract to reconnect with Cadillac. Alvan Macauley was amenable. Disappointed that Theodore MacManus hadn't written more of the Packard ads personally, he took the opportunity of a friendly separation to encourage his friend Austin F. Bement to form an agency with Packard as its client. Bement, who had been executive vice-president of the Lincoln Highway Association in which Macauley and Henry Joy had long been interested, brought with him E.J. Evans, the vice-president of Bassick-Alemite and a founder of the highway group.

The summer before, these two men had driven a 226 Packard Sport Model from Winnipeg to Victoria, British Columbia, over roadless terrain, using railroad tracks through tunnels and trestles for sixty-three miles of the seventeen hundred for the projected Canadian Highway. There had been a standing offer for fourteen years, a gold medal to be won by anyone accomplishing the first motor trip across western Canada, and Bement and Evans blazed the trail. They then presented the medal to Macauley for the Packard Hall of Fame. They had the

*Interestingly, "Doc" Hills—from his pleasant vantage within a company where the overload was at the factory—came out very forcefully in mid-January about the industry practice of overstocking. "Motor car dealers and distributors through their organizations and individually have been making so strenuous a protest against the system of manufacturers loading them up with cars during low selling periods that results are in sight," Hills said. "At least promises are being made that it will not be done again." He was optimistic. But as any student of motoring history during the Twenties knows, those promises were, oft as not, ill kept.

Packard background, they were a perfect choice for Packard advertising.

The first Bement advertisement appeared in *The Saturday Evening Post* on March 7th, 1925. It included an illustration of the new 326-333 car and a good deal of nostalgic name-dropping of great Packard models past, but didn't bother to designate the Packard model being advertised nor its new features. That would await the *Post* ad of June 13th and the *National Geographic* (and other consumer magazines) for July—six months after the models had come into being!—and even then the advertisement seemed to be daring the reader to pick out the salient points in a veritable sea of copy. "Words . . . so full of subtle flame," as Francis Beaumont had said several centuries before.

Still, despite Packard's reluctance to talk about them, the changes were significant. First was the Bijur chassis lubrication system, which was soon to be adopted by several other automobile manufacturers. A detailed description of it had appeared in *Automotive Industries* of February 12th, 1925, together with illustrations which anyone in the know would have recognized as the application drawings for the Packard chassis, though no mention of Packard was made. Essentially, the Bijur system consisted of an oil reservoir with a single stroke hand pump forcing oil through a system of copper tubing to the various chassis points requiring periodic lubrication. The distinctive feature of the Bijur over other systems then available was the use of metering fittings at the outlets to control the amount of oil each lubricated point received. And too, its inventor, Joseph Bijur—lately of an automotive electrics business which had supplied ignition and starter-generator systems to Packard among others—used the device of brass tubing coils to bridge from axles and

Pages preceding: General Billy Mitchell in his Packard Eight 236 Sport Model. On these pages, the Third Series Packard Six, introduced with the Second Series Eight in February 1925. Above: Model 333 Convertible Coupe with body by Dietrich. Below from the left: Model 326 Five-Passenger Coupe, Model 333 Club Sedan and 333 Four-Passenger Sedan with body by Dietrich.

Second Series Packard Eights. Above left: Model 236 Runabout. Above right: 236 Holbrook Coupe and 243 Dietrich Convertible Coupe, each a Series Custom car. Below left: Model 243 Four-Passenger Sedan, a Series Custom by Dietrich. Below right: Model 243 with special custom-built coachwork by Willoughby.

springs to the frame and elsewhere where relative motion had to be considered.

At first forty-five points were lubricated by the Bijur but this was down to thirty by April 1926 through consolidation and simplification. Among other factors, the drive torque arm to the rear axle was then eliminated as improvements in steel springs were sufficient to convince Colonel Vincent that he could now go with Hotchkiss drive.

The Bijur system probably got its biggest boost—and Packard took happy promotional fact of it—through Lieutenant Leigh Wade, he of round-the-world flying fame, who with his personal Packard Eight Seven-Passenger Touring Car and colleague Linton Wells, trekked from Los Angeles to New York City "without once allowing either the motor or the car to come to a stop." Since Wade, with A.A.A. sanction for the trip, agreed to observe all laws "except when under police escort," one assumes he did halt whenever one of the few stop signs told him to. Still, such a trip was a first, it was said, and had been possible only with a Packard, Wade averred, because of the car's "mere pull of a plunger" lubrication—and the fact that not once did the oil have to be changed.

Which brings us to the Skinner Oil Rectifier, an idea patented by one R.S. Skinner. It has often been assumed that it was merely a still, heated by the exhaust manifold, which vaporized the gasoline and water out of the crankcase oil. The word "rectifier" inferred that the oil was made right after it had gone wrong. Actually the operation was more preventive than curing.

The owners manuals are ambiguous in that they advise that "the oil rectifier is designed to maintain the viscosity of the [oil] by a process of distillation. . . ." But what it was really designed to do was draw off raw gasoline and waters of combustion, which would otherwise pass down the cylinder wall, before they got into the crankcase to dilute the oil. Likewise it would draw off oil which would pass up the cylinder wall, on its way to the combustion chamber, before it could get that far. These were most desirable functions. But apparently Skinner had not quite perfected his idea. The Rickenbacker company which had introduced the device in May of '24 had a bushel of troubles with it. As B.F. Capwell, who handled Rickenbacker sales in New York, recalled: "The principle was fine, but the float valve that was supposed to open and return the rectified oil to the crankcase would sometimes carbon up and stick. At those times everything went into the intake manifold and you laid a smoke screen all over town!. . . Sometimes a sharp blow to the side of the tank would do the trick but more often it wouldn't." The engineers at East Grand Boulevard would have second thoughts about the Skinner Oil Rectifier too, despite Leigh Wade's enthusiastic endorsement.

Packard was much more successful in another area. For years front wheel wobble had plagued motorists. Better known as shimmying, after a popular vibratory dance of the time, the immediate remedy, performed

Custom-built Seven-Passenger Stationary Town Cabriolet on a 243 chassis.

at first symptom, was to yank the steering wheel hard to one side. If the steering mechanism was worn, the only relief might be to stop the car and start all over again. Balloon tires, being less firm and with a tendency to give with the bounce of the car, created a wobble of somewhat different characteristics. Colonel Vincent had noticed that if the front end of a standing car was bounced up and down, the steering wheel would oscillate. Customarily, front springs were anchored at the front, with the shackle at the rear, allowing fore-and-aft give when the spring flexed and flattened. The motion of the front axle, then, was in a segment of a circle with the front spring anchor as a center. But the steering drag link had its center at the lower end of the steering gear arm close to the rear spring mount, its front end performing a segment of a circle opposite to that of the axle. The difference in the geometry of the two circle segments was taken up in the steering knuckle lever, causing the front wheels to be deflected from side to side with every bounce. Hence the shimmy.

Packard fixed that by locating the fixed end of the front springs at their rear end close to the end of the steering gear arm to make the two circular paths coincide, or nearly so. This both mitigated the shimmy and resulted in less "wheel fight" when driving rough roads. As part of the revision of the front suspension, the axle was mounted atop the springs; that is, the springs were underslung. Thus the main spring leaf was connected direct to the axle for a more positive relationship with less chance for shifting or unsteadiness. The former axle had been a drop center type, this one was in the shape of a shallow vee.

Balloon tires and disc wheels came together, the first allowing the second. Wire wheels were not in the picture; discs were *au courant*, the modern look. They were Budd-Michelin "All Steel" type. Interestingly, Packard did not then do what General Motors and others did—provide natural finish wood wheels, especially on sporty models. Their bigger tires and resultingly smaller wheels, with fatter, stubbier spokes, gave an appearance quite different from the spindly wood-spoked wheels of the type Packard was abandoning. Yet Packard was to use no more wood until offered as an option on the Sixth Series models for 1929.

Double bar bumpers front and rear were standard equipment on both Six and Eight, mounted on perches or pads integral with the frame. This feature, plus the revised suspension, called for a new frame design, now with side members eight inches in depth. Cross members were more firmly connected, and now motor supports had four bolts each instead of the former two. All in all, this new Packard was a considerably more substantial car—which was saying something.

The bore of the Six motor was increased to three and a half inches, for a displacement of 288.6 cubic inches. The N.A.C.C. horsepower rating was now 29.40, effectively under the 30.0 figure where license rates in many states jumped. Developed horsepower of the Six was now up to a solid eighty.

The crankshaft bearings of the Six were enlarged to be the same diameter as the Eight, the mains 2⅜ and the crank pins 2⅛ inches. There were crankshaft counterweights at the center and end bearings, and the crankshaft was no longer rifle-drilled but each main supplied oil by a tubing manifold in the crankcase thence through drillings to the crankpin bearings.

The cam rocker levers, so characteristic to the Packard motor, were revised to provide a roller as a cam follower. Such a roller had been used in the first 116 Sixes but in succeeding models had been changed to a boss which had sliding contact with the cam. Concern with cam wear had brought the roller back, larger, and set into a cast rocker lever. The camshaft was larger too. Mid-model the levers were changed to a formed sheet metal design which was lighter and more economical to produce.

Bodies from the preceding models were continued with no appreciable change, even in color—but there were more of them. The Club Sedan for one, a four-door, close coupled car with no rear quarter window but a separate fitted trunk on the rear platform deck. Mounted on the 133-inch Six or the 143-inch Eight chassis, and priced respectively at $2725 and $4890, these Club Sedans were the only five-passenger bodies, other than custom cars, to be mounted on the longer wheelbases—and were the result of a public demand for a more distinctive sedan seating five. The result was a sporty look, and the new model proved popular.

Even more distinctive was a coupe by Holbrook. First offered only on the Eight, it had the "Holbrook" windshield, the lower half sloping forward, the upper half sloping back, the corner post of the bottom section extending up and forward to support the front corners of the visor. This was the only custom-bodied car priced and listed in the factory specifications—at $5775—a trial balloon lofted by Packard to test the idea of merchandising custom cars.

Packard black and white advertisement from the March 1925 issue of **House & Ga**

(Color advertising from this period is featured in the Appendices art portfolio.) A Series Custom Eight 243 Stationary Town Cabriolet by Dietrich.

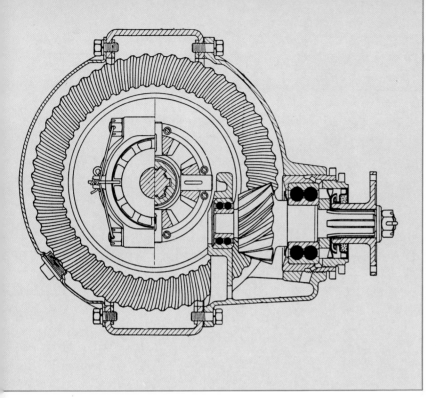

Vertical section through differential and hypoid gears of new Packard axle.

A new Four-Passenger Coupe was also introduced, on the 126- and 136-inch wheelbases, its difference from the other such coupe already in the lineup being that the integral rear deck compartment was truncated for a trunk—a separate one, that is—on a platform as on the Club Sedan. Whether the former body style was discontinued at the introduction of the new one, we know not. We do know the new style was not continued into the next model, and the old one came back (if indeed it ever went away). The new Coupe was shown in folders issued later in the model year to the exclusion of the older type—but this writer has never seen one in the flesh, nor in photographs, and it appears Packard might better have called it the Chimerical Coupe. Chimerical or no, it should not be confused, however, with the *Five*-Passenger Coupe already in the line, which was arranged like the typical two-door coach of the day.

Packard had, traditionally if reluctantly, always made special colors available to those who insisted. Now the company loosened up a bit more. In July and August of 1925, full-page Packard advertising offered "Your Choice of Color and Upholstery" on the Eight: There were two options, "First—to select from numerous combinations, artistically created and ready for early delivery [and] Second—to specify anything obtainable in beautiful colors and fine fabrics with due allowance for the time necessary to produce . . . . Packard feels complimented that the great majority are pleased to take the Packard Eight in standard paint and trim, but realizes there are always those who want the unusual." And there were more of them now too.

A body finish that would last more than a season or two had long been desired. It came, a du Pont development called Duco, a pyroxylin lacquer introduced on the General Motors Oakland of 1924. It was sprayed on, dried almost instantaneously and reduced the painting process to a few hours rather than many days. It would not check or craze or dull as varnish finishes always did. If it became oxidized or dull in the weather, it could be polished to original brightness or better. If such polishing wore through the color surface, it could be resprayed over the old, after a rubbing, without the necessity of removing the old paint down to bare metal. It seemed almost too good to be true. And, most important, lacquer brought with it a phenomenal color range.

Packard tread cautiously at first. Its option plan was appropriately greater in cost, and the option available only on the Eight. Some customers, admiring the special color jobs on showroom floors, were chagrined to find they would have to dip into their purses to pay for something similar. There was a genteel revolt against the staid, even common, blue paint on the Packard closed cars and a criticism of the standard, time worn, Dust Proof Gray on the open versions. "Look at Buick!" cried Packard prospects. "Why can't the Packard Six look as classy as a Buick? It costs a lot more."

They certainly had a point, and it was well taken by Packard. In 1926 the company went to lacquer generally, and in January of that year new set of standard color schemes was adopted. Two-tone combinations had become popular, especially on open cars, which now were generally of the sporting variety. Packard featured such schemes on all its models, save for the Seven-Passenger Touring which remained Dust Proof Gray and scarcely a sporting car. The Phaeton and Runabout (the beautiful Sport Model had been dropped about this time) were Plymouth Gray (darker) above the belt line, Pilgrim Gray (lighter) below and on the wheels; the striping was Flamingo Carmine, with fenders and aprons black. Closed cars, which had not the raised belt line lending itself to two-toning, were Westminster Gray striped with Ivory White, with body above the belt black as were fenders and aprons. The result in both cases was dignified and aesthetically appealing, and gave Packard a new look distinguishable from the ubiquitous Dust Proof Gray and blue of yore.

The standard line of Packard bodies was generally considered to be handsome and in fulsome good taste. The body engineer in charge was Archer L. Knapp, though Alvan Macauley and Jesse Vincent were frequent, and welcome, kibitzers. Knapp avoided the popular body

Motor improvements made in 1926—note slot in piston and slipper extension to open and shut vacuum orifice in cylinder wall for withdrawing scavenged oil.

moldings then running over hood and field, the leather-covered tops, the fake landau bars and the elliptical or odd-shaped quarter windows. Fads were not a Packard prerogative. And Knapp had some quite specific ideas about coachwork and who was qualified to do it, as witness his comments from 1925: "Judging from my experience, what is needed is not an artist, but a real body designer, or I should say car designer, as it is necessary nowadays to design a vehicle as a whole, in order to have harmony of lines in the entire car. This man may not necessarily be a mechanical engineer capable of designing motors or detailed chassis parts, but he must have a combination of mechanical skill and knowledge coupled with a certain artistic ability and sense of proportion in vehicle designing. This is usually obtained only by long practice and knowledge of body and car construction. The ability to make beautiful lines, or pictures for magazine advertisements, is not all that is necessary to make a good body design."

The idea of automobile design—or styling, a word not in use then—was in a transitional state, and those whose task it was to cloak a chassis were not perforce among the most highly regarded or recompensed members of a company hierarchy. This was true throughout the industry, as a few figures, in Packard's case, might demonstrate. During 1925 "Doc" Hills, the fellow in charge of distribution, received a raise in salary from $1041.66 semi-monthly to $1250, E.F. Roberts in charge of manufacturing was upped from $1250 to $1500, Colonel Vincent in charge of engineering was in that range as well. Archer Knapp got a raise too—from $200 to $250 semi-monthly.

The status of body design then might be put in perspective also by reference to J.J. Cole, president of the Cole Motor Car Company, who in 1923 announced a "novel method in body design" for his new cars. Instead of laying out the job on a drafting board, a clay model was molded over the previous year's body. That way, he advised, it was possible to visualize clearly and inexpensively just what the new body lines would be. And, only then, was the idea taken into the drafting room. Cole, an expert modeler, was said to have donned overalls himself and assisted in the working out of the new idea.

Harley Earl had been working in clay too, but doubtless he did not do a clay mockup prior to Cole's. He was about to join General Motors. . . .

257

Packard meantime was thinking custom. In the spring of 1926 board director Frederick M. Alger would return from Europe having purchased five custom bodies—three Labourdettes and two Kellners—for the company's edification. Custom coachwork, of course, was scarcely new to Packard, most of it originating in the New York branch of Packard or in Earle Anthony's distributorship in California. But the New York arrangements made by Gordon C. Parvis of that branch often were drawn upon by other branches and dealers in the East and Midwest. Parvis knew the custom body builders, almost all of whom were in the East, and his influence and success with the specialized carriage trade now led Packard to present a line of custom-bodied cars through headquarters to all dealers. Horace Potter coordinated this work at Detroit and in late 1925 the Packard factory offered the array. The bodies had been ordered by Packard in "series," a limited number contracted for, to be finished to the customers' orders. The client of course had complete freedom as to color and upholstery—and some cars were ordered with special modifications, as for example one Fleetwood Town Cabriolet sporting special fenders with an extra set of guards just ahead of the rear doors, reminiscent of an old victoria.

Each style could be had on the Six (333) as well as on the Eight (243) chassis, save for the aforementioned Holbrook coupe initially on the 136-inch Eight chassis but now on the 126-inch Six as well. These included:

Two-Passenger Coupe, Style No. 281
  Body by Holbrook

Four-Passenger Sedan Cabriolet, Style No. 6413
  Body by Judkins

Five-Passenger Stationary Town Cabriolet, Style No. 1177
  Body by Dietrich

Two-Passenger Convertible Coupe, Style No. 1222
  Body by Dietrich

Four-Passenger Sedan, Style No. 1176
  Body by Dietrich

Five-Passenger Stationary Town Cabriolet, Style No. 3509
  Body by Derham

Five-Passenger Stationary Town Cabriolet, Style No. 1509
  Body By Fleetwood

Seven-Passenger Inside Drive Limousine Sedan, Style No. 2711
  Body by Holbrook

A formidable collection certainly, advertised in the May 1926 issue of *Ladies' Home Journal* as "Original Creations by Master Designers."

All Packard models, standard or "original," underwent revision and simplification in braking in late 1925 with the adoption of the Bendix system. The planetary gear system by which the service brake pedal

Miss Marjorie Dork, noted "Beauty Specialist" of the Twenties, gracing the Fourth Series Six Model 426 Runabout she purchased in New York City.

stepped up the braking pressure was eliminated, and the brake linkages were now being equalized front to rear only. Rear service brakes were changed from external contracting to internal expanding type. Both rear and front brakes were now of three-shoe design, cam operated, and it followed that the parking or hand brake operated internally on the same bands. Vincent strongly opposed any brake, even a "set brake," on the transmission or driveshaft. The term "emergency brake" for the hand brake still meant exactly that to the public; a broken axle or driveshaft would render a transmission brake useless. Among other changes was revision (finally!) to one-piece windshields on both open and closed cars, and the elimination of the torque arm to the rear axle, after motor number 75,000 on the Sixes, after March 1926 on the Eights.

The only change in Packard's financial picture was a good one, a very good one. The company report for the fiscal year ending August 31st, 1925 showed Packard with its greatest sales, production and earnings year in history. A total of 24,246 cars was produced—doubtless some of the Sixes seeing service as taxicabs, Packard's board authorizing management "to transact such business at a maximum discount of ten percent off the regular list price" at its meeting of March 31st. Sales totaled $60,475,989 (up nearly $15 million), with net earnings at $12,-191,081 after taxes, a whopping increase compared to the previous year's $4,805,174. Company assets of nearly $30 million were three and a half times current liabilities—this ratio despite the purchase and retirement of all outstanding preferred stock at $110 per share plus interest, the sum of $12,780,446 having been required to accomplish that. Common stock was authorized to be increased $50,000,000—Packard was soon to be one of the most widely held corporations in the world.

Nineteen twenty-five had been a great year for the entire industry. Cadillac had facelifted, pricing its new five-passenger sedan on the 132-inch wheelbase at $3195, on the 138-inch wheelbase $4150. Buick increased the bore on the Master Six to three and a half inches, the same as the Packard Six, and priced its five-passenger sedan at $1495. It is a bit strange in retrospect that GM provided no car between Buick and Cadillac. Packard had driven its Six right in there—and prospered.

Nearly four million cars rolled off American assembly lines in 1925; over a million and a half were scrapped, and that worried some industry observers. Again there was the bugaboo of saturation. Charles W. Nash thought it had arrived already, stating so when Packard was striving manfully to keep up with orders already on hand. Ned Jordan said the saturation point would be reached only when cars were built so they would never wear out and when style ceased to be an element in buying. Alvan Macauley had worried, "What does it matter if there are still plenty of people to buy automobiles if they have no place to use them? The big cities of the country, and particularly New York must face this question. Already the men whose overwhelming task it is to struggle with New York's traffic problems are seriously discussing the restriction of automobiles and the limitation of taxicabs." They're still discussing it today, a half century later.

Packard missed making the list of the ten largest producers of motorcars in America by one in 1925, though doubtless the company was not dismayed. Alvan Macauley paid his personal taxes, $53,531; and Henry Ford and his son Edsel paid theirs, $2,608,808 and $2,158,056 respectively. The Ford Motor Company had to ante nearly $16.5 million to the Federal government, Packard provided $751,862, Hudson $1,120,587, Dodge $2,450,843. General Motors an estimated $5,000,000. These were prosperous times. The next fiscal year for Packard was even better. Gross sales totaled $77,363,954; net profit $15,843,586.

Packard was sure of itself, perhaps even a little cocky, but never arrogant. Packard carried its pride with aplomb. Advertising themes included "Born in the Lap of Luxury," "The Ambassadors' Choice," "When You Arrive in a Packard. . .," "Distinguished by Illustrious Patronage," "At Home in Any Environment," "Serving America's Aristocracy." And perhaps the most self-assured of all—that full-page advertisement with no illustration and no signature whatsoever, but merely the words in large italic, "Now! More than ever—Ask the Man Who Owns One."

He was probably waiting for his car to be delivered. And it mattered

Also from 1927, Brigadier General Bird W. Spencer and his Six 433 Sedan.

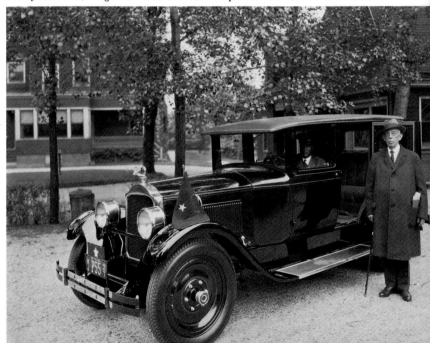

Archer L. Knapp's domain, the body drafting rooms in the mid-Twenties.
Page opposite: The Babel letter, and "satisfying the vogue for color" in 1927.

not who he was, Packard's policy was unswerving in dealing with each customer alike. When Captain Lowell H. Smith and Lieutenant Leslie P. Arnold, two fliers of the U.S. Army around-the-world flight in the flagship *Chicago* were each offered any car they wished as a gift from the Windy City, they both chose the Packard Eight Sport Model. Though several makes of cars had been offered to the city at no cost for this purpose, and others at discount, the Packard company had, before its selection by the fliers, told the organizing committee a Packard car could be purchased for full price and not a penny less. And that is the way the two cars were bought. On the other hand, the company did feature the Packard selection by the airmen in full-page advertisements picturing plane, one of the cars and the two recipients—and whether Packard reimbursed the City of Chicago for the publicity is not known.

With deliveries on some models taking up to four months after sale date in 1925, there was bound to be pressure, cancellation threats and other cajolery tried to effect an earlier arrival of the desired car. Again Packard was adamant, no favoritism. From the coast, Earle Anthony vice-president George R. Bury carefully advised his salesmen that deliveries had to be made in sequential order, with no exceptions: "We would much rather have a man's respect and lose his business than have his business and lose his respect."

Nineteen twenty-six would prove as healthy as 1925 for the industry, though the wringing out within it which had characterized the early years of the decade continued. The newcomer and dropout figures for the period are telling:

Year	Entering	Exiting	Remaining
1921	5	1	88
1922	4	9	83
1923	1	14	70
1924	2	15	57
1925	0	8	49
1926	1	6	44

Mortality had been a full fifty percent during the half-dozen years, but in 1926, with half the number of manufacturers, car production would almost triple. Cadillac continued to do well with its V-8, the 200,000th produced sold to airplane and engine builder Glenn Curtiss. Buick, Kissel, Studebaker, Peerless, Dodge and others were oversold. Pierce-Arrow restored its $8.00 annual dividend on its preferred stock, the first since 1921, though there were no prospects for paying the arrears. Rickenbacker was in trouble, reorganizing and attempting to entice the public fancy with a streamlined sport sedan. Rollin filed for bankruptcy. Chrysler added the Imperial Six to its line, for which it claimed 92 hp and 80 mph, and with which it hoped to compete with the Packard Six. Oakland's new Pontiac was a sterling success. But the new Stutz Vertical Eight with Safety Chassis was not, at least commercially. Oldsmobile put chrome on its radiator shell and other bright work instead of nickel. Billy Durant had his Flint Junior Six—with a Packard-shaped radiator.

Across an ocean Ettore Bugatti was building a mammoth car he would call the Royale, fitting his first chassis with a seven-passenger touring car body from Packard. The company didn't fear the competition. Only six Royale chassis were ever built.

Considerably more of the new Packards introduced in August of 1926 would be made, of course, and this time the company was not dilatory with the announcement. There were full-page ads "Introducing the improved Packard Six"—and the reader was advised that "Today's Packard Six will out-perform . . . any Packard car ever built with one exception . . . today's Packard Eight." The Eight was heralded as "And *Now* the Boss of the Road," though one had to read well into the copy to discover that it was indeed the Eight being spoken of, in deference

probably to Packard Six purchasers who might think likewise of their chosen car.

Although this promotion might seem considerably more high-key than the year previous, again there was not one word of the improvements to the cars themselves. Ned Jordan had long been saying the public wasn't interested in "mechanical chatter"—and Packard and Austin Bement agreed wholeheartedly. With the new models announcement, too, their advertising blazed forth in full color.

Previously, Packard's most artistic ads had been the lovely vignetted wash drawings, on gray background highlighted in Chinese white, by Frank Quail. But Quail had been a MacManus man, and left with him; Bement's black and white wash drawings were amateurish by comparison. But now, with color, the Bement agency really came into its own. The basic layout idea was: a tinted background; a dominant color

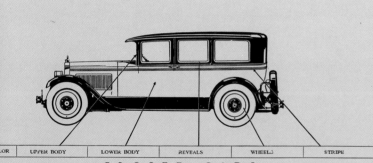

OLOR	UPPER BODY	LOWER BODY	REVEALS	WHEELS	STRIPE
			C L O S E D C A R S		
A	Black	Westminster Gray	Westminster Gray	Westminster Gray	Coronado Tan
B	Black	Packard Blue	Packard Blue	Packard Blue	Gold
C	Black	Morocco Maroon	Morocco Maroon	Morocco Maroon	Gold
D	Black	Sheffield Green	Bakst Green	Sheffield Green	Pistache Green
E	Sage Brush Green, Deep	Sage Brush Green, Deep	Pigskin Brown, Light	Pigskin Brown, Light	Derby Red, Light
F	Black	Algerian Blue	Algerian Blue	Algerian Blue	Flake White
G	Black	Ching Blue	Bambalina Blue	Bambalina Blue	Fawn Gray
H	Black	Ambato Green	Ambato Green	Ambato Green	Flake White
J	Black	Chicadee Green	Chicadee Green	Chicadee Green	Gold
K	Copra Drab	Chicle Drab	Chicle Drab	Chicle Drab	Platinum
L	Thrush Brown	Coot Brown	Coot Brown	Coot Brown	Oriole Red
M	Moleskin, Deep	Beige Brown, Light	Beige Brown, Light	Beige Brown, Light	Cream, Light
N	Killarney Gray	Dundee Gray	Dundee Gray	Dundee Gray	Flake White
P	Morocco Maroon	Morocco Maroon	Pigskin Brown, Light	Pigskin Brown, Light	Runabout Red, Deep
Q	Bolling Green	Ambato Green	Pigskin Brown, Light	Ambato Green	Orange, Double Deep

dy Belt, Upper Cowl and Bonnet, Drake Green

			O P E N C A R S		
S	Helldiver Gray	Partridge Drab		Helldiver Gray	Tanager Scarlet
T	Black	Black		Black	Oriole Red
U	Thrush Brown	Coot Brown		Thrush Brown	Woodpecker Red

rendering of the car located centrally;* a framed painting above in color, illustrating the theme word; type copy below, led by the theme word; the name PACKARD at page bottom; "Ask the Man Who Owns One" suitably placed.

The theme words or "attributes" were important, and there were a lot of them: Performance, Grace, Distinction, Acceleration, Quality, Comfort, Pride of Possession, Safety, Flexibility, Precision, Beauty, Prestige, Reputation, Luxury, Silence, Charm, Power, Enduring, Leadership, Balance, Dependability, Color, Simplicity, Service.

Of the twenty-four ads in the series, twenty-two pictured the Eight, though descriptions applied equally to both cars. As, for example, the advertisement called "Acceleration," which was the closest Packard came to supplying specifics: "Excess power, lithe and fluid as steam, giving a top speed of 75 miles an hour in the largest closed model of the Packard Six and 80 miles an hour in the Eight. . . . Brake action is still quicker and as sure." No reference, of course, was made to the new braking system.

Consider, too, the first ad in the series, displaying a phaeton in two tones of soft blue with wheels soft yellow, and even fenders and aprons in color. One might have expected the text to describe the illustrated car or say something about color options. But not a mention about that. The theme word was "Performance"—"The top speed of Packard cars is too great for safe use anywhere off a speedway. But the power is there—reflected in a new standard of traffic agility and hill-climbing ability—the marvel of new owners." The painting illustrating "Performance" featured a sartorially resplendent rider atop a rearing horse held in check by a groom. The setting was an aristocratic iron gateway

*It should be noted that the colors used were rather imaginative, having nothing to do with standard color options, but everything to do with attractively keying the car to the accompanying painting.

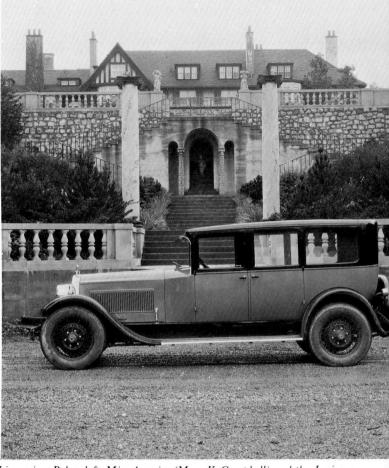

Third Series Packard Eights, introduced August 1926. Above: Model 343 Limousine. Below left: Miss America (Mary K. Campbell) and the Junior Prom Queen of Ohio State University in a Model 336 Runabout. Below right: Gilda Gray and her Model 336 Phaeton. These cars carried the wire wheel option.

with a yellow Packard roadster in the background. Or was it a Buick?

Austin Bement commissioned a variety of artists to do the paintings, all of which—save one—remained on the walls of the Packard offices until the depredations of 1956 when, reportedly, most were destroyed. They vary in artistic merit, some with an ethereal or romantic quality, others more commercial and of the modern genre. "Distinction" presented an elegant group in formal attire in an opera box. "Pride of Possession" was a lovely woman admiring her jewelry. "Flexibility," with more imagination, presented a Seventeenth Century swordsman flexing his long, narrow rapier. "Precision" was an elderly craftsman checking a connecting rod on a gauge. "Silence" was an Indian guiding a canoe over still water; "Leadership" a knight in armor astride a white horse leading his standard-bearing hordes into battle. "Balance," less imaginatively, was two children on a see-saw. "Service" was the poorest: a U.S. mail plane heading in a dive for a lighted hangar door. A crash would have been inevitable, Packard men with aviation experience should have vetoed that one.*

But the best ad, and by far, was that ferocious tiger crouched to come straight at you. It was done by famed animal painter Charles Livingston Bull—and it illustrated "Power." Later, in 1935, Alvan Macauley presented the painting to Frank J. Navin, owner of the Detroit Tigers, the team which had just won the American League baseball pennant.

After the first two ads appeared, Alvan Macauley, who always read every word of copy before approving it, suggested using the phrase "The Restful Car." It was thereafter variously placed, until Bement who, along with others through the years, had thought Packard should have a coat of arms, brought back the composition using the Packard radiator shape with ribbon scrolls below on which the slogan "Ask the Man Who Owns One" appeared. On the field or core of the radiator, "The Restful Car" now was placed. The device, the form of which was first used in 1924, continued on the ads for a year, and then two years later was reinstated with various legends thereafter.

The Packard radiator shape had been used as a device since the early days of 1905. In 1908 it was placed on a triangular panel of acanthus leaves and became an advertising insignia used for many years. It appeared on the Second Series Twin Six headlamp rims in 1916 and as a center bumper clamp insignia in 1923; its last use in an advertisement was apparently in January 1924. As a decal, covered with celluloid, it

---

*The "Service" ad is interesting for another reason. It pictured a roadster with disc wheels not of the type used on that model, but the Disteel conical discs adopted for the next. Illustrators worked from factory photographs, and this roadster apparently was trying out the new wheels for management when the photograph was taken. This sort of "error" happened with some frequency.

was incorporated into the enameled cloth tire covers of early Twin Sixes and was used that way as late as 1928. It was not, however, adopted as *the* official Packard insignia. When the matter was broached in management or board meetings, the consensus was that the radiator shape itself was sufficient, and no insignia need be added. That is, no insignia so far had been suggested or suggested itself as so appropriate that it deserved a place of honor. But one would, in a couple of years.

Packard's impressive color promotion caught Cadillac by surprise. The marque's advertisements had more often portrayed an aristocratic woman or a patrician scene, or merely the Cadillac crest or a detail of a radiator cap, than the car itself—and entirely in black and white. But four months after the inauguration of the Packard series, MacManus put the Cadillac into color, and in announcing its new Model 314-A in August of 1926 also widely touted available color options—"50 Body Styles and Types, 500 Color Combinations"—which of course Packard had begun promoting the year previous. Another ad noted with pride "Cadillac is, today, outselling all cars, at or above its price, by two to one"—careful phrasing making this true, but eliminating altogether the Packard Six. There was no doubt Cadillac was sensitive about Packard competition. As well it should have been. Packard had handily acquired the lead in the fine car field and was holding on to it steadfastly. And its advertising campaign was the envy of the industry, none other would hold interest for as long a period as Packard, all the way into 1932.

Nor was Packard reluctant to spend money to accomplish that. During 1926 the company spent $709,160 on national magazine advertising to Cadillac's $472,130. Only Chevrolet and Buick spent more ($972,144 and $970,534); Lincoln spent a mere $256,260—but then Henry Ford never liked advertising much.

Packard was spending money at the factory too. To build the new models 426-433 and 336-343, the plant was completely revised and re-equipped at a cost of almost three million dollars, the previous year's production halted for two months to effect the changes. Formerly, the chassis had been assembled, then taken out for road testing, brought back and the body mounted. Now a continuous production line, starting with the frame, followed through to the completion of the car. Then it was given its road test.

Included in the new equipment installed was a battery of gear cutting and lapping machines for the brand-new hypoid gears of the rear axle, Vincent's engineers collaborating with the Gleason Gear works in the design of the necessary machinery. Hypoid gears were a significant automotive development, and although Packard never mentioned them in advertising, the trade press covered the subject thoroughly. Leslie Gillette of *Automotive Industries* wrote:

"Hypoid gears resemble bevel gears, but the axis of the pinion is offset from the axis of the gear and does not intersect it. The tooth action of the gears combine the rolling action of spiral bevel gears with a sliding action along the entire face of each tooth. Another way of expressing [this] is by comparing the action of a sled runner passing over a rough surface where the runner tends to ride over the surface smoothly. The sliding action of hypoid gears has the effect of smoothing out the tooth engagements and hence they tend to run more smoothly than spiral gears.

"On the new Packard cars, the axis of the pinion is offset two inches below the axis of the gears . . . the drive for the rear axle is not through the center of the differential housing carrier as is customary, but is set considerably below. . . . With this type of axle design the end thrust on the front bearing is reduced considerably and longer life for all axle parts is claimed because of the smoother operation. . . . Adjustment and maintenance of hypoid gears is very similar to that of spiral bevel

gears. . . . Packard is the first automobile company to put [them] into regular production."

In addition to being quieter, another advantage was the possibility of lowering the body floor, since the driveshaft would be lower, and thus allowing a lesser overall car height. Packard would not take advantage of this until the next model, however; it would require a new frame layout and new basic body proportions, and Packard preferred caution. It was possible that the very new and still almost experimental gear machines might prove unable to produce in quantity with the required accuracy, forcing a retreat to the former spiral bevel gears. Hence the Packard wariness, and hence too the reluctance to include mechanical specification changes in advertising, and even in catalogues.

Packard's policy of evolution meant that it never made many changes

Very Ivy League and very Packard, an Eight Model 343 Seven-Passenger Touring Car grandly parked in front of a Princeton University dormitory in 1927.

at once, yet for this model series the number was greater, and more noticeable, than in any prior model change since 1922.

Spectacular improvements in engine performance were made in both Six and Eight. Or, as the Packard board minutes of January 27th, 1926—seven months before introduction of the new cars—understated, "the engineering department was meeting with considerable success in improving the activity of the Six and that these improvements when applied to the Eight will show an increase in its power." The bore of the Eight was increased ⅛-inch (to 3½) to correspond to the Six. The low speed torque of both was such that the car could walk along at two miles an hour in high gear. The brake horsepower of the improved Six was now 81 at 3200 rpm (equivalent to the old Eight!) and the Eight was up to 109 hp at 3200. Road performance improved correspondingly, and apparently Packard had been modest in advertising speed maximums. Leslie Gillette wrote that he drove an Eight at 86 mph "without any feeling of unsteadiness" and because of road conditions he wasn't pressing the car. "The acceleration from 50 mph seemed to be as quick as accelerating from 20 mph," Gillette continued. "A speed of 58 mph was attained in second gear without any undue noise arising from the transmission, while the car kept in a straight line when the brakes were applied hard at 75 mph showing perfect equalization of the 'new' internal shoe four-wheel brakes."

Aluminum pistons, a redesign of the combustion chamber and new manifold layout were had with the new Packard engines. Colonel Vincent had wanted to use aluminum pistons for some time. The first Single Eights had been so equipped, as we've seen, until warpage, piston slap and wear militated the change to conventional cast iron after a few months. The pistons with the slipper appendage used with the Skinner Oil Rectifier had required cast iron in any case for strength of the slipper. Now, using aluminum, with a reinforcing Invar steel strut, the piston shape was conventional and the pickup line for the rectifier was omitted from the cylinder wall. The device was continued a while, however, but it received its oil from the line going to the oil pressure gauge. Its efficacy was questionable now as it became merely a still to boil out the volatile matter from the crankcase oil. Packard soon decided it was easier simply to encourage more frequent oil changes which most Packards likely as not were given anyway. So the oil rectifier was dropped about November 1926, without so much as a goodbye. And the Packard owner was advised to change the oil every 1000 miles in summer, 500 winter (previously it had been every 2500 miles). No one apparently cared much. Oil was cheap, about a quarter a quart.

Turbo-head was the name Packard gave its new combustion chamber design. The old chamber had a flat form, slightly higher over the valves; the new form was domed over the valves and over to the midline of the cylinder bore. Over the other half of the cylinder bore it was flat, flush with the top of the cylinder, and therefore very close to the top of the piston at its highest position. Thus the initial stage of the explosion was concentrated on half the piston, increasing as the piston traveled down, and a more even piston pressure was obtained making a smoother power curve. Also, the domed shape produced much more complete combustion through the mixing of the gases. The spark plug was in the center of the dome. This one change in cylinder heads accounted for the major part of the spectacular power increase in the motors, and Packard continued to use this general shape head in its six- and eight-cylinder cars as long as it made them.

Increased power demanded new manifolds. Heretofore, the intake manifold had been entirely within the cylinder block, only the exhaust manifold was exposed—this presented a neat appearance and satisfied Vincent's penchant for simplicity. The new manifolds were combined in one casting and, not being confined to the block, the intake manifold had considerably larger passages. Intake gases passed through a chamber in the exhaust manifold to become heated—and the venerable Fuelizer disappeared.

For evenness in engine power, a tube connected the front section of the intake manifold to the rear section, thus equalizing manifold depression or vacuum. On the Eight, firing order was changed from 1-3-2-5-8-6-7-4 to 1-6-2-5-8-3-7-4. This spread the power impulses over the length of the crankshaft which was supposed to reduce some motor vibration. More noticeable, however, was a quieter exhaust as the flow was more evenly distributed in the manifold passage and did not "pile up" in bunches.

Crankshafts were heavier of course, and the increased power of the motors allowed higher rear axle ratios. These cars would never appear to labor at speed. Optional ratios were available for different wheelbases, body weights and expected road conditions:

	Low	Standard	High
Six	5 to 1	4-2/3 to 1	4-1/3 to 1
Eight	4-2/3 to 1	4-1/3 to 1	4 to 1

Many other changes there were throughout. Two-plate clutches with four friction surfaces superseded the multiple disc with five driving plates, the decreased weight purportedly making shifting easier due to lesser momentum. Leaves were added to the springs to prevent "hitting bottom," and frame cross members were beefed up, with Watson Stabilizers added as standard to the Six.

Engine appearance was given attention. Nickel plated acorn cylinder head nuts, nickeled priming cups and large nickel plated knurled spark plug nuts provided sparkle against the darker green enameled cylinder blocks and heads and the black enameled piping, tubing and rods. The sandblasted aluminum crankcase and front end cover were emphasized by the aluminum paint on the iron transmission case. It was a handsome motor, and Packard was proud of it.

But for those owners who never lifted the hood—paying others to perform that chore and whatever followed it—more noticeable than any of the revisions hitherto mentioned was the new Packard's outside look. The changes were subtle—and began with the Packard *carte d'identité*. The radiator shape was altered, not the exterior silhouette, but the interior frame shape surrounding the core. The cusps that had been there from the first Model L of 1904—though some few did not have them—were removed and an arched curve substituted. Now, for Packard, this was a cataclysmic move, and doubtless the result of much deliberation.

The open cars changed very little, though a tear might have been shed for the passing of the beautiful Sport Model with its place taken by the Five-Passenger Touring Car, promptly renamed the Phaeton. The closed cars were given the continuous belt molding now, and the tops were lower and extended forward over the windshield in an integral visor. A couple of new ideas were tried and quickly discarded, viz., the elimination of door pockets and substitution of small compartments with doors placed in the front seat backs on sedans (the pockets were back in four months)—and the replacement of the pivoted foot rail by a pair of movable carpeted hassocks (the foot rail was back in four months).

Full crown, one-piece fenders were featured on the Eight, the Six continued with two- or three-piece paneled fenders. But the headlamps on the Six were reshaped to full drums of cylindrical shape, a smaller variation of those on the Eight.

Since Packard was advertising so extensively in color, it followed that the cars themselves should be colorful too. The new Six was introduced in standard colors as follows: for open cars, body and bonnet above molding and wheels, Helldiver Gray; body and bonnet below molding, Partridge Drab; striping on body, bonnet and wheels, Tanager Scarlet. And for enclosed cars, body and above upper belt molding and body moldings, Black; bonnet and body below upper belt molding and wheels, Packard Standard Blue striped with Gold, or Westminster Gray striped with Old

When not breaking flying records, French ace Dieudonné Coste preferred traveling in a Packard, here an Eight Model 336 Five-Passenger Phaeton.

Ivory; all other chassis parts, Black.

And if that didn't appeal, the prospect was handed the chart illustrated on these pages, which reflected not only the admirable range afforded, but also the ingenuity of the fellow who came up with the names for all those new colors. There was, it appeared, something for everyone.

For the Eight, the standard color for closed cars was Westminster Gray, as for the Six. The Touring Car for seven passengers was given the "S" scheme noted on the Six chart. But the Phaeton and Roadster, even in standard, would appear in a masterwork of color which might sound haphazard to read but was most effective and tasteful in practice, for example, a Roadster fondly recalled by the writer: body and bonnet above molding, Arizona Gray; body and bonnet molding (only), Brewster Green Light; body and bonnet below molding, Munster Gray (lighter); wheels, Taupe Coral Gables Gray; striping on body and bonnet, Robin's Egg Blue, striping on wheels, Coach Painter's Green Light; fenders, splashes and other chassis parts, Beige Gray. It was quite something.

The new colors, the new cars were selling well; and the new produc-

tion lines had the happy effect of allowing Packard to reduce prices on the Six once again. This was done March 1st, 1927—and the lineup with new and old prices was as follows:

Model 426 (126-inch wheelbase)	Body Number	8-2-26	3-1-27
Phaeton (5)	301	$2585	$2250
Runabout (2-4)	302	$2685	$2350
Sedan (5)	303	$2585	$2250
Model 433 (133-inch wheelbase)			
Sedan (7)	304	$2785	$2450
Sedan-Limousine (7)	305	$2885	$2550
Club Sedan (5)	306	$2725	$2390
Coupe (4)	307	$2685	$2350
Touring (7)	300	$2785	$2450

The separate trunk Coupe was gone, as was the Five-Passenger Limousine and, as mourned already, the Sport Model. All closed cars now were on the longer wheelbase, except the price leader, the Five-

Borne majestically in Packards, H.R.H. the Prince of Wales on the left, and Queen Marie of Roumania about to enter her parade 343 Seven-Passenger Touring.

Passenger Sedan. Total model year production of the Sixes was 25,355 cars—and though there are no figures on the Five-Passenger Sedans this included, an educated guess would be that body style outsold all others combined. Russ Westover, the creator of the comic strip's "Tillie the Toiler," bought one and promptly wrote Packard in sheer delight, the indefatigable "Tillie" having taken the letter of course. And the charming letter reproduced herein of F.E. Babel to Edwin E. Squires testifies to the car's popularity in rural areas, Broken Bow, Nebraska being some eighty-one miles from the larger metropolis of Grand Island.

The Eight's lineup was similar to the Six, though no price reductions were sent the way of the larger car:

Model 336 (136-inch wheelbase)	Body Number	8-2-26
Phaeton (5)	291	$3750
Runabout (2-4)	292	$3850
Sedan (5)	293	$4750
Model 343 (143-inch wheelbase)		
Sedan (7)	294	$5000
Sedan-Limousine (7)	295	$5100
Club Sedan (5)	296	$4890
Coupe (4)	297	$4750
Touring (7)	290	$3950

Dropped were the Five-Passenger Coupe and the Five-Passenger Limousine, and the Holbrook Coupe was transferred to the Custom department which was flourishing. Production of the Eights for the model year was something less than 5000; various records are in error, but the motor numbers ran from 220,000 to 224,999. More accurate calendar year production figures bear out this approximation.

Packard was riding high. Everything was going right. When Marie of Roumania arrived in America during 1926, the first visit paid America by a reigning queen, she was squired in a Packard. And in Uruguay when H.R.H. the Prince of Wales arrived there for a tour, he too saw the country courtesy of the car from East Grand Boulevard.

Leaders of the democratic sort bought Packards instead. "Better than one out of every five governors of the United States is a Packard owner," boasted *The Packard*, among them Alfred E. Smith of New York and, of course, Alvan T. Fuller of Massachusetts. Chief Justice of the Supreme Court William Howard Taft had his Packard—and "three Associate Justices and a former Associate Justice have cast a Packard ballot for their personal cars." As had Secretary of State Frank B. Kellogg, Speaker of the House Nicholas Longworth, Secretary of the Navy Curtis D. Wilbur and other assorted "men to whom are entrusted the administration of affairs affecting more than one hundred millions of people." No fewer than a dozen United States diplomats and ambassadors chose Packard.

"Even a man who doesn't ordinarily look an aristocrat suddenly becomes one when driving a Packard," wrote Tony Sarg of marionette fame. From Tucson, Arizona popular novelist Harold Bell Wright, the "Dickens of Rural Delivery Routes," advised that previous to Packard ownership life had been "just one motor thing after another . . . But from the very hour I began using Packards I have known only automobile peace . . . . Why, I can ride in a Packard and think out a story at the same time—even though Mrs. Wright is driving. That may or may not be a benefit to the dear public, but it certainly is to me." Broadway producer Winchell Smith allowed, "Realizing that I don't know a blessed thing about machinery, I have no hesitation in saying that the Packard is the greatest motor car on earth! I have an English car, known the world over, which can't begin to do what my Packard does—so my chauffeur says, and he knows all about machinery. The Packard handles so easily and simply that I can drive it—and I can hardly drive a nail!"

By now the Packard was ubiquitous in Hollywood, "the universal choice of the cinema world," so *The Packard* said—with such luminaries among owners as Ruth Roland, Colleen Moore, Lew Cody, Hope Hampton, Rod La Rocque, Reginald Denny, Wallace Beery, Buck Jones, Conway Tearle and May McAvoy. Starlet Pauline Starke purred that "A keen Packard plays a leading role in the super-production 'The Life of Pauline,' [this yet another of the promotions staged by the irrepressible Earle C. Anthony] but it's a great co-star. It never talks back nor gets upstage, but I will admit it takes lots of attention away from me." A Packard Roadster starred with Jason Robards and Rose Blossom in Warner Brothers' *White Flannels* of 1927. And over at Metro-Goldwyn-Mayer, a Packard studio transportation car had been specially equipped and pressed into service for the filming of the great chariot race in *Ben-Hur* two years earlier.

Nor were such feats of fancy peculiar only to Tinseltown. In Tucson champion bulldogger Homer Roack leapt from the running board of his Packard and threw a steer in record time. "You shore don't need spurs with that cyar," he drawled, "she just gits up and gits herself." In circles more chic, the Packard was even more in evidence; seven members of the Westmoor Polo Club (Hartford, Connecticut) were proud Packard owners, though they chose to play the game with their ponies.

"Born in a Packard, Borne in One Still," enthused Cornelius Vanderbilt, Jr., when he purchased his fifteenth example of the marque. And the Packard was much in evidence in New York City, whenever anyone of import came to town, as the car which carried the notables through the streets in ticker tape triumph: French aces Coste and Bellonte; General Diaz, hero of the Piave; General Foch; Lloyd George; Commander Byrd; the Graf Zeppelin's Dr. Hugo Eckener. And most spectacularly, in 1927, Charles A. Lindbergh, when he returned from Paris.

Ah yes, Packard was riding high.

…he reception in Omaha in 1927, Colonel Charles A. Lindbergh and a Second Series 236 Packard Eight.

CHAPTER THIRTEEN

A SPLENDID
TACTICAL POSITION

The Six Model 526-533, The Eight Model 443

July 1927-August 1928

The Sixth Series Models 626-633, 640, 645

August 1928-August 1929

AUTHOR: L. MORGAN YOST

In its issue of July 30th, 1927, *Automobile Topics* reflected upon Packard, presenting a lucid picture of the marque as it was viewed in trade circles of that day. It merits quotation.

"Frequent recurrence of rumors that the Packard Motor Car Company is about to enter into some sort of merger," the article said, and it should be interpolated that such rumors were as recurring as rain, "is eloquent testimony to the independent and prosperous status of that concern. Otherwise, it may mean very little. The fact is that this Company is not only self-sufficient but that it gives good promise of continuing to grow more independent and even more prosperous as time runs on, as it is in a splendid tactical position.

" 'Packard prestige' has always been a phrase to conjure with and nothing has ever been permitted to dim the luster of the name. Continued pioneer work in aero and marine engineering, and the undiminished vogue of the straight eight as a style leader have kept the concern in the forefront of the industry. In addition, the fact that the shorter wheelbase six has successfully entered the moderate price class has placed Packard products within the reach of a very much wider market. . . . Notwithstanding the fact that the Company is without low-priced lines and has no ambitions in the quantity market, therefore, it is able to maintain a condition of stable equilibrium through conservative management, and a continued appeal to selective buyers."

Indeed. Probably the only event which had given Packard pause prior to the introduction of its new lines that same month had occurred four months previous. Cadillac brought out the LaSalle.

The LaSalle no doubt represented the strongest outside influence upon Packard in finalizing its new Six, for it was a new car which competed directly. That had not been the original Cadillac plan but the LaSalle's $2000 target was missed and what was hit—$2495-$2685—put it in the smaller Packard's class, though not as closely as Cadillac hoped. Packard had been up to its old tricks again: Its price reductions ($2250 for Five-Passenger Sedan) had come a few days before the LaSalle debut. The LaSalle's wheelbase was 125 inches, with no seven-passenger models; Packard's volume five-passenger was 126 inches, all other closed cars on a 133-inch wheelbase.

But if the LaSalle lost in price competition and wheelbase, it was ahead of the Packard in cylinders—eight of them in a 90° vee, 303 cubic inches and 75 hp. It was a snappy car which could outperform the Packard Six, though the *stock* top speed of both, over 70 mph, was similar. (The word stock is emphasized because that famous 95.3 mph GM Proving Ground run of the LaSalle was put up by a roadster stripped of muffler, top, windshield and fenders, and equipped with a high compression head, high lift cam and 3.5 to one rear end ratio. The car, incidentally, was driven by Will Rader who a decade before had broken records at Sheepshead Bay with a Liberty-engined Packard.)

Still, performance figures and technical specs were not where the LaSalle shone; its real radiance came from its styling, very much along chic European lines (read Hispano-Suiza), the first mass-produced car in America created by a genuine stylist. The influence of Harley Earl and the GM Art and Colour department he created would be prodigious.

One might have ventured then that the LaSalle would prove formidable against its competitors, principally the Chrysler Imperial 80, Jordan Great Line Eight, Franklin 11-B—and, most emphatically, the Packard Six. It didn't. The car from East Grand Boulevard had two advantages: its price and its name. During 1927-1928 some 26,807 LaSalles were produced, a commendable beginning. But that didn't approach Packard. Although the model years of the two cars didn't coincide and thus exact figures are not available, it can be estimated with assurance that during the same period Packard produced approximately 52,000 Sixes—about twice the LaSalle figure. And the LaSalle was never to catch up.

Packard's conservative course was serving it well, as Alvan Macauley related, with a few figures, to stockholders at the close of the fiscal year in August 1927:

	Three years 1925-1927	Nine years 1916-1924
Earnings	$39,778,166	$39,449,824
Average earnings per year	13,259,722	4,383,314
Percent of earnings to sales*	18.9	9.8
Earnings applicable to common dividends	39,091,173	32,037,305

Pages preceding: Packard DeLuxe Eight Model 645 Sport Phaeton (Dietrich).
These pages, the Fifth Series Six. Above left: The Speaker of the House
Nicholas Longworth and his Model 533 Touring Car. Above: Rocketry pioneer
Max Valier and his 526 Phaeton in Germany. Below: 533 Runabout prototype.
Above right: A 526 Runabout specially equipped for fire chief in Butte, Montana.

Dividends paid—cash	22,006,770	18,101,941
Plant expenditures	20,623,723	36,268,006
Depreciation taken	12,951,563	25,715,434
Percent of earnings to plant investment	57.0	36.5
Percent of earnings to invested capital	29.0	11.0

*Included profit from sales, Branch profits, interest on investments, rents and miscellaneous gains.

Equally telling were the statistics narrating the price history of the Packard Six, that car now being made available "to the public at much less than half its introductory price"—viz., $4950 for the Model 116 Five-Passenger Sedan introduced September 1st, 1920; $2285 for the same body style in the Model 526 introduced July 1st, 1927.

And Alvan Macauley was thinking greater advantages than that, further price reductions still, in a letter dated November 3rd, 1927 in which he explained the necessity of expansion in retail facilities and the advantages of two daily shifts: "Double-shifting our Six divisions will enable us to supply our present Six cars to the public at a reduction in price of more than $300.00, provided we can market twice as many cars. . . . Four months ago I directed the Distribution Department to accomplish a 50% increase in our retail distributing facilities, feeling that we would need them to move the 3000-a-month program we had undertaken. Despite a good deal of pressure from me, the expansion so far in salesman numbers is just over 14%. I feel, however, that we should double-shift the factory even in the face of uncertainty as to the extent to which we can expand our Six sales. . . . In the first place, a number of competing companies in price classes just below us have double shifted. Buick, Nash, Chrysler, Cadillac, as I am informed, are all equipped for double shift and operate on a double shift basis at least part of the year. In other words, competitors in the price class towards which we are heading, have already double shifted."

The letter reflects Packard thinking regarding the future course of its more moderate-priced line, but the company would soon have a corporate change of mind about what the car itself should be. And for the moment it tabled as well the idea of double-shifting.

For 1928, however, Packard was all set—with a line of Sixes (526-533) and Eights (443) introduced July of 1927. The figures, as before, referred to the series (fifth for the Six, fourth for the Eight) and the wheelbase length, the Eight now being offered only on the 143-inch chassis.* The cars came out strong, with appearance changes giving an

impression of greater massiveness than previous. Radiator shells were thicker, drum headlamps were bigger, the car itself lower. The hood louvers on the Eight gave way to door vents. Particularly striking was the Phaeton, with sturdy big wheels covered but not obliterated by fenders which repeated their circle and boasted a well rounded protective depth. At the rear the body nestled comfortably between the fenders. The color panel on the doors below the belt line, however, was an acquiescence to pervading style. The car might have been handsomer without it.

Interestingly, perhaps the color panel had been a last-minute decision. The first advertisement to appear for the 1928 Six (in the August 6th, 1927 issue of *Saturday Evening Post*) illustrated a phaeton with a simple belt molding sans color panel. Conceivably, when the painting was commissioned for the ad that was how the model was envisioned.

The new closed bodies were provided the continuous belt molding

---

*These model designations have proved a Packard perplexity through the years. They were inaugurated, as we have seen, with the Six 126-133 (First Series, 126- and 133-inch wheelbases) introduced in 1922, followed by the Eight 136-143 (First Series, 136- and 143-inch wheelbases) introduced in 1923, and the Second Series Six 226-233 introduced in 1924. Thereafter, new models of both Six and Eight were introduced simultaneously, i.e. the 326-333 and 236-243 in February of 1925, which helped some, but not entirely since series numbers were still not marching in step. Packard would solve all this, finally, for 1929 simply by skipping a Fifth Series Eight altogether, and designating all models the Sixth Series.

Which leaves only the perplexity of model year. Some authorities have

stated positively that Packard did not have model years, only model numbers. The difficulty, then and now, is that there is no wieldy term for the cars produced in a model run including both Sixes and Eights. To refer to them, for example, as the Packards 426-433-336-343 (which looks more like a number one might direct dial in phoning Madagascar) is cumbersome in the extreme—when they might just as logically be called the 1927 models. Likewise the now-new 526-533-443 cars as 1928 models. And they were that, at least to their owners. True, a Packard ad from January of 1926 appearing in *The American Review of Reviews* noted the company's preference for designating "no yearly models," but rest assured that from 1927 on, Packards were referred to by year and continued to be so until the end.

Stage star Alexander Gray and his Model 443 Seven-Passenger Touring Car; world champion (bantamweight) boxer Bud Taylor and his 443 Standard Runabout.

from radiator to rear which first appeared the previous year. Earlier in 1927 Ray Dietrich at the "Body Session" attendant to the Society of Automotive Engineers seminar meetings noted that stronger single belts—rather than the double then in vogue—would improve body design and advocated a wide molding at the sill line with a rounded body top for a look of lowness. Dietrich, Inc. was to become design consultant to Packard later that year, and would incorporate these features in the line of semi-custom Packards in the series to follow. Packard design in the meantime would include the *au courant* double belt, but with a curved top, especially the rounded rear contour, already in accord with Dietrich's thinking.

If the Six was Packard's bread-and-butter line, its relationship to the Eight might be viewed metaphorically as salt to pepper. Packard made more money on each Eight sold, but the company sold four times as many Sixes. The Six rode on the prestige of the Eight, and the Eight was possible because of the production and dealer facilities of the Six. In these contemporary days when a Chevrolet can cost as much as a Cadillac, one might tend to forget the price differential between the Packard lines. The Packard Eight Club Sedan, for example, listed at $4950, the Six Club Sedan at $2685. Now that was a difference! The Eight Runabout (rumble seat roadster) listed at $3975 while the 533 Six of that body style listed at $2385 and the shorter 526 Six runabout at $2275. Why two runabouts with the Six engine? Quite a few more of the shorter ones were sold. Many purchasers of a Six were striving, perhaps even overreaching, to get a Packard, and the $110 made the difference. It was often preferred for city use where parking was an increasing problem, and

many home garages of the time were too short to take a larger car in any case. Then, why did Packard not drop the longer Six runabout? Simply because it used the same body as did the Eight 443, which was ten inches longer. Packard had the body and the longer Six chassis, and it was no problem to combine them for those who wanted a more impressive car but at a Six price. The use of the same bodies on different models—with the adjustment taken care of in hood length—had been a Packard practice throughout the Twenties and would continue for some years to come.

It didn't work out always, however. The increment number was ten inches, allowing bodies from 133-inch wheelbase Sixes to be used on 143-inch Eights, likewise from the 126-inch wheelbase Six to the 136-inch Eight—but the latter chassis size had been dropped for 1928 and the five-passenger sedan body used on the 526 Six would not fit on the Eight's 143-inch chassis, so that body style was simply no longer available in the Eight line. It did no harm, however, most customers in that price stratum preferring the Club Sedan anyway, which body did fit either chassis.

Seven body styles were included in the 443 line at first but two more—coupe and convertible coupe, each with a rumble seat—were added in January 1928. Both had been in the Six line, on the 126-inch wheelbase, since the previous July. These were the first convertible coupes in the regular Packard line, all previous convertibles having been custom cars, usually by Dietrich. Because of the differences in body space on the 126- and 143-inch chassis, these styles were of different sizes on Six and Eight, the added length for the latter being in the rear deck.

The adoption of hypoid axles in the previous model year, together with a new double drop frame and smaller twenty-inch wheels brought

The Fourth Series Packard Standard Eight was introduced March 1st, 1928, this Model 443 Five-Passenger Phaeton carrying a $3650 pricetag at that time.

the Packard two inches closer to earth for 1928. The change to Disteel wheels was made for more than appearance reasons though those were important. With previous models, wire wheels had been a rather obscure extra, as different brake drums had to be installed to accommodate them. Now, wire or wood artillery wheels could be installed on the same hubs as the discs, merely by using the correct length of wheel bolts or studs. The twenty-inch wheels took 32x6.75 tires, save for the 526 models which carried 32x6.00 and were not available with wood wheels. Initially, spare disc wheels were secured by a lock plate having a winged handle, these appearing in some of the earlier ads and catalogues. But thieves learned they could force these off with a big pipe wrench, so the flush type keyed plug (Oakes lock) covering the bolt was quickly substituted.

Side-mounted spares had been a seldom purchased extra on the previous model. This year they were optional on the Sixes, available initially only on the left side of 533 models, later symmetrically on both 526 and 533 Sixes. When the 443 debuted it was with the two fender-mounted spares as regular equipment but without provision for optional rear-mounted spares. Requests for the latter must have been numerous, as an additional catalogue in March 1928 introduced the 443 "Standard Models" with them. (This "Standard" nomenclature is often confused with the car to be introduced for 1929, the smaller "Standard Eight.") Interior trim was simpler, body color selections limited to "a broad selection of beautiful combinations"—but not as broad as the other 443's. As Alvan Macauley wrote his stockholders, the new Packards were "standard in design and therefore lower in cost." And the price was concomitantly lower too, significantly. Annual model production averages for Eights had been under 5000 since 1923. With the addition of this new "Standard" model for 1928, Eight production swept to 8000.

Prices had been decreased on the 1928 Eight once before the introduction of the Standard version, and were lowered again on some body styles at that time, as set forth below, with closeout prices for the Standard line included:

Model 443	Body Number	7-1-27	1-3-28	3-1-28
Phaeton (5)	311	$3975	$3875	$3875
Runabout (2-4)	312	$3975	$3875	$3875
Coupe (2-4)	318	—	$4150	$3950
Coupe (4)	317	$4950	$4450	$4250
Convertible Coupe (2-4)	319	—	$4250	$4050
Club Sedan (5)	316	$4950	$4450	$4450
Sedan (7)	314	$5150	$4450	$4450
Sedan-Limousine (7)	315	$5250	$4550	$4550
Touring (7)	310	$4050	$3975	$3975

Standard Model 443	Body Number	3-1-28	closeout 7-9-28
Phaeton (5)	381	$3650	$2925

Runabout (2-4)	382	$3650	$2925
Coupe (2-4)	388	$3550	$3000
Coupe (4)	387	$3750	$3300
Convertible Coupe (2-4)	389	$3650	$3100
Club Sedan (5)	386	$3750	$3500
Sedan (7)	384	$3750	$3500
Sedan-Limousine (7)	385	$3850	$3600
Touring (7)	380	$3550	$3025

ustom designs on the Fourth Series Eight Model 443, seen clockwise from above: Sedan-Cabriolet by Judkins; Inside Drive Limousine by Holbrook; Town Car Derham; Sedan, Convertible Sedan and Two/Four-Passenger Coupe by Dietrich.

Closeout prices, incidentally, were negotiable, especially after the new models hit the scene. An original bill of sale dated 9-11-28 noted "One Packard Eight—Model 4-43 DeLuxe Phaeton . . . $2650, Extra tires and tubes $92.00. Transportation: At Factory." ("DeLuxe" meant side-mounted spare equipment—not the "Standard" model.)

All Eights delivered for the 1928 model year were equipped with drum cowl lights and nickeled cowl bands at the rear of the hood, on the Sixes these were a $45 extra and could be had with or without side-mounted spares. The radiator shell, as well as all bright work on 1928 models, was nickel plated. Later 1928 cars could be had from the factory with chromium plating on special order, and many owners of these cars refurbished them a few years later replating the nickel with chrome, which helped update the car. Following Oldsmobile's lead for 1927, most manufacturers had adopted chromium plating by 1928. Conservatively, Packard delayed in this until the 1929 models.

Engineering changes for 1928 were minimal. As Frank W. Diver, manager of the Packard Motor Company of Wilmington (Delaware), wrote prospective clients: "There are several cars in the Packard Eight price class and most of them will last for a long time—but, name a single one, other than the Packard Eight, that does not face a radical motor change, long before Hoover or Smith or whoever is elected moves out of the White House." (In Washington, President Coolidge had already chosen not to run.)

New to this model was the cylinder bore lubrication system, a tubular oil manifold alongside the cylinders with passages drilled into each cylinder bore. Connected with the choke control, oil would flow only when the carburetor choke was in operation. Thus, the raw gasoline from overchoking did not wash off the oil film from the cylinder walls. Not only did this cut down on cylinder wear but it also maintained the piston ring seal to reduce dilution of crankcase oil. In a way it accomplished part of the job expected from the late, unlamented Skinner Rectifier.

The Six's motor, given the four-point mounting that the Eight had had from the beginning, was set at an angle to accomplish a straight line drive to the axle when the car was loaded—with front mounts on rubber blocks. An oil filter was fitted and a breather installed on the motor chain housing. Gear ratios were modified, on the 526 decreased from 4-2/3 to

Where Packards were sold in New York City: The emporium at 61st Street and Broadway, and the super-elegant showroom across town on Park Avenue.

4-1/3, remaining 4-2/3 on the 533 and 4-1/3 on the 443 Eight save for the open models on which 4.07 was adopted.

With more attention given to smoothness at higher speeds and to eliminating shimmy, provision was made for balancing wheels by means of studs evenly spaced, inside the wheel rims, which carried washers to be removed or added. This device was not provided on wire or wood wheels, because the studs could not be hidden as they were by disc wheels.

Nor could Packard hide its price reductions from irate owners who had purchased at the higher prices. This was beginning to cause something of a problem. In mid-July 1928 supervisor of districts J.W.

Loranger sent to all Packard distributors and dealers a copy of a letter written by Alvan Macauley to one such disgruntled owner, suggesting that it "should be a distinct help to you in answering inquiries of the same kind." The letter was indeed a model of decorum. "I have your telegram of July tenth . . . in which you charge a lack of good faith and some other things that I believe are not justified," Macauley commented in part to R.C. Menendez of Jamaica, New York. "Your telegram states you have recently, and before the price reduction, bought a car. I am sorry, of course, your purchase was not delayed and that you are, therefore, for the time being, not pleased at having purchased. But please have this in

In Miami, Florida, a Sixth Series Model 645 Dietrich Roadster highlights the showroom of Packard Miami Motors, Inc., photographed during 1929.

mind, that it is our duty to the public to make price reductions when and as we can. No matter when we announce a price reduction there would, on the average, be 130 patrons who the day before would have purchased cars. No matter when we fixed the date of the announcement of a new model there would, inevitably and invariably, be those who had recently purchased. Even if we antedated the price reduction a week, or a month, or any period prior to the date of the announcement, there would still be back of that antedated period, the same number of those who just escaped being included within the price reduction." It was a problem the solution for which Macauley had not yet divined, though he proffered that a "workable suggestion" from Mr. Menendez "would be most gratefully received by us." Mr. Menendez couldn't come up with one either.

The object of the gentlemen's ire was the sweeping price slash made to the Six line on July 9th, 1928, in conjunction with reductions to the "Standard" 443. This was a genuine Packard clearance sale, in anticipation of a new model to be introduced later that summer, the new cars to be "identical in size and similar in appearance [to the Six but with] enough mechanical changes to classify them as new models." True, assuredly.

The price story for the 1928 model year Six might be set down as follows:

From the September 22nd, 1928 issue of **The Saturday Evening Post,** *the first use of the Packard crest set against an illustration of the new radiator design. The Sixth Series Standard Eight for 1929: President Culter of Colgate University and his Model 633 Sedan; Toledo (Ohio) Horse Show ladies and a 633 Runabout.*

Model 526	Body Number	7-1-27	closeout 7-9-28
Phaeton (5)	331	$2275	$1975
Runabout (2-4)	332	$2275	$1975
Coupe (2-4)	328	$2350	$2050
Convertible Coupe (2-4)	329	$2425	$2125
Sedan (5)	323	$2285	$1985
Model 533			
Phaeton (5)	321	$2385	$2085
Runabout (2-4)	322	$2385	$2085
Touring (7)	320	$2485	$2185
Sedan (7)	324	$2685	$2385
Sedan-Limousine (7)	325	$2785	$2485
Club Sedan (5)	326	$2685	$2385
Coupe (4)	327	$2685	$2385

Arithmetically, if Packard was thinking subtraction in price during this era it was also thinking addition in custom coachwork. This year, as last, Packard issued a fine color catalogue of designs created for the company by a number of firms. Most of these were formal cars to be chauffeur driven, others suitable for family use, others still created to fill the coming demand for cars adaptable for town or country, for club or touring. The convertible—open or closed at will—was not a new idea, but it required development to be practical, weather tight, easy to operate and at the same time handsome. The custom firms had done the experimenting—often at the expense of the client—to bring such bodies to the point where they could be produced at the factory in quantity. In the meantime they were hand built and while done in series—several or a dozen of a single design—changes and improvements were often made from one to the next. And they could be modified to order.

There were twenty designs in the catalogue for 1928, all shown on the 443 chassis though most could be ordered on the 133-inch Six. Rollston had an all-weather cabriolet, a formal style with open driver's seat which could be roofed and enclosed with windows in inclement weather—one of nine of that type offered, two by Rollston, five by Dietrich and two by Holbrook. There were three inside-drive limousines by Holbrook and one by LeBaron, with a Judkins sedan-limousine and sedan-cabriolet completing the list of formal cars. Dietrich had a sedan and a stationary coupe as well as two convertible cars, one a sedan, the other a coupe with rumble seat, Dietrich having already attained preeminence in the design of convertible cars and soon to carry the art to perfection. Perhaps the most striking design of the lot, however, was the Sport Phaeton by Holbrook, a sleek black car with polished aluminum hood and belt molding, a bright orange red for wheels, undercarriage and upholstery.

In addition to the work of these five coachbuilders, the Packard catalogue also illustrated the nameplates of three others: Derham, Murphy and Fleetwood. Fleetwood was soon to be exclusive to General Motors but that company had built bodies for Packard since early Twin Six days, along with Holbrook, Judkins and Derham.

Custom-bodied Packards had been winning prizes at concours d'elegance in Europe for years, garnering firsts at Vichy, Aix-les-Bains, Wiesbaden, Neuenahr, Trier, Baden-Baden, Oporto and Monte Carlo. And Packard's own design efforts on its chassis gathered a share of the laurels too. One Captain G.R. Edie, U.S. Navy, Retired, had written the company of a delightful experience he had while driving through Le Touquet, France, in his new Packard Eight touring car in 1924, the town crowded with automobiles: "I asked a policeman what it was all about," he wrote. "He said I could not stop to see the show, as there was no place to park. Then I said, 'My car is muddy, for I have come from Fontainebleau, but I will go in the show to park my car.' They gave me a number. The best I could do was to take a rag and wipe off the nickel and clean up the engine a bit. . . . The committee came . . . then retired to deliberate. . . . My number was called, to receive first place in touring cars. . . . I received a jewel case and a bronze plaque, the first I gave to my daughter, but I should be glad to send you the plaque if you would like to have it."

Whether Packard accepted the offer is not known. But the designer of that particular car, of course, was Archer L. Knapp, who retained his body engineer position at Packard throughout this era, although gradually now his department was being enlarged. In 1927 Raymond B. Birge, formerly general manager of LeBaron, joined the company. His task was to develop and supervise the new "Custom Body by Packard" operation that Alvan Macauley was anxious to establish in order to bring to Packard part of the profit in custom cars which usually went to the custom body firm.

Birge was not primarily a body designer save from the manufacturing and structural standpoint and consequently he invited someone else to Packard—Werner Gubitz, who had been a renderer or pictorial body man for Dietrich. Dietrich had tried to persuade R.L. Stickney, the renderer par excellence, to follow him to Detroit when Murray Body Corporation set Dietrich up in business as Dietrich, Inc., but Stickney would not leave New York so Dietrich had hired Gubitz to do watercolor rendering and studies of body designs. Of him, Dietrich recalls, "He was a good man but not of Stickney's calibre"—this in reference to his delineation work. Perfectly true, but Stickney was never a designer as such, while Gubitz, after joining Packard, developed a styling sense and progressed to become chief of design for Packard in the Thirties under Ed Macauley, son of Alvan, who would become manager of Styling.

Young Macauley's position at Packard at this time, however, was considerably less grandiose. As Fred A. MacArthur, who joined Packard Body Engineering late in 1928, remembers, "Ed . . . was a sales guide in the showroom on the main floor. He arrived at work every morning—on time—on the Boulevard bus because his father would not allow him to have a car." MacArthur had been hired by Archer Knapp because "they were interested in an individual capable of developing the surface of an entire body model [shown twelfth size on a sketch made by Werner Gubitz]."

Other manufacturers, Cadillac in particular, were being watched with care. The LaSalle, the Jordan Tomboy, the Little Marmon among others focused attention on smaller quality cars. And Packard made serious studies for a six with 117-inch wheelbase, in essence a 526 chassis shortened nine inches. It was a simple matter to make one up, but the choppy ride and reduced body space did not appeal to management. Gubitz produced drawings of several body styles, two of which survived the big postwar cleanup, those being a phaeton and convertible coupe. Performance of the car was excellent, of course, and this study would ultimately lead to the 626 Speedster using the big eight-cylinder motor in the shortest standard chassis.

But, for the moment—with the LaSalle growing in size each year and the others proving less than signal successes—Packard dropped the idea of the little quality car. Certainly its cost would have been so minutely less than the standard Six line that it could not have been a price leader. Besides, the Depression had not yet arrived . . .

But what would not go away—all through 1928—was the "whirring of tongues," as *Automobile Topics* put it, regarding Packard's imminent merger with another company, or combination of companies, those mentioned most often being Nash, Hudson and Chrysler. The magazine conjectured on the subject: "Mergers between concerns as prominent as Packard and Nash, however would be not at all to the liking of such men as Charles W. Nash and Alvan Macauley, or to others associated in the management of these two concerns, for the simple reason that they are independently organized, independently minded, and making eminently satisfactory progress, with no more bankers sitting around the table than the law actually requires."

That may have been true then, but a couple of years earlier the merger idea was entertained from one corner, as related in a confidential memo Alvan Macauley wrote to his board on October 19th, 1926, following a meeting with the president of Murray Body:

"Mr. William Robert Wilson . . . was here most of the morning . . . Talked first of our relations with the Murray Body Company; then about the proposed Guardian Bank; and finally, without previous notice, sprang this on me:—

"That he had recently been to see Mr. Nash and had discussed with him possible combinations of companies. Mr. Nash said that he was not interested in most existing companies but had a high regard for Packard and felt that it would afford better combination opportunities than any other company; and, as I gathered, that he could be favorably disposed

toward such a combination.

"Mr. Wilson wanted to know if we would consider it. Told him that I knew of no single one of the directors who was not satisfied with the present Packard situation or who desired a combination with anyone; that I was perfectly satisfied that no Packard stockholder would consider disposing of his Packard holdings on any basis involving an exchange of stock; that I believed that the directors representing the majority stockholders would not even consider any proposition unless it were a very favorable one involving a purchase of the company's shares for cash. And that I knew of no stockholder who was favorably inclined to even that move.

"I went on to tell him that we were approached a number of times recently by people wanting to put several companies together, and that in order to avoid being possibly misrepresented, I had told them all, what I would have to tell him, viz., that we are not interested. Here the interview ended."

And, Alvan Macauley added a postscript, "I asked Mr. Wilson during the course of the conversation what were his views as to the advantages that might accrue from a consolidation. He was unable to give me any that appealed to reason, though he talked about insuring the continuity of management and other things that seemed to me not to have a great deal of weight. . . ."

Neither Macauley nor anyone else at Packard had changed their minds about the matter by 1928, and finally a bit bored with the recurring rumors, the company issued a definitive statement over Macauley's signature in July and to buttress the point featured the letter in full-page ads headlined "PACKARD IDENTITY WILL ENDURE" and noting in part, "We have made our own way from the beginning. We have created a position for ourselves and a reputation that is distinctive and unique. We do not intend to surrender either . . . very definitely, we do not intend to lose our identity through any merger, combination, or consolidation, now or hereafter." Bold words, and boldly meant. Nineteen twenty-eight, of course, was the year an ailing Pierce-Arrow merged—with Studebaker.

Packard's net earnings for the fiscal year ending August 1st, 1928 were a healthy $21,885,416 on a total sales of $94,677,390. This was a robust increase from the year previous when $11,743,498 was earned on $71,659,188—a proportionate profit almost doubled from a total sales one-third higher. Assets of the company rose during the year from $61,044,632 to $75,177,324. Foreign business was moving briskly, now up to about $5,000,000 annually with the marque represented by selling organizations numbering 233 in sixty different countries throughout the world. And domestically the company was delighted to discover through a survey it conducted that a large majority of Packard cars sold of late had gone to owners who previously drove another manufacturer's product, fully two-thirds of the cars traded in on new Packards were other makes. And once sold on the Packard motorcar, the company believed, an owner would stay sold.

Why merge? Why indeed.

But why not, on the other hand, celebrate the Packard tradition and independence as elegantly—and in essence intimately—as possible? Packard decided to do exactly that. The stimulus came March 20th, 1928. That day James Ward Packard had died, having been preceded in death five years by his brother William Doud Packard. With the passing of the company founders, Packard management—along with Austin Bement—concluded that a memorial would be appropriate, and what better place to put it than on the Packard motorcar. Apparently in preparation for the policy announcement to come, Packard placed full-page eulogy advertisements in several magazines for August 1928, with James Ward Packard's portrait, the inscription "The World Never Knew Him" and text reflecting upon "the quiet, kindly gentleman and scholar upon whose wisdom, taste and foresight the organization was founded." Interestingly, however, but typically Packard, the first appearance of the Packard family crest and coat of arms in an advertisement—the September 22nd, 1928 issue of *Saturday Evening Post*—did not mention the source of the crest; its drawing was simply placed against an illustration of a new radiator design (no mention of that made either) and the textual reference read only, "Twenty-five years ago Packard adopted a distinctive style of hood and radiator design. Changed slightly in dimensions as powerplant needs have increased, it is still distinctly Packard."

Interestingly, too, the new Packard emblem was not featured on illustrations of cars in all ads thereafter, some unadorned radiators appearing as late as March of 1929; presumably four-color printing plates had been made up before the new emblem was official. But official it was, and presented as such in advertisements for October 1928. The heraldry was explained: " . . . Gules, a cross lozengy between 4 roses or. A pelican in her piety . . . " Not quite correctly though. The description "4 roses or (gold) had originally been "4 roses argent (silver)." It had seemed best, however, to have all the metal "or" including the crest, for production purposes and to contrast with the chrome of the radiator. The shield remained "gules (red)." Over the years liberty would be taken with the Packard crest design; this first version remains the best. Not everyone would approve of it initially, however; to some devotees of the marque an emblem was un-Packard, and imitative of other motorcars. But it was genuine, in an era when all manner of spurious crests or contrived shields attached themselves to the radiators of other cars—and it would remain as long as the Packard motorcar, appropriately.

Retirements from the Packard Motor Car Company that late summer of '28 numbered two. The first was "Doc" Hills, who left the firm "to

Above: Model 640 Custom Runabout. Below: 633 Standard Phaeton, with Dorothy Mackaill, Charles Delaney and director William Beaudine, during filming of Hard To Get. *This photograph from 1929 carried a note on the back indicating that the Packard motor was too quiet to pick up on the Vitaphone. The sound heard in the film was not Packard's: "A 'double,' consisting of an electric fan and a piece of cardboard" was used instead.*

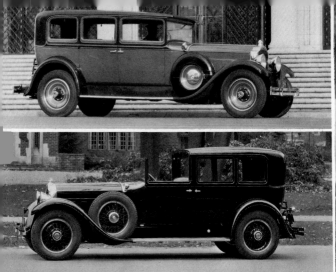

Model 640 Packards for 1929: Gary Cooper and the Phaeton he bought from Earle Anthony, the All-Weather Town Car and the Seven-Passenger Sedan by Dietric

enjoy the leisure he so well deserves." As the press reported, "His successor has not been announced although following Packard's wise policy of promoting from within the ranks, it will probably be someone now associated with the Company." It was. One week later, on August 25th, Hebar Wallace Peters was appointed vice-president of distribution. Peters, a graduate of Cornell University and its secretary for two years prior to joining Packard in 1916, had served the company successively as office manager, general manager of the Detroit branch and vice-president and general manager of the Chicago organization. The shoes "Doc" Hills left to be filled were big ones.

The second retirement was the Packard Six, after eight years and nearly 154,000 units built. Its successor was proclaimed September 15th, 1928, although it wasn't called that. All the advertisement said, in small type, was, "With the presentation of the new Standard Eight with cylinders in line, Packard offers the consummation of thirty years of skilled artisanship. Lithe, graceful as a seabird, and with the potential strength of an ocean liner, it is a fitting companion for the Packard Custom Eight—which has so firmly established itself in the fine car field."

That was it—not another word in all the national magazine advertising that entire model year; indeed of the twenty-seven periodical ads Packard placed, only three even illustrated the new Standard Eight.

The press knew it was important though, "another stroke of far-reaching consequences," *Automobile Topics* said in a lengthy article that also offered the comments, "A strong point from the competitive angle . . . is that Packard is still aiming above the popular-priced field [the new cars ranged from $2435-$2835] and will continue to be a stabilizing in-

fluence in the industry, instead of introducing a radical and disturbing departure. As for the new line itself, its official disclosure disposes of rumors of a small eight in the two thousand dollar class. It also substantiates the promise of a few weeks ago, when prices on the six-cylinder line were materially reduced, that a new car of materially enhanced value would be offered before long. This frank method of dealing with the public and the trade not only enabled the dealers to get into splendid condition to handle the new car in volume, but also protects recent purchasers against any of the rancor that has so often followed the abrupt introduction of new models and general mishandling of publicity associated therewith by some of the other manufacturers." Obviously *Automobile Topics* hadn't heard from R. C. Menendez.

The magazine did not venture to say definitively that the Standard Eight was a replacement for the Six, though A.F. Denham of *Automotive Industries* dared to suggest it, apparently a bold move on his part since it was a full two months later—in late October—before Packard alluded to that fact officially. And then *Automotive Industries* allowed demurely that "this move has been expected since production of the Six was stopped several months ago after a large bank of cars had been run off the assembly lines and stored against future demands, but an announcement was not forthcoming until this week." The Packard Motor Car Company liked guessing games.

This, of course, worked to the company's advantage. Carefully dripped news leaks were a promotional tool, and Packard was a master at them. Prior to the Standard Eight's coming, the company whispered the news hither and yon, which might have prevented prospective buyers from rushing to another showroom, say to purchase a LaSalle.

And now the new Packard was here. It looked a lot like the Six, intentionally so, "to obviate the high obsolescence which would otherwise be incurred," as the irrepressible Mr. Denham reported. Differences were more in appointments than basic line, though radiator and headlamp configuration provided a recognition point. The radiator shell had a narrow frontal frame with cusps returned, whereas the 1928 shell had surmounted the core with a simple arch. New built-in thermostatically-operated radiator shutters extended, in simulation, down into the vee-shaped apron. The motometer was gone from the radiator cap, replaced by a temperature gauge on the dashboard. Parabolic headlamps were new and elegantly simple, though they would survive this model year only; perhaps they were too Rolls-Royce-like to please the Packard arbiters. From the rear it was practically impossible to differentiate the new Standard Eight from the former Six, save for the bumpers which like all the brightwork on the new car received chromium plating.

The big difference, of course, was the engine. It was of the same design as the larger eight, sharing a stroke of five inches, but with bore reduced to 3-3/16ths allowing a shorter block and enabling this unit to fit into the space of the former six with only a slight indentation of the firewall. The pump at the front of the block had to be compressed, leaving no space for the Alemite fitting to grease the fan and water pump bearing, this solved by providing a hole in the fan hub to receive an Alemite fitting which would have to be removed and a pipe plug screwed in. "Important," warned the *Information Book*. "Do not leave the Alemite fitting in pulley as it tends to throw the assembly out of balance." A small point to dwell upon, perhaps, but it was a clue to big trouble. The fan belt could not be replaced except by loosening and tilting the radiator forward, rather a chore. Packard was soon aware of its mistake and changed the pump location mid-model to a left side position on the bottom radiator hose. The following year the engine would be relocated, twin fan belts installed and the redesigned pump put back in its original position.

The Standard Eight had a displacement of 320 cubic inches, a rated 32.5 hp and a developed 90. Its larger brother, substantially unchanged from the year previous, was rated at 39.2 with a developed 105 from a cubic inch displacement of 384.8. The two motors were of like quality with interchangeable parts wherever a size difference would not prevent it. The cylinder wall lubricating manifold operated coincidentally with the choke was continued, although the rubber insulated engine mounts were dropped in favor of a rigid four point suspension. The transmission, being farther back into the driver's compartment in both cars, came up for redesign too. In the smaller Packard, the engine was longer than the Six, and in the larger Packard, the wheelbase was—at 140½ inches —two and a half inches shorter than its predecessor. To avoid shortening of bodies, the dimension was absorbed partly in hood length, the shift lever then moved forward from the top of the transmission case to a plate on the bell housing, angle mounted—the result being more room in the front compartment than heretofore. A spring controlled vibration-damper mechanism to prevent synchronized vibration of engine and transmission was incorporated in the Long clutch, the smaller car with a single dry plate, the larger a double with four contacting surfaces. Brake drums on both were enlarged to sixteen inches.

The new shock absorbers, replacing the Watson Stabilators, were Packard designed—and unsuccessful. The body of the shock absorber was mounted on the axle adding to the unsprung weight. It was of the rotating vane type, double-acting with a device giving more resistance on the rebound. No provision, however, was made for service adjustments, replacement instead recommended, which resulted in many of these units being used after they had "frozen up," giving a hard ride—so hard in fact that there were frequent cases of crystalizing and breaking of front frame horns. Often the shock absorbers were discarded or replaced with snubbers or the later Delco piston type mounted on the frame.

A happy accident had seen to the adoption of the "loose trunnion" mount for the rear end of the left front spring. During testing, one of the cars seemed to be free of wheel fight and shimmy when others were not, over the same test road. Examination showed that the left front spring rear mount was loose. This led to the design of a rocker mount held in place by four short compression springs, with the shackle at the front as previous, and road shock absorbed by the limited fore and aft movement allowed by the "loose trunnion" before it was transmitted to the steering gear. Although the "loose trunnion" and other changes had been incorporated to eliminate shimmy, and each had brought improvement, it would be the later adoption of independent front wheel suspension that would really lick the problem.

The springs were given a lower rate action for a softer ride—concomitant with the new shock absorbers. The seat cushions were redesigned and contoured with the result that—if the shock absorbers were working properly—the 1929 Packards rode more luxuriously than before. Front springs on all models were thirty-eight inches long and two inches wide, with rear springs two and a half inches wide by fifty-six inches long on all models, save one.

Actually there were three Packard models for 1929, or more, depending upon how one categorizes them. The Standard Eight in its two wheelbase sizes, carrying designations 626 and 633, is best considered one model. The larger Eight with the 140½-inch wheelbase borrowed the non-custom bodies from the previous 443, received the numerical designation 640 and was dubbed the Custom Eight, which made no sense at all (at least logically) since the custom and semi-custom bodies would now be mounted on a new 145½-inch wheelbase car—with sixty-two-inch rear springs—which carried the designation 645. When the latter arrived—a bit after the 626-633 and 640—it was called the DeLuxe

Eight which didn't make much sense either, but by then the name "Custom" had already been usurped.

On the date the presence of the 1929 Packards was let be known—"announced" seems scarcely the word—the Standard Eights were less than two hundred dollars in excess of the Six's price before that famous clearance sale. The Custom 640 Eight was priced at $700 less, for most body styles, than the 443 models it replaced, this by design as the 645 DeLuxe Eight would be higher priced to cover the upper price brackets.

And then Packard did it again, lowered prices on its new Standard Eight line mid-model. The changes are noted below, with the original prices of the corresponding Six of the year before included for reference:

	626 Body Number	Six 526 7-1-27	626 8-1-28	626 3-4-29
Sedan (5)	333	$2285	$2435	$2275
Coupe (2-4)	338	$2350	$2510	$2350
Convertible Coupe (2-4)	339	$2425	$2585	$2425

	633 Body Number	Six 533 7-1-27	633 8-1-28	633 3-4-29
Phaeton (5)	351	$2385	$2535	$2375
Runabout (2-4)	352	$2385	$2535	$2375
Touring (7)	330	$2485	$2635	$2475
Sedan (7)	334	$2685	$2735	$2575
Sedan-Limousine (7)	335	$2785	$2835	$2675
Club Sedan (5)	336	$2685	$2735	$2575
Coupe (4)	337	$2685	$2735	$2575

The mid-year reductions, as can be readily seen, brought prices of the Standard Eight to figures equal to or below those of the Six of the previous year. This, and doubtless the addition of two cylinders, contributed to Standard Eight production for the model year of some 43,130 units, about 1380 more than the Six had enjoyed the annum previous.

The larger Packard lines were equally as prosperous, in this case due to the newness of price as well as the design appeal when Dietrich's fresh styles became available. Ray Dietrich's assignment at Packard was a line of semi-custom cars for the DeLuxe Eight, and for this he had requested some chassis changes, the first of which was the longer 145½-inch wheelbase. The rear frame was shaped to gain space for a deeper rear seat cushion, Dietrich designed a metal shroud to cover the rear frame horns and gasoline tank, and up front he made the radiator and hood an inch and a half higher, and the hood two inches wider at the dash.

This, and Dietrich's bodies, made for a whole new look. No longer was there the double belt line but a wide molding at the top of the door

Packard enjoyed its international celebrity, as these photographs from the company files attest. Above: General Augusto C. Sandino and his men in July 1929, the caption noting, "General Sandino has attracted attention by his operations against the U.S. Marines in the vicinity of Nicaragua. He is here shown on his flight from Nicaragua to Mexico City." Below: The Six 526 Sedan sold to "Chinese War Lord Chang-Kai-Shek . . . This car is to be used in Ningpo where the alleylike streets must be widened and straightened to accommodate it." Page opposite: A 443 Club Sedan posed before the Russo-Japanese War memorial arch at Kudan Hill in Tokyo.

panels which, narrowing at the windshield, extended along the hood to the radiator. All open cars and the Two/Four-Passenger Coupe carried Dietrich, Inc. body plates, while the other closed cars carried the new "Custom Made by Packard" body plate. There were no convertible styles in this line. The DeLuxe Eight cars could be had in any color or combination desired and with a wide upholstery selection. Other features were dual side mounted spare wheels, trunk rack, adjustable driver's seat and leather spring covers. The windshields of the open cars would fold forward to lie flat over the cowl. The Sport Phaeton had a rear seat cowl and folding windshield, the Phaeton was the same body sans cowl and windshield.

The price relationship between the Custom and DeLuxe models is defined herewith, vis-à-vis the pricetags of the previous 443 model.

	Custom 443 3-1-28	640 Body Number	Custom 640 8-1-28	645 Body Number	DeLuxe 645 9-1-28
Runabout (2-4)	$3875	342	$3175	372	$4585
Phaeton (5)	$3875	341	$3175	371	$4585
Coupe (2-4)	$4150	348	$3250	378	$5385
Sport Phaeton (5)	—	—	—	373	$4935
Touring (7)	$3975	340	$3275	370	$4585
Convertible Coupe (2-4)	$4250	349	$3350	—	—
Coupe (4) (5 on 645)	$4450	347	$3750	377	$5735
Club Sedan (5)	$4450	346	$3750	376	$5785
Sedan (7)	$4450	344	$3750	374	$5785
Sedan-Limousine (7)	$4550	345	$3850	375	$5985

And then there was the Individual Custom line, these cars often built in

other coachbuilders' plants, although the Dietrich designs generally emanated from the Packard Custom body plant. His 645 Individual Customs carried the same design characteristics as the DeLuxe Eight bodies, with those on the 640 chassis of chaste design without moldings on body or hood. The array provided in this Packard grouping, with style numbers indicated, was as follows, all on the 645 chassis unless noted otherwise:

Convertible Coupe (2-4)	1600	by Dietrich
Convertible Victoria (5)	1601	by Dietrich
Convertible Sedan (5)	1602	by Dietrich
All-Weather Cabriolet (7)	1900	by LeBaron
All-Weather Landaulet (7)	1901	by LeBaron
All-Weather Cabriolet (7)	1902	by LeBaron
Sedan-Limousine (7)	1904	by LeBaron
Sedan-Limousine (7)	1905	by LeBaron
All-Weather Town Car (7)	1907	by LeBaron
All-Weather Brougham (7)	1908	by LeBaron
All-Weather Town Car (7)	1909	by LeBaron
All-Weather Cabriolet (7)	7509	by Rollston
All-Weather Town Car (7)	7509 BD	by Rollston
All-Weather Cabriolet (7)	1584	by Dietrich (640 chassis)
All-Weather Landaulet (7)	1585	by Dietrich (640 chassis)
All-Weather Town Car (7)	1586	by Dietrich (640 chassis)

Prices on the Individual Custom line varied according to fittings, some touching five figures. Packard's price range for the year thus traveled from $2275 all the way up to $10,000.

The Autocar, in its road test of the new model Packard, commented briskly that it even had a personality, "if a machine can have such a thing—which brings it on to a rather different plane from the normal, mass-produced American machine." And it didn't look upon the Packard as expensive, "it is, indeed, inexpensive regarded as a large, luxurious town carriage and touring car combined.... It can be maneuvered at extraordinarily low speeds, accelerated and handled generally in traffic without any real thought of the gear change...on the

Hoover and Roosevelt, the President of the United States in Washington, the Governor of New York in Pittsburgh in a Model 640 Seven-Passenger Touring Ca

open road the big car has the power of travelling right up to a high speed [circa 70 mph] without fuss, without suggestion that the engine is doing much work, without harshness, yet with plenty still in reserve." The magazine did cavil that "right up at the maximum speed on top it is possible to hear the fan, and when the engine is accelerating there is a certain carburetter hiss, but neither of these factors is exaggerated, and the power unit as a whole is quiet." And it did not like the upright front seat "which makes one believe that the American driver must be built on rather different lines from his European *confrère*"—and suggested such additions as an armrest for the rear seat, a rear window-blind that could be lowered from the driver's seat and a bit more room for the driver, among other ideas on an Ask the Man Who Tests One theme.

The Men Who Bought Them, and the Women too—Packard-New York staged an enormously successful Women's Week, with tea and dancing and "particular stress . . . laid upon color combinations and appointments to please the feminine fancy"—numbered 49,698 for calendar 1928, with 1929's model year at 54,992 units, this to prove the most

533 Phaeton ready to take aeronaut Hugo Eckener to a ticker tape parade, 1929.

successful in company history. During 1928 Cadillac sold 18,134 cars bearing that name, plus 18,755 LaSalles. Lincoln had slipped a little to 6027, while Peerless dropped twenty percent to 7751. A struggling Pierce-Arrow, now under Studebaker, sold but 5733 cars. Others in this class sold even fewer. And some of the foregoing had begun thinking multi-cylinders.

But not Packard. For its 1929 catalogue the company would come out four-square for the engine it already had, commenting pointedly that "today we find twenty leading motor car manufacturers in this country using the straight-eight motor while the number offering the V-type has dropped from thirty to four. And in Europe, the original home of the V-type motor, the V-type motor has been completely displaced by the straight eight." Packard had started something with its straight eight, the company concluded, and it was happy to see others following suit after its benevolent assist to the industry.

Nineteen twenty-nine looked good, Alvan Macauley said in March that year in an address before the National Automobile Chamber of Commerce, of which he was president. This was *after* a rather portentous stock market slump in early February, which had followed a year of incredible escalation. All motor stocks suffered likewise, but they rose again before month's end. The Packard stock performance might dramatically be set alongside competing companies in its field:

Date	Packard	Auburn	Chrysler	GM	Hudson	Studebaker
1/1/27	37	69	43	—	54	54
1/1/28	62	120	63	138	83	60
2/5/29	143	147½	113½	84½	89	95½
2/8/29	129	139	101	79½	84	85

Macauley was not alone in failing to recognize the danger ahead. Few did—or at least said so publicly. Colonel Leonard P. Ayres, vice-president of the Cleveland Trust Company, whose annual forecast was generally respected by the industry, was one of the exceptions. On December 13th, 1928 he had told the Cleveland Automobile Manufacturers and Dealers Association that the coming year would decide the contest for supremacy and survival in the automobile industry. "Automobile production will reach record breaking proportions in the first and second quarters of the new year," he predicted. "It will be this production and the efforts of manufacturers and distributors to market the product which will bring the greatest competitive struggle in the history of the industry. The industry has a capacity of 7,000,000 cars, for a market that has shown repeatedly that it is able to absorb annually about 4,500,000 cars." And, he suggested, "The wise automobile dealer will strive to do all the business he can in the first two quarters, will try to change cars for spring delivery into immediate delivery, and will try to

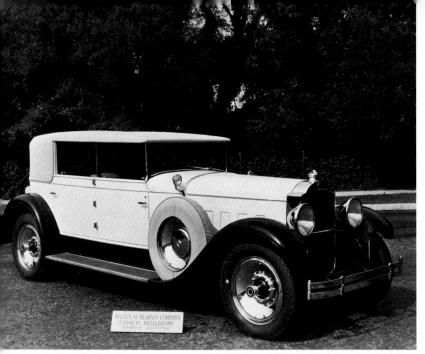

*The Model 645. Above: With Convertible Sedan custom coachwork by Murphy.
Below: The Convertible Victoria by Dietrich in the Individual Custom series.
Page opposite, clockwise from above left: The Sedan-Limousine owned
by Governor William G. Conley of West Virginia; a Runabout photographed
in the Swiss Alps; the Convertible Coupe by Dietrich in the Individual
Custom series; a Five-Passenger Sedan with custom coachwork by Willoughby;
the Phaeton, one of the Packards in the Royal Garages of Spain and
belonging to S.A.R. el Principe de Asturias, "son of the recently deposed
King Alfonso XIII." Note special bumper and Lalique glass comets on fender.*

approach July 4th with the lowest inventory of used cars which is possible."

Who listened? Not many.

For Packard what 1929 portended was what for the company actually happened—for the first nine months of the year. Trade magazine headlines told the story: "Packard Earnings Show Big Increase" from January 2nd, "Packard Earnings Reach New Record" from March 23rd, "Packard Earnings Rise to $23,433,684" from June 29th, "Packard Net Near Entire Former Year" from August 24th, "Packard Motor Assets Increase to $79,812,653" from August 31st, "Packard Sets Delivery Mark" from September 14th, "Packard Deliveries and Sales Top Last Year" from September 28th.

The company's unprecedented sales volume had demanded further plant expansion in a complex which already contained seventy-nine buildings. The program had involved the expenditure of nearly $10 million annually for new machinery and equipment, and the rearrangement of facilities for more efficient use. A new aluminum foundry, an addition to the stamping plant, and a complete rebuilding of the main factory power plant had just been completed. The successful development of the new radial diesel aircraft engine under the direction of Captain Lionel M. Woolson had meant another new building for its manufacture, and the 645 DeLuxe "Custom Made by Packard" cars were selling so well that four stories had to be added to the custom body plant to match production to sales. There were 13,500 people now working for the Packard Motor Car Company, and one might wonder if any among them guessed what lay just ahead.

And who among new Packard owners did? Did Norman Rockwell in his studio in Westchester, New York: did Walter A. Strong, publisher of the *Chicago Daily News*; did Samuel H. Collom, president of the U.S. Lawn Tennis Association; did Joseph Lodge, ice boating sportsman of the prize-winning *Duce-II*; in Hollywood did "the nephew of Rupert Hughes and the industry's youngest producer"—as *The Packard* referred to the young man named Howard; did Mervin LeRoy, Buck Jones, Tom Mix, Bebe Daniels or Corinne Griffith who could convert her Packard limousine "into a corking dressing room big enough to accommodate herself and maid, so that on location she has no need for the usual messy make-up tent provided for the cast?" And did Knowlton L. "Snake" Ames who had pioneered the end run and the spiral punt for the Princeton Tigers football team—or the presidents of universities throughout the country who were contentedly motoring in Packards?

There were the dire predictions, it is true, but those who gave them were regarded as Cassandras. Automobile industry sales for the first quarter of 1929 reached 833,525 units, a hefty 49.9 percent increase over 1928 and 35.6 percent above 1927. How could anything be wrong with business so good? But the stock market continued uneasy.

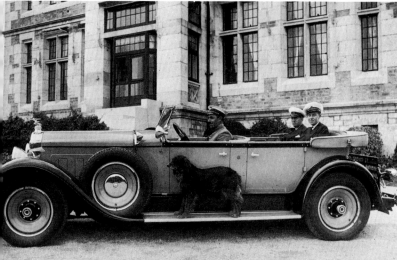

CHAPTER FOURTEEN

NOBODY KNOWS HOW LONG THIS DEPRESSION WILL CONTINUE

The Seventh Series

August 1929–August 1930

The Eighth Series

August 1930–August 1931

AUTHOR: L. MORGAN YOST

Fiscal 1929 had been a record year for the Packard Motor Car Company. Net sales were $107,542,000, net profit $25,912,000, both figures the highest ever. Packard stockholders received a whopping $17,234,000 in dividends. Never again would such an incredible profit year be realized.

The Seventh Series Packards were introduced in this heady atmosphere, announced to the press on September 12th, 1929, though priced as of August 20th, and as usual many sales were made before the public introduction. Many more were made in the days after, and as Alvan Macauley reported, September proved "the greatest month in our history." And October looked just as good, in the beginning.

The catastrophe began with a gigantic sell-off on the New York Stock Exchange. Some 12,894,650 shares were sold on a tobogganing market on October 24th. Bargain hunters stayed the decline for a day or two, but October 29th—when 16,410,000 shares were sold for whatever they would bring and many more were offered with no takers—spelled ruin for thousands of investors. After two more days of panic selling, the market was ordered closed for Friday and Saturday. Headlines screamed disaster and newspapers were filled with stories of suicides.

Still, it didn't seem that all this was formidable enough to alter Packard's course. Although declaring it "foolish to deny that the recent debacle has had no effect on Packard sales," sales manager R.E. Chamberlain told his men to grasp the "real opportunity to capitalize on the sound investment represented in the purchase of a Packard car. . . .

Pages preceding: In mid-September 1929, Packard veterans from East Grand Boulevard and the company branches met for a few days of relaxation at the Seaview Golf Club near Atlantic City. Pictured, from the left, seated: M.A. Cudlip, J.W. Tarbill (Cincinnati), E.F. Roberts, Lee Eastman (New York), R.B. Parker (Philadelphia), Alvan Macauley, Alvan T. Fuller (Boston), H.W. Peters (Chicago), I.L. Berk (Pittsburgh). Standing: B.C. Buff (Packard Export), R.C. Kilgour (Toronto), W.S. Pickell (Detroit), C.M. Fiske (Cleveland), J.E. Hansen (Rochester), L.R. Mack (Albany), Oscar Coolican (Washington, D.C.), K.C. Wettstone (Cleveland), Jesse Vincent, Earle Anthony (Los Angeles), Roy Chamberlain. On these pages, clockwise from the right, Packards for 1930: 733 Phaeton, 726 Five-Passenger Sedan, 733 Seven-Passenger Touring, 745 Club Sedan, 740 Seven-Passenger Sedan, 740 Phaeton, 740 Roadster. The Roadster is shown in a scene from the film, A Show Girl in Hollywood, in which it was prominently featured.

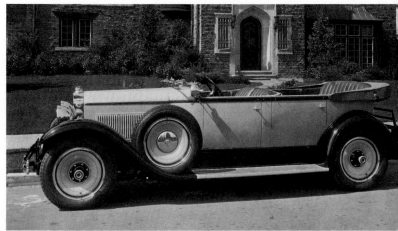

no one can put his finger on anything that resembles in any way shape or manner a panic. Although the practice of stock buying has grown considerably more popular, yet away from the big stock market centers the rise and fall of quotations excite but relatively little interest. . . . The percentage of those paying cash for their Packards is high, some 70 percent*—which means that people who are in the habit of paying cash for Packard cars pay cash for most other things and hence are not so likely to have been caught short."

Nevertheless, sales in December dropped to 1537 units, well below the

---

*Now Chamberlain was perhaps privately relieved that the Packard clientele had not tended more to time-payment purchases.

previous December's 2302. (The final figures for both years were 49,698 for 1928, 47,855 for 1929.) In November Alvan Macauley had been appointed one of twenty members of the executive committee of the National Business Survey Conference organized to recommend a future course of action for the business community. Julius Barnes, the chairman, in a masterpiece of equivocation hardly excelled since, advised, "A preliminary study . . . indicates that there is nothing to cause further timidity or hesitation, but, rather, warrants confidence in the early optimism in the early stabilization of business activity without justifying optimism before the close of the test period of the next few months."

Packard's vice-president of distribution H.W. Peters was a bit more succinct; in mid-December, allowing that "the normal seasonal decline

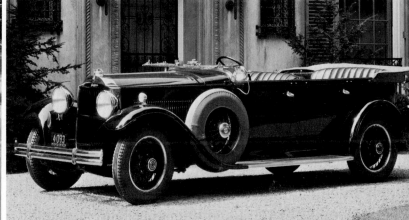

Seventh Series Individual Customs, from the top: 745 Brewster Convertible Sedan, 745C LeBaron Sedan-Limousine, 745C Rollston All-Weather Town Car.

of business has been somewhat accentuated by the market break," he declared that Packard would continue its substantial production. In March of 1930 in a letter to stockholders detailing the interim period from August 31st to December 31st, 1929—Packard changed to a calendar fiscal year on January 1st, 1930—Alvan Macauley said simply, "Contrary to the experience of many companies following the stock market crash in October 1929, our operations have been profitable during each subsequent month and to date."

The Packard record looked so good, there seemed no inordinate cause for alarm:

Fiscal Year	Net Sales All Operations Dollars/Thousands	Profit after Taxes All Operations Dollars/Thousands
1925	60,476	11,115
1926	77,354	15,844
1927	71,659	11,743
1928	94,677	21,885
1929	107,542	25,912
Interim four months	27,734	4,725
but . . . ahead lay		
1930	57,690	9,034
1931	29,987	-2,909

And there were other signs. Buick had laid an egg for 1929 with a car which earned the sobriquet "pregnant Buick," at a time when that adjective was not usually heard in polite circles. It was greatly altered for 1930—and for '31 Buick abandoned its six-cylinder engine to go to a straight eight, the first in the GM family. Buick would now be breathing down Packard's neck. By 1931, with the Depression growing deeper, and the market still going down in spurts, Packard felt the competition keenly. In 1930 Packard produced 28,386 cars, in '31 only 12,922.

Late in 1929 Cord had followed Ruxton into the marketplace with the novelty of a front wheel drive car. Ruxton produced only a handful, Cord more. But the times made for hesitation. No buyer could afford a mistake on an unproven product. That fact, as much as the word being passed regarding the Cord's less-than-admirable performance and handling, led to the withdrawal of the L-29 from the market. At the time there seemed to be little connection between Cord and Packard but the engineer who designed the former, Cornelius Van Ranst, had been hired by the latter and would be at work trying to come up with something profitable as Packard sales slowed down to a trickle.

Cadillac was not flourishing either. But it had the blockbuster of a new, high priced, very prestigious, limited production car with a V-16 engine. The timing of its introduction, January 1930, was inopportune, but it had been developed prior to the crash—and besides, everyone expected the Depression to be over soon anyway. The car reflected great

The 745 Brewster car modified for Alvan Macauley, reflecting the Louis XVI period with its French walnut and tulipwood paneling and hand-carved moldings.

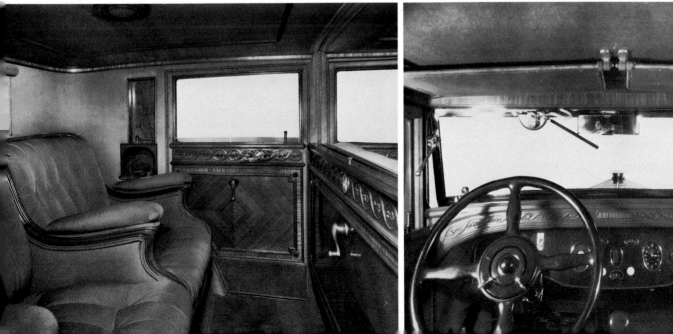

glory on Cadillac, which did Packard no good. Trade journals extolled its engineering and design, the finesse of the V-16 with its 5.5 compression ratio (high for the time) and its 170-185 horsepower on tap, its two complete fuel systems, and the synchromesh transmission which had been fitted to all Cadillacs and LaSalles since August of 1928. Cadillac was giving Packard pause. And with good reason, for though Cadillac was hurting, it would not be as much as Packard, comparatively:

Calendar Year	Cadillac-LaSalle Production	Packard Production
1929	36,598	47,855
1930	22,559	28,386
1931	15,012	12,922
1932	9,153	9,010

The car Packard was selling then might seem a bit *démodé* compared to some of its contemporaries. But the Packard clientele had ever possessed a notable attribute: seeming blindness to the competition, a loyalty every other maker envied. Packard was averse to the untried, a Packard was made to be good for years, an effective sales point which the company enhanced with a catalogue on the notion of renewing the cars. "Once a Packard—Always a Packard" was its title, and its theme, "why not consider yourself in the position of one who bought his Packard new and drives it today for the years of good service still in it? You can put yourself on a par with him because your used Packard will still be distinguished in beauty, luxury and comfort."

The Seventh Series Packards were new looking. Ray Dietrich had modified the theme of his 1929 645 body styles to cover the entire 1930 line. They were lower and more fleet with the appearance of the Twenties left behind. The same bodies were now used on the 733, the 740 and the 745 models, with wheelbases at 134½ inches, 140½ inches and 145½ inches respectively, the dimensional difference in each case being taken up in hood length. What was all that extra space doing under the hood of the 745? Nothing at all. The motor was the same as the 740 but it was mounted five inches rearward with a sheet metal shroud extending back from the radiator surrounding the fan to keep the air on course. (Some early 745 cars were shroud-less and the fan was mounted on an extended shaft close to the radiator.) In manufacturer's parlance, the "body space"—the horizontal distance from firewall to center of the rear axle—was the same for all three cars: 93⅞ inches. For those custom bodies where more body space was desired, the 745C chassis was used, the long 145½-inch wheelbase but with the engine mounted close to the radiator as on the 740. The hood was the same length as the 740 but an inch and a half higher, the same as the 645, providing five more inches for more spacious interiors in seven-passenger sedan-limousines, town cars and cabriolets.

The Packard Motor Car Company goes diesel: Lionel Woolson checking an engine on dynamometer (below), Jesse Vincent with a test plane (above) and the company exhibiting at a national aeronautical show (page opposite).

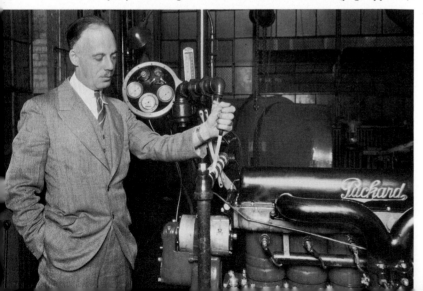

Aside from hood length, the 745 cars were distinguished by a barbed spear head formed into the leading end of the hood side molding. The 745C and the 740 hood moldings had rounded ends with a small arrowhead striped on in paint. Both 745 and 745C had new and long sweeping front fenders following the vogue.

Other changes included a half-melon shaped headlamp design and the omission of cowl band and sidelights on brackets. The new parking lamps were fender mounted, though they were an accessory on the Standard Eight where the parking lights were incorporated into the headlamps. Those for the larger Eights had a heavy rib with the profile of the Packard radiator shape placed on top. The same "Packard shape" was used in the center part of the three-lens taillamp, flanked by the stoplight and back-up light. The long wheelbase 745 and 745C had a new radiator spout design, also used on the Speedsters, about which more anon. The cap was triangular with two curved sides, the flat side to the front, the base of the spout extending down the front of the radiator tank to form a background for the usual oval crest. As before, this new cap was held in place by a wire bail; it would be retained this one model year only. Accessory mascots might be mounted on any of the caps: the goddess, called "DeLuxe" in the catalogue, or the Adonis, the first now familiarly known as the "doughnut chaser," the latter the "sliding boy."

Non-shatter laminated glass was adopted for the windshield and all

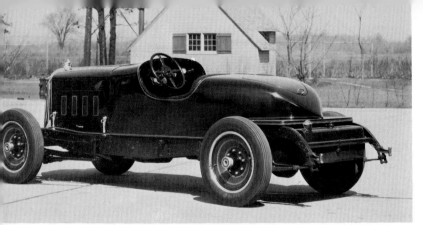

windows, glove compartments were installed on each side of the instrument board. The driver's seat was now adjustable, and steering wheel position could be changed, though it was a service operation. Adjustable sun visors and a map light on the instrument board were added.

Wood or wire wheels were optional to the disc, and dual side-mounted spares were also optionally available on the Standard Eight and 740. The 745 carried two extra wheels as regular equipment, either in fender wells or on a double-wheel carrier at the rear, the latter making for an exceptionally long and impressive car, especially since the long sweeping fenders were not then interrupted.

For 1930 all Standard Eight cars were on the 134½-inch wheelbase, save for the price leader, the Five-Passenger Sedan, on the shorter 127½-inch wheelbase and designated as model 726. Both 726 and 733 were one inch longer than formerly, and that inch was put where it was needed, at the front of the motor for a redesigned water pump. Not only were the fan and pulley given enough space but the drive was now by twin fan belts. Packard had heard so much about the inept design of that part in the 1929 Standard Eight that the company wanted it clearly understood the fault had been entirely eliminated. The double fan belt arrangement was also applied to the larger Eights, though they had not been subject to such criticism. The motor thermostat was eliminated, dependence for temperature control being entirely with the thermostatically controlled radiator shutters. Other than that, engine modifications for the new model were few.

A new carburetor, Detroit Lubricator No. 51, was adopted, still updraft. Fuel supply was retained by vacuum tank, though on the larger Eights a vacuum pump was installed after January 1930, this pump not being, as many suppose, unique to the Speedsters. It was a reciprocating piston device which assisted the vacuum tank at high speeds, was mounted on the front chain cover and driven off the camshaft by an eccentric—and was offered for installation on any 1930 Packard as a service operation. The piston tire pump formerly on the transmissions of the Eights fell by the wayside, as filling stations became ubiquitous.

The most important mechanical change was the four-speed transmission, which was to be retained in the Eighth Series and into the early Ninth. The shift pattern was the usual for the three regular gears; the fourth was an extra low, usually called low-low, reached by pushing the shift lever firmly to the left against a spring-loaded stop, then to the rear. Many who bought these cars second- or third-hand never were aware of the extra low. It was not a performance four-on-the-floor box in today's sense: It was adopted in order to use ratios more in keeping with improved engine torque for ordinary driving, without foregoing the availability of extra power for special purposes. The change made getting under way easier, but the extra low was almost useless.

The transmission housing was still cast iron painted aluminum, not cast aluminum as many believe. The new floor boards, oddly enough, might be singled out for mention as well. The sloping toe board on the 1928 and '29 Packards had been cast aluminum in pyramid pattern, the level portion linoleum bound in aluminum. The rear compartments were carpeted, even in the rumble seats. With the Seventh Series, however, both front and rear were entirely carpeted, which diluted the masculine quality of the car. That, doubtless, was the idea, for more and more women were driving.

As in the Sixth Series, the Standard Eight hoods had louver vents while the larger Eights had four doors in each side of the hood, now equipped with small chrome knobs so they could be opened without raising the hood. An accessory hood was available for the Standard Eight, with three doors, giving the car more of the appearance of the larger Eights. Windshields on all open cars folded forward, stanchions and all, to lie flat on the cowl.

Prices for the Standard Eight line, with increases mid-model year in three cases, were as follows:

Model 726	Body Number	8-20-29	1-13-30
Sedan (5)	403	$2375	$2485
Model 733			
Coupe (2-4)	408	$2525	
Coupe (5)	407	$2675	
Convertible Coupe (2-4)	409	$2550	
Phaeton (4)	401	$2425	
Sport Phaeton (4)	431	$2725	
Roadster (2-4)	402	$2425	
Touring (5-7)	400	$2525	
Sedan (5-7)	404	$2675	$2785
Club Sedan (5)	406	$2675	
Sedan-Limousine (5-7)	405	$2775	$2885

Prices on the misnomered Custom 740 line—within fifty dollars of those on the previous 640's—are compared herewith to the long wheelbase 745, which had the same bodies but full options:

	Model 740		Model 745	
	Body No.	8-20-29	Body No.	8-20-29
Coupe (2-4)	418	$3295	428	$4785
Coupe (5)	417	$3650	427	$5100
Convertible Coupe (2-4)	419	$3350	429	$4885
Phaeton (4)	411	$3190	421	$4585
Sport Phaeton (4)	441	$3490	451	$4885
Roadster (2-4)	412	$3190	422	$4585
Touring (5-7)	410	$3325	420	$4585
Sedan (5)	413	$3585	423	$4985
Club Sedan (5)	416	$3750	426	$5150
Scdan (5-7)	414	$3785	424	$5185
Sedan-Limousine (5-7)	415	$3885	425	$5350

The Speedster Series. Page opposite: Colonel Jesse Vincent's special roadster which provided the inspiration and the 734 Speedster motor showing vacuum pump, finned exhaust manifold and double-barrel carburetor. The 626 Speedster Runabout and Phaeton (above); the 734 Speedster Runabout and Phaeton (below).

The five-passenger sedan was back in these lines after a two-year absence, carrying its own body—the short wheelbase 726 wasn't long enough—though all other bodies, as mentioned, were the same for 733-740-745, the difference being in trim, paint options and upholstery. The premium put on five inches of car length and some broader options for the 745 was not trifling—around fourteen hundred dollars. Though these cars carried the highly prized "Custom Made by Packard" on the lower cowl, they were really production cars with owner's choice of color and trim, and produced to order. And the factory always had some already on hand with distinctive paint and trim for those who did not wish to wait five or six weeks.

Many of the Individual Custom bodies offered for '29 were re-offered for 1930. Brewster was new to the line with very crisp low designs, one of which—a Style No. 7813 sedan-limousine—Alvan Macauley had modified into a personal car for himself with a special wood paneled and carved interior, and individual lounge chair seats in the rear. The Individual Custom roster for 1930, with asterisk indications of those retained from the previous year, was as follows:

Body Maker	Body Type	Style No.		Chassis
LeBaron	All-Weather Cabriolet	1900	*	745C
LeBaron	All-Weather Landaulet	1901	*	745C
LeBaron	Sedan-Limousine	1904	*	745C
LeBaron	Sedan-Limousine	1905	*	745C
LeBaron	All-Weather Town Car	1907	*	745C
LeBaron	All-Weather Town Car	1909	*	745C
Brewster	All-Weather Cabriolet	7812		745
Brewster	Sedan-Limousine	7813		745
Brewster	Convertible Sedan	7815		745
Brewster	All-Weather Landaulet	7934		745
Brewster	Sedan-Limousine	7936		745
Rollston	All-Weather Cabriolet	7509	*	745C
Rollston	All-Weather Town Car	7509BD*		745C
Dietrich	Convertible Sedan	1602	*	745
Dietrich	Convertible Victoria	1711		745

The 745C bodies carried over needed no modification to fit the hood dimensions, as the 745C hood was the same size as that of the 645. Chassis of both these types, as well as the 733, were supplied to these coachbuilders and to such others as Derham, Brunn, Murphy, Judkins, Waterhouse and Willoughby for special custom bodies if so ordered by a customer.

LeBaron published a beautiful catalogue with Stickney renderings in color of two additional custom bodies on the 745C chassis handled through Packard, the first a close-coupled, four-passenger, four-door convertible sedan with individual bucket seats and a special metal trunk affixed to the rear; the second a convertible roadster, with a top which folded into a well abaft the front seat, neatly covered—almost flush—by a Burbank boot, presaging the similar arrangement by Dietrich for the 1932 production lines.* (Fifty of these LeBaron convertible roadsters were built.) The why of these two additions may have been LeBaron's awareness that its contributions to the 1930 Packard Individual Custom line suffered by comparison to the sleek Brewster and Dietrich submissions. LeBaron's formal cars stood tall, literally, some two inches higher than Brewster's designs. There were, of course, some customers who preferred a high roof in this era when top hats were still being worn on elegant occasions. Still, LeBaron probably felt a little image-rescuing was in order.

Packard, at least publicly, did not feel rescue measures of any sort necessary yet. In mid-April 1930 Alvan Macauley reported the company would adhere "as closely as possible to a constant level of factory operation throughout the year, regardless of the irregularities of the market." But, privately, he was a little worried. He wrote his directors on May 12th that "we are in the midst of curtailing expenses because of our belief that business will not greatly improve before the beginning of next spring"—curtailments to include compacting manufacturing operations into a five- rather than six-day week, which "I am sorry to say, will result in the release of perhaps 2000 additional employees. All salaries in the factory and offices have been readjusted accordingly."

By May 12th, however, he was able to report "the first promising sales news in a long time"—the delivery in New York of fifty-seven cars over the previous weekend. Then on May 28th Packard reduced prices on all cars $400, pending the introduction of the new models. Doubtless this was a sales-generating ruse, because the changes to come were not so substantial as to depreciate the 1930 cars greatly.

Packard's steady market, especially for the larger cars, was the repeat customer, many of whom had two-, three- or four-year schedules for turning in the old Packard for a new one. The sales force was now encouraged to go after owners of other cars in the lower price ranges and step them up to a Packard. "Two-thirds of those who buy the Packard Standard Eight," ads said, "give up other makes of cars. Thousands prefer to buy out of income. Your used car will be accepted as cash and if of average value will more than make up the down payment on a new car." The idea was that the prospect purchase his Packard without

---

*To fold the top snugly into the well, the frame member that spanned the door opening was hinged in the center to fold horizontally so the folded top was a more compact package. Today it is often erroneously called a "three-position top," as in the half-opened position it suggests a victoria top, never the original intention, and the sloppy roll of cloth would never have been tolerated as a finished product.

recourse to his savings, spreading payments over three or four months only and leaving investments intact. Some of these "investments," of course, were in common stocks which, it was hoped, and expected, would soon rise again in value. Few people thought the Depression would endure much longer.

Packard's ambitious aviation program seemed to confirm that, at least. Captain Lionel M. Woolson, with Packard's Engineering Division since January of 1919, had developed the company's diesel-type radial nine-cylinder aero engine—and by early 1930 it had received widespread attention via a number of highly successful demonstration flights. Woolson was a go-getter; during a week of Government tests he had a cot moved into his office and his meals sent in to remain as close to the project as possible—but he loved flying above all. As Alvan Macauley would remember, when Woolson's work neared completion, "I earnestly endeavored to get him to allow someone else to do the [air] testing, but he sturdily maintained that it was part of his work and that it was the reward he sought for his hours at the drafting table in the testing laboratory." By early April the Packard Diesel program was so far along that a special sales manager was placed in its charge: Macauley's son Edward, who had been apprenticing as assistant to H.W. Peters. But on the 23rd of that month during a flight from Detroit to New York—in a blinding snowstorm near Attica—a Packard-Diesel-engined Verville crashed. Its three occupants were killed; one of them was Captain Woolson. A saddened Alvan Macauley pledged to make the Packard Diesel "the success his vision pictured it." But without Woolson's inspiration the project lost its spark and, with the Depression, its momentum. Soon nothing more would be heard of it, and Edward Macauley would transfer his energies to Packard styling.

Colonel Jesse Vincent's energies betimes were speedster oriented. Probably the opening of the million-dollar Packard Proving Grounds at Utica (see Appendices) in 1927 had occasioned it. The Colonel relished speed, racing his Packard-powered hydroplanes repeatedly to adventure and victory. On land, speed was more difficult, the roads of Michigan crowded, twisted—and patrolled. With Utica in operation, however—in the charge of the Colonel's brother Charles—Jesse Vincent could move as fast as he wanted, or at least as fast as his Packards would let him. At the Master Salesmen's Convention there in August of '28, the Colonel "showed what real speed looks like" in a 443 Rollston sedan—about 85 mph. That was incentive enough for a faster Packard, to satisfy the Colonel, to use the track for publicity purposes and to take advantage of the advertising value of speed.

So Vincent had a special car built. It used a Fourth Series chassis with a tapered-tail racing-type body, sans fenders, windshield, bumpers, lamps and other impedimenta. It was driven in 1928 by Colonel Charles Lindbergh, on a visit to look over the aviation engine, and in 1958

Lindbergh wrote of the experience: "I drove the car several times around the track, at a little over 100 mph, if my memory is correct. . . . I believe the average was 109 mph, and that the car had averaged 128 mph with its regular driver." About twenty years later R.M. Williams, a Packard company veteran of some two decades, saw the roadster in the Proving Grounds garage, wanted to buy it, but was told Colonel Vincent was keeping it there because of its history. No trace of it remains now, nor any details or specifications.

This car was undoubtedly a basis for the 1929 limited production 626 Speedster Eight though, as mentioned before, the experimental 117-inch wheelbase six was a step in that direction as well. Some references have miscalled it the 634 Speedster and some Packard information books have incorrectly given its wheelbase as 134 inches, by retroactive inference from the better known 1930 Model 734 Speedster.

One lone example of the 626 Speedster remains, a rumble-seat roadster. It was sold in Chicago, the purchaser insisting on a speed

Monobloc Twelve, 1929; Packard paint shops, circa 1930. (Note striping tool.)

capability of 100 mph. He went to the factory to prove it himself and did—adequately—then accepted the car, and it was delivered on October 10th, 1928. The factory billed Buresch Motor Sales—the Packard dealer—$3825 for the car, and the new owner paid Buresch $5000 plus $250 for chrome-plated wire wheels and $10 for the DeLuxe (Goddess of Speed) ornament.

At first glance the car looks like any other 1929 roadster, but a second look shows the hood to be longer in proportion to the short rear deck. The chassis is the shorter of the two Standard Eights—126½ inches—fitted with a 640 Custom Eight motor, with high compression head, a high-lift camshaft, and metric spark plugs, developing 130 hp at 3000 rpm. A vacuum booster pump aided the vacuum tank when the reading fell below seven, this pump available on no other 1929 Packard. Rear axle ratio was 3.31 to one. A muffler cutout was provided.

To make the speedster body, a production Runabout was modified by removing a section fourteen inches long from the back of the front seat to the front of the rumble seat opening, eliminating the golf club compartment. Body type number was 392. The weight of the new car was 3830 pounds, compared to 4285 pounds for the stock 640 Runabout—455 pounds can make a difference. Furthermore, the catalogue stated, "As minimum head resistance is essential for maximum speed, no specifications are accepted for DeLuxe equipment, [side-mounted spares], windshield wings, etc., for these special cars." A phaeton body, numbered 391, was also available at the same price, $5000.

The Colonel had his fast car but very little publicity was provided it. Perhaps only seventy to seventy-four were built. A few sedan models of the 626 Speedster were produced as well, but not catalogued, one of them driven by Tommy Milton from Miami to Los Angeles at an average speed of 50 mph, which in those days was good enough to be noticed.

The performance of the 626 Speedsters had highly satisfied Packard management but there remained some objections which led to a revised line for 1930. First, the shortened 640 bodies, the Phaeton and especially the Runabout, looked stubby and high. They lacked the fleet lines that made cars look fast, the Cord, Auburn, Kissel and Black Hawk, for instance. Furthermore, the 1930 Packards had new bodies with the refined Dietrich influence and did not lend themselves to alterations. And, the short body space—only 79⅞ inches—was just not enough to be comfortable, especially for a sedan.

Packard needed a glamour car to counteract the attention Cadillac's V-16 was getting. A full line of really fast cars, it was thought, would do it. Instead of selecting the 726 chassis, as before, Packard modified the longer Standard Eight chassis of 134½ inches, and put a DeLuxe Eight motor in it—with significant modifications this time to provide free breathing passages. The cylinder block casting was different from that in the other 1930 Packards; the faces to which were bolted the inlet and ex-

haust manifolds were not vertical in a plane but rather at 45 degrees on a tent-shaped protrusion allowing more interior space and larger openings to the manifolds since they did not have to be crowded into a straight line. The exhaust openings were on the upper face of the tent, the inlet on the lower, with exhaust and inlet manifolds separate. The intake riser was heated but not connected to the exhaust manifold. The stove chamber was opened to the exhaust ports of the two center cylinders by passages inside the block, exhaust gases did not circulate through it. The exhaust manifold was straight line to the rear, its top surface with cast and machined longitudinal fins for cooling. Exhaust valves were increased to 1⅝ inches in diameter, the same as the inlet valves.

The carburetor, unique to the 734 Speedster, was a Detroit Lubricator dual throat updraft. A muffler cut-out was operated by a foot pedal in the driver's compartment. A vacuum pump, much like that used on the 626 Speedster, was piston type operated by an eccentric on the front end of the camshaft and connected between the inlet manifold and the vacuum tank.

With the standard compression ratio of 4.85 to one and standard spark plugs, the engine delivered 125 hp at 3400 rpm, compared to 106 hp at 3200 rpm for the production version used in the 740 and 745 models. For superior performance, a high compression head, 6.0 to one, with metric plugs, could be had, which required anti-knock fuel but provided the bonus of 145 hp at 3400. In its catalogue, the company recommended the low compression head and a 4.0 to one gear ratio. But most of the open

A Packard takes on the Dark Continent. In 1931 Prince Eugene de L

models were sold with the high compression head and a 3-1/3 to one gear ratio, providing a car that would readily exceed the century mark. For rapid acceleration and use in the hills, a gear ratio of 4-2/3 to one was available. The different gear ratios and cylinder heads were optional at no difference in cost.

Most Speedsters, but not all, were equipped with a tachometer mounted on the instrument board, driven from the distributor shaft. Again the purchaser was warned, "As minimum head resistance is important for maximum performance, the addition of accessories and extra equipment is discouraged." Not quite as uncompromising as the pronouncement in the 626 Speedster catalogue, but nevertheless usually heeded. The cars were provided with one rear spare only, save the Runabout, familiarly called the boattail, for which, "because of its graceful streamlined torpedo design, the spare wheels are necessarily mounted forward."

Speedster bodies were about three inches narrower and considerably lower than bodies in the regular lines, the windshield on the open cars was lower as well and did not fold forward. All bodies were designed and built in the Packard custom shops and carried the "Custom Made by Packard" plate on the lower body panel.

Best known is the Speedster Runabout (Body No. 422), the boattail design, which usually had staggered front seats to give the driver more elbow room, but was available also with seats straight across. Its capacity was two and no more, and baggage had to be carefully selected to fit into the tiny compartment in the narrow tail. The Phaeton (Body No. 445), for four passengers made a great touring car—for two—using the tonneau for luggage. There was no rear deck or windshield and at speed a rear-seat passenger would be gasping for breath.

The Victoria (Body No. 447), a four-passenger, close-coupled coupe, was for the family desiring a closed Speedster without the seeming formality of the Sedan. It had a smallish rear compartment for luggage, although with its full complement of passengers there was no more space inside for anything. The Sedan (Body No. 443) had ample leg room in the rear seat, even enough for a bag or two, but a width for only two rear-seat passengers comfortably.

These four comprised the catalogued line but there was demand for a roadster with greater capacity so a rumble-seat variation (Body No. 452) was added later, very sleek and low, but without the commanding distinction of the Runabout. At least one coupe with a rumble seat was built but it was not generally offered. Price for Runabout and Phaeton was $5200, for Sedan and Victoria $6000.

Complete choice in colors and upholstery was provided, with disc or wire wheels available at the same price, and the same triangular radiator cap as the 745 models. The chassis could also be purchased for mounting of special coachwork. *The Packard* illustrated a body by Kirschhoff so obliterating the Packard features that only the wire wheel hubs remained identifiable. Another, by Thompson, was given a rounded radiator shell (as was the Kirschoff), cycle fenders and low pointed body.

Belgium chose his Model 833 for motoring across the Sahara, an expedition which, with the occasional assistance of the natives, went smashingly.

The 734 Speedsters were introduced in January 1930 but were not carried into the next model year, which remains an enigma since changes in other models for the 1931 Eighth Series were minor save for the engines—for which the Speedster was the prototype. The Speedster line, again, simply was not promoted, for whatever reason remains a mystery as well. Some city branches ran local newspaper ads, but of national advertising there was precisely none. There is no certainty as to the number built, 140 is a reasonable guess, of which at least twenty-two remain extant.

Two very distinctive—and very different—special Packards also issued forth from the company about this time, one widely publicized, the other not. Indeed the latter—the Monobloc Twelve—has long been considered a figment of someone's imagination, but it was real enough. An experimental straight twelve with cylinders cast in one block, installed in the 145-inch chassis and fitted with a convertible victoria body by Dietrich, very much like the 745 Style No. 1711, the car was turned over to Warren Packard, son of William Doud Packard. As Warren's widow, now Mrs. Edward Cope Smith, remembers, "[it] just appeared one day in 1929 and that Sunday we drove to church in it." It was resplendent: orange body, silver fenders and aprons, body moldings also silver—the family called it the "Easter Egg." The hood was *very* long, and because of this the body was placed farther back in relation to the rear wheels, so much so that the door came within a few inches of the rear fender. Body space must have been very cramped. Ray Dietrich has stated that a factory building at Murray had been set aside to make the Dietrich bodies for the car when it went into production. That consideration was given to production is indicated by several Werner Gubitz styling drawings for a "12-45," one of them a four-door sedan indicating a rear fender cutting two-thirds of the way across the rear door. Production never came, of course, doubtless one reason being that sedans or formal cars would have been impossible on the chassis.

No factory data on the car, nor any photographs of its motor, have since been discovered. The Warren Packard family used the car for a number of months, including a 1500-mile round trip to Quebec in the summer—and Mrs. Smith remembers it as wonderfully smooth and quiet, and trips as uneventful except for the crowds that gathered round. Warren Packard died that same summer in a plane crash on August 26th, the first day of the Packard Master Salesmen's Convention in Detroit in which he was participating. Shortly thereafter the Packard company bought the car back, removed and destroyed its engine, put an eight-cylinder in its place and reportedly sold it for export where it would not be so noticeable.

The other special Packard couldn't have been less unnoticeable either—and it too was destined for export—a snow white 740 limousine delicately striped in pink. A white automobile in those days was quite un-

Packards for 1931. The 845 DeLuxe Seven-Passenger Sedan, the 840 Indivi[...]

heard of—"That's the color of milk wagons!" But no milk wagon this. It was built for His Highness, the Maharaja Sahib of Porbander, India. It was for his wife, the Maharini—and she was a very demanding lady. The interior was a delicate pink, rather like the ashes of roses, the hue discovered after months of searching and inspecting samples that might please Her Highness, with a *voila!* finally given. Packard's task was to duplicate the material of the lady's slipper. The company did, in a specially woven mohair by Chase Velmo, complemented by a rug of deep mohair pile giving the appearance of soft fur. Not everyone was roughing it in the Depression.

Packard's overseas sales had continued high . . . comparatively. In 1930 the company exported one-third the total number of cars among all the eighteen marques selling for $2000 or more. Packard advertising tried to pretend the Depression wasn't happening, although one ad in February of 1930 strayed far enough from the romantic to provide price ranges of the three lines. "Luxurious Transportation" through the ages was the theme early in the year, with paintings illustrating gondolas, palanquins, Tally-Hos, galleons, horses, elephants, coaches and carriages of all types. In the fall the theme was "For a Discriminating Clientele," depicting fine things by fine people from fine ages past: china by Wedgewood, portraits by Holbein, charts and maps by Mercator, jewelry by Boehmer, music by Mozart, tapestries by Goya, furniture by Duncan Phyfe, and on and on.

tom Convertible Victoria (Dietrich), the 826 Standard Five-Passenger Sedan.

And, of course, the new Packard line—designated 826-833-840-845—which the company began building in August. The hubcaps were larger, steering wheels had three spokes rather than four, fenders were a bit deeper, running boards thicker, the bumper clamps plain, not paneled. The long sweeping front fenders of the 745 were now installed on the larger Eights, the 840 and 845, both of which had the same hood length, the long hood of the 745 having been dropped. With the shorter hood length, the car doors overlapped the rear end of the fenders next to the running board so six chrome strips were placed on the fender to protect against inadvertent stepping. The misnomered "Custom" tag for the 740's was dropped, all large Eights now being called DeLuxe. The 740 and 745 had been separate lines at different price levels, the new 840 and 845 were in one line now, with the longer wheelbase merely being used for seven-passenger sedans and limousines. Despite the larger bodies, these cars were over $1000 less in price than their 745 counterparts, about $400 more than the 740 models.

Eighth Series Packards had considerably more get-up-and-go than their predecessors, the Standard Eight developing 100 hp, the large Eight 120, the block from the 734 Speedster engine with its larger exhaust and inlet ports being largely responsible. The intake manifold was the same general type as on the Speedster but made in three sections, with a cylindrical heater chamber in the center which connected with the exhaust ports of the two center cylinders. Thus, all mixture from the car-

buretor was preheated and entered the ports through much larger passages. The exhaust manifold was straight as on the Speedster but not finned—and set higher to allow space for the stove on the inlet manifold.

To accommodate the more volatile fuels then in use, the vacuum tank gave way to a Stewart Warner fuel pump operated by a cam on the front end of the timing chain cover. The new fuel pump had no vacuum booster as there did not remain such demands on manifold vacuum as a source of energy, merely the windshield wiper and the new type vacuum-operated Bijur chassis lubrication system which no longer had the old hand pump. The daily chore of pulling the chassis lubricator handle was eliminated, and the reminder to refill was gone too—the old pump would fall free from the hand if the reservoir was empty. A float gauge on the metal tank under the hood now had to be watched. The hood latches were concealed with a mere handle exposed; gone now was the old familiar spring plunger type.

Prices for the Standard Eight—which generally remained as before—and the DeLuxe Eight—which changed were as follows:

Model 826	Body Number	8-14-30	6-23-31
Sedan (5)	463	$2385	$2150
Model 833			
Coupe (2-4)	468	$2525	$2175
Coupe (5)	467	$2675	$2295
Convertible Coupe (2-4)	469	$2550	$2250
Phaeton (4)	461	$2425	$2175
Sport Phaeton (4)	481	$2725	$2395
Roadster (2-4)	462	$2425	$2125
Touring (5-7)	460	$2525	$2325
Club Sedan (5)	466	$2675	$2345
Sedan (5-7)	464	$2725	$2475
Sedan-Limousine (5-7)	465	$2885	$2575
Convertible Sedan	483	$3445	$3125
Model 840			
Sedan (5)	473	$3795	$3200
Coupe (2-4)	478	$3545	$2900
Coupe (5)	477	$3850	$3250
Convertible Coupe (2-4)	479	$3595	$2900
Phaeton (4)	471	$3490	$2990
Sport Phaeton (4)	491	$3790	$3200
Roadster (2-4)	472	$3490	$2800
Touring (5-7)	470	$3595	$3195
Club Sedan (5)	476	$3950	$3200
Model 845			
Sedan (5-7)	474	$4150	$3500
Sedan-Limousine (5-7)	475	$4285	$3600

The 833 Convertible Sedan was priced out for the 1931 line, but it would

The 840. Walter Damrosch and his Touring Car on Park Avenue, Jack Holt and his Phaeton on location for a film; Clifton Webb and his Convertible Sedan.

not appear in the catalogues.

Neither would many of the Eighth Series cars appear on the road. Sales were down, down, down all year. To provide a hoped-for push up, the company decided to introduce its new 1932 Ninth Series cars early, on June 17th, 1931. That left hundreds of the Eighth Series still in stock, at the factory and in dealerships. Only 12,105 Standard Eights and 3345 DeLuxe Eights had been built, but even with the production reduced from the year previous, the oversupply was serious. When introducing the new 1932 line, Packard included the Eighth Series in salesmen's handbooks, and it provided dealers free of charge a facelifting kit to give the Eighth Series the look of the Ninth—outside horns, special vee radiator shell front grille and headlight bar, and the twin taillights and bumpers from the Ninth Series. It was a desperate move to clear the merchandise.

Things were decidedly not good at Packard. Even Alvan Macauley had turned pessimistic. In his letter of December 19th, 1930 to members of the Packard Senior League, he said, "Nobody knows how long this depression will continue. I have no way to predict definitely the course that our business, or business generally, will take from now on." But he remained convinced Packard would be among the first to show signs of restoration when conditions improved. Would that it had been that easy. The company was still in an excellent cash position. If it were merely a matter of waiting out a lull in business, Packard could do it. But attitudes were changing. A holding pattern wasn't the answer.

No matter what the Packard people would work out for the future, they still had to rid themselves of the stock on hand. Prices on the oversupply of Eighth Series Standard Eights were reduced again on September 17th, 1931. A customer with the means could have the cars at the new listed prices, or better—and a frenzied salesman might throw in the spare tire, or even tire covers or the wire wheel option. It was a buyers' market. Never had new Packards sold for so little, as witness: Sedan (5) $1885, Coupe (2-4) $1985, Coupe (5) $2150, Convertible Coupe $2075, Phaeton $2050, Sport Phaeton $2250, Roadster $1985, Touring $2150, Club Sedan $2150, Sedan (5-7) $2250, Sedan-Limousine $2350, Convertible Sedan $2600.

Packard's plan of building the Individual Custom bodies in-house reached its final stage in 1931, too far into the bad times to be of much help. Custom bodies, especially of the formal type, were just too conspicuous for people to buy—and in a counter measure, the company offered them on the 833 chassis as well as on the more expensive 840. No Packard Individual Customs were offered on the 845, though a few of these longer chassis were used by independent makers.

The Packard salesmen's handbook for 1931 advised, "De luxe equipment can be installed on the 840 chassis, but cannot be used (with custom bodies) on the 833 chassis due to interference between the front doors and the spare tires, except in the case of the Packard Cabriolet Sedan-Limousine. . . . In this body the doors are hinged at the front and clear the tires when the doors are opened." The DeLuxe equipment referred to dual side-mounted tires. The term had been used since 1928 and fell into a mix-up when Packard named its large car the "DeLuxe Eight." One had to contend then with a DeLuxe DeLuxe Eight.

The previous experience of Raymond Birge, "who was formerly General Manager of LeBaron, Inc., at Bridgeport, Connecticut and is now Chief Body Engineer for the Packard Company," was touted in the handbook as well, Packard wishing to emphasize that these were actually custom bodies, albeit built in the Packard factory. There were nine "Individual Custom Cars" shown in folio, the first two, the convertibles, were by Dietrich, the others carried the "Custom Made by Packard" plates. Prices for the cars, with single rear spare wheel, were as follows:

	Style No.	833	840
Convertible Victoria	1879	$4275	$5175
Convertible Sedan	1881	$4375	$5275
All-Weather Cabriolet	3000	$4850	$5750
All-Weather Landaulet	3001	$5050	$5950
All-Weather Town Car	3002	$4975	$5875
All-Weather Town Car Landaulet	3003	$5175	$6075
Cabriolet Sedan-Limousine	3004	$4490	$5390
All-Weather Sport Cabriolet	3008	$4850	$5750
All-Weather Sport Landaulet	3009	$5050	$5950

The All-Weather Town Car was somewhat comparable to the standard Sedan-Limousine, save for the open front. Mounted on the 833 chassis, the former listed at $4975, the standard body at $2885, a difference of $1890. It is small wonder then that Alvan Macauley had been so insistent that profits from custom-made cars remain with the company. He had simply not reckoned with the deepening Depression that would soon wipe out almost all of the custom body shops, including Packard's.

Yes, the times were changing. Doubtless a few years hence H.F. Olmstead, of Packard's advertising department, would not have written as he did now to a reporter on the New York *Sun* who had glowingly reviewed the new Packards: "Well sir, I think we certainly have got to do something about this. That piece ought to rate two or three DeLuxe Packards with nothing less than full-livered (sic) chauffeurs and footmen." Just about the nicest thing that happened to Packard in all of '31 was its inclusion as an example of the creative spirit in American intellectual and aesthetic life by the Hampshire House on Central Park South in New York City. Into its cornerstone, among other artifacts, went poetry by Benét, a play by O'Neill, a novel by Hemingway, and photographic representations of a painting by Benton, a sculpture by Zorach—and a Packard town car.

CHAPTER FIFTEEN

WE ALL
THOUGHT IT WAS
A SNAPPY CAR

The Light Eight

January 1932–December 1932

The Ninth Series

June 1931–December 1932

AUTHOR: L. MORGAN YOST

Packard had its new Ninth Series cars and a new general sales manager by mid-June 1931. Two weeks prior to the dealers' meeting it had been announced that R.E. Chamberlain was leaving Detroit to become the Packard distributor in Buffalo, and although the company went to considerable lengths to point out that the new post was one of the most important distributorships in the Packard selling organization, it was apparent that Chamberlain had been shuffled off to Buffalo. The new sales manager, J.W. Loranger, was a Packard veteran of some twelve years. Macauley obviously thought he was the man to get Packard sales moving again, but alas he could not foresee that failing health would force Loranger to retire soon after his appointment. Fortunately, Macauley had had another thought. It was a go-getter by the name of Max M. Gilman, vice-president of sales for Packard-New York. He was given a prominent place on the program for the big dealers' meeting.

Management fears of a small turnout, with scores of dealers staying home to attend to the seemingly more urgent business of selling all those Eighth Series cars that remained on their showroom floors, proved unfounded. "It was expected about 400 would attend," the *Automotive Daily News* reported, "but some 800 Packard distributors and dealers visited the factory and looked over the new lines, following which approximately 400 of the cars were driven over the road to various branches and salesrooms." *A.D.N.* had the figures a bit off but the point was well made. Actually almost 600 attended and more than 300 cars were driven away. What brought many of the dealers to Detroit was the expectation—or fear—of something radically different, this the result of the presence on Packard's payroll of C.W. Van Ranst. But, as *A.D.N.* noted on June 20th, "None of the surprises that have been hinted at will be found in the line. There is no front-drive or free-wheeling say those who have seen the cars."

That publication seems to have been persona non grata at the Packard plant, for on that same June 20th date both *Automotive Industries* and *Automobile Topics* carried full descriptions and illustrations of the new cars—as well as the reassuring news that, noted the latter journal, although "not only modernized in appearance, but invigorated with revised concepts of automobile engineering . . . [they essay] no deviation from [Packard's] conservative and well-planned course of progress. . . . Contours are more comfortably filled out. The effect is a little less severe than that of the most recent Packards, yet it holds that peculiar refinement which has distinguished this line for many years, and which likewise has many times successfully defied attempts at competition."

The new look consisted of many nuances, with no single outstanding change though the slight vee front of the radiator was immediately identifiable to Packard watchers. The emblem was moved down to the crank hole cover, the bail removed from the lowered radiator cap. Windows were straight topped, not arched as before, and the wide molding at the belt had a new contour as did the window reveals. On closed cars the visor over the windshield was omitted, the windshields had a seven degree slope to avoid reflections. The body base mold curved down rearward from the firewall resulting in a narrower splash apron. The new design of the fender battery box was repeated as a toolbox on the left side. The Eight (formerly Standard Eight) now had hood vent doors,

Pages preceding: The Light Eight during demonstration at Washington-Hoover Airport, 1932. Below: An Eighth Series Sedan with Ninth Series conversion Alvan Macauley taking Jesse Vincent (left) and Eddie Roberts for a ride in the Ninth Series DeLuxe Eight Model 904 Sedan-Limousine at the Packard Proving G

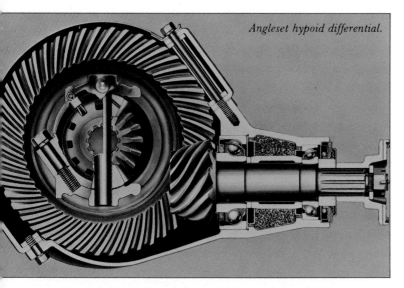

Angleset hypoid differential.

single bar bumper while the DeLuxe Eight was equipped with a new type front bumper with "harmonic stabilizers" on the ends, this an option on the Eight.

The stabilizers were a development of Clyde R. Paton whom Jesse Vincent had brought from Studebaker in 1930 as chief experimental engineer. As Paton recalled later, "Though Packard was the leader in the luxury car market, I found the riding quality harsh and jolty. The engines bolted solidly to the frame were harsh and noisy. The radiator, hood and front fenders shook and vibrated at shimmy speeds." This appraisal of Packard was harsh, too, but Paton had been hired to improve the car and his forte at Studebaker had been in the field of chassis and ride improvement. He had been the first to make stroboscopic study of shimmy on chassis dynamometer rolls which revealed the true nature of the phenomenon and had pioneered in the use of rubber for chassis and motor mounts. (Packard had used the latter for 1928 but without notable results.)

"Naturally we wanted the reduction in operating noises which floating the engine in rubber would give in our new cars," Paton commented at the introduction of the 1932 models. "However, we simply could not sacrifice the . . . front end stability which [could be lost by the use of rubber motor mounts on the long chassis. The rigidly mounted motor had braced the frame against twisting.] The 'Packard Stabilizer' . . . is operated on the tuned mass principle and to oppose any tendency for the development of frame or body torsional vibration, which it has been found is the type of vibration constantly occurring, even when a car is being driven over relatively smooth pavements. [The action of the

which made it less distinguishable from DeLuxe models, and hopefully more appealing to prospects in the lower—for Packard—price range. All cars now had sweeping fenders, with dual trumpet horns mounted under the headlamps gracing the DeLuxe models and optional on the Eights. "Custom Equipment" was the new term for dual spare wheels in the fenders, plus trunk rack and full rear bumper and, on the Eight, fender lamps (which were standard on the DeLuxe). The Eight carried a wide

e long wheelbase chassis for the Ninth Series. The DeLuxe models featured the "harmonic stabilizer" bumper as standard; it was optional on the Standard Eight.
he embryonic X-bracing, the two-piece driveshaft with universal joint at the crossing of the X; the shorter wheelbase Packard Eights featured a one-piece driveshaft.

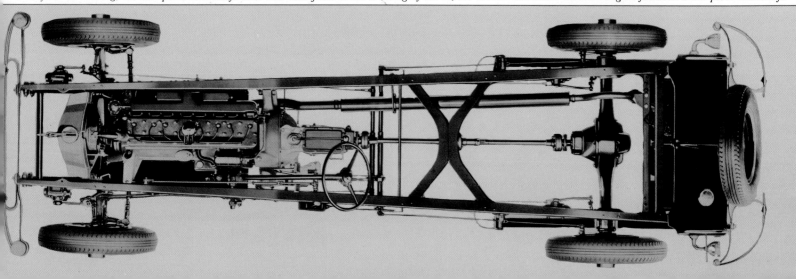

Clockwise from top left: 902 Convertible Victoria; 904 Individual Custom Convertible Victoria, Stationary Coupe and Convertible Roadster; 903 Coupe-Roadster.

Stabilizer] is as simple and as certain as the heavy pole that holds the tight rope walker in balance. At each end of the bumper is a small weight supported between two sets of specially designed springs in an oil tight housing. Initial lubrication is furnished for the life of the car. Construction is rugged and the Stabilizer is practically indestructible. The weights and springs are so designed that they are instantaneously and automatically brought into action to neutralize shocks reaching the car frame. They work in combination with the new Ride Control device and with the system of cross-tying and mounting the radiator in rubber to use its mass and weight of the water as an effective dampener against chassis disturbances."

Though Paton obviously steadied things in the Packard automobile, it is equally apparent that he shook things up in Packard Engineering. By July of 1932 he would be promoted to chief engineer, with Al Moorhouse resigning to become a consulting engineer. Chief chassis engineer J.R. Ferguson would be moved up to assistant chief engineer.

That intriguing new device called "Ride Control," of which Paton made note, was perhaps best described by a writer for *The New Yorker* in its July 11th, 1931 issue: "If you ask the man who has ridden in one of the new Packards, I'll wager the first thing he speaks about is the Ride Control. This is the name of a new gadget [a knob to the left of the steering wheel] that regulates the shock-absorbers, loosening the tension for smoothly paved streets, setting it at medium for average roads, or snugging it tight for fast driving on rough going. I tried it out on the Farm, as they call that stretch of Twelfth Avenue in the Fifties where new drivers are taught the rudiments of shifting gears and new cars are tested by the critical. Packard has its own testing ground on the roof of its service station in Eleventh Avenue, with concrete cobblestones and staggered blocks of cement that are guaranteed to conjure up all the squeaks and rattles in any car; but I think the Farm has a wider range of rough going. The Ride Control, however, made that road—even when I crossed the railroad tracks—seem smooth." In technical terms, this control moved sleeve valves in the shock absorbers which opened or shut orifices metering the flow of fluid and thus controlling the response of the shock absorber. Otherwise, the shock absorbers were the same Delco-Remy as before.

Packard frames were new too, a double drop design with the second drop on the front beginning at the dash and curving rearward, with the apron and lower body mold following this frame contour and allowing a 1½-inch lower body mounting. Heavy X-bracing reinforced the frame in mid-location. The three-speed-with-extra-low transmission now provided synchronizing for second and high gears—at long last, Cadillac having scored handsomely with its synchromesh several years earlier. The transmission case was changed to aluminum alloy to reduce weight, and gear teeth were reshaped to render them more quiet. Within six

months, however, this new transmission would be superseded by yet another newer one, again a three-speed, but fully synchronized, fully quiet, and again in an iron case.

Clutch refinements included mounting the pedal on the frame instead of the engine to eliminate telegraphing of motor vibrations and rumble to the driver. Rear axle tread was increased to 59 inches, front to 58 9/16ths, primarily to give greater body width but also to increase stability on the long wheelbase.

Engine refinements boosted power to 110 bhp at 3200 rpm for the Eight, 135 at 3200 for the DeLuxe Eight. The standard compression ratio was raised to 6.0 to one, with lower and higher compression ratio cylinder heads available at extra cost. An automatic-advance type distributor was adopted with a new timing curve and was provided with a hand two-position adjustment for retarding the spark at the distributor when hand cranking became necessary. But most owners never knew it was there and the hand crank was no longer furnished in the tool allotment anyway. (It could be had as an extra.)

The oil manifold interconnected with the choke for cylinder wall lubrication was dropped, the piston slot changed from the thrust side to the opposite face to reduce chances of piston slap due to cocking of the piston in the bore. The manifold hot spot was made integral with the exhaust manifold to increase heat flow and reduce the warming-up period, and a combination AC air cleaner and intake silencer was adopted.

Refinements were to be had, too, in fan, muffler, accelerator travel, carburetor air vanes—and, outside, double radial sweep windshield wipers with concealed motors were fitted, these replacing the horizontal sweep wipers which had given trouble on the Eighth Series cars. Inside, interiors were even more luxurious, with "airplane type" round-faced instruments grouped on a central panel with an engine-turned finish. Indeed, details throughout the new Packards had been given the touch of freshness which, it was hoped, would prove sales generating.

"As modish as Matisse in painting," "as late as Georg Jensen in silver," "as modern as an architectural design by Frank Lloyd Wright," "as recent as Debussy in music," "as new as Brancusi in sculpture"—Packard promotion was struggling to overcome that impression of the old-fashioned which its competition had long been anxious to attach to it. The traditional approach had lost its cachet. The time honored didn't seem to have much place in a world where upheaval was becoming the norm.

And yet there were limits, there was that very fine line. The public in 1932 was not interested in the radical, front wheel drive, for example. The idea of enticing the populace by startling it wouldn't work. Development, yes, an unproven idea, no. Synchromesh transmission, yes; GM had developed and used it even before the stock market crash, and Packard had now fitted it belatedly. Free wheeling, maybe. It was said to save gasoline and the effort of using the clutch pedal except to start, but it also meant more use of the brake when slowing down, contrary to the usual driving habit of allowing the motor to act as a decelerator. Packard wasn't yet convinced of its merits, at least publicly.

With the Ninth Series cars the Packard model numbering system was revised, eliminating the indication of wheelbase by the last two digits. The Eights were now Models 901 and 902 with wheelbases of 129½ and 136½ inches respectively. The DeLuxe Eights were Models 903 and 904, with wheelbases of 142⅛ and 146⅛ inches (the fractions to be dropped hereafter in references to these cars). Vehicle numbers were merely the body type number plus the production run number of that type; thus 506-14 meant the fourteenth Club Sedan on the 902 chassis. The lineup for the Eight, with prices, was as follows:

Model 901 (129 inches)	Body Number	6-23-31	1-9-32	6-1-32
Sedan (5)	503	$2485	$2250	$2350

Model 902 (136 inches)	Body Number	6-23-31	1-9-32	6-1-32
Coupe (2-4)	508	$2675	$2595	$2795
Coupe (5)	507	$2795	$2745	$2945
Coupe-Roadster (2-4)	509	$2650		$2850
Phaeton (4)	501	$2650		$2850
Sport Phaeton (4)	521	$2950		$3150
Sedan (5)	543	$2685		$2885
Sedan (5-7)	504	$2885	$2835	$3035
Club Sedan (5)	506	$2775		$2975
Convertible Sedan (5)	523	$3445	$3250	$3450
Sedan-Limousine (5-7)	505	$2985		$3185
Touring (5-7)	500	$2775	$2500	$2700
Convertible Victoria (5)	527	$3395	$3195	$3395

The show time price cuts on some models were made coincident with the debut of two brand-new Packards to be soon discussed. Packard was already talking about them a lot, internally, although the plans had not been divulged at the June 1931 dealers' meeting. Even Alvan Macauley couldn't be sure then what the company would be introducing for the January show: Neither of the new production cars was a reality, even experimentally, that summer. The price boosts the following summer were made simply because the price cuts hadn't worked. The thought now was that the number of sales lost at the slightly higher figure would be more than offset by the higher prices per unit. There just was not enough volume available to make money in any Packard line in 1932.

And that included the DeLuxe Eight, whose price story was as follows:

Model 903 (142 inches)	Body Number	6-23-31	1-9-32	6-1-32
Coupe (2-4)	518	$3725	$3150	$3350
Coupe (5)	517	$3850	$3350	$3550
Coupe-Roadster (2-4)	519	$3750	$3250	$3450
Phaeton (4)	511	$3690	$3290	$3490
Sport Phaeton (4)	531	$3990	$3590	$3790
Sedan (5)	513	$3845	$3245	$3445
Club Sedan (5)	516	$3890	$3395	$3595
Convertible Sedan (5)	533	$4550	$3895	$4095
Touring (5-7)	510	$3795	$3395	$3595
Convertible Victoria (5)	537	$4495	$3825	$4025

Model 904 (147 inches)	Body Number	6-23-31	1-9-32	6-1-32
Sedan (5-7)	514	$4150	$3495	$3695
Sedan-Limousine (5-7)	515	$4285	$3695	$3895

Interchangeability between Eight and Deluxe Eight in seven-passenger Sedan and Sedan-Limousine bodies was no longer possible, Models 902 and 903 sharing a 93⅞ths-inch body space, but the long-wheelbase 904 had 98⅜ths. The Convertible Sedan and Victoria bodies had been moved from the Individual Custom line into the production category, though they were made in the Dietrich shops of Murray Body Corporation. By that time, however, Ray Dietrich was out.

Happily, the Individual Custom line was not. It included:

Model 904	Body Number	6-23-31
Stationary Coupe (2-4)*	2068	$5900
Convertible Coupe (2-4)*	2071	$6050
Sport Phaeton (4)*	2069	$5800
Convertible Sedan (5)*	2070	$6250

Convertible Victoria (4)*	2072	$6150
Cabriolet, All-Weather (5-7)	4000	$6850
Landaulet, All-Weather (5-7)	4001	$7250
Town Car, All-Weather (5-7)	4002	$6850
Landaulet, Town Car, All-Weather (5-7)	4003	$7250
Limousine, Sedan, Cabriolet (6)**	4004	$6850
Sport Sedan (5)**	4005	$6850
Brougham, All-Weather (5-7)**	4006	$6850
Limousine Sedan (6)**	4007	$6850
Cabriolet, Sport, All-Weather (5-7)**	4008	$6850
Landaulet, Sport, All-Weather (5-7)**	4009	$7250

Model 904 Individual Custom Packards for 1932, clockwise from above: The All-Weather Town Car, Sedan-Limousine, Sport Sedan, All-Weather Landaulet.

The single asterisk cars, by Dietrich, with their distinctive vee windshields, were regarded by many as his masterpieces. *Automobile Topics* found the Stationary Coupe the most striking: "Its windshield is set with such a rakish angle that it is almost possible for the driver to look straight up in the air." The double asterisk cars denote styles which would not be fitted on the twelve-cylinder chassis when it became available in April 1932.

The number of body styles overall was overwhelming, fewer of them might have cut down production costs substantially. Instead Packard offered an embarrassment of riches in a depressed year. Perhaps even H.W. Potter, the new manager of the Individual Custom Car Department, recognized that. He decided to have the cars' pictures taken: "For those distributors and dealers who are unable to stock individual custom cars we feel that the actual photographs will be of tremendous sales value

Light Eight testing in Colorado Springs. On the photo on the right was noted: ". . . rounding a hairpin curve with a twenty percent grade, this entire trip

inasmuch as they will eliminate any doubt in the prospect's mind as to how the cars will look." Prospects were few, however.

Meantime Packard dealers were having sufficient trouble simply trying to rid themselves of the old Eighth Series cars . . . still, six to eight months after introduction of the Ninth. Packard had offered updating "kits" to help move them, one item being a vee grille to affix in front of the flat radiator. Then, to bring the appearance of the two series together, the same type grille was offered as an accessory for the Ninth Series cars. The new bumpers and trunk racks could also be installed on the older cars.

Macauley observed in March of 1932, "It is notable that during the year [1931] we delivered to Packard customers 25.4 percent more cars than we produced during the year, due to the fact that we determined to reduce our stock of finished cars at the factory and in distributors' hands to the minimum. . . . At this [time], although so soon after the announcement of our new models, we have only 331 noncurrent cars of any kind, anywhere, that are unsold—an insignificant number." But the "insignificant number" becomes significant when it is remembered that the cars were all a year or so old by that time, production having been stopped months before the introduction of the Ninth Series in June of '31. There had been trouble with stale batteries on these old-new cars.

The new models to which Macauley referred were two, the first, as he announced at a distributor meeting at the Hotel Roosevelt in New York at show time, "is no stranger. It is a brand new, strictly up-to-date Twin Six motor which we have designed to interchange in our highly developed DeLuxe chassis; so that from now on you can go to your DeLuxe clientele and offer them the DeLuxe chassis of both chassis lengths equipped with either Twin Six or DeLuxe motors, with all of our current bodies and of course with custom bodies as well."

The second model was a new car altogether.

Minutes of the Packard board of directors, September 23rd, 1931,

reveal the state of uncertainty with which the company approached the New York automobile show in January, that date having just been set to announce the new car. Management had been talking about a smaller, lower-priced Packard for years,* but now the struggle to come up with one had Engineering working nights. Let the minutes tell it: "The president reviewed our engineering development program from the inception of the X-127 and stated that now we find it will be advisable to use the present 901 motor in the X-127 chassis; that the X-127 motor after further development may be used in the Tenth Series Standard Eights which may also use the X-127 front and rear axle, transmission, et cetera, for the advantage of interchangeability and improved results . . . that the X-127 car will be announced at the time of the New York automobile show; that our loss in January of next year will probably be about as large as the previous year but that February manufacturing

---

*For example, board minutes for December 9th, 1925 include the following details: "The president said that our present cars and the light eight experimental car were tested with a competitive car and that these tests showed that the light eight lacked performance as a result of which we are building a more powerful light eight motor to obtain satisfactory results. The president said that the engineering department had started work on a çar to be sold in a lower price class, probably $1500-$1700 for the five-passenger sedan. Such an addition to our present line of cars was considered very important and after full discussion a motion duly supported and carried, management was authorized to proceed as soon as possible with experimental cars, keeping in mind the advisability of having three eights for an ultimate line of cars." By 1927 thoughts had changed a bit, and the 117-inch wheelbase Six was built in prototype. But business was so good and the plants so busy that it was carried no further. The real feeling then was against a small car for the Packard Motor Car Company—or at the very least against any real urgency to getting it into production quickly.

...le in high gear. This turn is much steeper and more difficult than picture shows."

schedule calls for 1000 of the X-127 and 2500 in March and monthly thereafter if they can be sold in that volume and if in addition to this volume our present other lines total 1500 a month we may be able to show an annual profit of $10 to $14 million."

The X-127, of course, was the Light Eight which, it was hoped, would be the savior of Packard's fiscal integrity. The X-127 motor intended for the Light Eight never was brought to production though its development continued. It was given a glance when the idea of the $1000 Packard was born a little later but dismissed as being too costly for that job.

There was a certain desperation at Packard now, as illustrated in the board minutes of December 23rd, 1931: "The president reported . . . that we are releasing the Packard Light Eight and the new Packard Twin Six for production . . . without having completely tested them against possible difficulties in design or proved them for satisfactory owner operation." But "recognizing this hazard," it was decided to proceed in any case. For three months, testing went on with a vengeance, two Packards traversing the traffic of downtown Detroit twenty-four hours a day for weeks on end, another car circling about in a steady grind under the glaring sun of Death Valley, yet another mountain climbing in California, another still on a transcontinental test run—all this in addition to the Packard Proving Grounds activity which was proceeding twenty-four hours a day as well.

The Light Eight—or 900 Series as it came to be called in service letters, shop or owner's manuals, though never in advertising or literature—was the first new car Packard had brought out since 1923. Both mechanically and artistically, it was the most carefully designed production car built by Packard up to that time. And if quietly apprehensive, Packard was plainly proud publicly of what it had done.

And especially how quickly it had been done, the introduction of two completely new cars within six months of the Packard Ninth Series line. As Alvan Macauley told his distributors, "We have never been called

upon to accomplish this before. It is a record-breaking performance and may be an indication to you of the resources of the Company. It should prove to you, if you ever had any doubts, the power of your company in this depression. . . ."

In the news release accompanying the Light Eight's introduction, H.W. Peters noted that "we have taken full advantage of today's conditions to build for today's necessities." And Alvan Macauley, while praising to the fullest the company's new Twin Six, conceded that of the two new cars, he considered the Light Eight "in many ways the more important. . . . We have not built the new car to supersede our Ninth Series cars. Far from it. Our whole plan would be frustrated if that were the result. Our present clientele have been educated to, and prefer, the conservative dignity of our present lines. We have hoped and we believe that the new car will have a special appeal to people *who have never been Packard owners* and who are more in favor of the youthful and modern appeal that we believe we have designed into it."

The radiator shell was the starting point for all Packard design. This one was typically Packard but with a difference. The sides swept down and forward, meeting at a point in the splash apron. And *that* was news. Some called it the snow plow front. The splash apron was one with the fenders, there was no tubular cross brace connecting the frame horns at the front, and no cross bar to support the headlamps. Here was smooth simplicity, integrally designed. To achieve the front end sans cross member, the frame was redesigned—or perhaps the frame had been redesigned and the new front end resulted. The new K member produced a stable front end in any case. Though Packard first used X-bracing, centrally located in the new 901-2-3-4 frames, for the 900 the X extended more fore and aft. In addition the two rear cross members were tied together. The side channel rails were eight inches deep of 5/32nd-inch steel—all this producing a more rigid frame than any previous Packard had enjoyed.

High body sides and low windows were the vogue, and the Light Eight had them. The rear deck blended into the gas tank shroud. The single bar bumpers were sympathetic to the body lines. Contours and fender sweeps were graceful. Withal, it was a masterpiece of design by Packard's great and largely unheralded stylist, Werner Gubitz.

The Bijur lubrication system was not incorporated because the Light Eight had rubber-mounted spring shackle bolts and oilless bushings which left only ten points requiring manual lubrication, a mere half dozen more than with a Bijur lubricated chassis. This was intelligent simplification, evidence of the hand of Clyde Paton.

The engine was the same as in the Standard Eight, save for minor points, chief of which was in the cylinder head which had a frontal projection to contain a thermostat in the gooseneck to the radiator. (The 900 did not have thermostatically controlled radiator shutters.) The 900 air

cleaner was provided with a metal jacket surrounding the exhaust manifold from which a thermostatic damper allowed warmed air to be fed to the carburetor as needed. This same damper automatically controlled the inlet of cool air in hot weather directly from the front bonnet door which opened to the front for this purpose.

Ease of operation was stressed during these times when even more women were driving as a family necessity and more men were driving more miles and scarcely desirous of being fatigued by it. There is no denying that previous Packards took real muscle to steer, to declutch and to shift. That was all changed with the 900 which had a new worm and sector steering gear with a higher ratio, also an automatic clutch as standard equipment. A red knob on the steering wheel cut the latter in or out. When the accelerator was released the manifold vacuum actuated a piston that operated the clutch release lever; it disengaged at speeds below eight miles an hour or so and the reengagement of the clutch when accelerating was not as smooth as a good driver would wish. Consequently many never used it. It was discontinued the year following.

The clutch itself was new, too—a single plate type mounted in the flywheel. It was smooth and without chatter and even without the automatic feature in operation, it was much easier to negotiate than those in previous Packards.

Heretofore a whine or grind of gears was the norm when a car drew away from the curb. If a young man wanted to leave his girl's house without awakening her parents he started in high gear—if he had enough torque. Some transmissions had ugly rasping characteristics. Others, and especially Packard, had a singing, rising crescendo that fairly cried out quality. This would be no more, not only the sound of gears but that of the clash which some drivers never overcame. The silent shift and the easing into the next bar of musical gears had been the mark of the expert, one he had to forego when silent gears and synchromesh shifting "provided a sure quiet shift that required no skill on the part of the operator to avoid clashing." Such was progress.

The 900 had a three-speed, fully synchromesh transmission. It was a beautiful mechanism. So easy, yet so positive, it slid from gear to gear, even back and forth without embarrassment, and its soft rubber lever knob absorbed even the transmitted hum. Naturally it was considered prudent to incorporate this new transmission into the larger Packard Eights as well—and this was seen to.

To the rear of the new 900, the Angleset hypoid differential—another Packard first—allowed a lower body mounting, and more contact of gear teeth, for better wear, quietness and strength. Brakes were two shoe, cable operated, of mechanical design, the handbrake operating the same shoes. Wheels were steel disc for 17x6.50 tires, with wire wheels optional at a small extra cost. The traditional Packard fender-mounted battery box was gone, with the battery mounted under the front seat, removable only from below, however.

Interiors of the Light Eight were restrained and tasteful, the Coupe-Roadster upholstered in leather, the closed cars in wool broadcloth. The instrument board was finished in dark walnut on metal, an oval raised panel in the center carrying the simple, round-faced and businesslike instruments. The needle-type speedometer was flanked on the right by gasoline and oil pressure gauges, on the left by ammeter and motor temperature. The gas gauge was electric, not fluid. The choke button balanced the cigar lighter below. Way off to the left was a little button looking rather like a Moore push pin—that was the starter button, operating a relay. The time honored position for the throttle on the steering wheel sector was usurped. Orbiting the horn button now were two mysterious round balls, one bright chrome, one bright red—the light switch and the automatic clutch control.

And that was the Light Eight, all 4000 pounds of it. The Standard Eight (the "Standard" cognomen was revived with the introduction of the Light Eight), by comparison, weighed in at 4600 pounds. Which made quite an edge for the Light Eight, and reason enough for the Packard people to write in 1933, "Last year with the exception of the Twin Six, the Light Eight provided the swiftest acceleration. We all thought it was a snappy car."

It was snappy enough to appeal to youngsters. The first one this writer saw in a showroom was a convertible with apple green fenders and aprons and a beige body. Colors? There were standard colors, of course, but variations were available at $45 for the body, $45 for fenders and chassis parts. What fun you could have for $90!

Light Eight prices, comparative to similar Standard Eight body styles, were as follows, the Light Eight available only in the four styles listed, all on a 127¾-inch wheelbase:

	Body Number	Light Eight Model 900	Standard Eight Model 901	Model 902
Sedan (5)	553	$1750	$2250	$2685
Coupe-Sedan (5, two-door)	563	$1795		$2745
Coupe (2-4)	568	$1795		$2595
Coupe-Roadster (2-4)	569	$1795		$2650

The prices were inviting. As Alvan Macauley had told his dealers before advising them of the figures, ". . . we decided to do a daring thing. We decided to build a car that ought to sell for $2200 and to boldly offer it to the public at a medium car price, in the hope and belief that the public will appreciate what we have done and will learn the difference between the quality characteristics of our Light Eight and other cars. And we counted on your enthusiasm being such that you could carry the message home with conviction. . . . If the volume-response is not satisfactory, we shall not be able to keep the price at the figure we shall announce. We

The Light Eight. Page opposite from the top: The Sedan and Coupe-Sedan models, Al Jolson posing with his Light Eight. Above: The Coupe, with non-folding top.

have arbitrarily priced it where it should sell in large quantities at a profit to you, even in these times. The uncertainty, and I frankly admit it, is whether it can be sold at its price at a profit to the Company. . . ."

It couldn't. The prices quoted were competitive with the large Buick 90. However, Packard, having tooled up for this completely new car—save for its motor—soon found the Depression was surging as wickedly as ever and that modest sales made it necessary to raise prices at mid-year to $1895 for the sedan and $1940 for the other body styles. (Standard Eight prices were increased too.)

Some refer to the 900 Light Eight as the forerunner of the One Twenty. No such thing. Its price class was one step below the 901-902, $1750 compared to $2250. At its introduction in 1935, the One Twenty sedan listed at $1060, the volume Senior sedan at $2385. And the fact is that the 900 should have been priced higher. Even the mid-year increase did not make the car profitable. The volume just was not there in 1932. Another year or two might have told another story.

But this was not another year. And Packard was making mistakes, right down the line. Advertising and early catalogue promotion for the Eight and DeLuxe Eight referred to "Continental models"—a term which did not take. The logic of it was understandable. Packard's foreign business remained impressive, easily outdistancing the competition in overseas markets. In Rio de Janeiro, for instance, in 1932 there were 24 Pierce-Arrows, 152 Cadillacs, 167 Lincolns and 305 Packards. King Alexander I of Yugoslavia had purchased six Packards, each carrying a special traffic light with red and green lenses which, when lighted, gave warning to traffic officers that the royal right of way be immediately given. Chiang Kai-shek, "the guiding military genius behind the Chinese defense of Shanghai," had a special armor-plated variation, with special seating and running board room for six guards and their submachine guns. And in Windsor, Ontario, with more ceremonial dignity—on October 1st, 1931—Alvan Macauley had symbolically installed the finishing hubcap on the first Packard to roll off the assembly line in the company's new Canadian plant.

But the Bement agency's attempt at an advertising tie-in on the

...ckards on their way to the Orient; one of the cars in Yugoslavia's Royal garages.

"World Supremacy" theme—the series portraying Packard in countries of Europe, Japan, Greece, China, Egypt, Argentina, India and Canada—though colorful, simply did not impress American buyers. Earlier in the year there had been better color ads of the cars without distracting backgrounds, and that idea was used again with the Light Eight, in non-color ads this time, boldly portraying the cars in pencil drawings and getting down strictly to business in the copy.

This was good and effective promotion, and makes one wonder why Alvan Macauley asked Austin Bement about this time to find a replacement for his agency. Bement did as Macauley asked. After investigating and interviewing, he recommended Young and Rubicam. The character of Packard advertising was to change. No longer would there be the consistency of former years. The first Young and Rubicam ad was nothing if not startling. It was a painting of the gate to the Packard Proving Grounds. A car was entering. The caption—"The Packard You Never See." The text began, "These gates are about to close on a new Packard the world will never see. For . . . the car that is passing through them is going to be deliberately destroyed." The response was overwhelming. Many wrote objecting to the destruction or offering to test the car themselves after 50,000 miles on the track. That particular ad appeared in *Fortune*'s issue of October 1932, then had a second insertion in January of 1933, an unprecedented move at the time. Just how many Packards it sold is questionable.

In March of '32 advertising manager F.H. McKinney, with twenty Packard years behind him, entered his twenty-first with additional duties, as head of a newly created sales promotion department. Already he was talking in such terms as "strongest announcement advertising campaign," "by backing its new cars in this forceful manner Packard is keeping step with the rest of the industry," "shaking the public loose from its old cars" and "whipping into shape this very complete program." All this sounded strangely un-Packard. So, too, did just about everything Max M. Gilman said. Gilman, who is best profiled in the chapters devoted to the One Twenty, became Packard's vice-president of distribution in August, replacing—or as the press said, "severing"—in that post sixteen-year Packard veteran H.W. Peters. Upon his departure, Peters expressed uncertainty as to his plans for the future. Eventually he returned to the life academe, becoming provost of Cornell University in 1938.

The Light Eight survived Peters at Packard by only a few short months. Although manufacturing vice-president E.F. Roberts might caption his memos, "Ride Back To Prosperity In A New Motor Car," it would not be the Light Eight. Only 6750 of the cars were built before the model was discontinued in December. Some 7659 Ninth Series Standard Eights were produced from June 1931 to December 1932—for a Light and Standard Eight total of 14,409. Eighth Series Standard Eight production had been 12,105, though it had taken a long time to sell the cars. Still, the Light Eight obviously accomplished very little in the way of sales boosting. Indeed Alvan Macauley chastised his distributors and dealers for not selling more of the Standard and DeLuxe Eights to old customers, noting that records indicated salesmen were demonstrating the Light Eight too often when they should have been showing the Standard or DeLuxe cars. Even Al Jolson bought a Light Eight—scarcely for reasons of economy.

Although profits eluded the company, Packard continued to lead the fine car field in sales. No other fine car manufacturer was making money either, but that was scant consolation. During calendar year 1932, Packard built only 9010 cars: 557 Twin Sixes, 6622 Light Eights, 1831 Standard and DeLuxe cars. Most Ninth Series Standard and DeLuxe cars had been produced during the latter part of 1931 and had been stockpiled. Of these two models, a total of 1655 DeLuxe Eights and 7659 Standard Eights was built.

The Light Eight might appropriately be termed a success-failure. Certainly it did give added impetus to the formulation of plans for a lower priced car which could be sold in volume yet not take sales away from the luxury lines. The Light Eight patently had too many of the good qualities of the Standard Eight, to which some good qualities of its own were added—performance, ease of handling and modern looks—at a price too close to the Standard Eight. It really didn't set up a new price field. It merely shaved off a bit of the present one. But it was important as a strong and positive directive, perhaps a do-or-die directive.

CHAPTER SIXTEEN

ALWAYS THERE IS THAT GREAT RESERVE OF POWER

The Tenth Series

January 1933-August 1933

The Eleventh Series

August 1933-August 1934

AUTHOR: L. MORGAN YOST

Alvan Macauley needed time to think. The rush to get the Light Eight and the Twin Six into production had taxed the resources of both the Packard company and the Packard men. Macauley promised his engineers a respite to work things out, to consolidate, to evaluate carefully what had been accomplished and what needed to be done. True to his word, he delayed introduction of the next series Packards, the Tenth, until January 1933.

It was a bad month. The prosperity that optimists had long felt was just around the corner appeared to have moved down to the next block. President Herbert Hoover had lost the country's confidence—and then the election to Franklin Delano Roosevelt in November 1932. Year's end was tense. Enthusiasm for Roosevelt was mixed with uncertainty as to what he would—or could—do to instill confidence, to turn things around. There was strong feeling that Hoover should leave office at once so Roosevelt could get on with his program. Tradition would be served, however. The inauguration would be held on the authorized day, March 4th, 1933.

It was in this interim period of bewilderment and doubt that the new Packards for 1933 were presented. Of them, Max Gilman said, "If I had my way I'd put a chip of wood on the shoulder of every bonnet with an invitation to competitive cars to knock it off." Still, it didn't seem likely that many would be sold.

Reports from the field were not encouraging. Economic conditions, and customers' desires to avoid ostentation, combined to make Packard showrooms rather lonely places. The agency in Monterey, California reported, "During the year 1930 we delivered thirty new Packards. Of the thirty owners all are still driving their Seventh Series cars, with the exception of two, one of whom traded his in on a Light Eight, the other on a 901 Standard Eight." From Cook County (Chicago and suburbs) came a census in 1933 of what had happened to the sixty-five Packards just *one* salesman had sold during 1928: "Two owners have moved away from Chicago. Three have died. Three have disposed of their cars and now own no automobiles at all. Six have traded in their Packards on other makes—a surprisingly small number in an era of shifting fortunes and positions. Eight have replaced their 1928 Packards with new Packards. But here is the most amazing thing. Forty-two of the sixty-five owners, or two out of every three, are still driving their original 1928 Packards."

It wasn't really so amazing. Though it was, for Packard, a haunting paradox. Long life had been the marque's strong selling point, Packard owners were now effectively demonstrating its truth. The company was confident these owners would buy a new Packard—but when? It was this backlog of "some day" sales that Gilman would be tackling with the Tenth Series. Were these owners of older Packards to try out the new Packard, sales could be made. It was the company's own veteran cars as

well as the competition's new cars that Gilman was eager to have prospects compare with the Tenth Series. He asked sales outlets to keep strict records of the demonstrations each salesman made, the prospect's present car and the model demonstrated. He analyzed the totals, usually finding—he said—that the salesman underestimated the purchasing power of the prospect in trying for an easy "price" sale.

To make the point with sledge-hammer ferocity, he had published in *Inner Circle* one photograph of two very dissimilar cars. The caption read: "It is a big jump in ownership from the smallest and cheapest car manufactured to a Packard Twin Six, but J.D. Addison . . . induces Capital City prospects to take the leap enthusiastically. Hence the 'long and short' of this picture is a Twin Six Coupe-Roadster and its trade-in, an Austin Coupe. A sound selling policy, that of suspecting more people of being Packard prospects, eh, Addison?"

How many Austin owners were out there with the means to trade up to a Packard? Even Max Gilman must have had qualms about that—but a brave front wedded to a frontal assault, that was the way he was convinced Packard should go. The new Tenth Series was introduced with a flourish. In New York—and again at Chicago, Boston and Philadelphia—the cars were shown, alongside the Packard Hall of Precision (an exhibit featuring fixtures, tools, precision gauges and instruments used in the manufacture of Packard cars), a miniaturization of the Packard Proving Grounds dramatizing the testing the new models received, the nostalgia of Packard's first Model A on display—plus the motors which had powered speed boats to victory in the Gold Cup and President's trophy races, and the *Miss America X*, also a Packard Diesel aircraft engine which the company was already tending to forget, but which looked good anyway. In toto, the effect was spectacular, a company on top of the world, "Another Packard Triumph," as *Inner Circle* heralded, which enticed visitors at the rate of about 200 every hour, "huge crowds that came early and stayed late."

"We have three lines this year instead of four," Packard said. The Twin Six was called that no more, the lapse of a decade had obscured its meaning—"No, it's not a six, it's a twelve. Twin Six, get it?" Apparently, not everyone did, so Packard's top line became simply the Twelve. The Light Eight seemed to vanish altogether. The company mentioned it not at all, but in truth it was actually combined into the Standard Eight line, which once again had the "Standard" dropped from its name.

In 1932 there had been but one Standard Eight 901 body style, the five-passenger sedan, on the shorter 129½-inch wheelbase. This year the four body styles which had comprised the 900 Series Light Eight were carried through to the 1001 Eight chassis, on the 127½-inch wheelbase of the 900. These four were now Packard's lower price leaders, with the onus of the "Light Eight" name deleted—as well as that car's styling distinction. "Front ends are once more . . . of the massive-appearance type," Athel F. Denham wrote in *Automotive Industries*. "The frontal appearance of the radiators for all Tenth Series cars is now uniform," Packard said.

The cars were neither as chic nor as modern looking as the Light Eight, though the Packard rationale was logical enough. To have given its successor a similar look for more money might not have settled well in the marketplace. Moreover, a commonality of styling between Eight and Super Eight—the new name for the old DeLuxe—made for upper echelon democracy, for prestige rub-off, which Packard encouraged.

Chassis and frame were redesigned, though the new frames for the entire line were closer to the old 900 pattern than to the predecessor Ninth Series. Gone, however, was the rubber-mounted spring shackle system of the 900 which had eliminated the Bijur chassis lubricator and which, time would tell, was more practical and long lasting. The double drop of the Ninth Series frame was smoothed out and car height averaged down by changing to seventeen-inch wheels on all lines. Disc wheels were dropped in favor of wire wheels to assist in attaining the intense quiet that was Packard's goal. Tire manufacturers, incidentally, had to develop new and quieter tread designs since the lower sound level rendered the old ones noisy.

The bullet design headlamps of the Light Eight and Twin Six were now on the entire Tenth Series, and wheelbase lengths were redisposed. Hood lengths on Super Eight and Twelve were identical, that on the Eight six inches shorter. As before, the same standard bodies were used on all three cars, on the 1002, 1003 and 1005 chassis. The 147-inch chassis was dropped from the Super Eight line, the seven-passenger cars being reassigned to the 142-inch chassis. A table might better illuminate:

Series	Wheelbase	Name	Remarks
1001	127½	Packard Eight	four bodies from 900 series
1002	136	Packard Eight	thirteen body styles
1003	135	Packard Super Eight	one body style (five-passenger sedan)
1004	142	Packard Super Eight	thirteen body styles
1005	142	Packard Twelve	eleven body styles
1006	147	Packard Twelve	two body styles (closed seven-passenger), plus customs

With no 147-inch chassis available on the Super Eight, the Dietrich custom cars, and others, originally designed for the 1932 DeLuxe Eight could no longer be had on the succeeding shorter Super Eight chassis. This had the effect of forcing those who had the wherewithal to buy a custom to go to the Twelve, which presumably they would do willingly.

Pages preceding: Model 1101 Eight Five-Passenger Sedan for 1934. This page, from the top, Super Eight Packards for 1933: 1004 Seven-Passenger Sedan, 1004 Formal Sedan (142-inch wheelbase); 1003 Five-Passenger Sedan (135-inch).

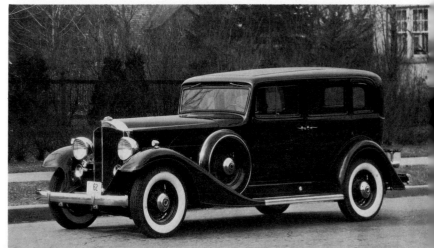

Windshield slope on closed cars was increased, the former fold-forward windshield on open cars made rigid. Bodies were insulated against noise, heat and cold, all closed examples equipped with a highly touted new system of window ventilation control. Consisting of a pair of pivoted panes positioned to scoop air in or to deflect and exhaust as with today's vent windows—the driver simply pushing his hand through the middle to signal, the two panes pivoting out like a pair of French doors—Packard called the result "Motoring's Latest Contribution to Health and Comfort." And promptly dropped it the following year. Usually the panes would not stay in position, the vertical joint leaked badly, the pivoted windows were in the way when one wished complete openness, or to rest his arm on the window sill—and the whole thing was a good idea which just could not be made to work.

The lower car frames generally allowed higher body side panels, and window sill lines were raised to match the higher radiator and bonnet, resulting in less window height. Such was the fashion then—and perhaps not a particularly good idea, cars of this era might have been more graceful and sleek had they been sectioned two or three inches—but *la Mode* must ever be served.

"The boxes for battery and tool boxes were removed from the fenders, and skirts have been added," ballyhooed Packard. This was disappointing to many, the former location kept acid and dirt out of the car. Packard had thought of that too, and was inspired to the notion that the battery would not have to be in the car if it were installed from below, under seat or floorboards. That proved unfortunate enough on a lift, and for the owner or roadside mechanic it was impossible, devastating to shirt or shampoo. The former, and awkward, appearance of the battery boxes below the fender would have been mitigated by the fender skirt which was added for 1933.

Packard fenders were now braced through headlamp brackets to the radiator, thence to the other side through a rod concealed behind the louvered grille. The old cross bar lamp mounting was gone. Double diagonal bracing from the top of the radiator to the dash gave rigidity to the front end structure.

New too was the horsepower developed by the eight-cylinder engines. The 900-901-902 had boasted 111 bhp, the new 1001-1002 was up to 120; the 903-904 had 135, the 1003-1004 developed 145. And, Packard said, perhaps a bit sheepishly, "this year the entire line is faster than the Light Eight with the one exception of the 1002 Packard Eight which is only a fraction (.4 of a second) behind the mark established by the Light Eight. You can welcome an opportunity to pit any one of the new cars against a competitive car in the matter of snappy getaway."

In England *The Autocar* found that "the maximum acceleration possible is of a most valuable order" (0 to 50 in 15.6 seconds at Brooklands) and speeds in the eighties (a maximum of 88 mph was

Super Eight Packards, introduced to the public during the first week of January 19

reached with facility) were simply so much good fun. "Ordinary hills are taken in a quiet, sweeping rush if the driver chooses; with the throttle back the car creeps silently and majestically through the streets of a town, and always there is that great reserve of power, a most pleasing thing."

The biggest factor in the increased horsepower was the dual down-draft carburetor system, with new manifolds having free curves which minimized sharp elbows. A ten percent reduction in fuel use was also claimed, one reason for this being the automatic choke provided.* A smaller flywheel for greater flexibility, finned caps on the connecting rod bearings and deeper radiator cores were among other engine refinements.

In a booklet entitled "How a Motor Car Breathes," Jesse Vincent explained—with all the patient understanding of a schoolmaster lecturing a student and all the charming metaphoric reference of a nanny telling a story to her charge—how the spectacular improvements in the Packard performance came about. It merits quotation in part. In racing engines, he explained, additional air and mixture could be rammed into the cylinders by superchargers, but this was not practical for automobiles in normal use. And he went on:

"Packard has succeeded in packing more air into the cylinders in another and more simple way. Actually there is an increase in the compression pressures although there has been no increase in the compression ratio. . . .

"Air rushing into a cylinder in the motors of the new Packard Eight

---

*These improvements were offered owners of Eighth and Ninth Series Eights and the 734 Speedsters. The manifold faces of these cars had been angled, allowing these later manifolds and carburetors to be installed. Thus, owners of these vehicles could enjoy a new car sensation for a relatively small outlay. And, conceivably, some new Packard sales may have been delayed by this offer. Sometimes one wonders if the company might not have been *too* good to its customers.

Pictured from the left, the 1004 Coupe-Roadster, priced at $2870; the 1004 Club Sedan, priced at $2975; and the Convertible Sedan, priced at $3590.

finds no place to hesitate on the way. There is an uninterrupted passage from the outside atmosphere straight through to the openings of two cylinders at one end of the manifold and the same to two other cylinders at the other end. The four center cylinders are served with a separate 'breathing' pipe, or manifold, this being done through the use of a duplex carburetor.

"Vacuum starts a veritable hurricane of air rushing toward a cylinder when the piston of that cylinder starts down on its intake stroke. That this rush of air actually reaches hurricane force can be appreciated when it is known that it is traveling at a speed of 74 miles an hour with the car running 80 miles an hour.

"Soon after the piston of the 'breathing' cylinder reaches the bottom of its suction stroke, the vacuum, of course, ends. However, the column of air is still traveling 74 miles an hour. Naturally it has plenty of what engineers call inertia force.

"In the Packard motors, this force itself is utilized. By means of a new camshaft the intake valve is caused to remain open after vacuum has completed its job. Through this open valve the inertia force of the 74-mile-an-hour 'gale' rams in still more air by compressing that already in the cylinder.

"Then as the valve snaps shut, the 'hurricane' comes forcibly up against unyielding iron and steel. Just like a rubber ball striking a brick wall, it bounces back. This rebound starts it away in a hurry in the opposite direction and toward another cylinder whose intake valve has just opened for its 'breath.' The rebounding air actually gets behind the air coming in from the carburetor and, through its rebound force, urges it along to greater speed.

"Engineers have tried to obtain such results before by harnessing the inertia force of the rushing air and gas mixture in the intake manifold. They could do so in a four-cylinder motor, but in motors of more than four cylinders their previous efforts have been largely balked . . . because before suction stops in one cylinder of a multi-cylinder motor it has

started in another, [resulting] in suction from one cylinder operating against the inertia force of the mixture traveling toward the previously opened cylinder. So far as breathing is concerned the Packard eight-cylinder motor has been made into two four-cylinder motors [with] a separate manifold and a separate carburetor for each. . . .

"It should be plain to anyone that air at low temperatures is heavier than air expanded by heat. It would therefore follow naturally that the cooler the air going into a motor the greater the weight of oxygen that can be packed into the cylinders. . . . However, this air has an important job to do. It must furnish a means of transportation from the carburetor to the cylinders for the gasoline. . . . And cold gasoline just stubbornly refuses to vaporize and climb aboard and be taken for a ride unless it can travel in comfortable warmth. . . . Before, it has always been thought necessary to heat up the 'conveyance'—the air—and then to keep both the 'conveyance' and the 'passenger,' cozily warmed until the destination, or cylinder, was reached. Wrong, in principle, as it was known to be, it was thought that the 'passenger' had to be coddled all the way on the trip.

"A most important feature in the new Packard carburetion system arises from the discovery that if the gasoline can be heated sufficiently it is not reluctant to venture out and it will stay aboard with no effort to climb off on the way, if its conveyance is just reasonably warm. This is the 'cool mixture' so long sought by the industry and now found in the new Packards. . . . Here is the point where the downdraft carburetor is effective. Immediately below each barrel of the double carburetor there is a hot plate which applies heat to the reluctant gasoline to get it started on its way when the motor is cold."

If Jesse Vincent was mightily pleased with the Packard engine's carburetion, Clyde Paton deserved to be equally so for its quiet. A new three-point motor suspension cushioned any slight vibrations—thanks to Mr. Paton—and a more efficient fan operated at a slower speed for even more enhanced serenity. As *The Autocar* reported, a Packard driver was "hardly conscious . . . of the existence of the engine . . . the most prominent noise is that of the air stream, and this is an impression gained with few cars indeed."

Because its vacuum-operated mechanism had not proven popular, the Packard clutch had received attention. It was now a single plate. The former double plate used on the larger cars had not worn well and was difficult to adjust. Previously, however, a single-plate clutch had been an untenable idea for larger cars because the strong engagement springs necessary made for a prohibitively heavy pedal pressure. In this improved clutch in the heavier Super Eight and the Twelve, the pedals and all operating mechanism were mounted on anti-friction bearings. This brought approximate pedal pressure down from forty-five pounds on the then-new two-plate type of the Ninth Series to twenty-eight pounds on the now-new single plate. It was said the Packard clutch, because of other detail improvements, would last three times as long as the former clutch—and it was delightfully smooth. Packard also provided an automatic clutch control at a nominal cost should a customer desire it. Doubtless few did.

Clyde Paton's attention to ride coupled with the experience of assistant chief engineer Ferguson, whose specialty was chassis design, brought a redesign of front and rear springs, for balance, more clearance or "jounce" space. Shock absorbers were improved. Steering too was made easier, through change in ratio and attention to bearings. The Angleset hypoid rear axle was adopted for all cars.

Brakes were of the Bendix-BK vacuum booster type, the same as used on the Twin Six in 1932. The system was of the "reaction" type in which a small portion of the power was reflected back against the pedal so the operator had a feel for the braking pressure. A Brake Selector knob on the instrument panel allowed the driver to choose the amount of power assist he wanted, and allowed one as well to become accustomed to power braking gradually so to avoid inadvertent "jamming on" of the brakes. The brake shoe and drum mechanism was new to the Eights, though it had been in use on the Light Eight and Twin Six. Levers and the ball-jointed operating shaft to the front wheels were abandoned after nine years in favor of cable-in-conduit controls, not only a simpler system but also providing improved equalization through freedom from the effect of axle roll or movement caused by spring action or braking itself. The Packard brakes were rattle free, needed no attention, were easier to adjust and worked just as efficiently in reverse.

Demountable wood wheels, or even steel discs, could be had at extra cost, all with drop center rims. Black tires were standard; one did not then see as many white walls as he would today at a classic meet.

There was no doubting that the Packards for 1933 were highly refined, carefully developed and beautifully manufactured automobiles. It was a real pity that more people could not or would not buy them. The lineup of the eight-cylinder lines was as follows:

Body Style	Body No. 1-5-33		Body No. 1-5-33	
	Eight Model 1001 127½-inch		Super Eight Model 1003 135-inch	
Sedan (5)	603	$2150	653	$2750
Coupe-Sedan (5)	602	$2190		
Coupe (2-4)	608	$2160		
Coupe-Roadster (2-4)	609	$2250		
	Model 1002 136-inch		Model 1004 142-inch	
Coupe (2-4)	618	$2350	658	$2780
Coupe (5)	617	$2440	657	$2980
Coupe-Roadster (2-4)	619*	$2380	659	$2870
Phaeton (5)	611	$2370	651	$2890
Sport Phaeton (5)	621*	—	661	$3150
Sedan (5)	613	$2385	673*	—
Sedan (5-7)	614	$2455	654	$3090
Club Sedan (5)	616	$2390	656	$2975
Convertible Sedan (5)	623	$2890	663	$3590
Convertible Victoria (5)	627	$2780	667	$3440
Touring (5-7)	610	$2390	650	$2890
Sedan-Limousine (5-7)	615	$2550	655	$3280
Formal Sedan (5-7)	5613*	—	5673*	—

The asterisked cars were neither shown nor mentioned in the catalogue. They were available nevertheless. The Formal Sedan was introduced on February 9th and carried a $3085 pricetag for Eight, $3600 for Super Eight. On April 3rd prices were raised on the two Club Sedans to $2470 and $3055 respectively. This covered a new standard equipment metal trunk contoured to the rear body shape, though removable, with a suitcase and hatbox to fit, available as accessories.

On March 4th Packard carried Franklin Roosevelt to the Presidency, a fleet of the cars from East Grand Boulevard motoring in the procession to the Inaugural. This great nation will endure, FDR insisted, there was only one thing to fear—"fear itself, nameless, unreasoning, unjustified terror. . . ." And it was rampant. Packard Motor Car Company common stock was down to two dollars a share, from 196 in early 1929, though there had been a five for one split later that year. Banks from coast to coast were suffering, borrowers could not repay loans, much of their collateral was worthless or nearly so, and a bank foreclosure might mean only another problem property to be handled. To provide a breathing spell and time to work out reconstruction measures, just two days after his inauguration, President Roosevelt closed all banks in the country. Some 4004 of these institutions had either closed before March or did not reopen for business after the moratorium, with some $3,590,975,000 in deposits lost. By now the life savings of many families had been wiped out, as had the lives of many companies throughout the country.

Packard treasurer Hugh Ferry was instrumental in the working out of money difficulties in Detroit, where banks had been closed earlier—on February 14th—by state edict. Most of the company funds were invested in government or other safe securities, Packard would not be forced to the wall. With the moratorium, Ferry had cash brought in from New York so Packard could meet its payrolls. This was a bit out of the ordinary, at a time when school teachers were getting scrip and many workers checks they could not cash, or nothing at all.

In 1931 Packard had lost $2,909,000 on net sales of $29,987,000 in 1932 $6,824,000 on $15,516,000. A modest profit of $506,433—reinvested in the business—was seen in 1933 on $19,230,000 sales, but 1934 would see a further plummet, a loss of $7,291,000 on sales of only $14,619,000 (though the preponderance of the loss was tooling for new models). Dividends on common stock of $6,746,000 had been paid in 1931, out of surplus built up over previous years—but none would be forthcoming in 1932, 1933, 1934 or 1935. Uncertainty reigned.

In his report to stockholders in March of 1933, Alvan Macauley's best news was the company's solidarity despite all, and the fact that "registration of new cars of all makes throughout the U.S. last year [1932] were 57.5 percent of those registered in 1931, whereas Packard registration [was] 68 percent." Slim comfort.

Impressive nevertheless were the luxury car registrations elicited from Chicago's North Shore suburbs: Cadillac 960, Cord 27, Duesenberg 10, Franklin 299, LaSalle 911, Lincoln 548, Pierce-Arrow 204, Rolls-Royce 18, Stutz 83—Packard 2481. Kenilworth, Illinois—Chicago branch advertising manager Don Elrod said—boasted one Packard to every 2.2 "native white families"—to differentiate from those families of chauffeurs and gardeners who lived in quarters on the premises of the Packard owners. But there weren't enough Kenilworths in the country to help the company much.

Packard advertising was vacillating now. Many of the ads seemed not to belong to Packard at all. Save for examples like "HUSH!," that striking painting by Peter Helck of a Twelve Victoria reflected in a deep blue lily pond which, as one reader wrote, "told the entire Packard story of beauty, quality, simplicity, elegance, refinement and distinction." Other ads picked up the theme of precision—and were quite effective. A lot of others weren't.

The dark days of 1933 were brightened by the Century of Progress Ex-

ge McManus, creator of "Bringing Up Father," said Maggie and Jiggs really agreed on just one thing, "when it concerns motorcars, Packard is the only car to buy."

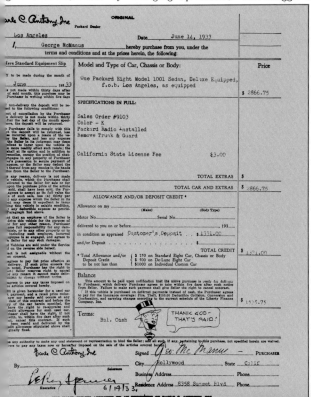

The Super Eight 1104 Club Sedan for 1934, the first year for the built-in trunk.

position in Chicago, attended by millions from all over the world who saw the development of the motorcar exemplified by a magnificent Packard Twelve chosen for the postion of honor in the big rotunda of the Transportation Building.

In this same dark year Alvan Macauley had to cope with the Blue Eagle of the National Recovery Act, administered by the U.S. Department of Commerce, which set up price and wage standards intended to stabilize industries and competition and bring a return of employment and prosperity. As president of the National Automobile Chamber of Commerce, Macauley was a leader in the formation of regulations for the automobile industry, and Packard was the first to sign the NRA Motor Car Code. As it turned out, the Code worked to the greater disadvantage of those companies producing higher priced cars—undoubtedly one of the factors reinforcing Packard's resolve to produce a smaller car . . . and quickly—but in May of 1935 the NRA was declared unconstitutional in any case. By that time conditions had improved in the country and whether the NRA was a contributory factor to the recovery became a matter for academics to debate.

In the meantime Packard sales were eked out. Alvan Macauley's equanimity in the face of it all was admirable, as gently lampooned by Hy Vogel, a cartoonist for the Detroit *News*, who accompanied a caricature

of Packard's president with the ditty following:

> The ancient equipage of state
>   Was gilded, bossed and lacquered;
> Its counterpart of modern date
>   Is probably the Packard.
>
> Macauley runs the show out there
>   With skill that none can question.
> Depressions don't get in his hair
>   Or ruin his digestion.

Which was exactly the impression Alvan Macauley wished to convey, of course. Behind the scenes much might be happening, but out front, on stage, there had to be the aura of Packard peace and serenity. And Packard class. When the company took to the airwaves, initially, it was Macauley-like all the way. "Well loved and beautiful classical compositions" were heard on the Blue Network of the National Broadcasting Company, these being overwhelmingly desired—so Packard studies suggested—by Packard owners and prospects. The company had contacted one of its satisfied owners, Dr. Walter Damrosch, and arranged with him to conduct his seventy-five-musician orchestra in a series of forty-five-minute radio programs. There was some cultural latitude allowed: "Instead of the 'high hat' compositions usually associated with symphonic orchestration the programs . . . feature the best liked of the well known, and popular light classics, tempered with a 'surprise' number or two—for instance, a lovely old ballad in symphonic arrangement with a beautiful voice floating out unannounced on the refrain. . . ."

But the result, alas, proved to be neither great symphony nor popular, or so the failure to attain high ratings suggested. Still, Alvan Macauley was pleased; he thought he was bending to the will of the broader masses. Max Gilman would show him how to bend even further.

For the moment, however, Gilman was busy with plans for the introduction of the Eleventh Series Packards, aware of the sales impetus a new model might afford. He went all out. In August 1933 it was a delighted Macauley who welcomed the largest gathering of Packard men in the history of the company to the curtain raising on the new cars at the Detroit Masonic Temple. The Temple was the largest in the world, and it filled quickly with nearly a thousand Packard distributors and dealers and salesmen. To a man they appeared pleased that the new cars looked and handled very much like the Tenth Series. There wasn't much sense in revising a good thing.

Not extensively anyway. On the Eleventh Series, the fenders extended downward at the front, almost to the bumpers, which were new and wider, tapered to each side with a slot simulating a double-bar bumper. (Some purchasers had the stabilizer bumpers from the new Twelve fitted to their Eights.) There were a few other minor appearance changes: new hood door handles replacing the knobs, new "feathered" radiator caps, left taillight combined with gas filler cap, new running board design, higher front seat backs and more luxurious upholstery throughout including concealed curtains for the three rear windows. Conventional roll-up windows plus a crank-adjustable vent on the front windows were fitted. Underneath, motor oil was cooled by circulation of water from the radiator around a cellular core through which the oil passed, and an oil filter was fitted.

There was some reshuffling of wheelbase lengths in the Eights, as the table following indicates. The bodies held over from the Light Eight for 1933 were abandoned and the Five-Passenger Sedan reverted to the 129-inch wheelbase. In 1933 all remaining Eights had been on the 136-inch chassis but now the Seven-Passenger Sedan and Limousine were removed to the 141-inch wheelbase for reasons of room and impressiveness. Similarly, those two bodies in the Super Eight line were returned to the 147-inch wheelbase on which they had been for 1932, with Super Eights and Twelves once again sharing the same chassis lengths for the same bodies.

Prices represented a two-hundred dollar advance for each body type over 1933 and, unlike the Tenth Series, the Eleventh had a clearance sale. "A downward revision of the price structure in the high-price class was commenced this week when both Packard and Pierce-Arrow made drastic cuts," *Automobile Topics* reported at the time. Pierce-Arrow was really struggling by now. In Packard's case, it was simply a matter of clearing the salesrooms for introduction of the considerably revised Twelfth Series. The Eleventh lined up as follows:

Body Style	Body No.	8-21-33	6-21-34
Model 1100 Eight (129 ½ inches)			
Sedan (5)	703	$2350	$1970
Model 1101 Eight (136 inches)			
Coupe (2-4)	718	$2550	$2140
Coupe (5)	717	$2640	$2140
Coupe-Roadster (2-4)	719	$2580	$2180
Phaeton (5)	711	$2570	$2170
Sport Phaeton (5)	721	—	—
Sedan (5)	713	$2585	$2135
Club Sedan (5)	716	$2670	$2270
Convertible Sedan (5)	723	$3090	$2690
Convertible Victoria (5)	727	$2980	$2580
Formal Sedan (5-7)	712	$3285	$2885
Touring (5-7)	710	$2590	$2190
Model 1102 Eight (141 inches)			
Sedan (5-7)	714	$2655	$2300
Sedan-Limousine (5-7)	715	$2790	$2430

	Body No.		
Model 1103 Super Eight (135 inches)			
Sedan (5)	753	$2950	$2350
Model 1104 Super Eight (142 inches)			
Coupe (2-4)	758	$2980	$2390
Coupe (5)	757	$3180	$2480
Coupe-Roadster (2-4)	759	$3070	$2380
Phaeton (5)	751	$3090	$2390
Sport Phaeton (5)	761	$3350	$2650
Sedan (5)	773	—	—
Club Sedan (5)	756	$3255	$2555
Convertible Sedan (5)	763	$3790	$3190
Convertible Victoria (5)	767	$3640	$2990
Formal Sedan (5-7)	752	$3800	$3100
Touring (5-7)	750	$3180	$2480
Model 1105 Super Eight (147 inches)			
Sedan (5-7)	754	$3290	$2690
Sedan-Limousine (5-7)	755	$3480	$2780

As before, the Sport Phaeton had tonneau cowl and windshield, the Phaeton did not. The Eight Sport Phaeton was not, however, illustrated in the catalogue, on the theory that the body style made it a second or third car for a wealthy family which might be enticed instead to buy the more expensive Super Eight Sport Phaeton. If that failed, the Eight could be ordered from the factory—as a favor.

In addition, the custom styles were returned to the Super Eight line, some being the same bodies originally introduced for 1932. The Dietrich designs were modified and a new hood supplied, extending back to the windshield and equipped with slanting vent doors repeating the slant of the rear hood line—an adaptation of the similar treatment of the Century of Progress Exposition Packard. All Custom bodies offered on the Twelves could be had now on the Super Eight, save for the LeBaron Sport Runabout, Style 275, and the Sport Coupe by Packard, Style 264. (These two were actually on the 135-inch Super Eight chassis but with a Twelve engine.) The Custom cars were not, of course, afforded clearance prices, and their lineup was as follows:

Model 1105 Super Eight	Body No.	8-21-33
Coupe, Stationary, (2-4), Dietrich	4068	$5445
Convertible Runabout (2-4), Dietrich	4071	$5365
Convertible Sedan (5), Dietrich	4070	$5800
Convertible Victoria (5), Dietrich	4072	$5345
Sport Sedan (5), Dietrich	4182	$6295
Cabriolet, All-Weather (5-7), LeBaron	858	$5450
Town Car, All-Weather (5-7), LeBaron	859	$5450
Sport Phaeton (5), LeBaron	280	$7065

"What the Boys Who Sell Them Think of the New Eleventh Series

Packards" heralded the *Inner Circle* in September of '33. They liked them. From Packard-Indianapolis, T.E. Byrne offered the opinion that anyone not on a driving acquaintanceship with the new car " 'ain't seen nuthin.' It actually performed so smoothly and quietly that I could almost hear my watch tick at 60 miles per hour." From Packard-Pittsburgh, F.E. Bishop allowed that, despite initial fears the increased wheelbase and concomitant weight gain of the 1100 and 1105 might affect performance, "comparative tests which we conducted here have allayed our apprehension in this direction." In England, *The Autocar*

took the 1100 to Brooklands and correlative figures to the '33 car tested the year previous showed an increase in acceleration, 0 to 50 in fourteen seconds flat, and a mean timed speed a full five miles an hour faster. The new cars were easily the performing equals of their predecessors.

At sixty, at seventy, or even a healthy eighty plus, the owner of one of the new Eleventh Series Packards could, if he wished, hear something besides the sound of his watch. It only took a turn of the knob. Charlie Vincent told this story: "In 1929 Earle Anthony, Milton Tibbetts and I were selected to interview executives of various radio companies with the

idea of persuading them to build for Packard a very high grade radio to be installed in our cars. Earle was to do the introducing because he knew many of them, I was to supply technical knowledge, and Tibbetts was to do the bargaining. After talking with Western Electric and several other possible sources, we visited David Sarnoff, then president of RCA and famous because he had been the radio operator who handled the shore end of the traffic when the *Titanic* was sunk by an iceberg. He was a rather small man sitting at an enormous desk in the middle of a large room and obviously very much in charge. After listening to us, he

The 1934 Eight 1101 Coupe-Roadster (left); the 1101 Five-Passenger Sedan at Brooklands for a road test by The Autocar; *a custom-bodied Super Eight shown by the daughter of racing driver Felice Nazzaro at a 1934 concours in Italy.*

remarked that he would be happy to send an engineer to the Proving Grounds to work with us but then added, 'I fear you will be wasting your time and money because automobile radio will never be a success. I have tried one and think they will soon be prohibited by law.' "

Packard thought otherwise, cheerfully spreading the news that fully fifty owners had sets especially installed during the first six months of 1929. By early 1931, the Packard Service Letter, addressed to service stations throughout the country, advised, "Undoubtedly you are interested in learning about what is being done in the construction of Packard bodies so that radio equipment can be added. We have found that the wire netting used in the roof of closed cars provides a very satisfactory antenna. . . ." What the factory had done was merely leave a larger gap, one and a half inches, between the wire netting roof reenforcement and the metal side panels, which acted as a ground. This was the sum total of the radio provision. The "B" battery was usually made up of sixteen large dry cells stored wherever space could be found—and that wasn't easy. In the writer's 1930 phaeton, it was in the compartment at the toe space of the rear seat, with the control head attached to the steering post. This radio was not a Packard accessory; the company did not approve one for use until April 1932, a Packard DeLuxe which retailed at $89.50 installed. Packard dealers also handled a much less sensitive or selective radio which retailed for $39.95, not installed. Both were steering post models with the works above the toe board, were made by Philco—Packard stayed with Philco to the end—and it was the DeLuxe version which Packard chose when committing itself wholeheartedly to the radio idea with the Eleventh Series cars.

Claiming the distinction of being "the first automobile builder to give full recognition to the radio receiving set as a desirable feature in the modern car"—and getting no argument—Packard's cars for 1934 were completely engineered for radio, this involving "a specially designed instrument board, shielded wiring and lead-in wires, change in coils to prevent interference, a larger air cooled generator and other such engineering features." And—who but Packard would have thought of it—the removable panel for the dial and controls of the set followed the "characteristic profile of the Packard radiator, and becomes an ornamental detail in cars whose owners do not require the set." But by July of 1934 the company reported that fully thirty-five percent—a very healthy percentage—of all Packards being delivered were equipped with radio. "It's no longer just a fad," the company concluded.*

---

*It was only natural that owners of 1933 and 1932 Packards would want the new built-in look of the 1934 radio. With a minimum of alteration to the mounting panel, the 1934 instrument panel could be installed on those cars. For further updating, the 1934 front fenders could be installed on the 1933 cars. Both these alterations were covered in the Packard Service Letters.

Equally fortuitous, Packard's foreign business continued to flourish—and indeed provided the company's happiest news throughout these bad years. Not that the going was always easy. The Depression hadn't hurt Packard's export greatly, but revolution occasionally played havoc instead. In Spain the company's distributor was a woman who had secured her job by taking export manager B.C. Budd to the royal garages in the mid-Twenties and showing him the "nothing much . . . in evidence but a number of Cadillacs in various stages of disintegration." By the end of the decade she had made Packard a royal favorite, and indeed the "pathetic leave-taking of the Queen from Spain, when she was forced to leave the country" was accomplished in a long retinue of cars from East Grand Boulevard. "With the overthrow of the government," Budd noted solemnly in a memorandum to Alvan Macauley, "there were several difficulties to be faced, least of which was the starting to build a business all over again. Having been more or less aligned with the Royalist government, she was naturally in disfavor with the Revolutionists." But the lady discovered that even overthrowers of governments could be enticed into Packard ownership—"happenings

The Packard Engineering blueprint room and experimental garage photographe
August 1933. Alvan Macauley shaking hands with Ossip Gabrilovitch and
Dr. Walter Damrosch, leaders of the symphony orchestra for the Packard radio

that all go to make life exciting in the export department."

In Japan, where comparative serenity reigned in royal circles, no fewer than seventy-three Packards were in use in the Imperial household, or by governors of prefectures, members of peerage, prominent statesmen, et al. "The Shah of Persia; the Sovereign Sultans of Langkat and Djokjakarta, in the Dutch East Indies; the Agha Khan, the visible head of the Moslem World and a ruler of an Indian State, as well as thirty-seven more of these fabulously wealthy Rajahs and Princes of India; the Presidents of most of the South and Central American Republics; statesmen and noblemen without number [including the racing driver Count Carlo Felice Trossi]—you could continue the list indefinitely." All were Packard owners. And in London where "you will strain your eyes in vain looking for a Lincoln, a Cadillac or a Pierce-Arrow," there were fifteen hundred Packards strolling the Strand. "Rest your finger anywhere on the slowly revolving globe and there you will find Packard," a company catalogue boasted in 1934, adding a phrase that seems particularly poignant now: "For, like the British Empire, the sun never sets on this fine car."

CHAPTER SEVENTEEN

FULSOME HARMONY WITH THE STREAMLINE MOTIF

The Twelfth Series -- August 1934 - August 1935

The Fourteenth Series -- August 1935 - September 1936

The Fifteenth Series -- September 1936 - August 1937

The Sixteenth Series -- September 1937 - August 1938

AUTHOR: L. MORGAN YOST

Pages preceding: Photographed in 1936, Earle Anthony's showroom in Los Angele

With salutary news from foreign shores continuing to arrive at East Grand Boulevard, Packard determined that the company was ready for a change in fortune on this side of the Atlantic, or Pacific, as well—and set about to prepare for it. Already there were signs that turnaround from the depths of the Depression worldwide might be in the offing, and in fulsome good spirit the company leased more space than ever it had before for the 1934 automobile show at New York City's Grand Central Palace. Behind the scenes even bigger things were happening.

Two matters weighed most heavily on the Packard agenda—new styling and a new small car . . . for the lower-priced field. The former would be seen to first. In early 1932 Alvan Macauley's son Edward had been named head of the newly created Packard styling division, and in February he announced the appointment of Alexis de Sakhnoffsky as consulting art director to the company. Actually, by that time, de Sakhnoffsky was already at work, the Packard board minutes noting that he had been engaged for "two days each week, for a period of three months, beginning January 25th, 1932, at the rate of $800 monthly." That was a tidy sum for "part-time" employment in those days, but the Packard company was expecting a lot from de Sakhnoffsky, though the results of his efforts would not be immediately revealed. Dietrich's legacy of designs continued with modification through the 1934 models, providing for some types a style life of five years.

De Sakhnoffsky's assignment was to change things, the creation of a new and different theme but one which would retain the characteristic Packard identity. One essence of his design ideas—the long hood stretching from radiator to windshield which he had used extensively in Europe—would be in evidence on several Packard custom bodies for 1934, most notably the Dietrich Convertible Sedan. (Ralph Roberts of Briggs and LeBaron had anticipated Packard by incorporating the extension of the hood to the windshield into the 1932 DeSoto and Chrysler Custom Imperial.) Other de Sakhnoffsky ideas would await the new Twelfth Series.

Critical of the prevailing narrow car hoods which forced a reverse curve into the body sides at the cowl in order to expand to the required width at the front compartment, de Sakhnoffsky preferred to taper the hood uniformly so it would blend into the body volume without undue curvature. His object was to attain the ultimate body-of-a-piece that his predecessors had been working toward, but had not yet fully accomplished. Development of this design theme would be carried out by Werner Gubitz, following de Sakhnoffsky's short tenure at Packard.

It was Ed Macauley's task to reconcile the new small Packard, then in its early developmental throes, to the appearance of the larger models. The decision to provide a styling marriage between what would soon be called the Junior and Senior Packards was well thrashed out by management. The new Twelfth Series Senior cars were to be the launching pad for the new small car. Four months would elapse between their introduction and Packard's entry into the lower-priced field, and it was felt this interval would serve to acquaint the public with Packard's new look and provide for an orderly assimilation of the new car into the Packard Motor Car Company family.

Already word was out that it was coming. And a lot of owners were not sure they liked the idea. Letters to the company revealed the desire that the new car not look like "their" Packard—or that it even be called a Packard at all. One alternate suggestion coursing the rumor rounds, even gaining some credence, was "Packette." But Packard's mind was already made up. The company had looked at the figures. It had to have a small car, and that car had to be a Packard, a Packard One Twenty as it turned out.

There just was not enough fine car business to be had. Whether the men at Packard were aware of it or not—and probably they were—Cadillac was considered a candidate for the automotive graveyard in 1934, but was given a reprieve, much to the later satisfaction of General Motors. The subsequent success enjoyed by the marque would likely have been impossible had Packard been able to remain in its exclusively fine car position, for never again would Cadillac have the strong competition in its field that Packard had given it. Interesting is a comparison of new car registrations, Packard versus Cadillac-LaSalle, for the six years prior to the One Twenty.

	1929	1930	1931	1932	1933	1934
Packard	44,636	28,318	16,256	11,058	9,081	6,552
Cadillac-LaSalle	35,226	23,340	18,019	10,117	7,618	10,081

For 1934 the LaSalle was a lower-priced straight eight which naturally drew more sales—7195 of them. But still Cadillac didn't make bundles of money, it was being carried by General Motors. The Packard Motor Car Company had to carry itself, of course.

Much of the company's loss during 1934—$7.3 million—was attributable to tooling for the new models: $3,541,500 for the One Twen-

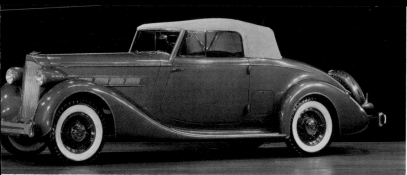

ckwise from above left, Packards for 1935: 1201 Club Sedan, 1201 Coupe-Roadster, 1201 Victoria, 1201 Phaeton, 1204 Formal Sedan, 1201 Five-Passenger Coupe.

ty, $1,559,975 for the Twelfth Series. These items were charged off in their entirety rather than capitalized, a method of bookkeeping which the Internal Revenue Service no longer recognizes. As Alvan Macauley explained, Packard remained in a "strong financial position . . . despite substantial losses." In July of 1934 cash and marketable securities were valued at $14,636,963, compared with $15,161,361 the New Year's Day previous. Much of the so-called loss incurred had been offset by the new liquidity of frozen bank accounts and the rise in prices of stocks and bonds held. The $15 million still on hand was actually left over from the great profits of the Twenties, plus capital remaining from sale of common stock. For the ten years 1925-1934, profits had exceeded dividends paid by $3,717,000, though no dividends were paid in 1932, 1933 or 1934—nor would any be paid in 1935. In the main, Packard investments had been wise. The board of directors, and treasurer Hugh Ferry, pointed with pride to Packard's lack of indebtedness. No money had to be borrowed for the development or tooling up for the new models, nor for the radical plant conversion planned. And that was an accomplishment hardly equalled in those depressed days.

Hardly equalled either—in the light of previous Packard history— were the widescale changes being made among Packard personnel during this period.

Roy Chamberlain was called back from Buffalo in 1934 to take general-sales-manager charge of the Senior contingent, promoting it as the prestige line, and laying the groundwork for the One Twenty campaign. Loranger had left for health reasons, and F.H. McKinney, who had been given sales manager responsibility, was now relieved of that, to devote full efforts to advertising and sales promotion. William Packer, schooled in high-pressure sales at Chevrolet, was brought in to handle that department for the One Twenty, which he would do so well that he would be made general sales manager by 1936, which moved Chamberlain down to assistant sales manager in charge of the eastern division. That same year M.A. Cudlip, after eighteen years as Packard's secretary, left the company, and Hugh Ferry added that post to the one he already had as company treasurer.

341

Chrome plating department of the Packard Motor Car Company, photographed in 1935, with a worker handling gingerly one of the world's most famous radiator s

Engineers and efficiency experts were brought in by the score. And one afternoon in 1934 Max Gilman called a production man who had retired from General Motors two months previous, and offered him the job of setting up production lines for the One Twenty. George Christopher left his Ohio farm right away and got down to work in Detroit. The magnitude of his accomplishment will be detailed later; sufficient here to relate that the Senior lines would be consolidated into one of the two main production buildings (the other reserved for the One Twenty), and never-the-twain-should-meet requirements planned for each. Many of the factory workers of the old line would, however, be transferred to the

new as a nucleus to train the new force—and this depleted the man-per-car ratio in the Senior plant, a situation Christopher made up for at least partially by adding more specialized machinery and methods to the more traditional *modus operandi* of Packard fine car production. Manufacturing vice-president E.F. Roberts was nearing sixty by now, forty of those years having been spent with the Packard Motor Car Company. He longed to retire and did not relish the prospect of having the driving responsibility for the new Packard mass production. He agreed to stay on until Christopher was established at the company, leaving finally in July of 1935 for a trip around the world and a well-earned retirement.

Christopher immediately took Roberts' old post.

Another significant change in management put Max Gilman in one of the seats that Alvan Macauley had occupied for so many years. In May of 1934 Gilman, then just forty-five and already a vice-president, was also made general manager of the company. "In addition to [his] wealth of field experience," the announcement stated, "Mr. Gilman's sympathetic understanding of distributor and dealer problems proved of such aid to President Macauley in conducting the affairs of the Company in the last ten years that added recognition and responsibilities have now been given him by action of the President and the Packard Board of Directors." Implicit in this was relieving Macauley of the day-to-day pressure of overseeing and carrying out the operation of the manufacturing, sales and engineering divisions. Henceforth he would be, as *Fortune* magazine would so aptly put it, Packard's "flywheel rather than its spark plug." Max Gilman was now number two man, certainly the most significant personnel change to have occurred at the company in a long time, perhaps ever. It was clearly a recognition that the traditional way of cultivating a clientele was no longer entirely viable. Not many years before, the incomparable "Doc" Hills had said, "We expect a Packard man to be well spoken, well poised, and just a bit retiring." At the very least, and rather obviously, that last personnel requisite was fast being changed.

But not the basic Packard philosophy, certainly not by Alvan Macauley. While maintaining that the One Twenty was very important to Packard, he vowed that Packard would in no way be abandoning the high-priced field: "It has been our experience over a period of more than thirty years, that, with a return to more prosperous conditions, [the tendency for the public to buy lower-priced cars] will be checked, since there is no indication of people financially able to buy the best in motor cars, or, for that matter, any other product, having permanently lost their desire to do so."

More prosperous times appeared to be on the way—and Packard had its new Twelfth Series, introduced again in Detroit's mammoth Masonic Temple in August of 1934. Nearly four thousand distributors, dealers and service managers attended. They drove away thereafter in the demonstrators—covering a total of 196,435 miles without so much as a tire puncture—and once in the showrooms the response to the new cars was quite overwhelming. "Sales resulting from the public introduction of the new models," Packard reported, "have carried the bank of unfilled orders to the highest point they have reached in the last four years, so that it may be necessary to put the factories on both night and day work."

Mechanically, all three Senior cars, the Eight, the Super Eight and the Twelve, were refined. Aluminum cylinder heads were made standard, which with increased compression ratios—6.5 to one on the Eight, 6.3 on the Super Eight—raised developed horsepower at 3200 rpm to 130 and

Polishing the bottom radiator plate of one of the Twelfth Series Packards for 1935.

150 respectively. This added horsepower—and the ever improving road conditions throughout the United States—encouraged faster sustained speeds by drivers, and resulted in another change Packard thought wise. The poured babbitt metal connecting rod bearings used generally produced fatigue problems and required replacement after hard use. Under severe strains, with improper lubrication, they would melt or "burn out," on Packards as well as other cars. Packard's new copper-lead, steel-backed bearings were a remarkable improvement, the result of several years' research, development and testing by company engineers and metallurgists, under William H. Graves who would later become

vice-president of engineering. The thin layer of the alloy bonded to a steel shell produced a bearing that would stand a higher temperature and speed than any metal previously used, and which could be replaced more easily and accurately. The old scraping and fitting of bearings was now a process consigned to history.

A standard Packard sedan had been run wide open for 25,000 miles on the Proving Grounds track, with stops only for gas, oil and change of drivers. It aroused considerable comment in the industry, and in retrospect might be said to have heralded the long-lasting automobile engine as we know it today. As *Automobile Topics* reported: "Although high-speed runs for long distances have been made before, they generally were accomplished with cars in which gear ratios had been changed to slow down engines to 3000 rpm or less. Even the grind of the Indianapolis race is mild by comparison with the Packard test, inasmuch as the distance there is only 500 miles and in making each lap the engines are shut down four times for curves." After the test the Packard engine was dismantled, measured for wear and displayed unassembled at the Masonic Temple meeting.

Further refinements were to be found in the oil filter and cooler, the automatic choke, austenitic exhaust valves, generator, et al. And the frame-body-motor relationship was revised by moving the motor forward about two inches and pulling the front axle back the same distance. Combined with softer front spring rates, the result was a much better ride both front and rear. Ride Control was retained. The frame was considerably stiffened by extending the X-member to form boxed side rails. The long-characteristic tubular front cross member was eliminated, as the radiator with its cross member below was moved forward, allowing wheelbases to be shortened two inches on the Eight, three on the Super Eight—at the same time increasing body space. The Eights were now 127, 134 and 139 inches, while Super Eights were 132, 139 and 144. (The Twelves were 139 and 144.)

Welded spoke wire wheels were standard on all chassis, though wood wheels or convex steel wheel covers for the wire wheels could be had at extra cost, the latter proving quite popular as they minimized the cleaning problem. Tires were 7x17 low pressure 6-ply black, with white walls optional.

The redistribution of motor weight and the new frame went hand-in-hand with the biggest news of all, the completely new appearance of the cars, as great a change as that between the Second and Third Series Twin Sixes way back in 1917. What *The Autocar* called "the fashionable swept effect" and *Automobile Topics* "fulsome harmony with the streamline motif" was the point of departure, though up front the Packard identity remained. The shouldered radiator was there, but it was sloped back about five degrees. Its shell was lacquered body color, the louvers chrome plated. The new bullet-shaped headlamps and the

fenders were lacquered the same color as the body too, the latter deeper, skirted and the rear fenders of pontoon shape. Body sides extended down to the running board and followed its gentle curve. The spare tire—unless side mounts were ordered—was carried concealed in a compartment in the sloping rear panel, also a new feature. All sedans had a single slope rear, with no integral trunk bulge except on the Club Sedan.

The spear which for five years had accented the side of the hoods was raised to become the edge arris of the hood shoulder shelf, which carried back past the windshield, and windows, and died into the body surface. Thus the trademark shoulder, which had formerly dwindled before it reached the rear of the hood, became a strong unifying feature of the entire body design. Many of the open and convertible cars carried Dietrich body plates though they were not custom cars in any way. But . . . it did help sales.

Interiors were wider and more spacious and more quiet, one reason for the latter being the increased use of wood in the body frame, some 250 pounds of it. This was a quality feature stressed by Packard at a time when more manufacturers were going to all-steel construction, which was considered to be noisier and "tinnier." The instrument board was of new design, all round faces being contained in a wide oval frame with the radio panel in the center. The hand brake was relocated to hang from the cowl, freeing floor space to allow use of the wider front door. Unfortunately, the front doors were hinged at the rear to allow the front edge to follow the windshield slope. A hinge arrangement that would solve this problem seemed to have eluded the body men.

The Eight, Super Eight and Twelve were distinguishable mainly by the different style hood louvers in each, though one could read the hubcaps if the car were standing. As before, the same bodies were used on all cars with but trim differences. The hood of the Eight was five inches shorter than that of the Super Eight or Twelve. Withal, these were monumental automobiles which could not fail to impress, guarantors of the prestige which it was hoped would carry the new small car to success. The Packard One Twenty was introduced January 5th, 1935. In a word, it was a smash.

Smiles broke out at East Grand Boulevard, and in April a gala gala—which is the most fitting way to describe it—was held to celebrate Alvan Macauley's twenty-five years with Packard. It was supposed to be a surprise party, but as the press reported, "the affair was not altogether a surprise to President Macauley, who became suspicious because of the abnormal number of out-of-town distributors drifting into town." Reporters from the national news media began drifting into Detroit, too. Alvan Macauley suddenly became news, he made the cover of *Time* later that year. "At sixty-three," that magazine said, "President Macauley with his high forehead, his thin white hair, his rimless eyeglasses and his square-jawed face could, if he would, get a job in Hollywood playing

The Packard Eight powerplant for the Twelfth Series and the 1935 model year. Note such improvements as the new manifolding and down-draft carburetion.

parts as a typical U.S. tycoon. He detests people who jingle coins and he shrinks from the sight of gold teeth. His voice is seldom raised, his temper never lost." There wasn't much now happening at Packard about which tempers might be lost. The view through Macauley's rimless eyeglasses was rosy.

All this was largely through the blessing of the One Twenty, of course, although Packard went to great lengths to give pats on the back to its Senior cars as well. In March of '35 the company released the news that for the three months previous, Packard registrations in its higher price lines were 43.5 percent ahead of the same period the year before. In May the *Inner Circle* reported that "demand for Twelfth Series cars has kept pace with the rapidly mounting sales [of the One Twenty]." In July Packard revealed a six months' production of 17,816 of the latter and 3561 of the Senior cars—and a half-year net profit of $290,460. "In this showing of profits," Alvan Macauley pointed out, "we must not fail to give due credit to the sales of Twelfth Series cars. They are an extremely important element in enabling us to make a record that we can view with considerable satisfaction."

Packard was becoming strong. If the One Twenty was helping the Senior cars—and/or vice versa—it was, however, nailing the coffin shut

on the Packard Diesel program. "Because of the magnitude of the job of bringing out a car in a new price field," Macauley advised, "we decided to concentrate on that job and hold the Diesel engine project in abeyance." And there it would remain until it died.

In August, again, came the new Senior Packards. They weren't the Thirteenth Series. Somebody at Packard must have been superstitious. But for minor details, the Fourteenth Series for 1936 was a repeat of the Twelfth Series for 1935. A recognition point was the greater slope of the radiator and the modification of the fender fronts to blend with it. In addition, the Delco-Remy ignition system with octane selector was installed, and clutch throw-out bearings were of the permanently lubricated type although to make absolutely sure they were hooked up to the Bijur system too.

This new era of Packard styling had obviously assisted in revitalizing company sales, but it did complicate matters for the custom body builders who were having a difficult enough time of it anyway. So much of the Packard ensemble was prescribed before the body designer could begin; the radiator and hood dictated the body shape and volume at the cowl, the fenders and running boards controlling much of what remained, leaving little opportunity for the body designer to make his own statement. Some attempts were made by LeBaron, Derham, Rollston and others, but precious few they were. Most of the coachwork plates were on modified bodies, as for example the LeBaron Town Car and Cabriolet appearing in the list following for the Twelfth and Fourteenth Series. The Town Car was revised from a Seven-Passenger Sedan, with removal of the roof over the front compartment, remodeling of front doors and windshield and the addition of a portable top. Similarly, the Cabriolet was modified from the Formal Sedan. The full lineup was as follows:

Body Style	1935 Eight Type No. 8-30-34		1936 Eight Type No. 8-10-35	
127-inch wheelbase	Model 1200		Model 1400	
Sedan (5)	803	$2385	903	$2385
134-inch wheelbase	Model 1201		Model 1401	
Coupe (2-4)	818	$2470	918	$2470
Coupe (5)	817	$2560	917	$2560
Coupe-Roadster (2-4)	819	$2580	919	$2730
Phaeton (5)	811	$2670/$2870	911	$3020
Sport Phaeton (5)	801		901	
Sedan (5)	813	$2585	913	$2585
Club Sedan (5)	816	$2580	916	$2580
Formal Sedan (5-7)	812	$3285	912	$3285
Convertible Victoria (5)	807	$3100	907	$3200
Cabriolet, LeBaron (5-7)	195	$5240	295	$5240
139-inch wheelbase	Model 1202		Model 1402	
Sedan (5-7)	814	$2755	914	$2755
Business Sedan (5-8)	814	$2630	914	$2630
Limousine (5-7)	815	$2890	915	$2890
Business Limousine (5-8)	815	$2765	915	$2765
Convertible Sedan (5)	863	$3200/$3300	963	$3400
Touring (5-7)	810	—/$3170	910	$3270
Town Car, LeBaron (5-7)	194	$5385	294	$5385

Body Style	1935 Super Eight Type No. 8-30-34		1936 Super Eight Type No. 8-10-35	
132-inch wheelbase	Model 1203		Model 1403	
Sedan (5)	842	$2990	943	$2990

Super-Eight Packards: Left, the 1500 Touring Sedan; below, the 1404 Coupe-Roadster purchased by comedian Bob Hope; the 1404 Club Sedan.

139-inch wheelbase	Model 1204		Model 1404	
Coupe (2-4)	858	$2880	958	$2880
Coupe (5)	857	$3080	957	$3080
Coupe-Roadster (2-4)	859	$3070	959	$3070
Phaeton (5)	851	$3190/$3390	951	$3390
Sport Phaeton (5)	841	$3450/$3650	941	$3650
Club Sedan (5)	856	$3170	956	$3170
Formal Sedan (5-7)	852	$3800	952	$3800
Convertible Victoria (5)	847	$3760/$3860	947	$3860
Sedan (5)	853			
Cabriolet, LeBaron (5-7)	195	$5670	295	$5670
144-inch wheelbase	Model 1205		Model 1405	
Sedan (5-7)	854	$3390	954	$3390
Business Sedan (5-8)	854	$3265	954	$3265
Limousine (5-7)	855	$3580	955	$3580
Business Limousine (5-8)	855	$3455	955	$3455
Convertible Sedan (5)	883	$3910/$4010	983	$4010
Touring (5-7)	850	$3690	950	$3690
Town Car, LeBaron (5-7)	194	$5815	294	$5815

On these pages: The 1402 Eight Seven-Passenger Sedan during and after the 15,000+ miles it was run at the Packard Proving Grounds in November 1935.

The double figures for open cars for 1935 represent the initial pricetag together with the revised price as of May 21st, 1935. Those desiring an open car in the Thirties had to pay increasingly more for it.

If the Fourteenth Series was largely a mirror of the Twelfth, the Packard Motor Car Company sought to make it newsworthy anyway, in a nifty promotional stunt whose author, alas, is unknown. A Packard Eight Seven-Passenger Sedan was pulled from the assembly line at random in November of '35 and taken to the Proving Grounds. At the very instant that, in New York, the National Automobile Show opened its doors to the public, the car was started around the track, stopping for the usual gas, oil, change of drivers and tires—but coming to a complete halt only when the show closed its doors seven days later. Meantime, at the Packard exhibit at the show, a model of it was running around a miniaturization of the Proving Grounds, with teletype machines flashing the news of what was happening at Utica on a screen for all show visitors to see. When it was all over, the big Packard had put up 15,432½ miles, an endurance run the company claimed was "the most severe ever undertaken"—and the little Packard had drawn spectators by the thousands to the company display at the show.

Still, it remained the One Twenty which continued to make the big news. Packard's dealer network was expanding so fast now that the factory could barely keep up with it. Men skilled in sales and long out of work during the Depression's worst years were flocking to the Packard standard. And one very important veteran came back as well. The new Packard dealer for Lafayette, Indiana would be—it was announced in

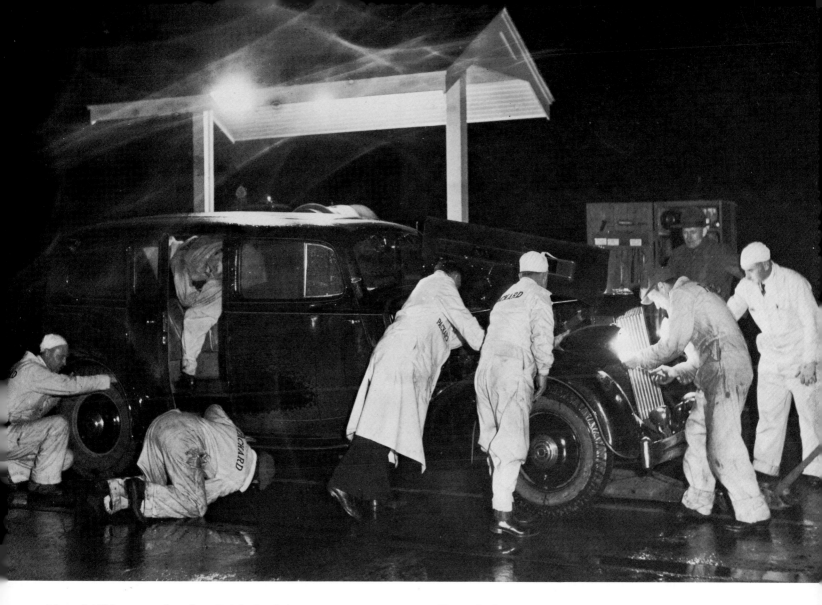

May of 1936—none other than Ralph De Palma, operating his dealership under the Packard distributor at Indianapolis, one Preston Tucker.

In the face of all this, it was an almost plaintive Alvan Macauley who counseled his sales people that "our Senior line is still the backbone of our prosperity. These cars must not be forgotten or neglected in the glamor of the striking success of the One Twenty. . . ."

Net profit for the year 1935 turned up an impressive $4,315,622. During the first six months of 1936, earnings jumped to $3,520,128. By late summer a $5 million expansion program to double Packard's productive capacity was announced, and late fall saw the company declaring yet another stock dividend bringing the total for the year to $6,750,000—the first dividends not paid out of surplus since 1930. By year's end Packard's profits totaled $7,053,220.

One good success deserved another, Packard reasoned, and the company's biggest news for model year 1937 was the addition of a six-cylinder car to the Junior line. The Senior cars, unfortunately, had contributed little to Packard's fiscal strength.

A little clever paring was done at the top with the introduction of the new Fifteenth Series. Three Senior cars were too many. So the Super Eight was dropped from the line. But the public was not made aware of it, quite the contrary, for the new model was given the same name as the old—or, as Colonel Vincent explained, "The new Super Eight embodies all the fine qualities of the former Packard Eight and the former Super Eight plus the new mechanical features of the Twelve." Which freely translated meant that the former Eight now became the Super Eight—wheelbase, engine and all—and it and the Twelve were given parallel mechanical, chassis and body improvements. It was an astute marketing move. Instead of using the old sales trick of giving less for more with a name change, Packard gave more for less, setting the prices of the new Super Eight fifty dollars lower than the prices of the former Eight.

Perhaps the company felt it had no choice. A look at a few figures had proven sufficient cause for alarm. As Bill Packer admonished his sales organization at the introduction of the '37's: "Now for the Senior cars. . . . Packard was outsold by its nearest competitor during 1936 for the second time in twelve years. Granted that we had certain handicaps which are now overcome, the fact remains that our Senior car business was affected mostly by division of effort. [The sales people] flung their effort to the big volume and . . . our big car business suffered from neglect. . . . From today on every Packard outlet is going to do its share of the Senior car job . . . because the success of the Packard One Twenty . . . [and of the six-cylinder car] . . . are built on the foundation of Packard fine car leadership. . . . The statement is made repeatedly that we are not in on Cadillac deals and Cadillac is not in on ours. To me, that means only one thing—we have not been working Cadillac owners and as a result, when they do come into the market they give Packard no consideration."

There it was, perhaps said a bit more brusquely than the company would have said it before—but it was precisely right. Packer thought the problem had been solved with the '37 model "finer cars at lower prices . . . [plus] every feature you men in the field have asked for." But Cadillac for '37 had not stood still either. First, the LaSalle again had a V-8, the 322-cubic-inch unit of the 1936 Cadillac 60, and it was priced in the Packard One Twenty range. With its added power and length (124-inch wheelbase), it was more of a "big car" than the One Twenty which now was in its third year with the same general appearance. If nothing else, the LaSalle was a strong feint designed, probably not inadvertently, to keep Packard salesmen glued to their Junior Packard endeavors.

For 1937 Cadillac would produce 13,629 of its Series 60, 65, 70 and 75

cars—more than twice the Super Eight production of 5793. Clearly something had sparked GM's premier division, and it was more than the new and larger 346-cubic-inch V-8. Stand a 1937 Senior Packard next to a 1937 Cadillac. The Cadillac looks like a newer car, the Packard lamentably out of date—and the company would make few appearance changes for yet another two years. The best news for Packard Senior lines for '37 would be the Twelves, their production total of 1300 being twice that of 1936 and contrasting handsomely to Cadillac's total of 523 of its twelve- and sixteen-cylinder cars for 1937.

"Where is the Fine Car Going?" was the enigmatic title of a booklet Packard distributed that year—and the answer was that it was going places: "America's oldest and largest fine car maker is projecting its

Packard abroad, at automobile shows in Johannesburg, South Africa and Pre

plans upon a forecast of still greater demand for the finer type of automobile.'' The plans for '37, apparently, hadn't called for much change beyond the "every feature you men in the field have asked for" of which Bill Packer spoke.

This included adoption of the independent front suspension which had been a hallmark of the One Twenty from the beginning. The steering linkage was redesigned with central lever control to conform to the geometry of the new suspension. And new too were hydraulic brakes, with centrifuse drums, two shoes for each wheel. The Bijur system was dropped; because of the use of rubber and sealed bearings and the design of shackles and other parts, lubrication points were reduced to fifteen.

Though of the same general design, the Super Eight and Twelve frames and running gear were not identical, the Twelve of course being somewhat heavier construction largely because of the longer wheelbase available. Wheelbases for the Super Eight were 127, 134 and 139 inches; for the Twelve, 132, 139 and 144 inches.

Bodies remained identical, save for trim. The new front-hinged front doors, as introduced on the 1936 One Twenty, were a definite plus; the previous front-opening type had been egregiously dangerous. The built-in "bustle" trunks were now standard on all sedan-type bodies, which made them now "Touring Sedans." The spare tire—except when side-mounted spares were specified—was carried on the bottom of the trunk with a shelf over for luggage. Though they were presented in dimensional drawings in the Salesmen's Data Book, all phaetons were abrupt-

hoslovakia (1936 and 1935 respectively)— and Amelia Earhardt and a '35 Super Eight Phaeton during ceremonies in New York opening Brooklyn Day in September.

ly dropped from the line. Radiators were somewhat narrower and consequently more graceful. New bumper designs were adopted, the stabilizer type no longer being available. Neither were wire wheels, save on the Twelve, standard wheels now being a disc design using 7.50x16 tires, with a steel spoke wheel design as an option. Instrument panels followed the pattern of former models, with throttle and light switches now relocated there from the steering wheel which retained only the horn button.

The Super Eight, as noted, retained the Eight's powerplant, a fine performing motor now developing 135 hp. Though quite a few veteran Packard owners decried the loss of the bigger engines, they were reassured after a demonstration. Many of them traded in their aging big Eights on the new Super Eight, although it was observable that many of them traded in on the One Twenty as well.

The lineup for '37 was as follows:

Body Style/Wheelbase	Type No.	9-3-36	12-24-36	8-9-37
Model 1500 (127 inches)				
Touring Sedan (5)	1003	$2335	$2480	$2630
Model 1501 (134 inches)				
Coupe (2-4)	1018	$2420	$2565	$2715
Coupe (5)	1017	$2510	$2660	$2810
Coupe-Roadster (2-4)	1019	$2680	$2830	$2980
Club Sedan (5)	1016	$2530	$2680	$2830
Formal Sedan (5)	1012	$3235	$3400	$3550
Convertible Victoria (5)	1007	$3150	$3310	$3460
Touring Sedan (5)	1013	$2535	$2685	$2835
Cabriolet, LeBaron (5-7)	L-394	$4850		
Model 1502 (139 inches)				
Touring Sedan (5-7)	1014	$2705	$2860	$3010
Business Sedan (5-8)	1014B	$2580	$2730	$2880
Limousine (5-7)	1015	$2840	$2995	$3145
Business Limousine (5-8)	1015B	$2715	$2870	$3020
Convertible Sedan (5)	1063	$3350	$3515	$3665
Town Car, LeBaron (5-7)	L-395	$4990		

The LeBaron cars, each available with collapsible rear quarter, had their prices raised January 1st, 1937 to $5050 for Cabriolet, $5190 for Town Car. And it will be readily noted that all of the "finer cars at lower prices" inched up in price as the model year progressed. This was the case industry-wide. "Car Price Increase Spreading Rapidly," *Automobile Topics* headlined during the summer of '37 as virtually everyone fell in line once Ford decided to ask more for its car. A clearance sale wouldn't be considered, the '38 models would be priced higher yet.

Packard's spectacular sales gain from 1934 to 1937 was, quite literally, the talk of the industry. And with good reason, as witness the Packard new car registrations in the United States for those years: 1934, 6552; 1935, 37,653; 1936, 68,772; 1937, 95,239. Export added another eight percent. The Senior line was the sole contributor to the 1934 total of course, but had added a very small part in the succeeding years. Model year production of the Seniors was 6894 for 1935, 5985 for 1936, 7093 for 1937.

There were a few high spots. From California, Earle Anthony proclaimed that more than a hundred of the "best known stars in the motion picture world own and drive large Packards." From points north, south, east and west came bulletins from the Count and Countess Frederick Wilhelm von Keller who were "Super-Eighting 'Round the World." From Japan, so *The New York Times* reported on February 7th, 1937, came an order for fourteen—more!—Super Eights for the Imperial family.

And in the summer of '37, Alvan Macauley hit a hole-in-one at the Detroit Country Club, using a No. 6 iron, with Henry E. Bodman and Truman H. Newberry as witnesses. Which was as pleasant an episode as the ratification—just weeks previous—of the pact between the United Auto Workers and Packard. After "some protest and outbursts of dissatisfaction," as *Automotive Industries* reported, Packard employees had voted to accept the pact negotiated by the UAW, which Max Gilman called "a workable agreement which does not place the company at a disadvantage with its competitors." Indeed, many of its competitors were experiencing significantly tumultuous labor problems in comparison.

From his office at East Grand Boulevard, meantime, George Christopher had come to a conclusion regarding the Senior line for 1938. Why build two different chassis for two big cars that were so nearly alike in design and appearance? In 1932, when the Twin Six was introduced, it was a matter of choice of powerplant—eight or twelve—in the DeLuxe chassis. Why not do it again? The twelve-cylinder engine weighed about 750 pounds more than the eight, so Engineering had beefed up the Twelve chassis to take care of the load. Betimes *both* chassis frames had been redesigned to the point where they were the stiffest manufactured anywhere. If the long-wheelbase Twelve were eliminated, the Super Eight chassis would carry the Twelve very nicely, with some attention to cross members and bracing. Also, using the same wheelbases for like bodies on the two cars would allow standardization of fenders, hoods, running boards, steering linkage, et al. And so the deed was done. Save for such differences as required by the Twelve's heavier weight, the chassis for Super Eight and Twelve were identical for 1938.

The Junior lines—both the eight- and six-cylinder—were lengthened by seven inches, this putting the former at the same wheelbase size—127 inches—as the short-wheelbase Super Eight sedan. Prescience suggested a merger, which indeed would happen for '39. But for the nonce the

Super Eights, 1937: Page opposite, 1500 Touring Sedan and 1501 Club Sedan. Above and below: The 1501 Coupe-Roadster, Touring Sedan and Formal Sedan.

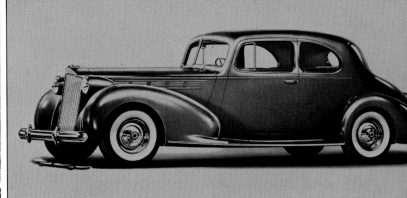

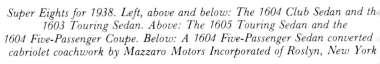

Super Eights for 1938. Left, above and below: The 1604 Club Sedan and the 1603 Touring Sedan. Above: The 1605 Touring Sedan and the 1604 Five-Passenger Coupe. Below: A 1604 Five-Passenger Sedan converted cabriolet coachwork by Mazzaro Motors Incorporated of Roslyn, New York

Senior cars were still trying it alone, and looking pretty much the same as before. The major appearance changes were new pontoon style front fenders, split vee windshield with center chrome strip running up to overlap the roof, and the continuous radiator shutters in a shell set more to the vertical, all characteristics found in the new Junior lines. The Junior designs were all new, entirely revised body shells—and to many most disappointing. To make matters worse, the new Cadillac 60 Special arrived soon thereafter, carrying a new low, suave body that was, in a word, pacesetting. It was in the price range of the Super Eight, its distinction and custom-built appearance made the Senior Packards look stodgy—and Packard management was already well aware that, for 1939, the Senior Eight was destined to adopt the body shell of the Junior cars. The dies were cast—and could not be changed. This situation would soon set other wheels in motion.

But, for now, there wasn't much to do but sell the cars, or try to. The Super Eight for 1938 lineup was as follows:

Body Style/Wheelbase	Type No.	9-29-37	10-11-37	10-26-37
Model 1603 (127 inches)				
Touring Sedan (5)	1103	$2790		
Model 1604 (134 inches)				
Coupe (2-4)	1118	$2925		
Coupe (5)	1117	$2965		
Convertible Coupe (2-4)	1119	$3210		
Club Sedan (5)	1116	$2990		
Formal Sedan (5)	1112	$3710		
Convertible Victoria (5)	1107	$3670		
Touring Sedan (5)	1113	$2995		
All-Weather Cabriolet/ Rollston	494			$5790
Model 1605 (139 inches)				
Touring Sedan (5-7)	1114	$3165		
Business Sedan (5-8)	1114B	$3035		
Limousine (5-7)	1115	$3305		
Business Limousine (5-8)	1115B	$3180		
Convertible Sedan (5)	1143	$3970		
All-Weather Cabriolet/ Brunn (5-7)	3087			$7475
Touring Cabriolet/ Brunn (5-6)	3086			$7475
Town Car/Rollston (5-7)	495			$5890

Note the shift in model numbers, last year's 1500 becoming this year's 1603, this the result of the Juniors having been brought into the fold. The Six was now Model 1600, the Eight (formerly One Twenty) was 1601, with the 148-inch wheelbase variation 1602.

The custom array was distinctively handsome. The Brunn cars, in a somewhat sporting vein with collapsible rear quarters, were new, and the Rollston formal cars, also available with collapsible rear quarters, were continued similar to the LeBaron types of the previous year. In addition Rollston produced three town cars for the Junior Packard Eight chassis. There had been a few custom bodies by other makers on the One Twenty chassis, but none previously sponsored by Packard. The upgrading of the Eight and the blurring of it into the Super Eight was inherent in these new offerings.

Ironically, this idea was not carried through into advertising. The Junior cars were featured in *The Saturday Evening Post, Collier's, Time, Life* and *The New Yorker.* Senior car advertising appeared in *Fortune, Country Life, Horse and Horseman, Sportsman, Spur, Stage, Town and Country* and *Yachting.* Perhaps the bifurcation was ill advised. Omitting the Senior cars in the popular magazines lost sight of one factor Packard was doing its utmost to maintain in all its public pronouncements, that, as Alvan Macauley said, the Junior Packard success rested largely upon the "tradition, prestige and reputation" which had been long established by the Senior cars. How would a *Post* reader know that the Super Eight and Twelve were out there upholding the Packard social position when the *Post* reader often never saw the *Fortune* ads?

Packard tried to pretend that all was going well with its Senior cars. "It is scarcely news that the past few years witnessed an enforced retreat from distinguished living," a brochure for '38 noted. "But it is, perhaps, news and surprising news to many that the art of fine living is decidedly more than back on its feet—that actually it is challenging the records of all previous years." But the truth was more nearly approached by the British *Sussex Daily News* whose automotive writer deemed the Super Eight "worthy to retain the marque's proud position of being numbered among [the] slowly diminishing aristocracy of fine cars . . . cars of international repute, representing the culmination of engineering experience and skill, and the alpha and omega of luxurious road travel." An era was passing. Packard's prestige cars were losing money, a lot of it.

Nineteen thirty-seven had seen more Packards produced than in any previous year in the company's history, although less money was made in doing it—$3,052,212—this due to the Junior line redesign, and the backtracking into economic doldrums the year had also seen. Nineteen thirty-eight would show the recession, or "depression within a depression"—or however one wishes to term it—unrelenting, and Packard production would total but 50,260 units, less than half the 1937 figure. The company would lose $1,638,000, the first red ink in four years. And during the model year, a dismal 2478 Super Eights and 566 Twelves would leave the lines. It was becoming a luxury for Packard to maintain the Senior cars. Decisions, reluctantly, were in the making.

CHAPTER EIGHTEEN

THE END
OF AN ERA

The Seventeenth Series--September 1938-August 1939

The Eighteenth Series--August 1939-September 1940

The Nineteenth Series--September 1940-August 1941

The Twentieth Series--August 1941-February 1942

AUTHOR: L. MORGAN YOST

The loyalty of the distributors is a fine thing to see," Alvan Macauley wrote in a friendly letter to Henry E. Bodman on May 19th, 1938. "A few are prosperous, some are broke, and the balance partly so." Adolf Hitler had invaded Austria two months before, but in America any forebodings of war were muted by the continuing concern about the economic recession. By late September, when the new Packards were introduced, British Prime Minister Neville Chamberlain had a piece of paper assuring "peace in our time," Hitler had the Sudetenland, and the economy remained this country's principal worry.

"Packard, entering its 40th year, is still unmistakably sturdy in its four types," commented *Time* magazine in its appraisal of the new car scene. But anyone with prescience might have sensed something else. Four types there were, two Juniors and two Seniors, but one of the latter was by now receiving only scant attention. A *Fortune* advertisement read, "The Packard Super-8, Now Only $2035. A Great Companion Car for the 1939 Edition of The Famous Packard 12"—but the twelve-cylinder car was not illustrated, nor would it ever be in an advertisement again. It was practically unchanged from 1938, save for a new steering column gearshift, an enamelled emblem on the sides of the hood, and radiator louvers alternately painted body color and chromed. This last superficiality was also used on the Super-8's as a mark of Senior Packard distinction. Otherwise the Super-8 looked very much the same as the One Twenty, save for trim differences.*

Its engine, carried through from '38, had a few changes. The water pump was new, permanently lubricated, packless, with double rows of pre-loaded ball bearings on the shaft which in turn carried a new asymmetrical fan with two of the blades serrated to reduce noise. Small end connecting rod bearings were fully cylindrical, burnished to size. Cylinder heads were again cast iron: Aluminum by now was going into defense production for the war no one really wanted to think was coming.

It was a good engine, with 130 horsepower, lots of torque and a livelier performance than any previous Packard eight. The preceding year's Super Eight, on the 127-inch wheelbase with the same motor, weighed 4530 pounds; the new Super-8 weighed 3930. The One Twenty, with its short-stroke high-speed straight-eight of 120 hp, tipped the scales at 3605 pounds, and its performance was lively, too—indeed, many drivers would claim it the superior of the Super-8 for 1939.

Looking at the two cars with the same wheelbase, the same all-steel

bodies and frames, and most chassis components, and identical redesigned constant mesh transmissions with the new steering column shift, it was difficult to justify the extra cost of the Super-8 on the basis of trim alone. Each had the fifth shock absorber, mounted in the rear stabilizer linkage, which dampened transverse vibration and greatly improved riding and handling. Optional solenoid-operated overdrive was available to each. Both had the Packard look from the front, and both had the characterless bodies which had been carried through from the 1938 Junior cars. Seven-passenger sedans and limousines on a wheelbase of 148 inches could be had in the Super-8, but so could they in the One Twenty. (Catalogued custom bodies were available only on the Twelve.) The most individual feature of the Super-8 was its price, at $2035 a considerable reduction from the $2790 tag on the 1938 short-wheelbase sedan. But any interest that might excite was diminished with a look at the $1295 pricetag of the One Twenty.

The choice of body styles on the Super-8 was diminished too, by more than half, fifteen for 1938, now only six for '39, comprising:

Super-8's from East Grand Boulevard for model year 1939. Pages prece[d]
The 1703 Touring Sedan is put through its paces at the Proving Grounds in [U]

*And, as the One Twenty, this Senior Packard suffered the company penchant for alterations in designation. The change to a hyphen and a numeral in "Super-8" for model year '39, however—unlike the dallying with designation for the Junior Packards which happened almost yearly and haphazardly—might have been pre-planned, as the new designations for Senior cars for 1940 would seem to indicate.

Body Style/Wheelbase	Type No.	9-20-38	5-1-39
Model 1703 (127 inches)			
Club Coupe (2-4)	1275	$1955	$1650
Convertible Coupe (2-4)	1279	$2180	$1875
Touring Sedan (5)	1272	$2035	$1732
Convertible Sedan (5)	1277	$2435	$2130
Model 1705 (148 inches)			
Touring Limousine (5-8)	1270	$2600	$2294
Touring Sedan (5-8)	1271	$2460	$2156

Some 3962 Super-8's would be produced, fifteen hundred more than the year previous, but they were decidedly different, and lower-priced, cars. One, however, was special. Nineteen thirty-nine was Packard's fortieth anniversary, symbolized in the genealogy of gems by the pigeon blood ruby. The company painted a Super-8 convertible coupe that color, plating all its bright work in gold, and sent it on a tour of dealers' showrooms.

Clockwise from above left: The 1703 Convertible Coupe, the Touring Sedan, the Convertible Sedan, the Convertible Coupe with special drophead coupe top.

Alvan Macauley was nearing an anniversary as well, his thirtieth with the company. He was sixty-seven years old now. At the April 17th, 1939 Packard board meeting, he announced the personal decision he had made, adding that "my interest in the company's affairs will not lessen in the least but I do want to be relieved of the operating responsibilities which Mr. Gilman's long association with Packard so admirably equips him to assume." Henceforth Max Gilman would be the president of the Packard Motor Car Company, Alvan Macauley would be its chairman of the board.

This changing of the guard—which was big news in the industry—had actually been presaged several years before and any reluctance Macauley or the Packard board felt in the appointment of Gilman as president was publicly well concealed. Macauley's personal choice as his successor had been M.A. Cudlip, secretary and vice-president of the company and a gentleman with whom he and the board were more at ease than the often abrasive and abrupt Gilman. But, in 1934, when the hard-charging Gilman was elevated to vice-president and general manager, Cudlip recognized that the path to Packard's presidency was closed to him. He asked Macauley's help in securing employment elsewhere and resigned in 1936 to join the McLouth Steel Company. Thus the Gilman appointment could now be made without the embarrassment of a concomitant Cudlip resignation.

The Packard board's membership was increased to six to include Gilman in the select circle of Alvan Macauley, Truman Newberry (brother-in-law to Henry Joy and one of the original stockholders of 1903), James T. McMillan (trustee of the estate of another original stockholder, Phillip H. McMillan), Robert B. Parker (distributor for Philadelphia) and Henry E. Bodman (of the company's legal counsel).

The month following, the Packard company had a new advertising manager: Hugh W. Hitchcock, who had come to East Grand Boulevard in 1922 as a clerk in the factory advertising department, later serving as editor of Packard publications and, since 1933, as assistant advertising manager. Possibly it was he who totted up these figures and saw that they were widely promoted: Among personages identified as Packard owners were three kings, one queen, two sultans, four princes, three princesses, two royal courts, fifteen cabinet ministers, thirty-one legation members, thirty ministers, seventeen ambassadors, and other officials of thirty-nine countries. In Canada a Packard Super-8 phaeton was used to squire H.M. King George VI and Queen Elizabeth during their Dominion tour in June (with a Packard Twelve to take over when the Royal couple visited Washington, D.C.) And in Detroit a rather amusing order was received from far-off India: "The Maharajah weighs 280 pounds," the instructions read. "He has two brothers who always travel with him. One weighs 325 pounds and the other 350. In addition the car will carry five other passengers. The Maharajah will use the car to travel between his native capital and Bombay. No other motor cars are driven through this section. There are no roads. The Maharajah's car travels the greater part of the distance between his home and Bombay along elephant trails and across the open country. As compared with other parts of the route, the elephant trails could be considered good roads. He travels at from seventy to ninety miles an hour." Packard sent him a Super-8 limousine, and Hitchcock sent the news to *The New York Times*.

But the maharajah there, the prestige buyer here, the Senior cars now being sold in the wee thousands failed to justify the luxury treatment the cars were receiving at Packard. At least to manufacturing doyen George Christopher's view. Why all that factory space to produce an embarrassingly few cars? For model year 1939 the Super-8 moved over to the Junior car assembly line, leaving the Twelve alone in the gargantuan Senior car plant. This was but prelude. With production of '39 models exceeding demand during this recession year, a stockpile was created to take care of early sales. The lull resulting provided the opportunity to close down and revamp all production facilities. And it carried with it the decision to drop the Twelve. Had the Twelve been continued, a complete redesign would have been necessary; already the car was suffering alongside Cadillac's V-16, not so much in performance as in appearance. And to maintain or set up a new assembly line for a model whose yearly sales had diminished to fewer than five hundred did not make sense.

And so the space taken up for the Twelve was transformed into a new conveyer assembly line a sinuous mile and a half in length, the old Junior car area metamorphosed into the body and stamping plant, and across East Grand Boulevard between the two buildings a bridge was erected for convenient transport of materials. All Packard cars would now be made in a single new, big, efficient plant. George Christopher's dream had come true at last.

Everything was ready for the 1940 model line. Again there were four Packards, two Juniors and two Seniors. The latter were now called Super-8 One-Sixty and Custom Super-8 One-Eighty. One-Sixty meant something, it was the developed horsepower of the brand-new engine to be used in both Senior cars. One-Eighty meant only One-Sixty with

better quality upholstery, trim and appointments—an exercise in rhetoric hopefully to ameliorate any public feelings of loss over the Twelve. As its replacement, the One-Eighty would be considerably lower priced than the Twelve had been, but substantially higher priced than the One-Sixty. Under the Packard roof, Christopher's facilities allowed price reductions all around; now, in the new plant, would be produced Packards ranging from $867 to $2855 plus the chassis for custom bodies produced by outside coachbuilders on the One-Eighty, some of them with pricetags as high as $6300.

That these cars were every bit as good as the Packards preceding was demonstrated by a spectacular show at the Proving Grounds at 1940 model unveiling time in August of 1939. Packard sales people, four thousand strong, saw the vehicles race up steep ramps on two wheels, plunge off at break-neck speeds, leap eighty feet through space over a truck, land on all fours with a terrific impact. After a post-torture inspection by engineers, the test cars were sold—presumably at a discount—to factory employees. They were entirely sound. Of note, too, among these introductory festivities was the speedway race staged between a 1939 Twelve and a 1940 One-Eighty. The new car won, easily. It was a sort of the-king-is-dead-long-live-the-king spectacle.

But to cite an akin metaphor, the Emperor's new clothes—as the little boy of fairytale fame commented—weren't there. The new Packards weren't naked, they just weren't new. The same body shells begun for '38 were carried through into 1940, with but few revisions. On the Senior cars, a narrow, more rectangular chromed frame was placed around the ovoid windows and the rear quarter window was enlarged, these changes mitigating the unappealing porthole effect. The radiator had a softer look. The shell, body color, extended forward an additional five inches, for a more impressively long look to the hood, the top surfaces curving down to meet the chromed frame of the radiator shutters. This extra length allowed the hood to taper to a narrower radiator front, the cooling area then augmented by flanking grilles in the "catwalks." Longer bullet-shaped headlamps incorporating sealed beam units for the first time nestled close to the fender valley, with miniatures on the fender crowns serving as parking lights; side mounts were enclosed in a one-piece cover. The few distinguishing marks between One-Sixty and One-Eighty included hood louver grille design, hubcaps and radiator emblems, the One-Sixty carrying the "flying lady," the One-Eighty the pelican. All this notwithstanding, the new Packards—all of them—looked rather shopworn.

Apparently word of disappointment over Packard styling had reached management. It was a ticklish situation, Packard's head of styling being the son of Packard's chairman of the board. And it was resolved to Packard's satisfaction when Alvan Macauley reported to the board, without mentioning son Edward by name, that an independent fact-

finding organization had shown pictures of all American cars, identifying names and marks concealed, to a random sample of people with the question, "what car is the best looking?" In the survey, "using the methods of Dr. George Gallup, and checked by that famous statistical investigator," the Packard received more favorable votes—"by a substantial margin"—than any other car. Subsequent history would demonstrate that polls need not always be accurate, but this one had the pleasant result of making everyone at Packard feel better—at least for the moment. For the long run, management would be making other decisions.

Packard was absolutely sure of one thing now, however, widely touted in advertisements: "With its 160 horsepower, [the One-Sixty] is the most powerful eight-cylinder motor built for passenger car use in America today." And that was exactly right, as this chart demonstrates:

	Cyls.	HP - RPM	C.I.D.	Torque - RPM	C.R.
Packard One-Sixty and One-Eighty	8	160 - 3500	356	292 - 1800	6.45:1
Packard One Twenty	8	120 - 3600	282	225 - 1700	6.41:1

Cadillac V-8	8	135 - 3400	346	250 - 1700	6.25:1
Cadillac V-8	8	140 - 3400	346	270 - 1700	6.70:1
Cadillac V-16	16	185 - 3600	431	324 - 1700	6.75:1
Lincoln 12	12	150 - 3400	414	312 - 1200	6.38:1
Buick (large)	8	141 - 3600	320.2	269 - 2000	6.25:1
LaSalle	8	120 - 3500	322	234 - 1800	6.25:1
Hudson	8	128 - 4200	254	198 - 1600	6.50:1
Chrysler	8	137 - 3400	323.5	260 - 1600	6.80:1

Only the Cadillac V-16 was more powerful, the big Lincoln was in its last year, and the Cadillac V-8 developed its 140 using the high compression head, with 135 standard. Both Junior and Senior Packards had a 6.85 compression ratio option as well, which added another five horsepower.

The new One-Sixty engine was designed along the same lines as the One Twenty, but with a few important differences. It was larger, of course—3 ½ by 4 ⅝ inches compared to 3 ¼ by 4 ¼—and had nine main bearings as opposed to the One Twenty's five. (In the U.S. market, only

er-8's for 1940. Page opposite: 1803 Touring Sedan. Above: 1807 Formal Sedan and 1803 Convertible Sedan. Below: 1803 Club Sedan and 1805 Touring Sedan.

the Nash Ambassador and the Studebaker President equaled the Packard's nine main bearings.) And the new Packard had silent hydraulic, zero clearance valve tappets such as used only on Cadillac-LaSalle and Lincoln. Packard's tappets, a new development by Wilcox-Rich, not only contributed to long valve life but also eliminated periodic tappet adjustments.

As in the One Twenty, the pistons were aluminum, the cylinder heads cast iron, and the block and upper half of the crankcase one iron casting, the aluminum crankcase having died with the old engine. The angleset valves in the L-head design allowed the valve to be closer to the cylinder bore for greater turbulence and more complete combustion.

With 1940 models came the availability of Econo-Drive, an overdrive unit brought into operation with the momentary release of the accelerator at any speed over 21 mph, this resulting in a 27.8 percent reduction in engine speed for the same road travel speed. Flooring the accelerator returned the unit to direct drive. The quiet floating sensation at speed, the fuel economy and alleviated motor strain made this a popular option.

The all-steel bodies, made in the Packard plant, had the same basic shell for the Junior Packards and the 127-inch Super-8's. Of course, all body styles were not used on all chassis, the long wheelbase eight-passenger bodies having been discontinued in the One Twenty line pursuant to the new, lower prices on the Super-8 One-Sixty. No station

The accommodations provided passengers in the 1940 Model 1807 Formal Sedan.

wagon, incidentally, was ever offered by Packard on the One-Sixty or One-Eighty chassis, though Hercules, for example, would build them on special order. The high-priced One-Eighty carried but two models on the 127-inch chassis, one of these a smart convertible coupe at $4570—about which more anon—which did not enjoy the power-operated top mechanism that was standard on the convertible coupes in the other lines, including the Six at $1087. Nineteen forty was the last year for trunk racks on the Senior cars, as it was on the Juniors. Seat cushions in the One-Sixty had a "foundation of luxury springs with a pad of soft foam rubber sponge, 1 ⅝ inch deep for the cushion top," while on the One-Eighty there was a "foundation of Marshall springs, with a thick pad of soft foam sponge rubber topped by soft, luxurious down cushions." This is where some of the extra money went.

As successor to the regal Packard Twelve, the One-Eighty assumed the enameled hubcap emblems of the former flagship in the same size and design, with the appropriate lettering executed in champlevé, not cloisonné as has been frequently noted.

The use of the word "Custom" in the One-Eighty designation rendered confusion—as it had in 1929 and '30—since in reality most of the cars were production models. The line did, however, have a number of genuine custom bodies to offer. Of these, the formal cars by Rollson were generally 1940 variations of the bodies on the 1939 Twelve, more modern, if less dignified. More exciting were the cars from an American who had been in Paris but was now in California.

Howard "Dutch" Darrin had already established himself as purveyor of swank custom bodies to cinema stars and related luminaries. His first Packard, a roadster on the One Twenty chassis in 1937, had led to similar efforts mostly on 1938 and '39 One Twenty chassis using the convertible coupe or coupe as a basis. Sectioning and altering on succeeding orders, Darrin developed a style which created sufficient enthusiasm in Los Angeles to interest Packard in Detroit, though not initially enough to convince management of the wisdom of adding the cars to the Packard line. For that there was need for a little Darrin-do. Surreptitiously Dutch managed to have his pilot car parked at the Packard Proving Grounds when a big dealer meeting was in session. Huzzahs were heard all round. Here was a car that would bring hordes of people into Packard showrooms, the dealers said. Packard gave its approval. The first advertisement for the new collaboration, in *Fortune* for the Darrin Custom Sport Sedan, acknowledged that "it is virtually a request car—built for those who look to Packard to provide the exceptionally fine car, to create the newest, the finest, the most luxurious in motor car transportation." And perhaps to make them forget the Twelve as well.

Advertising in *Fortune* continued monthly, with some ads placed in *The Saturday Evening Post* too. "Glamour Car of the Year! (Of course, it's a Packard!)" read a headline for the Darrin Convertible Victoria.

Gene Krupa was enticed; he bought one and while drumming away at the Hotel Sherman in the Windy City, he had Packard-Chicago paint the car in the "standard Krupa color, Packard cream with red wheels."

The Darrins were the first Packards to omit running boards. At least one of the early Victorias sported them, but others of his California specials had rocker panels flush with the door, and on the production victoria cars the door itself extended down over the frame with no panel or molding visible. That was a daring concept; indeed, the absence of running boards themselves was looked upon askance in some sections of the industry.

The Darrin sedan showed the influence of the 1938 Cadillac 60 Special, the top being a separate entity from the body, while the trunk was integral with it. The graceful gentle swayback of the door line shown in the ads, however, became almost straight when built, losing much of the appeal. In the convertible variation, it was probably the handsomest ever to come on the market, possessing none of the bulk usually found in that type of body.

The Victoria was built for the 127-inch wheelbase and was also available on the One Twenty at $3800. Aside from insignia, smaller bumpers, non-moveable grille and metal dash on the One Twenty, it was difficult to tell them apart, as all Darrins had sectioned and lowered radiators and hoods, and special narrow hood louvers. For this reason of lowness, side-mounted spare wheels could not be supplied; they "would

definitely detract from the appearance."

Another detraction which became apparent under road use was the unstable front end. P.S. de Beaumont, an engineer at Packard then, has related that Darrin removed the heavy frame cross member under the radiator in order to lower that unit, substituting a thin strap which provided no strength to the fender braces, this resulting in a wobbly, vibrating front end at speed. It was de Beaumont's job to design a reinforcing kit which was sent out to all dealers who had sold Darrins with instructions that it be installed at factory expense. Today the word for all this would be "recall."

Darrin arranged to have the 1940 Victorias built in the old Auburn plant at Connersville, Indiana. In his shop in Los Angeles he built the prototype Sport Sedan, towed it to Indiana to be trimmed and painted for its introductory showing. Later, the pilot Convertible Sedan was built at Connersville. Both these sedans were on the 138-inch chassis and could borrow no body frame or panels except hood center panel and trunk lid from the production cars—and for this reason, they were the most expensive vehicles in the Packard line. There was an attempt made to produce a Darrin sedan using standard radiator and hood, and based on production doors, running boards and other parts, but only two were built. Two, at most, of the sedan models pictured in the catalogue were produced, perhaps as many as twelve of the Convertible Sedan (of which nine still exist), while the Victorias probably numbered up to fifty.

…oled by Mechanical Refrigeration in Summer," said Packard in February 1940, the dashboard control and the necessary apparatus under the hood pictured below.

The Darrin Packards. Above left: A very early four-door, the first one run up by Dutch to indicate to Packard what he could do. Above right: A 1939 Victoria.

The Darrins, and all the other Senior Packards, provided a lineup for 1940 as follows:

	Type No.	8-8-39	2-5-40	7-1-40
SUPER-8 ONE-SIXTY				
Model 1803, 127 inches				
Business Coupe (2)	1373	$1524	—	—
Club Coupe (2-4)	1375	$1595	$1605	$1614
Convertible Coupe (4)	1379	$1775	$1787	$1797
Club Sedan (5)	1376	$1717	$1732	$1740
Convertible Sedan (5)	1377	$2050	$2065	$2075
Touring Sedan (5)	1372	$1632	$1647	$1655
Model 1804, 138 inches				
Touring Sedan (5)	1362	$1895	$1910	$1919
Model 1805, 148 inches				
Touring Limousine (5-8)	1370	$2154	$2169	$2179
Touring Sedan (5-8)	1371	$2026	$2041	$2051
CUSTOM SUPER-8 ONE-EIGHTY				
Model 1806, 127 inches				
Club Sedan (5)	1356	$2228	$2243	$2243
Convertible Victoria, Darrin (5)	700	$4570	—	—
Model 1807, 138 inches				
Touring Sedan (5)	1342	$2395	$2410	$2422
Formal Sedan (5-6)	1332	$2825	$2840	$2855
All-Weather Cabriolet Rollson (5-7)	694	$4450	—	—
Convertible Sedan, Darrin (5)	710	$6300	—	—
Sport Sedan, Darrin (5)	720	$6100	—	—
Model 1808, 148 inches				
Touring Limousine (5-8)	1350	$2654	$2669	$2683
Touring Sedan (5-8)	1351	$2526	$2541	$2554
All-Weather Town Car Rollson (5-7)	695	$4575	—	—

If the new Packards, excepting the Darrins, were not cool—in the street lingo sense of the word—on the outside, the company decided to make them so on the inside. "Cooled by Mechanical Refrigeration in Summer" read a footnote to an advertisement appearing in February 1940. There was a home-appliance ring to the phrase, but then Packard was the first manufacturer in the industry to offer air conditioning on an automobile, so the quandary about what to call it was understandable. The company decided on Weather-Conditioner. It was bulky. The evaporator and heater plenum chamber were combined into one and installed in the trunk compartment under the package shelf, with a continuously operating compressor mounted up front on the right side of the engine near the water inlet. Thus the faster a car was driven the cooler it became; there was no clutch or automatic disconnect and it was recommended the drive belt be removed when cool weather came. But this did not solve a problem. There was no thermostat, a three-speed switch on the dashboard controlling the fan which blew the cooled air forward out of the package-shelf grille directly onto the soon-to-be-stiff necks of rear-seat passengers. And, even with the fan turned off, the cold air from the coil would merely drop into the floor area by gravity. The price for all this was a reasonable $275—the frequently bruited thousand-dollar figure is a myth—but, still, keeping cool in the summer

Above left: A 1940 Sport Sedan, one of two built in an attempt by Packard at using stock parts. Above right: The Darrin Convertible Victoria for 1941.

and not too warm in the winter was scarcely a can't-miss proposition, and customers generally gave the idea the bye, if they could. A snafu developed here as well. Special insulation for cars so equipped was provided at the factory but, although noted in Packard literature as "factory installed," the refrigerating unit itself was actually fitted into the car by Bishop & Babcock in Cleveland, and in theory vehicles ordered with it were shipped there, the unit was installed and then the cars were forwarded to the dealers. In practice, however, some cars showed up at dealerships with unordered air conditioning—and in order to rid themselves of the cars, dealers discounted the units substantially. Cooling the air was an expensive experiment all around for Packard, and although continued (but with separate heaters) as an option until World War II, it was dropped thereafter until 1953. Packard engineer W.H. Graves has estimated that about two thousand units were installed.

More successful certainly for Packard was the 1940 model year itself. Production was up from 46,405 in 1939 to 98,000—with 5662 One-Sixty models sold as compared to 3962 of the previous Super-8's, and 1900 One-Eighty models as opposed to the 446 Twelves in its last year of production. All this was to the good, but the figures were deceptive. Cadillac had overtaken Packard in fine-car leadership. The appearance identity between Junior and Senior Packards—in addition to the styling finesse of the Cadillac vis-à-vis the cars from East Grand Boulevard—provided dealers for General Motors' "Standard of the World" with pungent sales arguments. Here some further figures were more revealing. For model year 1940, GM produced 24,130 LaSalles and 13,046 Cadillacs; Packard's statistics were 28,138 for the One Twenty, 7562 for the One-Sixty and One-Eighty. In this spirited, and traditional, rivalry, the LaSalle had lost out to the One Twenty . . . but

Cadillac won convincingly over the Super-8's.

Industrywide, the figures were no more reassuring to Packard either. The company's 1940 sales had increased 14.7 percent over 1939. But the gain industry-wide was 27.8 percent. Clearly Packard was slipping.

Among the logical recourses the company had was the creation of a new car, one which would be separate from the established lines, one which if successful could chart a new course for the company, but if not could be eased out without damaging the traditional Packard product. Work had already begun on such a car, a fact which Packard spent the remainder of 1939 and all of 1940 denying. No, company officials told *The New York Times*, Packard was always experimenting but no new model was forthcoming. And when rumors became even more prevalent, these same officials leaked the news to *Automobile Topics* that plans for a new car—on which $350,000 had purportedly been spent in preliminary work and die production—would, for the time being, be shelved. The Clipper arrived in April 1941.

Meantime, war was raging in Europe. Alvan Macauley, as president of the Automobile Manufacturers Association, announced that the leaders of the American industry were unanimously opposed to U.S. entry in the war: "The experience of the past has clearly demonstrated that the destiny of an industry such as this one lies in the enrichment of the lives of the people, not in destruction. Boom conditions based on manufacture of war implements have proven equally as ruinous to industry as to the welfare of the average man." But Packard was soon in the defense business, building marine engines for the Navy, contracting to produce aircraft engines for both Britain and America, ripping up parts of the new plant for these endeavors, putting automotive body dies and presses under tarpaulins, and in general preparing for an American

The "Photo Gallery," as Packard called its archives, in 1940; Hugh Ferry conferring with Alvan Macauley that same year, Life *magazine, October 21st, 1940.*

war that, as day passed day, seemed increasingly inevitable.*

For the moment the automobile business had to go on, with the introduction of the 1941 line in September 1940. Mechanical changes were few for the Super-8—new motor mounts in larger rubber cushions, new steel-backed connecting rod bearings, a low pressure (four-and-a-half pounds standard; twelve pounds for cars with air conditioning) cooling system, an oil bath cleaner among the noticeable refinements. Certainly more noticeable was the new Packard look. Packard had finally concluded that appearance just had to be the key to sales success. Chassis changes were incorporated mainly to accommodate the styling. The suspension was dropped to allow lower floors without a driveshaft tunnel, greater front and rear overhangs called for redimensioning of frames. Although wheelbases remained the same, overall length of the cars was increased about five inches. The radiator was again moved forward, two-and-a-half inches this time, and the hood was uninterrupted from windshield to chrome-trimmed Packard grille, giving the impression of immense length. The radiator shell no longer appeared as an entity; hinged at the center, the hood tops lifted up like lids, the

---

*After storage for a while, the dies were then sold to various buyers including the Soviet Union where the ghost of the Packard later appeared as the ZIS. This disposal of the dies was not as reckless as it might appear. Briggs had supplied some body panels for the regular Packard line beginning in 1938, and that company was able to fill the breach by producing all Packard bodies from June 1940 on, most of these the new Clipper shells. Panels for the other lines had been stockpiled to last until Clipper styling could take over—a gamble on Packard's part. But endure the stockpiled panels did—until car production was shut down with America's entrance into the war.

sides remaining in place. The massive hood side grilles were gone—ventilation being taken care of entirely through louvers under the fenders—and in their place was a narrow chrome band incorporating the hood latch handle. Newly contoured fenders met the hood sides with little declivity, the headlamps now having been inset into the fenders—and this, for Packard, was news! At first the headlamp bezels were painted body color, later chrome plated. Meretricious perhaps were the over-stressed parking lamps which rode piggyback on the headlamps, the new chrome, plastic and gold feather hood ornament (though the "doughnut pusher" was available at $6.75 and the pelican at ten dollars), and the four stainless steel strips on each fender, which last two features more than a few owners had removed. The familiar Packard spearhead, now in stainless steel, headed a stainless molding which extended along the belt and around the rear of the body on closed cars articulating the top and, when desired, the two tones of the color scheme.

Two-tone color schemes had been impossible with the old body and its lack of a demarcation line. Now they were back, together with single color schemes and further selections in upholstery materials, in striped or plain pattern broadcloth or Bedford cord. If desired, "Multi-tone" options could be had, the leading edges of the seat cushions and upper part of the backs in a darker shade than the remainder, and in convertibles the darker portion might be leather, the lighter, cloth—with all interior hardware to match.

Again there was a distinct resemblance among Junior and Senior Packards, the two Super-8's were identical to each other save for trim and appointments. The 127- and 138-inch wheelbase models were available with or without running boards—a decision that could be reversed after delivery, if desired. Cars without running boards were

LINCOLN-ZEPHYR JACKET COPIES RADIATOR GRILL.   PURSE IS FROM INSIGNIA

AUTOMOBILE DESIGNERS SKETCH FALL

Marketing the annual array of feminine fashions is a constant series of deeply plotted stunts known to the trade as "promotions." Last month the dress and automobile industries put their heads together, hatched the joint promotion shown here. They asked the men who designed the body styles for the new 1941 automobiles to create dress styles to go with them.

Since there are certain structural differences between the chassis designed to accommodate the feminine form and that for the internal combustion engine, the stylists got most of their ideas from such surface features as radiator grills, hub caps, bumpers, upholstery, took others over into accessories. While some of the finished ensembles had but a tenuous connection with the cars, conceptions like the "Packard hood" were notably successful.

... (ABOVE) FOR EVENING DRESS (BELOW) TAKES WINGS FROM RADIATOR

...AC DRESS, BY HARLEY EARL, IS MADE OF STREAMLINED SILVER RAYON   PACKARD'S RADIATOR OUTLINE APPEARS ON GREATCOAT.   BUTTONS COPY EMBLEM

equipped with rear fender gravel protectors, black rubber on One-Sixty closed cars, chrome on the convertible and all One-Eighty models.

Windows were all larger, squared out and outlined by stainless steel beads, with the rear window glass curving to the contour of the body and eliminating the need of the divider strip. Plastic materials, new to the industry and capable of being molded and colored in almost any way a designer might wish, were used more extensively by Packard this year in the new instrument boards, particularly the centrally located radio grille and the ash tray. Unfortunately, the plastics idea needed further development, as severe warpage, cracking and discoloration sometimes appeared after two or three years, depending on the exposure to heat and sun. More successful were the new triple-tone horns with their melodious organ tones commanding respectful attention without offending. And Packard, incidentally, was now the only American company offering sidemount fenders. Hydraulically operated power windows were featured in One-Eighty closed cars. Wood again was used for interior window molding on all closed One-Eighties; 1940 models had featured wood-grained metal moldings.

Aero-drive was the new name for the optional overdrive unit mounted to the rear of the transmission, and it gained a partner dubbed Electromatic clutch. Though reminiscent of the vacuum clutch used first in the 900 series of 1932, the new version did not itself depress the pedal when in use. Yet the driver could utilize the pedal at any time, to shift to a lower gear, for example, or when starting the motor in cold weather. In regular driving, one would go through the gears in the usual manner but without touching the pedal. The clutch would disengage by manifold vacuum when the accelerator was released, except when in high gear above ten or twelve miles an hour. This did away with the free wheeling in high gear that many had found objectionable a few years earlier. It also provided, in combination with the Aero-drive, a type of semiautomatic transmission which Packard presented as an answer to the fluid drive transmission then offered in Chrysler cars. In city stop-and-go traffic, both shifting and tiring clutch operation could be eliminated, the literature promised, with the shift lever placed in second gear and left there. Depressing the accelerator would move the car forward and at speed the momentary release of the accelerator would bring the overdrive into operation which, in conjunction with second, would approximate high gear. At the next stoplight, the foot would naturally be removed from the accelerator to operate the brake, automatically cancelling out the overdrive and making ready for the sequence to be repeated.

The catalogue was quite specific this year: "Because all Packard One-Eighty models are custom cars, each is illustrated in this brochure with suitable equipment. . . ." Thus all body styles—five by Packard and six by independent coachbuilders—were presented as cars for special order. Production of the Senior cars would be down for the 1941 model year,

3525 units of the One-Sixty and a mere 930 of the One-Eighty. With numbers like that, the One-Eighty might have been seen as a custom car whether it was indeed that or not.

For 1941 the Darrin Convertible Victoria and the Sport Sedan shared the hoods and radiators of the other Senior cars; Packard was still recovering from the problems the cut-down variations of 1940 had brought. The side notch of the Victoria was now incorporated into the door itself rather than resulting from the articulation of door and body panel. The result, all in all, was a dilution of an inspired design, but was much more practical from a customer standpoint—and it remained one of the most striking convertibles around. The top was still manually operated—and very temperamental—and the Victoria did not have automatic windows, though the Sport Sedan did, in the Data Book at least. The Sport Sedan was illustrated and listed therein as available on the 138-inch chassis but, it is believed, only one was built, and for a Packard company official. A Darrin convertible sedan was not offered. The Victorias were built by Sayers and Scoville of Cincinnati, makers of hearses, ambulances and special bodies, and it is thought that thirty-five were produced of the '41 model. Fifteen of the '42—similar, save for side grille, wheels and hubcaps—have been confirmed to have been built.

The Rollson Cabriolet and Town Car—devised by altering standard sedan bodies—were restyled to conform to the new hood and body lines and came off with greater distinction than previously. LeBaron produced two stunning new offerings, the Sport Brougham and the Limousine, the latter available as a seven-passenger sedan if desired. The Sport Brougham, with its sweeping curve roof line meeting the body belt above the center of the rear wheel opening (rather than behind it), provided a close-coupled look, and with its lengthy rear deck, long hood and four (not six) large side windows, presaged a direction in which the luxury sedan was headed. The distinctive lines of both these LeBaron cars, with their square-cut, chrome-trimmed window openings, were architecturally most pleasing, for which a few discerning customers were willing to pay the extra $2600 over the One-Eighty Seven-Passenger Sedan by Packard— or $3000 over the One-Sixty with the same body.

Some few of the elite ordered individual custom bodies as well. Mrs. Alta Rockefeller Prentice had Rollson build a One-Sixty convertible sedan for her—a tall car from the belt up, yet with the long length, on the 148-inch wheelbase, it carried very well. All mention of Packard was deleted, even on the hubcaps, a common request of the very rich, especially those from Philadelphia. The spear and molding, normally bright, were painted the body color, a very dark green, with fine gold striping. By its very understatement, the car was impressive.

Another special car was made for Ed Macauley. Basically it was a Darrin victoria: its convertible top replaced with a metal half-top, coupe-de-ville style, with sweeping landau irons; the hood gold-chrome-plastic ornament removed; the long parking lights painted-out body color, the door handles replaced by a push-button type à la Lincoln Continental. Ed Macauley added a removable clear plexiglass top for the driver's section. This beautiful car did not long remain in this configuration, however, as Macauley would spend the war years revising the hood, the grille, the wheels, the bumpers, even turning the landau irons upside down at one point. He called the result the Phantom, and stopped traffic around Detroit whenever he took it out for a spin. Some of the experimentation with the Phantom would ultimately be seen in the postwar Twenty-Second Series, successor to the Clipper design.

For 1941, and the Nineteenth Series, the lineup was as follows:

	Type No.	9-16-40	6-26-41
SUPER-8 ONE-SIXTY			
Model 1903 (127 inches)			
Business Coupe (2)	1478	$1594	$1639
Club Coupe (4)	1475	$1709	$1754
Convertible Coupe (4)	1479	$1892	$1937
Convertible Coupe, DeLuxe (4)	1479 DE	$2067	$2112
Convertible Sedan (5)	1477	$2180	$2225
Convertible Sedan, DeLuxe (5)	1477 DE	$2405	$2450
Model 1904 (138 inches)			
Touring Sedan (5)	1462	$2009	$2054
Model 1905 (148 inches)			
Touring Sedan (7)	1471	$2161	$2206
Touring Limousine (7)	1470	$2289	$2334
CUSTOM SUPER-8 ONE-EIGHTY			
Model 1906 (127 inches)			
Convertible Victoria, Darrin (5)	1429	$4550	$4595
Model 1907 (138 inches)			
Sport Brougham, LeBaron (5)	1452	$3500	$3545
Sport Sedan, Darrin (5)	1422	$4750	$4795
Cabriolet, All-Weather, Rollson (7)	794	$4650	$4695
Formal Sedan (6)	1432	$3045	$3090
Touring Sedan (5)	1442	$2587	$2632
Model 1908 (148 inches)			
Touring Sedan (7)	1451	$2724	$2769
Touring Limousine (7)	1450	$2868	$2913
Touring Sedan, LeBaron (7)	1421	$5300	$5345
Touring Limousine, LeBaron (7)	1420	$5550	$5595
Town Car, All-Weather, Rollson (7)	795	$4775	$4820

It wasn't a particularly good year for the industry. The war in Europe was more distracting now than ever. One of the few exercises in levity was presented in *Life* magazine, a promotion sponsored jointly by the automobile and fashion industries, whereby the men who designed the body styles for the new 1941 automobiles created dress styles to complement them. "Since there are certain structural differences between the chassis designed to accommodate the feminine form and that for the internal combustion engine," said *Life*, "the stylists got most of their ideas from such surface features as radiator grilles, hubcaps, bumpers, upholstery. . . . While some of the finished ensembles had but a tenuous connection with the cars, conceptions like the 'Packard hood' were notably successful." Alone among American marques, Packard had retained its traditional radiator and straight-hood concept.

After that design competition, the automotive stylists went back to the drawing board for the industry's 1942 models. There would be little change generally, this holding true for Packard as well, for several very good reasons. First, the defense work preempted the efforts of the management and factory. Second, both the regular lines and the Clipper were new for 1941 and had been well received. Third, the government put the brakes on new tooling for civilian products and placed reduced production quotas on all manufacturers, effective August 1941, the month the new 1942 models were to be announced. The quota policy was seen as indicative that the question now was not *if* America would enter the war but *when*.

"For 1942 Clipper Styling comes to the entire Packard line" was the

Nineteenth Series for 1941 "at the 11th Avenue Preview" in New York. Above: One-Sixty 1904 Touring Sedan and One-Eighty 1907 LeBaron Sport Brougham.

headline. Except for convertible coupes which retained the old styling, the Clipper took over the One Twenty and the One Ten, but on a shortened 120-inch wheelbase. The former 127-inch frame was given to the new Clipper Super-8 One-Sixty and One-Eighty. As was Packard practice, the wheelbase difference was evidenced in the hood length, the bodies being identical but for trim. Furthermore, a new two-door "fastback" Clipper Club Sedan was added to all lines. All national advertising had been concentrated on the Clippers since May 1941, except for those ads extolling the company's war efforts. Although seldom noted, horsepower for the Senior Series cars was up to 165 for 1942.

The Convertible Coupe and the Darrin Victoria were the only non-Clipper models remaining on Super-8 127-inch chassis; the LeBaron Sport Brougham and Darrin Sport Sedan were dropped. Added to the One-Sixty line were a business sedan and limousine on the 148-inch wheelbase. Obviously the non-Clipper body styles were planned only for the low production cars, to coordinate the limited number of bodies available with the number of sales made. Once the bodies were gone, so would be the models. The most noticeable difference on these cars for 1942 was the change to horizontal bars in the flanking grilles to follow the general pattern of the Clipper front-end treatment. There were larger dish-type hubcaps, with the word "Packard" and the model identification omitted from the hubcap medallions. It was the first year as

well for turn indicators, 1941 models having been wired for them although they were never installed by the factory. Nineteen forty-two Senior Packards also featured the electric windshield wipers the Junior cars had had since 1940. There was an accelerator pedal starter and the wiper control was located at the windshield, reducing the knobs on the lower dashboard by two. The lineup for '42 was as follows:

	Type No.	8-25-41	10-1-41	11-29-41
SUPER-8 ONE-SIXTY				
Model 2003 Clipper (127 inches)				
Club Sedan (6)	1575	$1635	$1678	$1753
Touring Sedan (6)	1572	$1695	$1739	$1814
Model 2023 (127 inches)				
Convertible Coupe (5)	1579	$1795	$1842	$1917
Model 2004 (138 inches)				
Touring Sedan (6)	1562	$1905	$1954	$2029
Model 2005 (148 inches)				
Touring Sedan (5-7)	1571	$2050	$2103	$2178
Touring Limousine (5-7)	1570	$2175	$2231	$2306
Model 2055 (148 inches)				
Business Sedan (5-7)	1591	$1900	$1949	$2024
Business Limousine (5-7)	1590	$2025	$2077	$2152

"Never Was Quality So Important," headlined Packard. "This is a year for farsighted buyers. It is a year when careful selection of a new motor car— with Quality guiding the choice—is bound to pay larger-than-usual returns...." Packard was perhaps more right than even it realized; the year was 1942. Although Clipper styling and Clipper promotion were obviously the company's principal concern, a nod was given the traditional Senior cars. Among them were, above from the left: The One-Sixty 2023 Convertible Coupe; the Custom One-Eighty 2007 Formal Sedan; the Custom One-Eighty 2008 Limousine with body by LeBaron. Below, from the left: The One-Sixty 2005 Touring Sedan; the Custom One-Eighty 2006 Special Convertible Victoria with body by Darrin; the One-Sixty 2004 Touring Sedan; the Custom One-Eighty 2008 Sedan.

CUSTOM SUPER-8 ONE-EIGHTY
Model 2006 Clipper (127 inches)

Club Sedan (6)	1525	$2115	$2169	$2244
Touring Sedan (6)	1522	$2215	$2271	$2346

Model 2006 Special (127 inches)

Convertible Victoria, Darrin (5)	1529	$4595	$4708	$4783

Model 2007 (138 inches)

Formal Sedan (6)	1532	$3050	$3126	$3201
Touring Sedan (6)	1542	$2465	$2527	$2602
Cabriolet, All-Weather, Rollson (7)	894	$4875	$4995	$5070

Model 2008 (148 inches)

Touring Sedan (7)	1551	$2550	$2614	$2689
Touring Limousine (7)	1550	$2675	$2742	$2817
Touring Sedan, LeBaron (7)	1521	$5545	$5681	$5756
Touring Limousine, LeBaron (7)	1520	$5795	$5937	$6012
Town Car, All-Weather, Rollson (7)	895	$4975	$5097	$5172

Some 2580 One-Sixty and 672 One-Eighty (mostly non-Clipper) cars would be produced. On December 7th, 1941, the Japanese attacked Pearl Harbor. On New Year's Eve, automobile sales effectively ceased.

Thereafter sales could be made only to those persons who could show a priority order of wartime necessity. On February 7th, 1942, all passenger car production in the United States was halted by government wartime emergency order.

It was the end of an era for Packard. Postwar all was changed, it was changing already. In April 1942, George T. Christopher was made president and general manager of the Packard Motor Car Company. A few weeks earlier, Max Gilman had driven his Packard into an unlighted street excavation. The accident was unfortunate for more than the simple fact of it; riding with him was the wife of a representative of Packard's advertising agency. While Gilman was still in the hospital, Alvan Macauley asked for and received his resignation as company president. The couple eventually secured divorces and married, and Gilman joined General Tire and Rubber Company as general manager, rising subsequently to its presidency. Perhaps a love affair should not have been cause for Gilman's severance from Packard, but scandal, the unseemly, was anathema at East Grand Boulevard. The action taken was very Alvan Macauley, it was very Packard—at least Packard as it was. Packard as it would now be was a different thing altogether. At the company's helm was a man who had never liked all that "goddam senior stuff." Fortunately, for those who admire the classic era Packards today, others at Packard had not all shared in that view.

MOTOR CARS FROM THE COMPANY

Color Portfolio II
1925-1938

1925 Model 326 Six with roadster coachwork by San Francisco Auto Sheet Metal Works

1927 Model 426 Six Sedan

1928 Model 443 Eight Runabout

1928 Model 443 Eight Runabout

1928 Model 443 Eight Club Sedan

1928 Model 533 Six Runabout

1930 Model 740 Custom Eight Phaeton

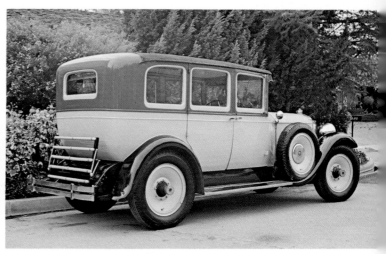
1929 Model 626 Eight Sedan

1929 Model 640 Custom Eight Roadster

1929 Model 645 DeLuxe Eight Sport Phaeton by Dietrich

378

1930 Model 740 Custom Eight Phaeton

1930 Model 733 Standard Eight Phaeton

1930 Model 734 Speedster Eight Runabout

379

1930 Model 734 Speedster Eight Phaeton

1930 Model 734 Speedster Eight Runabout

1930 Model 740 Custom Eight Phaeton with accessory bumpers by Packard

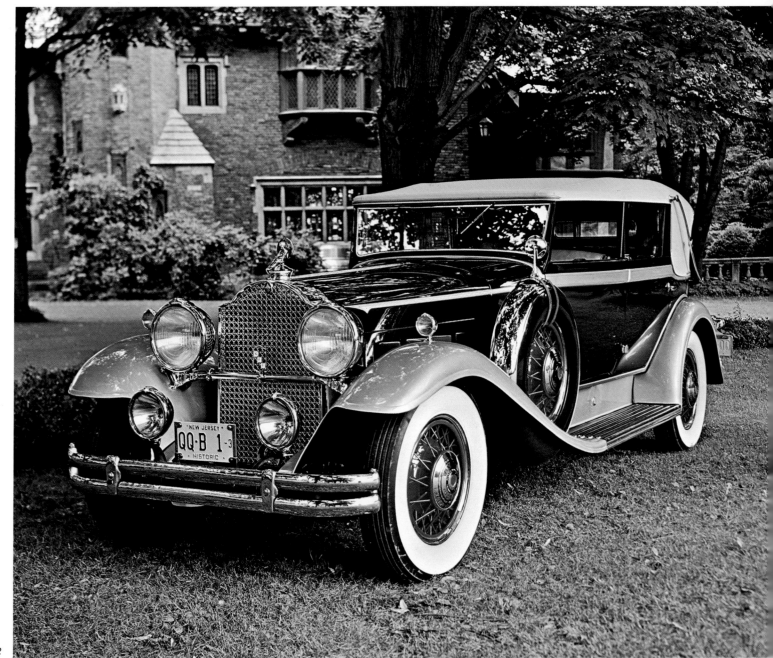

1931 Model 840 Individual Custom Eight Convertible Sedan by Dietrich

1930 Model 733 Eight Phaeton

1931 Model 840 Custom Eight Coupe

1931 Model 845 DeLuxe Eight Victoria by Waterhouse

Experimental Twelve-Cylinder Front Wheel Drive Car, 1932

1931 Model 840 DeLuxe Eight Phaeton

1931 Model 840 DeLuxe Eight Sport Phaeton

1932 Model 900 Light Eight Coupe-Roadster

1933 Model 1002 Eight Phaeton

1932 Model 906 Twin Six Individual Custom Convertible Victoria by Dietrich

1933 Model 1005 Twelve Convertible Victoria

1934 Model 1106 Twelve Sport Coupe by Packard

1934 Model 1104 Super Eight Phaeton

388

1934 Model 1107 Twelve Touring

1934 Model 1107 Twelve Coupe-Roadster

1934 Model 1108 Twelve Sport Sedan by Derham

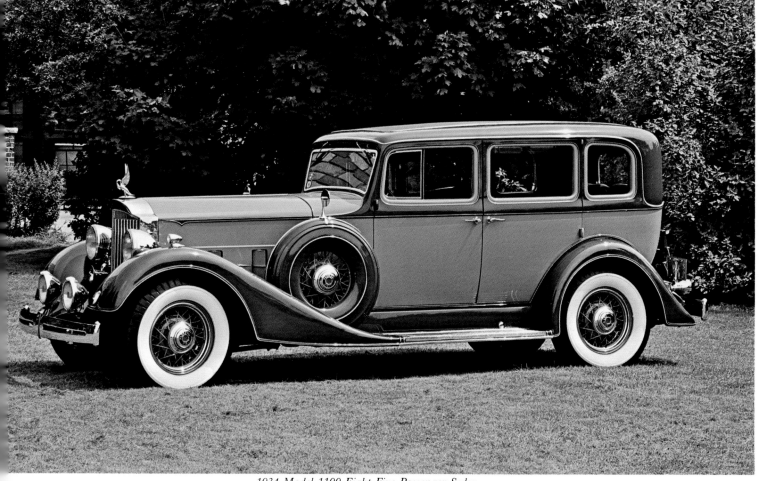

1934 Model 1100 Eight Five-Passenger Sedan

1935 Model 1201 Eight Convertible Coupe

1936 Model 1408 Twelve Convertible Sedan

1935 Model 1201 Eight Two/Four-Passenger Coupe

1935 Model 1207 Twelve Limousine by Brewster

1937 Model 1507 Twelve All-Weather Cabriolet by LeBaron

1936 Model 1404 Super Eight Two/Four-Passenger Coupe

1937 Model 1501 Super Eight Club Sedan

1937 Model 1507 Twelve Victoria

1937 Model 120-C One Twenty Touring Sedan

1937 Model 115-C Six Convertible Coupe

1938 Model 1600 Six Two-Door Touring Sedan

1938 Model 1601-D Eight DeLuxe Touring Sedan

Owner and Photographic Credits

1925 Model 326 Six with roadster coachwork by
San Francisco Auto Sheet Metal Works
Owner: Beverly Ferreira   Photograph by Rick Lenz

1927 Model 426 Six Sedan
Owner: Charles McConnell   Photograph by Rick Lenz

1928 Model 443 Eight Runabout
Minden Automotive Museum   Photograph by Rick Lenz

1928 Model 443 Eight Runabout
Owner: Robert R. Hannaford
Photograph by Henry Austin Clark, Jr.

1928 Model 443 Eight Club Sedan
Courtesy of Frederick C. Crawford Auto-Aviation Museum
Photograph by Henry Austin Clark, Jr.

1928 Model 526 Six Runabout
Owner: Peter Brown
Photograph by Henry Austin Clark, Jr.

1930 Model 740 Custom Eight Phaeton
Formerly A.N. Rodway Collection
Photograph by Russel W. Berry

1929 Model 626 Eight Sedan
Owner: Dr. Leon Weissman
Photograph by Marc Madow

1929 Model 640 Custom Eight Roadster
Owner: Shelley D. Vincent
Photograph by Don Vorderman

1929 Model 645 DeLuxe Eight Sport Phaeton by Dietrich
Owner: Don E. Weber
Photograph by Henry Austin Clark, Jr.

1930 Model 740 Custom Eight Phaeton
Owner: Bob Kieffer
Photograph by Don Vorderman

1930 Model 733 Standard Eight Phaeton
Owner: W.E. Blakesly
Photograph by Richard M. Langworth

1930 Model 734 Speedster Eight Runabout
Formerly A.N. Rodway Collection
Photograph by Russel W. Berry

1930 Model 734 Speedster Eight Phaeton
Owner: Tom Mix   Photograph by Don Vorderman

1930 Model 734 Speedster Eight Runabout
Owner: M.H. "Tiny" Gould
Photograph by L. Scott Bailey

1930 Model 740 Custom Eight Phaeton
Courtesy of J.K. Lilly III
Photograph by Henry Austin Clark, Jr.

1931 Model 840 Individual Custom Eight
Convertible Sedan by Dietrich
Owner: Robert Turnquist
Photograph by Don Vorderman

1930 Model 733 Eight Phaeton
Owner: Bill Montigel   Photograph by Rick Lenz

1931 Model 840 Custom Eight Coupe
Owner: Bob Butke   Photograph by Rick Lenz

1931 Model 845 DeLuxe Eight Victoria by Waterhouse
Owner: Shelley D. Vincent
Photograph by Henry Austin Clark, Jr.

Experimental Twelve-Cylinder Front Wheel Drive Car
Harrah's Automobile Collection
Photograph by L. Scott Bailey

1931 Model 840 DeLuxe Eight Phaeton
Owner: J.K. Griffith
Photograph by Don Vorderman

1931 Model 840 DeLuxe Eight Sport Phaeton
Owner: Art Schreiber   Photograph by Stan Grayson

1932 Model 900 Light Eight Coupe-Roadster
Owner: Dr. Gerald Dahlen   Photograph by Rick Lenz

1933 Model 1002 Eight Phaeton
Owner: William H. Herrman
Photograph by Don Vorderman

1932 Model 906 Twin Six Individual Custom
Convertible Victoria by Dietrich
Owner: Robert DeForest
Photograph by Don Vorderman

1933 Model 1005 Twelve Convertible Victoria
Owner: Tom Lester
Photograph by Henry Austin Clark, Jr.

1934 Model 1106 Twelve Sport Coupe by Packard
Owner: John Linhardt
Photograph by Henry Austin Clark, Jr.

1934 Model 1104 Super Eight Phaeton
Owner: Paul Rutherford
Photograph by Henry Austin Clark, Jr.

1934 Model 1107 Twelve Touring
Owner: Ruth Dougherty
Photograph by Richard M. Langworth

1934 Model 1107 Twelve Coupe-Roadster
Owner: Ed Blend   Photograph by Stan Grayson

1934 Model 1108 Twelve Sport Sedan by Derham
Owners: Mr. and Mrs. Kenneth Vaughn
Photograph by Rick Lenz

1934 Model 1100 Eight Five-Passenger Sedan
Owner: Richard Masters
Photograph by Richard M. Langworth

1935 Model 1201 Eight Convertible Coupe
Owner: John W. Morrison
Photograph by L. Scott Bailey

1936 Model 1408 Twelve Convertible Sedan
Owner: Richard M. Edwards
Photograph by Rick Lenz

1935 Model 1201 Eight Two/Four-Passenger Coupe
Owner: Frank R. Miller, Jr.
Photograph by Rick Lenz

1935 Model 1207 Twelve Limousine by Brewster
Owner: Lewis S. Smith, Jr.
Photograph by Don Vorderman

1937 Model 1507 Twelve
All-Weather Cabriolet by LeBaron
Owner: John C. Turner
Photograph by Henry Austin Clark, Jr.

1937 Model 1501 Super Eight
Two/Four-Passenger Coupe
Owner: Dr. Howard M. Miller
Photograph by Strother MacMinn

1937 Model 1501 Super Eight Club Sedan
Owner: William Kranz
Photograph by Henry Austin Clark, Jr.

1937 Model 1507 Twelve Victoria
Owner: Irving B. Linden
Photograph by Rick Lenz

1937 Model 120-C One Twenty Touring Sedan
Owner: James A. Cook   Photograph by Rick Lenz

1937 Model 115-C Six Convertible Coupe
Owner: W.W. Walmsley   Photograph by Rick Lenz

1938 Model 1600 Six Two-Door Touring Sedan
Owner: Paul Mack   Photograph by Rick Lenz

1938 Model 1601-D Eight DeLuxe Touring Sedan
Owner: L.J. Ruppert   Photograph by Rick Lenz

CHAPTER NINETEEN

MULTI CYLINDERS AND A NEW, INADVERTENT LUXURY CAR

Engineering the Twin Six and the Twelve,

The Ninth through

Seventeenth Series 1932-1939

AUTHOR: C. A. LESLIE, JR.

Alvan Macauley couldn't have been more explicit. "If it is ever said that Packard in bringing out the Light Eight is stepping down to a lower price field," he counseled his distributors, "our Twin Six is the answer." The date was January 9th, 1932. The place: the Hotel Roosevelt in New York City. The occasion: the introduction of the latest and most refined addition to an already extensive Packard luxury car line.

It was a dismal day, cold, with overcast skies giving way sporadically to a drizzling rain—a gloomy, if apt, metaphor of the nation as the Great Depression rolled on unchecked. It was an inauspicious time to introduce a new all-out luxury car. And if on the face of it, the Twin Six appeared simply as Packard's answer to the multi-cylindered—and equally ill-timed—opposition from Cadillac, Auburn, Lincoln, Pierce-Arrow, Franklin and Marmon, it was a case of appearances deceiving. Even Macauley's Twin-Six-as-answer-to-Light Eight admonition didn't tell the whole story. The situation was more complicated than that.

Packard's management was zealously competent, hardly the sort to rush pell-mell into production of a car for which the tenor of the times seemed to predestine commercial disaster, nor was Packard the sort to "me-too" in the luxury field, the company was a leader not a follower in that arena. Two factors are revealing here: First, the big Ninth Series invitational showing in mid-June of 1931 had been heartening to the company. Initially Packard had thought of cancelling the meeting "because of the expense it would incur on distributors and dealers, with times as hard as they've been." Finally, the decision to go ahead was made, and attendance had proved even better than expected, company executives viewing this as an indication better times were on the way. Second, the multi-cylinder idea wasn't a new one for Packard. The company had thought in two figures before any of the johnny-come-latelies now on the market—and Packard was perpetually nostalgic. "Looking backward at the car ahead" had been the theme in *The Packard* when the first Twin Six was introduced in 1915. That precise phrase would be used again in 1932, the company presenting its new Twin Six in a retrospective reverie of literature extolling the accomplishments of those halcyon-day twelve-cylinder automotive, marine and aircraft engines. Thus, with Packard convinced—however wrongly—that prosperity was around the corner, and with the natural and potent selling point of Packard's early leadership in the multi-cylinder arena, it could scarcely be considered foolhardy for the company to launch its new luxury car that dismal Saturday during the first month of 1932.

The Twin Six made its debut with the Light Eight, giving the impression, as *Automotive Industries* said, that "Packard plays for [the] High-Low Market." This was true, but it had not been intended. The Twin Six had started as a project aimed at a much less expensive Packard, moreso than even the Light Eight.

Pages preceding: The Twin Six as it resulted, with the Eight and Light E

Of the two new cars, it was plain that the Light Eight was the more important to the company. The Twin Six was very much second fiddle, Macauley advising dealers that they could now offer their clientele the DeLuxe Eight chassis with a choice of Twin Six or DeLuxe Eight engines. What was this marvelous new V-12 engine doing in an eight-cylinder chassis? The answer is fascinating in the extreme.

Automotive manufacturing had for some time reflected continuing increases in the market penetration of lower-priced cars. Because of the Model T, the trend had grown even during the prosperous Twenties. By 1925 low-priced cars (selling for $1000 or less) garnered 69.4 percent of the total market. By 1929, at the height of the economic curve, this percentage had increased to 81.5. After the stock market crash, it climbed to 83.7 percent, then to 85.5 percent for 1931. The average wholesale price of passenger cars declined from $949 in 1920 to only $590 in 1930.

From a marketing standpoint, the Packard Motor Car Company had, of course, remained aloof from these developments in the lower-priced field. And why not? The luxury segment of the market, though small percentagewise, was a lucrative one—and, while the battle for sales was savage, Packard consistently set the pace. Luxury cars ($3000 and up) had always been its mainstay—with rare exceptions such as the early Twin Six of 1915-1916 and the postwar Sixes of 1922-1923, and even

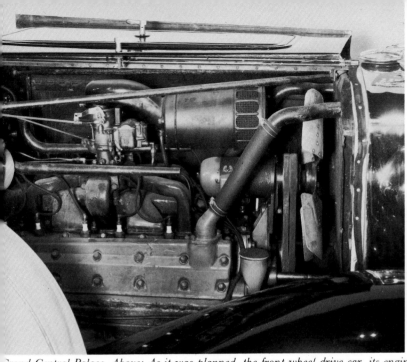

Grand Central Palace. Above: As it was planned, the front wheel drive car, its engine (shown with EE-3 carb) and dash resembling ultimate Ninth Series.

these were far from low-priced automobiles.

Still, the Packard board minutes indicate that at least latent interest in changing the Packard policy was manifest during the Twenties, if only experimentally. A degree of shift first occurred publicly in January 1925, when Packard gambled on a price cut that dropped many of its models into the upper-middle ($2000-$3000) price bracket which then accounted for 3.7 percent of the market. The move was successful, the *Automotive Daily News* remarking in September that Packard had "closed its fiscal year . . . with the largest profits, greatest sales, and most comfortable cash position of any year in its history." Entering the upper-middle bracket enormously broadened Packard's sales base, though even this segment would drop from 5.4 percent of the market in 1921 to 2.7 percent by 1929.

An increase in automobile production overall allowed Packard production to soar in the Twenties *despite* a declining market share for higher-priced cars. Enough engineering refinements and minor styling changes were offered to satisfy its conservative clientele. "Packard sales have been showing steady growth since the end of 1921," said *Automobile Topics.* "In the six year period of 1921 to 1927, there has been spent for property additions and betterments $27,800,000." Packard registrations for 1927 were 31,211 units and "approximately 90

percent represents the Company's six cylinder model."

By 1927, of course, rivals had followed Packard's drive into popular-priced fields. That same year, for example, Cadillac registered only 18,-397 cars, but also introduced the LaSalle, over 11,000 of which were registered through December. At the top of the automotive scale, both Cadillac and Marmon would be thinking about many cylinders for extravagant super-luxury motorcars. Not Packard. To offset its low-profit Six, however, the company approved a new luxury model of its Eight for debut in late 1928, the 645 with a "Custom Made by Packard" tab.

Nineteen twenty-nine—a checkered year. Two weeks before the New Year's Eve ushering in what most people thought would be another twelvemonth of unparalleled prosperity, Colonel Leonard P. Ayers, as noted earlier, had given his annual financial forecast. Citing the current seven-million-car industry capacity for a market that history had thus far shown to have an absorption capacity annually of 4.5-million vehicles, he wasn't as optimistic as most. The increased capacity had been the result of strenuous efforts by manufacturers to meet the demand during Ford's shutdown pursuant to the changeover from Model T to A. But now the Model A was out, the Ford plant was back in business—and Ayers predicted a competitive struggle greater than the industry had ever before known, suggesting concentration on sales during the first two *401*

Twin Six prototype show chassis, with Eight hubcaps and steering wheel. Further differences: eighteen-inch drop center rims (changed to snap-ring tire retainer for production), cable-operated two-shoe Bendix brakes and wide-based X-bracing (not phased in until 1933), battery box location (moved to right-hand fender as on Eights for production). Neither the EE-3 carburetor nor the oil filter was fitted on the prototype. The photograph at right shows an extra pedal operating an on-off valve for the vacuum clutch cylinder, subsequently discarded for a fully automatic system keyed to the accelerator via an elaborate vacuum cont

quarters and approaching the Fourth of July with the lowest possible inventory of used cars. He also noted the trend of wealthy automobile buyers toward the purchase of "light inexpensive cars," this following the rather new idea among medium-priced vehicle manufacturers that color and style just might be attractive selling points.*

Chevrolet had won the sales race in 1928, just as it had in '27 when, mid-year, Henry Ford discontinued the Model T. Overall, industry sales had been improved thirty percent over 1927. Buick, down 15.2 percent, was hanging on to a shaky third place, Willys-Overland's Whippet had gained 95.2 percent and jumped up to fourth. Packard's increase had been 37.4 percent. But Lincoln was down 5.8, Pierce-Arrow 1.7, Peerless 20.6. Cadillac was off 1.4 percent, while LaSalle was up 68.7.

Nineteen twenty-nine proceeded just as Colonel Ayers had predicted. First quarter sales were 49.9 percent above 1928. Packard continued to set the pace with all-time records for luxury cars. Cadillac continued to

slide, as did Lincoln, Pierce-Arrow; Peerless was treading water. The LaSalle made Cadillac's total respectable, and the Roosevelt was giving a boost to Marmon. Ford had overtaken Chevrolet.

Wall Street was uneasy. March 26th had seen a record selling wave of 8.2 million shares in one business day, but thereafter the market had settled down for the summer. Packard introduced its Seventh Series in August; on the 28th of that month newspaper headlines screamed, "Stock Floor Is Bedlam As Billions Lost." It was just the beginning. Stock liquidation waves swept the market on September 5th, and again on the 26th, and again as October began, during which month Cadillac president Lawrence P. Fisher announced that the year following his "company will in all probability place on the market a sixteen-cylinder super motor car." On Thursday, October 24th, a record 12.9 million shares were traded on Wall Street, erasing the March 26th mark; a week later the figure was 16.4 million and the day would be forever remembered as "Black Tuesday."

Cadillac duly rolled with its new V-16 for 1930. "While present design and construction in motor cars have attained a degree of excellence supplying any real need," said Lawrence Fisher, "there are a few motorists willing to pay for the 'ultra,' regardless of price." The sixteen was not built for a sales blitz, but with the hope that enough of its prestige would rub off on the other Cadillacs to justify its existence. Its 452-cubic-

*Ironically, the day prior to Colonel Ayres' forecast—on December 12th, 1928—the Packard board had authorized Macauley "to provide such additional facilities as may be needed for production of [the low-priced experimental car carrying code number 717] as soon as possible." At the board meeting following two weeks later, however, the authorization was rescinded.

inch engine (3 by 4 inches, 165 bhp at 3400 rpm) sported a compression ratio of 5.7 to one—low by Packard standards—and though of antiquated design in many ways, i.e., its separate crankcase and block type construction with updraft carburetors, it nevertheless employed a unique hydraulic valve silencing system that was outstanding in its day.

Good initial acceptance of the new super-luxury Cadillac was enough to raise a few eyebrows on East Grand Boulevard—but not enough to forestall Cadillac's sales slump following the stock market crash, and by mid-1930 V-16 sales had dwindled to a trickle. Packard, confident of maintaining its position of leadership, had refrained from the hasty marketing of a competitive "ultra" car and so avoided such a serious disappointment. The company did, however, augment its "Custom Made by Packard" bodies with the introduction of Models 734 and 745, the former designated the Speedster.

During the first quarter of 1930, with the overall car market down by seventeen percent over the same quarter of 1929, Packard registrations fell by over thirty percent. For April they were half of the April 1929 figure. "Problems, very serious ones, have confronted our distributing organization, dealers and salesmen," said Alvan Macauley. That statement was the crux of a decision to embark on a program which would produce for 1932 the Light Eight and, inadvertently, the Twin Six.

Packard, Macauley knew, had the production capacity and technical expertise for major extensions of its line. Experience and the new wave of economic torpor seemed to point in the direction of a downward line expansion. To help solve his problem, Macauley could assuredly count on crack engineers: Jesse Vincent, of course, and chief engineer Al Moorhouse, chassis engineer J.R. Ferguson, body engineer Al Knapp, custom body engineer Ray Birge, service engineer R.M. Williams, retired racing driver Tommy Milton as development engineer. And the latter would prove influential in convincing Vincent to add an outside consultant: Cornelius Willett Van Ranst.

Van Ranst was an engineer with vast engine and drive train experience, having spent his early years with Duesenberg, then with Louis Chevrolet designing Monroe racing cars, and producing the Frontenac overhead valve racing head for Model T Fords. His reputation as a front wheel drive specialist had been secured when he and Tommy Milton developed and built the fwd Detroit Special racing car for Russell C. Durant, son of the General Motors founder. The advantage of this car over the popular Miller then in vogue was that it could be shifted while the car was in motion. (The Miller used a ring gear and pinion mounted ahead of the transmission gears in the power train; being in such a high torque area, it was almost impossible to shift gears at speed.) Milton, recently retired from racing and working for Packard, had been talked into driving the Detroit Special at the 1927 Indianapolis 500.

Despite considerable manifolding problems, he managed to finish

eighth, and the ease of operation of the car was called to E.L. Cord's attention by Leon Duray. Cord hired Van Ranst to work with Duray, Harry Miller and Leo Goossen in building a prototype front wheel drive Cord automobile, using the Auburn motor and transmission components and as many of Harry Miller's patented parts as could be fitted.

After the production Cord L-29 was announced in July of 1929, Van Ranst left for Chrysler. Milton rejoined Packard, and when his employers decided the time had come for a new car, he convinced them that it should be a front-drive vehicle of Van Ranst's design. On June 25th, 1930, the Packard board approved the project. Van Ranst later

Prototype Twin Six engine: Note six-bladed fan, vertical plugs, DDR-3 carburetor, absence of oil filter and snorkel tube to pick up warm air from the crankcase

recalled that he and Milton "made a deal with Macauley: I signed a contract to design and develop a twelve cylinder front wheel drive prototype. Though I later went to work for Packard, this was purely a contractual agreement."

In this contract was the Twin Six born—but not as the "ultra" it turned out to be. Not at all. According to Van Ranst, the proviso was that "we were supposed to get [the new car] down into the Buick price range." Exactly what convinced Packard that front wheel drive was the way to go is not recorded. The company had at least given it cursory thought some years before—the board minutes for June 3rd, 1925 included among recent appropriation expenditures: "one Miller car with front wheel drive for $15,000 to be used for experimental purposes in a study of the commercial value of its new features." The following week management was authorized to reach an agreement with Harry A. Miller for services as a consulting engineer. Moreover, Packard was aware of the performance image of a car driven by its front wheels, having extended to Leon Duray the courtesy of the company's as-yet unfinished proving grounds track for a most successful high speed record run in a Miller—on June 14th, 1928. And Van Ranst could be persuasive. He was convinced "a unit power plant and drive train is more economical to manufacture than a conventional unit with a driveshaft."

In breaking with its tradition of evolution rather than revolution in motorcar design, Packard was able to take advantage of the industry's latest developments. Some of these were innovations by Packard while others belonged to its suppliers or even the competition. "When we began the design," admitted Macauley, "we bought one or more of each of the popular cars on the market and selling from $1200 and up. We took them to pieces and studied their design. . . . We analyzed every part and feature of all these cars for the purpose of taking from them everything of good they contained."

The front wheel drive Ruxton and the L-29 Cord were on the market by mid-1929, and Gardner had followed with an advanced prototype for its six-cylinder engine. At the same time, Archie M. Andrews was trying to convince Hupp to join the fwd bandwagon. The Gardner, with its driveshafts exiting from the center of its transmission, undoubtedly influenced Van Ranst's overall layout for his Packard project. And a small bore twelve could be made shorter than a large bore eight for a more compact engine compartment, which in turn might add a degree of lightness and provide better handling. Said Van Ranst, "They wanted something fast and they wanted a radical change in design." Later he remarked, "Buick had come out with their eights and they would beat the pants off a Packard, and of course they sold for a lot less." The large Buick eight, Packard's target for the new twelve, had a bore of 3-5/16 and a stroke of 5 inches, giving 344.8 cubic inches. Packard's new engine was to be placed in a car having a price range of between $1500 and $2000—right alongside Buick.

It might seem improbable that an engineering team as proficient as Packard's would call in an outside designer for a ground-up project. Cornelius Van Ranst's son Nicholas provides one answer: "I think Colonel Vincent wanted Dad because he was considered one of the outstanding engine men in the world at the time, a genius, but not a businessman. He was one of the few who was able to put something exactly on a drawing board and have the tool shop make it and have it do as well or better than he said it would do when he drew it." In any case, Packard Engineering was never closed to people with good ideas, although Nicholas Van Ranst admits the influence of Milton was strong: "Tom was my [father's] closest and only friend from the time he started in the racing business. Milton won his first race in a Monroe, which Dad had designed, and this is where they got together. Milton . . . wasn't an engineer. He was more of a promoter and a get-the-job-done type of fellow. I think that's why he was valuable to Packard. He could recognize good design and he certainly knew automobiles. He was innovative to a great extent—it was Milton for example who installed an Allison engine in the Hackercraft boat, and my dad designed the manifolding and transfer cases for its counter rotating twin screws."

"We were given a corner of the engineering building," Cornelius Van Ranst would later reflect, "and left pretty well alone." Collaborating with him were the Storey brothers, Frank "Long" Storey as assistant chassis engineer, Edward "Short" Storey in charge of the engine section. With few restrictions by Packard on design or components, Van Ranst was able to achieve what he considered ideal weight distribution for proper traction: "We found it necessary to place sixty percent of the weight over the front wheels."

By one of those quirks of fortunate fate for which automotive historians live, Van Ranst's prototype front wheel drive Packard has survived and is owned today by Harrah's Automobile Collection. Van Ranst, who during his tenure at Packard used the car on occasion as personal transportation, identified it at a Classic Car Club meet a number of years ago when it was owned by Greg and Gerry Fauth. The appearance of the car had come as quite a surprise to him since he had wistfully watched it pass through the factory gates on its way to the chopping block in 1935. Somehow that ignominious end had been avoided, however, and the car later became the property of the Thompson Products Museum (now the Frederick C. Crawford Auto-Aviation Museum) in Cleveland. "We bought [it] from a young man in the service for about $250," Thompson's former curator Ruth Sommerlad remembers, "but there was no identification on it. We had correspondence with Packard about the car, but they either had no records or didn't want to acknowledge it, because they made no claim for the car whatsoever."

The Packard front wheel drive prototype bristled with ingenuity. Built on a 138-inch wheelbase, its center frame brace was an "X" member extending from the frame rear axle kickup to the front of the engine block, a modified and shortened version of this configuration becoming standard production for the Light Eight in 1932, and throughout the line beginning with the Tenth Series. The dropped rear axle had an "H" cross section with the rear springs mounted on top of the axle rather than the usual location beneath the axle housing. The springs were positioned outside the frame, allowing it to ride much lower with only a trace of rear frame kickup. The flywheel cover at the front of the engine served as attaching points for the front motor mount. Beneath the car were primary pivots for the cantilevered front springs. The inverted nine-leaf main spring extended twenty-seven inches to the rear of the primary pivot where it was coupled to an extension of the rear engine mount—and extended fifteen inches forward of the primary pivot where it was affixed to the lower portion of a de Dion front axle. The upper portion of the front axle was stabilized by an unequal length parallel arm pivoted to the frame. Power was transmitted to the front wheels through double universal joints on each side of the transmission.

The transaxle case contained a unique two-speed transmission and two-speed axle. As Greg Fauth has described it, "first and second gears are on one side. As you cross neutral, you change axle ratios, and third and fourth are on the other side." The shift pattern, was "very unusual," according to Ken McDowell who, with his brother, also owned the car at one time. "It has the conventional 'H' shape and low gear is in its regular position. But second, instead of being where you'd expect it, is halfway between low and neutral. So you put it in gear like you would any car, then accelerate and lift the shift lever about two inches for second. Then you go on up into neutral and over and up into third, then down into fourth. Reverse is in the conventional position." Fourth gear was more suitable as an overdrive. Greg Fauth has remarked that "we were never able to use fourth . . . in town."

It was the bizarre transaxle that caused all the front wheel drive's problems. A basic design flaw emerged: If second gear was not fully engaged when the clutch was released, the sliding gear was spit back into first or up into reverse with an occasional shelling of gear teeth. Fauth's experience was typical: "You let your clutch out and kind of hope you happen to be in gear because the lever goes beyond the engaged position. Second gear detent is very difficult to feel as you shift, and if it was halfway between gears when you let out the clutch, you tore up the transmission. When we obtained the car, it had a broken transmission case because some gears had been jammed. We made new gears for it twice before we were through."

April 1931 brought design revisions to the transmission, but these were insufficient to cure the problem. A complete redesign seemed the only solution. Unfortunately, April also brought a forty-one percent drop in Packard registrations, compared to a twenty-two percent increase in Cadillac's. With its greatest rival now within nine points in the production race, it was imperative that Packard react quickly. The Ninth Series Eights had been in production at the rate of 975 cars per month beginning in January, thus enough would be on hand at new-car introduction time in June. Immediately following their introduction, and almost a year to the day after the project was authorized, Macauley reported to the board that the "M & V Car may prove to be in the $3500 price field and more complete testing might show wisdom of later going into production."

The new V-12 engine had proved much more satisfying to Cornelius Van Ranst than the front wheel drive's problem-beset transaxle. Its number of cylinders had been a carefully-arrived-at decision. "We were trying to get out of that little twelve the same horsepower that Buick was getting out of its eight," said Van Ranst. Later Packard Engineering would couch its reasoning in official parlance: "because of the demand for greater power without a sacrifice to smooth, efficient operation . . . Cylinder bores in excess of 3½ inches—in the case of in-line engines—produce prohibitive lengths, roughness and other undesirable features . . . The only way to get more power is to increase the piston displacement and the breathing capacity of an engine. A large eight would mean larger cylinders, more severe power impulses and much heavier reciprocating parts than used in the [Packard Twin Six]. These items produce lower engine speed, greater roughness, much more vibration and would result in an absence of stay-put ability that has been secured with our present design . . . The smoothness and power of the [Twin Six] cannot be duplicated by any engine of fewer cylinders."

As Van Ranst designed it, the V-12 placed its integrally cast blocks at a 67° angle, "selected to make the power plant as compact as possible while leaving adequate room for a horizontal [zero lash] valve mechanism within the Vee," so *Automotive Industries* quoted, "and to eliminate the synchronous periods which occur frequently in multi-cylinder engines designed for equal firing intervals." Proving grounds tests, Van Ranst said later, indicated that it could be driven "50,000 miles without doing a valve job." Van Ranst was particularly proud of his zero lash valve system, but other engineers preferred to attribute the quietness of the new engine to "the use of a perfectly balanced, heavier crankshaft." They did, however, concede that the valve system "prevents any valve clearance at all times and removes the cause for much noise in the former [1915-1923] Packard Twin Six engine."

With a 3⅜-inch bore and 3½-inch stroke, the engine displaced 375.74 cubic inches and produced 150 brake horsepower at 3600 rpm, well above the target Buick eight's 344.8 cubic inches which produced only 104 brake horsepower. Particularly significant is the fact that the prototype V-12 displaced less, not more, cubic inches than the DeLuxe Eight's 384.85. This gives strong credence to Van Ranst's assertion that

the engine was intended for a car smaller than existing Packards. However, a major restriction on engine size was the lack of cooling capacity, since the transmission passed beneath the radiator, limiting the size of the latter. Van Ranst designed the hood side panel with a large door that could be opened outward, better allowing air to circulate.

Part of the twelve's 150 bhp could be attributed to the new engine's improved breathing, achieved by using a downdraft carburetor pioneered by Chrysler in 1928 with the D and DD Bendix Stromberg series. A redesigned and improved version of this carburetor, the DDR-3, was available to Packard. (It had originated with the Marmon Sixteen program.) The fuel induction system, again according to Engineering, was "designed to take fullest advantage of down draft carburetion and as a result would have: 1. Greater horsepower; 2. Better gas distribution; 3. Better economy; 4. Greater smoothness; 5. Greater acceleration; and 6. Higher top speed." Van Ranst called the prototype "the fastest passenger car in the country" and claimed that proving grounds tests showed the original car to lap consistently at 110 mph, although "considerable mileage was registered on the chassis before the body was placed on it."*

Van Ranst may also be given credit for the design of the prototype's body. The four-door, center-opening sedan, with its rather novel dropped beltline, bore a marked resemblance to the L-29 Cord the drive train of which Van Ranst had only recently engineered. Forest R. McFarland, an employee in the experimental machine shop during this period, later observed emphatically, "It was all Van Ranst's baby." Said Van Ranst: "Only the people in Packard Styling were working with me. We were trying to do everything we could to show the advantages of front wheel drive; to make it low slung and racy looking, but with a lot of passenger room inside."

But a front wheel drive Packard was not to be. A complete redesign of the transmission would take time—and the company could not afford the luxury of that. Packard was faced with a dilemma. To render to naught all the development work done thus far was perhaps not that dastardly to contemplate, but it would be a sad waste to forget the new and very exciting twelve-cylinder engine that had resulted from it. The company decided not to do that—and instead to think conventionally with regard to chassis.

---

*How many prototypes were built may perhaps ever remain a mystery. Van Ranst himself said three in 1958, but a decade later had revised that to just the single one. Still, upon his first re-encounter with the car, he exclaimed, "This has to be the one Styling worked with." Conceivably there was more than one; when Fauth purchased the car now in the Harrah collection, it had only 2500 miles on the odometer, a figure he was sure was correct.

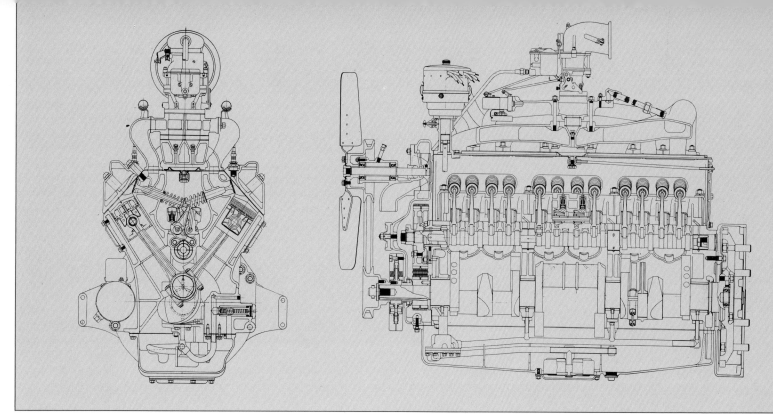

Prototype (left) with first-style EE-3 carb. Production engine (above and below) with four-bladed fan and dual-rod choking system. Note EE-3 below with air horn to air cleaner adapter and snorkel tube, later replaced by elbow air horn above.

Interestingly, some preliminary photos of the twelve in a conventional chassis were labelled "900 Series" in the files of Packard Photographic. Conceivably, its use may have been contemplated for what ultimately became the Light Eight—but probably not for long. Packard's *raison d'être* for a V-12 in a lower-priced car had been simply that it was feasible so long as it was front wheel drive. Van Ranst had argued convincingly that a front-drive set-up was markedly cheaper to produce than conventional drive—and since eighty percent of a total Packard's cost was in its chassis, it had all seemed beautifully possible. But when front wheel drive flopped, the idea of a V-12 in a pleasantly popular priced Packard flopped with it. But there was an alternative, an obvious one. The twelve, perhaps the most finely engineered engine in the industry at that time, could easily be used elsewhere. Thus the final nail was driven into the front wheel drive coffin on October 14th, when Macauley reported that he had "revised the agreement with Milton and Van Ranst, paying them $10,000 for the use of their twelve cylinder motor and any other parts of the M & V car for adaptation to our deluxe chassis because the developing and testing of the M & V car will require more time than we can spare to meet competition." The referenced chassis were those of

142 ⅛ and 147 ⅛ inches currently in use on the DeLuxe Eights.

On the face of it, the plan might work well. Practical considerations to the contrary, Packard perhaps did not relish being out-ultra-ed by its rivals. And, moreover, the Twin Six as a super luxury car, introduced with the Light Eight, would provide a very proper rejoinder to anyone who might suggest that the latter signified a new Packard marketing policy. The decision, perhaps, just made itself. Packard played it for all it was worth. As its News Service would announce "For Release After 12 o'clock, noon, Saturday, January 9, 1932," the new car "enters that exclusive and limited production field where the last word in motoring luxury is demanded and where prices are correspondingly higher."

But the question was, would it be ready in time? On November 25th authorization was given to mount two Type 514 seven-passenger sedan bodies upon 147 ⅛-inch chassis equipped with the new twelve (designated X-378) motors. One of these would be used for the New York show, the other assigned to the Proving Grounds for further testing by Charlie Vincent.

All of its engineering preparations and backtracking had exacted their toll on the car. Still, as the public filed into the Grand Central Palace on January 9th, paying their seventy-five cents each to view the new cars on display, there it was, in space A-14, the Twin Six, with the Light Eight, surrounding a glistening show motor in the center of the display—flanked by Hudson, like a poor courtier in space A-8, glowered at by Cadillac across the aisle at A-13. But the Twin Six on display was not the Twin Six that would go into production.

Engineers Cornelius Willett Van Ranst (left) and Thomas Willard Milton.

Aside from glittering generalities, little was said by Packard about the car. Colonel Vincent, in his speech to sales personnel talked attributes, not specifics. "I should like to point out . . . [the] characteristics that make it a superior motor . . . ," he hedged. "But I understand that shortly you will receive this information in detail." Alvan Macauley, that same day releasing price and delivery information to the press, allowed that Light Eight shipments would commence March 1st, "the Twin Six about a month later." The "month later" saw a Packard news release affirming that orders were healthy, "many . . . from persons who owned the Packard Twin Six of a decade ago"—and that "production on the car is just getting under way." By the middle of May, Packard reported that shipments had begun "around April 10th"—and that new orders were "coming in at a faster rate than deliveries." During that week the first Twin Six, a 4007 Sedan-Limousine, had been delivered by the Detroit branch to J.B. Ford, president of Libby-Owens-Ford Glass Company. Though this body style was catalogued for use only on the Eight DeLuxe, Packard was not about to let formalities interfere with a sale.

The reason for the glittering generalities at the show was simple. The engine on display was the small displacement 150 hp unit from front wheel drive development days. It would not power the Twin Six. The chassis beneath the body of the car on display bore similarities to the one that would carry the production Twin Six, although it was not exactly the same. But the Twin Six *had* made it to the show.

Meanwhile, back in Engineering, the men of Packard were dealing with the exigency of it all. Much work remained. Two distinctly different sets of parameters had been presented, the first for the prototype, the second for the production car. The original concept had been a small displacement, relatively high-revving engine for use with a four-speed gearbox in a medium-weight car providing outstanding high speed performance. This was Van Ranst's baby. By many standards, his L-29 Cord had been a blooper, with inadequate traction due to improper weight bias, and though speedy to the eye when at curbside, the Cord was a disappointment in performance, with a top speed of only 80 mph. For a designer who had cut his engineering eyeteeth on flat-out racing cars, such disappointments were intolerable the first time, impossible the second. With Packard, Van Ranst was determined to eradicate his Cord experience, hence those 110 mph laps at the Proving Grounds with the prototype. It could go.

But when the Packard engineers, led by Clyde Paton, put the twelve into the DeLuxe chassis, as Van Ranst commented, "they weren't able to get it above 85 mph." And that was trying hard. So the concept changed. What would be sought now was a larger displacement, medium-revving engine for use with a three-speed gearbox in a luxury car that would outperform its competition.

In any case, 376 cubic inches was not enough to project the twelve as the luxury car it had become, with a pricetag of almost $1000 more than the 385-cubic-inch DeLuxe Eight. So, about a week after the New York show, Packard quickly changed the specs. The January 16th, 1932 issue of *Automotive Industries* reported that "the bore is now 3-7/16 inches instead of 3⅜, as was the former plan." This change brought displacement to 389, which looked a little better vis-à-vis the DeLuxe Eight.

A few days after one of the cars so engined was built, it was delivered to Charlie Vincent at the Proving Grounds. He was preparing for a trip to California at the time, and decided to take the new car along, together with a DeLuxe Eight as back-up in case of a breakdown. "You can imagine my disappointment when I found that as a hill climber, in high gear of course, the new twelve was not nearly as good as the old eight," he recalled. "Production had already started on the new engine because it had been considered thoroughly tested by Tommy Milton and J.G. [Vincent] assumed I would find it satisfactory. But when I called Macauley and asked him to call a telephone conference of all concerned, Jesse agreed to my suggestion that the stroke be lengthened."

That was the only alternative. In its front wheel drive configuration, the engine had been deliberately designed with a short overall length to keep it out of the driver's lap. With conventional drive, the transmission usually fits behind the firewall since it is beneath the floorboard; in front wheel drive, the entire engine and gear train must fit ahead of the firewall. The center-to-center distance between adjacent siamesed cylinders of the Twin Six precluded a bore above 3-7/16 inches to maintain adequate cylinder wall thickness for overbore—a proper safety fac-

tor—and for adequate cooling. So four inches became the stroke. This raised displacement to 445.5 cubic inches, horsepower to 160 at 3200 rpm—and, most important, provided torque of 322 pound-feet at 1400 rpm. "Usually little is said of engine torque," Packard would comment, "but we believe it is of greater interest than maximum horsepower to most people, since it is torque that provides acceleration . . . The new Twin Six produces remarkably fine torque and it is this engine characteristic that gives the big luxurious Packard Twin Six cars their great acceleration. . . ."

Eight days after he had delivered his suggestion to the factory, Charlie Vincent got the new engine out on the West Coast: "Naturally I lost no time having it installed in my test car and took off for the test hills. As I reached the outer limits of Los Angeles where the traffic was light, I kicked the throttle wide open from low speed and looking in the rear view mirror saw black marks on the pavement that almost duplicated those made from a quick stop. I knew then that the engine performance problem was licked. When I reached the long grade on Swartout Canyon I found that my speed was limited by the curves rather than by the grades. [It] was the most pleasant to drive of any car I had driven to date." Subsequent proving grounds testing showed the Twin Six capable of repeated laps at the ninety mark "and certain body types under the most favorable conditions will do in excess of 100 miles per hour." All was well.

Packard then took direct aim at those other multi-cylindered motorcars in the marketplace. "We say without reservation . . .," the company

Clyde Paton, protégé of Barney Roos in his Studebaker days, at his Packard desk, after joining the company in 1930 as chief experimental engineer.

challenged, "[that] over accurately measured highway or track, the Packard Twin Six will out-perform any of its production built recognized competitors of the same price class."

Packard's competitors were, of course, the Cadillac V-16 (the company paid scant attention to Cadillac's smaller V-12) and the Marmon Sixteen. Of the two, the Marmon would probably come closer to running the Packard Twin Six a horse race. The Cadillac, with its 45^0 vee cylinder banks, was confined to relatively mediocre performance throughout its life because of its antiquated updraft carburetion. And, as good as it was, the Marmon Sixteen still lacked the sophisticated refinement of valving and induction of the Packard Twin Six. The Packard company could well afford to boast.

For ease of comparison, the Packard Twin Six specifications in prototype and production form are listed herewith:

	Prototype*	Production
Bore	3 ⅜ inches	3 7/16 inches
Stroke	3 ½ inches	4 inches
Displacement	375.74 cubic inches	445.5 cubic inches
Horsepower	150 at 3600 rpm	160 at 3200 rpm

And for the reader's ease in the discussion to follow, it should be mentioned here that only during its introductory year (the Ninth Series) was the car referred to as the Twin Six. For 1933, the Tenth Series, the designation became simply Packard Twelve. And that car would incorporate a number of changes which the rush to production had not allowed the Twin Six. There is something to be said for the luxury of a little relaxation.

The Packard engineers' raptures about their new engine were inspired less by its specifications than the induction system it incorporated, providing an entirely new concept in carburetion and manifolding. In October of 1930, when Van Ranst signed his Packard contract, the Cadillac V-16 had been on the market for ten months, and the Marmon Sixteen was almost ready for its debut. This gave Packard the advantage of commencing its design where its competition had left off. Marmon had a similar design advantage over Cadillac which, as we've seen, it parlayed in the introduction of the Bendix-Stromberg DDR-3 downdraft carburetor in its Sixteen. This was a plain tube, dual fixed venturi type and was considered the foremost design of its day. Still, in spite of its dual 1 ½-inch diameter bore, the main venturi of this unit had to be restricted to 1-1/32 inches to increase air velocity at the main jet for improved low end performance, imposing a severe breathing limitation on

high speed operation of the huge 491-cubic-inch Marmon engine.

Being the best available, the DDR-3 had found favor with Van Ranst when the Packard idea was front wheel drive, proving ample for the high-revving, small displacement twelve when coupled with the four-speed transmission. Van Ranst, accustomed to flat-out performance, was not one to worry about low end torque or smoothness at idle. But when the plan changed to a three-speed transmission and the heavy DeLuxe chassis, shortcomings were revealed so severe as to dictate further refinements. The plain venturi type carburetor just would not cut the mustard. And the changes required were so extensive that an entirely new carburetor resulted. It would be called the EE-3.

Basic to it was the addition of an auxiliary within the main venturi, the main discharge jet now protruding into the auxiliary, the increased air velocity of which served to better vaporize fuel at low and medium as well as high speed operation. The new carburetor, like the DDR-3, also had a 1 ½-inch dual throat, but now encompassed 1-3/16-inch venturii for adequate breathing of the 445.5-cubic-inch engine. For the Twelfth and subsequent series, the crankshaft was stroked from four to four-and-a-half inches, bringing displacement to 473.3 cubic inches and horsepower to 175 at 3200 rpm. It then became necessary to open up the venturii to 1-5/16th inches in diameter.

The DDR-3-equipped small prototype engine at the New York show, and also the early style EE-3 carburetor with a vertical air horn, were equipped with a vent tube leading from the engine valve area into the top of the carburetor for preheating the fuel/air mixture. When the well-known elbow-type bowl cover and air horn was phased into production early in the Ninth Series, the vent tube was deleted and a small breather, placed opposite the distributor, was used to relieve vapor pressure built up in the engine and to supply an air inlet for the crankcase draft tube.

In a farsighted action, Packard purchased the 1926 Church Patent No. 1,583,959 relating to the interconnection of choke and throttle on a carburetor to provide for fast idle during engine warmup with the choke being utilized to enrich the fuel mixture. Stromberg Motor Devices was issued a license under this patent in March 1930, stipulating a royalty of $0.01 per carburetor. DD type carburetors provided only manual choking, while the more sophisticated EE types were designed for use with an automatic choke. Unfortunately, the Stromberg Model "B" choke unit available at the advent of the Twin Six did not provide for fast idle, only for movement of the choke butterfly from fully closed at 70^0 to fully open at 120^0. The choke unit was mounted on the front of the intake manifold, with its thermostatic coil spring sitting directly above the exhaust manifold. This basic induction system, with refinements, would serve the Twin Six and Twelve throughout its entire existence. The first of the refinements would be the application of Packard's Church patent, which would come with the Tenth Series via the Model "C" automatic

---

*The prototype engine was designated X-378 rather than 376 as one might suppose. This may be due to an overbore of .010, bringing the bore to .385 instead of .375 for the 378-cubic-inch displacement.

choke and would remain for the duration of the Twelves.

If the new production carburetor proved a design advance on the one designed for the prototype, and it did, the same cannot be said for what happened to the distributors in the production Twin Six. Van Ranst's original design used two six-cylinder distributors, one for each engine bank. This was the delicate touch of a fine artisan who had been down this path before and who knew exactly what he wanted. The twin Delco-Remy distributors were mounted on each side of the camshaft drive gear and next to the firewall, resting—for easy access—on seven-inch stand pipes where independent adjustments could be made to fine tune each bank. The distributor caps still had to be removed to set the dwell angle, but the amount of timing advance could be varied without removing the distributor cap or stopping the engine, requiring only the use of a timing light to adjust the spark advance.

But, then, the engine was modified for use in a conventional drive car—and Packard engineered in a few difficulties. These came via an Auto-Lite No. IGO-4001 distributor, with a six lobe cam operating two breaker arms with independent points and condensers for each bank of cylinders. The right bank of cylinders was fired by the fixed arm and point plate resting on the distributor base plate; the timing on the left bank was controlled by points mounted on a movable subplate, the latter allowing the firing interval to be adjusted. For 1933 the distributor became IGO-4001-A, with an altered advance curve to match the redesigned valve cam. With the next model—the Eleventh Series, when optional high and low compression heads were offered—still another version was available, IGO-4001-A being retained for the high compression heads, with IGO-4002-A mated with the regular and low compression varieties.

The Twin Six engine was put into production with cast iron heads, the same as the prototype. In the former, however, the spark plugs were placed vertically at the top of the heads, but with the engine refinements to produce more power, the combustion chamber was redesigned and the spark plugs repositioned closer to the center of combustion where water passages in the head would provide better plug cooling. Although Packard had used optional high compression heads since the Seventh Series on the Eights, these would not be introduced on the Twin Six. Only one ratio, 6.0 to one, was offered. With the Eleventh Series, the company phased in aluminum heads with compression ratios of 6.0 and 6.8 to one and phased out the cast iron.

As the company said, "... the degree of silence necessary in Packard's finest motor car precluded any possibility of employing conventional construction in the valve gear." To eliminate the annoying rattle of the mechanical tappet, as well as to draw abreast of the competition, there would be a change made—to the noiseless, zero-lash hydraulic system. Though comparatively ancient in origin, hydraulic valve silencing had

Sam Rockwell, of the Detroit branch, delivering the first production Twin Six (a Sedan-Limousine) to the home of J.B. Ford in April 1932.

not found general favor within the industry, due to high manufacturing cost. Two proven methods were available to Packard: the direct acting hydraulic tappet and the more elaborate indirect system as used on the Cadillac V-16, though this valve system carried an automatic penalty as well, the license agreement with General Motors costing Packard one cent per valve per engine. A more thorough analysis of the Cadillac system would have saved the company a subsequent redesign, but Packard in its haste didn't initially have time for that.

The Twin Six, with its 67^0 blocks, modified "L" heads and 320^0 valve angle, lent itself to a compact and efficient silencer configuration. For the valve take-up mechanism to function properly, friction had to be at a minimum. Packard took a big stride in that direction by replacing Cadillac's bronze sleeve with needle bearings.

The system itself is best described with the rocker arm roller at rest on the cam lobe heel and the valve closed. The spring-loaded plunger, pressing against the small arm of the eccentric bushing, rotates it counterclockwise to bring the rocker arm into contact with the cam lobe on one end and the valve stem on the other. With the cranking of the engine, the cam exerts pressure on the eccentric bushing, causing it to rotate clockwise, overcoming the spring of the plunger and forcing the plunger up to the end of its travel. Further cam rotation will partially open the engine valve. Oil in the meantime has been pumped into the top of the plunger cavity. As the cam lobe passes its high point and drops away releasing the pressure on the eccentric bushing, the spring-loaded plunger is forced down, opening the check valve and allowing oil to fill the unit. With the unit reservoir filled, the eccentric bushing is prevented from turning and the full lift of the cam is transmitted through the rocker arm to the valve stem which is lifted off its seat. The plunger piston is fit into the housing bracket with .0015 to .0025 clearance, this providing a path through which oil can escape from the reservoir as the engine warms up and the components expand.

But, binding in the hydraulic system or in the eccentric bushing would cause the valve system to malfunction. Clearance of the piston in its housing was critical for proper bleed-off of the oil. During opening of the valve, the oil was subjected to very high pressure—and wear increased the clearance between the hardened piston and its cast iron housing, allowing excess oil to escape. When this happened, valves would not open to their full design height and the engine lost power. At high speeds, the system was subject to pump down, as the check valves did not stay open long enough for oil to be drawn into the reservoir to replace that lost through the clearance gap.

To control fit in assembly, Cadillac made its plungers in four hand-fitted sizes, and to minimize pump down, used a long plunger—and, in final design, a double spring to return the plunger more quickly. Packard used a dashpot and a piston on the end of the check valve stem, this delaying the closing of the check valve and allowing more replacement oil to be drawn into the reservoir. But, so sensitive was the system that uneven torquing of the hold down bolts—and warpage through engine stress under heavy loads—would cause the aforementioned binding of the plunger in its housing. And the "silent" valve system became noisy. Packard immediately ordered a redesign for the Tenth Series. The company's solution to the problem was quite ingenious. The engineers merely isolated the high pressure hydraulic system by incapsulation and then let the capsule float in the housing bracket. The spring plunger was extended in length and the check valve seat placed on a close fitting inner sleeve. Clearance was held between .0007 and .001 inches with components being selectively fitted. Housing clearance was no longer critical since the housing was removed from the high pressure system. With occasional flushing to remove oil sludge, the new units were troublefree for the life of the engine.

The change from front wheel drive to DeLuxe Eight chassis, and from lower displacement engine to higher, decreed a concomitant change in cooling as well. Radiator core size was limited to the 21-inch width and 22½-inch height of the DeLuxe Eight. Some relief was obtained by increasing core thickness from the Eight's 3½ inches to 4¼ inches for the Twin Six. There simply was not enough time, however, to place into production a new body allowing for a taller and larger radiator. And the Twin Six engine, while only sixteen percent larger than the Eight, required almost twice as much coolant capacity (11.5 gallons to 6.5) to maintain a reasonable temperature level.

The coolant system, as it was, would prove adequate under optimum conditions, but as the system aged, again, overheating could be expected. In anticipation of this, Packard engineers devised an expansion tank.

Tenth Series prototype chassis, featuring many '32 prototype elements; note dual fan belts, new exhaust manifold shank, radiator expansion tank and AC fuel pu

This necessitated a sealed system with an overflow line leading from the top of the radiator neck down the outside of the radiator and into the expansion tank. As the coolant became hot, it expanded into the tank; as it cooled, the resulting vacuum drew the coolant back into the radiator. The expansion tank was fitted with a small stand pipe—open to the outside air—which served as an overflow exit for excessive expansion. (For the Sixteenth Series a pressurized filler cap was interposed between the radiator and overflow line, increasing the normal boiling point by twelve degrees.)

The Tenth Series, however, found a redesigned cooling system with two distinctly different radiator sizes for the Packard line. The revision included a new water pump impeller and housing, with the addition of a radiator fan shroud to increase cooling efficiency. With this, coolant capacity was dropped to ten gallons, the reduced flow and shrouded core providing for better heat transfer and a slightly cooler engine. The heat problem was eventually solved through the use of aluminum heads, whereby the engine ran consistently 10^0 or more cooler.

The fuel pump on the Twin Six was a Stewart Warner Model 407, a mechanical pump with a single diaphragm; with the Tenth Series, this changed to an AC pump having dual diaphragms, the second being a vacuum booster to operate the windshield wipers when engine vacuum dropped at high speed or in accelerating.

Actually, although horsepower on the models preceding had not been advertised as other than 160, the Tenth and Eleventh Series Twelves were slightly more powerful than the Ninth Series Twin Six. Initially in-

velfth Series engine, with three-point suspension and new oil temperature system.

experienced at cam design for use with hydraulic silencers, Packard engineers had run a very conservative cam acceleration rise and fall, based more on the ramp required for solid lifters. For 1933, however, they speeded things up with a more rapid cam rise and fall for a longer duration of valve opening thus giving better fuel/air induction and exhaust scavenging. And since the valve system had zero lash, there was no contact shock on the valve and the tendency for valve bounce was greatly reduced.

The DeLuxe Eight chassis was, as we've seen, pressed into service to house all the foregoing mechanical bits. But, a look under the Twin Six prototype car at the New York show reveals a good many advanced features which would not be incorporated in the production Twin Six, but would be ready for the Tenth Series Twelve arriving a year later. Again, there was the element of time. Packard didn't have it. Among these features to become part and parcel of the Tenth Series were: drop center wheel rims in contrast to the Twin Six's snap ring type, front frame drop replaced by taper type construction, a wide based "X" frame center brace, the battery located beneath the driver's seat, Gemmer worm and roller steering gear replacing the Packard-built worm and sector for the Twin Six, Spicer needle bearing type universal joint and one-piece tubular propeller shaft.

When the Twin Six was announced, its rear axle was described by *Automotive Daily News* thusly: "[It] has the appearance of being turned upside down, with the forward side inclined upward. The pinion gear drive of the hypoid gears is located below the center. This construction contributes to dropping the height of the body." Packard called the result Angleset—but did not provide it to the Twin Six in every case. The Light Eight was given production priority, and the larger car phased in with the regular DeLuxe Eight rear axle. Then it got the Angleset too . . . sometimes. The Parts Service List does not differentiate by frame serial number which cars have which axles, indicating that use was probably indiscriminate.

In both types of rear axles, however, the same gear ratios were available: 4.06:1, 4.41:1, 4.69:1 and 5.07:1. The standard ratio for closed cars was the 4.69:1; for open and convertible models, the 4.41:1—with dealers and customers ordering the options suitable for their local territory. The maximum horsepower of the Twin Six was reached at 3200 rpm, but engine revolutions could go upward to about 4200 before breathing limitations, valve float and lifter pump down began to take their toll of horses. With 4200 as the practical limit to revs, the top speed with each gear ratio was: 5.07:1, 81.33 mph; 4.69:1, 87.91 mph; 4.41:1, 93.50 mph; 4.07:1, 101.31 mph. The lower ratios were used mostly in the open cars where acceleration was not unduly penalized compared to the heavier sedans—and a higher top speed could be reached. Who would want to spend the Packard price for a sport

The Fifteenth Series and i.f.s., with motor sitting back behind cross member; the Sixteenth Series brought motor forward onto cross member.

phaeton only to have a sedan run off and leave it on the highway?

Another change. Although the front wheel drive Packard was fitted with hydraulic brakes, and the prototype Twin Six with a Bendix two-shoe cable and conduit mechanical type, the production Twin Six would arrive using the same three-shoe brake system as the 740-745, 840-845 and 903-904. This system was used in conjunction with the Bendix-Perrot Control—and to bring the big beast to an easy halt with a minimum of effort, engineers installed the Bragg-Kliesrath system of vacuum assist. For the Tenth Series in 1933, Packard also placed an aux-iliary vacuum control valve on the dash so sensitivity could be controlled by the driver, but by 1935 decided this was superfluous. Although the vacuum power assist was retained for the life of the Twelves, no dash regulator was used after 1934. And the power system would, of course, be redesigned for the hydraulic brake system to be used on Fifteenth and subsequent series.

Nineteen thirty-two was a big year for free wheeling. Studebaker had started the ball rolling two years earlier, with Auburn, Pierce-Arrow, Hupp and others joining in for 1931. For '32 Buick pioneered an elaborate automatic clutch it called "Wizard Control," while Cadillac's was dubbed "Controlled Free Wheeling." Chevrolet chimed in with a straight free wheeling concept using a coil spring wrapped around a shaft behind the transmission; when the accelerator pedal was released, the unit acted as an overriding clutch allowing the car to coast. More sophisticated units used a vacuum cylinder for disengagement while gears were changed, some of these automatic and others manually operated using the vacuum cylinder to supply the power. Nobody was quite sure where to put the activator control. Buick, Cadillac and LaSalle located an auxiliary pedal betwixt brake and clutch; Chrysler and Lincoln went for a push-pull knob on the dash.

Packard wasn't initially sure what it should do about the matter either. The Ninth Series Eights introduced in June of '31 were sans free wheeling, the company settling instead for a new aluminum-cased four-speed gearbox with synchros on third and fourth, the synchros courtesy of General Motors at $1.25 per transmission. With the Light Eight and Twin Six at show time, however, came the new three-speed gearbox with synchros on second and third, and an automatic clutch—an idea passed along then to the Standard and DeLuxe Eights as well.

At first, Packard toyed with a foot controlled pedal, similar to the Cadillac unit, which needed to be depressed each time the clutch was disengaged. The early prototype Twin Six chassis used this version, but the decision to go fully automatic was reached prior to production and specifications called for "Finger Control Free Wheeling" with activator on the steering column as standard equipment.

The automatic clutch control mechanism consisted of a vacuum cylinder linked to the clutch release lever and connected to the intake manifold through an accelerator-operated control valve and a transmission shaft rod motivated selector valve. When the control lever was in the down (off) position, the clutch could be operated conventionally, when up (on) the automatic clutch came in. Instructions to owners advised that the "change from automatic to conventional clutch operation or vice versa may be made instantly at any time at any speed by changing the position of the control lever."

When the accelerator pedal was fully released, the vacuum supply plunger connected the engine vacuum to the cylinder and disengaged the clutch. After the shift to second or third gear, the clutch was re-engaged by depressing the accelerator pedal, the rate of clutch re-engagement being proportional to the amount of gas given the engine. The transmission selector valve assisted in controlling the rate of clutch engagement.

Packard suggested the clutch be used manually when taking off in low gear from a standstill and applying automatic for second or third. The unit was so sensitive that the slightest pressure on the accelerator pedal instantly engaged it, causing a lurching, neck snapping start that no respectable Packard driver could permit. Many Packard owners left

driving chores to their chauffeurs generally, and found upon the occasional taking of the wheel themselves they had a little trouble. Premature application of the accelerator pedal during shifting engaged the clutch before the gears were fully shifted—and that was grating both to ears and gears. After a few such shifts, many owners turned the control off and forgot about it. Packard, in an effort to ease the problem, redesigned both the accelerator control valve and the transmission selector valve late in the Ninth Series run—and this worked at least well enough for the company to offer the automatic clutch as an option on the entire line of Tenth Series cars. But sales didn't work equally as well, and the device was deleted from the catalogue at the end of the Tenth Series.

The clutch in the Twin Six was a Long 29A double disc dry type, borrowed directly from the DeLuxe Eight 903-904, but this was replaced in the Tenth Series Twelve by a spring cushioned single disc clutch. Centrifugal assist on the pressure plate helped to ease clutch pedal pressure to some extent on the Tenth Series cars without the automatic clutch. With the horsepower increase for the Twelfth Series Twelve, a new heavier pressure plate was required which used heavier springs, and for the ease of lady drivers, Packard was prodded into a power assist unit for the Twelfth Series which was continued throughout the life of the Twelves.

Of all the chassis components from the DeLuxe Eight given to the Twin Six, one of the most highly touted was the harmonic front end stabilizer which has been described earlier in this book. It all began innocently, but soon turned into a parts man's nightmare.* While the principle of operation was straightforward enough, it was not a cure-all for an inadequately braced frame. Front end dance persisted, and the Packard Service Letter dated December 1st, 1932 offered solid brackets in place of the front rubber mountings, cautioning, ". . . there will naturally be a slight decrease in motor smoothness." This was obviously a stopgap, devised to use the motor casting to strengthen the frame.

It was back to the drawing boards, and for Tenth Series cars the wide based "X" frame center brace appeared—and two more versions of the stabilizer bumper were added. For 1934 came bullet caps to the ends of the bumpers—and four versions of the harmonic balancer, each "tuned" to a different body series: one for open models, one for closed models, one for the LeBaron town cars and another for export cars. Then, for 1935, design changes in the front fenders made it necessary for Packard to

---

*Basic research on this unit had been undertaken by Clyde Paton during his tenure at Studebaker and a cross-license agreement for "Anti-Shimmy Methods or Devices of the Bob-Weight Type" was established between Studebaker and Packard in April 1931. Paton, protégé of Studebaker's estimable Delmar G. "Barney" Roos, had become Packard's chief experimental engineer in October 1930. It had been Roos and Paton as well who had pioneered free wheeling at Studebaker.

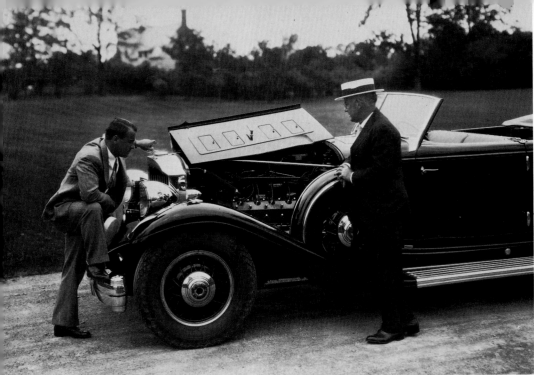

Gene Sarazen and Alvan Macauley examining the innards of Gene's Ninth Series Twin Six Dietrich Convertible Sedan. Donning knickers and wielding a golf c

flatten out the bumper impact bars to allow the bumpers to ride in front of the fenders, and the frame was further braced by an inner box channel, with the addition of three-point suspension for the motor. For the year following, the Fourteenth Series, Packard went mad with stabilizers, five versions for the front bumper and another eight for the rear bumpers—all this in an attempt to provide the Senior Packards a ride comparable to the new One Twenty. Fortunately, for 1937, the i.f.s. engineers won out and sanity returned to bumpers at Packard, the company introducing its Safe-T-fleX independent front wheel suspension on the Fifteenth Series with helical springs and a simple stamped front bumper—and no stabilizers. They were gone forever, after a career that can only be called checkered.

The same cannot be said for the Twin Six or Twelve. Notwithstanding the refinements and changes that came with the years, from the first to the last, the big Packard was essentially the same animal. It could go—fast. It could perform—phenomenally. It could stop—well. Granted, it did get only about nine miles to a gallon, but anyone able to afford twelve cylinders and a Packard during the Depression doubtless didn't consider that a controlling factor in the purchase of a motorcar.

In England, *The Autocar* was vastly impressed, though few of the big

Packards would find their way across the Atlantic. In fact, the magazine had to borrow a car from a new owner for its road test in 1936 which meant that it could not be "put through the more extreme tests, though it may be mentioned that a quarter-mile was covered on Brooklands at 92.78 mph by stopwatch. The twelve-cylinder engine is wonderfully smooth and quiet, and even though in the circumstances the usual range of figures was not recorded, obviously the acceleration is altogether out of the ordinary, especially in the higher ranges of speed, in spite of a total weight of not less than 55 cwt. (5500 pounds) with petrol in the tank (0.80 lb. per cc)."

No similar impressions of driving the big Packard appeared in an automotive periodical in the United States. The Twin Six's performance prowess had been early demonstrated in this country, however, and in one of the more curious speed tests ever visited upon a motorcar. It was, indeed, the sort of promotional gambit associated with the devil-may-care decade that preceded the car's introduction, and not the Threadbare Thirties into which it debuted, though perhaps the madcap nature of it all provided a whimsical reprieve from most of what filled the news columns in those days.

The event received extensive coverage in the *Detroit News*. It was a

...zen takes on Jesse Vincent and the Twin Six Speedster at the Proving Grounds in July of 1932 in what was perhaps Packard's most unusual match race.

Tuesday in July of 1932, the day the Twin Six raced a golf ball. The latter belonged to Gene Sarazen, the British Open and National Open champion, and a Packard owner of eleven years standing. He was in town, casually visiting with Jesse Vincent, Alvan Macauley and Harold Olmstead—golfers all—when the subject turned to the speed of a golf ball when traveling through the air. Various opinions were offered. Bullet-like, Sarazen said. Colonel Vincent suggested maybe 60 mph on leaving the tee, and added that in full flight a Twin Six (the Macauley Speedster, of which more later) could beat it. They all went out to the Proving Grounds thereafter to check this out.

"The race between the golf ball and the motor car was plainly visible to all who watched," the *Detroit News* reported. "Impelled by the force of Sarazen's unerring swing the ball shot out in front of the car. . . . Then its slowly spending force became apparent against the relentlessly speeding car which Col. Vincent's foot was keeping unvarying at 120 miles an hour. There was a space of many yards when the car and ball were racing on even terms. [Indeed Jesse Vincent would afterwards comment that the ball was so close to him he could have reached out and grabbed it.] Gradually the car pulled away, its wraith-like length moving out in front of the little white sphere. . . . The time for the ball for

230 yards of flight was 4.5 seconds. The car's time for the same distance was 4.1 seconds."

Five times more the test was made, confirming the results of the first effort—which proved to Sarazen "that it is the speed with which the clubhead hits the ball, as much as the timing of the stroke, that gives distance on drives." And though it didn't tell Packard anything it didn't know already about the Twin Six, the afternoon had been fun.

Certainly a more serious endeavor at the Proving Grounds was the testing "Certificate of Approval" which accompanied every Twin Six and Twelve Packard produced through the Twelfth Series. It was signed by Tommy Milton and Charlie Vincent and testified that the car had been driven 250 miles, conforming "to the best Packard standards in acceleration and maximum speed, in control including steering, speed changes and brakes, in roadability and riding qualities, and in all adjustments necessary for . . . all riding and driving conditions."

And if the care exercised in seeing to it that the Twin Six or Twelve under the skin was exemplary, no less finesse was put to the task of providing it coachwork that could but enhance the whole. The majesty, the beauty of the car, and all the factors revolving thereon, is a story in itself.

417

CHAPTER TWENTY

CLOAKING
THE ULTIMATE
IN CONVEYANCES

Twin Six and Twelve Coachwork,
The Ninth through
Seventeenth Series 1932-1939

AUTHOR: C. A. LESLIE, JR.

Packards had always been regarded as regal and stately motorcars, this despite the firm's reluctance to accord the vehicle's body anything more than secondary consideration. The company's management team was headed primarily by engineers and mechanics, with enough salesmen on hand to move the merchandise. Coachwork was a necessary evil to sell the chassis, upon which Packard lavished all its talent. The ratio of chassis to body price for standard production cars was about four to one, and for this reason Packard had gladly made chassis available to independent coachbuilders such as Brewster, Fleetwood, Holbrook, Judkins and LeBaron for custom bodies, and in the post-World War I era sublet much of its production body requirements to Anderson, Buffalo, Pullman, Towson, Wilson and, later, Briggs. But turning over that business to outside vendors violated the company's integrated-manufacturer credo, placed it at the mercy of the body builder, and sent considerable profits the vendors' way which otherwise would have been Packard's. Consequently, a "fixed policy" would be devised to bring coachbuilding close to home.

To keep abreast of production requirements, the factory had expanded to cover eighty-eight acres of ground by October of '29, when the stock market crash and its aftermath brought a screeching halt to the building program. Body shops comprised twenty-five percent of the factory area, this twenty-two acre facility lying to the south of East Grand Boulevard bound by Palmer Avenue on the north, reaching to Frederick Avenue on the south, bordered by Concord Avenue on the east and the Michigan Central Railroad Beltline on the west. Prior to 1923, this had been the site of Packard truck manufacturing.

During the week of June 19th, 1931, Packard's distribution personnel were invited to mecca to see the new Ninth Series Eights and DeLuxe Eights, with the most magnificent array of production and Individual Custom bodies ever to grace the chassis of a single marque. The times were bad, of course, and Packard dealers had showrooms-full of the Eighth Series cars still. Facelifting kits would be provided these and, with the new Ninth Series, the Packards listed as current for sales purposes in the Information booklet issued June 15th comprised production bodies numbering one for the 826, eleven for the 833, nine for the 840, two for the 845, one for the 901, twelve for the 902, ten for the 903, two for the 904; plus Individual Customs numbering nine each for the 833 and 840 and fifteen for the 904. All of this added up to eighty-one different body styles, a fantastic number. And the Twin Six hadn't even arrived yet.

Even more amazing, each of these body styles was derived from designs by Raymond H. Dietrich, and all the bodies not produced in the Packard factory were made by Dietrich, Inc. or its parent company, the Murray Corporation of America.

The ultimate sheathing of these Eights, the Twin Six and later Twelves is a memorable episode in Packard Motor Car Company annals. It all began in 1913 when an ambitious nineteen-year-old apprenticed himself to Brewster & Company of New York City as a draftsman for automobile bodies. Ray Dietrich was required as well to attend the Mechanics Institute on 44th Street where he was taught the fundamental principles of construction and the system of surface development for body contours. After graduation in 1917, he left Brewster to work for Billy Durant who had plans to bring out a new enclosed-bodied Chevrolet. As Dietrich recalled, "I would sit in with the engineers and sketch their ideas . . . I laid out a complete Chevrolet car in perspective so that I could hand it to somebody and say, 'Well, you assemble it like that.'"

Dietrich's subsequent return to Brewster and the resulting close association with a fellow designer, Thomas L. Hibbard, led to formation of LeBaron Carrossier at 2 Columbus Circle, "the only address in New York City that couldn't be forgotten . . . just like 10 Downing Street. We were on the fourth floor, Fleetwood was on the sixth. Ernst Schebera gave us our first job, to design and make a working draft of a Packard town car to be built in Fleetwood, Pennsylvania." It led to others.

In the spring of 1923, Hibbard set sail for Europe to firm up LeBaron's business on imported chassis, and decided to set up shop there. In New York, Dietrich allied himself with Roland Stickney, who handled LeBaron's illustrations, and Ralph Roberts, who managed the office—and early in 1924 with C.W. Seward in Bridgeport, Connecticut. LeBaron, Inc. was the name given the new firm, and Bridgeport was its new home. "It worked very well," Dietrich remembers. And Detroit noticed.

In the motor city at that time a farsighted financier by the name of Allan Shelden was busy creating an empire. Its cornerstone was the J.W. Murray Manufacturing Company, a supplier of sheet metal stampings to the industry, the "King of the Stampers," as it was then known. Shelden convinced James R. Murray, son of the founder, and Jerome E.J. Keane, of the investment banking firm of Keane, Higbie & Company and like Shelden a member of the board of Murray, that his idea of a unified company for the manufacture of bodies for the automobile industry was a good one. And on November 15th, 1924, the Murray Body Corporation was brought into being. Then, with the corporate shell formed, Shelden set about filling it with concrete assets: stock, of course, and more facilities. First came Towson Body Company, successor to the Anderson Electric Car Company, it being the largest supplier of Lincoln production coachwork and, to a lesser degree, Packard; the adjacent C.R. Wilson Body Company south of Clay Avenue, this firm's history dating back to carriage-making days and now, under the presidency of C. Haines Wilson, a successful volume supplier of bodies at competitive prices. Lastly, there was J.C. Widman & Company at 14th Avenue and Kirby Street, a small firm which began in 1905 with furniture and fur-

Pages preceding: The Twelfth Series Twelve Seven-Passenger Sedan for 1935. Above: The Dietrich 645, its single wide raised belt molding characterizing [ ] open cars through the Eleventh Series and, with the recessed window reveals [a]nd a higher waistline, all closed cars through the Ninth. Below: The Dietrich [Sp]ort Sedan 845 for Alvan Macauley, its semi-flush windows, sloping windshield [a]nd visorless top predicting styling for Tenth and Eleventh Series closed cars.

nishings, this leading in 1915 to the manufacture of automobile bodies. The company's second generation, Charles H. and C. David Widman had refocused efforts, however, so that now the firm concentrated largely on supplying window glass to other body building enterprises.

On January 2nd, 1925, these companies combined with Murray to become the coachbuilding empire Shelden had envisioned—almost. One thing was missing: a custom body division. On the advice of Edsel Ford, president of the Lincoln Motor Company, Shelden attempted unsuccessfully to lure LeBaron into the fold. Only one vote at LeBaron had been in the affirmative, and the man who cast it thereupon set out for Detroit. The doors of Dietrich, Inc. were opened February 12th, 1925, with Murray Body Corporation footing the bills.

Custom body building in Detroit was new, and Ray Dietrich moved quickly. "Within about five or six months we developed bodies, produced them, were shipping them, but all this was for Lincoln," he remembered. "Now Packard came into my picture. I was called upon one day to go over and see Mr. Alvan Macauley." Macauley asked for an invitation for himself, and his staff, to visit Dietrich and see what he was doing. "We'd like to work with you and have you do work for us," Macauley said.

Packard meanwhile was rapidly becoming disenchanted with its vendor body building program. Firm contracts for specific quantities of bodies had led to disputes and costly cancellation charges with Anderson, Pullman and Buffalo whenever car production diminished and bodies were no longer required. A switch to Briggs brought complaints of poor quality with higher prices sought as more rigid controls were instituted by Packard.

Gradually more body fabrication was brought in-house and, on October 14th, 1925, board minutes noted, ". . . it was decided to build all of our own bodies when, and as, arrangements can be made to that end."

The Twenty-First Annual Automobile Salon was approaching—November 15th—and Dietrich was ready: "We were going into the Salon this time fortified with a sales organization. While the others were showing foreign cars, I had Lincolns and Packards. Previously they had not been in the Salons much." The Packard Motor Car Company was also recognizing the potential of the custom body business. While setting production records almost daily with its standard fare, the company noticed too that its output of chassis for custom bodies had zoomed. To capitalize upon the increased demand, Packard set up a special custom body sales division that same November with Horace Potter, formerly of the sales staff of the company's Detroit branch, placed in its charge.

The company's production body design and styling remained a function of Engineering under the jurisdiction of Archer L. Knapp who had risen through the Packard ranks to become "Chief Draftsman Body Art Department" in May 1917 under L. Clayton Hill. (Hill, an engineering graduate of the University of Michigan, had joined Packard's engineering division in 1911 and would leave in 1920 to become assistant general manager of the Society of Automotive Engineers during Jesse Vincent's tenure as president of that august organization.) In October 1925, Knapp was given a new title: "Body Engineer." No creative stylists were retained by Packard at this time, the company relying instead on its body sources and the factory parroting their efforts for in-house coachwork. Realizing the importance of styling to sales, however, Packard was having second thoughts about originating its own designs.

Meanwhile, at Murray, Allan Shelden had proven himself a good empire builder but a bad production specialist. Inefficiencies in manufacturing had resulted in most body contracts being taken at a loss. There was red ink all over the place, and Murray sought the protection of the Federal courts. On December 3rd, 1925, the Guardian Trust Company of Detroit took over as receiver for the Murray operation, and a former Packard official became part of the Murray-Dietrich axis. The president of Guardian Trust was William Robert Wilson, formerly personal assistant to the Dodge brothers and later president of Maxwell—but more important from the Packard-Dietrich relationship was his (Wilson's) assistant: Frederick R. Robinson. Robinson was a man whose creden-

tials with Packard were impeccable. Beginning with the company in 1911 as chief accountant, he was one of the incorporators—together with Henry Joy, Sidney Waldon, Alvan Macauley and H.H. Hills—of the Packard Motor Sales Company of Detroit in 1913. Robinson also served as secretary and treasurer of that firm, and succeeded Phillip H. McMillan in 1919 in those positions for the Packard Motor Car Company until his resignation was "regretfully accepted" in November 1923. His association now with the Murray Body Corporation through the Guaranty Trust Company would provide Murray with a direct link to Alvan Macauley and others in Packard's upper echelon.

Ray Dietrich meantime had skillfully avoided the stigma of Murray's bankruptcy by leaving the Murray premises and moving across the street, although the effect was merely cosmetic, since he remained under Murray's control, dependent upon it for financing. On December 19th, 1925, having been impressed with what he had seen during his recent visit to Dietrich and needing to establish a more definitive hallmark of body styling, Alvan Macauley signed Ray Dietrich as "Body Critic" for his company. Dietrich's association with Packard, however, was to be on a consulting basis, and thus not conflict with business as usual back at Dietrich, Inc.

From the left: Horace Potter, who in 1925 was placed in charge of Packard's newly created special custom body sales division; Ray Dietrich who that same

In Ray Dietrich, Macauley found an amalgam of talents seldom assembled in a single individual. His background at the American Banknote Company eminently qualified him as a line sketch artist, while his four years at Mechanics Institute had further developed his ability in drafting, illustrating, air brush technique, surface development of body contours, preparation of working drawings for detail parts and construction supervision. All this combined with twelve years practical experience, a natural creative ability and a finely-honed knack for salesmanship. Packard, providing a large-scale commercial outlet for this talent, was bound for unparalleled heights. With the postwar recession of the early Twenties now history, people were purchasing high-priced custom-bodied cars at an ever increasing rate. For Packard, today's Dietrich custom body would become tomorrow's production body. One such body, a Style No. 1176 four-passenger sedan, was mounted on a 243 chassis (Vehicle No. 216155, Motor No. 216001) for Macauley's personal use during the following season.

During 1926, on the heels of record profits, Packard launched a program to increase body production from sixty to a hundred units per day. Only two bodies remained outside, these to Briggs, the Four-Passenger Coupe and the Five-Passenger Club Sedan. In 1927, at

Dietrich, Inc., orders overwhelmed facilities—"it can't be done, not in this space!"—and Holden Avenue beckoned. At number 1331 stood the old Leland Lincoln plant, which had become Ford property with that company's takeover of Lincoln and was now being used as a warehouse. "I went to see Mr. Edsel Ford," Dietrich remembered, "and I explained the situation to him. . . . He said, 'I'll tell you what I'll do, I'll let you have the building . . . for four hundred thousand dollars . . . and you can name how you want to pay for it.' " From its portals would emerge all future Dietrich bodies.

Elsewhere in the city, and to counteract the advantage of Murray (now reorganized as Murray Corporation of America), with its custom body division in Dietrich, John H. French, the president of Briggs, succeeded where Sheldon had failed and in February brought LeBaron to Detroit. Subsequently, William Robert Wilson, his proposed Packard-Nash merger having failed, made an ill-advised attempt to combine Murray and Briggs, an idea which appeared headed for success until Henry Ford heard about it. Both Briggs and Murray were suppliers to Ford, the former for Ford bodies and parts, the latter mostly for Lincoln production bodies and, through Dietrich, Inc., custom bodies for that marque as well. A merger of Briggs and Murray would not only have lessened the

hired as Packard's "Body Critic"; Archer Knapp, celebrating twenty-five years of service in 1935; Count Alexis de Sakhnoffsky, who came aboard in 1932.

competition on Ford components but now would also have affected the custom body program at Lincoln (and Packard) by bringing together two of its largest custom body suppliers: Dietrich and LeBaron. Henry Ford didn't like that at all. As the press tactfully put it, he "exerted influence to nip the [proposed Briggs-Murray] combine in the bud." "Within a two-week period," Dietrich remembered, "Ford pulled every die, every form, and every piece of construction out of Murray Body." Wilson had not anticipated such a violent reaction. According to Dietrich, "there was a deal made and everybody patched up their differences. Ford Motor Company recommended a man to be placed in Murray by the name of Clarence Avery."

For the Packard-Dietrich relationship, nothing could have been better, as another vital link was forged in the chain of former Packard men now aligning themselves with Murray. Charles H. Widman had become Murray's sales manager and brought in as his assistant none other than Packard's former body engineer, L. Clayton Hill. Hill was to generate far-reaching effect on the fortunes of both Murray and Dietrich, Inc.—and on the misfortunes of Ray Dietrich.

Meantime the Packard Motor Car Company had decided to hit the custom-bodied car market with a bang. On May 11th, 1927 at the company's Broadway and 63rd Street showroom in New York City was opened a special exhibit of nine custom-styled Packards by six coachbuilders: Dietrich, Fleetwood, Holbrook, Judkins, LeBaron and Rollston.

By that time, with the Ford Model A program nearing production, Edsel Ford had taken the time to flex a corporate muscle or two and seize more absolute control over Murray via Clarence W. Avery, formerly chief development engineer for Ford. As of October 12th, Avery became the power behind the Murray throne, signaling the beginning of the end for Wilson, as soon as his court approved contract was fulfilled. Together with Clayt Hill, Avery would eventually ring down the curtain on Ray Dietrich as well. For the moment, however, Dietrich wasn't to be trifled with; the custom body business looked too good and obviously he was the most valuable asset Dietrich, Inc. possessed. Ray Dietrich was to prove likewise for Packard.

Packard board minutes for December 21st, 1927 noted that "Macauley reported . . . 'the development work on the new Packard Eight 645 series was progressing' and exhibited preliminary designs for some of the bodies." These were totally new body styles emanating from the pen of Ray Dietrich, and Dietrich, Inc. would enjoy the fruits of production for six of the nine body types. Dominant theme of the new design was a raised beltline (2¾ inches wide on closed and convertible models, two inches in open cars) encompassing the cockpit area with a one-inch extension of the beltline running forward to the radiator shell. The closed models were given recessed window reveals, thus raising the

Ninth Series Twin Sixes for 1932. Above and below: The Coupe-Roadster, its new dash panel finishing plate and steering wheel which set the pattern for future cars, the left-hand lever the light switch, the right to actuate the automatic clutch; the ride control lever is to the left of the steering column. Right above and below: The Seven-Passenger Limousine and Seven-Passenger Sea

lower edge of the window opening to give a more massive but less boxy appearance. More pleasing proportions resulted from the use of a longer wheelbase with the same overall height providing suitable headroom as well as the look of a lower profile. This new body series was designated the 645 (purists insist 6-45 but Packard used both designations and for the sake of uniformity the hyphen will be omitted here) DeLuxe Eight—and would become the styling basis for all enclosed car bodies through the Ninth Series, all open car bodies through the Eleventh Series, all Individual Custom bodies through the Tenth Series, as well as the LeBaron town cars for the Tenth and Eleventh Series.

Although catalogued as production models, each 645 body (excluding Individual Customs) was tagged with either a "Custom Made by Packard" or a "Dietrich, Inc." body emblem. The result, in effect, was a pseudo-custom, with special trim, upholstery and other minor deviations from the standard norm—including a premium pricetag. For example, a 645 Seven-Passenger Sedan with a "Custom Made by Packard" plate brought $2000 over its 640 equivalent, while a Two/Four-Passenger Coupe with the Dietrich name was worth $2100 more than its 640 standard companion. Thus, by the use of a professional stylist, hanging on a few accessories and adding a "custom" body plate, Packard was able to get twice as much for the 645 as it could for the 633, and fifty percent above the price of a 640. That was a *very* nice markup. Due credit has never been given the Packard sales staff for its extraordinary accomplishment in marketing these cars. The result had to be an ultimate in merchandising.

Most body parts for the 645 cars carrying a Dietrich, Inc. body plate were furnished by Packard, with a similar arrangement later being made with Murray Corporation to complete convertible sedans, victorias and phaetons for Packard's production series. The status of these bodies as they left the Packard plant bound for either Murray or Dietrich varied from time to time. Generally, however, Packard fabricated all major components and, except in rare instances, skinned the wood skeleton before turning the bodies over for final fitting, trimming, upholstery, painting and mounting on a chassis.

These cars were not the first to come from Packard's Custom Body Shops, however, that distinction falling to the 443 Custom, followed by early production 640 Custom models, all this resulting from Packard's decision in November 1927 to segregate Six and Eight production. Sixes, generating up to ninety percent of production, retained the regular body shops, buildings numbered 31 through 38 east of Bellevue Avenue. Eight production was moved to Building No. 5, a seven-story structure in the center courtyard of the original factory site, under the management of H.J. "Jack" Crain, a Packard veteran having started in 1911 as a clerk in the mechanical department.

Opposite the regular shops on the west of Bellevue were the saw tooth

The standard production Twin Six, Model 905: Franklin Delano Roosevelt and his Seven-Passenger Touring; Tommy Milton in Detroit with his Phaeton and Gene Sarazen at the Packard Proving Grounds with a Convertible Sedan.

stamping sheds also housing the dies and sheet metal stock. New fabrication techniques instituted for the 645 body called for larger body panels, deeper compound curves, and less welding to complete the body sections. The massive presses required to handle the up-to-thirty-ton dies mandated a new facility, Building No. 92 at the south end of the sheds, the first floor of which was completed in the summer of 1928.

Production of the 640, preceding the 645 by several months, began in the custom shops but was moved to the regular body shops in late October when it became apparent after early previews that the 645 would far exceed sales expectations and allocated production space. A month after the December debut of the 645, four additional floors were given to Building No. 92 for welding and finishing of the metal parts before conveying them to final assembly.

"Custom Made by Packard" thus became a permanent part of the scene as Dietrich's designs were initiated for the Eighth Series, these being designated "Individual Customs." They are not to be confused with full customs on Packard chassis by Brewster, Dietrich, Judkins, Holbrook, LeBaron, etc., but fall instead into the semi-custom category, that name indicating limited production models.

In May 1929 overtures were made to Raymond B. Birge, formerly head of LeBaron's Bridgeport body plant, to take over the Packard Custom Body Division. Birge would do so—a month before the market crash, his tenure at Packard thereafter abbreviated as he became a casualty of the Depression.

As for Dietrich, matters at the factory never looked better for him, but changes in the front office portended adversity. In September of 1929, Clarence W. Avery became president of Murray Corporation, upon the certainly-not-unexpected resignation of William Robert Wilson. Avery tightened the reins on Murray—and Dietrich, Inc. Over Dietrich's strenuous objection, Clayt Hill was moved into the vice-presidency of Dietrich, Inc. To this day, Ray Dietrich explodes at the mention of his name: "Nothing but a lackey for the S.A.E., ask anyone, they'll tell you, that's all he was." His animosity is understandable; in mid-1930 Avery appointed Hill president of Dietrich, Inc., relegating the man for whom the company was named to a seat on the board of directors. Of Avery, Dietrich remains somewhat more charitable: "He was a thorn in my side. He was not an easy man to deal with. Each time he advanced into a higher position, he became a little tougher . . . I tried to keep away from him as much as possible. If I saw him coming over to my plant, I would always try to be very busy . . . Avery was trying to use force, not to get me out of the organization but to capture my brain. . . Here we had the irresistible force of Dietrich meeting the immovable object of Avery. It was always nip and tuck."

With the appearance of the Seventh Series bodies, Dietrich designs permeated all Packard production models. The "Custom Made by

Packard'' label was transferred from the 645 to the 745, with some 740's tossed in for good measure. And a completely new model, the 734 Speedster Series, was also made in the new custom body facility.* Outside body builders remained the only source of catalogued Individual Custom bodies.

The Sixth Series had seen an entirely new body design instituted for "Custom Made by Packard." The Seventh Series by contrast, except for the very limited Speedster Series, found standard bodies taken from the regular production line to be finished by the Custom Body Division and so labeled. The main onslaught would come with the Eighth Series. In preparation, the entire Custom Body Division was placed directly under the Engineering Division rather than Manufacturing. To accomplish this, a separate trim department and woodworking department was installed in Building No. 5 during March 1930. Sheet metal stampings still originated in No. 92 but body framing, indigenous to each style of the Eighth Series Individual Customs, and finalizing were completed in No. 5. For yet greater efficiency, the Engineering Division was relocated into this facility the following August.

With the Eighth Series introduction that month, all specialty body builders except Dietrich were out of the Individual Custom Body Catalogue. The new 3000-numbered series—confined, with one exception, to the town car style—represented an entirely new concept in body building for Packard, and supplanted the variety of this style previously built by Brewster, LeBaron and Rollston as Individual Custom Packards.

Prior to this, the Individual Custom body divulged its parentage through chassis, radiator, bonnet and instrument panel, all furnished by Packard, with the body itself, however, retaining the character of the coachbuilder. Now, with the 3000 series, Dietrich styling was propagated throughout the entire Packard line. In the Eighth Series, there were three distinct types of Dietrich styles in the production line, viz., open, convertible and enclosed body. The new Individual Custom town cars built by Packard reflected a merger of the Dietrich convertible and enclosed body styling. Quite obviously, to maintain compatibility among all Packards catalogued by the factory, only Dietrich designs would suffice. His personal offerings were a convertible victoria and convertible sedan.

The reason for this change in Packard policy was also obvious. Not

---

*Beneath the ever sedate and ever proper exterior of Alvan Macauley perhaps lurked a more adventurous soul. In mid-November 1929, the second production 734 Speedster motor was installed in vehicle number 180810, a 740 Custom Club Sedan, for the personal use of Packard's president. This factory hot-rod probably produced some startled looks at stoplight grands prix on East Grand Boulevard.

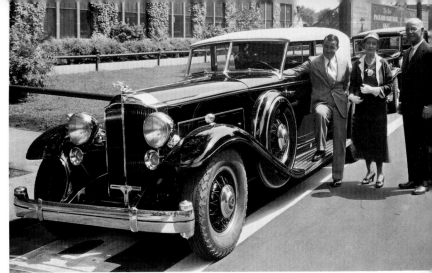

Alvan Macauley, Mrs. Sarazen and the omnipresent Gene upon taking delivery of his Model 906 Individual Custom Dietrich Convertible Sedan in 1932.

only had the depressed economy taken its toll of high-priced custom cars, but prior planning had decreed that henceforth "Custom Made by Packard" would appear on the stately all-weather town cars which had been conceived in a more prosperous era when it appeared that a large volume of these types could be marketed. This action would bring to Packard coffers the profits heretofore traveling to satellite coachbuilders. The fact that, now, factory production had nosedived, along with profits, only made it more imperative for the company to try for every available production dollar.

Any of the Packard chassis were available to the custom body builder, however, for mounting of their own special bodies, although primarily the long 845 chassis would be requested. It was on one such that Dietrich mounted his Sport Sedan which would presage most of the design elements of the Tenth and Eleventh Series Packard closed cars. The first of these (845-1 Motor No. 188001) supplanted Alvan Macauley's 740 hot-rod Club Sedan.

The Ninth Series arrived in June of 1931. And Packard remained Packard, Great Depression or not. As Alvan Macauley mused around this time, with equal parts candor and pride, "Some other kind of car might conceivably have as fine a motor, as fine axles, as good a steering . . . yet it wouldn't be a Packard. Its roadability might be as good as ours. It might be as safe. . . . Yet, you could ride in it blindfolded and know immediately that it wasn't a Packard. You would have no trouble sensing the fact that it lacked . . . what I call the personality of Packard cars. Personality is the combination of characteristics that make you like one car better than another without knowing exactly why."

But one of the indefinable somethings that made up the personality of the Ninth Series Packards could not be sensed blindfolded. It had to be seen. And it comprised five all-new Individual Custom bodies by Dietrich. As in the past, these designs were portentous, the styling to be integrated into future production bodies.

The Twin Six arrived in January 1932, six months after the Ninth Series line of Eights, or in April, putting the time at nearly a year, if one uses the date the new twelve-cylinder cars were actually rolling out of the factory. Whatever the month—and whatever the rush to production—they were the lucky recipients of the Packard evolution in style which had preceded and which, to romantics, might seem to have taken place simply in anticipation of this "ultimate" in conveyances to emanate

The Twin Six Macauley Speedster, first version, with teardrop taillamps which would later be used, in an inverted form, in Packard's Sport Coupe.

Version two, with extended pontoon fenders, wheel discs, vee-shape taillamps and instrument panel finishing plate also found on the "Car of the Dome."

from East Grand Boulevard.

The fifteen Individual Custom body styles offered in the 904 DeLuxe Eight line were reduced to nine for the Twin Six 906 chassis, though the complete group of ten 903 and two 904 DeLuxe Eight production styles was offered on the Twin Six Model 905 and 906 lines. One striking variation between Twin Six and DeLuxe Eight in the Ninth Series

appeared inside the cars. In the latter—and the Eight as well—a new instrument board with dark walnut finish set off the black tooled instrument finishing plate. For the Twin Six, however, there was an entirely different instrument board finishing plate, as well as new instruments which would set the styling trend for succeeding Tenth and Eleventh Series panels, featuring an antiqued grey background setting off the

Minor revisions, right, to version number two included the front pontoon fenders; then the updating with 1935 appointments, above and below.

The man behind it all, Ed Macauley, photographed in the Speedster during 1933. Macauley had grown up around fast cars, and his penchant for them never waned.

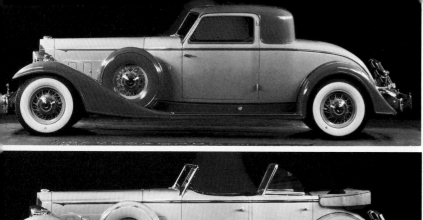

chrome-plated grained rings surrounding each instrument. The first production run for the Twin Six, it should be noted, had finishing plates which were engine tooled, then plated chrome over nickel with a clear lacquer protective coat. Instruments were black faced with chromed pointers and a raised tan band carrying appropriate black numerals. The four-inch clock, a Waltham eight-day hand wound dual main spring type, rested to the right of the panel, balanced by the 120 mph speedometer on the left. Top center was the twenty-five-gallon gas gauge the alternate connection of which indicated engine oil level. To the left was a seventy-five-pound oil gauge with an engine temperature gauge to the right. The 20-0-20 ammeter rested at the bottom of the panel between the hand throttle on the left and the cigar lighter to the right.

The Twin Sixes available in the Ninth Series, with passenger capacities in parentheses, and prices as of introduction and mid-year, were as follows:

Body Style/Wheelbase	Type No.	1-9-32	6-1-32
Model 905 (142 ⅛ inches)			
Touring (5-7)	570	$3895	$4395
Phaeton (5)	571	$3790	$4290
Sport Phaeton (5)	581	$4090	$4590
Sedan (5)	573	$3745	$4245
Convertible Sedan (5)	583	$4395	$4895
Club Sedan (5)	576	$3895	$4395
Coupe (5)	577	$3850	$4350
Convertible Victoria (5)	587	$4325	$4825
Coupe (2-4)	578	$3650	$4150
Coupe-Roadster (2-4)	579	$3750	$4250
Model 906 (147 ⅛ inches)			
Sedan (5-7)	574	$3995	$4495
Sedan-Limousine (5-7)	575	$4195	$4695
All-Weather Cabriolet (5-7)*	4000	$7550	
All-Weather Landaulet (5-7)*	4001	$7950	
All-Weather Town Car (5-7)*	4002	$7550	
All-Weather Town Car, Landaulet (5-7)*	4003	$7950	
Stationary Coupe, Dietrich (2-4)*	2068	$6600	
Sport Phaeton, Dietrich (4)*	2069	$6500	
Convertible Sedan, Dietrich (5)*	2070	$6950	
Convertible Roadster, Dietrich (2-4)*	2071	$6750	
Convertible Victoria, Dietrich (4)*	2072	$6850	

*Indicates Individual Custom series.

At the introduction of the Twin Six, Alvan Macauley had advised distributing personnel that "we have made large and far-reaching reductions in the price of all the DeLuxe line. It is to you alone that we must look for the volume of sales necessary to continue the . . . pricing of all our products at the favorable figures we have decided upon."

As the foregoing chart indicates, the favorable figures did not long remain so. Sales of the "Custom Made by Packard" bodies, particularly, were somewhat less than sensational and as far as can be determined, only one production run was ever made. The highest chassis number recorded by the Packard Twin Six Association is 906-21, the "21" figure comprising all types of custom bodies whether built by Packard, Dietrich, or others, rebodied cars included. The economy being as it was, and Packard's optimistic pronouncements to the contrary, the company may have anticipated a less-than-stampede rush to the Twin Six. Still, the sales figures must have been a disappointment.

For Ray Dietrich, the Ninth Series Packards must have been bittersweet too. He had conceived them within the tumult of political machinations at Dietrich-Murray, and hardly had they been born when he was summarily ousted from the company. It was early in 1931. "When the final reckoning came, I was surprised at the accounting," Dietrich would remember. "I didn't even want to stamp the check afterwards. Avery and I didn't part bad friends, but we didn't part good friends . . . ."

L. Clayton Hill was now fully in charge at Dietrich, Inc. And at Packard—following the New York show in January 1932—Edward Macauley was placed in charge of the new factory styling division. Dietrich's opinion of Macauley—"he was no designer, he was a playboy"—may have been the reason he was not retained as Packard's styling consultant after his ouster from Dietrich, Inc.

The "Sparks from Detroit" column in the *Automotive Daily News* edition of January 23rd, 1932 carried the announcement. "Hot off the griddle comes [word] from Count Alex de Sakhnoffsky, that he has just signed as a body stylist for Packard, specializing on the Twin Six. The ink was hardly dry on the contract when the column office was advised that the Count will continue his affiliation with Studebaker and Hayes Body. As we know him, he is one of the elite when it comes to body designing, and the industry is familiar with his work . . . ."

The Macauley-de Sakhnoffsky combination was to play a dominant role in the unification of Packard's body styling. Previously, there was no correlation between open, closed or convertible design—and the custom field had been wide open. Macauley would exercise his new authority to change all this and eventually coordinate Packard's body styling so that phaeton, convertible, sedan or town car would each contain the same design elements. The final result was a combination Dietrich-de Sakhnoffsky design.

Something of what might have been expected was telegraphed by de Sakhnoffsky in recounting his background: "Early in the Twenties, I started developing design of bodies with false hoods. I found that though the actual distance from the radiator to the front door remains the same,

Twelves for 1933. Page opposite, from the top: Dietrich Stationary Coupe; the Dietrich Sport Phaeton; the LeBaron All-Weather Town Car; the interior of the Dietrich Convertible Sedan, all these cars in the Custom Series, Model 1006. Above: The 1005 Coupe-Roadster with stationary top built for Alvan Fuller that was the forerunner for the Eleventh Series Stationary Coupe. Below: The 1005 Coupe-Roadster, gracing the Packard booth at the show in Milan, Italy.

by extending the hood almost to the windshield, the effect of length is considerably increased. At that time most of the deluxe chassis came to the coachbuilder with short hoods. These were generally narrow at the dash, and the blending of such hoods to wide bodies necessitated ugly ogee curved surfaces in plan view. By discarding the short hoods, we were free to lengthen and widen them and carry the flowing lines into the body.''

This idea first revealed itself in the Packard that was Edward Macauley's pet. Whatever may have been Macauley's qualifications as a designer, the ex-diesel engine salesman knew what he liked, and that was a fast sporty car. He grew up during the days when Henry Joy, Jesse Vincent, his father and the Packard factory all supported racing with a fervor. With this background, it was only natural that his choice for personal transportation now would be a very racy looking car.

"We used to call [it] the 'Brown Bomber'," engineer Forest

McFarland remembered. Today it is called the "Macauley Speedster," although Vincent was behind the wheel when it raced the golf ball. It was a highly developed version of a 734 Speedster that was progressively refined and altered at Macauley's caprice. The body (Type 442) today is commonly referred to as a boattail speedster, but Packard defined it as a two-passenger runabout with staggered seats and fishtail streamlining. Parentage of the Macauley Speedster was very subtly announced with a "Custom Made by Packard" medallion embellishing the lower cowl.

But almost every adjunct to the body was changed between 1932 and 1935, resulting in many intermediate versions as various elements were modified or replaced. The earliest configuration unearthed to date heralded the new dimension of de Sakhnoffsky's "false hood" married to the new split windshield design expropriated from the Dietrich Individual Custom styling. Twin Six hubcap medallions hailed the new engine under its hood, Ninth Series appointments abounded, including Twin Six headlamps and mounting brackets, bumpers, snap ring wheels and a vee radiator shell modified to conform to the very low profile of the 734 body. The instrument board finishing plate was typical of the Twin Six production unit, save for tachometer replacing clock. Auxiliary instruments reflected Edward Macauley's aircraft background: Visible to the left of the horn button was an aircraft recording tach, while to the right of the sub-panel was an altimeter and small vacuum gauge. Above each set of auxiliary instruments was a pull-out lamp for illumination. Pie-shaped windows rose out of door slots to provide the wind protection usually afforded by windshield wings. Mounted on the windshield center post was a bulb-type thermometer.

The staggered seating of the original Runabout was now side-by-side configuration, and the removal of the side-mounted spares provided an uninterrupted sweep of the front fenders. George Moore of Milford, Michigan remembers, "When I lived on Somerset and Harper, I used to see Edward Macauley drive by in his Speedster. It was a golden brown and had a transparent bubble top." Cliff Bailey, a former employee in the Packard garage, recalls, "The Prince Brothers Body Shop on Larned Avenue in Detroit did the modifications to the body and fenders, but the mechanical work was done in the Packard experimental shop."

Modification to the Speedster in 1933 saw pontoon fenders on the rear, full wraparound and skirted fenders on the front, new taillamps and a new instrument panel whose finishing plate would paceset the styling for the Eleventh Series production cars. The bead trimming the rear wheel openings had been dropped to the bottom edge of the rear fender and feathered out beneath the trailing edge. This trimming bead and the pointed front fender was a finishing touch used by Macauley on his Speedster, as well as a subsequent dual cowl phaeton and several sport coupes built by Packard on an 1106 chassis. It was lacking, however, on the Eleventh Series LeBaron Speedster and Sport Phaeton,

Page opposite: Loading up in Detroit and after setting up in Chicago for the Century of Progress Exposition. Above: The Transportation Building. Below: Admirers crowd around the "Car of the Dome" during the Exposition.

Across the top, from the left: The basis of the "Car of the Dome," the 1933 Model 1006 Dietrich Sport Sedan; the car as updated at the time of introduction of the Eleventh Series, now with bumper caps, new front fenders and a bail radiator cap; and the third and final version, with Eleventh Series rear bumper, taillights and spears on hood and cowl vent doors, as delivered to new owner, Mrs. Thomas M. Flanagan.
Left and below: The car as seen at the Exposition. Its dash panel with integral radio control head would be adopted throughout the Eleventh Series. Passenger amenities were grand. The "quite futuristic" cabinet, Packard said, "is made of highly polished burled Carpathian Elm as is the rest of the wood interior trim of the car. . . . Most unusual modernistic indirect lighting fixtures are set in each rear quarter. . . . Between the two cabinets at the bottom is a grilled loudspeaker for the radio. Just above this is an electric clock and above is a folding smoking case. . . ."
Dressing table vanity boxes, all cups and containers were gold, naturally.

as well as the Dietrich Convertible Victoria with pontoon fenders mounted on an 1108 chassis, all of which had flush exteriors. From the design elements of these front fenders would evolve the front fenders for the Packard One Twenty and the Senior Packards on the Sixteenth and Seventeenth Series chassis.

The pontoon style rear fenders, sans wheel covers, were phased into production on the Twelfth Series as Macauley's styling division grew in power. Other innovations reaching production status were the front bumper end caps, on the Eleventh Series. Also new was the radiator ornament depicting an elongated teardrop within a ring, matching the shape of the door handles. Packard subsequently used the new radiator ornament on the Speedster Dual Cowl Phaeton, as well as the 1106 Sport Coupe by Packard, and allowed LeBaron to affix it to its Eleventh Series Speedster Runabout and Sport Phaeton.

While Speedster-izing was ongoing, of course, the Tenth Series Packards arrived. Previously, at the introduction of the Light Eight and Twin Six on January 9th of '32, Alvan Macauley had assured the Packard distributing organization, "We do not intend to announce new models until . . . next December or early January. I haven't time to tell you the reasons for reaching this conclusion . . . but the decision has been reached for excellent reasons . . . ." Obviously, Macauley was privy to the fact that it would be some time before the Twin Six reached production status, and it would have been quite unwise to bring a car to market in May and supersede it in August. So, true to his word, the Tenth Series cars didn't arrive until the dealer preview at New York's Astor Hotel on Friday, January 6th, 1933.

Edward Macauley had his say about the Tenth Series too. Sent abroad to study automobile design on the Continent and to attend the Paris and London shows of 1932, he arrived back to report, "After driving the best cars in every country visited and after covering their mechanical developments, I can without exaggeration say that our Tenth Series cars are far above the best offered in Europe today in all-around performance, riding comfort and styling."

Early prototypes for the Tenth Series were proclaimed Twin Six and had skirtless fenders, but by production time, Packard changed its mind about both fenders and designation. The new car was called the Twelve, and it came in two wheelbase sizes, the 1005 at 142 inches and the 1006 at 147 inches, and on the latter were Packard's custom styles, the word "Individual" dropped to become simply Packard Twelve Custom Cars. Slow sales had left enough of the 4000 series Individual Custom bodies in stock to justify their reissue, but sales of catalogued custom bodies would now be limited to the Twelve chassis only, as the factory endeavored to force its moneyed clientele to move up a notch and drop another thousand dollars into the Packard till. The Tenth Series lineup was as follows:

Body Style/Wheelbase	Type No.	1-6-33
Model 1005 (142 inches)		
Touring (5-7)	630	N.A.
Phaeton (5)	631	$3790
Sport Phaeton (5)	641	$4090
Sedan (5)	633	$3860
Convertible Sedan (5)	643	$4650
Formal Sedan (5-7)	5633	$4560
Formal Sedan (5)	5633A	N.A.
Club Sedan (5)	636	$3880
Coupe (5)	637	$3890
Convertible Victoria (5)	647	$4490
Coupe (2-4)	638	$3720
Coupe-Roadster (2-4)	639	$3850

The Eleventh Series for 1934, from the left: 1107 Phaeton; 1108 Dietrich Convertible Victoria; 1107 Club Sedan; 1108 Dietrich Convertible Roadster.

Model 1006 (147 inches)

Sedan (5-7)	634	$4085
Sedan-Limousine (5-7)	635	$4285
All-Weather Cabriolet (5-7)*	4000	$6030
All-Weather Cabriolet, LeBaron (5-7)*	D-758	$7000
All-Weather Landaulet (5-7)*	4001	$6250
All-Weather Town Car (5-7)*	4002	$6080
All-Weather Town Car, LeBaron (5-7)*	D-759	$7000
All-Weather Town Car, Landaulet (5-7)*	4003	$6250
Sedan-Limousine, Cabriolet (6)*	4004	$6000
Sport Sedan (5)*	4005	$6000
Sedan-Limousine (6)*	4007	$6045
Stationary Coupe, Dietrich (2-4)*	3068	$6000
Sport Phaeton, Dietrich (4)*	3069	$5875
Convertible Sedan, Dietrich (5)*	3070	$6570
Convertible Runabout, Dietrich (2-4)*	3071	$6085
Convertible Victoria, Dietrich (4)*	3072	$6070
Sport Sedan, Dietrich (5)*	3182	$7000

*Indicates Custom Cars series   N.A. = not available

Packard's enclosed bodies for the Tenth Series ballooned into a more rounded style, taking on the characteristics of the Dietrich Custom 845 Sport Sedan. Despite an increased windshield rake angle, yon-lean-and-hungry look for Packard had disappeared forever in favor of the billowing body and skirted fenders. The change in body styling which eliminated the recessed window reveal was not without some merit, as window glasses were brought more nearly flush with the outside body surface, resulting in a claimed fifty percent reduction in noise level over the Ninth Series bodies. Photographs of the prototype Tenth Series cars depict side windows with conventional roll-up side window glass. Competitive pressure, however, forced adoption of a no-draft window ventilation system, the least expensive being under Dole Valve Company patents. Of dubious benefit it was discarded after the Tenth Series in favor of Fisher no-draft, with appropriate tribute to General Motors after a threatened infringement suit.

Providing perhaps more problems were the "Custom Made by Packard" bodies, none of which appeared in the Information booklet issued by the company on January 7th of '33. In an effort to move this unforeseen surplus of factory-built custom bodies, prices were dropped $1500 across the board.

The double-drop frame of the Ninth Series had given way to a smooth tapered frame for the Tenth. Consequently, to adapt Ninth bodies to Tenth frames required a wood wedge filler block affixed to the existing

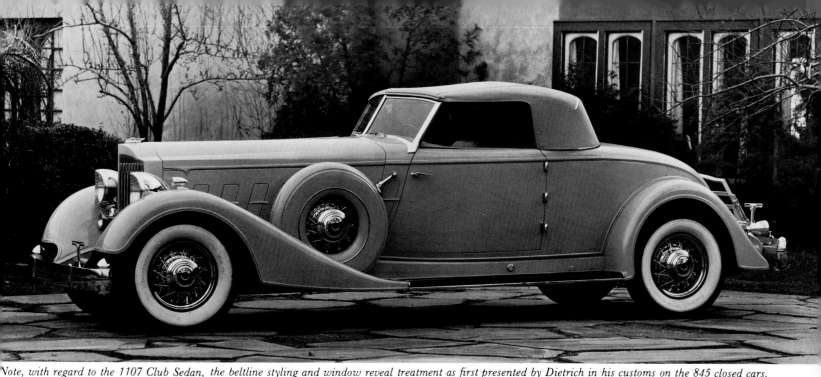

Note, with regard to the 1107 Club Sedan, the beltline styling and window reveal treatment as first presented by Dietrich in his customs on the 845 closed cars.

frame rail and a sheet metal wedge welded to the lower cowl on each side. Few bodies received this treatment. Expediency, and the fact that sales volume in 1932 of open and convertible body types was not sufficient to justify a new tooling program for new body styles, resulted in only the necessary tools being made to build cowls that would fit the new frames for these cars, which retained the thirty-six-inch-high radiator of the Ninth Series.

Packard again instituted the pseudo-custom program, however, in conjunction with the Tenth Series convertible victoria and sedans. The cowls, dash, windshield and many other parts—furnished by Packard—were identical to the Coupe-Roadster which was built in-house—and, as in the past, the balance of the work to complete the bodies was farmed out to Dietrich, Inc.

There were, of course, the true custom-bodied cars for the Tenth Series, as the foregoing chart indicates, most of these from Dietrich, Inc. as well. Of the All-Weather Cabriolet and All-Weather Town Car by LeBaron, the *Inner Circle* stated, "In their development . . . Packard engineers . . . supervised the engineering and construction." From their exterior appearance, these cars could well have borne the "Custom Made by Packard" label, so closely did they resemble the Ninth Series Packard-built Individual Customs.

One of the Dietrich customs must be singled out for special attention: the Sport Sedan, Style 3182, the first of the Dietrich customs made to be compatible with the tall radiator. Its higher beltline molding blends gracefully with the 37½-inch high radiator phased in with Tenth Series closed cars. Although featuring all-new sheet metal stampings, it reflected the styling of the Ninth Series Dietrich Individual Customs with its standard bonnet and extra long cowl. And it was this car, after Packard factory modifications, which was destined to become perhaps the most famous Packard of all time.

Preparations were under way for the Century of Progress Exposition in Chicago. Opening day was to be Saturday, May 27th, 1933. The giant dome of the Travel and Transport Building would rise above the rest of the structures at the Exposition to a majestic twelve-story height, and beneath the dome would be examples of the "earliest and the most modern examples of all types of transportation." Upon its unveiling at the Exposition, the modified Dietrich Style 3182 Packard would be awarded by an art jury the honor of representing motor car transportation, would be "selected as the highest expression of the industry that has civilized the world and the only motor car in the unusual display of the finest examples of personal transportation that mankind has been able to produce." Actually, there would be two Packards on display: the Model 437

A, the first Packard ever built, which would appeal to exposition visitors with a fondness for history—and this last word in Packards, a car that verily cried out unabashed luxury and was guaranteed to cause mouth-watering among the legions of spectators journeying to the dome for a welcome respite from the travail of those depressed days.

The car was a delicate blending of ingredients from Dietrich and de Sakhnoffsky, with dashes of flavor from Edward Macauley and Packard. Dietrich, of course, wasn't around when the cauldron was stirred. As he confided, "When this design was sold to Packard, I had no idea it would be used for the Chicago Exposition Car." And by the time it went on display, he was in his new quarters on the sixth floor of the Chrysler Engineering Building, where he had charge of exterior design for Walter Chrysler.

One of the most striking refinements to the car was the application of the de Sakhnoffsky false hood to increase the apparent length, this further accented by the addition of a rear-mounted spare tire. The hood swept all the way from radiator to rakishly sloping vee windshield, with another contribution to jaunty appearance being the sloping "A" door post with matching slant to vent doors and rear edge of the bonnet sides. Also added were the double pivoted front door glasses of Packard's ventilation system. All body hardware was heavily plated with gold, even the steering column and all instruments on the dashboard.

The Eleventh Series Packards debuted on August 21st, while the Chicago Exposition was still in progress, and the company tried very hard not to make them seem anticlimactic. Actually even the Car of the Dome, as the Exposition Packard came to be known, was afforded a little updating in August, company mechanics working nights in Chicago affixing full wraparound front fenders, front bumper end caps and a new bail radiator cap. With the close of the 1933 edition of the Exposition on November 12th, the car was returned to the factory for more complete updating to Eleventh Series specifications.

The standard production lines saw a continuation of the bodies offered in the Tenth Series, with the addition of the new instrument board (from the Macauley Speedster, also adopted on the Car of the Dome), new rear bumper and a relocation of gas filler cap. The big news for the Eleventh Series came in the custom body offerings. All custom-bodied Packards, except the pseudo-customs and those rebodied from earlier years, now sported the 37 ½-inch tall radiator and all—save style 4002—carried the de Sakhnoffsky false hood.

One last reprieve was given to the "Custom Made by Packard" label when, on December 6th, 1933, the board approved $3300 for "three 1106 chassis less fenders, radiator, running board, bonnet—etc., for mounting three sport coupe bodies being built in the Engineering Department." Work such as this, and the Car of the Dome, was ac-

complished on the first floor of Building No. 5, equipped for "handling

jobs that cannot be shown to outside vendors."

The introduction of this styling pacesetter at the January 1934 New York automobile show was concurrent with a similar 500 K Mercedes-Benz Autobahn Kurier making its debut at the 1934 Berlin show. The Eleventh Series custom catalogue included five models by Dietrich, four by LeBaron, and the "Sport Coupe by Packard." Its styling offered a blend of the de Sakhnoffsky false hood, simple Dietrich waistline, split windshield of the Car of the Dome, and the pontoon fenders of the Macauley Speedster. Though lacking the elegance which would have been afforded if constructed on a long wheelbase chassis, the car was nonetheless most attractive. The high waistline and low top broadcast the styling of the soon-to-be Packard One Twenty.

Unlike the Macauley boattail and Speedster Phaeton, the Sport Coupes were not one-off jobs, but offered on a full semi-custom catalogued basis. This was reflected in the superior quality of workmanship compared to that found on the previous two Macauley Speedsters, particularly the Phaeton where obvious irregularities were in evidence in the hand-wrought fenders and splasher panel. The front fenders, though, reflect the Macauley touch, with a trace of a point at their front edge and a bead outlining the wheel opening and leading edge, likewise the rear fenders with bead trimming and contours identical to the boattail.

ge opposite, from the top: Two views of Packard's 1106 Sport Coupe; the Mercedes Autobahn Kurier which it resembled; the 1106 LeBaron Runabout Speedster. w: 1108 LeBaron Sport Phaeton, differing from the Packard-built version in the smooth edge employed completely around wheel openings, and the absence of points the leading edge of the front fender and a bead around the bottom of the rear fender wheel opening. Further, the running board did not attach to the front fender.

Packard Twelves for 1935. From the left, the interior of a 1207 Formal Sedan, the 1208 Convertible Sedan, the 1208 LeBaron All-Weather Town Car.

Three Packard Twelve Sport Coupes remain extant. One of these was updated with 1935 appointments in keeping with its sister car, the final version of the Macauley Speedster boattail, thus closing the final chapter on "Custom Made by Packard." Many other types would, of course, emanate from Macauley's styling division but these would be only on an experimental or prototype basis.

In somewhat desperate straits for sales of custom bodies for the Eleventh Series, Packard made most of them available on the 1105 Super Eight chassis of 147-inch wheelbase, as well as the 1108 Packard Twelve chassis. In addition to a reissue of the two LeBaron Town Cars, two new open types were introduced, the Sport Phaeton for both the Super Eight and Twelve 147-inch wheelbase and the Speedster Runabout on 135-inch wheelbase 1106 chassis but available only with a Twelve engine. These represent a radical departure from the usual LeBaron styling, reflecting instead the de Sakhnoffsky false hood and the pontoon fenders of the Macauley Speedster. Ed Macauley was calling the shots more forcefully now, and conforming all Packards to a single theme. Also conforming to Packard's new styling concept was the entire line of custom bodies emerging from the portals of 1331 Holden Avenue, where Clayt Hill still held sway, although teetering on the brink of disaster. The entire line of Dietrichs now were equipped with the de Sakhnoffsky false hood. Dropped from the line was the Sport Phaeton, one of the most beautiful of Dietrich styles, but, in view of the vanishing market for open cars, it would have taken more tooling to convert this body style than prospective sales could possibly justify. The Sport Phaeton was the only Dietrich Custom with all doors front hinged, all others being hinged on the "B" post; to use the new false hood necessitated changing hinge location on the front doors to conform. Tooling on the LeBaron Sport Phaeton could be shared with its Sport Runabout, resulting in better amortization per unit. Consequently, all open custom models were taken over by LeBaron, Dietrich retaining a stranglehold on the convertibles.

Prices for the Packard Twelves of the Eleventh Series are indicated below in the complete lineup of cars as introduced August 21st:

Body Style/Wheelbase	Type No.	8-21-33
Model 1106 (134⅞ inches)		
Sport Coupe by Packard (4)*	—	—
Runabout Speedster, LeBaron (2)*	275	$7746
Model 1107 (141⅞ inches)		
Touring (5-7)	730	$3980
Phaeton (5)	731	$3890
Sport Phaeton (5)	741	$4190
Sedan (5)	733	$3960
Convertible Sedan (5)	743	$4750
Formal Sedan (5)	732	$4660
Club Sedan (5)	736	$4060
Coupe (5)	737	$3990
Convertible Victoria (5)	747	$4590
Coupe (2-4)	738	$3820
Coupe-Roadster (2-4)	739	$3850
Model 1108 (146⅞ inches)		
Sedan (5-7)	734	$4185
Sedan-Limousine (5-7)	735	$4385
All-Weather Cabriolet, LeBaron (5-7)*	D-858	$6155
All-Weather Town Car, Dietrich (5-7)*	4002	$5695
All-Weather Town Car, LeBaron (5-7)*	D-859	$6155
Stationary Coupe, Dietrich (2-4)*	4068	$6185
Convertible Sedan, Dietrich (5)*	4070	$6555

441

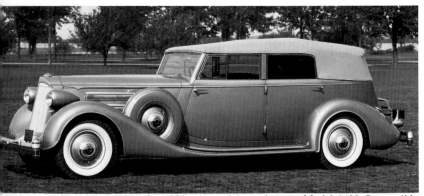

Packard Twelves for 1936, pictured from the top: Model 1408 Convertible Sedan, Model 1407 Sport Phaeton and Model 1408 Seven-Passenger Sedan.

Convertible Roadster, Dietrich (2-4)*	4071	$6100
Convertible Victoria, Dietrich (4)*	4072	$6080
Sport Sedan, Dietrich (5)*	4182	$7060
Sport Phaeton, LeBaron (4)*	280	$7065

*Indicates Custom Car Series

"An appearance more Packard than ever . . . cunningly [blending] the undying lines of Packard identity into a design that is pleasingly modern," said the brochure of the Twelfth Series Twelves introduced in August of 1934. What this meant was an all-new era for Packard bodies. Gone, utterly, was the individuality long associated with custom styles, as each carried the de Sakhnoffsky false hood coupled with the simple Dietrich beltline design from the Ninth Series Individual Customs. Front fenders of the Senior Packards had a full front wraparound extending to the lower edge of the front bumper, while an exaggerated rearward sweep extended to the middle of the front door. The rear fenders reflected the pontoons of Macauley's boattail of 1933. The side splash panels disappeared as the body extended down to the running boards. The front opening doors from the Ninth Series Dietrich Individual Customs permeated the entire line of production bodies.

Packard had many things on its corporate mind in 1934, but most of them were directed to the new One Twenty. Little thought was given to the large expensive models, least of all to limited production semi-custom jobs or open cars whose sales were approaching zero. When the body shops were commandeered to produce the One Twenty, Senior body production was banished to Packard's Siberia, north of Grand Boulevard—and Dietrich, Inc. took over fabrication and assembly of the open bodies in addition to the Convertible Victoria and Convertible Sedan, as pseudo-customs, while LeBaron retained the Town Car business. Not since the days of the 645 had Packard turned over its open models to an outside vendor for completion and, history repeating itself, these cars again bore the Dietrich label.

The Twelfth Series Twelves, with prices, were as follows:

Body Style/Wheelbase	Type No.	8-30-34
Model 1207 (139 ¼ inches)		
Phaeton (5)	831	$3990
Sport Phaeton (5)	821	$4290
Sedan (5)	833	$3960
Formal Sedan (5)	832	$4660
Club Sedan (5)	836	$4060
Coupe (5)	837	$3990
Convertible Victoria (5)	827	$4790
Coupe (2-4)	838	$3820
Coupe-Roadster (2-4)	839	$3850
All-Weather Cabriolet, LeBaron (5-7)*	L-195	$6290

Above: The 1407 Coupe and 1407 Coupe-Roadster. Below: The 1407 LeBaron All-Weather Cabriolet shown during Ladies Week at the Detroit showroom.

Model 1208 (144 ¼ inches)		
Touring (7)	830	$4490
Convertible Sedan (5)	873	$4950
Sedan (7)	834	$4285
Limousine (7)	835	$4485
All-Weather Town Car, LeBaron (7)*	L-194	$6435

*Indicates Custom Car Series

There was, meanwhile, trouble at 1331 Holden Avenue. With high-priced bodies in continuing lesser demand, dwindling profits had been visited upon Dietrich, Inc. By July of 1935, Clarence Avery had begun dropping the final curtain on the company. On August 4th, it was all over, not quite ten-and-a-half years after it began. Dietrich, Inc. was simply allowed to perish with the expiration of its corporate term. Even this action, however, did not signal the end of Dietrich bodies at 1331 Holden. The name was too valuable an asset for Murray to surrender, and for two more years that company would continue to make bodies with the Dietrich tag.

The fortunes of the Packard Twelve were suffering as well. The Fourteenth Series cars had little new to offer except revised front sheet metal to allow a more distinct slope to the radiator. Three-point suspension of the engine was continued after Packard settled Chrysler's threatened patent infringement suit for a seventy-five-cents-per-engine royalty. No longer would the Twelve receive the special 250-mile test at Utica, the Packard Proving Grounds being reserved for more important development testing. The mini-test track at Harper and Elliott, with its cobblestone road section to test and cure body and chassis squeaks, would have to suffice for the Twelve. In many ways the Fourteenth Series marked the end of an era, with the demise of mechanical brakes and the solid front axle utilizing the Delaunay-Belleville patented spring shackle for the rear hanger of the front spring.

Prices of the Fourteenth Series remained stable, however, varying little from the Twelfth Series preceding. (There had, of course, been no Thirteenth Series.)

Body Style/Wheelbase	Type No.	8-10-35
Model 1407 (139 ¼ inches)		
Phaeton (5)	931	$4190
Sport Phaeton (5)	921	$4490
Sedan (5)	933	$3960
Formal Sedan (6)	932	$4660
Club Sedan (5)	936	$4060
Coupe (5)	937	$3990
Convertible Victoria (5)	927	$4890
Coupe (2-4)	938	$3820
Coupe-Roadster (2-4)	939	**$3850**

All-Weather Cabriolet, LeBaron (5-7)*	L-294	$6290
Model 1408 (144 ¼ inches)		
Touring (7)	930	$4490
Convertible Sedan (5)	973	$5050
Sedan (7)	934	$4285
Sedan-Limousine (7)	935	$4485
All-Weather Town Car, LeBaron (7)*	L-295	$6435

*Indicates custom cars

Of the Fifteenth Series introduced in September 1936, Packard waxed eloquently on the virtues of its Senior line: ". . . the new models include Packard Safety Plus bodies of hardwood and steel, new Double Trussed frames, which are over 400% more rigid than before, the exclusive Safe-

Packard Twelves for 1937. Above: 1506 Touring Sedan (132 ¼-inch wheelbase). Below: 1507 Coupe (139 ¼ inches). Right: 1508 Convertible Sedan (144 ¼).

T-fleX independent front wheel suspension, built-in trunks, and Servo Sealed hydraulic brakes.'' Previously, with minor exceptions, the big Eight and Twelve engines were offered on the same wheelbases. For 1937 the small Eight became the Super Eight available only on the shorter chassis. Anyone now wishing a long-wheelbase car had to purchase a Twelve engine. This brought happy days for Packard Twelves; production doubled, from 682 for the Fourteenth Series Twelves, to 1300 for the Fifteenth.

Custom cars offered were the LeBaron All-Weather Cabriolet and All-Weather Town Car from the previous two years. Wheelbase for the Twelve Town Car was 144 inches, for the Cabriolet, 139 inches. The same bodies mounted on five-inch-shorter wheelbases respectively were offered with the Super Eight engine. Chassis for these cars followed

Henry Ford's famous dictate regarding the Model T, unless of course one was willing to pay extra for a color other than black.

The custom car business having become increasingly unrewarding, Packard discontinued the separate sales outlet devoted to it, and Horace Potter took a new job as fleet sales manager. New assembly lines and body drops were installed on the first floor of Building Nos. 11, 12 and 16 for both Senior and Junior cars to accommodate the panel delivery, station wagon, convertible coupes and Dietrich convertible sedans. Packard Twelve body styles and prices were as follows:

Body Style/Wheelbase	Type No.	9-3-36
Model 1506 (132 ¼ inches)		
Touring Sedan (5)	1023	$3490

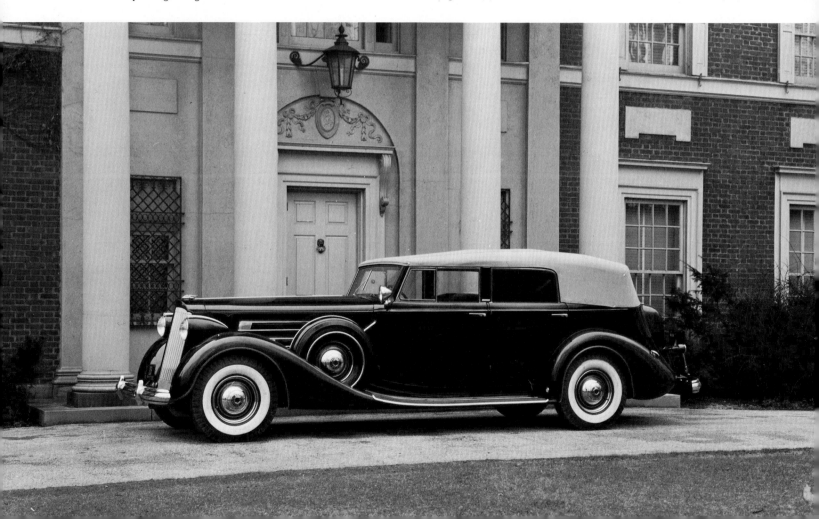

Model 1507 (139 ¼ inches)

Touring Sedan (5)	1033	$3560
Formal Sedan (6)	1032	$4260
Club Sedan (5)	1036	$3660
Coupe (5)	1037	$3590
Convertible Victoria (5)	1027	$4490
Coupe (2-4)	1038	$3420
Coupe-Roadster (2-4)	1039	$3450
All-Weather Cabriolet, LeBaron (5-7)*	L-394	$5700

Model 1508 (144 ¼ inches)

Convertible Sedan (5)	1073	$4650
Touring Sedan (7)	1034	$3885
Touring Limousine (7)	1035	$4085
All-Weather Town Car, LeBaron (5-7)*	L-395	$5900

*Indicates custom cars

There had by now been a formidable shift of emphasis at Packard. A dash of the old with a lot of the new had proved to be the right combination as the high-production Packard crew imported from General Motors' Buick-Olds-Pontiac divisions resurrected the company from the doldrums of the early Thirties. Christopher, Smith, Slack, Packer, et al. could not completely drive the Senior cars from the roster, however, since to do so would have incurred the wrath of Packard veterans in decisive positions who equated the high dollar car with high dollar profits and clung to the belief that the old days might return. Overall Packard production, from a low of 4800 units for model year 1933, had soared to more than 122,500 for 1937. The balance sheet for the latter volume reflected a paltry profit of $2.5 million. Some Packard people could recall when 50,000 units brought profits exceeding $20 million.

The unusually high sales of the re-engineered Fifteenth Series Twelve were enough to bring visions of grandeur to proponents of the Senior line. And sufficient also to justify a complete redo of the Senior cars from the "A" post forward. The Sixteenth Series, introduced in September 1937, found styling implementation throughout the line based on features from the 1106 Sport Coupe "Custom Made by Packard."

Superior handling associated with the new independent front suspension allowed the front wheels to be tucked a few inches rearward without disturbing body space. By comparison, a 98.88-inch body space on the Ninth Series Twin Six required a 147.13-inch wheelbase, while a 100.75-inch body space rested comfortably on the 139.38-inch wheelbase of a Sixteenth Series Twelve. Condemned by this action, however, was the long sweeping front fender instituted with the 745. The billowing pontoon-type front fenders now on the Senior cars, while not graceful, at least made them consistent with those of the Junior models. The transition from a flat windshield to a vee style brought not a murmur from the third floor of No. 13, this in marked contrast to the change from the sacred flat radiator to a slight vee for the Ninth Series which had required approval from the board of directors.

The demise of the Dietrich label saw a realignment of body types, with Rollston and Brunn filling the gap for Packard custom cars. The entire line of Sixteenth Series Twelves was as follows:

Body Style/Wheelbase	Type No.	9/10/37
Model 1607 (134 ⅜ inches)		
Formal Sedan (5)	1132	$4865
Touring Sedan (5)	1133	$4155
Club Sedan (5)	1136	$4255
Coupe (5)	1137	$4185
Coupe (2-4)	1138	$4135
Convertible Coupe (2-4)	1139	$4370
Convertible Victoria (5)	1127	$5230
All-Weather Cabriolet, Packard Rollston (5-7)*	494	$6730

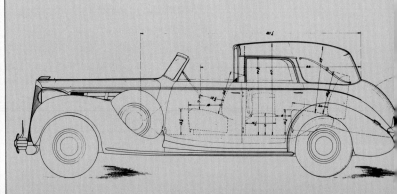

Left and center: The 1938 Model 1607 Touring Sedan and drawing for the 1608 Brunn All-Weather Cabriolet. Right from the top: The 1607 Convertible Co

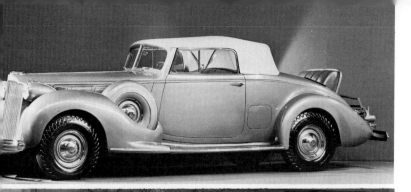

Model 1608 (139 ⅜ inches)

Body Style/Wheelbase	Type No.	9/20/38
Touring Sedan (7)	1134	$4485
Sedan-Limousine, Touring (7)	1135	$4485
Convertible Sedan (5)	1153	$5390
All-Weather Town Car, Packard Rollston (5-7)*	495	$6880
All-Weather Cabriolet, Brunn (5-7)*	3087	$8510
Touring Cabriolet, Brunn (5-7)*	3086	$8510

*Indicates custom cars

War clouds gathering abroad would soon turn lights out all over the world and at the same time draw the curtain on Packard Twelves. The Seventeenth Series Twelves, introduced in September 1938, were merely a continuation of the previous year's cars with minor exceptions, one of these being a steering-column gearshift lever replacing the cane shift. Originally planned for use with the Evans Vacuum Shift mechanism (dubbed Handishift by Packard), this feature failed to reach production status. The Twelve lineup for 1939 comprised the following:

Body Style/Wheelbase	Type No.	9/20/38
Model 1707 (134 ⅜ inches)		
Formal Sedan (5)	1232	$4865
Touring Sedan (5)	1233	$4155
Club Sedan (5)	1236	$4255
Coupe (5)	1237	$4185
Coupe (2-4)	1238	$4185
Convertible Coupe (2-4)	1239	$4375
Convertible Victoria (5)	1227	$5230
All-Weather Cabriolet, Packard Rollston (5-7)*	594	$6730
Model 1708 (139 ⅜ inches)		
Touring Sedan (7)	1234	$4485
Sedan-Limousine, Touring (7)	1235	$4690
Convertible Sedan (5)	1253	$5395
All-Weather Town Car, Packard Rollston (5-7)*	595	$6880
All-Weather Cabriolet, Brunn (5-7)*	4087	$8355
Touring Cabriolet, Brunn (5-7)*	4086	$8355

*Indicates custom cars

1608 Rollston All-Weather Town Car; the 1939 1708 Brunn Touring Cabriolet.

And they were the last Packard twelve-cylinder automobiles the world would ever see. Insofar as this chapter in the history of the marque was concerned, the word "Car" would henceforth be dropped from Packard Motor Car Company. In the years to follow, a steady stream of Packard Twelve motors would flow from East Grand Boulevard, destined for aircraft and marine application. Their use in air and sea conveyances would reach the same supreme heights of excellence as had the magnificent Packard Twelve motorcars. Appropriately so.

447

CHAPTER TWENTY-ONE

INTO A NEW
AND UNTRIED
MIDDLE GROUND

The One Twenty

1935-1936

AUTHOR: RICHARD K. PHILLIPS

Black Thursday. As irrevocably as the end of the First World War had changed the face of America, so would the events following October 24th, 1929. It didn't seem so at first. The Wall Street Crash and the plummeting in value of what, ironically now, were called "securities" didn't affect the mass of America. Earlier depressions had spent themselves in a matter of months, so might this one. But it didn't. The Great Depression was very real and very hard. There was no sign of recovery.

In a few months the banks began to close, wholesale farm prices collapsed. By March of 1930 an estimated 3,500,000 workers were unemployed, a year later the figure was 8,000,000, a year after that 12,-500,000. By March of 1933 unemployment was estimated by the National Conference Board to be an incredible 14,586,000.

There were bread lines and soup kitchens. Men who had sold stocks and bonds were now selling apples. Men who had honed advertising phrases to a fine polish were now shining shoes. Around the nation's industrial cities, shanty towns grew up. Miners in Arizona homesteaded under bridges of the Salt River. In Arkansas the desperate sought refuge in caves. In the bed of the drained reservoir near the Obelisk in New York City's Central Park, more of the homeless congregated; policemen, "with apologies and good feelings on both sides," arrested them for vagrancy. They probably didn't mind. Jail meant a bed and a roof over their heads. Several hundred homeless unemployed women in Chicago spent their nights in Grant and Lincoln parks—they were frightened and begged to be taken in somewhere. There was fear throughout America. From Youngstown, Ohio; from Birmingham, Alabama; from Seattle, Washington—mayors cried out that local relief problems were unmanageable. In Detroit the Department of Public Welfare was "unable to provide even groceries for a bare sustenance diet to the families under its care"—it owed $800,000, its cash on hand was but $8000. Americans were stunned, frustrated, angry . . . beaten. The mood of the country was ugly. There was talk of revolution.

Even those Americans who were not devastated by the Depression were suffering. Every sector of the country's life was affected. The state of Georgia closed 1318 schools, other states did likewise; school terms in Findlay and Cuyahoga Falls, Ohio were cut back to seven months, Akron hung on until early May. There were a quarter million fewer marriages in 1932 than in 1929, the birth rate dropped. Sable coats from Bergdorf Goodman were selling at forty percent discount, and Babe Ruth accepted a cut of $10,000 in his annual salary. Steel plants were operating at twelve percent capacity, rail shipments were halved—the automobile industry was limping at one-fifth pre-Crash levels.

On March 7th, 1930 President Hoover had said the crisis would be over in sixty days and that "the invisible hand of a nation's economy" was not to be tampered with. But after several years of ever worsening

Pages preceding: Nineteen thirty-four, early in the year, work begins in earnest.

conditions, the economy had become just that, ever worse. In 1932 Franklin Delano Roosevelt strode unto the national scene. He took that "invisible hand" of the nation's economy, and he shook it, he tampered. "Prosperity," he proclaimed, "was just around the corner." But America wondered where the corner was and how long would be required to reach it.

The events of these years could but have vast repercussions at East Grand Boulevard in Detroit. From his presidential desk Alvan

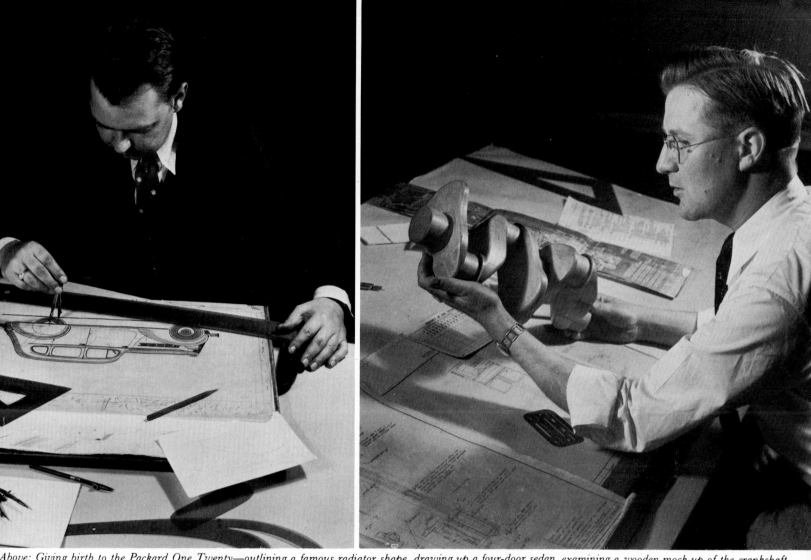

Above: Giving birth to the Packard One Twenty—outlining a famous radiator shape, drawing up a four-door sedan, examining a wooden mock-up of the crankshaft.

Macauley might survey the Packard scene with at least personal satisfaction. The "only gentleman in the automobile business" had put his gentle hand upon the marque and skillfully guided it to a position of both real and prestige leadership in its selective market, one that will probably never again be duplicated. For four years his car had outsold General Motors' Cadillac by a ratio of three to one. In 1928 his company's three million shares of common stock had risen to a high of $163.00 per share, before splitting five to one. In 1929 his organization had a net worth of

$63,000,000 and year-end earnings of $25,000,000. And there was that name, that Packard name, as distinguished as Tiffany's, as American as "Black Jack" Pershing, as solid as the Rockies, as well-known as Babe Ruth's.

But this was 1933, and the sixty-year-old Macauley was facing the most serious challenge of his seventeen years with the Packard Motor Car Company. For the unhappy facts were these, as revealed by the five-year report of his company's operations:

THE PACKARD ONE TWENTY

Introducing the One Twenty for 1935. The Sedan (above), Touring Sedan (below). Right: Mr. and Mrs. Elliott Roosevelt taking delivery of their Convertible Coupe; the One Twenty opening the baseball season in Los Angeles; the Sport Coupe model.

Year	Dollar Sales Volume	Net Income/Net Loss
1929	$107,542,000	+$25,183,000
1931	$29,987,000	-$2,909,000
1932	$15,516,000	-$6,824,000
1933	$19,230,000	+$506,433

The absence of figures for 1930—generally unavailable from any automobile company—was due partly to bank failures; the Packard company lost $656,295.27 in closed banks. Nineteen thirty-three's statistics were deceptive; the company that year made more money on its Government bonds than on its own operations.

The outlook was bleak. Packard stock had slid to under two dollars a share. The fine car market, loosely identified as vehicles with pricetags in excess of two thousand dollars, was down to two percent of total automobile sales. Packard would sell 9081 cars in 1933, a handsome 38.4 percent of the luxury car market, but a dismal six-tenths of one percent of all domestic sales.

Nineteen thirty-four didn't promise to be much better, indeed it would prove even worse, with yet another devastating net loss. What was Packard to do? With history's handy hindsight, one can explore the options or lack of them available to the company.

Question. Should Packard have continued with the Model 900, this car at $1800 effectively breaking the $2000 price barrier? Answer. The Model 900 was indeed a smaller, less expensive, high quality product, an undeniable bargain, one of the best Packard ever offered. But inching under the $2000 mark was not the answer. Eighteen hundred dollars was still too high a price to effectively stimulate sales.

Question. Could the company have leaned on any diversified subsidiaries to carry it through the storm? Answer. No, Packard had none.

Question. Should Packard have further upgraded its product in an attempt to secure an even larger portion of the luxury car market? Both Cadillac and Marmon were offering V-16's, for example. Answer. How much further could Packard improve its automobiles, given the state of the art in 1933? Its Twelve was an incredibly fine car. To design and tool up for an addition of four more cylinders would have been a fanciful frivolity that was, at best, both unnecessary and wasteful.

Question. Should the company have simply hung on, continuing to produce its high quality lines, gambling that the luxury trade would be back in force in a year or two? Answer. There was no indication whatsoever that this would come to pass, indeed that the high-priced market would ever return to pre-Depression levels. Moreover, to have proceeded as before would have been analogous to doing nothing, and Packard management was responsible not only to itself but to its employees and stockholders. There were 107,000 of the latter; next to General Motors, Packard was the most widely owned automobile company in the nation.

Question. Should Packard have more fully explored the areas of cost cutting in its operations and production? Answer. That would have helped only minimally. The company's Liberty engine experience during World War I had impressed upon Macauley the automated assembly concept and through the Twenties he had brought this practice gradually into play at Packard. Massive cost cutting in the area of production would only have made the high quality Packard a lesser car—and that couldn't even be considered.

So there was Packard in 1933, a company geared to making one product to meet a selective portion of one market. And the Depression had effectively taken its market away, or at the very least diminished it to the extent that the company was now its virtual captive, and survival was a question mark. But Packard had another option.

"Into [a] new and untried middle ground Packard cast its fortunes," the company would say. "A new era was born. In the depths of depression Packard placed all her rich store of tradition and prestige upon the table and bet it against a new car for the lower priced field."* Alvan Macauley put it more succinctly in his report to stockholders published on March 27th, 1934. The recent general improvement in the automobile market, he said, benefited principally those manufacturers of lesser-priced cars and Packard was about to join them, "to provide a greater use for our manufacturing facilities, by marketing a wider range of products for the benefit not only of the public but our distributors and the company as well. . . . We started some time ago the development of this lower priced car. The results are encouraging. We cannot say at this time when these new cars will be available. We still have research and development work to do, but we are forging ahead with a great deal of energy and enthusiasm. When we believe that they are as perfect as we know how to make them, and superior to the price class competition they

---

*"Lower priced field" is misleading, but that was the phrase Packard used most frequently in advertising and internal memoranda. Indeed, as the board minutes of May 16th, 1934 indicate, Packard even went to the superlative: "The president showed the board a clay model of our lowest priced SX-car and discussed with the board its design and the progress of our development work. . . ." The Packard company, however, clearly had no intention of competing with Ford, Chevrolet or Plymouth—and thus "medium" or "popular" priced would be more accurate. The term "lower priced" will be used hereafter only when citing the Packard company in direct quotation. Doubtless Packard's use of the term was simply to indicate a price range below its Senior models.

will have to meet, we intend then to get their manufacture under way."

The press carried the news in April.

The junior eight model idea was already several years old; before Wall Street's crash Macauley had loftily discussed a $28 million expansion program aimed at broadening Packard's lines. Now, with some general guidelines in mind, and a more modest $6.2 million fund allotted, came the awesome task of designing, engineering, testing, costing, producing and marketing a type of automobile totally unfamiliar to the company. Alvan Macauley decided he needed help.

Enter Max Gilman, initially as vice-president of distribution, within a few months as general manager, Macauley relinquishing to him his old title. Gilman had been a Packard man since 1919, when he sold the company's trucks in Brooklyn. From there he had traveled to Packard accessories, handling same for Packard's New York distributorship, and up the ladder to the vice-presidency of sales in that operation. He was a tough, shrewd and aggressive businessman who, through the years, had come to be known around Detroit as "that hardboiled guy in New York." It was a description he relished; among his favorite pastimes in the latter city, it was said, was cruising the streets in an old used touring car in search of cabbies whose driving offended him. Upon spotting one, he would urge it dexterously into an El pillar—and be off in search of another. In Detroit he wouldn't have time for such vigilant merry-making. He was a rough diamond, as utterly unakin to Alvan Macauley as a V-8 Ford to a V-12 Packard, but his credentials had to be respected. If what he said rankled and often embarrassed the dignified Packard management, he was nonetheless a man who could get things done. And at East Grand Boulevard now there was a lot to do. Max Gilman was Alvan Macauley's ramrod.

The venerable Jesse Vincent remained his vice-president of engineering, and he, together with chief engineer Clyde Paton, were already immersed in the project. And they decided they too needed help. Paton, an active and respected member of the Society of Automotive Engineers, suggested several fellow members to assist in developing and costing their new design in terms of high volume production, a process Packard people knew little about. On March 1st Earl H. Smith had joined up. He had previously been with Pontiac as assistant chief engineer, in which position he had been instrumental in the design of that company's 1933 eight. Effecting an organization and developing the program by which the new Packard would be brought into being was his charge. Assisting him was Erwin L. Bare, from Hupp, whose domain was the new Packard bodies—and E.A. Weiss, a Willys graduate, whose realm was the chassis. Other young lions came, mostly from General Motors, to teach Packard secrets it had never had the need to know before. By late in the first quarter of 1934 they had invaded the sacrosanct Packard engineering department to study the Vincent-Paton guidelines. And a department away, in the cost division, Edwin H. Johnson (also formerly with Pontiac and renowned as a cost engineer) stood at the ready, with six assistants, each a specialist (in machine shop procedures, in sheet metal, in body building, in trim, in accounting, in car weights).

The original management target called for a Packard weighing no more than 3000 pounds and destined to sell for approximately $850. The new men of Packard looked at what the old men of Packard had come up with and said it couldn't be done. Both weight and price goals would have to be modified. There was the expected clash: cost experts versus management. Each time the former group would remove or modify a design or component, the latter would insist it not be altered since same was *de rigueur* for a Packard, regardless of its price. Yes, all wool upholstery was required in closed cars. Of course, leather seat cushions should be offered in the Convertible Coupe. Obviously, all "loose" body parts had to be painted in sets to ensure a color match. Incontrovertibly, Colonel Vincent wanted aluminum pistons. And so on. Packard found itself able only to compromise to a certain extent—and no further. If the car had to be priced a hundred or so more dollars than others in the price class at which it was aimed, then it would simply be so priced. That case was closed.

Meanwhile the company had ended its search for the man to produce the new Packard. All that had gone before would prove valueless without someone having the finesse to put the car into true mass production, again an area in which Packard experience was lacking. Enter now George T. Christopher, as assistant vice-president (under E.F. Roberts) for manufacturing, and production manager for the new venture. He was six feet tall, weighed 190 pounds, "had a friendly twinkle in his eyes," so *Motor News* would report, "and a cigar in his hand is as much of him as the glasses on his nose." *Fortune* magazine would find him "sandy skinned, muscular and profane"—it became his wont to refer to Packard's prestige line as "that goddam senior stuff." A production man's production man, he was the son of an Indiana coal miner, had a mechanic's background and an engineering degree. Cost control he regarded as a religion. At Oldsmobile, at Pontiac, at Buick, he had practiced it with a zealot's fervor. He would do no less at Packard.

Shortly before Christopher's arrival, Macauley had consolidated the assembly of the Senior lines in one of the two main production buildings, leaving the other facility—previously the Senior body plant—gutted and ready for layout with the equipment necessary for the Junior line. Actually, the benefits derived from this were two-fold: First, production of the Senior line could now be streamlined resulting in some increased efficiency, and second, Christopher had a completely empty space in which to perform his magic, concerning himself only with the physical size limitations of the building. Into this he pulled together—and in only

Chassis assembly in the new Junior Packard

ninety days—what was then one of the most compact and efficiently mechanized automobile production plants in the industry.

"If you have not been through the Packard factory in recent years," Joseph Geschelin reported in the *Automotive Industries* issue of November 3rd, 1934, "a visit today will astonish you . . . Apart from the familiar walls on Grand Boulevard, the plant is entirely new inside. Some inkling of the change must have been sensed when Packard announced to the public its plan for a general house cleaning but only those in the inner circle knew the whole story." The Seniors in one building—the Main Division, as it was called—and the Juniors in another, and seldom would the twain meet; there seemed no way of blending the varying methods of assembly in the same facility. Both Senior and Junior groups would, however, utilize common facilities in iron foundry, aluminum foundry, forge shop, plant engineering and maintenance factory, woodworking mills, chemical and testing laboratories, heat treating departments, stamping factory, die shop, power house, engineering research and testing laboratories, metal finishing and plating plant and the service department.

This left the Junior plant to manufacture its own engines, transmissions, steering gears, rear axles and countless chassis parts. All this would be done on the first floor of the Junior plant, and the operation was to prove remarkably effective. Even such things as complete baskets of fully lapped and mated transmission components would be delivered by conveyor to the individual assembly point. The finest and most modern equipment was brought in for grinding, milling, broaching, burring, tapping, and the thousands of other operations necessary to the manufacture of an automobile. And Macauley and Christopher insured their investment by insisting all new equipment be flexible enough to adapt to various production changes that would develop through future model years. Packard had long been noted for its contributions to machine shop practices: It would contribute again with its new Junior car project.

On the second floor was the body assembly operation. Major body components would be routed from the stamping plant, again by conveyor, then fitted, welded, washed and painted in one continuously moving line. Loose body parts—fenders, splasher panels and hoods, for example—were to be moved in single car sets to their respective paint areas. Trimming and upholstering work would be done on the second floor as well—with all efforts directed to the ever consuming "body drop" where car body would disappear from view to join up with its chassis on the first floor. Withal, it was quite something.

Quite something too, for Packard, was the new sales manager Alvan Macauley hired for the Junior line: Bill Packer, the popular, brash and hefty fellow who had high pressured sales so effectively for Chevrolet. In a day when Chrysler Corporation refused to allow its executives to take

The One Twenty engine—in manufacture, on test stands, and being fitted to frame.

Mounting the grille-fender assembly, One Twenty bodies in the spray booths.

to the air and General Motors did so only reluctantly, Bill Packer owned and flew his own plane—which from Packard's point of view was probably a plus, for his early mission was in the field. What Packer called "fast closing and intelligent closing pressure" would be a new strategy for most Packard dealers, schooled through the years in the Macauley soft sell and velvet glove approach. But what had served a dealer well with the lap robe trade would scarcely be effective in Packard's new arena. Installment selling, too, would have to be encouraged, heretofore accounting for only a third of Packard's sales, as against the industry's two-thirds.

Another challenge awaiting Packer was to pick up the pieces of the company's sales outlets. The distributor network had held together solidly through the early years of the Depression, but of late there had been slippage. Packer would reverse the trend, bringing in over 1200 new dealers in three years. By 1939 he would treble the field network over pre-Junior Packard days.

Everything up to now had cost money, a lot of it, which Macauley had forthrightly spent—some $3,541,500 already, nearly half of Packard's net loss for 1934 and nearly eighteen percent of the company's working capital reported the year before. It was a very large gamble.

The new car was introduced the first week of January 1935. The company's survival depended upon its success.

In its show edition, *Packard News* bannered "Weather 120⁰ AND EVERY DEGREE A PACKARD ONE." That was the new Packard's name, the One Twenty, that figure the car's wheelbase length. It was, compared to its senior brothers, a small Packard. But by contemporary standards, it wasn't truly a small car. In its original seven body styles, the vehicle dry weighed from 3385 to 3515 pounds, and each was in excess of sixteen feet in length.

The One Twenty foundation was a massive rigid frame, the U-shaped channel center X-bracing reinforced at its juncture, both top and bottom, by two heavy riveted gusset plates. The outer four ends of this X-frame ran out to, and were both riveted and welded to, six-inch-deep (9/64-inch thick) U-channel side rails. The closure formed by this double U-shaped combination provided a sturdy front frame box member which extended forward to the front cross member. Working rearward, at approximately the bell housing location, was a second, removable member. Further to the rear, a Z-type section joined the side rails just behind the frame kick-up. From this third member, two channels ran parallel to the side rails and tied into a final U-channel cross member at the rear. This entire assembly resulted in a twist-free structure with a generous safety factor to meet the intended loadings the car would encounter.

At the front of this frame, Packard engineers hung their first mass-produced independent front suspension. They named it "Safe-T-fleX" and boasted that it was "the result of years of development work during which all of the best designs of both Europe and America had been carefully analyzed and judged." *Automotive Industries* said that it "differs from other designs" and called it "outstanding"—*The New York Times*, with a bit less restraint, called it "unique." But whatever it was called, the fact that it was a triumph, in those days when successful designing of i.f.s. was still something of a black art, is of little doubt.*

Basically, Safe-T-fleX was of the parallel-arm/coil-spring school of suspension design. The upper arms were double acting Delco shock absorbers bolted to the frame side rails; the singular lower arms were mounted at the front cross member by means of a rubber-type frictionless bearing at the inner end. At the outer ends, two steel rods—called torque arms—ran rearward and their rear ball-type tips were enclosed in hollow rubber spheres bolted to the bottom of the frame side rails at approximately the cowl. These arms were designed to protect the alignment of the front wheel spindle from braking loads and rear-driven impact and seemed to be a key in guaranteeing the happy fact of front-end low maintenance enjoyed by One Twenty owners. As for the torque arms, this was doubtless an example of overengineering by a company new to the i.f.s. business—though it is interesting to note that the stabilization concept is still in use today on certain four wheel drive Ford trucks.

The One Twenty's steering gear was Packard's own design, a worm and roller affair, with a ratio of 18.4 to one providing a light feel by contemporary standards. The car had a surprisingly short turning radius: 19.5 feet. The differential employed was based on Packard's well-known 45° Angleset hypoid principle with standard ratios of 4.36 to one or 4.54 to one (depending upon body style).

Rear suspension was by semi-elliptic, ten leaf, 1¾-inch by 54-inch rear shackled springs. They were heavily greased during assembly, then wrapped in canvas and finally covered in lightweight terneplate metal jackets. Double-acting rear Delcos were used and tied together by a ride stabilizer bar to hold body roll to a minimum.

The One Twenty was one up on its more prestigious companions being put together in that other building in utilizing Packard's first commercially offered hydraulic brakes. These were internal expanding concept, providing a total surface area of 182 square inches and were troublefree from the beginning.

The engine was typically Packard, basically an L-head in-line eight (3¼ by 3⅞ bore and stroke) displacing 257 cubic inches and developing 110 hp at 3850 rpm, with 203 foot-pounds of torque at 2000 rpm,

---

*This writer's One Twenty has put up better than 200,000 miles and the only known service to its front end through the years has been king pin rebushing; the entire assembly still runs shimmy free with excellent patterns of tire wear.

The body drops and the One Twenty thereafter moves on to final assembly.

Driving away the 1935 One Twenty (above); the 1936 being driven away (below). Page opposite: Shipping the One Twenty (the '36 model at the top, '35's below).

through a fully counterbalanced 90-pound crank. With its full floating aluminum pistons, austenitic exhaust valves, Packard-Ricardo aluminum head (in either 6.5 to one or optional 7.0 to one compression ratios), it proved to be another quiet, smooth running Jesse Vincent creation. At the Proving Grounds in Utica, Charlie Vincent was keeping his brother honest, to the extent that the in-line in question had to prove itself more acceptable than some V-8's under consideration for a time for the One Twenty.

Like other mechanical aspects of Packard's new Junior, the engine design was straightforward, sufficiently sound to endure, with only slight modifications, up through the 1947 model year. By today's standards, this eight would be considered understressed and "detuned," but this has proved a blessing to the collector who will find it long lived and, as an added fillip, comparatively easy to work on. Indeed, the only point of complaint might be that, because the engine is so low placed in the chassis, straightening up after working on the distributor, for example, can be a rather painful experience.

The One Twenty's power was fed back through a soft ten-inch single plate dry disc clutch to a rugged three-speed transmission. Shifting through the long floor cane was both smooth and positive. Positive, too, was the external Packard identification. Styling left no doubt as to the manufacturer of this car. There, on the One Twenty, was the familiar grille and red hexagonal hubcaps, and above the grille a hood ornament was placed, resembling the yet-to-come Buick bullet and ring idea, but *sans* ring.* Delicately cast chrome-plated louvers were sited at the frontal edge of the hood's side panels, and small chrome moldings followed the tops of the teardrop headlights to terminate at their rear tip. When viewed closely at the leading edges, these tiny moldings revealed a diminutive image of the V-shaped Packard grille.

Internal examination of the body revealed Packard's continued belief in the harmonious structural benefits of wood and steel construction. Floor sills and roof rails were made of selected hardwoods, while rumble seat lids and wheel cover lids (on some models) also depended upon wood support.

Bodies—offered in nine lacquer colors—were anchored to chassis at twenty-four points for further stiffness and were heavily insulated for blessed quiet. Interiors were all-wool broadcloth, with tasteful nickel

*This was available for the introductory model year only. Later Junior Packards might be seen with the standard "Baled Feather" ornament—or the pelican or the Goddess of Speed, the latter probably more appropriately. Both the latter mascots were accessories, of course, and available at dealerships for both Junior and Senior lines. Although the pelican was designed specifically for the Senior cars (and was in use before the Juniors arrived), one would doubt that a dealer ever refused to sell one to a One Twenty buyer requesting it.

and black hardware. All wool deep pile carpets were found in the rear seat area of sedans, while a heavy rubber mat was used up front. Such details as a rear foot rest, robe rail, assist straps, dome light and other convenience items were also seen to in the new One Twenty.

Body styles (with passenger capacities in parentheses) and prices (at the time of introduction in January 1935) were as follows:

Business Coupe (2)	$ 980
Convertible Coupe (2-4)	$1070
Sport Coupe (2-4)	$1020
Touring Coupe (5)	$1025
Sedan (5)	$1060
Club Sedan (5)	$1085
Touring Sedan (5)	$1095

Although a few exhibition models had been built earlier for automobile shows, actual production—so Max Gilman told *The New York Times*—would commence the week of January 20th. By the second week in February came the announcement that the cars had begun rolling off the assembly line, the very first one driven off—with a promotional fanfare, of course—by Detroit mayor Frank Couzens. In the meantime, F.H. McKinney was coming up with some rather provocative advertising—often utilizing cartoon themes—along with this-is-it-America themes.* And Alvan Macauley was overseeing that the car would be worth all the hoopla Packard was creating for it.

In a memo dated February 15th, 1935 and relating to a conversation of the day before, Macauley advised Charlie Vincent: "You are the only judge as to when a new product has been sufficiently tested. We will want you to talk over with us your plans, but in the long run I want you to be able to say that you had ample opportunity to test new product. This may seem expensive at the start, but what we must do is to cut down to the very minimum service allowances for returned parts, labor costs and what not, after cars have been delivered. It is absolutely essential that we find out the weak point of our cars at the earliest possible moment and to that end we are authorizing Mr. Page to place immediately in the Harper Garage up to ten of the new cars in the hands of selected men." And, as an afterthought almost, Macauley appended, "This refers, of course, to the Packard One Twenty." Not that Charlie Vincent would have any doubt.

Nor anyone else for that matter. The new Packard was a smash, phenomenally. Ten thousand orders had been received before a single car

---

*In advertising, incidentally, the model name was often given in figures as "120," although brochures and catalogues and management memos generally spelled the number out, as it shall be here.

was ready for delivery. By the end of May, Packard had retailed 2844 more cars than it had during the entire preceding calendar year, and the next month's end saw a second assembly line installed in the One Twenty plant in an attempt to catch up with unfilled orders. George Christopher was quite beside himself. (He would remain there for almost a year; by April 1st of 1936 Max Gilman would still be reminding him of unfilled orders, some 7500 of them now—and Christopher would struggle manfully to increase production from 240 to 342 units per day.)

As a newcomer in this price field, Packard of course had started dead last; by the end of 1935 the company had rocketed to third place. The competition, just as naturally, had not been caught unaware. Cadillac had reduced prices on its LaSalle to $1225 (down from $1495 of the year previous) and doubled 1934 LaSalle sales to 11,775 for 1935. But Packard more than doubled LaSalle, with production of 25,000 of its new car, and that figure reached by September model changeover time.

In its cover story on Alvan Macauley in early November of 1935, *Time* magazine itemized the reasons the man was smiling: In that year's first nine months his company produced 31,987 cars, a staggering 760.75 percent increase over the same period in 1934; during that same nine months Packard made $776,000, the twelve-month of 1934 had seen a loss of $7,290,000; Packard's 15,000,000 shares touched a high the week previous of 7½, the previous year's low being 2¾, with Macauley, as holder of 339,245 shares, increasing his net worth by $1,500,000; the new One Twenty was effectively the reason for all the foregoing; plans for 1936 called for 9000 Senior Packards and 70,000 Juniors, which would better the best previous Packard year of 1928 during which some 50,000 cars had been produced. Actually, *Time* should have waited a month or so. As it happened, Packard would exceed the 1928 figure in 1935, producing 52,045 cars. No other automobile company in America could approach the magnitude of this Packard growth year. As Alvan Macauley understated, "We look with confidence to the year ahead of us . . . We feel that we are in a splendid position to share in any improvement in general prosperity." But this gentle man of Packard did offer a bit of a boast: "We do not believe a quicker job of getting into profitable production with a new car was ever before accomplished." He was probably right.

Understatement, tinged with equal parts enthusiasm, came the One Twenty's way as well, via England where the idea of testing and reporting on new car performance was a studied art. "A £500 PACKARD," headlined *The Autocar*, noting in its initial report that "it is naturally to be expected that manufacturers possessing so good a reputation will not prejudice their name by putting out a smaller and less expensive car with a lower standard of manufacture." By road test time a few months later, the magazine was convinced that Packard had not done so. Viewing comparisons with the bigger Packards odious but inevitable, *The Autocar* concluded by saying, "In short, anyone knowing the make and its reputation can scarcely give higher praise to this new [model] than to say that it feels a Packard in its whole behaviour on the road . . . more particularly in the way it does its work than in what it actually achieves in performance, excellent though that is in relation to the engine size and to a weight which, in Packard style, is fairly heavy, giving a solid kind of car that feels roadworthy. The performance, indeed, is far more than ade-

quate. The maximum speed . . . closely approaches a genuine 85 mph. Points that matter much more are the extremely easy traveling up to as much as 65 to 70 mph, with the engine all but inaudible, and certainly not felt." The magazine did cavil about the speedometer reading, "unduly high, due possibly, it is understood, to some error in the gearing of its drive, following a change made in the rear-axle ratio during the final development of the model. Certainly some such explanation seems

Bill Packer, his plane and his selling program. Max Gilman, looking rather smug—and understandably so—beside a Touring Sedan (120-B) for 1936.

Feature and
SELL
Down Paymen

WINDOW SIGNS
NEWSPAPER ADS
RADIO SPOT
ANNOUNCEMENTS
DOWN PAYMENT AND
MONTHLY PAYMENTS ON

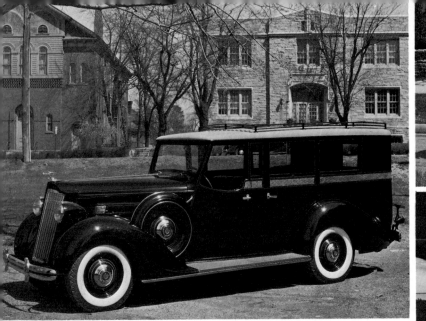

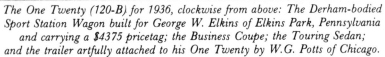

The One Twenty (120-B) for 1936, clockwise from above: The Derham-bodied Sport Station Wagon built for George W. Elkins of Elkins Park, Pennsylvania and carrying a $4375 pricetag; the Business Coupe; the Touring Sedan; and the trailer artfully attached to his One Twenty by W.G. Potts of Chicago.

reasonable, since the error was beyond normal practice.''

Quibbles aside, *The Autocar* assessment was, of course, rather well received at East Grand Boulevard. Indeed a Packard salesman wrote the magazine telling it like it was: "Perhaps it was the nervous tempo of a typical American morning sales conference—that hotbed of synthetic enthusiasm which is anathema to the British temperament; perhaps it was this writer's British sub-consciousness, he having lived half of his life there. What matters? *The Autocar* Road Test of August 9th being passed round slowly subsided, to be superseded, now by approving chuckles alternating with broad grins, and then by blank astonishment as the quaintly phrased and coolly technical report gradually assumed intelligible form. . . . Such eloquence, with no direct sales appeal! Such effort, and no apparent sales objective! The idea of the One Twenty standing squarely on its own merits, without the aid of good old American bombast, was simply incomprehensible. . . . The charm of this report, to the American who knows his Packard One Twenty, lies quite as much in its quaint phraseology as in the novel reactions it produces. Lulled into a totally strange awareness of poetry in motion as your reporter gracefully pours out the attributes of a car which to us is just 'a honey of a wagon,' we stand aghast at the designation of an engine that is 'entirely happy,' brakes that are 'not fierce,' and a car that feels 'in one piece.' " Aghast maybe, but utterly delighted as well.

Equally pleasurable was the report of the motoring correspondent for *The Times* of London: "The engine, like the whole machine, is silky in its smooth running. There is never any sign of harshness, laziness, or complaint. All the controls—except the hand brake, which is only needed for parking—have that feeling of lightness combined with progressive positiveness in operation which proves the car of quality and tradition. The clutch made no objection to the standing start tests and was not heavy to work. The change-speed lever is well placed, and straight-through changes can be made simply and without a sound. The steering is just what I like—a fairly low ratio but very light and consistently so throughout a lock exceptionally wide yet always firm and steady enough to give accuracy and a feeling of confidence."

American automotive journalists did not, alas, bother with performance critiques on new cars in those days—though a few magazine reports did allude to the One Twenty's admirable fuel consumption, ranging from 21 mpg at 20 mph to 12.5 mpg at 70—but that was a matter solved by Packard promotion in publishing excerpts from the letters of satisfied One Twenty owners, one from each of the forty-eight states. A sampling might suffice. From Lloyd Simon of Tucson, Arizona: "the acme of perfection at the price." From Florence Cagle of San Francisco: "I like my One Twenty because it starts so quickly, runs so smoothly and parks so easily. In fact, I like everything about my new Packard." From W.J. Weaver of Bridgeport, Connecticut: "It has worlds of power and rides

like a cradle." From Fred V. Chute of Chicago: "Full of pep, speed and comfort. Satisfaction with a capital 'S'." From Samuel S. Boyd of Portland, Maine: "Expressed in a few words: the car of effortless ease." From Dr. A.C. Erdman of Kansas City, Missouri: "You certainly did me a great favor, selling me the Packard 120. Intend buying another for my wife." From D. Wort of Kearney, Nebraska: "The 120 gets me there—like the man on the flying trapeze—with the greatest of ease." From Richard W. Brown of Concord, New Hampshire: "My 120 is fast and has a very good getaway, so good in fact that the Motor Vehicle Department are interested in this machine for police work." From John Barton of Sioux Falls, South Dakota: "It's a knockout. The more I drive it the better I like it."

The One Twenty for 1936 (introduced in September of '35 and designated 120-B by the factory) was even nicer. Packard's engineering group had done its homework well on the introductory car and the new one debuted with only a handful of mechanical refinements. Most significant among these was an increase of ⅜-inch in stroke to bring cubic inch displacement to 282, with brake horsepower developed at 3800 rpm up nine percent to a coincidental "120." This created a new slogan—"a horsepower for every inch"—and resulted, as *Time* magazine said, "in the sales-point, odd for Packard, that the new One Twenty cars can 'run away from a Ford.' " With the increase, the standard rear axle ratio was reduced ten percent from 4.54 to 4.09. Although the 4.54 remained available as an option, the 4.09 in conjunction with the larger engine provided a smoother, more tractable combination offering longer engine life and increased fuel economy.

An improvement too was the new cellular radiator, designed for a twenty percent increase in cooling efficiency. Minor refinements were also effected in the accelerator linkage, clutch facing, gearshift lever mechanism and coil spring rate.

Outwardly, the new One Twenty did away with the rear-hinged "suicide" front doors, and added heavier bumpers with guards. Color selections were up to fifteen, and an entirely new body type—the Convertible Sedan—was introduced, bringing One Twenty offerings to eight, as indicated below with prices as of the September 1935 introduction:

Business Coupe (2)	$ 990
Convertible Coupe (2-4)	$1110
Sport Coupe (2-4)	$1030
Touring Coupe (5)	$1040
Sedan (5)	$1075
Club Sedan (5)	$1090
Touring Sedan (5)	$1115
Convertible Sedan (5)	$1395

Writing in the Chicago *American* of the new One Twenty after a week's drive in a demonstrator, automotive journalist Herbert D.

Tommy Milton and the One Twenty Convertible Coupe pacing the 500 in May

Wilson allowed, "I formed a very definite opinion of the car—namely, that Packard engineers have attempted in their second model . . . to perfect every detail of the car. . . . In this attempt they have been notably successful, for the 1936 model is keen to look at and a joy to drive."

The Autocar editors tried this new Packard too, and were as impressed as the year previous; the car traveled at sixty "in a way which suggests it could keep up the speed all day if the roads permitted and tire neither the occupants nor itself. Still at 70 the driver can feel that everything is happy, and in consequence, ground may be covered rapidly when so required. Yet, by contrast, it is a beautiful 'pottering' car, being so soft, so easily controlled, and needing so little attention from its driver." On Memorial Day Tommy Milton was the driver and a One Twenty Convertible Coupe the pace car for the 1936 Indianapolis 500.

By now George Christopher was Packard's vice-president of manufacturing, taking over that post when E.F. Roberts retired in July of 1935. And, in January of '36, Bill Packer was appointed general sales manager, his new position, *The New York Times* intimated, the result of his "noteworthy record in charge of . . . the low-priced Packard line." The first six months of 1936 saw Packard with net earnings of $3,520,-128, a considerable jump from the $290,460 for the corresponding period of 1935. By August Max Gilman was announcing an ongoing company expansion program, at a cost in excess of $5,100,000, to double the

United Airlines' pilots preferred the One Twenty, Packard discovered; one Captain Sullivan posed with his, models from Bonwit Teller with a Convertible Sedan.

production capacity of the Packard plant.

Meanwhile advertising manager F.H. McKinney was being expansive too, and excessive, or so a lot of Packard people thought. "We have an Episcopalian reputation," McKinney said, "and we want to do business with Methodists." He thought the air waves might help, and with a little caution at first advanced Packard sponsorship of Walter Damrosch and the NBC Symphony, followed by a series of radio programs headlined by opera, concert and movie star Lawrence Tibbett (who also was shown in print ads congenially behind the wheel of his One Twenty Convertible Coupe). With the new car for '36, however, McKinney really let loose. With Young & Rubicam's assistance, he snared Fred Astaire—described in *Automotive Industries* as a "popular entertainer with diversified talents as a singer, actor, instrumentalist and light comedian"—as host for an hour series to be sponsored by Packard and broadcast over "the N.B.C. red network, Tuesdays from 9:30 to 10:30 p.m., Eastern time." It was a grand idea, Astaire had the savoir faire to complement perfectly the Packard image. But McKinney was determined the introductory Packard program should be a blockbuster and so enlisted the services of a comedian of immense popularity, but one who also spent a good deal of time joking about his old Maxwell. Jack Benny was a favorite of Max Gilman's, but not of the aesthetic Alvan Macauley. *Fortune* magazine reported that the first broadcast of

Packard's new hour was sufficiently disheartening for Macauley "as to shroud his office in gloom for days." The "less controversial" Charlie Butterworth was substituted for comedy interludes on subsequent hours but, so *Fortune* commented, "to Mr. Macauley (and perhaps to some old Packard-owning families) the whole thing still seems distressingly infra dig. The weekly difficulty of confecting a show that will command a national audience and still pass Packard's rigorously imposed standards of taste caused it to be known in Hollywood, where it is produced, as 'the grief program.' It will probably be a long time before Packard is really at home in mass appeals."

That may have been true, but Packard assuredly was feeling very much at home with its new-found good fortune, courtesy of the One Twenty. Sales for calendar year 1936 totaled 83,226 units, an increase of 37,701 or 82.8 percent over 1935. The company now ranked ninth among American motorcar producers, up from eleventh in 1935 and eighteenth in '34. Profits for 1936, at $7,053,220, were more than double the 1935 figure. The company produced 54.4 percent more cars, and there were 35.0 percent more dealers selling them. As a 1936 Packard brochure rather smugly noted, "a late and unlamented depression brought us all face to face with critical questions"—and Packard was convinced it had answered them well. Moreover, if '36 was good, 1937 promised to be even better. The One Twenty now had a baby brother. 467

CHAPTER TWENTY-TWO

A COMPANY HEADED FOR PROSPERITY

The Junior Packards

The Six and One Twenty

1937-1942

AUTHOR: RICHARD K. PHILLIPS

On September 3rd, 1936, at the Masonic Temple in Detroit, was gathered together what the press called "one of the largest conventions ever held in the history of the automobile industry." More than 4000 men of Packard—from the company sales and service organizations throughout the United States and Canada as well as six foreign countries—amassed there to see the new Packards for '37 and to hear an enthusiastic Alvan Macauley proclaim good times for America and American business for the coming year. "We are accelerating our pace, preparing you for the buying trends of a company headed for prosperity," he exulted. The next day nearly 3000 Packards destined for use as sales demonstrators left East Grand Boulevard—"the largest driveaway of cars ever held," the press also said—for points north, south, east and west, and a hoped-for sales year such as Packard had never before experienced.

The Packard optimism was unalloyed, and much of it centered around a brand-new automobile, "The Car That Will Turn Its Price Class Upside Down," as the brochures proclaimed. In company jargon it was known as the 115-C, the figure denoting the car's wheelbase, the alphabetical letter correlating with that of the new model for its bigger-cylindered brother. For sales and promotional purposes, however, it was called simply the Packard Six.

The new car zeroed in on the target that had been missed by the One Twenty. "A Packard for $795," the ads ballyhooed. "Beyond doubt the most astonishing motor car value ever offered." Competitors then, and historians today, might cavil on the quintessential truth of the latter, but one fact was readily apparent. This was the lowest-priced Packard ever produced. It put the company where the action was, in bumper-to-bumper competition with various models of Pontiac, Oldsmobile, Hudson and Nash Ambassador, among others. The costing fellows at Packard had got their car, and the traditionalists' compromises essentially numbered two, each one a cylinder.

Mechanically, and logically, the Six was closely related to the One Twenty. The frame design was the same concept (though five inches shorter), Safe-T-fleX independent front suspension was employed, four wheel hydraulic brakes installed, and the transmission was the same rugged box proven roadworthy in the One Twenty. (Standard rear axle ratio was 4.36 to one, with the 4.54 available optionally.)

The engine was simply a six-cylinder edition of the One Twenty's eight, an L-head in-line displacing 237 cubic inches and developing 100 brake horsepower. The stroke at 4¼ inches was shared with the bigger car, while the bore at 3-7/16 inches, was slightly larger. Bell housing, timing gear cover, oil strainer, vibration damper, both oil and water pumps, among numerous other components, were borrowed from the One Twenty.

And borrowed too were the looks of the car, the Six bearing more than

a familial resemblance. Actually, from the cowl back, the same basic body shell was used, with major differences in hood and front fender panels which were five inches shorter and bumpers and bumper over-riders which were lighter—and minor differences in chrome trim and interior accoutrements. Among the latter, cost-cutting was effected by the absence of wool broadcloth upholstery, a trip-set on the speedometer and chrome trim on the dashboard. Tires were smaller, and no side-mounted spare was available. Save for the front hood louver, remaining ventilation ports were sheet metal stampings, as opposed to the chrome-plated ornamental hood louvers on the One Twenty. Such concessions to economy in the Packard Six resulted in a model lineup with introductory prices as follows:

Business Coupe (2)	$ 795
Sport Coupe (2-4)	$ 840
Touring Coupe (5)	$ 860
Sedan (5)	$ 895
Club Sedan (5)	$ 900
Convertible Coupe (2-4)	$ 910
Touring Sedan (9)	$ 910
Station Wagon (8)*	$1295

*introduced mid-model year

The new Packard sold like the popular radio program of that era. It was "Gangbusters." During its first model year, some 65,401 Sixes were delivered to new owners, better than fifty percent of whom—a survey by the company revealed—had been former drivers of the "low-priced five" cars. As *Fortune* noted, "Packard was now offering their caviar at less than $1000 a throw"—and it was obvious the buying public had developed a taste for it.

One small problem arose. Alvan Macauley reported to his directors at the board meeting of September 16th, 1936, "that residents in the vicinity of our foundry are complaining about the fumes and noise emanating from the foundry where our capacity has been increased to take care of the production of the new Packard Six. . . . Some of them have approached us offering their property for sale. Others have been threatening court action." It was a situation amicably resolved. To avoid unpleasantness, and to provide for additional space "for parking . . . until it might be needed for manufacturing," the Packard board decided "to just go ahead and buy."

The Six was, the company averred, "a Packard through and through." The One Twenty was now "the luxury car of the lower priced field." The latter for the '37 model year—at the factory it was called the 120-C—was minimally changed from its predecessor. The U-channel members in the frame were altered to I-beams, reportedly increasing frame stiffness some four times over conventional design. (Packard's

ges preceding: The Packard Motor Car Company of New York showroom, with the One Twenty Touring Coupe on center stage, photographed November 1936. bove left: The 1937 Touring Sedans (120-C and 138-CD) compared. Above right: The Packard Six Business Coupe. Below: The One Twenty Touring Sedan.

Above: Bill Packer photographed in Detroit with his personal 1937 One Twenty; on the Pacific Coast, California girls posing with a '37 Convertible Coupe.
Below: Frank McKinney checking over promotion plans; Charles Butterworth and Fred Astaire entertaining radio listeners for Packard over the NBC Red Netw

engineering department obviously had a fixation about solid feel.) And gone in the '37 version was the four-lobe double breaker distributor in favor of the single breaker concept. Outwardly, the new One Twenty was deceptively similar in appearance to its predecessors. But to put it in the collector's parlance, the restorer of a 1937 One Twenty Convertible Coupe, for example, with a comparable 1935 model as a parts car would find the following body parts not interchangeable (some, however, adaptable with modification): bumpers, front fenders, grille, radiator shell, hood, windshield, dashboard, doors, rumble seat lid, left rear fender and hubcaps. Indeed, only the running boards and right rear fender could be directly exchanged, surprisingly.

Another surprise for the One Twenty of '37 was the addition of three models—designated 120-CD, the latter letter denoting deluxe and the cars including as standard equipment such niceties as automatic radiator shutters, sponge-backed carpets, full Marshall springs in the seats, banjo spoke steering wheel, clock, deluxe radiator ornament, extra quality trimming and white wall tires—all for an additional two hundred ten dollars over the comparable 120-C. The One Twenty lineup, with prices effective as of January 1937 (save for the station wagon introduced mid-model year) was, thus:

Model 120-C

Business Coupe (2)	$ 945
Sport Coupe (2-4)	$ 990
Touring Coupe (5)	$1010
Sedan (5)	$1045
Club Sedan (5)	$1050
Convertible Coupe (2-4)	$1060
Touring Sedan (5)	$1060
Convertible Sedan (5)	$1355
Station Wagon (8)	$1485

Model 120-CD

Touring Coupe (5)	$1220
Club Sedan (5)	$1260
Touring Sedan (5)	$1270

A further addition followed in July, two new seven-passenger cars (the Touring Sedan at $1835 and the Touring Limousine at $1985) on a new wheelbase for the One Twenty, 138 inches—these cars designated 138-CD. Interestingly, that latter Junior Packard was priced roughly three hundred dollars more than certain models of the Cadillac Sixty series.

There were other interesting comparisons to be made. And Packard provided a number of these in its series of publications called "Promotional Pointers," produced for the edification of Packard salesmen—and concomitantly Packard prospects. Indignant at an obviously GM-sponsored pamphlet espousing the Oldsmobile L-37 Eight

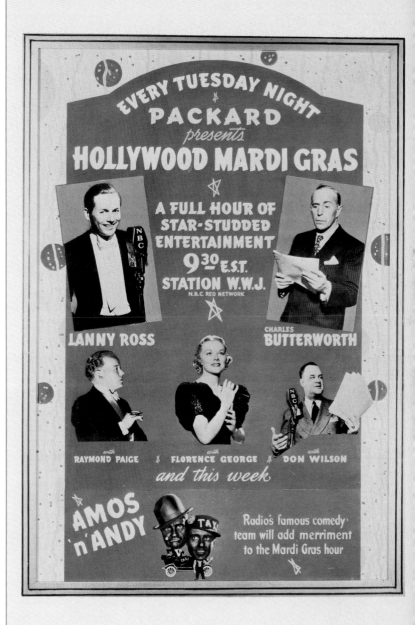

Alvan Macauley, Fortune *suggested, found it "distressingly infra dig," but selling a popular-priced car dictated sponsorship of popular entertainment.*

The Packard One Twenty engine and chassis, as introduced in September 1936.

as a "greater all-around value at a substantially lower price" than the 1937 One Twenty, Packard countered with its own booklet, carrying on its front page photographs of the front ends of both cars to make an aesthetic point courtesy of "the Most Famous Radiator Contour in the World." There was, as they say, no comparison. As for performance, though Oldsmobile was boasting of speeds in the nineties attained at Milford, Packard's experience at Utica showed the L-37 with a maximum only 1.85 mph faster than the One Twenty. At its maximum of 86.8 mph—Packard noted dryly—the Oldsmobile speedometer registered 96.5. "We do not claim that all Oldsmobile speedometers are 'enthusiastic,' " Packard continued, "nevertheless this example indicates how confusing are speed claims based on speedometer readings or mileage figures based on 'long' reading odometers."

Regarding fuel consumption, the faster the two cars were driven the less was the differential in gasoline used—at 60 mph the Oldsmobile registered at 14.2 mpg, the One Twenty at 13.7 mpg—the difference "less than twenty dollars in ten thousand miles of driving." And the Packard didn't use nearly as much pavement to halt in panic stops—128 feet from 60 mph, while the Olds used 165.5.

Likewise the Oldsmobile Six—"the car that has everything," Olds said; a "slightly immoderate" claim, Packard countered—was shown to

474

Safe-T-fleX independent front suspension, shown here on the 1937 chassis.

be outpointed by the Packard Six in "38 examples of Packard's plus quality."

And the poor LaSalle suffered even more ignobly, juxtaposed with the 1937 One Twenty. It was higher in price (by $115), lower in acceleration (0-60 in 20.15 seconds, as contrasted with the One Twenty's 19.8), featured an "enthusiastic" speedometer that overrated the LaSalle's maximum speed potential, and "slightly larger brakes" which nonetheless did not cause the LaSalle to stop any faster than the One Twenty. Further, Packard pooh-poohed, the LaSalle since its inception had been a "car of uncertain caste. . . . for reasons best known to the Cadillac Company," its design concept varying "erratically" from year to year with engine, wheelbase and price changes which "we are not criticizing . . . but we do feel more than a little pride in the progressive constancy that has marked Packard action during the same interval." So much for the competition.

Nineteen thirty-seven was a landmark for Packard. The company produced some 109,518 cars during that calendar year—approximately ninety percent of these the Juniors. Never again in its history would the company have such a prolific twelve months.

Clearly, however, Packard expected to in 1938, for the Junior cars incorporated what *MoToR* called "a variety of improvements" for that 475

Above: Factory drawing of a proposed One Twenty Sport Coupe for 1937.
Below: A station wagon special produced on the '37 One Twenty (120-C) chassis.

model year. Chief among these was the adoption of completely redesigned all-steel bodies, set on wheelbases seven inches longer, the Six up to 122 inches, the One Twenty up to 127. The latter suggested a name change and the "senior" Junior was now called the Packard Eight.

While more inches would be his, the Packard customer this year wouldn't be allowed quite the same variety in body style—the company perhaps now settling on those which had proved most effective—the Six down to five selections, the Eight to nine, as follows, with prices as of July 1937:

	Packard Six	Packard Eight
Business Coupe (2)	$1025	$1160
Club Coupe (4)	$1070	$1205
Touring Sedan* (5)	$1090	$1225
Touring Sedan** (5)	$1120	$1255
Convertible Coupe (4)	$1180	$1295
Convertible Sedan (5)	—	$1575
Touring Sedan Deluxe (5)	—	$1465
Touring Sedan*** (7)	—	$1875
Touring Limousine*** (7)	—	$2025
* = two-door   ** = four-door   *** = 138-inch wheelbase

The cars were heavier (3425 to 3525 pounds in the Six, 3550 to 4245 in the Eight) and noticeably roomier inside, with seat cushions widened for generous increases in shoulder room, and head room front and rear also augmented. In club coupe and convertible coupe guise, the double rear seat lower cushions could be folded up and concealed behind their respective hinged back cushions, for a helpful supplement to trunk baggage space. Outwardly, styling was rounder and softer, following the industry

Below: The Packard Six Station Wagon, introduced during mid-model year 1937

trend. The windshield was divided by a chrome strip running the length of the hood and up into the roof and the teardrop taillights, as featured the previous three model years, had been revised to small vertical units mounted on the lower crown of the rear fenders.

Mechanically, there were numerous refinements. Both Eight and Six employed pressure lubricated mushroom tappets, an external oil filter was introduced to improve upon the function of the crankcase strainer, and a new Tocco-hardened camshaft was utilized. Modifications to the aluminum alloy head of the Eight made for an increased compression ratio of 6.6 to one, with an optional 7.05 to one available.

A sixteenth of an inch was added to the Six's bore, bringing cubic inch displacement up to 245; the 100 brake horsepower figure remained as before, but low speed torque was improved. The standard cast iron head of the Six offered a compression ratio now of 6.52 to one but, like the Eight, a 7.05 to one aluminum option was available.

Underneath both cars, the 45⁰ Angleset differential was eliminated, no longer necessary with the wheelbase lengthening. Completely redesigned were the rear springs whose leaf ends formed into cups at strategic points of which were pads of live rubber plus rubber insulating of spring brackets and shackles—"which provides," *MoToR* said, "a remarkably level ride"—and a rear lateral stabilizer was added to assist the action of the rear roll control bar. Further engineering effort had been directed toward engine cooling, with a heavier water pump, new fan design, an increase in radiator capacity, and cooling tunnels incorporated into the front fenders to assist in expelling heated air out and under the fenders—all of which, Packard asserted, made for " 'desert-mountain' cooling in everyday operation."

In England, *The Autocar* tested the new Six (for some reason, it had not done so with the original) and liked it a lot. The gear change was found "pleasing," though not often necessary to use, the Packard Six performance being a standout on top gear: "It can hold top smoothly in slow traffic, without the thought arising that the engine or transmission is being ill-treated. On a journey the occasions for using the gear lever are few and far between, except when the car has actually been brought to rest. Indeed, it can be started smoothly on top gear, though such a practice is naturally not to be encouraged regularly." The car traveled from 0 to 50 in 15.8 seconds, with a maximum timed speed over a quarter mile of 77.59 mph, a fine performance certainly.

Packard Junior owners were enthralled. Harry Bailey of Spruce Pine, North Carolina wrote that ". . . I know you are interested in knowing just what the Packard Six will do on the highways. On my recent tour of Florida I drove 2028 miles, my gas consumption was 18¾ miles per gallon . . ." And H.O. Farlin of Reading, Pennsylvania said that his Six was his thirty-second automobile and "it has proven to be the cheapest car 'miles per dollar' I ever drove." The Eight got letters too, as from James H. Rolling of Utica, New York: ". . . Last December I turned in my first One Twenty for a new 1938 model. This proves more than anything else the regard I have for the Packard car—as I have never repeated on any car before, and I have been driving since 1914. . . ."

In California, meantime, Earle Anthony was noticing that the Junior Packards were becoming as "popular with movie folk" as the Seniors. And on the East Coast, Young & Rubicam was rounding up a new roster of entertainment worthies for Packard's radio efforts. "HAVE SECURED FOLLOWING GUEST STARS FOR FIRST FOUR PACKARD PROGRAMS

The Packard Six, crafted into a special panel delivery car for an exclusive Detroit shop, and the station wagon-cum-sedan delivery for mail toting at the plant.

With a wheelbase increase for the 1938 model year to 127 inches for the One Twenty (or Eight, as it was called this year), interiors were made conspicuously roomier, as witness the Convertible Coupe, above and left.

STOP"—Y & R's telegram of August 26th, 1937 read—"SEPTEMBER 7 AMOS AND ANDY IN THEIR FIRST MAJOR GUEST APPEARANCE DURING THEIR EIGHT YEARS ON AIR STOP SEPTEMBER 14 MARX BROTHERS MASTER CRAFTSMEN OF NONSENSE WHO HAVE SMASHED BOX OFFICE RECORDS FOR YEARS STOP SEPTEMBER 21 PHIL BAKER THE OLD ACCORDION MAN AND ONE OF BROADWAYS AND RADIOS BIGGEST ATTRACTIONS STOP SEPTEMBER 28 BURNS AND ALLEN SENSATIONAL COMEDY TEAM STOP THESE TOPLINERS OF ENTERTAINMENT WORLD PRESENTED IN ENTIRELY NEW AND DIFFERENT WAY ASSURE SUPREMACY IN VARIETY PROGRAMS FOR PACKARD." F. H. McKinney was delighted. But, sadly, Packard's major domo of advertising and sales was to leave the company suddenly. In June of 1938, after a brief illness, he died at his home in Birmingham, Michigan. The Junior Packards had lost one of their most enthusiastic boosters.

Nineteen thirty-eight wasn't a happy year at the company for another reason. Sales were down. But the fault wasn't Packard's. In the final months of 1937, the economy of the country, after the rally of the few years preceding, had begun to slip again. Industry-wide, automobile production for '38 dropped nearly forty-eight percent below that of 1937. And at Packard, a few more than 50,000 units left the factory, ninety percent of them the Junior models. Their volume muscle provided desperately needed income, but not enough to prevent the company from

experiencing its first annual loss since the introduction of the One Twenty: some $1,638,317.

Part of that loss, however, could be attributed to a massive reorganization of Packard production facilities. The demand for the Junior models since inception had overtaxed the capability of the still-young One Twenty factory. As a result, it was converted into a body plant for all Packard models, bodies now to be carried across a new conveyorized bridge to the main plant for assembly. All units of Packard operation were consolidated in one gigantic, unified facility. Although not married in production, the Juniors and Seniors would now be living together.

Alvan Macauley remained optimistic. On September 19th, 1938 Packard salesmen had again been summoned to Detroit, together with about 250 automobile editors and writers. "During the model year just closed," Packard's president commented, "the industry strove to gear production as closely as possible to sales. As a result it is now well situated to throw its weight into the balance to better business conditions generally." And Packard, he felt, had just the cars to do it. Reginald M. Cleveland, reporting for *The New York Times*, told of "some remarkable demonstrations of riding safety and comfort, attributed to improvements in stabilization and springing" that were staged at Utica for the benefit of the Fourth Estate. And three million dollars worth of the new 1939 Packards were piloted out of Detroit the next day in yet another "largest driveaway the automotive industry has known."

Logic notwithstanding, the One Twenty name was back for the bigger of the Junior cars, and it now shared a common body with the Super Eight. The days of amortizing a multi-thousand-dollar steel body die over a handful of Senior models were fast passing, throughout the industry. The complete lineup, with prices effective September 1938, was as follows:

Augmenting trunk baggage space, the double rear seat lower cushions could be folded up and concealed behind their respective hinged back cushions, this a feature of both Convertible Coupe and Club Coupe, the latter above.

	Packard Six	One Twenty
Business Coupe (2)	$1000	$1200
Club Coupe (4)	$1045	$1245
Touring Sedan* (5)	$1065	$1265
Touring Sedan** (5)	$1095	$1295
Convertible Coupe (4)	$1195	$1390
Convertible Sedan (5)	—	$1700
Touring Sedan (7)	—	$1805
Touring Limousine (7)	—	$1955

* = two-door   ** = four-door

Both Six and One Twenty were substantially the same outside as those for 1938 and standard body offerings remained as before. Most changes were inside and underneath, perhaps the most noticeable of these being the new remote control gearshift lever—coyly called Handishift—under the steering wheel,* although the cane shift was still available if desired. Also new as an option was Packard's first commercially offered over-drive, called Econo-Drive, which garnered praise from *The Autocar* in its road test of the new Six: "No matter what its price, a car could scarce-ly run more quietly and more smoothly, with less evidence of mechanism working. According to the road and the wishes of the driver, 30, 40, 50 or 60 mph on the overdrive are little different as far as suggestion of effort is

---

*The Handishift has been much maligned. The difficulties arose when the rubber grommets at each end of the two idler arms connected to the steering column became excessively worn. When this happened, the movement of the Handishift lever would not correspondingly move the internal sliding gears of the transmission and sloppy, lost motion would result. The rubber grommets were eventually replaced by Packard part number 351589—a kit of new steel shift idler lever bushings—which reduced the wear and thus the problem.

concerned." A point of interest: Both Six and One Twenty could be ordered with a mechanically driven tachometer, Part No. 335909, available only in 1939, and for perhaps no other reason than to offer visual proof of the fourth gear's function to the Econo-Drive owner.

Further engineering efforts were again directed to the rear suspension. The entirely new 1938 rear leaf spring concept was extensively modified for '39. As obsessed as they were with rigidity of frame, Packard engineers were concerned also about car ride. In addition to redesigned rear springs, the transverse link, connected between one frame side rail and the opposite extremity of the rear axle, was now a two-way hydraulic shock absorber. This "fifth" shock was programmed to dampen side shake vibrations as well as reduce wheel dance and oversteering effects. For enhancement of silence in operation, the water pump fan was redesigned and the "repackable" water pump was dropped in deference to a new, permanently lubricated, self adjusting packing version.

"Oh, all cars are pretty much alike today," said the fellow peering out from the photograph in a Packard booklet of 1939 comparing its Six with another "deservedly popular [leader] in the lower medium price field." Because this particular piece of literature was the most typical of all the Packard-versus-competition promotions during these years, it will be quoted at length, as reflective of what was becoming a new Packard tradition—the no-words-minced critique of a marketplace foe vis-à-vis

Junior Packards for 1938, clockwise from above: The Six Touring Sedan; the Eight Touring Sedan; and Eight Touring Limousines (on the 148-inch wheelbase).

the Junior Packard. In this case, the enemy was the Buick Forty. "Here is a revealing profile view of both cars: of the two—doesn't the Packard appear the better poised, the more majestic?... The Packard [trunk] compartment is neatly divided into two sections. Buick, presumably for cost reasons, has omitted the serviceable shelf, which keeps the luggage from becoming scuffed by rubbing on the spare tire.... Probably in an effort to reduce costs ... Buick this year has cut off its frame at the rear axle ... leaving a 35 inch body overhang ... Buick's greater over-all length is likely to make parking more difficult, and will certainly not improve maneuverability in traffic ... [and] does not, as one might suppose, result in more passenger space than Packard for the Packard interior is actually 2½ inches longer from dash pad to the front of the rear back seat cushion ... As months of ownership roll past, we believe that buyers will prefer ... the Packard speedometer which can be read at a glance—to Buick's novel but hard-to-read arrangement in 15 mile steps.... Buick's slightly lower cost may also be partly attributable to the new design of the rear quarter windows. Instead of pivoting as they do in Packard, they slide. Instead of creating an exhaust for smoke and stale air as in the Packard ... the Buick window sends it straight back into the face of the passenger...." And there was, of course, no comparison between the engines or the suspension. The Packard stopped faster (by 57 feet from 60 mph) and was less thirsty (16.5 mpg for the Six, 19 for the Six with Econo-Drive, to 14 for the Buick). Packard conceded the latter was somewhat quicker, 85.35 mph against the Packard's even 80—but "if we interpret performance in terms of an athletic decathlon ... wherein each event like pole vault, broad jump, low hurdles, is given a certain number of points, you will find ... that Packard outstrips its rival in the total—producing the best all around performance in its price

480

class." And providing a precisely figured $122.50 more value for the money than the Buick Forty.

In Packard's booklet limning the two cars the company deemed "tops" in the medium-price/quality-car field—the One Twenty and the LaSalle—Packard zeroed in on a facet of the Junior Packard's evolution which some historians in retrospect have suggested was less than commendable. Style identity was what Packard called it; a lack of progress in style, a loss of modernity by '39 has become the conclusion of contemporary critics of the One Twenty. But, from the vantage of that era, Packard argued its point forcefully: "LaSalle has had no lasting identity of its own . . . look at the 1938 LaSalle as compared with this year's model! About the only similarity is in the name . . . and who can be sure that a sudden fanciful style change won't make the 1939 LaSalle a style orphan—perhaps, before another year passes by?"

The merit of that argument notwithstanding, the year 1939 passed rather well for Packard. More than 75,000 cars departed East Grand Boulevard and the company earned a modest but real net profit of $545,-867, which doubtless would have been higher save for losses incurred in gearing the company for defense contracts.

By now Alvan Macauley had removed himself to the Packard board chairmanship and that "hardboiled guy from New York" was the company's new president. Max Gilman felt comfortable in his new chair, George Christopher continued his lordship of manufacturing and Bill Packer was now vice-president of distribution—these gentlemen, unquestionably, having risen in the Packard corporate galaxy with the star of the Junior models. And that star really shone in model year 1940, with over 90,000 of the new Junior cars sold.

Packard had been the first in the field to introduce its new models, on August 8th of '39, and Max Gilman promised that they would be accompanied by the "largest volume of newspaper advertising" the company had ever placed. Price reductions all around, with $120 and $150 off the Junior lines, were effected—and although these doubtless mattered not at all to Hedy Lamarr, she bought a One Twenty Convertible Coupe anyway. And it was that model, incidentally, which was the first prize in Packard's widely promoted "Photograph America's Most Beautiful Car—and Win It!" contest.

Whether the superlative represented utter truth in advertising probably depends upon the eye of the beholder, but there can be little doubt that the new Packard Junior models were beauties. Press comment ran along the lines of "more attractively styled," but that didn't say enough, the tall, narrow Packard grille being both flanked and complemented by smaller fender grilles, the teardrop headlights previously mounted on pods now lengthened and settled down directly onto the fenders. Outboard of these units, which incidentally utilized sealed beams, torpedo-shaped parking lights were affixed to the fender crowns.

A Junior Eight for 1938, with rather fetching custom coachwork by Rollston.

Tradition was served, but these new Packards indeed looked all-new.

For no other reason apparently than to be congruent with the One Twenty (and the newly designated Senior models), the Six was renamed the One Ten, and both One Ten and One Twenty were frequently hyphenated. The lineup, with One Ten prices effective as of September 1939 and One Twenty prices as of January 1940, was as follows:

	One Ten	One Twenty
Business Coupe (2)	$ 867	$1038
Club Coupe (4)	$ 924	$1095
Club Sedan (5)	—	$1217
Convertible Coupe (4)	$1087	$1258
Convertible Sedan (5)	—	$1550
Touring Sedan* (5)	$ 944	$1115
Touring Sedan** (5)	$ 975	$1146
Station Wagon	$1195	$1397
Darrin	—	$3800
Deluxe Club Coupe (4)	—	$1145
Deluxe Convertible Coupe (4)	—	$1299
Deluxe Club Sedan (5)	—	$1292
Deluxe Touring Sedan* (5)	—	$1225

* = two-door   ** = four-door

An overhanging boss in the cylinder head extending down close to the open intake valve and thus providing a more streamlined flow of mixture into the cylinder was the principal modification to the One Twenty's engine; the One Ten was unchanged. The Warner Gear overdrive was new, an all-electrical unit eliminating the centrifugal governor principle used in 1939. And once again the Packard engineers had played with the rear suspension, eliminating the fifth shock absorber, modifying the

481

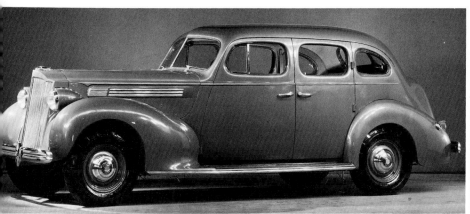

The 1939 One Twenty Touring Sedan and its interior (above); a 1939 Six Convertible Coupe gracing a Packard sales meeting in Omaha, Nebraska (below).

remaining two and moving the rear sway bar to the front of the vehicle.

The 1940 Packard, the company advertised, "spoils you for all other cars." The following year Packard thought it necessary only to tag the new models as "the Class of '41." Restyling again came the Junior models' way, and it was artfully crafted. As *The New Yorker*'s reporter noted—and here obviously was a man in tune with Packard's own thinking—"I always marvel at the way Packard manages to adapt its peculiarly individual lines to the changes in automobile styles. This year its radiator is narrower than ever and the flanking auxiliary grilles on the fronts of the fenders are considerably wider, yet the continuity of Packard design is still reassuringly there." The headlights were now fully incorporated into more highly crowned fenders, and four speed-line chrome moldings were delicately employed behind the front and rear fender wheel openings on the deluxe versions of both Junior models. Those long, graceful hood louvers from the 1940 versions were shortened for '41 but now doubled also as hood releases. And the divided rear window was replaced by a single softly curved and tempered one-piece section.

Two new ideas—which, again, Packard was first to commercialize in the industry—were also made available on the Junior line: air conditioning and two-tone paint schemes. The latter was offered in seven combinations, with twice that many single tones on the Packard charts. Running boards, which the industry was trying its best to do away with, could be ordered if desired—and should a buyer be unable to make up his mind, they could be added by the dealer on two hours' notice.

The Packard distributor for Guadalajara (also a White agent) preparing to drive his order of five trucks and five '39 Junior Packards back to Mexico.

Most significant for '41 was the enormous expansion of the One Ten line; in 1940 it had outsold the One Twenty by better than two to one, so a little augmentation seemed in order. Five deluxe body versions were added, while One Twenty choices were reduced to eight, the lineup as follows, with prices as effective September 1940:

	One Ten	One Twenty
Business Coupe (2)	$ 907	$1112
Club Coupe (4)	$1000	$1205
Touring Sedan* (5)	$1024	$1230
Touring Sedan** (5)	$1056	$1261
Convertible Coupe (4)	$1175	$1377
Convertible Sedan (5)	—	$1723
Deluxe Club Coupe (4)	$1038	—
Deluxe Touring Sedan* (5)	$1084	—
Deluxe Touring Sedan** (5)	$1116	—
Deluxe Convertible Coupe (4)	$1209	—
Station Wagon (8)	$1231	$1436
Deluxe Station Wagon (8)	$1291	$1496

* = two-door ** = four-door

Mechanical changes were minimal. A new thin-wall bearing was introduced for rods and mains, while a rustproof austenitic steel alloy was adapted for use in engine valves to alleviate the valve hang-up experienced by owners who operated their Packards only occasionally.

In Detroit, radiators being assembled for the 1940 Junior Packards; in Los Angeles, Barney Oldfield accepting delivery of his 1940 One Twenty Touring Sedan

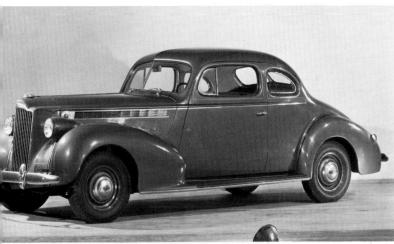

From the top: 1940 One Twenty Club Coupe, Convertible Sedan, Touring Sedan.

The Junior Class of '41 graduated nearly 73,000 units from East Grand Boulevard, fewer than the year previous, but then the Junior Packards had competition. First, from the Packard company's ever increasing military production. And second, from a new kid on the block. Fortunately the newcomer was a relative. It was called a Clipper.

So well received was the Clipper in its introductory '41 version that it was utilized for all six- and eight-cylinder Junior body styles for 1942 save station wagon, convertible sedan and convertible coupe. The former two were summarily dropped, but the One Ten and One Twenty were kept alive in new versions of the latter. Both incorporated long horizontal side grilles extending out from the center grille under the headlights (similar to the Clipper but not of the same cast construction). The Junior Packards also borrowed the flat dish-shaped wheel covers adapted by the entire Packard line in 1942. At introduction the new convertible coupes sold for $1385 and $1495 respectively, the highest prices ever for a standard model of the Junior Packard.

Less than five months after production began, it ended—abruptly. Pearl Harbor saw to that. Production totaled 30,524 units for the abbreviated model year.

And one is left now only with retrospect and a question which, historically, should never be asked. Did the One Twenty and the Six kill the Packard company? No, of course not. What would have done that, had the Juniors not intervened, was the Great Depression and the change in America's way of life it brought. Among luxury marques, Marmon,

Where Packard always did well, a One Twenty in the Gilmore-Yosemite, 1939.

A 1941 One Ten Touring Sedan in Packard's Cold Room and on the sand and gravel roads of the Proving Grounds, above; the One Ten Station Wagon, below.

Pierce-Arrow, Peerless, Stutz, Duesenberg did not survive the decade of the Thirties, most indeed went under early. Cadillac and Lincoln persevered by virtue of being sheltered by broad-based corporate umbrellas. Packard, although still a rich company during the Depression's early years, was an undiversified independent, held captive in a product policy aimed at less than two percent of the total automotive market. It couldn't have made it—as sometimes contended—in that market alone until the advent of military contracts brought more money into the company coffers. Senior car production from 1935 to '42 approximated 42,-000 units, less in eight model years than the company had produced during just one pre-Depression season, 1929. The figures are telling.

What carried Packard through the Depression was a model line which competed with a full forty percent of all domestic cars sold in the United States. What carried Packard through the Depression were the 479,500 Junior cars produced—and sold—during the dark days of the Thirties.

But should they perhaps not have been called Packards? Should they have looked otherwise than the Seniors? Should they have been other cars altogether? That is a question that shall probably ever be debated, and there will never be a simple answer. Committing a major portion of its working capital to successfully establishing itself in a new market, the Packard company obviously thought its most prudent course was to trade on the marque's prestigious name and widely acclaimed styling. Packard

The 1941 One Twenty Touring Sedan, above; the non-Clipper Juniors for '42 comprised only convertible coupes and taxis, the One Twenty of the former below left.

management, too, might have taken a hindsight look at what had happened to other companies which had taken the diversification plunge. Marmon's Roosevelt was a failure, the Studebaker product named for that company's president Erskine hadn't long survived, and in less than a fortnight of months the Reo Motor Car Company had become convinced that the problem with its Wolverine was less the car than the fact that the buying public didn't think it was a Reo—and promptly called the new model that for '29. Would a Macauley—and the idea of using the Packard president's name was broached but he wouldn't permit it—or some appellation conjured from the animal kingdom have sold as well as a Packard? We'll never know.*

A more interesting question, and one more readily contemplated with at least some answers resulting, is where—had Packard survived to this

day—these smaller Packards would compete in the contemporary industry. It is, at the very least, a tantalizing project, though changing market tactics of the companies still on the scene make it merely an academic exercise. Still, the basal automotive marketing programs of the Seventies can be considered a map, upon which might be overlaid the Packard marketing philosophy of the late Thirties. Where would the Juniors be? The Six would probably compete in the senior model range of the Dodge and the Pontiac. The One Twenty would be in league with the big Buicks and Oldsmobiles. And the Senior Packards? Given the industry pricing structure of the late Seventies, they would doubtless be priced well in excess of $20,000.

Idle speculation, certainly. For the fact shall ever remain that the Six and One Twenty did not survive the Forties, nor the Packard company the Fifties. And the former should not be blamed for the latter.

The business of business can be likened to an endless relay race, with hurdles representing the obstacles that must be cleared to stay in the race, the runners the management people who must decide how most effectively to clear those hurdles. They can only run so long before tiring (or retiring) and passing the baton to new and fresh runners. During the Thirties, Alvan Macauley and his team faced hurdles of devastating proportion, and they surmounted them and continued the race. Only later would the baton be dropped.

---

*Significantly, Cadillac's LaSalle—which endured longer but was finally withdrawn in favor of an inexpensive "Cadillac"—never sold in the numbers of the Junior Packards. This might indicate that Packard's decision to use its own name was indeed a prudent one ... before the war. After it, however, when any marketing philosophy the company desired could have been set up, conceivably retaining the Packard name for its lesser-priced cars was not so wise a choice. This possibility will, of course, be pursued in chapters following.

CHAPTER TWENTY-THREE

A NORMALLY TALL
MAN CAN EASILY
SEE OVER IT

The Clipper,
The Nineteenth and the Twentieth Series

1941-1942

AUTHORS: GEORGE HAMLIN AND DWIGHT HEINMULLER

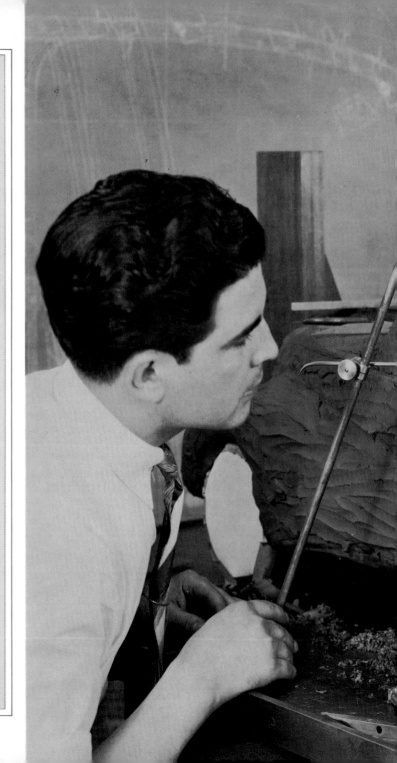

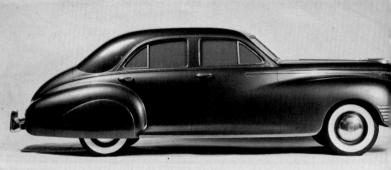

The middle and late Thirties marked a fast-paced evolution in automotive styling, the transition from the severe, traditional lines of the classic era to ever more sophisticated forms of streamlining. The culmination of this trend, though it was delayed five years by World War II, was the envelope body of the early postwar period, which rapidly came to dominate the industry. Students of the age have often pointed, with some justification, to the pioneering role of the swept-fender 1947 Studebaker, Kaiser and Frazer cars, and indeed these were the first to truly evidence the look of the future. Kaiser-Frazer had no prewar dies to amortize by building obsolete designs after peace had returned, and Studebaker bravely scrapped its old stampings almost immediately, scooping the rest of the industry with its radically different Loewy/Exner-designed cars of 1947.

But historians usually overlook the fact that literally everyone in the automobile industry had swept-through fenderline, envelope-bodied cars on their drawing boards before Pearl Harbor. Had the war not intervened, many might have been in production as early as 1943 or 1944. All such ideas had their roots in the first tenuous steps toward aerodynamics, i.e., the Airflow Chryslers and DeSotos; had progressed through milder forms like the Loewy-designed 1939 Studebakers, the Willys American and GM "Turret-Top" cars; had scored several stunning successes, like John Tjaarda's beautiful Lincoln Zephyr; and suffered failures, like the bizarre "shark-nose" Graham. Every company took part in the exercise in one form or another, but it had to be one of the surprises of the decade that the most advanced form of streamlined design before the global war emanated from those staunch traditionalists at East Grand Boulevard. It was the 1941 Packard Clipper.

Nine years earlier Packard had dipped its feet into the stream with the shovel-nosed Light Eight, but it hadn't fared well in the marketplace—and the company was not inclined to wade further into radical design. Succeeding models including the One Twenty were conservative.

Packard of course had built its house on many firm pillars, not the least of which was styling continuity. John Reinhart, whose thirteen-year career at the company began in 1938 and who was primarily responsible for the design of the Twenty-Fourth Series, has commented, "Packard never had any particular year when they'd decide to change a car, never had any cycles of any kind like the Big Three. They'd just carry on until sales started falling off."

Falling off was precisely the phrase. After setting an all-time record in 1937 with its first 100,000-car year, Packard had sold half that number in recession year 1938, and only marginally bettered its performance for 1939. The $3 million profit of '37 had turned into a $1.5 million loss the following year, followed by a modest $500,000 profit in 1939—scarcely enough to live on. Worse, Packard sales were concentrated heavily in the 490 production car, or lower-priced field, while Cadillac was chipping in-

Pages preceding: Clipper development, the quarter-scale clay model taking shape Above: Buick resemblance in Styling's sketch for update of the traditional lines (top) gave way to Clipper concept and the completed quarter-scale clay (bottom). Below: The 1941 Clipper prototype, the stripe would be deleted and script on rear deck added in production version. Right: The 1941 production Clipper.

creasingly more percentage points away from its old rival in the luxury bracket. Styling, in this brave new world of Airflows, Airstreams and Zephyrs, was obviously one of Packard's biggest problems. Packard designs were not keeping pace with the industry when they absolutely had to—a new experience for a company which never before had to meet styling competition.

The longevity of Packard's conservative designs is at least partly explained by the fact that Edward Macauley, head of styling and Alvan's son, was not a designer *per se*. His primary qualification for the position was his parentage. Nepotism is the bane of any large business enterprise, and there were undoubtedly others better suited for the task. The younger Macauley would remain director of styling from 1930 through 1955. Significantly, he was never named a vice-president and never held a seat on the board of directors.

It should not be assumed, however, that Ed Macauley was incompetent. He was a fine coordinator and administrator, a good manager of his department. He had a good "eye" for design and was personally responsible for Packard's offering some of the finest custom bodies during the Thirties. He knew, and insisted upon, quality. And—this appears to have been a family tradition—Edward was universally liked, even by those who disagreed with him; he was always referred to as a gentleman

in a field not noted for a preponderance of same. But the reality remained that Macauley was not a stylist, and toward the end of the Thirties he seemed to lose much of his enthusiasm for styling, taking less of a role in the development of show and idea cars than he had earlier.

Its lack of new designs notwithstanding, Packard continued to be an important factor in the luxury car market, as that market was to it. Packard engineering remained legendary. The company had on its payroll one of the finest groups of automotive engineers ever assembled—remarkable for a company which never held more than six percent of new car sales and primarily attributable to the recruiting prowess of Jesse G. Vincent. Forest R. McFarland, who joined Packard Engineering in 1924 and served in various capacities including chief research engineer until 1955, later noted: "Colonel Vincent was a brilliant man who commanded great respect in the field of automotive engineering, and [he] had over 200 patents to his name. He was a good picker, and didn't have many around him that weren't smart." In short, Packard did not have to look for talent, the talent came to Packard.

Styling, which came under the aegis of Engineering, shared these high standards, but its forte was the old school of design. Werner Gubitz, as second in command, had arrived in 1930, and was largely responsible for the traditional line and form, the consistency from year to year that

marked the classic Packard philosophy. But that formula would not meet the need for the new, innovative designs a competitive industry was demanding, and Styling's disability was magnified by the lack of a strong man at the top. Packard had no Harley Earl, as did Cadillac, no John Tjaarda, as did Lincoln via Briggs. Earlier this lack had been of minimal import, but depression had turned the world of commerce upside down, and it was becoming clearer with every sales report that a completely new design must be commissioned to supplement the existing line of cars.

The limitations of Packard's own styling section were obvious, so Alvan Macauley and Jesse Vincent took an equally obvious route: They went outside for ideas. This was considered good business; even if the in-house team eventually won a design competition, the cross-pollination from several schools of thought could only improve whatever product finally emerged. In the search for a brand-new Packard look, the company's own designers and engineers would of course have final authority, and would oversee and coordinate the entire operation. Ed Nowacky, a stylist under Gubitz, recalls that a crash program was begun in the summer of 1939 which was to be completed within a year—no small task. President and general manager Max Gilman continually admonished the staff, "We must look modern." And he meant it to be in time for the 1941 model year.

Early into the project, at Packard's request, Briggs Manufacturing became involved on a consultant basis. Briggs' policy was to maintain its own design department as a "gesture of good will" toward its clients, of whom Packard was one, along with Ford and Chrysler at the time. According to Alex Tremulis, with Briggs in 1937 and again in 1939, the purpose of this studio was to offer "the fresh outside viewpoint . . . to augment each company's styling activity."

Nor did Macauley and Gilman stop there. George Walker, then head of the independent firm of Walker Associates, recalled that the two came to his office in Detroit to enlist his aid as well. (Walker's company later strongly influenced the production Clipper dashboard.) Freelance designer Bill Flajole was also asked to offer his concepts. Last, although scarcely least, came Howard A. "Dutch" Darrin.

Darrin, who had returned to the United States from Europe in 1937 to establish an independent coachbuilding studio and shop in Hollywood, California, had rarely been in agreement with Packard management about the course of company styling, and output of the Darrin semi-customs Dutch had been building since 1938 had been punctuated by figurative handfuls of pulled hair when the respective ideologies clashed. Despite this, Darrin's talents were highly respected at Packard, and the passage of time had usually borne out his arguments with the company over the soundness of this or that design or method of construction.

Darrin believes the first long-distance call from Gilman about the new car project came in early 1940, by which date he says, "Packard was so afraid of GM they couldn't see straight." Darrin was asked to design a new car, with the proviso that it be done in ten days! It is interesting to speculate on the Boulevard's reasons for this absurd deadline. Perhaps Briggs, Walker, Flajole or Packard Styling had come up with something by then, which Macauley had thought less than perfect, warranting an alternative by Darrin. The deadline purportedly was to meet Ed Macauley's itinerary plans for a concurrent West Coast trip, though it is difficult to believe Packard expected anything serious from Dutch in such a short period.

Darrin nevertheless accepted the assignment, along with a fee of $1000 a day, saying he thought he "could establish enough lines for a full- and quarter-scale model" in the time allowed. "It was a terribly rushed job," he recalls. "The irony of the thing was the fact that I never got paid! I was pleased with the result, and am sorry now that I let them talk me out of paying *something* for it. Packard's purchasing agent Jim Marks said to me, 'Now Dutch, you know the real money is in your custom Packards. So let's up your order for them by a substantial amount.' This they did, and then later they quietly canceled it. What could I do?" What he had already done was submit a quarter-scale proposal for an all-new Packard to Ed Macauley on time, and Ed promptly took it back to Detroit.

By now a lot of talent was at work on the project. In addition to Briggs, Walker, Flajole and Darrin, the in-house team of Gubitz, Reinhart, Nowacky, along with Howard Yeager and Phil Wright, was well under way. Wright had joined Packard in 1939, after nearly three years at Briggs, from which company he brought along those ideas he had originally applied to a Chrysler styling contest and which now would be melded into the overall Packard styling effort. Little came of Flajole's project, while the Walker ideas were submitted to Packard for study. Ed Macauley, meanwhile, shipped the Darrin quarter-scale clay to Briggs, asking that templates be taken from it and a full-scale clay built for further study.

Alex Tremulis, in a 1971 letter to Darrin, recalls his first look at Dutch's small model. "I shall never forget the shocker one morning as I entered the Briggs showroom, which was always kept under lock and key, and saw a beautiful quarter-scale model in clay of a Packard proposal. None of us in Styling knew where it came from or who was responsible for its execution. I picked up all the marbles in the guessing game by simply stating that only one man in the world could have designed this model. One, it had all the fingerprints of . . . Darrin. There was the downward swept beltline and an inimitable Darrin blind quarter, with a Darrinized notch-back roof flowing into a beautifully swept rear luggage compartment. Two, it had a front fender flow that had the characteristic Darrin . . . angle. . . . It was a real shocker to all of us. Our approach at Briggs sort of emulated the straight-through beltline

Page opposite and above: The 1941 Clipper on road and track at Proving Grounds. Below: The Clipper's eight-cylinder powerplant and a test car in the Cold Room.

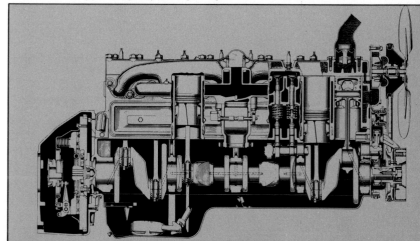

of the Buick-Olds-Pontiac torpedo body which if anything would have only flattered General Motors by our sincere form of imitation. My first impression [of the new quarter-scale clay] was that it's too beautiful to be a production car and that it's no doubt a custom one-off Packard proposal . . . Several hours later John Tjaarda informed us all that indeed it was a Darrin proposal." But Tremulis' biggest surprise occurred subsequently when he learned that the model was being seriously considered for production.

When the blown-up model arrived at Packard it was, of course, subjected to design-by-committee, but the results were not at all disastrous—and to many they were pleasing. Gubitz and his aides made only a few changes: They raised the beltline slightly, eliminating in the process any downsweep except at the rear; they decreased the size of the rear window and shortened the front fender sweep; they accentuated the enclosed running boards and increased the capacity of the trunk to meet competitive requirements. Some of the ideas the Gubitz team had been working on at the Boulevard were incorporated into the final design, and possibly some from the Walker proposal. Darrin, in a memoir in AUTOMOBILE *Quarterly*, remarked that the "original Clipper design called for a sweeping front fenderline that carried right on through the doors to the rise of the rear fender, similar to the custom Clipper I built later for Errol Flynn. But Packard shortened the sweep to fade away at mid-door. This was done as a hedge because no one knew if the through-fenderline would sell." Dutch never did appreciate the enclosed running board: "It was all very sad in the end because Packard styling vandalized the design by throwing on huge gobs of clay along the wheelbase . . . The Clipper never recovered."

It must be remembered, of course, that Darrin considered any vestige of a running board anathema; others do not share his revulsion to the Clipper rocker treatment. Without this arrangement the rear fenders would have been the typical pontoons of the period, beginning with naught and jutting out from the body along their lower leading edge, and it was from this era that Packard was attempting to escape.

The Clipper would lie comparatively unnoticed on the discard heap of history for many years; only recently has the car received belated recognition as one of the significant designs of its day, and as a result the exercise of "placing credit for the design" has become more important. When introduced, Packard said that "three world-famous designers tackled the job," referring apparently to Darrin, Walker and the House of Briggs—Phil Wright being part of the company staff. But of the three, Darrin held the only claim to being "world-famous." Credit for the Clipper, however, has tended to lie until now principally with Gubitz and Yeager, because Gubitz directed Packard Styling and placed final approval on all designs regardless of their origin. While the Clipper remains a tribute to Gubitz' insight—as does his restraint in revising the design—this does not mean credit for the car can properly be attributed to Werner Gubitz himself.

Certainly Briggs did not originate the Clipper. That company's designs of the period and the testimony of employee Tremulis confirm this. The latter estimates that at least eighty percent of Darrin's original thinking in the quarter-scale model survived the modification process. Darrin has viewed Packard's reneging on the $10,000 payment as unfortunate primarily from the standpoint of historical accuracy rather than from the resulting shortfall in the Darrin Retirement Fund. However, acceptance of such payment would not in itself have attested to principal responsibility because no one ever denied that Darrin had spent ten days preparing some proposal.

While others certainly contributed, only Howard Darrin can be awarded the lion's share of the Clipper design. In addition to the evidence cited, there is, finally, the Packard introductory statement comparing the Clipper with its "custom-built parent." The statement referred not to the Packard Walker, nor the Packard Briggs. It referred to the Packard Darrin.

"Skipper the Clipper," coaxed Sales as the new car debuted in April 1941 and, simultaneously, a color portrait enclosure was sent to all stockholders in the 1940 annual report. Said Gilman in the latter, "Our new model cars, introduced in the fall of 1940 . . . have been well received by the public. However we determined that the addition of a newly styled Packard car to our line, which would represent a distinct departure from Packard styling, was a desirable forward step toward further increasing the demand for our cars."

Increase demand it did. There were 72,855 Packards manufactured for 1941, and 16,000 of them were Clippers, despite the seven-month production penalty due to their 1941½ introduction. The public was electrified, and contemporary observers were nearly unanimous in concluding that the car was (1) outstandingly beautiful and (2) a totally unexpected surprise from Packard.

The Clipper was over a foot wider than it was high—the widest car then in production—and it made a success of the integrated fender design. "One is immediately impressed with the low, wide lines of the whole car," said Packard. "A normally tall man can easily see over it." The Clipper had so many new features that ninety-two of them were included in the Clipper Data Book. So few parts interchanged with the regular line that a separate parts book was issued.

Significant departures for Packard were found in the Clipper body. The bonnet, the grille and each quarter panel/fender were formed of a single piece of metal. The bonnet could be lifted from either side or removed entirely if desired. Both doors were hinged at the front, and the vent window in the rear door replaced the conventional sixth window. The gasoline tank incorporated a new "Ventalarm" to warn when the tank was within one gallon of being full—to avoid splashing fuel onto the fender, the automatic pump nozzle having not yet been invented. The battery was moved from its usual underseat location to a position under the bonnet where it became easier to service, and where voltage loss due to long cables was minimized. The new trunk lid was counterbalanced by a spring, eliminating the conventional snaplatch.

Starting the Clipper involved another innovation. The starter switch was mounted on the side of the carburetor and was actuated not by a conventional dash button but by depressing the accelerator to the floor with the ignition on. This system, which endured through 1953, appealed to Buick as well, though no other manufacturers are known to have used it. (For a brief period unique starter locations became an industry fad, Studebaker's and Nash's turning up under the clutch pedal.) But Packard's system eliminated the need to set the automatic choke by momentarily flooring the accelerator, assured proper accelerator position for efficient starting, and proved remarkably free of operating difficulties.

Clipper body construction was significantly different from what had gone before. From dash to trunk lid, the roof was a single piece of seamless steel, and the floor pan had only one welded seam from toe board to trunk floor. Door hinges were concealed, door latches were rotary. At the same time Packard elected to hold with the basic powerplant of the One-Twenty, the 282-cubic-inch unit, with increased compression allowing the Clipper five added horsepower. An electric oil gauge was adapted from the Super Eight, and the block was mounted on a new removable cross member at the rear.

With the new body and old engine came a brand-new chassis, beginning with a totally new frame of double-drop construction, which brought the floor pan closer to the ground without infringing on road clearance. The engine was mounted further forward than on the One-Twenty, and the rear shock absorbers were mounted at an angle to assist the fifth shock absorber in controlling sidesway.

Clipper front suspension was entirely contrary to the rest of the line, and eventually replaced the older system totally. The lower frame eliminated the need for long torque arms, as in previous Packards, while the linkage between the Pitman arm and steering brackets was of a double-link design, incorporating a cross bar and idler arm with two cross tubes to permit independent wheel movement. The older style, referred to as "cross steering," had transmitted Pitman arm movement directly to the steering connections by means of two tie rods. Other mechanical features introduced earlier, such as Electromatic, Aero-Drive and air conditioning, continued to be available on the Clipper.

The 1941 Clipper was priced between the One-Twenty and One-Sixty, and cannot really be considered part of either line. Effective June 1941, the prices for standard four-door sedans were as follows:

Clippers for 1942. Above: The Eight Special. Below: The One-Sixty (the script missing on this prototype would appear on production cars) and the One-Eighty.

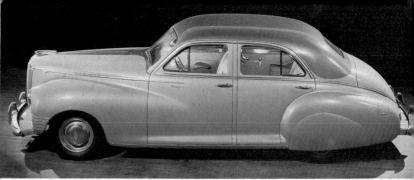

One-Ten	$1076
One-Twenty	$1291
Clipper	$1420
One-Sixty	$1795
One-Eighty	$2632

The breakdown above provides dramatic evidence of two emerging factors in Packard's overall picture. First, the Clipper was never a low- or even medium-priced car, even at introduction. The Cadillac 61, for example, was at this time selling for $1445. Second, the spread between the bottom and top line Packards did not approximate the traditional company pricing norm and the gap had been closed principally by the higher-priced cars moving downward rather than the lower-priced ones moving up. Packard management had alluded to this in a *Fortune* interview as early as 1937, and these facts illustrate the rapidly changing nature of the automobile industry, as well as the improved technology available to makers of lower-priced cars. The day when you could buy a Packard and be guaranteed to go farther, faster, quieter than anyone in a car costing half or even a third as much had simply vanished. This was of course true for Lincoln and Cadillac too. But the difference, insofar as the success of the product was concerned, would be measured in each company's salesmanship.

Nineteen forty-one proved a good year for Packard, the company out-producing Cadillac and LaSalle combined and earning $2,061,323. The Clipper look obviously pointed the way to the future—Darrin and Derham later built convertible versions of it—and work began im-

Further Twentieth Series Clippers for 1942. Pages preceding: The four-door sedan One-Eighty (center), One-Sixty (above right) and Six (below right). This page: The Clipper wearing its Defense Trim of painted grille and hubcaps with a two-toned variation (above left); the Darrin convertible for Errol Flynn.

mediately on expanding the theme for the 1942 models. Clipper styling was offered in four lines: There was a Clipper Six sedan for $1250, a Clipper Eight sedan for $1305, a Clipper One-Sixty sedan for $1814, a Clipper One-Eighty sedan for $2346. In the lesser-priced lines it was difficult in fact to find a non-Clipper; the only such bodies were for convertibles and commercial cars. This means that the convertible was the only passenger car being built in Six and Eight lines which did not offer Clipper styling. Likewise, in the One-Sixty and One-Eighty series, the emphasis for standard-wheelbase cars was Clipper, non-Clippers among those vehicles consisting of 138- and 148-inch wheelbase limousines, formal sedans and touring sedans, as well as Rollson and LeBaron customs. Or they were convertibles, the One-Eighty version being by Darrin.

In this line expansion of the Clipper, Packard did a good deal of tinkering with Darrin's original idea. For example, there was now a two-door fastback body, the junior Clippers had foreshortened front fenders and were set on 122-inch wheelbases, and to meet competitive challenges two-tone paint jobs were again available. None of these alterations produced paeans of praise from Darrin, but by now he was accustomed to Packard and he understood the automobile business pretty well. The cars' two-toning was certainly a monument to questionable taste, with the second color running arrow-like down the hood, over the top, and neatly wrapping under the backlight, following body creases. In the two-door, which being a fastback lacked the crease below the rear window, the second color went lower, to the beltline, on to the upper half of the doors and all the way around the deck lid.

The 1942 Clippers were further altered for model year distinction: The horizontal grille bars now wrapped completely around the front fender to the wheel openings on the Senior cars, the front bumper was moved closer to the grille, the parking lights were enlarged and the instrument panel was changed from horizontal to circular dial format. In addition, Clippers received the standard 1942 wheel covers, flatter than those offered previously and without the Packard name. This pie plate design, except for one minute modification around the edge, would remain through 1950, though the Packard name would return for 1946.

Production figures for the different bodies are not available, only line statistics (2580 One-Sixties of all descriptions, for example) being retained for 1942. However, Clippers predominated in the lower-price range while the traditional styling remained more popular among One-Sixties and One-Eighties, due to the manner in which the cars were marketed. Largely because of this (and because the Clipper was revived in 1953-1957 for a junior line of cars), the name has gained a connotation of "cheaper Packard" in much the same way as Zephyr means "cheaper Lincoln." This unfortunate and mistaken impression is a disservice to the body design as well as to the design genius which saw it built. It has been said that the Clipper, intended as a medium-priced car, could never

be upgraded to a luxury car. Yet it *was* a luxury car in all the best aspects of, for example, the Lincoln Continental, differing from other Packards only in line of style. The 1941 One-Sixty four-door model 1472 was priced at $1795 against the 1942 One-Sixty Clipper model 1572's $1814. Some representative body measurements also assist in demonstrating the Clipper's luxury-car status:

Dimension	1941 1472	1942 1572 Clipper
Length (inches)	206	215
Width (inches)	74	76
Height (inches loaded)	68	64
Front hiproom (inches)	50	58
Rear hiproom (inches)	48	51
Front headroom (inches)	37	37
Rear headroom (inches)	37	37
Trunk capacity (ft³)	17.8	17.2

No direct comparison with the One-Eighty models is possible because there was no One-Eighty sedan on the 127-inch wheelbase in 1941; there was a 1940 club sedan, however, which had similar measurements and was priced at $2243, vis-à-vis $2346 for the 1942 Clipper One-Eighty.

Allowing for equivalent price, greater interior dimensions in all respects, identical engine and drive train, equivalent trunk capacity, and equally sumptuous interior and exterior fit and finish, one must either accept the validity of the One-Eighty and One-Sixty Clippers as luxury automobiles or conclude that only sidemounts can make a prestige car.

After the war the Clipper idea of flow-through fenders, supported by the designs of Kaiser-Frazer and Studebaker, would quickly reshape the design concepts of the industry. By this yardstick, introducing the Clipper in 1941 put Packard miles ahead, but the promise of the car was never fulfilled.

In retrospect we can see that the Clipper's introduction was a tragic case of bad timing. Nineteen forty-one was shaping up as one of Packard's best years, and 1942 showed even greater promise. If the $3 million profit of 1937 was not equaled or surpassed in 1941, thought the company, surely it would be in 1942. But the problems of the world thwarted expectations.

The Clipper was late in the showrooms, and about the time its sales began to move in August 1941, automobile production was curtailed because of the threatening international situation. Defense orders helped the profit picture, but defense is a notoriously tricky business to depend upon. On December 7th, 1941, the Japanese bombed Pearl Harbor; on December 8th, the United States was at war. On February 9th, 1942, Packard automobile production was suspended altogether. Packard had lost a giant lead on its competition and, as 1946 and 1947 would later prove, the early momentum of the Clipper was gone forever.

CHAPTER TWENTY-FOUR

IN THE NATION'S DEFENSE

Packard in World War II

AUTHORS: GEORGE HAMLIN AND DWIGHT HEINMULLER

In August 1941, off the coast of Newfoundland, the President of the United States met the Prime Minister of Great Britain in talks which were to form the basis of the Atlantic Charter. During the conference the two attended worship services on the deck of a destroyer, joining their naval forces under muted cannons in singing "Onward Christian Soldiers." "I chose the hymn myself," said Winston Churchill, who thought it poignantly appropriate. "It was a great hour to live." Perhaps it was at that moment when Churchill became assured of ultimate victory. For now it was more than evident that, very soon, the United States of America would be at war.

Wars are not conveniently scheduled for the civilian segment of any country's population, however, and the American entry into the greatest war of all could not have come at a worse time for Packard. It scuttled the Clipper momentum and, worse still, resulted in the gutting of a plant that had only recently been admirably reequipped—for the building of automobiles.

Max Gilman had begun talking about "increasing the demand for our cars" early in the Thirties, and concomitant with the 1933 decision to enter the medium-priced field came a move to overhaul production capabilities and improve efficiency—largely encouraged by board member and legal counsel Henry Bodman. In assessing Packard's greatest wartime setback—the revamping of its plant for defense production—it is helpful to review history briefly.

Max Gilman, it will be recalled, had been brought to Detroit as distribution vice-president by Alvan Macauley, Macauley subsequently turning over to him his own position of general manager. Gilman in turn hired George T. Christopher out of retirement from General Motors to be the new assistant vice-president for manufacturing in 1934, and Christopher brought in others, like himself experts in low-cost production, from GM, Ford and Chrysler. Christopher's influence was to be significant at Packard from that point, through the war and beyond.

Said *Fortune* of George Christopher in January 1937, "His passion for low-cost production has an echoing passion for low-priced cars, and in all ways open to him he exerts a strong downward pressure on pricing, so that he can make more cars, so that he can make each car cheaper, so that he can make more cars." On April 22nd, 1942, the board of directors voted to name Christopher president and general manager, succeeding respectively Macauley—who moved up to board chairman—and Gilman, who resigned after suffering severe injuries in an automobile accident the previous January.

By now, Christopher and his team were veterans. Their first step, in 1934, had been to revamp the plant for volume production. Whereas Henry Ford, less than a decade earlier, had converted his plant from one model to another by completely shutting down for half a year, Christopher performed similar transmogrification while car production

maintained full steam; it was not an easy task, and it took nearly five years. Slowly and painfully production flow was improved. Lines were retracked during the periodic model-change shutdowns, bottlenecks were broken, the small freight trains of parts and completed cars criss-crossing East Grand Boulevard were eliminated. Congestion had become so acute that traffic signals had to be installed to ease things; Christopher solved the difficulty by building bridges, the most famous of which was the one connecting the two plants over the Boulevard itself. By 1940 George Christopher had created one of the most efficient sub-assembly layouts in the industry; the Eighteenth Series cars shared enough components to put everything on one assembly line—achieving Christopher's long-anticipated goal at last.

None of these changes was inexpensive, but it was expected that the 1941 and 1942 models would be able to pay the bill. Then came the war, and the whole operation had to be painfully disassembled, pushed outside, and stored wherever there was room.

With the cessation of car production, Packard undertook a program of service improvement to keep its dealerships busy. Incentives and promotions were offered to induce people to bring their cars in for maintenance, and the Service Letter series continued uninterrupted. But there were no cars, and for a while not enough parts. From time to time the government would permit the company to run needed items when the demand grew acute, but the war years proved harrowing to Packard motorists as well as other car owners. Those who kept their automobiles faced gasoline rationing, tire rationing, speed limits designed to save both, along with a parts and anti-freeze shortage. Drivers of air-conditioned Packards could find no Freon. The company offered devices to hold spare tire covers in place in the wheel wells when there was no tire or wheel underneath—six-wheel equipment was "wasteful"—but many covers were simply welded into place, to the ultimate detriment of future collectors.

New fortunes were made by people, notably dealers, who had seen what was coming and collected large stocks of new and used cars privately titled—dealer-owned cars were subject to controls and sale to "essential customers." Then there were the wartime scrap drives, which resulted in the extinction of many classic era cars to the apparent benefit of no one on the front lines. Public resentment against such programs grew in direct relation to revelations of their inefficiency, such as the dumping of gasoline into rivers (gasoline itself was never in short supply, the reason for rationing it being to conserve tires), or the burying of tons of scrap because it was found of no advantage to the war effort other than providing a good feeling to the people who contributed. But no serious challenge ever appeared to the rationing and controls, even in the face of widespread black markets.

Having been in the military engine business since 1940, Packard was

Pages preceding: General Omar Bradley, General Dwight David Eisenhower and a Packard staff car, somewhere in France, the photograph taken August 13th, 1944.
Above: The last production Packard leaving the line, February 9th, 1942, with George Christopher on the right; and taking billboard notice of the war effort.
Below: Preparing for military production, the old factory in the background at the right and the new aircraft motor assembly building undergoing construction.

Horse Power for the Navy—Six of the Navy's new "Elco" patrol torpedo boats, streaking through coastal waters at close to a mile a minute. Each of these swift, hard-hitting Water Wasps is powered by a trio of 1350 horsepower Packard marine engines, churning up a total of 4050 horsepower!

Somewhere in England—A squadron of Spitfire fighting planes lined up for action. Packard, chosen to build—by the thousands—the famous aviation motors which have been so thoroughly battle-tested in the Spitfire and Hurricane fighters, recognizes this assignment as a tribute and a challenge to Packard precision production.

Packards for the Army—Just a part of a Packard fleet, over three blocks long, recently delivered to the Army for service as Staff cars. Land transport, too, must have swift, dependable performance—and these roomy, 160-horsepower Packard Super 8's answer all of those major requirements with plenty of power to spare.

Sisters under the skin

On land, sea, and in the air, Packard-built power plants are answering today's emphasis on the need for swift, powerful, and dependable performance.

Thanks to 42 years of experience—with almost every type of engine, for almost every type of mobile equipment—Packard has been ready and able to undertake assignments calling for superfine precision production.

Fortunately, too, Packard is big enough to fulfill its responsibilities to national employment and prosperity—to give defense clear right of way and carry on with regular car production at the same time.

All of Packard's traditional skill in engineering, production and craftsmanship are embodied in every new 1941 Packard that "rolls off the line". Once you enjoy the superb

performance it combines with amazing dependability and all-round economy—you'll want a Packard for your own. $907 to $5550, delivered in Detroit, State taxes extra.

PACKARD

ASK THE MAN WHO OWNS ONE

Advertisement from Collier's, *the April 5th, 1941 issue (above); aircraft test day at the Proving Grounds, 1941 (right); the M4A4 medium tank, 1943 (below).*

deeply committed to defense production by the time the 1942 cars were announced. Consolidated net earnings, largely on the strength of the defense orders, were three times those of 1940 despite a car production decrease of 10,000 units. Earnings rose to nearly $5 million for 1942, with ninety-six percent of the firm's capability devoted to defense.

For a brief period between the announcement and curtailment of the '42's, Packard tried to convince people cars could live alongside military hardware. "Despite its enormous defense assignments," said the Packard News Service in August 1941, "Packard has been able to maintain essential, though curtailed, production of motor cars . . . of particular significance, in a defense world of 'curtailments' and 'substitutions,' is the fact that Packard quality has in no way suffered by reason of replacement materials. While manufacturing in smaller quantity than the larger motor car companies, Packard has maintained its standards while preparing for substitutes when and if required by the government.

"Tooling for cast-iron pistons has been made ready and Packard engineers are prepared to swing over whenever it becomes necessary. For many months the engineering department has been conducting severe tests on a new type cast-iron piston. Both on the road and in dynamometer tests these pistons have shown unusual success. Engineers are convinced that if substitution becomes necessary it will be accomplished without any change in power output."

All of this was fine while the nation remained out of the war, but after Pearl Harbor, there was no point in pretending cars could go on. And as the cars disappeared, the Boulevard turned to one of its most significant wartime products, the Merlin aircraft engine. Originally designed by Rolls-Royce, the Merlin engine had been adjudged unsuited to mass production by Ford, that company among American manufacturers having first accepted a contract for its production. In addition to the technological complexities of the unit, Ford saw flaws in the government contract and wisely, from its own standpoint, elected to pass. Packard, for many years proudly identified as "Master Motor Builders," accepted the contract after a thorough reworking by counsel Bodman into "Plancor 1," a document which would serve as a production standard for some time to come. A plant for the building of the aircraft engine was to be equipped at once—it was, and was known later as the "ten-month miracle."

"During the latter part of 1940," stated Packard in its annual report for that year, "the Company accepted the assignment of producing 9,000 Rolls-Royce aircraft engines. Under present contracts, 6,000 engines are to be built for Great Britain and 3,000 for the United States. Stockholders' interests were carefully considered [because] the estimated cost of plant expansion, machines, equipment, tooling, etc., is more than $35,000,000 [and] the value of the engines to be produced will probably exceed $165,000,000. . . . Three new buildings for aircraft engine

production are approaching completion. Altogether about 1,000,000 square feet of floor space will be devoted to building these engines."

The engine plant was an addition to the factory, bordered by Concord Avenue on one side and on the other by what is now the Edsel Ford Freeway. The building was to house the new engineering and styling offices as well. Packard had "some 1600 employees working full-time on aircraft engine processing, plant layout, tool making, material processing and control. . . . In addition several thousand employees in vendors' plants are working on orders we have placed with them for machines, tools, engine parts, etc. . . . We estimate that we will require 14,000 production employees for the aircraft engine division when we reach full production . . . plans schedule the first production engine to be built on July 20."

Colonel Vincent prepared an enormous report on the Merlin engine program, only two copies of which are known to exist. Quoting from the late Forest McFarland's copy: " . . . the Rolls-Royce Merlin Aircraft engines which originated in 1935 were being assembled by the 'hand method' in England and when the American Government completed negotiations with Great Britain for manufacturing rights certain manufacturers in the United States rejected it as being too complicated to manufacture on a mass production basis." From Vincent's report it is evident that no such repugnance existed at Packard; further, it is significant that on the day the Boulevard was contacted about building the Merlin the plant was turning out Packard cars at the rate of 6391 per month, and was also producing marine engines for PT boats.

"As I write," said Vincent, "I think back over the years I spent exclusively in the Aircraft Engine Division. I am inclined to believe it has been the most interesting of my varied engineering career. I appreciate the unusual opportunity that I had to become intimately acquainted with and have had a part in producing the Packard-Built Rolls-Royce Merlin Aircraft Engine which has won for itself the honor of being the best liquid-cooled engine in existence." Many fail to realize the incredible feat Packard accomplished in producing this engine, on a mass basis, while making all the refinements Vincent described.

"On Monday, June 24, 1940," continued Vincent, "Mr. Gilman and I called on Mr. Knudsen [William S., president of General Motors, who on May 28th, 1940 became Commissioner for Industrial Production] at his home in Grosse Isle." Knudsen came straight to the point: Would Packard build the Merlin? "Mr. Gilman told Mr. Knudsen that the PMCC would be very glad to consider any proposal which he cared to place before us."

As a result of this and subsequent meetings Packard agreed in a memorandum to duplicate the Merlin XX engine, with the understanding that Packard would redesign some units for mounting U.S. standard pressure-type carburetors, hydromatic propellers and propeller governors, vacuum and fuel pumps, generators, tachometer drives and miscellaneous fittings to accommodate U.S. aircraft.

"I was told to go full speed ahead," wrote Vincent, "because we had been assured by Mr. Knudsen that we would be given a contract." Blueprints were transferred from Ford, Vincent hired personnel. ". . .we did not want to take on this job unless we could be assured of the goodwill and cooperation of the Ford Motor Company. We were assured. It was made clear to us, however, that they would not consider the making of any of the parts for us. It took a few days to inventory the drawings and parts at the Ford factory and arrange for their delivery to Packard." Vincent prepared an outline for Gilman on June 29th, advising him of the design and redesign program.

Early on it became apparent that the differences between the U.K. and U.S. Merlin engines would involve more than simple bolt-on components. The Ford blueprints, as approved by the Army Air Corps, specified a one-piece cylinder block for example, but when a coordinating team of Rolls-Royce engineers arrived on August 2nd they brought drawings for a new two-piece block which they desired "for improved performance and production considerations." Such major differences were not allowed by the contract that, as promised, had been tendered Packard, so Vincent was forced to rectify the situation through long and tiresome negotiations.

"From the latter part of October, 1940 until the latter part of March,

The Rolls-Royce Merlin engine in production in the new aircraft motor assembly building (above) during October 1943; the 50,000th built (below), October 1944.

1941," he wrote, "I was busily engaged working with representatives of the British Air Commission and our British (engineering) consultants, Messrs. Barrington, Ellor and Reid in an endeavor to arrive at definite decisions covering details of construction desired for British engines which would not be the same as corresponding parts of U.S. Air Corps engines. I found this to be a very tedious job because the situation was constantly changing and it was becoming more and more evident that it was going to be necessary to furnish the British with engines which would be installationally interchangeable with RR-built engines." Finally Vincent prepared a specification for the needed modifications, though it was not accepted by the government until October 1941. In the meantime Packard held to schedule by releasing drawings to the Manufacturing Department—minus "certain parts required for the British type"—by the end of November 1940. "During the time that we were making the drawings of the basic engine, it was necessary to have in mind the accessory equipment which we thought might be required by both governments." It must have been quite a twelve months.

While the British had Packard build what became the model V-165-1 Merlin engine with a two-piece block, back in England Rolls-Royce was carrying on with the old one-piece block model 28. The contretemps forced Packard to do enormous additional design and development work to assure interchangeability on British aircraft, including complete layouts and design studies. And that wasn't the end of it.

506 "In copying the RR drawings," Vincent continued, "it was necessary

for us to reverse all projected views and include much production information not found on the British drawings." During this process, Packard discovered that the British drawings of important and expensive castings did not correspond with current production parts being shipped from England. Rolls-Royce later confirmed Packard's suspicion: The British had not included changes in castings! Col. Vincent patiently narrated: "We immediately took steps to revise our drawings of important cast aluminum parts, and this, of course, made it necessary to rework all patterns, which were practically completed." That little item caused a delay of six weeks.

Then there were the Whitworth problems. Packard was unable to find complete engineering information on these U.K. threads and found it necessary to improvise: Measurements were taken from a British-built engine and experimental taps, dies and thread gauges were made. There was no choice—Packard's usual sources had more U.S. standard work than they could handle as it was, and were loath to take on additional work in which they were unfamiliar. Other automotive sources aggravated the situation because of their lack of expertise "in producing the highly specialized parts required for aircraft engines."

There were people problems as well, a wide divergence of opinion, for example, as to how important engineering items should be handled; whether to follow American or British shop practice; what kind of carburetion to use; how to establish accurate production schedules, and reconcile production of two different engines; what kind of special tools, jigs and fixtures to obtain; how to train personnel (the best employees from the automobile division were transferred); what kind of tests to employ; what to do about reworking the patterns for the new aluminum castings. Vincent summed up his three greatest problems as "The difficulties encountered in converting British drawings and establishing satisfactory shop practices to eliminate much of the British hand fitting . . . the necessity of duplicating British Whitworth threads . . . [and] establishing satisfactory material specifications to cover each part" of the Merlin engine. Around this time Mr. Churchill was telling his wartime partners that they would "find in the British Empire good comrades, with whom you are related by many ties—law, language, literature." But evidently not by Merlin engines.

Reading Vincent's report in its entirety, one can receive only a single impression: Vincent never felt the Merlin was a job Packard should not have undertaken. Quite the contrary, he seems to have relished the whole unbelievable thing. No problem was too much for him to handle, and he seemed to proceed with the assumption that if Packard didn't have the talent necessary to make the Merlin a success, nobody did. Most likely he was right.

With preliminaries out of the way, a period of modification began to ensure greater efficiency. "Rolls-Royce did have an excellent engine," Forest McFarland would remember, "and what we did were refinements [to the] number of moving parts, cost, horsepower. We eliminated scuffing of the reduction gears and cam followers, improved the lubrication of the magneto gears, and designed the supercharger for the Suffix-5 engine. The blower was a two-stage, two-speed device, [one speed was] really an overdrive. I had experience with overdrive and the patent is in my name." In the course of the supercharger development McFarland also devised and patented a new type of fail-safe driveshaft spline. "On everything I went to the British," continued the engineer. "They invited me to design the last reduction gear modification, but they appreciated it, and their inspector appreciated it." It required a little diplomacy, to make some of these changes, "but it worked out fine. The British would never have thought of it; they were good engineers, though."

Pilot model Merlins were tested in August 1941, and complete units were used in Mustang P-51, Mosquito, Lancaster, Warhawk and Hurricane fighter aircraft. Secretary of the Treasury Henry Morgenthau visited the plant in 1943 and summed up Packard's effect: "Only Packard had the nerve to tackle it, and the job I see done is remarkable."

Packard employees became enamored of the project, caught up in patriotic fervor, and the hard drive to produce. They even collected enough money to pay for a P-51B fighter, and named it the Sky Clipper. By war's end 55,523 Merlin engines were built. In the face of this remarkable record of engineering and production, it is puzzling indeed why many wartime historians persist in referring to the Merlin as a "Rolls-Royce" engine. Rolls received the credit, but Packard saw to it there was something to receive credit for.

East Grand Boulevard also became involved with military marine engines, the first examples of which were shipped in March 1940. Packard engines had, of course, long been used in marine applications, but they were usually adapted from aircraft—and occasionally passenger car—powerplants. Ross Taylor, who was Marine Engine Division project engineer from 1942 to 1947, was closely involved with design and development of Packard's V-12 marine unit, which began life with a government contract in 1939. This agreement provided for a redesign of the famous Gar Wood engine that had won Packard so many trophies decades before. Nomenclature for this engine was 2M—apparently the Gar Wood version had "1" tacitly set aside for it posthumously—but it never evolved beyond the experimental stage. Because of its racing design it proved unacceptable for Navy use.

The practice of suffixing marine engine nomenclature with the displacement in cubic inches commenced with the next design (and continued through 1957, including diesels). This was the 800-horsepower model 3M 1500, first marine unit actually used in the field. It evolved directly to the 4M 2500, a 1200-horsepower version which powered 85-

and 104-foot PT boats built by Elco, Higgins and Vosper, as well as Army and Navy rescue boats.

The 4M 2500 was essentially the engine on which the armed services was to depend throughout the war, though it was eventually supercharged and thereby upgraded to 1800 horsepower. Three or four of the units were used in a single PT boat, and those craft could hit 41 knots, or about 47 mph. Packard was fond of pointing out that the horsepower developed by each cylinder of the PT engine was greater than that of the entire prewar Six.

Packard conducted schools, attended by the Allied fleets, in which factory instructors using Packard equipment taught operation, care and maintenance of the 4M 2500. The courses were very necessary, because the engine came in seventeen configurations—they were all the same basic engine, of course, and modifications were generally minor, such as the special fresh water piping distinguishing the Type W2 from the Type W1. Specifications of the 4M 2500 included:

Form	60 degree Vee
Fuel	100 octane gasoline
Rotation	right-hand
Starter	24 volt
Generator	28 volt, 75 ampere
Bore & Stroke	6 ⅜ by 6 ½ inches
Piston speed	2600 fpm (average)
Displacement	2490 cubic inches
Dry weight	2950 pounds net
Spark advance	36 degrees ($\pm$ 1) BTDC
Valves	four per cylinder

During the war a PT squadron engineering officer wrote Packard, calling the 4M "the most nearly perfect marine engine of its type." Recommended overhaul intervals were continually extended and, in emergency situations, postponed indefinitely without breakdown or undue wear. The Navy ordered 808 PT boats altogether, and 774 were actually completed before the war ended. Of those, seventy were war losses, 219 were transferred to Russia under Lend-Lease, 481 were sold or scrapped after the war—and many are still in daily use. The remaining four were transferred to the Republic of Korea in 1952.

Late in the war the Navy placed orders for a larger, more powerful version of the PT engine, this time a sixteen-cylinder model. The new powerplant, designated 1M 3300, developed 2500 horsepower and was the largest and most powerful ever built by Packard. It was intended for use in larger PT boats but by the time development and production were under way the war had ended. The few models built were assigned to Navy training craft, and some may have seen service in Korea.

Neither the Navy nor Packard left the PT boat business after the war.

Orders were placed with the Boulevard for a number of the 1800 hp engines (of improved design), for spare parts for earlier engines, and for the new V-16. Four new PT's of experimental design were built in 1950-1951 by four different shipbuilders; each had a different hull design, all of aluminum, and were larger than the wartime PT (ninety tons displacement instead of thirty). Each boat was powered by four Packard marine engines developing 10,000 shaft horsepower per boat, and each was capable of forty-two knots in spite of the larger displacement. But the Navy decided they were not fast enough, and the craft were stricken from the Navy list in November 1951. Two were converted to fast PT boats (PTF's) by removing the torpedo tubes to lower weight and increase speed. In this configuration they would cruise at forty-five knots, and were recommissioned in 1952. Ultimately, however, the Navy decided the PTF was outdated, and the boats were stricken again in 1965 to be expended ignominiously as targets—unfortunately so as it turned out. Under the influence of events in Southeast Asia, the Navy was later to reverse course and build more PTF's.

In November 1945, Christopher intimated that Packard would be making civilian adaptations of its marine engines. They were to include, he said, marine and industrial applications, and smaller models would be built with fewer cylinders for use in heavy-duty trucks and off-the-road equipment. Two civilian marine engines were in fact released, but they were merely revised passenger car powerplants: the 1M 245 (Six) and 1M 356 (Super Eight). They featured a reverse gear and a reduction gear, and saw respectable sales and long service lives.

Packard's last marine engine program was undertaken under a $20 million Navy contract in the early Fifties. A group of sixty-one nonmagnetic fleet minesweepers (MSO's), launched between 1952 and 1958, was powered by two Packard diesel marine engines each. The units were made of nonmagnetic stainless-steel alloy and developed 2280 hp through two shafts and controllable-pitch propellers: They moved the MSO's, which displaced from 665 to 750 tons each, at 15.5 knots. Twelve coastal minesweepers (MSC's) were also equipped two each with Packard diesels, developing 1200 shaft horsepower. These were of wooden construction, built for lowest magnetic attraction, the Packard engines again of nonmagnetic alloy. Some of each series of minesweeper were powered instead by GM diesel engines, these having only two-thirds to three-quarters the horsepower of their Packard counterparts.

Development of the minesweeper engines, named the Series 142 Diesel, began in 1951, the nomenclature designating that each cylinder displaced 142 cubic inches regardless of cylinder count. Packard called the engines "a new concept in Diesel . . . design," and they were. Making them nonmagnetic was a major challenge. Until then, no technology existed in this area, so Packard found it necessary to create it. The result was a complement of five engines, the first experimental and

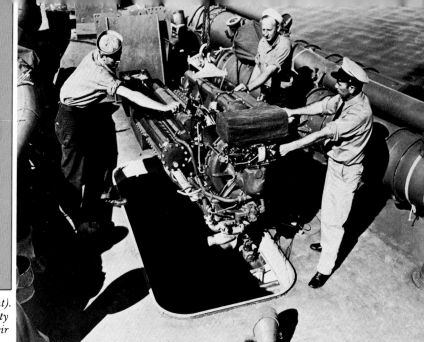

The 4M 2500 marine engine (above) and being installed in a Navy PT boat (right). Wartime propaganda photograph (below) carrying the caption: "PT boats, mighty midgets of the U.S. Navy—hurled over the water at an unbelievable speed by their super-charged engines that attest to the designing genius of Colonel Vincent."

the last four production:

Series	Configuration	Cubic Inches	Horsepower
1D 850	six cylinders in line	852	300
2D 850	six cylinders in line	852	300
1D 1135	eight cylinders in line	1136	400
1D 1700	V-12	1704	600
1D 2270	V-16	2272	800

Packard's lengthy report on this project claimed the company had now "given the Navy a complete family of engines which, Packard believes, will ably fulfill rigid demands for serviceability and yet weigh one third per horsepower less than other Diesels of their type . . . Diesel engines Packard is now building for Navy applications approach 5 pounds per HP as compared with 16-20 pounds per HP average for other Diesels used by the Navy . . . In order to accomplish light weight with compactness and high speed, Packard used aluminum in place of cast iron and steel. One of the major features of these engines is that all models are built around a standard cylinder design which makes for complete interchangeability of parts . . . with the crankshaft for both 6-cylinder and V12 identical. Basic design is standardized and the entire family of engines incorporates tremendous advantages of interchangeability.

"Perhaps the most difficult feat achieved in the new design [is that] the cylinder heads are made of high resisting alloy steel, are precision cast, and contain intake and exhaust ports and valve nests . . . It is the largest such unit ever produced in quantity.

"At present all of Packard's Diesel engine production is for the Navy, although additional military as well as marine, industrial and auto-motive applications are being studied for future development."

Packard began building the Series 142 Diesels at the Boulevard, in the "old" Merlin building, which after Packard's demise would become the property of Essex Wire, the diesel operation moving to Utica after the Detroit production stoppage in 1954. Full production was achieved in 1953, only two years after development began following the phase-out of PT boat engines. Engine development was strictly in-house done entirely by Packard engineers. Only one other company, Continental Motor, might have had the same abilities. Comments Ross Taylor, "people felt that Continental and Packard were the engineering culture of Detroit."

Unfortunately, Packard's expertise was not enough to dissuade the Navy from rushing the 142 Diesels into service without adequate development time. The Navy pressed them into use over Packard's objections and, predictably, they have since required more frequent overhauls than the norm and are difficult to keep in tune. The Navy began phasing them out in the early Seventies, although the replacement program was halted by tightened budgets.

Packard was involved in many other wartime projects of less note than those described already—"We even went to making shells for ordnance, 37-40 mm, in the old press shop on the other side of the Boulevard," remarks plant manager Dick Collins—and some programs resulted in major property expansion. In 1943 Packard took over a modern $5 million war plant in Ohio, naming it the Toledo Division, where many vital precision parts for engines built on the Boulevard were constructed. During 1944 this plant was expanded in order to carry out a program with the Army Air Corps, which had asked Packard to handle advanced aircraft engine development. Simultaneously, flight installation and test laboratories were designed for a new building at the Army Air Base at Willow Run, next to the Ford bomber factory. Construction began in December 1944. In these two facilities, both government-owned, research projects continued after the war, mainly on jet engine design. Operations finally ceased in early 1949, when the Air Force terminated the jet engine research contracts and closed the Toledo laboratory.

In 1950 Packard began negotiations with the Air Force for the production of J-47 turbojet engines. The contract was awarded in early 1951, Packard acquiring fifty-five acres adjacent to its Utica test track to erect a factory. The contract was one of the largest placed in Detroit up to that time, and Packard had high hopes for it. The J-47, a General Electric development, was used in the F-86, XF-91, B-36, XB-51, B-45 and B-47 aircraft, but its contribution to Packard's profit picture turned out to be insignificant, and the factory was turned into a parts, engine and transmission facility in 1954.

It is more than a little ironic, incidentally, to reflect on Packard's experience in defense work. Certainly the government did Packard no favors in return for extraordinary service in three wars. The most blatant case, of course, was the sacrifice Packard made in the Liberty engine program during the First World War, submerging corporate identity and interests in order to move the United States out of a position of gross inferiority in aircraft engines in less than a year. For this performance Packard received inferior, unequal contract treatment; Vincent had felt so strongly that Packard was victimized he so wrote the Aircraft Production Board—with no apparent success. Once again, two decades later, Packard was taking it on the chin for flag and country, diverting efforts toward Merlin, PT and military diesel projects at the expense of its principal business, long before it had to.

Packard was still involved in defense work after leaving the Boulevard in 1956, though by then the business belonged to Curtiss-Wright. What government work Studebaker-Packard had in 1956 was given over completely to that company under terms of the financial agreements that saved S-P; to handle this work, which Curtiss-Wright saw as the most promising aspect of S-P's business, a new corporation known as Utica Bend was formed. This company comprised the best properties of both Packard (Utica, Michigan) and Studebaker (Chippewa, Indiana), but

George Christopher and Lt. Commander (former Packard marine engine worker) Alan R. Montgomery. The ZIS, using Senior Packard body dies, in production in Russia.

operated for the betterment of Curtiss-Wright, not Studebaker-Packard. Ross Taylor, who was there at the time, recalls that "those who were working for Packard were suddenly receiving checks from Utica Bend." The employees were laid off from S-P and rehired in place by Utica Bend, which in Utica at least consisted of the same people who had been there all the time.

Roy Hurley, president of Curtiss-Wright, took an active interest in Utica Bend and tried to expand its markets, but without notable success. One day he got caught behind a Greyhound bus, decided such vehicles ought to be capable of greater speed, and started a program to market the 300 hp Packard diesel for buses! Taylor remembers that the engineers told Hurley the marine engine was unsuited to this application, but C-W's president insisted it could "shorten the time with Greyhound buses." Greyhound apparently agreed with the engineers.

From 1941 through 1945, Packard had produced for the Allied governments 67,626 marine and aircraft engines. This war work accounted for approximately ninety-nine percent of total sales volume for the period. The Packard annual report for 1944 pointed out to stockholders some "outstanding events" that had occurred in that last full year of the war: Two transcontinental speed records were set with Packard-built Merlin engines, one by a Mustang from Los Angeles to

New York in six hours thirty-one minutes, the other by a Mosquito from Labrador to Great Britain in six hours forty-six minutes. Packard-powered motor torpedo boats spearheaded the D-Day attack on the beaches at Normandy. The employee-donated Sky Clipper completed forty-eight missions over Nazi-occupied Europe, and the 50,000th war engine was completed on October 14th. Packard was understandably proud of its achievements and contributions to the war effort. From an original order for 9000 Merlin engines in late 1940, the Boulevard produced 55,523, the last on September 20th, 1945. Peak wartime production and sales were achieved in 1944 at $456 million. The 1945 figure, by contrast, was $217 million.

It should be mentioned too that the Henney Motor Company of Freeport, Illinois also contributed to the defense program. Since Packard was not producing chassis, Henney, like others in the field, was unable to make any commercial vehicles. Ray Laible, the Henney engineer in charge of chassis tooling, explains that the company was producing instead certain parts for the Merlin engines such as auxiliary supercharger shafts. Some of the assignments coming from Packard required very close tolerances, i.e., $\pm.0002$ inch. Laible relates this was "quite a change from the body business," but that it kept Henney afloat during the war. The firm also produced bomb caps for A.O. Smith and Blaw Knox, Jeep

You'll gross more—and _Net_ more— with Packard Marine engines!

● Tony Danielovich, Astoria, Oregon.

● John Tarabochia, Astoria, Oregon.

● D. S. Tarabochia, Skamokawa, Wash.

● **Just ask this _family_ who own them**

HERE'S a good idea of how Packard Marine power appeals to the operators of fast gillnet boats . . .

Martin Bajocich of Seattle, Washington, installed a 150-HP Packard Marine Eight in his 30-foot gillnetter, the _Donna B_, pictured above. What he learned about Packard efficiency was so good he quickly passed it along to three of his relatives, shown at left. Now all four of them gross more—and _net_ more!

Talk with experienced operators like these. Then, see your Packard Marine Engine dealer. Get his propulsion recommendation for your own boat!

Two great engines—standard-equipped with built-in finger-tip gear control.

100-HP MARINE SIX   150-HP MARINE EIGHT

Packard MARINE ENGINE DEPARTMENT

PACKARD MOTOR CAR COMPANY, DETROIT 32, MICH.

ASK THE MAN WHO OWNS ONE

Advertising Packard marine wares in fishing and boating magazines, fall of 1948.
Center: Marine usage passenger-car engines, the Six converted to the 1M245,
the 356 Super-8 to 1M356; marine engine exhibit at 1949 New York boat show.
Right: The Packard 2D-850 diesel marine unit (above), the 1D-1700 (below).

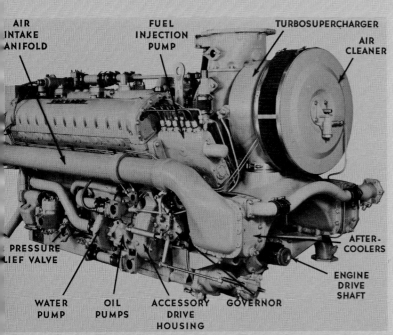

AIR
INTAKE
MANIFOLD

FUEL
INJECTION
PUMP

TURBOSUPERCHARGER

AIR
CLEANER

PRESSURE
RELIEF VALVE

AFTER-
COOLERS

ENGINE
DRIVE
SHAFT

WATER
PUMP

OIL
PUMPS

ACCESSORY
DRIVE
HOUSING

GOVERNOR

trailers, wooden assault boats, pontoons for temporary bridges, and formed-and-threaded tubing, some of which was made by Eastman Kodak under a Henney subcontract.

Packard's wartime income appeared enormous, but when the accounts were finally complete the company had earned only 1.2 percent on its combined 1941-1945 business. And it emerged from the war with its factory a shambles and its proving grounds a total loss. The latter had been leased to Chrysler for the testing of tanks, which destroyed the concrete surface in less than three years. In repairing the test track, commented a July 1947 edition of *Packard News*, there were three alternatives. "First the entire track could be ripped up and a new one built. Second, the track could be merely resurfaced. But Roy Stougaard, head of Packard's Field Building and Real Estate Department, chose the third way of rebuilding the test track: resurfacing the test track first with a black material known as black-top and then covering that perfect black surface with a 6-inch slab of concrete.

"A unique and forward looking engineering method was employed at this point. It has captured the interest of state highway commissions all over the U.S.A. and particularly the watchful eye of the Commission for the Design of Public Roads, Washington, D.C. For in this new Packard design only 10 contraction joints replace 230 . . . These 10 joints are entirely on the curves." Packard was revolutionizing the paving industry: ". . . besides this interesting construction detail, the concrete surface slab is laid over the black-top, unbonded and free to move separately from the black base . . . In October of 1946, the Packard test track was reopened for use in testing Packard automobiles. It stands today as the fastest track in the world. Rebuilt, the track is now valued at $2 million."

The notation on Packard's original request for bids on the job vividly tells the story of how scrupulous the company was to rebuild the track to the highest specifications possible. That notation read: "ANY CONTRACTOR WHO DOES NOT HAVE THE EQUIPMENT, THE PERSONNEL, THE TYPE OF SUPERVISION AND PERSONAL INTEREST TO ASSURE HIM OF PERFECTION AND ACCURACY IN PERFORMING THIS JOB SHOULD STOP AT THIS POINT AND RETURN THE PLANS TO THE PACKARD MOTOR CAR COMPANY."

In Packard's favor at war's end was a net worth of $109 million, including $33 million in cash. While it earned only $1.1 million during 1945, the company had no outstanding debt. During 1945, 301 new dealer contracts were signed, bringing the total to 1793, and 1500 applications were on hand for additional franchises. In short Packard was in very good financial condition. It could turn again to its primary product, and could succeed therewith, provided no false steps were taken during the unprecedented and confusing market conditions that lay ahead. But the income arising from World War II would never compensate Packard for the setbacks the war had caused, setbacks whose effect would be felt now, five years after they occurred.

CHAPTER TWENTY-FIVE

CIVILIANS
AGAIN

The Twenty-First Series

1946–1947

AUTHORS: GEORGE HAMLIN AND DWIGHT HEINMULLER

While the war had lasted, its winning was paramount. Nonetheless, the phrase "just as soon as the war is over" was frequently heard at East Grand Boulevard. Postwar planning for automobiles was continued throughout the conflict by a small cadre whose members, Packard insisted, were working "in off hours, with no interruption of war effort." But the hard-won victories of efficiency by Christopher and his team had been entirely lost after the factory was laid out for defense work.

New dealers continued to be signed on, although some were lost as the hostilities continued. The V-J Day figure of 1793 was the largest in Packard's history, and to that body George Christopher offered many rosy promises. One was his intent to build 200,000 cars yearly, the equivalent of peak production on two shifts, Christopher believing the pent-up demand for new cars at the end of the war would warrant this output. Many dealers took him at his word, making irrevocable cash commitments based on his expectations.

Plans were laid too for a greatly increased workforce. Peak peacetime employment had totaled around 12,000; management now planned for up to 28,000. From a wartime high of 41,000, the personnel roll had settled to about 10,000 by the end of 1945. But this was only temporary, it was felt, pending the swing into full-time automobile production. Packard's distribution system was revised, organized by zone as opposed to the prewar concept of many area distributors, with the distribution system for Canadian and export markets significantly expanded as well. But it would be a long time before all the new dealers and zone managers would have enough cars for sale to honestly justify their existence.

In the reconversion of its plant Packard faced a monumental task, considerably greater, for example, than did Ford or Willys, where motor vehicles had continued in production during the war for military purposes. Packard, by contrast, found itself on V-J Day with large volumes of war material in process, sizeable commitments to vendors and subcontractors, and a reconversion estimate of $1.5 million.

The situation was not wholly unexpected, of course. Throughout 1945 there was careful planning to determine which areas would be freed from defense work first. As space was abandoned, the maintenance force attempted to prepare it for the reinstallation of automobile machinery. On September 12th, 1944, anticipating the need for postwar expansion, a plant on Hern Avenue was purchased and another on Milwaukee Avenue was leased, though the following year Packard decided the Hern plant was expendable, and sold it. Real estate was evaluated as well, Packard purchasing some buildings which the American and British governments had erected on its property at the start of the war, and selling distribution properties it owned in London and New York. At the same time, war inventories were reduced according to plans worked out in advance with government agencies, and Packard began to subcontract some defense work to other firms which found themselves with a

Pages preceding: As early as mid-January of 1943, while World War II was still ongoing, Packard was planning its postwar plant layout. From the left:

decreased workload. More than $35 million in raw material, semi-completed products and finished items was disposed of through such measures. Finally, better than 200,000 government-owned machines, tools and similar equipment with a value of about $110 million were removed from the Boulevard plant and disposed of.

When the removal task was well along, work began on the relocation or reinstallation of some 3200 Packard-owned machines which had been suitable only for automobile production and therefore had been stored for the duration of the war—usually outdoors. The gear was in deplorable condition by 1945. According to Dick Collins, chief plant engineer at the time and a Packard employee from 1933, the badly weathered equipment was the main reason for Packard's postwar production delay. "You couldn't visualize . . . the condition of that machinery," he recounts. "We [had] sprayed it with Cosmoline and the motors were wrapped with weather protection, but the moisture got in. We'd bring in machines, and the motors and electric controls all had to be overhauled. The government paid the company to do this, but the time required was what got us down. We really didn't get rolling until '47 or '48."

Machinery salvage and defense reductions notwithstanding, if Packard was ever to meet Christopher's 200,000-car goal, a new final assembly line would be needed. Construction of a building to house one began on September 13th, 1945, and the first body was mounted there on October 19th—before the roof was complete. Improvisation was fre-

quent throughout the early production process. Engines, for example, were run in test cells quickly converted from the Merlin line. A dribble of 2722 cars emerged in late 1945, all Clipper Eight four-door sedans. There were enough handicaps without attempting a model mix.

The early months of 1946 were heartbreaking for Packard. The entire industry was experiencing difficulties; with demand for consumer goods at an all-time high, many labor unions chose to make demands of their own. During the war, self-interest had been frowned upon, although unauthorized work stoppages were not unknown and Packard experienced thirty-two of them in 1945, before automobile production started. Labor standards throughout the country—and in the auto industry in particular—had become lax during the war years, and all manner of casual practices had been condoned in order to Whip The Axis. Point man for the auto industry was gigantic General Motors. The unions shut GM down tight during the winter of 1945-1946, and the settlement finally reached there set the industry pattern. Minor strikes were experienced at other factories as the individual companies negotiated with the United Auto Workers, but in general the GM lead was followed—except at Studebaker. South Bend management elected instead to provide its workers particularly generous terms—bad judgment for which Packard would have to pay nine years later. But at the time Packard had worries of its own.

The Boulevard's brand-new twin assembly line operated only nine

Reconversion work began in the plant yard in May 1945, though there was still debris to be cleared in June; the new production line was ready by October.

days in the first quarter of 1946—holding production to less than 2000 units—primarily because of a fifty-five-day wait for a strike-delayed supply of main and connecting rod bearings. The Boulevard itself experienced a seven-day stoppage later in the year, due to the unauthorized walkout of its maintenance force. Strikes occurred in forty-seven supplier plants, the worst of which was at Briggs in September, closing Packard for a week due to lack of bodies. Briggs closed again in December to reorganize, and Packard lost another eight working days.

Now the 1941 agreement whereby Briggs had talked Packard out of the body business was revealed for what it was: a disaster with a long fuse. William H. Graves, who served Packard for forty years in various capacities, ending with a board seat as vice-president of engineering, recalls how it happened. "Briggs told Mr. Macauley that they could build bodies cheaper than we could. This was the first very serious mistake. If we couldn't build bodies cheaper, we had no business being in the auto business. But Mr. Macauley didn't realize that, and Briggs began. As soon as they got the business they started raising prices, until pretty soon they were more expensive than if Packard had built the bodies. That was the worst mistake we ever made, as all companies were pretty largely producing their own bodies. I used to argue with Jim Marks, who was purchasing agent . . . he took a lot of machinery out. I said if we can't build our own stuff we shouldn't be building! But he dwindled the tooling and would have something done outside, and we would get away from it."

The Briggs problem was only smarting in 1946, costing Packard thirteen working days. In 1954, however, it would force Packard to spend money it didn't have to get back into the body business. And in the meantime, Briggs bodies were built with hidden pockets which trapped moisture and produced rust—another distinctive and unneeded headache. But above and beyond these problems, the single biggest bottleneck for the entire industry remained the shortage of sheet steel.

Not only was there an unprecedented demand for the metal among auto manufacturers, but from hundreds of other industries as well. To complicate matters, the steel producers were hampered by strikes, worn-out machinery, and materials shortages of their own. But the steel shortage hit Packard hardest. Most of the competition had its traditional sources—Ford, for example, with its own moderate-sized foundry—but three of Packard's prewar steel suppliers, which had produced sixty percent of the Boulevard's prewar requirements, now had changed hands. Packard found itself forced to buy up odd lots of steel from as far away as Austria—and to fight for every ton. Even Kaiser-Frazer, the fledgling firm which had not even been in business before the war, had an easier time, because Henry Kaiser had contacts everywhere and knew where a lot of uncommitted resources lay. Kaiser sometimes had steel *flown* into Willow Run, and became so proficient at finding it that Nash, Hudson, Studebaker and Ford came to K-F for help. But nobody was helping Packard.

The 1946 annual report best summarized the supply situation: "While it is always our desire to improve our industry position, it is not always possible to be first in that improvement. For example, suppliers of critical materials—unable to meet unprecedented demands in 1946—allocated only a percentage of their products . . . . This penal-

From the left: Surveying the wartime testing damage done to the Proving Grounds track in early September 1945, with the resurfacing begun the following September.

ized Packard sharply.

"But, despite this handicap, we produced 42,102 cars in 1946. This output was 62.9% of our 1941 volume. The industry as a whole in 1946 produced 57.8% of its 1941 volume. We also produced a higher percentage of Eights and Super Eights to Sixes. Thus, we increased our dollar sales volume to the maximum allowed by the restricted supplies of materials."

Still, this was not the end of Packard's postwar dilemma. Difficulties arose in dozens of areas. A factor of some importance was Packard's practice of manufacturing virtually everything in one large building, unlike other manufacturers who utilized many smaller ones and thus could convert the plants expeditiously one at a time. All this brings the realization that Packard's 1946 volume lead over the rest of the industry was rather a remarkable feat. Various tricks came into play, of course. Parts substitutions were common, heater switches were used in lieu of dash light switches, alternate suppliers of many components were found. Serial it and get it out the door! At one point Packard was shipping cars without bumpers, a new owner finding himself driving a shiny automobile with a wooden plank mounted on the bumper supports. New bumpers were shipped on back-order by August 1946, whereupon the dealers exchanged them for the planks.

The annual report said of the labor situation, "Your company entered into an agreement June 7, 1946, with local 190, UAW-CIO covering hourly rated employees. It extends for a period of one year . . . During March, 1946 the Company increased wages 18½ cents an hour and salaries 15%." Other labor problems were pressed for solution: "Pend-

One month later, in October, the test track, valued at $2 million, would reopen.

ing in federal courts are suits for $44 million in alleged 'portal-to-portal' wages and demands claimed by present and former employees of the main Detroit plant [and] the Toledo plant. Also pending . . . were suits for $1,765,000 in alleged 'super-seniority' wages" claimed by employees at both locations.

Thus Packard weathered the disappointments of the first full year of peace. Of the 42,102 vehicles assembled, 30,883 were '46 models, the rest '47's. Not surprisingly, the books ended in the red, but the loss was not as high as it might have been ($3.9 million), and management confidently looked ahead to 1947. The public, meanwhile, was looking ahead to one hundred percent postwar automobiles which, thus far, Packard and most others weren't supplying.

Speculation about the looks of the "new postwar cars" had been rife as the war drew to a close. It needn't have been. Like the rest of the industry, it was no secret that Packard would build the same cars in 1946 as it had in 1942, and the company in fact announced this intent as early as 1943. Other manufacturers were more coy, but any student of the industry knows that dies are needed to produce sheet metal for new designs and that no one was ordering any new car dies during the war. For model year 1946, most manufacturers managed to effect a few bolt-on changes; for Packard this involved placing a new center grille on the Clipper to match its side grilles, and adding a new license plate bracket. The most noteworthy aspect of the 1946 line perhaps, to traditionalists at least, was the fact that it consisted only of Clippers.

The thrust before the war had been to phase out the old and phase in the new. For Packard the new was the mid-year 1941 Clipper which, by 1942, dominated the line. Although Clipper sales in the One-Sixty and One-Eighty lines were smaller proportionately than sales of "traditional" models, this was due to a larger number of models offered on the latter, plus the fact that expensive coachwork was provided only on the old chassis. It was clear that the days of the older styled cars were numbered, though apparently not to everyone.

During the war the Roosevelt Administration approached Packard with the proposal of selling its older model dies to the Union of Soviet Socialist Republics. The Russians had always been great fanciers of Packards, and needed automobile dies for civilian production. Naturally if they could obtain existing dies rather than manufacture new ones, they could save a lot of money.

Packard had been operating before the war with two entirely different types of automobiles and every intention to phase out the older models as soon as possible. The dies for these cars had already been in use three years, though one of those years was truncated, and would not be indefinitely valuable. Packard itself had outdated the dies with its own Clipper. The opportunity to sell them to the Russians must have been held a rare opportunity at the Boulevard, and at the same time it provided some smoothing of the war effort at a time when the Allied machine could benefit by it. Thus the deal was made, the dies went East, all of them, One-Ten, One-Twenty, One-Sixty and One-Eighty.

Enthusiasts today mourn their loss, placing the onus for many of Packard's subsequent setbacks on this sale and—by association—on Roosevelt himself. This is unjustified. If the Soviets had not received what the Boulevard regarded as relics, the dies would have become part of the wartime scrap melt. Packard may have suffered at the hands of the Roosevelt Administration—aside from problems stemming from the war, its share of the official White House fleet had fallen—but the sale of the old dies to the U.S.S.R. was no disservice to the company.

The Russian version of the 1942 Packard bore a striking likeness to its ancestor, though the hood ornament was a flying red star, the grille outline was altered, the engine was low-powered and of Soviet manufacture and the familiar notched hood had disappeared. It was a state favorite for many years. Named the ZIS (pronounced "zees"), the People's Packard was a monument to Joseph Stalin: The three letters are the initials of Russian words meaning "factory" (Z), "in honor of" (I), and Stalin. When the dies finally wore out the Russians would return to Packard for further styling inspiration, but by then more than a decade had passed, and the car would be named ZIL, Stalin having been deemphasized. The "L" honored the vehicle's Russian designer.

Having made the decision to stand or fall after the war with the Clipper, and having backed that decision with the disposal of any alternative, Packard had to market a full product line on a design which had been tooled for only two body styles—a two-door sedan (doubling in 1942 as a business coupe) and a four-door sedan, each on two wheelbases. This was tolerable only in the short run. Styling was quickly busy expanding the Clipper concept into other body types. Bodies which had not been tooled for Clipper styling in 1942 included convertibles, taxicabs, funeral and rescue vehicles, limousines and long-wheelbase sedans, formal sedans and catalogued custom cars.

The prewar taxicab had had a special chassis as well as a special body, so this gap was closed temporarily with the Clipper Six. Formal sedans and catalogued custom cars were simply dropped, in forthright admission that an era had ended. (Most coachbuilding houses had ceased to exist by the end of the war, though Derham of Rosemont, Pennsylvania remained, and executed a few attractive custom Clippers on individual order—not factory-commissioned.) Funeral and rescue equipment and convertibles would not be available in Clipper guise, principally because there wasn't time. Henney began work on Clipper commercial vehicles, but stopped when it realized a facelift was in the offing for 1948, and waited instead for that year's Twenty-Second Series.

The only line additions produceable in a reasonable period of time were limousines and long-wheelbase sedans. Henney, being relatively

idle, was called upon to build them. That company was ideally suited to the work, for it had been producing special bodies for Packard since 1935. One car each was planned in the Super and Custom lines, but all were ultimately marketed as Customs. The Freeport, Illinois firm took "in the white" bodies from Briggs, converted and trimmed them appropriately, building 3081 long-wheelbase Twenty-First Series cars in all, although never publicly claiming credit for them.

The Twenty-First Series line of cars, spanning the 1946 and 1947 model years, was therefore complete: Clipper Six club and touring sedan; Clipper Six taxi—sedan and partition type; Clipper Eight touring sedan; Clipper Eight DeLuxe club and touring sedan; Super Clipper club and touring sedan; and Custom Super Clipper club and touring sedan, limousine and seven-passenger sedan. The cars differed from the Twentieth (1942) Series only in detail, the most obvious being the aforementioned new center grille. Instrument panels were slightly modified through a change in numeral style, and 1942's small ridge was removed from the wheel covers. Prewar two-toning was also revised, the rear deck and upper doors now painted the top color on four-door as well as two-door sedans.

From the day the original Clippers had left the drawing board, they had been altered by Packard Styling—two-toned, made into club sedans, lengthened into limousines, cut short in front for Junior cars, bestowed with outside accessory sun visors, customized into convertibles, cobbled into taxicabs with roof lights and trunk racks. It is a tribute to Darrin's basic design that with all the tinkering, the integrity of the Clipper's lines remained intact.

It had not been easy to get the Twenty-First Series onto showroom floors. Indeed the only Packards available through April 1946 were Eights. Six production began in April, Super Clippers rolled in May, Custom Super Clippers, taxicabs and long-wheelbase cars in June.

Flagships of the line, the Custom Super Clippers were finished with an elegance befitting the name of Packard. Equipped with the nine main bearing, 356-cubic-inch engine, the Customs were whisperquiet and smooth on the road, and their performance ranked with the best of the day. All-wool interiors, deep "Mosstred" carpets and a total of seven interior courtesy lights were installed. Upholstery was done in tan, maroon, blue or green, and a unique headliner placed its seams fore-and-aft instead of side-to-side, solely "to add to the feeling of spaciousness and luxury." The Custom's chromed wheel covers were emblazoned in rich cloisonné—a long-time tradition.

Many optional features of the Custom were also provided on the remainder of the Twenty-First Series: roof-swivel or vacuum-powered antenna, indicator light for overdrive, fresh air heater, and underseat heater. Turn signals were available, albeit invisible on bright days, and the Electromatic vacuum-operated clutch was simplified. Other features of a mechanical nature which set the cars apart were a fifth shock absorber on the rear axle; Packard's well-tested, durable transmission and rear axle; electric windshield wipers and the whistling "Ventalarm" gas-filler signal. In an era when nothing special was needed to sell cars, Packard was making its cars special anyway.

The classic seller's market for automobiles lasted through 1948. New cars of any make, any type—and any quality—were in such short supply that any producer could sell literally anything he could build. Henry Kaiser took full advantage of the situation, and the firm he founded with Joseph W. Frazer found itself eighth in the industry and first among independents for model years 1947 and 1948. But Packard's experience was largely disappointing—production of the Twenty-First Series totaled only 80,660 units. The company which had talked of 400,000 cars in two full production years had failed to deliver, and the irony was that had those cars been built, they would have all been sold.

Automobile dealers were besieged, often by faithful regulars who wanted a new car, and wanted it immediately. Waiting lists were *de rigueur*, and genuine customers were given preference—though some agents moved people up on the list for less honorable reasons. Many impatient would-be buyers offered under-the-counter premiums for early delivery, and some dealers themselves demanded such gratuities. Whitewall tires, which were for all purposes unobtainable, were improvised with the help of white paint; if one customer was unwilling to pay for the ersatz whitewall, there was always another who would. The Office of Price Administration disallowed price increases, so many dealers stocked up on higher-priced models on which there was a greater net. Because accessories were not price controlled, countless cars were ordered with the full complement of factory options, some of them useless, all of them uniformly overpriced. Fog lights, tissue dispensers, exterior sun visors and other such ephemerae proliferated on immediate postwar cars. At some agencies one couldn't buy a car without a tissue dispenser, and the dispenser sold for up to fifteen dollars.

Some Packard dealers tried all these tricks, and, unfortunately, appear to have invented others of their own. To the extent that such practices cost future sales, they contributed to Packard's eventual end. To the extent that this chicanery was performed by desperate men who would not ordinarily have considered it—had the promised 200,000 cars a year been produced, for example—the responsibility can be laid in part to the golden oratory of Packard management. By proclaiming that Packard should be capable of a magnified production, gearing commitments to that production, and prodding dealers into acting upon it, George Christopher bought himself a sadly demoralized dealer force that would ill serve the company.

Still part of the Twenty-First Series, the 1947 models were introduced on November 11th, 1946. Changing the series number merely to accom-

Peacetime production returns to East Grand Boulevard, the first postwar Packard motorcar shown at the body drop—the date, October 26th, 1945. The kit car Clipper (below), partially assembled and crated for export.

The Twenty-First Series for 1946-1947. Above: DeLuxe Clipper two-door.
Below: Two-door Clipper Six. Center: Custom Super Clipper four-door.
Right above: Clipper Six four-door. Right below: The DeLuxe Clipper
four-door for 1947, with the revision of two-toning to the window line,
'46 being the only year in which four-door sedans featured two-toning
which extended down the trunk lid (this always a feature of two-door sedans).

modate a new model year was something Packard had been doing for a decade—reluctantly, because it had never been The Packard Way. But the company had acquiesced to industry resolutions for model year designations since 1935, and 1947 was no exception. There was neither the inclination to shut down for a model change nor the need to make any alteration to the Clipper line, which would sell with or without it. Further, a facelift had already been scheduled for 1948. The 1947 Clipper was therefore identical to the 1946 Clipper, save for the reversion of two-toning to the 1941-1942 style: Top colors were no longer applied to four-door trunk lids and window frames.

Granting that revising external appearance simply for model year differentiation is not necessary, it is nonetheless useful for technicians to be able to tell one year car from another. The device Packard settled upon was the body number, and because serial numbers were made up of body plus production numbers, that implied a serial change. For years body designations had lagged behind series designations because the former had not been changed annually; Eighth Series cars, for example, used chassis designations in the 800's and body designations in the 400's. This lag continued, four years behind, until 1936. Then, because the Thirteenth Series was skipped, the lag became five years—body 903 was on chassis 1400 and body 917 was on chassis 1401. This brought Packard

Above and below: The Super Clipper four-door sedan for model year 1946. Interestingly, Packard Styling had decreed that the word "Clipper" must always appear on the car door. Therefore,,depending upon which side of the car you were viewing, it was either a "Super Clipper" or a "Clipper Super."

Fiorello LaGuardia appraises his retirement gift from presidency of U.S. Conference of Mayors; right, Custom Super Clipper limousine and sedan interior.

into 1946 with chassis numbered in the 2100's and bodies numbered in the 1600's. Finally in 1947 the company simply caught the body numbers up with the chassis numbers.

This juggling explains why a 1946 Custom Clipper four-door, for example, is body style 1622, while the same model in 1947 became body style 2122. The chassis designation in both cases is 2106, because it did not change with the model year. Packard chassis numbers did not appear in the serial numbers unless an outside builder mounted a custom body. Then the chassis was serialed without knowledge of the type of body to be

mounted on it. No one was providing custom bodies on Twenty-First Series chassis, so adding a model year designation to the chassis numbers was not warranted. The limousines and long sedans which Henney was building were treated as production cars, and sold through Packard.*

---

*It is also important to note that the production numbers and engine serials continued without interruption through the entire Twenty-First Series—straight across the 1946-1947 model-year change. Production numbers of the 1947 models thus often appear inordinately high.

524

For 1947 the standard Clipper Eight (chassis 2101) was dropped, and all 1947 Eights were DeLuxe Clippers, selling for about seventy dollars more than the 1946 "standards." Also for 1947 the Six engine was redesigned and all Sixes got positive crankcase ventilation, formerly used only on taxicabs. At about the same time another offshoot of taxi technology became available to the regular line—an accessory trunk rack. This throwback to an earlier age was made optional on all Clipper four-doors, though few installations were made. A practical addition to a taxicab, the trunk rack was unsuited to Clipper styling and on a family sedan it was mud-ugly. Furthermore, installation was irrevocable, as it involved cutting the trunk lid.

It is interesting from the standpoint of history to compare the 1947 lines of Packard and its traditional rivals, Cadillac and Lincoln. Some important marketing tendencies are revealed.

PACKARD			CADILLAC			LINCOLN		
Custom Super (148' w.b.)			Seventy-Five (136" w.b.)					
2151	7 pass. sedan	$4504	7519	4dr sedan	$4471			
2150	7 pass. limo.	$4668	7523	7 pass. sedan	$4686			
			7523L	Business sedan	$4368			
			7533	Imperial sedan	$4887			
			7533L	Business Imp.	$4560			
						Continental (125" w.b.)		
						57	coupe	$4662
						56	cabriolet	$4746
Custom Super (127" w.b.)			Sixty Special (133" w.b.)					
2122	4dr sedan	$3449	6069	4dr sedan	$3195			
2125	club sedan	$3384						
Super Clipper (127" w.b.)			Sixty-Two (129" w.b.)			Lincoln (125" w.b.)		
2172	4dr sedan	$2772	6269	4dr sedan	$2523	73	4dr sedan	$2554-$2722
2175	club sedan	$2747	6207	club coupe	$2446	77	club coupe	$2533-$2701
			6267	convertible	$2902	76	convertible	$3143
DeLuxe Clipper (120" w.b.)			Sixty-One (126" w.b.)					
2112	4dr sedan	$2149	6109	4dr sedan	$2324			
2115	club sedan	$2124	6107	club coupe	$2200			
Clipper Six (120" w.b.)								
2182	4dr sedan	$1937						
2185	club sedan	$1912						
Overdrive, $82			Hydra-Matic,		$186	Automatic overdrive,		$96
Electromatic clutch & o/d, $112								

Most obvious is the incidental weak position of Lincoln. Its Continental was not at all comparable to the long-wheelbase Packards and Cadillacs selling for the same price, and Lincoln met the competition only in the middle ground around the $2700 mark. Packard at first glance seems well arrayed against Cadillac, but further study indicates this was not really the case. Weaknesses were apparent in Packard's position which would have strong effects on its sales in the post-seller's market—and on its standing in the eyes of the general public.

Firstly, Cadillac had literally cornered the top prestige bracket with five models of long-wheelbase cars. Packard's only "plus" in that area seems to have been its extra foot of wheelbase, whereas Cadillac was offering top-line models to suit a variety of needs, eclipsing Packard at least psychologically as the leading purveyor of automotive luxury. Cadillac also offered the popular Fleetwood-bodied Sixty Special, promoting its limousine features and long wheelbase, and its attractive selling price of about $200 to $250 below the approximately comparable Custom Super sedans.

Second, Cadillac by now was dominating the volume luxury market with its Sixty-Two and Sixty-One models. Aside from the relatively expensive Super Clipper, Packard simply had no answer in this field to Cadillac, or Lincoln for that matter. The latter even offered two trim versions of four-door sedan and club coupe, and a convertible to rival Cadillac's. Packard was unable to market a convertible—again more of a psychological setback than a business reverse, but one that was nevertheless important from the selling viewpoint. Cadillac also had the advantage of totally clutchless Hydra-Matic, while the best Packard could offer was its Electromatic clutch.

Finally, Packard appears strongest in the market for which it was probably least known, a leftover effect from the prewar Junior Clipper and before that, the One Twenty. For the time being, Packard's availability outside the luxury price class helped sell cars, but in the long run it severely damaged Packard's luxury standing. Years later many hundreds of thousands of dollars would be spent by the company trying vainly to recover its lost image. The reasoning which produced the One Ten and One Twenty before the war saved Packard's life but that same reasoning applied *after* the war, when the company could have written its own ticket to any place on the market, would ultimately prove a serious mistake.

The year 1947 saw a rise in production to 55,477 units (of which 35,-336 were 1947 models) and a loss of $1.5 million (which was turned into a $1.1 million profit through a tax refund based on carryback of the 1946 operating loss). But Packard still had no bank loans, no preferred stock or bonds outstanding, and a working capital of $34.7 million. Perhaps the magical figure of 200,000 cars was possible—only the foundry and transmission/rear axle operations needed additional capacity by the end of 1947. Yet, talk of 200,000 had diminished by now, predictively as history would prove, for peak production would never rise to much above half that figure.

It was unfortunate that the Clipper, born with such great promise, died as it did, a warmed-over prewar car, its freshness and impact destroyed by a four-year hiatus, spending its last model year marking time for the facelifted 1948 cars to come. Even more ignominiously, the Clipper endured its last two months of production life being built alongside the first of the new models: the long-awaited 1948 convertible.

CHAPTER TWENTY-SIX

ONE GUESS WHAT NAME IT BEARS

The Twenty-Second and
the Twenty-Third Series 1948-1950

AUTHORS: GEORGE HAMLIN AND DWIGHT HEINMULLER

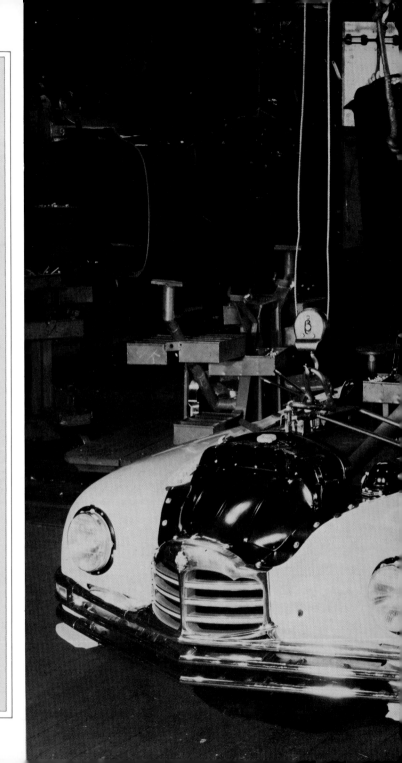

The 1948 Twenty-Second Series, introduced in the form of a Super Eight convertible in mid-1947, personified what many later referred to as the "bathtub look," which was not exclusive in those days either to Packard or the automobile industry. Industrial designers had universally decided, it seemed, that the round and the streamlined belonged to the future, and this theme strongly dominated the design of every consumer product from jukeboxes to refrigerators. Some automotive stylists were more influenced by the trend than others, notably those at Nash-Kelvinator, whose 1949-1951 cars were probably the most amorphous ever to leave a showroom. Packard was a relative newcomer to the councils of High Style, but was determined not to be left behind: Its version of the bathtub look resulted in a controversy which still rages among enthusiasts of the marque.

In 1947, however, other controversies prevailed at East Grand Boulevard, involving who would henceforth command Packard's destiny. The company was drifting nearly rudderless. Henry Bodman, who had been instrumental in pushing Packard into the Clipper program and was largely responsible for the Merlin contract, elected to retire. Alvan Macauley remained chairman of the board, but his influence and activity were on the wane. He had probably stayed on overlong, though his leadership had seen Packard at its pinnacle. To a considerable degree, in fact, history may judge that Packard's own influence directly paralleled that of Alvan Macauley. Nevertheless, by 1947, new leadership was clearly required.

On April 19th, 1948, Macauley finally retired as board chairman—at age seventy-six. George Christopher assumed complete control as president, the chairmanship not being filled after Macauley's departure. Christopher had a better automotive background than his colleagues on the board, and his production expertise had helped bring the company back from the brink of fiscal disaster before the war. But his abilities were narrowly based. An old automotive hand, Christopher had great plans for Packard, but his presidency would be marked more often by failure and must be ranked as one of the climacterics of the company's postwar history. He was simply not the man to lead Packard to new heights. Instead he led it to the Twenty-Second Series.

"A lot of us at Packard styling wanted to advance the Clipper design," says then-chief stylist John Reinhart—"keep the thin nose and sweeten the thing, and make it into a very aerodynamic car. We called this idea the 'needle nose.' But [management] wanted a lower, fatter profile, so we had to work out some of those great tremendous front ends . . . I liked the Clipper very much, a whole lot better than the '48. It would have lasted another two years without a doubt. But they said not to do it, and you have to follow management's dictates." The correctness of Reinhart's position is recognizable in hindsight. At the time, however, there was a virtual styling revolution raging all over Detroit. Studebaker's new postwar design, the new Kaisers and Frazers, and even the radical Tucker were all having their effects on customers, and those who depended on customers. As Packard management doubtless

Pages preceding: The Twenty-Second Series in production. These pages: Ed Macauley's Phantom as it evolved from 1941 to 1946, the car as originally delivered below.

knew, there would shortly be a new Hudson, a new Nash, and totally new 1949 designs from the Big Three. And though the war had halted its production for three years, the Clipper already was a five-year-old design.

The major work on Twenty-Second Series styling was done at Briggs under Al Prance, the styling chief. Originally conceived as an inexpensive rework of the Clipper, the job involved filling in the sides of the car with clay from fender to fender to make the vehicle more "up to date." This technique resulted in doors several times thicker than they needed to be, and produced no noticeable cost saving: The only panels salvaged from the job were the top stamping and the deck lid.

Overseeing the work at Briggs on behalf of Packard was Edward Macauley. At the time he was driving a custom-built Packard known as the Phantom, or (at East Grand Boulevard) the "dog car." Originally built in 1941 by Hess & Eisenhardt, the Phantom began life as a One-Eighty Darrin-esque landaulet with a transparent roof panel over the driver, pushbutton doors and dummy landau irons. Contrary to some versions of Packard history, the Phantom did not resemble in the slightest the Twenty-Second Series as first built, and it followed—instead of led—the bathtub school of Packard styling. Macauley did try out his "mouth organ" grille on this car in 1944, and a highly modified version of that grille appeared on the 1948 cars, but otherwise the 1944 "dog car" bore little similarity to the Twenty-Second Series and continued to feature separate fenders.

Above, the Phantom receives a new grille, hood and wheelcovers, the auxiliary lamps are moved and the landau bars upended. Moving closer to a "bathtub" look below, the car sports flow-through fenders, the contemporary wheelcovers and a new hood ornament, with the nameplate removed and the landau bars upended again. At the bottom, the Phantom finale, with nameplate, new taillights and wheelcovers, Twenty-Second Series rear bumper, and no hood ornament.

Here with new paint, parking lights removed, John Reinhart-designed plastic roof.

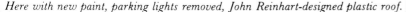

The Clipper facelift originally planned for the Twenty-Second Series. The heavier front end and recessed headlights (left) evolved to a more streamlined look (right).

Macauley's custom served as a sort of personal laboratory of styling ideas, and over the years saw many interesting engineering features such as a twelve-cylinder engine, special highway horns, power brakes and trunk lid, and an eight-stack exhaust pipe. Some items used on the car eventually saw production in subsequent Packards: a glove drawer (1951), automatic transmission (1949) and instrument warning lights (1951). There were also items that Packard never used but others did: front seat armrest (Imperial), vanity compartment (Studebaker), and reclining seats (Nash).

By the time the Twenty-Second Series was being worked up at Briggs, Ed Macauley's ever-changing Phantom had been nicknamed, due to its color, the Brown Bomber. It had a front bumper and hood line that could be adapted to the Clipper, as well as the lower grille outline of the Twenty-Second Series to come. Final responsibility for the design of the 1948 Packard goes to Briggs for the body, Macauley for ornamentation. Reinhart, who under Macauley designed the grille, summed the car up by saying it was "in tune with the times, but it sure wasn't very attractive."

Attractiveness, of course, is largely a matter of taste, and the 1948 Packard was actually awarded a disproportionate number of styling awards: "Fashion Car of the Year" gold medal from the Fashion Academy of New York; "Finest and most beautiful car in the show," for the Super Eight convertible, at Cacuta, Colombia; the Concours d'Elegance prizes from automobile shows at Caracas, Luzerne, Sofia and Monte Carlo; and the "Grand Prix," for the Super Eight, at Rome. But opinion was far from unanimous on the part of the public and the automotive trade writers—one recalls that the irrepressible Tom McCahill effectively summed up the "cons" by calling the car a "goat." The subjective nature of aesthetics notwithstanding, the fact remains that the Twenty-Second Series Packards were controversial, especially

among designers who are presumably trained to be relatively objective about such matters. A good many people did not like the way they looked in 1948, and a good many still do not.

Yet there was no denying that the new car was a Packard. "ONE GUESS WHAT NAME IT BEARS!" was the headline on a widely distributed advertisement which omitted the word Packard altogether. (The marque name was also not to be found anywhere on the exterior of the Custom series.) But the cars had plenteous Packard identity: From the rear they were still similar to the famous Clipper. They used wheelcovers with hexagon centers and a cloissoné emblem on the Custom, the Packard family crest was back on the grille after a long absence, and the outline of the grille was easily recognizable. Temporarily absent was the sweepspear, which had so long decorated the edges of Packard hoods—it would return in mid-1949 for another four-year run. The lineup for 1948 was as follows:

Chassis 2220 Six Long-Wheelbase
Model 2280 New York Taxi

Chassis 2240 Six
Model 2282 Four-Door Sedan, export only
Model 2286 Four-Door Taxi

Chassis 2201 Eight
Model 2292 Four-Door Sedan, $2275
Model 2293 Station Sedan, $3425
Model 2295 Club Sedan, $2250

Chassis 2211 DeLuxe Eight
Model 2262 DeLuxe Four-Door Sedan, $2543
Model 2265 DeLuxe Club Sedan, $2517

Proposed new lines were added to production '42 car photo by artists in 1944.

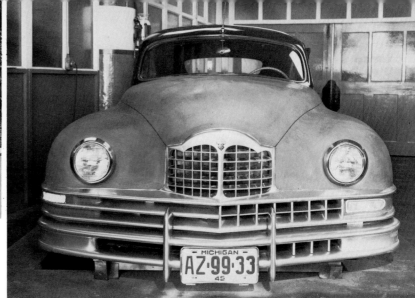

Ultimately, production prototypes with a completely revised fuselage and flow-through fenders (below), and the Custom Eight front end (above), emerged.

<u>Chassis 2202 Super Eight</u>
Model 2272 Four-Door Sedan, $2827
Model 2275 Club Sedan, $2802

<u>Chassis 2232 Super Eight Convertible</u>
Model 2279 Convertible Victoria, $3250

<u>Chassis 2222 Super Eight Long-Wheelbase</u>
Model 2276 Seven-Passenger Limousine, $3650
Model 2277 Seven-Passenger Sedan, $3500
Model 2270 DeLuxe Seven-Passenger Limousine, $4000
Model 2271 DeLuxe Seven-Passenger Sedan, $3850

<u>Chassis 2206 Custom Eight</u>
Model 2252 Four-Door Sedan, $3750
Model 2255 Club Sedan, $3700

<u>Chassis 2233 Custom Eight Convertible</u>
Model 2259 Convertible Victoria, $4295

<u>Chassis 2226 Custom Eight Long-Wheelbase</u>
Model 2250 Seven-Passenger Limousine, $4868
Model 2251 Seven-Passenger Sedan, $4704

Mechanically, the Twenty-Second Series cars were nearly identical to the Twenty-First, and the model lineup remained the same with Six, Eight, Super Eight and Custom Eight—although the Six was now available only as an export sedan or taxicab. The six-cylinder engine was rapidly becoming synonymous with low-powered, low-priced cars, and regardless of its merits Sales decided there was limited utility in its retention. This was probably a correct decision for a car in Packard's class; at General Motors, for example, the six would shortly be consigned only to Chevrolet, and the lack of a V-8 would later prove to be one rock upon which the Kaiser-Frazer enterprise foundered.

Summer 1947, the first Twenty-Second Series car, a Super Eight convertible, at the body drop and on the line, alongside Twenty-First Series Clippers.

The "standard" Eight was offered in a basic and deluxe version two- and four-door sedan, plus one new body style, the Station Sedan. The latter was another example of Ed Macauley going ten rounds with Common Sense, and Common Sense coming out the loser. Against the advice of his colleagues, Macauley brought out this expensive automobile ($3425 at introduction, only $275 less than the two-door Custom Eight) with Packard's least expensive eight-cylinder engine (288 cubic inches, 130 horsepower). It represented a large investment in tooling, special panels being required for the roof and quarters. The body was all-steel, an early application of this principle to station wagons (but second to Willys-Overland), and Macauley trimmed it with generous panels of

white ash which required semi-annual varnishing. The tailgate structure was all wood and of two-piece design hinged at top and bottom, a configuration to become standard in the industry for many years. A folding bracket was mounted on the tailgate to display the license plate when the gate was down. The rear opening was quite small, however, and the car was rather impractical as a utility vehicle, albeit a highly interesting one that is today prized by collectors.

The 288 engine represented only a slight increase—six cubic inches—from its predecessor, but was significant as a change in engineering philosophy. The displacement came about through the use of a 3½-inch piston in *all* Packard engines: the unchanged six and the

356-cubic-inch nine main bearing Custom Eight, and the new 327-cubic-inch Super Eight.

Twenty-Second Series Super Eights were unique: They not only used their own 145 hp engine, a different unit than the Customs, but were mounted on a shorter 120-inch wheelbase. Their lineal predecessors, the One-Sixty and Super Clipper, were basically the same mechanically as their more expensive 1948 stablemates, though with less costly trim. But for the Twenty-Second Series alone, the Super Eight became a car midway between the standard and Custom versions. The Supers comprised the largest single model lineup in some time, with seven body styles available on three chassis. The standard passenger cars were the club and touring sedans on 120-inch wheelbases, while a new 141-inch wheelbase mounted the first Super Eight limousines and seven-passenger sedans in years. There was a standard and deluxe version of each long wheelbase.

The Super Eight did look more or less like the lower-priced Packards, with identical grille and sheet metal and only minor differences in ornamentation—many owners found this objectionable and said so. But there was no mistaking the Custom.

For the Custom Eight, Packard pulled out all the stops. To a model line that in 1947 had consisted of two- and four-door sedans and seven-passenger sedan and limousine were added a commercial chassis and a convertible victoria—the latter, at $4295, the highest priced production car of its day, exclusive of limousines. Glorious brochures in full color were created for the Custom. The car was distinguished by an eggcrate grille and similar rear motif, a newly styled pelican hood mascot (optional on lesser models), a double bar of bright metal along the lower body panels, and traditional cloisonné wheel cover emblems. Inside, the cars were as distinctively crafted as the previous Custom Super Clipper, though one feature from the latter—Amboyna burl garnish molding overlays—had given way to universal application of pearwood graining. But the graining was more abundant, covering nearly a quarter of each door panel, and the leather bolsters on the seat frame were carefully pleated to match the design of the bedford cord upholstery. As before, Customs were equipped with foam-backed cut-pile Mosstred carpets, duck down-filled seat backs and seat cushions adjustable for firmness, six interior courtesy lights and the distinctive woolen headliner with fore-to-aft seams. On the convertible, hydraulic window lifts and seats were standard, while on closed cars window regulator handles consisted of ten intricately combined individual pieces if hydraulics were not specified.

Chassis equipment matched the luxury of the Custom body. The fifth shock absorber was continued, along with the 356-cubic-inch engine, the latter now curiously rated at 160 horsepower instead of its former 165—and the most widely admired transmission in the industry with its nine roller bearings, which compared favorably to Cadillac's six.

Above: The first Packard and the millionth (a 1948 Super Eight), with George Christopher standing and Alvan Macauley at the tiller. Below: George Woodside and Henry Schryver (who worked on the first Packard), Hugh Ferry flanking Mrs. M.C. Summers and Mrs. Oliver Gardner (niece and sister of James Ward) as plaque is unveiled in Warren on site where first Packard was built in 1899.

The coin minted by Packard on the occasion of its golden anniversary in 1949.

Packard's Electromatic clutch option continued to be available, but was not compared very favorably to Hydra-Matic, which Cadillac had had since before the war. Packard engineering was already at work on that problem.

The introduction of the new Twenty-Second Series was spaced between the Super and Custom convertibles on July 25th, 1947 and the rest of the line about two months later. A commercial chassis had been placed on the market early too, and for the same reason as the convertibles: Packard had been devoid of these body types when its competition was offering them. Never tooled for hearse, ambulance or convertible production before the war, the Clipper's lack of these body styles was painful in the face of Packard's former leadership in commercial bodies and traditionally higher than average proportion of convertibles. Clippers, as mentioned earlier, continued to be available alongside the new body styles until the rest of the 1948 line appeared. Some $1.5 million was spent on tooling and engineering the convertible alone, and Christopher finally found a use for his double production line.

Packard's production line was one of the most modern material-handling conveyor operations in the world. New from ground up since the war, it represented an investment of $25 million. The line was controlled by teletype and carefully synchronized, with parts flowing to cars from both sides on three levels of factory operation. It was Christopher's finest achievement and was easily capable of serving Packard's needs—too easily as it turned out—into the foreseeable future.

The rest of the Twenty-Second Series was introduced on September 8th, 1947, prices ranging from $2250 for the Eight club sedan to $4868 for the Custom limousine, and a smattering of offerings from custom body producers still hanging on despite depression, warfare and the coming of the envelope body. Most custom-bodied Twenty-Second Series Packards were executed by Derham and Henney, with an occasional

Campaigning for the same job, and doing it in the same car (a Custom Eight convertible), Thomas Dewey and Harry Truman on parade during the '48 presidential race.

one-off venture from such foreign coachbuilders as Worblaufen of Germany and by Ramseier of Switzerland.

In the 1948 calendar year, 98,897 Packards were built, the second best year on record. (Nineteen thirty-seven had been, and would remain, the best ever with 109,518.) Total production for the 1948 model year was 95,495, but that was not the last of the Twenty-Second Series.

The industry was entering a period of feverish annual model revision—but Packard wasn't convinced of its wisdom. Its 1947 cars, for example, were identical to the 1946's, and the seller's market obliged the company's conservative approach. This policy was retained: When the 1948 model year was finished, the 1949 Packards were announced on November 1st, 1948, but the lines simply kept rolling and the Twenty-Second Series was continued without a single change.

This did present an identity problem. Packard serial numbers had been based on body designation since the Ninth Series, but in 1947 the body designation was keyed to the series designation, which at that time was "21." Thenceforth, if the series didn't change with a new model year, the body designation didn't either, and thus for 1949 Packard serial numbers would not reflect model year information. In order to distinguish the 1949's, a "-9-" was inserted between the body and serial numbers on vehicle identification plates. For example, the last 1948 Custom convertible was (body-serial number) 2259-3105, and the first 1949 version was 2259-9-3106. Bare chassis serial numbers were suffixed too—commercial chassis 2213 became 2213-9, for example—so cars by outside body makers could also be identified as to model year.

Packard earnings for 1948 rose to $15 million, a great improvement over the scant million of 1947. The cars covered a sizable portion of the market, on five wheelbases, with four engines and eight body types. It was easy to be convinced that things had never looked better. But in reality the company's prospects had seldom been worse.

The public's division over what Sales called "Free Flow Styling" was also reflected at the Boulevard. Christopher argued that Packard could not afford to replace the bathtub design for some time, others believed that not only could it be replaced but, more important, it must be. "The Packard president," said *Fortune*, "was the kind of production man that other production men brag about, but as a president he was so much sand in the gears. He irritated his colleagues by pinchpenny policies that varied from a refusal to paint the ladies' lavatory (it hadn't been redecorated in a decade) to an insistence [not to produce] a completely retooled car. He infuriated the dealers first by lack of production, then by eager publicity about the 1948 car when they had a six-month inventory of old-style 1947's on their hands, and finally by unfilled promises of a bigger output of the 1948 model."

Christopher, the magazine continued, "had taken a tour around the country and, no doubt feeling that Packard's Golden Jubilee called for a bit of ebullience, promised everybody—dealers and stockholders alike—that the company would be making 200,000 cars a year in 1949, over twice as many as in 1948. Many of the dealers spent money expanding their establishments but by mid-1949 it was clear that far from producing 200,000 cars, Packard would only shade its 1948 output . . . What was happening was clear also to the directors and some of the principal stockholders: over a period of twenty-four months the number of dealers resigning had reached 500."

The much-discussed good cash position of Packard after the war was really the only tangible the company had going for it. This strength of the company was an historic one, earned by Packard, Joy, Gubitz, Vincent, Macauley, men who were now gone or soon leaving. Recent management had neglected a traditional Packard practice: building for the future. Thus, as the firm entered its golden anniversary year of 1949, no one knew for sure what lay immediately ahead.

The anniversary clearly called for a celebration, however. Among automobile manufacturers, only Studebaker was older, and only the Packard remained of the forty marques which had been shown at the first New York Automobile Show back in 1900. An all-new line of 1949 Packards would have been the most festive way to celebrate, but there weren't any new Packards. So the company settled for a mild facelift, called it the Twenty-Third Series, and with fanfare announced the only automatic transmission ever developed by an independent manufacturer—Ultramatic.

Packard had been experimenting in this field as long as anyone in the industry. GM's Hydra-Matic was not the first automatic transmission on the market but it was the first commercially successful one and made a lasting impression on buyers. Doubtless, too, it spurred Packard toward further development of its own version.

At the Boulevard, chief research engineer Forest McFarland had begun work on a torque converter featuring a centrifugal clutch in the middle Thirties. (He later said he "didn't like it much.") At least two others at Packard—Tommy Milton and Cornelius Van Ranst—had also worked in the field but without visible results, and two outside sources—Sunstrand of Wisconsin and a Windsor, Ontario firm—had approached Packard with their own proposals. Of the latter McFarland noted, "we did quite a bit of fooling around with them [but] finally gave up." Though some progress was made on gearing work, it was the autumn of 1944 before Vincent and McFarland were released from the Merlin program to begin concentrating on what became the Ultramatic.

McFarland was determined that his transmission would be a major improvement on contemporary technology. "When Hydra-Matic came out," he commented, "it had a total of eight mechanical shifts. While it was convenient and rather ingenious in terms of gearing, it required a godawful number of shifts on the road. Back in the early Forties I patented a torque converter job, an Ultramatic forerunner but [with] more shifts than the Ultramatic. It had four shifts, and if we'd worked on it we could have cut it down from four to two because I did a great deal of gearing work on it."

Of course Ultramatic was far from a one-man show. McFarland worked under Vincent's general cognizance and direction, and working with him were development project engineer Warren Bopp and automotive division staff engineer Herbert Misch, the latter to become vice-president of engineering some years later. All those involved ran tests with two-speed gears, then installed test units in 1946 Clippers for further development of the torque converter and gearing. "If we had more time," said McFarland, "we would have had a three-speed job, but knowing the amount of work you had to do with clutches and so forth, we stuck with this two-speed job and had the converter [arranged] so you could kick down into ordinary gear. This wasn't as good as a second

536

Chief research engineer Forest R. McFarland; cutaway drawing of Ultramatic transmission, introduced in the Twenty-Third Series during mid-May of 1949.

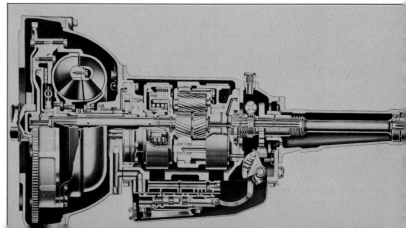

speed [for kickdown] but it did a good job.''

The new Ultramatic was a good job from many standpoints. A torque converter like Buick's Dyna-flow, it marked a significant departure from the Hydra-Matic principle of multi-gear changes with power applied through a simple non-torque multiplying fluid coupling. A two-element coupling, having no gear reduction, needs the extra gearing behind it (Hydra-Matic was a four-speed) to cope with the characteristics of a piston engine. But Packard's torque converter was a new development, combining two turbines with a pump and a reactor to produce torque multiplication, or gear reduction, *within the unit*, no external gearing being required. Packard didn't use any external gears—and neither did Buick with its Dyna-flow—though both Packard and Buick did put in a manually selected low gear behind the torque converter, to cope with extraordinary situations such as a sandy road surface or hard pulls. In ordinary driving there was never a need for the low range.

In addition to its torque converter, which predicted the eventual evolu-

tion of all other automatics, Ultramatic had other features unique unto itself. The converter had higher internal torque multiplication than any rival automatic, and this resulted in better acceleration. Secondly, McFarland had added a direct-drive clutch to the final product.

The direct-drive clutch was the single most distinguishing feature of Ultramatic—then and now. It was an eleven-inch cork-faced unit running in transmission fluid like Hudson's cork clutch, actuated automatically by a combination of vehicle speed and driver throttle pressure. Once engaged—and engagement was so sure that most drivers thought of it as a gear change—the torque converter was no longer in use. All power was transmitted through the clutch, for lower operating temperatures, greater fuel economy, and improved deceleration.

In its day, Ultramatic was the perfect transmission. Borg-Warner later used its direct-drive clutch principle in its own unit (sold to Studebaker until 1956, and to Jaguar for many years thereafter). So did GM's own transmissions for buses. In 1974, under pressure for greater

Twenty-Second Series Packards were produced in greater numbers than any lines previous, although with a six-month longer production life, from 1948 to mid-1949. Above, the Eight in touring and club sedan models. Below, the Station Sedan, the car for suburbanites, and the Super Eight convertible for more sporting drivers.

fuel economy, manufacturers began taking another look at Ultramatic's principles, Chrysler having direct lock-up back on the road by 1978. In the matters of durability and performance, Packard's transmission was unrivaled until the horsepower race of the middle Fifties. *Consumer Reports*, never easy to please, rated Ultramatic highly, in 1952 as a "Best Buy." *Popular Science* said it worked "like a dream," that Packard's version could "give all other transmissions aces and deuces and still pace the field."

It is interesting to look back on the comments of *Motor Trend*, a magazine later in the vanguard of those demanding small and sensible cars, but in Packard's day one fully enamored with Hamtramck Hotrods. As early as 1952 it lamented the absence of a kickdown in direct-drive, whereby Packard might reach "today's standards of performance." In 1953 *Motor Trend* mentioned "a loss of fuel economy when accelerating at low speeds" as the price one paid for keeping the throttle down. In 1954, with the horsepower race in merry full swing the recommendation was: " . . . wind up till you're at 50 mph [in Low range]; then drop into High (it corresponds to Drive in other automatics). You'll have skipped the torque converter part of the range—it no longer adds much push to the engine's own thrust at that speed—and you're in direct drive." And you're also cutting your fuel economy almost in half. But those were the Fifties.

Motor Trend did, however, recognize that Ultramatic's goal was convenience and smoothness rather than stump-pulling power takeoffs when it summed up Ultramatic in 1953: "The greatest advantage is, of course, that it eliminates the usual gear shifting, and replaces it with unusually smooth acceleration. Acceleration whine is at a minimum, and our test car was free of the clanks and clunks so often heard in automatics . . . . This transmission has no hill-holding or anti-creep features, but it

The Twenty-Second Series. Left: Custom Eight limousine (above), sedan (below).

has an uncommon feather touch, and is extremely sensitive in operation, making the car easier to park than most automatic-drive cars.''

Something like $3 million was spent in 1949 on preparing and building new Ultramatic production facilities—over and above research and development costs. For tooling, the tab was $8.5 million. No other independent manufacturer was ever able to muster the engineering expertise required to develop its own automatic transmission, and no other company of Packard's size ever attempted it. But to Packard's engineering staff it was just one more job well done, and if not exactly done on time—other units were on the market well ahead of Ultramatic—it was done better.

Said McFarland, "We had more power in the converter (than Dyna-flow) and a 3.54 rear axle ratio versus Dyna-flow's 3.9. Dyna-flow was not a direct lock-up, while Hydra-Matic locked up in various degrees and in a Cadillac you'd get up to 5-6 mph and then go right into second, then third. [Hydra-Matic] gave a pretty good account of itself but it wasn't too smooth, whereas we had a beautifully smooth job.''

Smoothness over lightning acceleration was a choice Packard made based on a certain philosophy which, while sensible in retrospect, probably wasn't as marketable at the time. McFarland recalled that then-chief Cadillac engineer Ed Cole and Cadillac's general manager Jack Gordon "came over and wanted to ride in an Ultramatic Packard. Cole admitted it was beautiful for smoothness except that he said 'we've given our customers the performance we have in Hydra-Matic and we can't step back to this.' I think Cole made the logical answer." When McFarland was asked if Packard really wanted great performance, he said his company "didn't go all out but the performance was there . . . . When you went into first or second you were right in gear, whereas with others you'd get a clunk." And for a given axle ratio Ultramatic outper-

formed Dyna-flow through its fast-acting clutches. McFarland: "They were lovely.''

Of Buick, McFarland recalled that "Oliver Kelly and his gang over there did a nice job. We were good friends. For the time [Dyna-flow] was good, but I felt it had too much slip. It just seemed to me that I was in second gear all the time. Col. Vincent couldn't stand it either." About Chrysler, McFarland said its engineers "examined our transmissions and some of them told me ours was by far the quietest of anything they had ever found—they figured this was because we had bigger gears. Now, they were bigger, but we had learned an awful lot about making quiet gears, and we had applied it to the problem.''

After Ultramatic appeared Packard became involved in a lawsuit arising over allegations by a French inventor named Fleishel, who claimed he owned the rights to a hydraulic regulation valve in the Packard transmission. McFarland had met this "interesting" gentleman but had suspected his integrity, and reported his meeting with vice-president and patent counsel Milton Tibbetts. Fleishel later also sued GM, Hudson and Borg-Warner, trying, as McFarland said, to "make a clean sweep of the industry"—evidently other companies had been doing some inventing of their own, particularly on valves of different operating principles. The situation was reminiscent of the infamous Selden patent, in which an inventor claimed royalty rights on all self-propelled gasoline vehicles because he had invented one earlier.

In court, Fleishel's attorney tried to trick McFarland with the opening question: "Mr. McFarland, isn't it true that you could have made the Packard valve out of the Fleishel valve by merely exchanging the ports?" McFarland replied, " . . . when you say 'merely' you talk about a slight change in degree. But it is not a slight change in degree, it's an entire change in principle—from a valve you can move back and forth to a valve

m the left: Custom Eight convertible; Super Eight all-weather town car with body by Derham; Super Eight four-door convertible with body by Worblaufen of Germany.

that, once it makes its shift, is irreversible. So they are two entirely different valves." No more questions were asked, and McFarland remembered that Packard's counsel asked him, "Do you want me to kiss you now or when we get back to the hotel?" Packard won the lawsuit.

With Ultramatic ready, it was time for Packard's Golden Anniversary. Because the celebration could hardly be postponed until 1950, a new Twenty-Third Series was introduced midway in the 1949 model year, on May 2nd. Body and chassis numbering was changed again: The "-9-" suffix was dropped and body/chassis numbers became conventional again with designations in the 2300's. Hence there were two distinct 1949 models—both the 2201-9 and the 2301, for example, are 1949 Packard Eights. At 148,633 units, the Twenty-Second Series scored the highest production total for any Packard line, albeit with the advantage of six extra months of life.

Changes for the Twenty-Third Series were minimal. The rectangular taillights, which had started life on the 1941 Clippers, were replaced by oval units on all but the commercial cars and Station Sedans, the metal trim on the side was revised to a single piece of brightwork at mid-door, and the rear window was enlarged. A Packard nameplate, never found on previous Custom Eights, appeared on the front fenders, and the traditional barb or spear shape reappeared on the side molding after having temporarily disappeared on the Twenty-Second Series. The open front bumper was closed in.

Minor changes were also made to interiors: Twenty-Third Series brake and clutch pedals were round (rectangular pedals would return in 1951) and Ultramatic was standard on the Customs and shortly optional on the rest of the line. The Custom itself lost some distinction with a less luxurious interior and a conventional left-right seamed headliner. The Six was eliminated, and the long-wheelbase Custom sedans and limousines were no longer offered, while the Super Eight models were considerably rearranged.

The Super Eight shake-up was significant because it represented an upgrading of the car. Whereas the Twenty-Second Series Super Eight was basically the same vehicle as the Junior lines, the Twenty-Third Series version shared sheet metal and wheelbase with the Custom. This, of course, represented a dilution of the latter, but the move was inevitable because Custom production was too limited (12,685 Twenty-Second Series models) for production man Christopher to continue justification of separate sheet metal. All Twenty-Third Series limousines and seven-passenger cars were designated Supers and placed on the 141-inch wheelbase chassis, putting Packard out of the 148-inch wheelbase field for several years.

Upgrading the Super to a larger chassis required a new grille too, whereas the Twenty-Second Series Eights and Super Eights had shared the same front end. The old Super grille was too small and could not be used with the new sheet metal, so the Super received a new fluted grille of its own with double-height parking lights. The Eight and Custom Eight retained their previous grilles, the latter with double-height parking lights like the new Super.

The Super's new grille presented an opportunity to interchange some parts with the Custom, which appealed to Christopher, so a new model was introduced called the Super Deluxe—a Super with a Custom-type eggcrate filling—at $86 above the basic Super price. This gave the customer a car that looked like a Custom for $1231 less, but simultaneously caused Customs to look more like Supers. At the same time, the Custom club sedan was dropped. Results were predictable: Custom sales for the Twenty-Third Series slid to 1825 units. The 1949 Twenty-Third Series therefore was heavier in the Super line, lighter in the Custom, as indicated below.

Chassis 2301 Eight
Model 2392 Four-Door Sedan, $2249
Model 2393 Station Sedan, $3449
Model 2395 Club Sedan, $2224
Model 2362 Deluxe Four-Door Sedan, $2383
Model 2365 Deluxe Club Sedan, $2358

Chassis 2302 (Convertible 2332) Super
Model 2382 Four-Door Sedan, $2633
Model 2385 Club Sedan, $2608
Model 2372 Deluxe Four-Door Sedan, $2919
Model 2375 Deluxe Club Sedan, $2894
Model 2379 Convertible Victoria, $3350

Chassis 2322 Super Long-Wheelbase
Model 2370 Seven-Passenger Limousine, $4100
Model 2371 Seven-Passenger Sedan, $3950

Chassis 2306 (Convertible 2333) Custom
Model 2352 Four-Door Sedan, $3975
Model 2359 Convertible Victoria, $4520

Sales for 1949 were respectable at 116,955 units in both series, 104,-593 for the calendar year. But some disturbing trends were visible. Aside from lessening demand for Customs, the Station Sedan was not selling well and 1950 would be its last year. Packard had evidently foreseen this, because Twenty-Third Series Station Sedans were unchanged from the previous lot, receiving none of the modifications the other cars did. In fact, evidence indicates that Twenty-Third Series Station Sedans were actually leftover Twenty-Second Series cars (they bear bumpers and engine numbers from the latter.) Again the new model year was declared at Packard's convenience, this time on October 1st, and again the current series continued without interruption, just as the series before it. The serial number trick employed to distinguish the 1950 cars from the

Proposals advanced for Twenty-Third Series facelift included tack-on-bumper-guard/taillights, Continental-like bustle and 1946-1947 Cadillac mimicry. Finally revision from oblong to oval taillights was deemed to be the most meritorious change. Similarly, new front-end ideas never proceeded beyond clay model.

The Twenty-Third Series Packard for 1949-1950. Above, left and right: Eight sedan and Super sedan. Below: Custom convertible and Super Deluxe sedan.

1949's was "-5-" inserted in the vehicle identification number. For 1950, though, the Six returned for a limited engagement in thirteen New York-style taxicabs, and the limousines disappeared completely—only four had been sold during the 1949 Twenty-Third Series.

The Six thus ended its fourteen-year run for Packard. It had been responsible for a good deal of income during that time, and it had been refined year by year, including an extensive rework in 1947, so by 1950 it was a very good powerplant indeed. But a six-cylinder Packard was now an anachronism, a hindrance to sales in eight-conscious 1950. It was not, however, scrapped. In the late Forties an executive of White Motor Company was impressed by a test ride in a six-cylinder Packard, and the engine had a reprieve for six years (1950-1955) in the White 3014 cab-over-engine truck, as well as the model 3015. But the larger White engine was also employed in these trucks, and more successfully. The Packard Six had never really been a truck engine. It was dependable, smooth and serviceable, but not all that powerful.

When the 1950 model year ended, the sales figures totaled 106,457 Twenty-Third Series cars, of which 42,640 were '50 models—poorest sellers of the bathtub Packards. Profit for the year—with a big boost courtesy of the 1951 models—was down to $5,162,348. Management meetings were getting rather more turbulent.

Chief engineer William Graves had made himself heard in the Office of the President by refusing to rework the bathtubs any further. In 1949 Graves told Christopher that if that was demanded he'd rather quit, then took a ten-day vacation along the Gulf of Mexico. When he returned, he found Christopher had capitulated and work had been ordered to begin on a brand-new 1951 Twenty-Fourth Series Packard, but this did not entirely satisfy the stockholders and directors, who had seen profits drop alarmingly. After a lively board session in October 1949, Christopher retired to his Ohio farm. His parting words, according to *Fortune*, were

542

that "farming is a damned sight easier than the auto business—you don't have so many bosses on a farm." It was the last Packard saw of George Christopher, his resignation was effective December 31st, 1949, and his successor was Hugh Ferry.

Ferry had been with Packard for forty years—board minutes as early as 1917 record his receiving frequent promotions in the accounting department—and had been elected most recently to positions as a director and treasurer. His forte was finance, and he did not see himself as the right man to run the company. "I just wasn't fit for the job," he said, "and I knew it." Ferry felt his best option was to find a successor as soon as possible, and in the summer of 1950, at the Detroit Athletic Club, he approached one James J. Nance of Hotpoint. Results were inconclusive—Ferry got what is now called a "definite maybe"—but Packard's president was optimistic and told a local banker friend about Nance. The banker happened to have a friend on the board of General Electric, which owned Hotpoint, and word of the encounter reached GE's president. That worthy hastened to Nance with a pep talk and an offer of certain financial arrangements which precluded Nance's giving Ferry's offer further consideration. Hugh Ferry would have to keep looking.

By the end of the Twenty-Third Series, Packard had fallen short of most of its goals. Production delays, marketing a full line of similar cars all bearing the same name but competing in widely scattered price fields, poor pricing policies and unfortunate styling had cost the company so heavily it would take a miracle to save it—though few realized or wanted to realize this fact. There remained that comforting cash in the bank, enough to carry on for years.

The dwindling base of the independents was perhaps best summarized by Hickman Price, export vice-president of Kaiser-Frazer, as quoted in Richard M. Langworth's *Kaiser-Frazer: Last Onslaught on Detroit:* "I was young and I was brash, and I had a whole lot of ideas. One of them was that in the automobile business—although this had not been proven at that stage at all—the big ones got bigger and the little ones went out of business. My influence, such as it was, was that no we can't [do things on a small scale], it won't work. We may have a period of three or four years—I remember putting 1950 as the terminal date—in which we can sell everything we can make, and hopefully we can price the things at a level where we can make a good profit. But that isn't going to be enough, because it isn't enough volume, and it isn't enough business, really, in this industry. That was Hudson's experience ultimately, and I was sure it would happen to us." Among others.

Packard had devoted a significant percentage of its manufacturing to lower-priced cars, even though it could have sold as many vehicles as it could build in *any* price class. The company could make only so many cars, and it made more money per car on luxury models than on junior versions. Why then did Packard continue its prewar policy of building inexpensive models? The reason, and the blame, can be laid largely at George Christopher's door, for it was Christopher as president who frittered away Packard's place in the luxury field at a time when Packard had a golden opportunity to recover that place—perhaps to assume it as never before since the Roaring Twenties.

Christopher was blinded by stubbornness. Obsessed with mass production and his two-lines-around-the-clock idea, he lost sight of the real strengths of the corporation. Compounding this miscalculation was the marketing of Twenty-Second and Twenty-Third Series cars with controversial and largely unpopular styling. Cadillac, meanwhile, had concentrated *only* on luxury cars, and had conceived really good postwar styling in its 1948 models with their famous uplifted rear fenders, which brought distinction to the rear of the automobile for the first time. Packard was selling cars to people who bought them only because they were available, and because after the war many of them—i.e., farmers, factory workers and returning servicemen—had more money to spend than they ever had before. They may have bought Packards because they had always wanted them. But they were buying a legend, and they would not buy again.

The Packard legend was many-faceted, of course, and among the factors contributing to it was the glamour of so many of its customers: the ultra-rich, the Hollywood stars, the highly placed politicians, the miscellaneous celebrities. The large cadre of people of what might be unkindly termed as the "ordinary sort" and who had saved for years to buy a DeLuxe Eight after the war would not enhance the Packard image—nor provide the publicity-generating news stories that celebrity purchases did. It is true that in 1949 the *Wall Street Journal* and other metropolitan dailies did give extensive coverage to the purchase by the United Auto Workers executive board of a Packard sedan for its president Walter Reuther. (It was promptly armor plated, though union spokesmen denied this "was inspired by any renewed threats on Reuther's life." The year previous he had narrowly escaped death in an assassination attempt.) But such stories would be occasional now, certainly not comparable to the prewar days of the marque when it seemed—and was widely touted by the company—that a Packard was *the* conveyance for the Very Important Person. But to be elite, perhaps by definition, is to be fickle. When a favored product becomes commonplace, the elite will generally desert it, summarily switching allegiance to a new favorite. The mystique that was Packard's during the glory years was, by this period, in danger of being irretrievably lost.

It was going to take quite a car to reverse the forbidding course set for the Fifties at East Grand Boulevard. But a worthy attempt was going to be made, one that would sweep away the bloated designs of the Christopher era with a new, crisply modern look of elegant dignity. Packard would call it "Contour Styling."

CHAPTER TWENTY-SEVEN

ALL-NEW CONTOUR STYLING

The Twenty-Fourth and
the Twenty-Fifth Series

1951-1952

AUTHORS: GEORGE HAMLIN AND DWIGHT HEINMULLER

Work on the all-new 1951 Packard, begun in the middle of 1949, resulted in a car very much in keeping with the times—a low hood, a great deal of glass, unprecedented interior room and four-fender visibility. Credit for the design can be placed squarely with John Reinhart, Packard's chief stylist, who had replaced Werner Gubitz during 1947.

There had always been plans for a Twenty-Fourth Series Packard, but it wasn't always going to look as it finally did. In the latter part of 1948, Briggs began facelift experiments of the bathtub body style, with results that were uninspiring and, in some cases, absurd. Briggs tried to save the doors, beltline and hood of the earlier car, until Graves finally rebelled in 1949, at which point Reinhart and his staff were allowed to begin with a fresh sheet of paper. Edward Macauley was still director of styling, but with his father retired was becoming steadily less influential.

Pages preceding: The 400, 300 and 200 photographed at the Proving Grounds.

The evolution of the Twenty-Fourth Series Packard involved a major battle of the beltline. Reinhart believes that had he been able to lower it just another inch and a half, the end result would have been far more pleasing. But Engineering was more concerned over the cost of glass than the price of sheet metal tooling. Reinhart feels that the final design "was bottom heavy. I wasn't particularly happy with it, but then I hated every design I ever made anyway. You never get what you really want because you have to compromise; the thing could have been a lot better looking had we the option of altering the glass along with the sheet metal."

High beltline or not, the 1951 Packard was an instant hit. The Society of Motion Picture Art Directors said it "embodies the most advanced concepts of automotive styling," and favored Packard with its top award. Automotive writers were impressed, particularly with the extraordinary visibility. Shipments from the factory during the fourth quarter of 1950 were double those of the previous year, and reached 12,000 during October. By the end of 1950, 40,179 1951 models had already been built, forty percent of that production having occurred in the final three months of the year.

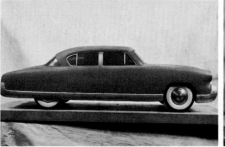

Above: New lines, slab sides, with the production windshield and grille emerging.

Despite a $1.5 million loss for the first three quarters, the Twenty-Fourth Series turned calendar 1950 into a $5.2-million profit year.

The total offering was reduced for 1951 from thirteen to nine models, primarily because of a de-emphasis of the high-priced models: Only two cars were offered in the Senior lines. The model lineup was designated numerically, like the One-Ten through One-Eighty cars before the war. Flagship was the Patrician 400, its name hearkening back to the days when the company published lists of "The Packard Four Hundred" owners to reinforce its hold on the luxury market. Lesser models were designated the 300 and 200.

The 200 line, on a 122-inch wheelbase, was offered in standard and deluxe trim. Standard powerplant was the same 288-cubic-inch eight as before, though a 327 c.i.d. engine could be ordered. A business coupe was

Above, from the left: First restyle attempt involved Twenty-Third Series facelift.

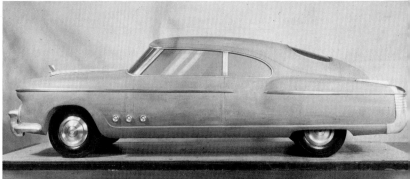

Above and top: By 1948 new lines evolved, borrowing a General Motors theme.

Above and right: More embellished variations on the slab-sided theme. Below, from the left: The full-scale clay model as it neared production form late in 1949.

Above: The 1951 200 two-door sedan and the 300 four-door sedan. Right: The Twenty-Fourth Series Packards on display at the Chicago Automobile Show in 1951.

available for the first and last time since the war, along with standard and deluxe two- and four-door sedans, a convertible, and Packard's first hardtop. Packard had not been in the vanguard of those producing the latter style, but the design came off particularly well, and since all hardtops had to have a special name in those days Packard called its the Mayfair. The convertible and the Mayfair were originally designated as 200 Deluxe cars, with the 288 engine, toothless grilles and uninspiring interior trim. But they were not ready at the time the rest of the Twenty-Fourth Series was, and while body and chassis engineering neared completion, someone took another look at the market in which these two cars would be competing. As a result, some changes were made after only a very few cars had been built. From that point forward, the convertible and Mayfair wore fresh makeup, grille teeth, even the pelican as standard equipment—and the engine was changed from 288 to 327. And it was thus that these models bowed to the public on March 16th, 1951. The Mayfair was priced at $3166.59, the convertible at $3200.58—more expensive than the 300 and only $286 less than the Patrician 400. Eventually the chassis on which these two models were built came to be known as the "250."

As the top-selling line the 200 accounted for 71,362 of 100,713 units for the model year. It was distinguished from more senior 1951 Packards by the lack of teeth in its grille, a one-piece rear window, a speed line in the rear fender sheet metal and vertical taillights—for the average buyer this provided little distinction and probably served to limit sales in the 300 and 400 categories. The 250 models looked like the 200's, but had the grille dentalwork of the 300/400.

The 300 line, successor to the Super Eight, was powered by the 327-cubic-inch, 150 hp engine and used a 200 body shell stretched five inches amidships for greater rear-seat legroom, resulting in a 127-inch wheelbase. Its rear fenders had no speed line, and its taillights were a four-unit "bug eye" design which persisted through 1954. Rear fender edges were capped with a plated fin; interiors, while not as austere as the 200's, were not competitive with other manufacturers—the floor coverings, for example, were rubber mats with fabric inserts instead of full carpets. The 300 rear window differed from the Junior cars in wrapping around to the rear edge of the back door through the use of a curved glass section at each side, giving a total glass area for this model of 3132 square inches. This was not the best in the business—the new 1951 Kaiser had 3541 square inches—but can be favorably compared to every other American car. Buick, for example, had 2858 square inches of visibility, DeSoto 2364, Nash 2802, Hudson 2805. A commercial chassis in the 300 line also became available in early 1951.

Packard's heritage was best recalled in the Patrician 400 model, although it was available only as a four-door sedan—which probably limited its appeal. Standard equipment included Ultramatic, cloisonné wheel-cover medallions, individual hassocks for rear seat passengers, Wilton carpets and carefully plated appointments. Its exterior was marked by two trim items which have not worn well, however—large chrome guards at the lower edges of the rear fenders and stainless steel decorations on each side above the rear wheels. The latter was ephemerae similar to that provided by Buick, which had originally used the term "Cruiserline Ventiports" for the decorations. Packard's term was ventiports too, but just as Buick's became known as portholes, so Packard's have come to be called "bottle openers." They were also used

to adorn the 250 models.

It was abundantly clear that under Christopher and Ferry, Packard had been slowly allowing its best cars to cheapen appreciably. The carpets were no longer Mosstred, interior woodgraining was visibly less extravagant, and partway through the year the cloisonné emblems gave way to painted ones on the wheel covers. In addition the big 356-cubic-inch Custom Eight engine was gone, replaced by a nine main bearing version of the 327 rated at 155 horsepower. The reasoning behind this move is obvious: Due to the increased compression ratio of the nine-main 327, Packard engineers were able to offer an engine of only five horsepower less than the 356 without the latter's high production costs and significant weight penalty. The weight advantage alone compensated for the five lost horses, and enabled the efficiency experts to base the entire 1951 line on two engine blocks, the 288 and the 327. Compression ratio options resulted in differences of rated horsepower: The 288 was 135 hp, or 138 with high compression (which in turn was standard with Ultramatic), while the 327 was rated at 150 hp standard and 155 with high compression, again standard with Ultramatic.

It has been often said that the Twenty-Fourth Series marked a significant change in Packard marketing philosophy in that models were now based on body styles rather than powerplants. This is a reasonable characterization of the 1951's, but was by no means something new. Just as the 1951 Patrician 400 was for all purposes a custom version of the 300, so had the 1946 Custom Super Clipper been a luxury version of the Super; so too had the 1940 One-Eighty been a custom One-Sixty. In each case these pairings used the same body shell and powerplant. The only real change was the use of special names, Mayfair and Patrician, for the hardtop body style and top-line sedan. Other than the Clipper in 1941, Packard had not given names to its cars before—only designations based on some aspect of design, wheelbase, engine, whatever.

But the 1951 models departed from many former traditions. The new low silhouette and horizontal grille format, while retaining the time-honored radiator outline that had characterized Packards for nearly half a century, represented a totally new car. The 1951 had little in common with the 1950 from the frame up—in fact Packard issued a service letter advising dealers to cease immediately their practice of raising a car by the center of the frame X-member. The new frame was simply too light to support the weight of the car at that one point only.

The luggage compartment of the new Packard contained over thirty cubic feet, and the front suspension was changed from knee-action shock absorbers to airplane type shocks with upper control arms. Electric radio antennas, rear window wipers and defoggers, twin back-up lights, rear compartment speakers for signal-seeking radios became available on Packards for the first time, and all models featured a useful pull-out glovebox drawer instead of the conventional glove compartment. Igni-

Page opposite: The new 1951 Twenty-Fourth Series convertible and some of the men who would sell it, at the Milwaukee auto show. Above: The convertible, and the Mayfair, were originally designated as 200 Deluxe cars, although both ultimately would be placed on a chassis which came to be known as the 250. Below: The 1951 Mayfair. Bottom: The 1951 Patrician 400 four-door sedan.

tion switches were lighted, a T-handle parking brake appeared, and warning lights replaced gauges for amps and oil-pressure monitoring.

Hydraulic power windows were available in 1951 as an option on both hard- and soft-top cars. Also available on non-convertible cars for the first time was a hydraulic power seat, while continuing options included a windshield washer, fresh air heater, spare tire valve extension and underhood light. Missing now were the Electromatic clutch and Packard's traditional roof antenna. Points of ready identification on the 1951 models included a three-pointed star motif on the deck handle ornament, the "Packard" name spelled out in block letters on the hood, and the last of the upright pelicans as a hood ornament.

Reception of the 1951 Packard was good, even with *Mechanix Illustrated*'s Tom McCahill, who had abhorred the 1949's. McCahill wrote enthusiastically about the new cars' Ultramatic drive, high compression engines and "continental hood line reminiscent [he became carried away here] of the Italian Cisitalia's. Thanks to it 'the man who owns one' no longer requires a transfusion of giraffe blood before he can see his right front fender from the driver's seat." McCahill traveled to the Packard Proving Grounds for his test of a 200 and a 400 model, and actually pushed the 200 to an indicated 102 mph after a couple of laps. The 200, he said, was a fine performer: "I have never driven an American car at actual speeds above 95 that handled better and showed less high-speed stress. . . . The steering was firm and the car was as confident on the curves as Charles Boyer. . . . Zero to 60 in high all the way took 17 seconds flat but zero to 60 starting in low and shifting to high after 50

miles per hour averaged 14.2 seconds, which is really peeling the wind. [It was, in addition, really peeling the Ultramatic, but the factory did not discourage the practice.] There is no sign of acceleration flattening out until well after 80. Zero to 70 averaged 19.1 and zero to 80 averaged 24.4 seconds. Fifty from zero took 10.3, which shows that in a 30-mile stretch from 50 all the way through 80, the 200 picks up at the rate of better than two miles an hour per second. This car is big, comfortable, fast and luxurious and my personal favorite of the line."

McCahill's 400 easily exceeded a true 100 mph, "held the curves like glue and showed no distress whatsoever at 100 and no signs of overheating, even though this speed was maintained for some time. . . . Zero to 60 averaged 13.4 seconds, using Low and Drive [which] puts the big Packard right up with the best whiz-kids on the roads. . . . I headed for the 39 percent grade hill climb, a real pip. In both Packards I stopped halfway up, put on the brake and then started off again just as easily as though the road was perfectly flat. . . . The comfort of these big Packards is pretty hard to top. I rode in the back seat and felt like a Dowager Duchess on the way to the King's Grouse Shoot. . . . Though these new Packards are the lowest from ground to roof in Packard history (62½ inches), your ears will be perfectly safe while wearing a top hat for occasions of state, political gatherings or a mobster's funeral."

McCahill also pointed out a neat improvement in fuel mileage—so much for those who say it never mattered in the Fifties—which had been explained to him at the Proving Grounds. "The automatic spark advance has been set ahead ten percent in the low 20 to 30 mph range,

Always interested in looking competitive at a stoplight grand prix, when Ed Macauley's Brown Bomber became dated, he had this speedster built during 1952.

where most driving is done, and this advance flattens out to normal at higher speeds. The carburetor has been leaned down to further economy but this has not affected performance in the least. . . ."

"In summing up," said the tester, "Packard is back and cooking on three front burners. These are good automobiles, big, fast and capable. I'm glad to say they also have a touch of that old glamour that the big, open Eights had in the twenties, when I was in college owning a fifty-dollar crate and dreaming that someday I'd have a Packard."

For many people that someday came in 1951: The Twenty-Fourth Series made a lot of money and its model-year total of 100,713 stood as the third highest in Packard history. But the money picture was deceptive because Packard now ranked next to last in an industry that had become geared to mass production at an extraordinary level. Packard was about to discover that if production slipped below 50,000 cars a year, it could not make a profit. Before the Depression that figure would have meant a bonanza—but Packard had approached it only once, in 1928.

Ferry realized that the company's good gray image needed a little sparkle, and an opportunity arrived to acquire some in early 1952. Having recently completed a sizeable limousine order on Lincoln chassis for President Truman, Charles Russell Feldmann of Henney suggested that his company's first-rate designer Richard Arbib might produce something special for Packard for automobile show exhibition. On February 15th, 1952, Ferry concurred in a written agreement. Packard had earlier shipped a 1951 250 convertible, serial number 2469-3630, to Henney at Freeport, and Arbib had been tinkering with it all winter.

Now this vehicle was to be a real show car, on very short notice—the International Motor Sports Show would open at New York's Grand Central Palace on March 29th. "We had quite a gang on that job," Feldmann recalled. "We worked days, nights and Sundays." By March 10th work had proceeded sufficiently and Henney general manager Preston Boyd advised Bill Graves that the conversion was nearing completion. But time was still pressing: "You mention the possibility of changes to the mechanism or operating parts of the car to enhance its value," he wrote Graves. "At the moment there is no change that we propose to make on this one conversion that we are working upon other than perhaps to lower the steering column and to lower both front and rear springs in order to give the car the setting that Mr. Arbib desires. . . . In addition, we are putting on wire wheels for display purposes only, which we are cobbling out of some old wheels."

In another letter to Graves on the same date, Boyd advised Packard's chief engineer that owing to "the other production parts that we have ordered from time to time with which to make this conversion . . . a number of parts that we have removed from your standard job [will] be returned to you for whatever disposition you see fit. . . . We are going to have to rework the springs front and rear, in order to get the overall height down the way Mr. Arbib wants it. We are also going to have to lower the steering column and have already lowered the radiator core. In addition, we are equipping this car with wire wheels that we are making from an old set, and at a considerable cost, I might add."

The wires were only part of a very ambitious conversion. The 250 was

It sported the 1953 rear bumper, '52 crest, '51 Packard lettering, the '52 grille with '53 bumper guard panel, and a scoop borrowed from the Pan American.

The interior of the Pan American. Note both its opulence and lack of rear seat.

sectioned down, and lowered further through its suspension—to the point where it could not be taken to New York on a conventional auto transporter. The back seat was eliminated and the top boot—which was empty—completely concealed by a metal lid. A front center armrest was used, and the interior (even the steering wheel, door handles and dash knobs) was set off in top-grain oyster white leather. The hood received a functional airscoop and a Hudelson-Whitebone continental spare tire was fitted to the rear, along with round taillights to match the front parking lights. The grille was basically a 1952 motif, with a mesh pattern insert.

Henney met its deadline. The car, called the Pan American, was sent to New York on March 24th, and an elaborate publicity orgy ensued. All the photos were carefully posed to hide the fact only two wire wheels had been finished—the other two were shipped and installed just before the show—and a gala introduction followed on opening day. The Pan American was said to have a four-barrel carburetor, was rated at 185 horsepower, and came away with the first-place trophy "for outstanding automotive design and engineering achievement." And Packard found itself with hundreds of requests for the car from its dealers and the public.

Some production of Pan Americans was definitely planned—at least by Henney. On March 13th Preston Boyd wrote that he had mentioned

to Packard "the necessity of having some sort of a tentative price . . . Of course, one of the chief problems is to know how many [Packard] wants to run or commit itself for, which will be a determining factor as to what should be done in the way of tools, dies, jigs and fixtures with which to produce in the most economical manner . . . if it is to be offered with wire wheels it will mean complete tooling for production of these, which will be rather costly." (The wheels eventually selected were bought from Kelsey-Hayes, cutting costs considerably.)

"Also the top," continued Boyd. "There has nothing whatsoever been done as far as the convertible top is concerned and that means a complete engineering, tooling and production setup with which to produce . . . In my estimation it will be cheaper in the long run to tool for certain panels rather than to cut, solder and finish the way we had to do on this one . . . [And] Packard has the problem of determining whether or not the car can be made runnable in the low down condition in which it is going to be shown—and that involves springs, shock absorbers, proper bounce allowance, to say nothing of air cleaners, four-jet carburetors and whatever they may want to put on it." Four-barrel carburetors were a comparatively recent development; this and other correspondence suggest that an operating four-barrel carb with a Packard manifold was not fitted to the car until the Twenty-Sixth Series, which did have such equipment.

By May of 1952 Boyd had a cost estimate ready for Feldmann. "The work that we performed on converting the Packard convertible into the Packard Pan American stands on our books as of this moment at $9,-882.66 [including] direct labor charges. . . . If we were to sell the car today we would have to have [including overhead and Arbib's salary] $18,262.92." (The car was sold, at what figure is unclear, to the Macauley family who drove it for some time, eventually cobbling it up with Fifty-Fifth Series trim. It is now owned by a collector in Florida.)

The question of producing more Pan Americans persisted, mainly through Feldmann's efforts. On July 31st, 1952, he wrote Packard about "further inquiries" he had received concerning the car and requests for prices and delivery dates. "Not knowing your policy with regard to the marketing of the Pan American, I was unable to present the pertinent details requested." Henney did receive a go-ahead on five additional Pan Americans, but Packard was apparently reticent about going further. Feldmann persisted, though—"Don't you think it remarkable that interest in this sports car is still so keen?" he asked Packard in his letter.

While the company was deciding on a course of action for the Pan American, Henney's Arbib had busily engaged in yet another project, the Monte Carlo, a conversion from two 1952 Mayfair hardtops which Packard had sent Henney in early September, complete with 1953 style bumpers, headlight rims, fender and body moldings, deck lid ornaments and grilles. The Monte Carlos had wire wheels, exterior spares and hood scoops like the Pan American, but the body speedline was eliminated and the tops were changed to a semi-town car configuration with removable solid panels or fabric over the driver. These cars were billed to Packard at $9,095.36 each, and Henney tried to sell them for limited production too, but without success.

While the Pan American never saw more than six units and the Monte Carlos not even that, they did ultimately serve an important function. The decision was made in late 1952 that neither car in its existing form would be placed in production, but Feldmann and company had planted certain ideas, and in October 1952 Packard decided to build a limited production special sports convertible which in due course became the 1953 Packard Caribbean. The first move in that direction was to ask Henney for a quote on 200 scooped hood panels of standard configuration. "We will find ways and means to handle it if they see fit to give us this order," Boyd wrote Feldmann in October. Henney quoted $155 each for the hood panels, although Mitchell-Bentley ultimately got the job—and the Caribbean project was under way. But other matters were brewing both within and without Packard's spheres of influence that would not be as pleasantly solved nor as easily executed.

On June 25th, 1950, armed forces of North Korea had crossed the 38th parallel separating it from the South in a widely spread invasion. At the United Nations, the Soviet delegation made the tactical blunder of walking out of the Security Council in rage over the on-going arguments therein, and without a Russian veto the United Nations labeled North Korea an aggressor and voted in favor of armed intervention. What this meant was a multi-national force in reality largely composed of Americans; the United States became involved in the war on June 30th.

In its opening stages the Korean conflict proceeded rather badly from the U.S. point of view, and the government once again began to pressure civilian industry regarding military necessity. Many businessmen feared automobile production might be halted again, as in World War II, but this never happened. Strategic materials were placed on quota, however, and auto output was cut by nearly twenty percent, each manufacturer given an assigned production quota based on past performance. With its dismal 1950 record this could have spelled disaster for Packard, but for once the Boulevard got a break: The government realized output that year was abnormally low and granted Packard a five percent increase. The restrictions nevertheless hampered Packard in many ways, as witness the severe cutback on the civilian nickel supply.

Because nickel was a needed constituent in the chrome-plating process, a shortage of it made for less durable bright trim. Many 1952 Packard trim parts, such as windshield and belt moldings and wheel shell covers, were made of stainless steel and presented no difficulty, but plated pieces, with no nickel content, were subject to speedy deterioration. A coat of clear synthetic enamel was baked onto finished parts, but it was

The Richard Arbib-designed and Henney-built Pan American show car, from '52.

easily scratched or rubbed off, and at this point rapid pitting began. Such parts were referred to as "Defense Chrome," and included the license plate lamp, taillamp housings and fins, headlamp doors, trunk handle, rear window molding clips, hood ornament and grille, fender shields and rear stone guards. Bumpers, door handles, ventwing frames and radio antennas were judged to require nickel, and it was used on those parts. "We are supplying chrome in accordance with national emergency regulations," said Packard, so "our usual policy with regard to replacements does not apply." Translation: The owner was on his own with these parts. And good luck.

Other than Defense Chrome, the 1952 Twenty-Fifth Series introduced on November 1st, 1951, saw few external changes. The business coupe, reborn the year before, was now gone forever, and the new Deluxe 200's received vertical grille bars. Packard's bottle openers were redesigned and made optional on nearly all models (four to a side standard on 400's) and side moldings were extended from mid-door to door edge. The Packard name was removed from the hood and the family crest reappeared on the grille. Minor changes were given the bumper guards and trunk handle, while a new wheelcover of ribbed design became available, for the 1952 model year only. Packard's pelican hood ornament now had a new racy look, with wings trailing back instead of held boldly upright. Those who specialize in nonsense often say that when the bird folded its wings the end was in sight. Actually some of Packard's most exciting days were yet to come.

The significant changes in the 1952 cars were hidden from immediate sight. For sharpening up the interiors, Styling retained fashion designer Dorothy Draper, to ply "her rare talent for combining daring originality with comfortable practicality." Draper did not really accomplish the miracles attributed to her, but she did add a touch of harmonious color to the cars, the Patrician 400 versions being particularly well done. The importance of the Draper-styled 1952 interiors lies not with the execution itself, but rather with Packard's recognition of the changing nature of public demand. And the company was only beginning; in coming years it would dazzle the buyers with the opulence of Packard upholstery.

A second major development for 1952 was mechanical: Packard now offered Bendix's vacuum-assisted Treadlevac power brake system, calling it "Easamatic." The advent of power brakes was a milestone for the industry; there had been such units before, during the Thirties, though they were not the same. Easamatic was a complete unit with master cylinder, operating mechanism and power booster integrated into a single assembly, which Packard offered at a reasonable price and even sold as a kit for field installation in 1951 and other 1952 cars. Retrofit of previous models had always been a tradition at Packard, resulting for example in many 1935-1939 models with sealed beam headlights.

But there was another reason for allowing Easamatic to be fitted to 1951 Packards: Too many of them were left in dealer stocks when the '52's were announced. This oversupply cut into Twenty-Fifth Series production, in fact, and only 62,921 of the latter were built. Whereas nearly half of the 1951 cars had been produced in 1950, only a third of the 1952 cars were built in 1951. And just at the time sales caught up with production, a five-week steel strike brought Packard to a halt, which threatened 1953 production because of the past-performance government quota policy. Fortunately, the government was giving favored treatment to the small producers, and no reduction was imposed. This was a blessed relief at a critical time, when demand was moving up again, though the government wasn't always so obliging—within a year Packard would lose a promising defense contract.

The defense contract was for jet engines, and in pursuit of it Packard acquired a 325,000-square-foot plant on Mt. Elliott, a short distance from East Grand Boulevard, which quadrupled forge production for the airplane engines. A new 780,000-square-foot plant adjoining the Utica proving grounds was also completed and tooled up—and about $17 million, including a new Utica parts facility, was spent on the jet program. As 1952 closed, Packard's prospects in this field looked bright. With jet engines and the marine diesel program, 1952 sales to the government totaled $69 million. This would be an important part of the

Packard picture for whomever Hugh Ferry recruited as the company's new president. His search ended in May of 1952.

In his two-and-a-half years as Packard's president, Ferry had made his first priority finding a replacement for himself. He had retained his former position as treasurer together with the presidency, a rather unusual combination among top executives of major corporations. Packard virtually ran itself during this period, as Ferry talked to potential candidates intermittently.

The untimely departure of Max Gilman and the abrupt leavetaking of George Christopher had combined with Packard's lack of a development plan to render the company bereft of any rising young stars. One opportunity to add to its corps of up-and-coming executives had fizzled in 1948: In February that year Macauley had offered George Romney a position as executive vice-president and member of the board.

During the war Romney and Macauley, the latter as president of the Automobile Manufacturers Association, had worked together, although they had not seen each other since. Macauley was evidently impressed with Romney's ability, because his offer included a $50,000 salary and the promise that within two years he would succeed Christopher, who was talking again of retirement. (Christopher's departure was expected; it was merely his timing that was in doubt.) A contract was drawn up and Ferry was informed that "we are hiring George Romney."

According to Tom Mahoney, in *The Story of George Romney*: "Macauley's successor as president of AMA and Romney's boss was George W. Mason, president of Nash-Kelvinator. He was then vacationing in Bermuda. Romney telephoned him he was resigning from AMA to go with Packard. 'Now look, George,' Mason spluttered through the phone. 'Wait until I get back. I'd like to talk with you.'

"When Mason got back, he offered Romney a job at Nash-Kelvinator. It was neither as high nor as definite as the Packard offer . . . . He would spend a year or longer if necessary to learn everything about the company. After that, Mason would see what he could do about a top executive job for him." As Mahoney notes, Romney explained that "the decision would probably determine my last employment and vocational opportunity. The answer was definite. I knew I should take the least flattering offer."

It is difficult to conjecture how Packard's future would have changed had Romney's decision been otherwise—although surely it would have been affected. The result now was that it was 1952, there was no Romney to take over, no one else particularly interested in the job, and Ferry was still looking for a replacement. At one point he offered the position to Bill Graves, who declined it. But one of his earlier candidates had not forgotten Packard completely: James J. Nance, who had initially been approached in the summer of 1950, but who had been persuaded by his superiors to remain at Hotpoint.

In the meantime, the fortunes of the leading independent automobile manufacturers were being altered drastically. Studebaker was losing money so rapidly that, metaphorically, the company was rather like the man who didn't know his throat had been cut until he tried to shake his head. Nash sales were slipping, together with Packard's. "Hudson was for sale and being shopped, that was no secret," Nance told *The Packard Cormorant* in 1976.* "Everybody in the automobile industry knew Queen Wilhelmina owned eleven percent of Hudson and wanted to sell." Into this maelstrom stepped Nash's George Mason. It was Mason's grand design to put together a fourth full-line company, one bigger than Chrysler Corporation. He foresaw an American Motors producing Studebakers in the Chevrolet-Pontiac class, Nashes in the Oldsmobile class, Hudsons in the Buick class, Packards in the stratosphere—as well as a line of Studebaker trucks. He got nowhere with Studebaker because he could not talk amicably with Harold Vance. A common problem apparently; in the mid-Thirties Vance had forced the resignation of chief engineer Barney Roos, one of the ablest engineers the business ever knew, whose presence would have helped Studebaker in many ways. In any case, Mason could not build his empire so long as Vance was in charge at Studebaker.

Mason had therefore begun preliminary talks with Nance, whom he knew to be under continuing consideration by Packard, and the two developed their plan. "We agreed," Nance recounted in *The Packard Cormorant*, "that Mason would take the Hudson-Nash end, and I would put Studebaker-Packard together, then we'd fold the two pieces together into one company." Nance was slated to be its president once Mason had everything running smoothly. "I wouldn't have gone into it," said Nance, "just to take over Packard."

And thus Nance let Ferry know he wasn't as happy at General Electric as he had been. Ferry leapt into the saddle and renewed the chase. When Nance made his second trip to Detroit early in 1952, he toured the plants, interviewed the board, appraised the 1952 product, and made two suggestions "regardless of whom you might hire." First, commission a full-scale study of the company by a team of management consultants. Second, institute an executive retirement plan. Among the reasons Packard was becoming moribund was that older executives were hanging on, as Alvan Macauley had, because their only security was their paychecks— there was no pension, although a retirement plan had begun operation in a very limited fashion the year before. Nance left the meeting with a salary offer of $150,000 plus a sizable stock option, and the board did adopt a full retirement plan. Following the plan's approval by the stockholders, 383 employees were retired on pension.

*Mr. Nance's comments are used with permission, from an interview copyright J.J. Nance, 1976.

*Above: The '52 Twenty-Fifth Series 300 four-door sedan and 200 two-door sedan.
Below: Dorothy Draper, who assisted in the design of Packard's 1952 interiors.*

Most of the changes for the Twenty-Fifth Series models for 1952 were wrought inside or underneath, viz., the Draper-styled interiors and the adoption of Easamatic.

Nance meanwhile made up his mind, and gave notice at Hotpoint on May 7th, 1952. A story was floated about that the primary reason behind Nance's decision for Packard was that he had reached a dead end at Hotpoint following a General Electric reorganization in 1951. "It was," says Nance with a smile, "a cover story." The grand plan was not going to be made public prematurely, so Nance merely left Hotpoint for Packard. Upon his departure, General Electric purchased 25,000 shares of Packard stock—*Fortune* magazine termed this "the kind of compliment that counts."

Nance was a new broom, but he represented another in a long tradition of specialists who came to the company to do a particular job: Packard, the inventor; Joy, the empire builder; Macauley, the executive; Vincent, the engineer; Christopher, the production genius. Each in his time contributed a specific skill to build, and sometimes to save, the Packard Motor Car Company. In 1952 the company had everything it needed except sales. Enter Jim Nance, the salesman.

"Your Directors feel fortunate in securing 51-year-old James J. Nance as your newly elected President and General Manager," wrote Ferry in the 1952 stockholders report. "In addition, Mr. Nance has been chosen a Director." Nance was taking over a company which boasted $15 million in cash and almost $46 million in working capital, a cash position so good that few employees, either high or low echelon, thought anything could be wrong with Packard. Their complacency soon became apparent.

For the first three weeks of his incumbency Nance opened his door to everyone in the company. From fledgling machinists to sexagenerian vice-presidents they arrived, with opinions seldom straying from the optimistic. "What if the company does have a capacity of 150,000 cars a year—it's making profits on the 70,000 it turns out, isn't it?" "Isn't the future pretty rosy, with 25-35 percent of Packard capacity assigned to

defense work like the jet engine contract?" "Packard's engineering will always pull the company through."

At that point Nance established an unofficial organization called the Key Man Group, and invited its 150 members to a dinner and address at the close of his first month. "Nance has a bit of the revivalist speaker about him," said *Fortune*, "and he was at his best that night." This assessment of Nance is universally shared. Irrespective of private opinions about the man, everyone who knew Nance never forgot him. The most frequently heard description of him is "spellbinder." Several people have noted that "he could charm the birds out of the trees." But charm wasn't Nance's intention that night.

"I like to win," he began, "and I *don't* like a good loser. Any guy who loses good doesn't go on my team. I like a fellow who likes to win and is willing to fight to win and willing to work to win, and I like a challenge, and that's why I'm here at Packard.

"The greatest problem facing Packard today, in my opinion, is that of gross profit." The company was operating on a six-percent profit margin and Nance felt little imagination was needed to project Packard's position should the rumored five-percent industry-wide price reduction become reality. "Now the easiest thing to do . . . is to ask the sales department to put the price up to where the margin is automatically taken care of. *That* is not dynamic pricing." To Nance, dynamic pricing meant gauging the market, setting a price to achieve necessary volume, then pressing sales strategy to meet the objectives. This had never been Packard's strong suit. Pricing also largely depended upon, as Nance said, "planning for costs." That meant in the engineering department, not simply trimming a design after its completion.

Then Nance spoke of revitalizing the vendors, of taking advantage of their engineering and creative development. "If big companies like

With minor styling revisions, including a racier hood ornament, from the left: The 1952 convertible, 200 Deluxe four-door sedan, Mayfair hardtop, Patrician 400.

General Motors are going to make all their parts, then they have to support all the engineering and development work that makes that possible. If we are going to buy those parts, then as part of that purchase price we are paying for engineering ideas and developments; we should insist on getting them." Nance used radios as an illustration. He had long envisioned a radio with three kinds of tuning—pushbutton, manual, and selector bar—but no such unit was on the market, though Packard had offered the "wonder bar" radio in 1951. Nance took the idea to GM's Delco Division and found that "these guys had this thing all ready to go. If we hadn't asked them for it, you know where it would have been now—on a Cadillac. Now it will still be on a Cadillac, but by heaven we'll be out four or five months ahead of them."

Next Nance addressed the subject of outside parts. "I'm just old-fashioned enough to believe that in the manufacturing business there is only one basic commodity on which you make a profit: human effort. Now the Packard labor content on our automobile has sunk to an all-time low of roughly thirty percent. The more labor content taken outside of our plants, the less competitive we become. It's a vicious circle that makes it harder and harder for you to compete. Now we are going to initiate a program of taking a good look at every part we buy and set up standards to show where it becomes feasible and profitable for Packard to make that part—and anyone who wants to take a part out of this plant from now on will have to sell *me!*" *That* was a breath of fresh air. Would that it had been wafted about when the disastrously shortsighted decision was made to give the body business away in 1940.

"To the man in his forties or over," Nance boomed on to an audience which possibly didn't want to hear what was coming, "Packard stands for quality. He still thinks of it as a quality car, an impression he got as a young man. But to the younger person of say thirty-five, *Packard doesn't stand for anything.* Now you ask the man in the street today, whether he is twenty-five, fifty or seventy-five, what Buick stands for and you'll get a pretty universal answer: it's a good solid automobile in the upper middle price class. You ask what Cadillac stands for and every kid on the curbstone can tell you, 'That's the best, mister.' Now we're supposed to be in three of the five price classes, competing in the top bracket, for example against Cadillac, the big Buick, and the two Chryslers, and we're getting a miserable *3½ percent* of that business. Packard! Three and a half percent!

"Now we must make a decision, gentlemen. And whatever that decision is, I'll be damned if I'm going to be in a horse race and get left at the quarter pole. Let's get in or get out. If we are going to make a quality car, then let's get in the race, and if we are going to abandon the field, then by God let's do it with *honor.* Not by default."

His position clearly stated, Nance proceeded therefrom to reorganize all company operations—some called the process "thunder and lightning." Office lights were turned on earlier and burned later, and the plants became noticeably cleaner. "Only part of that stuff coming out of the Packard stacks is smoke," said one observer. "The rest is Nance."

The president organized an operating committee that met each Monday so, as Nance said, "the men police themselves and I don't have to spend my time checking up. Nobody wants to make a poor showing in front of his colleagues." Surveys were undertaken of employees, dealers, supervisory personnel and vendors. A cost review committee was set up, as was a Watch List to ensure that important suppliers did not run out of any necessary raw material. A foreman's program was instituted to provide special business training and cash incentives for superior work. New people, many of them eager to follow their former boss from Hotpoint, came to Packard to fill positions left by the pensioned ancients. *559*

Nance conducted neither personal recruiting nor a wholesale housecleaning, and worthy Packard people were allowed to remain. "I say in all candor," he told them, "that where you go is entirely up to you." But after Nance's arrival, Packard was a changed company.

"For twenty years we haven't developed any organization of sales managers with experience in hard selling," Nance said. "This company has been just successful enough to be lulled asleep. It will have to be shaken out of its lethargy and made to realize that you can't stand still. There's no dead center in this industry, no status quo. The automobile business is the fastest track there is; to succeed in it you've got to keep moving." On styling, Nance said Packard should be conservative, favoring "good lines that are architecturally correct." On the existing

models: "Too much of a gamble for a company like Packard—it was lucky to show up in blue ink, it could also have come red. Packard should never put out anything as radical as that 1951 design." He was also adamant about meeting deadlines, especially on the vital defense work. "If you're on schedule, you're pretty hard to cancel. But, brother, if you're not on schedule, you're a sittin' duck." Prophetic words; defense contract cancellations would shortly become a painful subject on the Boulevard.

At the top echelon, the new team included marketing vice-president Fred Walters, from Oldsmobile; financial vice-president and treasurer Walter Grant, from Hotpoint; procurement vice-president Albert Behnke, from Hotpoint; manufacturing vice-president George Reifel of Packard; engineering vice-president William Graves; Packard's George

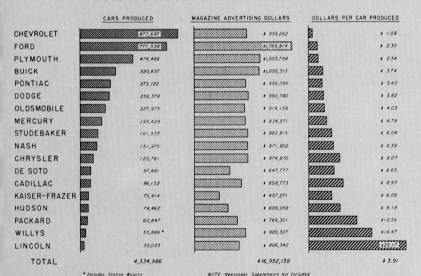

A revealing chart, from Packard files, noting its heady advertising expenditures. As Hugh Ferry (left) departs, James J. Nance (right) moves in, looking confident.

PASSENGER CAR ADVERTISING IN MAGAZINES
DOLLARS PER CAR PRODUCED — 1952

	CARS PRODUCED	MAGAZINE ADVERTISING DOLLARS	DOLLARS PER CAR PRODUCED
CHEVROLET	877,697	$ 959,262	$ 1.09
FORD	777,538	$1,789,814	$ 2.30
PLYMOUTH	474,466	$1,203,788	$ 2.54
BUICK	320,837	$1,200,315	$ 3.74
PONTIAC	273,122	$ 936,096	$ 3.43
DODGE	259,378	$ 990,780	$ 3.82
OLDSMOBILE	227,975	$ 919,156	$ 4.03
MERCURY	195,429	$ 934,571	$ 4.78
STUDEBAKER	161,533	$ 982,815	$ 6.08
NASH	151,975	$ 971,802	$ 6.39
CHRYSLER	120,761	$ 974,870	$ 8.07
DE SOTO	97,481	$ 647,777	$ 6.65
CADILLAC	96,152	$ 858,773	$ 8.93
KAISER-FRAZER	75,414	$ 457,271	$ 6.06
HUDSON	74,462	$ 609,058	$ 8.18
PACKARD	62,847	$ 789,321	$12.56
WILLYS	55,886 *	$ 920,327	$16.47
LINCOLN	32,033	$ 806,342	$ 25.17
TOTAL	4,334,986	$16,952,138	$ 3.91

* Includes Station Wagons   NOTE: Newspaper Supplements Not Included
SOURCE: Automotive News—January 5, 1953; 1952 Publishers' Information Bureau (Advance Release)   Compiled by Pathfinder Research Dept.   (P) A-4, 1/53

'52 AUTO ADS—Pathfinder has put out this chart, showing the number of passenger cars produced by leading makers, amount spent on magazines and ad dollar per car in 1952. In addition, the magazine made a color chart on how much each spent in each magazine and number of pages. Ford lead in **pages** (about 170) and dollars ($1,789,814). The **Saturday Evening** Post had the most pages (226) with Time running second (166) and Life third (165). But Life got the most revenue ($4,405,470), SEP had $4,315,039 and Time $1,697,759. A total of $16,952,138 was spent for about 1,602 pages. Page and dollar breakdown is for 47 magazines, newspaper sections not included. **Source: Publishers Information Bureau and Automotive News.**

Brodie as vice-president of Coordinating Operations (Defense); industrial relations vice-president Wayne Brownell. (Reifel, however, was replaced before year's end by Ray Powers, who had come from Lincoln and whose advice to Nance would later be held as generally poor.)

"Make no little plans," became the Nance credo. "They lack the magic to stir men's souls." Nance increased the advertising budget, pushed the dusty Pan Americans onto the fairground circuit to stimulate customer interest and, once the decision had been made to stay in the upper price bracket, launched an attack on it which had dramatic results. Eventually he planned to devote thirty percent of the company's output to this class, and he was successful, though production for 1955 and 1956 hardly proved the statistical base Nance had in mind. Nevertheless,

Packard built 84,082 cars in those two model years, and 24,371 of them were in the top bracket. Company advertising, he said, had been "bleeding the Packard name white," referring as it did to the modest price of a 200 model. Consequently, advertising took a decided turn toward the luxury market, and some layouts began to rival the famous Packard ads of the golden years.

Production in the last quarter of 1952 was double the previous year's, net sales were up from $178 million to $234 million (due mostly to defense contracts), property acquisition had been impressive, dealers had stopped deserting, and the company was poised for some remarkable forward strides. But what of the Packard tradition?

Among the sins of which Nance would be accused during those early months of reorganization was "destroying the past," specifically, the disposal of tons of parts and literature relating to the older models. Such an act, if committed in the manner folklore tells it, would justify the language which has been used to denounce Nance, to wit, references to "insensate vandalism" and comparing the man to "the barbarous Turks." But many months of research in the process of writing this history has uncovered no evidence that (1) Nance ordered the destruction, (2) Nance was aware of the destruction, (3) the destruction was all that widespread, or (4) it occurred at all.

If Nance had been so blindly dedicated to snapping Packard's link with its golden past, would he have commissioned the classic-grilled Request in 1955 and come within an ace of releasing it for limited production; hosted the Classic Car Club and promoted Packard's heritage in publicity; released a brochure in 1956 entitled "The Living Legend" and highlighted such hallmarks as the hexagon and the pelican; allowed Product Planning to toy with the idea of a 1957 Twelve for so long, approved a vertical grille for the 1957 line, or posed the 1957 prototype alongside a 1942 One-Eighty for publicity photographs?

In assessing the overall situation, it is useful to remember that in 1952 Packard moved *all* parts to a new facility in Utica. During operations of this type, older, slow-moving parts are more likely to be scrapped than normally—and many of them were. The Utica facility was a side benefit of the jet engine contract, Ferry having seized the opportunity to erect two new buildings there at essentially the same time. Nance did not order either of them, though he was to be accused later of building various new factories, including these two.

Thus it is virtually certain that Nance had nothing whatsoever to do with destroying Packard's past. On the other hand he had much to do with rescuing the present, and things looked more promising after his first year in office than they had for a long time. The doldrums were left behind in a wave of enthusiasm and activity. Packard's new president had done everything right.

So far.

CHAPTER TWENTY-EIGHT

AMERICA'S NEW
CHOICE
IN FINE CARS

The Twenty-Sixth and
the Fifty-Fourth Series

1953-1954

AUTHORS: GEORGE HAMLIN AND DWIGHT HEINMULLER

The industry was quick to recognize that Nance really did mean everything he said and that Packard had, indeed, roused out of a long nap to become a competitor with which to reckon. The Twenty-Sixth Series Packards for 1953 represented the best attempt that could be fielded with a three-year-old car, and sales were brisk from introduction day.

Because the war in Korea remained, National Price Administration (NPA) allocations still threatened to disrupt the program. Packard had not sold its allowable number of cars during the first six months of 1952, and was in danger of having its share cut again. The only way to avoid that was to make up for it in the last quarter of 1952 under a carryover provision. Nance took advantage of this to boost Twenty-Sixth Series production and called upon his dealers to sell. To a large extent this was successful, and though sales would not hit Nance's goal of 135,000, they continued at a good pace.

The restyled 1953 line received the usual good reviews, and deserved them all. To the basic Reinhart 1951 body was applied—after some flirting with the typical atrocious alternatives—a modest cosmetic job which, unlike a typical industry facelift, served mainly to accentuate the design's good points.

Reinhart had left in 1951, when the 1953 program was getting under way, and was replaced as chief stylist by Richard A. Teague, still under director of styling Edward Macauley. As his talents came to be highly utilized by Nance, Teague would exert increasingly more influence over the look of production Packards. The 1953 design was dictated by the shape of the basic shell; Teague put a new grille on the product but it had to fit the same hood and fender stampings used in 1951. The old bumpers were retained, but another bar was added to the tops to give them a more massive appearance—a compromise Teague speaks of through gritted teeth today. The major change, however, was the adaptation of the sharp-cornered Mayfair/convertible windshield to the entire sedan line.

The first evidence of Nance's "thunder and lightning" in product planning was the line separation of the Twenty-Sixth Series. Less than a year earlier, he had told Packard's movers and shakers they must decide if the company was going to attempt to return to the luxury market Christopher had abandoned. That decision in the affirmative, Nance began reversing programs which had nearly eclipsed the Packard name in the high-priced field. In the process, the groundwork was laid for correcting what the writers believe was a mistake dating back nearly twenty years: Nance planned the removal of the Packard nameplate from the medium-priced cars.

Marketing the One Twenty and the even less expensive Six was a maneuver into uncharted territory, and no one at the time had been entirely sure what effect the Packard name would have on the cars, or on the company. As was observed at the time, the name was used for the ready cash it could bring in—and in this it was successful.

But what if the One Twenty had not been called a Packard? Using the LaSalle example, most likely sales would have suffered. Conversely, however, Packard cars in the higher-priced brackets might *not* have suffered. In any case, Nance intended to find out. He called for introduction of a new name, one which could later be upgraded to a make in its own right, to get the Packard nameplate up where it belonged. The new name chosen was "Clipper."

Resurrecting the Clipper name for the medium-priced cars was good for public recognition. It bore Packard's patina, and had favorable connotations from the standpoint of sales. It was a good, snappy word that would stand on its own merits as a marque, it had a ring of history and, as Sales put it, "the sniff of the sea." Its only negative aspect would be in retrospect, for the name now gives a connotation of a less expensive car, which earlier Clippers certainly were not. But such factors seldom influence sales departments—the Clipper was dead, long live the Packard Clipper, direct replacement for the 200 line.

The standard Clipper main line was available in two body styles, a two-door sedan (which doubled as the Sportster at a $261 premium) and four-door sedan. Prices ranged from $2544 to $2805, wheelbase as before was 122 inches, and the power was again provided by the 288-cubic-inch eight, now upgraded to 150 horsepower as Packard's contribution to the horsepower race. The high compression of V-type configurations was coming into prominence, but a Packard V-8 was still some years away so Engineering made the best it could of the old 288. The Clipper Deluxe, with the same body as the other Clippers, received instead the 327 engine now rated at 160 horsepower, and offered a two-door at $2691 and a four-door at $2745.

Clipper styling featured an enlarged backlight, elimination of the rear fender speed line, and a new grille. The latter dispensed with the inner work of the previous year, and instead used a simple bar running to two large parking lights at the sides and wrapping back to the front of the wheel opening. A new impact bar was designed for both front and rear bumpers, and the headlight rims were deeper. On the Deluxe Clippers, a full-length stainless steel strip incorporated a Packard crest at approximately the two-thirds point. The Deluxe models also had a chrome taillight extension, about three times longer than the extension used on the 1952 Senior models. It was obvious from this production change that the effect sought was one of greater length and bulk, which was just what 1953 customers wanted.

Added to the Clipper line was a new commercial product, the Henney Junior, a financial disaster for Henney (the story behind this episode is presented in the commercial bodies section of the Appendices) but one that fit ideally Packard's line-dividing policy. The Henney Junior was, like the other Clippers, powered by the 288 engine.

The former 300 line was now known as the Cavalier and, while the former 250 hardtop Mayfair and convertible still held their 122-inch wheelbase, Nance officially upgraded their designation to Senior cars. They still had the Junior series vertical taillights, and carried the same side trim as the Clipper Deluxe, but the 1954 models would see the end of such practices. The Cavalier has always suffered from schizophrenia because it never carried its name in bright metal either in 1953 or 1954, though it sometimes wore the "300" designation on its roof quarters on '53 cars. The new front window enhanced its looks, though the old *rear* window treatment now became a bit of an embarrassment, and was carefully hidden in sales materials. The Cavalier also received a stainless steel slashmark up front instead of the traditional Packard spear, which

was now relegated to Clippers. The following year would see it disappear for all time.

Both Cavalier and Mayfair/convertible used the same 327 engine as before, but with 8.0 to one compression as in the Clipper Deluxe, providing 180 horsepower with four-barrel carburetion. No significant driveline changes were made. Henney commercial cars continued to share drivetrain with these cars, though the four-barrel was optional. Later in the model year a special of limited production was added, though mechanically it was the same as the convertible. Inspired by the Pan American, it took another Latin name as the Packard Caribbean.

The original Pan American, which was too low and lacked an operating top, was entirely unsuited for production. But because public

Pages preceding: Jim Nance's personal 1953 Clipper and Caribbean. Below: The Nance team, photographed in the early summer of 1953, clockwise from the left: R.E. Bremer, A.H. Behnke, G.H. Brodie, G.C. Reifel, F.J. Walters, J.J. Nance, W.R. Grant, D. Norton, W.H. Graves, W.B. Hoge, R. Blythin, P.A. Monaghan.

reaction to it had been favorable, Nance had been persuaded to offer a close relative. Dick Teague did the detail work, mainly adding Senior Series taillights, cutting out rear wheel openings and outlining them with brightwork. The Caribbean was a full six-passenger car, of course, which made it more practical than the Pan American, but in its first year it was not the definitive luxury model it later became—even Ultramatic was optional. It shared the five main bearing engine and all mechanicals with—indeed in the beginning was simply made over from—the convertible. Though Henney had wanted the business, as earlier noted, Packard ultimately shipped completed convertibles to Mitchell-Bentley of Ionia, Michigan, for rendering into Caribbeans. The model was announced in January and deliveries began in March, with 750 units dispatched, not a bad record for a car with a $5210 pricetag. The Caribbean's clean design (no speed lines, lightning bolts or two-tones, no Caribbean nameplate) was well received.

Essentially the car was aimed at the market Buick had created with the Skylark, and it came in at $400 less than the Buick. But Nance's attack on the luxury market was based on much more than this specialty model; the top-line cars broke out of the sedan-only mold and received some exciting variations.

Like the 300, the Patrician lost its numerical designation for 1953 but because the hardware was well along before the decision was made, the number 400 remained on Patrician rear roof quarters. Joining the four-door sedan now was a stablemate built by Derham and called, logically, the Packard Derham. In the two years previous, the Rosemont, Pennsylvania coachbuilders had produced several special Packards on a one- or two-off basis, with and without divider windows, with and without curved divider glass, with and without Derham's traditional oval backlight. But Packard had not catalogued a custom-bodied car since 1942 and thus the Derham represented both a new departure for the company and an evocation of the past. The cars were assigned the model number/body designation 2653, although in reality they were converted Patricians and therefore carried 2652 numbers. The initial order was for twenty-five units, but as usual additional cars were made for private individuals. The catalogued version featured flat center divider glass, small rectangular backlight and leather top.

And still Nance was not finished. Earlier he had decided Packard would again offer long-wheelbase sedans and limousines. Such cars had last been available in the 1949 Twenty-Third Series and sales, at a grand total of four units, had been worse than poor. But Packard's "comeback" in the luxury market wouldn't be complete without them, so Henney was commissioned to build these models on a 149-inch wheelbase. As Nance announced to the trade press: "A short time ago when Packard announced its return to the fine-car field with a beautiful new line of superb automobiles, America had for the first time 'a new choice in fine cars.' At the same time, Packard promised that new custom limousines and sedans

In 1953 the Packard Motor Car Company hosted a meeting of the Classic Car Club, with the Pan American and Caribbean leading the parade at the Proving Grounds.

would be produced to round out the most complete selection of fine automobiles in America. Today that promise is fulfilled; these handsome new eight-passenger custom limousines and sedans, for personal or corporate use, are available and can be ordered now through Packard dealers, everywhere." With these cars Henney, anonymous producer of long-wheelbase sedans and limousines for Packard since 1946, finally achieved overdue recognition: On the rear door post was a cloisonné medallion proclaiming "Body Styled and Built by Henney."

The top of the line—Patrician, Derham formal sedan, and Henney "Executive sedan" and "Corporation limousine"—were priced at $3740, $6531, $6900 and $7100 respectively and all used the nine main bearing 327-cubic-inch engine, still rated at 180 bhp with four-barrel carburetor. All models had similar styling to the Cavalier, but the Patrician retained its chrome rear fender guards. All non-Clipper Packards used a fluted grille insert, a new trunk medallion and, save for the convertible and Mayfair, the same bulging horizontal taillights of 1951-1952. Back-up lights were moved under the taillights to accentuate width, and plain wheelcovers of the 1951 type replaced the ribbed versions available in 1952.

These detail revisions provided the only styling news for 1953, because the main focus had quickly shifted to a totally revitalized new Packard which Nance originally hoped to have on the market in 1954. Once the realities of automobile lead times became obvious, he settled for 1955,

though this change did not come so late as to disrupt key planning. There were no anguished meetings over the subject.

In engineering, the 1953's offered several new developments. In addition to the four-barrel carburetion there was now power steering, air conditioning was back after an eleven-year hiatus, and Nance also got his three-way radio. All of these new options were critical in Nance's prestige program. Prewar air-conditioning of Packards had been a luxury item which doubtless didn't much impress Christopher after the war. But by 1953 Cadillac and others were offering it and Packard had to follow suit. Its new unit was Frigidaire, like Cadillac's, built by GM. The evaporator case remained in the trunk with cold air outlets behind the back seat, like Packard's original unit, and the compressor still ran continuously through two belts which the owner removed in the winter. Turning the unit off merely short-cycled the Freon. There was one change in design: The evaporator incorporated no heater, as the prewar 1940 version had.

Power steering, on the other hand, was all Packard's, and it was a good system. GM's Saginaw was early in the field and had captured a degree of public fancy, but it had two serious drawbacks: a preload of some seven pounds which the driver had to overcome to put it into operation, and a linkage exposed to all the force of the power unit. The preload was designed to retain "road feel," but wasn't the most admirable idea GM ever had. Dubbed "you pull first" by the automotive press, the

In 1953, too, Packard advertising reflected the concerted, if ultimately unsuccessful, attempt by management to separate the Clipper from the Packard motorcar line.

Saginaw had a habit of taking over at inopportune moments, and under road conditions such as glare ice had been known to send vehicles off the road. The exposure of linkage to the power unit was a flaw shared with Chrysler, which was advertising its power steering as "full time"; the slightest nudge could turn the wheel full lock with the car at a standstill. Until Packard's power steering unit came along, systems of the day were mainly bolt-on operations. Saginaw's unit, for example, was affixed to the steering column, as was Studebaker's short-lived mechanical assist. Thus a 90-pound woman twisting the steering wheel on television commercials was doing as much damage to the linkage as a 300-pound linebacker wrenching the same wheel if the car was not moving. Packard's answer was to put the power linkage down on the frame, and have it act *directly* on the steering geometry. This arrangement eventually became a standard.

In publicizing its engineering advances, Packard was taking a leaf from Buick's book: In the early days of Dyna-flow, that transmission had sold well because if the customer didn't want it he had to special-order the car. By energetically promoting power brakes and steering, Ultramatic and three-way radio, Packard received high acceptance for these options. The power brakes in 1953 were priced at $39.45, the steering $195, Ultramatic (which began at $225 in 1949) was $199.

General reaction to the 1953's by the automotive press was cautious approval. *Motor Trend* was disappointed with the Packard performance in those days of onrushing horsepower from Chrysler, Ford and GM, but admitted that the name still "means luxury, sturdiness and prestige to many people. Regardless of what car they own now, those people who remember Packard in the pre-horsepower-race days may return to the fold *if* the company improves performance in its cars. As it is now, 'regular' Packard buyers buy the car not for high performance, but for the other fine features the car offers them. Many new buyers would be attracted to it because of these features *and* improved performance . . . Whether Packard makes the grade is not so much a matter of the competition meeting the challenge, but of Packard being able to back it up."

Nance was trying manfully to back Packard up. Luxury field penetration increased a few percentage points during the early months of the 1953 model year, and in May 1953 a five-year plan was undertaken to restore the company to a "sound status" by 1958. Said Nance, "Our targets are set, our blueprints drawn." The plan was designed to give Packard "long-range strength" to keep the company out of trouble, and to make it "heavy enough in the next five years so that emergency steps won't have to be taken again."

So far, nobody could argue with the statistics. In less than a year Nance had turned Packard into a new company, one preparing to take on the competition with gusto. In the first quarter of 1953, net profit was $3.5 million, compared to $1.3 million for the same period in 1952. Sales

rose 182 percent to $124 million, and pre-tax earnings, at $10 million, were the best in Packard history. The factory was producing 10,000 cars a month, and money was rolling in so handsomely that company officials began worrying about the possible imposition of an excess-profits tax!

While Packard carefully watched dealer inventories and the industry-wide sales picture, the dealer organization itself was strengthened by adding more franchises and weeding out weak ones. In an attempt to reach the 1946 peak of 2000 dealers by September 1st, 1954, 140 agencies had been added by the autumn of 1952. In 1953 200 marginal dealers were removed and in the first five months of that year, 400 were added, bringing the June total to 1700. "Company stores," the bane of the retailers, were instituted in key market locations, to be sold to independent operators once they were fully established and making money.

Nance was everywhere, coaxing, directing, cajoling and cheering his team. New ways were being found to increase the labor content of the finished product; the engineering staff was doubled, to promote new styling and engine developments; management was under study to avoid duplication of authority and to better integrate operations; personnel were watched to see who would be likely candidates for advancement. Jim Nance had little time for anything not Packard. When an invitation arrived for him from presidential assistant Sherman Adams to attend a business conference in the White House, it was accepted, as an internal memorandum noted, "to keep Mr. Nance's name on the list [but] it

Below: Twenty-Sixth Series 1953 convertible and Clipper Deluxe four-door sedan.

should be watched to cancel on the day of the meeting." He was really moving now. Morale was high—and then, something went wrong.

Without warning, in mid-1953, the market softened. The entire industry suddenly found itself producing at a rate that could not be justified by sales. An unfortunate underpinning of the Nance program was that its success depended on no lessening of the strong demand for cars, and when inventories suddenly mounted, production had to be quickly curtailed to avoid a pile-up. A minor setback, but one that couldn't have come at a worse time, was a reduction in the delivery schedule (though terminal dates were extended) for the jet engine program. The company ultimately marketed only 90,277 Twenty-Sixth Series cars, and about 75,500 for calendar 1953. These figures were far short of the anticipated 135,000, but net earnings remained stable at $5.4 million, and the threat of a pile-up was relegated to a corner of the corporate mind by the simultaneous start of Nance's great modernization program.

The aim of this program was "to place Packard in a more competitive position through lowered operating costs and afford the Company an opportunity for greater flexibility in its manufacturing operations." The project really got under way in 1954, and Nance planned it to be complete by the beginning of 1955 production. To finance it Nance completed an agreement with fourteen major U.S. banks for a $20 million line of credit. Packard had not generally been at ease with regard to borrowing money, but no one was worried—the firm had had credit

Rather flamboyantly showcasing its new cars at the factory, with the Mayfair (above) and the Cavalier (below). The Patrician four-door sedan (on the right).

Packards built by Henney Motor Company on the 149-inch long wheelbase, the 1954 "Corporation limousine" (above) and the 1953 "Executive sedan" (below). Also from model year 1953, the formal sedan by Derham (pictured at the bottom).

agreements before, primarily for defense work, and the new agreement just replaced the former defense program.

One interesting sidelight of the 1953 model year was the Packard Balboa, which won another prize—the *Cars* magazine award for Design, Safety and Comfort. Below the beltline it looked like a Caribbean, though it carried a 2631 chassis number instead of the Caribbean's 2678. But the Balboa's main feature was what Dick Teague called a "canopy top," featuring a rear overhang and a reverse slanting rear window. Packard said the Balboa's main purpose was safety: "Such driving hazards as optical distortion, accumulation of snow and rain are eliminated by the reverse angle of the rear Picture Window . . . Since the rear Picture Window can be lowered or raised at will, draft-free ventilation is an added benefit."

A production version of the Balboa, occasionally referred to as "Balboa-X" in literature, was considered for 1954 but the project was abandoned. The design *idea* wasn't, well into the clay model stage for the 1955's, and of course it did appear in production on the Mercury Turnpike Cruiser of a few years later. In 1953 it was brand-new, though, and the red and white Balboa made a striking appearance. Packard said the car was done entirely in-house, though there may have been Mitchell-Bentley input evident in the lower panel sheet metal work. And as a matter of historical accuracy it should be added that the literature was incorrect in claiming the rear window would be powered—it was never powered, and never lowered at all, for it had no place to go and was set solidly in place.

Though the basic body shell would endure, 1954 was the last model year for the original Reinhart styling. With the major rework scheduled for 1955, Packard just played the Detroit game of changing the product enough for model identification: large hooded headlamp doors, back-up lights integrated into Senior Series taillight housings, revised bumper guards which shortened the product. (Model for model, the 1953 Packards had been the longest ever built.)

One change for 1954 was the end of the traditional series nomenclature. Since the Teens, Packards had been designated by series: there were five series of 48's and three series of 38's in the 1912-1915 Packard Six period, three series of Twin Sixes, then a First Series Six in 1920 and a First Series Eight in 1922. In 1928 Packard found itself building a Fifth Series Six and Fourth Series Eight, but the anomaly ended with the discontinuance of the Six, and the Eight skipped a number to become the Sixth Series Packard. This numerical order, skipping the Thirteenth Series, had continued through the Twenty-Sixth Series of 1953. Someone, possibly Nance, finally had tired of trying to remember which series accompanied which year, and the cars were now firmly tied to model year designations anyway, so designating the 1954 models the "Fifty-Fourth Series" blended common sense with tradition.

(Nance would do the same thing to Studebaker's model designation system after the companies combined.)

To his Clipper line Nance gave renewed attention. New for '54 was the Clipper Special, a $2544 model with the 288 engine, in two-door form, along with a four-door at $50 additional. These were price leaders, with a minimum of standard extras, excluding even turn signals except where required by law. A commercial Clipper also used the 288 engine.

Next came the Clipper Deluxe, again available as a two-door sedan, four-door sedan and Sportster, the latter the same as the year previous: a two-door Deluxe Clipper with flashy trim. It didn't provide significant model distinction, but helped compensate for Packard's hardtop shortage, and 3672 Sportsters were sold in 1953 and 1336 in 1954.

The top-line Clipper Super was really the same as the Deluxe, sharing stampings, wheelbase, and drivetrain including the 327 engine, now rated at 165 horsepower. Supers included two- and four-door sedans and the first Clipper hardtop, named Panama. At $3125, the Panama filled a large gap in the Clipper line. There could have been a Clipper convertible too, without excessive tooling cost, for the Packard Convertible (now with capital "C") was already on the short wheelbase. But none was ever offered.

The 1954 Clippers showed growing evidence of Nance's philosophy of line separation.* They were on their own 122-inch wheelbase, with overall grille differentiation, and had their own taillight which was visible from the sides and became known around Styling as the "sore thumb." All models—Special, Deluxe, Super—were *Clipper* models, and the Packard name was placed discreetly on the corner of their trunk lids, more as a signature than a marque. Carrying the separation theme to details, 1954 Clippers had *black* hexagons with red borders in which a script "Packard Clipper" appeared—a reversal of the traditional scheme. "You will notice," cooed Advertising, "that the CLIPPER retains the regal 'Packard look.' This is Packard style, that stays in style." The push to establish the Clipper name was on, and the cars were always referred to by that name, or at least "Clipper by Packard."

Along the same lines was a significant change in the Packard models. Whereas the convertibles and Mayfair hardtop had been advanced only the year before to co-equal status with the Cavalier, for 1954 they passed beyond that to the next price bracket, at $3827 for the hardtop (now

---

*He was not, however, entirely satisfied yet. In a friendly letter to a Packard owner who had written him on the subject, Nance replied, "I share much your same feeling about the need for a greater difference of appearance between our Packard and Clipper lines. As you so clearly indicate, this is a real problem to challenge the stylists' ingenuity but it is having close attention in our forward planning." And the result would appear for '55.

Tony Curtis, Janet Leigh, Don Taylor and a Caribbean, photographed in '53. The prize-winning Packard Balboa from '53, with its "canopy top" rear overhang and reverse slanting rear window which quite obviously could not be rolled down.

named Pacific), $3935 for the Convertible, and $6100 for the Caribbean. Still equipped with the 327 engine and five main bearings, the 1954 Cavalier sold for $3344 and was rated at 185 horsepower, its side trim changed to two horizontal strips separated at the rear by three smaller strips. The Cavalier, as the 300, had started out in 1951 as a Patrician with less expensive trim, but for 1954 it was significantly different, comparable to Cadillac's Model 62 vis-à-vis the 60 Special. The '54 Cavalier was the only Senior Packard with the 327 engine, and there would be no 1955 equivalent.

The 1954 Patrician was a highly refined product, with new dash, new interiors including the option of nylon matelasse, and a new engine (shared with the convertibles and Pacific) of 359 cubic inches. This was a bored and stroked (3 9/16 by 4 ½) version of the 327, with compression boosted to the highest in the industry—despite the growing number of competitive V-8's—at 8.7 to one. It was rated at 212 bhp with four-barrel carburetion, and was truly the ultimate development of the in-line eight, with aluminum alloy cylinder head and the highest horsepower Packard ever pulled from such an engine, without supercharging. Originally a 1954 Derham had been listed as well, but it did not make the catalogues, although many 1954 Packards went through the Derham shops for private or dealer conversions.

The limousine and eight-passenger sedan carried Patrician nameplates for 1954, though Ultramatic was not standard, as on the former. Henney built only thirty-five limousines and sixty-five eight-passenger sedans in the last production year for these cars.

Nance was stuck with the 122-inch wheelbase for the Caribbean, Pacific and Packard Convertible, but in every other way he upgraded their image mightily. They used the new 359 engine and the Pacific/Convertible had taillights identical to other Senior Packards. This change was not simply a matter of installing new lights because the fenders were still those of the preceding three years. Consequently a bright metal pod was tacked onto the sides of the fender to allow it to accept the wider taillight.

The 1954 Caribbean now emerged as a complete luxury vehicle, loaded with extras and powered by the biggest Packard engine. Still equipped with wire spoke wheels, scooped bonnet and continental tire carrier, the 1954 Caribbean did not have wide cut-outs on the rear wheels, as the 1953 models. Instead there was a two-toning strip, added to accentuate length, which received mixed reviews. Caribbean sales were down to 400 for 1954, but figures on a specialty car like this are not meaningful. Usually the vehicle is a loss item, each sale representing a contribution to "image" but not to profit. A sales figure as arbitrary as 400 indicates only that Nance decided to build that quantity.

All Senior Packards featured a new dash which rid Packard of what had been criticized as austere in the past—the three-dial layout of 1951-1953. Electric four-way power seats were offered, and the air conditioner fresh air scoops could now be shut off from the inside. The pelican/cormorant (the latter designation had been in common usage at the Boulevard since the late 1930's) remained unchanged in 1954. New were an inside-control rear view mirror option, tubeless tires (later standard, an industry first), and electric windshield washers. The commercial car line from Henney was also equipped with the nine main bearing engine, which had not been the practice since 1950. There was a particularly well-styled landau funeral coach and flower car, and Henney also produced a one-off "Super Station Wagon," a twelve-seater on an ambulance chassis, featuring air conditioning, rear conference table, and the industry's first rear-facing seat. The company had planned to market this model, along with a camper to be called the Flying Sportsman. But Henney was in deep financial trouble and these plans died—notwithstanding the repeated public announcements to the contrary—with the cessation of automobile production in Freeport in 1954.

The now-annual Packard experimental or show car for 1954 was the fiberglass-bodied Panther Daytona, powered by the 359 engine but supercharged via a McCulloch centrifugal blower (like the concurrent Kaiser Manhattan) which would reappear on the 1957 Packards and 1958 Packard Hawk. With 275 horsepower on tap and equipped with Ultramatic, it was clocked at 131.1 mph at Daytona Beach, and won the "Motorsport merit award for excellence of design in the American Luxury Car Field classification" at the International Motor Sports Show in New York.

The Panther marked Packard's first contact with Creative Industries Inc., a Detroit firm specializing in one-off cars for automotive styling studios. Officials at Creative recall that no more than five Panthers were made, two of which were later fitted with 1955 taillights (one with a fiberglass hardtop at Mitchell-Bentley).

The Panther was originally called Gray Wolf II, recalling the historic Packard racing car, but the name was changed before it appeared in public. Aside from 1954 Clipper taillights, it borrowed little from current production, the front bumper strongly resembling the forthcoming 1955 version, albeit upside down. Packard was anxious to evaluate the fiberglass body; Chevrolet and Kaiser-Willys already had such bodies in regular production. The Panther was also the first Packard with a wraparound windshield. Of the car's styling Dick Teague states, "I didn't think of it as a benchmark at the time, but it was fiberglass, supercharged, and unique." He has also noted occasionally that there are things he'd revise if he were doing it today, but this is a Teague characteristic: "Every time I see the Predictor," he told the Packard Automobile Classics national convention in 1971 about that later show car, "I want to change something about it."

Engineering advancements continued beyond the 1954 engine. Early

With a major design revision planned for 1955, Packard elected to change its cars for 1954—the last model year for the original Reinhart styling—only enough to differentiate them from the Packards of the previous season. Some of the ideas tossed about in Styling are reflected in the photographs on this page. Obviously the changes considered were of the strictly "bolt-on" variety and thankfully most of them would not reach production. Ultimately, large hooded headlamp doors, back-up lights integrated into the Senior Series taillight housings, and minutely altered bumper guards would compose the basic change for model year '54. The biggest revision perhaps was in nomenclature. The Twenty-Sixth Series for 1953 was not followed by the Twenty-Seventh for 1954, but instead by the Fifty-Fourth, which made rather marvelous good sense.

With Neil Brown holding on to its left rear fender, the last Packard—an air-conditioned model—arrives at the body drop at East Grand Boulevard. Below: A Chrysler executive presents Brown the "key" to the Conner plant.

in Nance's tenancy, Bill Graves had spoken with him about another matter: "If we want to stay on top by 1955, we'll have to put some money into retooling the Ultramatic to add direct drive to our torque start." Ultramatic, known more for smoothness than zip as we have seen, wasn't as mushy as Dyna-flow, the original ungeared torque converter transmission, but it did not approach the performance of Hydra-Matic. When Chevrolet's Powerglide and Chrysler's Powerflite appeared, they combined torque converters with a geared start, and Chrysler's subsequent Torque-flite went beyond this to a three-speed. Packards operated in High were hard put to keep up in an all-out acceleration contest. Starting in Low and shifting to High was only half-heartedly sanctioned by Packard, and was certain to shorten the life of the high-range clutches. So Graves and company went to work on a method of accommodating the flashy driver by having Ultramatic shift itself from low to high before it locked up into direct drive.

A special governor kit for 1954 did cut down drastically on the time required for the high-range clutches to engage once the unit was put into High, and essentially did away with engine flare on manual upshifts. By late 1954, a Gear-Start Ultramatic was in production with two "Drive" ranges, one the same as the former High (converter start only), the other a low-gear start which would shift to high. G-S Ultramatic also featured an easy-reading dipstick sprouting from the transmission oil pan. This transmission was a reasonable success, though it needed refinement, and many parts were later incorporated into 1955's Twin Ultramatic.

Packard had outlasted the unexpected mid-year slump in 1953, and had launched the 1954's proclaiming some optimism, but it had hardly placed the new cars in dealer showrooms before another unpleasant surprise hit—the loss of Briggs' bodymaking facilities. The decision in 1940 to give its body business to Briggs, which was also supplying Chrysler and Hudson at that time, had been a costly mistake from the start. Now it was compounded. In December of 1953, shortly after the death of Briggs' founder, the family found itself faced with ruinous inheritance taxes and put the whole operation up for sale. Chrysler bought Briggs and promptly served notice it was not willing to continue the production of Packard bodies.

"Your management has under consideration plans for bodies in future years," Nance wrote calmly in the 1953 annual report. "In the meantime we have arranged with Chrysler Corporation to produce Packard bodies until these plans can be finalized." But a change was going to cost a lot of money—money that had been earmarked for other work.

Meanwhile, sales of the 1954's were plunging. "Every time a road man came around I asked him some time in the visit when we were going to get a V-8," Sante Fe, New Mexico dealer Henry Lawrence would remember. "I suspect every other dealer did the same." Despite all the refinements in the Fifty-Fourth Series, selling an in-line engine in an era when the V-8 was becoming all the rage was not easy. The in-line eight, once an industry mainstay, had powered two cars other than Packard in 1953: the Pontiac and, in ohv format, the Buick Special. For 1954 the roster was reduced to Packard and Pontiac. (No U.S. in-line eights have been manufactured since.) "We have no choice," Nance growled, "even though there's no news in a V-8. Making one is the only road to a modern car. Everything follows the product." Nobody really knows what this last sentence meant, but the rest of the statement was clear enough, and a V-8 engine—already under way for some time—was absolutely necessary in time for the '55 models.

Other engineering developments and a major restyling effort were also planned for 1955, so the low sales of the '54's didn't cause that much concern. Total 1954 model production was only 31,291 units, the least for any series since the Eleventh of 1933-1934.

Part of the 1954 sales decline had nothing to do with Packard. A major battle had developed between the industry's two major powers when Henry Ford II announced he intended to make Ford number one again or break it in the process. Because dealers received shipments whether they wanted them or not, Ford prices were discounted drastically; the cars had to be moved out before the next truckload arrived. GM retaliated, and the pitched battle continued through the end of 1955. "This development," said Packard in its annual report, "served to point up the advantages of the full-line producers and the disadvantages of the single-line or independent producers." Nance had been planning such a full-line producer from the beginning, and it was clearly time to move.

In early 1954, word was passed that Packard might merge with the Studebaker Corporation of South Bend, Indiana. George Mason had by this time put Nash-Kelvinator and Hudson together to form American Motors, and it was Nance's turn to make up his half of the Grand Plan. Neither Nash nor Hudson was very sound and the merged companies faced a confusing future of dealer overlaps, model disarray and duplicated efforts. Studebaker, for that matter, appeared not much interested in merging with anybody—*Iron Age* reported that the company "remained aloof in South Bend." Nance admitted that Packard was at least approachable. And he had been given clearance by his board to work out any changes that would improve Packard's position.

On April 6th a report, which had been commissioned a year earlier from the management consulting firm of Lehman Brothers Inc., was issued on the "Benefits of a Merger" between Studebaker and Packard. It called the potential grouping "a dignified combination of the two best names in the independent field. The combined lines are essentially complementary and non-competitive [unlike Hudson and Nash]. Studebaker covers the low- and low-medium-priced fields; Packard covers the upper-medium and high-priced fields. In addition, through the Studebaker truck line, the merged Company would be represented in the

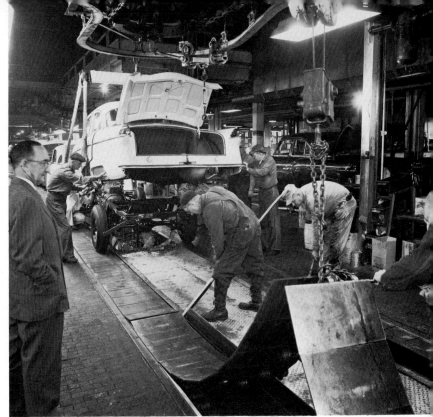

A stripe-suited Clare Briggs watches the last Clipper proceed down the line at East Grand Boulevard, followed by workers ripping up the conveyor in its wake.

low-priced and high-volume segment of the trucking industry."

The report also stressed the larger financial and management resources resulting from merger, and the chances to achieve lower unit costs through greater volume, more models, interchangeable parts, better purchasing power, East and West Coast Studebaker assembly plants and dual dealerships. Studebaker's good standing in the export field (seven percent of total production) was mentioned as an outlet for Packard.

On May 4th Lehman issued a follow-up, "Suggested Basis of Consolidation," proposing that for technical reasons the consolidation "take the form of an acquisition by Packard of Studebaker's assets. This will not, however, preclude the [new firm] from having all the characteristics of a merged company."

But the Studebaker-Packard combination was no merger, in spite of the repeated use of that designation by automotive historians and publications. In an agreement dated June 22nd, the terms stated: 575

Fifty-Fourth Series for 1954: The Caribbean (above), the Patrician (above right) and Convertible (below right) which was now designated with the "c" capitalized.

"Packard desires to purchase, and Studebaker desires to sell . . . all the property and assets of Studebaker, including its name, business and good will, in exchange solely for shares of Packard voting stock and assumption by Packard of substantially all liabilities of Studebaker." Finances were complicated by the fifteen million shares of stock outstanding at Packard, second only to General Motors, which would finally be replaced in a reverse split leaving the shareholders with only three million. Studebaker Corporation would be paid 3,542,187 shares of new stock for its business, with 8,457,813 shares valued at $10 assigned to the treasury—ready money for trading in the process of acquisitions and diversification.

Prior to approval of all this by the Packard stockholders, Jim Nance answered a few questions for columnist Sylvia Porter, and her resulting article in the *New York Post* in July delighted him. Apologizing that "lawyers and financiers had my time so chewed up" that he had not been able to grant a lengthy interview, he wrote Miss Porter: "I should mention that perhaps the most gratifying thing about your column is that you see in the 'merger' a benefit for the people who choose cars. You know that to be successful that is what it has to have. And your saying so hastens the time when we shall have it." Having Miss Porter in his corner was helpful. Her column was widely syndicated and doubtless read by many Packard shareholders.

With stockholder approval, on October 1st, 1954, Packard purchased Studebaker. The name change was immediate: Studebaker-Packard Corporation. The board was enlarged from eight to fifteen, comprising both previous boards except for Jesse Vincent who had retired. Nance was president, the board chairman was Studebaker's Paul Hoffman, and former Studebaker president Harold Vance was chairman of the executive committee.

Not everyone was happy. Out in Sante Fe, Packard dealer Henry Lawrence was convinced this was "a 'Shotgun Wedding' as all of the Packard men I knew did not care too much for Studebaker, and the

Studebaker men felt the same way about Packard." Even more disgruntled was Fred H. Rush, a member of the Packard Management Group who now quit that body in disgust and prepared a twenty-four-page report for stockholders regarding the "sellout terms" of the Studebaker-Paackard agreement. It questioned decisions as various as the salaries of top-ranking Packard personnel and the reason the name Studebaker preceded Packard's in the new corporation, and quoted financial columnists in various newspapers and business magazines who had not been as sanguine about the Studebaker-Packard marriage as Miss Porter was. Apparently some Packard stockholders felt likewise, as a sampling of replies from them when Nance asked for their approval indicates: "The Studebaker people manipulated Pierce Arrow so it's no more, so be careful," from Great Neck, New York; "If Packard's present management thinks they have a sinking ship what good would it do to tie it to another sinking ship?" from Elkhart, Indiana; "How dumb do you think people are?" from Davenport, Iowa; "I recommend that you go back to Hotpoint and manufacture curling irons and washing machines," from Washington, D.C.

It was Rush's idea to rally stockholders—"one dollar from each [of you] will build an invincible fighting machine . . . "—and oust the "liability that the Packard Motor Car Company can ill-afford." But Jim

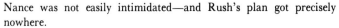

Clippers for 1954: The Sportster (above left) with grille surround experimentally painted white by Styling, the Deluxe club sedan (below left), the Panama (above).

Nance was not easily intimidated—and Rush's plan got precisely nowhere.

Nance had officially stated that the rationale behind the Studebaker purchase was to broaden market coverage and to better face costs in accord with the Lehman reports. Nineteen fifty-five, most analysts agreed, would decide whether it would pay off. Unaware of the overall Nance/Mason plan, some observers noted that the "little three" of Studebaker-Packard, Kaiser-Willys and AMC was still too little. The six independents had fallen from ten to five percent of the market, and in 1954 too, Chrysler had dropped from over twenty-one percent to as low as eleven. In effect, there was now only a Big Two. And, it was thought, Studebaker-Packard had a fair shot at outdistancing Chrysler, if everything proceeded smoothly. But that depended largely on Studebaker.

Founded in 1852 by Henry and Clem Studebaker as a small blacksmith and wagon shop in South Bend, the family venture was pushed into prominence by another brother, John Mohler Studebaker, who had been building wheelbarrows in the California gold fields and returned east in 1857 with a large injection of cash. Amassing assets of over $200,000 in the next fifteen years, the partnership became the Studebaker Brothers Manufacturing Company in 1868, and in 1911

Studebaker Corporation, by which time it was the largest vehicle works in the world. Electric car production had begun in 1902, followed in 1904 by the first gasoline car, built in cooperation with the Garford Auto Company, and later E-M-F. Automobiles gradually outstripped wagons and with business booming after World War I, Studebaker sold its horse-drawn enterprise, becoming the only wagon maker in America which successfully made the transition to the horseless age.

Everything proceeded well for Studebaker until the Depression. In 1928 the company had chosen to broaden its line by acquiring Pierce-Arrow, and the timing couldn't have been worse. Pierce-Arrow was already ailing, and after the Wall Street crash, Studebaker spent vast sums of money in an attempt to restore it to competitive health, including the development of a twelve-cylinder engine. Further measures were equally unsuccessful. President Albert R. Erskine introduced two cheaper cars, one named after himself and another named Rockne, after the famous Notre Dame football coach; both cars died horribly. Then he attempted to merge with White after buying ninety-five percent of that firm's stock, but was blocked by a minority group of White stockholders. Erskine had compounded his management errors by continuing to issue dividends in the face of continued losses, and had misread the staying power of bad times. On March 8th, 1933, Studebaker went into receivership. Shortly thereafter Albert Erskine committed suicide.

The new management team included production vice-president Harold Vance, sales and advertising vice-president Paul G. Hoffman. Pierce-Arrow was sold for $1 million cash, and a new Studebaker Corporation was formed on March 9th, 1935, with Vance as chairman and Hoffman president. This team accomplished an economic miracle, culminating with the introduction of the successful Champion in 1939; in 1941 Studebaker emerged from receivership and declared a dividend. Prewar production reached 133,855 units.

Resuming production postwar with a good cash position and a $12 million loan, Studebaker astounded the industry and the public with the

577

modern styling of its 1947 model. Sales zoomed, the truck line was expanded, but Hoffman left temporarily in April 1948 to head the Marshall Plan, and in a short time Vance undid most of Hoffman's good work. Probably the most visible error was the airplane-styled 1950-1951 line, a pet project of Vance and styling consultant Raymond Loewy. Though Loewy had some highly successful industrial designs behind him—the red and white Lucky Strike package and the Coldspot refrigerator, in addition to the '47 Studebaker—and was to have more successes later, he had reached a nadir with the 1950-1951 Studebakers. Though they didn't immediately effect sales, they nose-dived in value as used cars. And that was not the only bomb ticking.

During the war Studebaker had lost control of its production costs. When peace came, the larger companies suffered long and painful strikes to bring their costs under control, but Studebaker took an easy way out and settled with the United Auto Workers on the union's terms. It is true that the workforce was largely local, and tended to look upon Studebaker as its own, but the labor population had doubled during the war and the newcomers and outsiders valued the union more than the company. Just as Erskine had stubbornly insisted on continuing to issue dividends, Vance insisted on keeping Studebaker strikeless, as historically it had always been, and settled for low work standards, attributing part of the $5 million decrease in profits in 1950 to establishment of high standards for the 1950 line.

By the time Studebaker's radical and beautiful 1953 "European Look" was introduced, costs were completely out of control. That year ended with a profit of $2.7 million, less than half of one percent of sales—management had scheduled too many sedans and too few sporty coupes, resulting in the sales debacle—and the first four months of 1954 didn't even see manufacturing costs covered. The South Bend workers now made history by voting themselves a pay cut, although it was not enough, and this entire disquieting economic climate had induced Studebaker to begin merger discussions with Packard early in 1954.

Why did the Packard board agree to buy such a loser? Apparently, the answer at least partly may be laid to a lack of concern. Several directors described the purchase as "an act of faith," termed it a "friendly deal" where neither board asked for an outside audit of the other's figures. Lehman Brothers and others made no independent investigations because they had no underwriting responsibilities. Mutual Benefit Life, in the course of its agreement to lend money to the new company, made no realistic inquiries, nor did Metropolitan.

Nance worked out a careful program for the new Studebaker-Packard Corporation which anticipated a $9 million loss in 1955, a smaller loss in 1956, with profitable operations beginning late that year on the strength of the new common-shelled 1957 model line he had commissioned immediately after the purchase. He predicted solid profits in 1958, with about four percent of the market. It was all out of the question, as Nance would find out. But it seemed like a good idea at the time.

Accurate appraisal of Studebaker's situation was not the only major roadblock to "America's Fourth Full-Line Company." Nance had emphasized many times that the defense business was critical, and up to the time of the preliminary agreement between Studebaker and Packard there was a fair amount of it. Packard had the marine engine and J-47 airplane engine contract, and Studebaker was building military trucks and complete J-47 engines. Then came another undeserved bad break for Nance: It was named Charles Wilson.

A former head of General Motors, Wilson had become Secretary of Defense in the new Eisenhower administration. In his new job he had to manage Defense without any wars to fight after Korea ended, and in an attempt to cut costs he called for a "narrow-based procurement policy." Cynics were quick to point out that as far as the auto industry was concerned, the narrow base largely rested with Wilson's old friends at General Motors.

Charles Wilson probably had no idea of the damage he did to Studebaker-Packard, but Nance estimated that the loss in defense work was about $426 million. In 1956, when the situation had become clearly desperate, Wilson claimed that he would be in an "untenable position" if he favored S-P with any defense work over its competition.* Studebaker Division was caught with a New Jersey plant which had been used only for defense work, and Packard had a similar one in Utica.

The mid-1953 sales downturn, the loss of Briggs as his body builder, the purchase of flimsy Studebaker, the loss of the defense business. Was there anything else? Yes, there was, and it came when Packard's chief financial officer Walter Grant went to South Bend to study the Studebaker accounts. He returned to Nance's office ashen-faced: Instead of the 165,000 figure quoted in the agreement papers as the break-even point, the figure that had to be met was 282,000!

This was not the level of production to which Studebaker had been accustomed. In fact, the all-time record had been only 334,554 units in 1950. Nance received Grant's estimate with alarm, Studebaker with skepticism. Hadn't Studebaker made profits for years at less volume?

The difference lay in work standards. Whereas Hoffman, shortly after returning to Studebaker from the Marshall Plan, had brought wage rates back into general agreement with the industry, Studebaker's and Grant's estimates of work standards varied widely. In fact, Grant pegged Studebaker's costs at nearly double the industry average, and Grant had always been very accurate. Nance and Grant did finally succeed in get-

*The government later provided such help for American Motors, with a $20 million tax rebate, and Lockheed, with a large loan guarantee—without listening to any criticism.

Page opposite: Jim Nance, Paul Hoffman and Harold Vance, September 1954.
Clare Briggs photographed with a Clipper Super from model year 1954.
Above: Vice President Richard M. Nixon checking his notes on a Caribbean.
Below: Mrs. Henry B. Joy going out in the last production 1954 limousine.

Packard's experimental/show car for 1954, the supercharged and fiberglass-bodied Panther Daytona (originally Gray Wolf II), designed by Richard Teague.

ting the costs down at Studebaker, but it took the better part of the next twelve months.

Now Nance really had troubles. The first two years had gone so well, he and everyone else had begun to believe the long-sought miracle was taking place and that nothing could stop Packard. But in just a few months the market for cars had shrunk, the market for defense products had disappeared, South Bend was faced with runaway labor costs, the body supply was tapering off. About the first two problems even Nance could do nothing, and Grant had set about doing whatever could be done with the third. Nance was left with the fourth—a source of bodies—and a wrong move here had the potential of sinking the whole company. What would he do?

The choices were: Find another body maker, lease new premises to build Packard bodies, or bring the body operation back into the East Grand Boulevard plant. Finding another body maker was out of the question—Briggs had been the last in the field. Though a few companies like Budd had done miscellaneous stampings, none was capable of a full-scale program. No major company was interested in making bodies for an independent, and none of the smaller ones had the capacity—with the

possible exception of American Motors.

The AMC option had been explored before the formation of Studebaker-Packard. AMC had wanted to buy the Clipper V-8 for its larger models, and during these negotiations George Mason mentioned the possibility of assembling Packard body components at the Nash plants in Kenosha, Wisconsin. Although Mason subsequently suggested the plan be dropped because of excess handling and freight costs from Kenosha to Detroit, to Packard the idea remained workable if enough costs could be cut out of it, and so Graves got together again with Mason to work out common body dimensions for a possible joint body venture between the two firms. A study to determine if the unit body construction used by Nash might be a stumbling block indicated this not to be a problem. But the death of George Mason and the ascendance of George Romney at AMC brought a rethink by the latter, and while uncertainty reigned, the time for a decision came and went.

In the meantime, the Briggs loss had sealed Hudson's fate. Hudson had, of course, been Briggs' other big customer when Chrysler took over, and while it was equipped to do stampings (and in fact did some for S-P), it could not make bodies. Beginning with the 1955 models, Hudson

No more than a handful were made, two of them subsequently updated (as above) and wearing 1955 taillights and a Creative Industries badge on the rear fender.

bodies were produced by Nash, parting company with the old "step-down" body, the resulting car to be referred to as a "Hash" by disappointed Hudson partisans to the present day.

In a way, Packard's fate was also sealed by the loss of Briggs, because in coping with it, Nance botched his most crucial decision. He leased a former Briggs plant on Conner Avenue. This would not have proven a major obstacle in itself, but Nance compounded the situation by relocating the entire Packard assembly line at Conner, a move which afforded the opportunity to modernize his assembly line, but it cost millions and returned no benefits.

A lot of history would have changed had Packard never left the body business in the first place, but hindsight offered no consolation in 1954. Still, Nance might have bailed himself out had he elected to reinstitute body building at East Grand Boulevard where, after all, it had been done before, rather than order the third total tear-up since 1934.

In the broader view, Nance had never really learned how to retrench. It was a skill he should have developed for this incredible business in which, as Joseph W. Frazer had said about his similar experience at Willow Run, "there's so much money going out the window every day that if you're not careful, you'll lose your shirt." When all the money was gone, and the Packard Detroit empire lay in ruins, many would come to wish that—just this one time—James J. Nance had passed up the opportunity to move ahead, to modernize, and to expand.

The final blow of the year was almost an anticlimax. When George Mason died, Nance did not immediately suspect that the four-marque American Motors plan would die with him. But it did. AMC's new president, George Romney, at first delayed, then decided against it for all time. Nance and Studebaker-Packard were caught flatfooted. Romney proposed instead a "love without marriage" arrangement of mutual cooperation but most attempts in this direction would be unsuccessful.

In the meantime, Nance was stuck with his new purchase: Studebaker. "I don't think they could have made it alone," Nance told *The Packard Cormorant.* "I wouldn't have wanted them if I didn't see them as part of a bigger picture. Their labor costs were substantially out of line." The proposed full-line, four-marque company would have needed Studebaker's entrée to the lower and lower-middle price classes, but Nance didn't need that now. Still, need it or not, he had it, and management set about making the best of a bad deal.

581

CHAPTER TWENTY-NINE

LET THE
RIDE DECIDE

The Fifty-Fifth Series

1955

AUTHORS: GEORGE HAMLIN AND DWIGHT HEINMULLER

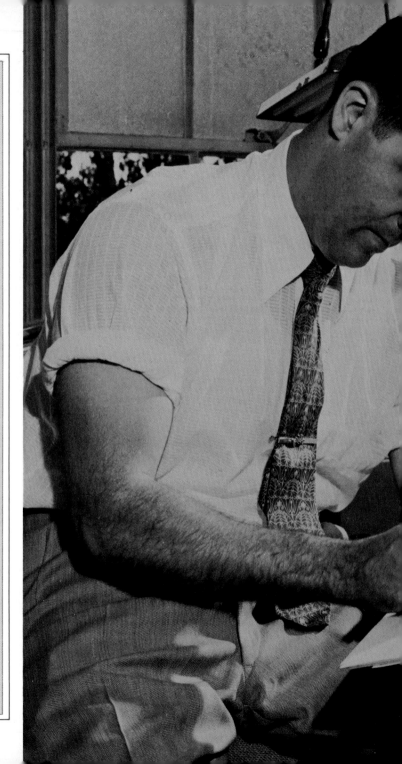

The Packard series numbered fifty-four had ended. Studebaker-Packard faced at least that many problems. It had a labor difficulty at South Bend, a new body plant to create, a new assembly line to arrange, a radical new model to build. But the latter, Packard's Fifty-Fifth Series, was a major achievement, rendered more so by the troublesome straits in which the company found itself. It featured new styling, a new V-8 engine, and a truly revolutionary torsion bar suspension.

In the matter of design, the 1955 cars were the first to bear more than a smattering of the ideas of Richard A. Teague, though he had previously done the Balboa and Panther Daytona, and some work on the 1953-1954 models. Teague competed in the '55 styling with certain outside organizations—Sundberg-Ferrar among them—and won, and his work was basically complete by April 1954. To the basic 1951 body shell he grafted a new wraparound window, keeping pace with the competition; he added a new grille and new side trim, returning to the eggcrate motif in the former; and at the last possible minute—and in record time at which he still marvels today—he replaced the bulging taillights of 1954 with what Packard called the "cathedral" lamps.

Other than the doors and roof panel, about which little could be done,

Teague had at an early point rendered the new '55 well nigh unrecognizable over 1954—except for the taillights, which were to have been carried over. But, as Teague recalls, "Nance said the only stale part of the '55 was the rear end and if we could come up with something else, we should.

"It was on a Friday afternoon before Easter 1954. Nance had wandered back to Styling with his nodding disciples and bright young Ford escapees and, I think, Ray Powers—a sort of shirtsleeves, 'let's look at the cars' thing. I remember that he said we could live with the doors, but we need a new look in the tail area. 'Goddammit, Teague,' he said, 'you're a bright guy, why don't you come up with something and I'll see you next week?' This was like 5 p.m. Friday, so I took a bunch of junk home in case I got time to work something out. Nance didn't much care about routine lead times—it was like April, and the car had to be built in the summer and be ready by fall!"

"I lived in Rochester and it was Easter Sunday," Teague continued. "I didn't feel like going anywhere. I drew this thing up, and I knew it was impossible, there was no time, but JN wanted it so . . . I whipped it out in about four hours."

For all Nance cared, it might have taken weeks of research. "I was a

Pages preceding: Dick Teague at work, the small scale clay model using an entirely new front end and sheet metal. These pages: The 25,000-mile Patrician.

Contest **AAA** Board
of the
American Automobile Association
Washington, D.C.
◄ CERTIFICATE OF PERFORMANCE ►

The undersigned Certify in the name of the
Contest Board, American Automobile Association
that

AN EXPERIMENTAL PACKARD 4-DOOR SEDAN, EQUIPPED WITH A PRE-PRODUCTION
1955 ENGINE, WAS DRIVEN ON THE PACKARD PROVING GROUND, UTICA,
MICHIGAN FROM OCTOBER 21 THROUGH OCTOBER 31 TO ESTABLISH
THE FOLLOWING PERFORMANCE:

TOTAL DISTANCE TRAVELED	25,000 MILES
TOTAL ELAPSED TIME	238 HRS. 41 MIN. 49.3 SEC.
AVERAGE MILES PER HOUR	104.737

Sanction No.
9273A

Planning the 1955 Clipper, the proposal by Sundberg-Ferrar, below;
Packard Styling's own proposal, incorporating all new sheet metal, above.
Page opposite: The early attempts, from circa July 1953, at changing
the marque's facial expression—on the Clipper, above center and right; and
on the Packard, as shown above left and in the three photographs below.

big hero, J. Pierpont Teague. 'Goddammit, that's it,' Nance said when he saw the sketch, 'put that sonofabitch on the car!' It was ridiculous. But we eyeballed it and I mothered or fathered it and it turned out. The thing involved cutting off the end of the bumper and fender and was a monster job around the exhaust pipes, but he was in love with that taillight. I never saw a guy get so hooked on a design, and he gave me a $250-a-month raise, which was 33 percent, and a trip to Europe.

"We had used the '54 double bumper because Nance had wanted it to look heavier; we had had the bumper since 1953. I put that abortion on the '54's; we were trying to come up with something new and get a heavier bumper look. For 1955 we blended in exhaust ports, and that helped give it a fresher look. But it was the only time before or since that I can recall there's been such a fantastically quick creation of a design unit on an automobile."

The taillight treatment blended well with the rest of Teague's work, and the entire facelift was so successful that many still think the 1955's received an entirely new body. This effect was amplified by the complete reorganization of the product line further emphasizing the difference between a Packard and a Clipper. At the bottom was the Clipper Deluxe ($2586), offered only in four-door form, with minimal ornamentation, inexpensive upholstery and standard suspension. Next came the Super four-door and Panama hardtop ($2686, $2776) on the same 122-inch wheelbase as the Deluxe; both models were powered by a 327-cubic-inch V-8 of 225 hp. Top of the line was the Custom four-door sedan and Constellation hardtop ($2926, $3076), powered by a 352-cubic-inch, 245 hp engine and optional torsion bar suspension. The latter, at $150 extra, proved so popular it was offered on Supers later in the year. All Clipper hardtops used a downward sweeping side molding in two-tone versions; Super and Custom sedans received this treatment later in the year. There were vertical barred grilles bearing the Clipper's ship's wheel, along with 1954's Clipper "sore thumb" taillight mounted atop a clear back-up lens and blended into the rear fender. Clipper bonnets spelled out that name plainly, and the only place the word "Packard" appeared was in a small piece of script on decklids, a "Body by Packard" plate on seat frames, and "Packard Clipper" on Deluxe hubcaps, left over from 1954. Other changes further differentiated the cars: Clippers were on a wheelbase five inches shorter than Packards, used smaller tires and non-interchangeable wheels, and Clipper electrics were Auto-Lite, versus Delco for Packards. Finally, carburetion was Carter (it was Rochester on the Packard) and power steering was Monroe (on Packards it was Bendix).

The Packard line was reduced to a Patrician sedan, a Four Hundred hardtop, and a Caribbean convertible, priced respectively at $3890, $3930 and $5932. The 352-cubic-inch block of the Clipper Custom was used, but the Rochester carbs gave the Packards 260 horsepower, and

275 in the Caribbean. Automatic and the new torsion suspension were standard, although the latter was treated as a mandatory option, to the ire of some dealers. On the Caribbean, literally everything was standard save air conditioning and wire wheels; with the former option Packard became first to achieve the dubious distinction of an air-conditioned convertible.

One design idea that didn't make it appeared on a special 1955 show car Packard called the Request, the result of many letters from customers asking for a return to Packard's classic vertical grille. Nance commissioned a number of clays in which Teague explored possibilities; finally Teague built such a car for the spring 1955 round of auto shows. He took one of the first Four Hundred hardtops, and had Creative Industries in Detroit accomplish the transformation. Aside from the tall grille, the Request also employed Caribbean side treatment, wire wheels and twin antennas, and a special bronze and white color scheme.

The Request was a success in its early appearances, and sales vice-president Clare Briggs suggested that production car styling move in its direction. Product Planning's Roger Bremer noted to Nance in February that, "We intend going over the implications of this survey [of public reaction] to reach a conclusion as to whether or not the classic front end should have any part in our Program for future models." Ultimately the idea was dropped. (Although a future show car and the proposed 1957 line did have vertical grilles, they were not the classic variety, and those close to Nance had their doubts that the public would really take to an idea twenty years old. Had it been 1965 instead of 1955, perhaps the notion would have been better received.)

Various authoritative and non-authoritative reports have circulated for years as to the Request's ultimate fate. The facts are that it was taken

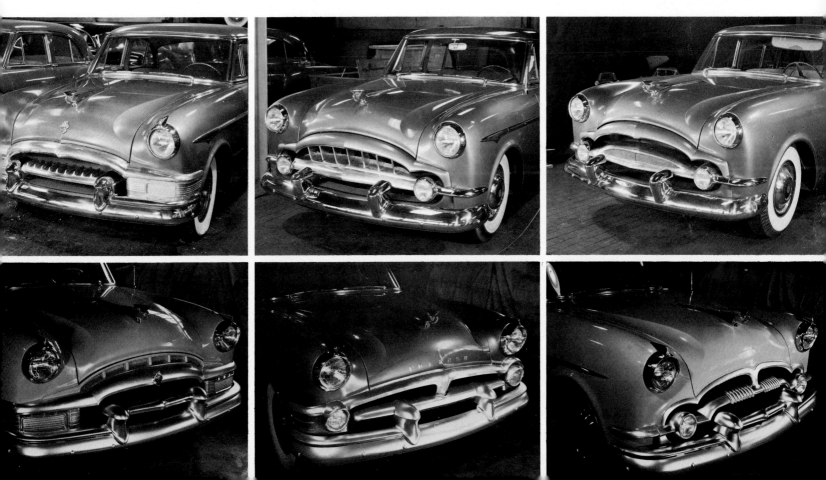

out of the company on a property pass during the confusion in late 1956, and was involved in a front-end collision by its taker-out. The front end was partially reworked and the vehicle, after lengthy outside storage, was purchased by a collector in 1974 and restored to its 1955 state.

Styling was only one of Packard's hit news items for 1955, however. At least as important was the new V-8 engine—Packard's first. The company had experimented with the configuration before, during the One Twenty project, but had never in its entire half century built one as a production unit. Now in 1955, engineers created one of the better V-8's ever built which would prove itself over millions of miles with no major shortcomings.

A lot of rumors had circulated regarding how radical the new Packard powerplant would be, so many pundits were disappointed when they finally saw that it broke no new ground. It did feature a unique intake manifold, offering freer breathing than competitive engines, but little more technical innovation save its displacement, which was by comparison enormous.

The Packard V-8 was introduced at 327/352 cubic inches and went to 374 the following year but, according to engineer Graves, it "had at least 400 in it." The use of later technology, such as cylinder siamesing, would have pushed this to over 500 had the necessity arisen. The engine rapidly established itself in such diverse fields as drag racing and motor boating with some quite impressive power being developed: Packard had seen the horsepower race coming and had determined to design in the capability for more performance.

The new engine had performance aplenty. And Packard dramatized it in a highly unusual publicity stunt. A strictly stock car, one of the early prototype Patricians, was tuned up and sent out to the Proving Grounds for a durability run of 25,000 miles—approximately the circumference of the earth. Under the supervision of the American Automobile Association, which Packard requested, the car was thus to be driven around the world as fast as possible, with no stops for repairs. Teams of drivers ran the Packard for days, around the clock, pausing occasionally for tire, oil and fuel servicing. The final average speed, including all pit stops, was computed to 104.737 mph. This made for good ad copy, although the feat set no records because the Packard test track was not a certified course for the purpose.

The engineering significance of this run should be emphasized, however; such performance from a *stock car* was not commonplace. When, a few years later, Mercury ran a car 100 miles an hour for 100,000 miles at Daytona, many industry insiders sniffed that the car, equipped with a super-high rear axle, had performed "roughly equivalent to a good 48-hour dynamometer run." But the Packard demonstration was made with a production car having no special equipment other than such ephemerae as rally lights and hood straps. The car

was put on tour with all grime carefully preserved and a sign on the windshield next to a bad break: The sign read, "PHEASANT."

The only design flaw of any notice in Packard's new engine was occasional oil starvation. The V-8 used overhead valves and hydraulic lifters, oiled by a pump incorporating a vacuum booster, early versions of which could suck air and starve the engine at high speeds—and, when the engine had considerable mileage on it, cause vacuum leaks. Either way, the process made for noisy lifters due to bubbles in the oil and, if ignored, eventually damaged lifters. The American Motors people chose, with the engines they bought from Packard, to stay with the conventional placement of a vacuum booster pump—attached to the fuel pump—and overall results were better. The oil pump was improved as production continued, as were the valve spring seats, which sporadically broke at extremely high rpm. On balance, however, the new engine was a tough and reliable unit—years later *Motor Trend* described it as "very healthy"—and its near total lack of troubles in its teething year was rarely achieved in the industry: Packard could still call itself the Master Motor Builder.

Back of the new V-8 was Packard's latest automatic, still based on the rugged unit of 1949 but refined from 1954's Gear-Start variety and known now as Twin Ultramatic. Like Gear-Start, it had a "D" range instead of High, with two positions. In the first, the transmission operated as usual, starting out in 1:1 ratio plus torque converter, locking into direct drive when the vehicle came up to speed. In the second "D" range, the unit started in low, later shifted to 1:1 and still later locked into direct, affording mid-Fifties acceleration of which the new V-8 was easily capable. Forest McFarland, with help from former Chrysler engineer John Z. DeLorean, was principally responsible for the new transmission, which was now made in Packard's just-modernized Utica plant along with engines and rear axles. Manual transmissions and overdrives, both by Borg-Warner, were still available, but on Clippers only, though some conversions were placed on Packards for insistent customers.

Packard did its best to encourage traffic light grands prix by adding special vanes to torque converters of Caribbeans and Four Hundreds to give them still snappier performance. Twin Ultramatic was a good transmission, but over the years proved insufficient to the V-8's torque characteristics, and its life could be considerably curtailed with inadequate service or poor owner treatment—always a threat in cars everywhere. A steady diet of full throttle starts caused slippage, failure to follow the fluid-change interval resulted in further slippage and, sometimes, corrosion. Manual shifting while under way, bypassing the governor, made for premature clutch wear, and when unfamiliar hands adjusted the transmission they usually overlooked linkage adjustment—which was yet another cause of slippage. Many mechanics failed to replace the bushings in the transmission which were so critical to the maintenance of proper operating pressures—sometimes because of ignorance, other times because it added to shop costs.

Such developments did not bode well for Twin Ultramatic. It was not nearly the disaster some like to think it, but admittedly it did not project the usual high standard of Packard engineering. Properly set up and well serviced, it was capable of reliability as admirable as any, but it was simply unforgiving of lapses. In 1955 it was Packard's weakest link and caused innumerable service problems; many officials eventually came to think the old Ultramatic should have been abandoned that year, and proprietary Hydra-Matic purchased instead, as Lincoln had done.*

But Twin Ultramatic, V-8 and new styling aside, one feature of the Fifty-Fifth series stood out, and it probably was responsible for better than half the revived enthusiasm for Packards that year—Torsion-Level suspension. In this, Packard scored a first among American cars. No other domestic had it, or had ever had it, although it had been featured in the past on prototypes. As for interconnecting the front and rear wheels, which Packard did, this was simply unheard of.

The basic advantage of a torsion bar is in its reaction to road jounces. Whereas a conventional spring puts the force of a bump right back into the car—because there is no way to contravene the laws of physical action and reaction—a torsion bar takes the bump force and dissipates it winding up against an anchor point. This twisting motion is not received by the vehicle, though it can be felt to a small degree. Packard carried the concept a step further by connecting the front and rear wheels to the same

---

*It should be noted that a Twin Ultramatic in service today has a much higher life expectancy than one in service a quarter of a century ago, because it can benefit from greatly improved transmission fluids and widely available accessory oil coolers. Heat and fluid deterioration were Twin Ultramatic's enemies, in addition to drag racing.

Below: The 1955 Clipper nearing production. Above: The 1955 Packard in Spring 1954, with Teague's cathedral taillights added but side trim not yet in final form.

torsion bar on each side, loading it in opposite directions and forcing any upward force at one end to be transmitted as a downward force to the other—there was no anchor point on the torsion bars.

Though Forest McFarland noted in a paper for the SAE that Packard had had patent coverage on torsion bars connecting front and rear wheel suspensions since the early Thirties, the concept of interconnection on the Hutchison patent, for example, would have proved unworkable. He perhaps mentioned previous efforts because the '55 unit came from outside Packard, an invention of William D. Allison, who had been with Hudson on a consulting basis through the Motor Research Corporation of Detroit. The entire system was developed in a six-week marathon session by Allison and a team of moonlighting designers he hired after signing the initial contract with Packard on December 12th, 1951.

Allison's work with the system stemmed from his Hudson days ten years earlier. In 1941, he says, he "was asked to interconnect a full-sized car with coil springs and cables. We worked on that for months before we stopped at the advent of World War II. The car was, however, com-

Clay model showing early version of the classic grille for the Request show car.

pleted, and had an automatic leveling system using torsion-bar springs where the main springing in front was, and extra-long coils connected by cables to the rear of the vehicle." The car was finally stripped for parts during the war, and survives only in photographs.

Allison continued to develop his idea, eventually going to full torsion springing. But Hudson decided it was not in a position to finance further development, and elected to let Allison pursue his concept independently on his own time. Allison thereafter began showing a small model around the industry (including Packard)—not with any success.

"In 1950," he recalls, "I decided to build what I called the cyclecar—a lightweight car with torsion-bar suspension. I proceeded to do that in the winter of 1950-1951, using heavy-duty bicycle wheels and an Indian motorcycle engine, welding up the frame and assembling the chassis components as I went along. I made the torsion bars myself. The ⅝-inch diameter coil spring steel was provided by Eaton Spring. I struggled into the wee hours one morning, came up with two torsion bars and took them the next day to Commercial Heat Treat in Detroit, where the bars bowed because of the method they used in treating them. A friend at Hudson straightened them on a press. They were then shot-peened and installed into the cyclecar's chassis, still with a slight bow."

Allison first showed the cyclecar to Studebaker. "They were very impressed, and on their proving grounds we ran away from a Studebaker in it! I heard one engineer say that the cross-country road at the proving grounds would tear it up and I was a little apprehensive. They told me it was kind of rough and to take it easy because they didn't want me to hurt myself. Well, we ran over a five-inch bump and I asked the engineer if there were any higher. He said no, so I opened it all the way up. The Stude behind us went up onto the shoulder and eventually the engineer noted with a few choice words that it was not able to keep up with us!" But Studebaker didn't offer to buy the idea—it was still doing well at the time, and torsion bars had already been passed up by Studebaker for cost reasons in 1945.

Allison hit the road again, showing the cyclecar to Ford, Chrysler, GM and Kaiser. Once again, in August 1951, he journeyed to the Packard Proving Grounds in Utica, where McFarland, Herb Misch and chief engineer Bill Graves awaited him. That afternoon, the break Allison had hoped for finally came. "They drove it, had an engineering meeting, and later that afternoon Mr. Graves asked if I could make a big car ride like that. It was a very exciting afternoon."

More meetings, questions and tests followed. McFarland at one point led the way to a severely humped Detroit intersection, taking it in a Packard with the cyclecar behind. "I saw daylight under his wheels," Allison says, "after we went over the first cross street. It was a nasty bump but the cyclecar came through it perfectly." Shortly thereafter, in December, an agreement was signed and Allison was given a 1951

Packard on which to put his new suspension.

The prototype, known as A-1, was completed in five months, and costs were eased by the contribution of some parts by vendors who hoped to get future business. Hupp Corporation contributed the leveling device, for example, and Maremont made the torsion bars for a nominal fee. Packard tested the car for about a year after its completion, and when Nance came aboard in June 1952, the orders came to proceed with development. This was exactly the sort of thing which appealed to Nance—something to really one-up the opposition.

Allison, who was still officially a Hudson man, had a very understanding employer; Hudson gave him a leave of absence coupled with six months' salary and insurance benefits so he could go to work for the competition! "They were very good to me," he noted, "it would never happen again. I told them what I was doing and that I had this opportunity with Packard. They told me they felt they were not in a position to develop it and assumed it would be available to them if they wanted it. . . . It's really unheard of in the industry."

The next test car was the A-2, a 1953 model, followed by ten experimental 1954's. In January 1954, Nance gave the go-ahead for introduction of the system on the 1955's. Eleven of the twelve experimental cars, incidentally, were destroyed, but Allison himself drove the last one for many years until an irreplaceable experimental component snapped and dropped the car onto its haunches one night in his driveway, after which it too was scrapped.

Some minor roadblocks did occur on the way to production, one of which involved the level compensator. The twelve-volt ignition system was a late change for 1955, and someone had forgotten to tell Allison about it, so he had to convert; converting meant a more powerful compensator motor but Allison feels it resulted in excess corrosion in his control box. "We were only able to get the motor built that quickly by using existing components. Delco-Remy worked with us and came up with the best motor for the job in the time we had, a generator housing, generator armature and commutator. They wound a new field winding, one clockwise and the other counterclockwise . . . It did the job. It weighed

Dick Teague, Bill Graves and the Request—with classic grille, Caribbean side treatment, wire wheels, twin antennas and a special bronze and white color scheme.

more than I wanted it to—we were testing much lighter motors, starter types, but they were very noisy and ran up to six or seven thousand rpm."

Allison had wanted special front-end components to handle his suspension, but Packard insisted on maximum use of existing tooling to simplify parts stockpiling and production inventories, as well as to cut costs. Another developmental change involved torque reaction from the driving wheels, formerly transmitted to the car by rear leaf springs, which had to be channeled elsewhere. A pair of torque rods were added, locating the rear axle and transmitting these forces; they served to hold down the rear end during braking and pick it up during acceleration, reducing dive and squat. A similar technique later would appear on the front-drive Oldsmobile Toronado. Other cars, such as Chevrolet, Buick and Nash, which used coil rear springs, went a different route and adopted torque-tube rods, but the people at East Grand Boulevard re-

jected these as noisy and complicated.

Critical to the system's refinement was the electric leveling device. Because the suspension had no anchor points on the frame, the 1955 Packard was free to rock back and forth, coming to rest where its center of balance was compensated by the bars' reaction force. If this did not happen to be at a point at which the car was level, something would have to change—and even if it did, slight load changes could throw it entirely off. The leveling device was a heavy-duty electric motor with two-way winding, connected through a gearbox to the rear suspension by two short torsion bars. This could load the car's suspension in either direction and bring the car back to level in a very short time. Refinements were added to the leveler itself: a seven-second time delay, for example, to keep it from trying to compensate for minor bumps. Further, the leveler was turned off by running the control circuit to a third contact on the brake light switch—because braking could easily continue for more than seven seconds. A manual switch under the dash also permitted the owner to change a tire without interference from the Torsion-Level system. Finally, limit switches inside the control unit stopped the motor at either end of travel, in the event the owner loaded the car too heavily or forgot to use the flat-tire switch.

Some skeptics shook their heads at all those switches—there were seven of them, counting solenoids and control box—but overall the reaction to Torsion-Level suspension was excellent. *Auto Age* judged Packard the best handling car of 1955 and, in fact, "the best car of the year . . . its combination of brakes, steering and far superior suspension not only give it the edge in handling but mark it as *the* car for '55. [Auto experts have] been complaining for years that we didn't have one really stable American car. Now at last Packard has broken the ice and come up with a new feature that is more than just another sales gimmick."

The Packard had wowed the populace, all right. Floyd Clymer found its handling characteristics "different from any other car . . . for stability, both front and rear ends have independent stabilizers . . . You can drive into a corner at high speed with this car and the body remains almost level . . . It was the most comfortable ride I've ever had with a feeling of security at all times." Said *Car Life*, the suspension was "a great contribution to the world's motor industry . . . at least one manufacturer realizes that the conventional coil and leaf springs leave much to be desired. . . . Not only is the 1955 Packard safer than many of its contemporaries, but it is much more comfortable." *Motor Trend* said that "Everything else dims by comparison with ride . . . Test crew couldn't tell when driver deliberately steered car over projecting manhole covers on road under repair. What a fantastic ride!"

"With a year of development it would have been more reliable," Forest McFarland noted. "You never expect your first to be your best." But Torsion-Level was remarkably trouble-free from the start, and

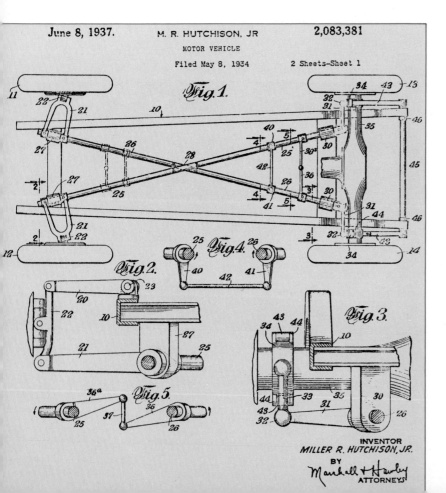

June 8, 1937.

M. R. HUTCHISON, JR

2,083,381

MOTOR VEHICLE

Filed May 8, 1934

2 Sheets-Sheet 1

Fig. 1.

Fig. 2.

Fig. 4.

Fig. 3.

Fig. 5.

INVENTOR
MILLER R. HUTCHISON, JR.
BY
Marshall & Hawley
ATTORNEYS

though a few early control boxes were subject to corrosion or stone damage, these conditions were soon corrected. Certainly it worked as intended—and it was a mighty challenge to the opposition by the company Nance had said was going to once again battle Cadillac for supremacy.

Just to be sure, the executive staff turned out one day with a new Patrician, a Lincoln and a Cadillac, along with Allison's cyclecar. The entourage went to a railroad crossing in Detroit, an intersection known at the time for the grim efficiency with which it dealt with vehicles attempting to cross it at more than 10 mph. Allison charged across in the cyclecar, making a straight-line transit, the bicycle wheels going up and down madly but the body remaining level. Next came the Lincoln and Cadillac. Severe damage was done to the Lincoln after brief airborne transit; the Cadillac bounced around wildly but managed to hold together. Then the new Patrician sailed across, level as a canoe. Allison's invention had decisively proven itself "under fire." Incidentally, owning a Patrician in Detroit might still come in handy—that railroad crossing has never been repaved.

Torsion-Level was offered in different ways because Packard was not convinced the market would swallow it whole.* It was standard on the Caribbean, a required option on the Patrician and Four Hundred, optional at $150 on Clipper Customs. This meant it was necessary to stock more parts. "There was a difference of opinion in Packard management on how many would sell," says Allison. "It was brand-new, a big gamble and they decided to hedge their bets. First they weren't going to put it on the Clipper at all, then they decided to offer it on the Custom at additional cost. The decision was made to build 25 percent of the Clippers with torsion bars [but] three months later the dealers were ordering Torsion-Level on 75 percent of their cars." Thus the system was later made available on Clipper Supers.

"We found that those familiar with automotive engineering were ex-

*Jim Nance had also apparently worried some about what to call this Packard advance and decided to get outside advice. He had recently called upon Studebaker veteran (then a consulting engineer) "Barney" Roos for help in another area—to provide him "a personal and confidential memo on your observations of the Studebaker engineering department, as to how it is now set up; how, in your opinion, it should be set up; and your evaluation of the personnel in the various areas"—and now he also asked Roos for suggestions for a name for the Packard suspension. After taking a ride with Bill Graves and Forest McFarland, Roos decided that "putting it mildly [the] torsion-bar suspension is completely startling in the ride it produces," and therefrom he "worked like a beaver with the encyclopedia and dictionary" and came up with Wing Flight, Wing Action, Wing Glide, Aero Flight, Level Ride, Level Glide and Level Flight. Ultimately, someone else came up with something better.

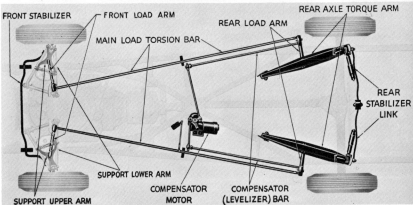

A patented "torsion-level" idea from Packard in the Thirties, page opposite. Engineer William D. Allison and a sketch of the Torsion-Level components of the Fifties, above; and winding the torsion bars at the Conner plant, below.

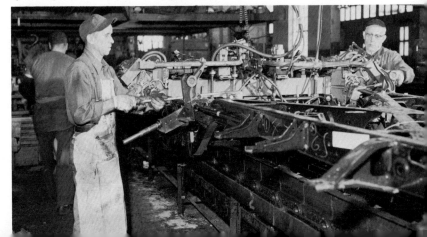

cited," said Nance about the new suspension, "but we knew our selling job was to the public. To them torsion suspension was a mystery, and we had complicated this dramatic change still further by including a load levelizer or compensator . . . To emphasize that all this was a tremendous advancement in riding comfort and automobile construction, we decided to take our merchandising and advertising out of the realm of super-adjectives." Packard conducted clinics for sales/service people and the public on the system, and constructed display chassis, detailed literature and publicity. Dealers pushed the theme, "Let the Ride Decide," which was shortly teamed with "Take the Key and See." Some demonstration cars sped around with signs on the rear daring others to "follow this car."

The results were favorable: Packard sales were up strongly over 1954. Other manufacturers began advertising about ride and suspension for the first time in memory. Said Buick, "to be completely honest, there are some bumps *nothing* can level out completely." GM accelerated research and eventually offered air suspension, which was plagued with ills, though a hydraulic leveling idea turned up later on GM cars. Chrysler elected to provide torsion bars on the front of its 1957 line—without reference to Packard but nevertheless a tribute—calling the product Torsion-Aire. Initially, Chrysler had planned to introduce Torsion-Aire in 1955, but after hearing about Packard's all-wheel torsion bars shortly before the new '55's appeared, decided to delay the offering of the front-wheel system. "If only they hadn't found out," moaned one Packard executive, "we could have advertised that our system was twice as good."

Packard's 1955 advertising was sufficiently dismal without adding that lame theme to it. Nance fulminated: "The attitude of our group in advertising, promotion and sales planning is the most desultory I have ever seen. Always late. No forward planning. Routine thinking—do everything like the other fellow—when obviously we must be ingenious to get more for our dollar." Nance had a good point—a page in *Life* cost Packard the same as it cost General Motors, but on a per car basis the tab was much higher.

And the company had done little to promote its product as "the" luxury automobile. The previous "New Choice in Fine Cars" theme died after a short run, and 1955 really had no theme at all. The lack of direction arose partly from frequent changes in ad agencies. After years with Young & Rubicam, Packard had switched to Maxon in 1953, then to Ruthrauff & Ryan for 1955. In 1956 it would go to D'Arcy, which carried the Studebaker account for several years thereafter. Ruthrauff & Ryan's days were numbered early: In an April 25th memo, Nance noted: "The proof of the June advertisement on the Clipper just passed over my desk. It is one of the weakest, most ineffectual ads I have ever seen. It literally has nothing; no selling copy and poor art. Our Clipper advertising has absolutely nothing. It doesn't establish Clipper as a separate

594

Below: Packard Patrician, "the newest entry in the luxury car field for 1955.

The 1955 Clipper (left from the top): Custom sedan (with early side trim), Panama and Constellation hardtops. Above: Packard Caribbean and Four Hundred.

line of cars; it doesn't present it as a series of Packard models. In short it goes nowhere against strong advertising of its competition, like Buick."

Packard's television advertising was mediocre as well. At the time of the Studebaker acquisition it sponsored the "Martha Wright Show" on ABC, which had a pitiful share in the ratings. Later S-P sponsored the "TV Reader's Digest," again to a small audience.

The company's audience of dealers was disgruntled for another reason. In a March 1955 memo, Nance told Sales that dealers "are very critical, confused and disgusted with the number of organization changes that have been made over the past three years in the factory sales organization." He was seeking to restore confidence by reducing or eliminating changes in zone managerships and confronting those district or zone people who were not concerned with the well-being of dealers. Restoring confidence in Packard clients was vital too: "The attitude of our whole factory sales organization toward a customer is the worst I've seen in my thirty years of selling."

The state of the union with Studebaker was little better. When Nance and the board authorized Walter Grant to get Studebaker's costs down, nobody had expected the union to rush willingly to more work for the same pay. Nobody was disappointed. On January 20th, 1955, South Bend workers walked out. During that year there were eighty-five wild-cat work stoppages and the company was shut down for thirty-six working days. It took nearly a year to get South Bend work standards in line with the rest of the industry. Also, Grant's alarming financial estimates were vindicated. Studebaker had claimed a break-even point of 165,000 vehicles, Grant 282,000. Studebaker Division finished the 1955 calendar year with 138,472 units and a whopping loss. Packard approached 60,000 and was in the black. For the time being.

Meanwhile the new Conner Avenue plant was wreaking havoc.

Transfer of final assembly operations began September 16th, 1954, the last piece was to be put in place on October 17th and the first 1955 Packard completed November 1st. The rest of the industry told Nance it could never be done, but it *was* done. Not, however, with a great deal of class. Typical was the massive concrete slab that turned up in the middle of the floor while the line was being installed. It was not supposed to be there. It couldn't be there. But it *was* there. Nothing could be done except detour the line around it.

Veterans called Conner a "crackerbox"—compared to three million square feet at East Grand Boulevard, it offered only 760,000—and plant manager Dick Collins questioned the move from the first. "Conner was too small," he notes. "We always said whoever figured out the square footage must have been crazy because you could never come up with it unless you counted the closets and everything else." So why was Packard doing it? Why take time off from production, spend the enormous amounts of money, risk the shakedown problems to leave a huge building standing empty and paying taxes a short distance away? There was only one reason that Nance and the planners gave: The Boulevard was a multi-story layout and Conner was not; Conner was "more efficient." Had they been historians they might have pointed out that a one-story layout was what Henry Bourne Joy had originally wanted at East Grand back in 1903.

But now it was 1954, and things were different. Collins approached manufacturing vice-president Ray Powers with his doubts: "I said I was with them, I just thought it was the wrong move: 'The engine and transmission plant is okay and we already have the facility to put out the new cars. I'm apprehensive that if we make the move we'll not be able to meet production.' He said, 'You've got your orders.' So I carried the orders out and started to make the move to Conner. That was the last time the conveyors ever moved at the Boulevard."

The poor old Boulevard plant. Gutted in 1934-1939, laid out for Christopher, gutted once more in 1942, built up from scratch in 1945-1946, it was now gutted again. Its sin was that it was an old, multi-story building. But never had production delays been encountered there, while delays would be common occurrences at Conner Avenue. Trucks laid over for days—always at full driver salary—waiting to unload in a cramped dock area that still holds the auto plant lightweight record, or simply because there was no room to store the materials inside. There was space for only a single production line. There was a miscalculation at the point where frames entered the line and too many manual operations had to be put in to get them started.

All this took its toll on Packard, and put introduction of the 1955 models months behind the competition, setting the dealer force at a disadvantage at exactly the time when people were becoming anxious to own one of the wonderful cars they were hearing about. In the end, the Conner production vexations resulted in a cutback of the entire 1955 model program:

Ray Powers shows Nance a sketch of Conner, above; production begins there, rig

	January Program	April Program	Final Production
Clippers	46,870	42,958	38,414
Patricians	13,230	12,192	9,127
Four Hundreds	10,290	9,695	7,206
Caribbeans	945	500	500
	71,335	65,345	55,247

Capacity at the Boulevard had been 100 cars an hour on two shifts, about the industry average. At Conner the maximum was fifty cars an hour, though production was half that because of the poor layout and cramped space. "They felt that twenty-five an hour would do and that labor costs would be less," says Collins. "Actually the concept was entirely wrong; they should have stayed at fifty an hour on one shift at the Boulevard. But they felt that labor costs at fifty an hour were too high. Actually, we did make twenty-five cars an hour but none would pass inspection [owing to] defects of workmanship, poor assembly, poor quality on every aspect of the automobile."

Powers was quickly apprised of the dilemma. "I am shocked by the report from the Sales Department of the snowballing of product complaints," he wrote manufacturing manager Neil Brown in January 1955. "Such things as loose wires, loose assembly, non-functioning items such as radios, clocks and windshield wipers and generators, are a little hard to understand. The fit-up on doors, deck lids and interior mouldings has also received severe criticism." Powers took corrective steps, but it would be months instead of days before anything was accomplished. Manufacturing reported to Nance in late February that "two out of five

cars are up to quality typical of the industry"—and this was an *improvement*.

Nance himself was well aware of the situation. On March 7th he wrote Powers, "I was terribly disappointed at the condition in which our cars are still coming through. One Patrician was so bad I couldn't begin to itemize all the things wrong with it, but suffice it to say it was literally necessary to use a crowbar to get one of the rear doors open . . . . Really, Ray, it was horrible, and not one of the cars on the load I saw unloaded was anywhere near what it should have been." Again on March 17th, Nance wrote, "The poor quality apparently has caught up with us with both the public and our dealers, and shipments arriving in the field as late as yesterday indicate no improvement in the quality. 23 cars out of 44 delivered to Bankston yesterday had to go into the shop before they could be delivered to either dealers or the customers. They report that the cars upon arrival were loaded with inspection slips indicating what was wrong, but the corrections had not been made . . . Bankston's cost of fixing up cars to date is averaging $85 per car."

More complaints followed. Nance later advised Powers, "Dealers' orders are being ignored and we are still shipping whatever we want to build. We got away with this, of course, for several months, but now that the dealers have got their samples, we can't do this any more, because the cars must be delivered to customers . . . we just can't go on shipping cars

at our own discretion. For example, [Chicago] just got in a shipment of cars. Out of seven Patricians they received six in solid blue. The dealers generally are complaining that we send out too many green cars . . . We are going to have to fill orders as they are received."

By the end of March a new "conditioning line" was set up for the Packards at Conner. Its purpose was to fix all the mistakes, clean, touch-up and tune, install floor mats, recheck instruments and accessories. It was sheer patch work. And it wasn't enough. Warranty expenditures on the '55's were running $30 per car and had mounted to over $45,000 by April. On the 1954's, warranty expense had been less than $15 per car.

In the throes of all this, on April 19th, Nance discussed with Powers the possibility of moving the sub-assemblies out of Conner and back into the Boulevard—either temporarily or permanently. Powers either talked him out of it or Nance himself decided against the move. But he was becoming desperate, for things were not improving. It was too late to have reservations about the move now—Packard was stuck with Conner and nothing could be done for years.

To Herb Misch, who would relieve Graves as engineering vice-president later that year, Nance wrote, "If we are going to re-establish Packard and start cutting into the Cadillac business, we are going to have to come up with a quality automobile. I have discussed this problem with manufacturing people and it is their opinion that we can build quality cars on the same line as the Clipper but that the Clipper will probably suffer a cost penalty. This, of course, will be cheaper than to set up two lines until our volume is substantially increased." The irony here was that Nance had had a two-line setup at the Boulevard, and had walked away from it. "The decibel level on our cars is entirely too high and is not even comparable to the high-priced cars, let alone the Cadillacs." He was also still concerned about minor assembly, "the detail of the car. Not only in the trim but all the detail of the body work. There are entirely too many ragged edges.

"It is essential that we get [the improvements] done on the balance of the '55 cars . . . We have to show marked improvement to compensate with our dealers for the poor quality up to date and, if we are going to hold the dealers and keep them in the business, we must convince them by the quality of the car that we are really serious about producing a fine car." Nance was adamant about the corrective measures being completed for the Fifty-Sixth Series, and Misch responded with a detailed list of 120 engineering changes that would improve quality, covering everything from paint to quarter panel fit to improved door checks.

Quality did improve, but by that time it was very late in the game. Nance eventually wrote Powers, "I just drove a new Patrician. The improvement in quality is very encouraging. It is by far the best built of all the cars I have had of the '55 models." The date of the memorandum was August 26th.

597

Production at Conner during 1955. Veterans called the plant a "crackerbox."

Studebaker-Packard's businesses outside the automotive field were, however, prospering, comparatively. One such was the Aerophysics Development Corporation, S-P's only non-automotive subsidiary at the time, though it would diversify widely in the late Fifties under guidance of Curtiss-Wright. ADC, a California-based firm, was expanding and offered possible entrée into the burgeoning field of guided missiles. By the end of 1955 its workforce had risen to 400, its monthly sales to nearly $500,000, and it had contract work with the Army, Air Force, Sandia and Chrysler. If properly nurtured, Aerophysics Development Corporation would prove profitable to Studebaker-Packard, though not enough to offset auto losses.

Another profitable area was sales of engines to outside buyers, always a Packard mainstay. The primary customer here was American Motors, which was using the 327-cubic-inch Clipper engine and Twin Ultramatic in its top-line Nash Ambassador and Hudson Hornet. Though sputtering by now, attempts at cooperation between AMC and S-P along a broad range of reciprocal purchases for their mutual benefit were still being pursued. The proposal for common bodies hadn't worked out, and the purchase of air-conditioning components was post-

East Grand had boasted a total of three million square feet, four times that of the Conner facility. As these photographs indicate, things were rather cramped there.

poned until AMC could tool for compressors—which never eventuated. A trade program had been proposed on engines, with a Studebaker V-8 to be sent to AMC in return for one of its F-head sixes. Studebaker had been planning such an engine, but canceled its tooling in anticipation of placing this business with AMC. Nothing happened for awhile because AMC did not respond with interest in the Studebaker V-8, and finally on September 16th George Romney declined to furnish the six on any basis. Sending 40,000 engines to Studebaker would, said Romney, leave AMC short on its expected Rambler requirements. Packard had also asked AMC to bid on engine blocks and miscellaneous stampings, but the bids were always high and the lead times extraordinary. Though Packard did give Hudson an oil pan contract and other minor work, Hudson's price was not low. Ultimately, Walter Grant summed up the AMC situation to Nance:

"It would appear that Studebaker-Packard has tried to keep a spirit of cooperation with AMC but substantial progress was being made up until Mr. Mason's death and that since that time the progress of the program has been very uncertain." Some have accused Jim Nance of alienating American Motors by focusing his program on bringing as much work as

possible into his own plant. This view ignores the fact that a company the size of Studebaker-Packard must always source thousands of parts outside. AMC, in addition, was pursuing development of its own "AM Special" V-8, which would be ready in 1956. When it was, the company quickly stopped buying the Clipper engine. The entire situation might be summed up very simply. Packard had apparently gone out of its way to cooperate with American Motors; AMC cooperated only at its own convenience.

Also in 1955 came the question of the future of Packard custom cars. Packard's former supplier, Henney, had gone down in 1954 after a financial drubbing resulting partly from some ill-timed expansions. Charles Russell Feldmann, the tireless financier who had purchased Henney in 1946, had used the firm in his various enterprises, picking up a steel company and an electric plant, and then made a try for Reo Motors. He was rewarded with a strike at the electric company, a lawsuit over the steel acquisition, and a stockholders' rebellion at Reo. Henney sales dipped at the same time. A program for a junior line of commercial cars turned into a bad loss item, and Feldmann spent most of 1954 cleaning up his inventory, minimizing his losses and, essentially, bailing his way out with what was left of Henney's money. When he closed the old firm in 1954, Packard was without a supplier of long-wheelbase customs and commercial cars.

Nance expended considerable effort to adding some specialty cars to the line in 1955.* Product Planning, however, was not enthusiastic, although one 1956 Patrician was sent over to Derham for conversion into a formal sedan for Nance's use. Nance did not insist, but rather suggested that Product Planning consider the possibilities. "We still get quite a few letters on the subject, and I am also beginning to get inquiries from people who now own the eight-passenger cars. Several of them have indicated that they are quite upset about the fact that they are being left 'orphans,' with nothing to trade for. . . . It occurred to me that there might be a possibility of our picking up the trade name of one of the famous coach builders, such as Darrin—most of whom I understand have already gone out of business. It might be that we could use something of this kind down the road on a super deluxe model and merchandise it in a way comparable to the Fleetwood."

Darrin, of course, was very much in business, and around the same time was working up a striking proposal based on his Kaiser Darrin, but with four seats and a longer wheelbase. Its grille was in the classic Packard idiom, and its doors slid both forward and backward on tracks, allowing entrance to either front or back compartment. A detailed report on this car was submitted to Bill Graves, but it was just another idea that didn't make it; Packard didn't have the money anyway.

It may seem curious that a president would be asking subordinates to consider his ideas. Nance, however, had worked assiduously to set up the Product Planning division, and granted Bremer real authority even if it meant that he, Nance, had to plead his case for such as limousines. Nance bombarded Bremer with memos all year, dealing with many ideas for Product Planning's consideration: a record player, inspired by Chrysler's Highway Hi-Fi; a driveshaft-mounted parking brake, again like Chrysler's (Nance and Tex Colbert, Chrysler's president, were close friends); a front center armrest for the Patrician; a hardtop in the Clipper Deluxe line; a regular Packard convertible in addition to the Caribbean; torsion-bar suspension for Studebaker cars and trucks; the Packard Request; marketing of the Volkswagen transporter line in the United States (that wouldn't have been a bad idea!); and minute details including the shape of the Studebaker instrument panel. Product Planning was charged with working closely and effectively with Engineering and Styling, and the relationship appears to have been a good one. The emphasis on styling had been increasing, and before the '56's appeared it

---

*A detailed discussion of this, and the history of Packard's commercial cars, appears in the Appendices.

600

ascended to the vice-presidential level among departments.

As styling vice-president Nance brought chief designer William Schmidt in from Lincoln-Mercury. This spelled the final departure of Edward Macauley, and from all indications he went along quietly. With the new regime, Styling was no longer under the auspices of Engineering, but Bill Graves eased the way by saying to Schmidt, "Now usually designers, stylists and engineers don't get along too well, but I want you to tell me anything you think we should have on our cars. We'll do our damnedest to get it for you." Schmidt, who recalls this statement, adds that "You don't divorce styling from engineering. It's an intermingled thing and you have to work closely with them."

Now Styling had new prominence and a new, expanded organization. Dick Teague was made director of Packard Styling and Duncan McRae, from Ford, became director of Studebaker Styling. The latter change meant easing out Raymond Loewy, who was under a ten-year contract at South Bend with seven years still remaining, but the pain of his departure was lessened by a cash payment in the neighborhood of a million dollars. Nance had succeeded in unifying the styling of the company, and Schmidt joined the S-P commuter club hopping back and forth between Detroit and South Bend in the company DC-3.

The expense of Loewy's severence was just another small drop in a huge bucket. It is easy to picture Jim Nance standing at his office window about this time, gazing into a future that seemed bleak and contemplating the difficulties besetting his program. Its weaknesses had now become apparent—the plan had depended heavily on freedom from setbacks, and Nance had had enough of those to bedevil the best talent. Everything was coming unglued. Packard had lost its body supplier and had been forced to get back into the body business abruptly. The start-up costs at Conner Avenue had been high—too high. The defense business, on which the cash flow really depended, had been snatched away and handed to the competition, which scarcely needed it. Quality control at Conner was elusive, the customers and dealers in near rebellion over it. The cars could not be produced fast enough to fill initial orders, nor to make significant amounts of money. Studebaker had turned into a financial albatross. Packard had lost its only supplier of specialty vehicles. And the great four-way merger, the proposition that had brought Nance to Detroit in the first place, was off.

Jim Nance had been an outsider in the automobile business, and he had brought with him many other outsiders—probably too many. A fresh outside viewpoint is a priceless asset, but so is inside expertise. There was too much earn-while-you-learn in the upper levels of management, and some of the advice Nance was given was irretrievably bad.

For model year 1955, Packard production was 55,247 cars, 16,833 of which were non-Clippers and two-thirds of which had been equipped with Torsion-Level suspension. For calendar 1955, Studebaker-Packard

Continuing proposals for Packard from Darrin included a sports car, above, with a nicely executed classic style grille, and a four-seat roadster which incorporated sliding doors, these being originally proposed in 1941 (below).

would lose $29,705,093 after tax credit, which figure bears an uncomfortable proximity to the start-up tab for the Conner plant, the best example of the bad advice proffered Jim Nance. Still, the Packard Division had turned a profit overall, which was some basis for optimism. But everything was going to have to go well in 1956 for the optimism to be justified.

That would not be easy. The industry had just experienced its first seven-million-car year, but the figure stood as a production record—not a sales record. Dealers were surveying the vast quantities of new cars practically dumped upon them, wondering how to move them out before the 1956 models appeared. When they did, Packard dealers would be among the hardest hit, being close to margins anyway, even under normal circumstances.

Nineteen fifty-six was going to be a hard year, probably a decisive one. What *Fortune* termed "the next rough bump on S-P's downhill ride" was definitely not provided for. And it was to coincide neatly with the introductory date of the Fifty-Sixth Series.

CHAPTER THIRTY

THE HOUSE
FALLS

The Fifty-Sixth Series

1956

AUTHORS: GEORGE HAMLIN AND DWIGHT HEINMULLER

The '56 was called "The Greatest Packard of Them All," and it carried unusual significance for a transition design. Newly refined with all sorts of ideas from the Product Planning Division, the '56's represented the make or break point for the marque—perhaps the most significant single models since the introduction of the One Twenty back in 1935. The Fifty-Sixth Series had to keep the company afloat.

At last in 1956, the Clipper was officially on its own, at least for a while. Nance had been trying for months to induce Sales to cease thinking of it as "a tail on the kite of the Packard"—and he deplored Clipper advertising as showing "a complete lack of imagination and vision as to our objectives." In August 1955, he had written Dan O'Madigan in Sales that "the only excuse for us having the Clipper is to get volume to support the factory and our dealer organization . . . even though there has been considerable compromise in our thinking as against our original planning, we are still selling *two* lines of cars."

The Clipper's evolution as a separate make had not been without confusing results. "*Wards*," said Nance, "are now reporting Packards and Clippers as two separate lines of cars; the franchises are physically split, although nothing much is being done about it in field application; but most importantly, we have involved ourselves in a tooling program for the company on two separate lines . . . expediture for facelifting the '56 cars is twice what it was [in past similar years] because we are face-lifting *two*—not *one*—lines."

Emphasizing the Clipper's new independence were the change of the division's name to the Packard-Clipper Division, availability of "Clipper" as well as "Packard" and "Studebaker" dealer signs, a new ad agency (D'Arcy), specific notifications to the trade publications and state licensing agencies. Few of the states actually complied with Nance's request—Chrysler was having the same trouble at the time with Imperial and AMC was still trying to identify the Rambler as a make instead of a model of Nash.

After much soul-searching and not a little indecision, the Packard name was removed from Clippers altogether. But even Nance was having second thoughts about this as late as September, when he asked Bremer what was planned. Bremer responded, "Have been advised that you agreed with R. Laughna [Purchasing and Production Control] that name be removed. Personally, I do not concur, but was not contacted." Perhaps Bremer scored a point—on January 6th, 1956, Packard script re-entered production for the Clipper deck and in March it became available as an add-on kit to be installed on previous Clippers free of charge. This marked the death of the short-lived attempt at marketing

Pages preceding: The Clipper for 1956 presented to Pacific Coast Packard dealers in the Fairmont Hotel, San Francisco, on October 25th, 1955.

the Clipper on its own. In its wake, Nance commented that "drifting without a policy is deadly, as evidenced by Packard's fatal mistake of doing so since 1938."

The 1956 Clipper lineup was identical to that of 1955, save for the deletion of the "Panama" name on Super hardtops. Initially Torsion-Level suspension was available on the Deluxe and a mandatory option on the Custom, but on May 1st it was made standard on all Packards and Clippers. Prices were up slightly: The Deluxe sedan was $2731, the Super sedan and hardtop $2866 and $2916, the Custom sedan and Constellation hardtop $3069 and $3164.

Styling revisions for 1956 consisted of new "fish mouth" taillights (later more common on hot-rodded customs than road-going products of Studebaker-Packard), a slight shuffle of brightwork, dual exhaust ports in the rear bumpers, fender skirts for the Constellation and wrapped parking lights. The wide downward-sweeping color band on two-tone models of 1955 was replaced by a straight band. The power came from the same basic 352-cubic-inch unit as used by the 1955 Custom, with two-barrel carburetion for 240 horsepower on the Deluxe and Super, four-barrel and 275 for the Custom—improvements realized through a new, higher compression ratio of 9.5 to one.

The 1956 Packard line was the peak development of Reinhart's old

From the left: R.P. Laughna at his desk; in Packard Styling, Dick Teague showing Bill Schmidt an idea car; Herb Misch. Above: Jim Nance, still cheerful.

style of 1951. The beltline had always been too high—Reinhart had complained about it six years before—but the car appeared so lavish that this was generally overlooked. The grille gained a silver mesh (which later became gold) and the headlight shrouds were extended—to a point where they were vulnerable in the slightest collision. As with the Clipper, minor trim was revised or shuffled. The deck lid was squared off and the 1951 contours removed from the rear window. The deck handle/ornament of 1954-1955 gave way to a new circle and "V" motif which Teague had come up with "in an effort to create a timeless symbol akin to the star of Mercedes-Benz." To avoid having too many "V's," the small gold ones were deleted from the taillights.

Inside, Packards featured a sweep-second hand clock, thicker dash padding and reversible seat cushions on the Caribbean showing leather on one face and bouclé cloth on the other. Color schemes and fabrics were entirely new and the most luxurious since perhaps the Twenty-Second Series—and the seats were more comfortable. (Nance had told Powers in March 1955, "In my judgment our seats are not soft enough, certainly not as compared to General Motors.")

A new model in the 1956 Packard line was the Caribbean hardtop, complete with Hypalon vinyl-covered roof, at $5495—$500 below the corresponding convertible. Nance himself had seen to this offering, and in 1955 had pushed the idea of "Caribbeanizing" Four Hundred hardtops at dealer level, which was actually done in a few rare cases. Caribbeans again came with every possible option except chrome wire wheels ($325 extra), air conditioning ($567) and Twin Traction limited-slip differential ($44). The four-door Patrician was the least expensive Packard at $4160, and the 1956 Four Hundred followed at $4190.

Again power was up, following overall industry trends, through a bore increase to 4 ⅛ inches, resulting in 374 cubic inches, highest in the industry. Horsepower was 290 in the Patrician and Four Hundred, 310 in the Caribbean—a convenient five horsepower above Cadillac's Eldorado. Compression ratio also set a new record at an even 10.0 to one.

Twin Ultramatic for 1956 was mildly refined and beefed to cope with increased horsepower. (The '56 transmissions would turn in a better record than their predecessors.) A linkage change eliminated the tendency to stick in "Park" on grades, the shift pattern was changed, kickdown from direct drive was inhibited, and the case was aluminum alloy. The rear axle was the area of greatest change, however, as Packards now had flanged axles and limited-slip "Twin Traction" differential out of Dana (Spicer), a standard offering on cars of today. *Motor* dedicated "Twin Traction" to the "forgotten man—that fellow who must drive in all kinds of weather," and Packard claimed that eighty percent of the torque might be applied to one wheel in certain cases.

Twin Traction was an advance in automotive safety—of the preventive kind. In the mid-Fifties, safety witnessed a short period of popularity. Kaiser had plunged into it heavily back in 1951 with a padded dash, recessed instruments, right-hand emergency brake and pop-out windshield; Ford had followed with deep-dish steering wheels and positive door locks in 1955, and Nash had been the first car to offer seat belts—in 1951—although they had been hastily withdrawn the following year after dealers said customers thought them a tacit admission of an unsafe car. But all these *anticipated* accidents, like the safety equipment of today. Twin Traction was designed to *prevent* them, along with other Packard features like side marker lights, wrapped parking and taillights, and optimum nighttime visibility through the automatic leveling system. In addition Packards featured such passive devices as a thickly padded dash, optional seat belts and dished steering wheel.

To keep the children inside, there was also an electric door lock for four-door models, controlling all four locks through a button on either side of the dashboard. It sold for $30, or was included with electric window lifts at $108—it wasn't given much publicity, however, and a lot of other companies "invented" it later.

Tying up the list of 1956 mechanical changes, manual shift was again available on the Patrician and Four Hundred—if the customer really wanted it, the manual requiring a special driveshaft and a special factory order. (Packard had always been willing to provide nearly anything a client desired, and tradition was being served in this case.) Torsion-Level was rewired and simplified, the electric system went to negative ground, and pushbuttons were used to control the automatic transmission.

Nineteen fifty-six was a big year for pushbuttons, particularly on automatics. Chrysler products had them, on the extreme left of the dash, and before the decade ended Rambler, Mercury and Edsel would try them as well as Packard and Clipper. The version from Conner Avenue placed the buttons to the right of the steering wheel—where one normally reached for the quadrant lever—held there by a metal arm, with the messages relayed to the transmission by an electric motor. Dubbed "Touch-Button Ultramatic," it was a $52 option.

The pushbuttons showed careful thought: The neutral, park and reverse buttons, for example, were disabled by hydraulic pressure when the car was moving at more than a walk, and the starter would operate only if the park or neutral button was pushed. Just before introduction an automatic park relay was incorporated which put the transmission into "Park" whenever the ignition was turned off. It was an inexpensive, useful system, and created showroom traffic at modest cost. Nance loved it. While at Hotpoint he had made the "pushbutton kitchen" the dream of every housewife. If pushbuttons helped sell stoves, he may have reasoned, they'd help sell cars. He was right.

Studebaker-Packard managers said the company was embarking on "The Bold New Idea." It would work, if the money held out. The "Idea" was that "cars can be built on modern production lines without sacrificing craftsmanship . . . our goal must be to build not the most cars but the best cars . . . individuality of design and true pride of workmanship are not dead, but alive." Beneath the public relations tenor of the statement, the thought was to give each of the cars a personality. This had been lacking for some time. The key was a combined drive by Product Planning, Engineering and, most of all, Styling.

In the latter department the results were evident. Styling command had been unified under Schmidt, who knew how to run things in the face of limited resources and tight money. Both the South Bend and Detroit studios were streamlined and modernized, morale was high, models were being considered, completed and put into the hopper for future production. A program had been developed for the sharing of sheet metal among 1957 Studebakers, Clippers and Packards, plus a new line of small Studebaker pickups to carry the designation (as in prewar days) of Coupe Express.

Schmidt assessed his staff as "the top styling management team in the industry," and granted some salary raises to its members in South Bend, after assuring Nance this was necessary to hold the talent and "the loss of two or three qualified people creates a very definite problem as well as opening our 'doors of security.' " Of the Packard product, Schmidt saw it as "second to none in appearance and in a time span that is unheard of in the Styling industry. It is our intent to go even further in the future." Schmidt was optimistic; the 1956 cars were of necessity reworked from shells dating back as early as 1951, and his studio would never get a new unit on the road—with one exception. It was the Packard Predictor.

The Predictor was intended to do just what its name implied—forecast Packard's ideas, as well as those of the industry. Comments Schmidt, "I was brought in to do a new redesign, a new car, all the planning, interchangeability; to lay out the lines and determine the styling. Within three months we had hired some eighty people"—and work progressed around the clock.

Styling of the Predictor, on a Clipper chassis, was principally the work of Dick Teague. The car had all the mechanical features of contemporary Packards plus a powered "tambour" roof, retractable headlights and a power rear window. It was primarily a styling exercise, though it was operative, for several dealers drove it, if only around the block, during its tour of the country. Literature, however, claimed the Predictor was equipped with transaxle and independent rear suspension—actually it was not.

What it did have was enough: swivel seats, overhead control switches, narrow-stripe whitewalls, vertical grille, hidden headlights, sculptured sides, reverse-slanted power rear window—and, of course, tail fins. "I am still sensitive about those fins," recalls Teague. "I never did like them that much. But the chiefs would keep dropping by, and they'd say, 'Put some fins on 'er, Teague,' so on they went. Fins were on the way in, and

New for 1956: "Twin Traction" differential, below; pushbuttons, above.

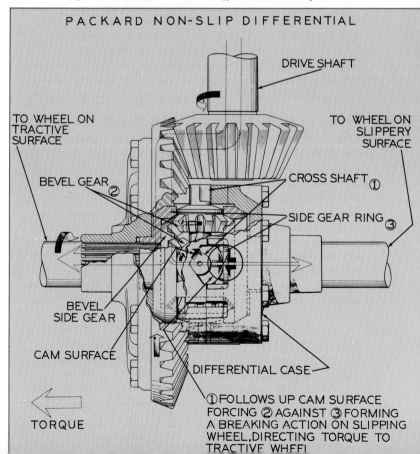

PACKARD NON-SLIP DIFFERENTIAL

DRIVE SHAFT

TO WHEEL ON TRACTIVE SURFACE

TO WHEEL ON SLIPPERY SURFACE

BEVEL GEAR ②

CROSS SHAFT ①

SIDE GEAR RING ③

BEVEL SIDE GEAR

CAM SURFACE

DIFFERENTIAL CASE

TORQUE

① FOLLOWS UP CAM SURFACE FORCING ② AGAINST ③ FORMING A BREAKING ACTION ON SLIPPING WHEEL, DIRECTING TORQUE TO TRACTIVE WHEEL

everybody knew it.''

Although the styling was entirely an in-house project, the Predictor itself was built by Ghia, possibly in response to Bremer's earlier suggestion that the Italian company be asked to do something. Work was begun there in September 1955, and the car was received in New York on December 29th. "We were working through the winter holidays trying to get the Predictor ready for the 1956 Chicago Auto Show," recalls Schmidt. "The union came in with complaints about required notice for holidays, overtime, etc. I called for a meeting of the higher-ups and the vice-president of the union came over; and I gave the only speech of my life, saying 'the whole future of Packard lies in this car. If it goes over big it will make all the difference in the world for thousands of workers so you'll have to give us a moratorium to get this done. What I'm asking is to take all the styling people out of the union.' They said they couldn't do that because of their elected positions within the union. I said it was only common sense. They took a vote and I'll be darned if they didn't okay it! I agreed we'd come back a year later if the cars were doing well. They asked that we not publicize it, though, as they'd never done it before.''

There was plenty to do on the Predictor. As received, it was equipped with Italian electrical components of an inferior grade—the car caught fire the first time a window was operated—and it had to be rewired by Creative Industries. (This was Creative's last job for the company; Schmidt had been phasing out its input in favor of his new in-house team and had previously transferred five of his people from "on-site" locations at Creative back to Packard.)

The Predictor was not the savior its makers hoped it would be. It was, however, very well received at the time, and today provides an interesting metal study of styling trends and a visible statement of the direction in which Packard was heading. It remained company property long after the closing of the Detroit facilities, and was later stored in a back room at Studebaker Plant No. 8 until it was deeded, with the balance of the Studebaker Automobile Collection, to the City of South Bend.

Meanwhile, the production 1956 models were on the way to dealers. For the first time in many years, Nance said, sales agencies would "get off to an even start with competition on any given model year in both timing and product. Until they got the V-8 and other improvements, they had been, for the past five years, at a disadvantage productwise, even though the cars were announced at the proper time." But, there was one potential difficulty.

"Our success," said Nance, "will depend on getting rid of the balance of our 1955's without resorting to distress-merchandising tactics . . . . Not only is it costly and non-profitable to both dealer and factory, but further, it depreciates the Packard reputation."

Another change in sales tactics was advised by Nance in August 1955. "Insofar as the Packard line is concerned, let's forget Cadillac and go

Above: The 1956 Clipper Custom sedan. Below: The Clipper Deluxe sedan. On the right: The Clipper super hardtop produced during model year 1956.

after Chrysler and Lincoln, who are not nearly as formidable competition. Chrysler has proven in 1955 what can really be done through good sales promotion and sales management . . . . Certainly we want to continue to hammer away at Cadillac business but we might be realistic and concede that Cadillac has the prestige situation sewed up tight, and will have for several years to come, even though we continue to make inroads. I'll settle for half the performance that Chrysler is doing in that price field.'' Three years before, Nance had said he'd be damned if he'd be in a horse race and be left at the quarter pole—but even Nance had to now face reality.

"We are running into difficulties due to obstructionist attitude, indifference, or poor organization on the part of the vendor," Bremer wrote Nance about pushbutton shifting on July 25th, 1955. "It does not appear that we will have sufficient quantities of these transmissions available until late October." The vendor, Auto-Lite, eventually did speed up its deliveries, but Packard was never happy with the quality;

and as a parting gift Auto-Lite destroyed the tooling for the units while Studebaker was attempting to make a new run in the early Sixties to meet service shortages in the field.

"The outlook for the special seats in the Caribbean is rather disappointing at this time," continued Bremer, "due to an inertia in determining where the seats are going to be trimmed, who will engineer the design, etc. We are doing everything possible to bring all the loose ends on this one together." He wouldn't succeed—Caribbean production was delayed for three weeks, and when it did begin it was with Four Hundred seats. This cost Packard $15,000 in recalls, and to complicate the situation the company decided the seats remained—despite Nance's admonitions—too hard. No-charge soft cushions were offered—and more money flowed out.

In November these incidents were followed by a major accident: The new flanged rear axle failed during breakdown tests. The fault lay with Dana's Spicer, which did not meet the agreed-upon specifications, but

Packard had to bear the cost, which was impoundment of every vehicle in stock, on showroom floors, or in transit—some $20 million worth— while Dana ran off new axles. Part of the financial price paid was recovered through a $43,000 settlement with Dana, but the loss in public confidence was irrevocable. And Dana was only beginning.

Spicer had anticipated being ready to supply "production quantities" of Twin Traction differentials in December, and agreed to ship 300 by then. The actual shipment was closer to 200, and the units were not as rugged as Packard differentials had been in the past—many had to be replaced by conventional units. These two back-to-back adversities were of a nature not commonplace in Packard history; they would never have occurred in earlier years, when ideas were evaluated for as long as a decade before being put into production.

And at the same time there were certain business distractions, notably a costly suit with Pan American World Airways over ownership of the name Clipper which Pan Am had used for its airliners since 1931. When

Packard introduced the Clipper model in 1941, the air line had not objected, and in 1946, in fact, had published an advertisement showing both plane and car. But now Pan Am sought to extend its trade name to surface transportation of passengers and freight to and from airports; because Packard was using the Clipper name for passenger cars, Pan Am filed suit in February 1955. The litigation later spread to the names Pan American, Constellation, Panama and Caribbean. Packard had stumbled onto a whole nest of sensitive appellations, and the suit ground on interminably, ultimately to be dropped after a dying Packard eliminated all the names by 1958.

There was also a patent dispute with General Motors over nine transmission features. Years before, the industry had adopted a patent sharing agreement, although Packard had not been a signatory to it because the company had a first-rate engineering staff and sufficient patents of its own with which to trade. General Motors had for some time "winked" at violations or possible violations of its patents, but in 1955 this policy was abruptly changed. GM now intended, Graves wrote Nance, "to retain unto themselves new developments made by their research and engineering departments until such time as the commercializing advantages thereof have been utilized to the fullest by General Motors. When no commercializing advantage is left in a development, they say they will be willing to grant licenses at reasonable royalty rates to other members of the industry."

Packard was included in the GM offensive with the transmission infringement charges in June 1955. The company's patent department was already busy enough with Pan Am, but now had to analyze the latest problem. The canny Graves put some people to work to ascertain if GM was violating any Packard patents—a trade-off was the easiest route to a settlement.

A few silver linings peeped through the clouds, however; AMC increased its engine orders (for a while) with the Utica plant, and the use of the Clipper engine and Ultramatic in the 1956 Studebaker Golden Hawk increased volume, though it did not help the balance and handling of that particular model; it was much too heavy. At the time the Golden Hawk was respected for its straight-line performance, which the Packard engine generously provided it, and this acclaim rubbed off to Packard's benefit on its own cars.

Nance was also getting some defense work again, a J-57 jet engine parts contract, and a little missile work for Studebaker. But it was scarcely more than a pittance compared to what had come Nance's way before.

Overall, the outlook remained gray. Schedules at Conner Avenue would be cut after the sales people reported diminished demand for the 1956's. D'Arcy had not evolved a solid advertising program. All this must have been frustrating for Nance, who had been chosen by Packard particularly for his sales ability, and there is no question that he was now

Above: The 1956 Executive hardtop. Below: The 1956 Executive sedan. Right above and below: The Four Hundred hardtop and Patrician sedan.

feeling decidedly pessimistic. "With the failure by a wide margin of meeting our October forecast of operations," Nance wrote Bremer in November, "it is perfectly obvious that everything possible is going to have to be done to get this thing turned around—and fast. [We must] get the business operating in the black [and] get the operations in line to come closer to the targets that we gave to the financial institutions of a break-even point of 65,000 units and a $10 million profit at 80,000 units . . . . Our problem is one of still reaching to hit the goal."

No goals were being hit. Compared to 1955, 1956 sales were a dribble, and an irony—because finally the Conner Avenue plant was beginning

get stock in the hands of our dealers . . . I assume the pressure is on the sales department to get all franchised dealers equipped with display models. Secondly, experience has shown that our dealers must have a total stock in the high selling season of at least 12,000 units to generate 6-7,000 units in sales. It is an axiom that dealers won't sell them, if they don't have them."

There was enough turmoil from within, more came from without. Lincoln-Mercury suddenly began an undeclared "open season" on Packard dealers—approaching them to change franchises. A letter of complaint was sent by Packard, and in reply Lincoln-Mercury offered the assurance that there had been no basic change in its recruitment policy. Still, Laughna wrote Nance that "dealers in Washington, Philadelphia and New York have been approached by Mercury representatives to change franchises. In fact, [one zone manager] states that every one of his dealers of any size has been solicited." Vultures, it seemed, were gathering.

Next came cash flow. A finance committee of Studebaker-Packard directors formed on a routine basis to borrow $50 million against the expected tooling up costs for 1957's new common body (about $30 million of the total) ran into resistance from the insurance companies backing the corporation. This was a distinct and most unpleasant surprise. Said *Fortune*, "Just fifteen months and twenty-five days after its formation, Studebaker-Packard faced bankruptcy. The finance committee promptly became a rescue committee."

The committee's first recommendation was to scale down all plans, and double-quick. One of the first thoughts: delay the new 1957 program. Nance wrote Laughna in March, "it is almost a 'must' that we facelift the present Clipper and get it out the first of October, to keep your dealer organization from dying on the vine before you get the new Packard in December. You can probably drop the present [1956] Clipper line after you get into production on the Packards . . . we might introduce as a second line . . . the small Clipper. Whether this should be built at South Bend or Detroit will have to be ascertained . . . . I want you . . . to get this low end of this new Packard line down in price . . . engineer to a price target on the low side and then beef the car up for the big model for the senior line, à la Chrysler."

While these plans took root, cutbacks were invoked pending disposal of the huge stock of unsold cars. Business management was told by Nance, "We sweat and strain to produce and price our car competitively and then our dealers get $200 to $300 more than competition. On limited volume, of course. In January, Studebaker dealers 'creamed' the deals for a Variable Net of $374, while Chevrolet dealers were about $100, so we are advised by a good source. And Packard dealers had a higher Variable Net—believe it or not—this January than a year ago." Although the goliath of General Motors has been cited by some as the source of

to be sorted out. By year's end the zones were heavily overstocked, a fact which Nance thought prudent to keep a secret from his dealers, whose noses were attuned from long experience to sniffing disaster. "I suggest," Nance wrote Laughna of Purchasing and Production Control on February 6th, "that you retrieve all copies of these [sales] figures and take them out of circulation, for obvious reasons. Please send me instead, a program predicated on moving a wholesale domestic minimum of 60,000 units for the calendar year of 1956 . . . 60,000 is our required minimum to keep from incurring horrendous losses in this division.

"We will never achieve anywhere near the sales we need if we do not

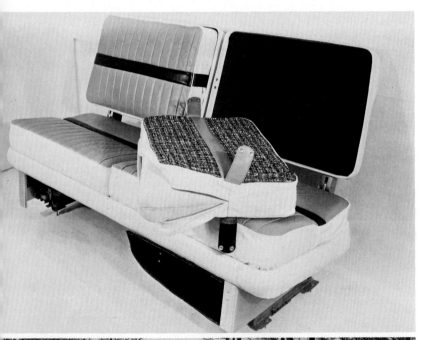

The 1956 Caribbean, and its unique leather-and-bouclé reversible seat cushions.

Packard's predicament, obviously the company's dealers were contributing massively to it themselves.

"Our dealers are not facing up to market conditions," Nance continued. "Since our dealer body, as a whole, has a breakeven point substantially below that of the factory, they bleed us to death, and have been doing it—at least I can speak for Packard—for years." He could have easily spoken for Studebaker, too. Its dealer force was notorious for holding out for the full sticker price while the competition madly discounted to maintain volume.

By the middle of March, Nance's plan to build Clippers in Detroit, to hold the dealer body together, was abandoned. "It is definitely impossible from a tooling, lineup, material handling and inventory view point," wrote Laughna, "to assemble both a Face Lift Clipper and the 1957 Packard at the Conner plant. Assuming we started the production of the 1957 Clipper Face Lift on August 1, 1956, we would have to discontinue its production on September 30, 1956 [with] the production of 7600 units at a tooling cost of over one million dollars."

It would seem that a market so flooded with unsaleable Packards and Clippers did not need another model, but on March 5th one came—probably out of sheer momentum. This was the Packard Executive, for "the young man on the way up," a Clipper Custom with Packard front end and modified side trim. It retailed for $3465 and $3560 as four-door sedan and hardtop respectively, $400 more than a Clipper Custom but up to $695 less than a Senior Packard. This was obviously a return to the practice of "selling the Packard name" on a cheaper car, an idea that had worked in 1935 but which Nance himself had said was "bleeding the Packard name white" in 1952. The Executive further demoralized the field force, and with its introduction the Clipper Custom was no longer produced. The Executive sold as fast as it was produced—2815 units were built—but its invitation "to enter the luxury car class now—at a modest investment" was a clear signal to anyone with eyes that something was very wrong on East Grand Boulevard.

The word was fast getting round—in the papers, in the media, all over Detroit, at the dealerships. Nance alluded to "the recent unfavorable publicity" in late March in his report to the board, and candidly told S-P's directors that further emergency action was going to be needed. One hundred top dealers were brought to Detroit for a conference, Torsion-Level was folded into standard list prices, D'Arcy accelerated advertising, specifically trying to soften the "orphan" publicity beginning to be heard. At Product Planning, with the hope of saving a million dollars, the Ford passenger car seat was being adapted for the planned 1957 models. And that wasn't all Packard hoped to get from Ford.

In March 1956, discussions were opened on the possibility of using Lincoln bodies for 1957 Packards, hanging the Packard sheet metal on fronts and rears. Teague was put to work on proposals—a super-quiet

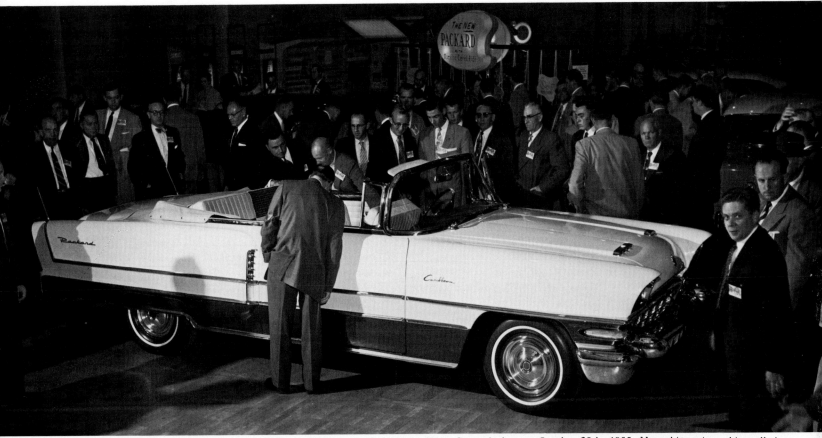

The Terrace Room of the Fairmont Hotel where the 1956 Caribbean was first shown West Coast dealers on October 25th, 1955. Note thin-stripe whitewall tires.

assignment in a locked room. Henry Ford II indicated willingness to supply Nance with whatever he needed, Nance sent Graves to Dearborn to confer with Ford engineers.

Graves came back disillusioned. Evidently Henry Ford's amicability did not transcend to lower levels—Graves hadn't even been allowed to inspect material. Nance gave up on the idea. On March 30th, however, Bremer suggested that perhaps Ford would sell truck cab stampings, "because styling is not of as great significance." But nothing came of that either; the 1957 Studebaker trucks were warmed-over 1956's, (which meant re-warmed-over 1949's); and so they continued until 1964.

With every conventional money-saving, sales-creating, publicity-massaging method already tried, there was nothing left to do now but ac-tivate the doomsday machine—a drastic, unprecedented, total reorganization, or even a total departure from the automobile business. A consultant firm, Ernst & Ernst, was called in to make studies in this regard. Three plans were worked up by April 9th:

Plan I: Moving the Packard-Clipper Division to South Bend. This consisted of Studebaker continuing unchanged in the low-priced field, but dropping the President series; Packard continuing as planned for 1957, on 125- and 130-inch wheelbases; deletion of the Clipper name entirely; continuance of the Conner plant; disposal of the Utica plant. As an alternative, Plan I-B delayed the new Packard until September 1958, and the new Studebaker until April 1957.

Plan II: Packard Discontinued. In this program, Studebaker's market

coverage would be expanded, the 1956 Packards would be given a "fast build-out" to get rid of them; the Utica plant would be sold; and the demise of the Packard make would be announced on May 1st, 1956. As an alternative, Plan II-B called for outright sale of the Packard-Clipper Division, assets and properties to a new owner "who would continue to produce the Packard line." One wonders where anyone with cash in hand might have been found for that.

Plan III: Complete Liquidation of the Properties and Assets of Studebaker-Packard. If this had been adopted, it would have been the biggest industrial collapse in the history of the United States. The plans forecast continued losses as a result, with $45 million the smallest 1956 estimate. The attrition in labor would have been enormous, further magnified through every S-P dealership in the field.

Among these options, Plan I received little consideration. Studebaker, Ernst & Ernst noted, "cannot accommodate the larger Packard bodies. Revamping these facilities to build Packard would be costly and would reduce the hourly productive rate. The Chippewa Plant could provide sufficient floor space . . . [but it is] not available for auto operations because of defense operations in the missile field." Ernst & Ernst estimated the costs of Plan I would be about $23 million and would require from seven to eight months. The Utica plant, the disposal of which would mean the end of Packard engines (proprietary units were estimated to cost $500,000 a year), would net $20 million. Significantly, the abandonment of Utica was basic to all three plans—it simply couldn't be worked into any system of survival or liquidation.

No one on the S-P board was ready to accept any of these recommendations—yet. Other avenues were being pursued, among them merger

The Predictor, its swivel seats (above), its sliding roof (right), Bill Graves behind the wheel (below). Ultimately narrow whitewall tires would be fitted.

with or purchase by Ford, GM, Chrysler, Litton Industries, International Harvester, Textron, General Dynamics, Curtiss-Wright. Royal Little of Textron decided that S-P was not only too big, it was in need of more help than he could provide. Ford said it would be bad business to keep S-P in business for two years and then abandon it when Ford's new "E" (for "Experimental," not "Edsel," although that was ultimately its name) car was ready—by which time it would need the dealer force. An insurance company offered to give Nance working capital if he could get General Motors to endorse the loan—which GM declined to do. GM financial officer Albert Bradley proffered his regrets, noting that if S-P was successful GM would be charged with gobbling up the industry, and if S-P failed GM would be blamed for that, too.

A team was dispatched to Washington to seek aid in that direction. There was none. Defense Secretary Wilson again talked about the "untenable position" he would be in if he helped. The word from Treasury Secretary George Humphrey, whom Studebaker-Packard also approached, was equally discouraging.

By early 1956, dealers were dropping out at about twenty a month. In December 1954, S-P had had 2178 of them, including exclusives and duals—by February 1956, the figure was down to 1523. At that rate, 465 more dealers could be expected to leave by year's end, and Laughna admitted to Nance on April 10th that this was likely. "With the current unfavorable publicity and circulation of numerous rumors, our dealers are starting to definitely question our announcement date of our 1957 models."

Laughna then desperately pushed for firm word on the '57's. "The continued delay of publishing definite information will increase the difficulty of maintaining our dealer strength. At the same time, we realize that notifying our dealers that our 1957 models will not be introduced until February [another delay had just occurred in the 1957 program] will also have an adverse effect." He recommended a booklet be issued illustrating the new models and explaining the reasons for the delay, or identifying new models by series instead of model year.

While Laughna worried about how to face the dealers, Nance had to face the even more concerned stockholders. But he couldn't tell them much. "I am sure that you will recognize that premature public discussion could seriously jeopardize plans. [We] have faced unusual difficulties, undertaken tasks which seemed overwhelming and carried on in trying circumstances with a degree of business and technical competence, loyalty and devotion to duty which probably never will be fully realized."

Nance concluded his report by assuring stockholders that every effort was being extended in their interests. Of course the average stockholder had no stake in the Packard *car*, merely the company. In the past, firms like Graham-Paige and Peerless had turned to sports promotions and breweries to find their way out of automotive doldrums. Nance appears

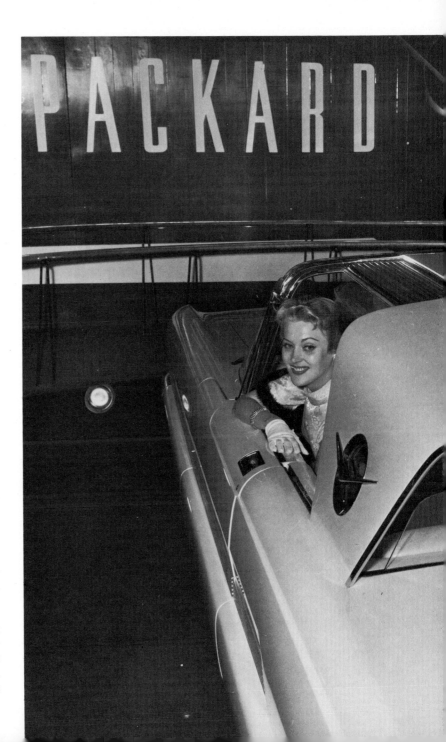

to have made a genuine effort to save the car as well as the company.

Gradually the remaining options began to disappear. Tex Colbert of Chrysler wrote Nance on April 20th, "When we examine our own situation, forward planning and the effects on Chrysler's corporate structure, we are unable to see any way that the merger or acquisition you propose could be fitted into our plans to the mutual advantage of our companies and their stockholders." Chrysler had of course recently expanded its line to five makes of cars including Imperial, and the lines S-P could offer were not complementary.

On May 30th, all S-P commitments were frozen and advertising was cut back. Laughna knew that D'Arcy was going to ask why. He queried Nance in early June about which answer he should give them—a temporary analysis of the financial position, contemplated shutdown, financial negotiations, or "none of your business." It is not recorded which of these tasty options Nance recommended; in any case D'Arcy would not have to wonder long.

In May another doomsday plan arrived from Robert Heller & Associates: "Program for the Liquidation of the Automobile Business." This followed the last of the merger negotiations, which expired on April 27th and was presented orally at a board meeting in New York. It foresaw a total loss of $108 million in the process of closure, nearly $7 million more than S-P was worth, and would have left the company with a cash deficiency of over $19 million.

The Heller report recommended a temporary counter-attack—announce S-P's intent to stay in the auto business, but simultaneously start laying off personnel and selling facilities. Then, in the summer and fall of 1956, end the production of Packards, Clippers, Studebaker cars and trucks, one line at a time. Finally, in October, make the news of closure public, and reduce the company to a defense division and corporate shell.

Again S-P was able to dodge ultimate disaster—this time not through its own doing but with sudden help from the outside. On May 8th, Curtiss-Wright was reported to have made a new offer—a management agreement, more defense work, the stocking of S-P dealers with Mercedes-Benz products. The board snatched at it as the only viable alternative to complete collapse.

The May 8th board meeting adjourned just long enough for conferences with Curtiss-Wright and Packard's bankers. The latter asked for one additional condition—a ninety-day note for an additional $15.3 million in cash. Curtiss-Wright accepted it, and the bank advised that if C-W stayed on board the note would be renewed indefinitely.

Exactly what Curtiss-Wright hoped to gain by the deal was in doubt, although it was obvious that S-P would be a good tax write-off for a profitable firm. In any event the C-W entry was a signal to some—Graves, Powers and Bremer all resigned, and the board minutes recorded that if the C-W agreement was finally concluded, Nance

wouldn't be far behind them.

Meanwhile, Nance stayed aboard to try to run the automobile business. Typical of these trying days for him was the following letter—"Dear Mr. Nance: The finest car I ever owned was a '51 Packard. Because I intend to own another some day, I am sending you the enclosed $5. I hope you won't resign. I hope you get the loan you need." To which Nance replied, "Under stress of present conditions it was a pleasure to have your note and 'pledge' toward your future Packard. Thank you very much for your sentiments. We have been extremely gratified to have many similar and sympathetic expressions from the public, all of which have added impetus in our unrelenting efforts toward an early solution to our problems."

The exchange was heartwarming, but it bore no weight in the continuing press of events. Everyone in the center of the whirlwind knew it was nearly over. Packard, great and wonderful, fifty-year-old Packard, was doomed in its existing form: None of the expert proposals had even considered saving it at the expense of Studebaker, with its annual sales of 350,000 to Packard's 75,000.

The first draft of the Curtiss-Wright management agreement with Studebaker-Packard was dated May 28th, 1956 and was effective the following day. It called for additional defense work, revision of the borrowing agreements, additional funds, distribution rights for Daimler-Benz vehicles. S-P accepted C-W's management and operation of its business in return for expenses and a stock option. It was really a fairly decent agreement, considering the hard facts—and it was the only feasible hope of the company's staying in the auto business.

The idea came to be known in Detroit as the "Joint Program." The Heller Associates doubted it would be more than a holding action, and revised their doomsday plan down to $60 million for dissolution—on the basis of more complete information. There was some doubt in June if Curtiss-Wright would even be able to place the Joint Program in operation because S-P's business wasn't going to be worth enough. A June 4th board meeting was continually interrupted by phone calls from Roy Hurley, president of Curtiss-Wright. Eventually Hurley advised that the Joint Program might be possible *if* S-P would transfer various assets to a wholly-owned subsidiary. This was, as Cannon Ball Baker would have said, "the kicker," the string attached to Curtiss-Wright's intervention.

Studebaker-Packard by now had no choice but to acquiesce. Two of its best facilities were placed into a new corporation, Chippewa and Packard's plant in Utica. Hurley also had S-P put the Aerophysics Development Corporation into the pot, and the whole combination eventually became known as the Utica Bend Corporation.

James J. Nance asked to be relieved as president "substantially with the initiation of the program." He told the board on June 4th that, as they knew, there was no place for him in the Joint Program with Curtiss-

Wright, although he would cooperate in every way possible to initiate the program, even staying on for thirty days in an advisory capacity. "I spent several months at the plant even after I was off the payroll," Nance said later in an interview, "on my own time and my own expense in helping my key boys get located. I think as a result of that I have very loyal alumni. We went through that situation together."

In the midst of all the financial negotiations, the Packard automobile almost died unnoticed. The Conner Avenue plant had been on a four-day week, but on June 22nd had worked its first Friday in some weeks, completing 120 cars. There had been 162 to go, so the workforce came back the following Monday. On that sad day, June 25th, 1956, twenty-four Clippers and eighteen Packards were run through the body drop and completed. Altogether, there had been 28,835 cars built for the 1956 model year—18,482 Clippers, 10,353 Packards.

After that, it was all downhill. Cleanup of assembly operations was completed the next day, production material was moved to the Boulevard. The Utica plant was wound down—it finished the year's production on June 22nd but continued to run service units through most of July. The lot rented from Hudson was vacated by July 3rd. That month, too, the Packard Proving Grounds were closed.

By this time 700 employees had been released and Nance was on a program to cut expenses "and yet not create a panic situation." Styling and Engineering were retained intact at the Boulevard, as agreed with Curtiss-Wright—their abandonment would have created chaos. But the whole Boulevard operation was simply on a mark-time basis.

On July 16th Bill Schmidt notified Nance that Styling had completed the 1957 Packard and Clipper and was ready to release them for production—almost doggedly, those who loved the cars were still hanging on. "We have also completed a detailed interchangeability program chart and a proposed body program and timing chart, which includes extensive cost studies," Schmidt said. "Because the personnel here at the Packard Division have completed their design programs and I would like to keep them busy until the negotiations under way have reached a conclusion, we will begin work immediately on a full-size clay model of the Studebaker Golden Hawk, in which we will study the possibilities of carrying through on a new body or a facelift body the major design features of today's Hawks."

On July 25th Hurley let it be known that he intended to recommend continuance of the auto business, but only at South Bend. On July 26th the S-P board ratified the Joint Agreement, and Nance and Hoffman submitted their resignations, which were "accepted with regret." Harold Churchill of Studebaker was elected president, and the roll of vice-presidents was reduced (from a high of eleven in 1955) to three.

Thus ended James Nance's stewardship of "America's Fourth Full-Line Automobile Producer." His work will ever be debated, as in the

Clipper facelift ideas for 1956 which, thankfully, never made it into production.

past, sometimes with authority, sometimes not. He has been accused of personally destroying the greatest of America's automotive names, at least the greatest for the longest time. But he cannot, in any fair way, be totally blamed for what happened. Three of the factors that brought about his and Packard's downfall were not of his doing, nor under his direct control: the withdrawal of the defense business by Charles Wilson in 1954, the irresponsible financial estimates furnished Nance on the condition of Studebaker, and the demise of the Briggs Body Company with attendant costs to Packard. Factor number four, the decision to move automobile production to the Conner Avenue plant was, however, mostly Nance's.* But Jim Nance, like us all, was human, and he simply made a mistake. One suspects that many a lesser man would have rendered Packard into oblivion far sooner than he did, and with more of a whimper than the roar Nance gave to Packard in those last, ironically bittersweet years of 1955 and 1956—an outstanding product, a dying enterprise.** Let the Fifty-Fifth and Fifty-Sixth Series Packards be James Nance's memorial.

As for Paul Hoffman, the outcome was a bitter pill indeed. He had seen Studebaker in the best of times, then down for the count in the Depression, then back from the grave and thriving. He left the company for only a few brief years, and in that time it plunged to the depths again. Hope had shone briefly with the Packard takeover, and now here was disaster at the door once more. The Studebaker automobile would live yet awhile, to die in 1966. Paul Hoffman died eight years later.

In accord with the C-W contract, Chippewa and Utica were leased to Curtiss-Wright, which paid for them in advance. Utica Bend Corporation was sold to C-W for cash, and with it departed S-P's defense contracts. S-P received favorable revision of borrowing agreements and the Daimler-Benz franchise in the U.S.

Since Curtiss-Wright would not officially take over the company until September 1st, more time-making was called for. At the August 6th board meeting Churchill called the fate of the Packard "one of the most serious problems now confronting the Corporation." A decision was promised within thirty days on the marque's fate. In the meantime the long overdue shrink-back of styling was begun and arrangements com-

---

*There were other setbacks, of course but, comparatively, these were minor and in themselves did not contribute to Packard's undoing as the combination of the four factors mentioned did.

**Nance's later career was flushed with success; after a stint at Ford, he went on to a Cleveland banking career which was one of the most distinguished in that city's history. He has never wished to look back on Packard; and he never had to. The big thing he learned, Nance said, "was the reason I welcomed the opportunity to run a bank. You can't do anything without money . . . sooner or later everybody ends up at the bank."

Further styling ideas for 1956 which also fortuitously failed to materialize.

menced to "dual" all dealerships. Numerous details had to be attended to: Laughna pointed out that vendors would not hold tooling since no renewal business was in the works—this meant spare parts had to be run off quickly, while the tooling existed.

On August 20th, Churchill announced that he felt the best solution to the Packard question was to continue the name on an interim model through 1957 to be built on the Studebaker President Classic chassis with the 1957 Golden Hawk engine (Studebaker's 289, supercharged by McCulloch, with 275 horsepower). It might be called the Executive, but would sell for $150 less than the 1956 version, and it would cost $1.1 million to tool. Directors approved and the work was begun for a projected January 1957 announcement.

Parts began being shifted from Detroit to South Bend—a good many of them being lost in the process. S-P tried to cancel its five-year lease on the Conner Avenue plant, to which Chrysler vigorously objected, although it did agree to a sub-lease. By now the once-great plant on East Grand Boulevard was nearly deserted. Total employment of the Packard-Clipper Division had been 4309 on June 17th, but 1443 production people were terminated when the last car was built at Conner Avenue. Another 1228 left when clean-up was complete, and the deac-

tivation of Engineering meant the end of the line for 321 more. Utica Bend transfers totaled 118, and Sales laid off 680. Some of these people found work with other auto firms, notably Packard's great cadre of engineers—most did not, at least not right away. The streets were already full of former Packard employees who had departed in earlier waves. The closing down of the company added to woes already resulting from the demise of Hudson—the combination spelled economic decline for a whole section of Detroit.

Tucked away in the Boulevard plant was one last enclave—the Styling Department. Dick Teague refers to this period as "the last days in the bunker." They were not pleasant ones. "We were the last guys around. It was a ghost town, and we were 'way in the back on Concord Avenue at the old Rolls-Royce engineering section [at the present location of the Edsel Ford Freeway]. Styling was the last to go because I think those who were manipulating us thought there was some chance. You knew goddam well the end was close, but you kept hoping for the life raft. Rumors? My God, you wouldn't believe the rumors that circulated: Everybody from Universal CIT to Ford was buying us out. The '57 running prototype was there. . . ."

The prototype for 1957 represented an all-new car. It was created un-

der the original program and constructed by hand, and many hoped it would save the marque. Herb Misch pointed out that if something was available to show the bankers and Curtiss-Wright they might still get approval to build it. The vehicle was ready for tooling, although by this time it would require a record effort to get it on the road for the 1957 model year, and late at that.

The '57's suspension was highly refined—though Allison had joined International Harvester when his consultant's contract had expired, an alternative to accepting a full-time job at Packard which was, as it happened, the right decision. At I-H Allison developed a torsion bar suspension for trucks but the project did not succeed because fleet owners weren't willing to spend the extra money for the sake of driver comfort. Allison agrees that the refinements for 1957 were good ones. They were accomplished by Forest McFarland, John DeLorean and Herb Misch and would have set new standards of comfort, roadworthiness and reliability. DeLorean even tinkered briefly with a hydraulic leveling device, but it proved more costly than the existing system and was dropped. When DeLorean later went to Chevrolet as a vice-president and then president, the hydraulic leveler reached production there.

The 1957 V-8 engine and Twin Ultramatic also had many   *619*

refinements. Those responsible claim the transmission would have been "the best ever." The engine was bored out further, to 440 cubic inches according to Graves, and the entire vehicle represented a pinnacle of effort in the eyes of the men who had prepared it. The car was not pretty—its body was only a rough mock-up; Teague had its final lines on paper. It was known as Black Bess. The day now came when Black Bess was all of Packard that remained.

Said Teague, "the '57 prototype was a mule. It looked like it had been made with a cold soldering iron and a ball peen hammer. And it was, in an extremely short time, a last-ditch effort to come up with some money for die models. The doors opened but it was a very spartan mule. But engineered well it was, and it was the one and only ever built.

"The dough we had in it was hard to come by at that time. Herb Misch had put it together. There wasn't anything old on it except the V-8 and that was modified; the torsion bar suspension was entirely different although of the same concept . . . and the Ultramatic was upgraded. It was ugly, and if we had shown it to Curtiss-Wright we'd have had to show it to them blindfolded because if they saw the car instead of clays and drawings they wouldn't have loaned us a dime. It's flowers on the grave now, but it might just have saved Packard.

"When [Packard] really appeared to be finished, in the fall of '56, nobody was around. We were all on the payroll but every Friday the department you saw in action last week would be gone. Those big yellow carts would come through and they'd take all the files. The cart would come down, the files would be pulled out and dumped upside down, the file drawer would be put back in and a few weeks later they would have an auction [for] office equipment."

Asked if there was anyone to give the authorization for the destruction of the corporate files, Teague says, "there was nobody there who had the authority to say *don't* do it. The contents went to the powerhouse across the bridge and it would all be burned. Nance has been much maligned because of this but, of course, he hadn't been around for months. [He] was intensely interested in the cars. He came in with all kinds of publicity and his reputation. He didn't want to see the company go downhill but he couldn't be concerned with that historical file, it was just done by accident, an automatic kind of happening."

Finally the tumbrells rolled for old Black Bess. "Misch said 'find it' and we brought it up to a sort of styling showroom where we had the finished clay models and full-size plasters. It was there a day or so. Then Herb called and said, 'you might as well carry out the order. I can't do it myself, I'm going to make you the executioner. Cut the thing up; we are going to get rid of it, it's all over.' So I called Red Lux, an old welder in the studio, who had been there since the cornerstone. There were two or three other cars in the studio, including another black one, a Clipper. I said, 'OK, it's official, cut the black one up.' This welder had been there since he was a kid, and was hanging on by his thumbnails. I came back around 4 p.m. and he was just finishing. The pieces were lying all around like a bomb had gone off. It was probably the dirtiest trick I ever played but I said, 'My God, Red, what have you done? Not this one, man, the one over in the corner!' The poor guy had to have had a strong heart, because if he didn't he would have died right there. His face drained, and when I told him I was just kidding he chased me around the room. You've got to have a sense of humor in this business."

Teague was sent to South Bend to work on the 1957 Packard Clipper, tooling for which was formally approved on October 4th. The last board meeting held in Detroit was on October 31st, 1956—exactly fifty-three years, eight months and twenty-six days since Henry Bourne Joy had convened the first board meeting there in 1903.

The Boulevard plant eventually became host to a myriad businesses, as well as to the government's Defense Contract Administration. Its new owners rented whatever space was rentable, most of it on the ground floor or facing East Grand Boulevard. The Mount Elliott plant was eventually sold, some portions of the Boulevard facilities were marketed as complete entities, and Curtiss-Wright took over everything at Utica. The Utica facilities were eventually purchased intact by Ford, including the test track. The Conner Avenue plant, a financial albatross to the end, was sub-leased and finally received the fate it so richly deserved: It was razed in the Sixties.

Production at Conner; the Hypalon top being fitted to a Caribbean hardtop.

CHAPTER THIRTY-ONE

THE LAST OF
THE MARQUE

The Fifty-Seventh and
the Fifty-Eighth Series

1957-1958

AUTHORS: GEORGE HAMLIN AND DWIGHT HEINMULLER

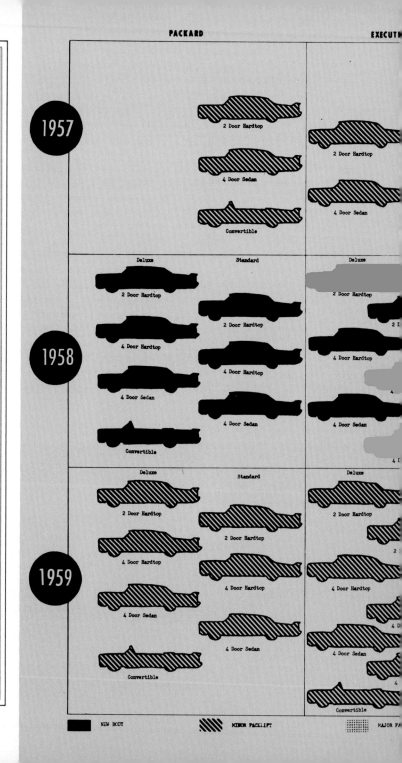

PROPOSED PRODUCTS

| CLIPPER | STUDEBAKER SEDAN | | | STUDEBAKER HAWK | TRUCK |

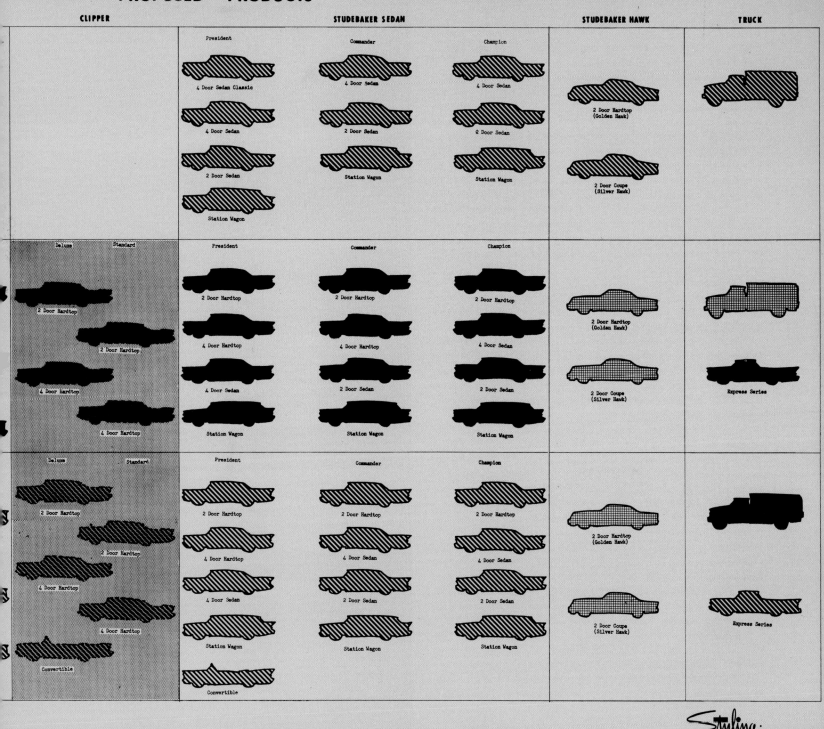

CLIPPER

Deluxe   Standard
2 Door Hardtop
2 Door Hardtop
4 Door Hardtop
4 Door Hardtop

Deluxe   Standard
2 Door Hardtop
2 Door Hardtop
4 Door Hardtop
4 Door Hardtop
Convertible

STUDEBAKER SEDAN

President
4 Door Sedan Classic
4 Door Sedan
2 Door Sedan
Station Wagon

Commander
4 Door Sedan
2 Door Sedan
Station Wagon

Champion
4 Door Sedan
2 Door Sedan
Station Wagon

President
2 Door Hardtop
4 Door Hardtop
4 Door Sedan
Station Wagon

Commander
2 Door Hardtop
4 Door Hardtop
2 Door Sedan
Station Wagon

Champion
2 Door Hardtop
4 Door Sedan
2 Door Sedan
Station Wagon

President
2 Door Hardtop
4 Door Hardtop
4 Door Sedan
Station Wagon
Convertible

Commander
2 Door Hardtop
4 Door Sedan
2 Door Sedan
Station Wagon

Champion
2 Door Hardtop
4 Door Sedan
2 Door Sedan
Station Wagon

STUDEBAKER HAWK

2 Door Hardtop (Golden Hawk)
2 Door Coupe (Silver Hawk)

2 Door Hardtop (Golden Hawk)
2 Door Coupe (Silver Hawk)

2 Door Hardtop (Golden Hawk)
2 Door Coupe (Silver Hawk)

TRUCK

Express Series

Express Series

Styling
DIVISION OF STUDEBAKER PACKARD

The 1957 Packards were introduced during the last days of January that year. The company had been putting out word of this late debut for some time, but few knew what to expect. Pre-announcement releases were impressive: "The new and different Packard Clipper sedan is two inches lower, 300 pounds lighter and twenty percent better in acceleration and performance than previous Packard Clipper cars. Representing a major move toward parts and body interchangeability, a two-year goal of the company, the new Packard Clippers are the first to be made in South Bend, Indiana, following the company's consolidation of all automobile manufacturing there. The pioneer auto company will concentrate its Packard program for 1957 in the medium price field which has accounted for eighty percent of Packard sales during the last two years." One look at the photograph which accompanied this press release, however, brought the reader up short with the certain knowledge of how the "parts and body interchangeability" had been accomplished.

It was a Studebaker.

It was, be it said, a particularly *good* Studebaker, with a 275 hp engine, Twin Traction option, many standard equipment features and a luxurious interior with a scaled-down Packard style dash. It was fitted with Studebaker's variable-ratio steering, finned brake drums, variable-rate coil springs. Teague had carried over the 1956 Clipper taillights and resurrected 1955's hood ornament and lettering, with side trim reminiscent of 1956. There was a station wagon model, the first on a Packard since 1950, and prices were right: $3212 for the sedan, $3384 for the wagon.

But public reaction was not good. The car was in no way a Packard, or anything like one. Gone were the torsion bars, the mighty 352 and 374 V-8's, the pushbutton transmission. Calling it Packard Clipper, though, assured some optimists that a big Packard was coming along behind it, if patience could be endured. The dealers did not discourage this notion; and a goodly number of them believed it too. Many company people had not really given up.

The *real* interchangeability program, now entirely out of the picture, would have given people who like Packards a lot more to cheer about. Despite the common body shell, the Fifty-Seventh Series Packard was to have had an identity all its own, while Clipper and Studebaker would be more similar, sharing some outer panels. This program was modified many times, postponing some new tooling and shuffling the lines around before being canceled altogether. Its original shape is discussed here.

Initially there were to have been three different wheelbases: 120 inches for Studebaker, 125 inches for Clipper, 130 for Packard. Four different models comprising four- and two-door sedans, four-door hardtops and wagons were proposed for the Studebaker Champion, Commander, Regal and President. Clipper was to retain its three Deluxe,

624

Pages preceding: "Styling Proposed Body Program" from circa March 1956, the grid-lined cars indicating a major facelift, the diagonal-lined a minor facelift, the solid a new body. These pages: Proposed '57 models derived from the common body program. The Clipper, above; the all-new Studebaker, below; the Patrician four-door hardtop and the Caribbean, above right; the Four Hundred, opposite.

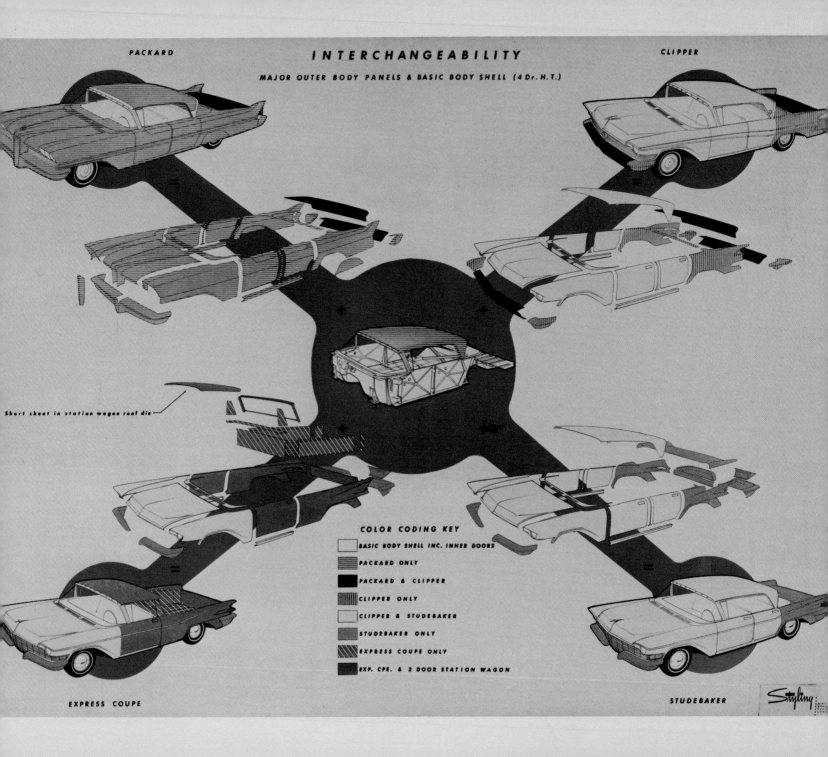

INTERCHANGEABILITY

MAJOR OUTER BODY PANELS & BASIC BODY SHELL (4 Dr. H.T.)

PACKARD

CLIPPER

Short sheet in station wagon roof die

COLOR CODING KEY

- ⬜ BASIC BODY SHELL INC. INNER DOORS
- ▨ PACKARD ONLY
- ⬛ PACKARD & CLIPPER
- ▥ CLIPPER ONLY
- ⬜ CLIPPER & STUDEBAKER
- ▨ STUDEBAKER ONLY
- ▨ EXPRESS COUPE ONLY
- ▨ EXP. CPE. & 2 DOOR STATION WAGON

EXPRESS COUPE

STUDEBAKER

Styling

Super and Custom lines with the same model mix as Studebaker but no wagon. Packard would have used the four-door sedan and two hardtops, plus a convertible and limousine derived from the tooling of other models. A 1957 interchange chart shows:

Packard (standard, deluxe versions)	four-door sedan
Packard (standard, deluxe, Caribbean)	four-door hardtop
Packard (standard, deluxe, Caribbean)	two-door hardtop
Packard (deluxe, Caribbean versions)	two-door convertible
Packard (Caribbean only)	limousine

The above lineup would have required one basic front end tooling, three roof panels, three doors, two door frames and two rear quarter panels. For the limousine Packard would either locate a supplier or do the work itself, modifying the rear doors and roof panel. It seems unlikely that it would have been marketed as a Caribbean.

Predictor styling was apparent in these cars: quad headlights, a narrow upright grille in the Packard classic outline, a restyled and refined cathedral taillight, a reverse-slant back window and a stainless steel strip fore to aft. Clippers and Studebakers were more "Fifties modern," having fins and appendages in profusion. In addition, the Studebaker Coupe Express was evolved from the same shell, which would have put S-P in the passenger-car-styled pickup business with the El Camino and Ranchero.

Inclusion of Studebaker in the interchange program survived partway through 1955. Bremer wrote Nance on June 30th that "Styling and Engineering, together with [Product Planning], thoroughly evaluated the possibility of reworking the clay model originally considered for our 1956 and 1957 Studebaker model [done by Loewy Studios]. Styling felt that it would be impractical to rework this model and end up with a satisfactory composite vehicle that would be competitive in line with anticipated competitive developments. Moreover, after checking into timing factors, it was determined that an extensive amount of engineering work would still have to be done to cover the styling changes considered necessary and this situation purportedly would have offset the timing advantages indicated earlier."

At this point Styling came up with its "one-plus" body program, to include Studebaker, and Bremer said if the entire program failed "we will then divert to a program of 'face lifts' for the 1957 models."

By the latter part of 1955 clays had been completed on the hardtop and sedan models, engineering was proceeding satisfactorily, and Budd had taken on the work for the doors of all models. Minor problems were encountered, the most serious of which was "the alignment of tool sources and the assignment of parts and assemblies . . . the tool shop program has reached an abominable status never before known in the industry."

Bremer wrote Nance that he assumed the funds for the interchange program would be forthcoming in September 1955. They were appropriated, in token amounts, just enough to keep the program moving. By now, of course, the last act was nearing and losses were mounting.

Bill Schmidt in a memo to Nance on November 1st, 1955, said he was pleased with the 1957 Packard thus far: "Such major things as the impressive size, the refined good taste, the modern yet classic feel of the car have been designed into the basic structure." Schmidt noted traditional identification themes as the classic-shaped Packard grille, the textured metal side molding, the tall taillights, rear quarter flare and flush intersection of windshield and backlight glass planes to their respective sheet metal areas. He also mentioned that the deck line carried through the backlight into the metal package tray, "visibly lengthening the extent of the rear deck," although this was no first: Dutch Darrin had done it with the 1951 Kaiser six years before.

About the Clipper, Schmidt said it was a car "of a different nature . . . that should speak of speed, far-reaching design . . . in the Mercury-Olds market with a definite appeal to the younger set . . . Our biggest problem with this automobile [is in] hiding the fact that the body is the same as that of the Studebaker," which Schmidt said was itself very clean, easily facelifted and competitive.

Styling wasn't the only grand plan abuilding in those days—over at Engineering there was talk of a twelve-cylinder powerplant. Product Planning's Dick Stout, writing in the February 1962 issue of Packard Automobile Classics' *The Cormorant*, described this engine. "Essentially, it would be a 90 degree V-12, built on the new V-8 tooling. The manufacturing group proposed to do this by means of long blocks, bored first with eight cylinders; moved, and the added four bored. The crankshaft would have 30 degree split-throws to permit in-step firing. Bore and stroke would be the same as the 320-cubic-inch Clipper engine of 1955, for a resulting 480-cubic-inch total . . . just about the same as the 473-cubic-inch Twelve of 1935 to 1939 . . . So far as the writer knows, drafts were not laid out for this engine, unknown problems might have deterred it, but at least the project had steam behind it in early 1956."

Engineering sources agree that despite stubborn rumors to the contrary, a reincarnated Twelve never reached drawing-board stage. Nance, however, took a personal interest in the program and Bremer kept him informed. The end of the idea actually came a little earlier than Stout remembered, at a meeting held on July 21st, 1955. On August 1st Bremer wrote Nance that the minutes of that meeting noted "further consideration of the V-12 engine for the 1957 models will be discontinued, principally because of inherent workloads on Engineering and the fact that available equipment cannot be practically utilized, thereby necessitating heavy capital outlays. Although I know you read the minutes of the meeting, I felt it was important enough to bring this specific section to your attention, in view of your past interest. . . ."

Proposed 1957 interchangeability chart.

Above: Black Bess, the prototype in metal for the never-produced 1957 line of big Packards, and the last Packard built in Detroit.
Right: The Studebaker-based Packard Clipper country sedan and town sedan. Below: The town sedan interior.

By April 1956, no fewer than eight plans for future lines were being considered, involving the interchangeable body shell idea:

Plan 1: Total cost $50 million
1957: facelifted Studebaker, new common shell Packard and Clipper.
1958: new Studebaker from common Packard/Clipper shell.

Plan 2: Total cost $15 million
1957: facelifted Studebaker, Clipper dropped, Packard on Lincoln shell.

Plan 3: Total cost $47.3 million
1957: facelift of all 1956 models with no common shell until 1958.
(Questionable if dealer organization could survive with this.)

Plan 4: Total cost $44.5 million
1957: new Studebaker, facelifted Packards and Clippers.
1958: new Packard/Clipper on 1957 Studebaker shell.

Plan 5: Total cost $44.5 million
1957: facelifted Studebaker/Clipper, Packard on Lincoln shell.
1958: facelift of Studebaker/Packard, Clipper using Studebaker sheet metal.

Plan 6: Total cost $38.6 million
1957: facelifted Studebaker, new Clipper, Packard on Lincoln shell.
1958: new Studebaker, facelifted Packard and Clipper.

Plan 7: Total cost $51.3 million
1957: facelifted Studebaker, new Clipper, facelifted Packard.
1958: new Studebaker/Packard, facelifted Clipper.

(Noted, "very costly in total tooling.")

Plan 8: Total cost: $48.3 million
1957: facelifted Studebaker/Clipper, new Packard on two wheelbases.
1958: new Studebaker/Clipper, facelifted Packard.

The main purpose of this exercise in futility was to provide *something* in the way of a new car plan for the dealers in 1957 with a minimum of expense. Studebaker-Packard felt that its dealer organization would not hold together unless it had something new that year. It was clear by then that the original program would not have worked owing to the cost involved, and the plan finally recommended was number seven, which would have given dealers a new Clipper in 1957 with a December announcement, following facelifted Packards and Studebakers in October.

Before Ford declined to furnish Lincoln bodies, Nance had tried to tie in this connection. Teague's work-up for this alternative "had standard Lincoln doors and greenhouse, and we'd hang Packard bits on the front; and it was quite a good-looking vehicle."

While Teague was at work on the Packard ideas, Duncan McRae had been given the same job for Studebaker—this time on the new 1957 Ford body. McRae, who had helped mold the outstanding 1951 Kaiser and who later went to Ford, had been recruited by Roger Bremer and moved from Creative Industries to South Bend, where his first unpleasant job was "to hasten the departure of the Loewy personnel." McRae had barely set up his studio and put the common body program into motion from the Studebaker side of the house when the money began thinning out and he found himself on the Ford project. As had the Lincoln proposal, this idea died; McRae says that he later learned "the 1957 Ford and our Studebaker proposal had too much in common."

With the escape routes blocked, S-P marketing turned its entire 1957 output on two styles of facelifted Studebakers, and the role of Packard Styling ground to a halt. Teague, Schmidt and many on their staff left to work for William Schmidt Associates, as consultants to Chrysler. Teague recalls the period as "the worst year and a half I ever spent. After that I went to American Motors as assistant director of styling in September 1959. I saw the '60 Rambler, and I almost walked out the front door. It looked like it was chiseled out of marble with a square roof. . . . An English stylist who was there with me said, 'My God, Dick, it looks like a ruddy ordnance vehicle.' "

What was left of Packard—and Studebaker—was now operating under Curtiss-Wright aegis; much of the management had passed back to the hands of South Bend people, but Roy Hurley was the real power. "Hurley has never headed a car division of a major auto company," said *Fortune*, "but he is about to have the time of his life showing his old Detroit friends what Roy Hurley can do in their damned business." Hurley's major auto company had lost $95 million during the first half of 1956; he now trimmed its net worth from $119 million to $23 million. The balance represented the defense business which C-W now controlled, plus the Detroit holdings that were being sold off in haste, plus the Studebaker Los Angeles equipment, sold at auction late in 1956.

One of Hurley's first programs was diversification. Through just such a program he had reduced C-W's dependence on defense work to about half its total income. He made no progress for the first two years, except to set up Mercedes-Benz according to his original proposals to S-P. But he kept at it, and in the meantime he advised the world that if S-P didn't soon turn in a good profit, "a lotta people will just get fired."

Studebaker people may have thought they had it rough before. Now they had Hurley. "Who are you going to fire this week?," one executive is reported to have asked him glumly during a visit. His interests, of course, lay first with Curtiss-Wright, but that did not preclude his hoping for S-P's success. The tax write-offs it provided could not continue forever, and C-W could expect generous treatment by the government if it could secure S-P's good health. But in doing his job Hurley shattered a lot of nerves, and for many he came in right on top of Nance, the first dose of "thunder and lightning." Said one Studebaker veteran, "We felt like an occupied country."

The 1957 Packard Clipper, though named with tradition in mind, was only a holding action, and the future of the Packard car remained in doubt throughout much of 1957. There was a very real interest in South Bend in seeing it return, for nobody had any illusions about being able to resurrect the marque once it had actually departed. If only it could somehow be glued together until a new, big Packard could be brought into production . . .

Hurley did not deny such speculation, and may have favored the resurrection of Packard himself. But there was a big obstacle in the way: S-P profits. They had to appear, and quickly. If a future was to be built, Studebaker sales had to be escalated. Until then Packard would have to wait. Sales did rise occasionally in the years ahead, but never long enough or well enough for Packard to have a chance. Further barriers to such a revival were physical: South Bend lacked big car assembly lines, though innovation might have solved this problem—the later Avanti was built in a separate plant, for example.

When S-P scored a net loss of $11 million for 1957, it became obvious that no big Packard would be forthcoming in the near future. Packard sales for 1957's model year totaled 4809, of which 3940 were the sedan. Nineteen fifty-eight would have to see another Packard holding action. This time, it would be wholly different. Churchill said the coming year would give Packard its own unique personality again. There was no doubt about that—unique was a most apt description.

Responsibility for the general 1958 Packard lines rests with Roy Hurley. According to Duncan McRae, Hurley "had seen a Ferrari during one of his European trips and asked me to attempt to use the design theme on a Hawk. It was my opinion that we were doing a one-off special job for him, and I still believe that was the original intent." But shortly the design was ordered into production as the Packard Hawk. Around South Bend, it was called the Hurley Hawk.

The 275 hp supercharged hardtop was mechanically identical to the Studebaker Golden Hawk. McRae added a fake continental tire to the deck and a large downward slope to the hood with a wide mouth encompassing black mesh grillework and prominent bumper. The Packard coat of arms appeared on the continental tire hub, there were hexagons on the wheel covers, and the interior was nicely done with leather upholstery and white-on-black instruments set into Studebaker's engine turned dashboard. There were even padded exterior armrests to lean on, nice on a summer day. But the Packard Hawk was a bizarre vehicle. At $3995 more people by far disliked it than admired it, and total sales were only 588.

The 1958 line comprised three other Packards. Studebaker had come up with a graceful new hardtop roof (used only in 1958) which had, according to one stylist, been lifted in nearly every line from DeSoto; this was offered in Packard Hardtop guise for $3262. There was also a sedan, at $3212, and a wagon at $3384. None of the three "family" type vehicles had superchargers, and each was equipped with fourteen-inch wheels. But they were all very uniform. One looked about as bad as the other.

"It was felt that somehow we must come up with a vehicle with twin headlights," says McRae, "since that was the industry trend. And since there was no money for fenders, we came up with a pod design that, looking back today, seems ridiculous; but in the short period of time that was available, it seemed to give us something new-looking. The rear fins were also tacked on the old quarter panels and we only hoped to survive until our new small car could be introduced." The faithful 1956 Clipper taillights rode again, this time in a double fin, one up and one out. The hood ornament was replaced by a single scoop, and the Clipper name and helmwheel were retired forever.

As in 1957, the 1958 cars were mechanically good machines, but they would not sell well as Packards because they weren't Packards. The large front grille-scoop had been combined with a long side sweepspear to give the car every millimeter of apparent length McRae could muster, but a 116-inch wheelbase (sedan and hardtop) was no way to turn out a Packard. Only 2622 altogether were built, and production was so low that no "Packards" were built in Canada at all.

When the 1958 model year ended, Studebaker-Packard had barely survived. But the 1959 Lark compact was to be completely different, compact in size and clean in design, and that year at least, S-P would turn a profit. Without Packard. The announcement of its departure came July 1958. Curtiss-Wright's departure was not far behind: The management

Clockwise from above left: Harold Churchill, Sherwood Egbert, Roy Hurley.

Above and below: As the news releases from the public relations department of Studebaker-Packard phrased it, the "1958 Packard Hawk, V-8 supercharged 289-cubic-inch engine generating 275 hp, with luxury leather interior."
Right: The 1958 Packard station wagon, hardtop and four-door sedan models.

agreement was terminated in October, ending an unproductive $65,000-a-month drain on S-P's limited finances.

It was all so very anticlimactic. The 1957 and 1958 "Packards" would not have been introduced at all had not a "big Packard" been held out as a possibility. They were worthy enough as cars, for their time, but as the company had said many years before, "Only Packard Can Build a Packard."

The old organization had been killed off in stages: first by turning it into a production car firm; next by dropping all handwork in the Senior cars; next by ceasing to manufacture large cars at all; finally by dropping the nameplate, which was merely an act of mercy.

To the news that it would never be built again, The Man Who Owned One reacted with disbelief. Even now, people simply refused to accept the inevitable. "We'll just keep driving the old one until some new ones are available," many said. Story after story circulated about the new, large Packard ready "in a year or two," and many waited for the announcement which never came.

Most rumors contain a grain of truth, of course, and there were some efforts to restore the marque to the ranks of the living. An S-P executive let it be known that sales success with the new Studebaker Lark would be followed by further development of the Hawk, and as soon as *that* became profitable, company attention would be turned to Packard. He even speculated as to whether it would have sidemounts! Another serious attempt at revival came from the outside, when a group approached Harold Churchill in 1960 with a proposal to import some 100 to 130 Facel Vega Excellence sedans from France, to be fitted with leftover Packard 374 engines, and a Packard grille, and to sell in the $14,000 range. Churchill was ready to go when Daimler-Benz objected—the Mercedes-Benz 300 model would have to compete against it.

The last chance for a revival came when Studebaker's later president Sherwood Egbert tinkered with name ideas for a new grand touring car in 1961-1962 and considered Packard, as well as Pierce-Arrow, to which S-P was entitled out of previous adventures. The name chosen was,

The Packard Stati

however, Avanti.

While the Packard name sank deeper into history, the company was getting along fairly well without it. The Lark's introduction turned fortunes around to a $28.5 million profit in 1959, though the entry of the Big Three automakers into the compact market in 1960 assisted in slashing this to less than $1 million in 1960 and only $2.5 million in 1961. Meanwhile, Hurley's diversification was showing results: The company began to pick up profitable firms, including Cincinnati Testing Labs (plastics and space research), and Gering Plastics in 1959. In 1960 it added Gravely Tractors, Clarke Floor Machine Company, and D.W. Onan & Sons (generators). In 1961 came Chemical Compounds Company (STP).

By the time Harold Churchill resigned as president, on September 2nd, 1960, he was a hero in South Bend and Studebaker-Packard was making solid progress. Some have said he was no hero to the company board, since he refused to scuttle the auto business which was not making profits that were at all significant. The new president, Clarence Francis, characterized himself as too old for the job and did not want to permanently deal with hostile stockholders. He immediately embarked on a talent hunt, and six months later S-P had hired its third mover and shaker since 1952. This time it was going to suffer an overdose.

Sherwood Harry Egbert came from McCulloch Motors, and was hailed in the 1960 annual report as a man with "a remarkable record of accomplishment [who] should give the Corporation the type of dynamic leadership so necessary in our present challenging situation." Egbert took over with an iron hand, running the company in a personal style. He pushed diversification so hard that Studebaker eventually ended up owning an airline, and he forced Studebaker's name into every headline imaginable with a display of record-setting Bonneville runs. He was himself responsible for a host of options and models, in some cases setting a pace that the auto industry was still attempting to match ten years later. He put Studebaker into the diesel truck business and into sporty cars, and drove his Avanti around South Bend with gusto, occasionally run-

ning publicity-getting duels with the local police. He took his coat off to fight with strikers in front of a picketed gate. He was a dynamic president, in many ways resembling James Nance.

For awhile it appeared that Egbert had pulled it off. The big billboard at the South Bend exit of the Indiana East-West Toll Road read "Studebaker: Flying High!"—and the company was doing well despite a crippling strike in January 1962.

In a notice to stockholders of the annual meeting to be held on April 26th, 1962 came Egbert's recommendation for the future of Packard: There wasn't going to be any. To be successful the company would concentrate on one product. "There will be presented to the meeting a proposal to change the name of the Corporation to Studebaker Corporation. The Board of Directors of the Corporation has given this proposal extended consideration and believes such a change would be beneficial to the Corporation and its shareholders. The Corporation's present name was assumed in 1954 upon the combination of the businesses of Packard Motor Car Company and The Studebaker Corporation. In 1958 production of the Packard car was discontinued. The present corporate name has become anachronistic as a result of the termination of the Packard car production and is a hindrance to the development of a new and more vital corporate image. If the proposed change of name is approved, the manufacture of vehicles in South Bend, Indiana, would be conducted by what would be called the Studebaker Division of the Corporation."

The length of time required to irrevocably kill the word Packard may have been indicative of its strength. Many criticized the change, though it was difficult to see a good reason for retaining the Packard name, with market conditions then existing and the problems facing the company. It would have been rather like waving a bloody shirt in front of the customers; the auto buyer does not wish to be associated with failure.

Still a ghost remained, in the form of a Michigan corporation, the Packard Motor Car Company, twice removed. A profit of $2.6 million was made by Studebaker in 1962, but not by automobiles, which had

The Packard Hardtop

The Packard 4-Door Sec

shrunk from over four-fifths of the total business in 1959 to barely more than half. While the subsidiaries had been originally acquired as a means of propping up the car business, they now began to look more attractive as a primary *raison d'être*. About this time it was observed that not one person on the company's board owned a single share of Studebaker stock. Members shrugged this off with the rationale that, being directors, they were expected to have some business sense.

The 1963 Studebakers were disappointing sellers and the Avanti suffered from production problems and consequent unavailability; Egbert had to settle for a mild facelift for 1964, despite ambitious plans for several unique new vehicles with Brooks Stevens, the Milwaukee industrial designer. Egbert could hold the board at bay only so long as he could keep selling cars, and in November 1963, he resigned. The new president was Byers Burlingame, formerly the comptroller. This time there would be no more nonsense: The automobiles would have to go.

Car and Driver later referred to Burlingame as "the undertaker." Though few believed it at the time, this was his role exactly. His first move was the celebrated closing of the South Bend plant just before Christmas of 1963. Automotive operations except for the engine plant, forge and minor stampings were transferred to the company's facilities in Hamilton, Ontario, with the stated hope that this plant would be able to show a profit on low volume as it had done for many years.

Byers Burlingame had been with Packard since 1925, but if anyone expected a sudden re-emergence of the marque under his presidency, the anticipation was doomed to disappointment. The 1963 loss had been $16.9 million, and the cost of closing the South Bend plants totaled $64 million. Burlingame's job was to turn in profits and rid the company of the cars as soon as practical if they could not make a profit.

The Hamilton plant had operated profitably on 8000 units yearly, and Burlingame said, "We have decided to live with the sales we have." But once Hamilton was forced to assume all the overhead expense of the automotive division, it was incapable of running in the black. With that, the Studebaker automobile was as washed up as the Packard before it. The Canadians under Gordon Grundy were making a good-faith effort and had no intention of stopping, but of course they had no research and development of any kind whatsoever, no engineering or styling departments at all. On Friday, March 4th, 1966, the end came; typically for this board, the news media had the story before the Hamilton plant did. While the radio was carrying the announcement, the assembly lines were still moving in Canada.

Now at last Studebaker was free to make real money. Burlingame had accomplished his assignment with cool efficiency. The South Bend plants were sold off and, in a series of mergers with Wagner Electric and Worthington, the company stepped away from automobiles to become a faceless conglomerate: Studebaker Worthington Inc. This was, ironical-

ly, exactly what S-P board director Abraham Sonnabend had had in mind a half decade earlier when, during a stormy 1960 board meeting, he had attempted a takeover with the intention of eliminating car production. Losing to Egbert then, he had left the board bitterly. Now the board was willing to try his approach, though Sonnabend wouldn't be present to run it. Simultaneously with the arrival of the millennium, in 1967, Burlingame stepped down as S-W president: "Quarterly dividends of 25 cents per share were commenced on the Corporation's common stock."

The fall of both Studebaker and Packard proves that a borderline company can endure only so many shakeups by new personalities from the outside. Studebaker's money problems came from the failure of an established product line to sell for little good reason. Packard's problem was different; certainly there weren't enough customers in 1954 and 1956, but two such years over time would not sink a strong company. It took many reverses from 1929 to 1956 to do that.

Obviously, had not the errors of the Forties been made, the problems of the Fifties, even arriving simultaneously as they did, would not have loomed so large. And it is plain that Nance was the victim of irretrievably bad advice from Ray Powers and his manufacturing people who, caught up in the then-current fad for one-story factory layouts, sold him on the flawed Conner Avenue plant. Further, seen from a distance, it may justifiably be said that the insurance companies, by refusing S-P the financing it had considered routine, killed Packard as surely as if they had used a gun.

Packard has been called "the car we couldn't afford to lose." The observer of today, considering all the company's strengths, can only ponder the tragic reverses that lost the company for us all. But thanks largely to those enormous strengths, maintained for such a long time, Packard has passed magnificently into folklore. There are more Packards on the road today than any other automotive "orphan" except Studebaker—which out-produced Packard by two or three or four to one—and among collectors it still remains, as ever, the "soft spoken boss of the road." Enthusiasts of the marque have happier thoughts to ponder than the company's heartbreaking end, thoughts of James Ward Packard, tinkering with his ideas; of Sidney Waldon, bouncing over the snows from Detroit to Chicago in Gasoline Gus; of Henry B. Joy who always had to "do something, even if it's wrong"; of Jesse Vincent, the sterling engineer, who brought us the Twin Six; of Alvan Macauley, the very personification of Packard for nearly forty years; of Gubitz, the classic designer; of the great engineers like Van Ranst, McFarland, Graves; of Dick Teague and Bill Schmidt, laboring away in "the last days in the bunker." But observer and enthusiast alike usually end up pondering the ultimate question: Did it really have to happen?

No. It did not have to happen.

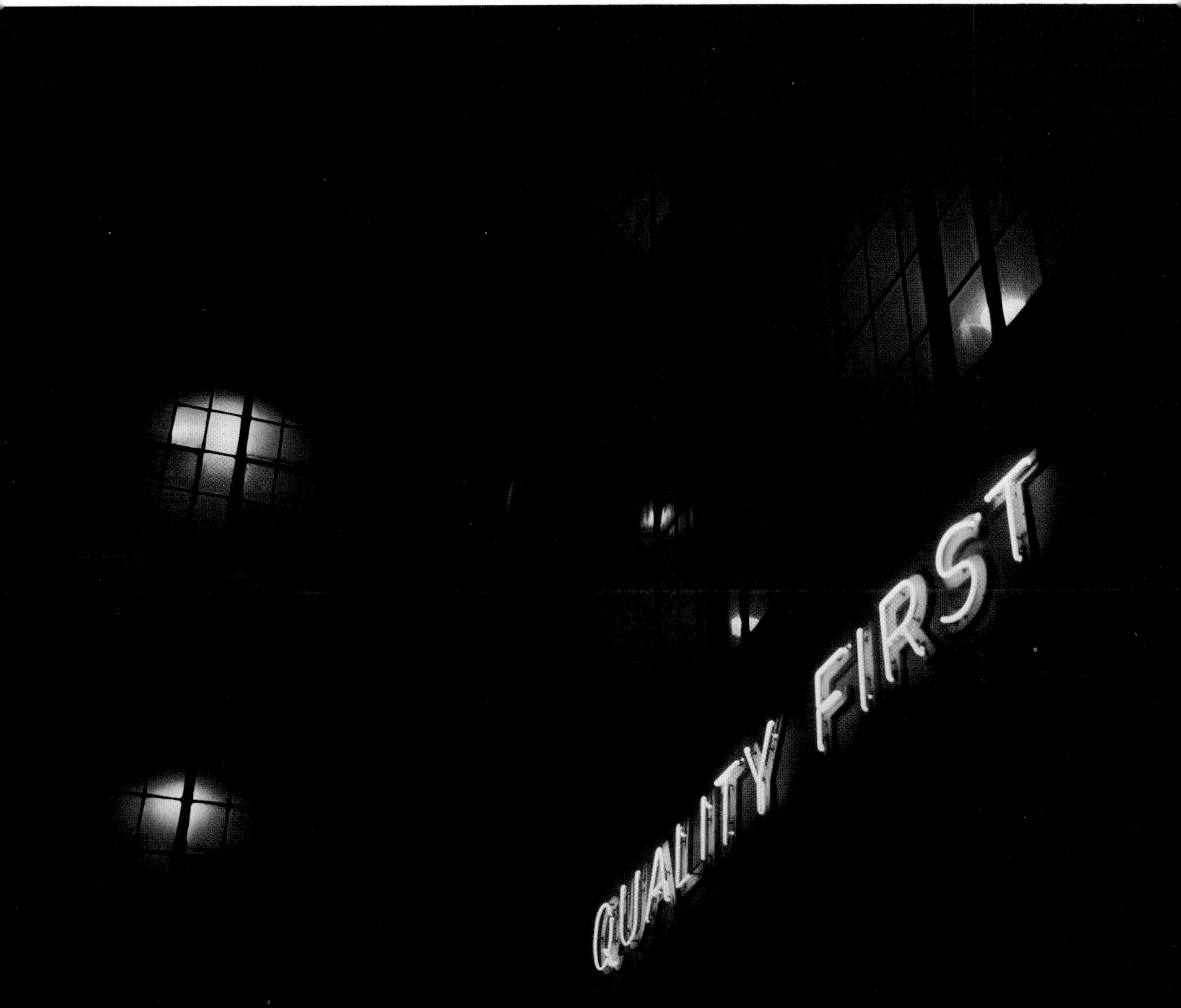
QUALITY FIRST

MOTOR CARS FROM THE COMPANY

Color Portfolio III
1938-1958

1938 Model 1608 Twelve Touring Cabriolet by Brunn

637

1938 Model 1608 Twelve Phaeton by Derham

1938 Model 1608 Twelve All-Weather Cabriolet by Brunn

639

1939 Model 1703 Super-8 All-Weather Panel Brougham by Rollson

1940 Model 1808 Custom Super-8 One-Eighty Touring Sedan by Bohman & Schwartz

1940 Model 1800 One-Ten Club Coupe

1939 Model 1708 Twelve Touring Limousine

1940 Model 1806 Custom Super-8 One-Eighty Convertible Victoria by Rollson

1940 Model 1807 Super-8 One-Eighty Convertible Sedan by Darrin

1941 Model 1906 Super-8 One-Eighty Convertible Victoria by Darrin

1941 Model 1901 One-Twenty DeLuxe Touring Sedan

1941 Model 1903 Super-8 One-Sixty Club Coupe

1941 Model 1901 One-Twenty Station Wagon

1941 Model 1900 One-Ten Station Wagon

1941 Model 1906 Custom Super-8 One-Eighty Convertible Victoria by Bohman & Schwartz

645

1941 Model 1951 Clipper Touring Sedan

1942 Henney-Packard Ambulance

1947 Custom Super Clipper Touring Sedan

647

1947 Custom Super Clipper Touring Sedan

1948 Eight Station Sedan

1949 (Twenty-Third Series) Eight Club Sedan

1952 Patrician 400 Touring Sedan

1952 250 Convertible

1952 Pan American Show Car by Henney

1954 Patrician Touring Sedan

1953 Mayfair Hardtop

1954 Pacific Hardtop

656

1955 Caribbean Convertible

1955 Clipper Custom Constellation Hardtop

1955 Four Hundred Hardtop

1956 Executive Touring Sedan

1956 Patrician Touring Sedan

1956 Caribbean Hardtop

1957 Clipper Country Sedan

1958 Hardtop

Owner and Photographer Credits

1938 Model 1608 Twelve Touring Cabriolet by Brunn
Owner: William Walker
Photograph by Henry Austin Clark, Jr.

1938 Model 1608 Twelve Phaeton by Derham
Formerly Ellenville Motor Museum
Photograph by Henry Austin Clark, Jr.

1938 Model 1608 Twelve All-Weather Cabriolet by Brunn
Owner: Phil Hill
Photograph by Strother MacMinn

1939 Model 1703 Super-8 All-Weather
Panel Brougham by Rollson
Owner: Joseph Zacher
Photograph by Richard M. Langworth

1940 Model 1808 Custom Super-8 One-Eighty
Touring Sedan by Bohman & Schwartz
Owner: Roger Morrison
Photograph by Rick Lenz

1940 Model 1800 One Ten Club Coupe
Owner: R.L. Derbyshire
Photograph by Rick Lenz

1939 Model 1708 Twelve Touring Limousine
Owner: Duncan Langton
Photograph by Rick Lenz

1940 Model 1806 Custom Super-8 One-Eighty
Convertible Victoria by Rollson
Formerly Paul Haynes Collection
Photograph by Henry Austin Clark, Jr.

1940 Model 1807 Super-8 One-Eighty
Convertible Sedan by Darrin
Owner: William Parfet   Photograph by Rick Lenz

1941 Model 1906 Super-8 One-Eighty
Convertible Victoria by Darrin
Owner: Tom Mix   Photograph by Don Vorderman

1941 Model 1901 One-Twenty DeLuxe Touring Sedan
Owner: Dr. Gerald Dahlen   Photograph by Rick Lenz

1941 Model 1903 Super-8 One-Sixty Club Coupe
Packards International Motor Car Club
Photograph by Rick Lenz

1941 Model 1901 One-Twenty Station Wagon
Owner: Walter E. Gosden
Photograph by Henry Austin Clark, Jr.

1941 Model 1900 One-Ten Station Wagon
Owner: Duncan Langton   Photograph by Rick Lenz

1941 Model 1906 Custom Super-8 One-Eighty
Convertible Victoria by Bohman & Schwartz
Owner: Charles M. Hackbarth
Photograph by Rick Lenz

1941 Model 1951 Clipper Touring Sedan
Owners: Mr. and Mrs. Jeff Spellens
Photograph by Rick Lenz

1942 Henney-Packard Ambulance
Owner: Stanley Zimmerman
Photograph by Rick Lenz

1947 Custom Super Clipper Touring Sedan
Owner: Terry J. Knoepp
Photograph by Rick Lenz

1947 Custom Super Clipper Touring Sedan
Packard Automobile Classics
Photograph by Bud Juneau

1948 Eight Station Sedan
Owner: Walt Beck   Photograph by Rick Lenz

1949 (Twenty-Third Series) Eight Club Sedan
Owner: Robert Langton   Photograph by Rick Lenz

1952 Patrician 400 Touring Sedan
Owner: Jim Smyth
Photograph by Stan Grayson

1952 250 Convertible
Owner: George Miller
Photograph by Richard M. Langworth

1952 Pan American Show Car by Henney
Owner: John Hodgman
Photograph by Don Vorderman

1954 Patrician Touring Sedan
Packards International Motor Car Club
Photograph by Rick Lenz

1953 Mayfair Hardtop
Owner: Russ Barton   Photograph by Rick Lenz

1954 Pacific Hardtop
Owner: Al Roush   Photograph by Bud Juneau

1955 Caribbean Convertible
Owner: Ernie Snyder
Photograph by Stan Grayson

1955 Clipper Custom Constellation Hardtop
Packards International Motor Car Club
Photograph by Rick Lenz

1955 Four Hundred Hardtop
Owner: Richard Ryan
Photograph by Don Vorderman

1956 Executive Touring Sedan
Packards International Motor Car Club
Photograph by Rick Lenz

1956 Patrician Touring Sedan
Owner: Frederick Mauck
Photograph by Rick Lenz

1956 Caribbean Hardtop
Owner: Paul Sternbach
Photograph by Richard M. Langworth

1957 Clipper Country Sedan
Harrah's Automobile Collection
Photograph by Rick Lenz

1958 Hardtop
Owner: Robert R. Mitchell
Photograph by Rick Lenz

APPENDIX I

THE BIGGEST
PACKARDS
OF ALL

Motor Trucks

from the Company

AUTHOR: JOHN B. MONTVILLE

The idea came from Henry Joy. Having seen examples on the streets of Detroit early in 1903, he quickly wrote James Ward Packard in Warren that here was an automotive application "that will not be subject to seasons as in the purely pleasure vehicle." The major sales of the latter were in the spring and summer months. He was looking to a vehicle which would enjoy an almost year-round market. He wanted Packard to build a truck.

James Ward did, and the result—a delivery car on a 1903 Model F chassis with a handsomely executed "Packard Motor Car Co." legend painted on its rear quarter— was used around the factory for various errands. Later that spring, regarding one of the more shadowy vehicles in Packard's history, Joy wrote James Ward of his "okay to make up a few more M machines, one of them to be in the form of a delivery wagon." Whether this was done is moot, the Model M had posed problems from the beginning. Decidedly, however, James Ward Packard's interest in the commercial field was never more than superficial, and it was only after the company move to Detroit in late 1903 that Henry Joy could himself move on the idea of placing Packard among the ranks of truck manufacturers.

As the new factory was being sorted out, Joy had another truck built and put into company service. Accepting loads of up to 1 ¾ tons, it was a strange-looking vehicle, its driver's seat located on the right about midway between front and rear, surrounded on three sides by a flat bed body. With a special frame of channel steel supported by full-elliptic springs at the rear and semi-elliptics up front, it was powered by a two-cylinder (Model G), mid-mounted engine though, *The Automobile* noted, most of its other components were adapted from the single-cylinder Model F automobile. The truck was fitted with pneumatic tires and could achieve 20 mph fully laden. Next came a cab-over-engine design with coil pipe radiator, a photograph of this truck indicating that it used a two-cylinder engine, reinforced wood frame and dual solid tires on the rear wheels. This vehicle was built entirely in Detroit and had a "No. 3" painted on it, which would appear to indicate it as Packard's third commercial vehicle. Its capacity was approximately two tons and, like its predecessor, it was used around the factory.

Henry Joy recognized that, with literally thousands of horses in daily delivery service in every major city in the country, the potential for commercial motor vehicle sales was almost unlimited. But he recognized as well that the going would not be easy. Sales could not be made without extensive demonstrations; most owners of horse-drawn delivery equipment had to be convinced of immediate savings before investing their capital in what was then considered an unproven product. Only 700 motor trucks were produced industry-wide in 1904, a year which saw better than 22,000 passenger cars leave American factories.

Pages preceding: A Packard demonstrator bus crosses Woodward Avenue in Detroit.
Above: The experimental "engine-under-floorboards" truck built in 1904.
Left: The TA chassis, indicating armored wood frame, Model N automobile transaxle used as a jackshaft and transmission, and platform springs, an early automotive carryover from wagon-building practice.
Below: The Model TA 1½-ton capacity truck, introduced in late 1904, with stock stake-sides body by Packard.
Right, from the top: Several mining companies purchased TA's to haul high-value silver ore from rugged mine sites to local concentrators or shipping points; the early fleet sale of five identical units to the New York branch of a national express firm; a TA fitted with chemical tanks and fire-fighting gear by James Boyd & Brother of Philadelphia.

Thus, now anxious to enter the field, Henry Joy had his engineers work up a vehicle which he thought could most effectively demonstrate to potential customers the wisdom of horseless delivery service. It was the 1½-ton TA, the first prototypes of which were produced in late 1904, with commercially available versions following early in 1905, several of them quickly put to use as demonstrators in the Detroit area. That summer Packard advertised its wares in the special commercial vehicle edition of *The Horseless Age*. Better than a dozen manufacturers were represented in the issue; three of them chose to insert large double-page advertisements: Oldsmobile, Knox—and Packard. Once committed, Henry Joy liked doing things in a big way.

With a short ninety-four-inch wheelbase and sharp-cutting angles of the front wheels, the Packard Model TA was an easy truck to negotiate in tight spaces and therefore highly suitable for city delivery service. Although a stake-sides platform body proved popular, the diversity of individual users prompted Packard to sell the TA chassis separately, at a list price of $2500. By mid-1905 firms in Chicago, Buffalo, Baltimore and Boston were using TA's in fair quantity; the Adams Express Company of New York ordered a fleet of five, quite an order in those days; and the first export fleet (of three) was purchased by a mining company in Honduras for hauling gold and silver the ninety miles between the mines and the capital city of Tegucigalpa. Other TA's were sold for fire fighting and sightseeing purposes.

The Model TA's principal power train components were identical to those of the 28 hp Model N touring car, but the TA used only two cylinders as opposed to the automobile's four, and was rated at fourteen horsepower. Its midships-mounted jackshaft (the touring car's transaxle) drove a pair of side chains which, combined with gear reduction, gave the TA speeds of three, eight and twelve miles an hour in its three forward gears. Its frame was armored wood; wooden artillery wheels and solid tires were fitted.

The use of so many standard Packard parts was a boon with regard to maintenance, and the TA's removable seat panels provided easy engine access whether the truck was fully loaded or empty. There was much to admire in the TA, but in its design Packard made one significant error, unwittingly it seems, as witness the naïveté of the following statement appearing in *The Automobile* for March 28th, 1905: "The manufacturers express the belief that wear and tear on the motor and power transmitting mechanism will be less in a commercial vehicle than in a pleasure car, the truck not being subjected to the shocks occasioned by driving over rough roads at high speeds; and as the parts were built for the more severe service, their ability to stand the commercial work is considered excellent."

That conclusion did not take into account the fact that, as a measure of

durability, the TA's modest speed capability was almost completely mitigated by the dead weight of its payload. The propensity of most owners to overload their trucks was, perhaps, a decisive factor in Packard's decision to replace the TA. Wooden frames, even those braced with steel, did not provide much of an overload factor; all that was claimed for the 3000-pound Packard truck was that it had successfully carried as much as 4000 pounds without showing signs of stress.

While the TA was prominent in the trade press of 1905, little was heard of it thereafter, apparently because by 1906 Packard was at work on its successor, a more substantially built model with a higher capacity rating. Nineteen-seven saw the first prototype of this new truck; 1908 marked its final testing. The pilot model was in daily service as a Packard plant truck for nearly two years. Meanwhile, Packard truck sales slowed perceptibly.

The commercial vehicle industry itself grew slowly during this period, with only about 800 and 1000 trucks produced respectively in 1906 and 1907. Partially this was due to the Panic of '07. With credit tight, potential truck purchasers had to weigh the benefits of acquiring new models against short-term expenses. And coupled to poor economic conditions were the realities of a costly new product still in its developmental period with few manufacturers underwriting the costs of that development.

Fortuitously, the Packard TA's successor began production in the fall of 1908, just at the time of a revival in business confidence. The new model was named the TC, indicating that an interim design "TB" may have been tried and rejected, though the writer has been unable to discover any record of it. The TC had a nominal capacity of three tons, twice that of the TA, plus a much larger overload factor. (By 1908 most manufacturers had increased this safety margin after experience in the field, in order to avoid undue warranty claims.) Its frame was structural steel, many times stronger than the TA's armored wood. The location of its engine, up front, provided ease of access, and the use of the now-traditional Packard radiator and hood design presented a clean-cut appearance and made the vehicle identifiable as a Packard.

The new truck used the 24 hp engine of the Model S, its four cylinders cast in pairs. It was equipped with an Eisemann magneto and storage battery and coil, these together providing a more-than-adequate switch-starting ignition system. A three-speed transmission was combined with a jackshaft for double-chain drive, similar to the TA, but with service brakes located at the ends of the jackshaft and emergency brakes on the rear wheel drums. Because solid tires had been found to encourage excessive shakes and rattles at higher speeds, the engine was provided a governor so that the TC could not exceed 12 mph.

Initially, a flat bed body with hardwood floor and short stake sides was offered as standard with the TC chassis. The total price was $3850 and included finishing in Packard Blue for the body, driver's seat, engine hood and chassis frame, with cream yellow striping. The wheels were cream yellow with blue striping.

As noted, the TC's arrival was opportune. Many mercantile houses were snapping out of the recession by the end of 1908, with the desire for new delivery equipment and the means to purchase it. This business up-surge marked the beginning of the end for horse-drawn delivery. At the conclusion of the new century's first decade, the motor truck was clearly

Left, from the top: "Indestructable" steel wheels on a Model TC; the TC chassis with stock Packard stake-sides body and paint scheme; a TC for Peoples. Below: A TC owned by a Chicago wholesale food supply house; a Model Thirty passenger car rebuilt as a light delivery truck and bought by the Burroughs company.

the choice of the progressive merchant and manufacturer.

Truck production doubled between 1908 and 1909, with 1500 units being built industry-wide during the former year, 3300 during the latter. Two large department stores—Marshall Field in Chicago and John Wanamaker in New York—were quick to adapt the Packard TC for their delivery needs. Wanamaker's equipped their Packard trucks with a rather unique nesting or "false" body, consisting of a simple latticework frame with floor, which slid into the truck's van body from a large cart. The loading of the false body took place on various floors in the store; it was then taken down in an elevator and pushed into the van body of the waiting truck. This avoided blockages of sidewalks and awkward or excessive handling of bulky or expensive goods.

The TC truck well filled delivery needs of many businesses: Express services, breweries, furniture stores, food stores and building supply firms were among its best customers. Many moving and storage companies in the larger cities also began using van-bodied Packard trucks. From an initial run of twenty-seven for the last months of 1908, production at East Grand Boulevard reached 110 units in 1909, then jumped to 411 for 1910.

In addition to the TC chassis, the popular Model Thirty passenger car chassis also achieved a fair degree of success as a commercial appliance. The city of Detroit, for example, used a fleet of the cars as police patrols, and the Detroit Fire Department fitted out a Thirty as a squad car for the quick transport of manpower to the scene of a fire. Moreover, by about 1912, the company had embarked upon a program of rebuilding their old Model Thirty passenger cars for resale in commercial form. A special thirty-six-page catalogue was issued, illustrating what were called "Packard renewed cars for light delivery service." Already a cash register firm was using such vehicles, the company noted, which were rebuilt with extra heavy rear springs to provide carrying capacities of up to a ton, and answered the need for speedy delivery trucks of moderate capacity. Not coincidentally, this program would also provide for Packard a rather unique way to solve the ever-present trade-in problem.

With the outlook for their commercial division bright, the Packard Motor Car Company had begun early looking for opportunities to demonstrate the prowess of their vehicles. During the summer of 1909, a TC was lent to the Army for war maneuvers held in Massachusetts, and during a particularly wet and rainy period demonstrated its ability to reliably haul both supplies and men. Earlier in the same year another three-ton chassis had been fitted with a rapid-fire automatic three-pound cannon—said to be the largest automatic gun in the world—and proved suitable as a firm but mobile gun mount. But the Army was slow to adopt motor trucks on a wide basis. It would require a national emergency to change its thinking.

Perhaps the most outstanding and successful of Packard's truck demonstrations was the transcontinental run of a three-tonner in July and August 1911. The vehicle was fitted with a "prairie schooner" style body, complete with bowed canvas top, and carried a complete camping outfit, barrels of gasoline and oil, a fresh water supply and all sorts of rigging equipment for the rough passage. Walter T. Fishleigh of the Packard engineering staff was in charge, commanding a crew of two men from the experimental department, E.L. Burnett and Arnold Haener.

Leaving New York on July 8th, the Packard reached San Francisco on August 24th, forty-six days later. This had not, of course, been a run for a speed record, but it had been an adventure brimming with arduous challenges. Said Fishleigh: "We had heard about the Bitter Creek (Wyoming) bridge. It would not support a real heavy touring car. We stood on end as we went down into this canyon, then lugged rocks from the bridge pier, built a foundation for a skid bridge of our own, then strained every fiber in that truck as we jammed her up the vertical opposite bank, inch by inch with skids and blocking and all the human ingenuity we had with us." The rope and windlass came in handy on another occasion, west of Rawlins, when the crew lashed the vehicle to a telegraph pole to prevent it falling into a canyon after the approach to another bridge had caved in under it. Further obstacles in the western and some midwestern states included deep sand, potholes, sharp rocks, ruts, steep hills and washouts which measured up to twenty-five feet across. The enormously strong TC survived them all. There had not been a single mechanical breakdown, not a single component replacement (save for tires). It was with considerable pride that the Packard Motor Car Company advertised "the first motor truck to cross the continent entirely under its own power."*

Since its introduction as the TC in 1908, the three-ton chassis had been gradually improved, most of the changes involving modifications to the engine control and braking systems. In 1911 the Model TD succeeded the original, with a fully enclosed governor unit (on the TC the connecting shaft to the throttle was not enclosed nor was the governor sealed to prevent tampering), and the jackshaft service brakes were changed from internal expanding to external contracting. Front fenders also appeared on the new models. And appearing soon thereafter as well

---

*There was a reason for that particular wording. On March 1st, 1911, a 4½-ton Saurer truck had reached San Francisco from Denver, Colorado and, after demonstrating its virtues in various western states en route, was shipped back to Pueblo, Colorado for a reverse trip to New York City, where it arrived on August 2nd. Though the Saurer Motor Company immediately claimed this as a "first," it was not a continuous run, hence the Packard qualification, "under its own power."

Page opposite, from the top: The record-breaking transcontinental Packard, 1911; a Packard "five-tonner," 1912; a three-ton capacity truck of that era. Above: Another "three-tonner," most probably a Model ATD from 1912.

were two new trucks, the ATD and ATN, models shrouded in some mystery, though it is known that they were three-ton vehicles, both were built in 1912, and the ATN used a smaller 25.6 hp four-cylinder engine while the ATD used the TD's 32.4.

According to available figures, the industry nationwide turned out 10,681 trucks in 1911 and 22,000 in 1912, again a doubling of production in just a year's time. Packard truck volume rose handsomely as well, from 774 in 1911 to 1159 in 1912. By now the company had established itself as an important factor in a quickly growing market. Its sales during one month in 1912, reported *The Horseless Age*, "totaled 213 vehicles, amounting in value to $800,000. This is an increase of 24 per cent over the best previous total for a month's business, and said to be a world's record for actual sales to users of motor trucks." Packard also claimed its trucks were used in over 150 lines of business and in over 200 cities.

This marked acceptance of the three-ton model encouraged Henry Joy to broaden the line. A two-ton Model 2A had arrived in 1911, a five-ton Model 5A in 1912. These new models were similar to each other, and their progenitor, with the traditional Packard radiator and hood styling, as well as the combined transmission and jackshaft with chain drive. The 2-A used the 26.4 four while the hefty 5-A employed a four rated at 40 hp. All chain-drive Packards featured right-hand drive, with brake and gear levers mounted to the outside of the frames. Prices with standard equipment at the beginning of 1913 were $4500 for the 5-A, $3400 for

Above and below: Testing the prototype worm-drive Packard in the West during the summer of 1914. Note the Lincoln Highway poster attached to the body, which was the route the truck followed as closely as possible after leaving Detroit.

the 3-A (nee ATD) and $2800 for the 2-A (which with minor modifications had now become the 2-B). By now, too, all Packard trucks used a high-tension ignition system, the change from the low-tension type identified by a large coil box on the dash. The high-tension system used a magneto but did not depend on a coil for regular running, although a round coil recessed in the dashboard was used to assist in starting. In 1914 Packard rounded out its heavy-duty chain-drive truck line with the introduction of four- and six-ton units, most likely designated 4-A and 6-A respectively, the former priced at $3550, the latter $4300, both prices excluding bodies.

Increased demand for motor trucks after 1911 naturally attracted increasing numbers of manufacturers into the field of established marques like Packard, Knox and Mack. Three of these newcomers were firms known for high quality automobiles—Pierce-Arrow, Locomobile and Peerless—and they distributed their commercial vehicles through extensive dealer networks. The Pierce-Arrow heavy-duty truck introduced in 1911 used worm drive, which Pierce claimed was more efficient and trouble-free than chain. Whether this was completely true was a matter of dispute, of course, but worm drive's silence and lack of exposed moving parts were good selling points, and chain drive began to decline after 1912. The Packard Motor Car Company could not help but notice.

By 1913 Packard Engineering was working on a new series of worm-driven trucks, the first models of which were extensively tested during the summer of 1914. Officially introduced early in 1915, the line was designated with the letter "D," and ostensibly constituted a further expansion of the tonnage range with seven different models of one, one-and-a-half, two, three, four, five and six ton capacities. But, while the five- and six-ton worm drive units were announced and listed in several truck catalogues, no detailed specifications were ever printed and, as it turned out, the extra-heavy worm-drive Packards were not introduced until late 1916, as part of a new series of models.

This apparent jumping of the gun in announcing a complete line of worm-drive trucks before they were ready was most likely a public relations decision. Interestingly, in a statement published in *The Commercial Vehicle* issue of January 15th, 1914, H.D. Church,* Packard's chief engineer for trucks, defended the use of double-side-chain drive for trucks with capacities of two or more tons, noting twelve reasons (simplicity, durability, efficiency among them) for its superiority over other types of drive, including worm. The investigation into worm drive was probably a management decision based on the desire to reflect a modern image. Henry Joy's legendary penchant to always "do something" contributed as well. Then the inevitable production problems, coupled with the tremendous demand for the three- and four-ton chain-drive models, doubtless delayed final introduction of the 5-D and 6-D until they were about to be superseded by the corresponding models in the E series and, consequently, they were simply never produced.

While not radically different in appearance from its chain-drive predecessor, the new Packard "chainless" truck represented an almost complete break with past engineering practice. Every component—save wooden artillery wheels, structural steel frames and radiator shape—was changed. New were monobloc four-cylinder engines, service brakes on the driveshafts just behind the amidships-mounted transmission, and worm-drive rear axles with large torque arms pivoted to the front of the differential housing. Another important change was the placement of the steering wheel, brake and gearshift levers on the left side of the cab. The D series saw a repositioning of electric and carburetor controls on a pedestal-mounted console placed just below the steering wheel near the dashboard, this arrangement clearing the dash and steering wheel of a number of switches and levers and bringing them all within easy reach of the driver. The dashboard now presented an almost clear expanse, save for an oil pressure gauge mounted in the center. The only other gauge was a motometer mounted in its accustomed place on the radiator cap, in direct view of the driver. Rear spring hangers on the frame were outboard mounted so that chassis height could be lowered, allowing easier loading and unloading. Extra cost equipment included electric self-starting and lighting systems and power take-off attachments for the transmission whereby the engine could drive a winch, pump or a dump body hoist. The new Packards offered engineering refinements while at the same time presenting a clean design and the rugged construc-

---

*Although the writer has seen Mr. Church referred to as "Harold" in various historical publications, there can be no confirmation that this indeed was his name. Which is probably exactly what the gentleman would have wished. As *The Packard* joshed in its Autumn 1914 number: "Hamm, Hamilcar, Harlo, Hermann, Hubert, Hernando, or is it just plain Henry? We don't know. He signs his requisitions 'H.D. Church' and firmly refused to divulge for publication the label sprinkled upon him at the christening font." To the people at East Grand Boulevard, he was "Heavy Duty Church," and he came to his Packard post eminently qualified. He had attended Boston Tech, directed the building of the Waltham Manufacturing Company's light delivery trucks and was chief engineer at Mercer before joining Packard around 1912. And, incidentally, he—together with his colleague F. Van Z. Lane—would be among the engineers snatched from Packard for the empire Emlen S. Hare was planning in his reorganization of the Locomobile, Simplex and Mercer companies in 1920. Subsequent to that corporate debacle, he served in engineering posts for Kelly-Springfield Trucks, Chevrolet Motor Company, White Motor Company and Winton Engine Corporation.

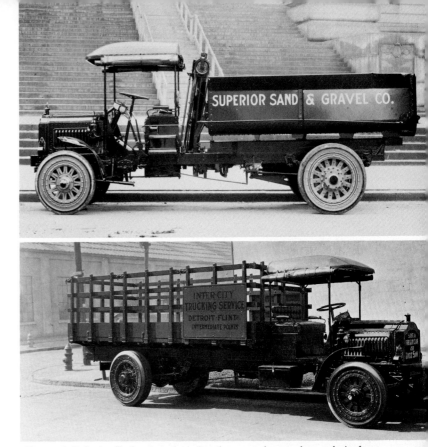

Above: A D Series Packard; note pedestal-mounted control console in front of steering gear, and brake and shift levers mounted on the left-hand side. Center: An E Series, with Sewell cushion wheels and "pro-truck" radiator slogan. Below: A popular utilization of the E Series, as a furniture mover.

tion established with the chain-drive vehicles. Their introduction was, as it turned out, perfectly planned, exactly on time for the Allied effort in World War I.

With increased massing of huge armies in northern France and parts of central Europe, motor transport took on a vital role in supplying the millions of troops involved. At first the British and French governments commandeered privately owned trucks and buses to help rush troops and supplies to endangered sectors of the front. By 1915, however, large contracts for military vehicles were placed with both European and American manufacturers.

Packard was the recipient of a number of orders during that year and in 1916 from England, France and Russia, amounting to several thousand army trucks. Domestic demand, increased at the same time, pushed factory output for 1915 to 4000 units, far exceeding the automobile production of 2645. In order to meet commitments, a 377,000-square-foot addition to the truck shops was built that year, located at the south end of the property, although in reality this plant enlargement had been dictated earlier, when a large backlog of orders caused Packard trucks to be turned out on a three-shift basis during the summer of 1914.

It was not long before America's booming export business in war materiél for England and France brought protests from the Central Powers, Germany and Austro-Hungary, the latter threatening to sink any ships carrying instruments of war to belligerent nations. The torpedoing of the Cunard liner *Lusitania* in May 1915, with the loss of many prominent U.S. citizens, helped stir up a war psychosis in America which favored the Allies. By 1916 "preparedness" had become an important concern in the United States. The fervor contributed to a precipitous incursion into Mexico by a large motorized American military force in the spring of 1916 to deal with the insurrectionist Pancho Villa, who had been raiding towns north of the border. The incident was to further dramatize the virtues of Packard trucks.

Early in March 1916, raiders believed connected with Villa had crossed the border and attacked the town of Columbus, New Mexico, burning several buildings and killing American citizens. Since Mexico had been suffering from an on-going revolution for several years and its political power was fragmented, the government in Mexico City did not have the force to stop Villa. American protests led to a call for unilateral U.S. action and an expeditionary force was gathered in late March. This resulted in the first large purchase of commercial vehicles by the U.S. War Department, which placed orders for immediate delivery with Locomobile, Jeffery and Packard.

The Packard Motor Car Company was by then in a good position to supply the trucks. Within a day twenty-seven of them were loaded on railroad flat cars for shipment to Texas. As part of the order, Packard supplied drivers and mechanics to accompany the trucks, accomplished by a call for volunteers at a mass meeting held at the factory. And Henry B. Joy supplied himself.

Packard's irrepressible president joined the expedition to hunt down the Villa forces as several columns of trucks entered Mexico from their base at Columbus. He was there, he said, to get a first-hand look at "the problems of motor transport," but he did not miss the opportunity to photograph Packard trucks in service for leading Detroit and New York newspapers.* The expedition proved to be a wild goose chase, for Villa never was located, but it did prove the inherent value of motor transport to the War Department, and by July over 700 Packard trucks were in American military service. Also in service was U.S. public opinion, by now keyed up to accept the country's open involvement in the Great War, which would come in April 1917.

Meanwhile, Packard had launched a moderate national advertising campaign domestically to promote its worm-drive models which was carried through 1916 and 1917. A house organ, *Packard Truck Digest*, was begun in March 1916 to illustrate and explain what the company product was doing in the service of owners. And newspapers and magazines carried pictures showing activities of Packard military trucks overseas, where they were by now serving on most European fronts.

To accommodate the ever increasing demand for trucks of all sizes, Packard enlarged its D series to include a 1 ½-to-1 ¾-ton model, and the one-tonner was now rated as a 1-to-1 ¼-ton vehicle. The prices for these two smallest models were $2500 and $2200, with standard equipment. Few were built, however, due to their relatively high prices and the huge call for larger models by the military and civilian markets. But in any guise the D series trucks had received considerable in-use testing since their announcement in 1915, testing which gave engineers data which under normal circumstances would have taken years to accumulate. The result was a new four-speed truck transmission for the line having a very low first, or "creeper" gear, and a direct drive fourth. The night and day operation of the truck plant was, however, allowing speedy amortization of D-series design and tooling costs, and it permitted management to unveil its brand-new E series late in 1916.

This series chiefly represented modifications to the previous line. While the transmission was still mounted amidships, the gear lever was moved to the driver's right, extending from the center of the cab floor. The emergency, or parking, brake lever remained at the driver's left side

---

*Ironically, this would be one of the last such "Packard trips" for Henry Joy. That summer he turned over the company presidency to Alvan Macauley, retaining the chairmanship of the board. The year following he left Packard altogether following a dispute with company directors.

*Page opposite: Packard truck production, on a three-shift basis by 1916.
Above: Progressive assembly methods, 1917, for Packard truck building; Packard army trucks being uncrated and assembled at a port in France.
Below: Half-track mockup. A few worm-drive Packards were so fitted, but such crawler units did not really become popular until World War II.*

at the edge of the cab. The shifting of the gear lever provided better driver access, and a left-hand running board was added to take advantage of it.

The E series featured a thermostat for better temperature control during extreme climatic conditions, and an odometer was standard equipment on all models. Made available as a $180 option, factory installed, was a special Packard-Bijur cranking/lighting system employing dashboard and rear lights. On the five- and six-ton models, cast steel disc wheels were standard, and Packard continued to offer a standard flat bed body with removable low slatted sides. Other body designs were available from the Hopkins Manufacturing Company of Hanover, Pennsylvania—and this company was recommended, and illustrations of its designs included, in the Packard truck catalogue.

Sales had reached an impressive 92,130 for the truck industry in 1916, and at Packard the total was an encouraging 5092. In 1917, the economy stimulated by American entry into the war, the figures were 128,157 and 7116 respectively. The 1917 E series consisted of seven models of various tonnage capacities: 1-to-1 ¼, 1 ½-to-1 ¾, 2-to-2 ¼, 3-to-3 ½, 4-to-4 ½, 5-to-5 ½, and 6-to-6 ½.

The American entry into World War I was the first real test of domestic manufacturing and transportation capabilities since the Civil War. Diversion of many parts of heavy industry to shipbuilding and armament manufacture, coupled with an already booming civilian economy, put a severe strain on the railroads' ability to provide the equipment and manpower with which to move freight. Shortages of

World War I. On the bloody Macedonian front. A convoy parading down Washington Boulevard in Detroit en route to an Eastern port and then the war zone.

Five- and six-ton worm drive Heavy Service Packards (above and below) were introduced in 1916. An army surplus Packard (center) converted to peacetime use.

freight cars became epidemic during 1917, creating such concern that Congress voted for federal operation of the railroads through the U.S. Railroad Administration from 1918 to 1921.

A major outgrowth of the rail crisis was the increased use of motor trucks to haul less-than-carload freight shipments between nearby towns and cities, especially where good roads allowed such activity to be profitable. But solid tires limited speeds. Goodyear Tire and Rubber Company decided to tackle this problem, and developed a line of pneumatic commercial vehicle tires, demonstrating them on a fleet of Packard, White and Mack trucks. This "Wingfoot Express" program was begun during 1917, and the Packard-White-Mack fleet served not only to expedite the delivery of Goodyear tires to the market and to bring raw materials back to the plant, but also to dramatize the long-distance hauling capabilities of pneumatic-tired motor trucks.

The railroad bottleneck also encouraged mass driveaways by auto dealers from factories to home markets, and by late 1917 the government had applied the same idea to military vehicles. The most obvious route from Detroit to Atlantic coast ports was through Toledo, Cleveland, Warren, Pittsburgh, Philadelphia and Baltimore—and December 14th found a convoy of thirty Packard army trucks leaving East Grand Boulevard on the first such journey. It arrived in Baltimore on the 28th. Poor roads kept the pace to about fifty miles a day, the convoy being held up for a total of three days en route. But all trucks arrived safely and brought with them a sixty-ton payload of spare parts. The success of this first convoy led to many more. America rode around the railroad bottleneck on rubber tires.

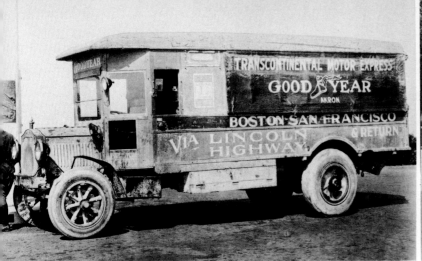

One of the Goodyear Wingfoot Express E Series Packards (above left) at the Betsy Ross Monument in San Francisco during a transcontinental run in 1918. Boom conditions at factories brought worker transport problems. Packard, among others, started its own bus service, doubtless a feeder to nearest street car line.

To Packard's H.D. Church goes the credit for the perfecting of worm-drive Packard trucks and for their practical military applications. Indeed Church served on the Army board responsible for preparing truck specifications for the war effort, his appointment to that post having been made by a former Packard engineering veteran and now S.A.E. president, Russell Huff. Under Church, Packard became the single largest producer of Army trucks for the Allied war effort, and the company built at least 6000 of them for U.S. forces alone. "Behind the Guns! Backbone of Army Transport," the company boasted in an advertisement of August 1917.

The war's end in November 1918 brought a feeling of tremendous optimism in the industry. The war had shown the skeptics what trucks could do and sales of the vehicles had grown almost tenfold in five years, from 24,900 in 1914 to 227,000 in 1918. Packard management showed a deep interest in furthering development of its truck line through both improved engineering and accelerated sales efforts.

For the 1919 E series, the 1-to-1¼ ton model was dropped and the list prices for standard equipped trucks were: 1½-to-1¾ ton, $3200; 2-to-2½ ton, $3600; 3-to-3½ ton, $4350; 4-to-4½ ton, $4550; 5-to-5½ ton, $5450; 6-to-6½ ton, $5700. A clean looking coupe cab and pneumatic tires on wooden spoked wheels were offered as options. The growing popularity of the pneumatic truck tire induced Packard to develop several models specifically for it, and these were tested and approved for production by late 1919.

Pneumatic-tired models were announced early in 1920 in one-and-a-half-, two- and three-ton capacities. Because of the larger diameter of the air-filled tires, and their higher speed capabilities (almost double that of solids), more power was consequently required. This was accomplished simply by moving the engines of one or two models down from the heavier to the lighter units. For example, the new three-ton Model EY used the same 40 hp engine as the five-ton Model EF.

Another important change for 1920 was a larger radiator, now a cast iron shell with separate header tank and bearing the die-cast Packard logo. (Plain, brass-bound radiators were last used on 1919 models.) Metal spoked wheels with demountable rims and a Kellogg tire pump, driven from a power take-off on the transmission, were standard equipment. Other .than the revisions in engine and radiator sizes, the pneumatic-tired models had the same construction as the solid-tire vehicles in frame and drive train.

The major drawback of the pneumatic-tired '20 models was their pricetags, averaging about a thousand dollars more than each version's solid-tired counterpart. The increase was due to the larger engines, special steel wheels and huge (and costly) pneumatics. In fact, high replacement cost of pneumatics caused many truck owners to stick with solid tires long after pneumatics had demonstrated their improved mileage and speed capabilities.

During World War I a Freight Transportation Department had been established by Packard to assist truck owners in economical operations, a service rendered not only in response to the transport crisis but in the hope of insuring customer satisfaction with a product of quite high initial cost. Packard recommended the National Standard Truck Cost System as a method for owners to oversee operating expenses. In 1919 the house

Above: A "trailer-bus" operated by the City of Detroit. Above right: The EF, Packard's largest truck, did not have a pneumatic-tired counterpart; a pneumatic-tired EX. Right: A trolley bus under test, 1921, and under its hood (far right).

organ *Freight Transportation Digest* was introduced to acquaint owners with the services of the new department, this publication superseding the *Packard Truck Digest*.

Transportation engineer F. Van Z. Lane spelled out Packard's "scientific approach" to truck selling, and probably surprised a good many colleagues at East Grand Boulevard by frankly stating that his company was "prepared to analyze, engineer and recommend the adoption of the best transportation system for any requirement. Perhaps the answer will be steamboats, possibly railroads exclusively. At all events it will be strictly the best that the freight transportation engineer . . . can devise to do the work most satisfactorily, all things considered."

Shortly thereafter, in 1920, an announcement was made that tonnage ratings by Packard would be discarded. A Packard transportation

678 representative would study the needs of the prospective truck purchaser,

and work performed, not the capacity of the unit, would be the deciding factor in truck size. Since all Packard trucks were essentially heavy duty vehicles having structural steel frames, this marked a major change to a more flexible policy toward product usage. Although capacities were no longer stated, general ratings can still be estimated from the specifications given for the Packard truck line in 1920.

Basically there were three capacity ranges, all sizes designated with the E prefix. The lowest was the EC, basically a two-ton unit priced at $3700. Its pneumatic-tired counterpart was the EX, capable of 30 mph versus the EC's 14 mph, and selling for $800 more.

The second capacity range was three to four tons, and for such load the ED was offered at $4450. Its pneumatic-tired alternative was the EY, at $5500, with a top speed of 24 mph, double the ED's.

The largest haulage unit was the solid-tired EF, offered to satisfy the needs of truckers carrying five- to six-ton loads but possessing a huge overload factor allowing burdens of up to eight tons. Because of its size the EF was restricted to only 11 mph, had steel disc wheels as standard and no pneumatic-tired counterpart. It listed at $5500. (No pneumatic-tired counterpart was produced in that capacity range by Packard's competitors either; pneumatics hadn't reached that capacity stage in their development and demand for them was lagging in any case.)

Meanwhile the industry offered other developments. "The Stage-Coach Comes Back—Motorized" headlined *The Literary Digest* in July of 1921, noting that in California alone approximately 1100 "motor-stages" were "traveling the highways of the State on regular schedules." The motor bus idea attracted a number of truck manufacturers which offered such models, usually on medium-duty truck chassis of one- to three-ton capacity and initially with only slight modifications although later special drop-frame models were developed. Packard made available slightly revised versions of its EC and EX trucks as motor bus chassis during 1921. Few were sold.

But, also in 1921, the city of Toronto decided to compare-test motor buses with straight mechanical and electric drive, as well as a new trolley bus. Packard was selected to supply the latter, for which was used a highly modified ED chassis. The order for four models called for Brill bodies and Westinghouse traction equipment in place of the normal engine and transmission. Testing of the Packard trolley bus took place under the auspices of the Detroit Department of Street Railways, and the product was pronounced satisfactory. In June 1922, the twenty-nine-passenger trolley buses were placed in service; all had received final assembly work by the Packard Ontario Motor Car Company.

Some Packards also found their way into fire departments. The company had never itself built fire-fighting appliances for its vehicles, but its Special Equipment Department prepared chassis using apparatus of firms specializing in such products. With nearly all fire apparatus sales resulting from "lowest competitive bid," it is not surprising that few Packards entered that service. Most of those which did used bodies and pumps supplied by the Northern Fire Apparatus Company, and were sold to a few communities in the East and Midwest.

For the most part the Packard company did not zero in on any specific vocational market; the nearest it had come was probably in the moving and storage field. Of course Packard had opened a large specialty market during the war, but that ended in 1918, and many of its military vehicles were sold as surplus or given to local and state road commissions in the early Twenties. Peace was found to have a disastrous effect on new truck sales. The Army surplus had been dumped on the market at an inopportune time, too, when the economic downturn in late 1920 cut capital spending. Most truck builders registered sales losses of over fifty percent in 1921.

PACKARD TRUCK PRODUCTION

The following figures represent those prepared by the Packard Motor Car Company as part of its official historical record.

Year	Units Built	Year	Units Built
1902	1	1913	967
1903	1	1914	1,381
1904	10	1915	4,000
1905	40	1916	5,092
1906	—	1917	7,116
1907	1	1918	5,930
1908	27	1919	6,668
1909	110	1920	5,907
1910	411	1921	1,331
1911	774	1922	2,145
1912	1,159	1923	466

NOTES: The company was most likely in error—a common occurrence in Packard historical records—regarding 1902 production. All available evidence indicates the first Packard commercial vehicle was built early in 1903 in Warren. Regarding the decidedly low production for the years 1906-1907, it might be noted that this represented the period during which Packard was developing the TC model truck, following the company experience with the TA which had indicated extensive design modifications were wise. Packard records the figure of 43,538 units as the total truck production over the two decades the company was in the commercial vehicle business. Doubtless not all prototypes or experimental vehicles are included in that figure.

Dramatically highlighted, the famous radiator shape on an early 1920's truck.

The postwar recession hit Packard similarly. Truck production plunged to 1300 units for 1921, and even with 1922 witnessing a rise to slightly over 2000, the handwriting was on the wall when dealers began to complain about the factory's forced allocations of trucks based on the number of passenger cars sold. The difficulty in maintaining a high truck-sale-percentage was heightened at the dealer level when in 1919 the passenger car line was broadened to include a new Single Six, which would soon sell quite well. Packard could and did diminish its output of trucks, but this idled facilities designed for more prosperous times.

Packard trucks were quality products with most models selling for as much as a thousand dollars more than similar models built by the so-called "assemblers," who purchased most of their components from outside sources. Competition heightened in the diminished truck marketplace after the war. In 1920 about 200 companies produced over 200,000 commercial vehicles, although these figures are misleading because they represent mostly light delivery types built by Ford, Dodge and Chevrolet. Packard was competing with such quality marques as Mack, White and Pierce-Arrow.

A group of Heavy Service Packards with full trailers carrying a consignment of California-grown citrus fruit to Los Angeles for steamship shipment to England.

White dropped its automobile line by 1919 to specialize in commercial vehicles, a move which could only further intensify the competition Packard faced. Peerless, in 1919—and Locomobile in 1922—had gone the other way and given up trucks to concentrate on automobiles. Evidently the economics of specialization was militating against those companies trying to sell both high grade cars and trucks through the same dealer network. Only Pierce-Arrow, of the above mentioned, would continue to do so after 1923. Packard would follow the Peerless and Locomobile lead.

The Packard decision to cease commercial vehicle manufacture was based on the exigencies of the marketplace more than any other factor. Management realized that the days of large government orders for military vehicles had passed. At the same time, the company was drastically revising its automotive thinking by phasing out the large, expensive, hand-built Twin Six and pouring its efforts and plant facilities into the new, less expensive Single Six and a straight eight. There didn't seem to be room any longer—in a figurative and literal sense—for Packard to think about trucks. Though not a major factor, dealer morale promised to improve as well by the removal of commercial vehicles. So, in effect, it was a "package decision"—and, economically, a logical one.

In 1937 a *Fortune* magazine article about Alvan Macauley and his company noted that "it was easier to abandon trucks because the increasingly tough competition—Mack, White, et al.—was forcing such big discounts to fleet buyers that Packard could no longer make a profit on them. Mr. Macauley also recalls that trucks were growing too heavy to consort in showrooms with automobiles that were growing annually sleeker."

Such were the hard facts of it. The Packard Motor Car Company had taken an active part in truck development during the pioneer period for the industry. Sales growth had, until the postwar period, been excellent, even with a moderate advertising budget. Then the corporate axe fell. Because it had to. Perhaps Packard regretted having to make that decision. In that early summer of 1923, the company did not say precisely that it was abandoning the truck market. Instead the announcement noted only that "plant facilities of the Packard Motor Car Co. are now being devoted exclusively to the manufacture of passenger cars. . . ."

681

TESTING
THE PRODUCT

The Packard
Proving Grounds

AUTHOR: MENNO DUERKSEN

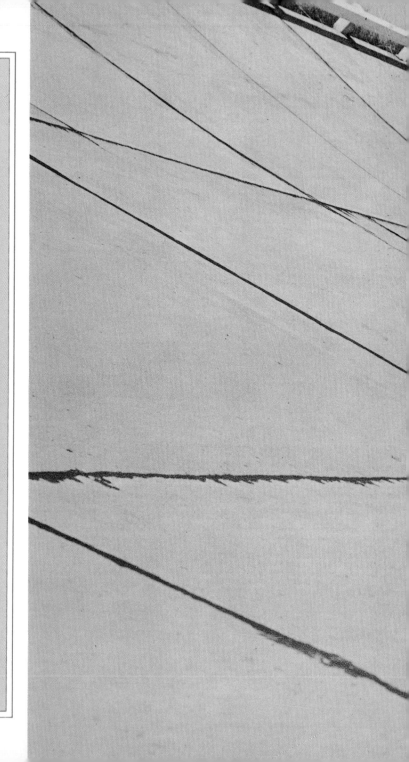

Just weeks before, he had charged his Miller Special round Indy for a lap at 124.018 mph—a record in the 500 that would endure nine years. Now, on June 14th, 1928, Leon Duray took the same car to another 2½-mile oval—in Michigan. The track was paved, though the facility was as yet incomplete. Its lack of a guard rail on the banked turns might have daunted some racing drivers. It did not Leon Duray. He took the Miller out and set a world's closed-course record at 148.7 mph, which gladdened both Duray and the Miller racing people—and allowed the owner of the new facility to claim it as the "World's Fastest Speedway."*

The track was at Utica, some twenty miles to the north of Detroit. Its owner was the Packard Motor Car Company.

Packard, of course, had not built the oval in order to entice the Indianapolis 500 to Utica.** Setting a record there, however, made news—and allowed promotional mention of the track's principal pur-

pose. It was but part of the new Packard Proving Grounds, designed to test the performance and stamina, even the souls, of Packard motorcars coming off the assembly lines at Detroit.

The proving grounds idea was a relatively new one to America. In the early days of the industry, public avenues and roads had sufficed for such testing as there was. Crank it up and send it for a spin of a few miles on streets around the factory—that was about the extent of it for cars fresh off the line. Prototypes were usually tested further—for thousands of miles sometimes, to Chicago, to New York, wherever.

Gradually, limited facilities were built near their plants by some manufacturers, the Dodge Brothers, for example, coming up with a test hill and a small board track around 1915. But it was Henry Joy who that same year had a better idea. He walked into a Packard board of directors meeting and announced, "I've just bought a field"—which he explained would be used for construction of extensive testing facilities. Eyebrows

shot up. Why?, everyone said. Why buy land when one had the whole country in which to test cars? Joy mentioned that it could also be used for another notion that intrigued him—aviation and getting his company involved in that nascent industry.

Still, the board was unconvinced, so the land was sold, eventually becoming Selfridge Field, a U.S. Army Air Force base—and the proving grounds idea lay dormant for nearly another decade, until steadily mounting traffic congestion, speed laws and outraged cries from the citizenry dictated a little fresh rethinking. In 1924 General Motors opened its gigantic proving grounds at Milford, thirty miles west of Detroit, and soon thereafter the Packard Motor Car Company concluded as well that Henry Joy had been right all along.

Alvan Macauley, now Packard president, found the necessary land near Utica***—no longer could it be had in the sprawling industrial center around Detroit—the eventual 640 acres bisected by a highway,

*Miller's record, and the "Fastest Speedway" title, would stand for twenty-four years, until the building of Monza postwar in Italy.

**Interestingly, however, the commercial possibilities of the track were not overlooked by Packard. "Speedway racing and other outdoor events" were noted in board minutes of 1927 as possible future programs for the facility and during the same month Leon Duray was making his record at the track, an appropriation of $150,000 was authorized for preparing the speedway for racing. By December 1928, however, a proposed race was postponed "in view of the heavy development work ahead"—and the idea was dropped thereafter, doubtless another casualty of the Wall Street crash and its aftermath.

***Initially, in November 1925, 400 acres were purchased a couple of miles south of Milford, but for a reason which history does not record, that site was deemed unsuitable, was subsequently sold "at its increased value," and the land at Utica acquired instead, in increments beginning with 340 acres.

Pages preceding: Four Packards coursing the Proving Grounds track in 1933. Page opposite: Construction of the track ongoing at Utica during 1927. Below: Inaugurating the track, June 1928, last-minute checking out of the Miller by mechanics before Leon Duray went out to break a world's record. Below right: Practice dashes on the oval, the Packard company captioning this photo, "Leon Duray and Norman Batton coming out of curve at 140 mph." Above right: A Packard Speedster and a Packard Diesel plane "race" in '29.

leaving 504 acres on one side of the road, this area to be where the major Packard activities were to be centered. Albert Kahn, Inc. was contracted to design and supervise construction of the facilities. Principal among these, of course, was the speed track. As James B. Forman, one of the men who would be employed at Utica, recalls, the result was a beauty: "The track was so perfectly banked that you could drive into the curve at either end full throttle (about 100 mph) and take your hands off the steering wheel and the banking would guide the car around the curve and onto the straightaway. The drivers liked to initiate the new people on the test crew by demonstrating this."

In addition to the track, there was the lodge, a residence for the proving grounds manager and his staff, shops and testing laboratories, hills of varying gradations, plus mile upon mile of gravel, dirt and sand roadways. Workmen scattered boulders the size of watermelons along some roads, shoveled loads of sand into muck holes on others, devised a devilish stretch with railroad ties embedded crosswise at one-foot intervals, built up hills so steep a car might seemingly bound into the blue when topping the crest. Though some of this had the look of a medieval torture rack, the whole was couched in a beautifully landscaped and utterly grand setting. It had to be. Packard had a rather plush reputation to protect.

These were Packard's golden years. The marque was outselling every other luxury car built in America—indeed the world. And Packard profits were as lush as its products; the company barely missed the better-than-a-million dollars that was expended outfitting Utica.

Put in charge at the Packard Proving Grounds was one Charles H. Vincent, a man whose career had included being test driver and mechanic for Thomas-Detroit shortly after the turn of the century and later experimental engineer at Ferro Machine and Foundry in Cleveland, and with Hudson in Detroit during Super Six development days. He was a well-trained, self-educated engineer, and he was Jesse G. Vincent's brother—which factors combined to bring him to Packard in 1916. Save for a brief sojourn to work for a bank in Tulsa and to set up a Packard-Reo agency in Arizona, both of which failed during the depression following the end of World War I, he would remain at Packard through 1947.

At Utica with him, of course, was the redoubtable Tommy Milton, hired in April 1927 at an annual salary of $7500, $2900 more than Charlie Vincent was making at the time—and a figure reflective of Milton's stature in the automobile field, his celebrity as a racing driver and his position as ramrod of the Packard Proving Grounds project. Day-to-day operation of the facility was the charge of Charlie Vincent; overall inspiration was provided by Milton.

Initially, the Packard Proving Grounds were not independent of Detroit, but were rather an adjunct to the engineering department then headed by chief engineer Al Moorhouse. (Brother Jesse had by now moved up to vice-president in charge of engineering.) This system proved not to work at all well, as one rather costly mistake demonstrated. Charlie Vincent remembers:

"It was during the period when Packard was phasing out production

The Proving Grounds personnel, 1933; Charlie Vincent with his radio set; aerial view of the Proving Grounds and its two-and-a-half mile concrete oval track.

The handsomely landscaped entrance to the Utica facility; the spacious accommodations of the Lodge; Eleventh Series Packards parked in front of the garage.

Clockwise from above left: A 1938 Packard Six with the towing dynamometer; a Super Eight being looked over, and technicians checking the electrics in the garage, July 1938; a 1934 Packard with the Proving Grounds' "fifth wheel"; an Eleventh Series car torn down for shop inspection, August 1933.

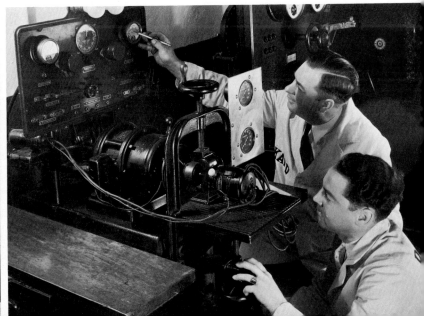

Clockwise from above: Charlie Vincent, J.A. Gilroy and H.F. Olmstead with an Eleventh Series prototype at the Timing Stand (1933); Packards under test, in the sandtrap (1932), on sand and gravel roads (July 1937), over "The Hump" (1932); on the track, a Henney funeral coach (1935), a speedster and sedan (1929).

of six-cylinder engines in favor of the straight eights [the 626-633 models]. Due to some miscalculation either by the purchasing department or the sales department, about $250,000 worth of frames for six-cylinder cars had been carried over from the year before and management was most anxious to salvage these if possible.

"To accomplish this and still find room for an eight-cylinder engine, Moorhouse had designed a new and very thin water pump that required a minimum of space between the cylinder block and the radiator. Shortly after starting high speed tests, the fan belts began to fail and when I reported this, he sent out special fans that had been cut down in diameter to reduce the load on the belts. His feeling was that no customer would drive at high speed long enough to wear out the belt. With this combination, the cars completed their 25,000 miles tests with only one or two failures and the model went into production.

"Unfortunately, the radiators were also a bit small that year and in many sections of the country it was necessary to install larger than usual fans, this being a common remedy in those days. In every case where the larger fan was installed and in many cases where the regular fan was used, the water pump bearings failed in a few thousand miles. After these pumps had been redesigned a few times and each car campaigned [called back for repair] that many times, it was necessary to design a full-sized pump and mount it on the left side of the crankcase on a special bracket. The fan problem was then solved by mounting it on a special bracket where the thin water pump had been located. All this redesigning and campaigning ran into a lot of money—about five million, as I recall."

A five-million-dollar loss to save a quarter of a million dollars is not the way to run a business. Alvan Macauley quickly decided that the Packard Proving Grounds should be independent of, not responsible to, Engineering (as had always been the case at Milford with General Motors). And Charlie Vincent would be Lord of the Grounds.

Thereafter, any new car or any new feature had to have Proving Grounds approval, in addition to an okay from Engineering and

A Junior negotiating the sand and gravel (August 1938), a Henney funeral coach at "The Hump" (March 1935); a One-Twenty ride demonstration (August 1940

Distribution and other departments involved in the overall scheme of Packard production—or as Alvan Macauley admonished vice-president of manufacturing E.F. Roberts in a memo, "There should be separate certificates because it is intended that each . . . shall pass upon the proposed improvement, particularly from the standpoint of his own department."

Charlie Vincent liked that a lot. And he was happy too to be given authority to slip into the Detroit plant whenever he wished and "kidnap" any car off the assembly line for a go at the Proving Grounds. During the early weeks of production on any new model, at least five such purloined Packards were taken to Utica, to be driven 250 miles for operational evaluation and then thoroughly inspected for workmanship. Subsequently, one of them would be taken a thousand miles for quality checking, both full throttle on the track, plus round after round on the torture roads. Another car might put up 2500 such miles, yet another made to endure 25,000. On at least two occasions, a Packard was driven

A One-Ten taking on what Packard called its "rough roads" in July of 1940.

at top speed, day and night, for the seven days required to reach 15,000 miles, as effective as any test possible of performance and stamina.

All this resulted in a goodly many Packard miles being racked up, both on experimental and pre-production cars, as year passed year. During 1933 alone, the company reported, test driving at Utica totaled 769,573 miles—a distance more than thirty times around the world at the equator. For the first four years of its production, *every* Twin Six or Twelve produced was driven 250 miles at the Proving Grounds in a break-in test including maximum speed checks and a thorough inspection, with a certificate signed by Milton and Vincent issued thereafter and a sticker with the acceptance date glued to the side of the right glovebox behind the instrument panel—or the car was returned to the factory for correction of any defect or weakness noticed. Every new owner got both his car and the "graduation" certificate.

No one was ever killed at the Packard Proving Grounds, indeed no one was ever injured—a fact in which Charlie Vincent took the greatest pride. In fifteen years, and millions of miles, there were, as he remembers, "no [serious] accidents . . . During that same period GM had several men killed at their proving grounds. At one time while we were testing tires for Goodyear . . . one man drove steadily at top speed just to blow tires. He did this constantly for three months and never had any trouble when the tires blew."

Nor did Charlie have any trouble maintaining his autonomy. In 1937, when his brother requested experimental facilities at the Proving Grounds, Alvan Macauley lectured in a memo reply: "One thing that you didn't make as clear as I think it should be, is that C.H. Vincent is to remain boss of the outfit; that he is to issue or continue in effect the necessary rules; that they are to be respected by the Engineering Division; and that in any case of divided opinion, C.H. Vincent's direction is to prevail. I think this is quite necessary in order that the Proving Grounds be left entirely separate and supreme . . . I don't think any doubt should be left as to our intentions in this respect."

None ever would be—the Colonel's and his brother's realms remained kingdoms apart. Jesse Vincent's efforts would, of course, bring him renown such as Charlie would never enjoy—but the latter was apparently unbothered by this. As he has reminisced, "I doubt that any two brothers ever got along better in spite of the fact that we were entirely different kinds of people. We both inherited our mechanical ability from our maternal grandfather but Jesse was the genius who loved to create new things while I was the man who could make them work. He was a decided extrovert while I am, and always have been, a real introvert, with lone wolf tendencies. But during the seventy-three years we were on this planet together, I do not think a harsh word ever passed between us."

In fact, one might suspect Jesse was rather pleased that, as everybody at Packard said, Charlie was keeping him honest out at the Proving Grounds. And the Detroit factory had reason too to be grateful for Utica. For the honesty of Packard cars owed a great debt to Charlie and his men who totted up miles by the millions and were very hard to satisfy.

At the Proving Grounds, from the left: a Twenty-Second Series taxi, a 1942 Clipper, a Twenty-Third Series Custom, a 1952 Mayfair, a 1953 Patrician.

APPENDIX III

THE
PROFESSIONAL
PACKARD

Commercial Bodies
on Packard Chassis

AUTHOR: GEORGE HAMLIN

Hearses and ambulances were among the last conveyances to enter the horseless age, lagging considerably behind the use of automobiles in pleasure motoring and for other commercial applications. There were reasons, the matter of dependability for one—and, for another, the consideration of respectable, quiet operation, this particularly important in the funeral business. These two prerequisites would seem to have favored marques like Packard, but luxury-car chassis were very costly.

The earliest funeral coaches were built by individual funeral directors, mounting bodies on motorized chassis available commercially. Beginning about 1909 the manufacture of funeral equipment was begun by various carriage and wagon producers building the complete vehicle in their facilities. Some companies, however, utilized manufactured chassis, and some of these chose Packard—as often as not a Packard truck chassis. By the 1920's the industry began to swing generally to manufactured chassis, and Packard benefited. The A.J. Miller Company of Bellefontaine, Ohio was featuring Nash and Packard chassis exclusively by 1926; other firms favoring Packard included Knightstown (Knightstown, Indiana), Eureka (Rock Falls, Illinois), Silver Knightstown (Knightstown, Indiana) and Superior (Lima, Ohio). No one chassis captured an overwhelming percentage of the funeral and rescue car business in those days, but a good share of it was going to Flxible-bodied Buicks and Superior-bodied Studebakers. Cadillac, later to dominate the field, did not make a serious effort at marketing a special chassis until the very late Twenties.

Packard's frontal assault on the commercial-car business came in 1935, with the offering of "A" or commercial versions of three chassis: 120A (One Twenty), 1200A (Eight) and 1203A (Super Eight). The 120A was expected, as was the One Twenty itself, to bring in the lion's share of the business, and it did. Many leading body builders offered hearses and ambulances on this specially-suited chassis, which was a solid value. Not only was it a Packard at a lowered cost, but it was a special chassis which did not need to be stretched or otherwise modified—and its customers included Superior, Silver-Knightstown, A.J. Miller, Knightstown, Eureka (Sterling, Illinois), Cunningham (Rochester, New York), Mitchell (Ingersoll, Ontario) and Henney (Freeport, Illinois). It was Henney which was to provide Packard's future in the commercial-car business.

Established in Cedarville, Illinois in 1868, with a subsequent move to Freeport, John W. Henney & Company had worked at acquiring a reputation in its field in much the same way Packard did—building up to a standard, not down to a price. The firm was assisted in this by the vast numbers of dedicated Swedish craftsmen who had emigrated to the Rock River area to work for John Deere, the Vermont-born blacksmith who had himself traveled there in the mid-1830's, proceeded to revolutionize farming and, within three decades, become the world's largest manufacturer of steel plows. Many of these craftsmen would work for Henney, building the beautiful hand-carved hearses and ambulances which attracted wide attention to the company. Henney prospered, and in 1916 built its first motorized hearse.

For over fifteen years Henney produced its own chassis and became the leader among those in its field building complete vehicles. Ultimately

the company decided to turn to other manufacturers for chassis, concentrating itself on bodies, and again establishing an enviable reputation for quality and innovation. Henney was early to offer the side-servicing coach under the Heise patent, and its three-way table became an industry standard, the company selling it to many other manufacturers. In 1928 it won a head-to-head competition among the leading ambulance builders sponsored by the U.S. Bureau of Standards, and in 1929 came up with the avant-garde offering of an airplane ambulance. In 1931 Henney was producing bodies for mounting on Reo chassis by the National Casket Company (which marketed the result as the National-Henney-Reo), and by 1935 was building a Henney Arrowline series on Pierce-Arrow chassis and a Henney Progress series on Oldsmobile chassis.

Now, Freeport and East Grand Boulevard moved closer together. Although Henney had built Packards previously, their numbers had not been large. With the introduction of the Packard 120A early in 1935, however, Henney announced an 800 series on that chassis, a 1400 series on the Packard 1200A chassis and a 1500 series on the Packard 1203A. Deviating from past practice, either at the insistence of Packard or in recognition of the strength of the marketing power of the Packard name, Henney offered the new product with both names and used the Packard grille, nameplate and hubcaps. "The combined craftsmanship of two experienced motor vehicle builders," Henney announced, "has achieved a series of funeral cars possessing outstanding value—cars that can be sold at moderate prices. More funeral directors than ever before can have the satisfaction and advantages of HENNEY ownership. If you have been seeking a funeral car that furnishes convenience, prestige, and depend-

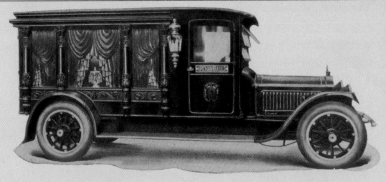

Pages preceding: Henney-built 1935 Model 1203A Super Eight ambulance.
Clockwise from the top: Station coach built on a Six chassis, circa 1913;
hearse bodied by August Schubert Wagon Company on a Twin Six chassis, 1921;
ambulance in use in the Philippines, 1927; A.J. Miller-bodied fleet of
DeLuxe Eight ambulances sold by Packard-Detroit to Kiefer Hospital, 1930;
station coach built on a Third Series Twin Six chassis and sold in 1922.

Above: Seventh Series Packard, with Ninth Series bumper (mounted upside down) and rather flamboyant lines for a funeral car, built in California, 1932.
Below: More sedately, a Model 1102 Packard Eight of 1934 bodied by Henney.

able operation at low cost, the Henney Eight Hundred is the car." Henney had tied its wagon to the same star Packard had: a moderately priced vehicle to see it through the Depression. Prices of the Henney 800 series ranged from $2250 to $2450.

From East Grand Boulevard in 1936 came a continuation of commercial chassis for the One Twenty (120BA), the Eight (1400A) and Super Eight (1403A). Henney was already Packard's major customer, and the use of its chassis by other body makers began to taper off.

Henney technology continued to pace the industry. During this period the company introduced the Elecdraulic, a system of hydro-electric casket table operation still used under the original name years later by Henney's competition. In 1937, concurrent with Eureka, Henney offered the first flower car, and that year too made available a steel roof on the 120CA chassis, which Packard itself had not yet been able to do. The development of the roof had created problems, however, and Henney apologized that it was not stamped in one piece. "Because of the difficulty of obtaining sheets of body steel large enough, and the prohibitive cost of dies needed to mould the entire roof in one piece," said a factory brochure, "attempts to duplicate the passenger car all-steel top for hearse or ambulance use have been unsatisfactory. [Technology would ultimately make this possible.] So-called one-piece, all-steel tops, which have been made by welding several pieces of metal together, in our tests have proved unsatisfactory." Henney's answer was the "articulated roof," formed separately from the rest of the car in about the same dimensions as a fabric roof insert, the roof section then bolted in place against an angled rubber seal.

Another Henney development of 1937, and again used under the original Henney trademark by the competition for many years, was Leveldraulic, a manually-controlled hydro-electric device which leveled the car from side to side while it was parked at the curb for loading. This development eliminated the display of isometrics previously necessary by those loading a side-servicing hearse, which negated a certain entertainment factor, but then funeral services are not supposed to be entertaining.

By 1938 funeral and rescue vehicles on Packard chassis by body makers other than Henney were for all purposes unavailable. There are two versions as to the why of this. The first is provided in a 1953 brochure prepared by the A.J. Miller Company which states that in the fall of 1937 Packard "served notice that Miller must discontinue use of all chassis other than Packard," and that while its Packard sales had been strong in the late 1920's, they had fallen off upon the entry of Cadillac and LaSalle into the field and "Miller, therefore, refused the Packard demand." (Miller eventually standardized on Cadillacs and Oldsmobiles, was finally bought by Wayne Works and merged with its old rival Meteor in 1956.) Verifying the Miller version of the Packard

Above: 1934 Miller-Packard town car limousine hearse. Below: Eureka-Packard ambulance, circa 1931. Right: Ambulance for New York hospital, October '34.

exclusiveness demand is difficult in the extreme; variations on the story abound. One fact and several assumptions might be noted, however. Indisputably, Packard sales had not fallen off in the late Thirties; commercial Packards were leading the pack during that period. And presumably, if Packard had served such a demand, on Miller and/or the entire funeral-and-rescue body industry, it would have been contrary to all that we know about Alvan Macauley, it would have been short-sighted from a sales standpoint, and it would have been in violation of anti-trust legislation.

Solid evidence supports version number two, that the exclusiveness demand came not from Packard, but from Henney. According to former Henney counsel William A. Alfs, "It was the other way around. We had Packard under exclusive contract not to sell commercial chassis to any other body maker." That agreement was among the exhibits relating to Packard's purchase of the Studebaker Corporation in 1954, and it was still in force. Dated January 16th, 1936, it could be canceled by either party upon thirty days' notice. Willard Hess, co-founder of the rival firm

Hess & Eisenhardt, agrees with Alfs: "Packard never gave us any ultimatum like that. Henney landed that agreement. We all [in the industry] thought that was a real ten-strike for John Henney."

In retrospect, the agreement was probably a mistake on Packard's part and likely contributed to Cadillac's eventual dominance of the market. A funeral director might have five or six firms selling him on the advantages of that chassis, as against one Henney dealer extolling Packard's. Even Brantford Body, which could use Packard because it was Henney's Canadian sales outlet, was also using other chassis.

This is not to imply that the Henney-Packard marriage was all bad, quite the contrary. During the good years it was the best duo in the industry. Offering the finest engineering and craftsmanship available in both bodies and chassis, Henney-Packard was usually in the forefront of style and innovation as well. Mechanical air conditioning became available on the commercial Packards for 1938; the first air-conditioned ambulance was a Henney-Packard delivered to the Kreidler Funeral Home in McAllen, Texas. And over one-third of all professional cars

Funeral coaches on the One Twenty chassis, from the top: 1935 Superior end-loader; 1936 Henney three-way; and 1935 Cunningham art-carved.

built in this period were on a Packard chassis.

In 1939 two new landau models were introduced: Henney's 897 Utility Car and the 898 Three-Way Funeral Coach. These vehicles were built along the lines of a custom landaulet passenger car, with fabric false folding top and dummy bow joints, and with side windows lowered and both front and rear doors closed onto the same post. They almost resembled four-door convertibles. For the truly style-conscious, Henney produced the Super Formal, a custom-built design with extra-large rear windows in a heart-shaped configuration, the glass at the lower point of this window expanse reaching halfway to the street.·

The Packard 1701A chassis carried a price of $1080, the coachwork of the Model 897 cost $1170, for a total pricetag of $2250—the same as the 1935 Model 805 service car. Some 1939 options included: stainless steel interior, flower car, $60; spare tire, right-hand fender well in lieu of partition, $28; sixth wheel, left-hand fender well, $24; Leveldraulic, $150; Elecdraulic, $360.

In 1940 the 800 and 1500 series were abandoned, and Henney adopted a model-designation system that was to remain through 1954: one based on model year. (It would take Packard almost a decade and a half to see the merit of this idea.) Henney offered cars in three series. The ambulances available, for example, were the 4094 on the 1801A (One-Twenty) chassis; the 14094 standard and 24094 deluxe on the 1803A (One-Sixty) chassis. The 1- and 2-prefix system of designating the standard and deluxe line was used through 1950 in Freeport.

Packard meantime was building another commercial car itself at East Grand Boulevard. Since 1935 Junior Packards had enjoyed good sales as taxis, and the company had long offered taxi-service components (i.e., special clutches) for these cars. By 1940 Packard was testing the taxi waters in earnest, customer acceptance was favorable and company advertising in 1941 claimed that taxi passengers frequently requested a Packard cab. It was thus decided to offer two purpose-built taxis for 1941. Perhaps still another market in the specialty transportation field could be cornered.

The new taxis were of two wheelbases. The conventional-sized sedan was put on the regular 1900 One-Ten chassis, and the car was designated T1482 to distinguish it from the regular 1482 sedan. For the New York City market, a stretched chassis (T1900) of 133-inch wheelbase was introduced. Both these taxis were specially equipped with heavy-duty equipment and an offset driver's partition. (The T1482 could be had at lowered cost without the partition; when the partition was installed, there was also a rear-facing auxiliary seat at the driver's right.) The long New York version, the T1462, was equipped with a sliding sunroof over the rear compartment. This car was continued in 1942 as the 1584; the shorter sedan was dropped.

Specific production and other data are difficult to obtain for Packard taxis. As is well known, Packard did not bother to retain production figures by body type until 1953. Furthermore, a subsidiary named Packard Federal Corporation was set up to market these cars and no PFC records have been discovered. Beyond that, because the vehicles were not sold directly by Packard, no pricing information has been found other than for 1946-1947. Nor did Packard place sufficient stress on this aspect of its business to assign a distinct chassis and body type until 1942. Finally, if any examples of these cars exist today, they are not widely known.

Packard's taxicab adventure is of interest, however, particularly for the fact of the company's embarking upon it. The regulations for New York City taxicabs had formed a formidable obstacle for many years. This was not a market that a company simply entered. New York's police commissioner published a stringent list of requirements that had to be met, and that list was amended frequently. The requisite interior measurements were too generous for most ordinary cars; the distance from driver's partition to the top rear seat back, for example, had to be sixty inches minimum. No front seat was permitted other than for the driver, and this lost revenue space meant that most operators would make up the difference by choosing a car equipped with auxiliary rear seats. Among other requirements which had to be built in before a hack could work the streets of New York were the following: The vehicle had to have four doors; grab handles on the rear pillars and a trunk rack at the rear were mandatory; a built-in trunk was prohibited, this compartment welded shut to allow only space for a spare tire (a rule finally waived in 1952); the driver's partition had to feature a lighted ID card and inch-thick leather-covered sponge-rubber crash pad; the interior had to be fully washable; the roof light had to be integrated with the taxi meter control; there had to be rear door finger guards and a rear license plate mounted just below the backlight.

Faced with this array of requirements, obviously no auto maker contemplated the New York market casually. In fact it was regulations such as these which contributed to the success of companies like Checker and Yellow, the latter a General Motors subsidiary that Checker eventually defeated in the marketplace, a fate to which GM had not, and has not since, grown accustomed.

But Packard seemed anxious somehow to provide a little bit of everything in the commercial line. By this time the range was formidable, most carrying Henney bodies. Included were three-way limousine funeral coaches, limousine combination hearse/ambulances, limousine rear-loading funeral coaches, landau utility cars, landau three-way funeral coaches, landau rear-loading funeral coaches, ambulances, service cars, flower cars, combination sedan/ambulance invalid coaches, tax-

Above and below: 1938 Henney-bodied Model 1601A Eight with church truck.

icabs, airport limousines, and a line of vehicles specially suited for military service such as heavy-duty and field ambulances. Available with a new ambulance were such standard options as air conditioning, electrically-operated cot fasteners, baby bassinets, Pullman-type (pull-up) curtains, all types of seating options, inhalators, tools and emergency implements, stainless steel lavatories with cup dispensers, ice water and 175-degree hot water. Very little, in fact, which was available to the funeral and rescue service thirty years later was not available on commercial Packards of the immediate prewar years. On the 1942 chassis

Henney had even begun to offer a line of civilian-defense ambulances, styled along the lines of van trucks.

The outbreak of World War II and the accompanying stoppage of civilian vehicle production, of course, put an end to the commercial Packards as well as the pleasure cars. Packard diverted its energies to aircraft and marine engines, offering many subcontract jobs to Henney to keep the unemployment lines in Freeport from getting out of hand. With the war's end, and because the vehicles Packard and Henney had built before its onset had given such a good account of themselves, East Grand

Sightseeing coach on a 1934 Twelve chassis; 1939 airport limousine by Henney for American Airlines; 1937 by A.J. Miller for United Airlines.

Boulevard broke with its usual practice and mentioned commercial cars in a passenger-car brochure produced for the 1946 Clipper Eights.

"Early in the war," it was noted, "we presented a Packard fleet to the American Ambulance Corps in Great Britain. Then came the London Blitz. . . . For four and a half years, those Packard ambulances were in constant service, speeding through the bomb-pocked and rubble-blocked streets of London. After Britain had emerged safely from its ordeal, this message reached us from the head of the Ambulance Corps: 'Please accept our grateful thanks and congratulations on the excellent performance these cars put up.' To which the Packard service director in London added: 'Every time we saw these cars for routine service check-ups, they looked as good, and performed as well, as they did the day we turned them over.' "

War's end found the Packard Motor Car Company squeezed from several directions. The test track had to be completely rebuilt, as did much of the factory itself. Other auto makers, particularly those building vehicles during the war, had a head start on machinery installation. The steel shortage was acutely felt at East Grand Boulevard and, finally, Packard found itself without the vehicles which had constituted the basis for all its prewar commercial cars, the early or "conventional" styled One-Ten, One-Twenty and One-Sixty. Entering the postwar market with only cars of Clipper design, the company had to forego many of the products which had never been tooled for such styling in 1942, among them the convertibles, limousines, catalogued custom cars, formal sedans—and commercial vehicles of all types including taxicabs, funeral and rescue equipment, and airport buses. Packard elected to plug the taxicab gap early, using as a basis the 120-inch Clipper Six.

The new taxi was ready in June 1946. There were two models, essentially the same car with different interiors, the 1684 (partition type) and 1686 (sedan type) in 1946, becoming the 2184 and 2186 for 1947. These cabs, no longer available with the prewar sunroof, featured instead a vacuum-operated power rear window by Trico. They were equipped with metal frames around the side window glass, vinyl headliner, and positive crankcase ventilation (to cope with prolonged idling, not air pollution). A trunk rack was available, and in the partition model there was a new two-passenger right front seat, front-facing, which was hinged on the right and swung away for passenger entry from the back door. Early models had an outside-mounted hood release. There was a roof light available with the Packard name prominently displayed for independent operators who desired the Packard identification. Prices ranged from $1831 at introduction to nearly $2500 by the end of 1947, although prices were actually lowered briefly during 1946.

In the meantime work was under way in Freeport on the new Packard professional cars. Initially Henney had intended to market a Clipper-based line, and two handbuilt prototypes, a hearse and an ambulance, were cobbled up out of miscellaneous prewar and postwar Clipper parts. A brochure was printed, and a photograph appeared in the 1945 Packard annual report. But the project suffered continuing delays, induced by the steel shortage and the necessity for entirely new tooling. That this was anticipated is indicated by a brochure title, "Worth Waiting For." Said Henney: "Regardless of rumors to the contrary, enough new funeral vehicles cannot be produced, for some time, to meet the tremendous pent-up demand for them. Sheet steel, body hardware, tires, trim fabrics and numerous other materials are not yet being manufactured in quantities to make possible full production schedules. You may be sure, however, that just as soon as all necessary materials become available, better, finer and entirely new HENNEY-PACKARD vehicles will be offered for your approval."

But retooling takes time, and ultimately only Studebaker was able to get newly-styled cars into showrooms in 1946 (as 1947 models). Henney simply couldn't make it; even the cars used for the prototypes were mostly of 1942 derivation. To add to the complexity of the undertaking, Packard was reworking the Clipper so extensively for 1948 that any product Henney could market would be outdated at just about the time it was offered. (Packard was planning to introduce the 1948 styling fairly early in 1947.) Therefore Henney, upon the occasion of the sale of the company from John W. Henney to Charles Russell Feldmann, announced that no 1946 models would be produced, all efforts instead being "devoted to tooling for an entire new line of 1948 models [the deliveries of which] will start early in 1947."

In the interim the only funeral/rescue equipment built on the Packard chassis was a one-off by John Little of Ingersoll, Ontario, using a Clipper limousine. Little's efforts were, however, nearly all handwork and made scant impact on the market. It was the 1948 Henney which was to put Packard back into the funeral and rescue business. "The graceful sweep of HENNEY-PACKARD postwar styling (unmarred by protrusions or appendages) presages changes in automobile contours that rapidly are becoming the vogue," it was heralded. "You do not have to wait until next Fall or next year to get true postwar styling and postwar engineering. Present . . . models provide you with both."

By skipping the Twenty-First Series, Henney had scored a coup by offering new styling long before its competition could. In less than a year Henney sold over 1500 vehicles and was leading the industry again. It should be noted as well that, in taking a bye on the 1946 and 1947 model years, Henney had neither lost all that much time nor all that much money. The 1948 models were, as noted, on the street early in 1947. Further, Packard had come to Henney's aid again by giving it the contract for the 1946-1947 Clipper limousines and seven-passenger sedans.

Henney was to return the favor by giving Packard its Pan American show car five years later on a crash schedule which enabled Packard to scoop the industry at the Motor Sports Show in New York. The two companies had always worked well together.

The marketing strength of the Henney-Packard was considerable, and in this regard it is illustrative to compare Henney's price structure with that of the rest of the industry. Far from being a budget item, the commercial Packard by Henney was a comparatively expensive product. For 1948 the following prices were posted for standard ambulances with limousine styling: Miller Cadillac, $5408; Meteor Cadillac 76-481, $5711; Superior Cadillac, $5785; Flxible Buick B22-748 Premier, $5804; Eureka Cadillac, $5863; Henney Packard 14894, $6119; S&S Cadillac 48293 Deluxe Parkway Victoria, $6485.

The Henney line continued basically unchanged through 1950. In addition to the regular line, the company delivered another first: a mobile television studio to WOW-TV in Omaha, Nebraska.

In the meantime, Packard had decided to plunge once more into the taxicab business. Faced with the loss of the prewar 133-inch wheelbase chassis, the company had initially stayed out of the New York market even though it had a 148-inch chassis in production. (Apparently that wheelbase would have been a little too much for Manhattan traffic.) But a new Super limousine was in the line for the Twenty-Second Series, on a 141-inch wheelbase, which was not quite so formidable to maneuver. Equipped as always with the six-cylinder engine, the new taxi was designated the 2280, and 1316 of them were sold before the bottom fell out of this market. The 1949 version (designated 2280-9) sold only twenty-five units, all of them built in late 1948. One more short run of New York taxis for the 1950 model year (designated 2340-5) was made in late 1949, but the 141-inch wheelbase was not being used in the Twenty-Third Series car other than for this limited engagement (thirteen copies) and a briefer run of 1949-model Super limousines (four copies)—both orders probably made up out of spare stock as specials.

Alongside the New York model, the sedan-type taxi continued, with a slightly better sales record. The 1948 version (designated 2286) was, as

Above left: 1938 funeral car at Forest Lawn, Los Angeles. Clockwise from above right: Henney, 1939, town car funeral coach, flower car, funeral car, ambulance. Note Art Deco decorative metalwork carrying Henney name, this being the Henney answer to the more elaborate art-carved coaches popular during this era.

in 1947, a taxi-ized version of the regular 2282 export Six sedan. It continued in 1949 as the 2286-9 and was dropped for the Twenty-Third Series. Sales for 1948 were 1356; sales figures for 1949 were mixed with the export Six sedan statistics and total 682 for both models. There was no longer a separate partition taxicab model; instead the sedan model could be had with an optional driver's partition.

Eventually the New York regulations were relaxed and that market changed. Meanwhile, taxicabs became low totem and luxury marques got out of the business. Packard did offer one more workhorse-level commercial car in 1951, the 2498 business coupe in the 200 line. Thereafter, however, especially with Nance's coming aboard in 1952, the emphasis switched to luxury vehicles, both pleasure and commercial.

In 1951 Henney restyled its Packard commercial line for what was to be the last time. The new cars were designated part of the 300 line and used the five main bearing engine, for reasons which are not clear. The nine main bearing engine was to return to Packard commercial cars in 1954. The new Packard styling by John Reinhart was executed in what

was to prove a timelessly efficient layout, and it offered the Henney people numerous advantages, company literature boasting of the room in the driver's compartment and the overall quality of the body design.

Henney had by this time contracted for some first-rate styling talent of its own—in the person of Richard Arbib. Arbib had had previous experience with General Motors, Republic Aviation and such industrial clients as United States Rubber, Argus, Union Pacific, Benrus, Simca, Tidewater Oil, International Nickel, and Swank. In addition to the commercial Packards from 1951-1954, Arbib was responsible for the 1952 Pan American and several other show Packards. His work on the Twenty-Fourth Series commercial Packards was responsible for both favorable response and good sales (401 units in 1951). The rear side windows wrapped around to the back and interiors were offered in an astonishing rainbow of reds, greens, yellows, oranges and blues. In addition, the customer was invited to offer his own ideas and "the full cooperation of our Design Department in working out such suggestions is always available."

Taxicabs: 1941 One-Ten; 1946-1947 Clipper Six, with partition-style body.

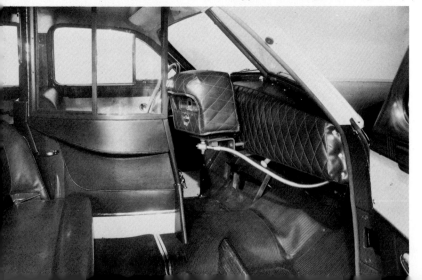

Postwar inflation had had its effect on prices; the basic 5194 Packard ambulance listed at $7260, the landau 5104 at $7470. Another change had slowly come too; the market was shifting to other body builders and other chassis. In 1951, for example, the industry produced 4177 funeral cars and ambulances, of which 2140 were on the Cadillac chassis. Henney sales, and therefore Packard sales, totaled 401. Part of this was due to firms entering the field with lower-priced chassis: Acme Pontiac, Economy Chrysler, Barnett Pontiac, Memphian Chrysler and DeSoto, National Chevrolet and Pontiac, Siebert Ford. The rest was due to the continuing onslaught of the Cadillac name. When sales industrywide slackened the following year to 2622, both Cadillac and Packard held their own fairly well, but this meant 1771 Cadillacs and only 320 Packards. Cadillac was putting great effort into the professional cars, recognizing their prestige value in continuous exposure.

For the 1953 model year there was a commercial Clipper to join the Packard. Called the Henney-Packard Junior at Freeport, it was a shorter economy vehicle built on a 127-inch wheelbase. Equipped with the 288-cubic-inch engine and the Clipper grille, it came in a two-door version only and could be had as a combination car or a straight ambulance or rear-loading funeral coach. It was designed as a price leader and fit in ideally with the Nance policy of separating the Packard from the Junior line, now named Clipper.

The new commercial Clipper was planned to appeal to volunteer fire departments, low-budget funeral homes, Civil Defense organizations and other economy markets. An order for 256 Juniors was immediately placed by the Defense Department and the Henney plant figured its costs on a projected production total of 500 units, committing itself to that many chassis and body kit units. The price was set at $3333 and everything looked good . . . for a while. But the target price had been unrealistic. Even before the first Junior could be delivered, the price was raised to $3533 and finally, on December 31st, 1952, it went to $3883. Junior sales were stopped cold, understandably since the final delivered price, including a ten-percent federal tax and a few essential options, had reached $4700—directly competing with such vehicles as the Barnett, National or Economy conversions which offered greater loading length than the Henney Clipper.

Henney was in over its head with the Junior and was badly hurt. The order for 500 chassis and body kits was accepted, but only 380 of the vehicles were built and sold for 1953. (Two of these, prototypes, were actually sold as 1952 models with rounded windshields, 1952 grilles and other 1952 items.) The remaining 120 units were marketed as 1954's. The Henney Clipper had failed.

This alone did not spell unmitigated disaster. Other products would pay the bills in 1953. In addition to the Clippers, there were 166 commercial Packards, 150 eight-passenger Packard sedans and limousines, and 596 crash bodies (some at Freeport, some at Oneida in Canastota, New York). Work was also begun on three mobile brokerage buses for Merrill Lynch, on chassis by Marmon-Herrington. The crash trucks, also on Marmon-Herrington chassis, were to become Henney's principal business very shortly. The industry produced 3034 funeral and rescue vehicles in 1953: Cadillac's share was 1949, Packard's 546.

Henney was in trouble. By 1954 other body makers began circulating stories that there would be no Henney line that year. Feldmann felt obliged to put on a high-powered display at the '54 shows to counter these rumors, and prepared an impressive number of brochures for the trade. At the same time the company was quietly shutting down in a most insidious manner. No work, for example, was being done on development of bodies for the new 1955 Packards, and that work should have been started if there was going to be a Henney body with wraparound windshield, cathedral taillights, new trim and new bumpers. Meanwhile, Feldmann began seeking other non-Packard business that did not have long-term obligations. "From sports car to limousine or station wagon, on your chassis," said one advertisement, "our organization stands ready to meet your desire for the ultimate on wheels." Eventually

Twenty-Second Series taxis: New York, sedan, sedan interior (optional partition).

ROSTER OF PACKARD TAXICABS, 1941-1950

Model Year	Chassis	Wheelbase (ins.)	Body No.	Type	Weight (lb.)
1941	1900	122	T1482	Sedan	3250
	T1900	133	T1462	New York	3950
1942	2030	133	1584	New York	3980
1946	2130	120	1684	Partition	3730
			1686	Sedan	3670
1947	2130	120	2184	Partition	3730
			2186	Sedan	3670
1948	2220	141	2280	New York	4460
	2240	120	2286	Sedan	3735
1949	2220-9	141	2280-9	New York	4460
	2240-9	120	2286-9	Sedan	3735
1950	2320-5	141	2340-5	New York	4460

NOTES: Prices are available for only two model years: 1946 when prices decreased mid-year, $1952-$1838 for the Partition, $1831-$1725 for the Sedan; and 1947, when they increased, $2069-$2465 for the Partition, $1945-$2341 for the Sedan. Known production figures are the following: 1316 and 1356 for the 1948 New York and Sedan respectively; 25 for the New York in 1949, and 13 for the New York in 1950. Total production of the 2240-9 chassis in 1949 (including the 2282-9 export sedan) was 682 units.

Henney did secure a missile-trailer contract from the Department of Defense, but this work alone would not keep the Freeport plant open. Something was going wrong with Feldmann's empire.

C. Russell Feldmann was a tireless financier, one of the last of the old-school tycoons, and this was his first reversal in a string of successes dating back over thirty years. Starting as an office boy in an auto dealership, Feldmann had moved rapidly into the higher echelons of business, owning his own firm by 1919 at age twenty-one. By 1928 he had purchased, reorganized and sold three companies: Winton Engine, Victor Peninsular and, interestingly enough, Henney. ("My friend," was his opening remark when interviewed for this book, "I'll bet you never met anyone who bought the same company twice.") In 1928 he founded the Transitone Automobile Radio Corporation and sold controlling interest to Philco two years later, securing his future nicely; in bibliographic material into the 1960's he continued to refer to himself as "the man who first put a radio into an automobile."

The intervening years had seen Feldmann acquiring and selling such companies as Simplex Radio, Foster Machine, International Machine Tool, Detrola, Newport Rolling Mill and Strong, Carlisle and Hammond. He had been chairman of the National Union Electric Corporation since 1946 and owner of Henney since 1947. In late 1953 Feldmann had bought, through Henney, the Eureka Williams electrical firm in Bloomington, Illinois—and in April of 1954 he took the first steps toward acquiring Reo Motors for himself. But Feldmann was now in a predicament. He had disposed of his holdings in Newport (by then renamed Newport Steel Corporation) in 1950 after being approached by a moneyed consortium looking to benefit from the steel shortage. He shortly thereafter found himself the defendant in a suit brought by the other Newport stockholders, who contended that under terms extant, they should have been offered first refusal on the stock. The suit dragged on for some time, and when Feldmann eventually lost it, all kinds of things were going wrong at once. Reo's stockholders launched a counterassault on his takeover try, the victorious parties in the Newport case had to be paid, and the losses on the commercial Clipper were combining with dwindling sales across the board in Freeport; the plant which had once been the industry leader with nearly 2000 cars per year had recently been operating on a small fraction of that volume.

Feldmann, unaccustomed to this sort of treatment, went on the defensive. He began to retrench, first by assigning to Bohn Aluminum his option on Reo. That purchase would have cost him $16.5 million, and he no longer had access to the money. (Reo eventually ended up the property of White, was combined with Diamond T after the 1967 models in order to cut costs, was sold off in 1972 and finally failed in 1975.) And at some point Feldmann realized that he would have to get out of the Henney

business too, and rebuild his empire from the base of National Union Electric. Henney offered no financial assistance in its weak condition.

With regard to Henney, many of its setbacks in the early 1950's stemmed from the fact that the Packard chassis was a liability in some circles because the competition offered a V-8. Indeed Freeport's sales were largely on the strength of its own craftsmanship rather than its Packard chassis. Feldmann recognized this. The 325 commercial Packards and Clippers built for 1954 shared a total market of 2880 units; Cadillac's share was 1756. From nearly forty percent in the late 1930's, the Packard market penetration in professional cars had dropped to around nine percent; the decline of the Packard commercial car paralleled that of the Packard pleasure car. Feldmann determined to get out of the Packard business and did. While exploring a few other tentative ideas on other chassis, he also began closing the Freeport plant systematically and irretrievably.

Packard was pretty well cast adrift in an unfriendly sea by this move. The company had not furnished chassis or kit cars to any other producer of professional car bodies for years, and by 1954 these makers were comfortably settled in with other lines. Eureka, Hess & Eisenhardt (S&S), Meteor, A.J. Miller and Superior, representing the bulk of the industry, were happily competing with each other on Cadillac chassis. Moreover, the number of such firms was on the decline: Miller and Meteor would soon merge, Eureka close. Other smaller companies did conversion work on various chassis, but never on Packards, were not equipped to do so and in general had customers who preferred cheaper products.

The demise of commercial Packards after 1954 has often been ascribed to the car's torsion bars, but this is not a compelling reason. Although installation was a little tricky, winding equipment used in mass production was not required in a low-volume shop; an inexpensive tool enabled dealers to do it locally. The engineering effort would have been negligible, and Packard had already adapted the bars to two wheelbases and two markets (domestic and export). "I was approached about the bars for the commercial chassis," recalls Bill Allison, "but nothing ever came of it. There would have been no difficulty in making longer bars, because it has been done with a Mack truck." Further, there was no requirement that Torsion-Level be used for the long-wheelbase cars anyway.

Still, the long association of Packard with the estimable house of Henney probably worked to East Grand Boulevard's disfavor. Had Packard made available a commercial V-8 with torsion bars at that time, probably only Henney could have built it. It should be noted that Henney's approach to commercial car production was more comprehensive than the norm. While other builders began with a driveable chassis (front end sheet metal and all running gear assembled), Henney had discontinued this practice some time earlier, accepting from Packard only a

Clipper funeral coach from 1946 mounted on '42 chassis; the WOW-TV field car from 1948; Twenty-Second Series funeral coach with landau styling by Henney.

HENNEY-PACKARD COMMERCIAL CAR PRODUCTION, 1935-1954

No records were retained by Packard of prewar commercial chassis production. Where a prewar figure is given, it represents an estimate of Henney bodies only, based on an analysis of several hundred Henney vehicle plates on cars in service, in the hands of collectors or in scrapyards. The figures are rough because, during those years, not all commercial Packards were Henneys and not all Henneys were Packards. Prior to 1935 serial-plate analysis is completely inconclusive because quantities were fewer and manufacturers intermixed chassis frequently.

Model Year	Packard Chassis	Packard Lines	Production
1935	120A, 1200A, 1203A	One Twenty, Eight, Super Eight	—
1936	120BA, 1400A, 1403A	One Twenty, Eight, Super Eight	750
1937	120CA, 1503A	One Twenty, Super Eight	1300
1938	1601A, 1603A	Eight, Super Eight	800
1939	1701A, 1703A	Eight, Super Eight	1000
1940	1801A, 1803A	One Twenty, One Sixty	1200
1941	1901A, 1903A	One Twenty, One Sixty	
	1903AB	One Sixty Airport Limousine	1200
1942	2001A, 2003A	Eight Special, One Sixty	300
1946	—	Custom Clipper prototype	2
1948	2213	Custom Eight	1941
1949	2213-9	Custom Eight, Twenty-Second Series	220
	2313	Custom Eight, Twenty-Third Series	160
1950	2313-5	Custom Eight	244
1951	2413	300 model	401
1952	2513	300 model	320
	2633	Prototype Junior	2
1953	2613	Packard	166
	2633	Clipper	378
1954	5413	Packard	205
	5433	Clipper	120

Henney-Packard passenger and show cars are not noted in this list. These included one Monte Carlo on a 1948 chassis, one Pan American on a 1951 chassis, five Pan Americans on 1952 chassis, two Monte Carlos on 1952 chassis, and all long-wheelbase sedans, taxis and limousines from 1946 to 1954. One 1954 senior ambulance was converted into the 1954 Super Station Wagon, Model 5460-S.

kit and doing all assembly work itself. Thus Packard did not actually produce a completed commercial chassis that a body-only shop could use.

And now Henney was not going to assemble anything. Feldmann did not even seem interested in selling the stock he had. Toward the end of the 1954 model year, Henney had put together thirty chassis which had not yet had bodies mounted. Sales manager Newell Steinmetz advised Feldmann to cut the price $500 for quick sale; there was already a percentage cut in effect on the 1954 products and such a program would have resulted in the least loss. No, said Feldmann, send them back. This process took months and cost thousands of dollars, because all thirty chassis had to be disassembled before Packard would accept the parts.

Many of Feldmann's decisions were inexplicable to his associates, and he is widely accused today of running his company into the ground. Certainly he had enough financial worries for any one man during 1954. He did not announce the end at once. On January 18th, 1955, he said only that the Freeport plant would close; by August he had moved key equipment and personnel to the Oneida plant in Canastota. On the 17th of that month he pledged in a letter to his dealer force "to continue our design and development work at Canastota—and work toward a super-fine 1957 Henney." He did conduct discussions with other automobile companies, Lincoln among them; Henney had done Lincolns before, for the Truman White House. He also had stylist Arbib work up ideas for Ford taxis and, doubtless what would have been an ultimate of some sort, a Thunderbird ambulance. In the end, however, Feldmann did nothing.

Meanwhile, faced with both the challenge of manufacturing a commercial chassis and finding someone willing to use it, Nance attacked the matter in December 1954, after attending to the Studebaker purchase. He pointed out the importance of such products to Roger Bremer of Product Planning. Bremer replied in February: "We are now doing some work with the Bristol Motor Company of England on the possibility of 'Rolls-Roycing' the limousine. I believe this company, the Spohn or Ghia companies of Germany and Italy, respectively, would be the only possibilities for production, since labor costs are inordinately high in this country, and because of our specific experience with Henney."

The subject was not reopened until March, when Nance asked Bremer if it would be possible "for us to put some custom-built bodies—built by Derham, etc.—on our Patrician chassis, to add a few numbers to our line and give us some added class? What about a brougham? If not immediately, could they be factored into the '56 line? Also, what are the possibilities of limousines for '56?" Bremer investigated and immediately responded: "It would be possible to put some custom-built bodies by Derham on our Patrician chassis and using basically the present body shell. As you know, this has been done in the past by the application of either a vinyl or leather covering over the roof,

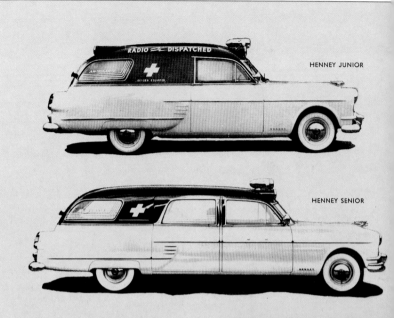

Left: Henney ad from 1954. Henney cars, from the top: 1951 combination hearse/ambulance; 1953 Model 2613/5394 ambulance; 1954 Henney Super station wagon.

with a closed-in quarter panel and a backlight of reduced size. Generally this treatment has been confined to limousine vehicles (by Derham and, copying them, Cadillac), and our attempt to accomplish the same effect might be interpreted as ersatz. Moreover, the price to accomplish this would run anywhere from $300 to $1200.

"With regard to the brougham," Bremer continued, "it is assumed that you are referring to a model similar to Cadillac's which is a misnomer, as was their term Coupe de Ville. If you are referring to the conventional limousine without a roof over the driver's seat, I doubt whether our cars could be adapted practically to this." Richard Arbib had, in fact, had Henney make two such vehicles in 1953, but Bremer apparently did not know about them. There was little difficulty with a hardtop, but a limousine would have involved considerable structural modification.

"With regard to limousines," Bremer went on, "as we have advised, this is currently under consideration with Bristol Motors of England. We have not received a final answer due to the absence of their people who are now in Australia. I am sure we do not want to get into another Henney fiasco, and doubt that we have the Engineering personnel available to take this on with the Superior or other similar outfit." Neither Bremer nor Nance was amenable to another exclusive contract arrangement, nor were they contemplating great numbers of cars—just enough to lend luster to the name, as Lincoln did later with Lehmann-Peterson and Imperial with Ghia. Bristol bodies were superbly hand-crafted and might well have filled the bill, but the idea never proceeded beyond the proposal stage. No commercial V-8 Packards have been confirmed to exist today.

And so the professional Packard died with the Henney Motor Company. Like so many other aspects of the Packard saga in the last years, the demise of the professional Packard left in its wake enough controversy to fuel many an argument; most Henney alumni believe that Packard elected to leave the business, while Packard alumni say the decision originated with Henney. As for the latter, Feldmann changed the Oneida name to Henney, which was merged with Eureka Williams on February 28th, 1958. Both Henney and Eureka Williams were merged into Feldmann's National Union Electric Company of Stamford, Connecticut (now Greenwich) in 1960. The Henney name was revived briefly on a line of electric cars made by Eureka Williams in its Bloomington plant during 1960-1961, but the new Henney Kilowatt, a converted Renault Dauphine body with most available engine and trunk space occupied by batteries, was the victim of a battery technology unequal to the task of propelling a modern car. (Only a hundred were produced, fifty-eight of them sold to utility companies for promotional purposes.) The Henney name is today owned by National Union Electric. Charles Russell Feldmann died in December 1973.

APPENDIX IV

PROMOTING
THE PRODUCT

Catalogue of Packard

Advertisements 1900-1958

— ◆ —

Packard Advertising Art:

A Portfolio in Color

AUTHORS: ROGER ABBOTT AND BOB ZIMMERMAN

The following listing of advertisements represents the preponderance of Packard's advertising efforts from the turn of the century in Warren to the late Fifties and the company's last days at East Grand Boulevard in Detroit. The listing was compiled as a reference for Packard historians and collectors, most of whom doubtless shall wish to refer to it with regard specifically to the period or motorcar of their particular interest. A general perusal of the entire listing, however, is suggested for another reason. It provides a grand tour through Packard's history. A company's advertising reveals a lot about the company itself—and about its reactions to the forces of social change in the various eras of its life. In this advertising list, Packard is seen stressing the structural quality and achievements of its product during the automobile's earliest era, when the automobile was so new that any company venturing into the marketplace developed an almost defensive posture or a bombast aimed at convincing the skeptical. As the automotive idea itself gained prominence, Packard became more self-assured, more assertive, more apt to stress the peripheral advantages of ownership. And then Packard went to war, patriotically. Therefrom, when the Twenties were ready to roar, so was Packard. The supreme confidence of the company during those years is evident in its advertising, displaying not only the strength of its position within the industry but the hauteur of its place in the market. Then Packard met the challenge of the Great Depression, when the social parameters changed and the focus of its promotional efforts of necessity had to change too. There followed war again. Then the last desperate years, the struggle to stay alive, the obvious lack of focus in advertising themes, the lack of assurance this implied. It's all here. What follows is more than a list, it is history.

NOTES REGARDING LIST REFERENCES AND CODES. This compilation is arranged chronologically by calendar year and issue date. Model year introductions generally occurred sometime during the previous calendar year, and the initial appearance of advertisements for the new models is noted. The first reference in each individual listing represents the illustrated subject of the advertisement and is followed by an identifying quote from the advertisement itself. Advertisements appearing in full color are referenced in one of two ways: either by noting the color of the motorcar which illustrates the advertisement or by the words "in color." It should be mentioned that all *National Geographic*, *MoToR* and *American Motorist* advertisements appeared in black and white only. And it should be noted as well that the listing includes a scattering of advertisements published by companies other than Packard but which used a Packard as their subject. In those cases the company placing the advertisement is indicated. Following the identification of the advertisement are references to the magazine or magazines in which the advertisement appeared and the issue date (s). For reasons of readability, the full or an identifying title of the magazine is given in many cases. In others, code initials are used—as follows:

AC = *American City*; ATJ = *Automobile Trade Journal*; AT = *Automobile Topics*; Auto = *The Automobile*, which became *Automotive Industries* in 1918; CATJ = *Cycle and Automobile Trade Journal*; CLIA = *Country Life in America*; CW = *Collier's Weekly*; GH = *Good Housekeeping*; HA = *The Horseless Age*; H&G = *House and Garden*; HB = *House Beautiful*; LHJ = *Ladies Home Journal*; LD = *The Literary Digest*; MA = *Motor Age*; McC = *McClure's Magazine*; MW = *Motor World*; NG = *National Geographic*; SA = *Scientific American*; SEP = *The Saturday Evening Post*; T&C = *Town and Country*; VF = *Vanity Fair*. As noted above, the magazine, *The Automobile*, evolved into *Automotive Industries*. It might be noted as well that *Collier's Weekly* later became simply *Collier's*, *Country Life in America* simply *Country Life*. For a short period in the late Thirties, following merger with *The Sportsman*, the latter magazine was also known as *Country Life and The Sportsman*. It might be mentioned, too, that the *Life* magazine of the years preceding 1936 was an altogether different periodical, published in Chicago, from the large-format pictorial publication begun by Henry Luce in New York that year.

1900

Packard Special, 'Packard Gasoline Automobiles'—HA, October 10

Special and standard models, 'Packard Gasoline Automobiles'—HA, November 7

1901

Model C, 'All Features Thoroughly Tested' —HA, February 27 and April 3

Model C, 'Packard Gasoline Automobiles' —Auto, July

Model C, 'NY-Buffalo Endurance Run' —HA, September 18

all text ad, 'Packards . . . Built for Combined Reliability'—CATJ, November 7

Model F, 'An American Creation' —HA, November 13 and 20

Model F, 'Ask the Man Who Owns One' —MA, October 31; CATJ and AT, November; HA, December 4

Model F, 'Not to know all about the . . .' —MW, December 12

1902

Model F, 'Packard Automobiles' —HA, March 5

Model F, '100 Miles on 3-2/3 Gallons' —HA, April 30

Model F, 'A Mile in 50 Seconds' —HA, May 28

Model F with tonneau, 'An Examination' —HA, June 18

Model F with tonneau, 'Ask the Man Who Owns One'—HA, September 3

Model F, 'Packard's Perfect Record' —MW, December 11

Model F with tonneau, 'Contest Records' —CATJ, December

1903

front and side views, 'We have the proofs . . .' —Scribner's, January

Model F, 'The Evidence'—HA, January 29

rear ¾ view, 'You don't have to select a boulevard . . .'—Harper's, February

front and side views, 'Packard the verdict . . .'—Scribner's, February

Model F front and side, '$2500 Packard' —HA, February 11

Model F with tonneau, '13 First Class Certificates'—MW, February 19

man at wheel, 'He writes of Packard' —Harper's, March

car held by giant hands, 'The Apex of Perfection'—McC, April

Model F side view, 'You Should Own a Packard'—HA, April 1

side view, 'Packard the Machine Ahead' —SEP, April 25 (first Saturday Evening Post ad)

side view with Uncle Sam, 'Packard 1903 Model F'—Harper's, May

touring, 'Putting It Mild'—Auto, May 9

side view, 'Packard the Car Ahead' —SEP, May 16

front silhouette, 'The Car Ahead' —CW, May 23

Model F side view, 'They All Say the Same' —HA, May 27

side view with Gibson Girl, 'Packard 1903 Model F'—McC, June

front view in outline, 'Packard Records' —Collier's, June 13 (first Collier's ad)

side view, 'Ask the Man Who Owns One' —SEP, June 20

runabout, 'It does not take an expert . . .' —Auto, June 20

touring, 'Packard cars hold a line of public records . . .'—Auto, June 27

front view in outline, 'The Packard Motor Car'—Collier's, June 27

Model F side view, 'The Name a Sufficient Recommendation'—HA, July 1

Model F, 'S.F. to N.Y.'—MW, July 16

Model F, 'Across the Continent' —HA, July 22

Model F, 'Across Desert and Mountain' —HA, August 5

Model F trip, 'The Itinerary and Schedule' —MW, August 13

Model F trip, 'The Carburetter' —MW, September 3

Model F trip, 'The Motor' —MW, September 10

Model F, 'Old Pacific's Replacements' —HA, September 16

Old Pacific-Gray Wolf, 'Packard Motor Car Co.'—CATJ, November

Thirty coupe, 'Packard Motor Cars 1911'
—Collier's, August 20

coupe, '1911 Packard Thirty'—Everybody's,
Scribner's and CLIA, August

fore-door limousine, 'Packard Motor Cars
1911'—Collier's, September 10

Thirty limousine, 'Packard Motor Cars
1911'—Life, September 29;
Harper's, September

touring, 'Packard Motor Cars 1911'
—Century and CLIA, October

stake truck, at Marshall Field's, 'Packard 3
Ton Trucks'—Life, October 13

touring, 'Packard Motor Cars 1911'
—Collier's, October 29

fore-door landaulet, 'Packard Motor Cars
1911'—Collier's, November 19

fore-door landaulet, '1911 Packard Thirty'
—Century, McC and American, November

fore-door limousine, '1911 Packard Eighteen'
—Century, December

truck, 'Packard Motor Trucks'
—Collier's, December 3

limousine, 'Packard Motor Cars 1911'
—Collier's, December 17

Eighteen landaulet, 'Ask the Man Who
Owns One'—Life, December 22

truck, 'Packard Motor Car Company'
—Collier's, December 24

1911

forge shop at Packard—Detroit Fenestra
Window Company—SEP, January 7

coupe, 'Packard Motor Cars 1911'
—Collier's, January 21

truck, 'Packard Motor Trucks'
—Collier's, January 28

close-coupled touring, '1911 Packard Thirty'
—CLIA, February; Century, Munsey's and
MA, circa February

close-coupled touring, 'Packard Motor Cars
1911'—Collier's, February 18

truck, '100 Per Cent of all Trucks'
—Collier's, February 25

Thirty brougham, 'Ask the Man Who Owns
One'—Collier's, March 11

truck, 'John Wanamaker'—MoToR, April

Six phaeton, 'Packard Motor Cars 1912'
—Life, April 27

Thirty touring, Eighteen landaulet,
Six phaeton, 'Large line of open . . .'
—Collier's and LD, April 22

Thirty touring, Eighteen landaulet, 'Chassis
in three sizes . . .'—SEP, April 22

listing, all models, 'Packard 30, Packard 18,
Packard Six'—CLIA, May; McC, circa May

phaeton, 'Packard Motor Cars 1912'
—Collier's, May 20

truck, 'Piano Delivery'—Collier's, May 13;
SEP, May 27; MoToR, June

Six phaeton, 'Chassis in three sizes . . .'
—Review of Reviews, June

Thirty phaeton, 'Chassis in three sizes . . .'
—CLIA, June

truck, 'Yamen Yerbe'—SEP, June 3;
Collier's, June 10

service, 'For all owners . . .'—SEP, June 17

**Six touring (1912), 'Ask the Man Who Owns
One'—Collier's, June 24**

Broadway auto exchange, 'Supreme Verdict'
—SEP, July 1

truck, 'American Express'—SEP, July 22;
Collier's, July 29

truck, 'Used in 174 Cities'—SEP, August 12

Six touring, 'Packard Motor Cars 1912'
—Review of Reviews, August

Six touring, 'Sold Exclusively through
Packard Dealers'—Collier's, August 19;
SEP, August 26

touring, 'Elton Hotel'—SEP, September 16

phaeton, 'The Prevailing Car'—Collier's,
September 9; SEP, September 16

truck, 'First Continental Trip'—Collier's,
September 23; SEP, September 30

truck, 'N.Y.-S.F. Trip'—MoToR, October

Six phaeton, 'Packard is the prevailing . . .'
—CLIA, October

phaeton, 'Boss of the Road'
—Collier's, October 28

touring car, 'Boss of the Road'—Life,
October; Liberty and Century, November

phaeton, 'Packard Six'
—Collier's, November 11

truck, 'The Supreme Test'
—Collier's, November 18

Six phaeton, 'Pride of the Boulevard'
—Century, December

limousine, 'Packard Six'
—Collier's, December 23

1912

people scene, 'The Limousine'
—MoToR, January

Anheuser Busch stake truck, 'Packard trucks
are used . . .'—MoToR, January

limousine, 'Packard Six'—MoToR, January

brougham, 'Packard Motor Car Company'
—Collier's, January 20

touring, 'Packard Six . . .'—Auto, January 25

touring, 'Dominant Packard Six'
—Collier's, January 27; CLIA, February;
Everybody's, circa February

Six touring (three-color printed ad)
—The International Studio, February

truck, 'Packard trucks are used . . .'
—Life, February 8

four cars scene, 'Fifth Avenue'
—Collier's, February 17

factory, 'The factory . . .'—Life, February 29

hood ornament, 'The Dominant Six'
—SEP, March 23

touring, 'The Packard is the best cash asset'
—CLIA, April 1

hood ornament, 'The Packard is the best cash
asset'—SEP, April 6

Six, 'The safest car for fast . . .'
—Life, April 11

touring, '60 miles an hour'—Life, April 25

touring, 'Just as cash in the bank'
—Life, May 9

Six, 'The Dominant Six'—Collier's, May 25

cable splicing truck, 'Used in 154 lines'
—Life, June 6

touring, 'Packard 48 for 1913'
—Collier's, June 22; Country Life, July 1

touring, 'The Packard 48 Line'
—Collier's, July 13

touring, 'In the Packard 48 for 1913'
—Harper's and CLIA, July; Life, June 20

touring, 'Its dominance on the road . . .'
—SEP, July 20; Collier's, July 27;
CLIA and McC, August

truck, 'Five-Ton Truck'
—Collier's, August 17

touring, 'The New 38'
—SEP and Collier's, August 31

Six, 'Seven Thousand Men'—SEP,
September 14; Collier's, September 21

Model 38 touring, 'Pullman comfort'
—CLIA, October 1; Collier's, October 5;
Harper's, October

truck, 'American Express'
—Collier's, October 26

landaulet, 'Packard Left Drive 38'—Collier's,
November 9; Life, January 9, 1913

Model 38 touring, 'The Answer'
—LD, Collier's and SEP, November 30

1913

landaulet, 'Packard Left Drive 38'
—Life, January 9

truck, 'A Logical Answer'—LD, January 11;
HA, January 22

control panel, 'Answered by the Packard 38'
—NG, February

control panel, 'Packard Six Carriages'
—CLIA, February

phaeton and touring, 'Packard Six Carriages'
—Collier's, February 1

truck, 'Has Run Three Years'—HA, April 2

touring, 'Packard left drive motor carriages'
—CLIA and NG, April

truck, 'Oscar Daniels Company'
—HA, May 7

scene in Rome, 'Packard 38 Phaeton'
—CLIA, May; Theatre and NG, June

touring, 'The Gentlewoman's Motor
Carriage'—MoToR, May

Model 38 phaeton, 'Road Comfort'
—CLIA and Suburban Life, June

truck chassis, 'Study the Price of Parts'
—HA, June 4

Model 38 motor, 'Three Hundred Hours'
—MoToR, July

truck, 'Kaufman Brothers'—HA, July 30

scene in Paris, 'The Packard Phaeton-
Runabout'—LD and CLIA, August

phaeton-runabout, 'Packard Service'
—MoToR and NG, August; LD, June 7

ring and pinion, 'New Packard Worm Bevels'
—SEP, August 16; LD, September 13;
Travel and MoToR, September

Chicago to Detroit record, 'Boss of the Road'
—CLIA and Harper's, October;
SEP, September 13

all text ad, 'Packard Two-Thirty-Eight'
—HA, October 15

special touring, 'A New Packard for $3350'
—HA, November 12

Model 2-38 limousine, 'London'
—NG, October; McC, December

Model 2-38 limousine, 'Packard enclosed
bodies typify . . .'—CLIA, December

1914

limousine, 'Cathedral'—Collier's, January 10

all text ad, 'Record Shipments for 1913'
—Auto, January 22

Model 2-38 phaeton and 4-48 touring,
'Boss of the Road'—SEP, February 14

Model 2-38 coupe, 'All works of taste must
bear . . .'—Harper's and NG, February

Model 4-48 salon touring, 'Boss of the
Road'—McC, March

English commentary, 'The Other Sort of
American'—SEP, March 7

worm bevel, 'A silent and fully efficient . . .'
—HA, March 11

limousine, 'Prestige'—Leslie's, April 16

brougham, 'Three Window Type'
—MoToR, May

all text ad, 'Safety First—Left Drive'
—Auto, May 14

touring scene in Rotenburg, 'Easiest way to
tour'—CLIA, April; LD, May 30

touring scene, 'Packard in the Austrian
Tyrol'—NG, June

truck, 'Quality in Motor Trucks'
—MoToR, July

Model 3-38 touring, 'You can get a
Packard in September'—Collier's, August 1;
LD, July 11

limousine with cab sides, 'Beauty is a human
necessity'—NG and Travel, September

Model 3-38 touring, 'Announcing the 3-38
and 5-48'—American, September

Model 3-38 phaeton, 'New Packard'
—SA, September 5

salon brougham, 'New Packard 3-38'
—Collier's, September 26

salon brougham, 'Packard Made in
America'—LD, October 10; NG, October;
SA, October 3; Everybody's, November

brougham, '3-38'—SA, October 3

Model 5-48 touring, 'A blend of . . .'
—SA, November 7

1915

all text ad, 'The All American Car'
—World's Work, January

salon brougham, 'Builders of the Packard'
—Collier's, February 20; LD, February 27;
CLIA, March

truck, 'New Model'—AT, February 27

touring, 'Keep Gasoline, Oil . . .''
—Collier's, March 20

front view, 'If you want a car'
—AT, March 27

truck, 'This ends the last doubt . . .'
—SEP, April 10

all text ad, 'Packard responsibility'
—LD, April 24

all text ad, 'Packard new model trucks'
—LD, May 8

touring cars in desert, 'Traveling First Class'
—Travel, May

Packards (1899 and 1915 Six), 'Success built
on public good will'—LD, May 29;
MoToR, June

phaeton, 'Announcing the Packard Twin
Six'—SEP, June 5; SEP, June 12;
Collier's, June 19; NG, June; CLIA, July

motor, 'The Packard Twin Six'
—LD and SEP, June 26; Collier's, July 17

touring, 'Innumerable'
—LD, July 10 and August 21

distributor, '24,000 sparks a minute'—Delco
—SEP, July 14

718

all text ad, 'The only grand prize . . .'
—Collier's, August 21; NG, August

touring, 'The only grand prize . . .'
—LD, July 24

salon brougham, 'Twin Six Enclosed Cars'
—Collier's, September 18

Twin Six limousine, 'Public Interest'
—LD, September 11; NG, October

overhead platform truck, 'Forty cities
employ . . .'—AC, October

all text ad, 'The name Packard conveys a
definite measure . . .'—Life, October

all text ad, 'Packard new type chainless . . .'
—AC, November

dump truck, 'For every municipality'
—AC, December

Twin Six landaulet, 'Eager power
under perfect control'—NG and
Harper's, December

1916

Twin Six limousine, 'The distinctive lines'
—CLIA and MoToR, January

truck, 'Hauling problems simplified'
—Collier's, February 26; SEP, March 4

roadster, 'Every superiority'—The
Independent, January 24; Collier's,
January 29; NG, February; CLIA, March

all text ad, 'Right of Way'—Leslie's,
March 30; NG, April; SEP, April 1

touring, 'Distance has no frontier'
—Auto, April 20; SEP, May 6;
Collier's, May 13; CLIA, June

touring, 'Packard Twin Six'
—Collier's, May 13

landaulet—Hess Bright Ball Bearing
Company—Auto, June 29

front view, 'In plain speech'—Auto, June 1;
Leslie's, June 8; Collier's and SEP, June 10;
NG, June

all text ad, 'A fifty per cent savings'
—AC, July

trucks, 'War's test is the test'—AC, August

Twin Six touring (Second Series), 'And here
now is a new fulfillment'—NG and
Review of Reviews, August; Collier's and
SEP, August 19; Auto, August 24;
CLIA, September

trucks, 'Emergencies'—AC, September

biplane and motor, 'Steady! It's Smoothest'
—NG, September; SEP, September 9;
Collier's, September 16

touring car and truck, 'Matched'—LD,
September 23; AC and System, November

light bulb, 'More from Less'
—SEP, October 7; Collier's, October 14

trucks, 'More'—AC, October

limousine, 'Range extenders'
—NG, October; Country Life, November;
The Independent, October 9

smoke stacks, 'Waste'—SEP, October 28;
Collier's, November 4; NG, November

landaulet, 'Year round and everywhere'
—SEP, November 18; Vogue, December 15

work truck, 'Cut the budget'
—AC, December

ammunition, 'Seven Sizes'—
LD, December 16

limousine, 'Quality Folk'—NG, December;
The Independent, December 25;
CLIA, January 1917

1917

stake truck, 'Night and Day'—AC, January

gondola, 'Afloat'—NG, January

trucks, 'The little fellow'—LD, January 20

chariot, 'Dominant'—
NG and CLIA, February

gear, 'Pull-Continuous'—AC, February

truck, 'Far'—LD, February 17; AC, March;
Leslie's, March 1

forest scene, 'Wanderlust'—NG and
CLIA, March; Vogue, March 15

touring, 'Quick blade and a strong one'
—Collier's and SEP, March 3

truck, 'Bridge the gap'—LD, March 24

flat bed truck, 'Hauling economy'—AC, April

touring car by pool, 'Reflections'
—Country Life, April

truck, 'Circles'—LD, April 21

sailing ship and phaeton, 'Economy!
Cheapest Power Is . . .'—Collier's and
The Independent, April 21; SEP, April 28;
NG, April

touring scene, 'Adventure'—NG, May

touring, 'If it isn't an Eastman'
—Eastman Kodak—SEP, May 12

touring, 'A woman's choice'
—Country Life, May

touring, 'Swinging'—Country Life, June

dump truck, 'Range and economy'
—AC, June

truck, 'Now Money Counts!'—LD, June 2

touring, 'Old methods . . .'—SEP, June 16;
Century, July

truck, 'Long Life—Low Cost'—LD, June 23;
System, July; AC, December

dump truck, 'City hauling cheap'—AC, July

truck, 'Where the Flag Goes'—LD, July 21

Model 3-35 touring, 'A New Creation'
—SEP, August 4; Collier's and
LD, August 11; NG, August

double decker bus, 'Safe—quiet—
economical'—AC, August

dump truck, 'A Yard Ahead'
—AC, September

street flusher, 'Full Time'—AC, October

landaulet, 'What Is Security Worth?'
—Collier's, September 8;
Vogue, September 15

limousine, 'Why Do Women Knit?'
—Collier's, October 13; Harper's, November

landaulet, 'Within Lies Beauty'
—Vogue, November 15;
Collier's, November 17; NG, October

fire truck, 'On the Spot'—AC, November

truck, 'Your own freight line'
—LD, November 17

limousine, 'New York's fighting mayor'
—Motor Life, November

1918

two ton-truck, 'Double Duty'—AC, January

all text ad, 'Packard's hand is set to help'
—The Independent, January 19

truck, 'Priority Freight'—LD, January 19;
System, February

flatbed truck, 'All four have done . . .'
—AC, February

all text ad, 'Help Win the War'
—Collier's, February 9

stake truck with trailer, 'Hauling Economy'
—AC, March

all text ad, 'Cars of Character'
—LD, March 2; Collier's, March 9

limousine, 'Boots in smart combinations
—Cousin's Shoes—Vogue, March

trucks, 'Army Packards'—LD, March 16;
Leslie's, April 6; System, April

flatbed truck, 'Proved in Service'—AC, April

all text ad, 'What's Back of Your Packard'
—Collier's, May 11

all text ad, '$5000 for the Best'—AC, May;
LD, May 18; System, June

dump truck, 'Repeat Orders'—AC, June

motor, 'Twin Six Quality'—Collier's, June 8;
LD, June 15

all text ad, 'Packard Twin Six Announcement
of Policy'—Collier's and LD, July 20

all text ad, 'Is your hauling cost . . .'
—AC, July; System, August

dump truck, 'Cut the Cost'—AC, August

truck, 'Save a Freight Car'—SEP and
Leslie's, August 10

all text ad, '1760 Packard Trucks'
—LD, November 30; Leslie's, December 7;
Collier's, December 14; SEP, December 21

all text ad, 'Truck Efficiency Test'

Twin Six touring, 'Owners live, move . . .'
—Country Life, June; VF, July

touring, 'Better operation and appearance'
—Gier Tuarc Wheel Company
—SEP, June 24

Twin Six Special touring, 'An hour or a day'
—SEP, July 8; Country Life, July

dump truck, "Decision to buy . . .'
—LD, July 15

Single Six coupe, 'Retail sales of the new
Packard . . .'—SEP, July 22

Twin Six touring, 'Naturally there
attaches . . .'—Country Life, August

Single Six sport touring, 'The value of this
new Packard . . .'—SEP, August 5

Single Six runabout, 'There is a deeper
significance . . .'—SEP, August 19

flatbed truck, 'The main facts . . .'
—LD, August 19

sedan, 'Twin Six owners are . . .'—SEP,
September 2; Country Life, September

Single Six touring, 'Anywhere but
in America . . .'—SEP, September 9

all text ad, 'Packard Re-Discovers America'
—SEP, September 16

Single Six sedan, 'Packard has now
proved . . .'—SEP, September 23

moving van, 'The main facts . . .'
—LD, September 23

coupe, 'With the Advent of the Single Six'
—SEP, September 30; NG, November

Single Six sedan, 'Even a year ago . . .'
—SEP, October 14

sedan, 'With the Single Six . . .'—SEP,
October 21; Atlantic Monthly, November

dump truck, 'Wherever you go . . .'
—LD, October 21

Single Six sedan, 'There is one pleasant
phase'—SEP and Country Gentleman,
October 28

custom limousine, 'There is nothing . . .'
—Vogue, November 1

touring, 'To speak of the Twin Six . . .'
—SEP, November 4

all text ad, 'Reputation'
—SEP, November 11; Vogue, December 1;
H&G, Country Life and NG, December

Single Six coupe, 'Packard has given . . .'
—SEP, November 18

Twin Six touring, 'There is nothing in all
the generality . . .'—SEP, October 7;
Country Life, October; NG, November

custom limousine, 'To speak of the
Twin Six . . .'—Country Life, November

logging truck, 'One in every . . .'
—LD, November 18

Single Six sedan, 'Packard Salesmen Are . . .'
—SEP, November 25

Single Six sedan-limousine, 'One pleasant
phase'—LHJ, December

Single Six sedan, 'There is one important
respect . . .'—SEP, December 9

Single Six coupe, 'Of all cars,
the ambitious . . .'—SEP, December 16

dump truck, 'Packard . . . preference'
—LD, December 16

Single Six limousine, 'It is evident
that most . . .'—SEP, December 23

Single Six sedan-limousine, 'The invitation
to you . . .'—SEP, December 30;
MoToR, January 1923

1923

woman with Packard, 'Trust your own
thoughts . . .'—NG, LHJ, H&G and
Country Life, January; Vogue, January 1;
T&C, January 15; SEP, December 2, 1922

Six sedan, 'The purchase of a Packard'
—SEP, January 6

Six sedan, 'The thousands who . . .'
—SEP and LD, January 13; H&G and
Vogue, February

all text ad, 'The universal desire for Packard'
—SEP, January 20

Packard and horses, 'Trust your own
thoughts . . .'—SEP, January 27;
NG, LHJ, HB and Country Life, February

Six coupe, 'The average . . .'
—SEP, February 3

radiator and headlights, 'Packard probably
represents the first and only case . . .'
—LD and SEP, February 10

coupe, front of lamp post, 'In addition
to its other . . .'—SEP, February 17;
Vogue, H&G and NG, March

all text ad, 'Twin Six and
Single Six . . . with Delco Ignition'—Delco
—LD, February 17

Six sedan, 'People so universally take for
granted . . .'—SEP, February 24;
Country Life, March

coupe, 'Trust your own thoughts . . .'
—LHJ, March; SEP, March 3

Six coupe, 'To realize the pronounced . . .'
—SEP and LD, March 10; T&C, March 15

Six sedan, 'Whenever you are disposed'
—SEP, March 17

Sedan and coupe behind lamp post, 'The
heaviest production . . .'—SEP, March 24;
LD, April 7; Country Life, April; Vogue,
NG and H&G, May

sedan, in mirror, 'Trust your own
thoughts . . .'—SEP, March 31; LHJ, April

Six sedan, 'Unconsciously we have all . . .'
—SEP, April 7

Six radiator, 'For twenty-three years . . .'
—SEP, April 14

Six sedan, 'Whenever you are disposed'
—Vogue, H&G and NG, April

Six touring and coupe, 'Public appreciation'
—SEP, April 21; Country Life, May

Six sedan-limousine, 'Public confidence'
—SEP, April 28

Six coupe and sedan, 'American women'
—LHJ, May

Six coupe, 'Nearly three years . . .'—LD and
SEP, May 5; Vogue and H&G, June

all text ad, 'The Packard Motor Car Co.'
—SEP, May 26

Six, 'A success which has endured'
—SEP, June 2

Six sport touring, 'Because it was a Packard
. . .'—SEP, May 19; NG, June; LD, June 2

Six sedan, 'Those who buy . . .'—SEP,
May 12; LHJ and Country Life, June

Six touring and roadster, 'The number
of . . .'—SEP, June 9

Eight touring car, two-page ad,
'Announcing the . . .'—SEP, June 16

Six sedan, '. . . had its origin'—SEP, June 23

Eight touring car, 'The Packard Motor
Car Company'—SEP, June 30;
NG, LHJ, Country Life and Vogue, July

touring car, racing locomotive, 'Is it not
strange . . .'—SEP, July 7

Six coupe and touring, 'Any Packard
salesman . . .'—SEP, July 14

Six sport touring and sedan, 'Packard Single
Six offers . . .'—SEP, July 21

Eight sedan, 'Those who ride in . . .'
—SEP, July 28; Vogue, LHJ, Country Life,
NG and H&G, August

Six, 'Among the thousands . . .'
—SEP, August 4

Six sport touring, 'Those who graduate from
lesser cars . . .'—SEP, August 11

sedan and coupe, front of yacht, 'Everyone
feels so sure . . .'—SEP, August 18

Six touring, 'It is fine to be able to feel . . .'
—SEP, August 25

roadster, 'The striking thing . . .'
—Vogue, NG and LHJ, September;
Country Life, September and October

Six coupe, 'If you are seeking . . .'
—SEP, September 1

all text ad, 'There are certain important
things . . .'—SEP, September 8

Six sedan, 'Because it has always . . .'
—SEP, September 15

Six limousine, 'If you have . . .'
—SEP, September 22

all text ad, 'It has to be a pretty good

Yankee car . . .'—SEP, September 29;
NG, LHJ, H&G and Vogue, October

Six sedan-limousine, 'What is the net . . .'
—SEP, October 6

Six headlights, 'There are wise people . . .'
—SEP, October 13

Six coupe, 'Never cost me a dollar . . .'
—SEP, October 20

all text ad, 'Ten simple reasons . . .'
—SEP, October 27

Six sedan, 'Perhaps the prettiest
compliment . . .'—LHJ, November

coupe, 'The Packard Single Eight'
—NG, Vogue and Country Life, November

Six limousine, 'A comfort in traffic'
—SEP, November 3

all text ad, 'Possession of a Packard'
—SEP, November 10

club sedan, 'New principles in Packard
Straight Eight'—NG, Country Life and
H&G, December; SEP and
Vogue, December 1

touring car, front of ocean liner, 'There is
a deeper . . .'—SEP, November 17;
LHJ and Nation's Business, December

Eight sedan, 'Why owners are enthusiastic'
—LD, December 8; SEP, December 15;
Country Life, Nation's Business, Vogue and
H&G, January 1924

1924

Six touring, 'For twenty-four years . . .'
—American, January

Six coupe, 'The car ideal of most women . . .'
—LHJ, January

all text ad, 'A new improved model . . .'
—NG, January; LD, January 5;
SEP, December 29, 1923

Six sedan, 'Can you afford to overlook . . .'
—SEP, January 26

Fuelizer, 'Only Packard owners know . . .'
—SEP, January 12; Life, January 17; Vanity
Fair, Vogue, Nation's Business, H&G,
American and NG, February

Six sedan, 'Improvements women appreciate'
—LHJ, February

Six sedan, 'Can you afford to overlook . . .'
—Country Life, February (same text as SEP
January 26 ad, different illustration)

Eight sedan, 'Only Packard can build a
Packard'—SEP, February 9;
Life, February 14; Vogue, American, H&G,
NG and Nation's Business, March

Six touring, 'Superior performance . . .'
—SEP, February 23; LD, March 1;
American, April

Eight sedan, 'You feel at once . . .'
—Country Life, March;
Nation's Business, April

Six coupe, 'To design and build . . .'
—SEP, March 8; Life, March 13

Eight sedan, 'Women appreciate . . .'
—LHJ, March; H&G, April

coupe, 'Every woman will delight . . .'
—Vogue and LHJ, April

Eight limousine, 'Only Packard can build
a Packard'—SEP, April 5; Life, April 10;
Country Life and NG, April

Six coupe, 'Day-to-Day Experience . . .'
—SEP, April 19; LD, April 26

sedan, 'Only Packard can build a Packard'
—Harper's and LHJ, May

sedan, 'Those Who Possess . . .'—NG and
Nation's Business, May

Eight coupe, 'Because the Packard . . . is
a product'—Vogue, H&G and
Country Life, May

Eight touring, 'Simplicity'—SEP, May 3;
Life, May 8; LD, May 24; Vogue, July 1;
Country Life, July

Six touring, 'The Packard . . . is built'
—SEP, May 17

Six touring, 'Why women are loyal to . . .'
—LHJ, June

Six touring, 'Only Packard can build a
Packard'—SEP, June 14; LD, June 21

Eight motor, 'Simplicity'—SEP, May 31;
Life, June 5; H&G, Country Life, Vogue and
Nation's Business, June

Six touring, 'Only Packard can build a
Packard'—SEP, June 28; H&G, July;
Life, July 3

Eight touring, 'Supreme'—SEP, July 26;
Life, July 31; H&G, Country Life and
Harper's, August

Six touring, 'Who are buying . . .'
—SEP, July 12; LD, July 19; Vogue and
Nation's Business, August

Six coupe, 'Thousands of men . . .'—SEP,
August 9; LD, August 16; Life, August 28

Six touring, 'The Used Car Evil'—SEP,
August 23; Nation's Business, September

Eight limousine, 'Incomparable'—
Vogue, September

limousine, 'The car men are waiting for'
—SEP, September 20; H&G and
Country Life, September

sedan, 'The Packard owner knows'
—MA, August 28; SEP, September 6;
LD, September 13; Life, September 25;
Nation's Business, October

coupe, 'The rejuvenation of motoring . . .'
—Vogue, H&G and Country Life, October

touring, 'The Packard you buy today'—SEP,
October 4; American Motorist, October

Six touring, 'Brings 44% of its cost . . .'
—SEP, October 18; Life, October 23

limousine, 'Distinction'—Vogue, H&G and
VF, November

coupe, 'The Packard Six owner knows . . .'
—SEP, November 1; Life, November 20

coupe, 'Depreciation'—SEP, November 29

limousine, 'Ten years ago . . .'
—SEP, November 15; Vogue, H&G and
NG, December

Six sedan, 'Two kinds of men'
—SEP, December 13; Life, December 18

coupe, 'There are two kinds of
good cars . . .'—SEP, December 27;
Life, January 15, 1925

1925

Eight limousine, 'Europe's Choice'
—H&G and MoToR, January;
SEP, January 10; AT, January 17

sedan, 'A man is known . . .'
—SEP, January 24

Eight roadster, 'Motor Car
Manufacturers . . .'—Strom Ball Bearing
Manufacturing Company—SA, January

Six limousine, 'A Tale of Two Cities'
—Vogue, January; SEP, April 4;
NG and H&G, May; Life, May 7

touring, 'Your 1925 Packard . . .'
—Vogue, H&G and NG, February

Six coupe, 'For twenty-five years . . .'
—SEP, February 7; Life, February 12

Eight touring, 'Round the world fliers . . .'
—SEP, February 21; Vanity Fair, H&G,
Vogue and NG, March; Life, March 12

Six sedan, 'Long life chassis demand . . .'
—SEP, March 21

front view, 'Of a Distinguished Family'
—SEP, March 7; Life, April 9;
Vogue, NG, VF and H&G, April

Six sedan-limousine, 'Precision is protected'
—SEP, April 18; Vogue and NG, June;
Life, June 4

Eight sport touring, 'From the diary . . .'
—SEP, May 2; H&G, June

Six runabout, 'A flood let loose'
—SEP, May 16

Eight sedan, 'The luxury of roominess'
—SEP, May 30

Six sedan, 'Gratifying a national desire'
—SEP, June 27

all text ad, 'Again Packard pioneers'
—SEP, June 13; Life, July 2;
Vogue, NG and H&G, July

motor, 'Packard Marine Engines'
—Motor Boat, July 10

car, plane, boat, 'Supreme—air, land and
water'—AT, July 4; SEP, July 11; Life,
July 30; Vogue, NG and H&G, August

Six sedan, 'The car of youth'
—SEP, August 8

side view, 'Packard Presents a Club Sedan'
—AT, August 1; SEP, August 22

Eight sedan, 'Your choice of color and
upholstery'—SEP, July 25; Life, August 27;
T&C, September 15; Vogue, HB, Country
Life, Atlantic Monthly, NG, Theatre, Asia,
SA and H&G, September

Gold Cup race, 'Packard Engines Win . . .'
—Motor Boat, September

Six sedan, 'The Packard . . . is a conquest
car'—SEP, September 5; LD, September 12;
Vogue and H&G, October

Eight touring, 'Seven days without a stop'
—SEP, September 19; Life, September 24;
LD, September 26; Country Life, SA, Asia,
NG and HB, October

front view, 'Packard Six owners are loyal'
—AT, September 26; SEP, October 3; LD,
October 10; Life, October 22; Spur,
November 1; Country Life, NG, Theatre,
HB, SA and H&G, November

airplane and boat, 'New Laurels'
—SEP, October 31; LD, November 7;
Life, November 19

seaplane, 'Endurance'
—Aviation, November 9

Eight limousine, 'A new measure of fine car
excellence'—SEP, November 28; LD,
December 5; Life, December 17; Vogue, HB,
Country Life and H&G, December

front view, 'Mastery of Power'
—SEP, October 17; LD, October 24;
Asia and NG, December

Six sedan-limousine, 'What is the price
of . . .'—SEP, December 12; LD,
December 19; Vanity Fair, January 1926

aero engine, 'Versatility'
—Aviation, December 21

sedan with Brewster body, 'This Year's
Salon . . .'—American Leather Producers,
Inc.—VF, December

1926

Six sedan, 'How often do you buy a war
tax?'—SA, Country Life, NG, Theatre, HB,
Asia, H&G and Sunset, January; SEP,
November 14, 1925; LD, November 21, 1925

Six sedan, 'Distinction, Beauty, Comfort'
—LHJ, Vogue and GH, January

Eight club sedan, 'Born in the Lap
of Luxury'—LD, January 2; Outlook,
January 9; SEP, December 26, 1925

Six club sedan, 'Serving or Selling'
—LD, January 16; SEP, January 9;
Life, January 14

sedan-limousine, 'And now at Monte Carlo'
—SEP, February 20; LD, February 27;

Country Life, NG, Sunset, HB, Asia, H&G
and Theatre, April

sedan-limousine, 'The Ambassador's Choice'
—SEP, January 23; LD, January 30;
Country Life, Vogue, H&G, Sunset, GH,
Asia, HB, LHJ, NG, VF and SA, February

sedan, 'Serving with distinction'
—SEP, February 6; LD, February 13;
H&G, Country Life, NG, Asia, HB,
SA and Sunset, March

all text ad, 'Now, more than ever'—SEP,
March 6; Life, March 11; LD, March 13

all text ad, 'The secret of owning a Packard
car'—SEP, March 20; LD, March 27

front view, 'When you arrive in a Packard'
—Vogue, LHJ, Asia and GH, March

club sedan, 'The prestige of a great name'
—Vogue, LHJ and GH, April

Eight limousine, 'Distinguished by Illustrious
Patronage'—SEP, April 17; LD, April 24;
Life, May 6; Sunset, June

all text ad, 'Are you paying for a Packard?'
—SEP, May 1; LD, May 8

club sedan, 'Original Creations by Master
Designers'—Vogue, GH and LHJ, May

Six sedan, 'The Packard mile costs less'
—SEP, April 3; Life, April 8; LD, April 10;
Country Life, NG, Sunset, Asia, H&G,
Theatre and HB, May

touring, 'The Navy and Army . . .'
—SEP, May 29; Life, June 3; LD, June 5;
Country Life, SA, Asia, NG, Theatre, H&G
and HB, June

roadster, 'The satisfaction of Packard
ownership'—SEP, May 15; LD, May 22;
Vogue, GH and LHJ, June

Eight touring, 'The greatest Packard of
them all'—SEP, June 12; LD, June 19

touring, 'The high position . . .'
—Vogue, GH and LHJ, July

front ¾ view, 'At Home in Any
Environment'—SEP, June 26; Country Life,
HB, Sunset, Theatre, H&G, Asia, SA and
NG, July; Life, July 1; LD, July 3

Packard factory door, 'For a year Packard
has asked'—SEP, July 24; LD, July 31

touring car, 'Serving America's Aristocracy'
—SEP, July 10; LD, July 17; Life, July 29;
Country Life, SA, Sunset, NG, Theatre,
H&G, VF, Asia and HB, August

front view, 'The hallmark of excellence'
—Vogue, LHJ and GH, August

dual cowl phaeton, 'Exploring deluxe . . .'
—SEP, August 6

Six roadster, 'Introducing the improved . . .'
—LD, August 14

sedan, 'And now the boss of the road'
—SEP and LD, August 21; Life, August 26

boat race, 'Again Packard makes clean
sweep'—Motor Boat, September 25

club sedan, 'Beautiful in its simplicity'
—American Leather Producers, Inc.
—Asia, September

touring (green), 'Performance'—LHJ, Asia,
Sunset, HB, Theatre, H&G, Vogue, SA,
American, Country Life and NG, September;
Life, September 3; SEP, September 4; LD,
September 11; Mentor, January 1927

sedan (maroon), 'Grace'—
SEP, September 18; LD, September 25;
Mentor, NG, H&G, Sunset, American, LHJ,
Theatre, Asia, HB and Vogue, October;
Life, October 21

sedan (green), 'Acceleration'
—SEP, October 2; LD, October 9

cabriolet (three-tone), 'Distinction'
—SEP, October 16; LD, October 23;
SA, Sunset, HB, NG, Asia, H&G, Country
Life, LHJ, American, Theatre and Vogue,
November; Life, November 18

sedan (blue), 'Pride of Possession'
—SEP, November 13; LD, November 20;
NG, Theatre, HB, Vogue, H&G, Theatre,
LHJ and Country Life, December

opera coupe (tan and brown), 'Quality'
—SEP, October 30; LD, November 6;
Asia, Mentor, Sunset and American,
December; Life, December 16

opera coupe (tan), 'Comfort'
—SEP, November 27; LD, December 4

sedan, 'Safety'—LD, December 18;
SEP, December 25

1927

sedan (blue), cabriolet (maroon), runabout
(gray), 'The finest Packards ever built'
—Nitro-Valspar Paints—SEP, January 8

sedan (blue), 'Beauty'—SEP, January 8; LD,
January 15; Country Life, LHJ, Theatre,
Vogue, H&G, HB and NG, January

club sedan (tan and brown), 'Precision'
—SEP, January 22; LD, January 29; Asia,
Sunset, American, SA, February; Life,
February 10

club sedan (red and black), 'Flexibility'
—LD, January 1; SA, Sunset, Asia and
American, January; Mentor, September
1926; SEP, December 11, 1926

opera coupe (green and gray), 'Reputation'
—SEP, February 19; LD, February 26; Life,
March 10; SA, Asia, Sunset and American,
March

sedan (green), 'Prestige'—SEP, February 5;
LD, February 12; Country Life, HB, Vogue,
LHJ, Theatre, NG, VF and H&G, February

opera coupe (yellow and black), 'Luxury'
—LD, March 12; Country Life, NG,
Theatre, LHJ, H&G, Vogue and HB,

March; SEP, March 5

sedan (blue and green), 'Silence'
—SEP, March 19; LD, March 26;
Life, April 7; Sunset, SA, American,
Mentor and Asia, April

sedan (purple), 'Charm'—SEP, April 2;
LD, April 9; Country Life, HB, Vogue,
H&G, LHJ, Theatre and NG, April

sedan (green), 'Enduring'—SEP, April 16;
LD, April 23; T&C, Country Life, NG, HB,
Theatre, H&G, LHJ and Vogue, May

touring (black and orange), 'Power'—SEP,
April 30; Life, May 5; LD, May 7; Sunset,
SA, Asia and American, May

aero engines, 'For more than a quarter . . .'
—Aviation, May 16

touring (brown and orange), 'Balance'
—SEP, May 28; LD, June 4;
Sunset, SA, Asia and American, June

club sedan (black and blue), 'Leadership'
—SEP, May 14; LD, May 21; Life, June 2;
AT, June 4; LHJ, Country Life, HB, Vogue,
Theatre and H&G, June; American, July

club sedan (red and green), 'Color'
—SEP, June 25; LD, July 2;
Life, July 28; Sunset and Asia, July

aero engine, 'Performance'
—Aviation, July 11

roadster (yellow and blue), 'Service'
—SEP, July 23; LD, July 30

touring (cream and red), 'Dependability'
—SEP, June 11; LD, June 18; Country Life,
NG, Vogue, LHJ, Theatre, H&G and HB,
July

convertible coupe (red), 'Simplicity'—SEP,
July 9; LD, July 16; Country Life, LHJ,
Vogue, NG, Theatre, HB and H&G, August

touring (orange and sand), 'Enduring Style'
—SEP, August 6; LD, August 13; Life,
August 25; Asia, Sunset and America, August

motor (443) in color, 'Engineering'
—SEP, August 20; LD, August 27

touring (green), 'To create a Packard . . .'
—SEP, September 3; LD, September 10;
Life, September 22; Country Life, GH, HB,
Asia, H&G and Vogue, September

Six sedan (green), 'Four hundred years . . .'
—SEP, October 1; LD, October 8;
AT (b&w), October 22

Eight sedan (green and black), 'Packard
requires in upholstery . . .'—LD,
September 24; SEP, September 17; Life,
October 20; T&C, Asia, GH, Country Life,
NG, HB, Vogue and H&G, October

Eight 443 all-weather town car (red and
black), 'In leather selection . . .'
—SEP, October 15; LD, October 22; Asia,
NG, Country Life, HB, GH, Vogue and
H&G, November; Life, November 17

Six coupe (sand and green), 'Those who

design . . .'—SEP, October 29;
LD, November 5

motors, 'Master Motor Builders'
—LD, November 12; SEP, November 19;
MoToR, January 1928

Eight 443 sedan (blue and black), 'Few jewel
collectors'—SEP, November 12; LD,
November 19; Vogue, H&G, GH, Country
Life, HB, MoToR and T&C, December

Eight 443 opera coupe (green), 'In exterior
finish . . .'—SEP, December 10; LD,
December 17

men working on car, 'Thirty-One Men'
—LD, November 26; SEP, December 3

Six convertible coupe (grey), 'In one
generation'—SEP, November 26;
LD, December 3; Asia and NG, December;
Life, December 15

Eight 443 convertible sedan (dark blue,
Dietrich), 'Cultured women . . .'
—SEP. December 24; LD, December 31;
Vogue, Asia, Country Life, NG, HB, and
H&G, January 1928; GH, February 1928

1928

Eight 443 club sedan (yellow), 'The master
cabinetmakers'—SEP, January 7;
LD, January 14; Country Life, HB and
H&G, February

all text ad, 'Packard Eight prices reduced'
—LD, January 14

Eight 443 sedan (brown and yellow),
'Through the Ages'—SEP, January 21; LD,
January 28; Asia, SA and NG, February

sedan (red and cream), 'Packard die cutters'
—SEP, February 4; LD, February 11;
SA and NG, March

Six convertible coupe (blue), 'Packard body
designers'—SEP, February 18;
LD, February 25; Vogue, HB, Country Life
and H&G, March

touring (red), 'Packard quality begins . . .'
—SEP, March 17; LD, March 24; Asia and
NG, March

Eight 443 opera coupe (red and green), 'The
life of many Packard parts'—SEP, March 3;
LD, March 10; H&G, Country Life, HB,
Vogue and GH, April

Eight 443 convertible coupe (red and black),
'Since man first applied wheels'—SEP,
March 31; LD, April 7; T&C, Country Life,
GH, Vogue, HB and H&G, May

Eight 443 roadster (black), 'Packard
crankshafts, gears, axles . . .'
—SEP, April 14; LD, April 21;
Asia, MoToR and NG, May

Six sedan (green), 'The mixing and
application . . .'—SEP, May 12;
LD, May 19; Country Life, GH, HB, Vogue
and H&G, June

Eight 443 sedan (orange and black),
'The famed beauty . . .'—SEP, April 28;
LD, May 5; Asia and NG, June

Eight 443 sedan (blue and black), 'Back of
Packard's acknowledged . . .'—AT, June 2;
SEP, June 9; LD, June 16; MoToR, June;
Country Life, HB, Vogue and GH, July

Eight 443 club sedan (purple), 'Packard has
made . . .'—SEP, May 26; LD, June 2;
Asia, NG and MoToR, July

Eight 443 convertible sedan (green),
'Precision is strictly . . .'—SEP, July 7;
LD, July 14

Eight 443 touring (blue), 'Each succeeding
model . . .'—SEP, June 23; LD, June 30;
Country Life, HB, Vogue and GH, August

Eight 443 dual cowl phaeton (orange and
black), 'Packard's characteristic lines'
—SEP, July 21; LD, July 28; NG, MoToR
and Asia, August

Eight 443 opera coupe (black and red),
'The Slender, Graceful . . .'—SEP, August 4;
LD, August 11; NG, September

all text ad, 'Packard identity will endure'
—SEP, August 4

Eight 443 sedan (green) two-page ad,
'Achievement'—SEP, August 18;
LD, August 25; Asia, Theatre, Vogue and
Country Life, September

portrait, 'James Ward Packard'
—LD, August 18; SEP, August 25

sedan (red and black), 'Luxury for the second
owner'—Liberty, September 8

626 sedan (blue), 'One reason I always buy
a Packard'—SEP, September 15;
LD, September 22; Vogue, H&G, HB and
Country Life, October

radiator and coat of arms, 'Twenty-five
years ago Packard adopted . . .'—SEP,
September 22; MoToR, January 1929

sedan, 'Serves the second family . . .'
—Liberty, October 6

645 dual cowl phaeton (red), 'I suppose I
have owned . . .'—SEP, September 1;
LD, September 8; MoToR, Theatre, NG and
American Motorist, October

633 sedan (red and black), 'My experience is
that the best . . .'—SEP, September 29; LD,
October 6; Asia, NG and Theatre, November

sedan (blue and black), 'Even those who have
been brought up . . .'—SEP, October 13;
LD, October 20; Country Life, HB, Vogue
and H&G, November

club sedan (green), 'Gules, a cross lozengy'
—SEP, October 27; LD, November 3; T&C,
Asia, H&G, Country Life, HB, Theatre and
NG, December

club sedan, 'A better buy used . . .'
—Liberty, November 3

cabriolet (orange), 'Packard beauty, of
course'—SEP, November 10;

LD, November 17

sedan (black), 'Packard has always designed
. . .'—SEP, November 24; LD, December 1

sedan (blue), 'Second owners too enjoy
prestige'—Liberty, December 1

sedan (black and brown), 'Each Packard in a
famous succession . . .'—SEP, December 22;
LD, December 29

sedan (black), 'Why not buy a good used
car?'—Liberty, December 29

1929

opera coupe (purple), 'Packard, like its
patrons'—Country Life, T&C, Asia, NG,
Vogue, H&G, Theatre and HB, January;
SEP, December 8, 1928

opera coupe (purple), 'Packard knows that
. . .' SEP, January 5; LD, January 12

convertible sedan (blue), 'Packard was
born to occupy . . .'—SEP, January 19;
LD, January 26; H&G, HB and
Country Life, February (Country Life ad
mislabelled January in magazine)

club sedan, 'Its prestige never wanes . . .'
—Liberty, January 26

sedan (green), 'Packard men bear the
imprint'—SEP, February 2; LD, February 9;
Theatre, NG and MoToR, February

sedan, 'Ownership Changes . . .'
—Liberty, February 23

sedan (red), 'The romance of exploration . . .'
—SEP, February 16; LD, February 23;
Theatre and NG, March

club sedan (black and red), "The first
Packard was built in the '90's . . .'
—SEP, March 2; LD, March 9; HB,
Country Life, H&G and Vogue, March

dual cowl phaeton (blue and orange),
'Packard has ever looked beyond . . .'
—SEP, March 16; LD, March 23; Asia,
NG, Theatre and American Motorist, April

sedan (green), 'Real beauty is unchanging
. . .'—SEP, March 30; Country Life, HB,
H&G and Vogue, April; LD, April 6

sedan (brown), 'Packard enjoys a
priceless . . .'—SEP, April 13; LD, April 20;
Country Life, H&G and HB, May

opera coupe (red and green), 'From its
inception . . .'—SEP, April 27; Theatre,
Asia, NG and MoToR, May; LD, May 4

roadster (orange and black), 'Packard men
are carefully chosen . . .'—SEP, May 25;
LD, June 1; NG, Theatre and American
Motorist, June

roadster (1926), 'You have better control'
—Ethyl Corporation—LHJ, June

sedan (blue), 'The discriminating public . . .'
—SEP, May 11; LD, May 18;
Country Life, H&G and HB, June

club sedan (tan), 'The log of Packard
achievement . . ."—SEP, June 8,
LD, June 15; NG and Theatre, July

dual cowl phaeton (yellow and green),
'Where taste and discernment . . .'
—SEP, June 22; LD, June 29;
HB, H&G and Country Life, July

coupe (black), 'Quality craftsmanship . . .'
—SEP, July 6; LD, July 13;
Country Life, HB and H&G, August

dual cowl phaeton (blue), 'Packard has
always aspired . . .'—LD, July 27;
SEP, July 20; NG, Asia, MoToR and
Theatre, August

sedan (red), 'Reputation is the most treasured
. . .'—SEP, August 24; LD, August 24;
Country Life, H&G and HB, September

cabriolet (black), 'Packard dealers are
ambassadors . . .'—SEP, August 3;
LD, August 10; NG, Asia and
Theatre, September

sedan (purple), 'Packard owners today enjoy
. . .'—SEP, August 31; LD, September 7;
Country Life, Harper's, H&G and HB,
October

all text ad, 'What Price-Class?'
—SEP, September 7; Time, September 9;
LD, September 14; NG, October

745 sedan (brown and orange), 'Packard
luxury is mental . . .'—SEP, September 14;
LD, September 21; Asia, Theatre and
T&C, October; MoToR, November

all text ad, 'You are paying for a Packard'
—SEP, September 21; Time, September 23;
LD, September 28; NG, November

740 club sedan (blue), 'That Packard is the
greatest'—SEP, September 28;
LD, October 5; Arts & Decoration,
Country Life, HB and H&G, November

all text ad, 'Philadelphia records prove it'
—SEP, October 5; Time, October 7;
LD, October 12

sedan (blue), 'The Packard Standard Eight
. . .'—SEP, October 12; LD, October 19;
Asia and Theatre, November

all text ad, 'The New Packard Eights . . .'
—SEP, October 19; Time, October 21;
LD, October 26

745 sedan (red), 'The New Series Packard
. . .'—SEP, October 26; LD, November 2;
T&C, Asia and Theatre, December

all text ad, 'Confirmed by owners in Atlanta'
—SEP, November 2; Time, November 4;
LD, November 9; NG, December

740 opera coupe (green and black),
'Packard luxury has never been . . .'
—SEP, November 9; LD, November 16;
HB, H&G and Country Life, December

all text ad, 'Cleveland owners find it true'

—SEP, November 16; Time, November 18;
LD, November 23; NG, January 1930

740 sedan (green), 'Packard luxury, once
enjoyed'—SEP, November 23;
LD, November 30; Asia and
Theatre, January 1930

all text ad, 'Proved by owners in Kansas
City'—SEP, November 30; LD, December 7

745 sedan (red and black), 'Packard luxury
goes deeper . . .'—SEP, December 7;
LD, December 14

745 sedan (red), 'In thirty years devoted to
. . .'—SEP, December 21; LD, December 28;
Country Life, HB, H&G, Arts & Decoration
and American Motorist, January 1930

1930

740 opera coupe (green and blue),
'The Packard Custom Eight . . .'
—SEP, January 4; LD, January 11;
Asia, Fortune and Theatre, February

745 town car (black), 'No finer personal . . .'
—SEP, January 18; LD, January 25;
HB, Country Life, Arts & Decoration and
MoToR, February; Vogue, February 15

745 club sedan (blue), 'Packard builds three
. . .'—SEP, February 15; LD, February 22;
Fortune and Theatre, March

745 convertible coupe (blue), 'Packard
pioneered the straight eight . . .'—SEP,
February 1; LD, February 8; Country Life,
HB, H&G and American Motorist, March

745 sedan (black and green), 'That the
Packard Eight . . .'—SEP, March 1;
LD, March 8; HB, H&G, Country Life
and American Motorist, April

745 sedan (red and black), 'Each year
Packard has . . .'—LD, March 22; SEP,
March 15; Asia, Fortune and Theatre, April

engine, 'Radial Diesel Aircraft Engine'
—Aero Digest, April

745 coupe (black and red), 'Three years
ago . . .'—SEP, March 29; LD, April 5;
Vogue, HB, H&G, Country Life and
Arts & Decoration, May

733 sedan (green), 'This spring people are
weighing . . .'—SEP, April 12; LD, April 19

745 dual cowl phaeton (yellow), 'From its
first . . .'—SEP, April 26; LD, May 3;
Asia, Fortune, American Motorist and
Theatre, May

745 roadster (orange), 'Among Packard
owners . . .'—SEP, May 10; LD, May 17;
Country Life, H&G and VF, June

diesel engine, two-page ad, 'To give new
impetus to flight'—SEP, May 17

sedan (purple), 'The Packard Standard
Eight'—SEP, May 24; LD, May 31;
Theatre, Fortune, Asia and
American Motorist, June

745 convertible coupe (green), 'Packard
owners keep their . . .'—SEP, June 7;
LD, June 14; Vogue, H&G and
Country Life, July

all text ad, 'Packard Standard Eight'
—LD, June 7

745 sedan (black), 'Packard engineering
leadership . . .'—SEP, June 21;
LD, June 28; Theatre, Fortune,
Country Life and Asia, July

740 club sedan (cream and blue), 'If you
are looking forward . . .'—SEP, July 5;
LD, July 12

745 opera coupe (green), 'Everyone knows
that . . .'—SEP, July 19; LD, July 26;
HB, H&G, American Motorist and
Country Life, August

745 touring (green), 'Many motorists . . .'
—SEP, August 2; LD, August 9;
Fortune, August; Theatre, September

740 roadster (blue), 'The luxury and
distinction'—SEP, August 16; LD, August 23

745 touring (blue), 'Throughout the
centuries . . .'—SEP, August 30;
T&C, Fortune, Country Life and
H&G, September; LD, September 6

convertible coupe (green), 'Packard families'
—SEP, September 13; LD, September 20;
Country Life and H&G, October

826 sedan (rose), 'Most popular of all . . .'
—SEP, September 27; LD, October 4;
Fortune, October

sedan (blue and brown), 'Packard owners
everywhere . . .'—SEP, October 11;
LD, October 18; Fortune, November

town car (purple), 'The patronage of
the discerning . . .'—SEP, October 25;
LD, November 1; Country Life and
H&G, November

sedan (green), 'The luxury of Packard
transportation'—SEP, November 8;
LD, November 15; Country Life, December

club sedan (red and black), 'In all
Packard's thirty years'—SEP, November 22;
LD, November 29; Fortune, December

Towle amphibian, 'Powered by Twin
Packard Diesels'—Aviation, December

sedan (green & black), 'The world of
discrimination . . .'—SEP, December 6; LD,
December 13; Country Life, January 1931

opera coupe (orange), 'Families of taste . . .'
—SEP, December 20; LD, December 27;
Fortune, January 1931

1931

town car (black), 'A whole generation . . .'
—SEP, January 3; LD, January 10;
Fortune and The Sportsman, February

sedan (green), 'Owners of the new Packard . . .'—SEP, January 17; LD, January 24; Country Life, February

sedan (blue), 'The Packard Seven-Passenger . . .'—SEP, January 31; LD, February 7

coupe (blue and yellow), 'The Packard DeLuxe may be . . .'—SEP, February 14; LD, February 21; Country Life, March

club sedan (rust), 'The designing and building . . .'—SEP, February 28; LD, March 7; Fortune and The Sportsman, April

sedan (tan), 'Packard leadership . . .' —SEP, March 14; LD, March 21; Country Life, April

town car (blue), 'The first Packard car was . . .'—SEP, March 28; LD, April 4; Country Life, May

opera coupe (maroon), 'To own . . .'—SEP, April 11; LD, April 18; Fortune, May

sedan (green), 'Packard has been the supreme . . .'—SEP, April 25; LD, May 2

roadster (yellow), 'Passing fads or fancies' —SEP, May 9; LD, May 16; Fortune and Country Life, June

touring (tan and brown), 'Ownership of a Packard car . . .'—SEP, May 23; LD, May 30; Fortune and Country Life, July

Bellanca Pacemaker, 'Performance of the Packard Diesel'—Aero Digest, June

club sedan (black), 'The Packard Eight is a unified . . .'—SEP, June 6; LD, June 13

sedan (green), 'The continued patronage . . .' —SEP, June 20; LD, June 27

convertible coupe (blue), 'Those Who Select . . .'—SEP, July 4

Ninth Series front view (blue), 'To you who appreciate . . .'—LD, July 11; SEP, July 18; Fortune and Country Life, August

sedan (maroon), 'The newly announced Packard cars . . .'—LD, July 25; SEP, August 1; Fortune and Country Life, September

Super Eight (yellow), 'The new Coupe-Roadster'—LD, August 8; SEP, August 15

DeLuxe Eight (green), 'In the new convertible victoria . . .'—LD, August 22; SEP, August 29; Fortune and Country Life, October

Standard Eight (blue), 'In the new Packard Eight sedan . . .'—LD, September 5; SEP, September 12

all text ad, 'A dollar for dole'—LD, September 12; Time, September 14; Forbes, September 15

DeLuxe Eight (black), 'The new Packard Sport Phaeton . . .'—LD, September 19; SEP, September 26

DeLuxe Eight limousine (brown), 'Discriminating owners of the new Packard . . .'—Time, October 10; SEP, October 10

DeLuxe Eight sedan (blue), 'Jugo-Slavia' —LD, October 17; SEP, October 24; Fortune and Country Life, November

DeLuxe Eight sedan (brown), 'Switzerland' —Time, November 2; SEP, November 7

opera coupe (turquoise), 'Japan' —LD, November 14; SEP, November 21

town car (green), 'Paris' —Time, November 30; SEP, December 5; Fortune, December

Standard Eight sedan (red), 'Canada' LD, December 12; SEP, December 19; Fortune, January 1932

1932

DeLuxe Eight coupe (blue), 'Greece'—SEP, January 9; Time, December 28, 1931

DeLuxe Eight club sedan (blue and brown), 'Egypt'—LD, January 9; SEP, January 16; Fortune, February

sedan (green), 'China'—Time, January 25; SEP, January 30

all text ad, 'The New Packard Light Eight' —ATJ, January

sedan, 'The New Packard Light Eight' —ATJ, February

Super Eight sedan (blue), 'Argentina' —LD, February 6; SEP, February 13

all text ad, 'Packard for 1932' —SEP, February 6; LD, February 13; Time, February 15

Light Eight sedan, 'Announcing the New . . .'—SEP, February 20; LD, February 27; Time, February 29

DeLuxe Eight club sedan (blue and yellow), 'India'—Time, February 22; SEP, February 27; Fortune and H&G, March

Light Eight sedan (blue and green), 'England'—LD, March 5; SEP, March 12; Fortune and H&G, April

Light Eight full line, two-page ad, 'The New . . .'—SEP, March 5; LD, March 12; Time, March 14

Light Eight full line, two-page ad, 'See and Drive . . .'—SEP, March 19; Time, March 28

stationary coupe (blue, Dietrich), 'Italy' —Time, March 21; SEP, March 26

Light Eight sedan, 'With the new . . .' —SEP, April 2

Light Eight convertible coupe (yellow), 'Spain'—LD, April 2; SEP, April 9; Fortune and H&G, May

Standard Eight sedan (green), 'Germany' —Time, April 18; SEP, April 23; LD, April 30

Twin Six sedan (blue), '. . . A Familiar Name'—Time, May 16; SEP, May 21; LD, May 28; Fortune and H&G, June

Light Eight sedan (yellow), 'These are days of unusual . . .'—Time, June 13; SEP, June 18; LD, June 25; Fortune and H&G, July

Twin Six dual cowl phaeton (red), 'The new Packard . . . develops'—Time, July 11; SEP, July 16; LD, July 23; Fortune, H&G and Vogue, August

Standard Eight club sedan (blue), '. . . as Packard builds it . . .'—Time, August 8; SEP, August 13; LD, August 20; Fortune, September

Gold Cup winner, 'Only Motor That Could Beat a Packard'—Motor Boating, September

rear view, in color, 'The Packard You Never See'—LD and SEP, September 17; Time, September 19; Fortune, October and January 1933

front view (maroon), 'The Step That Only Packard Takes'—SEP, October 8; LD, October 15; Time, October 17; Fortune, November

Packard mat, 'It may never again be so easy to become . . .'—LD, October 1; Time, October 3; SEP, October 15

Man and woman, 'Maybe it's time to talk . . .'—SEP, November 5; LD, November 12; Time, November 21

Gar Wood and boat, 'Gar Wood' —LD, October 29; Time, November 7; SEP, November 12; Fortune, December

front view closeup, 'It may never again be so easy to become . . .'—LD, December 3; Time, December 5; SEP, December 10

1933

all text ad, 'The family invisible' —Time, January 9

Twelve sedan (blue), Super Eight victoria (orange), Eight sedan (red), two-page ad, 'This Is What Packard Has Done . . .' —Time, January 30; LD, February 4; SEP, February 18; Fortune and H&G, February

Packard on test track (green), 'Where Packard and Nature . . .'—Time, February 13; LD and SEP, February 25

Twelve victoria reflected in pool (tan), two-page ad, 'Hush'—Time, February 20; Fortune and H&G, March; SEP, March 11 (one-page)

man seated in library, 'I'm not going to wait any longer'—Fortune and H&G, April; Time, April 3

1903 Packard, 'Buy your car in '33 the way they did . . .'—LD, April 22; Time, April 24; SEP, May 13; Fortune, May

all text ad, 'Stability'— Time and Forbes, May 1

Super Eight club sedan, 'To the man who almost owns one'—LD, May 20; Time, May 22; SEP, May 27

Standard Eight sedan (green), 'Into the Years'—Fortune, June

Super Eight sedan, 'What's this chip of wood doing . . .'—LD and SEP, June 17; Time, June 19

touring models, 1927 and 1933, 'Ask them both . . .'—LD, July 8; SEP, July 15; Time, July 17; Fortune, July

Super Eight sedan, 'How did you happen to buy a Packard?'—Fortune, August; Time, August 21

Packard dealers, 'On Monday, August 21 . . .'—LD, September 2; Time, September 4; Fortune, September

Eight club sedan, Super Eight coupe-roadster, Twelve sedan-limousine (1934), two-page ad, 'With these new cars . . .'—SEP, September 9; Time, September 11

Twelve sedan, 'Packard urges you to borrow . . .'—LD and SEP, September 16; Time, September 18; NG and Fortune, October

engineers in quiet room, in color, 'Where silence . . .'—SEP, September 30; Time, October 2; Fortune, November

Standard Eight sedan, 'Why pay the price . . .'—SEP, October 7; Time, October 9; NG, November

engineer checking wood, in color, 'This piece of wood . . .'—SEP, October 21; Time, October 23; Fortune, December

engineer with light-ray machine, in color, 'How wide is red . . .'—SEP, November 18; Time, November 20

engineers and components, in color, 'Only in Packard and Rolls-Royce' —SEP, December 16; Time, December 18; Fortune, January 1934

1934

all text ad, 'Ask the man who . . .' —MoToR, January

Twelve town car (maroon), two-page ad, 'More than thirty years ago . . .' —SEP, January 13

man and woman, 'The first step . . .' —SEP, February 3; Time, February 5; Fortune, February

Twelve club sedan (red), 'The day that was years in the making'—SEP, February 24; Time, February 26; H&G, March

Twelve dual cowl phaeton (yellow), 'Ask your friends that own them' —SEP, March 10; Time, March 12; Fortune, March, H&G, April

Twelve convertible sedan (red), 'Rest'—SEP and New Yorker, March 24; Time, March 26; Fortune, April

Ohio
Automobile
Co.
Warren, Ohio

Eastern Department
The Adams McMurtry Co.
114 Fifth Avenue
New York

Promoting the Packard. During the Warren years, the catalogue for the Models B and C published during 190 on the left, the booklet announcing the new Model F of 1902 on the right. And, from East Grand Boulevard in Detroit, the frontispiece illustration from the catalogue introducing the Model Thirty for 1908 shown below.

Model Thirty catalogue art from 1912; promoting the Twin Six; The Packard cover of the January 1921 issue.

The PACKARD

Motor Show Number

REPRINT FROM
THE PACKARD
Announcement Number

POWER

The soft purr of the Packard motor hardly hints its vast reserve power. Yet a touch of the accelerator and the great car leaps forward with the eagerness of a living thing.

In its swift response to the driver's will lies the promise of superb and sustained performance. Mile after mile through the starts and stops of the crowded city, hour after hour on the long pull of the mountain grade, the Packard proves superior to all requirements —Packard power now reigns supreme.

Packard design—widely imitated but never equalled—has long been recognized as an outstanding combination of smartness, beauty and comfort. And Packard power —now unsurpassed in any motor car— offers matchless traffic agility, hill climbing ability and, when emergency demands it, *speed*.

Packard distinction—Packard power! A combination of qualities which has restored to many thousands of new owners their waning zest in motoring.

PACKARD

Flexibility · · To say that the improved Packard Six now has forty per cent more power, does not adequately impress its truly remarkable performance.

To add that even the largest closed models, fully loaded, will easily reach 75 miles an hour does not sufficiently explain the enthusiasm of new owners. For few men wish to use such speed.

But translated in daily use, this surplus power, this capability of great speed, means supreme flexibility—a thrilling, effortless response to the driver's will—a lithe agility in traffic and on hills, previously unknown. It means easy, restful driving—the constant delight of smooth, silent motion which recaptures the lost zest of motor travel.

With this matchless new performance added to its traditional comfort, beauty and distinction, the improved Packard Six is converting new thousands to the economy of fine car ownership.

PACKARD

*The "Attributes" campaign, 1926-1927; illustration
from "The Ambassador's Choice" dealer letter of 1926.*

The Gates of the Palais de l'Elysée

SERENE— *as the course of a yacht*
on moonlit waters

The inside-fold illustration gracing the dealer's letter which introduced the 1929 Packard Eight, the caption copy for the "Packard Shock Absorbing System" that was the principal promotional theme of the letter conveying further the feeling of the artwork: "calm—placid—unruffled by Road-sway or shock."
The cover of **The Packard** *from winter 1930, the painting by Manning de V. Lee of Commander Byrd's welcome home, in a Packard of course. The "Luxurious Transportation" ad campaign of 1930 with its "For a discriminating clientele" variation. Returning to basics in promoting the 1932 Packard Sport Phaeton.*

HEROES' CARNIVAL

THE PACKARD MAGAZINE

For a discriminating clientele - -

THE MAN WHO OWNS ONE

ACKARD

Luxurious Transportation

The imperial coach which carried Napoleon and Josephine in their coronation, glittered with golden ornaments. Drawn by eight richly caparisoned steeds, it was the most luxurious vehicle of 19th century France

PACKARD

ASK THE MAN WHO OWNS ONE

Packard

The new Packard Sport Phaeton is a smartly beautiful car —trim and yacht-like in its lines, modish and modern in its entire conception. Folding windshields front and rear, with a counter-balanced cowl to protect the tonneau, make it virtually a double roadster. All four passengers enjoy the thrill of open air motoring in *complete* comfort. ¶ The Sport Phaeton is one of the three handsome open models that are available on either the Packard Eight or the Packard Eight De Luxe chassis. The others are the Phaeton and the Touring Car. All embody the many new features and refinements which have established the new Continental Series Packards as supreme in the field of luxurious transportation. ¶ The new Packard cars are longer in wheelbase, wider in tread. The Straight-Eight engine, now "floated" on rubber, is quieter, smoother, more powerful. The transmission is four-speed synchro-mesh—easy and silent. While the new and exclusive Packard Ride Control—which permits instant adjustment of shock absorbers from the dash—provides a degree of riding comfort that has never before existed in motor cars. ¶ The new Packards are truly the cars of tomorrow. Why not have one today?

ASK
THE MAN
WHO OWNS
ONE

The startling, dramatically effective "Hush!" advertisement, painted by Peter Helck, from 1933. On the page opposite, advertisements from Fortune *magazine. Above left and right: Campaigns along very social themes, featuring the Packard Twelve, from the April 1935 and August 1937 issues respectively. Below left and right: Taking the more popular approach in advertising the One-Sixty in July 1940 and introducing the Clipper in the May 1941 issue. On the page following, promoting the postwar Packard: Introducing the Custom Eight in* Town & Country, *December 1947; presenting the Custom Super Club Sedan in* Time *and* Newsweek, *July 22nd, 1946; an old format and "The New Packard" from* Saturday Evening Post, *May 23rd, 1953; the Caribbean in* Esquire, *June 1955.*

"Hush!"

There is a deeper significance in the quiet of the Packard Twelve motor than mere solace to your ears.

Such quiet is a reflection of standards so precise as to be almost incredible.

Would you believe that any manufacturer would carry the war against noise into the realm of inaudible sounds? Packard does so. By amplification—the same way sound is stepped up in your radio—Packard locates and eliminates noises that the human ear unaided could not hear.

Would you believe that any manufacturer could reduce even the noise of the wind as it rushes by? Packard has done so —by minutely studying contours, angles, moldings, and redesigning them.

Such examples are typical of the lengths to which Packard has gone to produce the quietest motor car ever built.

What does this quiet mean in comfort, in motoring pleasure? Take a Packard Twelve out on the road and open the throttle. In a trice you're going faster you've probably ever dared drive a ca fore. Yet you drive with a perfect sen security. For there's no snarl, no roar the motor to rasp your nerves. So is the whole car that you can con in normal tones while traveling a mil a half a minute. You ride relaxed. As melts into mile, you realize why Pac Twelve owners have been able to a thousand miles in a day without fat

Today's Twelve is not only Pac masterpiece—it is, we believe, the motor car ever produced in Ame A car that has withstood tests that broken other fine cars to pieces. A that offers years of the finest mot the world has ever known.

That's saying a great deal. But it' saying too much, and your Packard d would like to prove it to you. He w like to bring a Packard Twelve door, and have you drive this car were your own. Drive it over roa your own choosing, not his. Comp with every car you've ever known. (pare it with any other fine car 1933 offer you. Do this, and we know the car that will ever completely satisfy will be the Packard Twelve.

Prices begin at $3,720 at Detroit.

THE TWELVE
BY PACKARD
ASK THE MAN WHO OWNS ON

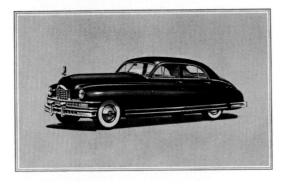

Twelve coupe-roadster (beige), 'Ask' —SEP, April 7; Time, April 9; H&G, May

circa 1909 touring (red), 'Maybe you were that boy'—SEP, April 21; Time, April 23; Fortune, May

Twelve sedan (blue), 'Packard's greatest invention . . .'—SEP, May 5; Time, May 7; Fortune, June

Twelve coupe (green), 'A famous slogan goes to work'—Time, May 21; SEP, June 2

Twelve front detail, 'Insurance you cannot buy'—Fortune, July

river scene, 'Stepping Stones' —Fortune, August

horizon, 'The Narrow Road' —Fortune, September

Twelve sedan (red) two-page ad, 'This is the new Packard for 1935'—SEP, September 8; Time, September 17; Fortune, October (one-page)

all text ad, 'America's oldest' —SEP, September 22; Time, September 24

Super Eight club sedan (yellow), 'The new 1935 Packard'—SEP, October 6; Time, October 22; Fortune, November

Eight sedan (green), 'What a Packard!' —SEP, November 3; Time, November 12; Fortune, December

all text ad, 'There has never been . . .' —Forbes, November 15

1935
senior roll of Packard distributors, 'These gentlemen . . .'—MoToR, January

all text three-page ad, 'The Packard 120' —Time, January 7; SEP and Collier's, January 12

all text ad, 'Above we have answered' —Forbes, January 15; SEP and Collier's, January 26; Time, January 28

Twelve sedan (red), 'Mr. Charles H. Morse' —SEP, January 19; Time, January 21; Fortune, January

Twelve club sedan (green), 'Mr. Edwin S. Webster'—SEP, February 9; Time, February 11; Fortune, February

One Twenty sedan (blue), 'This is the new low-priced . . .'—SEP, February 16; Time, February 18; Collier's, February 23

One Twenty sedan (orange), 'Mr. Houston, here are your answers'—SEP, March 2; Time, March 4

Twelve convertible victoria (blue), 'Mr. Morton C. Treadway'—SEP, March 9; Time, March 11; Fortune, March

One Twenty club sedan (red), 'We turn it over to you'—SEP, March 16; Time, March 18; Collier's, March 23

One Twenty sedan, 'Will service costs be low . . .'—SEP, March 30; Time, April 1

Twelve coupe-roadster (beige), 'Mr. A. Atwater Kent'—SEP, April 13; Time, April 29; Fortune, April

One Twenty touring sedan (blue), 'Packard's Fourth Dimension'—SEP, April 20; Time, April 22

Eight convertible sedan (red), 'Mr. D.M. Ferry, Jr.'—Time, May 20; Fortune, May

One Twenty, 'He's been like that . . .' —SEP, May 4

One Twenty (yellow), 'Why has Packard . . .'—SEP, May 11; Time, May 13

all text ad, 'Two questions . . .' —Forbes, May 15

One Twenty sedan drawing, 'Of the many things . . .'—SEP, May 18

One Twenty, 'He says he's trying to show . . .'—SEP, May 25

One Twenty touring coupe (green), 'What things appeal . . .'—SEP, June 1; Time, June 3

One Twenty, 'He's been acting that way . . .'—SEP, June 8

Twelve cabriolet (blue, LeBaron), 'W.K. Jewett'—Fortune, June; Time, June 17

One Twenty, 'He says it doesn't handle . . .' —SEP, June 15

Twelve sedan, 'I found out why' —Forbes, June 15

One Twenty convertible coupe (blue), 'Question: How Can I . . .'"—SEP, June 22; Time, June 24

Twelve front view, 'I found out why' —Fortune, July

cylinder heads—Alcoa Corporation —ATJ, July

One Twenty sedan, 'What the man who owns one . . .'—SEP, July 20; Time, July 22

Twelve, 'Let this 20-year-old ad . . .' —Fortune, August; Time, August 12

One Twenty club sedan, 'How the Packard 120 Stands'—SEP, August 10; New Yorker, August 31; Time, September 2; Fortune, September

One Twenty convertible coupe, 'Question: How do you like . . .'—SEP, August 31

One Twenty convertible coupe, 'Packard presents Lawrence Tibbett'—Newsweek and New Yorker, September 21; Time, September 23; SEP, September 28; Fortune, October

all text ad, 'If you are . . .'"—SEP, October 5; Time, October 7

Twelve limousine (red), 'Packard presents for 1936'—SEP, October 12; Time, October 14; Fortune, November

One Twenty sedan (red) two-page ad, 'Even Finer for 1936'—SEP, October 19; Time, October 21

One Twenty sedan (green), 'Now let us tell you . . .'—SEP, October 26; Time, October 28

front view 1936 models, 'Try to find its equal'—MoToR, November

One Twenty coupe (blue), 'Here are the facts'—Time, November 4; SEP, November 9

Twelve town car (blue, LeBaron), 'Symbol of a Nation's Preference'—Time, November 25; SEP, November 30; Fortune, January 1936

side view, 'Match Packard 120 against the field'—SEP, December 7; Time, December 9

One Twenty club sedan, 'If you want a car . . .'—SEP, December 14; Time, December 23

One Twenty club sedan (red), 'No Art, dear, you're not seeing things . . .'—Fortune, December; Time, December 16

One Twenty convertible coupe, 'For twenty years . . .'—SKF Bearings —Time, December 23

1936
One Twenty sedan, 'Match Packard 120 against the field'—SEP, January 11; Time, January 13

One Twenty club sedan, 'Before you buy' —SEP, February 1; Time, February 3

One Twenty touring coupe (red), '1936 will reward . . .'—SEP and Collier's, February 15; Time, February 17

Twelve sedan (red), 'First' —SEP, February 22; Time, March 2

Twelve club sedan (green), 'Grosse Pointe Prefers Packards'—Fortune, February

Twelve limousine (red), 'Washington Prefers Packards'—Fortune, March

touring sedan (red), 'An Open Letter to the Editors of Time'—SEP and Collier's, March 7; Time, March 9

Twelve town car (red), 'Solitaire'—SEP, March 14; Time, March 23; Fortune, July

two women, 'To the ladies . . .' —Time, March 16

One Twenty sedan (red) two-page ad, 'You can tell it's a Packard from here' —SEP and Collier's, March 28; Time, March 30 (one-page)

Twelve club sedan (blue), 'Chicago's North Shore Prefers Packards'—Fortune, April

One Twenty convertible coupe (blue), 'What happens after the honeymoon?' —Time, April 6; SEP, April 11

Twelve convertible victoria (blue), 'Birthright'—Time, April 13; SEP, April 18

One Twenty sedan (blue), 'A letter from Pottsville, Pa.'—Collier's, April 18; SEP, April 25; Time, April 27

Twelve convertible victoria (green), 'New York's Westchester Prefers Packards' —Fortune, May

One Twenty coupe (blue), 'Like father, like son'—Collier's, May 2; SEP, May 9; Time, May 11

Twelve limousine (red), 'Sacrifice'—SEP, May 16; Time, May 18; Fortune, September

One Twenty sedan (red), 'We invite you to . . .'—SEP, May 23; Time, May 25

Twelve convertible sedan (blue), 'Pasadena Prefers Packards'—Fortune, June

One Twenty sedan, 'One-Two-Three' —Time, June 15; SEP, June 27

Twelve sport phaeton (cream), 'A testimonial that has been lived . . .'—SEP, June 20; Time, June 22; Fortune, August

One Twenty sedan, 'Three steps that . . .' —Time, July 13; SEP and Collier's, July 18

Six sedan (blue), 'Any car that bears the name Packard . . .'—SEP, September 19; Time, September 21

Fred Astaire, 'Packard Presents . . .' —Time, September 21

Six sedan (green), One Twenty sedan (red), Super Eight club sedan (red), Twelve sedan (blue) five-page ad, 'For 1937 get the plus of a Packard'—SEP, September 12; Time, September 14; Fortune, October 8

One Twenty sedan (green), 'Again! The Car of the Year'—SEP, September 26; Time, September 28

Packard salesman, 'Man of the Year' —SEP, October 3; Time, October 5

Twelve sedan (green), 'Packard announces . . .'—Country Life, October

Six club sedan (red), 'From now on, son, you ride in a Packard'—SEP, October 17; Time, October 19

One Twenty sedan (red), 'You can't sell me . . .'—SEP, October 31; Time, November 2

invitation, 'Packard cordially invites . . .' —Forbes, November 1

One Twenty front view, 'Four reasons . . .' —MoToR, November

Super Eight club sedan, Six touring coupe, Twelve and One Twenty sedans, 'Four great new cars'—Forbes, November 15

Six touring coupe (green), Super Eight club sedan (brown), One Twenty and Twelve sedans (red, blue) two-page ad, 'Whatever you plan to spend for a car . . .'—SEP, November 14; Time, November 16

Twelve club sedan (maroon), 'For 1937 get the plus of a Packard'—Fortune and Country Life, November

Twelve sedan (blue), 'How Packard, with one epochal . . .'—Fortune and Country Life, December

1937

Packard factory bridge, in color, 'From this famous factory . . .'—Fortune, January

Six sedan, 'Reflections of a husband' —SEP, January 9; Time, January 11

James Ward Packard at desk, in color, 'His answer became a slogan'—SEP, January 23; Collier's, January 30

book, 'Why you should read this book' —SEP, January 30; Time, February 8; Collier's, February 20

Madison Square Garden, in color—Fortune, February; Country Life, January

Metropolitan Opera, in color—Country Life, February

One Twenty sedan, 'One day a week . . .' —GH, February

One Twenty sedan, 'Three reasons why women leave home'—Vogue, February 1

Six sedan (red), 'I'm keeping a promise' —Newsweek, February 6; SEP, February 13; Time, February 15; Collier's, March 6

Carnegie Institute, in color—Fortune and Country Life, March

One Twenty sedan (red), 'Three Great Firsts . . .'—SEP, March 13; Time, March 15; Collier's, March 20

Six sedan (tan), 'He wanted, she wanted . . .' —SEP, March 27; Time, March 29; Collier's, April 3; Life, April 5

all text ad, 'Packard plays host'—GH, April

Twelve and Six sedans, in color, four-page ad, 'This is the story of an Elk . . .' —Elks Magazine, April

flower shop, in color, 'Easter Sunday' —Fortune and Country Life, April

One Twenty sedan (red), 'But is this just another spring'—SEP, April 10; Time, April 12

Six sedan (red), 'The awakening of Mr. & Mrs. Rip van Winkle, Jr.'—SEP and Collier's, April 24; Time and Life, April 26

Six club sedan, 'Our chauffeur'—GH, May

Maryland hunt, in color, 'Whenever smart people gather'—Fortune and Country Life, May

One Twenty coupe, 'Love, honor and . . .' —GH, June; Vogue, May 1

Six coupe (green), 'We're tired of leading a second-best life'—SEP, May 8; Time, May 10; Collier's, May 15; Life, May 17

boy watching girl in antique Packard, in color, 'Reaching for the moon . . .' —SEP, May 22; Time, May 24

Six saloon, 'The Packard . . .' —The Autocar, May 28

One Twenty sedan, 'Look me over' —Vogue, June 1

Six convertible coupe (yellow), 'American campus'—Fortune and Country Life, June

Kids playacting a wedding, in color, 'And we're going to . . .'—SEP and Collier's, June 5; Life and Time, June 7

Six sedans (red and blue), 'Here we are . . . envying'—SEP, June 19; Time, June 21; Collier's, June 26; Life, June 28

Twelve (bronze), 'Southampton, Socially America's First Motor Car'—Fortune and Country Life, July

Twelve sedan (blue), 'Socially America's First Motor Car'—Fortune, Country Life and Stage, July

reprint of 1903 McClure's ad—Stage, August

Six sedan, "All I need is a cap' —GH, August; Vogue, August 1

Six sedan (red), 'We know what people are saying . . .'—Time, August 2; SEP, August 7; Collier's, August 14; Life, July 26

Six and Eight sedans (blue, red) two-page ad, 'And no other 1938 car . . .'—SEP, October 2; Time and Life, October 4; Collier's, October 9

Twelve sedan (red), two-page ad, 'For America's First Families'—Country Life and Fortune, October

Eight sedan (red), 'The man who buys . . .' —SEP, October 9; Life and Time, October 11

Eight sedan (green), 'Tear out these claims' —SEP, October 16; Time, October 18; Life, October 25; Forbes, November 1

Six and Eight sedans (blue, red) two-page ad, 'You'll think you stepped into the wrong . . .'—SEP, October 30; Time and Life, November 1

Six sedan (blue), 'And check these statements . . .'—SEP, November 13; Life and Time, November 15

Eight sedan (blue), 'We said the same thing . . .'—SEP, November 27; Time and Life, November 29

Packard dealership, 'Behind this radiator . . .'—MoToR, November

Twelve formal sedan (green), 'Bodyguard' —Fortune and Country Life, November

Six sedan, 'The opportunity that . . .' —MoToR, December

1938

Twelve sedan-limousine (purple), 'Social Mirror'—Fortune and Country Life, January

Eight sedan (blue), 'Are These Puffs . . .' —Time, January 10; SEP, January 15; Collier's, January 22

Twelve touring cabriolet (blue, Brunn), 'To men whose judgment the world calls good'—Fortune and Country Life, February

Six sedan (green), 'You're looking at a . . .' —SEP, February 26; Newsweek, February 28; Time, March 7

Six sedan (red) two-page ad, 'Here is a really new car'—SEP, March 19; Time and Newsweek, March 21; Collier's, March 26

all-weather cabriolet (black, Brunn), 'R.S.V.P.'—Country Life and Fortune, March

Twelve sedan (red), 'For Key Men' —Country Life and Fortune, April

Six sedan (blue), 'Our Packard pays us $39 . . .'—SEP, April 2; Time, April 4; Collier's, April 16

Eight sedan (red) and 1911 model, 'When heaven was at the corner . . .'—SEP, April 9; Time and Newsweek, April 18; Collier's, April 30

Six convertible coupe (red), 'How to lead a . . .'—SEP, April 23; Time and Newsweek, May 2; Collier's, May 14

Twelve coupe-roadster (green), 'We suggest . . .'—Fortune, Country Life and Stage, May

Six sedan (red), 'An old flame never dies' —SEP, May 7; Time and Newsweek, May 16; Collier's, May 28

man, woman and Packard Eight (red), 'Just for the fun of it'—SEP, May 21; Time, May 30

Six sedan (red), 'How big is a Packard income?'—SEP, June 11; Time and Newsweek, June 20

Twelve convertible sedan (yellow), 'Before you start for Newport'—Fortune and Country Life, June

Twelve convertible victoria, 'Dress Parade' —Fortune, July

Six sedan, 'Four things to tell your husband/wife . . .'—SEP, July 16; Time, July 25; New Yorker, August 6

Twelve sedan, 'Without frontiers' —Fortune, August

Twelve sedan, 'To a Packard born' —Fortune, September

Twelve sedan, 'Elected'—Fortune, October

Super Eight sedan (red), 'For 1939 Packard has created . . .'—SEP, October 15; Time, October 17; Collier's, October 29; Newsweek, October 24

Six and One Twenty sedans (tan, blue), two-page ad, 'Announcing Two New . . .'—SEP, October 8; Time, October 10; Collier's, October 15

Six sedan (blue), 'Test a 1939 Packard . . .' —SEP, October 22; Time, October 24; Newsweek, November 7

showroom, 'Why I'm going to . . .' —MoToR, November

Six sedan (green), 'Every traffic sign confirms it . . .'—SEP, November 5; Time, November 7; Collier's, November 19; New Yorker and Newsweek, November 21

Six sedan (red), 'Let these traffic signs prove . . .'—SEP, November 12; Time, November 14

Six front view, 'See the new 1939' —Forbes, November 15

Super Eight sedan, 'What's new about America's . . .'—SEP, November 19; Time, November 21

Super Eight sedan (red), 'You are cordially invited to inspect . . .'—Fortune and Country Life, November

Super Eight sedan (red), 'This is the new motor car you helped to design'—Fortune and Country Life, December

Six front view (red), 'Why these signs all say . . .'—SEP, December 3; Time, December 5

1939

Super Eight sedan (green), 'You are looking at two motor cars in one'—Fortune and Country Life, January

Six front view, 'Protected Investment' —SEP, January 14; Collier's, January 28

Super Eight sedan (yellow), 'This is 1939's most newsworthy merger'—Fortune and Country Life, February

Six front view (red), 'Three things a parking space can teach'—SEP, February 11; Time, February 13; Collier's, February 18; Canadian Home & Gardens, April

Super Eight sedan (green), 'One answer to two questions'—Country Life and Fortune, March

One Twenty and Six (blue, red) two-page ad, 'When you drive a Packard'—SEP and New Yorker, March 11; Time and Newsweek, March 13; Collier's, March 18

Six (blue), Washington Monument and Statue of Liberty, 'Three American Faces . . .'—SEP and New Yorker, March 25; Time, March 27; Collier's, April 1; Newsweek, April 3

Super Eight limousine (blue), 'How to get both . . .'—Time, April 3; New Yorker, April 8

Super Eight convertible sedan (yellow), 'One year ago this was impossible'—Fortune and Country Life, April

Six front view (red), 'These remarks point out three facts'—SEP, April 8; New Yorker and Collier's, April 15;

Time and Newsweek, May 1

One Twenty sedan (green), 'Packard wins beauty crown'—Time and Newsweek, April 17; SEP, April 22; New Yorker and Collier's, April 29

Super Eight convertible coupe (blue), 'More than meets the eye'—Fortune and Country Life, May

circa 1908 runabout, in color, 'I wanted to grow up and marry Mr. Washburn' —SEP, May 6; Collier's, May 13

Super Eight sedan, 'How many cars' —New Yorker, May 13; Time and Newsweek, May 15

Six front view, 'Packard completes . . .' —Time and Newsweek, May 22

Six sedan (blue), 'Something every new car buyer . . .'—SEP, May 20; New Yorker, May 27; Time, May 29; Collier's, June 3; Newsweek, June 5

Six front view, 'With its four-year plan completed . . .'—SEP, June 3; Fortune, July

Super Eight convertible sedan (maroon), 'The Packard you do not see'—Fortune and Country Life, June

front view, '3 figures that took 4 years' —Time, July 10; SEP, July 15; Newsweek, July 17

Packard plant bridge, 'This bridge . . .' —Fortune, August

One-Ten sedan (red) three-page ad, 'Announcing the new 1940 Packard' —SEP and New Yorker, September 9; Time and Newsweek, September 11; Collier's, September 16; Opinion, September

One-Ten sedan, 'Announcing the new . . .' —Forbes, September 1

One-Sixty sedan (red), 'Presenting the new master'—SEP and New Yorker, September 16; Time, September 18; Collier's, September 23

One-Ten coupe, 'Great things have happened'—SEP, September 30; Collier's, October 7

One-Twenty sedan, 'You'll fall in love . . .' —New Yorker, September 30; Time and Newsweek, October 2; SEP and Collier's, November 11

bank book, 'Let's take a bank book' —MoToR, October

One-Ten sedan, 'A Whole Auto Show' —Forbes, October 15

One-Ten sedan (green), 'Crossing tradition with chain lightning' —SEP, October 14; Collier's, October 21; New Yorker, October 28; Time and Newsweek, October 30

One-Sixty sedan (red), 'The engineer's engine'—New Yorker, October 14; Time, October 16; SEP, October 28

One-Eighty formal sedan (black) two-page ad, 'Introducing the 1940 . . .'—Fortune, October; Country Life, October (one-page)

One-Eighty sedan (blue), 'Don't follow the leader, drive it'—Fortune and Country Life, November

One-Ten front view, 'Doesn't anybody yawn anymore?'—SEP, November 25; New Yorker and Collier's, December 2; Time and Newsweek, December 4

One-Twenty sedan, 'What a car to drive anywhere'—New Yorker, November 11; Time, November 13; Newsweek, November 20; SEP, December 9

custom sport sedan (maroon, Darrin), 'Adventure for sale'—Fortune, December; Country Life, January 1940; this ad also distributed by Fortune in December with the copy 'For a fortunate few'

1940

One-Eighty limousine (green), 'To people who refuse to be second'—Fortune, January

One-Ten in showroom, 'When you cross this threshhold'—New Yorker, January 13; Newsweek, January 15; Time, January 22; SEP and Collier's, January 27

One-Twenty convertible coupe, 'Announcing the Picture Packard contest' —Life, January 15

One-Eighty club sedan (red), 'Here is your hope'—Fortune and Country Life, February

all text ad, 'How to sign yourself' —Automotive News, February 5

business card, 'To top flight automobile salesmen'—SEP, February 10

One-Ten coupe (green), 'Who's going to pick whose car?' —SEP and New Yorker, February 24; Time, February 26; Collier's, March 2

One-Eighty sedan (blue), 'Invitation to be spoiled'—Fortune and Country Life, March

One-Ten sedan (red), 'Doesn't a big car like that cost . . .'—SEP, March 16; Collier's and New Yorker, March 23; Newsweek, April 29

One-Twenty sedan (red), 'Standing or running'—Life, March 18; Time and Newsweek, March 25

One-Ten station wagon, 'The new Packard . . .'—New Yorker, March 30; Country Life, April

all text ad, in color, 'The fourth Packard owner'—SEP and Collier's, April 6

One-Sixty sedan (red), 'Come on . . . be a king'—Time, March 11; New Yorker, April 6; Fortune and Country Life, April

One-Ten station wagon, 'Newest and smartest . . .'—Country Life, March; Fortune, April

One-Eighty convertible victoria (blue, Darrin), 'Glamour Car of the Year' —SEP, March 30; Collier's, April 20; Fortune and Country Life, June

One-Ten sedan, 'Proof that Packard' —Forbes, April 15

One-Twenty sedan (green), 'Crowds other eights out . . .'—Life, April 1; Time, April 29

One-Sixty sedan (blue), 'Four wheeled amazement'—Newsweek and Time, April 8; New Yorker, April 20; Fortune and Country Life, May

One-Twenty sedan (cream), 'Can a car have personality?'—Life, April 15

One-Ten coupe (blue), 'It's happening on a thousand main streets'—SEP, April 20; Collier's, May 4

One-Twenty sedan (green), '. . . belies its thrift'—Life, April 29

One-Ten station wagon, 'The kind of station . . .'—Country Life, May

One-Ten (green), 'Start off by asking' —SEP, May 4; Collier's, May 25

One-Twenty family sedan (red), 'Car of the personal pronoun'—Life, May 13

One-Ten coupe (red), 'Ask the Man Who Owns One'—SEP, May 18

One-Twenty convertible coupe (blue), 'Meet straight eight enthusiast'—Life, May 27

One-Sixty sedan (red), 'Passport to seventh heaven'—Time, May 20; Newsweek, May 25; Fortune, July

One-Ten (red), 'Dialogue with thousands of dittos'—SEP, June 8

One-Twenty coupe (red), 'Choose a car' —Life, June 10

One-Ten sedan (blue), 'Let's Call on the Ainsworths'—SEP, July 13

air conditioning, in color, 'First with a really refrigerated car'—Fortune, August; SEP, August 24

front view, 1941 model, 'Gentlemen, meet a . . .'—MoToR, October

tanks, boats, plane and One-Sixty sedan, 'Historic Horsepower'—Fortune, October

One-Ten DeLuxe sedan (grey and red), 'Brimming with Beauty'—SEP, October 5; Life, Newsweek and Time, October 7; Collier's, October 12

One-Ten DeLuxe interior (in color), 'The year's . . . inside story'—SEP and New Yorker, October 12; Life and Time, October 14; Collier's, October 19; Newsweek, October 21; Fortune, November

One-Ten DeLuxe sedan, 'New from roof'—Forbes, October 15; U.S. News, October 18

One-Ten DeLuxe sedan (blue), 'Exciting as your first dollar'—SEP, October 26; Time, November 4; New Yorker, November 9

One-Ten DeLuxe sedan (green), 'Cuts your footwork in half'—SEP, October 19; Time, October 21; New Yorker, October 26; Life, October 28; Collier's, November 2; Newsweek, November 4

One-Ten station wagon, 'To build America's finest . . .'—New Yorker, October 19; Fortune and Country Life, November

One-Ten DeLuxe sedan (red and white), 'One mile free in five'—SEP, November 9; Time, November 18

One-Ten station wagon, 'The mystery of space . . .'—New Yorker, November 23; Country Life, December

One-Ten DeLuxe interior (in color), 'Luxury's lap is now on wheels' —SEP, November 23; Time, December 2; Fortune, December

tanks, boat, plane, One-Ten sedan, 'Historic Horsepower'—Life, December 2

One-Ten DeLuxe sedan (red), 'Full of surprises as a Christmas stocking' —SEP, December 7; Time, December 16; Fortune, January 1941

1941

planes, PT boat and engine, One-Ten sedan, 'Packard reports . . .'—U.S. News, January 10; Forbes, January 15

PT boat, 'Packard powers the water wasps' —Life, Newsweek and Time, January 13; SEP, January 18; Collier's, January 25; Fortune, February

One-Ten Special coupe (green), 'Packard makes this a great year for left feet' —Newsweek, January 27; New Yorker, February 1; Life and Time, February 3; SEP, February 8; Fortune, March

One-Ten sedan (red), 'A four-color picture of comfort'—Newsweek, February 17; Life, February 24; SEP, March 1; Time, March 3

One-Eighty convertible victoria (black, Darrin), 'What could it be but a Packard' —Newsweek, March 3; Collier's, March 15; New Yorker, March 22; Time, March 24; Woman's Home Companion and Fortune, April

boats, planes, army staff cars, 'Sisters under the skin'—Life, March 31; Collier's and SEP, April 5; Time, April 7

One-Ten station wagon, 'Costs so little more'—Country Life, April; New Yorker, April 19

One-Ten Special sedan, 'This little foot went to market'—SEP and Collier's, April 19

Clipper (red) three-page ad, 'A star is born . . . world premiere'—SEP, April 26; Time, Life and Newsweek, April 28; Collier's, May 3

Clipper (red), 'World Premiere'
—Fortune, May

One-Ten station wagon, 'The world's
worst . . .'—Country Life, May;
New Yorker, May 10

Clipper, 'Step into the future'
—U.S. News, May 9; Forbes, May 15

Clipper (green) two-page ad, 'First
streamlined car that considers . . .'
—SEP, May 10; Time, June 2

Clipper (blue) two-page ad, 'For both lookers
and riders'—SEP, May 24; Time, June 23

Clipper (green), '. . . first streamlined car'
—Life, May 19; Collier's, May 24;
Fortune, June

Clipper (red) two-page ad, '. . . first
streamlined car'—SEP, June 7

Clipper (blue), 'New beauty you'll . . .'
—Life, June 9

Clipper Six club sedan (red), 'For 1942,
Clipper styling comes to . . .'—Fortune,
October; Forbes, October 15 (b&w)

Clipper club sedan, 'News made to order'
—MoToR, October

Clipper Six club sedan, two-page ad, 'Even
the lowest priced Packard'—SEP, October 4;
Life, Newsweek and Time, October 6;
Collier's and New Yorker, October 11

Clipper sedan (green), 'How Clipper
beauty pays off'—SEP, October 18;
Life, October 20; Time, October 27;
Collier's, November 1; Newsweek,
November 10; Fortune, November

Clipper Special club sedan (blue), 'How
Clipper beauty adds up'—SEP, November 1;
Life, November 10; Time, November 17;
Fortune, December

Clipper Custom club sedan (red), 'Beauty
made to . . .'—SEP, November 22

1942

PT boat, 'In Action'—Life, March 16

service plan, 'Wartime service plan'
—SEP, March 21; Time, April 6

service plan, 'Packard owners, save . . .'
—SEP, April 11; Newsweek, April 20;
Collier's, May 2

PT boat, 'The American Monster'
—Newsweek, July 27; Collier's, August 8;
Life, August 10; SEP, August 15;
Time, August 17

P-40 Warhawk, 'Ask the Man Who Flies
One'—Collier's, August 29; Life, August 31;
SEP, September 5

Uncle Sam, 'Remember Miss America'
—Collier's, September 19; Life,
September 21; SEP, September 26

PT boat and plane, 'A word about . . .'
—MoToR, October

P-40 Warhawk, 'Born to come out on top'
—Collier's, October 10; Life, October 12;
SEP, October 17

war effort, two-page ad, 'The kind of story
Hitler hates'—Newsweek, October 26; Time,
November 2; Business Week, November 7;
Collier's and SEP, November 14; Forbes,
November 15; U.S. News, November 20;
American, January 1943

1943

car wrapped in bonds, 'Announcing the new
Packard . . .'—SEP and Collier's, January 9;
Life, January 18; Time, January 25;
Newsweek, February 1

De Havilland Mosquito, 'Who puts the buzz
in . . .'—SEP and Collier's, February 13;
Life, February 22; Time, March 1;
Newsweek, March 8

PT engine test, 'Sign language for a naval
victory'—SEP and Collier's, March 13;
Time, March 22; Newsweek, March 29

Lancaster bomber, 'OK for the 70,000th'
—SEP and Collier's, April 10;
Time, April 19; Newsweek, April 26

hand palm, 'The hand with a telltale touch'
—SEP, May 8; Life, May 24;
Collier's, May 22; Time, May 31;
Newsweek, June 7; American, August

Packard war worker, 'Packard takes care'
—MA, June

boats, planes, Clipper club sedan, 'Did you
know this family secret'—SEP, June 12; Life,
June 21; Collier's, July 3; Time, July 12;
Newsweek, July 26; American, September

P-40 and pilot, 'When life hangs on . . .'
—SEP, July 17; Life, August 2;
Collier's, August 14; Time, August 23;
Newsweek, September 13; American, October

P-51 Mustang, 'Up goes the Mustang
ceiling'—SEP, August 28; Life, September 6;
Collier's, September 25; Time, October 4;
Newsweek, October 11; American, November

aircraft, 'Seven good reasons . . .'
—MoToR, October

PT boat, 'Eleven men against 500'
—SEP, October 16; Life, October 25;
Collier's, November 6; Time, November 15;
American, December

airplane pilot, 'Engines too need oxygen
masks'—SEP, November 20; Collier's,
December 4; Life, December 6; Time,
December 13; Newsweek, December 20;
American, February 1944

letter from Malta, 'You're good if you can'
—MA, December

1944

war production, 'Packard reports to . . .'
—Business Week, January 29;
Forbes, February 1

all text ad, 'Quiz for plane-minded readers'
—Time, February 7; Collier's, February 12;
Newsweek, February 14; Life, February 21;
SEP, February 26; American, April

wartime survey, 'The backbone of our . . .'
—MA, March

Mustang P-51B, 'The newest thing in
umbrellas'—Collier's, March 18;
Time, March 20; Newsweek, March 27;
Aero Digest, April 1; Life, April 3

PT boat, in color, 'The split second . . .'
—SEP, April 1; Newsweek, April 17;
Time, April 24; Collier's, April 29;
Yachting, May; American, June

tank, in color, 'How Private Jim Thornbro
. . .'—SEP, May 13; Collier's, May 27; Life,
May 29; Time, June 5; Newsweek, June 12;
American, August

plane quiz, 'Packard'—Aero Digest, June 1

Private Charles Turner, in color, 'A JAP
Bayonet . . .'—SEP, June 17; Life, June 26;
Collier's, July 1; Time, July 17;
American, August

PT boat engine, in color, 'Men bet their
lives'—Yachting, July

John Yaksich, in color, 'He had to knock
out . . .'—SEP, July 29; Collier's, August 12;
Time, August 14

Mustang and Mosquito, 'Two record
breakers . . .'—Life, July 31;
Aero Digest, August 1

war headlines, 'Did you see this headline?'
—MA, September

Arthur Herbey, in color, 'Through as a
fighter?'—SEP, September 2; Time,
September 25; Collier's, September 30

PT boat engine, 'The Skipper Who . . .'
—Yachting, October

PT boat at dock, in color, 'Men bet
their lives on it'—SEP, October 7;
Collier's, November 4; Time, November 13;
American, December

PT boat engine, 'Letter of credit'
—Yachting, November

Leo Marzean, 'Marzean's still in the fight'
—SEP, November 4; Collier's, December 9

Clipper club sedan, 'How soon?'—Life,
November 27; Time, January 8, 1945

all text ad, 'Letter we prize'—Aero Digest,
October 15; Life, October 16; SEP,
December 9; Time, December 18; Newsweek,
January 15, 1945; Collier's, February 3,
1945; American, February 1945

1945

PT boat engines, 'Jobs the officers . . .'
—Yachting, January

right-hand drive ambulance, in color,
'Through the London blitz and robot
bombing'—SEP, January 20;

Life, January 29; Time, February 5;
Newsweek, February 12; Collier's,
March 17; American, April

war production, 'A special message'—Forbes,
February 15; Business Week, February 17

Clipper front end, last 1942 Packard built,
'Don't make the mistake of forgetting . . .'
—Time, February 19; SEP and Collier's,
February 24; Life and Newsweek, March 5

plane strafing locomotive, in color, 'Built to
forget'—SEP, March 24; Life, April 2;
Time, April 9; Newsweek, April 30;
Collier's, May 5; American, June

Clipper (green), 'What every motorist
can learn from a Mustang pilot'
—SEP, May 5; Life, May 7; Time, June 4;
Newsweek, June 11; Collier's, June 16;
American, August

Clipper (red), 'Two ways to be a patriot'
—SEP, June 16; Life, June 25; Time, July 9

PT boat, 'The PT boat that was half
submarine'—Life, July 23; SEP and
Collier's, August 4; Newsweek, August 13;
Yachting, August; Time, September 10;
American, October

Packards (1904 and 1942 models),
'Time makes good things better'—Texaco
—SEP, August 4; Life, August 13; Time,
August 20

bank, Packard Service, 'Presenting
a patriotic hoarder'—SEP, September 15;
Collier's, September 22; Life, September 24;
Time, October 8; Newsweek, October 15

Clipper club sedan, 1942 model (green),
'How good a guesser are you'—SEP,
October 13; Life, October 15; Collier's,
October 20; Time, October 22; Newsweek,
October 29; American, December

DeLuxe sedan, 1946 model (green-grey),
'Now for the first time'—SEP and
Collier's, November 17; Life, November 19;
Newsweek, December 3; Time, December 10

DeLuxe sedans, 1946 models (blue and grey),
'Brand new . . .'—SEP and Collier's,
December 15; Life, December 17

1946

DeLuxe sedan (green), 'If ever a car was
worth . . .'—Life, January 21; SEP and
Collier's, January 26

DeLuxe sedan (blue), 'No matter how you
look'—SEP, June 1; Life, June 10; Collier's,
June 22; Time and Newsweek, June 24

Custom Super club sedan (red), 'Never before
in Packard's history'—SEP, June 29;
Collier's, July 13; Time and Life, July 15;
Newsweek, July 22

factory assembly line, in color, 'The extra
Packard Clipper'—SEP, July 27; Collier's,
August 10; Life, August 12

Custom Super sedan (blue), 'For an Air-
Corps'—Time and Newsweek, August 19;
New Yorker, August 24

DeLuxe sedan (blue) with 1902 runabout and 1923 touring, 'When the Packard company . . .'—SEP, August 24; Collier's, September 7; Life, September 9

Custom Super sedan (green), 'For a commander'—Time and Newsweek, September 16; New Yorker, September 21

Super club sedan (red), 'Your eye tells you'—SEP, September 21; Life, September 30; Collier's, October 12

Custom Super sedan (blue), 'For a world-famed . . .'—New Yorker, October 19; Time and Newsweek, October 28

Super sedan (blue), 'Note to car-hungry'—SEP, October 19; Life, October 28; Collier's, November 9

Super sedan (green), 'For a successful man'—Newsweek, November 25

DeLuxe sedan (green), 'Two things you'll discover'—SEP, November 16; Life, November 25; Collier's, December 7

1947

Super sedan (blue), 'Ask the Man Who Owns One'—SEP, January 18; Life, January 27; Collier's, February 8

DeLuxe front view (blue), 'Speaking of red letter days'—Life, March 18; SEP, March 22; Collier's, April 12

Super sedan (blue), 'For an empire builder'—Time, March 24; New Yorker, March 29; Newsweek, March 31

Super sedan, (blue), 'For an executive'—Newsweek, April 21; Time, April 28

DeLuxe sedan (blue), 'A man has a right . . .'—SEP, April 26; Life, May 14; Collier's, May 24

Super sedan (green), 'For an airplane designer'—Newsweek, June 2; Time, June 9; New Yorker, June 14

Super Eight convertible (yellow), 1948 model, 'Top up . . . top down'—Time, August 25; Newsweek, September 1; New Yorker, September 6

Super Eight convertible (brown), 'Top up . . . top down'—Fortune, August

Super Eight convertibles (blue, brown) two-page ad, 'Packard proudly presents'—SEP and Collier's, August 2; Life, July 21

dashboard and steering wheel, in color 'Behind this wheel'—Collier's, September 27; Life, September 29; SEP, October 4

DeLuxe Eight club sedan (red), Super Eight convertible (blue), Custom Eight sedan (green), Station Sedan (brown) two-page ad, 'Three great new Packard eights'—SEP, October 18; Life, October 27; Collier's, November 8

DeLuxe Eight club sedan (red), Super Eight convertible (blue), Custom Eight sedan (green), 'Three great new Packard eights'—Time, October 20; Newsweek, October 27; New Yorker, November 1; Forbes, November 15 (b&w)

Custom Eight (green), 'The distinguished new . . .'—Fortune, November

DeLuxe Eight sedan, 'For a famous designer'—Harper's Bazaar, November

DeLuxe Eight sedan (red), 'Out of this world'—Life and Time, November 24; New Yorker, November 29; Newsweek, December 1; SEP and Collier's, December 6

Custom Eight sedan (blue), 'In all the world'—Fortune, December

DeLuxe Eight club sedan, 'For a mother of three'—Harper's Bazaar, December

1948

DeLuxe Eight sedan, 'For an outdoor girl'—Harper's Bazaar, February

DeLuxe Eight sedan (red), 'All this . . .'—Newsweek, February 9; SEP, February 14; Time, February 16; Collier's and New Yorker, February 28

Super Eight convertible (blue)—Borg-Warner—SEP, March 20; Fortune, October

Custom Eight sedans (blue, grey), 'The Ultimate'—Fortune, March

DeLuxe Eight sedan, 'For a professional'—Harper's Bazaar, April

DeLuxe Eight sedan (green), 'Rain or Shine'—Newsweek, March 29; SEP, April 3; Time, April 5; New Yorker, April 10; Life, April 12

Custom Eight convertible (red), 'A motor car such as . . .'—Fortune, May

Super Eight convertible and station sedan (yellow and brown), 'Designed by the Wizard'—Newsweek, April 26; SEP, May 1; Time, May 3; New Yorker, May 8; Life, May 10; Holiday, June

DeLuxe Eight sedan (blue), 'Measure Packard economy'—SEP, May 22; Collier's, June 5; Life, June 21

Station sedan (red), 'What a double'—Newsweek, May 24; Time, May 31; New Yorker, June 5; Holiday, July

DeLuxe Eight sedan, 'For a famous hostess'—Harper's Bazaar, June

Super Eight sedan (brown), 'The BIG Inside'—SEP, June 12; Time, June 21; New Yorker, June 26; Newsweek, June 28

Super Eight sedan (blue), 'Sedan for seven'—Fortune, July

Super Eight sedan (red), 'Why Packard owners call it . . .'—SEP, July 10; New Yorker, July 17; Time, July 19; Newsweek, July 26; Holiday, August

DeLuxe Eight sedan (blue-grey), 'Packard owners get a break'—SEP, August 14; Time, August 16; Newsweek and Life, August 23; New Yorker, August 28; Holiday, September

DeLuxe Eight sedan, 'For an editor'—Harper's Bazaar, August

Custom Eight sedan (red), 'Outstanding even among . . .'—Fortune, September

Custom Eight sedan (red), 'One guess what name . . .'—Time, September 13; SEP, September 18; Newsweek, September 20; Collier's and New Yorker, September 25; Life, September 27; Fortune, October

DeLuxe Eight sedan, 'For a decorator'—Harper's Bazaar, October

DeLuxe Eight sedan (blue), 'No wonder a Packard'—SEP, October 2

Deluxe Eight sedan, 'How a Packard changes'—SEP, October 16; Time, October 18; Newsweek, October 25; Collier's, October 30; New Yorker, November 6

DeLuxe Eight sedan (grey), 'Yes, you can quote me'—SEP, October 30; Life, November 8

Custom Eight sedans (blue and grey), 'A motor car designed'—Fortune, November

Super Eight convertible, 'For a debutante'—Harper's Bazaar, November

DeLuxe Eight sedan (red), 'Weather prediction'—SEP, November 20

1949

DeLuxe Eight sedan (red), 'How to make today's gas'—SEP, January 29; Life and Time, February 7; Newsweek, February 14; Collier's and New Yorker, February 26

Eight club sedan (green), 'Can you find the limousine'—SEP, February 26; Time, March 7; Life, March 14; Newsweek, March 28; Holiday, April

Eight sedan (blue), 'Why Packard owners buy'—SEP, March 26

Eight sedan (grey), '3 Guesses . . .'—SEP, April 9; Time, April 11; Collier's, April 23; Newsweek, April 25; New Yorker, April 30; Holiday, May

Eight sedan (blue), "It isn't what you pay"—SEP, April 30

Super DeLuxe sedan, Eight club sedan, Custom Eight convertible, Twenty-Third Series Golden Anniversary models, 'Presenting the distinguished new . . .'—MoToR, May

Eight and Super Eight sedans (green, red) and Custom Eight convertible (blue) two-page ad, 'Golden Anniversary Packards'—Collier's, May 28; Life, May 30; SEP, May 14 (three-page)

Custom Eight convertible (blue), 'Proudest achievement'—Time, May 16;

Newsweek, May 23; New Yorker, May 28; Holiday, June

Eight club sedan, "City X needs . . .'—Business Week, June 11

Super sedan (blue), 'A wonderful new hush . . .'—SEP, June 11; Time, June 13; Life and Newsweek, June 25; New Yorker, June 25; Holiday, July

Eight club sedan (red), 'You'll think the fuel gauge . . .'—SEP, July 9; Time, July 11; Newsweek, July 25; New Yorker, July 30

Eight club sedan, "City X-1 needs . . .'—Business Week, July 16

Eight sedan (blue), 'Designed for a roaming'—SEP, August 13; Time, August 15; Newsweek, August 22; New Yorker, August 27; Holiday, September

Eight club sedan, "City X-2 needs . . .'—Business Week, September 10

Eight club sedan (green), 'Are you guessing yourself?'—SEP, September 17; Life, October 3; Collier's, October 8

Super DeLuxe sedan (red), 'Road's Eye View'—Time, September 26; SEP, October 1; Newsweek, October 3; New Yorker, October 8

several views, in color, 'The last word in automatic . . .'—SEP, October 15; Time, October 17; Newsweek and Life, October 24; New Yorker, October 29; Collier's, November 5; Holiday, November

DeLuxe Eight sedan (red), 'How would your car rate?'—SEP, October 29; Time, November 7; Newsweek, November 14; New Yorker, November 19

Super DeLuxe sedan (red), 'Shiftless'—SEP, November 19

1950

Eight DeLuxe sedan (green), 'What do you miss most'—SEP, January 28; Time, January 30; Newsweek, February 13; New Yorker, February 25; Holiday, March

deburring barrel, 'The new wonder working machine'—Business Week, February 25

assembly line, 'Meet a new kind . . .'—Business Week, March 18

Eight club sedan (blue), 'There are 3 ways'—SEP, March 18; Time, March 20; Newsweek, March 27

Eight DeLuxe sedan (red), 'All these no's add up'—SEP, April 1; Time, April 10; Newsweek, April 17

Eight club sedan (blue), 'How many miles between . . .'—SEP, April 15

Custom Eight sedan and Super Eight, 'Quote'—SEP, April 29; Time, May 8; Newsweek, May 15

test track, 'Where is the world's . . .'—Business Week, May 13

Henney-Packards, 'The largest fleet operator' —Mid-Continent Mortician, May

Super Eight front view, 'I spent two weeks . . .'—SEP, May 20; Time, May 22; Newsweek, May 29

various model Packards, 'It's time you asked' —SEP, June 10; Time, June 12; Newsweek, June 26

Custom Eight models, 'Ask the woman who . . .'—SEP, June 24

baby in highchair and Packard toy, 'Meet our youngest boss'—Business Week, July 8

Patrician 400, 300, 200 sedan, 1951 models, 'New, all new Packard'—MA, September

Patrician (red) two-page ad, 'World Premiere'—SEP, September 16; Life, September 25; Collier's, October 7; Time and Newsweek, October 9

Patrician 400, 'Take a look' —Business Week, September 16

Patrician, 300 and 200 sedan (red, blue and green) two-page ad, 'A daring new concept' —Collier's, October 21; Life, October 23; SEP, October 28; Time and Newsweek, November 6

300 model, 'It's turning the . . .' —Business Week, October 28

300 model (blue), 'Everything here is new' —SEP, November 11; Time and Newsweek, November 20

Patrician (green), 'Never a car . . .' —SEP, December 9; Time and Newsweek, December 18

1951

Patrician, 'Ask the man who sells . . .' —Automotive News, almanac issue

300 model (green), 'For one who puts character'—SEP, January 20; Time and Newsweek, January 29; Collier's and New Yorker, February 17; Fortune, H&G, Atlantic, HB and Holiday, March

200 DeLuxe club sedan (blue), 'All it needs'—SEP, March 3; Time, March 12; Collier's, March 17; Newsweek, March 26

Patrician (red), 'So far ahead . . .' —SEP, March 31; Time, April 9; New Yorker, April 14; Newsweek, April 16; Collier's, April 21; Fortune, HB, Atlantic, H&G and Holiday, May

Convertible (yellow), 'Pride of Possession' —SEP, April 28; Time and Newsweek, May 7; New Yorker, May 12; Life, May 14; Holiday, June

200 Sedan DeLuxe (green), 'It's more than . . .'—SEP, May 26; Time, June 4; Newsweek, June 11; Collier's, June 23

Mayfair (maroon and cream), 'Wonderful Way'—SEP and New Yorker, June 23;

Fortune, Holiday, H&G, Atlantic and HB, July

Patrician (red), 'It has just one old-fashioned . . .'—Time, July 16; SEP, July 21; Newsweek, August 6; Collier's, September 1

Patrician, 300 sedan, 200 club sedan (red, green, blue), 'Now get the plus of . . .'—SEP, September 8; Collier's, September 22; Time, September 24; New Yorker, September 29; Life and Newsweek, October 1; Holiday, Fortune, H&G and HB, October

200 sedan (green), 'Portrait . . .' —SEP, October 13; Time, October 15; Collier's, October 20

Patrician 400, 1952 model, 'Surprise Package'—Automotive News, November 19; MoToR, November

Patrician (green) two-page ad, 'Fashion-Keyed'—SEP, November 17; Time, November 26; Collier's, December 1; Life, December 3

300 model (green), 'Overnight'—SEP, December 1; Time, December 10; Collier's, December 15; Newsweek, December 17

Patrician (green), 'Presenting Packard for 1952'—New York Times Magazine, December 2

1952

200 Deluxe sedan, 'In looks . . . in performance'—Automotive News, almanac issue

all text ad, ¼-page, 'Better in 70 ways' —Time and Newsweek, January 7, April 21 and October 13

all text ad, ¼-page, 'New for '52 Packards, Easamatic'—Time and Newsweek, January 14, May 19 and October 27

all text ad, ¼-page, 'Packard's exclusive Ultramatic'—Time and Newsweek, January 21 and September 29

all text ad, ¼-page, 'Famous Packard Thunderbolt'—Time, January 28 and June 2; Newsweek, January 28 and May 5

all text ad, ¼-page, 'More than 53%'—Time and Newsweek, February 4 and June 16

all text ad, ¼-page, 'Every Packard undergoes'—Time and Newsweek, February 11 and June 30

all text ad, ¼-page, 'Largest trunk space'—Time, February 18; Newsweek, February 18 and July 2

200 sedan (red, 1951 model) and roadster (blue, 1913 model)—Gulfpride—SEP, February 23

all text ad, ¼-page, 'Seats as wide'—Time and Newsweek, February 25 and July 21

all text ad, ¼-page, 'Packard Thunderbolt engine'—Time and Newsweek, March 3 and August 4

Convertible (red) two-page ad, 'New luxury ride'—SEP, March 1

200 Deluxe sedan (grey) two-page ad, 'America's most exciting'—Life, April 7; SEP, April 19

all text ad, ¼-page, 'Built like a Packard' —Time and Newsweek, March 10, April 14, May 12, June 9, July 14, August 11, September 8 and October 6

all text ad, ¼-page, '3046¾ square miles' —Time and Newsweek, March 17 and August 18

all text ad, ¼-page, 'New shockproof steering'—Time and Newsweek, March 24 and September 1

all text ad, ¼-page, 'Engineered to outperform'—Time and Newsweek, March 31, April 28, June 23, July 28, August 25 and September 22

side-servicing Packard-Henney funeral car, 'Everything is . . .'—Casket & Sunnyside, April

Patrician (blue) two-page ad, 'Engineered to outperform'—Life and Time, May 5; SEP, May 24

200 Deluxe sedan (grey) two-page ad, 'Proved in use'—Newsweek, June 2; Life, June 9; SEP, June 28

200 Deluxe sedan (cream) two-page ad, 'Big-car comfort'—Life, July 14; SEP, July 26

Packards (1912 and 1952 models), 'Today as yesterday'—Ethyl Corporation —Collier's, September 20; Life, September 22

motors, 'Packard Power'—Life, Time and Newsweek, November 3; SEP and Business Week, November 8; U.S. News, November 7; Forbes, December 1; Fortune and Dun's Review, December

Pan American and test track, two-page ad, 'Where Packard Quality'—Life and Newsweek, October 20; SEP and Business Week, October 25; U.S. News, October 17; Forbes, November 15; Fortune and Dun's Review, November

200 Deluxe, 'Packard is really . . .' —Automotive News, November 3

Patrician and Clipper, 1953 models, 'Here's the new . . .'—Automotive News, December 1

1953

Caribbean, two-page ad, 'For those who want . . .'—Time, January 5

Patrician, Convertible and Deluxe Clipper (red, green, blue) two-page ad, 'Two great new lines of cars'—Life and Time, January 26; SEP, January 31; Newsweek, February 2

Pan American, 'Designed and built by . . .' (Henney ad)—International Motor Sports

Show Program

Caribbean (yellow), 'Introducing . . . —Holiday, HB, Vogue and Fortune, February; Time, February 9; New Yorker, February 14; Newsweek, February 16; U.S. News, February 20

Clipper Deluxe club sedan (red), 'New big-car value'—Life, February 9; Time, February 23; SEP, February 28; H&G, March; Newsweek, March 9

Patrician (red), 'America's most advanced new . . .'—New Yorker, January 24; U.S. News, January 30; SEP, February 14; Life, February 23; Holiday and Fortune, March; H&G, April; Vogue, April 15

Cavalier and Clipper Deluxe sedan (blue, green) two-page ad, 'Introducing two great new lines . . .'—Life, March 16; SEP, March 28

Cavalier (blue), 'Outstanding in beauty' —Time, March 2; New Yorker, March 14; U.S. News, March 20; Newsweek, March 23; Holiday, April

Patrician, Convertible, Mayfair (black, green and red/bronze) two-page ad, 'From the oldest builder'—SEP, April 11

Cavalier (black), 'Now setting the trend . . .' —New Yorker, April 11; Newsweek, April 13

Clipper Deluxe sedan (blue) two-page ad, 'Here's America's new . . .'—Time and Life, April 20; Newsweek, April 27; SEP, May 9

all text ad, 'Packard keeps a promise' —MoToR, May

Patrician (blue), 'How long has it been . . .' U.S. News, May 1; SEP, June 20; Time, May 4 (b&w)

all text ad, 'Here's the story about the new Packard'—Time, May 18

Cavalier (black), 'America's new choice . . .'—SEP, May 23; Life, June 8

Clipper Deluxe sedan (green), 'This is the news . . .'—Life, May 18 (two-page ad); SEP, May 30 (one-page)

Clipper Deluxe sedan (blue/cream) two-page ad, 'The insiders call it . . .'—Life, June 15; SEP, June 27 (one-page)

front view, 'You can see the new . . .' —Time, June 22

several models, two-page ad, 'You can see the new . . .'—U.S. News, July 10

Cavalier (blue), 'A great new car with a grand . . .'—Time, July 27; SEP, August 1

side views, 'Packard's new program' —MoToR, August 1953

Clipper Deluxe sedan (green), 'See for yourself'—SEP, August 15

Patrician (blue), 'America's New Choice . . .' —Time, August 24; SEP, August 29

APPENDIX V

THE PACKARD
RECORD:
AIR, LAND
AND WATER

Cars and Motors from the Company

in Trials and Competitions

AUTHOR: CHARLES BETTS

The preponderance of Packard's official racing program was concentrated during the Liberty aero engine period. Racing per se was not generally a structural part of the activities at East Grand Boulevard prior to that time or subsequently. During the Warren years, reliability runs found the Packard company in attendance, the Model K Gray Wolf bridged the move to Detroit, and the company indulged in occasional speed forays during the early Detroit years. Private owners of Packards frequently campaigned their own cars, and with the opening of Indianapolis Motor Speedway and the emergence of the board track era, the Packard Motor Car Company often took to those venues to establish the Packard speed performance in non-competitive trials. Although a factory racing team was considered declassé for a marque of refined image by many in the Packard echelon, there can be no doubt that others of the men who built them were speed aficionados, doubtless the most dedicated of them being Jesse Vincent.

It was Vincent who championed the cause of the company's involvement in the 1915 Indianapolis 500. Packard purchased, rebuilt, rebodied and sponsored the Ralph De Palma Mercedes entered in that event. Vincent headed up the pit crew, and the Mercedes' winning margin was generally credited to its adoption of a Packard carburetor. And in 1923 it was Vincent who spearheaded the drive for a Packard Indy team, who announced its formation to the press, who supervised the design of the cars and gave overall direction to De Palma, who was in the pits during that unhappy afternoon as the cars failed to finish. Thereafter Jesse was content to confine the Packard name in public competition to motor boating. In private, at the firm's Proving Grounds, he could, of course, race his Packards against anything he wished—including a golf ball, which he did in 1932 with a special Twin Six speedster.

A Packard was the pace car for the Indianapolis 500 on three occasions. In 1915 Carl Fisher, founder of the track and a prominent Indianapolis Packard dealer, drove his custom-built 38 hp Packard Six, a snow white runabout which he also used to pace the field of the 1916 Fall Harvest Classic race at Indy. In the 1919 Indy 500 Jesse Vincent drove a Third Series Twin Six roadster, modified for the occasion by setting the motor back a few inches to achieve better balance for the high speeds required of pace cars. And in 1936 a One Twenty convertible coupe, with Tommy Milton driving, paced the 500, that year's event being the first occasion upon which the pace car was presented afterwards to the race winner, in this case Louis Meyer.

The listing which follows includes noteworthy events and performances. The turn-of-the-century reliability runs—which were races only when overzealous participants illegally made them so—are not included, nor are the city-to-city runs made in prototypes unless a specific record was put up en route. And, although doubtless numerous more Packard owners privately competed in speed events than are mentioned here, those recorded comprise the most notable victories or performances.

The Packard racing record, while not extensive, was impressive—and perhaps partly accounts for the fact that the adjective "staid" was seldom applied to a motorcar from East Grand Boulevard.

Note: On first mention, complete information is provided regarding the track on which an event was held; thereafter the venue only is noted.

1903

June 20th-August 21st.
San Francisco to New York.
Transcontinental record.
E.T. "Tom" Fetch of Packard and Marius C. Krarup of *The Automobile*, driving Model F named Old Pacific.
Elapsed time: 61 days.

September 5th.
Cleveland, Ohio.
Charles Schmidt, driving Model K Gray Wolf.
In practice, Schmidt skidded, tore out sixteen feet of fence, was thrown twenty feet and broke his ribs.

September 7th.
Grosse Pointe (Detroit, Michigan) one-mile dirt track.
Harry Cunningham, driving Model K Gray Wolf.
Finished 2nd to Tom Cooper in Ford 999 in five-mile race for Manufacturers Challenge Cup.

September 9th and 10th.
Grosse Pointe (Detroit, Michigan).
Harry Cunningham, driving Model K Gray Wolf.
Finished 2nd in five-miler, 4th in five-mile open; 1st in ten-mile open (averaging 55.56 mph, two cars participated, Oldfield crashed); 1st in ten-miler (only car entered).

September 19th.
Narragansett Park (Providence, Rhode Island) one-mile dirt track.
Charles Schmidt, driving Model K Gray Wolf.
Finished 1st in five-miler, :05:35, 53.73 mph; 3rd in another five-miler; 2nd in ten-miler.

October 3rd.
Empire City (Yonkers, New York) one-mile dirt track.
Model K Gray Wolf.
Charles Schmidt placed 2nd in ten-miler; Harry Cunningham 3rd in fifteen-miler.

October 10th.
Empire City (Yonkers, New York).
Harry Cunningham, driving Model K Gray Wolf.
Finished 3rd in handicap, 2nd in ten-mile open, 2nd in fifteen-mile free-for-all. With Schmidt driving, placed 3rd in fifteen-miler (behind Oldfield in Winton Bullet II and Henri Page in Decauville).

October 31st.
Brighton Beach (Brooklyn, New York) one-mile dirt track.
Albert Champion, driving Model K Gray Wolf.
Finished 3rd in ten-miler.
Notes: In a subsequent event that same day, Champion crashed into a fence.

1904

January 3rd.
Ormond-Daytona Beach (Florida).
One- and five-mile records.
Charles Schmidt, driving Model K Gray Wolf.
 One mile, 46.4 seconds, 77.6 mph.
 Five miles, 4:21.6, 68.8 mph.

August 8th.
Grosse Pointe (Detroit, Michigan).
1000-mile nonstop motor run.
Charles Schmidt, Sidney Waldon and E.F. Roberts, driving stock Model L.
Time: 29:53:37.6, 33.5 mph.

Notes: Seventy gallons of gasoline consumed, three of oil; twelve stops for tires, four for lamps, sixteen for gas, three for oil—for a total of twenty-nine stops. The first record attempt in June had resulted in a night crash at 228 miles.

August 26th.
Grosse Pointe (Detroit, Michigan).
Charles Schmidt, driving Model K Gray Wolf.
Ten-mile record.

October 8th.
Long Island, New York.
Vanderbilt Cup inaugural race (ten laps, 28.44-mile lap, 284.4 miles).
Charles Schmidt, with mechanic William McIldrid, driving Model K Gray Wolf, modified with two-passenger body and semi-elliptic front suspension.
Completed eight laps (227.52 miles), 5:50:27; approximately 39 mph. Finished 4th. Fastest lap: 36:19, 47 mph.

1905

circa May.
Wilkes-Barre, Pennsylvania.
Sidney Waldon, driving prototype Model S (or 24) during Michigan-Massachusetts testing.
Unofficially lowered the record for the "famous Wilkes-Barre Mountain," making the climb to the summit in 3:44, the previous record being 8:30.

May 27th.
Harlem (Chicago, Illinois) one-mile dirt track.
Jesse Ellingsworth, driving Model K Gray Wolf.
Finished 4th in five-miler; also 2nd in ten-miler on May 30th.

1906

circa May 15th.
Cincinnati Automobile Club Paddock Road Hill Climb.
O.F. Pogue, driving his Model S.

Pages preceding: Ralph De Palma and the 299 Liberty racer taking a practice lap at Indy, 1919. Above: Charles Schmidt campaigning the Gray Wolf. 743

Fastest time of the day, 1:01, a second faster than second-place car (another Model S) and five seconds faster than third-place Stearns.

November 6th.
Empire City (Yonkers, New York).
C.H. Embleton, driving his Model Thirty.
Finished 1st, 2:00:55, 49.6 mph, in 100-miler.

1907

August 9th.
Brighton Beach (Brooklyn, New York).
Stewart Elliott, driving his Model Thirty.
Finished 2nd, 2:12:03, 45.44 mph, in 100-miler.

September 14th.
Point Breeze (Philadelphia) one-mile dirt track.
Joseph W. Parkin, Jr., driving his Model Thirty.
Finished 1st, 2:02:26.8, 49.0 mph, in 100-miler for Keystone State Championship.
Notes: In twenty-five miler for runabouts, Wally Owen finished 1st, 33:05.8, 47.13 mph.

1914

June 20th.
Indianapolis Motor Speedway, two-and-a-half mile brick oval.
Non-competitive speed trial.
W.R. McCulla, Packard assistant research engineer, driving Models 5-48 and 3-38, each a stock phaeton.
Model 5-48: One hour covering 70 miles, 2362.8 feet for 70.447 mph. (Nonstop run, only three laps averaging under 70 mph, none less than 69.7 mph.)
Model 3-38: One hour covering 62 miles, 2244 feet for 62.425 mph. (One stop for oil; slowest running lap, 63 mph; fastest lap, the last, 67.8 mph during which a maximum of 71.4 mph was recorded on back straightaway.)
Notes: Trial conducted under supervision of the Automobile Club of America, cars timed and verified as stock by A.C.A. official Herbert Chase. Each car had already traveled more

than 7000 miles, having just completed a trek to Los Angeles and back. *The Automobile* reported that the trial settled "definitely the ancient contention that no stock touring car is capable of a speed of a mile a minute."

1915

June 26th.
Uniontown (Pennsylvania) annual hill climb, three-mile distance.
Charles Johnson, Uniontown Packard dealer, driving Six 3-38 nicknamed Greyhound.
Finished 1st in free-for-all, 3:27.4—nearly twenty seconds ahead of second-place Simplex, and bettering the previous year's time by thirty seconds.

July 10th.
Chicago Board Speedway (Maywood, Illinois), two-mile track.
Non-competitive speed and economy trial.
Ralph De Palma, driving stock Twin Six five-passenger touring car, and seven-passenger touring car.
Ten-mile run (one passenger, top down and windshield up) in 8:15, 72.7 mph.
Ten-mile run (six passengers, top and windshield up) in 8:38.4, 69.8 mph.
Notes: Trial timed and stock status confirmed by Chicago Automobile Club and American Automobile Association. In fifty-mile economy run (five passengers, top down, windshield up), the seven-passenger car consumed 3 gallons 95½ ounces of gasoline, averaging 13.3 mpg, so *Motor Age* reported, showing "unexpected economy for a twelve-cylinder car." The five-passenger Twin Six had been shipped direct from the factory, the seven-passenger was the car Henry B. Joy, as president of the Lincoln Highway Association, had recently driven to the Pacific Coast. It had been returned from San Francisco by train.

July 15th.
Chicago to New York.
Packard stockholder E.C. Patterson, driving his Twin Six.
Established new amateur record by covering the

1004 miles between the two cities without once stopping the car's engine, and cutting six hours off his time made in a similar run in 1914. The new record, 35 hours 43 minutes, averaging 28.11 mph.

November 2nd.
Sheepshead Bay (Brooklyn, New York) two-mile board track, Harkness Trophy day.
Non-competitive speed demonstration.
Jesse G. Vincent, driving a special Twin Six with racing body. According to *The Automobile*, "the car was standard except the timing was changed for higher speed; pistons were arched on top to give higher compression; a double Zenith carburetor was used and the rear axle gear ratio was to give 34 mph at a crankshaft speed of 900 rpm. Mr. Vincent says the crankshaft speed was 3000 rpm [equal to 113 mph] on the backstretch."
Two-mile lap in 1:10.52, 102.10 mph.
Notes: On November 8th, Rader drove the special Twin Six thirty-two laps in 37:29.4 for 102.42 mph. During that week, too, Henry B. Joy took the wheel for a few better-than-100 mph laps. When Mrs. Joy was apprised of this, she reportedly wired back: "Please slow down to 90 miles an hour."

1916

August 4th.
Indianapolis Motor Speedway.
Non-competitive speed run.
Willard Rader, driving prototype 299 Liberty-engined racer.
One lap of 2½-mile oval, timed by speedway general manager T.E. Myers, at 1:29.32 for 100.76 mph, establishing a new fastest-lap record for the Indy track.

1917

Notes: During the spring and early summer De Palma campaigned the 299 racer with varied results. On May 10th, at the Uniontown board track, he did not finish and was flagged 11th; a radiator leak on May 30th at the Cincinnati board track prevented him finishing; and on June 16th over the Chicago boards he finished 11th, averaging 91.05 mph. Following this was a series of match races with Barney Oldfield. At Milwaukee on June 25th, he finished 2nd in the ten-, fifteen- and twenty-five milers; at Detroit he beat Oldfield's Golden Submarine in those same events; and on July 14th, at the Indiana Fairgrounds, the tables were turned again, with Oldfield winning all three races. At Narragansett Park, Oldfield took the ten-and fifteen-milers, but De Palma cinched the twenty-five-mile feature on July 21st. A week later De Palma took the ten- and fifteen-milers, Oldfield the twenty-five. Meantime the 905 Liberty-engined racer was completed, and Willard Rader took it to Sheepshead Bay on July 14th for a shakedown, and put up six

miles at 120 mph unofficially, prior to the official trial which followed in two weeks.

July 27th-28th.
Sheepshead Bay (Brooklyn, New York).
Non-competitive speed trial.
Willard Rader, driving 905 Liberty racer.
Quarter mile in 6.90 sec., 130.43 mph.
Half mile in 13.95 sec., 129.03 mph.
Kilometer in 17.35 sec., 128.94 mph.
Mile in 28.76 sec., 125.17 mph.
Two miles in 57.81 sec., 124.55 mph.
Three miles in 1:26.6, 124.71 mph.
Four miles in 1:55.74, 124.42 mph.
Five miles in 2:24.66, 124.43 mph.
Ten miles in 4:50.88, 123.76 mph.
Notes: These marks broke all existing track records, previously held by the likes of Bob

Burman in the Blitzen Benz, Barney Oldfield in the Christie, Caleb Bragg in the Fiat. Intermediate new marks were established for six, seven, eight and nine miles.

July 28th.
Livonia (New York) Hill Climb, half-mile.
Fred Turner, driving his 48 hp Six.
Finished 1st.

August 11th.
Maxwelton (St. Louis, Missouri) one-mile dirt track.
Ralph De Palma, driving 299 Liberty racer.
Finished 2nd in match race to Oldfield in ten- and fifteen-miler; finished 1st in twenty-five miler at 71.92 mph.

August 18th.
Sheepshead Bay (Brooklyn, New York).
Ralph De Palma, driving 299 Liberty racer against Louis Chevrolet in a Frontenac and Oldfield in a Miller.
Twenty-mile event in 10:53 for 110.26 mph; thirty miler in 16:35.8 for 108.46 mph; fifty-miler in 27:22.2 for 109.61 mph. Chevrolet and Oldfield defeated in each event.

September 3rd.
Chicago Board Speedway.
Ralph De Palma driving 299 Liberty racer.
Fifty-miler: Finished 1st, 28:09.0, 106.57 mph.
Hundred-miler: Finished 3rd, 57:36.0, 104.17 mph.

September 22nd.
Sheepshead Bay (Brooklyn, New York).
Ralph De Palma, driving 299 Liberty racer.
Harkness Trophy (100 miles): Finished 2nd, 56:18.4, 106.5 mph. A stop for tires at forty-six miles deprived him of first.
Ten-mile heat: Finished 1st, 6:20.4, 94.64.
Ten-mile heat: Finished 1st, 6:11.6, 96.9 mph.

November 2nd.
Sheepshead Bay (Brooklyn, New York).
Ralph De Palma, driving 299 Liberty racer.
Speed test, ten miles at 113.7 mph.

De Palma and the 299 versus Howdy Wilcox and the Peugeot at Sheepshead Bay, July 4, 1919.

November 16th
Sheepshead Bay (Brooklyn, New York).
Non-competitive speed trial.
Ralph De Palma, driving 299 Liberty racer.
One hour: 110.0 mph.
Two hours: 219 miles, 109.5 mph.
Three hours: 320.9 miles, 106.9 mph.
Four hours: 426.8 miles, 107.2 mph.
Five hours: 522 miles, 104.4 mph.
Six hours: 616 miles, 102.8 mph.
Notes: Effective this date, the Packard racer
held all world's records from ten to 600
miles, regardless of class or free-for-all
classification for cars under 300 cubic inches.
The car used sixty-seven gallons of gasoline,
eight gallons of oil and underwent eight tire
changes during the record breaking.

1918

June 1st.
Sheepshead Bay (New York).
Ralph De Palma, driving 299 Liberty racer.
Harkness Trophy (100 miles): Finished 1st,
58:21.0, 102.8 mph.

June 26th.
Chicago Board Speedway.
Ralph De Palma, driving 299 Liberty racer.
Chicago Automobile Derby (100 miles):
Finished 8th. This was a handicap event, De
Palma starting last. Prior to race, De Palma
set a new one-lap record for the two-mile
track of 115.3 mph, bettering Resta's record
of two years previous by 2.1 mph.

746 *De Palma, 905 Liberty race car, Daytona, 1919.*

De Palma, 905 Liberty, Santa Monica, 1919.

July 4th.
Cincinnati Board Speedway, two-mile track.
Ralph De Palma, driving 299 Liberty racer.
Finished 1st, 57:02.0, 105.2 mph, in 100-miler.

July 28th.
Chicago Board Speedway.
Ralph De Palma, driving 299 Liberty racer.
Two-miler (standing start): Finished 3rd,
1:19.0, 91.1 mph.
Ten-miler: Finished 1st, 5:24.8, 110.8 mph.
Twenty-miler: 1st, 10:50.2, 110.7 mph.
Thirty-miler: 1st, 16:54.8, 106.42 mph.

August 17th.
Sheepshead Bay (New York).
Ralph De Palma, driving 299 Liberty racer.
Two-miler (flying start): Finished 1st, 1:05.6,
109.8 mph.
Ten-miler: Finished 1st, 5:23.8, 111.1 mph.
Twenty-miler: Finished 1st, 10:51.6, 110.4
mph.
Thirty-miler: Finished 1st, 16:31.2, 108.9 mph.
Fifty-miler: Finished 1st, 27:29.2, 109.1 mph.

1919

February 12th-17th.
Daytona Beach (Florida).
Non-competitive speed trial.
Ralph De Palma, driving 905 Liberty racer.
One mile: 24.02, 149.9 mph.
Ten miles: 4:09.31, 144.4 mph.
Fifteen miles: 6:48.75, 132.1 mph.

Twenty miles: 8:54.2, 134.85 mph.
One mile (standing start): 38.83, 92.71 mph, a
national record, unlimited class, which was
still standing in 1952.

March 15th.
Santa Monica (California) sixth annual road
race.
Ralph De Palma, driving 905 Liberty racer.
Prior to event, put up exhibition lap (7.396
miles) in 4:45.2, 93.38 mph. Car not allowed
in race because of single-seat configuration;
De Palma did not compete.

March 23rd.
Ascot (Los Angeles, California) one-mile
asphalt speedway.
Ralph De Palma, driving 905 Liberty racer.
Five-mile exhibition, 03:57.8, 75.7 mph.

May 30th.
Indianapolis 500.
Ralph De Palma, driving 299 Liberty racer,
with lowered body and Winterfront on
radiator, among other changes.
Finished 6th, 6:10:10.64, 81.04 mph. Had
qualified at 98.20 mph and started in outside
position in front row; led the pack until
engine lost a valve and a front wheel bearing
which were replaced in time-costly pit stops.

June 14th.
Sheepshead Bay (Brooklyn, New York).
Ralph De Palma, driving 299 Liberty racer.
Fifty-miler: Finished 1st, 26:23.40, 113.8 mph.

Joe Boyer, Jr., Packard Special, Indy 500, 1923.

In thirty-miler, finished 2nd to Mulford; in ten-miler, finished 4th (Milton won).

July 4th.
Sheepshead Bay (Brooklyn, New York).
Ralph De Palma, driving 299 Liberty racer.
Finished 2nd in ten-mile match race against Howdy Wilcox in Indy-winning Peugeot.

October 12th.
Cincinnati Board Speedway.
Ralph De Palma, driving 299 Liberty racer.
Forced out after 166 miles in 250-mile A.A.A. Championship Race.

Notes: The 905 Liberty racer was sold to the Countess Maria Avanzo for speed trials in 1921 at Fanoe Island, Denmark. Subsequent to that, it was returned to the U.S.A., its engine set up for display in the Packard company lobby, and its chassis, with revisions and a Stutz motor (later a Hupmobile), was used in dirt track events around Morristown, New Jersey. The 905 racer was sold in 1925 to Jesse Lasky of Los Angeles and converted to a speedster.

1921

March.
Buenos Aires to Rosario (Argentina) and return.
Gran Premio Nacional won by Mariano de la Fuente in a probably-much-modified Twin Six.

1923

May 30th.
Indianapolis 500.
Ralph De Palma, Dario Resta and Joe Boyer, Jr., driving three Packard Specials powered by dohc six-cylinder 122-cubic-inch engines with removable heads and three main bearings. The blocks spread over the wide gap of the center wide babbitt main, blowing the head gaskets and causing the retirement of the De Palma and Resta cars. (The Boyer car broke a pinion gear, the rest of the differential being caught up in the loose parts.) These engines had a very Miller and Offy look to them. All mechanical components were built in Detroit. Body, frame and assembly were seen to behind curtains at Earle C. Anthony's shops in Los Angeles, under De Palma's direction.

Notes: After the race the cars were secreted in the Packard factory. Subsequently they were ordered demolished. The De Palma car, however, was saved and modified. It was registered at the Detroit Fairgrounds in 1951, and later run on dirt tracks around Detroit.

1925

July 16th-23rd.
Los Angeles to New York.
Leigh Wade and Linton Wells, driving Packard Eight Touring Car.
Completed 3965 miles in 6 days 21 hours 50 minutes without stopping either the engine or the wheels. A puncture in left rear tire, west of Phoenix, Arizona was changed in forty minutes while the car traveled approximately one mile an hour downgrade with the jack on rollers.
Notes: Wade was one of the pilots in the Army round-the-world flight, while Wells was the aerial "stowaway" on that famous journey.

1926

April 27th-28th.
Pendine Sands (Wales).
One-mile straightaway record.
J.G. Parry Thomas acquired the V-12 400 hp Liberty-engined Higham Special after the death of its owner, Count Louis Zborowski, during the 1924 Italian Grand Prix. He installed Miralite pistons and a revised carburetion system with four Zenith carbs, replaced the scroll clutch with a multi-plate mechanism of his own design and renamed the vehicle Babs.
On April 27th, he broke H.O.D. Segrave's record by 17 mph, setting a new Land Speed Record of 169.30 mph for the flying kilometer; on the 28th, he raised the record to 171.02 mph for the kilometer and 170.624 for the mile.
Notes: On March 1st, 1927, in another record attempt at Pendine, Thomas was killed in a crash. Babs was subsequently buried in the Pendine sands; several years ago it was exhumed and has been partially restored.

1928

April 22nd.
Daytona Beach (Florida).
One-mile straightaway record.
Ray Keech, driving the White Triplex (the Triplex Special named Spirit of Elkdom and built by five mechanics over a two-year period for the Philadelphia wire manufacturer J.M. White). The vehicle was powered by three twelve-cylinder V-type Liberty engines, 500 hp each, arranged one in front, two in rear of cockpit. The car weighed four tons and cost $45,000 to build.
The south run was completed in 17.86 seconds for 201.56774 mph; the north in 16.63 for 213.90374—the average (and official record) being 17.345 seconds and 207.5526 mph.
Notes: The Triplex record was broken by Major H.O.D. Segrave on March 11th, 1929 at Daytona in the twelve-cylinder 925 hp Golden Arrow with a two-way average of 231.36246 mph. The next day Lee Bible, driving the Triplex, was killed in his attempt to take the record back; the car was completely demolished.

June 14th.
Packard Proving Grounds (Utica, Michigan) 2½-mile concrete speedway.
Track became world's fastest speedway (a title it held until the opening of Monza in Italy after the Second World War) when Leon Duray set closed-course one-lap record of 148.17 mph in a 91-cubic-inch front-drive Miller Special during inauguration ceremonies.

1937

May 30th.
Indianapolis 500.

747

Russ Snowberger driving a Packard-engined
front wheel drive special.
Completed sixty-six laps.

1951

November 20th-25th.
Pan-American Road Race.
Tuxtla to Juarez, Mexico; 1933 miles.
Jean Trevoux in a Packard, finished 5th,
22:22:17.0.

1952

November 19th-23rd.
Pan-American Road Race.
Tuxtla to Juarez, Mexico, 1933 miles.
Jean Trevoux in a Packard, finished 9th,
22:35:00.0, in Stock Car Division.

1953

August 27th.
Milwaukee (Wisconsin) one-mile dirt track.
Don O'Dell, driving a Packard.
Finished 1st, 2:04:13.502, 72.45 mph, in the
150-mile A.A.A. Stock Car Race.

1954

October 22nd-31st.
Packard Proving Grounds (Utica, Michigan)
two-and-a-half mile concrete speedway.
High speed stock car trial; 25,000 miles.
A Patrician prototype V-8 was driven the
distance with stops only for tires, gasoline
and oil and change of drivers at an average
speed of 104.737 mph.
Notes: Although supervised by the A.A.A., the
results did not represent an official record
because the Utica track was not certified for
this purpose.

November 19th-23rd.
Pan-American Road Race.
Tuxtla to Juarez, Mexico, 1908 miles.
Jean Trevoux in a Packard Special, finished
6th, 20:48:31.0, in the Large Sports Cars
Division.

748

Packard's involvement in aero engines began with a motor called Liberty, but it did not end when the war for which that engine was built was over. In 1920 William B. Stout, who had joined the company in December 1916, was named chief engineer of the aircraft division, and although he left the company within a few years to begin his own aircraft firm, his place at Packard was taken by the estimable engineer, Lionel M. Woolson, and work continued apace.

By the mid-Twenties, Packard was building five models of its Liberty-derived water-cooled V-12 aero engine. These powerplants featured aluminum slipper-type pistons and four valves per cylinder operated by overhead camshafts driven by bevel gears and shafts from the rear of the crankshaft. There were two sizes produced: the 1A-1500 of 500 (later 600) hp for the Navy and the 1A-2500 of 800 hp for the Army—both engines built in two forms, for direct drive and for geared drive.

By early 1928 the company was selling these engines to both American and foreign governments, a Packard representative even conferring with Raj Tafari, ruler of Abyssinia, on a possible airplane program for that country. In March two 800 hp Packard engines were fitted to Germany's Dorner Super-Wal, the largest seaplane (sixty-passenger capacity) in the world—and at the same time twenty-three 800 hp Packard-engined U.S. Navy planes were completing 250,000 miles of maneuvers at Guantanamo Bay, Cuba. *The Packard* noted that summer that "the well-known Packard script is flying overhead to the tune of 200,000 total horsepower" in Japan, Russia, Germany, Hawaii, the Philippines, Panama, China, Cuba and the United States. The only false note in the melody had come the year previous when the Navy requested of Packard a "super-speed engine" to capture the world's airplane speed record from France. By early summer of 1927 the project had garnered the cognomen "Mystery engine"; when it arrived in the fall it was called the "X"—the largest aircraft engine in the world, twenty-four cylinders in four banks of six each, 2775 cubic inches, 1250 hp at 2700 rpm (1500 hp supercharged). It was installed in a racing plane built by Kirkam Products of Long Island City, New York; although

Lieutenant A. J. Williams reportedly flew the machine at 322 mph, the flight was not timed officially nor was any flight subsequently, and the world speed record was not wrested from France.

Packard's energies in the meantime had become absorbed in its diesel engine program, the first application of diesel principles to aviation design. The diesel idea for an aero engine had been considered by the company—and the industry—for some time; such an engine, it was thought, would lessen the danger of explosion and would provide greatly enhanced economy as well. (Aviation fuel was then selling at 19.8 cents a gallon. Not only would diesel fuel be cheaper but its weight for any given cruising range was also considerably less, affording either an extended cruising range or a heavier payload depending upon the requirements of the aircraft.)

Actual work on the engine commenced in mid-1927. Associated with Lionel Woolson in the planning stages were Professor Hermann Dorner and Adolph Widmann. In September of 1928 the new nine-cylinder radial air-cooled 200 hp Packard Diesel was installed in a Stinson Detroiter monoplane for its first experimental test flights at the Packard Proving Grounds. Initially flying it were Walter Lees and Captain Woolson; subsequently Colonel Charles A. Lindbergh and Major Thomas Lanphier traveled to Utica to try it out themselves. The consensus all around was most favorable.

By the summer of 1929, Alvan Macauley announced that production would begin in the fall, when the company's new diesel engine plant would be ready. Capacity of the plant was 500 units per month, a production figure which was not to be realized. Although the company was the recipient for 1931 of the coveted Collier Trophy, awarded annually for the greatest achievement in aviation by the National Aeronautic Association, Packard's diesel program was destined to be short-lived, a casualty of the Great Depression and the tragic death of Lionel Woolson in a testing crash during 1930.

It would require another war for Packard to resume on a large scale the aero-engine activity that had begun with the Liberty. Among Packard records established in the air during the years of peace intervening were the following:

1920

February 27th.
McCook Field, Major Rudolph Schroeder, supercharged Liberty-engined Le Pere.
Altitude record of 33,112 feet, first flight exceeding 30,000 feet.

August 28th.
Pulitzer Trophy Air Races, Lieutenant C.C. Mosley, Verville-Packard.
Speed of 178 mph.
Notes: Packard called the feat the "record for all speeds made by any human being from one to thirty miles."

1921

March 15th.
Lieutenants John A. Macready and R.F. Langham, Liberty-engined Le Pere.
Soared to 30,000 feet, an altitude mark for plane carrying two people.

September 28th.
Lieutenant John Macready, Liberty-engined,
  Packard designed and built Le Pere.
Soared to 34,508 feet.
Notes: In 1923 Macready reached 36,800 feet,
  and in 1926, 38,704 feet—all official altitude
  records, winning for him the Mackay Trophy
  three times.

1922

October 12th-14th.
Selfridge Field, Lieutenant T.J. Koenig,
  Liberty-engined Le Pere.
Won Liberty Engine Trophy, averaging 128.8
  mph over 357-mile course at National Air
  Races, the Liberty event sponsored by the
  Packard Motor Car Company.

Aviation motor endurance mark of 300 hours
set, and "economy record for any gasoline
motor of 0.45 pounds per brake horsepower,"
for powerplant Packard was building for the
Navy for the airship Shenandoah. The
Shenandoah was originally fitted with six six-
cylinder 500 hp Packard aero engines, which
were run usually at 1000 rpm, producing
approximately 200 hp each. The pricetag of
these hand-tooled powerplants was $16,000
each. Ultimately one of the engines was
removed for the installation of radio equipment.
The dirigible made its first successful test flight
on September 4th, 1923. On September 3rd,
1925, it fell near Ava, Ohio en route from its
station at Lakehurst, New Jersey to St. Louis.
The last sentence in the Shenandoah's log read
"all engines operating perfectly." After the
crash, Gar Wood bought the five engines of the
Shenandoah and used them in his first Miss
America speed boats.

The airship Roma, built under American
contract in Italy, shipped to this country in
sections and originally fitted with six Ansaldo
engines, had two of the Ansaldos removed after
her first short test flight and replaced with 240
hp Packard Liberty units. On her first long
distance flight, December 21st, 1921, all four of

the Italian engines broke down and the test was
completed under power of the two Liberties.
Unfortunately, the ship had not been designed
to bear the stresses of the more powerful
American engines, and on February 21st, 1922,
while undergoing high speed tests at Langley
Field, the Roma began to break up in the air,
went out of control and crashed into a hillside.

1924-1925

Navy Seaplane PN-9, powered by two Packard
500 hp engines, endurance record for seaplanes,
28 hours 35 minutes 27 seconds. Record made
on forty-mile course over Delaware River, with
twenty-eight round trips at an altitude of 1000
feet. Previous record was 14 hours. Lieutenants
J.R. Kyle and C.H. Schildauer were the pilots,
with Charles Sutter, a Navy mechanic, and
Captain Woolson comprising the crew.

Navy Seaplane PN-9, distance record for
seaplanes, 1841 statute miles in 25 hours over
the Pacific Ocean, exceeding by 400 miles the
Navy's previous long distance record and twice
the distance covered in the longest "hop"
during the Army's flight around the world.
Piloted by Commander John Rodgers.

Army Huff-Daland plane, speed record for
single-motored bombing plane, 130 mph.

Walter Lees and Frederic A. Brossy, 1931.

1926

Lieutenant G.T. Cuddihy, Boeing-Packard
combat plane, 120 miles at 180.495 mph over
closed course.

1927

Lieutenants B.J. Connell and S.R. Pope, Navy
Seaplane PN-10, powered by two Packard 600
hp engines, seven world and twenty American
records for duration, distance, altitude and
speed with specified use loads, at San Diego,
California.

1929

First cross-country flight with diesel airplane,
providing "new world economy record for
internal combustion engines." During Detroit-
Langley Field (Virginia) trek, with Lionel
Woolson and Walter Lees aboard, the Packard-
engined Stinson "burned $4.58 worth of furnace
oil and covered 700 miles in six hours and fifty
minutes."

1931

American non-refueling airplane endurance
record, 73 hours 48 minutes, Packard-Diesel
Bellanca Pacemaker, exceeding previous record
by 14 hours 29 minutes. Pilots Walter Lees and
Frederic A. Brossy went up at 8:52 a.m. on
April 12th and came down at 10:40 a.m. April
15th. The total fuel supply cost for the trip was
$45.80. The following month Lees and Brossy
took to the air again, breaking the world record
(previously held by France) with a flight
duration of 84 hours 33 minutes.

1944

Two speed records set with Packard-built
Merlin engines, one by a Mustang from Los
Angeles to New York in 6 hours 31 minutes,
the other by a Mosquito from Labrador to
Great Britain in 6 hours 46 minutes.

The Packard Diesel and the Collier Trophy. Packard executives, from the left: Mr. Edwards, E.F. Roberts, H.W. Peters, Jesse Vincent, Mr. Page, Hugh Ferry, Frank McKinney, Frederic A. Brossy, Milton Tibbetts, Walter Lees, George Brodie, Edward Macauley, Alvan Macauley, Merlin A. Cudlip.

Above: Harmsworth Trophy winner and world record breaker, Miss America IX. Right: Jesse Vincent and Packard Chriscraft II; Miss America X.

In 1928 the Packard Motor Car Company boasted that its engines contributed to more existing world speed marks than those of any other manufacturer in the world. History does not record anyone objecting to that statement vigorously. Probably it was true and, more probable, most of those records were made on the water. All this was because Jesse Vincent liked to travel fast—wherever he was.

It was before the First World War when Packard first got its feet wet—a four-cylinder automobile engine of 1906 being adapted for a racing boat named Sparrow—but the company's real plunge into the world of motor boating came in 1922 when Jesse Vincent designed, had built and personally drove to victory his first Packard Chriscraft. Thereafter the Packard Motor Car Company got into marine manufac-

ture in earnest, developing from its 500 hp aero engine two marine units of formidable proportion. The first, for Gold Cup events specifying engines not to exceed 625 cubic inches, was a six-cylinder powerplant developing 260 hp at 2700 rpm. The second, for Sweepstakes events allowing 1250 cubic inches, was a twelve developing 550 hp at 2700 rpm. The Gold Cup Model IM-621 and the Sweepstakes Model IM-242 sold for $6000 and $12,000 respectively in 1925. Though the design remained generally the same, horsepower steadily rose and the name of the marine engine was changed in promotion copy to Twin Six when Packard decided to revive the designation for its new twelve-cylinder motorcar in 1932.

Packard's notable victories on water were the following:

1922

Colonel Jesse Vincent's Packard Chriscraft, Gold Cup winner.

1923

Colonel Jesse Vincent's Packard Chriscraft, Gold Cup winner.

Commander Harry B. Greening's Rainbow III, 1064 miles in 24 hours, a new record for boats of any type.

1925

Colonel Jesse Vincent's Packard Chriscraft II, Sweepstakes winner, 150 miles at 55.65 mph, a new record for boats of any type.

Colonel Jesse Vincent's Nuisance, 49.1 mph for 30 miles, a new record for Gold Cup boats.

Caleb Bragg's Baby Bootlegger, Gold Cup and Dodge Memorial Trophy winner.

1926

Victor Kleisrath's Rowdy, six miles at 64.7 mph, American record for displacement boats, any type, one to six miles inclusive.

George Townsend's Greenwich Folly, Gold Cup.

1927

Horace Dodge's Miss Syndicate, Sweepstakes and President's Cup winner.

Horace Dodge's Solar Plexus, Dodge Memorial Trophy winner.

George Townsend's Greenwich Folly, Gold Cup winner.

1928

Gar Wood's Miss America VII (two Packard 1100 hp motors), Harmsworth Trophy winner, this boat also establishing a new world speed record of 92.838 mph on Detroit River.

1929

Gar Wood's Miss America VIII, 93.123 mph, a new world speed record for both salt and fresh water, Miami, Florida.

1930

Gar Wood's Miss America IX, Harmsworth Trophy winner.

1931

Gar Wood's Miss America IX, Harmsworth Trophy winner, establishing a world record of 102.256 mph, the first to break the 100-mph mark.

1932

Gar Wood's Miss America X, Harmsworth Trophy winner, establishing a new world record of 124.915 mph.

Horace E. Dodge's Delphine IV, Gold Cup and President's Cup winner, at a record-breaking 59.21 mph.

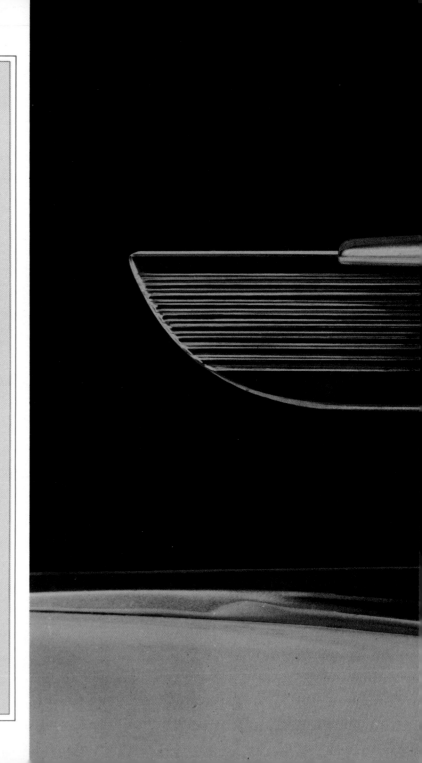

APPENDIX VI

THE HERALDIC PACKARD

Company Hood Ornaments

and Emblems

AUTHOR: W. C. WILLIAMS

Motometers from the left: 1912-15, 1915-16, 1917, 1918, 1918-28. Bail cap, 1929 6th Series.

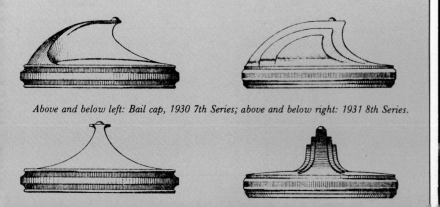

Above and below left: Bail cap, 1930 7th Series; above and below right: 1931 8th Series.

In its December 27th, 1911 issue, *The Horseless Age* announced that a new design had been adopted by the Packard Motor Car Company to distinguish its Six from the four-cylinder cars (the Thirty and the Eighteen) in the company's line. A special radiator cap with the figure "6" incorporated into its design was now to distinguish the six-cylinder cars built on East Grand Boulevard.

Thus began the long line of Packard ornaments gracing the radiator caps and hoods of the company's automobiles. This first special radiator cap design was patented by Packard, Design Patent 42,139 being issued October 27th, 1911. Henry B. Joy was credited with the design, and it was used through 1915 when a more practical motometer took its place. A double-six motif followed in 1917 for the firm's Twin Six models. But these small, pot metal ornaments were very delicate and did not survive the passage of time well, principally being replaced by the familiar motometer.

The Boyce motometer was a handy instrument, indicating to the driver the condition of his radiator coolant temperature at all times. A series of at least five different motometer faceplates was supplied by Packard during the period 1912 through 1928. A special motometer was needed for the company's automobiles because of the construction of the

Below: Bail cap, 1930, 734 and 745 models, Design Patent 81,713.

hinged radiator cap. Genuine Packard motometers have a slot in their base to fit over the fin on the cap, the temperature tube extension being especially short to clear the filler neck when the cap is tilted back to receive coolant. The Packard motometer was furnished in two thicknesses, a thin one for Sixes, a thick one for Eights and Twin Sixes.

Beginning in 1929, with the abandonment of the motometer for a dash-mounted heat indicator, the standard radiator cap furnished by Packard was a plain type with a raised rib and held in place by a bail wire. This plain bail cap, however, was infrequently seen since most owners preferred to decorate their cars with an appropriate deluxe mascot. The bail concept continued even after the radiator filler was relocated under the hood, and on 1941 and 1942 models the new wonder material called plastic was incorporated. The exception to the bail cap was a special mascot provided on the One Twenty, introduced in 1935 on Twelfth Series cars. It was designed by Howard F. Yeager, Design Patent 97,587 being issued November 19th, 1935.

With the advent of the streamlined design of the Clippers in 1941 and continuing through 1955, Packard designers followed the contemporary vogue and provided varying spears, fins and the like as standard ornamentation.

Below: Bail cap, 1938-40, 16th-18th Series, chrome-plated zinc, die cast.

Left: Bail cap, 1932-33, 9th and 10th Series. Right: 1934-37, 11th through 15th Series.

Left: One Twenty, 12th Series, 1935. Right: One-Twenty and One-Ten, 19th Series, 1941.

Left: Feather bail, 1941-42, 19th and 20th Series. Right: 1946-47, 21st Series, Clipper.

Left: 1949-50, 23rd Series, Junior models. Right: 1949 23rd Series, Golden Anniversary.

Left: 1951-52 Model 200 and 1953 Clipper. Right: 1955-56, 55th and 56th Series, Clipper.

From the top: 3rd-5th Series;
2nd Series Eight and 3rd Series Six;
6th Series, introduced for 1929.

The Packard ornament affectionately known as the Goddess of Speed or the doughnut pusher or doughnut chaser is the longest lived mascot in the history of the American automobile. From inception in 1926 to disappearance in 1950, the ornament underwent a series of changes, beginning as a beautifully proportioned art deco figure and ending with a resemblance more akin to a wheelbarrow but recognizable by the forward-thrusting wheel. Throughout her long life, the Packard goddess was the product of the Packard design department, and no prototypes nor other designs were allowed to interrupt her continuation through the years. Invariably, she was referred to as the Packard DeLuxe Emblem in the company's literature and design patents.

The Packard DeLuxe Emblem first appeared as an accessory held in place on the radiator cap by a threaded bolt, with no provision for a motometer. Patent application was made June 25th, 1926, and Design Patent 73,026 was issued July 12th, 1927. According to the patent papers, the designer was Joseph E. Corker and the patent was assigned to the Packard Motor Car Company. Used on a number of different caps and bases, the original design was retained through the Fifteenth Series in 1937, although it was not available on either the One Twenty in the Fourteenth and Fifteenth Series or the new Six introduced for 1937. For these cars, a new goddess was used, designed by Werner Gubitz. Patent application was filed May 27th, 1935, and Design Patent 95,526 was issued November 19th, 1937 for the design. Again, the patent was assigned to Packard. Because of its limited usage, this mascot is one of the rarest of the goddesses.

The goddess, used on a variety of bases, from 1937 through 1938 (the

Below: 1930 Models 734 and 745. Below right: 1937-38 15th and 16th Series.

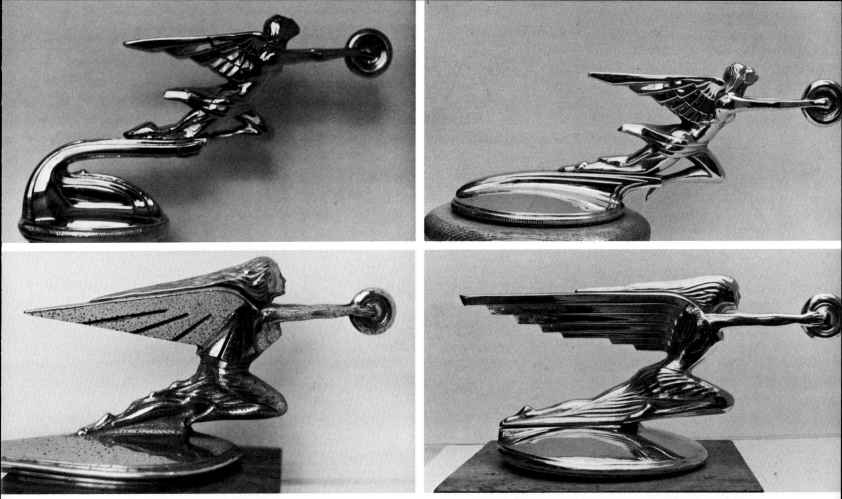

Above, clockwise from top left: 1930-31 7th and 8th Series; 1932-37 9th-15th Series; 1937 Super Eight; 1936-37 14th-15th Series One Twenty and Six.

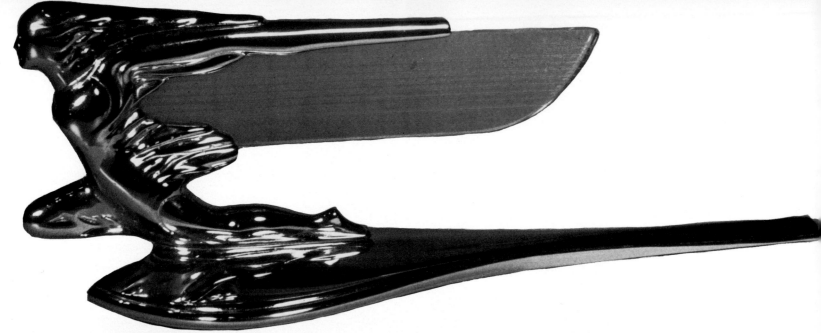

Above: 1939-40 17th and 18th Series, California model. Below: 1941-42 19th and 20th Series, non-Clipper base; above right, same mascot, Clipper base.

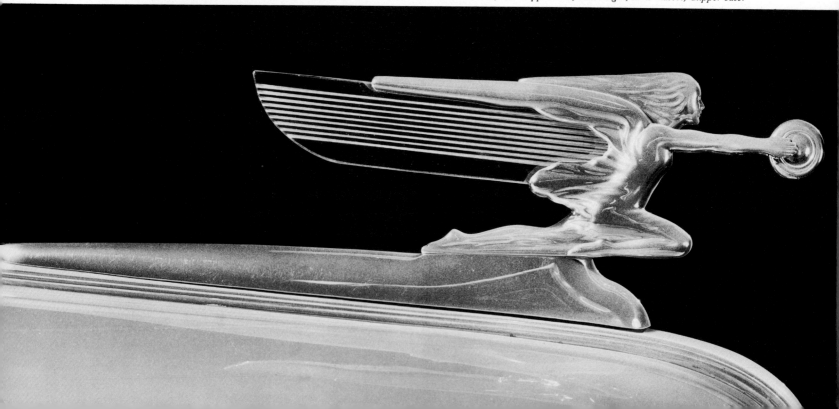

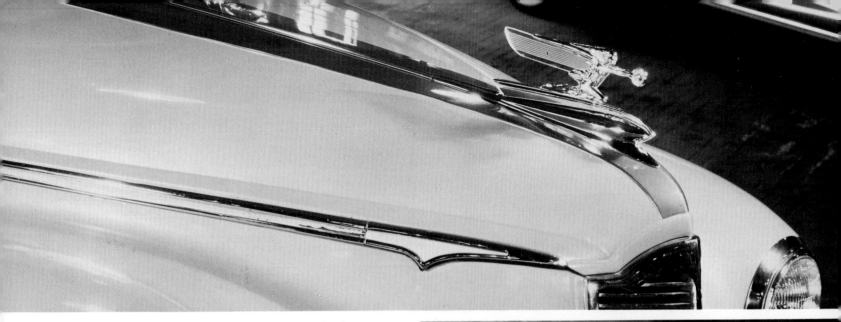

Fifteenth and into the Sixteenth Series) was also designed by Werner Gubitz, patent applied for March 13th, 1937, Design Patent 104,774 issued June 1st, 1937. Although the Super Eight of 1937 used this ornament, more often the previous design was seen.

The final design immediately recognizable as a Packard DeLuxe Emblem was the work of John D. Wilson, patent applied for October 11th, 1938 and Design Patent 114,358 issued April 18th, 1939, assigned to Packard. This goddess was used from 1939 through 1942 on Seventeenth through Twentieth Series cars. It is perhaps the most common Packard mascot and can be identified by the glass wing, which was usually decorated with horizontal grooves although it was available in 1940 with a plain, ungrooved wing. This design was also available in a very special model to California buyers. Perhaps Earle C. Anthony considered the forward thrust of the goddess as a potential danger to pedestrians, for he persuaded Packard to produce the lady without arms or wheel.

The passage of World War II brought a new, stylized look to the Packard goddess mascots which harmonized with the streamlined styling of postwar models. This design was the work of Howard F. Yeager, the patent applied for October 18th, 1946 and issued May 11th, 1948 as Design Patent 149,601. In use on the Twenty-First Series in 1946 and 1947, the goddess wore an apron, which was removed on Twenty-Second and Twenty-Third Series cars for 1948 to 1950. The demise of the Twenty-Third Series cars saw also the end of the famed goddess as Packard joined the rest of the industry in providing mascots of rather less esoteric design.

Above: 1946-47, 21st Series, with apron. Below: 1948-50, 22nd-23rd Series, without apron.

Daphne at the well, sliding boy and other designations to the contrary, this most pleasing Packard mascot's true name is Adonis, and it was generally found on sporty open cars. Legend tells that it was designed in France, manufactured in this country and represents a young girl of about eight to ten years of age. Patent papers, however, credit the design to Edward McCarten of New York City. Patent was applied for November 7th, 1928, with Design Patent 79,561 issued on October 8th, 1929. Adonis was introduced for the Sixth Series and was discontinued after December of 1932 with the introduction of the Tenth Series. The price of an Adonis was fifteen dollars, as contrasted to other Packard DeLuxe mascots which were available for ten dollars.

762

Adonis, from the left: 1929 Sixth Series, chrome-plated or silver-plated zinc, die cast;
for 1930, the Models 734 and 745, chrome-plated zinc, die cast, on a scroll pedestal;
for 1930-1931, Seventh and Eighth Series, chrome-plated zinc, die cast, on a scroll pedestal;
for 1932, the Ninth Series, chrome-plated zinc, die cast, and also on a scroll pedestal.

763

The graceful pelican was introduced in 1932 on Ninth Series cars and endured in various configurations until Packard designers decided to eliminate hood ornamentation altogether with the Fifty-Eighth Series for 1958. By 1955, however, all resemblance between the famous pelican or indeed any form of bird life had been lost completely. Historically, the pelican mascot was generally reserved for Super Eights and Twelves but after the demise of the latter car was used on all Senior Packards.

What to call the well-known bird has been an area of conflict among Packard people since the late 1930's when advertising first referred to it as a cormorant. Controversy—then and now—raged on the subject. "I have always been under the impression that our ornament was intended to carry on the tradition of the Packard family whose escutcheon carries the pious pelican," Hugh Ferry noted in an inter-office memo dated

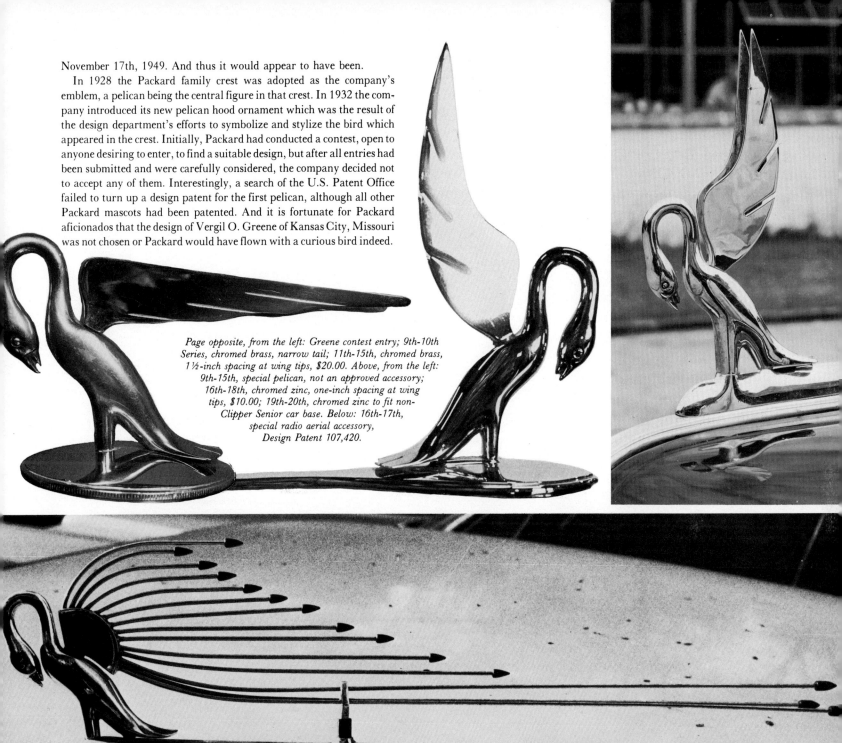

November 17th, 1949. And thus it would appear to have been.

In 1928 the Packard family crest was adopted as the company's emblem, a pelican being the central figure in that crest. In 1932 the company introduced its new pelican hood ornament which was the result of the design department's efforts to symbolize and stylize the bird which appeared in the crest. Initially, Packard had conducted a contest, open to anyone desiring to enter, to find a suitable design, but after all entries had been submitted and were carefully considered, the company decided not to accept any of them. Interestingly, a search of the U.S. Patent Office failed to turn up a design patent for the first pelican, although all other Packard mascots had been patented. And it is fortunate for Packard aficionados that the design of Vergil O. Greene of Kansas City, Missouri was not chosen or Packard would have flown with a curious bird indeed.

Page opposite, from the left: Greene contest entry; 9th-10th Series, chromed brass, narrow tail; 11th-15th, chromed brass, 1½-inch spacing at wing tips, $20.00. Above, from the left: 9th-15th, special pelican, not an approved accessory; 16th-18th, chromed zinc, one-inch spacing at wing tips, $10.00; 19th-20th, chromed zinc to fit non-Clipper Senior car base. Below: 16th-17th, special radio aerial accessory, Design Patent 107,420.

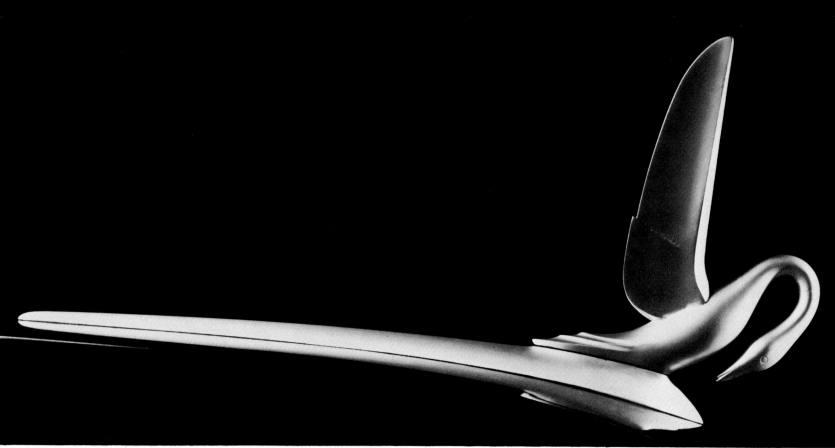

Above: 1948-1950 Twenty-Second and Twenty-Third Series, Design Patent 151,310. Below left: Twenty-Fourth Series. Below right: 1952 Twenty-Fifth Series, Packard line, $13.45.

At one point during the late Thirties, Earle C. Anthony whimsically suggested to company executives that Packard had designed a cormorant instead of a pelican, and referring to the bird as a cormorant became an in-house jest at East Grand Boulevard thereafter. By mid-1938, however, the jest ceased being that, when Packard's advertising department concluded that cormorant sounded more dignified than pelican and without management's approval published an accessory catalogue for the Seventeenth Series offering a cormorant ornament. The term was repeated in the 1940 Data Book, copyrighted by the company in August of 1939, in the back of which, under authorized and approved Packard accessories, is listed "Cormorant Radiator Emblem . . . $10.00."

Subsequently, Packard was deluged by cards and letters from owners whose personal family crests bore a pelican or who disapproved of the selection of the term cormorant to replace the beloved pelican in the Packard family crest. In due course—the wheels of corporate management turning ever slowly—Packard vice-president Milton Tibbetts issued a memorandum to the executive staff noting that the original designers had intended that the bird be a pelican and that is what it should be called. This was in 1949. By 1953 everyone at Packard had finally agreed that indeed it was a pelican, although by this time all argument was meaningless because the hood design for the Fifty-Fifth Series was finalized and one couldn't be sure if the bird thereon was a cormorant or a pelican or a pileated woodpecker.

While only the bail cap was furnished as standard equipment, Packard owners were offered a number of deluxe ornaments by the company (the DeLuxe Emblem, the Adonis and the pelican) to adorn their cars. In addition, there were a few other mascots available which had an association with Packard and although some were offered by dealers and not by the company itself, they deserve recognition.

In the Twenties an accessory to dress up the standard motometer was designed: a wraparound wreath surmounted by the figure "8." It was sold by Packard-Chicago. Originals of this ornament are very rare although it has been reproduced in brass. An additional motometer adornment was the Winged Motor Mascot sold for Third and Fourth Series cars as an approved Packard accessory at a price of four dollars.

In the Twenties, too, came the Earle Anthony peacock. During this period a few of the larger automobile dealers in the country, like Anthony on the West Coast and Greenlease Cadillac of Kansas City, Missouri, designed their own mascots and offered them to the public in lieu of the standard ornament or cap. Anthony, who was also in the custom body business on a small scale, chose the peacock as his trademark and bodies built by his company in Los Angeles bore a beautiful peacock in full color. The mascot, while not in color, was a carefully detailed representation of the bird, with the tail feathers illuminated at night by a small light bulb hidden in the bird's body and wired to the car's electrical system. Constructed of pot metal, few have survived.

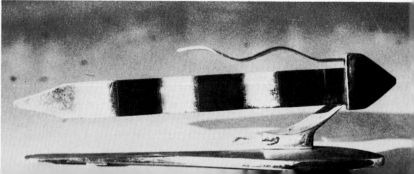

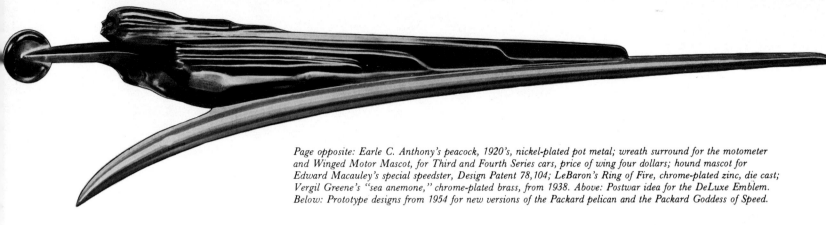

Page opposite: Earle C. Anthony's peacock, 1920's, nickel-plated pot metal; wreath surround for the motometer and Winged Motor Mascot, for Third and Fourth Series cars, price of wing four dollars; hound mascot for Edward Macauley's special speedster, Design Patent 78,104; LeBaron's Ring of Fire, chrome-plated zinc, die cast; Vergil Greene's "sea anemone," chrome-plated brass, from 1938. Above: Postwar idea for the DeLuxe Emblem. Below: Prototype designs from 1954 for new versions of the Packard pelican and the Packard Goddess of Speed.

In the Thirties, Ed Macauley decorated his special speedster with an unusual bail cap and sheet metal hound which had been designed by Henry C. Kenly. And a custom coachbuilder of great renown was also to adopt its own personal mascot: LeBaron with its Ring of Fire. Although not featured on all LeBaron products, this mascot was used on the beautifully styled bodies of the Tenth and Eleventh Series Packard. It was designed by Frederick A. Leisen and was issued Design Patent 92,-184 on May 8th, 1934. During the Thirties as well, Packard owners could buy the standard Packard cap which was especially made to accept the popular crystal mascots of René Lalique.

And then there was Vergil O. Greene, a prolific designer of mascots and an entrant in Packard's pelican contest. His mascots were usually riveted pieces of sheet metal taking the form of various birds. His designs lacked the grace and beauty of most ornaments of this era and have since quietly disappeared from the scene. In 1939 he proposed another mascot to designers at Packard which might be called a sea anemone. Fortunately, again, his design was not accepted. Neither, and fortunately too, were many of the mascots made up in the company's own design department for hood ornamentation on forthcoming series Packards and which never proceeded beyond the clay model stage.

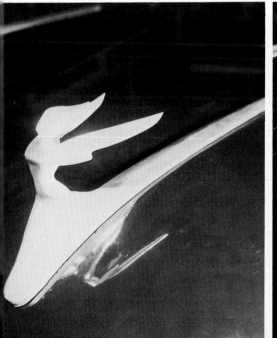

Body plates, from the top:
1907-10; 1911; 1912;
1913-14; 1930 734 and 745
custom body by Packard;
postwar body.

Script, 1904 through Sixth Series.
Above, from the left: radiator
emblems, 1929, 1930, 1931; 1929-31
6th-8th Series stone guard emblem
(no black cloisonné in oval).
Below: 1932 crank hole cover emblem.

Prior to 1929 the use of decorative emblems by the Packard Motor Car Company was almost nonexistent. Various body plates were employed in the early years but save for rare exceptions (i.e., the first Twin Sixes, the popular brass scripts), the cars were unadorned. Beginning with the Sixth Series in 1929, the company decided to honor the memory of its founding family by placing the Packard coat of arms on the radiator shell. The crest is described in heraldic terms as: Gules, a cross lozengy accompanied by four roses argent, a pelican in her piety. In commonplace terms, it translates thus: a cross of diamonds on a red field surrounded by four silver roses and surmounted by a pious pelican. The pelican was a revered bird and it was thought it fed its young by wounding its own breast, the young nursing on the mother's blood. The pelican in the Packard coat of arms is shown thusly. (It should be noted that for aesthetic and production purposes Packard chose to substitute roses or (gold) for roses argent.)

Literally hundreds of different emblems, scripts, body plates, et al. were used by the Packard Motor Car Company in its later years. The representative selection which follows presents a broad canvas and illustrates some of the more important of these ornamentations.

At top, from the left: radiator emblems, 1914-1915 Models 4-48 and 5-48; 1916 Twin Six; exported Packards, 1926. Above: Small script for export cars, through 1926, optional on domestic cars. Left: 1932 Ninth Series crank hole cover. Right, from the top: hub cap medallions, 1932 Ninth Series; 1933-1939 Tenth through Seventeenth Series; 1940-1941 Eighteenth and Nineteenth Series Custom Super Eight; 1942-1951 Twentieth through Twenty-Fourth Series for the Custom Eight, Custom Super Clipper and the Patrician 400.

Above, from the left: Crank hole cover emblems, 1933-1938 Twelve, 1933-1937 Super Eight and 1933-1937 Eight; One Twenty emblem, 1936-1937; Six emblem, 1937.

Above, from the left: Hood side emblems, 1939 Seventeenth Series Twelve; 1939-1940 Seventeenth and Eighteenth Series Super-8; 1940 Eighteenth Series One Twenty.

Far left: Hood side emblem for the 1940 Eighteenth Series One-Ten. Above: 1941-1942, Nineteenth and Twentieth Series hood side script. Left: 1941-1942, Nineteenth and Twentieth Series hood side emblem for the One-Eighty and One-Sixty.

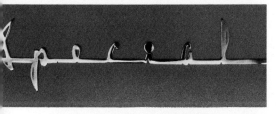

Left, from the top: 1941-1942 One-Sixty, 1941 One-Twenty, 1941 One-Ten Special DeLuxe, 1941 One-Ten Special; 1948-1950 Twenty-Second and Twenty-Third Series metal grille crest. Above: 1941 One-Twenty hood side emblem. Below: 1952 and 1954 Twenty-Fifth and Fifty-Fourth Series plastic grille crest.

From the top: 1941 One-Ten hood side emblem; 1955 Packard line vee and circle with crest; 1956 Packard line vee and circle; 1955-1957 Clipper grille emblem.

APPENDIX VII

THE PACKARD SPECIFICATIONS

Engineering and Coachwork

Data on the Cars

1899-1958

The selected specifications which follow encompass the Packard motorcar from the first Model A built in Warren, Ohio in 1899 to the last 58L assembled in South Bend, Indiana in 1958. The data in each case was contributed by the historians who authored the text narrative on the cars themselves. Represented is nearly sixty years of Packard automobile production, and it is the production Packard—as opposed to experimental or show or one-off cars—which is the focus here. These specifications have been prepared to provide a ready reference to various running changes and refinements made to Packards through the years and to offer additional data which in some cases would have been cumbersome to have been incorporated in the narrative. For complete descriptive data, the reader is referred to the index, which notes the sections of the historical text which relate to each production car.

This compilation is arranged both subjectively and chronologically, to wit, the Junior Packards of the 1930's and prewar 1940's are presented consecutively by model year, as is the Twin Six/Twelve. The introductory car of any new Packard series is given a full specification entry; cars ensuing are noted with regard to engine refinements, chassis refinements, et al. which were provided in that particular model year. The absence of data indicates no major changes occurred.

MODEL A
MODEL YEAR: 1899 • FIRST TEST RUN: NOVEMBER 6TH, 1899
ENGINE. One cylinder; suction intake, mechanical exhaust valves; fixed head, cast in one piece; 5 ½ by 6 inches, 142.6 cubic inches; 9 hp at 800 rpm. *Ignition:* jump spark. *Carburetor:* float feed. *Lubrication:* drip oilers on mains, piston and pin; grease cup on connecting rod. *Cooling:* flat copper sides on cylinder, circulating pump and radiator, capacity 4 gallons.
TRANSMISSION. Planetary with two forward speeds; center chain drive; geared as required for different localities. (First Packard had ten teeth on small drive sprocket off transmission, sixty-eight teeth on large rear axle sprocket, appearing to be 7 to 1 ratio.)
CHASSIS. *Frame:* 2" channel iron. *Suspension:* front, two half-elliptic leaf springs, back to back, transverse; rear, full elliptic leaf, both sides lengthwise. *Steering:* hinged spade handle lever, direct ratio. *Braking:* hand lever on transmission, foot pedal to brake band in center of rear axle. *Wheels:* bicycle-type tangent spoked wire wheels, 34x3 single-tube tires. *Track:* 56 ½ inches. *Wheelbase:* 71 ½ inches.
BODY. *Construction:* all wood. *Paint:* varnish, all black. *Interior:* top grade leather. *Standard fittings:* chime foot bell, tools and oiler, single lamp. *Lighting:* special solar auto light, center front. *Instrumentation:* double throw ignition switch. *Body types:* single-seat roadster.
PRICE RANGE. Single-seat roadster, $1200; with dos-a-dos seat, $1250; with dos-a-dos seat and top, $1325.

MODEL B

Model Year: 1900 • Introduced early Spring 1900

ENGINE REFINEMENTS. *Lubrication:* site drip on piston; main oiler drips on all other bearings except grease cup on connecting rod.

CHASSIS REFINEMENTS. *Wheels:* wire spoke wheels, 34x3 single tube tires. *Track:* 56 inches. *Wheelbase:* 76 inches.

BODY REFINEMENTS. *Paint:* varnish, choice of color. *Standard fittings:* bulb horn on spade handle lever, chime foot bell, tools and oiler. *Lighting:* solar self-generating gas light, center front. *Instrumentation:* double throw ignition switch, with two sets of batteries.

PRICE RANGE. Single-seat roadster, $1200; dos-a-dos seat option, $50; tops optional, $50 to $75.

MODEL C

Model Year: 1901 • Introduced November 1900
Motor Serial Numbers 29 to 140

ENGINE. One cylinder; suction intake, mechanical exhaust valves; fixed head, cast in one piece; 6 by 6½ inches, 183.8 cubic inches, 12 hp at 850 rpm. *Ignition:* jump spark with two sets of batteries. *Carburetor:* float feed. *Lubrication:* main oiler drips to bearings. *Cooling:* radiator with mechanical pump, capacity a little over 4 gallons.

TRANSMISSION AND CHASSIS. Same as Model B save for worm and segment steering, right hand steering wheel.

BODY. Same as Model B save for bulb horn on steering spoke and pair of oil Dietz auto lamps up front. *Body types:* single-seat roadster with dos-a-dos rear seat; four-passenger surrey; roadster with high rear seat facing forward.

PRICE RANGE. Roadster with dos-a-dos seat, $1500; tops optional, $50 to $75.

MODEL F

Model Year: 1902 • Introduced November 1901
Motor Serial Numbers 141 to 241

ENGINE. Same as Model C save for radiator capacity now at 5 gallons.

TRANSMISSION. Sliding gear with three forward speeds, center chain drive, spur gear differential.

CHASSIS REFINEMENTS. *Wheels:* wood artillery, 34x4 tires. *Wheelbase:* 84 inches.

BODY REFINEMENTS. *Standard fittings:* oil side lights and bulb horn. *Body types:* five-passenger rear entrance tonneau, removable to form two-passenger roadster.

PRICE RANGE. $2500 with tonneau, $2250 without tonneau.

MODEL G

Model Year: 1902 • Introduced late Summer 1902

ENGINE. Two cylinders; suction intake, mechanical exhaust valves; cylinders cast with head; 24 horsepower developed. *Ignition:* jump spark, twin coil and battery. *Carburetor:* one for each cylinder, float feed. *Lubrication:* mechanical oil pump. *Cooling:* rotary pump to 24-tube radiator, capacity 8 gallons.

TRANSMISSION. Sliding gear with three forward speeds, center chain drive.

CHASSIS. *Frame:* channel steel. *Suspension:* front, semi-elliptic; rear, two full-elliptic. *Steering:* worm and segment, right side steering wheel. *Brake:* contracting on differential drum and on transmission shaft. *Wheels:* wood artillery, 36x-4½ tires. *Track:* 56 inches. *Wheelbase:* 91 inches.

BODY. *Construction:* all wood. *Paint:* varnish, choice of color. *Interior:* tufted leather. *Standard fittings:* Deitz oil lamps up front. *Lighting:* oil. *Instrumentation:* Speed-O-Meter, site gauges for oil and gas. *Body types:* eight-passenger rear entrance tonneau, four-passenger surrey.

MODEL F

Model Year: 1903 • Introduced November 1902
Motor Serial Numbers 244 to 403

ENGINE REFINEMENTS. *Lubrication:* wick-feed gravity oiler. *Cooling:* circulation pump and coiling coils, capacity 6 gallons.

CHASSIS REFINEMENTS. *Braking:* two clamping on rear wheels, one on driveshaft. *Track:* 56½ inches. *Wheelbase:* 88 inches.

BODY REFINEMENTS. *Standard fittings:* oil side lights, self-generating center headlight. *Lighting:* Oil and gas.

PRICE RANGE. $2300 with tonneau; $2000 without tonneau.

MODEL K

Model Year: 1903 • Introduced November 1902

ENGINE. Four cylinders, automatic inlet valves, head cast separate from cylinders, 4 by 5 inches, 24 hp at 1000 rpm. *Ignition:* jump spark with batteries. *Carburetor:* float-feed. *Lubrication:* force-feed. *Cooling:* finned pipe radiator.

TRANSMISSION. Sliding gear with four forward speeds, bevel gear differential.

CHASSIS. *Frame:* armored wood. *Suspension:* front, semi-elliptic; rear, pair, semi-elliptic. *Braking:* two clamping on rear wheels, one on driveshaft. *Wheels:* wood artillery, 36x4 tires. *Track:* 56½ inches. *Wheelbase:* 92 inches.

BODY. *Construction:* aluminum over wood frame. *Paint:* varnish, choice of color. *Interior:* top grade leather. *Standard fittings:* bulb horn, oil sidelights and a pair of self-generating headlights; wicker baskets on side. *Lighting:* oil and gas. *Instrumentation:* site water and oil gauges; double throw switch. *Body types:* King of Belgian and standard rear entrance tonneau.

PRICE RANGE. $7300 with top; $7000 without top.

Packard Number One, Model A, 1899.

MODEL L

MODEL YEAR: 1904 • INTRODUCED NOVEMBER 1903 *
MOTOR SERIAL NUMBERS 501 TO 705

*The date on which production ceased is not known. The car was advertised into early 1905 and was built awhile alongside the concurrent Model N.
ENGINE. L-head four, 3 ⅞ by 5 ⅛ inches, 241.7 cubic inches; 22 hp at 900 rpm. *Crankshaft:* three bearings. *Ignition:* jump spark, battery with spark coil. *Carburetor:* float-feed. *Lubrication:* force-feed. *Cooling:* radiator capacity 6 gallons.
TRANSMISSION. Sliding gear on rear axle, with three forward speeds, bevel gear differential.
CHASSIS. *Frame:* overslung, pressed steel with cross supports. *Axles:* front, tubular; rear, live (solid). *Suspension:* front, inverted semi-elliptic transverse spring; rear, pair, semi-elliptic. *Steering:* worm and sector, wheel. *Braking:* two external clamping, two internal expanding on rear hub. *Wheels:* wood artillery, 34x4 tires. *Track:* 56 ½ inches. *Wheelbase:* 94 inches.
BODY. *Construction:* aluminum over wood. *Paint:* body Richelieu blue, black moldings with cream yellow striping; running gear cream yellow, black and blue striping. *Interior:* dark blue leather. *Standard fittings:* tools, lamps, tool kit, horn and tube, storm aprons. *Lighting:* oil lamps. *Instrumentation:* lights, sight feed oil, hand spark and throttle. *Body types:* tonneau.
PRICE RANGE. $3000.

MODEL N

MODEL YEAR: 1905 • INTRODUCED CIRCA NOVEMBER 1904 *
MOTOR SERIAL NUMBERS 1002 TO 1405

*Production of the car commenced in October, but Packard delayed its official announcement until later that year.
ENGINE. L-head four, 4-1/16 by 5-1/8 inches, 265.7 cubic inches; 28 hp at 900 rpm. *Crankshaft:* three bearings. *Ignition:* jump spark. *Carburetor:* float-feed. *Lubrication:* force-feed. *Cooling:* radiator capacity 6 gallons. *Note:* new carburetor design, single jet with auxiliary automatic inlet, warm water jacket.
TRANSMISSION. Sliding gear on rear axle, with three forward speeds, bevel gear differential.
CHASSIS. *Frame:* overslung, pressed steel with cross supports. *Axles:* front, tubular; rear, live (solid). *Suspension:* front, semi-elliptic transverse spring; rear, pair, semi-elliptic. *Steering:* worm and sector, wheel. *Braking:* two external clamping, two internal expanding on rear hub. *Wheels:* wood artillery, 34x4 tires. *Track:* 56 ½ inches. *Wheelbase:* 106 inches.
BODY. *Construction:* aluminum over wood. *Paint:* body Richelieu blue, black moldings with cream yellow striping; running gear cream yellow, blue striping. *Interior:* dark blue leather. *Standard fittings:* tools, lamps, tool kit, horn and tube, storm aprons. *Lighting:* oil lamps. *Instrumentation:* lights, sight feed oiler, hand spark and throttle. *Body types:* brougham, touring, roadster, limousine. *Note:* tonneau became side entrance, instead of rear.
PRICE RANGE. $3500-$4600.

MODEL 24 OR S

MODEL YEAR: 1906 • INTRODUCED SEPTEMBER 1905
MOTOR SERIAL NUMBERS 2003 TO 2729

ENGINE. T-head four, 4 ½ by 5 ½ inches, 349.9 cubic inches; 24 hp at 650 rpm. *Crankshaft:* three bearings. *Ignition:* jump spark with magneto, battery in reserve. *Carburetor:* float-feed, warm water, jacketed. *Lubrication:* force-feed. *Cooling:* radiator capacity 5 gallons. *Note:* Hydraulic governor added.

TRANSMISSION. Sliding gear on rear axle, with three forward speeds, bevel gear differential.
CHASSIS. *Frame:* overslung, pressed steel with cross supports. *Axles:* front, tubular; rear, solid (live). *Suspension:* front, pair, lengthwise, half-elliptic; rear, lengthwise, half-elliptic, outside frame. *Steering:* worm and sector, wheel. *Braking:* internal and external rear. *Wheels:* wood artillery, tires 34x4 front, 34x4 ½ rear. *Track:* 56 ½ inches. *Wheelbase:* 119 inches (runabout 108).
BODY. *Construction:* aluminum over wood. *Paint:* body Richelieu blue, black moldings with cream yellow striping; running gear cream yellow, blue striping. *Interior:* black leather. *Standard fittings:* two side, one rear oil lamps; tools; storm aprons; tire repair outfit; horn and tube. *Lighting:* oil lamps, acetylene available as option. *Instrumentation:* lights, sight feed oiler, hand spark and throttle. *Body types:* touring, runabout, limousine, landaulette. *Note:* body enlarged, storage area added.
PRICE RANGE. $4000-$5225.

MODEL THIRTY (U)

MODEL YEAR: 1907 • INTRODUCED AUGUST 1906
MOTOR SERIAL NUMBERS 3003-4134

ENGINE. T-head four, 5 by 5 ½ inches, 431.9 cubic inches; 30 hp at 650 rpm. *Crankshaft:* three bearings. *Ignition:* jump spark with magneto, battery for starting current. *Carburetor:* float feed, warm water, jacketed. *Lubrication:* force-feed. *Cooling:* radiator capacity 6 gallons. *Note:* top of cylinders and valve chambers flat, replacing dome appearance of year previous.
TRANSMISSION. Sliding gear on rear axle, with three forward speeds, bevel gear differential.
CHASSIS. *Frame:* overslung, pressed steel with cross supports. *Axles:* front, tubular; rear, solid (live). *Suspension:* front, lengthwise semi-elliptic; rear, lengthwise semi-elliptic. *Steering:* worm and sector, wheel. *Braking:* expanding and contracting on rear hub. *Wheels:* wood artillery, tires 34x4 front, 34x4 ½ rear (runabout 34x3 ½ front, 34x4 rear). *Track:* 56 ½ inches. *Wheelbase:* 122 inches (runabout 108).
BODY. *Construction:* aluminum over wood. *Paint:* body Richelieu blue, black moldings with cream yellow striping; running gear cream yellow, blue striping. *Interior:* black leather. *Standard fittings:* lamps, horn, tools, storm aprons. *Lighting:* oil lamps. *Instrumentation:* lights, sight feed oiler, hand spark and throttle. *Body types:* runabout, touring, limousine, landaulet.
PRICE RANGE. $4200-$5600.

Model 24 or S, 1906.

MODEL THIRTY (UA)
Model Year: 1908 • Introduced May 1907
Motor Serial Numbers 5006 to 6311

ENGINE REFINEMENTS. *Ignition:* jump spark with magneto, battery for reserve current.

CHASSIS REFINEMENTS. *Wheels:* tires 36x3½ front, 36x4 rear for runabout. *Wheelbase:* 123½ inches (runabout 108).

BODY REFINEMENTS. *Body types:* close-coupled introduced circa March 1908.

PRICE RANGE. $4200-$5650.

MODEL THIRTY (UB)
Model Year: 1909 • Introduced Summer 1908
Motor Serial Numbers 6481 to 7086
Motor Serial Numbers 7501 to 8999

ENGINE REFINEMENTS. *Cooling:* radiator capacity 5 gallons.

CHASSIS REFINEMENTS. *Wheels:* tires 36x3½ front, 36x4½ rear for runabout.

BODY REFINEMENTS. *Standard fittings:* headlamps, side and rear lamps; horn, tube, bulb; storm aprons; irons for extension cape cart top; tire repair outfit. *Lighting:* gas headlamps, two side and one rear oil lamps. *Body types:* demi-limousine added.

MODEL EIGHTEEN (NA)
Model Year: 1909 • Introduced Summer 1908
Motor Serial Numbers 9001 to 9801

ENGINE. T-head four, 4-1/16 by 5⅛ inches, 265.7 cubic inches; 18 hp at 650 rpm. *Cooling:* radiator capacity 4½ gallons. All other specifications same as Model Thirty.

TRANSMISSION. Same as Model Thirty.

CHASSIS. Same as Model Thirty with the following exceptions. *Wheels:* tires 34x4 (34x3½ front, 34x4 rear for runabout). *Wheelbase:* 112 inches (runabout 102).

BODY. Same as Model Thirty with the following exceptions. *Body types:* touring, landaulet, limousine, runabout.

PRICE RANGE. $3200-$4400.

MODEL THIRTY (UC)
Model Year: 1910 • Introduced Summer 1909
Motor Serial Numbers 10000 to 11999
Motor Serial Numbers 13001 to 13518

TRANSMISSION REFINEMENTS. Dry plate clutch replaced expanding flywheel clutch.

CHASSIS REFINEMENTS. Shock absorbers added as standard equipment.

BODY REFINEMENTS. *Standard fittings:* lamps; horn, tube, bulb; gas tank; tools; irons for carrying two extra tires. *Body types:* phaeton added.

MODEL EIGHTEEN (NB)
Model Year: 1910 • Introduced Summer 1909
Motor Serial Numbers 12001 to 12837

PRICE RANGE. $3200-$4500.

Model Thirty, 1907.

MODEL THIRTY (UD)
Model Year: 1911 • Introduced Summer 1910
Motor Serial Numbers 15001 to 15999
Motor Serial Numbers 16000 to 16884

CHASSIS REFINEMENTS. *Wheels:* wood artillery, 36x4½ tires.

BODY REFINEMENTS. *Paint:* body and door panels Packard blue striped with Packard gray; underbody, hood, radiator, frame, fenders, battery and tool boxes and moldings black; wheels, axles, springs, other running gear Packard gray striped with black. *Standard fittings:* gas headlights; two side and one rear oil lamps; horn; tools; jack; two extra demountable rims. *Body types:* coupe added.

PRICE RANGE. $4200-$5750.

MODEL EIGHTEEN (NC)
Model Year: 1911 • Introduced Summer 1910
Motor Serial Numbers 18801 to 19176

BODY REFINEMENTS. *Body types:* close-coupled and coupe added.

PRICE RANGE. $3200-$4700.

MODEL THIRTY (UE)
Model Year: 1912 • Introduced Summer 1911
Motor Serial Numbers 20001 to 23000

CHASSIS REFINEMENTS. *Wheels:* wood artillery, tires 36x4½ front, 37x5 rear. *Wheelbase:* 123½ inches (phaeton 129½; runabout 114).

BODY REFINEMENTS. *Standard fittings:* headlights; side and rear lamps; horn; tools; jack; rims for two extra tires; cape top and storm curtains on open cars; toilet cases on closed bodies. *Lighting:* gas headlights; combination oil and electric side and rear lamps. *Body types:* brougham added.

MODEL EIGHTEEN (NE)
Model Year: 1912 • Introduced Summer 1911
Motor Serial Numbers 26001 to 27000

CHASSIS REFINEMENTS. *Wheelbase:* 112 inches (runabout 108).

MODELS THIRTY AND EIGHTEEN

SIX (LATER 1-48)
MODEL YEAR: 1912 • SERIES: FIRST 48
INTRODUCED APRIL 1911 • CURRENT TO MAY 1912
MOTOR SERIAL NUMBERS 23001 TO 26000

ENGINE. T-head six, cast in three blocks of two, mechanical valves; 4½ by 5½ inches, 525 cubic inches; 74 hp at 1720 rpm. *Crankshaft*: four bearings. *Ignition*: jump spark by Bosch dual magneto, 6-volt battery reserve. *Carburetor*: Packard combined float-feed and automatic mixture regulation. *Lubrication*: complete force-feed by gear pump. *Cooling*: water cooled, centrifugal pump, belt-driven fan, capacity 6 gallons.

TRANSMISSION. Sliding gear, with three forward speeds, rear mounted; straight cut gears, aluminum housing, ball end thrust bearings; Packard multidisc clutch; rear axle ratio 3.27, optional 3.05 and 3.52.

CHASSIS. *Frame*: ladder, channel section pressed steel. *Axles*: front, steel tubing, roller bearings; rear, beam, tubes riveted to differential housing. *Suspension*: front, semi-elliptic leaf springs 40" long; rear, semi-elliptic leaf springs 56" long. *Steering*: worm and sector, right hand drive. *Braking*: two-wheel internal-expanding/external contracting. *Wheels*: wood artillery, detachable rims; tires 36x4½ front, 37x5 rear. *Track*: 56½ inches. *Wheelbase*: 133 inches (139 for phaeton and brougham; 121½ for coupe and runabout). *Overall length*: 183½ inches (189½ for phaeton and brougham; 172½ for coupe and runabout).

BODY. *Construction*: aluminum over white ash frame. *Paint*: Packard blue (striped gray) and black; axles cream yellow; optional body colors available. *Interior*: leather, broadcloth or goatskin on closed models. *Standard fittings*: sidelight bails on top of sidelights. *Lighting*: combination oil and electric side and taillamps, gas headlamps. *Instrumentation*: ammeter, fuel, oil gauges; speedometer and clock optional. *Body types*: touring (7), Imperial limousine (7), limousine (7), landaulet (7), Imperial landaulet (7), phaeton (5), close-coupled (5), phaeton-victoria (5), brougham (4), coupe (2), runabout (2). Weight range from 3500-4200 pounds.

PRICE RANGE. $5000-$6500.

2-48 (OR 1348)
MODEL YEAR: 1913 • SERIES: SECOND 48
INTRODUCED JUNE 1912 • CURRENT TO OCTOBER 1912 *
MOTOR SERIAL NUMBERS 35026 TO 37999

*Production gap from October 1912 to April 1913 during which the company produced no 48 models, this car thus technically "current" through March 1913.

ENGINE REFINEMENTS. Horsepower now 82 at 1720 rpm. *Ignition*: electric generator added, magneto moved rearward. *Carburetor*: acetylene primer added. *Lubrication*: auxiliary oiling system added, interconnected with throttle.

Model 2-48 or 1348, 1913.

Note: three-point motor support instead of four, water pump moved rearward.

CHASSIS REFINEMENTS. *Suspension*: rear, three-quarter elliptic leaf springs 53" long. *Track*: 56 inches. *Wheelbase*: touring car now on 139-inches.

BODY REFINEMENTS. *Construction*: wider and roomier bodies, thicker upholstery. *Standard fittings*: side light bails on sides. *Lighting*: electric headlamps, combination oil and electric side and taillamps. *Body types*: brougham (5) and coupe (3) added; close-coupled (5), phaeton victoria (5), brougham (4), coupe (2) dropped. Weight range from 4010 to 4560 pounds.

PRICE RANGE. $4650-$6050.

3-48 (OR 1448)
MODEL YEAR: 1914 • SERIES: THIRD 48
INTRODUCED APRIL 1913 * • CURRENT TO FEBRUARY 1914
MOTOR SERIAL NUMBERS 50026 TO 52000

*This model first shown in January, announced in March, and ultimately available in April.

ENGINE REFINEMENTS. *Ignition*: Bosch ZR6 dual-magneto, moved to left side. *Carburetor*: moved to left side. *Note*: engine turned 180⁰ from previous 48's for right hand exhaust, left hand drive, Delco electric starter-generator; flywheel diameter reduced.

TRANSMISSION REFINEMENTS. Spiral bevel gears.

CHASSIS REFINEMENTS. *Steering*: left hand drive. *Wheelbase*: 139 inches (121½ for runabout). *Overall length*: 202 inches for touring; 192 for phaeton; 180 for runabout.

BODY REFINEMENTS. *Construction*: touring, back windshield support rod behind cowl. *Paint*: forty-two color selections available. *Interior*: leather colors available, four reds, four greens, three blues, two browns, two grays, black. *Standard fittings*: side light bails on sides; brass trim optional. *Lighting*: electric headlamps, combination oil and electric side and taillamps. *Instrumentation*: new steering-column-mounted control panel. *Body types*: salon-limousine (7), brougham (4), salon-brougham (4), cabette (4) added; Imperial limousine (7), coupe (3), runabout (2), brougham (5) dropped.

PRICE RANGE. $4650-$6100.

4-48
MODEL YEAR: 1914 • SERIES: FOURTH 48
INTRODUCED FEBRUARY 1914 • CURRENT TO JUNE 1914 *
MOTOR SERIAL NUMBERS 63026 TO 66000

*Production gap from July to October 1914, with no shipments in July and August that year.

ENGINE REFINEMENTS. L-head six, cast in two blocks of three; 4½ by 5½ inches, 525 cubic inches. *Cooling*: radiator capacity 7⅜ gallons. *Note*: water jacketed intake header; ball-bearing carrying impeller and front gear thrust.

TRANSMISSION REFINEMENTS. Rear axle ratio 3.58, optional 3.28.

CHASSIS REFINEMENTS. *Braking*: seventeen-inch drums replacing former fifteen, swept area 453 square inches. *Wheels*: tires 37x5. *Wheelbase*: 144 inches all models. *Overall length*: 204¾ inches all models.

BODY REFINEMENTS. *Standard fittings*: no bails on side lights. Previous options now standard—speedometer, clock, klaxon horn, power tire pump, rear tire carrier, non-skid tires, gas tank funnel, extra lamps. *Lighting*: electric headlamps and sidelamps; combination oil and electric taillamps. *Body types*: cab sides

limousine (7), cab sides landaulet (7), standard limousine (6), cab sides limousine (6), landaulet (6), Imperial limousine (6), brougham (6), salon touring (6), phaeton (4), Imperial coupe (4), coupe (2), phaeton runabout (2) dropped. Weight range from 4310 to 5015 pounds.
PRICE RANGE. $4750-$6510.

5-48

MODEL YEAR: 1915 • SERIES: FIFTH 48
INTRODUCED OCTOBER 1914 • CURRENT TO CIRCA APRIL 1915
MOTOR SERIAL NUMBERS 78026 TO 78586

TRANSMISSION REFINEMENTS. Rear axle ratio, 3.11 optional.
CHASSIS REFINEMENTS. *Overall length*: 202¼ inches (touring 204¾).
BODY REFINEMENTS. *Lighting*: all electric, combination main and auxiliary lamps; tail/license lamp moved to top left rear, sidelamps smaller than 4-48. *Body types*: six-passenger special touring added.
PRICE RANGE. $4750-$6150.

1-38 (OR 1338)

MODEL YEAR: 1913 • SERIES: FIRST 38
INTRODUCED DECEMBER 1912 * • CURRENT TO FEBRUARY 1913
MOTOR SERIAL NUMBERS 38000 TO 42000

*Announced in August but problems with new combination starter-generator from Delco delayed deliveries until December.
ENGINE. L-head six, cast in three blocks of two; mechanical valves, all on the right; 4 by 5½ inches, 415 cubic inches; 60 hp at 1720 rpm. *Crankshaft*: seven bearings. *Ignition*: jump spark by Bosch dual-magneto; 6 volt battery for starting and reserve. *Carburetor*: Packard, float-feed, acetylene primer. *Lubrication*: force-feed by gear pump, auxiliary oiling system interconnected with throttle. *Cooling*: water cooled, centrifugal pump, belt-driven fan, radiator capacity 5½ gallons. *Note*: first use by Packard of electric starter.
TRANSMISSION. Sliding gear, rear mounted, with three forward speeds; straight-cut gears, aluminum housing, ball end thrust bearings; multi-disc clutch; rear axle ratio 3.8; optional 4.0 and 3.5.
CHASSIS. *Frame*: channel section pressed steel. *Axles*: front, I-beam with roller bearings; rear, beam, tubular, riveted to differential housing. *Suspension*: front, semi-elliptic leaf springs 40" long; rear, three-quarter elliptic leaf springs 51" long. *Steering*: first use of left hand drive. *Braking*: internal expanding, external contracting, fifteen inches. *Wheels*: tires 36x4½ front, 37x5 rear, spare sidemount. *Track*: 56 inches. *Wheelbase*: 134 inches (138 for phaeton and brougham; 115½ for runabout). *Overall length*: 175½ inches (179¼ for phaeton and brougham; 156¾ for runabout).
BODY. *Construction*: aluminum over white ash frame. *Paint*: Packard blue (striped gray) and black; axles cream yellow; optional body colors available). *Interior*: leather; Packard gray cloth on closed models. *Standard fittings*: on closed cars, silver-plated interior bright metal, sterling silver toilet articles; on divided cars, speaking tube, folding footrail, hat and parcel carrier. *Lighting*: combination oil and electric side and taillamps, electric headlamps. *Instrumentation*: dashboard control panel; oil, fuel, amps gauge; speedometer and clock optional. *Body types*: touring (5), phaeton (5), Imperial limousine (5), Imperial landaulet (5), limousine (5), landaulet (5), phaeton (4), brougham (4), Imperial coupe (4), runabout (2), coupe (2). Weight range from 3820 to 4510 pounds.
PRICE RANGE. $4050-$5400.

1-38 (OR 1438)

MODEL YEAR: 1914 • SERIES: FIRST 38
INTRODUCED FEBRUARY 1913 • CURRENT TO SEPTEMBER 1913 *

*Owing to the production practices of the Packard company, whether any of these cars were left after July is problematical. Further, because this model was simply a continuation of the 1338, the exact breakdown of motor serial numbers is not known.

2-38

MODEL YEAR: 1914 • SERIES: SECOND 38
INTRODUCED DECEMBER 1913 • CURRENT TO JUNE 1914 *
MOTOR SERIAL NUMBERS 53026 TO 56000

*Although no shipments were made in July and August 1914, this model may technically be considered "current" during those months.
ENGINE REFINEMENTS. L-head six, cast in two block of three. *Ignition*: Bosch duplex, enclosed wiring. *Lubrication*: all piping within crankcase, camshaft drilled to carry oil. *Cooling*: radiator braced from top of water outlet manifold, capacity 6 gallons. *Note*: hot water jacketed inlet manifold, mud webs cast integral with crankcase, siamesed exhaust manifold.
TRANSMISSION REFINEMENTS. Shift throws reduced; spiral bevel gears; rear axle ratio 3.9, optional 3.53.
CHASSIS REFINEMENTS. *Suspension*: front, raised front spring eyes; rear, underslung three-quarter elliptic leaf springs. *Braking*: drum diameters increased to seventeen inches, swept area 437 square inches. *Wheels*: spare tires carried at rear; 37x5 front tires optional. *Wheelbase*: 140 inches. *Overall length*: 198½ inches (201 on the touring).
BODY REFINEMENTS. *Construction*: driver's door added, tapering hood and cowl, cowl vent, window regulators in closed bodies. *Lighting*: electric headlamps/sidelamps; combination oil and electric taillamp; Bijur starting-lighting system, motor and generator separate; no bails on sidelamps. *Body types*: touring (7), Imperial limousine (7), salon-limousine (7), all-weather convertible (7), standard limousine (7), cab sides limousine (7), standard landaulet (7), cab sides landaulet (7), salon touring (6), special touring (6), standard limousine (6), cab sides limousine (6), landaulette (6), brougham (6), salon brougham (4), coupe (3) added; touring (5), Imperial limousine (5), Imperial landaulet (5), limousine (5), landaulet (5), brougham (4), Imperial coupe (4), coupe (2) dropped. Weight range from 4113 to 4818 pounds. *Note*: the seven-passenger all-weather convertible and the six-passenger special touring bodies were not built by Packard, the former being built by the Springfield (Massachusetts) Metal Body Company, the latter by Fisher.
PRICE RANGE. $3350-$5150.

3-38

MODEL YEAR: 1915 • SERIES: THIRD 38
INTRODUCED SEPTEMBER 1914 • CURRENT TO CIRCA APRIL 1915
MOTOR SERIAL NUMBERS 75026 TO 76999

ENGINE REFINEMENTS. Horsepower now 65 at 1720 rpm.
BODY REFINEMENTS. *Lighting*: now completely electric; combination main and auxiliary lamps; tail/license lamp moved to top left rear. *Body types*: six-passenger limousine with cab sides added. Weight range from 4163 to 4868 pounds.

TWIN SIX 1-25
Model Year: 1916 • Series: First
Introduced May 1915 • Current to August 1916
Motor Serial Numbers 80000 to 87787

ENGINE. L-head 60⁰ V-12, cast in two blocks of six; 3 by 5 inches, 424.1 cubic inches; 88 hp at 2600 rpm. *Crankshaft*: three main bearings. *Ignition*: battery, with automatic advance; Delco distributor; reserve auxiliary battery. *Carburetor*: Packard, pressure-fed. *Lubrication*: oil pump. *Cooling*: water cooled by double centrifugal pump, belt-driven fan; thermostat in pump housing; narrower, higher radiator; capacity 7½ gallons. *Note*: four-point engine mounts.

TRANSMISSION. Selective sliding gear, in unit, with three forward speeds; torque arm differential; spiral bevel gears; multi-disc clutch.

CHASSIS. *Frame*: channel section pressed steel, 6" deep. *Axles*: front, I-beam with roller bearings; rear, beam, tubular steel, semi-floating. *Suspension*: front, semi-elliptic longitudinal leaf springs; rear, platform, semi-elliptic leaf springs. *Steering*: worm and nut. *Braking*: two-wheel, internal expanding, external contracting, swept area 262 inches. *Wheels*: artillery, tires 36x4½ front, 37x5 rear. *Track*: 56 inches. *Wheelbase*: 125 inches.

BODY. *Construction*: aluminum over white ash frame. *Paint*: Packard blue with cream-yellow striping, wheels cream yellow with black striping. *Interior*: tufted leather. *Standard fittings*: nickel-plated exterior bright metal. *Lighting*: Bijur electric headlamps. *Instrumentation*: motometer, speedometer. *Body types*: touring (7), salon-touring (7), limousine (6), landaulet (6), phaeton (5), salon-phaeton (5), brougham (4), coupe (3), runabout (2). Weight range from 3910 to 4395 pounds.

PRICE RANGE. $2750-$4200.

TWIN SIX 1-35

Data for Twin Six 1-25 applicable to 1-35 with the following exceptions: *Wheelbase*: 135 inches. *Body types*: touring (7), salon-touring (7), Imperial limousine (7), salon-limousine (7), standard limousine (7), cab sides limousine (7), standard landaulet (7), cab sides landaulet (7), limousine (6), landaulet (6), brougham (4). Weight range from 4210 to 4715 pounds.

PRICE RANGE. $3150-$4800.

TWIN SIX 2-25
Model Year: 1917 • Series: Second
Introduced August 1916 • Current to August 1917
Motor Serial Numbers 125051 to 150000

ENGINE REFINEMENTS. Removable cylinder heads. *Cooling*: thermostat located at water outlet; revised circulation system; capacity 8½ gallons. *Note*: gas intake passages shortened.

CHASSIS REFINEMENTS. *Frame*: 7½" deep. *Wheels*: 35x5 tires. *Wheelbase*: 126½ inches.

BODY REFINEMENTS. *Construction*: two-inch lower body, fenders following wheel curve. *Interior*: softer upholstery springs, plaited leather. *Standard fittings*: forward-disappearing jump seats. *Lighting*: new Warner Lenz headlamps. *Instrumentation*: improved speedometer, Warner. *Body types*: four-passenger runabout added. Weight range 4150 to 4900 pounds.

PRICE RANGE. $2865-$4315.

TWIN SIX 2-35

Data for Twin Six 2-25 applicable to 2-35 with the following exceptions: *Body types*: four-passenger salon-brougham added; seven-passenger landaulet with cab sides and four-passenger brougham dropped. Weight range from 4440 to 4970 pounds.

PRICE RANGE. $3265-$4915.

TWIN SIX 3-25
Model Years: 1918-1919 • Series: Third
Introduced August 1917 • Current to August 1919
Motor Serial Numbers 150051 and up
Body Numbers 520000 and up

ENGINE REFINEMENTS. Horsepower now 90.

TRANSMISSION REFINEMENTS. Center shift lever.

BODY REFINEMENTS. *Instrumentation*: ammeter, oil and gas pressure gauges; speedometer and clock. *Body types*: salon-touring (7), limousine (7), landaulet (7), Imperial limousine (7), brougham (7), brougham (6), coupe (4) added; limousine (6), landaulet (6), brougham (4), coupe (3), runabout (2) dropped. Weight range from 4210 to 4860 pounds.

PRICE RANGE. $4800-$6900 (1918), $5200-$7350 (1919).

TWIN SIX 3-35

Data for Twin Six 3-25 applicable to 3-35 with the following exceptions: *Wheelbase*: 136 inches. *Body types*: seven-passenger salon-limousine dropped.

PRICE RANGE. $3255-$4915.

TWIN SIX 3-35
Model Years: 1920-1923 • Series: Third
Introduced August 1919 • Current to June 1923
Motor Serial Numbers 21000 to approximately 22300
Body Numbers 160130 to approximately 165662

ENGINE REFINEMENTS. Fuelizer added.

TRANSMISSION REFINEMENTS. Selective sliding gear, in unit, with three forward speeds; semi-floating differential; spiral bevel gears; rear axle ratio 4.36.

CHASSIS REFINEMENTS. *Wheels*: artillery, 33x5 tires on detachable rims.

BODY REFINEMENTS. *Body types*: touring (7), limousine (7), landaulet (7), salon-touring (7), Imperial limousine (7), brougham (7). Weight range from 4465 to 4845 pounds.

PRICE RANGE. $3850-$5500.

SINGLE SIX (116)
Model Years: 1921-1922 • Series: First
Introduced September 1st, 1920 • Current to April 20th, 1922
Motor Serial Numbers 26 to 8850

ENGINE. L-head, in line six, cast en bloc; 3⅜x4½ inches, 241.5 cubic inches; 52 hp at 2400 rpm. *Compression ratio*: 4.8. *Crankshaft*: seven bearings. *Ignition*: Delco distributor. *Carburetor*: Packard updraft with Fuelizer, hand choke. *Lubrication*: full pressure. *Cooling*: centrifugal pump on cylinder head, thermostat, radiator capacity 4⅜ gallons. *Note*: power tire pump.

TRANSMISSION. Selective, in unit, with three forward speeds, seven-plate eight-inch clutch, torque arm drive to center frame member, rear axle ratio 4.31; bevel gears.
CHASSIS. *Frame:* pressed steel, 7" deep, torsion tubes front and rear. *Axles:* front, I-beam, below spring, Elliot; rear, pressed steel, semi-floating. *Suspension:* semi-elliptic front and rear. *Steering:* opposed threaded worm and nut. *Braking:* rear only, drums 14⅜ by 2¾ inches, external contracting, swept area 236 square inches. *Wheels:* twenty-four-inch wood, 33x4½ tires. *Track:* 56 inches. *Wheelbase:* 116 inches.
BODY. *Construction:* steel on wood frame. *Paint:* varnished body, black baked enamel for superstructure, running gear, fenders, etc., Packard (dark) blue body. *Interior:* open cars, leather; closed cars, broadcloth (sedan front, leather). *Standard fittings:* shades in rear windows. *Lighting:* headlights with auxiliary lights, dashboard light, tail and license lamps, dome lights in closed models. *Instrumentation:* speedometer, gasoline gauge, ammeter, oil pressure gauge. *Body types:* sedan (5), coupe (4), touring (5), runabout (2).
PRICE RANGE. $3640 for touring (reduced to $2350); $4950 for sedan (reduced to $3350).

Model 126 Single Six, 1922-1923.

SINGLE SIX (126, 133)
MODEL YEARS: 1922-1923 • SERIES: FIRST
INTRODUCED APRIL 20TH, 1922 • CURRENT TO DECEMBER 27TH, 1923
MOTOR SERIAL NUMBERS 9000 TO 35942

ENGINE. L-head, in-line six, cast en bloc; 3⅜ by 5 inches, 268.4 cubic inches; 54 hp at 2700 rpm. *Compression ratio:* 4.8. *Crankshaft:* seven bearings. *Ignition:* Delco distributor. *Carburetor:* Packard updraft with Fuelizer, hand choke. *Lubrication:* full pressure. *Cooling:* centrifugal pump on front of block, thermostat, radiator capacity 4⅞ gallons. *Note:* power tire pump dropped.
TRANSMISSION. Selective, in unit, with three forward speeds, nine-plate eight-inch clutch, torque arm drive to center frame member, rear axle ratios 4.3 (for 126), 4.66 (for 133), either optional; spiral bevel gears.
CHASSIS. *Frame:* pressed steel, 7½" deep for 126, 8" for 133, torsion tubes front and rear. *Axles:* front, I-beam, below spring, Elliot; rear, pressed steel, semi-floating. *Suspension:* semi-elliptic leaf springs front and rear. *Steering:* opposed treaded worm and nut. *Braking:* rear only, external contracting, swept area 285 square inches. *Wheels:* twenty-four-inch wood, 33x4½ tires, disc wheels optional (standard on sport model). *Track:* 56 inches. *Wheelbase:* 126 and 133 inches.
BODY. *Construction:* steel on wood frame. *Paint:* varnished body, black baked enamel on fenders, etc., closed cars Packard blue, open cars Packard town car blue. *Interior:* open cars, leather; closed cars, broadcloth. *Standard fittings:*

shades in rear windows of closed cars, foot rest in rear. *Lighting:* headlights with auxiliary lights, dashboard light, taillight, dome light in closed models. *Instrumentation:* speedometer, gasoline gauge on tank, ammeter, oil pressure gauge, clock. *Body types:* touring (5), runabout (2), sport model (4), coupe (4), sedan (5) on the 126-inch wheelbase; touring, sedan and sedan-limousine, all seven-passenger cars, on the 133-inch wheelbase.
PRICE RANGE. $2485-$3350 for 126; $2685-$3575 for 133.

SINGLE EIGHT (136, 143)
MODEL YEAR: 1924 • SERIES: FIRST
INTRODUCED JUNE 14TH, 1923 • CURRENT TO FEBRUARY 1925
MOTOR SERIAL NUMBERS 200001 TO 208428

ENGINE. L-head, in-line eight, cast en bloc; 3⅜ by 5 inches, 357.8 cubic inches; 85 hp at 3000 rpm. *Compression ratio:* 4.51. *Crankshaft:* nine bearings. *Ignition:* Delco distributor. *Carburetor:* Packard updraft with Fuelizer, hand choke. *Lubrication:* full pressure. *Cooling:* centrifugal pump on front of block, thermostat, Winterfront on early production, radiator capacity 5½ gallons. *Note:* power tire pump.
TRANSMISSION. Selective, in unit, with three forward speeds, nine-plate eight-inch clutch, torque arm drive to center frame member, rear axle ratio 4.7, 4.08 (roadster and sport models); spiral bevel gears.
CHASSIS. *Frame:* pressed steel, 8" deep, torsion tubes front and rear. *Axles:* front, I-beam, below spring, Elliot; rear, pressed steel, semi-floating, spiral bevel gears. *Suspension:* semi-elliptic leaf springs front and rear. *Steering:* worm with babbitt nut. *Braking:* four wheel, finned fourteen-inch drums, internal expanding (later external contracting), swept area 324 square inches. *Wheels:* twenty-five-inch disc, 35x5 tires. *Track:* 56 inches. *Wheelbase:* 136 and 143 inches.
BODY. *Construction:* steel on wood frame. *Paint:* varnished body, black baked enamel on fenders, etc., closed cars Packard blue. *Interior:* open cars, leather; closed cars, broadcloth. *Standard fittings:* shades in rear windows of closed cars, foot rest in rear, cigar lighter. *Lighting:* headlights with auxiliary lights, dashboard lights, taillight, dome light in closed cars, tonneau light in open cars. *Instrumentation:* speedometer, gasoline gauge, ammeter, oil pressure gauge, clock. *Body types:* touring (5), runabout (2-4), sport model (4), coupe (4), coupe (5), sedan (5), sedan-limousine (5) on the 136-inch wheelbase; touring, sedan and sedan-limousine, all seven-passenger cars, on the 143-inch wheelbase. *Note:* bumpers front and rear.
PRICE RANGE. $3650-$4725 for 136; $3850-$4950 for 143.

SIX (226, 233)
MODEL YEAR: 1924 • SERIES: SECOND
INTRODUCED DECEMBER 27TH, 1923 • CURRENT TO FEBRUARY 2ND, 1925
MOTOR SERIAL NUMBERS 37000 TO 48917

ENGINE REFINEMENTS. Fuelizer dropped.
CHASSIS REFINEMENTS. *Axles:* front, reverse Elliot. *Braking:* four wheel, front internal expanding, rear external contracting, swept area 304 square inches. *Wheels:* wood, 33x5 tires, disc optional.
BODY REFINEMENTS. *Standard fittings:* cigar lighter. *Instrumentation:* gas gauge added to panel. *Body types:* on 126-inch wheelbase, runabout (2-4), coupe (5), sedan-limousine (5), touring sedan (5) added; runabout (2) dropped.
PRICE RANGE. $2750-$3450 for 226; $2785-$3675 for 233.

Model 443 Custom Eight, 1928.

SIX (326, 333)
MODEL YEAR: 1925-1926 • SERIES: THIRD
INTRODUCED FEBRUARY 2ND, 1925 • CURRENT TO AUGUST 1ST, 1926
MOTOR SERIAL NUMBERS 49501 TO 90463

ENGINE REFINEMENTS. Bore increased to 3½ inches, 288.6 cubic inches; 60 hp at 3200 rpm. *Lubrication:* Skinner Oil Rectifier added. *Cooling:* radiator capacity 4¼ gallons.
TRANSMISSION REFINEMENTS. Torque arm eliminated April 1926, revision to Hotchkiss drive.
CHASSIS REFINEMENTS. *Frame:* pressed steel, 8" deep, bumper perches added, with front and rear bumpers now standard. *Braking:* four wheel, internal expanding. *Steering:* worm and sector. *Wheels:* disc, 33x5.70 low pressure tires. *Note:* Bijur chassis lubrication system added, manual operation, 45 points, reduced to 30 points later in 1925.
BODY REFINEMENTS. *Paint:* pyroxylin lacquer introduced mid-model year. *Body types:* on the 126-inch wheelbase, phaeton (5) and separate-trunk coupe (4) added, though latter was dropped by year's end; club sedan (5) added on 133-inch wheelbase. Total of eight body styles offered in new "series" custom catalogue on 133-inch wheelbase.
PRICE RANGE. $2585-$2785 for 326; $2725-$2885 for production 333.

EIGHT (236, 243)
MODEL YEARS: 1925-1926 • SERIES: SECOND
INTRODUCED FEBRUARY 2ND, 1925 • CURRENT TO AUGUST 1ST, 1926
MOTOR SERIAL NUMBERS 208997 TO 219002

ENGINE REFINEMENTS. *Lubrication:* Skinner Oil Rectifier added. *Cooling:* radiator capacity 6 gallons.
TRANSMISSION REFINEMENTS. Multi-disc clutch, torque arm eliminated April 1926, rear axle ratio 4.66, 4.08 (roadster and sport models).
CHASSIS REFINEMENTS. *Axles:* front, reverse Elliot, axle above spring. *Braking:* four wheel, fourteen-inch drums, internal expanding, swept area 353 square inches. *Steering:* worm and sector. *Wheels:* disc, 33x6.75 tires, wire optional. *Note:* Bijur chassis lubrication system added, manual operation, 45 points, reduced to 30 points later in 1925.
BODY REFINEMENTS. *Lighting:* stoplight added. *Body types:* on the 136-inch wheelbase, Holbrook coupe and separate-trunk coupe (4) added, though latter was dropped by year's end; club sedan (5) added on 143-inch wheelbase. Total of eight body styles offered in new "series" custom catalogue on 143-inch wheelbase.
PRICE RANGE. $3750-$4850 for 236; $3950-$5100 for production 243.

SIX (426, 433)
MODEL YEAR: 1927 • SERIES: FOURTH
INTRODUCED AUGUST 2ND, 1926 • CURRENT TO JULY 1ST, 1927
MOTOR SERIAL NUMBERS 950007 TO 120407

ENGINE REFINEMENTS. Horsepower now 81 at 3200 rpm. *Carburetor:* Fuelizer dropped. *Lubrication:* Skinner Oil Rectifier dropped mid-model year. *Note:* aluminum pistons, turbo cylinder head, new manifold design and carburetor.
TRANSMISSION REFINEMENTS. Four-plate clutch, hypoid differential, rear axle ratios 4.66 standard, 5.1 and 4.33 optional.
CHASSIS REFINEMENTS. *Wheels:* disc standard, wire optional.
BODY REFINEMENTS. *Paint:* fifteen selections, closed cars; three selections, open cars. *Lighting:* stoplight added. *Body types:* on the 126-inch wheelbase, phaeton (5), runabout (2-4) and sedan (5) available, all other body styles (coupes, sedan-limousine, sport model and touring) dropped; on the 133-inch wheelbase, four-passenger coupe added.
PRICE RANGE. $2585-$2685 for 426 (reduced March 1st, 1927 to $2250-$2350); $2685-$2885 for 433 (reduced March 1st, 1927 to $2350-$2550).

EIGHT (336, 343)
MODEL YEAR: 1927 • SERIES: THIRD
INTRODUCED AUGUST 2ND, 1926 • CURRENT TO JULY 1ST, 1927
MOTOR SERIAL NUMBERS 220007 TO 224511

ENGINE REFINEMENTS. Bore increased to 3½ inches, 384.8 cubic inches. *Carburetor:* Fuelizer dropped. *Lubrication:* modified Skinner Oil Rectifier dropped mid-model year.
TRANSMISSION REFINEMENTS. Two-plate clutch, hypoid differential, rear axle ratios 4.33 standard, 4.66 and 4.1 optional.
CHASSIS REFINEMENTS. *Braking:* four wheel, sixteen-inch drums, internal expanding, swept area 364 square inches.
BODY REFINEMENTS. *Body types:* on the 136-inch wheelbase, phaeton (5), runabout (2-4) and sedan (5) available, all other body styles (coupes, sedan-limousine, sport model and touring) dropped and Holbrook coupe transferred to custom section; on the 143-inch wheelbase, four-passenger coupe added.
PRICE RANGE. $3750-$4750 for 336; $4750-$5100 for 343.

SIX (526, 533)
MODEL YEAR: 1928 • SERIES: FIFTH
INTRODUCED JULY 1ST, 1927 • CURRENT TO AUGUST 1ST, 1928
MOTOR SERIAL NUMBERS 125013 TO 166770

ENGINE REFINEMENTS. *Lubrication:* new cylinder bore lubrication system, with manifold pressure lubricating cylinder walls when choked; oil filter added. *Cooling:* radiator capacity 5 gallons. *Note:* revision from three- to four-point engine suspension.
TRANSMISSION REFINEMENTS. Two-plate clutch, rear axle ratios 4.33 (for 526), 4.66 (for 533), optional on either.
CHASSIS REFINEMENTS. *Wheels:* disc, with wire or wood optional, 32x6 tires on 526; 32x6.75 on 533.
BODY REFINEMENTS. *Body types:* on the 126-inch wheelbase, coupe (2-4) and convertible coupe (2-4) added; on the 133-inch wheelbase, phaeton (5) and runabout (2-4) added.
PRICE RANGE. $2275-$2425 for 526; $2385-$2785 for 533.

CUSTOM EIGHT (443)
STANDARD MODEL 443*
MODEL YEAR: 1928 • SERIES: FOURTH
INTRODUCED JULY 1ST, 1927 • CURRENT TO AUGUST 1ST, 1928
MOTOR SERIAL NUMBERS 225013 TO 232815

*This car, introduced March 1st, 1928, was a simplified version of the Custom Eight, not to be confused with the Standard Eight which would succeed the Six the following model year.

ENGINE REFINEMENTS. *Lubrication:* new cylinder bore lubrication system, with manifold pressure lubricating cylinder walls when choked; oil filter added. *Cooling:* radiator capacity 6¼ gallons. *Note:* rubber engine mounts.

TRANSMISSION REFINEMENTS. Rear axle ratios 4.33 for closed cars, 4.07 for open cars.

CHASSIS REFINEMENTS. *Suspension:* loose rear trunnion on left front spring introduced mid-model year. *Wheels:* disc, 32x6.75 tires, wire or wood optional. *Wheelbase:* 136-inch chassis dropped.

BODY REFINEMENTS. *Paint:* full options on Custom, limited selections on "Standard." *Standard fittings:* side-mounted spares on Custom Eight, rear spare only and simpler fittings on "Standard." *Body types:* phaeton (5), runabout (2-4), coupe (2-4) and convertible coupe (2-4) added to 143-inch wheelbase Custom; phaeton (5), runabout (2-4), coupe (2-4), coupe (4), convertible coupe (2-4), club sedan (5), sedan (7), sedan-limousine (7), touring (7) available in "Standard" Model 443, the same lineup as provided in the Custom Eight 443. Total of twenty designs (Rollston, Holbrook, Dietrich, LeBaron, Judkins, Derham, Murphy, Fleetwood) in custom coachwork catalogue.

PRICE RANGE. $3975-$5150 for production Custom 443; $3550-$3850 for "Standard" 443.

STANDARD EIGHT (626-633)
MODEL YEAR: 1929 • SERIES: SIXTH
INTRODUCED AUGUST 1ST, 1928 • CURRENT TO AUGUST 20TH, 1929
MOTOR SERIAL NUMBERS 233017 TO 276166

ENGINE. L-head, in-line eight, cast en bloc; 3-3/16 by 5 inches, 319.2 cubic inches; 90 hp at 3200 rpm. *Crankshaft:* counterbalanced, vibration damper, nine main bearings. *Ignition:* Northeast. *Carburetor:* updraft. *Lubrication:* full pressure plus pressure manifold to cylinder walls when choked. *Note:* design same as 640 but shorter.

TRANSMISSION. Selective, in unit, with three forward speeds, hypoid differential, single-plate clutch, rear axle ratios 4.38, 4.69 and 5.08.

CHASSIS REFINEMENTS. *Wheels:* disc, 32x6.00 tires on 626, 32x7.00 on 633. *Wheelbase:* 126½ and 133½ inches.

BODY REFINEMENTS. *Body types:* for the 626, sedan (5), coupe (2-4), convertible coupe (2-4) available; for the 633, phaeton (5), runabout (2-4), touring (7), sedan (7), sedan-limousine (7), club sedan (5), coupe (4) available.

PRICE RANGE. $2435-$2585 for 626; $2535-$2835 for 633 (at introduction).

CUSTOM EIGHT (640)
DELUXE EIGHT (645)
MODEL YEAR: 1929 • SERIES: SIXTH
INTRODUCED AUGUST 1ST, 1928 * • CURRENT TO AUGUST 20TH, 1929
MOTOR SERIAL NUMBERS 167001 TO 178879

*Applies to Custom Eight, DeLuxe Eight introduced September 1st.

ENGINE REFINEMENTS. 384.8 cubic inches; 106 hp at 3200 rpm. *Note:* rubber engine mounts dropped.

TRANSMISSION REFINEMENTS. Two-plate clutch, rear axle ratios 4.07 for open cars, 4.38 for closed cars.

CHASSIS REFINEMENTS. *Wheels:* disc, 32x7 tires, wire or wood optional. *Wheelbase:* 140½ and 145½ inches.

BODY REFINEMENTS. *Body types:* for the Custom Eight, runabout (2-4), phaeton (5), coupe (2-4), touring (7), convertible coupe (2-4), coupe (4), club sedan (5), sedan (7), sedan-limousine (7) available; for the DeLuxe Eight, runabout (2-4), phaeton (5), coupe (2-4), sport phaeton (5), touring (7), coupe (5), club sedan (5), sedan (7), sedan-limousine (7) available. Plus, in the Individual Custom line, thirteen designs (Dietrich, LeBaron, Rollston) on the 645 chassis, three designs (Dietrich) on the 640.

PRICE RANGE. $3175-$3850 for production 640; $4585-$5985 for production 645 (at introduction).

626 SPEEDSTER
MODEL YEAR: 1929 • SERIES: SIXTH
MOTOR SERIAL NUMBERS 166942 TO 167012

ENGINE. L-head, in-line eight, cast en bloc; 3½ by 5 inches, 384.4 cubic inches; 130 hp at 3200 rpm. *Crankshaft:* counterbalanced, vibration damper, nine main bearings. *Cooling:* radiator capacity 6¼ gallons. *Note:* differed from 640 motor in being equipped with high lift camshaft, high compression head, metric plugs and vacuum pump operating at high speeds; muffler cutout added.

TRANSMISSION REFINEMENTS. Two-plate clutch, hypoid differential, rear axle ratio 3.31.

CHASSIS REFINEMENTS. Same as Standard 626 save for the following. *Axles:* rear, differential case, driving gear and pinion. *Wheels:* disc, 32x6.00 tires, wire or wood optional. *Wheelbase:* 126½ inches.

BODY. *Construction:* wood and steel. *Paint:* lacquer, colors as ordered. *Interior:* leather. *Standard fittings:* same as 640. *Lighting:* same as 640. *Instrumentation:* vacuum gauge on most cars. *Body types:* runabout (2-4), phaeton (5), sedan (special). *Note:* based on shortened 640 bodies.

PRICE RANGE. $5000 and up.

STANDARD EIGHT (726, 733)
MODEL YEAR: 1930 • SERIES: SEVENTH
INTRODUCED AUGUST 20TH, 1929 • CURRENT TO AUGUST 14TH, 1930
MOTOR SERIAL NUMBERS 277013 TO 305283

ENGINE REFINEMENTS. Horsepower now 90 at 3200 rpm. *Carburetor:* updraft, Detroit Lubricator. *Cooling:* dual fan belts added.

TRANSMISSION REFINEMENTS. Four forward speeds, rear axle ratios 4.38, 4.69 and 5.08.

CHASSIS REFINEMENTS. *Wheels:* disc, 6.00x20 tires for 726, 6.50x20 for 733, wire or wood optional. *Wheelbase:* 127½ inches for 726, 134½ inches for 733.

BODY REFINEMENTS. *Body types:* sedan (5) only for 726; for the 733, coupe (2-4), coupe (5), convertible coupe (2-4), phaeton (4), sport phaeton (4), roadster (2-4), touring (5-7), sedan (5-7), club sedan (5), sedan-limousine (5-7) available.

PRICE RANGE. $2375 for 726; $2425-$2775 for 733.

CUSTOM EIGHT (740)
DELUXE EIGHT (745)
MODEL YEAR: 1930 • SERIES: SEVENTH
INTRODUCED AUGUST 20TH, 1929 • CURRENT TO AUGUST 14TH, 1930
MOTOR SERIAL NUMBERS 179001 TO 184000
MOTOR SERIAL NUMBERS 184501 TO 187508

ENGINE REFINEMENTS. *Carburetor:* updraft, Detroit Lubricator. *Cooling:* dual fan belts added. *Note:* vacuum booster pump added mid-model year.
TRANSMISSION REFINEMENTS. Four forward speeds, rear axle ratios 4.07, 4.38 and 4.69.
CHASSIS REFINEMENTS. *Wheels:* 7.00x19 tires. *Wheelbase:* 140½ and 145½ inches.
BODY REFINEMENTS. *Body types:* coupe (2-4), coupe (5), convertible coupe (2-4), phaeton (4), sport phaeton (4), roadster (2-4), touring (5-7), sedan (5), club sedan (5), sedan (5-7), sedan-limousine (5-7) available for both 740 and 745. Plus, in the Individual Custom line, fifteen designs (LeBaron, Brewster, Rollston, Dietrich). *Note:* The same bodies were now used on the Standard 733, Custom 740 and DeLuxe 745 models, the dimensional difference in wheelbase being taken up in hood length. Body space—93⅞ inches—was the same for all three cars. For custom bodies where more body space was desired, the 745C chassis was used, the long 145½-inch wheelbase but with the engine mounted close to the radiator as on the 740. The complete roster of six styles by LeBaron used the 745C chassis, as did Rollston for the two styles it offered; of the two Dietrich styles, one used the 745C, the other the 745; the five Brewster cars used the 745.
PRICE RANGE. $3190-$3885 for production 740; $4585-$5185 for production 745 (at introduction).

734 SPEEDSTER
MODEL YEAR: 1930 • SERIES: SEVENTH
INTRODUCED JANUARY 1930 • CURRENT TO AUGUST 1930
MOTOR SERIAL NUMBERS 184003 TO 184120

ENGINE. L-head, in-line eight, cast en bloc; 3½ by 5 inches, 384.8 cubic inches; 145 hp at 3400 rpm with high compression head. *Compression ratio:* 4.85 standard, 6.00 with high compression head. *Crankshaft:* counterbalanced, vibration damper, nine main bearings. *Carburetor:* dual updraft, Detroit Lubricator. *Note:* Differences from 740 motor included valve and manifold revisions, ribbed exhaust manifold, vacuum booster pump.
TRANSMISSION REFINEMENTS. Four forward speeds, rear axle ratios 3-1/3 and 4-2/3.
CHASSIS. Used Standard Eight chassis length of 134½ inches, extensively modified, with its own frame sides and intermediate cross channels, with front cross tube assembly from 633/733, rear cross tube and channel from 726/733, front axle and linkage of Sixth Series parentage, etc. *Braking:* finned brake drums. *Wheels:* 6.50x19 tires, wire or disc optional.
BODY. *Construction:* steel on wood. *Paint:* optional. *Interior:* optional. *Standard fittings:* same as 740. *Lighting:* same as 740. *Instrumentation:* tachometer available. *Body types:* runabout (2), boattail (4), phaeton (4), victoria (4), sedan (4) in catalogued line; roadster (4) added later. *Note:* Dealers and distributors had been advised of the first four body types in Trade Letter T-2448 on October 25th, 1929; they were advised of the roadster (called "another runabout") in Trade Letter T-2462 dated January 21st, 1930.
PRICE RANGE. $5200-$6000.

STANDARD EIGHT (826, 833)
INDIVIDUAL CUSTOM EIGHT (833)
MODEL YEAR: 1931 • SERIES: EIGHTH
INTRODUCED AUGUST 14TH, 1930 • CURRENT TO JUNE 17TH, 1931
MOTOR SERIAL NUMBERS 320001 TO 332111

ENGINE REFINEMENTS. *Carburetor:* fuel pump superseded vacuum tank. *Note:* valve and manifold arrangement of 734 adopted.
TRANSMISSION REFINEMENTS. Rear axle ratios 4.38, 4.69, 5.08 and 4.07. *Note:* Bijur system automatic, vacuum operated.
CHASSIS REFINEMENTS. *Wheels:* disc, 6.50x19 tires, wire or wood optional.
BODY REFINEMENTS. *Body types:* convertible sedan added on 134½-inch wheelbase 833; convertible victoria and convertible sedan by Dietrich and nine designs "Custom Made by Packard" (all-weather cabriolet, all-weather landaulet, all-weather town car, all-weather town car landaulet, cabriolet sedan-limousine, all-weather sport cabriolet, all-weather sport landaulet) available for Individual Custom Eight.
PRICE RANGE. $2385-$3445 for Standard Eight; $4275-$5175 for Individual Custom Eight.

DELUXE EIGHT (840)
DELUXE EIGHT (845)
INDIVIDUAL CUSTOM EIGHT (840)
MODEL YEAR: 1931 • SERIES: EIGHTH
INTRODUCED AUGUST 14TH, 1930 • CURRENT TO JUNE 17TH, 1931
MOTOR SERIAL NUMBERS 188001 TO 191345

ENGINE REFINEMENTS. *Carburetor:* fuel pump superseded vacuum tank. *Note:* valve and manifold arrangement of 734 modified.
TRANSMISSION REFINEMENTS. Rear axle ratios 4.38, 4.69, 5.08 and 4.07. *Note:* Bijur system automatic, vacuum operated.
BODY REFINEMENTS. *Body types:* sedan (5), coupe (2-4), coupe (5), convertible coupe (2-4), phaeton (4), sport phaeton (4), roadster (2-4), touring (5-7), club sedan (5) available for 840; sedan (5-7) and sedan-limousine (5-7) dropped on the 140½-inch wheelbase 840, these body styles being the only offerings on the 145½-inch wheelbase 845. The Individual Custom Eight 840 comprised the same designs as the Individual Custom Eight 833.
PRICE RANGE. $3490-$4285 for DeLuxe Eight; $5275-$6075 for the Individual Custom Eight.

STANDARD EIGHT (901, 902)
MODEL YEAR: 1932 • SERIES: NINTH
INTRODUCED JUNE 23RD, 1931 • CURRENT TO JANUARY 1ST, 1933
MOTOR SERIAL NUMBERS 340051 TO 347720

ENGINE REFINEMENTS. Horsepower now 110 at 3200 rpm. *Note:* compression raised to 100 pounds; air cleaner added.
TRANSMISSION REFINEMENTS. Four forward speeds at introduction, three with synchromesh introduced January 1933, vacuum operation of clutch added, rear axle ratios 4.41, 4.69 and 5.07 optional with four-speed transmission.
CHASSIS REFINEMENTS. *Frame:* double drop, X brace. *Suspension:* Ride Control. *Wheelbase:* 129½ inches for 901; 136½ inches for 902.
BODY REFINEMENTS. *Body types:* the roadster (2-4) became the coupe-roadster (2-4) and a convertible victoria (5) added for 902.
PRICE RANGE. $2485-$3445.

DELUXE EIGHT (903, 904)
INDIVIDUAL CUSTOM EIGHT (904)
MODEL YEAR: 1932 • SERIES: NINTH
INTRODUCED JUNE 23RD, 1931 • CURRENT TO JANUARY 1ST, 1933
MOTOR SERIAL NUMBERS 193051 TO 194708

ENGINE REFINEMENTS. Horsepower now 135 at 3200 rpm. *Note:* compression raised to 100 pounds; air cleaner added.

TRANSMISSION REFINEMENTS. Four forward speeds at introduction, three with synchromesh introduced January 1933, vacuum operation of clutch added, rear axle ratios 4.06, 4.41, 4.69 and 5.07 optional with four-speed transmission.

CHASSIS REFINEMENTS. *Frame:* double drop, X brace. *Suspension:* Ride Control. *Wheelbase:* 142⅛ inches for 903, 147⅛ inches for 904.

BODY REFINEMENTS. *Body types:* coupe (2-4), coupe (5), coupe-roadster (2-4), phaeton (2-4), phaeton (4), sport phaeton (4), sedan (5), club sedan (5), touring (5-7), convertible sedan (5), convertible victoria (5) available for 903, the last two mentioned having moved from the Individual Custom line of the year previous; sedan (5-7) and sedan-limousine (5-7) available for 904. The Individual Custom Eight 904 comprised five designs by Dietrich (stationary coupe, convertible coupe, sport phaeton, convertible sedan and convertible victoria) and ten designs "Custom Made by Packard" (all-weather cabriolet; all-weather landaulet; all-weather town car; all-weather town car, landaulet; sedan-limousine, cabriolet; sport sedan; all-weather brougham; limousine sedan; all-weather cabriolet, sport; all-weather landaulet, sport).

PRICE RANGE. $3725-$4550 for DeLuxe Eight at introduction (reduced to $3350-$4095 on June 1st, 1932); $5900-$7250 for Individual Custom Eight (no price reductions made for these cars).

LIGHT EIGHT (900)
MODEL YEAR: 1932 • SERIES: NINTH
INTRODUCED JANUARY 9TH, 1932 • CURRENT TO JANUARY 5TH, 1933
MOTOR SERIAL NUMBERS 360009 TO 366794

ENGINE REFINEMENTS. Horsepower 110 at 3200 rpm. *Cooling:* no radiator louvers, radiator capacity 4¾ gallons. *Note:* motor same as Standard Eight except head had provision for water thermostat.

TRANSMISSION. Synchromesh with three forward speeds, Angleset hypoid differential, single-plate clutch, vacuum operation as desired, rear axle ratios 4.36, 4.69 and 4.07.

CHASSIS. *Frame:* new X and K braces; 5/32-inch steel side channel rails, eight inches deep. *Suspension:* semi-elliptic, rubber-mounted spring shackles; no Bijur system. *Steering:* worm and sector, ratio 17 to 1. *Braking:* mechanical, internal expanding, fifteen-inch drums. *Wheels:* wire, 6.50x17 tires, disc optional. *Wheelbase:* 127¾ inches.

BODY. *Construction:* steel on wood. *Paint:* lacquer, standard colors and options available for $45 for body, $45 for fenders and chassis parts. *Interior:* broadcloth in closed cars, leather in convertible. *Lighting:* twin taillamps, optional fender parking lights. *Instrumentation:* speedometer, oil pressure and gasoline gauge, ammeter, temperature gauge; clock optional. *Body types:* sedan (5), coupe-sedan (5), coupe (2-4), coupe-roadster (2-4). *Note:* weight of Light Eight was 4000 pounds, six hundred less than the Standard Eight.

PRICE RANGE. $1750-$1795 at introduction; raised to $1895-$1940 effective June 1st.

EIGHT (1001, 1002)
MODEL YEAR: 1933 • SERIES: TENTH
INTRODUCED JANUARY 6TH, 1933 • CURRENT TO AUGUST 20TH, 1933
MOTOR SERIAL NUMBERS 370001 TO 373010

ENGINE REFINEMENTS. Horsepower now 120 at 3200 rpm. *Compression ratio:* 6.0 standard, 6.38 and 5.0 optional. *Ignition:* dual ignition coils added. *Carburetor:* dual downdraft, new sweep manifolds, automatic choke added. *Cooling:* smaller fan, deeper radiator core. *Note:* three-point motor suspension.

TRANSMISSION REFINEMENTS. Vacuum-operated clutch dropped, single-plate clutch, automatic clutch control available optionally, rear axle ratios, 4.36 standard, 4.69 and 4.07 optional; Angleset hypoid differential.

CHASSIS REFINEMENTS. *Frame:* new X brace. *Braking:* Bendix-BK vacuum booster, same as used on Twin Six in 1932. *Wheels:* wire, 17x7.00 tires, disc or wood optional. *Wheelbase:* 127½ inches for 1001, 136 inches for 1002.

BODY REFINEMENTS. *Standard fittings:* fender battery and tool boxes omitted. *Body types:* the four body styles of the former Light Eight 900 comprised the 1001 offerings; formal sedan added February 9th to 1002 line. *Note:* pivoted pane window ventilation control offered this model year only.

PRICE RANGE. $2150-$3085.

SUPER EIGHT (1003, 1004)*
MODEL YEAR: 1933 • SERIES: TENTH
INTRODUCED JANUARY 6TH, 1933 • CURRENT TO AUGUST 20TH, 1933
MOTOR SERIAL NUMBERS 750000 TO 751327

*Super Eight was the new designation for the former DeLuxe Eight.

ENGINE REFINEMENTS. Horsepower now 145. Other refinements same as Eight.

TRANSMISSION REFINEMENTS. Same as Eight.

CHASSIS REFINEMENTS. Same as Eight. *Wheelbase:* 135 inches for 1003, 142 inches for 1004, 147-inch wheelbase dropped.

BODY REFINEMENTS. *Standard fittings:* fender battery and tool boxes omitted. *Body types:* five-passenger sedan only available style for 1003; 1004 line expanded to comprise same body styles as available on the Eight 1002 including the formal sedan introduced February 9th. *Note:* with dropping of 147-inch wheelbase, customs now available only on the Twelve. Pivoted pane window ventilation control offered this model year only.

PRICE RANGE. $2750-$3600.

EIGHT (1100, 1101, 1102)
MODEL YEAR: 1934 • SERIES: ELEVENTH
INTRODUCED AUGUST 21ST, 1933 • CURRENT TO AUGUST 29TH, 1934
MOTOR SERIAL NUMBERS 374001 TO 379149

ENGINE REFINEMENTS. *Lubrication:* oil temperature regulator added.

CHASSIS REFINEMENTS. *Wheelbase:* 129¼ inches for 1100; 136¼ inches for 1101; 141¼ inches for 1102.

BODY REFINEMENTS. *Body types:* five-passenger sedan only available style for 1100, the former Light Eight bodies being dropped; the body styles formerly offered in 1002 now comprised 1101-1102, with the sedan (5-7) and sedan-limousine (5-7) the only two styles available on the long-wheelbase 1102. *Note:* cars completely engineered for radio.

PRICE RANGE. $2350 for 1100; $2550-$3285 for 1101; $2655-$2790 for 1102.

SUPER EIGHT (1103, 1104, 1105)
MODEL YEAR: 1934 • SERIES: ELEVENTH
INTRODUCED AUGUST 21ST, 1933 • CURRENT TO AUGUST 29TH, 1934
MOTOR SERIAL NUMBERS 752001 TO 753946

ENGINE REFINEMENTS. *Lubrication:* oil temperature regulator added.
CHASSIS REFINEMENTS. *Wheelbase:* 147-inch reinstated for 1105. Exact dimensions for line 134⅞, 141⅞ and 146⅞ inches.
BODY REFINEMENTS. *Body types:* sedan (5-7) and sedan-limousine (5-7) transferred from 142-inch wheelbase 1004 of 1933 to long-wheelbase 1105; custom styles returned to Super Eight 1105, all bodies available as on Twelve save sport runabout by LeBaron and sport coupe by Packard. *Note:* cars completely engineered for radio.
PRICE RANGE. $2950 for 1103; $2980-$3800 for 1104; $3290-$3480 for 1105; $5345-$7065 for customs.

EIGHT (1200, 1201, 1202)
MODEL YEAR: 1935 • SERIES: TWELFTH
INTRODUCED AUGUST 30TH, 1934 • CURRENT TO AUGUST 9TH, 1935
MOTOR SERIAL NUMBERS 385001 TO 390301

ENGINE REFINEMENTS. Horsepower now 130 at 3200 rpm. *Compression ratio:* 6.5 standard, 6.0 optional. *Ignition:* return to single coil. *Note:* aluminum cylinder head standard, copper-lead, steel-backed bearings.
TRANSMISSION REFINEMENTS. Rear axle ratios, 4.69 standard, 4.36 and 4.07 optional.
CHASSIS REFINEMENTS. *Frame:* stiffened by extending X to form boxed side rails, tubular front cross member eliminated. *Steering:* ratio 18.6. *Wheelbase:* 127 inches for 1200, 134 inches for 1201, 139 inches for 1202, 160 inches for commercial chassis 1200A.
BODY REFINEMENTS. *Body types:* LeBaron cabriolet added to and touring (5-7) and convertible sedan (5) dropped from 1201; business sedan (5-8), business limousine (5-8), convertible sedan (5), touring (5-7) and LeBaron town car (5-7) added for 1202.
PRICE RANGE. $2385 for 1200; $2470-$5240 for 1201; $2630-$5385 for 1202.

SUPER EIGHT (1203, 1204, 1205)
MODEL YEAR: 1935 • SERIES: TWELFTH
INTRODUCED AUGUST 30TH, 1934 • CURRENT TO AUGUST 9TH, 1935
MOTOR SERIAL NUMBERS 755001 TO 756540

ENGINE REFINEMENTS. Horsepower now 150 at 3200 rpm. *Compression ratio:* 6.3 standard, 6.0 optional. *Ignition:* return to single coil. *Note:* aluminum cylinder head standard, copper-lead, steel-backed bearings.
TRANSMISSION REFINEMENTS. Rear axle ratio 4.41.
CHASSIS REFINEMENTS. Same as Eight. *Wheelbase:* 132 inches for 1203, 139 inches for 1204, 144 inches for 1205, 165 inches for commercial chassis 1203A.
BODY REFINEMENTS. *Body types:* LeBaron cabriolet (5-7) added to and touring (5-7) and convertible sedan (5) dropped from 1204; business sedan (5-8), business limousine (5-8), convertible sedan (5), touring (5-7) and LeBaron town car (5-7) added for 1205. All other custom cars dropped.
PRICE RANGE. $2990 for 1203; $2880-$5670 for 1204; $3265-$5815 for 1205.

EIGHT (1400, 1401, 1402)
MODEL YEAR: 1936 • SERIES: FOURTEENTH
INTRODUCED AUGUST 10TH, 1935 • CURRENT TO SEPTEMBER 2ND, 1936
MOTOR SERIAL NUMBERS 390501 TO 394505

ENGINE REFINEMENTS. *Ignition:* Delco-Remy with octane selector.

SUPER EIGHT (1403, 1404, 1405)
MODEL YEAR: 1936 • SERIES: FOURTEENTH
INTRODUCED AUGUST 10TH, 1935 • CURRENT TO SEPTEMBER 2ND, 1936
MOTOR SERIAL NUMBERS 757001 TO 758360

ENGINE REFINEMENTS. *Ignition:* Delco-Remy with octane selector.

SUPER EIGHT
(1500, 1501, 1502)*
MODEL YEAR: 1937 • SERIES: FIFTEENTH
INTRODUCED SEPTEMBER 3RD, 1936 • CURRENT TO SEPTEMBER 9TH, 1937
MOTOR SERIAL NUMBERS 395501 TO 401336

*The "Eight" designation was dropped.
ENGINE REFINEMENTS. Bore now 3-3/16 inches, 320 cubic inches; 130 hp at 3200 rpm. *Compression ratio:* 6.5 standard, 7.0 optional. *Cooling:* belt-driven generator. *Note:* former Eight became Super Eight.
TRANSMISSION REFINEMENTS. Rear axle ratio 4.69.
CHASSIS REFINEMENTS. *Suspension:* front, Safe-T-fleX independent; Ride Control dropped; rear, semi-elliptic mounted in rubber bushings. *Braking:* hydraulic, centrifuse twelve-inch drums, no booster. *Wheels:* disc, 7.50x16 tires, steel spoke optional. *Wheelbase:* the former 132-, 139- and 144-inch wheelbase chassis of the Super Eight dropped, the 165-inch wheelbase for commercial chassis 1500A retained. *Note:* Bijur system dropped.
BODY REFINEMENTS. *Instrumentation:* throttle and light switches relocated to dashboard from steering wheel which retained only horn button. *Body types:* phaeton and sport phaeton dropped from 1501; touring dropped from 1502. *Note:* built-in "bustle" trunks standard on all sedan-type bodies.
PRICE RANGE. $2335 for 1500; $2420-$4850 for 1501; $2580-$4990 for 1502, these the prices at introduction, subsequently to be raised in December and again in August 1937.

SUPER EIGHT
(1603, 1604, 1605)*
MODEL YEAR: 1938: • SERIES: SIXTEENTH
INTRODUCED SEPTEMBER 10TH, 1937 • CURRENT TO SEPTEMBER 19TH, 1938
MOTOR SERIAL NUMBERS A500051 TO A502527

*Note shift in chassis numbers, the previous year's 1500 now 1603, 1501 now 1604, 1502 now 1605; the Junior cars carrying numbers 1600, 1601 and 1602.
ENGINE REFINEMENTS. Longer motor water jackets.
CHASSIS REFINEMENTS. Pressure-gun (5000-mile interval) lubrication.
BODY REFINEMENTS. *Body types:* Rollston all-weather cabriolet replaced LeBaron cabriolet for 1604; Rollston town car replaced LeBaron town car and Brunn all-weather cabriolet and touring cabriolet added for 1605.
PRICE RANGE. $2790 for 1603; $2925-$5790 for 1604; $3035-$7475 for 1605.

SUPER-8 (1703, 1705)
MODEL YEAR: 1939 • SERIES: SEVENTEENTH
INTRODUCED SEPTEMBER 20TH, 1938 • CURRENT TO AUGUST 7TH, 1939
MOTOR SERIAL NUMBERS B500001 TO B506023

ENGINE REFINEMENTS. Compression ratio: 6.45 standard, 6.85 optional. *Cooling:* new permanently lubricated packless water pump and asymmetrical fan, radiator capacity 5½ gallons. *Note:* cast iron cylinder heads.
TRANSMISSION REFINEMENTS. Same as One Twenty, three-speed constant mesh, steering column shift, overdrive available. Rear axle ratios, for 1703 4.36 standard (optional overdrive, out 4.54, engaged 3.28), for 1705 4.54 standard (optional overdrive, out 4.7, engaged 3.39).
CHASSIS REFINEMENTS. *Wheels:* steel disc, 16 x 7.00 tires. *Wheelbase:* 127 inches retained for 1703, 148 inches now for 1705, commercial chassis 1703A now on 148-inch chassis.
BODY REFINEMENTS. *Body types:* club coupe (2-4), convertible coupe (2-4), touring sedan (5), convertible sedan (5) available for 1703; touring limousine (5-8), touring sedan (5-8) available for 1705. All other body styles dropped. *Note:* all-steel bodies.
PRICE RANGE. $1995-$2435 for 1703; $2460-$2600 for 1705.

SUPER-8 ONE-SIXTY
(1803, 1804, 1805)
MODEL YEAR: 1940 • SERIES: EIGHTEENTH
INTRODUCED AUGUST 8TH, 1939 • CURRENT TO SEPTEMBER 15TH, 1940
MOTOR SERIAL NUMBERS C500051 TO C507697

ENGINE. L-head in-line eight, designed along same lines as One Twenty unit. 3½ by 4⅝ inches, 356 cubic inches, 160 hp at 3500 rpm. *Compression ratio:* 6.45 standard, 6.85 optional. *Crankshaft:* nine main bearings. *Ignition:* Auto-Lite. *Carburetor:* Stromberg. *Lubrication:* full pressure. *Cooling:* radiator capacity 5 gallons. *Note:* aluminum pistons, cast iron head, silent hydraulic zero clearance valve tappets.
TRANSMISSION REFINEMENTS. Rear axle ratios, for 1803 3.92 standard (optional overdrive, out 4.09, engaged 2.96), for 1804 4.09 standard (overdrive 4.36 and 3.15), for 1805 4.36 standard (overdrive 4.54 and 3.28).
CHASSIS REFINEMENTS. *Steering:* ratio 20.19. *Braking:* swept area 196 square inches. *Wheels:* steel spoke optional. *Wheelbase:* 138 inches for 1804.
BODY REFINEMENTS. *Lighting:* sealed beam headlamps. *Body types:* business coupe (2) and club sedan (5) added for 1803; touring sedan (5) only available style for 1804. *Note:* air conditioning available.
PRICE RANGE. $1524-$2050 for 1803; $1859 for 1804; $2026-$2154 for 1805.

CUSTOM SUPER-8 ONE-EIGHTY
(1806, 1807, 1808)
MODEL YEAR: 1940 • SERIES: EIGHTEENTH
INTRODUCED AUGUST 8TH, 1939 • CURRENT TO SEPTEMBER 15, 1940
MOTOR SERIAL NUMBERS CC500000 TO CC503000

These cars replaced former Twelve as flagship of the Packard line, and shared refinements with One-Sixty, rear axle ratios for 1806, 1807 and 1808, for example, being the same as for One-Sixty 1803, 1804 and 1805 respectively.
CHASSIS REFINEMENTS. *Wheelbase:* 127 inches for 1806, 138 inches for 1807, 148 inches for 1808, the same wheelbase lengths as the One-Sixty.

BODY REFINEMENTS. *Body types:* club sedan (5), Darrin convertible victoria (5) for 1806; touring sedan (5), formal sedan (5-6), Rollson all-weather cabriolet (5-7), Darrin convertible sedan (5), Darrin sport sedan (5) for 1807; touring limousine (5-8), touring sedan (5-8), Rollson all-weather town car (5-7) for 1808. *Note:* air conditioning available on sedans.
PRICE RANGE. $2228-$4570 for 1806; $2395-$6300 for 1807; $2526-$4575 for 1808.

SUPER-8 ONE-SIXTY
(1903, 1904, 1905)
MODEL YEAR: 1941 • SERIES: NINETEENTH
INTRODUCED SEPTEMBER 16TH, 1940 • CURRENT TO AUGUST 24TH, 1941
MOTOR SERIAL NUMBERS D500051 TO D505000

ENGINE REFINEMENTS. New motor mounts in larger rubber cushions; new steel-backed connecting rod bearings, new low-pressure closed cooling system (7½ lbs).
TRANSMISSION REFINEMENTS. Aero-Drive overdrive with Electromatic vacuum-operated clutch available. Rear axle ratio for 1903 3.92 standard (optional overdrive, out 4.36, engaged 3.15).
BODY REFINEMENTS. *Body types:* touring sedan and club sedan dropped from and DeLuxe convertible coupe and convertible sedan added to 1903. Airport bus 1903AB added. *Note:* 1903 and 1904 available without running boards if desired; two-tone color options; hydraulic window lifts on some bodies.
PRICE RANGE. $1594-$2405 for 1903; $2009 for 1904; $2161-$2289 for 1905.

SUPER-8 ONE-EIGHTY
(1906, 1907, 1908)
MODEL YEAR: 1941 • SERIES: NINETEENTH
INTRODUCED SEPTEMBER 16TH, 1940 • CURRENT TO AUGUST 24TH, 1941
MOTOR SERIAL NUMBERS CD500000 TO CD502000

ENGINE REFINEMENTS. Same as One-Sixty.
TRANSMISSION REFINEMENTS. Same as One-Sixty.
BODY REFINEMENTS. *Body types:* club sedan dropped from 1906; Darrin convertible sedan dropped from and LeBaron sport brougham added to 1907; LeBaron touring sedan and touring limousine added to 1908. *Note:* two-tone color options; hydraulic window lifts on some bodies.
PRICE RANGE. $4550 for 1906; $3045-$4750 for 1907; $2724-$5550 for 1908.

SUPER-8 ONE-SIXTY
(2003, 2004, 2005, 2023, 2055)
MODEL YEAR: 1942 • SERIES: TWENTIETH
INTRODUCED AUGUST 25TH, 1941 • CURRENT TO FEBRUARY 7TH, 1942
MOTOR SERIAL NUMBERS E500000 TO E504000

CHASSIS REFINEMENTS. *Wheelbase:* 127 inches for 2023; 148 inches for 2055. Clipper bodies on new wider frame for 2003.
BODY REFINEMENTS. *Body types:* Clipper club sedan (6) and touring sedan (6) for 2003 added; convertible coupe (5) for 2023; touring sedan (6) for 2004; touring sedan and touring limousine (each 5-7) for 2005; business sedan and business limousine (each 5-7) for 2055.
PRICE RANGE. $1635-$2175.

SUPER-8 ONE-EIGHTY
(2006, 2007, 2008)
MODEL YEAR: 1942 • SERIES: TWENTIETH
INTRODUCED AUGUST 25TH, 1941 • CURRENT TO FEBRUARY 7TH, 1942
MOTOR SERIAL NUMBERS CE500000 TO CE502000

BODY REFINEMENTS. *Body types*: Clipper club sedan (6) and Clipper touring sedan (6) added for 2006; Darrin convertible victoria (5) for 2006 special; formal sedan (6), touring sedan (6) and Rollson all-weather cabriolet (7) for 2007; touring sedan (7), touring limousine (7), LeBaron touring sedan (7), LeBaron touring limousine (7) and Rollson all-weather town car for 2008.
PRICE RANGE. $2115-$5795.

TWIN SIX (905, 906)
MODEL YEAR: 1932 • SERIES: NINTH
INTRODUCED JANUARY 9TH, 1932 • CURRENT TO JANUARY 5TH, 1933
MOTOR SERIAL NUMBERS 900001 TO 900584

ENGINE. Monobloc $67°$ V-12, modified L, cast iron detachable heads, zero lash automatic valve silencers, four-point rubber suspension; 3.4375 by 4 inches, 445.47 cubic inches; 160 hp at 3200 rpm; torque 322 lb/ft at 1400 rpm. *Compression ratio*: 6.0. *Crankshaft*: counterbalanced, heat treated drop forging with four removable steel-backed babbitted main bearings. *Ignition*: battery-powered, dual dash-mounted coil, double breaker Auto-Lite distributor with automatic centrifugal spark advance, 14 mm plugs. *Carburetor*: Stromberg dual downdraft, 1-3/16" diameter venturii, automatic choke, air cleaner and silencer. *Lubrication*: pressure feed by submerged gear pump to crankshaft, camshaft, piston pin bearing and valve rocker lever mechanism. *Cooling*: single belt crankshaft driven centrifugal water pump, copper down flow tubular core radiator, frame-mounted overflow expansion tank, four-bladed 21" unshrouded fan, thermostatic radiator shutters, radiator capacity 11½ gallons. *Note*: rods dropped forged with babbitted bearings; pistons aluminum alloy four-ring; Stewart Warner camshaft-driven mechanical fuel pump.
TRANSMISSION. Third, synchronized direct drive; second, synchronized constant mesh helical gears; first, constant mesh helical gears; reverse, sliding spur gears; cane shift. Double-plate clutch; vacuum-controlled free wheeling. Hypoid gearing, upright or angleset housing, Hotchkiss final drive. Rear axle ratios, open bodies 4.41; closed bodies 4.69; optional 4.06 or 5.07.
CHASSIS. *Frame*: double drop open channel pressed steel ladder type with X center brace. *Axles*: front, solid I beam with reverse Elliot ends; rear, semi-floating with spring propulsion, stamped banjo housing. *Suspension*: front and rear, metal covered semi-elliptic leaf springs. *Steering*: Packard worm and sector (ratio 17 to 1) to frame #900580; Gemmer worm and roller (ratio 18.6 to 1) from frame #900581. *Braking*: four wheel internal expanding vacuum boosted three shoe Bendix with front wheel Perrot control, swept area 402 square inches. *Wheels*: wire or wood demountable, 7.50x18 tires with rim flange retainer. *Track*: 59¼ inches. *Wheelbase*: 142⅛ inches for 905; 147⅛ inches for 906. *Note*: Bijur automatic lubrication; shock absorbers, hydraulic two-way, adjustable from front compartment.
BODY. *Construction*: metal panel stampings over wood skeleton. *Paint*: nitrocellulose lacquer, eleven standard selections, optional colors at no extra cost. *Interior*: closed cars, all wool broadcloth; open and convertible car, colonial leather. *Standard fittings*: twin horns, safety glass, rear foot rest, dual windshield wipers on closed cars, single windshield wiper on open cars, adjustable driver's seat, inside sun visors in front compartment, rear view mirror; rear center arm rest in closed and convertible cars. *Lighting*: dual fender lights, dual tail and stop lights, instrument panel reading light, automatic courtesy lights, spotlight on open cars, dome and quarter lights on closed cars. *Instrumentation*: heat indicator, speedometer-odometer, oil pressure, mechanical clock, ammeter, electric gas and oil capacity gauge, cigar lighter. *Body types*: on the 905 chassis—touring (5-7); phaeton (5); sport phaeton (5); sedan (5); convertible sedan (5); club sedan (5); coupe (5); convertible victoria (5); coupe (2-4); coupe-roadster (2-4). On the 906 chassis—sedan (5-7); sedan-limousine (5-7); all-weather cabriolet (5-7); all-weather landaulet (5-7); all-weather town car (5-7); all-weather town car, landaulet (5-7); stationary coupe, Dietrich (2-4); sport phaeton, Dietrich (4); convertible sedan, Dietrich (5); convertible roadster, Dietrich (2-4); convertible victoria, Dietrich (4). *Note*: on 906 chassis, all styles save sedan and sedan-limousine in Individual Custom series.
PRICE RANGE. $3650-$7950.

TWELVE (1005, 1006)
MODEL YEAR: 1933 • SERIES: TENTH
INTRODUCED JANUARY 6TH, 1933 • CURRENT TO AUGUST 20TH, 1933
MOTOR SERIAL NUMBERS 901001 TO 901548

ENGINE REFINEMENTS. Redesign of zero lash valve mechanism. *Carburetor*: automatic choke with fast idle. *Cooling*: dual belt drive, engine-mounted expansion tank, shrouded fan, radiator capacity 10 gallons. *Note*: clutch single dry plate 12-inch diameter, optional vacuum control free wheeling; A-C mechanical fuel pump with vacuum booster.
CHASSIS REFINEMENTS. *Frame*: tapered open channel pressed steel ladder type with wide based X centerbrace. *Steering*: Gemmer worm and roller, ratio 18.6 to 1. *Braking*: adjustable vacuum boosted two-shoe Bendix cable controlled. *Wheels*: wire or wood demountable, tires 7.50x17 drop center rims. *Track*: front, 60-5/16 inches; rear, 58-3/4 inches. *Wheelbase*: 142 inches for 1005, 147 inches for 1006.
BODY REFINEMENTS. *Paint*: sixteen standard selections, optional colors at no extra cost. *Standard fittings*: center arm rest in rear seat of open cars. *Lighting*: three filament headlight bulbs. *Body types*: on the 1005 chassis, formal sedan (5) and formal sedan (5-7) added; on the 1006 chassis, all-weather cabriolet, LeBaron (5-7); all-weather town car, LeBaron (5-7); sport sedan, Dietrich (5); sedan-limousine, cabriolet (6); sedan-limousine (6); sport sedan (5) added, all of these styles in the Custom Cars series.
PRICE RANGE. $3720-$7000.

TWELVE (1106, 1107, 1108)
MODEL YEAR: 1934 • SERIES: ELEVENTH
INTRODUCED AUGUST 21ST, 1933 • CURRENT TO AUGUST 29TH, 1934
MOTOR SERIAL NUMBERS 901601 TO 902587

ENGINE REFINEMENTS. *Compression ratio*: 6.0 with cast iron heads, 6.0 and 6.8 with aluminum heads. *Ignition*: engine-mounted coils. *Note*: cast iron and aluminum heads; clutch without vacuum assist.
CHASSIS REFINEMENTS. *Steering*: Packard worm and roller, ratio 18.1. *Wheels*: 7.00x17 tires for 1106. *Wheelbase*: 134⅞ inches for 1106, 141⅞ inches for 1107, 146⅞ inches for 1108.
BODY REFINEMENTS. *Construction*: metal window moldings. *Paint*: ten standard selections, optional colors at no extra cost. *Lighting*: backup lights.

Instrumentation: optional radio dial control head. *Body types*: speedster runabout (2) and sport phaeton (4) by LeBaron added; also 1106 sport coupe (4) by Packard; on special order, 1106 sedan (5), export left hand drive only. "Custom Made by Packard" all-weather cabriolet; all-weather landaulet; all-weather town car, landaulet; sedan-limousine, cabriolet; sport sedan and sedan-limousine dropped; all-weather town car finalized by Dietrich, Inc.; six-window formal sedan (production) and sport phaeton (Dietrich) dropped.
PRICE RANGE. $3820-$7746.

TWELVE (1206, 1207, 1208)
MODEL YEAR: 1935 • SERIES: TWELFTH
INTRODUCED AUGUST 30TH, 1934 • CURRENT TO AUGUST 9TH, 1935
MOTOR SERIAL NUMBERS 903001 TO 903857

ENGINE REFINEMENTS. Three-point rubber suspension; stroke increased to 4.250 inches, 473.31 cubic inches; 175 hp at 3200 rpm (180 at 3200 with high compression heads); torque 366 lb/ft at 1400 rpm. *Compression ratio*: 6.0, 6.25, 7.0. *Carburetor*: 1-5/16 diameter venturii. *Lubrication*: external crankcase oil filter and temperature regulator. *Cooling*: frame-mounted expansion tank. *Note*: aluminum heads only; rods, copper lead steel-backed insert bearings; clutch vacuum power assist.
TRANSMISSION REFINEMENTS. Rear axle ratios, 4.41 standard; 4.06, 4.69 or 5.07 optional.
CHASSIS REFINEMENTS. *Frame*: tapered open channel partially boxed pressed steel with wide based X centerbrace channels. *Track*: rear, 61 inches. *Wheelbase*: 139 ¼ inches for 1207, 144 ¼ inches for 1208, 132 ¼ inches for 1206 (short five-passenger sedan only).
BODY REFINEMENTS. *Paint*: eight standard selections. *Standard fittings*: radio aerial in all closed cars. *Lighting*: prefocused two-element headlight bulbs. *Instrumentation*: electric clock. *Body types*: Dietrich customs, LeBaron sport customs, sport coupe by Packard dropped. *Note*: front doors hinged at "B" post.
PRICE RANGE. $3820-$6435.

TWELVE (1406, 1407, 1408)
MODEL YEAR: 1936 • SERIES: FOURTEENTH
INTRODUCED AUGUST 10TH, 1935 • CURRENT TO SEPTEMBER 2ND, 1936
MOTOR SERIAL NUMBERS 904001 TO 904719

CHASSIS REFINEMENTS. *Wheelbase*: 132 ¼ inches for 1406; 139 ¼ inches for 1407, 144 ¼ inches for 1408.
BODY REFINEMENTS. *Paint*: thirteen standard selections.
PRICE RANGE. $3820-$6435.

TWELVE (1506, 1507, 1508)
MODEL YEAR: 1937 • SERIES: FIFTEENTH
INTRODUCED SEPTEMBER 3RD, 1936 • CURRENT TO SEPTEMBER 9TH, 1937
MOTOR SERIAL NUMBERS 905501 TO 906841

ENGINE REFINEMENTS. *Compression ratio*: 6.0 standard, 6.4 and 7.0 optional. *Ignition*: 10 mm spark plugs. *Lubrication*: pressure gun.
CHASSIS REFINEMENTS. *Axles*: front, independent front suspension with Elliot ends. *Suspension*: front, Packard Safe-T-fleX independent, helical coiled springs. *Braking*: servo sealed hydraulic vacuum booster. *Steering*: ratio 20.5. *Wheels*: steel disc, 8.25x16 tires. *Track*: front, 60 ¼ inches; rear, 61 inches. *Wheelbase*: 132 ¼ inches for 1506; 139 ¼ inches for 1507; 144 ¼ inches for 1508.
BODY REFINEMENTS. *Paint*: fourteen standard selections. *Lighting*: control on instrument board and foot switch. *Body types*: touring, phaeton and sport phaeton special order only. *Note*: front doors hinged at "A" post.
PRICE RANGE. $3420-$5900.

TWELVE (1607, 1607, 1608)
MODEL YEAR: 1938 • SERIES: SIXTEENTH
INTRODUCED SEPTEMBER 10TH, 1937 • CURRENT TO SEPTEMBER 19TH, 1938
MOTOR SERIAL NUMBERS A-600051 TO A-600620

ENGINE REFINEMENTS. *Cooling*: pressurized radiator cap.
CHASSIS REFINEMENTS. *Wheelbase*: 127 inches for 1606, 134 ⅜ inches for 1607, 139 ⅜ inches for 1608.
BODY REFINEMENTS. *Paint*: thirteen standard selections.
PRICE RANGE. $4135-$8510.

TWELVE (1706, 1707, 1708)
MODEL YEAR: 1939 • SERIES: SEVENTEENTH
INTRODUCED SEPTEMBER 20TH, 1938 • CURRENT TO AUGUST 8TH, 1939
MOTOR SERIAL NUMBERS B-602001 TO B-602497

TRANSMISSION REFINEMENTS. Column shift.
PRICE RANGE. $4155-$8355.

ONE TWENTY
MODEL YEAR: 1935 • SERIES: TWELFTH
INTRODUCED JANUARY 1935 • CURRENT TO AUGUST 9TH, 1935
MOTOR SERIAL NUMBERS X1526 TO X26701

ENGINE. L-head in-line eight; 3 ¼ by 3 ⅞, 257.16 cubic inches; 110 hp at 3850 rpm; torque 203 lb/ft at 2000 rpm. *Compression ratio*: 6.5 standard, 7.0 optional. *Crankshaft*: drop forged, high carbon steel, five main bearings. *Ignition*: double breaker distributor, Auto-Lite. *Carburetor*: Duplex downdraft, Stromberg EE-14. *Lubrication*: full pressure. *Cooling*: forced water, capacity 16 ½ quarts. *Note*: Export engine had 2⅞-inch bore.
TRANSMISSION. Packard-Selective Silent Synchronized, in unit, with three forward speeds; Packard-Hypoid Angleset differential; rear axle ratios 4.36 and 4.54 standard, depending upon body (4.7 on commercial chassis 120-A).
CHASSIS. *Frame*: taper pressed steel X-type double drop. *Axles*: front, reverse Elliot, Packard; rear, semi-floating, Packard. *Suspension*: front, independent parallelogram, Packard, Safe-T-fleX; rear, semi-elliptic multiple leaf. *Steering*: worm and roller, Packard, ratio 18.41 to 1. *Braking*: internal expanding, four wheel, hydraulic, effective area 182 square inches. *Wheels*: steel disc, sixteen-inch, steel artillery type optional. *Track*; front, 59 inches; rear, 60 inches. *Wheelbase*: 120 inches (158 inches for commercial chassis 120-A).
BODY. *Construction*: steel, wood reinforced. *Paint*: lacquer, nine selections. *Interior*: broadcloths, leathers, leatherettes. *Instrumentation*: speedometer; oil, fuel, amp, temperature gauges; odometer; tripset standard; clock optional. *Body types*: business coupe (Body No. 898), convertible coupe (899), sport coupe (895), touring coupe (894), sedan (893), club sedan (896), touring sedan (892).
PRICE RANGE. $980-$1095 (at introduction).

ONE TWENTY (120-B)
Model Year: 1936 • Series: Fourteenth
Introduced August 10th, 1935 • Current to September 2nd, 1936
Motor Serial Numbers X27501 to X82637

ENGINE REFINEMENTS. Stroke increased to 4 ½ inches; 3 ¼ by 4 ¼ inches, 282 cubic inches; 120 hp at 3800 rpm; torque 225 lb/ft at 2000 rpm.
TRANSMISSION REFINEMENTS. Rear axle ratios 4.09 standard; 4.54 and 4.7 optional (4.54 on commercial chassis 120-BA).
BODY REFINEMENTS. *Construction:* front doors hinging at front. *Paint:* fifteen selections. *Body types:* convertible sedan (Body No. 997) added.
PRICE RANGE. $990-$1395 (at introduction).

ONE TWENTY
(120-C, CD; 138-CD)
Model Year: 1937 • Series: Fifteenth
Introduced September 3rd, 1936 • Current to September 9th, 1937
Motor Serial Numbers X100001 to X150267

ENGINE REFINEMENTS. *Ignition:* single breaker distributor, Auto-Lite. *Carburetor:* Carter 366-S added as alternate. *Cooling:* radiator capacity 16-17 quarts. Packard data often shows cooling capacity as 20 quarts, but the figure above—for this year as well as the last—is correct.
TRANSMISSION REFINEMENTS. Rear axle ratios for the 120-C and CD, 4.09 standard, 4.54 and 4.7 optional; for the 138-CD, 4.54 standard, 4.36 and 4.7 optional; for the commercial chassis 120-CA, 4.54.
CHASSIS REFINEMENTS. *Frame:* taper pressed steel, I-beam X, double drop. *Wheelbase:* 138 inches for 138-CD.
BODY REFINEMENTS. *Paint:* fifteen selections. *Standard fittings:* for CD models only, rubber dimmer switch cap, lighter, special taillamp lens, radiator ornament, radiator shutter equipment, flexible steering wheel, nickel-plated steering column, wheel trim rings, lighter and ash tray (rear), mohair front carpet, arm rest rear, special cushions (Marshall), special gearshift knob, rear carpets and interior hardware. *Body types:* station wagon (Body No. 1070) added (body numbers for other body types now carried the "ten" prefix—i.e., the business coupe was 1098—body numbers to increase by one digit annually thereafter); on the 138-inch wheelbase 138-CD, a touring sedan (1091-CD) and touring limousine (1090-CD) available.
PRICE RANGE. $945-$1270 for 120-C and CD (effective January 1937); $1835-$1985 for 138-CD (effective July 1937).

SIX (115-C)
Model Year: 1937 • Series: Fifteenth
Introduced September 3rd, 1936 • Current to September 9th, 1937
Motor Serial Numbers T1501 to T67104

ENGINE. L-head in-line six; 3-7/16 by 4 ¼ inches, 237 cubic inches; 100 hp at 3600 rpm. *Compression ratio:* 6.3 standard, 7.0 optional. *Crankshaft:* drop forged, high carbon steel, four main bearings. *Ignition:* single breaker distributor, Delco or Auto-Lite. *Carburetor:* single barrel, downdraft, Chandler Groves. *Lubrication:* full pressure. *Cooling:* forced water, capacity 15 quarts. *Note:* Export engine had 3 ¼-inch bore.
TRANSMISSION. Packard-Selective Silent Synchronized, in unit, with three forward speeds; Packard Hypoid Angleset differential; rear axle ratios 4.36 standard, 4.54 optional.

CHASSIS. *Frame:* taper pressed steel, I-beam X, double drop. *Axles:* front, reverse Elliot, Packard; rear, semi-floating, Packard. *Suspension:* front, independent parallelogram, Packard, Safe-T-fleX; rear, semi-elliptic multiple leaf. *Steering:* worm and roller, Packard, ratio 18.41 to 1. *Braking:* internal expanding, four wheel hydraulic, effective area 168 square inches. *Wheels:* steel disc, sixteen-inch; steel artillery type optional. *Track:* front, 59 inches; rear, 60 inches. *Wheelbase:* 115 inches.
BODY. *Construction:* steel, wood reinforced. *Paint:* fifteen selections. *Interior:* broadcloths, leathers, leatherettes. *Instrumentation:* speedometer; oil, fuel, amp, temperature gauges, odometer standard; clock optional. *Body types:* business coupe (Body No. 1088), sport coupe (1085), touring coupe (1084), sedan (1083), club sedan (1086), convertible coupe (1089), touring sedan (1082), station wagon (1060).
PRICE RANGE. $795-$1295 (at introduction).

EIGHT (1601, 1601D, 1602)*
Model Year: 1938 • Series: Sixteenth
Introduced September 10th, 1937 • Current to September 19th, 1938
Motor Serial Numbers A300051 to A3222751

*One Twenty redesignated "Eight" this model year.
ENGINE REFINEMENTS. *Compression ratio:* 6.6 standard, 7.05 optional. *Carburetor:* Carter 366-S dropped as option. *Cooling:* radiator capacity 16 quarts.
TRANSMISSION REFINEMENTS. Rear axle ratios, 4.36 standard; 4.09, 4.54 and 4.7 optional; 4.7 on commercial chassis 1601A.
CHASSIS REFINEMENTS. *Braking:* effective area 182 square inches for the 1601; 232 square inches for the 1602. *Track:* front, 59-3/16 inches; rear, 60 inches. *Wheelbase:* 127 inches for the 1601; 148 inches for the 1602.
BODY REFINEMENTS. *Construction:* all steel. *Paint:* fourteen selections. *Body types:* 1601 club coupe (Body No. 1195), two-door touring sedan (1194), 1602 touring sedan (1191), touring limousine (1190) added; station wagon, touring sedan (138-inch wheelbase), touring limousine (138-inch wheelbase) dropped.
PRICE RANGE. $1160-$1465 for 1601 (effective July 1938); $1835-$1985 for 1602 (effective July 1938).

SIX (1600)
Model Year: 1938 • Series: Sixteenth
Introduced September 10th, 1937 • Current to September 19th, 1938
Motor Serial Numbers A1501 to A31660

ENGINE REFINEMENTS. Bore increased to 3 ½ inches; 3 ½ by 4 ¼ inches, 245 cubic inches; 100 hp at 3600 rpm; torque 195 lb/ft at 1400 rpm. *Compression ratio:* 6.52 standard, 7.05 optional. *Ignition:* single breaker distributor, Delco Remy.
TRANSMISSION REFINEMENTS. Rear axle ratios, 4.54 standard, 4.36 and 4.7 optional.
CHASSIS REFINEMENTS. *Track:* front, 59-3/16 inches; rear, 60 inches. *Wheelbase:* 122 inches.
BODY REFINEMENTS. *Construction:* all steel. *Paint:* fourteen selections. *Body types:* two-door touring sedan (Body No. 1184), club coupe (No. 1185) added; sport coupe, touring coupe, sedan, club sedan, station wagon dropped.
PRICE RANGE. $1075-$1235 (at introduction).

ONE TWENTY (1701, 1702)
MODEL YEAR: 1939 • SERIES: SEVENTEENTH
INTRODUCED SEPTEMBER 20TH, 1938 • CURRENT TO AUGUST 7TH, 1939
MOTOR SERIAL NUMBERS B300001 TO B319537
ENGINE REFINEMENTS. Torque 225 lb/ft at 1800 rpm. *Compression ratio:* 6.41 standard, 6.85 optional. *Carburetor:* Duplex downdraft, Stromberg EE-16. *Note:* aluminum cylinder head replaced by cast iron.
TRANSMISSION REFINEMENTS. Overdrive now available. Rear axle ratios, 4.36 standard; 4.09, 4.54, 4.7 and 4.9 optional; 4.54 standard with overdrive; 4.7 standard, 4.9 optional, 4.9 standard with overdrive for commercial chassis 1701A. Column shift introduced.
CHASSIS REFINEMENTS. *Track:* front, 59-3/16 inches, rear 60 inches for the 1701; front, 59-3/16 inches, rear 62½ inches for the 1702. *Wheelbase:* 127 inches for the 1701; 148 inches for the 1702.
BODY REFINEMENTS. *Paint:* seventeen selections. *Instrumentation:* Packard accessory tachometer available optionally.
PRICE RANGE. $1200-$1955 (at introduction).

SIX (1700)
MODEL YEAR: 1939 • SERIES: SEVENTEENTH
INTRODUCED SEPTEMBER 20TH, 1938 • CURRENT TO AUGUST 7TH, 1939
ENGINE REFINEMENTS. Horsepower now 100 at 3200 rpm, torque 195 lb/ft at 1500 rpm.
TRANSMISSION REFINEMENTS. Overdrive now available. Rear axle ratios, 4.54 standard; 4.36 and 4.7 optional; 4.7 standard with overdrive. Column shift introduced.
BODY REFINEMENTS. *Paint:* fifteen selections.
PRICE RANGE. $1000-$1195 (at introduction).

ONE-TWENTY (1801)
MODEL YEAR: 1940 • SERIES: EIGHTEENTH
INTRODUCED AUGUST 8TH, 1939 • CURRENT TO SEPTEMBER 15TH, 1940
MOTOR SERIAL NUMBERS C300001-C328320
ENGINE REFINEMENTS. Horsepower now 120 at 3600 rpm. *Cooling:* radiator capacity 18 quarts.
TRANSMISSION REFINEMENTS. Rear axle ratios, 4.09 standard; 4.36 and 4.54 optional; 4.36 standard with overdrive; 4.7 standard, 4.9 and 5.22 optional, 4.9 standard with overdrive for commercial chassis 1801A. *Steering:* worm and roller, Packard, ratio 20.19 to 1. *Braking:* effective area 171.5 square inches. *Wheelbase:* 127 inches (148-inch wheelbase dropped).
BODY REFINEMENTS. *Paint:* sixteen selections. *Body types:* club sedan (Body No. 1396), station wagon (1393) added; long-wheelbase touring sedan and touring limousine dropped.
PRICE RANGE. $1038-$1573 (at introduction).

ONE-TEN (1800)
MODEL YEAR: 1940 • SERIES: EIGHTEENTH
INTRODUCED AUGUST 8TH, 1939 • CURRENT TO SEPTEMBER 15TH, 1940
MOTOR SERIAL NUMBERS C1501 TO C64111
ENGINE REFINEMENTS. *Compression ratio:* 6.39 standard, 6.71 optional.

Model 1901 One-Twenty, 1941.

Carburetor: single barrel downdraft, Stromberg BXOV-26. *Cooling:* radiator capacity 17 quarts.
TRANSMISSION REFINEMENTS. Rear axle ratios, 4.3 standard; 4.55 optional; 4.55 standard with overdrive.
CHASSIS REFINEMENTS. *Steering:* worm and roller, Packard, ratio 20.19 to 1. *Braking:* effective area 158.5 square inches. *Track:* front, 59-3/16 inches; rear, 60½ inches.
BODY REFINEMENTS. *Paint:* sixteen selections. *Body types:* station wagon (Body No. 1383) added.
PRICE RANGE. $867-$1195 (at introduction).

ONE-TWENTY (1901)
MODEL YEAR: 1941 • SERIES: NINETEENTH
INTRODUCED SEPTEMBER 16TH, 1940 • CURRENT TO AUGUST 24TH, 1941
MOTOR SERIAL NUMBERS D3000001 TO D319000
ENGINE REFINEMENTS. *Carburetor:* Duplex, downdraft, Carter WA1. *Cooling:* radiator capacity 17 quarts.
TRANSMISSION REFINEMENTS. Rear axle ratios, 4.09 standard; 4.36 and 4.54 optional; 4.36 standard with overdrive; for commercial chassis 1901A, 4.7 standard, 4.9 and 5.22 optional, 4.9 standard with overdrive.
CHASSIS REFINEMENTS. *Wheels:* steel disc, fifteen-inch.
BODY REFINEMENTS. *Paint:* fourteen single selections plus two-tone combinations. *Body types:* club sedan dropped.
PRICE RANGE. $1112-$1723 (at introduction).

ONE-TEN (1900)
MODEL YEAR: 1941 • SERIES: NINETEENTH
INTRODUCED SEPTEMBER 16TH, 1940 • CURRENT TO AUGUST 24TH, 1941
MOTOR SERIAL NUMBERS D1501 TO D38000
ENGINE REFINEMENTS. Horsepower now 100 at 3600 rpm. *Ignition:* single breaker, Auto-Lite, Delco. *Carburetor:* single barrel, downdraft, Stromberg BXOV-26. *Cooling:* radiator capacity 15 quarts.
TRANSMISSION REFINEMENTS. Rear axle ratios, 4.3 standard; 4.55 optional; 4.55 standard with overdrive; for commercial chassis T1900, 4.54 standard.
CHASSIS REFINEMENTS. *Wheels:* steel disc, fifteen-inch. *Track:* front, 59-9/16 inches; rear, 60⅝ inches. *Wheelbase:* 133 inches for taxi chassis T1900.
BODY REFINEMENTS. *Paint:* fourteen single selections plus two-tone combinations. *Body types:* sedan taxi and New York taxi added.
PRICE RANGE. $907-$1291 (at introduction).

CLIPPER (1951)
MODEL YEAR: 1941 • SERIES: NINETEENTH
INTRODUCED APRIL 1941 • CURRENT TO AUGUST 1941
MOTOR SERIAL NUMBERS D400001 TO D418000

ENGINE. L-head, in-line eight; 3 ¼ by 4 ¼ inches, 282 cubic inches; 125 hp at 3600 rpm; torque 228 lb/ft at 1800 rpm. *Compression ratio:* 6.85 to 1. *Crankshaft:* drop forged, high carbon steel, five main bearings. *Ignition:* coil/battery, single BKR distributor, Auto-Lite 1GT 4502. *Carburetor:* two-barrel downdraft, Carter WDO-512-S. *Lubrication:* full pressure. *Cooling:* forced water, capacity 17+1 quarts.
TRANSMISSION. Packard-Selective Silent Synchronized, in unit, with three forward speeds, overdrive available; Packard-Hypoid Angleset differential; rear axle ratios, 4.09 standard; 4.36 optional; 4.36 standard with overdrive; 4.54 optional.
CHASSIS. *Frame:* taper pressed steel, double drop, box section side rail. *Axles:* front, reverse Elliot, Packard; rear, semi-floating, Packard. *Suspension:* front, independent parallelogram, Packard, Safe-T-fleX; rear, semi-elliptic multiple leaf. *Steering:* worm and roller, Packard, ratio 20.19 to 1. *Braking:* internal expanding, four wheel, hydraulic, swept area 171.5 square inches. *Wheels:* motor wheel, demountable disc. *Track:* front, 59 ¼ inches; rear, 60-5/16 inches. *Wheelbase:* 127 inches.
BODY. *Construction:* all-steel, integral fenders. *Paint:* lacquer, twenty-two selections including nine two-tone combinations. *Interior:* striped broadcloth in two combinations. *Lighting:* two-level sealed beam. *Instrumentation:* speedometer, oil pressure, radimeter, ammeter, gas gauge, odometer standard. *Body types:* four-door sedan (Body No. 1401).
PRICE RANGE. $1375 at introduction in April; price subsequently raised to $1420 effective June 26th, 1941.

EIGHT SPECIAL AND CUSTOM
(2001, 2011, 2021)
MODEL YEAR: 1942 • SERIES: TWENTIETH
INTRODUCED AUGUST 25TH, 1941 • CURRENT TO FEBRUARY 7TH, 1942
MOTOR SERIAL NUMBERS E300000 TO E321000

ENGINE REFINEMENTS. *Cooling:* radiator capacity 17 quarts.
TRANSMISSION REFINEMENTS. Rear axle ratios, 4.1 standard, 4.3 optional, 4.3 standard with overdrive for the 2001 and 2011; 4.09 standard, 4.36 and 4.54 optional, 4.36 standard with overdrive, 4.54 optional for the 2021; 4.7 standard, 4.9 optional, 4.9 standard with overdrive for the commercial chassis 2001A.
CHASSIS REFINEMENTS. *Track:* front, 59⅜ inches, rear 60-5/16 inches for 2021 and 2001A; front, 59 ¼ inches, rear 60-13/32 inches for 2001 and 2011. *Wheelbase:* 120 inches for 2001 and 2011; 2021 convertible coupe only on 127-inch wheelbase chassis.
BODY REFINEMENTS. *Paint:* fifteen selections including four two-tone combinations. *Interior:* antique, colonial grain leather and leatherette for 2021 convertible coupe; broadcloth for sedans. *Body types:* 2001 Clipper Special available as touring sedan (Body No. 1592), club sedan (1595) and business coupe (1598); 2011 Clipper Custom as club sedan (1515) and touring sedan (1512); traditional One-Twenty styling confined to 2021 convertible coupe (Body No. 1599) and 2001A commercial bodies.
PRICE RANGE. $1235-$1495 at introduction, prices subsequently being raised twice, effective October 1st and November 29th.

SIX SPECIAL AND CUSTOM
(2000, 2010, 2020, 2030)
MODEL YEAR: 1942 • SERIES: TWENTIETH
INTRODUCED AUGUST 25, 1941 • CURRENT TO FEBRUARY 7TH, 1942
MOTOR SERIAL NUMBERS E1501 TO E14000

ENGINE REFINEMENTS. Horsepower now 105 at 3600 rpm; torque 192 lb/ft at 2000 rpm. *Carburetor:* single barrel, downdraft, Carter WAI-530-S. *Cooling:* radiator capacity 15 quarts.
TRANSMISSION REFINEMENTS. Rear axle ratios, 4.3 standard, 4.55 optional, 4.55 standard with overdrive for 2000, 2010 and 2020; 4.54 standard for taxicab chassis 2030.
CHASSIS REFINEMENTS. *Track:* front, 59-19/32 inches; rear, 60-9/16 inches.
BODY REFINEMENTS. *Paint:* fifteen selections including four two-tone combinations. *Interior:* antique, colonial grain leather and leatherette for convertible coupe; broadcloth for sedans. *Body types:* 2000 Clipper Special available as touring sedan (Body No. 1582), club sedan (1585) and business coupe (1588); 2010 Clipper Custom as club sedan (1505) and touring sedan (1502); traditional One-Ten styling confined to 2020 convertible coupe (Body No. 1589) and 2030 taxicab.
PRICE RANGE. $1180-$1468 (at introduction).

CLIPPER SIX (2100, 2130)
MODEL YEARS: 1946-1947 • SERIES: TWENTY-FIRST
INTRODUCED APRIL 18TH, 1946 • CURRENT TO SEPTEMBER 7TH, 1947
MOTOR SERIAL NUMBERS F1501 TO F50999

Taxi 2130 introduced June 19th, 1946. All 1947 models introduced November 11th, 1946.
ENGINE REFINEMENTS. Six redesigned mid-year 1947, with new engine beginning at Motor Serial Number F35000.
TRANSMISSION REFINEMENTS. Rear axle ratio 4.3 standard.
CHASSIS REFINEMENTS. *Wheelbase:* 120 inches all models.
BODY REFINEMENTS. *Paint:* five selections, two additional special taxi colors; for 1947 two additional selections, one two-tone combination and two more taxi colors added; two-toning altered to include deck lid for 1946, two-toning mask line returned to crease below backlight for 1947. *Body types:* sedan taxicab and partition taxicab added; business coupe, New York taxi and convertible coupe dropped.
PRICE RANGE. $1461-$1838 (1946); $1679-$2465 (1947)

CLIPPER EIGHT STANDARD (2101)
CLIPPER EIGHT DELUXE (2111)
MODEL YEARS: 1946-1947 • SERIES: TWENTY-FIRST
INTRODUCED OCTOBER 19TH, 1945 • CURRENT TO SEPTEMBER 7TH, 1947
MOTOR SERIAL NUMBERS F300001-F309000

Models for 1947 introduced November 11th, 1946.
TRANSMISSION REFINEMENTS. Rear axle ratio 4.1 standard. Electromatic clutch revised.
CHASSIS REFINEMENTS. *Wheelbase:* 120 inches all models.
BODY REFINEMENTS. *Paint:* five selections, two-toning altered to include deck lid for 1946, two-toning mask returned to crease below backlight for 1947.

Body types: convertible coupe and commercial bodies (non-Clipper) dropped.
PRICE RANGE. $1570-$1869 (1946); $1816-$2149 (1947).

SUPER CLIPPER (2103)
MODEL YEARS: 1946-1947 • SERIES: TWENTY-FIRST
INTRODUCED APRIL 18TH, 1946 • CURRENT TO SEPTEMBER 7TH, 1947
MOTOR SERIAL NUMBERS F500001 TO F520000

Models for 1947 introduced November 11th, 1946.
TRANSMISSION REFINEMENTS. Rear axle ratio 3.92 standard. Electromatic clutch revised.
CHASSIS REFINEMENTS. *Wheelbase:* 127 inches all models.
BODY REFINEMENTS. *Paint:* five selections, same as 2101-2111. *Body types:* convertible coupe, commercial and long-wheelbase bodies, all non-Clipper bodies dropped.
PRICE RANGE. $1956-$2290 (1946); $2241-$2772 (1947).

CUSTOM SUPER CLIPPER (2106, 2126)
MODEL YEARS: 1946-1947 • SERIES: TWENTY-FIRST
INTRODUCED APRIL 18TH, 1946 • CURRENT TO SEPTEMBER 7TH, 1947

Long wheelbase 2126 introduced August 28th, 1946. Models for 1947 introduced November 11th, 1946.
TRANSMISSION REFINEMENTS. Rear axle ratio 3.92 standard. Electromatic clutch revised.
CHASSIS REFINEMENTS. *Wheelbase:* 127 for 2106, 148 inches for 2126.
BODY REFINEMENTS. *Paint:* five selections; one additional color (Packard blue) available on long-wheelbase cars only; another additional color (Cavalier Maroon) added mid-year; two-toning altered to include deck lid for 1946, two-toning mask returned to crease below backlight for 1947. *Body types:* limousine and seven-passenger sedan (by Henney) added on long wheelbase; all non-Clipper bodies, convertible victoria and other catalogued custom bodies dropped.
PRICE RANGE. $2544-$4496 (1946); $2913-$4668 (1947).

SIX (2220, 2240)
MODEL YEARS: 1948-1949 • SERIES: TWENTY-SECOND
INTRODUCED SEPTEMBER 8TH, 1947 • CURRENT TO MAY 1ST, 1949
MOTOR SERIAL NUMBERS G1501 TO G4100

ENGINE REFINEMENTS. 3½ by 4¼ inches, 245 cubic inches; 105 hp at 3500 rpm.
TRANSMISSION REFINEMENTS. Rear axle ratios 4.55 for taxi, 4.54 for New York taxi.
CHASSIS REFINEMENTS. *Wheelbase:* 141 inches added for New York taxi.
BODY REFINEMENTS. *Paint:* ten selections, one dropped in August 1948. *Body types:* New York taxi added; club sedan and partition-type taxi dropped.
PRICE RANGE. $2282 (sedan for export only, taxis sold by subsidiary, no prices available).

EIGHT (2201)
EIGHT DELUXE (2211)
MODEL YEARS: 1948-1949 • SERIES: TWENTY-SECOND
INTRODUCED SEPTEMBER 8TH, 1947 • CURRENT TO MAY 1ST, 1948
MOTOR SERIAL NUMBERS G200001 TO G203000

ENGINE REFINEMENTS. 3½ by 3¾ inches, 288 cubic inches; 130 hp at 3600 rpm; torque 226 lb/ft at 2000 rpm. *Compression ratio:* 7.0. Bore change rendered all engines identical, could use same piston.
TRANSMISSION REFINEMENTS. Rear axle ratio 3.9 standard.
BODY REFINEMENTS. *Paint:* ten selections, one dropped in August 1948. *Body types:* Eight touring sedan, club sedan and station sedan added.
PRICE RANGE. $2125-$3425.

SUPER EIGHT (2202, 2222, 2232)
MODEL YEARS: 1948-1949 • SERIES: TWENTY-SECOND
INTRODUCED SEPTEMBER 8TH, 1947 • CURRENT TO MAY 1ST, 1948
MOTOR SERIAL NUMBERS G400001 TO G43000

The 2232 convertible introduced July 25th, 1947.
ENGINE REFINEMENTS. 3½ by 4¼ inches, 327 cubic inches; 145 hp at 3600 rpm; torque 226 lb/ft at 2000 rpm. *Compression ratio:* 7.0. *Crankshaft:* five main bearings. *Carburetor:* Carter. *Cooling:* radiator capacity 20 quarts. *Note:* new 327 Super Eight derived from basic 288 block.
TRANSMISSION REFINEMENTS. Rear axle ratios, 3.9 for sedan, 4.09 for long wheelbase, 3.9 for convertible.
CHASSIS REFINEMENTS. *Wheelbase:* 141 inches for 2222, 120 inches for the others.
BODY REFINEMENTS. *Paint:* fourteen selections, five dropped in August 1948, four of them the introductory schemes for convertible only. *Body types:* convertible and four long-wheelbase cars added.
PRICE RANGE. $2665-$4000.

CUSTOM EIGHT
(2206, 2225, 2233, 2213)
MODEL YEARS: 1948-1949 • SERIES: TWENTY-SECOND
INTRODUCED SEPTEMBER 8TH, 1947 • CURRENT TO MAY 1ST, 1948
MOTOR SERIAL NUMBERS G600001 TO G612000

The 2233 convertible introduced July 25th, 1947, exact introductory date of the 2213 commercial type unknown.
ENGINE REFINEMENTS. Horsepower now 160 at 3600 rpm. Downgrading of horsepower remains unexplained.
TRANSMISSION REFINEMENTS. Rear axle ratios, 3.92 for sedan, 4.09 for long wheelbase, 3.92 for convertible.
CHASSIS REFINEMENTS. *Wheelbase:* 127 inches for 2206 and 2233; 148 inches for 2226; 156 inches for 2213.
BODY REFINEMENTS. *Paint:* fourteen selections, five dropped in August 1948, four of them the introductory schemes for convertible only. *Body types:* convertible and commercial cars added.
PRICE RANGE. $3625-$4868.

SIX (2320-5)
MODEL YEARS: 1949-1950 • SERIES: TWENTY-THIRD
INTRODUCED OCTOBER 1ST, 1949 • CURRENT TO DECEMBER 31ST, 1949
MOTOR SERIAL NUMBERS G1501 TO G1513

Packard's last use of the six, utilizing leftover Twenty-Second Series engines, most likely with leftover Twenty-Second Series bodies. Only the 141-inch wheelbase available. Export sedan and sedan taxi dropped.

EIGHT AND EIGHT DELUXE (2301)
MODEL YEARS: 1949-1950 • SERIES: TWENTY-THIRD
INTRODUCED MAY 2ND, 1949 • CURRENT TO AUGUST 1950
MOTOR SERIAL NUMBERS H200001 TO H290000 *

*Station sedans, leftover Twenty-Second Series production, carried G-prefix engine numbers.

ENGINE REFINEMENTS. A revision to 14 mm spark plugs in February 1950.
TRANSMISSION REFINEMENTS. Ultramatic two-speed torque converter with direct-speed lockup added as option.
BODY REFINEMENTS. *Paint:* eleven selections; one (Anniversary Gold) offered only on driveaway cars at introduction, not a regular option; eight colors dropped midway through 1950 model year; five additional colors added for 1950 model year. *Body types:* station sedans received no facelift.
PRICE RANGE. $2224-$3449.

SUPER
(2302, 2322, 2332)
MODEL YEARS: 1949-1950 • SERIES: TWENTY-THIRD
INTRODUCED MAY 2ND, 1949 • CURRENT TO AUGUST 1950
MOTOR SERIAL NUMBERS H400001 TO H416000

Engine and transmission refinements same as Eight.
CHASSIS REFINEMENTS. *Wheelbase:* 127 inches.
BODY REFINEMENTS. *Paint:* same as Eight. *Body types:* shared body with Custom; Super Deluxe series with Custom eggcrate grille; touring sedan, club sedan, limousine, long-wheelbase (141 inches) sedan added; standard and Deluxe version of long-wheelbase car dropped midway through the series, after 1949 model year.
PRICE RANGE. $2608-$3350.

CUSTOM
(2306, 2333, 2313)
MODEL YEARS: 1949-1950 • SERIES: TWENTY-THIRD
INTRODUCED MAY 2ND, 1949 • CURRENT TO AUGUST 1950
MOTOR SERIAL NUMBERS H600001 TO H603000

Engine and transmission refinements same as Eight.
BODY REFINEMENTS. *Paint:* same as Eight. *Interior:* headliner changed to transverse stitching vice fore-and-aft. *Body types:* all 148-inch wheelbase models and club sedan dropped.

200 (2401)
MODEL YEAR: 1951 • SERIES: TWENTY-FOURTH
INTRODUCED AUGUST 21ST, 1950 • CURRENT TO NOVEMBER 1951
MOTOR SERIAL NUMBERS J200001 TO J28000

ENGINE. L-head in-line eight; 3½ by 3¾ inches, 288 cubic inches; 135 hp at 3600 rpm; torque 230 lb/ft at 2000 rpm. *Compression ratio:* 7.0 standard, 7.5 optional. (Horsepower and torque figures for high compression head 138 hp at 3600 rpm, 235 lb/ft at 2000 rpm.) *Crankshaft:* five main bearings. *Ignition:* battery and coil, single breaker mixed make. *Carburetor:* Duplex downdraft Carter. *Lubrication:* full pressure. *Cooling:* forced water, capacity 20+1 quarts. *Note:* high compression head standard with Ultramatic.

TRANSMISSION. Three-speed Unimesh, overdrive, Ultramatic available. Rear axle ratios, 3.9 for standard Unimesh, 4.1 for overdrive, 3.54 for Ultramatic.
CHASSIS. *Frame:* pressed steel, I-beam X. *Axles:* front, reverse Elliot, Packard; rear, semi-floating, Packard. *Suspension:* front, independent parallelogram; rear, semi-elliptic, multiple leaf. *Steering:* worm and roller, Packard-Gemmer; ratio, gear, 20.4, overall, 28.3. *Braking:* internal expanding four-wheel hydraulic, swept area 171.5 square inches. *Wheels:* steel disc, 15x5 ½K tires. *Track:* front, 59.5 inches; rear, 60-23/32 inches. *Wheelbase:* 122 inches.
BODY. *Construction:* all steel. *Paint:* fifteen selections and two-tone combinations. *Interior:* broadcloth for sedans, leather and vinyl for convertible. *Instrumentation:* indicator lights used for battery and oil. *Body types:* business coupe, club sedan, touring sedan, convertible (the latter discontinued early in year, with 250 model substituted); deluxe versions available save for business coupe.
PRICE RANGE. $2195-$2616.

250 (2401)*
MODEL YEAR: 1951 • SERIES: TWENTY-FOURTH
INTRODUCED MARCH 16TH, 1951 • CURRENT TO NOVEMBER 1951
MOTOR SERIAL NUMBERS J400001 TO J425000

*The number 2431 has since come into common usage as the chassis number.
ENGINE. L-head, in-line, eight; 3 ½ by 4 ¼ inches, 327 cubic inches; 150 hp at 3600 rpm; torque 270 lb/ft at 2000 rpm. *Compression ratio:* 7.0 standard, 7.8 optional. (Horsepower and torque figures for high compression head 155 hp at 3600 rpm, 275 lb/ft at 2000 rpm.) All other specifications same as the 200 model.
TRANSMISSION AND CHASSIS. Same as 200 model.
BODY. *Construction:* all steel. *Paint:* fifteen selections plus two-tone combinations (hardtop only). *Interior:* leather and vinyl. *Instrumentation:* indicator lights used for battery and oil. *Body types:* convertible coupe and hardtop.
PRICE RANGE. $3166-$3391.

300 (2402, 2413)
MODEL YEAR: 1951 • SERIES: TWENTY-FOURTH
INTRODUCED AUGUST 21ST, 1950 • CURRENT TO NOVEMBER 1951
MOTOR SERIAL NUMBERS J400001 TO J425000

ENGINE. Same as 250 model.
TRANSMISSION. Rear axle ratios, 3.9 for standard Unimesh, 4.1 for overdrive, 3.54 for Ultramatic for 2402; 4.54 for standard Unimesh, 4.7 for overdrive, 4.36 for Ultramatic for commercial chassis 2413.
CHASSIS. Same as 250 model with following exceptions. *Steering:* worm and roller, Packard-Gemmer; ratio, gear, 22.3, overall, 30.9. *Braking:* internal expanding four-wheel hydraulic, swept area 208 square inches (292 for commercial 2413). *Wheels:* steel disc, 15x6K tires (16x5 ½F for commercial 2413.) *Track:* front, 60 inches, rear, 61-7/32 inches (59 ½ and 65-15/16 respectively for commercial 2413). *Wheelbase:* 127 inches (156 for commercial 2413).
BODY. *Construction:* all steel. *Paint:* fifteen selections plus two-tone combinations. *Interior:* broadcloth striped, rubber floor mat. *Instrumentation:* indicator lights used for battery and oil. *Body types:* four-door sedan plus commercial bodies.
PRICE RANGE. $2795-$3034 for sedans; $6460-$7920 for commercial cars.

PATRICIAN 400 (2406)

MODEL YEAR: 1951 • SERIES: TWENTY-FOURTH
INTRODUCED AUGUST 21ST, 1950 • CURRENT TO NOVEMBER 1951
MOTOR SERIAL NUMBERS J600001 TO J610000

ENGINE. L-head, in-line, eight; 3 ½ by 4 ¼ inches, 327 cubic inches; 155 hp at 3600 rpm; torque 275 lb/ft at 2000 rpm. *Compression ratio:* 7.8. *Crankshaft:* nine main bearings. All other specifications same as 200 model. *Note:* high compression head standard.
TRANSMISSION. Ultramatic standard, rear axle ratio 3.54.
CHASSIS. Same as 300 model.
BODY. *Construction:* all steel. *Paint:* fifteen selections plus two-tone combinations. *Interior:* solid-tone broadcloth with contrasting broadcloth insert. *Standard fittings:* Wilton carpets, rear center arm rest, hassocks. *Instrumentation:* indicator lights used for battery and oil. *Body types:* four-door sedan only.
PRICE RANGE. $3385-$3662.

200 (2501)
250 (2531); 300 (2502)
PATRICIAN 400 (2506)

MODEL YEAR: 1952 • SERIES: TWENTY-FIFTH
INTRODUCED NOVEMBER 1ST, 1951
MOTOR SERIAL NUMBERS K200001 TO K25000 (2501)
MOTOR SERIAL NUMBERS K400001 TO K424420 (2531 AND 2502)
MOTOR SERIAL NUMBERS K600001 TO K604169 (2506)

CHASSIS REFINEMENTS. *Track:* front, 60 inches; rear, 61-7/32 inches for 250 model.
BODY REFINEMENTS. *Paint:* twelve selections plus two-tone combinations for 200, 250 and 300 models. *Body types:* 200 business coupe dropped.
PRICE RANGE. $2424-$2695 for 2501; $3224-$3476 for 2531; $2795-$3034 for the sedans, $6650-$8090 for commercial cars 2513; $3689-$3737 for 2506.

CLIPPER (2601, 2633)

MODEL YEAR: 1953 • SERIES: TWENTY-SIXTH
MOTOR SERIAL NUMBERS L200001 TO L25000

ENGINE REFINEMENTS. Horsepower now 150 at 4000 rpm. Torque 260 lb/ft at 2200 rpm. *Compression ratio:* 7.7. *Ignition:* Delco.
TRANSMISSION REFINEMENTS. Rear axle ratios, 4.55 standard and overdrive, 4.1 Ultramatic for commercial chassis 2633.
CHASSIS REFINEMENTS. *Steering:* power steering available; ratio, gear, 18.6, overall, 22.5. *Track:* front, 59 ½ inches; rear, 65-15/16 inches for commercial chassis 2633. *Wheelbase:* 127 inches for commercial chassis 2633.
BODY REFINEMENTS. *Paint:* fourteen selections plus two-tone combinations. *Body types:* commercial cars added.
PRICE RANGE. $2544-$2805 for 2601; $3333-$3883 for 2633.

CLIPPER DELUXE (2611)

MODEL YEAR: 1953 • SERIES: TWENTY-SIXTH
MOTOR SERIAL NUMBERS L300001 TO L330920

ENGINE REFINEMENTS. Horsepower now 160 at 3600 rpm. Torque 295 lb/ft at 2000 rpm. *Compression ratio:* 8.0. *Ignition:* Delco. *Note:* 327 engine available in Junior line for the first time as standard; in all other respects this model shared specifications with 2601.
TRANSMISSION REFINEMENTS. Rear axle ratios, 3.9 for standard, 4.1 for overdrive, 3.23 for Ultramatic.
CHASSIS AND BODY REFINEMENTS. Same as 2601. *Body types:* two-door and four-door sedans added.
PRICE RANGE. $2691-$2745.

CAVALIER (2602)
PACKARD, MAYFAIR, CARIBBEAN (2631)

MODEL YEAR: 1953 • SERIES: TWENTY-SIXTH
MOTOR SERIAL NUMBERS L400001 TO L418552

ENGINE REFINEMENTS. Horsepower now 180 at 4000 rpm. Torque 300 lb/ft at 2000 rpm. *Compression ratio:* 8.0. *Ignition:* Delco. *Carburetor:* four-barrel Carter WCFB downdraft. (With two-barrel WGD installed on commercial chassis 2613, engine rated at 160 hp, torque 295 lb/ft.)
CHASSIS REFINEMENTS. *Steering:* power steering available; ratio, gear, 18.6, overall, 22.5. *Wheelbase:* 122 inches convertibles and hardtop (former 250).
BODY REFINEMENTS. *Paint:* fourteen selections plus two-tone combinations. *Body types:* Caribbean convertible added mid-year.
PRICE RANGE. $3244-$3486; $5210 for Caribbean; $6700-$8250 for commercial cars 2613.

PATRICIAN (2606)
PACKARD (2626)

MODEL YEAR: 1953 • SERIES: TWENTY-SIXTH
MOTOR SERIAL NUMBERS L600001 TO L607829

ENGINE REFINEMENTS. Horsepower now 180 at 4000 rpm. Torque 300 lb/ft at 2000 rpm. *Compression ratio:* 8.0. *Ignition:* Auto-Lite. *Carburetor:* four-barrel Carter WCFB downdraft.
TRANSMISSION REFINEMENTS. Rear axle ratios, 3.54 Ultramatic for 2606; 3.9 standard, 4.1 overdrive, 3.9 Ultramatic for 2626.
CHASSIS REFINEMENTS. *Wheelbase:* 148 inches for 2626.
BODY REFINEMENTS. *Paint:* fourteen selections plus two-tone combinations for 2606; all 2626 cars painted either black or dark blue. *Interior:* leather front compartment for limousine. *Body types:* limousine and Executive eight-passenger sedan on new 2626 chassis; a Derham formal sedan (converted Patrician with formal padded roof) on chassis 2606.
PRICE RANGE. $3740 for Patrician; $6531 for Derham; $6900-$7100 for 2626.

Model 2406 Patrician 400, 1951.

CLIPPER SPECIAL (5400, 5433)
CLIPPER DELUXE (5401)
CLIPPER SUPER (5411)
MODEL YEAR: 1954 • SERIES: FIFTY-FOURTH
MOTOR SERIAL NUMBERS M200001 TO M202000 (5400, 5433)
MOTOR SERIAL NUMBERS M300001 TO — — (5401, 5411)

Clipper Special was a new model designation devised to retain the 288-cubic-inch engine used only in this car. The former 2601 line, now the 5401, upgraded to the 327-cubic-inch engine chassis and renamed the Clipper Deluxe. The former Clipper Deluxe 2611, now the 5411, upgraded and renamed the Clipper Super.
ENGINE REFINEMENTS. Horsepower now 165 at 3600 rpm for the 5401 and 5411.
BODY REFINEMENTS. *Body types:* two-door and four-door sedans and Henney Junior available in Clipper Special line; Panama hardtop (the first Clipper hardtop) available in Clipper Super line.
PRICE RANGE. $2544-$2594 (5400); $4350 (commercial 5433); $3590-$3765 (5401, 5411).

CAVALIER (5402)
MODEL YEAR: 1954 • SERIES: FIFTY-FOURTH
MOTOR SERIAL NUMBERS M400001 TO M402638

ENGINE REFINEMENTS. Horsepower now 185 at 4000 rpm. Torque 310 lb/ft at 2200 rpm. The 327-cubic-inch engine was used in this Senior model only.
BODY REFINEMENTS. Successor to the 2602-2631-2613 chassis group of 1953, all body types save the Cavalier sedan were dropped from 5402 and moved to the new 359 engine.
PRICE RANGE. $3344.

PATRICIAN (5406)
PACKARD PATRICIAN CUSTOM (5426)
PACKARD, PACIFIC, CARIBBEAN (5431)
MODEL YEAR: 1954 • SERIES: FIFTY-FOURTH
MOTOR SERIAL NUMBERS M600001 TO M605618

ENGINE REFINEMENTS. 3-9/16 by 4½ inches, 359 cubic inches; 212 hp at 4000 rpm; torque 330 lb/ft at 2200 rpm. *Compression ratio:* 8.7. The aluminum-head 359 engine was the ultimate development of the flat-head straight eight design.
TRANSMISSION REFINEMENTS. Rear axle ratios, 3.54 Ultramatic for 5406; 3.9 standard, 4.1 overdrive, 3.54 Ultramatic for 5431; 4.1 standard, 4.55 overdrive, 3.9 Ultramatic for 5426; 4.54 standard, 4.7 overdrive, 4.36 Ultramatic for commercial chassis 5413.
CHASSIS REFINEMENTS. *Wheelbase:* 122 inches for 5431.
BODY REFINEMENTS. *Paint:* Pacific hardtop received mid-year option of two new colors available in single two-tone combination; commercial 5413 painted in enamel; all 5426 cars available only in mandatory dark colors. *Interior:* new matelasse option. *Body types:* the former 2631 chassis line, equipped with new 359 engine, moved to equivalency with Patrician; two convertibles and a hardtop added; Derham formal sedan dropped.
PRICE RANGE. $3827-$3935; $6100 for Caribbean; $5610-$5960 for 5426; $7150-$8208 for commercial cars (5413).

CLIPPER DELUXE AND SUPER (5540)
MODEL YEAR: 1955 • SERIES: FIFTY-FIFTH
INTRODUCED JANUARY 17TH, 1955
MOTOR SERIAL NUMBERS SAME AS VEHICLE SERIAL NUMBERS

ENGINE. OHV 90° V-8; 3-13/16 by 3½ inches, 320 cubic inches; 225 hp at 4600 rpm; torque 325 lb/ft at 2400 rpm. *Compression ratio:* 8.5. *Crankshaft:* counterbalanced cast steel, five main bearings. *Ignition:* battery and coil, 12-volt positive ground, Auto-Lite, *Carburetor:* Carter four-barrel downdraft. *Lubrication:* full pressure. *Cooling:* forced water, capacity 26+ ½ + ½ quarts.
TRANSMISSION. Synchromesh, overdrive, Twin Ultramatic available. Rear axle ratios: for the Deluxe sedan, 3.9, 3.59, 4.1 standard, 3.9, 3.54, 4.1 overdrive, 3.07, 3.23, 4.1, 3.9 Ultramatic; for the Super sedan and Panama hardtop, 3.9, 3.54, 4.1 standard, 3.9, 3.54, 4.1 overdrive, 3.23, 3.07, 4.1, 3.9 Ultramatic.
CHASSIS. *Frame:* channel side members plus X. *Axles:* front, reverse Elliot, Packard; rear, semi-floating, Packard. *Suspension:* front, independent parallelogram, coil; rear, semi-elliptic, multiple leaf. *Steering:* worm and roller, Packard-Gemmer; ratio, gear 22.3, overall 30.9; 18.2 and 22.0 respectively with power steering. *Braking:* internal expanding four-wheel hydraulic, swept area 191.8 square inches. *Wheels:* steel disc, 15x5½K tires. *Track:* front, 59.7 inches; rear, 60.0 inches. *Wheelbase:* 122 inches. *Note:* Torsion-Level suspension an option on Super sedan and Panama hardtop mid-year.
BODY. *Construction:* all steel. *Paint:* seventeen selections plus two-tone combinations. *Interior:* nylon, vinyl, leather, cloth options. *Instrumentation:* indicator lights used vice ammeter and oil gauge. *Body types:* sedan in Deluxe; sedan and Panama hardtop in Super.
PRICE RANGE. $2586-$2776.

CLIPPER CUSTOM (5560)
MODEL YEAR: 1955 • SERIES: FIFTY-FIFTH
INTRODUCED JANUARY 17TH, 1955
MOTOR SERIAL NUMBERS SAME AS VEHICLE SERIAL NUMBERS

ENGINE. OHV 90° V-8; 4 by 3½ inches, 352 cubic inches; 245 hp at 4600 rpm; torque 355 lb/ft at 2400 rpm. *Compression ratio:* 8.5. *Ignition:* Delco. *Carburetor:* Rochester. All other specifications the same as 5540.
TRANSMISSION. Same as for Super sedan and Panama hardtop.
CHASSIS AND BODY. Same as 5540. *Body types:* sedan and Constellation hardtop.
PRICE RANGE. $2926-$3076.

PATRICIAN, FOUR HUNDRED,
CARIBBEAN (5580)
MODEL YEAR: 1955 • SERIES: FIFTY-FIFTH
INTRODUCED JANUARY 17TH, 1955
MOTOR SERIAL NUMBERS SAME AS VEHICLE SERIAL NUMBERS

ENGINE. OHV 90° V-8; 4 by 3½ inches, 352 cubic inches; torque 355 lb/ft at 2400 rpm. Horsepower for Patrician and Four Hundred 260 at 4600 rpm; for Caribbean 275 at 4800 rpm. *Compression ratio:* 8.5. *Crankshaft:* counterbalanced cast steel, five main bearings. *Ignition:* battery and coil, 12-volt positive ground, Delco. *Carburetor:* Rochester four-barrel downdraft (for the Caribbean, two Rochester four-barrel downdraft). *Lubrication:* full pressure. *Cooling:* forced water, capacity 26+ ½ + ½ quarts.
TRANSMISSION. Twin Ultramatic, with two forward speeds plus direct

clutch; rear axle ratios, 3.07, 3.23, 3.54, 3.9.
CHASSIS. *Frame:* channel side members plus X; additional depth reinforcement for Caribbean. *Axles:* front, reverse Elliot, Packard; rear, semi-floating, Packard, with torque arms. *Suspension:* Packard full-length torsion bar (Torsion-Level) with automatic load compensator. *Steering:* worm and roller, Packard-Gemmer; ratio, gear 22.3, overall 30.9; 18.6 and 22.5 respectively with power steering. *Braking:* internal expanding four-wheel hydraulic, swept area 208.25 square inches. *Wheels:* 15x6L tires. *Track:* front, 60 inches; rear, 60.9 inches. *Wheelbase:* 127 inches.
BODY. *Construction:* all steel. *Paint:* seventeen selections plus two-tone combinations; Caribbean with four additional three-tone combinations one of which included a special eighteenth color. *Interior:* Jacquard, broadcloth, nylon, leather for the Patrician; nylon, leather, orchid boucle, patent leather for the Four Hundred; leather for the Caribbean. *Standard fittings:* everything standard on Caribbean save for wire wheels and air conditioning. *Body types:* Patrician sedan, Four Hundred hardtop, Caribbean convertible.
PRICE RANGE. $3890-$3930 for Patrician and Four Hundred; $5932 for Caribbean.

CLIPPER DELUXE AND SUPER (5640)
MODEL YEAR: 1956 • SERIES: FIFTY-SIXTH
INTRODUCED NOVEMBER 3RD, 1955
ENGINE REFINEMENTS. 4 by 3 ½ inches, 352 cubic inches; 240 hp at 4600 rpm; torque 350 lb/ft at 2800 rpm. *Compression ratio:* 9.5. *Ignition:* negative ground. *Carburetor:* two-barrel.
TRANSMISSION REFINEMENTS. Revision from traditional Packard hypoid differential to Packard-Spicer. Rear axle ratios, 3.54 and 4.09 standard; 3.54 and 4.09 overdrive; 2.87, 3.07, 3.31, 3.54 and 4.09 Ultramatic. Touch-Button Ultramatic introduced.
CHASSIS REFINEMENTS. Torsion-Level suspension available on Deluxe; made standard on all vehicles mid-year.
BODY REFINEMENTS. *Paint:* eighteen selections plus two-tone combinations; one additional color mid-year (soft pink) available only in combination with white. *Body types:* "Panama" name dropped from Super hardtop.
PRICE RANGE. $2731-$2916.

CLIPPER CUSTOM (5660)
PACKARD EXECUTIVE (5670)
MODEL YEAR: 1956 • SERIES: FIFTY-SIXTH
The Clipper Custom was introduced November 3rd, 1955 and was current to March 5th, 1956. The Packard Executive was introduced March 5th, 1956, current to June 25th, 1956.
ENGINE REFINEMENTS. Horsepower 275 at 4600 rpm. Torque 380 lb/ft at 2800 rpm. *Compression ratio:* 9.5. *Ignition:* negative ground.
TRANSMISSION REFINEMENTS. Refinements and rear axle ratios same as for 5640.
CHASSIS REFINEMENTS. Torsion-Level suspension made standard on all vehicles mid-year.
BODY REFINEMENTS. *Paint:* eighteen selections plus two-tone combinations; one additional color introduced mid-year (soft pink) available only with white as two-tone combination; this color not available on Custom, discontinued earlier. *Body types:* Executive sedan and hardtop available.
PRICE RANGE. $3069-$3560.

CARIBBEAN (5688)
PATRICIAN, FOUR HUNDRED (5688)
MODEL YEAR: 1956 • SERIES: FIFTY-SIXTH
INTRODUCED NOVEMBER 3RD, 1955 • CURRENT TO JUNE 1956
ENGINE REFINEMENTS. 4 ⅛ by 3 ½ inches, 374 cubic inches; torque 405 lb/ft at 2800 rpm. Horsepower for Patrician and Four Hundred 290 at 4600 rpm; for the Caribbean 310 at 4600 rpm. *Compression ratio:* 10.0. *Ignition:* negative ground.
TRANSMISSION REFINEMENTS. Standard and overdrive transmissions again available as regular options. Rear axle ratios same as for 5640.
BODY REFINEMENTS. *Paint:* eighteen selections plus two-tone combinations; Caribbean available with four additional three-tone combinations; one additional color for Patrician and Four Hundred mid-year (soft pink) available only with white as two-tone combination. *Interior:* reverse cushions, Jacquard/leather, available on Caribbean. *Body types:* Caribbean hardtop added.
PRICE RANGE. $4160-$4190 for Patrician and Four Hundred; $5495-$5995 for Caribbean

CLIPPER (57L)
MODEL YEAR: 1957 • SERIES: FIFTY-SEVENTH
Car introduced January 1957. Motor Serial Numbers began with LS 101.
ENGINE. OHV 90° V-8; 3.56 by 3.63 inches, 289 cubic inches; 275 hp at 4800 rpm; torque 333 lb/ft at 3200 rpm. *Compression ratio:* 7.5 standard, 7.0 optional. *Crankshaft:* cast iron, five main bearings. *Ignition:* coil and battery, 12-volt, negative ground. *Carburetor:* Stromberg two-barrel pressurized. *Lubrication:* full pressure. *Cooling:* forced water, capacity 17+1 quarts.
TRANSMISSION. Overdrive or Flightomatic, with four or three forward speeds respectively; Salisbury hypoid differential; rear axle ratios, 4.27, 3.92, 4.55 overdrive; 3.31, 3.07, 3.54 Flightomatic.
CHASSIS. *Axles:* front, reverse Elliot; rear, semi-floating. *Suspension:* front, independent parallelogram, variable rate coil (town sedan), coil (country sedan); rear, semi-elliptic multiple leaf, with helper leaves for country sedan. *Steering:* cam and roller, Ross, variable ratio; gear 20-22-20; overall 27.5-24.5-27.5. *Braking:* internal expanding four-wheel hydraulic, swept area 195.25 square inches. *Wheels:* 15x15 ½K tires. *Track:* front, 56-11/16 inches; rear, 55-11/16 inches. *Wheelbase:* 120 ½ inches for town sedan; 116 ½ inches for country sedan.
BODY. *Construction:* all steel. *Paint:* baked enamel, thirteen selections plus two-tone combinations. *Body types:* town sedan (four-door) and country sedan (four-door wagon) both a facelift of 1956 Studebaker President.
PRICE RANGE. $2933-$3384.

PACKARD AND HAWK (58L)
MODEL YEAR: 1958 • SERIES: FIFTY-EIGHTH
Motor Serial Numbers began with 58L-101.
ENGINE REFINEMENTS. Horsepower 225 at 4500 rpm; 275 at 4800 rpm for the Hawk. *Compression ratio:* 8.0 and 7.5; 7.5 and 7.0 for the Hawk. *Carburetor:* Carter four-barrel; Stromberg two-barrel pressurized for the Hawk. The Hawk was the only supercharged Packard for 1958.
TRANSMISSION REFINEMENTS. Rear axle ratios, 3.31 standard, 3.54 optional Flightomatic; 4.09, 3.54, 3.73, 3.92, 4.27 overdrive.
BODY REFINEMENTS. *Body types:* hardtop, Hawk hardtop added.
PRICE RANGE. $3212-$3995.

PACKARD POSTWAR PRODUCTION BODY/CHASSIS CHART

Because the data following was too complicated—indeed convoluted, in the memorable tradition of the Packard Motor Car Company—to include in the historical text portion of the book, it is presented here. The chart following, prepared by George Hamlin, represents numbers assigned to Packard chassis and bodies for the entire postwar production period. Chassis names are indicated in caps, and chassis numbers are shown in bold type. Body numbers listed directly below a chassis number are those marketed on that chassis either by Packard or Henney. When a descriptive note appears between columns, it indicates that nomenclature or wheelbase was changed.

	1946 Clipper 21st Series	1947 Clipper 21st Series	1948 22nd Series	1949 22nd Series	1949 23rd Series	1950 23rd Series
SIX 120"-wb Chassis	**2100**	**2100**	**2240**	**2240-9**		
Touring Sedan	1682	2182	2282	2282-9		
Club Sedan	1685	2185				
Taxi Chassis	**2130**	**2130**				
Partition Taxi	1684	2184				
Sedan Taxi	1686	2186	2286	2286-9		
SIX 141"-wb Chassis			**2220**	**2220-9**		**2320-5**
NY-type Taxi			2280	2280-9		2340-5
EIGHT Standard Chassis	**2101**		2201	**2201-9**	2301	2301-5
Touring Sedan	1692		2292	2292-9	2392	2392-5
Station Sedan			2293	2293-9	2393	2393-5
Club Sedan			2295	2295-9	2395	2395-5
EIGHT Deluxe Chassis	**2111**	**2111**	**2211**	**2211-9**		
Touring Sedan	1612	2112	2262	2262-9	2362	2362-5
Club Sedan	1615	2115	2265	2265-9	2365	2365-5
SUPER EIGHT 127"-wb Chassis	**2103**	**2103**	**2202**	**2202-9**	**2302**	**2302-5**
Touring Sedan	1672	2172	2272	2272-9	2382	2382-5
Club Sedan	1675	2175	2275	2275-9	2385	2385-5
Touring Sedan Deluxe					2372	2372-5
Club Sedan Deluxe					2375	2375-5
SUPER EIGHT 141"-wb Chassis			**2222**	**2222-9**	**2322**	
Touring Sedan			2277	2277-9		
Deluxe Touring Sedan			2271	2271-9	2371	
Limousine			2276	2276-9		
Deluxe Limousine			2270	2270-9	2370	

	1946 Clipper 21st Series	1947 Clipper 21st Series	1948 22nd Series	1949 22nd Series	1949 23rd Series	1950 23rd Series
SUPER EIGHT Convertible Chassis			**2232**	**2232-9**	**2332**	**2332-5**
Convertible Victoria			2279	2279-9	2379	2379-5
CUSTOM EIGHT 127"-wb Chassis	**2106**	**2106**	**2206**	**2206-9**	**2306**	**2306-5**
Touring Sedan	1622	2122	2252	2252-9	2352	2352-5
Club Sedan	1625	2125	2255	2255-9		
CUSTOM EIGHT 148"-wb Chassis	**2126**	**2126**	**2226**	**2226-9**		
Limousine	1650	2150	2250	2250-9		
7-Passenger Sedan	1651	2151	2251	2251-9		
CUSTOM EIGHT Convertible Chassis			**2233**	**2233-9**	**2333**	**2333-5**
Convertible Victoria			2259	2259-9	2359	2359-5
CUSTOM EIGHT Commercial Chassis			**2213**	**2213-9**	**2313**	**2313-5**
Landau 3-Way Hearse, Elecdraulic			14800	14900	14900	15000
Landau Combination Car			14801	14901	14901	15001
Landau 3-Way Hearse			14802	14902	14902	15002
Landau Rear Loading Hearse			14803	14903	14903	15003
Landau Ambulance			14804	14904	14904	15004
Limousine 3-Way Hearse, Elecdraulic			14890	14990	14990	15090
Limousine Combination Car			14891	14991	14991	15091
Limousine 3-Way Hearse			14892	14992	14992	15092
Limousine Rear Loading Hearse			14893	14993	14993	15093
Limousine Ambulance			14894	14994	14994	15094
Limousine Service Car			14895	14995	14995	15095
Limousine Flower Car			14896	14996	14996	15096
Limousine Utility Car			—	—	—	15097

	1951 24th Series	1952 25th Series	1953 26th Series	1954 54th Series
CLIPPER SPECIAL Chassis				**5400**
4-door Sedan				5482
2-door Sedan				5485
"200" Standard Chassis	**2401**	**2501**	CLIPPER **2601**	CLIPPER DELUXE **5401**
4-door Sedan	2492	2592	2692	5492
2-door Sedan	2495	2595	2695	5495
Sportster 2-door Sedan			2697	5497
Business Coupe	2498			
"200" Deluxe Chassis			CLIPPER DELUXE **2611**	CLIPPER SUPER **5411**
4-door Sedan	2462	2562	**2662**	5462
2-door Sedan	2465	2565	**2665**	5465
Panama 2-door Hardtop				5467
CLIPPER Commercial Chassis			2633	**5433**
"250" Chassis	**2431**	**2531**	**2631***	**5431**
Mayfair 2-door Hardtop	2467	2577	2677	PACIFIC 5477
Caribbean 2-door Convertible			2678	5478
2-door Convertible	2469	2579	2679	5479
"300" Chassis	**2402**	**2502**	CAVALIER **2602***	**5402**
4-door Sedan	2472	2572	2672	5472
"300" Commercial Chassis	**2413**	**2513**	**2613***	**5413**
Landau 3-Way Hearse, Elecdraulic	5100	5200	5300	5400
Landau Combination Car	5101	5201	5301	5401
Landau 3-Way Hearse	5102	5202	5302	5402
Landau Rear Loading Hearse	5103	5203	5303	5403
Landau Ambulance	5104	5204	5304	5404
Limousine 3-Way Hearse, Elecdraulic	5190	5290	5390	5490
Limousine Combination Car	5191	5291	5391	5491
Limousine 3-Way Hearse	5192	5292	5392	5492
Limousine Rear Loading Hearse	5193	5293	5393	5493
Limousine Ambulance	5194	5294	5394	5494
Service Car	5195	5295	5395	5495
Flower Car	5196	5296	5396	5496
Utility Car	5197	5297	5397	—
Station Wagon	—	—	—	5460-S

	1951 24th Series	1952 25th Series	1953 26th Series	1954 54th Series
"400" Chassis	**2406**	**2506**	**2606***	**5406**
Patrician Sedan	2452	2552	2652	5452
Formal Sedan (Derham)			2653	5453
PACKARD 149"-wb Chassis			**2626***	PATRICIAN	**5426**
Limousine (Henney)			2650		5450
7-Passenger Sedan (Henney)			2651		5451

*Indicates dropping of the designations: 200, 250, 300, 400.

	1955 55th Series	1956 56th Series	1957 57th Series	1958 58th Series
CLIPPER DELUXE SUPER CHASSIS	**5540**	**5640**		
Deluxe 4-door	5522	5622		
Super 4-door	5542	5642		
Super Panama Hardtop	5547	5647*		
CLIPPER CUSTOM Chassis	**5560**	**5660**		
Custom 4-door	5562	5662		
Custom Constellation Hardtop	5567	5667		
EXECUTIVE Chassis		**5670**		
Executive 4-door		5672A		
Executive Hardtop		5677A		
PACKARD Chassis	**5580**	**5680**	**57L**	**58L**
Patrician 4-door	5582	5682		
Four Hundred Hardtop	5587	5687		
4-door Sedan			57L-Y8	58L-J8
2-door Hardtop				58L-Y8
Station Wagon			57L-P10	58L-P8
Hawk Hardtop				58L-K9
CARIBBEAN Chassis		**5688**		
Caribbean Hardtop		5697		
Caribbean Convertible	5588	5699		

*Panama name dropped

APPENDIX VIII

THE
PACKARD
IN
PRODUCTION

A Roster of the Cars Built

1899-1958

In 1953 the Packard Motor Car Company published a compendium entitled *Historical Record of Packard Car Models, Specifications, Production, Serial Numbers and Retail Prices.* While an important reference work in most respects, historians have been aware for years that the volume contained some glaring inaccuracies. Since it is, however, the most substantive record the Packard company produced, it has been used as the basis for the listing herewith, with corrections made in those cases where errors occurred.

Obvious among these were Packard's figures for the years of production in Warren. Packard's compilation indicated one car built in 1899, no more than forty-three vehicles total for the years through 1903, and ignored altogether the Models G and K. (Amusingly, a half century after Henry B. Joy had enjoyed loathing the K so much, the Packard Motor Car Company was amiably insisting that it had never existed at all.) The figures herewith for the Warren years, thus, are completely new—and were gathered from sources contemporary to that period, viz., the diaries of James Ward and William Doud Packard and the Henry Joy papers. (It might be noted that conjecture remains as to whether the five Model A's noted for 1899 were actually completed that year; it is known definitely that production was begun but in that borning year of the Packard business whether the small Packard workforce found the time to finish all five cars is moot.)

Similarly, the figures for the early-to-mid-1920's—wherein again the Packard record of 1953 was grossly in error—were amended by fresh figures, these interestingly supplied by the Packard company itself in a chart prepared in 1936 ("Truck and Passenger Car Shipments by Calendar Year and by Model, 1904-1936") and unearthed recently in the National Automotive History Collection of the Detroit Public Library. Consulted as well for cross-checking purposes for the between-wars years were the following sources contemporary to that period: *Report on the Motor Vehicle Industry*, published by the U.S. Federal Trade Commission; *A Financial History of the American Automobile Industry*, authored by Lawrence H. Seltzer; the *Automotive Daily News Almanac* for 1936; the "Record of Packard Motor Numbers" from the *Packard Service Letter* of September 1st, 1938—as well as a compilation, apparently provided by Packard, in a lengthy article on the company appearing in *Steel* magazine, May 9th, 1949. Postwar figures subsequent to 1953 were acquired via a variety of documentary sources contemporary to the last years of the Packard Motor Car Company.

Throughout the preparation of this listing, the authors of the various sections of this book were consulted, provided figures themselves or verified the figures as presented here. The pages following represent the most complete compilation of the Packard production record ever published. It is as accurate as available figures made possible.

MODEL		UNITS
Model A	1899	5
Model B	1900	49
Model C	1901	81
Model E	1901	1
Model F	1902-1903	179
Model G	1902	4
Model K	1903	34
Model L	1904	207
Model N	1905	403
Model S	1906	728
Thirty (total units: 9,540)		
Model U	1907	1,128
Model UA	1908	1,303
Model UB, UBS	1909	1,501
Model UC, UCS	1910	2,493
Model UD, UDS	1911	1,865
Model UE	1912	1,250
Eighteen (total units: 2,278)		
Model NA	1909	802
Model NB	1910	766
Model NC	1911	360
Model NE	1912	350
Packard Six (total units: 9,569)		
Model 1-48 (Six)	1912	1,349
Model 2-48 (1348)	1913	1,000
Model 1-38 (1338 and 1438)	1913-1914	1,618
Model 3-48 (1448)	1914	1,499
Model 2-38	1914	1,501
Model 4-48	1914	441
Model 3-38	1915	1,801
Model 5-48	1915	360
Twin Six (total: 35,102)		
Series 1-25	1916	3,606
Series 1-35	1916	4,140
Series 2-25	1917-1918	4,950
Series 2-35	1917-1918	4,049
Series 3-25	1918-1920	4,181
Series 3-35	1918-1923	14,176
Single Six (total: 35,360)		
Model 116	1920-1922	8,800
Model 126	1922-1923	18,192
Model 133	1922-1923	8,368
Single Eight (total: 8,401)		
Model 136	1923-1925	3,507
Model 143	1923-1925	4,894
Six (total: 11,225)		
Model 226	1924-1925	8,094
Model 233	1924-1925	3,131
Eight (total: 7,912)		
Model 236	1925-1926	2,794
Model 243	1925-1926	5,118
Six (total: 40,358)		
Model 326	1925-1926	24,668
Model 333	1925-1926	15,690
Eight (total: 4,486)		
Model 336	1927	1,245
Model 343	1927	3,241
Six (total: 25,335)		
Model 426	1927	14,401
Model 433	1927	10,934
Six (total: 41,750)		
Model 526	1928	28,336
Model 533	1928	13,414
Eight Model 443	1928	7,800
Sixth Series (total: 54,992)		
Standard Eight 626	1929	26,070
Standard Eight 633	1929	17,060
Custom Eight 640	1929	9,801
DeLuxe Eight 645	1929	2,061
Seventh Series (total: 36,364)		
Standard Eight 726	1930	15,731
Standard Eight 733	1930	12,531
Speedster Eight 734	1930	113
Custom Eight 740	1930	6,200
DeLuxe Eight 745	1930	1,789
Eighth Series (total: 15,450)		
Standard Eight 826	1931	6,009
Standard Eight 833	1931	6,096
DeLuxe Eight 840	1931	2,035
DeLuxe Eight 845	1931	1,310
Ninth Series (total: 16,613)		
Light Eight 900	1932	6,750
Standard Eight 901	1932	3,922
Standard Eight 902	1932	3,737
DeLuxe Eight 903	1932	955
DeLuxe Eight 904	1932	700
Twin Six 905	1932	311
Twin Six 906	1932	238
Tenth Series (total: 4,800)		
Eight 1001	1933	1,881
Eight 1002	1933	1,099
Super Eight 1003	1933	512
Super Eight 1004	1933	788
Twelve 1005	1933	244
Twelve 1006	1933	276
Eleventh Series (total: 8,000)		
Eight 1100-1101-1102	1934	5,120
Super Eight 1103-1104-1105	1934	1,920
Twelve 1106-1107-1108	1934	960
Twelfth Series (total: 31,949)		
—Senior, 6,954; Junior, 24,995—		
Eight 1200-1201-1202	1935	4,781
Super Eight 1203-1204-1205	1935	1,392
Twelve 1207-1208*	1935	781
One Twenty 120-A	1935	24,995

*NOTE: Curiously Packard did not include the 1206 five-passenger sedan in this model year, nor would it in the Fourteenth, Sixteenth and Seventeenth Series Twelves to follow. This may explain the discrepancy in these years between engines produced as per motor serial numbers and cars produced as per the Packard figures, the thirty- or fifty-odd less of the latter in these cases representing the five-passenger short sedans.

Fourteenth Series (total: 61,027)
—Senior, 5,985; Junior, 55,042—

MODEL		UNITS
Eight 1400-1401-1402	1936	3,973
Super Eight 1403-1404-1405	1936	1,330
Twelve 1407-1408	1936	682
One Twenty 120-B	1936	55,042
Fifteenth Series (total: 122,593)		
—Senior, 7,093; Junior, 115,500—		
Super Eight 1500-1501-1502	1937	5,793
Twelve 1506-1507-1508	1937	1,300
One Twenty 120-C; CD; 138 CD	1937	50,100
Six 115-C	1937	65,400
Sixteenth Series (total: 55,718)		
—Senior, 3,044; Junior, 52,674—		
Six 1600	1938	30,050
Eight (One Twenty) 1601-1602	1938	22,624
Super Eight 1603-1604-1605	1938	2,478
Twelve 1607-1608	1938	566
Seventeenth Series (total: 46,405)		
—Senior, 4,408; Junior, 41,997—		
Six 1700	1939	24,350
One Twenty 1701-1702	1939	17,647
Super-8 1703-1705	1939	3,962
Twelve 1707-1708	1939	446
Eighteenth Series (total: 98,000)		
—Senior, 7,562; Junior, 90,438—		
One-Ten 1800	1940	62,300
One-Twenty 1801	1940	28,138
One-Sixty 1803-1804-1805	1940	5,662
One-Eighty 1806-1807-1808	1940	1,900
Nineteenth Series (total: 72,855)		
—Senior, 4,455; Junior, 51,800—		
One-Ten 1900	1941	34,700
One-Twenty 1901	1941	17,100
One-Sixty 1903-1904-1905	1941	3,525
One-Eighty 1906-1907-1908	1941	930
Clipper 1951	1941	16,600
Twentieth Series (total: 33,776)		
—Senior, 3,252; Junior, 30,524—		
Six 2000-2010-		
2020-2030	1942	11,325
Eight 2001-2011-2021	1942	19,199
One-Sixty 2003-2004-2005-		
2023-2055	1942	2,580
One-Eighty 2006-2007-2008	1942	672
Twenty-First Series (total: 80,660)		
Clipper Six 2100, taxi 2130	1946-1947	30,931
Clipper Eight 2101	1946-1947	6,526
Super Clipper 2103	1946-1947	9,726
Custom Super Clipper 2106	1946-1947	7,162
Clipper Eight DeLuxe 2111	1946-1947	23,234
Custom Super Clipper 2126	1946-1947	3,081
Twenty-Second Series (total: 95,495)		
Eight 2201	1948	12,782
Eight DeLuxe 2211	1948	47,807
Super Eight 2202	1948	12,921
Super Eight 2222	1948	1,766
Super Eight 2232	1948	7,763
Custom Eight 2206	1948	5,936
Custom Eight 2226	1948	230
Custom Eight 2213	1948	1,941
Custom Eight 2233	1948	1,105
Six 2220 taxi	1948	1,316
Six 2240	1948	1,928
Twenty-Second Series (total: 53,138)		
Eight 2201-9	1949	13,553
Eight DeLuxe 2211-9	1949	27,422
Super Eight 2202-9	1949	5,879
Super Eight 2222-9	1949	867
Super Eight 2232-9	1949	1,237
Custom Eight 2206-9	1949	2,990
Custom Eight 2226-9	1949	50
Custom Eight 2213-9	1949	220
Custom Eight 2233-9	1949	213
Six 2220-9 taxi	1949	25
Six 2240-9	1949	682
Twenty-Third Series (total: 63,817)		
Eight, Eight Deluxe 2301	1949	53,168
Super, Super Deluxe 2302	1949	8,759
Super, Super Deluxe 2322	1949	4
Super, Super Deluxe 2332	1949	685
Custom 2306	1949	973
Custom 2333	1949	68
Custom 2313	1949	160
Twenty-Third Series (total: 42,640)		
Eight, Eight Deluxe 2301-5	1950	36,471
Super, Super Deluxe 2302-5	1950	4,528
Super, Super Deluxe 2332-5	1950	600
Custom 2306-5	1950	707
Custom 2333-5	1950	77
Custom 2313-5	1950	244
Six 2320-5 taxi	1950	13
Twenty-Fourth Series (total: 100,713)		
200 model 2401	1951	24,310
200 Deluxe model 2401	1951	47,052
250 model 2401	1951	4,640
300 model 2402	1951	15,309
300 model 2413	1951	401
Patrician 400 model 2406	1951	9,001
Twenty-Fifth Series (total: 62,921)		
200, 200 Deluxe models 2501	1952	46,720
250 model 2531	1952	5,201
300 model 2502	1952	6,705
300 model 2513	1952	320
Patrician 400 model 2506	1952	3,975
Twenty-Sixth Series (total: 90,277)		
Clipper 2601		
four-door sedan	1953	23,126
club sedan	1953	6,370
Sportster	1953	3,672
chassis	1953	1
Clipper Deluxe 2611		
four-door sedan	1953	26,027
club sedan	1953	4,678
Clipper Commercial 2633		
Henney commercial bodies	1953	380
Packard 2631		
Mayfair hardtop	1953	5,150
Caribbean convertible	1953	750
Convertible	1953	1,518
Cavalier 2602		
Cavalier sedan	1953	10,799
Packard Commercial 2613		
Henney commercial bodies	1953	166
Patrician 2606		
Patrician sedan	1953	7,456
Derham formal sedan	1953	25*
Packard 2626		
Henney limousine	1953	50
Henney Executive Sedan	1953	100
Various chassis 2602-2606-2631	1953	9

*Made from completed Patrician sedans

MODEL		UNITS
Fifty-Fourth Series (total: 31,291)		
Clipper Special 5400		
four-door sedan	1954	970
club sedan	1954	912
Clipper Deluxe 5401		
four-door sedan	1954	7,610
club sedan	1954	1,470
Sportster	1954	1,336
Clipper Super 5411		
four-door sedan	1954	6,270
club sedan	1954	887
Panama hardtop	1954	3,618
Clipper Commercial 5433		
Henney commercial body	1954	120
Packard 5431		
Pacific hardtop	1954	1,189
Caribbean convertible	1954	400
Convertible	1954	863
Chassis	1954	1
Cavalier 5402		
Cavalier sedan	1954	2,580
Packard Commercial 5413		
Henney commercial bodies	1954	205
Patrician 5406		
Patrician sedan	1954	2,760
Packard 5426		
Henney Patrician limousine	1954	35
Henney Patrician sedan	1954	65
Fifty-Fifth Series (total: 55,247)		
Clipper Deluxe Super 5540		
Deluxe sedan	1955	8,039
Super sedan	1955	7,979
Super Panama hardtop	1955	7,016
Clipper Custom 5560		
Custom sedan	1955	8,708
Custom Constellation hardtop	1955	6,672
Packard 5580 chassis		
Patrician sedan	1955	9,127
Four Hundred hardtop	1955	7,206
Caribbean convertible	1955	500
Fifty-Sixth Series (total: 28,835)		
Clipper Deluxe Super 5640		
Deluxe sedan	1956	5,715
Super sedan	1956	5,173
Super hardtop	1956	3,999
Clipper Custom 5660		
Custom sedan	1956	2,129
Custom Constellation hardtop	1956	1,466
Packard Executive 5670		
Executive Sedan	1956	1,784
Executive hardtop	1956	1,031
Packard 5680		
Patrician sedan	1956	3,775
Four Hundred hardtop	1956	3,224
Caribbean 5688		
Caribbean hardtop	1956	263
Caribbean convertible	1956	276
Fifty-Seventh Series (total: 4,809)		
Packard 57L		
Clipper Country Sedan	1957	869
Clipper Town Sedan	1957	3,940
Fifty-Eighth Series (total: 2,622)		
Packard 58L		
sedan	1958	1,200
station wagon	1958	159
hardtop	1958	675
Hawk hardtop	1958	588

Photographs this section, from the left: Production at Conner Avenue, 1956; production at East Grand Boulevard, 1949; the Packard paint shops, 1909; Third Series Eights lined up for dignitary's entourage, 1926; One Twenty Packards ready for delivery, 1936; Packard Eights on their way overseas, 1930.

YEAR	MODELS	UNITS	TOTAL
1899	Model A	5	5
1900	Models B, C,		
1901	E and F	160	160
1902	Models F, G	154	
1903	Model K	34	188
1904	Model L	188	
	Model N	62	250
1905	Model L	19	
	Model N	341	
	Model S	121	481
1906	Model S	607	
	Thirty, U	352	959
1907	Thirty, U	776	
	Thirty, UA	627	1,403
1908	Thirty, UA	676	
	Thirty, UB, UBS	788	
	Eighteen, NA	339	1,803
1909	Thirty, UB, UBS	713	
	Eighteen, NA	463	
	Thirty, UC, UCS	1,428	
	Eighteen, NB	502	3,106
1910	Thirty, UC, UCS	1,065	
	Eighteen, NB	264	
	Thirty, UD, UDS	1,467	
	Eighteen, NC	288	3,084
1911	Thirty, UD, UDS	398	
	Eighteen, NC	72	
	Thirty, UE	1,072	
	Eighteen, NE	246	
	Six 1-48	733	2,521
1912	Thirty, UE	178	
	Eighteen, NE	104	
	Six 1-48	601	
	Six 2-48 (1348)	985	
	Six 1-38 (1338)	452	2,320
1913	Six 1-48	15	
	Six 2-48 (1348)	15	
	Six 1-38 (1338 and 1438)	1,161	
	Six 3-48 (1448)	1,302	
	Six 2-38	491	2,984
1914	Six 1-38 (1438)	5	
	Six 3-48 (1448)	196	
	Six 2-38	1,010	
	Six 4-48	441	
	Six 3-38	832	
	Six 5-48	139	2,623
1915	Six 3-48 (1448)	1	
	Six 3-38	969	
	Six 5-48	221	
	Twin Six 1-25	750	
	Twin Six 1-35	704	2,645
1916	Twin Six 1-25	2,856	
	Twin Six 1-35	3,436	
	Twin Six 2-25	1,989	
	Twin Six 2-35	2,364	10,645
1917	Twin Six 2-25	2,960	
	Twin Six 2-35	1,684	
	Twin Six 3-25	1,788	
	Twin Six 3-35	1,470	7,902
1918	Twin Six 2-25	1	
	Twin Six 2-35	1	
	Twin Six 3-25	1,518	
	Twin Six 3-35	1,221	2,741
1919	Twin Six 3-25	874	
	Twin Six 3-35	2,715	3,589
1920	Twin Six 3-25	1	
	Twin Six 3-35	5,193	
	Single Six 116	1,042	6,236
1921	Twin Six 3-35	1,310	
	Single Six 116	6,374	7,684
1922	Twin Six 3-35	1,944	
	Single Six 116	1,384	
	Single Six 126	7,685	
	Single Six 133	4,364	15,377
1923	Twin Six 3-35	303	
	Single Six 126	10,496	
	Single Six 133	4,004	
	Single Eight 136	912	
	Single Eight 143	1,783	
	Six 226	988	
	Six 233	411	18,897
1924	Twin Six 3-35	20	
	Single Six 126	11	
	Single Eight 136	2,507	
	Single Eight 143	3,065	
	Six 226	6,891	
	Six 233	2,604	15,098
1925	Single Eight 136	88	
	Single Eight 143	46	
	Six 226	215	
	Six 233	116	
	Eight 236	1,844	
	Eight 243	3,492	
	Six 326	16,904	
	Six 333	9,322	32,027
1926	Eight 236	950	
	Eight 243	1,618	
	Six 326	7,764	
	Six 333	6,368	
	Eight 336	650	
	Eight 343	1,911	
	Six 426	6,731	
	Six 433	8,399	34,391
1927	Eight 243	8	
	Eight 336	595	
	Eight 343	1,327	
	Six 426	7,670	
	Six 433	2,535	
	Six 526	15,911	
	Six 533	5,969	
	Eight 443	2,894	36,909
1928	Eight 343	3	
	Six 526	12,423	
	Six 533	7,444	
	Eight 443	4,904	
	Standard Eight 626	12,187	
	Standard Eight 633	7,305	
	Custom Eight 640	4,913	

YEAR	MODELS	UNITS	TOTAL
	DeLuxe Eight 645	519	49,698
1929	Six 526	2	
	Six 533	1	
	Eight 443	2	
	Standard Eight 626	13,883	
	Standard Eight 633	9,754	
	Custom Eight 640	4,853	
	DeLuxe Eight 645	1,542	
	Standard Eight 726	8,018	
	Standard Eight 733	5,987	
	Custom Eight 740	2,979	
	DeLuxe Eight 745	812	
	Speedster Eight 734	22	47,855
1930	Standard Eight 633	1	
	Custom Eight 640	35	
	Standard Eight 726	7,617	
	Standard Eight 733	6,528	
	Custom Eight 740	3,128	
	DeLuxe Eight 745	974	
	Speedster Eight 734	91	
	Standard Eight 826	4,074	
	Standard Eight 833	3,666	
	DeLuxe Eight 840	1,390	
	DeLuxe Eight 845	882	28,386
1931	Standard Eight 726	96	
	Standard Eight 733	16	
	Custom Eight 740	93	
	DeLuxe Eight 745	3	
	Standard Eight 826	1,935	
	Standard Eight 833	2,262	
	DeLuxe Eight 840	626	
	DeLuxe Eight 845	418	
	Standard Eight 901	3,554	
	Standard Eight 902	2,517	
	DeLuxe Eight 903	792	
	DeLuxe Eight 904	610	12,922
1932	Standard Eight 833	168	
	DeLuxe Eight 840	19	
	DeLuxe Eight 845	10	
	Light Eight 900	6,622	
	Standard Eight 901	367	
	Standard Eight 902	972	
	DeLuxe Eight 903	148	
	DeLuxe Eight 904	90	
	Twin Six 905	304	
	Twin Six 906	236	
	Eight 1001	21	
	Eight 1002	17	
	Super Eight 1003	2	
	Super Eight 1004	17	
	Twelve 1006	17	9,010
1933	Light Eight 900	128	
	Standard Eight 901	1	
	Standard Eight 902	248	
	DeLuxe Eight 903	15	
	Twin Six 905	7	
	Twin Six 906	2	
	Eight 1001	1,860	
	Eight 1002	1,082	
	Super Eight 1003	510	
	Super Eight 1004	771	
	Twelve 1005	244	
	Twelve 1006	259	
	Eight 1100-1101-1102	3,085	
	Super Eight 1103-1104-1105	1,156	
	Twelve 1106-1107-1108	525	9,893
1934	Eight 1100-1101-1102	2,035	
	Super Eight 1103-1104-1105	764	
	Twelve 1106-1107-1108	435	
	One Twenty 120-A	14	
	Eight 1200-1201-1202	2,103	
	Super Eight 1203-1204-1205	578	
	Twelve 1207-1208	336	6,265
1935	One Twenty 120-A	24,981	
	Eight 1200-1201-1202	2,678	
	Super Eight 1203-1204-1205	814	
	Twelve 1207-1208	445	
	One Twenty 120-B	20,313	
	Eight 1400-1401-1402	1,826	
	Super Eight 1403-1404-1405	648	
	Twelve 1407-1408	340	52,045
1936	One Twenty 120-B	34,729	
	Eight 1400-1401-1402	2,147	
	Super Eight 1403-1404-1405	682	
	Twelve 1407-1408	342	
	Six 115-C	23,518	
	One Twenty 120-C	16,199	
	Super Eight 1500-1501-1502	2,738	
	Twelve 1506-1507-1508	623	80,978
1937	Six 115-C	41,882	
	One Twenty 120-C, CD; 138 CD	33,901	
	Super Eight 1500-1501-1502	3,055	
	Twelve 1506-1507-1508	677	
	Six 1600	14,437	
	Eight 1601-1602	13,329	
	Super Eight 1603-1604-1605	1,828	
	Twelve 1607-1608	409	109,518
1938	Six 1600	15,613	
	Eight 1601-1602	9,295	
	Super Eight 1603-1604-1605	650	
	Twelve 1607-1608	157	

YEAR	MODELS	UNITS	TOTAL
	Six 1700	13,492	
	One Twenty 1701-1702	8,992	
	Super Eight 1703-1705	1,895	
	Twelve 1707-1708	166	50,260
1939	Six 1700	10,858	
	One Twenty 1701-1702	8,655	
	Super Eight 1703-1705	2,067	
	Twelve 1707-1708	280	
	One-Ten 1800	33,834	
	One-Twenty 1801	16,900	
	One-Sixty 1803-1804-1805	3,065	
	One-Eighty 1806-1807-1808	914	76,573
1940	One-Ten 1800	28,466	
	One-Twenty 1801	11,238	
	One-Sixty 1803-1804-1805	2,597	
	One-Eighty 1806-1807-1808	986	
	One-Ten 1900	21,670	
	One-Twenty 1901	9,697	
	One-Sixty 1903-1904-1905	1,801	
	One-Eighty 1906-1907-1908	472	76,927
1941	One-Ten 1900	13,030	
	One-Twenty 1901	7,403	
	One-Sixty 1903-1904-1905	1,724	
	One-Eighty 1906-1907-1908	458	
	Clipper 1951	16,600	
	Six 2000-2010-2020-2030	8,449	
	Eight 2001-2011-2021	16,584	
	One-Sixty 2003-2004-2005-2023-2055	2,067	
	One-Eighty 2006-2007-2008	591	66,906
1942	Six 2000-2010-2020-2030	2,876	
	Eight 2001-2011-2021	2,615	
	One-Sixty 2003-2004-2005-2023-2055	513	
	One-Eighty 2006-2007-2008	81	6,085
1945	Clipper Eight 2101	2,722	2,722
1946	Clipper Six 2100-2130	15,982	
	Clipper Eight 2101	3,804	
	Super Clipper 2103	4,924	
	Custom Super Clipper 2106	1,472	
	Clipper Eight DeLuxe 2111	14,611	
	Custom Super Clipper 2126	1,309	42,102
1947	Clipper Six 2100-2130	14,949	
	Super Clipper 2103	4,802	
	Custom Super Clipper 2106	5,690	
	Clipper Eight DeLuxe 2111	8,623	
	Custom Super Clipper 2126	1,772	
	Eight 2201	1,110	
	Super Eight 2202	2,555	
	Custom Eight 2206	453	
	Eight DeLuxe 2211	9,678	
	Custom Eight 2213	825	
	Six 2220 taxi	56	
	Super Eight 2222	24	
	Super Eight 2232	4,277	
	Custom Eight 2233	450	
	Six 2240	213	55,477
1948	Eight 2201	11,672	
	Super Eight 2202	10,366	
	Custom Eight 2206	5,483	
	Eight DeLuxe 2211	38,129	
	Custom Eight 2213	1,116	
	Six 2220 taxi	1,260	
	Super Eight 2222	1,742	
	Super Eight 2232	3,486	
	Custom Eight 2233	655	
	Custom Eight 2226	230	
	Six 2240	1,715	
	Eight 2201-9	6,005	
	Super Eight 2202-9	2,386	
	Custom Eight 2206-9	1,256	
	Eight DeLuxe 2211-9	11,574	
	Custom Eight 2213-9	120	
	Six 2220-9 taxi	25	
	Super Eight 2222-9	552	
	Custom Eight 2226-9	36	
	Super Eight 2232-9	706	
	Custom Eight 2233-9	119	
	Six 2240-9	264	98,897
1949	Eight 2201-9	7,548	
	Super Eight 2202-9	3,493	

YEAR	MODELS	UNITS	TOTAL
	Custom Eight 2206-9	1,734	
	Eight DeLuxe 2211-9	15,848	
	Custom Eight 2213-9	100	
	Super Eight 2222-9	315	
	Custom Eight 2226-9	14	
	Super Eight 2232-9	531	
	Custom Eight 2233-9	94	
	Six 2240-9	418	
	Eight, Eight Deluxe 2301	53,168	
	Super, Super Deluxe 2302	8,759	
	Custom 2306	973	
	Custom 2313	160	
	Super, Super Deluxe 2322	4	
	Super, Super Deluxe 2332	685	
	Custom 2333	68	
	Eight, Eight Deluxe 2301-5	8,502	
	Super, Super Deluxe 2302-5	1,183	
	Custom 2306-5	547	
	Custom 2313-5	44	
	Six 2320-5 taxi	13	
	Super, Super Deluxe 2332-5	330	
	Custom 2333-5	62	104,593
1950	Eight, Eight Deluxe 2301-5	27,969	
	Super, Super Deluxe 2302-5	3,345	
	Custom 2306-5	160	
	Custom 2313-5	200	
	Super, Super Deluxe 2332-5	270	
	Custom 2333-5	15	
	200, 200 Deluxe 2401	37,613	
	250, 300 models 2402	1,431	
	Patrician 400 model 2406	1,135	72,138
1951	200, 200 Deluxe 2401	38,389	
	250, 300 models 2402	13,878	
	300 model 2413	401	
	Patrician 400 model 2406	7,866	
	200, 200 Deluxe 2501	11,878	
	300 model 2502	1,626	
	Patrician 400 model 2506	963	
	300 model 2513	140	
	250 model 2531	1,335	76,476
1952	200, 200 Deluxe 2501	34,842	
	300 model 2502	5,079	
	Patrician 400 model 2506	3,012	
	300 model 2513	180	
	250 model 2531	3,866	
	Clipper 2601	6,548	
	Cavalier 2602	2,305	
	Patrician 2606	1,478	
	Clipper Deluxe 2611	4,475	
	Packard 2613	26	
	Packard 2631	997	
	Clipper 2633	180	62,988
1953	Clipper 2601	26,621	
	Cavalier 2602	8,494	
	Patrician 2606	6,003	
	Clipper Deluxe 2611	26,230	
	Packard 2613	140	
	Packard 2631	6,421	
	Clipper 2633	200	
	Packard 2626	150	
	Clipper 1954 models	5,688	
	Packard 1954 models	1,394	81,341

For calendar years 1954 through 1958, the breakdown of production into specific models is not known. Indeed, there are no figures extant prepared by the Packard Motor Car Company for calendar year production during these years. However, sources outside the company, but contemporary to the period, provided the following figures for the last years of the Packard automobile: calendar 1954, 27,583 units; calendar 1955, 69,667 units; calendar 1956, 13,432 units; calendar 1957, 5495 units; calendar 1958, 1745 units.

NOTE: Production by the Packard Motor Car Company by calendar year for 1899 through 1958 thus can be totaled as 1,614,005 cars. It is hoped, however, that this figure will not issue forth into history as the exact number of cars produced by Packard during its lifetime. The model year total for these same years, for example, is 1,-611,814 cars—a difference of two-thousand odd. It would appear the discrepancy revolves around the calendar/model year figures for the last years of the company, when record-keeping obviously was subordinated to survival. Packard record-keeping—as any historian of the marque knows—was haphazard in any case, but because a variety of figures were retained during the years prior to the mid-Fifties, these could be cross checked more easily. Doubtless the model year figure is the more accurate of the two total production figures.

PACKARD MOTOR CAR COMPANY EXPORT FIGURES

Although Packard automobiles were exported during the years prior to 1920 and in 1953 and 1954 as well, reliable figures are not available for those years. This listing represents the figures which could be substantiated, and includes Canadian production in the export total.

		Produced	Exports	Domestic
First Series (including 116)	1920-1925		1,470	42,291
Second Series	1923-1925		2,326	16,811
Third Series	1925-1927		2,455	42,389
Fourth Series	1926-1928		3,242	29,893
Fifth Series	1927-1928		4,906	36,844
Sixth Series	1928-1929		3,941	51,051
Seventh Series	1929-1930		1,932	34,432
Eighth Series	1930-1931		825	14,625
Ninth Series	1931-1932		558	16,055
Tenth Series	1933		609	4,191
Eleventh Series	1933-1934		837	7,163
Twelfth Series	1934-1935		4,268	27,621
Fourteenth Series	1935-1936		7,065	53,962
Fifteenth Series	1936-1937		6,675	115,918
Sixteenth Series	1937-1938		6,670	49,048
Seventeenth Series	1938-1939		5,457	40,948
Eighteenth Series	1939-1940		6,375	91,625
Nineteenth Series	1940-1941		2,115	70,740
Twentieth Series	1941-1942		1,655	32,121
Twenty-First Series	1945-1948		5,536	75,124
Twenty-Second Series	1947-1948		5,473	90,022
Twenty-Second Series	1948-1949		770	52,368
Twenty-Third Series	1949		1,920	61,897
Twenty-Third Series	1949-1950		1,030	41,610
Twenty-Fourth Series	1950-1951		3,712	96,600
Twenty-Fifth Series	1951-1952		1,773	61,148
Fifty-Sixth Series	1955-1956		408	28,427
Fifty-Seventh Series	1957		312	4,497
Fifty-Eighth Series	1957-1958		245	2,377

BIBLIOGRAPHY

BOOKS AND GENERAL PUBLICATIONS

Adams, Fred W., "The Saga of Packard: Some Notes on the First Half Century of America's Oldest Continuous Maker of Automobiles Under a Single Management." Detroit: Packard Motor Car Company, 1949.

Association of Licensed Automobile Manufacturers, *Hand Book of Gasoline Automobiles*. New York, annual editions 1904-1911.

Automobile Board of Trade, *Hand Book of Gasoline Automobiles*. New York, annual editions 1912-1913.

Automobile Quarterly, *The American Car Since 1775*. New York: Automobile Quarterly, Inc., 1971.

Boardman, Fon W., Jr., *The Thirties: America and the Great Depression*. New York: Henry Z. Walck, Inc., 1967.

Boylan, James, ed., *The World and the 20's*. New York: Dial Press, 1973.

Borth, Christy, *Masters of Mass Production*. Indianapolis: Bobbs-Merrill Company, Inc., 1945.

Branham, Ben P., *Branham Automobile Reference Book*. Chicago: Ben P. Branham Company, 1918-1938

Chilton's, various published manuals. Philadelphia: Chilton Book Company.

Detroit Institute of Arts, *The Legacy of Albert Kahn*. Detroit: Detroit Institute of Arts, 1970.

Dickey, Philip S., III, *The Liberty Engine 1918-1942*. Washington, D.C.: Smithsonian Institution Press, 1968.

Einstein, Arthur, "The Advertising of the Packard Motor Car Company, 1899-1956." Master's thesis, Michigan State University, 1959.

Epstein, Ralph, *The Automobile Industry*. Chicago: A.W. Shaw, 1928.

Greenleaf, William, *Monopoly on Wheels*. Detroit: Wayne State University Press, 1968.

Hendry, Maurice D., *Cadillac: Standard of the World, The Complete Seventy-Year History*. Princeton, New Jersey: Princeton Publishing Inc., 1973.

Jaffee, Morton, *Alvan Macauley: Automotive Leader and Pioneer*. Privately printed, 1957.

Langworth, Richard M., *Kaiser-Frazer: The Last Onslaught on Detroit*. Princeton, New Jersey: Princeton Publishing Inc., 1975.

Longstreet, Stephen, *The Canvas Falcons*. New York: World Publishing Company, 1970.

MacManus, Theodore, *Men, Money and Motors*. New York: Harper & Brothers, 1929.

————, *The Sword Arm of Business*. New York: Devin-Adair, 1927.

National Automobile Chamber of Commerce, *Hand Book of Gasoline Automobiles*. New York, annual editions 1914-1929.

Norman, Aaron, *The Great Air War*. New York: Macmillan Company, 1968.

Parker, John, "A History of the Packard Motor Car Company from 1899 to 1929." Master's thesis, Wayne State University Press, 1949.

Prendergast, Maurice (with Oscar Parkes), *Jane's Fighting Ships*. London: S. Low Marston and Company, annual editions World War II era.

Rae, John B., *American Automobile Manufacturers*. Philadelphia: Chilton Book Company, 1959.

Selden Patent Trial, Transcripts of Court Records and Exhibits, 1903-1911.

Seltzer, Lawrence H., *A Financial History of the American Automobile Industry*. New York: Houghton Mifflin Company, 1928.

Shannon, David A., *The Great Depression*. Englewood Cliffs, New Jersey: Prentice-Hall, Inc., 1960.

Sullivan, Mark, *Our Times: Over Here, 1914-1918*. Volume V, New York: Charles Scribner's Sons, 1933.

————, *Our Times: The Turn of the Century*. Volume I. New York: Charles Scribner's Sons, 1926.

————, *Our Times: The Twenties*. Volume VI. New York: Charles Scribner's Sons, 1935.

Turnquist, Robert E., *The Packard Story*. New York: A.S. Barnes & Co., Inc., 1965.

U.S. Department of Commerce and Labor, Bureau of the Census, *Census of Manufacturers: 1905; Automobiles, Bicycles and Tricycles*. Washington, D.C.: Government Printing Office, 1906.

U.S. Federal Trade Commission, *Report on the Motor Vehicle Industry*. Washington, D.C.: Government Printing Office, 1939.

U.S. House of Representatives, 76th Congress 1st Session, House Document No. 468. Washington, D.C.: Government Printing Office, 1950.

NEWSPAPERS, MAGAZINES AND OTHER PERIODICALS

American Architecture, American Review of Reviews, Auto Age, Automobile and Motor Review, Automobile Quarterly, The Autocar, The Automobile, Automobile Review, Automobile Topics, Automobile Trade Journal, Automotive Daily News, Automotive Industries, Automotive News, Car and Driver, Car Life, The Commercial Vehicle, Consumer Reports, Cycle and Automobile Trade Journal, Detroit Free Press, Detroit Journal, Detroit News, Detroit Sunday Times, Finish, Fortune, The Horseless Age, Illustrated London News, Iron Age, Ladies' Home Journal, The Literary Digest, McClure's Magazine, Mechanix Illustrated, Mill and Factory, Motocycle, MoToR, Motor Age, Motor Life, Motor News, Motor Trend, Motor Vehicle Monthly, Motor Vehicle Review of Cleveland, Motor World, National Geographic, National Service Manual, The New York Post, The New York Times, The New Yorker, The Packard Cormorant, Popular Mechanics, Popular Science, Printers Ink, Time, The Times (London), La Vie Automobile, Vintage Vehicles, Warren Daily Chronicle, Warren Tribune

PACKARD MOTOR CAR COMPANY PUBLICATIONS AND DOCUMENTS

Advertisements, Brochures and Catalogues; Annual Reports; Board Minutes; Data Books; Facts Books; Information Books; Owners Instruction Books; Parts Manuals; Shop Manuals; Service Counselors; Service Letters; Service Manuals; Service Technical Bulletins. Further to this were periodicals published by the Packard Motor Car Company: *Inner Circle, Freight Transportation Digest, The Packard, Packard News, Packard Truck Digest*. And in addition to the foregoing, primary source material including business and personal correspondence, diaries of Packard company principals, internal company memoranda, et al. was researched in the university, library and private collections hereafter noted.

RESEARCH COLLECTIONS

In addition to the private libraries of the authors of this book and the archives of *Automobile Quarterly* magazine, the following collections were researched:

Archives, Henry Austin Clark, Jr. Research Collection, Glen Cove, New York.

Archives, Frederick C. Crawford Auto-Aviation Museum, Cleveland, Ohio.

Archives, Harrah's Automobile Collection, Reno, Nevada.

Archives, Lehigh University, Bethlehem, Pennsylvania.

Archives, National Air and Space Museum, Smithsonian Institution, Washington, D.C.

Archives, Packard Electric Company, Warren, Ohio. (Included correspondence and minutes of the company, 1890 to date; William Doud Packard diaries, 1896-1903.)

Archives, State of Michigan, Lansing, Michigan.

Automobile Reference Collection, The Free Library of Philadelphia, Philadelphia, Pennsylvania.

Chrysler Collection, National Automotive History Collection, Detroit Public Library, Detroit, Michigan. (Included internal memoranda and competitive product comparisons.)

History Collection, Painesville Morley Library, Painesville, Ohio.

History Collection, Warren Public Library, Warren, Ohio.

Henry B. Joy Papers, Bentley Historical Library, The University of Michigan, Ann Arbor, Michigan.

Charles Brady King Collection, National Automotive History Collection, Detroit Public Library, Detroit, Michigan.

Packard Collection, National Automotive History Collection, Detroit Public Library, Detroit, Michigan.

James Ward Packard Diaries, Tom Summers Collection, New Jersey.

Studebaker-Packard Papers, George Arents Research Library, Syracuse University, Syracuse, New York. (Included Ohio Automobile Company and Packard Motor Car Company board minutes and correspondence.)

RESEARCH CONSULTANTS, PACKARD HISTORIANS, COMPANY PERSONNEL

During the years of their personal researches into Packard history, and in specific regard to this volume, the authors consulted scores of persons who contributed reminiscences, research data and historical or illustrative documentation which has been incorporated into this book. Further, during the course of the preparation of this book, many others came forward to volunteer further reminiscences and data. The list of sources which follows includes people who worked for or were involved with the Packard Motor Car Company during its lifetime; are the sons, daughters or other relatives of Packard company principals; are Packard historians with either general or especial expertise in various areas of the company's history; or are historians and archivists consulted for ancillary documentation with regard to the book's narrative:

William D. Allison, Howard Applegate, Richard Arbib, Clifford Bailey, Hyde W. Ballard, C. Richard Bell, Wayne Bellows, Alfred E. Benjamin, Donald Beyreis, Charles A. Blackman, David Blackmore, Robert Blackmore, Edward J. Blend, Jr., Duane Bohnstedt, Joseph Boyle, Roger Bremer, William Browning, Nelson R. Brownyer, E.A. Catlett, Mary Cattie, Harold Churchill, Henry Austin Clark, Jr., Richard Collins, Samuel J. Connor, Howard Darrin, Caroline Davis, Helen Deason, Enos Derham, Mrs. Enos Derham, Alexis de Sakhnoffsky, Raymond H. Dietrich, Arthur D. Dubin, Jim Edwards, Arthur W. Einstein, Jr., Don Elrod, Gerald W. Fauth, Charles Russell Feldmann, Earl Fenner, Wesley Fetch, Don Figone, Robert M. Finlay, James B. Forman, Roy Frailing, Truman Fuller, Truman Fuller, Jr., Harry T. Gardner, David Glass, Kenneth Gooding, William H. Graves, Gwil Griffiths, Peter Helck, Leslie R. Henry, Thomas Hibbard, Clarence Hibst, Ben Hickey, Hugh Hitchcock, Jr., David R. Holls, Douglas Houston, Jr., Thomas E. Jackson, Edward Jacod, David Johnson, Mrs. H.D.L. Johnston, Henry B. Joy, Jr., Arne Kesti, George D. Kirkham III, Gary Kulp, Robert Laughna, Charles Lytle, Kenneth L. McDowell, Forest R. McFarland, Strother MacMinn, Duncan McRae, Alvan Macauley, Jr., Edward Macauley, Jr., Tom Mahoney, Skip Marketti, James Marks, Thomas C. Marshall, Jr., Don Mumford, John Nagley, James J. Nance, Ed Nowacky, Warren Packard, Ron Paetow, Eleanor Paton, Isidor Peritz, Don Peterson, Thomas C. Phillips, Norman Pinnow, Barney J. Pollard, R.H. Poplawski, Al Prance, Harry Pulfer, James Quinlan, Richard Quinn, Robert H. Rand, Carolyn Kirkham Raymond, H. Jay Raymond, John Reinhart, George Romney, Fred A. Rouse, Belva Hatcher Sanford, Don Scheuring, William D. Schmidt, Ward Schryver, Robert Shape, Bradley Skinner, Mrs. Edward Cope Smith, William Snyder, Don Sommer, Ruth Sommerlad, Newell Steinmetz, Richard Stout, Mrs. Myron C. Summers, Ross Taylor, Richard Teague, George Tissen, Jack Trefney, Alex Tremulis, Bert L. Trillich, Jr., Jack Triplett, Robert Turnquist, Nicholas Van Ranst, Charles H. Vincent, George Walker, Erwin Weiss, Roger Turreff White, Henry Whiting, Robert M. Williams, Walter Williams, John M. Woods, John Young, Montgomery E. Young, Joseph Zewatsky.

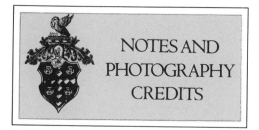

NOTES AND PHOTOGRAPHY CREDITS

CHAPTER ONE. 14-15, 17, 18 left and center, 19, 20, 21, 22: Terry Martin. 18 right: NAHC. 23, 26: Tom Summers. 24, 25: Frederick C. Crawford Auto-Aviation Museum.

CHAPTER TWO. 28-29, 30, 31, 34, 35, 36, 38 left, 39, 41, 47, 48 below: Terry Martin. 33 inset, 48 above left and right: NAHC. 33, 42: Long Island Automotive Museum. 38 right, 45, 46: Roger White.

CHAPTER THREE. 50-51, 56, 57 above, 59, 63: Terry Martin. 52-53 center: Tom Summers. 53 right, 54: NAHC. 57 below, 60, 62, 64: Long Island Automotive Museum. 60-61 center, 61 right: Duane Bohnstedt. 64-65 center, 65 right: Roger White.

CHAPTER FOUR. 66-67, 70 right, 86: Long Island Automotive Museum. 68, 70 left, 72, 73, 74, 75 above and center, 77 right, 79 above and below, 84-85, 86, 87 center and below: Terry Martin. 87 above: Charles Lytle. 88-89: Peter Helck. All other photos: NAHC.

CHAPTERS FIVE AND SIX. 90-91: John Reinhart. 92: C.A. Leslie, Jr. 94 left, 96-97 center, 98, 99, 101, 103, 105, 114: Long Island Automotive Museum. 95 right: Tom Mahoney. 124 above: Automobile Quarterly. All other photos: NAHC.

CHAPTERS SEVEN AND EIGHT. 132, 137, 139 above, 151, 155, 170 above: Long Island Automotive Museum. 133, 141: Don E. Weber. 140, 147: Richard Quinn. 142: Richard M. Langworth. 146: Bradley Skinner. 163 below: Strother MacMinn. 170 below: Tom Mahoney. All other photos: NAHC.

CHAPTER NINE. 174-175 center, 175 above and center, 189 above: Charles Lytle. 175 below, 189 center and above: Charles Betts. 188: Long Island Automotive Museum. 189 below: Bradley Skinner. All other photos: NAHC.

CHAPTERS TEN, ELEVEN AND TWELVE. 236: William Browning. 237 right, 252 above left and right and below right, 256, 267 left: Long Island Automotive Museum. 261: L. Morgan Yost. All other photos: NAHC.

CHAPTERS THIRTEEN, FOURTEEN AND FIFTEEN. 270-271, 291 center and below left and below right, 294 below right, 295 below left, 304: Long Island Automotive Museum. 290 above: Strother MacMinn. 292-293: Truman Fuller. All other photos: NAHC.

CHAPTERS SIXTEEN, SEVENTEEN AND EIGHTEEN. 338-339: Harry Pulfer. 358 below: William Browning. 364 left: David Holls. 367: L. Morgan Yost. 370, 371 above left and below and above right: Long Island Automotive Museum. All other photos: NAHC.

CHAPTERS NINETEEN AND TWENTY. 400-401: Douglas Houston, Jr. 422 center, 423 right: Automobile Quarterly. 435 above, 438 top and center above: C.A. Leslie, Jr. 483 center below: Marcus Clary. All other photos: NAHC.

CHAPTERS TWENTY-ONE AND TWENTY-TWO. 481, 486 bottom right: Long Island Automotive Museum. All other photos: NAHC.

CHAPTER TWENTY-THREE. 495 above, 498 above right: Theodore R.F. Hall. All other photos: NAHC.

CHAPTER TWENTY-FOUR. 500-501: Dwight D. Eisenhower Library. 509 above right: Richard Quinn. 509 below, 511 above left: Tom Mahoney. 513: Richard Teague. All other photos: NAHC.

CHAPTER TWENTY-FIVE. 522 above: Theodore R.F. Hall. 522 below right: Frank Pierce. 523 above left: William Browning. All other photos: NAHC.

CHAPTER TWENTY-SIX. 529, 539 left: John Reinhart. 534 below left: Tom Mahoney. 534 above center and right: Don Scheuring. 536 above: Dwight Heinmuller. 537 above left, 538 above and below left, 539 right, 542 above left and right: Richard M. Langworth. 537 below left, 538 below right: Eastern Packard Club. 537 above right: Howard and Shelby Applegate. 541 below right: Theodore R.F. Hall. 543 center: William Browning. All other photos: NAHC.

CHAPTER TWENTY-SEVEN. 546 below, 547 below: Donald Beyreis. 548 above left, 551 above and center, 557 center, 558 right: William Browning. 558 left: Howard and Shelby Applegate. All other photos: NAHC.

CHAPTER TWENTY-EIGHT. 565: Dwight Heinmuller. 570, 581: George Hamlin. 573 center right, below left and right: Donald Beyreis. 576 above right: William Browning. 577 below left and above right: Richard Quinn. 580: Creative Industries. All other photos: NAHC.

CHAPTER TWENTY-NINE. 582-583, 593 above and center: Dwight Heinmuller. 590, 594 above and above center, 595 left: Richard M. Langworth. 591: Richard Teague. 594 below: William Browning. All other photos: NAHC.

CHAPTER THIRTY. 605 below right: Dwight Heinmuller. 607 above, 611 above: George Hamlin. 608, 611 below: Richard M. Langworth. 609: Theodore R.F. Hall. 610 above: William Browning. 612 above and below: Anton Khropochnik. All other photos: NAHC.

CHAPTER THIRTY-ONE. 622-623, 624, 625: William D. Schmidt. 626: Dwight Heinmuller. 628, 629: Richard M. Langworth. 631 above right and below: Fabian Bachroch. 632 right, 633: George Hamlin. All other photos: NAHC.

APPENDIX I. 665 above left, center and below left and right, 666 above and below, 667 right, 668, 669, 671 above, 673 above and center, 676 center and below, 677 above left, 679 above: John B. Montville. 673 below, 679 center: Manning Brothers. 678 below: T.C. Vandegrift. All other photos: NAHC.

APPENDIX II. 687: Charles Betts. All other photos: NAHC.

APPENDIX III. 699 center right, 701 above and below left, 702 above: Bob Allen. 702 center, 706 above left, 708 below, 711 center, 712, 713: George Hamlin. 702 below: Howard and Shelby Applegate. All other photos: NAHC.

APPENDIX IV. 725, 726 above left, 727 above right, 729 right, 730, 731 above left and right and below left, 732 below left and right: Long Island Automotive Museum. 726 right and below left, 729 above left: Ron Paetow. 727 left: Roger Abbott. 729 below left: Automobile Quarterly. 731 below right: Theodore R.F. Hall. All other illustrations: NAHC.

APPENDIX V. 740-741, 745, 746 below left and right: Long Island Automotive Museum. 743: Theodore R.F. Hall. 746 above center: Vicente Alvarez, Bruce Craig. All other photos: NAHC.

APPENDIX VI. Hood ornaments from the collections following. 756 top left and below center right, 757 center above and below, 758 below right, 762 right, 764 right, 765 above center, 766 below left, 767, 768 above right and center right: Harrah's Automobile Collection. 756 top right: Bradley Skinner. 756 motometers, 758 above left, 763, 768 above left: W.C. Williams. 757 top right and left, 764 center: C.A. Leslie, Jr. 757 bottom right: George Hamlin. 758 center left: David Glass. 758 below left, 759 above and center right and left, 762 left: John Young. 760 above: Howard Vieen. 765 above left: Don Scheuring. Emblems, body plates, hub cap medallions: Pulfer & Williams. Photographs by W.C. Williams or courtesy of Harrah's Automobile Collection or the individual collectors. All other hood ornaments or decorations from historic photographs: NAHC.

APPENDICES VII AND VIII. 775, 776: Long Island Automotive Museum. All other photos: NAHC.

NOTE: The code letters NAHC refer to the National Automotive History Collection of the Detroit Public Library.

SUBJECT INDEX

Terry, F.S., 62
Textron, 615
Thaw, Harry Kendall, 135
Thomas, J.G. Parry, 747
Thomas, René, 150
Thomas Company, E.R., 46, 127
Thomas-Detroit Company, 686
Thompson coachwork, 305
Thompson Products Museum, 405
Tibbett, Lawrence, 467
Tibbetts, Milton, 102, 125, 245, 334, 335, 539, 767
Tidewater Oil Company, 707
"Tillie the Toiler," 269
Time magazine, 358, 462, 465
Times, The (London), 465
Titanic ocean liner, 335
Titusville & Pithole Plank Road company, 18
Tjaarda, John, 490, 492, 494
Torque-flite (Chrysler), 574
Torsion-Aire (Chrysler), 594
Torsion-Level (Packard), 588-594, 710
Touch-Button Ultramatic, 606
Townsend, George, 753
Towson Body Company, 420
Transitone Automobile Radio Corporation, 710
Trego, Frank, 138
Tremulis, Alex, 492, 493-494
Trevoux, Jean, 748
Triplex Special (land speed record car), 747
Trossi, Count Carlo Felice, 337
Truman, Harry S., 535, 553
Trumbull County, 16
Trumbull Manufacturing Company, 32, 43
Tucker, Preston, 349
Tucker automobile, 528
Turner, Fred, 745
"TV Reader's Digest," 595
25,000 Mile Test, 693
Twin Traction, 606, 609
Twin Ultramatic, 588-589, 598, 606, 619-621

Ultramatic, 536-540, 552, 568, 574, 610
Union Pacific Railroad, 707
Uniontown (Pennsylvania) hill climb (1915), 150, 744; (1917), 744
United Auto Workers, 353, 517, 519, 543
U.S. Express Company, 19
U.S. Railroad Administration, 676
U.S. Rubber Company, 707
USSR (Union of Soviet Socialist Republics), 366, 519-520
Utica (Packard factory), 556, 561, 579, 613-614, 616, 617, 621
Utica Bend Corporation, 510-511, 618, 619

Valier, Max, 273
Vance, Harold, 557, 576, 577, 578
Vanderbilt, Cornelius, Jr., 269
Vanderbilt Cup (1904), 82-83, 743

Van Ranst, Cornelius Willett, 296, 312, 403-404, 405-406, 408, 411, 536, 634
Van Ranst, Nicholas, 405
Verville-Packard aircraft, 303, 749
Victor Peninsular Company, 710
Villa, Pancho, 174, 672-673
Vincent, Charles Helm, 177, 178, 184, 185, 303, 334, 335, 408, 409, 417, 461, 462, 686, 692, 693, 695
Vincent, Jesse Gurney, 132, 154-157, 169-170, 175-177, 178, 180-184, 185, 186, 187, 190, 222, 223, 224, 242, 253, 256, 257, 265, 303, 304, 313, 328-329, 350, 403, 408, 409, 417, 422, 432, 433, 454, 491, 492, 505, 507, 535, 536, 539, 576, 634, 686, 742, 744, 753
Vincent Speedster (Fourth Series Special), 303
Vogel, Hy, 332
von Hamm, C.C., 123
Von Hamm-Young Company Ltd., 127
von Keller, Frederick Wilhelm, 353
Vosper PT boat, 508

Wade, Lt. Leigh, 253, 747
Wagner Electric, 634
Waldon, Sidney, 69, 70, 71, 76, 78, 79, 82, 88, 96, 98, 101, 103, 113, 114, 115, 117-118, 120, 124, 127, 130, 131-132, 133, 138, 141, 147, 160, 180, 183, 185, 422, 634, 743
Walker, George, 492, 493, 494
Walker Associates, 492
Wall Street Journal, 543
Walters, Fred, 560, 565
Waltham Manufacturing Company, 37, 671
Waltham tricycle, 37, 44
Wanamaker, John, 668
Ward's magazine, 604
Warhawk aircraft, 507
Warren, Ohio, 16, 37, 52, 64-65, 85-87
Warren *Daily Chronicle*, 23, 27, 32, 37, 83, 89
Warren *Tribune*, 20, 32, 39, 54, 64, 65, 78, 81, 82, 87
Washington Post, The, 183
Washington University, George, 131
Waterhouse coachwork, 302
Wayne Works, 700
Weather-Conditioner, 364
Webb, Clifton, 308
Weisell, Eli K., 16
Weiss, E.A., 454
Weiss, George, 25, 27, 30, 32, 34, 37, 39, 40, 42, 43, 44, 54, 57, 61, 62, 65
Weiss, Laura Furress, 27, 30
Wells, Linton, 253, 747
Western Toy Company, 40
Westinghouse Company, 19
Westinghouse traction equipment, 679
Weston-Mott, 58
Westover, Russ, 269
Wettstone, K.E., 294
Weymann coachwork, 232
Whipple, Harlan W., 58, 60, 61, 62, 71
White, J.M., 747
White, Roger, 30

White, Stanford, 135
White Flannels, 269
White truck and company, 542, 577, 671, 676, 680, 681, 710
White Triplex (land speed record car), 747
Whitman, L.L., 117
Wick, H.B., 62
Widman, C. David, 421
Widman, Charles H., 421, 424
Widman & Company, J.C., 420-421
Widmann, Adolph, 749
Wilbur, Curtis D., 269
Wilcox, Howdy, 747
Wilhelmina, Queen of the Netherlands, 557
Wilkes-Barre Mountain (1905), 104, 743
Williams, A.J., 749
Williams, R.M., 303, 403
Willoughby coachwork, 302
Willow Run, 510, 581
Wills, C. Harold, 185
Wills Sainte Claire automobile, 231
Willys American, 490; Willys Overland, 402, 532
Wilson, C. Haines, 420
Wilson, Charles, 579, 615, 618
Wilson, Herbert D., 465-466
Wilson, John D., 761
Wilson, William Robert, 282, 422, 423-424, 426
Wilson, Woodrow, 175, 187
Wilson Body Company, C.R., 420
Winged Motor Mascot, 768
Wingfoot Express, 676
Winslow, Rudolph, 55-56
Winterfront, 240
Winton, Alexander, 25, 27, 30, 92
Winton automobile and company, 25-27, 30, 32, 78, 79, 83, 118; Bullet, 81, 82, 742
Winton Engine Corporation, 671, 710
Wood, Gar, 750, 753
Woodside, George, 534
Woolson, Lionel, 191, 224, 290, 303, 749, 750
Worblaufen coachwork, 535, 539
World's Columbian Exposition (Chicago, 1893), 23
World War I, 174-191
World War II, 371, 499, 502-511
Worthington, 634
WOW-TV (Omaha, Nebraska), 706
Wright, Harold Bell, 269
Wright, Martha, 595
Wright, Phil, 493, 494
Wyman, George, 78

Yeager, Howard F., 493, 494, 757, 761
Yellow Cab Manufacturing Company, 245, 703
Young & Rubicam advertising, 323, 467, 477, 594

Zborowski, Count Louis, 747
Zeder, Fred, 244
ZIL automobile, 520
ZIS automobile, 366, 520

ILLUSTRATIONS INDEX

NOTE: Numbers in bold refer to photographs or illustrations in color.